THE
CAMBRIDGE
MEDIEVAL HISTORY

VOLUME III

THE
CAMBRIDGE
MEDIEVAL HISTORY

PLANNED BY THE LATE

J. B. BURY, M.A., F.B.A.

EDITED BY

H. M. GWATKIN, M.A.
J. P. WHITNEY, D.D.
THE LATE J. R. TANNER, LITT.D.
C. W. PREVITÉ-ORTON, LITT.D., F.B.A.

VOLUME III

GERMANY AND THE WESTERN EMPIRE

CAMBRIDGE UNIVERSITY PRESS

CAMBRIDGE

LONDON · NEW YORK · MELBOURNE

Published by the Syndics of the Cambridge University Press
The Pitt Building, Trumpington Street, Cambridge CB2 1RP
Bentley House, 200 Euston Road, London NW1 2DB
32 East 57th Street, New York, NY 10022, USA
296 Beaconsfield Parade, Middle Park, Melbourne 3206, Australia

ISBN 0 521 04534 7

First published 1922
Reprinted 1924 1930 1936
1957 1964 1968 1976

Printed in Great Britain
at the
University Printing House, Cambridge
(Euan Phillips, University Printer)

PREFACE.

THE first words in this volume must, of right and of piety, be about the late Editor, Henry Melvill Gwatkin. He had been one of the Editors from the first: he had brought to the help of the undertaking not only his own unrivalled mastery of the earlier period but also a singularly wide and accurate knowledge of history at large. This meant a great deal, and was generally known. But a constant colleague, in work which often called for large decisions and always for care in details, can speak, like no one else, of the time and trouble he freely spent even when he might sometimes have spared himself. Nobody else can know or judge of these things, and it is fitting therefore that I, who can, should pay the tribute of justice which memory demands. He had read with his usual care and judgment most of the chapters in this volume, and he was looking forward to their publication. But this he was not to see, although this volume owes him much. It will be difficult to fill his place in future volumes, for literary skill such as his is not so often added to an almost universal knowledge as it was with him. To me, after so many hours spent with him over the Medieval History, fellowship in our common work had grown into friendship, and during it I had learnt many things from him on many sides. All who knew him, and all who have read his own masterly chapters, will well understand the sadness which I feel as we give to the public part of a work in which he had shared and which owes him so much.

The volume was nearly ready when the War began, and, after delaying it to begin with, necessitated large changes in its plan and execution. Since the War ended other causes have, to the great regret of the Publishers and Editors, delayed it further, and for this long delay an apology is due to our readers. The fact that some chapters have, for these reasons, been long in type, has hampered both writers and editors and made it peculiarly difficult to make the volume uniform in scale and execution. To all our contributors, foreign and English, the Editors have been much indebted, and must here express to them most grateful thanks.

In a history which ranges over many lands but is written mainly for English readers there are, naturally and always, difficulties about names, whether of persons or places. In our special period these difficulties are unusually great. Personal names vary from land to land, and the same name appears in different forms: chroniclers and modern writers are a law to themselves, even if any law is to be found. Uniformity has been sought, but it is too much to hope that it has been reached. Certain rules have been followed so far as possible. Modern forms have been generally used where they exist, and earlier forms have been indicated. Names which are etymologically the same take different forms in Germany, France, Burgundy, Italy, and Slavonic lands. It has been thought proper in such cases to keep the local form, except for names which have a common English form. Thus the French Raoul is conveniently distinguished from the German Rudolf and the Jurane-Burgundian Rodolph. Familiar English names of continental towns are used where they are to be found in other cases the correct national and official names are used. Geographical names have special difficulties in this period, where boundaries and territories largely varied and were in course of growth. Accuracy, and, where needed, explanation, have been attempted.

Dr J. R. Tanner and Mr C. W Previté-Orton have been appointed Editors for Volume iv onwards. To them many thanks are due for services readily and plentifully given in this volume, although with no editorial responsibility. To Mr Previté-Orton especially it owes much, indeed almost everything. Without the care and skill brought by him to its aid, errors and omissions would have been much more numerous. Any merits which the work possesses should be ascribed largely to him, although defects must still remain. Professor J. B. Bury has always been ready to give us valuable suggestions and criticisms, although he also is in no way responsible for the work. In the Bibliographies Miss A. D. Greenwood, who has also prepared the Maps, has given the greatest help. And it should be said that the Maps had been printed before the long period of delay began. For the Index thanks are due to Mrs A. Hingston Quiggin and Mr T. F. T. Plucknett.

To some of our contributors special thanks are due for special kindness. Professor L. Halphen has been throughout a most courteous friend, and laid us under many obligations. Mr Austin L. Poole has been peculiarly ready to help us at need, and his father, Dr R. L. Poole, has often given us advice, naturally of the greatest value. Prof. A. A. Bevan and Dr E. H. Minns have given us expert guidance as to the proper forms of Oriental and Slavonic names. Many other historians, apart from the contributors, to whom we owe so much, have been of great service in various ways. And it is needless to say that to the staff of the University Press, working under peculiar difficulties caused by the war, we owe much for constant and unfailing help.

A general historical sketch has been added as an Introduction. It is in no way meant, however, as an outline of the history or as a summary of the particular chapters, but only as a general view of the period in its special characteristics and in relation to the ages which follow. It will also be seen that notes, short and significant, have been added as before where necessary: they are possibly more numerous than in preceding volumes, and two or three genealogical tables have also been given.

J. P. W.

July, 1921.

INTRODUCTION.

THE volume before this brought us to the death of Charlemagne, with whom in many senses a new age began. He, like no one either before or after, summed up the imperishable memories of Roman rule and the new force of the new races which were soon to form states of their own. Although we are compelled to divide history into periods, in the truest sense history never begins, just as it never ends. The Frankish Kingdom, like the Carolingian Empire, is a testimony of this truth. It cannot be rightly understood without a knowledge of the Roman past, with its law, its unity, its civilisation, and its religion. But neither can it be understood without a knowledge of the new conceptions and the new elements of a new society, which the barbarian invaders of the Roman West had brought with them. It was upon the many-sided foundation of the Carolingian Empire that the new world of Europe was now to grow up. Yet even in that new world we are continually confronted with the massive relics and undying traces of the old. The statesman and warrior Charles, the great English scholar Alcuin, typify some parts of that great inheritance. But how much the Empire owed to the personal force and character of Charlemagne himself was soon to be seen under his weaker successors, even if their weakness has often been exaggerated. Such is one side of the story with which this volume begins.

We of to-day, perhaps, are too much inclined to forget the moulding force of institutions, of kingship, of law, of traditions of learning, and of ideas handed down from the past. When we see the work of Charlemagne seeming to crumble away as his strong hand fell powerless in death, we are too apt to look only at the lawlessness, the confusion, and the strife left behind. In face of such a picture it is needful to seek out the great centres of unity, which were still left, and around which the forms of politics and society were to crystallise slowly. Imperial traditions, exemplified, for instance, in the legal forms of diplomas, and finding expression as much in personal loyalty to rulers of Carolingian descent as in political institutions, gave one such centre. The Christian Church, with its civilising force, had even a local centre in Rome, to which St Boniface, the Apostle of Germany, had looked for guidance and control. Other ancient cities, too, in which Roman civilisation and

Christianity had remained, shaken but still strong, did much to keep up that continuity with the past upon which the life of the future depended. But beneath the general unity of its belief and its organisation, the Church was always in close touch with local life, and therefore had its local differences between place and place. It had still much to do in the more settled territories which were growing up into France, Germany and England. On the borders of the Empire it had further fresh ground to break and new races to mould. Even within the Empire it was before long to receive new invaders to educate and train : Normans and Danes were to bear witness, before our period ends, to the spirit and the strength in which it wrought. As is always the case when two powers are attempting the same task in different ways and by different means, there was inevitable rivalry and strife between Empire and Church as they grew together within one common society. But such generalisations give, after all, an imperfect picture. Beneath them the details of ecclesiastical life, in Papacy, diocese, parish and monastery, are also part of the common history, and have received the notice which they can therefore claim.

But if political history and ecclesiastical history present us with two centres of unity in a tangled field, thought, literature, and art were no less distinctly, though in other ways, guardians of unity and fosterers of future life. They too brought down from the past seeds for the new world to tend. So their story also, with its records of inheritance, plainer to read, especially in its Byzantine influences, than those of politics or ecclesiastical matters, is an essential part of our task. Politics, Religion, and Thought in all its many-sided fields, summed up for the future Western world all the remnants of the past which were most essential and fruitful for generations to come. They were the three great forces that made for unity and, with unity, for civilisation.

Taking all this for granted, then, we pass to the separate history of the individual countries just growing into states. For a time, they grow within the common mould of the Empire, and Carolingian traditions bind them to the past. Dimly to begin with, but with growing plainness, the realms of France, Germany, Italy, Lorraine, and Burgundy are seen taking their later territorial and constitutional shapes. England lay somewhat apart, insular, and therefore separated from the Empire, but by this very insularity everywhere exposed to Northmen and Danes. Here, too, as on the continent, statesman-like kings and far-sighted ecclesiastics worked together. The growth of territorial unity is easiest of all to trace, for it can be made plain in maps. But the growth of unity of thought and interests, of constitutions and social forms, is harder to see and to express;

it is easier to estimate the work of Ecgbert, Edward the Elder, and Aethelstan than the more many-sided achievements of Alfred and Dunstan, or the more pervasive influence of the great Northern school which gave us Bede and Alcuin. But the peculiarity of England's position and history is most significant for constitutional growths, and it is, therefore, in connexion with English affairs that the origins of Feudalism are best investigated and discussed. Scientific history begins with the observation of resemblances and with classification by likeness. Then it passes on to detect differences, and to note their significance. Nowhere is there more need to remember these twin methods than in the study of Feudalism, where the Cambridge scholar Maitland was our daring and yet cautious guide. Processes and details which we notice in English history have their parallels elsewhere. If the centuries we traverse here have a large common inheritance, they also have at the same time, in spite of differences in place and character, something of a common history. What is said, therefore, as to the origins of English Feudalism also applies, with due allowance for great local differences, to Germany, France, and Italy ; even indeed to Spain, although there the presence and the conquests of the Muslims impressed a peculiar stamp upon its institutions.

The period with which we have to deal is more than most periods what is sometimes called transitional ; but this only means that it is more difficult than other periods to treat by itself. History is always changing and transitional, but keeps its own continuity even when we find it hard to discern. Breaches of continuity are rare, although in this period we have two of them : one, the establishment of the Moors in Spain, and the other, more widely diffused and less restricted locally, the inroads of the Northmen ending in the establishment of the Normans, whose conquest of England, as the beginning of a new era, is kept for a later volume. In many other periods some histories of states or institutions cease to be significant or else come to an end. Of this particular age we can say that it is specially and peculiarly one of beginnings, one in which older institutions and older forms of thought are gradually passing into later stages, which sometimes seem to be altogether new. The true significance, therefore, of the age can only be seen when we look ahead, and bear in mind the outlines of what in coming volumes must be traced in detail. This is specially true of the Feudalism which was everywhere gradually growing up, and, therefore, to understand its growth it is well to look ahead and picture for ourselves the system which forms the background for later history, although even here it is in process of growth and its economic and military causes are at work.

The dissolution of the Carolingian Empire ends its first stage with the Treaty of Verdun, following the Oath of Strasbourg. The oath is in itself a monument of the division between Romance and Teutonic languages, a linguistic difference which soon joined itself to other differences of race and circumstance. At Verdun Louis the German took most of the imperial lands in which a Teutonic tongue was spoken: Charles took mainly lands in which Romance prevailed. This difference was to grow, to become more acute and to pass into rivalry as years went by, and the rivalry was to make the old Austrasia into a debateable land; so that, for the later France and Germany, the year 843 may be taken as a convenient beginning in historic record of their separate national lives. Henceforth we have to follow separate histories, although the process of definite separation is gradual and slow.

At Tribur in 887 rebels deposed Charles the Fat, and next year the Eastern Kingdom proclaimed Arnulf; when his son Louis the Child died in 911, election and recognition by Frankish, Saxon, Alemannian (or Swabian), and Bavarian leaders made Conrad the first of German kings. In this process, unity, expressed by kingship, and disunion, expressed by the great tribal duchies which shared in later elections, were combined. And through many reigns, certainly throughout our period, the existence of these tribal duchies is the pivot upon which German history turns. To the king his subjects looked for defence against outside enemies: the Empire had accepted this task, and Charlemagne had well achieved it. But his weaker successors had neglected it, and as they made default, local rulers, and in Germany, the tribal dukes, above all, took the vacant place. But the appearance on all hands of local rulers, which is so often taken as a mere sign of disunion, as a mere process of decay, is, beneath this superficial appearance, a sign of local life, a drawing together of scattered elements of strength, under the pressure of local needs, and, above all, for local defence. If on a wider field of disorder the appearance of great kings and emperors made for strength and happiness, precisely the same was afterwards the case in the smaller fields. Here too the emergence of local dynasties also made for strength and happiness. Local rulers, then, to begin with, accepted the leadership in common local life. And they did so somewhat in the spirit with which Gregory the Great, deserted by Imperial rulers, had in his day boldly taken upon himself the care and defence of Rome against barbarians. So for Germany, as for France, the national history is concerned as much with the story of the smaller dynasties as with that of the central government.

But a distinction is to be noted between the course of this mingled central and local history in Germany and France. In France the growth of local order was older than it was in Germany; towns with Roman traditions were more abundant and life generally was more settled. In Germany a greater burden was, therefore, thrown upon the kings and, as was so generally the case with men in those days, they rose to their responsibilities. Accordingly the kingship grew in strength, and Otto the First was so firmly seated at home as to be able to intervene with success abroad. His Marches, as later history was to shew, served adequately their purpose of defence, and German suzerainty over the neighbouring lands became more real. The basis of his power was Saxony, less feudalised than the other duchies and peopled mainly by freemen well able to fight for their ruler. Otto understood, moreover, how necessary for strength and order was close fellowship in work between State and Church. Throughout his land the Bishops, alike by duty and tradition, were apostles of civilisation, and, on the outskirts of the kingdom above all, the spread of Christianity meant the growth of German influence, much as it had done under Charlemagne himself. To the Bishops, already overburdened with their spiritual charge, were now entrusted administrative duties. In England individual Bishops were counsellors of the king: in France Bishops, although later to be controlled by neighbouring nobles, had been a more coherent body than elsewhere, and the legislative authority of synods had been so great that the Episcopate had even striven to become the leading power in the realm. But it was characteristic of Germany to make the Bishops, with large territories and richly endowed, a part, and a great part, of the administration in its local control, working for the Crown and trusted by it, but with the independent power of Counts or even more: thus there grew up in Germany the great Prince-Bishoprics, as marked a feature of the political life as the tribal Duchies but destined to endure still longer. And furthermore, because of this close alliance between German Crown and German Episcopate, the later struggle between Church and King, which arose out of forces already at work, was to shake with deeper movement the edifice of royal power. Because of this special feature of German polity, the eleventh century strife between Pope and German King meant more for Germany than it did for other lands. And this was something quite apart from the revival of the Western Roman Empire.

Otto's political revival, with its lasting influence on history, was in the first place a bringing to life again of the Carolingian Empire. Like the earlier Empire it arose out of the needs of the Church at Rome: Otto the Great, like Charlemagne and his forerunners, had come into Italy, and Rome with the Papacy was the centre, indeed the storm-point, of Italian politics and strife. But Otto, unlike Charlemagne, was more a protector than a ruler of the Church, and here too, as on the political side of the

Empire, he set out from a distinctively German rather than from a general standpoint. His first care was rather with the German Church, needed as an ally for his internal government, than with the Papacy representing a general conception of wide importance. The new series of Emperors are concerned with the Papacy more as it affected Germany and Italy than under its aspect of a world-wide power built on a compact theory. The future history of the Empire in its relations to the Papacy turns, then, mainly upon the fortunes of the Church first in Germany and then in Italy: conflict arises, when it does arise, out of actual working conditions and not out of large conceptions and controversies. This is certainly true of our present period and of the Imperial system under Otto. Upon the Papal side things were very different. From it large statements and claims came forth: Nicholas I presented to the world a compact and far-reaching doctrine which only needed to be brought into action in later days; although, as a matter of fact, even with the Papacy, actual jurisdiction preceded theory. Ecclesiastics were naturally, more than laymen, concerned with principles (embodied in the Canon Law), of which they were the special guardians, and they remained so until Roman Law regained in later centuries its old preeminence as a great system based on thought and embodied in practice. Its triumph was to be under Frederick Barbarossa and not under Otto the Great, although its study, quickened through practical difficulties, began both in France and Lombardy during the eleventh century. To begin with, churchmen led in the realm of thought, and, when clash and controversy came, were first in the field. Laymen, from kings to officials, were, on the other hand, slowly forging, under pressure of actual need, a system that was strong, coherent, and destined to grow because it was framed in practice more than in thought. But for the moment we are concerned with the Empire and not with the Feudal system, to which we shall return.

The exact extent of St Augustine's influence upon medieval thought has been much discussed: to write of it here would be to anticipate what must be said later on. But it came to reinforce, if not to suggest, the medieval view of society, already held, though not expressed in the detail of Aquinas or Dante. Life has fewer contradictions than has thought, and in the work of daily life men reconcile oppositions which, if merely thought over, might seem insuperable. To the man of practice in those days, as to the student of St Augustine's *City of God*, Christian society was one great whole, within which there were many needs, many ends to reach, and many varied things to do. But the society itself was one, and Pope or Monarch, churchman or layman, had to meet its needs and do its work as best he could. This was something quite unlike the modern theories of Church and State, and it is only by remembering this medieval conception, which the late Dr Figgis so well expounded to us, that the course of medieval history can be rightly understood. Under such a conception, with a scheme arrived at by life rather than by thought, Pope or Bishop, Abbot or Priest, did secular things with no thought of passing into an alien domain. Emperor or King, Count or Sheriff, did not hesitate to undertake, apart, of course, from sanctuary or worship, what would seem to us specially the churchman's task. Here there were possibilities of concord and fellowship in work, which the great rulers of our period, whether clerical or lay, tried to realise. But there were also possibilities of strife, to be all the sharper because it was a conflict within one society and not a clash of two.

Only the preparation for this conflict, however, falls within our scope. But this preparation is so often slurred over that its proper presentation is essential. The medieval king, like Stuart sovereigns in England, was faced by a tremendous and expensive task, and had scanty means for meeting it. The royal demesne was constantly impoverished by frequent grants: to keep up order as demanded by local needs, and to provide defence as demanded by the realm at large, called not only for administrative care but also for money which was not forthcoming. It was easy to use the machinery of the Church to help towards order: it was easy to raise something of an income and to provide for defence by laying a hand upon church revenues and by making ecclesiastical vassals furnish soldiers. Most of all, horse-soldiers were needed, although to be used with economy and care, like the artillery of later days: their utility had been learnt from the ravages of the Danes, able to cover quickly large areas because of the horses they seized and used. Kings were quick to learn the lesson; knight-service grew up, and is recorded first for ecclesiastical lands in England.

It is therefore first in the estates of the Church that the elements of feudalism are noted in the double union of jurisdiction and knight-service with ownership of lands. Thus, beginning with the equally urgent needs of the crown and of localities, the elements of the Feudal system appeared and gradually grew until they became the coherent whole of later days. But its practical formation preceded its expression in theory. Its formation brought many hardships and opened the way to many abuses. An individual often finds his greatest temptations linked closely to his special capabilities and powers, and in the same way, out of this attempt to give the world order and peace, made by able rulers who were also men of devoted piety, sprang the abuses which called forth the general movement of the eleventh century for church reform. This was partly due to a revival within the Church itself, a reform both in diocesan and monastic life, beginning in Lorraine and Burgundy, and seen significantly in the rapid Western growth of Canon Law. But it was complicated and conditioned by politics, especially by those of Italy and Germany, imperfectly linked together by the Empire. Its history in the earlier stages is indicated in this volume, but must be discussed more fully along with the church policy of the great Emperor Henry III. Because its history under him is so closely joined to that of the wider period, reaching from the Synod of Sutri to the Concordat of Worms, it is left over for a later volume, although the purely political side of his reign is treated here.

To the German kingship, ruling the great German duchies, inevitably entangled in Italian affairs and in touch with warlike neighbours as yet heathen and uncivilised, fell the traditions of the Empire, so far as territorial sway and protectorship of the Papacy was involved. But to the growing kingdom of France there came naturally the guardianship of Carolingian civilisation. Mayence, Salzburg, Ratisbon, and Cologne to begin with, Hamburg and Bamberg at a later date, might be the great missionary sees of the West, but Rheims and the kingdom to which it belonged, together with the debateable and Austrasian land of Lorraine, inherited more distinctly the traditions of thought and learning. Paris, the cradle of later France, had a preeminence in France greater than had any city in its Eastern neighbour-land. So France with its older and more settled life from Roman and Merovingian days had, although with some drawbacks, a unity and coherence almost unique, just as it had a history more continuous. Yet even so it had its great fiefs, with their peculiarities of temperament and race, so that much of French history lies in their gradual incorporation in the kingdom of which Paris was the birthplace and the capital. And at Paris the varied story of Scholasticism, that is, of medieval thought, may be said to begin.

Thus the lines upon which later histories were to run were already being laid for France, Germany, and England, and for Italy something the same may be said. There to the mixture of races and rule, already great, was added now the Norman element, to be at first a further cause of discord, and then, as in France and England, a centre of stability and strength. The grasp of the Byzantine Emperors on Italy was becoming nominal and weak: the Lombards, with scanty aspirations after unity, were by this time settled. In Sicily, and for a time in the South, Saracens had made a home for themselves, and, as in Spain, were causing locally the terror which, in a form vaster and more undefined, was to form, later on, a dark background for the history of Europe as a whole. Rome, for all the West outside Italy a place of reverence and the seat of Papal jurisdiction, sinking lower but never powerless, was itself the playground of city factions and lawless nobles revelling in old traditions of civic pride. But above all the distinction between Northern and Southern Italy was becoming more pronounced. In the North, still subject to the Emperor, growing feudalism ran, although with local variations, a normal but short-lived course. The South, on the other hand, had drawn off into a separate system of small principalities, where inchoate feudalism was to be suddenly developed and made singularly durable by the Normans. But in the North and, as yet, in the South thickly strewn cities were the ruling factor in political life and social progress. For Italy, as for the other great lands, the period was one of beginnings, of formations as yet incomplete. Events on the surface were making national unity hopeless: forces beneath the surface were slowly producing the civic independence which was to be the special glory of later medieval Italy.

The fortunes of the Papacy in these centuries were strangely variable. It is a vast descent from Nicholas I (858–867), who could speak as if "lord of all the earth," to Formosus (891–896), dug up from his grave, sentenced by a synod, and flung into the Tiber. But the repeated recoveries of the Papacy would be hard to explain if we did not recall its advantages in the traditions of administration, and in the handling of large affairs in a temper mellowed by experience. Roman synods, as a rule, acted with discretion, and long traditions, both administrative and diplomatic, enhanced the influence of the Western Apostolic See; Gregory VII could rightly speak of the *gravitas Romana*. The Empire of Charlemagne opened up new channels for its power, and the weakness of his successors gave it much opportunity.

On the side of learning, as on that of Imperial rule, Rome had, however, ceased to be the capital. Not even the singular learning of Gerbert, furthered by his experiences in many lands, could do more for Rome than create a memory for future guidance. Before Gerbert's accession, however, the Papacy had undergone one almost prophetic change, which looked forward to Leo IX, while recalling Nicholas I. For a time under Gregory V (996–999), cousin and chaplain to the Emperor, the first German Pope, it had ceased to be purely Roman, in interests as in ruler. It took up once again its old missionary enterprise and care for distant lands. St Adalbert of Prague, who both as missionary and bishop typified the unrest of his day, wavering between adventurous activity and monastic meditation, had come to Rome and was spending some time in a monastery. He was a Bohemian by birth and had become the second bishop of Prague (983): besides working there he had taken part in the conversion of Hungary, and is said to have baptized its great king

St Stephen.   Commands from the Pope and Willigis of Mayence sent him back to his see, but renewed wanderings brought him a martyr's death in Prussia.   He had also visited Poland and there, at Gnesen, he was buried. Such a career reminds us of St Boniface, but there is a distinction between the two to be noted.   Boniface had always worked with the Frankish rulers, and had depended greatly upon their help.   Adalbert, on the other hand, looked far more to Rome.   Pope, German rulers, and even German bishops like Pilgrim of Passau, had independent or even contradictory plans of large organisation.   In Bohemia, Hungary, and Poland, the tenth century saw the beginning of national churches, looking to the Papacy rather than to German kings.   Thus were brought about later complications in politics, Imperial and national, which were to be important both for general history and for the growth of Papal power. But although Gregory was thus able to leave his mark on distant lands, and to legislate for the churches of Germany and France, he could not maintain himself in Rome itself: he was driven from the city (996), faced by an anti-Pope John XVI (who has caused confusion in the Papal lists), and was only restored by the Emperor for one short year of life and rule before Gerbert succeeded him.   The strength of the Papacy lay in its great traditions and its distant control: its weakness came from factions at Rome.

Gerbert, born in Auvergne, a monk at Aurillac, a scholar in Spain, at Rheims added philosophy to his great skill in mathematics.   As Abbot of Bobbio he had unhappy experiences.   For a time, through the favour of Hugh Capet, he held the Archbishopric of Rheims, where he learnt the strong local feeling of the French episcopate, in which his great predecessor Hincmar had shared.   Otto the Great admired his abilities: Otto II sent him to Bobbio: Otto III, his devoted pupil, made him Archbishop of Ravenna (998) and, a year later, Pope.   Moulded in many lands, illustrating uniquely the unity of Western Christendom, the foremost thinker of the day, yet on the Papacy he left no mark answering to his great personality.

Not even insignificant Popes and civic strife lessened Papal power as might have been supposed.   Benedict VIII (1012–1024) came to the throne after a struggle with the Crescentii: his father, Count Gregory, of the Tusculan family, had been *praefectus navalis* under Otto III, and had done much for the fortification of the city against the Saracens who had once so greatly harassed John VIII (872–882).   Benedict himself was dependent upon the Emperor for help against Byzantines, Saracens and factions in Rome itself.   He could not be called a Pope of spiritual influence, but he was an astute politician, and under him the

Papacy not only exercised without question its official power but also moved a little in the direction of church reform. As a ruler with activity and energy in days of darkness and degradation, he regained for the Papacy something of the old international position.

This administrative tradition in papal Rome is often hidden beneath the personal energy of the greater Popes and the growing strength gradually gained by the conception of the Papacy as a whole. Already we can see the effect of the union with the Empire, and of the entanglement with political, and especially with Imperial, interests, upon which so much of later history was to turn. Already we can see the growing influence of Canon Law, beginning, it must be remembered, in outlying fields, and then slowly centring in Rome itself. The letters of Hincmar, for instance, shew great knowledge of the older law, a constant reference to it and a grasp of its principles. The rapid spread of the False Decretals, in themselves an expression of existing tendencies rather than an impulse producing them, shew us the system in process of growth. Their rapid circulation would have been impossible had they not fitted in with the needs and aspirations of the age. They embodied the idea of the Church's independence, and indeed of its moral sovereignty, two conceptions which, when the ecclesiastical and civil powers worked in alliance, helped to mould the Christian West into a coherent society, firmly settled in its older seats and also conquering newer lands. But when in a later day the two powers came to clash, the same conceptions made the strife more acute and carried it from the sphere of action into the region of political literature.

One significant feature of this age of preparation demands special notice. St Boniface, when he laid the foundation of Church organisation in the Teutonic lands, had built up a coherent and united Episcopate. Joined to older elements of ecclesiastical life, it became, under the weaker Carolingians, strong enough to attempt control of the crown itself. Before the Papacy could establish its own dominion, it had to subjugate the Bishops: before it could reform the Church and mould the world after its own conceptions, it had further to reform an Episcopate, which, if still powerful, had grown corrupt. Constantine had sought the alliance of the Church for the welfare of the Empire because it was strong and united, and both its strength and unity were based upon the Episcopate. The Teutonic Emperors did the same for the same reasons, and now this Episcopate had to reconcile for itself conflicting relations with Empire and Papacy. And in establishing its complete control of the Bishops the Papacy touched and shook not only the kingly power but the lower and more local parts of a complicated political system.

Those results, however, belong to a later volume. For the present we are in the period of formation, watching processes mostly beneath the surface and sometimes tending towards, if not actually in, opposition among themselves. Thus, the Imperial protection of the Church, working superficially for its strength, tended, as a secondary result, to weaken and secularise it, and therefore in the end, to produce a reaction. And, when it came, that reaction was caused as much by the inner history of the leading nations as by the central power of Rome and the Papacy itself. It was one side of the complicated processes which, in the period dealt with here, moulded the Age of Feudalism.

It is well to recall the words of Maitland about Feudalism (*Domesday Book and beyond*, pp. 223–5). " If we use the term in this wide sense, then (the barbarian conquests being given us as an unalterable fact) feudalism means civilisation, the separation of employments, the division of labour, the possibility of national defence, the possibility of art, science, literature and learned leisure ; the cathedral, the scriptorium, the library, are as truly the work of feudalism as is the baronial castle. When therefore, we speak, as we shall have to speak, of forces which make for the subjection of peasantry to seignorial justice and which substitute the manor with its villeins for the free village, we shall—so at least it seems to us—be speaking not of abnormal forces, not of retrogression, not of disease, but in the main of normal and healthy growth. Far from us indeed is the cheerful optimism which refuses to see that the process of civilisation is often a cruel process ; but the England of the eleventh century is nearer to the England of the nineteenth than is the England of the seventh, nearer by just four hundred years." And again he says: " Now, no doubt, from one point of view, namely that of universal history, we do see confusion and retrogression. Ideal possessions which have been won for mankind by the thought of Roman lawyers are lost for a long while and must be recovered painfully." And " it must be admitted that somehow or another a retrogression takes place, that the best legal ideas of the ninth and tenth centuries are not so good, so modern, as those of the third and fourth." Historians, he points out, often begin at the wrong end and start with the earlier centuries, and yet " if they began with the eleventh century and thence turned to the earlier time[1], they might come to another opinion, to the opinion that in the beginning all was very vague, and that such clearness and precision as legal thought has attained in the days of the Norman Conquest has been very gradually attained and is chiefly due to the influence which the

---

[1] Maitland here refers to the Barbarian ideas and institutions, say from the seventh century onwards.

old heathen world working through the Roman church has exercised upon the new. The process that is started when barbarism is brought into contact with civilisation is not simple."

Here the great historian is speaking mainly of legal ideas and legal history which he taught us to understand. In a wider than a legal sense, it is the same process which this volume tries to trace and sketch. The steps and details of the process are to be read in the chapter on Feudalism and in the chapters on England. But once again it is here the preparatory stages with which we deal: the full process in English history, for instance, belongs to a later volume where William the Conqueror and his Domesday Book give us firmer ground for a new starting-point. But if it is more difficult, it is as essential, to study the stages of the more elusive preparation. It is the meeting-ground of old and new: the history in which the new, with toil and effort, with discipline and suffering, grows stronger and richer as it masters the old and is mastered by it.

In these centuries, even more than in others, it is chiefly of kings, of battles and great events, or of purely technical things like legal grants or taxes, of which alone we can speak, because it is of them we are mostly told. We know but little of the general life of the multitude on its social and economic side. For that we must argue back from later conditions, checked by the scanty facts we have. Large local variations were more acute: economic differences between the great trading cities of the Rhineland and the neighbouring agricultural lands around Mayence, or again the differences between the east and west of the German realm, had greater political significance than they would have to-day. Contrasts always quicken the flow of commerce and the tide of thought: travel brought with it greater awakening then than now. Hence thought moved most quickly along the lines of trade, which were, for the most part, those of Roman rather than of later medieval days. We know something of the depopulation due to wars, and of the misery due to unchecked local tyranny, which drove men to welcome any fixity of rule and to respect any precedent even if severe and rough. The same causes made it easier for moral and religious laws to hold a stricter sway, even if they were often disregarded by passion or caprice. Under the working of all these forces a more settled life was slowly growing up, although with many drawbacks and frequent retrogressions.

Under such conditions men were little ready to question anything that made for fixity and peace. The reign of law, the control of principles, were welcome, because they gave relief from the tumultuous barbarism and violence that reigned around. The past had its legend of peace: therefore men turned to memories of Roman law and of a rule supposed to be stable: thus, too, we may explain the eager study of old ecclesiastical legislation and the ready acceptance of Papal jurisdiction, even when it was in conflict with local freedom. The future, on the other hand, seemed full of dread, so men preferred precedent to revolution. In a world abounding in contrasts and fearful of surprise, strong men trained in a hard school were able to shape their own path and to lead others with them. So dynasties, like precedents, had peculiar value. And moreover from simple fear and pressing need, men were driven closer together into towns and little villages capable of some defence. In England some towns appear first, and others grow larger, under the influence of the Danes: in France it is the time of the *villes neuves*; Italy was thickly sown with *castelli*, around which houses clustered; in Germany, Nuremberg and Weissenburg, Rothenburg on the Tauber with other towns are mentioned for the first time now: it was a period of civic growth in its beginnings. Socially too men were drawn into associations with common interests and fellowship of various kinds, beginning another great chapter of economic history. Thus in these centuries men were beginning to realise, first in tendency and afterwards in process, the power and attraction of the corporate life. This was to be, in later centuries, one great feature of medieval society. The old tie of kinship, with its resulting blood-feuds, was already weakening under the two solvents of Christianity and of more settled local seats. The attempt to combine in one society conflicting personal laws, Roman or barbarian at the choice of individuals (expressed, for instance, in the *Constitutio Romana* of Lothar in 824) was causing chaos. Hence, in our centuries, society was seeking for a more stable foundation, and out of disorder comparative order arose. Dynasties, precedents, traditions, and fellowships for protection and mutual help had already begun to shape the medieval world as we shall see it later in active work.

This general view gives significance to the constitutional and ecclesiastical side of the history, but it gives it perhaps even more to the history of education, of learning and of art. The new races brought new strength, and were to make great histories of their own. But we see in our period how nearly all that brought high interests and ideals, nearly all that made for beauty and for richness of life, came from the old, although it was grasped with new strength and slowly worked out into a many-sided life beneath the pressure of new conditions. We have moved in a time of preparation, guided by the past but nevertheless working out a great and orderly life of its own.

TABLE OF CONTENTS.

INTRODUCTION.

PAGE

By J. P. Whitney, D.D.   viii

CHAPTER I.

LOUIS THE PIOUS.

By the late René Poupardin, Professor in the *École pratique des hautes études* of Paris.

Accession of Louis the Pious   1
First measures   2
Division of territory   3
Empire and Papacy   4
Constitutio Romana   5
Neighbours of the Empire   6
    Eastern frontiers   7
    The Saracens   8
    The Bretons   .   .   .   .   *ib.*
Divisio Imperii   9
Revolt of Bernard of Italy   11
Penance of Attigny   12
Judith   13
Family disunion ; Pepin's revolt   14
Disloyalty of Lothar   15
Revolt of Louis the German   16
Provisions for Charles the Bald   17
The Field of Lies   18
Restoration of Louis the Pious   19
Submission of Lothar   20
Death of Pepin of Aquitaine   21
Death of Louis the Pious   22

CHAPTER II.

THE CAROLINGIAN KINGDOMS (840—877).

By the late Professor René Poupardin.

Accession of Lothar   23
Battle of Fontenoy   24
Oath of Strasbourg   25
Treaty of Verdun   26
The Empire breaking up   28
The System of Concord   30
Conflicts and invasions   31

	PAGE
Weakness of the Concord	32
Affairs of Aquitaine and Brittany	ib.
Death of the Emperor Lothar	34
Growing disorder in the Western Kingdom	35
Fraternal quarrels	36
The divorce of Lothar II	38
Charles the Bald and his ambitions	40
Death of Charles of Provence	41
Triumph of Pope Nicholas I	42
Death of Lothar II	44
Contest for Lorraine	45
Partition of Meersen	ib.
Reign of the Emperor Louis II in Italy	46
Italian vassals	47
The Saracens sack St Peter's	49
Pope John VIII	50
Imperial coronation of Charles the Bald	51
Death of Louis the German	ib.
Assembly of Quierzy	53
Death of Charles the Bald	54

CHAPTER III.

THE CAROLINGIAN KINGDOMS (877—918).

By the late Professor RENÉ POUPARDIN.

Louis the Stammerer King of the West-Franks	55
Boso King of Provence	57
Charles the Fat in Rome	58
The Northmen	59
Union under Charles the Fat	ib.
Siege of Paris	61
Deposition of Charles the Fat	62
Final division of the Empire	ib.
Arnulf	64
Italian rivals	ib
The Formosan troubles at Rome	66
Death of Arnulf	68
Death of Louis the Child	69
Conrad I of Germany; the great Duchies	ib.

CHAPTER IV.

FRANCE, THE LAST CAROLINGIANS AND THE ACCESSION OF HUGH CAPET (888—987).

By Louis Halphen, Professor in the University of Bordeaux.

	PAGE
Accession of Odo	71
Carolingian Restoration	73
Charles the Simple in Lorraine	74
Raoul's usurpation	75
Hugh the Great	76
Louis d'Outremer	77
Feudal rebellions	78
Death of Louis d'Outremer	79
Lothair and Otto II	80
The last Carolingian	81
Theories of kingship	ib.
Hugh Capet	82
The king defends order and liberty	85
Royal impotence against the Northmen	ib.
Royal impotence against the Hungarians	87
The provinces provide their own defence	88
Rise of the great duchies	89
The March of Spain and Gothia	90
The Duchy of Aquitaine	91
Neustria and Flanders	ib.
The Duchy of Burgundy	93
The Duchy of Normandy	94
Break-up of the duchies	95
Neustria	ib.
Burgundy	96
Disintegration	97
Influence of the bishops	ib.

CHAPTER V.

FRANCE IN THE ELEVENTH CENTURY.

By Professor Louis Halphen.

	PAGE
Accession of Hugh Capet	99
Elimination of the Carolingians	100
Struggle with the Papacy	101
Weakness of the Capetian monarchy	102
Death of Hugh Capet	103
Consolidation of the dynasty	104
Energetic policy of Robert the Pious	105

	PAGE
Crisis at the death of Robert the Pious	107
Growing independence of vassals	108
Growth of Anjou	ib.
Philip I	110
Philip and Normandy	111
Church policy of Philip	113
Philip's last years	114
Precarious position of the first Capetians	115
Moral preponderance of the monarchy	116
Feudal disintegration in Anjou	118
Feudal anarchy in Normandy	120
The great fiefs: Flanders	121
Champagne and Blois	123
Burgundy	ib.
Anjou	125
A type of the great baron	ib.
Normandy	127
Brittany	128
Aquitaine and Gascony	ib.
Languedoc	130
Moral preponderance of the higher clergy	131
Fulbert of Chartres	ib.
Ivo of Chartres	132

CHAPTER VI.

THE KINGDOM OF BURGUNDY.

By Professor Louis Halphen.

A. The Kingdom of Burgundy down to the annexation of the Kingdom of Provence.

Rodolph I	134
Rodolph II	135

B. The Kingdom of Provence down to its annexation to the Kingdom of Burgundy.

Boso of Provence	137
Louis the Blind	138
Union of Provence with Burgundy	139

C. The Kingdom of Burgundy and its annexation to the Empire.

The German Protectorate	140
The Count Otto-William	141
German intervention	142
The succession to Rodolph III	143
The rival claimants	ib.
Success of the Emperor Conrad II	145
Independence of great vassals	146
Later history	147

CHAPTER VII.

ITALY IN THE TENTH CENTURY.

By C. W. Previté-Orton, Litt.D., F.B.A., Fellow and Librarian
of St John's College.

PAGE

Hungarian victory at the Brenta	148
Berengar I and Louis III	149
South Italy and the Saracens	ib.
Victory of the Garigliano	151
Anarchy of North Italy	152
Rodolph II and Hugh of Provence	ib.
Alberic of Rome	154
Hugh's alliance with Byzantium	155
Relations with Burgundy and Germany	156
Fall of King Hugh	157
Berengar II	158
First invasion of Otto the Great	159
The chronicler Liudprand	160
Pope John XII	161
Otto's second invasion	ib.
His imperial coronation	162
Subjugation of Rome and the Papacy	163
The Romano-Germanic Empire	164
The government of Italy	165
Otto's attempt to annex South Italy	166
Significance of Otto's reign	167
Otto II's failure in South Italy	168
Growth and danger of Venice	170
Rome and Italy during Otto III's minority	ib.
Otto III reduces Rome	172
Schemes of Otto III	173
Social changes and troubles	174
Revolt of Ardoin of Ivrea	175
Revolt of the Romans	176
Death of Otto III	177
Revival and permanent division of Italy	ib.

CHAPTER VIII.

GERMANY: HENRY I AND OTTO THE GREAT.

By Austin Lane Poole, M.A., Fellow of St John's College, Oxford;
Late Lecturer at Selwyn College, Cambridge.

Election of Henry I	179
Submission of Swabia and Bavaria	180
Conquest of Lorraine	181
Hungarian invasion of Saxony	182
Defensive measures	183
Campaigns against the Wends	184

	PAGE
Defeat of the Hungarians	185
Death of Henry I	186
Coronation of Otto the Great	187
Bavarian revolt; risings in Franconia and Saxony	188
The Rebellion of the Dukes in 939	189
Changes in the administration of the Duchies	191
War on the eastern frontier	ib.
Otto's intervention in French affairs	192
Situation in Italy in 950	194
Liudolf's disaffection and rebellion	195
Hungarian invasion	198
Defeat of the Hungarians in the Lechfeld	199
Peace restored in Germany	200
Otto the Great as Emperor	201
Spread of Christianity in the North	202
Death of Otto the Great	203

CHAPTER IX.

GERMANY: OTTO II AND OTTO III.

By Austin Lane Poole, M.A.

Accession of Otto II	204
Bavarian revolts	205
The War of the Three Henries	206
Otto II and Lorraine	207
Revolt of the Slavs	208
Accession of Otto III	209
The Regency	210
War on the eastern frontier	211
Ambitions of Otto III	212
His failure and death	214

CHAPTER X.

THE EMPEROR HENRY II.

By Edwin H. Holthouse, M.A., late of Trinity College, Cambridge.

Rival candidates	215
Recognition of Henry II	217
His earlier life and character	218
Revolt of Lombardy	220
Boleslav of Poland	222
Bohemia; the Babenbergs	223
Henry's first expedition to Italy	224
Recovery of Bohemia	225
Polish hostilities	226

	PAGE
Troubles on the West	227
Loss of Lausitz	228
Crystallisation of fiefs	229
Lessening resources of the Crown	230
The Church as an instrument of order	231
The Bishops	232
Protectorship of the Church	235
Reform of monasteries	236
Foundation of the see of Bamberg	237
War with the Luxemourgers	238
Fresh war with Poland	239
Civil wars in Lombardy	240
Henry's second expedition to Italy	241
His coronation as Emperor	243
Pacification of Lombardy	246
Peace with Poland	247
Expedition to Burgundy	248
Turmoil in Lorraine	ib.
Wendish and Saxon troubles	249
Benedict VIII in Germany	250
Henry's third expedition to Italy	251
Death of Henry	252

CHAPTER XI.

THE EMPEROR CONRAD II.

By Austin Lane Poole, M.A.

Choice of Conrad II	253
His formal election and coronation	254
The royal progress	255
The Burgundian question	256
Rebellion of Duke Ernest	257
Acquisition of Burgundy	258
The Eastern Frontier	260
Italy under Conrad II	263
Imperial coronation	264
The feudal edict of 1037	266
Proceedings against Archbishop Aribert	267
Affairs of South Italy	268
Conrad's death	269
Hereditary fiefs	270
Relations with the Church	271

CHAPTER XII.

THE EMPEROR HENRY III.

By Caroline M. Ryley, Newnham College, Cambridge.

	PAGE
Henry III's parents	272
His boyhood	273
His accession	275
The royal progress	ib.
Defeat in Bohemia	277
Submission of Bohemia	278
Burgundy	279
Hungary	280
The Day of Indulgence	281
Peace and Truce of God	282
Empress Agnes of Poitou	283
Godfrey of Lorraine	284
Submission of Hungary	285
Rebellion of Godfrey of Lorraine	286
Otto of Swabia	287
Germany at peace	288
Attempt at settlement in the West	289
Adalbert of Bremen	290
Henry, Emperor and Patrician	291
Germany and France	292
Fresh troubles in Lorraine	294
Birth of Henry IV	295
Hungary; Bavaria	296
Bremen and the North	ib.
Death of Leo IX	298
End of the reign	299
Břatislav of Bohemia	ib.
Casimir of Poland	302
Kings of Hungary	303
The Wends	304
Duke Godescalc	305
Henry's aims	306

CHAPTER XIII.

THE VIKINGS.

By Allen Mawer, Litt.D., F.B.A., Provost of University College in the University of London; late Fellow of Gonville and Caius College.

	PAGE
Early Scandinavia	309
Causes of Viking activity	310
Early raids on England and Ireland	311
The Danish kingdom	312
Preaching of Christianity	313
St Anskar	314
Viking raids on Frankish territory	315
Olaf the White	317

	PAGE
Ragnarr Loðbrók	318
Settlement of the Danelaw	ib.
The Vikings in France, Spain, Italy and England	319
The Siege of Paris	321
Founding of Normandy	322
Scandinavian kings in Northumbria	323
The Battles of Clontarf and Maldon	324
King Svein and King Knut	325
The Orkneys, Shetlands, Western Islands, and Man . . .	ib.
The Jómsvikings	326
The Swedes in Russia	327
Viking civilisation	328
Christianity and heathendom	329
Ideals of life and material civilisation	330
Ships	332
Trade and Social organisation	ib.
Influence in Ireland	334
Influence in Scotland, Man, and the Isles	ib.
Influence in Northumbria and the Five Boroughs . . .	336
Influence in East Anglia	337
Law and Society	ib.
The Northmen in Europe generally	338

CHAPTER XIV.

THE FOUNDATION OF THE KINGDOM OF ENGLAND.

By the late WILLIAM JOHN CORBETT, M.A., Fellow and Bursar of King's College, Cambridge.

Death of Offa. Beorhtric of Wessex	340
Anarchy in Northumbria. Coenwulf of Mercia . . .	341
Wales in the eighth century. Nennius	ib.
Coenwulf and Archbishop Wulfred. Beornwulf . . .	343
Ecgbert of Wessex. Conquest of Cornwall . . .	344
Battle of Ellandun. Ecgbert conquers Kent . . .	345
Ecgbert overthrows Mercia. Wiglaf restored . . .	346
Ecgbert and the Danes. Accession of Aethelwulf . . .	347
Character of the struggle with the Vikings	348
Aethelwulf's Donation. The Danes winter in England . .	349
Wales under Rhodri. Scotland under Kenneth . . .	ib.
Ingwar conquers Northumbria and East Anglia . . .	350
Halfdene attacks Wessex. Accession of Alfred . . .	352
Collapse of Mercia	353
Danes settle in Northumbria and the Five Boroughs . .	354
Guthrum renews the attack on Wessex	355
Battle of Edington. West Mercia submits to Alfred . .	356
Alfred's reforms. The Boroughs of Wessex . . .	357
Alfred's laws and literary activity	358
Alfred and Guthrum's Peace. Hasting's raids . . .	359
Death of Alfred. Edward the Elder	360
Edward attacks the Danelaw	361
Edward's reforms. Battle of Tettenhall	362
Aethelfleda, the Lady of the Mercians	363

PAGE

East Anglia and East Mercia submit to Edward 364
Edward and the Danes of Yorkshire 365
Reign of Aethelstan. Battle of Brunanburh 366
Aethelstan organises the midland shires . . . . . *ib.*
Reign of Edmund. Archbishop Oda 368
Reorganisation of the dukedoms. The shire-reeves . . . 369
Reign of Eadred. Final submission of the North . . . 370

CHAPTER XV.

ENGLAND FROM A.D. 954 TO THE DEATH OF EDWARD THE CONFESSOR.

By the late WILLIAM JOHN CORBETT, M.A.

Death of Eadred and accession of Eadwig 371
Accession of Edgar 372
Monastic Reform . . . . *ib.*
Oswald's Land Loans 375
Drift towards feudalism . . . . *ib.*
Edgar's administrative measures 376
Rise of ecclesiastical franchises 377
Reign of Edward the Martyr 378
Minority of Aethelred the Unready 379
Renewal of Scandinavian invasions 380
The Massacre of St Brice's Day 382
Svein of Denmark . . . . *ib.*
Restoration of Aethelred 384
Edmund Ironside . . . . *ib.*
Accession of Knut 386
His domestic policy . . . . *ib.*
His foreign policy 387
Harold Harefoot 389
Harthacnut . . . . *ib.*
Accession of Edward the Confessor 390
Edward's character . . . . *ib.*
Predominance of Godwin of Wessex 391
Edward's foreign advisers 392
Exile of Godwin 393
Return of Godwin 394
Flight of the foreigners . . . . *ib.*
Death of Godwin 395
War with Scotland . . . . *ib.*
Rivalry of Harold and Aelfgar 396
The succession problem 397
War with the Welsh . . . . *ib.*
Captivity of Harold 398
Northumbrian revolt. Fall of Tostig . . . . . *ib.*
Death of Edward the Confessor 399
Economic conditions under Edward . . . . . *ib.*
Contrast between East and West 400
The *Rectitudines Singularum Personarum* 401
The Tidenham evidence 404
The growth of seignorial courts; sake and soke . . . 405
St Edmund's Liberty 408

CHAPTER XVI.

THE WESTERN CALIPHATE.

By RAFAEL ALTAMIRA, Hon. LL.D., Professor Emeritus of Contemporary
Spanish History and Spanish Colonisation in the University of Madrid;
Judge of the Permanent Court of International Justice at the Hague.

	PAGE
Asturias and Navarre	409
'Abd-ar-Raḥmān I	411
The Umayyad Emirate	412
Muslim factions	414
'Abd-ar-Raḥmān II	415
Christians and Muslims	416
Mahomet I	417
Muslim civil wars	418
'Abd-ar-Raḥmān III	420
The Caliphate of Cordova	421
Rise of Castile	422
Almanzor	424
Fall of the Caliphate	427
The Christian kingdoms	428
Muslim Spain	
(1) races and classes	428
(2) administration and justice	429
(3) army and religion	431
(4) wealth and industry	432
(5) language and education	433
(6) literature and science	434
(7) books and libraries	435
(8) the Arts	436
Contact of civilisations	437
The Mozarabs	438
Government and classes in Leon and Castile	ib.
Aragon and Navarre; Catalonia	441

CHAPTER XVII.

THE CHURCH FROM CHARLEMAGNE TO SYLVESTER II.

By Professor LOUIS HALPHEN.

	PAGE
Louis the Pious and the Bishops	443
Aims of the Episcopate	445
Hincmar in the State	447
The Forged Decretals	448
Pope Nicholas I	449
Divorce of Lothar II	ib.
Photius	450
Pope, King, and Prelate	451
Decline of the Papacy	453
Ecclesiastical anarchy	455
Legend of the year 1000 A.D.	456
Cluny and reform	ib.
The *Peace of God*	457

CHAPTER XVIII.

FEUDALISM.

By the late Sir Paul Vinogradoff, Hon. LL.D., F.B.A., Corpus Professor of Jurisprudence in the University of Oxford.

PAGE

The feudal contract 458
Feudal reciprocity 460
Duties of vassals 461
Ministeriales; dominium 462
Subinfeudation; reliefs 463
The feudal nexus in politics 464
Private war and its remedies 465
Growth of franchises and immunities 466
Ecclesiastical advocates 467
Counsel and aid 468
Feudal Courts 469
Appeal of judgment 470
Feudal legislation . . . . *ib.*
The manor 472
The village community 473
Common fields 474
The demesne 475
Week work and boonwork 476
The villeins 477
Freeholders 479
Officers of the lord 481
Local administration 482
Survey of Europe 483
Precedence of England 484

CHAPTER XIX.

LEARNING AND LITERATURE TILL THE DEATH OF BEDE.

By Montague Rhodes James, Litt.D., O.M., F.B.A., Provost of Eton College, late Provost of King's College, Cambridge.

Boethius 485
Cassiodorus . . . . *ib.*
St Gregory the Great 487
Africa 488
Spain 489
Martin of Bracara . . . . *ib.*
Isidore of Seville 490
Julian of Toledo 493
St Valerius 494
Venantius Fortunatus 495

PAGE

Gregory of Tours and the decay of Latin 495
Virgilius Maro Grammaticus 497
Irish learning 501
Greek in Ireland 502
Adamnan 507
Early British learning 508
Theodore of Tarsus; Hadrian 510
Benedict Biscop . . . . *ib.*
Bede 511
Wanderings of manuscripts 512
Virgilius of Salzburg . . . . *ib.*

CHAPTER XX.

LEARNING AND LITERATURE TILL POPE SYLVESTER II.

By MONTAGUE RHODES JAMES, Litt.D., O.M., F.B.A.

Destruction of English learning 514
Paul the Deacon . . . . *ib.*
Alcuin 515
The Carolingian minuscule 517
Einhard . . . . *ib.*
Theodulf 518
Angilbert 519
Agobard; Raban Maur 520
Monastic libraries 521
Walafrid Strabo . . . . *ib.*
Classical knowledge; Spain 523
John the Scot 524
Sedulius Scottus 525
Glossaries 526
The Irish circle; mythographers 527
Anastasius the Librarian 528
Gottschalk 529
Notker; School of St Gall 530
Ekkehard; *Gesta Berengarii*; Hrotsvitha 531
Theology; *Libri Carolini* 532
Radbert and Ratramn; Hagiography 533
History 534
Geography and science 535
Gerbert (Sylvester II) . . . . *ib.*
Books in vernacular 537
Destruction of libraries 538

CHAPTER XXI.

BYZANTINE AND ROMANESQUE ARTS.

By W. R. LETHABY, sometime Professor of Design, Royal College of Art.

	PAGE
Early building	539
Domes	540
Early churches	542
St Sophia	544
Other churches of the period	546
Italian Byzantesque	548
Early art in books; mosaics and paintings	549
Roman art and its influence	551
The Barbaric element	554
The English crosses	555
Irish art	556
Beginnings of Romanesque	ib.
Sta Maria Antiqua	558
Romanesque among the Teutons	559
Architecture after Charlemagne	560
Beginnings of Gothic	564
Glass	565
Imagery and colour	566
Mosaics and painting	567

LIST OF BIBLIOGRAPHIES.

CHAPS.		PAGES
	Abbreviations	569—571
	General Bibliography for Volume III . .	572—582
I, II, III.	Louis the Pious and the Carolingian Kingdoms	583—586
IV.	France, the last Carolingians and the accession of Hugh Capet	587—588
V.	France in the eleventh century . . .	589—591
VI.	The Kingdom of Burgundy	592—593
VII.	Italy in the tenth century	594—603
VIII.	Germany: Henry I and Otto the Great . .	604—606
IX.	Germany: Otto II and Otto III . . .	607—608
X.	The Emperor Henry II	609—611
XI.	The Emperor Conrad II	612—614
XII.	The Emperor Henry III	615—617
XIII	The Vikings	618—624
XIV, XV.	England from A.D. 796 to the death of Edward the Confessor	625—630
XVI.	The Western Caliphate	631—635
XVII.	The Church from Charlemagne to Sylvester II	636—638
XVIII.	Feudalism	639—641
XIX, XX.	Learning and Literature	642—643
XXI.	Byzantine and Romanesque Arts . . .	644—645
	CHRONOLOGICAL TABLE OF LEADING EVENTS . . .	646—650
	INDEX	651—700

LIST OF MAPS

VOLUME III

28 a. The Western Empire 843.

28 b. The Western Empire 870.

29. France in 987.

30. North-Western France in the eleventh century.
   Inset: Environs of Paris.

31. Burgundy at the beginning of the eleventh century.

32. Italy at close of the tenth century.
   Inset: Rome, approximate plan before A.D. 1084.

33. Germany in the tenth and eleventh centuries.

34. Eastern neighbours of Germany in the eleventh century.

35. The Vikings.
   Inset: Ireland.

36. England circa A.D. 900.

37. Spain to illustrate the era of the Umayyads.
   Inset: Spain at the death of Alfonso I.

CHAPTER I.

LOUIS THE PIOUS.

It was at his winter home at Doué, early in February 814, that Louis of Aquitaine received the news of his father's death, which had been immediately sent to him by his sisters and the magnates who had espoused his cause. It is a difficult matter to discern through the self-interested encomiums of biographers and the calumnies set afloat by political opponents, the real character of the man who had now taken over the burdensome heritage left by the Emperor Charles. Louis, who was at this time thirty-six years old, was, in form and manners, a tall, handsome man, broad-shouldered, with a strong voice, skilled in bodily exercises, fond, as his ancestors were, of the chase, but less easily led away by the seductions of passion and good cheer. With regard to his mental qualities, he was a learned man, well acquainted with Latin, and able even to compose verses in that language, having some knowledge of Greek, and in particular, well versed in moral theology. He was modest and unassuming, of a usually gentle temper, and he constantly shewed himself capable of generosity and compassion even towards his enemies. His piety, to which he owes the surname by which history has known him from his own century to ours, appears to have been deep and genuine. It was shewn not only by his zealous observance of fast and festival and his prayerful habits, but by his sustained interest in the affairs of the Church. During the time he spent in Aquitaine the reform of the Septimanian monasteries by Benedict of Aniane had engaged a large share of his attention. Throughout his reign his capitularies are filled with measures dealing with the churches and monasteries. It must not be forgotten, however, that in that age Church and State were so closely connected that provisions of this description were absolutely necessary to good administration, and that it would thus be a mistake to look upon Louis as a mere "crowned monk." A king in Aquitaine from 781, and associated in the Empire in 813, he had become accustomed to the prospect of his eventual succession. Though the news of Charles's death took him by surprise, the new sovereign seems promptly to have made such arrangements as the circumstances required, for after having shewn all the signs of the deepest grief and ordered fitting prayer to be made for the repose of the soul of the dead, he set out on his journey for Aix-la-Chapelle in company with his wife and children and the chief lords of his party. He was doubtless uneasy as to what measures were being taken there by his father's former ministers, among them Wala, the grandson of Charles Martel, who had wielded so great an influence at the late Emperor's court. Such fears, however, were groundless, for hardly had Louis reached the banks of the Loire before the lords of Francia, hastening to meet him and take the oath of fealty to him, gave him an enthusiastic welcome. The famous Theodulf, Bishop of Orleans, having received timely notice, had even found leisure to compose certain poems for the occasion, hailing the dawn of the new reign. Wala himself came to meet his cousin at Herstall, before the Emperor, who was going by Paris in order to visit the celebrated sanctuaries of Saint-Denis and Saint-Germain-des-Prés, had entered Francia. Most of the magnates hastened to follow his example.

At Herstall the new Emperor made some stay. There was at the palace of Aix a clique of the discontented who relied, perhaps, on the support of Charles's daughters, and whose chief offence in the eyes of Louis seems to have been their disposition to pursue the dissolute way of life which had been customary at the court of the late Emperor. Wala, Lambert, Count of Nantes, and Count Garnier were sent on in advance to secure order in the palace and to seize upon any from whom resistance was to be feared. They were obliged to use force in carrying out their mission, and some lives were lost. After Louis, on 27 February, had made his solemn entry into Aix-la-Chapelle amidst the shouts of the people, and had taken over the government, he continued the same course, taking measures to put an end to the scandals, real or alleged, which for the last few years had dishonoured the court. His sisters, whose lapses from virtue, however, dated many years back, were the first to be assailed. After dividing among them the property due to them under Charles's will, he sent them into banishment at various convents. Nothing is known of the fate of Gisela and Bertha, but Theodrada was obliged to retire to her abbey of Argenteuil, and Rothaid to Faremoutier. The Jewish and Christian merchants also, who were found established in the palace, were summoned to depart from it, as well as the superfluous women not required for the service of the court. At the same time Louis kept with him his illegitimate brothers, Hugh, Drogo and Theodoric. But the arrangements made in the name of good morals were followed up at once by measures directed against the descendants of Charles Martel. In spite of the loyalty just shewn by Wala, his brother Adalard, Abbot of Corbie, was exiled to the island of Noirmoutier, while another brother, Bernier, was confined at Lérins, and their sister, Gundrada, at St Radegund of Poitiers. Wala himself, fearing a like fate, chose to retire to Corbie.

Apparently it was also a zeal for reform which inspired Louis at the first general *placitum* held at Aix in August 814 to decide on sending out to all parts of the kingdom *missi* charged with the duty of making inquiry into " the slightest actions of the counts and judges and even of the *missi* previously despatched from the palace, in order to reform what they found to have been unjustly done, and bring it into conformity with justice, to restore their patrimony to the oppressed, and freedom to those who had been unjustly reduced to servitude." It was a like anxiety which impelled him next year for the protection of the native inhabitants of the Spanish March, molested as they were by the Frankish Counts, to take those measures which are to be found among the provisions of certain of his capitularies.

At this *placitum* of Aix appeared the young king of Italy, Bernard, who came to make oath of fealty to his uncle. The Emperor received him kindly, bestowed rich gifts on him, and sent him back to Italy, having confirmed him in his title of king while reserving to himself the imperial sovereignty, as is shewn by the fact that even in Italy all legislative acts emanate exclusively from the Emperor. He it is also who, during Bernard's life, grants the confirmation of the privileges of the great Italian abbeys. At the same time Louis assigned as kingdoms to his two elder sons with much the same terms of dependence on himself two portions of the Frankish Empire which still retained a certain degree of autonomy, Bavaria to Lothar and Aquitaine to Pepin. Both were, however, too young to exercise real power. Louis therefore placed about each of them Frankish officials entrusted with the duty of governing the country in their names. As to the Emperor's latest-born son, Louis, he was too young to be put in even nominal charge of a kingdom so that he remained under his father's care.

In spite, however, of the " cleansing " of the imperial palace, Louis retained around him a certain number of his father's old servants and advisers, such as Adalard the Count Palatine, and Hildebold, Archbishop of Cologne. Some also who had been among his most faithful counsellors in Aquitaine followed him to Francia. Bego, the husband of his daughter Alpaïs, one of the companions of his youth, seems to have become Count of Paris. Louis also retained as Chancellor Elisachar, the chief of his Aquitanian clerks, a learned man and a patron of letters, to whom perhaps may be owing the remarkable improvement traceable at this time in the drawing up of the imperial diplomas. But the man who seems to have played the chief part during the early years of the reign was the Goth Witiza, St Benedict of Aniane, the reformer of the Aquitanian monasteries. The Emperor had lost no time in summoning him to his side at Aix, and a large number of the diplomas issued at this time from the imperial chancery were granted at his request. Benedict had at first been installed as Abbot at Maursmünster in Alsace, but the Emperor, evidently feeling that he was still too far away, had hastened to build the monastery of Inden in the woods around Aix-la-Chapelle and to set him at its head.

It was, no doubt, to the influence of the Abbot of Inden that the measures were due which were taken a few years later (817) to establish one uniform rule, that of St Benedict of Nursia, in all monasteries throughout the Frankish Empire. Other regulations were to be applied to the canons of cathedral churches, in order to complete the work formerly begun by St Chrodegang; and in a long capitulary, *de rebus ecclesiasticis*, the rights and duties of bishops and clerks were defined with the special object of preserving them from the secularisation of their property which had too often befallen them at the hands of the lay power, since the days of Charles Martel.

The Emperor's care for the interests of the Church, and the importance he attached to its good administration, were in harmony both with the traditions set up by Charles and also with the universal conception of an empire in which the civil and ecclesiastical powers were intimately connected, although the imperial authority could not be said to be subjected to that of the Church. As early as the first year of his reign, Louis had had occasion to shew that he intended in this matter to maintain his rights inviolate even against the Pope himself. A conspiracy among the Roman nobility against Leo III had been discovered and punished by that Pope. The culprits had been put to death without consulting the Emperor or his representative. Louis, conceiving that his rights had been infringed by these indications of independence, directed Bernard of Italy and Gerold, Count of the Eastern March, to hold an inquiry into the affair. Two envoys from the Holy See were obliged to accompany them to the Emperor bearing the excuses and explanations of the Pope (815). In the same year a revolt of the inhabitants of the Campagna against the papal authority was by order of Bernard suppressed by Winichis, the Duke of Spoleto. Leo III died on 12 June 816 and the Romans chose as his successor in the Chair of Peter Stephen IV, a man of noble family who seems to have been as much devoted to the Frankish monarchy as his predecessor had been hostile to it. His first care was to exact from the Romans an oath of fealty to the Emperor. At the same time he sent an embassy to Louis with orders to announce the election to him, but also to request an interview at a place suited to the Emperor's convenience. Louis gladly consented and sent an invitation to Stephen to come to meet him in France escorted by Bernard of Italy. It was at Rheims, where Charlemagne had formerly had a meeting with Leo III, that the Emperor awaited the Sovereign Pontiff. When Stephen drew near, Louis went a mile out of the city to meet him, in his robes of state, helped him to dismount from his horse, and led him in great pomp as far as the Abbey of Saint-Remi a little beyond the city. On the morrow he gave him a solemn reception in Rheims itself, and after several days spent in conferring about the interests of the Church, the ceremony of the imperial coronation took place in the cathedral of Notre-Dame. The Pope significantly set on Louis's head a diadem which he had brought with him from Rome and anointed him with the holy oil. The Empress Ermengarde was also crowned and anointed, and a few days later Stephen, accompanied by the imperial *missi*, again turned towards Rome, perhaps bearing with him the diplomas by which Louis confirmed the Roman Church in its privileges and possessions. Thus once more a seal was set upon the alliance between the Papacy and the Empire. At the same time, the subsequent relations of Louis the Pious with the Holy See shew the Emperor's constant anxiety for the observance of the twofold principle that the Emperor is the protector of the Pope, but that in return for his protection he has the right to exercise his sovereign authority throughout Italy, even in Rome itself, and, in particular, to give his assent to the election of a new pontiff. On the death of Stephen IV (24 January 817) Paschal I hastened to inform Louis of his election and to renew with him the agreement arrived at with his predecessors. The sending of Lothar to Italy as king with the special mission of governing the country, and his coronation in 823 at the hands of Paschal I, were a further guarantee of the imperial authority. Hence, no doubt, arose a certain discontent among the Roman nobles and even among the Pope's *entourage* which shewed itself in the execution of the *primicerius* Theodore and his son-in-law, the *nomenclator* Leo, who were first blinded and then beheaded in the Lateran palace, as guilty of having shewn themselves in all things too faithful to the party of the young Emperor Lothar. Paschal was accused of having allowed or even ordered this double execution, and two *missi* were sent to Rome to hold an inquiry into the matter, an inquest which, however, led to no result, for the Pope sent ambassadors of his own to Louis, with instructions to clear their master by oath from the accusations levelled against him.

On the death of Paschal I (824), as soon as the election of his successor, Eugenius II, had been announced to Louis, then at Compiègne, he sent Lothar to Italy to settle with the new Pope measures securing the right exercise of the imperial jurisdiction in the papal state. This mission of Lothar's led to the promulgation of the *Constitutio Romana* of 824, intended to safeguard the rights " of all living under the protection of the Emperor and the Pope." *Missi* sent by both authorities were to superintend the administration of true justice. The Roman judges were to continue their functions, but were to be subject to imperial control. The Roman people were given leave to choose under what law they would live, but were required to take an oath of fealty to the Emperor. The measures thus taken and the settlement agreed upon were confirmed in writing by the Pope, who pledged himself to observe them. On his death, and after the brief pontificate of Valentine,

Gregory IV was not, in fact, consecrated until the Emperor had signified his approval of the election.

Outside his own dominions, if Louis appears to have made no attempt to extend his power beyond the limits fixed by Charlemagne, he did at least exert himself to maintain his supremacy over the semi-vassal nations dwelling on all the frontiers of the Empire. For the most part, however, these races seem to have sought to preserve good relations with their powerful neighbour. The respect which, for the first few years of the reign, they entertained for the successor of Charlemagne is proved by the presence at all the great assemblies of ambassadors from different nations bearing pacific messages. At Compiègne, in 816, Slovenes and Obotrites appeared, and again at Herstall (818) and at Frankfort (823); Bulgarian envoys on several occasions; and in 823 two leaders who, among the Wiltzi, were contending for power, begged the Emperor to act as arbitrator. Danes were present at Paderborn (815), at Aix-la-Chapelle (817), at Compiègne (823) and at Thionville (831). Louis even received Sardinians in 815 and Arabs in 816. As to the Eastern Empire, the *Basileis* seem always to have shewn anxiety to keep on good terms with Louis. On various occasions their ambassadors appeared at the great assemblies held by him; at Aix (817) to settle a question concerning frontiers in Dalmatia; at Rouen in 824 to discuss what measures should be taken in the matter of the controversy concerning images; at Compiègne in 827 to renew their professions of amity. It may be added that it was a Greek, the priest George, who built for Louis the Pious the first hydraulic organ ever used in Gaul.

Even from a military point of view, the reign of Louis the Pious bore at first the appearance of being in some sort a continuation of that of Charles, under a prince capable of repelling the attacks of his enemies. In the north, the Danish race were at this time fairly easily held in awe. One of the rivals then disputing for power, Harold, having been driven out by his cousins, the sons of Godefrid, came in 814 to take shelter at the court of Aix. In 815 the Saxon troops with the Obotrite "friendlies" made an attempt to restore this ally of the Franks to the throne, under the leadership of the *missus* Baldric. Promises of submission were made by the Danes, and hostages were handed over, but this was the only result obtained. It was not until about 819 that a revolution recalled Harold to the throne, whence his rivals had just been driven. He retained it until a fresh revulsion of feeling forced him again to take refuge at the court of Louis. On the other hand, in concert with Pope Paschal, Louis had been endeavouring to convert the Danes to Christianity. Ebbo, Archbishop of Rheims, was sent on this mission. Setting out in company with Halitgar, Bishop of Cambrai, he united his labours with those of Anskar and his companions who were already at work spreading the Christian Faith in the district around the mouth of the Elbe, where

Saxons and Scandinavians came into contact with one another. The monastery of Corvey or New Corbie (822) and the bishopric of Hamburg (831) were founded to safeguard Christianity in the country thus evangelised. When in 826 the Danish prince Harold came to be baptised at Mayence with several hundreds of his followers, the ceremony was made the opportunity for splendid entertainments at which the whole court was present, and was looked upon by the circle surrounding the Emperor as a triumph. But attacks by way of the sea were already beginning against the Frankish Empire. In 820 a band of pirates had attempted to land, first in Frisia, and then on the shores of the lower Seine, but being beaten off by the inhabitants they had been forced to content themselves with retiring to pillage the island of Bouin off the coast of La Vendée. In 829 a Scandinavian invasion of Saxony had momentarily alarmed Louis, but had led to nothing. In short, it may be said that for the first part of the reign Louis's dominions had been exempt from the ravages of the Vikings, but the tempest which was to rage so furiously a few years later was already seen to be gathering.

The Slavonic populations which bordered Frankish Germany on the east were also kept within due bounds. In 816 the *heorbann* of the Saxons and East Franks, called out against the rebellious Sorbs, compelled them to renew their oaths of submission. Next year the Frankish counts in charge of the frontier successfully beat off an attack by Slavomir, the prince of the Obotrites, who, being made prisoner a little later and accused before the Emperor by his own subjects, was deposed, his place being given to his rival Ceadrag (818). The new prince, however, before long deserted his former allies, joined forces with the Danes, and unsuccessfully renewed the struggle with the Franks. The latter found a more formidable opponent in the person of Liudevit, a prince who had succeeded in reducing to his obedience part of the population of Pannonia and was menacing the Frankish frontier between the Drave and the Save. An expedition sent against him under the Marquess of Friuli, Cadolah, was not successful. Cadolah died during the campaign, and the Slovenes invaded the imperial territory (820). It was only through an alliance with one of Liudevit's foes, Bozna, the Grand Župan of the Croats, that the Franks in their turn were enabled to spread destruction through the enemy's country, and to force the tribes of Carniola and Carinthia, who had thrown off their allegiance, to submit afresh. Liudevit himself made his submission next year, and peace was maintained upon the eastern frontier till 827–8, when an irruption of the Bulgarians into Pannonia necessitated another Frankish expedition, headed this time by the Emperor's son Louis the German. By way of compensation, unbroken peace reigned on the extreme southern frontier of the dominions of Louis. The Lombard populations of the south of Italy continued to be practically independent of Frankish rule. Louis made no attempt to exert any effective sovereignty over them. He contented himself with receiving from Prince Grimoald of Benevento in 814 a promise to pay tribute and assurances of submission, vague engagements which his successor Sico renewed more than once without causing any change in the actual situation.

On the south-western frontier of the Empire a state of war, or at least of perpetual skirmishing, went on between the Franks and either the Saracens of Spain or the half-subdued inhabitants of the Pyrenees. In 815 hostilities had broken out anew with the Emir Ḥakam I, whom the Frankish historians call Abulaz. The following year the recall of Séguin (Sigiwin), Duke of Gascony, led to a revolt of the Basques, but the native chief whom the rebels had placed at their head was defeated and killed by the counts in the service of Louis the Pious. Two years later (818) the Emperor felt himself strong enough to banish Lupus son of Centullus, the national Duke of the Gascons, and in 819 an expedition under Pepin of Aquitaine resulted in an apparent and temporary pacification of the province. On the other hand, at the assembly at Quierzy in 820 it was decided to renew the war with the Saracens of Spain. But the Frankish annalists mention only a plundering raid beyond the Segre river (822), and in 824 the defeat of two Frankish counts in the valley of Roncesvalles, as they were returning from an expedition against Pampeluna. In 826 the revolt in the Spanish March of a chief of Gothic extraction gave Louis the Pious graver cause for disquiet. An army led by the Abbot Elisachar checked the rebels for the moment, but they appealed to the Emir ʿAbd-ar-Raḥmān, and the Muslim troops sent under the command of Abū-Marwān penetrated as far as the walls of Saragossa. At the Compiègne assembly held in the summer of 827, the Emperor decided on sending a new Frankish army beyond the Pyrenees, but its leaders, Matfrid, Count of Orleans, and Hugh, Count of Tours, shewed such an entire lack of zeal and interposed so many delays, that Abū-Marwān was able to ravage the districts of Barcelona and Gerona with impunity. The progress of the invaders was only checked by the energetic resistance of Barcelona, under Count Bernard of Septimania, but they were able, nevertheless, to withdraw unhindered with their booty. In 828, in another quarter of the Frankish Empire, Boniface, Marquess of Tuscany, was taking the offensive. After having, at the head of his little flotilla, destroyed the pirate Muslim ships in the neighbourhood of Corsica and Sardinia, he landed in Africa and ravaged the country round Carthage.

To the extreme west of the Empire, the Bretons, whom even the great Charles had never been able to subdue completely, continued from time to time to send out pillaging expeditions into Frankish territory, chiefly in the direction of Vannes. These were mere raids, up to the time when their union under the leadership of a chief named Morvan (Murmannus), to whom they gave the title of king, so far emboldened the Bretons that they refused to pay homage or the annual tribute to which they had heretofore been subject. Louis, having attempted in vain to negotiate with the rebels, made up his mind to act, and summoned the host of Francia, Burgundy, and even of Saxony and Alemannia, to gather at Vannes in August 818. The Frankish troops pushed their way into the enemy's territory without having to fight a regular battle, as the Bretons, following their customary tactics, preferred to disappear from sight and merely harass their enemy. The latter could do no more than ravage the country, but Morvan was killed in a skirmish. His countrymen then abandoned the struggle, and at the end of a month the Emperor re-entered Angers, having exacted promises of submission from the more powerful of the Breton chiefs. Their submission, however, did not last long. In 822, a certain Wihomarch repeated Morvan's attempt. The expeditions led against him by the Frankish counts of the march of Brittany or by the Emperor himself were marked only by the wasting of the country, and produced no permanent results. Not until 826 did a new system ensure a measure of tranquillity. Louis then recognised the authority over the Bretons of a chief of their own race, Nomenoë, to whom he gave the title of *missus* and who in return did homage to him and took the oath of fealty. But the union of Brittany under a single head was a dangerous measure. Louis was blind to its disadvantages, but they were destined to have disastrous results in the reign of his successor.

Events within the realm were to begin the disorganisation of Louis's government and ultimately bring about the disruption of the empire founded by Charlemagne. In July 817 at the assembly of Aix-la-Chapelle, the Emperor had decided to take measures to establish the succession, or rather to cause the arrangements already made by himself and a few of his confidential advisers to be ratified by the lay and ecclesiastical magnates jointly. The Frankish principle by which the dominions of a deceased sovereign were divided among his sons, was still too living a thing (it lasted, indeed, as long as the Carolingian dynasty itself) to allow of the exclusion of any one of Louis's sons from the succession. The principle had already been applied in 806, and Louis had in some sort recognised it afresh by entrusting two of his sons with the government of two of his kingdoms, while at the same time leaving a third in the hands of Bernard of Italy. But on the other hand, the Emperor and his chief advisers were no less firmly attached to the principle of the unity of the Empire, "by ignoring which we should introduce confusion into the Church, and offend Him in Whose Hands are the rights of all kingdoms." "Would God, the Almighty," wrote one of the most illustrious of the thinkers upholding the system of the unity of the Empire, Archbishop Agobard of Lyons, "that all men, united under a single king, were governed by a single law! This would be the best method of maintaining peace in the City of God and equity among the nations." And the wisest and most influential of the clergy in the kingdom thought and spoke with Agobard, because they realised the advantages which accrued to the Church from the government of a single emperor in a realm where Church and State were so intimately connected. Throughout these struggles, which disturbed the whole of the reign of Louis the Pious, the party in favour of unity counted in its ranks nearly all the political writers of the time, Agobard, Paschasius Radbertus, Florus of Lyons. They have been accused of defending their personal interests under cover of the principle, and it has been pointed out that often the so-called party of unity was nothing but the coterie which gathered round Lothar. It is probable enough that the conduct of the sons of Louis and of the principal counts who took part with each of them was dictated by motives purely personal, but if the more important leaders of the ecclesiastical aristocracy are found supporting Lothar, it must not be forgotten that Lothar stood for the unity of the Empire for which the Church was working.

However this may be, the arrangements made at Aix, after three days devoted to fasting and almsgiving in order to call down the blessing and inspiration of God upon the assembly about to be opened, might seem of a kind to reconcile diverse principles and interests. The title of emperor was conferred upon Lothar, who became his father's colleague in the general administration of the Frankish monarchy. His coronation took place before the assembly amid the loud applause of the crowd. The title of king was confirmed to his two brothers, and their dominions received some augmentation. With Aquitaine, Pepin received Gascony and the county of Toulouse, as well as the Burgundian counties of Autun, Avallon and Nevers. Louis took Bavaria which Lothar had held, with suzerainty over the Carinthians, the Bohemians and the Slavs. The rest of the Empire was, on the death of Louis, to revert to Lothar, who alone was to enjoy the title of Emperor. It is somewhat difficult to say what was to be the position of the young kings with regard to Louis the Pious. It is probable that in practice it was modified with the lapse of time and the age of the princes. Indeed Louis, who may from this time be called Louis the German, the name by which history knows him, was not put in actual possession of his kingdom until 825. On the other hand, the act of 817 dealt minutely with the relation in which the brothers were to stand towards one another after the death of Louis the Pious. Each was to be sovereign ruler within his own dominions. To the king was to belong the proceeds of the revenue and taxes, and he was to have full right to dispose of the dignities of bishoprics and abbeys. At the same time the Emperor's supremacy is ensured by a series of provisions. His two brothers are bound to consult him on all occasions of importance; they may not make war or conclude treaties without his consent. His sanction is also required for their marriage, and they are forbidden to marry foreigners. They are to attend at the Emperor's court every year to offer their *gift*, to confer with him on public affairs, and to receive his instructions. Disputes between them are to be determined by the general assembly of the Empire. This body is also to pronounce in case of their being guilty of acts of violence or oppression and having failed to make satisfaction in accordance with the remonstrances which it shall be the duty of their elder brother to address to them. If either of the two die leaving several lawful sons, the people shall make their choice among them, but there shall be no further division of territory. If, on the contrary, the deceased leave no legitimate son, his apanage shall devolve on one of his brothers. Supplementary provisions, derived, indeed, from the *Divisio* of 806, were added, forbidding the magnates to possess benefices in several kingdoms at once, but allowing any free man to settle in any kingdom he chose, and to marry there.

Such, in its main outlines, was the celebrated *Divisio imperii* of 817, which we may fittingly analyse, as its provisions were often to be appealed to during the struggle between the sons of Louis. Its object was to avoid every occasion of strife. Yet one of its earliest effects was to kindle a revolt, that of the young Bernard of Italy. He considered himself threatened, or his counsellors persuaded him that he was threatened, by one of the regulations of the act of Aix, laying down that after the death of Louis, Italy should be subject to Lothar in the same manner as it had been to Louis himself and to Charles. It is, however, difficult to see more in this article than a provision for the maintenance of the actual *status quo*. All our authorities agree in attributing the responsibility for the revolt less to Bernard himself than to certain of his intimates, the count Eggideus, the chamberlain Reginar (Rainier), and Anselm, Archbishop of Milan. The Bishop of Orleans, the celebrated poet Theodulf, was also counted among the young prince's partisans. The rebels' plan, it was said, was to dethrone the Emperor and his family, perhaps to put them to death, and to make Bernard sole ruler of the Empire. Ratbold, Bishop of Verona, and Suppo, Count of Brescia, who were the first to warn Louis of what was being plotted against him, added that all Italy was ready to uphold Bernard, and that he was master of the passes of the Alps. In reality, the rebellion seems in no sense to bear the character of a national movement, which indeed would hardly have been possible at this stage, and the numerous army, which the Emperor hastily assembled, found no difficulty in occupying the passes of Aosta and Susa. Louis in person put himself at the head of the troops concentrating at Châlon. Bernard was alarmed, and finding himself ill supported, made his submission, along with his chief partisans, to the Frankish counts who had pushed on into Italy, and surrendered himself into their custody. The prisoners were sent to Aix-la-Chapelle, and the assembly held in that town at the beginning of 818 condemned them to death. The Emperor granted them their lives, but commuted their punishment to that of blinding. Bernard and his friend Count

Reginar died in a few days in consequence of the torture inflicted (17 April 818). The young prince was not nineteen. Those of his accomplices who were churchmen were deposed and confined in monasteries. Theodulf, in particular, was exiled to Angers. It is probable that it was this rising in favour of a spurious member of his family which led the Emperor at this time to take precautionary measures against his own illegitimate brothers, Hugh, Theodoric and Drogo (later, 826, Archbishop of Metz), whom he compelled to enter monasteries.

The punishment suffered by Bernard, who was hardly more than a lad, was out of all proportion to the risk which he had caused the Emperor to run. It was an act of pure cruelty, and was generally and severely criticised at the time. Louis himself judged that he had shewn excessive severity. In 821 at the assembly at Thionville which followed the rejoicings on the marriage of Lothar with Ermengarde, daughter of Hugh, Count of Tours, he granted an amnesty to Bernard's former accomplices, and restored their confiscated property. At the same time he recalled from Aquitaine Adalard, another of the proscribed, and replaced him at the head of the monastery of Corbie. Next year at Attigny he took a further step in the same direction. He solemnly humiliated himself in the presence of the chief clergy of his kingdom, the Abbot Elisachar, Adalard and Archbishop Agobard, declaring that he desired to do penance publicly for the cruelty he had shewn both to Bernard and to Adalard and his brother Wala. The biographer of Louis the Pious compares this public penance to that of Theodosius. It was, in reality, extremely impolitic. The Emperor weakened himself morally by this humiliation before the ecclesiastical aristocracy, who looked upon the penance of Attigny as a victory won by themselves over Louis, "who became," says Paschasius Radbertus triumphantly, "the humblest of men, he who had been so ill-counselled by his royal pride, and who now made satisfaction to those whose eyes had been offended by his crime." His humiliation was also accompanied by measures taken to secure the protection of property belonging to the Church, and Agobard felt so sure of victory for the latter that he even meditated claiming the restitution of all the ecclesiastical property which had been usurped in preceding reigns. The penance of Attigny was one great political mistake of Louis; his re-marriage was another. Its consequences were to prove disastrous.

Louis's first wife, "his counsellor and helper in his government," the devout Empress Ermengarde, had died at Angers, just as her husband was returning from his expedition into Brittany (3 Oct. 818). The Emperor for some time gave himself up to despairing grief. It was even feared that he would abdicate and retire into a monastery. However, at the earnest request of his confidential advisers he decided on choosing a second consort "who might be his helper in the government of his palace and his kingdom." In 819 he chose from among his magnates' daughters that of Count Welf, a maiden of a very noble Swabian house, named Judith. Aegilwi, the new Empress's mother, belonged to one of the great Saxon families which had always shewn itself faithful to Louis. Contemporaries are unanimous in lauding not only the beauty of Judith, which seems to have had most weight in determining the Emperor's choice, but also her qualities of mind, her learning, her gentleness, her piety, and the charm of her conversation. She seems to have possessed great ascendancy over all who came in contact with her, especially over her husband. In 823 she bore him a son who received the name of Charles, and whom history knows as Charles the Bald. The *ordinatio* of 817 had contemplated no such contingency, nor had the confirmation of it which had been solemnly decreed at Nimeguen in 819. It was plain, nevertheless, that whether during his father's lifetime or after his death, the newborn prince would claim a share equal to that of his brothers. From this point onwards, the history of the reign of Louis the Pious becomes almost entirely that of the efforts made by him under the influence of Judith to secure to the latest-born his portion of the inheritance, and that of the counter-efforts of the three elder sons to maintain the integrity of their own shares in virtue of the settlement of 817, and of the principle of unity round which the partisans of Lothar rallied.

For some time events seemed to take the course provided for by the settlement of 817. Pepin was put in possession of Aquitaine on his marriage in 822 with Engeltrude, daughter of Theobert, Count of the *pagus Madriacensis*, near the lower Seine, and Louis the German was entrusted in 825 with the actual administration of his Bavarian kingdom soon after the assembly at Aix. But in 829, after the assembly of Worms, the Emperor, by an edict "issued of his own will" made a new arrangement by which his youngest son was given part of Alemannia with Alsace and Rhaetia and a portion of Burgundy, no doubt with the title only of duke. All these districts formed part of Lothar's portion, and he, though godfather of his young brother, could not fail to resent such measures. It appears probable that it was in order to remove him from court that at this juncture he was sent on a new mission into Italy. At the same time in signing charters he ceases to be designated by his title of Emperor. But it was necessary to provide a protector for young Charles, and for this office choice was made of Bernard of Septimania, who also held the Spanish March and received the title of Chamberlain. Son of a great man canonised by the Church, William of Gellone, friend of St Benedict of Aniane, great-grandson of Charles Martel, and defender of Barcelona at the time of the Saracenic invasion, Bernard was already in right of his birth and his valour as well as his position one of the chief personages of the Empire. Because he was chamberlain Bernard was entrusted with the administration of the palace and of the royal domains in general, and held "the next place after the Emperor." His rise to power seems to have been marked, more-over, by a change in the *personnel* of Louis's court. His enemies, through the mouth of Paschasius Radbertus, accuse him of having " turned the palace upside down and scattered the imperial council," and it is true that Wala and other partisans of Lothar were set aside from the administration of affairs to make way for new men, Odo, Count of Orleans, William, Count of Blois, cousin of Bernard, Conrad and Rudolf, brothers of the new Empress, Jonas, Bishop of Orleans, and Boso, Abbot of Saint-Benoît-sur-Loire (Fleury).

The displeasure of the magnates evicted from power or disappointed in their ambitions was shewn as early as the following year (830). Louis, perhaps by the advice of Bernard who was eager to strengthen his position by military successes, had planned a new expedition against the Bretons and summoned the host to meet at Rennes at Easter (14 April). Many of the Franks proved little disposed to enter on a campaign in spring, at an inclement season of the year. On the other hand, Wala secretly informed Pepin that hostile designs were being formed against him by Bernard, who under pretext of an expedition into Brittany meditated nothing less than turning his arms against the king of Aquitaine and stripping him of his possessions. Pepin was a man of energy, but also of levity and impetuosity, and under pressure, perhaps, from the Aquitanian lords who had gradually been substituted for the Frankish counsellors placed round him by his father, either believed, or feigned to believe the information, and came to an agree-ment with his brother Louis and the partisans of Wala and Lothar to march against the Emperor.

Louis the Pious, who was on his way to Rennes along the coast with Judith and Bernard, was at Sithiu (Saint-Bertin) when the news of the revolt reached him. He continued his journey as far as Saint-Riquier. But the time had gone by for the Breton expedition. The majority of the *fideles* who should have gathered at Rennes to take part in it had met at Paris and made common cause with the rebels. Pepin, after having occupied Orleans, had joined them at Verberie, N.E. of Senlis. Louis the German had done likewise. As to Lothar, he was lingering in Italy, perhaps to watch what turn events would take. But any resistance was impossible for Louis, because the whole weight of military force was on the side of the conspirators. The latter declared that they had no quarrel with the Emperor, but only with his wife, whom they accused of a guilty connexion with Bernard. They demanded therefore that Judith should be exiled and her accomplices punished. Louis, sending Bernard for refuge to his city of Barcelona, and leaving the Empress at Aix, went to meet the rebels, who were then at Compiègne and surrendered himself into their hands. Judith, who had set out to join him, fearing violence took shelter in the church of Notre-Dame at Laon. Two of the counts who had espoused Pepin's cause, Warin of

Mâcon and Lambert of Nantes, came up and forcibly removed her. After having detained her a prisoner for some time with her husband, they finally shut her up in a convent at Poitiers. Her two brothers, Conrad and Rudolf, were tonsured and relegated to Aquitanian monasteries.

In these circumstances, Lothar, dreading no doubt that he might be ignored if a division should take place without him, arrived at Compiègne and at once put himself at the head of the movement, his first step being to resume his title of joint-Emperor. Louis the Pious seemed inclined to dismiss Bernard and restore the former government. Lothar's desires went beyond this, and he surrounded his father with monks instructed to persuade him to embrace the religious life, for which he had formerly shewn some inclination. But Louis did not fall in with this project. He was secretly negotiating with Louis the German and Pepin, promising them an increase of territory if they would abandon the cause of Lothar. On their side, the two princes were no more inclined to be Lothar's subjects than their father's. The Emperor and his supporters succeeded in gathering a new assembly at Nimeguen in the autumn, at which were present many of the Saxon and German lords who were always loyal to Louis. The reaction beginning in favour of the Emperor now shewed itself plainly. Louis was declared to be re-established in his former authority. It was also decided to recall Judith. On the other hand, several of the abettors of the revolt were arrested. Wala was obliged to surrender the abbey of Corbie. The Arch-Chaplain Hilduin, Abbot of St Denis, was banished to Paderborn. Lothar, in alarm, accepted the pardon offered him by his father and shewed himself at the assembly beside the Emperor in the character of a dutiful son.

The assembly convoked at Aix-la-Chapelle (February 831) to pass definitive sentence on the rebels, adjudged them the penalty of death, which Louis the Pious commuted to imprisonment and exile, together with confiscation of goods. Lothar himself was obliged to subscribe to the condemnation of his former partisans. Thus Hilduin lost the abbeys he had possessed and was banished to Corvey, Wala was imprisoned in the neighbourhood of the Lake of Geneva, Matfrid and Elisachar exiled. At the same time the Empress, after solemnly clearing herself by oath from the accusations levelled against her, was declared restored to her former position. Her brothers, Conrad and Rudolf, quitted the monasteries in which they had been temporarily confined, and recovered their dignities. Contrariwise the name of Lothar again disappears from the parchments containing the imperial diplomas, the eldest son losing his privileged position as joint-Emperor, and being reduced to that of king of Italy, while in accordance with the promise he had made them Louis the Pious increased the shares of his younger sons in the inheritance. To Pepin's Aquitanian kingdom were annexed the districts between the Loire and the Seine, and, to the north of the latter river, the Meaux country, with the Amiénois and Ponthieu as far as the sea. Louis of Bavaria saw his portion enlarged by the addition of Saxony and Thuringia and the greater part of the *pagi* which make up modern Belgium and the Netherlands. Charles, besides Alemannia, received Burgundy, Provence and Gothia with a slice of Francia, and in particular, the important province of Rheims. Nevertheless, as these arrangements had no validity until Louis the Pious should have disappeared from the scene, they made little or no change in the actual position of the three princes, especially as the Emperor expressly reserved to himself the power to give additional advantage to " any one of our three above-mentioned sons, who, desirous of pleasing in the first place God, and secondly ourselves, should distinguish himself by his obedience and zeal" by withdrawing somewhat " from the portion of that one of his brothers who shall have neglected to please us." Yet the sentences pronounced at Aix-la-Chapelle were to be of no lasting effect. At Ingelheim, in the beginning of May, several of the former partisans of Lothar were pardoned. Hilduin, in particular, regained his abbey of St Denis. On the other hand, Bernard, though like Judith he had purged himself by oath before the assembly at Thionville from the accusations made against him, had not been reinstated in his office at court. On the contrary, it would seem that Louis the Pious made endeavours to reconcile himself with Lothar, perhaps under the influence of Judith, who was ever ready to cherish the idea that her young son might find a protector in his eldest brother. The Emperor was, besides, in a fair way towards a breach with Pepin. The latter being summoned to the assembly at Thionville (autumn 831) had delayed under various pretexts to present himself, and when he did resolve to appear before the Emperor at Aix (end of 831) his father received him with so small a show of favour that Pepin either feared or pretended to fear for his safety, and at the end of December secretly betook himself again to Aquitaine, disregarding the prohibition, which had been laid upon him. Louis decided to take strong measures against him and called an assembly to meet at Orleans in 832, to which Lothar and Louis the German were both summoned. From Orleans an expedition was to be sent south of the Loire.

But at the beginning of 832, the Emperor learned that Louis the German, perhaps fearing to share the fate of Pepin, or instigated by some of the leaders of the revolt of 830, was in a state of rebellion, and at the head of his Bavarians, reinforced by a contingent of Slavs, had invaded Alemannia (the apanage of Charles) where many of the nobles had ranged themselves on his side. Relinquishing for the moment his Aquitanian project, Louis summoned the host of the Franks and Saxons to muster at Mayence. The *leudes* eagerly responded to his appeal, and Louis the German, who was encamped at Lorsch, was obliged to recognise that he had no means of resisting the superior forces at his father's disposal. He therefore retreated. The imperial army slowly followed his line of march, and by the month of May had reached Augsburg. Here it was that Louis the German came to seek his father and make his submission to him, swearing never in future to renew his attempts at revolt.

Louis then turned towards Aquitaine. From Frankfort, where he was joined by Lothar, he convoked a new host to meet at Orleans on 1 September. Thence he crossed the Loire, and ravaging the country as he went, reached Limoges. He halted for some time to the north of this town, at the royal residence of Jonac in La Marche, where Pepin came to him and in his turn submitted himself to him. But, shewing more severity in his case than in that of Louis the German, the Emperor, with the alleged object of reforming his morals, caused him to be arrested and sent to Trèves. At the same time, disclosing his true purpose, he annexed Aquitaine to the dominions of young Charles, to whom the magnates present at the assembly at Jonac were required to swear fealty. Bernard of Septimania himself, whose influence excited alarm, was deprived of his honours and benefices, which were given to Berengar, Count of Toulouse. But the Aquitanians, always jealous of their independence, would not submit to be deprived of the prince whom they had come to look upon as their own. They succeeded in liberating him from the custody of his escort, and the Frankish troops, sent in pursuit by Louis, were unable to recapture him. The imperial army was obliged to turn northward, harassed by the Aquitanian insurgents, and their winter march proved disastrous. When Louis at length reached Francia again, leaving Aquitaine in arms behind him (January 833), it was only to learn that his two other sons, Lothar and Louis the German, were again in rebellion against him.

Lothar and Louis no doubt dreaded lest they should meet with the same treatment as Pepin. Moreover they could not see without feelings of jealousy the share of young Charles in the paternal heritage so disproportionately augmented. Again, Lothar had found a new ally in the person of the Pope, Gregory IV (elected in 827). The latter, though hesitating at first, had ended by allowing himself to be caught by the prospect of bringing peace to the Empire, and of securing for the Papacy the position of a mediating power. He had therefore decided on accompanying Lothar when he crossed the Alps to join his brother of Germany, and had addressed a circular letter to the bishops of Gaul and Germany, asking them to order fasts and prayers for the success of his enterprise. This did not hinder the greater number of the prelates from rallying round Louis who was at Worms where his army was concentrating. Only a few steadfast partisans of Lothar, such as Agobard of Lyons, failed to obey the imperial summons. The two parties seem to have been in no haste to come to blows, and for several months spent their time in negotiating and in drawing up statements of the case on one side or the other, the sons persistently professing the deepest respect for their father, and vowing that all their quarrel was with his evil counsellors. Things remained in this state until, in the middle of June, the Emperor resolved to go and seek his sons in order to have a personal discussion with them.

In company, then, with his supporters, he went up the left bank of the Rhine towards Alsace where the rebels were posted, and pitched his camp opposite theirs near Colmar, in the plain known as the Rothfeld. Brisk negotiations were again opened between the two parties. Pope Gregory finally went in person to the imperial camp to confer with Louis and his adherents. Did he exert his influence over the bishops who up to then had seemed resolved to stand by their Emperor? Or did the promises made by the sons work upon the magnates who still gathered round Louis? Whatever may be the explanation, a general defection set in. Within a few days the Emperor found himself deserted by all his followers and left almost alone. The place which was the scene of this shameful betrayal is traditionally known as the *Lügenfeld*, the Field of Lies. Louis was constrained to advise the few prelates who still kept faith with him, such as Aldric of Le Mans or Moduin of Autun, to follow the universal example. He himself, with his wife, his illegitimate brother Drogo and young Charles, surrendered to Lothar. The latter declared his father deposed from his authority and claimed the Empire as his own by right. He made use of it to share dignities and honours among his chief partisans. In order to give some show of satisfaction to his brothers, he added to Pepin's share the wide duchy of Maine, and to Louis's Saxony, Thuringia and Alsace. Judith was sent under a strong guard to Tortona in Italy, and Charles the Bald to the monastery of Prüm. After this, Pepin and Louis the German returned to their respective states, while the Pope, perhaps disgusted by the scenes he had just witnessed, quitted Lothar and betook himself directly to Rome.

Louis had been temporarily immured in the monastery of St Médard at Soissons. The assembly held by Lothar at Compiègne was not of itself competent to decree the deposition of the old Emperor, in spite of the accusations brought against him by Ebbo, Archbishop of Rheims. Lothar was forced to confine himself to bringing sufficient pressure to bear upon his father (through the agency of churchmen of the rebel party sent to Soissons) to induce him to acknowledge himself guilty of offences which rendered him unworthy of retaining power. But not satisfied with his deposition the bishops forced him besides to undergo a public humiliation. In the church of Notre-Dame at Compiègne in the presence of the assembled magnates and bishops, Louis, prostrate upon a hair cloth before the altar, was compelled to read the form of confession drawn up by his enemies, in which he owned himself guilty of sacrilege, as having transgressed the commands of the Church and violated the oaths that he had sworn; of homicide, as having caused the death of Bernard; and of perjury, as having broken the pact instituted to preserve the peace of the Empire and the Church. The document containing the text of this confession was then laid upon the altar, while the Emperor, stripped of his baldric, the emblem of the warrior (knight or *miles*), and clothed in the garb of a penitent, was removed under close supervision first to Soissons, then to the neighbourhood of Compiègne, and finally to Aix where the new Emperor was to spend the winter.

But by the end of 833, dissension was beginning to make itself felt among the victors. Louis's half-brothers, Hugh and Drogo, who had fled to Louis the German, were exhorting him to come over to the party of his father and of Judith, whose sister, Emma, he had married in 827. Louis the German's first step was to intercede with Lothar to obtain a mitigation of the treatment meted out to the imprisoned Emperor. The attempt failed, and only produced a widening of the breach between the two brothers. A reaction of feeling began in favour of the captive sovereign. The famous theologian Raban Maur, Abbot of Fulda and later Archbishop of Mayence (847–56), published an *apologia* on his behalf, in answer to a treatise in which Agobard of Lyons had just refurbished the old calumnies which had been widely circulated against Judith. Louis the German made overtures to Pepin, who was no more disposed than himself to recognise any disproportionate authority in Lothar, and before long the two kings agreed to summon their followers to march to the help of their father. Lothar, not feeling himself safe in Austrasia, went to Saint-Denis where he had called upon his host to assemble. But the nobles of his party deserted him in his turn. He was compelled to set Louis the Pious and young Charles at liberty and to retreat upon Vienne on the Rhone, while the bishops and magnates present at Saint-Denis decreed the restoration of Louis to his former dignity, reinvesting him with his crown and his weapons, the insignia of his authority. In charters and documents he now reassumes the imperial style: *Hludowicus, divina* repropiciante *clementia, imperator augustus*.

On leaving Saint-Denis Louis repaired to Quierzy, where he was joined by Pepin and Louis the German. Judith, who had been withdrawn from her prison by the magnates devoted to the Emperor, also returned to Gaul. Meanwhile Lothar was preparing to carry on the struggle. Lambert and Matfrid, his most zealous supporters, had raised an army in his name on the March of Brittany, and defeated and killed the counts sent against them by the Emperor. Lothar, who had rallied his partisans, came to join them in the neighbourhood of Orleans. There he awaited the arrival of the Emperor, who was still in company with his other two sons. As on similar occasions, no battle was fought. Lothar, realising the inadequacy of his forces, made his submission and

appeared before his father promising never to offend again. He was
obliged to pledge himself also to be content, for the future, with " the
kingdom of Italy, such as it had been granted by Charlemagne to
Pepin," with the obligation of protecting the Holy See. Further, he
was never to cross the Alps again without his father's consent. His
partisans, Lambert and Matfrid, were permitted to follow him into his
new kingdom, forfeiting the benefices they possessed in Gaul.

Next year (835) an assembly at Thionville again solemnly annulled
the decrees of that of Compiègne, and declared Louis to be " re-established
in the honours of his ancestors, henceforth to be regarded by all
men as their lord and emperor." A fresh ceremony took place at Metz,
when the imperial crown was again set upon his head. At the same
time the assembly at Thionville had decreed penalties against the bishops
who had deserted their sovereign. Ebbo of Rheims was compelled to
read publicly a formulary containing the acknowledgment of his treason
and his renunciation of his dignity. He was confined at Fulda.
Agobard of Lyons, Bernard of Vienne, and Bartholomew of Narbonne
were condemned as contumacious and declared deposed. The Emperor
attempted to take advantage of this returning prosperity to restore
some degree of order in the affairs of his kingdoms, after the fiery
trial of several years of civil war. At the assembly of Tramoyes (Ain)
in June 835 he decreed the sending of *missi* into the different provinces
to suppress acts of pillage. At that of Aix (beginning of 836) measures
were taken to secure the regular exercise of the power of the bishops.
A little earlier an attempt had been made to prevail on Pepin of
Aquitaine to restore the Church property which he and his followers
had usurped. But it is doubtful whether these measures produced any
great effect. On the other hand, a fresh peril became daily more
threatening, namely the incursions of the Scandinavian pirates. In 834
they had ravaged the coasts of Frisia, pillaging the sea-coasts as
they went, and penetrating at least as far as the island of Noirmoutier
on the Atlantic. Henceforth they reappear almost every year, and in
835 they defeated and slew Reginald, Count of Herbauges. In the
same year they plundered the great maritime mart of Dorestad on the
North Sea. Next year, 836, they again visited Frisia, and their king
Horic had even the insolence to demand the wergild of such of his
subjects as had been slain or captured during their piratical operations.
In 837 fresh ravages took place, and the Emperor in vain attempted to
check them by sending out *missi* charged with the defence of the coasts,
and especially by building ships to pursue the enemy. Horic even
claimed (838) the sovereignty of Frisia, and it was not till 839 that
hostilities were temporarily suspended by a treaty.

Nor was the internal peace of the Empire much more secure. Louis
and Judith appear to have reverted to the idea of a reconciliation with
Lothar, looking upon him as the destined protector of his young brother

and godson, Charles. As early as 836 negotiations were begun with a view to the renewal of amicable relations between the King of Italy and his father. But sickness prevented Lothar from attending the assembly at Worms to which he had been summoned. However, at the end of 837 at the assembly held at Aix the Emperor elaborated a new scheme of division which added to Charles's kingdom the greater part of Belgium with the country lying between the Meuse and the Seine as far as Burgundy. This project was certain to alarm Louis the German, whom we find at the opening of the next year (838) making overtures in his turn to Lothar with whom he had an interview at Trent. This displeased the Emperor and, at the Nimeguen assembly, June 838, he punished Louis by depriving him of part of his territory, leaving him only Bavaria. On the other hand, in the month of September young Charles at the age of fifteen had just attained his majority; such was the law of the Ripuarian Franks followed by the Carolingian family. He therefore received the baldric of a knight, and was given at Quierzy a portion of the lands between Loire and Seine. An attempt made by Louis to regain possession of the lands on the right bank of the Rhine met with no success. The Emperor, in his turn crossed the river and forced his son to take refuge in Bavaria while he himself after a demonstration in Alemannia returned to Worms, where Lothar came from Pavia to see him and went through a solemn ceremony of reconciliation with him.

The death of Pepin of Aquitaine (13 December 838) seemed to simplify the question of division and succession, for the new partition scheme drawn up at Worms utterly ignored his son, Pepin II. Apart from Bavaria, which with a few neighbouring *pagi* was left to Louis the German, the empire of Charlemagne was cut into two parts. The dividing line running from north to south followed the Meuse, touched the Moselle at Toul, crossed Burgundy, and having on the west Langres, Châlon, Lyons, Geneva, followed the line of the Alps and ended at the Mediterranean. Lothar, as eldest son, was given the right to choose, and took for himself the eastern portion; the other fell to Charles. After his father's death, Lothar was also to bear the title of Emperor, but apparently without the prerogatives attached to it by the settlement of 817. It was to be his duty to protect Charles, while the latter was bound to pay all due honour to his elder brother and godfather. These obligations once fulfilled, each prince was to be absolute master in his own kingdom.

Aquitaine was thus in theory vested in Charles the Bald, but several guerilla bands still held the field in the name of Pepin II. The Emperor went thither in person to secure the recognition of his son. Setting out for Châlon where the host had been summoned to meet (1 September 839) he made his way to Clermont. Here a party of Aquitanian lords came to make their submission to their new sovereign.

This did not, however, imply that the country was pacified, for many of the counts still maintained their resistance.

But Louis the Pious had now to renew the struggle with the King of Germany, who as well as Pepin was injured by the partition of 839, and had invaded Saxony and Thuringia. The Emperor advanced against him and had no great difficulty in thrusting him back into Bavaria. But as he was returning to Worms, where his son Lothar, who had gone back to Italy after the late partition, had been appointed to meet him, the cough which had long tormented him became worse. Having fallen dangerously ill at Salz, he had himself moved to an island in the Rhine opposite the palace of Ingelheim. Here he breathed his last in his tent on 20 June 840 in the arms of his half-brother Drogo, sending his pardon to his son Louis. Before his death he had proclaimed Lothar Emperor, commending Judith and Charles to his protection and ordering that the insignia of the imperial authority, the sceptre, crown and sword, should be sent to him.

The dying Emperor might well have despaired of unity for Charlemagne's Empire and have foreseen that the civil wars of the last twenty years would be renewed more fiercely than ever among his sons. As the outcome of his reign was unfortunate, and as under him the first manifestations appeared of the two scourges which were about to destroy the Frank Empire, the insubordination of the great lords on one side and the Norman invasions on the other, historians have been too easily led to accuse Louis the Pious of weakness and incapacity. He was long known by the somewhat contemptuous epithet of the Debonnaire (the good-natured, the easy-going). But in truth his life-story shews him to have been capable of perseverance and at times even of energy and resolution, although as a rule the energy was of no long duration. Louis the Pious found himself confronted by opponents, who took his clemency for a sign of weakness, and knew how to exploit his humility for their own profit by making him appear an object of contempt. But above all, circumstances were adverse to him. He was the loser in the long struggle with his sons and with the magnates; this final ill-success rather than his own character explains the severe judgment so often passed upon the son of the great Charles.

CHAPTER II.

THE CAROLINGIAN KINGDOMS (840–877).

THE death of Louis the Pious and his clearly expressed last wishes secured the imperial dignity to Lothar. But the situation had not been defined with any precision. The last partition, decreed in 839, had made important alterations in the shares assigned to the three brothers. Now what Lothar hastened to claim was " the empire such as it had formerly been entrusted to him," namely, the territorial power and the pre-eminent position secured to him by the *Constitutio* of 817, with his two brothers reduced to the position of vassal kinglets. To make good these claims Lothar had the support of the majority of the prelates, always faithful, in the main, to the principle of unity. But the great lay lords were guided only by considerations of self-interest. In a general way, each of the three brothers had on his side those who had already lived under his rule, and whom he had succeeded in winning over by grants of honours and benefices. Louis had thus secured the Germans, Bavarians, Thuringians and Saxons, and Charles the Neustrians, Burgundians, and such of the Aquitanians as had not espoused the cause of Pepin II. But it would be a mistake to see in the wars which followed the death of Louis the Pious a struggle between races. As a contemporary writes, " the combatants did not differ either in their weapons, their customs, or their race. They fought one another because they belonged to opposite camps, and these camps stood for nothing but coalitions of personal interests."

Lothar received the news of his father's death as he was on his way to Worms. He betook himself to Strasbourg, and in that town the oath of fealty was sworn to him by many of the magnates of ancient Francia who were still loyal to the Carolingian family and to the system of a united empire, being vaguely aware that this system would secure the predominance of the Austrasians from among whom Charles and Louis the Pious had drawn almost all the counts of their vast empire. But Louis the German, on his part, had occupied the country as far as the Rhine, and Charles the Bald was also making ready for the struggle. Lothar had not resolution enough to attack his two brothers one after the other and force them to accept the re-establishment of the *Constitutio* of 817. He first had an interview beyond the Rhine with

Louis, concluding a truce with him until a forthcoming assembly should meet, at which the conditions of a permanent peace were to be discussed. Then he marched against Charles, many of the magnates of the district between the Seine and the Loire joining him, among others Gerard, Count of Paris, and Hilduin, Abbot of Saint-Denis. But Charles, being skilfully advised by Judith and other counsellors, among them an illegitimate grandson of Charles the Great, the historian Nithard, opened negotiations and succeeded in obtaining terms which left him provisionally in possession of Aquitaine, Septimania, Provence and six counties between the Loire and the Seine. Lothar, besides, arranged to meet him at the palace of Attigny in the ensuing May, whither Louis the German was also summoned to arrange for a definitive peace.

The winter of 840–841 was spent by the three brothers in enlisting partisans and in gathering troops. But when spring came, Lothar neglected to go to Attigny. Only Louis and Charles met there. An alliance between these two, both equally threatened by the claims of their elder brother, was inevitable. Their armies made a junction in the district of Châlons-sur-Marne, while that of Lothar mustered in the Auxerrois. Louis and Charles marched together against the Emperor, proposing terms of agreement as they came, and sending embassy after embassy to exhort him "to restore peace to the Church of God." Lothar was anxious to spin matters out, for he was expecting the arrival of Pepin II (who had declared for him) and of his contingent of Aquitanians, or at least of southern Aquitanians, for those of the centre and north were induced by Judith to join Charles the Bald. On 24 June, Pepin effected his junction with the Emperor. The latter now thought himself strong enough to wish for a battle. He sent a haughty message to his younger brothers, reminding them that "the imperial dignity had been committed to him, and that he would know how to fulfil the duties it laid upon him." On the morning of the 25th, the fight began at Fontenoy[1] in Puisaye, and a desperate struggle it proved. The centre of the imperial army, where Lothar appeared in person, stood firm at first against the troops of Louis the German. On the left wing the Aquitanians of Pepin II long held out, but Charles the Bald, reinforced by a body of Burgundians who had come up, under the command of Warin, Count of Mâcon, was victorious against the right wing, and his success involved the defeat of Lothar's army. The number of the dead was very great; a chronicler puts it at 40,000. These figures are exaggerated, but it is plain that the imagination of contemporaries was vividly impressed by the carnage "wrought on that accursed day, which ought no longer to be counted in the year, which

[1] Much discussion has arisen over the identification of the place which Nithard calls Fontanetum. The various contentions are summed up in *Charles le Chauve* (Lot and Halphen), p. 29, no. 6. It is nearly certain that the Fontenoy in question is that situated in dép. Yonne, arr. Auxerre, cant. Saint-Sauveur.

should be banished from the memory of men, and be for ever deprived the light of the sun and of the beams of morning," as the poet Angilbert says, adding that "the garments of the slain Frankish warriors whitened the plain as the birds usually do in autumn." At the end of the ninth century, the Lotharingian chronicler, Regino of Prüm, echoes the tradition according to which the battle of Fontenoy decimated the Frankish nobility and left the Empire defenceless against the ravages of the Northmen.

In reality, the battle had not been decisive. Louis and Charles might see the Divine judgment in the issue of the fight, and cause the bishops of their faction to declare that the Almighty had given sentence in their favour, yet, as the annalist of Lobbes put it, "great carnage had taken place, but neither of the two adversaries had triumphed." Lothar, who was stationed at Aix-la-Chapelle, was ready to carry on the struggle, and was seeking fresh partisans, even making appeal to the Danish pirates whom he settled in the island of Walcheren, while at the same time he was sending emissaries into Saxony, to stir up insurrections among the free or semi-free populations there (the *frilingi* and *lazzi*) against the nobility who were of Frankish origin. His two brothers having again separated, he attempted to re-open the struggle by marching in the first instance against Louis. He occupied Mayence, and awaited the attack of the Saxon army. But on learning that Charles, on his side, had collected troops and was marching upon Aix, Lothar quitted Mayence and fell back upon Worms. Then, in his turn, he took the offensive against his youngest brother and compelled him to give back as far as the banks of the Seine. But Charles took up a strong position in the neighbourhood of Paris and Saint-Denis. Lothar dared not bring on a battle, so he fell back slowly upon Aix, which he had regained by the beginning of February, 842.

Meanwhile his two brothers drew their alliance closer, and Charles, with this object, had made an appeal to Louis. The latter went to Strasbourg, and there on 14 February, the two kings, surrounded by their men, had a memorable interview. After having addressed their followers gathered together in the palace of Strasbourg, and recalled to them the crimes of Lothar, who had not consented to recognise the judgment of God after his defeat at Fontenoy, but had persisted in causing confusion in the Christian world, they swore mutual friendship and loyal assistance to one another. Louis, as the elder, was the first to take the following oath in the Romance tongue, so as to be understood by his brother's subjects: "For the love of God and for the Christian people, and our common salvation, so far as God gives me knowledge and power, I will defend my brother Charles with my aid and in everything, as one's duty is in right to defend one's brother, on condition that he shall do as much for me, and I will make no agreement with my brother Lothar which shall, with my consent, be to the prejudice of my brother Charles." Thereupon Charles repeated the same formula in the Teutonic tongue used by his brother's subjects. Finally, the two armies made the following declaration each in their own language. " If Louis (or Charles) observes the oath which he has sworn to his brother Charles (or Louis) and if Charles (or Louis) my lord, for his part, infringe his oath, if I am not able to dissuade him from it, neither I nor anyone whom I can hinder shall lend him support against Louis (or Charles)." The two brothers then spent several days together at Strasbourg, prodigal of outward tokens of their amity, offering each other feasts and warlike sports, sleeping at night under each other's roofs, spending their days together and settling their business in common. In the month of March they advanced against Lothar, and by way of Worms and Mayence reached Coblence, where the Emperor had collected his troops. His army, panic-stricken, disbanded without even attempting to defend the passage of the Moselle. Louis and Charles entered Aix, which Lothar abandoned, to make his way to Lyons through Burgundy. His two brothers followed him. Having reached Châlon-sur-Saône they received envoys from the Emperor acknowledging his offences against them, and proposing peace on condition that they granted him a third of the Empire, with some territorial addition on account of the imperial title which their father had bestowed on him, and of the imperial dignity which their grandfather had joined to the kingship of the Franks. Lothar was still surrounded by numerous supporters. On the other hand, the magnates, fatigued by years of war, were anxious for peace. Louis and Charles accepted in principle the proposals of their elder brother.

On 15 June an interview took place between the three sovereigns, on an island in the Saône near Mâcon, which led to the conclusion of a truce. Louis made use of it to crush the insurrection of a league of Saxon peasants, the *Stellinga*, which the Emperor had secretly encouraged. In the month of November the truce was renewed, and a commission of a hundred and twenty members having met at Coblence, charged with the duty of arranging the partition of the kingdoms among the three brothers, the division was definitively concluded at Verdun, in the month of August 843. The official document has been lost, but it is nevertheless possible, from the information given by the chroniclers, to state its main provisions. The Empire was divided from East to West into three sections, and "Lothar received the middle kingdom," *i.e.* Italy and the region lying between the Alps, the Aar and the Rhine on the East (together with the Ripuarian counties on the lower right bank of the latter river) and the Rhone, the Saône and the Scheldt on the West. These made up a strip of territory about a thousand miles in length by one hundred and thirty in breadth, reaching from the North Sea to the Duchy of Benevento. Louis received the countries beyond the Rhine, except Frisia which was left to

Lothar, while west of that river, "because of the abundance of wine" and in order that he should have his share of what was originally Austrasia, he was given in addition the dioceses of Spires, Worms and Mayence. Charles kept the rest as far as Spain, nothing being said as to Pepin II, whose rights the Emperor found himself unable to enforce. This division at first sight appears fairly simple, but in reality the frontiers it assigned to Lothar's kingdom were largely artificial, since the border-line by no means followed the course of the rivers, but cutting off from the Emperor's share three counties on the left bank of the Rhine, allowed him in compensation on the left bank of the Meuse the districts of Mézières and Mouzon, the Dormois, the Verdunois, the Barrois, the Ornois with Bassigny, and on the right bank of the Rhone, the Vivarais and the Uzège with, of course, the whole of the transrhodanian parts of the counties of Vienne and Lyons. Each of the three brothers swore to secure to the other two the share thus adjudged to them, and to maintain concord, and "peace having been thus made and confirmed by oath, each one returned to his kingdom to govern and defend it."

The Treaty of Verdun marks a first stage in the dissolution of the Carolingian Empire. Doubtless it would be idle to see in it an uprising of ancient national feelings against the unity which had been imposed by the strong hand of Charlemagne. In reality, these old nationalities had no more existence on the morrow of the treaty than on the eve of it. It is true that the three ancient kingdoms of Lombardy, Bavaria and Aquitaine formed *nuclei* of the states set up in 843. But Lothar's portion included races as different as those dwelling round the Lower Rhine and those of central Italy. Louis, besides Germans, had Slav subjects, and even some Franks who spoke the Romance tongue. Charles became the ruler of the greater part of the Franks of Francia, the country between the Rhine and the Loire which was to give its name to his kingdom, but his Breton and Aquitanian vassals had nothing to connect them closely with the Neustrians or the Burgundians. The partition of 843 was the logical outcome of the mistakes of Louis the Pious who, for the sake of Charles, his Benjamin, had sacrificed in his interests that unity of the Empire which it had been the object of the *Constitutio* of 817 to safeguard, while at the same time it gave the younger sons of Louis the position of kings. None the less, the date 843 is a convenient one in history to mark a dividing line, to register the beginning of the individual life of modern nations. Louis had received the greater part of the lands in which the Teutonic language was spoken; Charles reigned almost exclusively (setting aside the Bretons) over populations of the Romance tongue. This difference only became more accentuated as time went on. On the other hand, the frequent changes of sovereignty in Lorraine have permanently made of ancient Austrasia a debateable territory. The consequences of the treaty of Verdun have made themselves felt even down to our own day, since from 843 to 1920 France and Germany have contended for portions of *media Francia*, the ancient home whence the companions of Charles and Pepin went forth to conquer *Gallia* and *Germania*. But in 843 France and Germany do not yet exist. Each sovereign looks upon himself as a King of the Franks. None the less, there is a Frankish kingdom of the West and a Frankish kingdom of the East, the destinies of which will henceforth lie apart, and from this point of view it is true to say that the grandsons of Charles, the universal Emperor, have each his country.

Even contemporary writers realised the importance of the division made by the Treaty of Verdun in the history of the Frankish monarchy. The following justly famous verses by the deacon Florus of Lyons sum up the situation as it appeared to the advocates of the *ancien régime* of imperial unity:

> Floruit egregium claro diademate regnum:
> Princeps unus erat, populus quoque subditus unus,
> . . . .
> At nunc tantus apex tanto de culmine lapsus,
> . . . .
> Cunctorum teritur pedibus; diademate nudus
> Perdidit imperii pariter nomenque decusque,
> Et regnum unitum concidit sorte triformi.
> Induperator ibi prorsus jam nemo putatur;
> Pro rege est regulus, pro regno fragmina regni[1].

For the old conception of a united Empire in which kings acted merely as lieutenants of the Emperor, was being substituted the idea of a new form of government, that of three kings, equal in dignity and in effective power. Lothar, it is true, retained the imperial title, but had been unable to secure, by obtaining a larger extent of territory, any real superiority over his brothers. He possessed, indeed, the two capitals of the Empire, Rome and Aix, but this circumstance did not, in the ninth century, carry all the weight in men's minds that has since been attributed to it. Besides this advantage in dignity was largely counterbalanced by the inferiority arising from the weakness of geographical position which marked Lothar's long strip of territory, peopled by varying races with varying interests, threatened on the north by the Danes, and on the south by the Saracens, over the whole of which it was barely possible that he could exercise his direct authority. As to the Emperor's brothers, they were naturally disinclined to recognise in him any superiority over them. In their negotiations with him they regard themselves as his equals (peers, *pares*). Beyond his title of king they give him no designation save that of "elder brother" and the very word *imperium* rarely occurs in documents.

---

[1] *Querela de divisione imperii* in *M.H.G., Poet. Lat.*, Vol. II. p. 559 et sqq.

Yet to say that the Empire has completely disappeared would be an exaggeration. One of the chief prerogatives of the Emperor is still maintained. It was his function not merely to safeguard the unity of the Frankish monarchy, but his duty was also to protect the Church and the Holy See, that is, to take care that religious peace was preserved, at all events, throughout Western Christendom, and, in concert with the Pope, to govern Rome and the Papal States. As Lothar had been entrusted with these duties during his father's lifetime, he would be more familiar with them than any other person. " The Pope," he said himself, "put the sword into my hand to defend the altar and the throne," and the very first measure of his administration had been the Roman Constitution of 824 which defined the relations of the two powers. These imperial rights and duties had not been made to vanish by the new situation created in other respects for the Emperor in 843. If Lothar does not seem to have given any large share of his attention to ecclesiastical affairs, on the other hand he is found intervening, either personally or through his son Louis, in papal elections. In 844 Sergius II, who had been consecrated without the Emperor's participation, met with bitter reproaches for having thus neglected to observe the constitution of 824. On his death (847) the people of Rome, alarmed at the risk involved in a vacancy of the Holy See while Saracen invasions were threatening, again ignored the imperial regulations at the election of Leo IV. But the latter hastened to write to Lothar and Louis II to make excuses for the irregular course taken by the Romans. In 855 the election of Benedict III took place, all forms being duly observed, and was respectfully notified to the two *Augusti* through the medium of their *missi*. The measures taken by Lothar against the Saracens of Italy were dictated as much by the necessity of defending his own states as by a sense of his position as Protector of the Holy See, but there were one or two occasions on which he appears to have attempted to exercise some authority on matters ecclesiastical in the dominions of his brother Charles.

It is at least highly probable that it was at his request that Sergius II, in 844, granted to Drogo Bishop of Metz, who had already under colour of his personal claims been invested with archiepiscopal dignity, the office of Vicar Apostolic throughout the Empire north of the Alps, with the right of convoking General Councils, and of summoning all ecclesiastical causes before his tribunal, previous to any appeal being made to Rome. This, from the spiritual point of view, was to give control to the Emperor, through the medium of one of his prelates, over ecclesiastical affairs in the kingdoms of his two brothers. But as early as the month of December 844, a synod of the bishops of the Western Kingdom at Ver (near Compiègne) declared, with abundance of personally complimentary expressions towards Drogo, that his primatial authority must be first of all recognised by a general assembly of the bishops concerned. Such an assembly, as may be imagined, never came together, and the Archbishop of Metz was forced to resign himself to a purely honorary vicariate.

Lothar met with no better success in his attempt to restore his ally, Ebbo, to his archiepiscopal throne at Rheims, whence he had been expelled in 835 as a traitor to the Emperor Louis, though no successor had yet been appointed. The Pope turned a deaf ear to all representations on Ebbo's behalf, and the Council at Ver entreated Charles to provide the Church of Rheims with a pastor without delay. This pastor proved to be the celebrated Hincmar[1] who for nearly forty years was to be the most strenuous and illustrious representative of the episcopate of Gaul.

Thus the attempts made by Lothar to obtain anything in the nature of supremacy outside the borders of his own kingdom had met with no success. They even had a tendency to bring about a renewal of hostilities between him and his youngest brother. But the bishops surrounding the three kings had a clear conception of the Treaty of Verdun as having been made not only to settle the territorial problem, but also to secure the continuance of peace and order. The magnates themselves were weary of civil war, and had, besides, enemies from without to contend against, Slavs, Saracens, Bretons and, above all, Northmen. They were of one mind with the prelates in saying to the three brothers " You must abstain from secret machinations to one another's hurt, and you must support and aid one another." Consequently a new system was established called with perfect correctness "the system of concord," of concord secured by frequent meetings between the three brothers.

The first of these interviews took place at Yütz, near Thionville, in October 844, at the same time as a synod of the bishops of the three kingdoms under the presidency of Drogo. Here the principles governing the " Carolingian fraternity " were at once laid down. The kings, for the future, are not to seek to injure one another, but on the contrary, are to lend one another mutual aid and assistance against enemies from outside.

The king most threatened at the time by enemies such as these was Charles the Bald. In 842 the Northmen had pillaged the great commercial mart of Quentovic near the river Canche[2]. In the following year they went up the Loire as far as Nantes which they plundered, slaughtering the bishop during the celebration of divine service. The Bretons, united under their leader Nomenoë, and not much impressed by an expedition sent against them in 843, were invading Frankish

---

[1] Hincmar, who was born during the first years of the ninth century, was at this time a monk at Saint-Denis and entrusted with the government of the Abbeys of Notre-Dame by Compiègne and Saint-Germer de Flay. But Charles had already employed him on various missions, and he seems for some years to have held an important position among the king's counsellors.

[2] Chapter XIII deals with the Vikings. They are therefore mentioned here only so far as is necessary to an understanding of the general history of the Frankish kingdoms.

territory. Lambert, one of the Counts of the March, created to keep them in check, had risen in revolt and was making common cause with them. On the other hand, the Aquitanians, faithful to Pepin II, the king they had chosen, refused to recognise Charles. An expedition which the king had sent against them in the spring of 844 had failed through a check to the siege of Toulouse, and through the execution of Charles's former protector, Count Bernard of Septimania, who was accused of treason. The Frankish troops, beaten by the Aquitanians on the banks of the river Agoût, had been forced to beat a retreat without accomplishing any useful purpose. The kings, who had met at Yütz, addressed a joint letter to Nomenoë, Lambert and Pepin II, threatening to unite and march against them if they persisted in their rebellion. These threats, however, were only partially effective. Pepin agreed to do homage to Charles, who in exchange for this profession of obedience recognised his possession of a restricted Aquitaine, without Poitou, the Angoumois or Saintonge. But the Bretons, for their part, refused to submit. Charles sent against them an expedition which ended in a lamentable defeat on the plain of Ballon, not far from Redon (22 November 845).

During the following summer Charles was compelled to sign a treaty with Nomenoë acknowledging the independence of Brittany, and to leave the rebel Lambert in possession of the county of Maine. A body of Scandinavian pirates went up the Seine in 845; the king was obliged to buy their withdrawal with a sum of money. Other Danes, led by their king, Horic, were ravaging the dominions of Louis the German, particularly Saxony. In 845 their countrymen had got possession of Hamburg and destroyed it. At the same time Louis had to keep back his Slav neighbours, and to send expeditions against the rebellious Obotrites (844) and the Moravians (846). Lothar, for his part, had in 845 to contend with a revolt of his Provençal subjects led by Fulcrad, Count of Arles. The friendly agreement proclaimed at Yütz between the three brothers was a necessity of the situation. It was nevertheless disturbed by the action of a vassal of Charles the Bald, named Gilbert (Giselbert), who carried off a daughter of Lothar I, taking her with him to Aquitaine where he married her (846). Great was the Emperor's wrath against his youngest brother, whom he accused, in spite of all his protests, of complicity with the abductor. He renewed his intrigues at Rome on behalf of Drogo and Ebbo, and even gave shelter in his dominions to Charles, brother of Pepin, who had again rebelled. Besides this he allowed certain of his adherents to lead expeditions into the Western Kingdom which were, in fact, mere plundering raids. He consented, however, in the beginning of 847 to meet Louis and Charles in a fresh conference which took place at Meersen near Maestricht.

Again the principle of fraternity was proclaimed, and this time it was extended beyond the sovereigns themselves to their subjects. Further, for the first time a provision was made which chiefly interested Lothar, who was already concerned about the succession to his crown. It was decided to guarantee to the children of any one of the three brothers who might happen to die, the peaceful possession of their father's kingdom. Letters or ambassadors were also ordered to be sent to the Northmen, the Bretons and the Aquitanians. But this latter resolution, save for an advance made to King Horic, remained nearly a dead letter. Lothar, who still cherished anger against Gilbert's suzerain, chose to leave him in the midst of the difficulties which pressed upon him, and even sought an alliance against him with Louis the German, his interviews with whom become very frequent during the next few years.

Nevertheless the position of Charles improved. The magnates of Aquitaine, ever inconstant, had abandoned Pepin II, almost to a man, and Charles had, as it were, set a seal upon his entrance into actual possession of the whole of the states which the treaty of 843 had recognised as his, by having himself solemnly crowned and anointed at Orleans on 6 June 848 by Ganelon (Wenilo), the Archbishop of Sens. Again, Gilbert had left Aquitaine and taken refuge at the court of Louis the German. There was no longer any obstacle to the reconciliation of Lothar with his youngest brother, which took place in a very cordial interview between the two sovereigns at Péronne (January 849). A little later, Louis the German, in his turn, had a meeting with Charles, at which the two kings mutually "recommended" their kingdoms and the guardianship of their children to one another, in case of the death of either. The result of all these private interviews was a general conference held at Meersen in the spring of 851 in order to buttress the somewhat shaky edifice of the *concordia fratrum*. The principles of brotherly amity and the duty of mutual help were again proclaimed, supplemented by a pledge given by the three brothers to forget their resentment for the past, and, in order to avoid any further occasions of discord, to refuse entrance into any one kingdom to such as had disturbed the peace of any other.

But these fair professions did little to alter the actual state of things, and the sovereigns pursued their intrigues against one another. Lothar tried to recommend himself to Charles by procuring for Hincmar the grant of the pallium. Louis the German, on the contrary, displayed his enmity to him by receiving into his dominions the disgraced Archbishop Ebbo, to whom he even gave the bishopric of Hildesheim. Meanwhile the Scandinavian invasions raged ever more fiercely in the Western Kingdom. In 851 the Danish followers of the sea-king Oscar, having devastated Aquitaine, pushed up the Seine as far as Rouen, pillaged Jumièges and Saint-Wandrille, and from thence made their way into the Beauvais country which they ravaged with fire and sword. Next year another fleet desisted from pillaging Frisia to sail up the Seine. Other hordes ascended the Loire, and in 853 burned Tours and its

collegiate church of St Martin, one of the most venerated sanctuaries of
Gaul. Some of the Northmen, quitting the river-banks, carried fire and
sword through the country to Angers and Poitiers. Next year Blois and
Orleans were ravaged, and a body of Danes wintered at the island of
Besse near Nantes, where they fortified themselves. On the other hand,
in 849, Nomenoë of Brittany, who was striving ever harder to make good
his position as an independent sovereign, and had just made an attempt
to set up a new ecclesiastical organisation in Brittany, withdrawing it
from the jurisdiction of the Frankish metropolitan at Tours[1], was again
in arms. He seized upon Rennes, and ravaged the country as far as
Le Mans. Death put an abrupt end to his successes (7 March 851), but
his son and successor, Erispoë, obtained from Charles, who had been discouraged by a fruitless expedition, his recognition as king of Brittany,
now enlarged by the districts of Nantes, Retz and Rennes.

Finally, the affairs of Aquitaine only just failed to rekindle war
between the Eastern and Western kings. The authority of Charles, in
spite of Pepin's oath of fealty, and in spite of the apparent submission
of the magnates in 848, had never been placed, to the south of the Loire,
on really solid foundations. In 849 he had been obliged to despatch a
fresh expedition into Aquitaine, which had failed in taking Toulouse.
But afterwards in 852 the chance of a skirmish threw Pepin into the
hands of Sancho, Count of Gascony, who handed him over to Charles the
Bald. The king at once had the captive tonsured and interned in a
monastery. But this did little to secure the submission of Aquitaine.
The very next year the magnates of the country sent envoys to Louis
the German offering him the crown, either for himself or one of his
sons, and threatening, if he refused it, to have recourse to the heathen,
either Saracen or Northman. Louis the German agreed to send one of his
sons, Louis the Younger, whom they might put at their head. But
Charles the Bald had become aware of what was intended against him,
for he is at once found making closer alliance with Lothar, whom he met
twice, first at Valenciennes and then at Liège. In the course of the
interviews the two sovereigns guaranteed to each other the peaceful
possession of their lands for themselves and their heirs. When they
separated, Aquitaine was in full revolt. Charles hastened to collect his

---

[1] The question of the Breton schism has given rise within the last few years to
keen discussion between M. M. R. Merlet (*La Chronique de Nantes*, Paris, 1896,
8vo, p. xxxix et sqq.); R. de la Borderie (*Histoire de la Bretagne*, tome ii. p. 480
et sqq.); Mgr. Duchesne, *Fastes épiscopaux de l'ancienne Gaule*, tome ii. p. 256 et sqq.);
L. Levillain ('Les réformes ecclésiastiques de Nomenoë' in the *Moyen Age*, 1901, p. 201
et sqq.) and F. Lot ('Le schisme breton du ixᵉ siècle' in *Mélanges d'histoire
bretonne*, Paris, 1907, 8vo, p. 58 et sqq.) especially with regard to the value of the
original narratives dealing with these facts. It seems certain that the Breton prince
set up a metropolitanate of Dol. But it is more doubtful whether he created bishoprics
at Tréguier and Saint-Brieuc, which continued as before to be abbeys the Abbots
of which held the rank of Bishops.

army, cross the Loire and march against the rebels, ravaging the country as he went, devastated as it already was by the troops which Louis the Younger had brought from beyond the Rhine. The news of a colloquy between Lothar and his brother of Germany excited the distrust of Charles the Bald, and abruptly recalled him to the north of Gaul, where he came to Attigny to renew the alliance previously made with the Emperor. Then, with his army he again set out for Aquitaine. But what was of more service to him than these warlike demonstrations was the re-appearance, south of the Loire, of Pepin II, who had escaped from his prison. At the sight of their old prince, the Aquitanians very generally abandoned the cause of Louis the Younger, who found himself forced to return to Bavaria. But it does not appear that Charles the Bald looked upon Pepin's power as very firmly established, for next year he gave a king to the Aquitanians in the person of his own son Charles (the Younger) whom he caused to be solemnly anointed at Limoges.

A few weeks earlier, Lothar, after having arranged for the division of his lands among the three sons whom the Empress Ermengarde had borne him, retired to the Abbey of Prüm. Here it was that on the night of 28–29 September 855, his restless life reached its end.

The partition which the Emperor Lothar I had thus made of his territories divided into three truncated portions the long strip of country which by the treaty of 843 had fallen to him as the lot of the eldest son of Louis the Pious. To Louis II, the eldest of the dead man's sons, was given the imperial title, which he had borne since April 850, together with Italy. To the next, Lothar II, were bequeathed the districts from Frisia to the Alps and between the Rhine and the Scheldt which were to preserve his own name, for they were called *Lotharii regnum,* *i.e.* Lorraine. For the youngest son, Charles, a new kingdom was formed by the union of Provence proper with the duchy of Lyons (*i.e.* the Lyonnais and the Viennois). For the rest, the two elder were discontented with their share, and in an interview which they had with their younger brother at Orbe attempted to force him into retirement in order to take possession of his kingdom. Only the intervention of the Provençal magnates saved the young prince Charles, and Lothar II and Louis II were forced to carry out the last directions of their father. But the death of Lothar I, whose position both in theory and in fact had fitted him to act as in some sort a mediator between his two brothers, endangered the maintenance of peace and concord. Charles, who was a feeble epileptic, had no weight in the " Carolingian concert." It was only the kind of regency entrusted to Gerard, Count of Vienne, renowned in legendary epic as Girard of Roussillon, which secured the continued existence of the little kingdom of Provence. Louis II, whose attention was concentrated on the struggle with the Saracens, had to content himself with the part of " Emperor of the Italians," as the Frank annalists, not without a touch of contempt, describe him. Only Lothar II, as ruler of the country where the Frank empire had been founded, and whence its aristocracy had largely sprung, might, in virtue of his comparative strength and the geographical situation of his kingdom, count for something in the relations between his two uncles. Thus at the very beginning of his reign we find Louis the German seeking to come into closer touch with him at an interview at Coblence (February 857). Lothar, however, remained constant to the alliance made by his father with Charles the Bald, which he solemnly renewed at Saint-Quentin.

The Western Kingdom was still in a distracted state. The treaty concluded at Louviers with King Erispoë (10 February 856) had for a time secured peace with the Bretons. Prince Louis, who was about to become Erispoë's son-in-law, was to be entrusted with the government of the march created on the Breton frontier, and known as the Duchy of Maine. But the Northmen were becoming ever more menacing. In the same year, 856, in the month of August, the Viking Sidroc made his way up the Seine and established himself at Pitres. A few weeks later he was joined by another Danish chief, Björn Ironside, and together they ravaged the country from the Seine to the Loire. In vain Charles, despite the systematic opposition of a party among the magnates who refused to join the host, shewed laudable energy in resisting their advance, and even succeeded in inflicting a check upon them. In the end, they established themselves at Oscellum, an island in the Seine opposite Jeufosse, near Mantes, twice ascending the river as far as Paris, which they plundered, taking prisoner and holding to ransom Louis, Abbot of Saint-Denis, one of the chief personages of the kingdom. On the other hand, Maine, in spite of the presence of Prince Louis, remained a hotbed of disaffection to Charles. The whole family of the Count Gauzbert, who had been beheaded for treason some few years before, was in rebellion, supported by the magnates of Aquitaine, where Pepin II had again taken up arms and was carrying on a successful struggle with Charles the Young. Even outside Aquitaine discontent was rife. Family rivalry intensified every difficulty. The clan then most in favour with Charles was that of the Welfs, who were related to the Empress Judith, the most prominent members of it being her brother Conrad, lay Abbot of Jumièges and of St Riquier, who was one of the most influential of the king's counsellors, and his nephews Conrad, Count of Auxerre, and Hugh, Abbot of St Germain in the same town. The relations of Queen Ermentrude, who were thrust somewhat on one side, Adalard, Odo, Count of Troyes, and Robert the Strong, the successor in Maine of young Louis whom the magnates had driven out, attracted the discontented round them.

Charles had reason to be uneasy. Already in 853, the Aquitanians had appealed to the king of Germany. In 856 the disloyal among the magnates had again asked help of him, and only the necessity of preparing for a war with the Slavs had prevented him from complying with their request. Charles the Bald attempted to provide against such contingencies. At Verberie near Senlis (856), at Quierzy near Laon (857 and 858), at Brienne (858), he demanded of his magnates that they should renew their oath of fealty. In 858 he thought he could sufficiently depend on them to venture on a new expedition against the Northmen, who had fortified themselves in the island of Oscellum. Charles the Younger and Pepin II of Aquitaine had promised their help. Lothar II himself came with a Lotharingian contingent to take a share in the campaign (summer of 858). This was the moment which Adalard and Odo chose for addressing a fresh appeal to Louis the German. The latter, who was on the point of marching anew against the Slavs, hesitated long, if we are to trust his chroniclers. Finally, "strong in the purity of his intentions, he preferred to serve the interests of the many rather than to submit to the tyranny of one man." Above all, he considered the opportunity favourable. Lothar's absence left the road across Alsace clear for him, and by 1 September 858 he had established himself in the Western Kingdom, in the palace of Ponthion. Here he was joined by such of the magnates as had deserted Charles the Bald before the fortified Northmen. Thence by way of Châlons-sur-Marne, he reached first Sens, whither he was called by its Archbishop Ganelon, and then Orleans, shewing plainly his intention of holding out a hand to the rebels of Le Mans and Aquitaine.

Charles, for his part, on hearing of the invasion, had hastily raised the siege of Oscellum, and was on the march for Lorraine. Louis, fearing to have his retreat to Germany cut off, retraced his steps, whereupon the armies of the two brothers found themselves face to face in the neighbourhood of Brienne. But the Frankish counts, whose support was essential for the final success of either party, had a deep and well-founded distaste for pitched battles; the question for them, was merely the greater or less number of " benefices" which they might hope to obtain from one or the other adversary. Recourse was consequently had to negotiation, when despite the numerous embassies sent by Charles to Louis, the latter shewed himself the more skilful of the two. By dint of promises, he succeeded in corrupting nearly all his brother's vassals. Charles found himself constrained to throw up the game, and retire to Burgundy, the one province where his supporters were still in a majority. Louis, seeing nothing to be gained by pursuing him thither, betook himself to the palace of Attigny, whence on 7 December he issued a diploma as king of Western Francia, and where he spent his time in dealing out honours and benefices to those who had come over to his side. But in order to make his triumph secure, he still had to be acknowledged and consecrated by the Church. The episcopate of the Western Kingdom, however, remained faithful to Charles, whether through attachment to the principles of peace and concord, or through dread of a new system founded on the ambitions of the lay aristocracy, who were ever ready to extort payment for their support out of the estates of the ecclesiastical magnates. Only Ganelon of Sens, forgetting that he owed his preferment to Charles's favour, had taken sides with the new sovereign, thus leaving his name to become in tradition that of the most notorious traitor of medieval epic. The bishops of the provinces of Rheims and Rouen being summoned by Louis to attend a council at Rheims, contrived under the skilful guidance of Hincmar to hinder the meeting from being held; protesting meanwhile their good intentions, but declaring it necessary to summon a general assembly of the episcopate, and demanding guarantees for the safety of Church property. The presence of Louis the German in the province of Rheims, where he came to spend the Christmas season, and to take up his winter quarters, made no difference in the Bishops' attitude.

However, Charles the Bald, with the help of the Abbot Hugh and Count Conrad, had rallied all the supporters that remained to him at Auxerre. On 9 January he suddenly left his retreat and marched against his brother. Many of the German lords had set out to return to their own country. The Western magnates, not seeing any sufficient advantage to be gained under the new government, shewed no more hesitation in deserting it than they had in accepting it. At Jouy, near Soissons, where the sudden appearance of his brother took Louis by surprise, the German found himself left with so small a proportion of his quondam followers that in his turn he was forced to retreat without striking a blow. By the spring of 859 Charles had regained his authority. Naturally, he made use of it to punish those who had betrayed him. Adalard lost his Abbey of Saint-Bertin which was given to the Abbot Hugh, and Odo lost his counties. What makes it plain that for the magnates the whole affair was simply a question of material gain, is that in the negotiations which Charles opened with Louis the point that he specially insisted on was that the latter, in exchange for the renewal of their alliance, should abandon to his discretion those magnates who had shared in the defection, in order that he might deprive them of their estates. The negotiations, moreover, proved long and thorny, despite the intervention of Lothar II. Synods and embassies, even an interview between the two sovereigns, in a boat midway across the Rhine, produced no results. It was not until the colloquy held at St Castor in Coblence on 1 June 860, in the presence of a large number of bishops, Hincmar being among them, that Louis and Charles succeeded in coming to terms. Charles the Bald promised to leave his magnates in possession of the fiefs which they had received from Louis the German, reserving his right to deprive them of those which he himself had previously bestowed on them. The oaths of peace and concord made in 851 at Meersen were again sworn to. Louis made a declaration to this effect in the German tongue, denouncing the severest penalties on all who should violate the agreement, a declaration afterwards repeated by Charles in the Romance language, and even in German as far as the more important passages were concerned.

Briefly, it was a return to the *status quo* as it had been before the sudden stroke attempted by Louis. A fresh match was about to be played, the stake this time being the kingdom of Lothar II.

From about 860 to 870 the whole policy of the Carolingian kings turns mainly on the question of the king of Lorraine's divorce and the possible succession to his crown. In 855, Lothar had been compelled by his father to marry Theutberga, a maiden of noble family, sister of a lord named Hubert whose estates were situated on the upper valley of the Rhone, and who seems about this time to have been made by the Emperor governor " of the duchy between the Jura and the Alps" corresponding roughly to French Switzerland of to-day. The marriage was evidently arranged with the object of ensuring for the young king the support of a powerful family. But before it took place, Lothar had had a mistress named Waldrada, by whom he had children, and this woman seems to have acquired over him an extraordinary ascendency, which contemporaries, as a matter of course, attribute to the use of magic. From the very beginning of his reign, Lothar bent all his energy towards the single end of ridding himself, by any possible means, of the consort chosen by his father, and raising his former mistress to the title and rank of a legitimate wife. Theutberga had not borne an heir to Lothar and seems to have been considered incapable of doing so, although this was not used as a weapon against her by her adversaries. On the other hand, it was the consideration which determined the attitude of the other sovereigns and helped to make the question of the Lorraine divorce, it may almost be said, an international one. If Lothar were to die childless, it would mean the partition of his inheritance among his relations, practically between his two uncles, for his brother Charles, epileptic and near his end, was in no position to interfere, while Louis II, himself without an heir, was too much occupied in Southern Italy to be a very serious competitor.

Hostile measures against Theutberga had been taken almost at the very beginning of the new king's reign. He hurled at his wife a charge of incest with her brother Hubert. But a champion nominated by the queen submitted himself on her behalf to the Judgment of God by the ordeal of boiling water. The result was the solemn proclamation of Theutberga's innocence, and Lothar II was obliged to yield to the wishes of his nobles and take back his wife. Hubert, for his part, had revolted, and under the pretext of defending his sister was indulging in acts of brigandage in the upper valley of the Rhone. An expedition sent against him by the king of Lorraine had produced no results. Thus the cession made (859) by Lothar to his brother Louis II of the three dioceses of Geneva, Lausanne and Sion had been designed, quite as much to rid the kingdom of Lorraine of a turbulent noble as to conciliate the good will of the Emperor. In the same way, Lothar had, the year before, attempted to win over Charles of Provence, by ceding to him the two dioceses of Belley and Tarentaise, in exchange, indeed, for a treaty securing to him the inheritance of his young brother, in the event, which seemed not unlikely, of the latter's dying childless. The conflict of 858–9 had displayed Lothar's anxiety to keep on good terms with both of his uncles by abstaining from interference on behalf of either. At the same time an active campaign was being kept up against Theutberga, organised by two prelates devoted to the king of Lorraine, Theutgaud, Archbishop of Trèves, and Gunther, Archbishop of Cologne. The latter even, with skilful treachery, contrived to become confessor to the persecuted queen. In January 860, Lothar thought himself sure enough of his position to convoke a council at Aix-la-Chapelle before which he appeared, declaring that his wife herself acknowledged her guilt, and petitioned to be allowed to take the veil. The bishops did not profess themselves convinced, and demanded that a fresh assembly should be held, to which were summoned foreign bishops and in particular Hincmar. But the latter did not respond to the invitation, and it was at a synod composed exclusively of Lorrainers, and again held at Aix, that Theutberga herself was present and read a confession, evidently drawn up by Gunther and his accomplices, in which she acknowledged herself guilty of the crimes imputed to her. On this occasion the bishops were obliged to accept as valid the declaration thus made by the queen and to condemn her. But they avoided coming to a decision on the point which lay nearest to Lothar's heart, viz. the possibility of his contracting another marriage. He was forced to content himself with the imprisonment of Theutberga without advancing any further towards the execution of his plans.

Some months later the dispute was re-opened. Hincmar stepped into the lists by putting forth his voluminous treatise *De divortio Lotharii,* in which he shewed clearly the weakness of the arguments used against Theutberga, and pronounced confessions extorted by constraint and violence null, while demanding that the question should be examined in a general council of the bishops of the Franks. The treatise of the Archbishop of Rheims was of exceptional importance, due not only to the reputation which he enjoyed in the ecclesiastical world as a theologian and canonist, but also to his political prominence in the Western Kingdom as the adviser of Charles the Bald. The latter thus took his place among the declared opponents of Lothar II's matrimonial policy. He gave further proof of this attitude by affording shelter in his kingdom to Hubert, who was forced to quit Lorraine, and to Theutberga, who had succeeded in making her escape. Lothar, indeed, retorted by offering a refuge to Judith, Charles's daughter, the widow of the old English king Aethelwulf; she had just arranged to be carried off by Baldwin Iron-arm, first Count of Flanders, son of Odoacer, whom she married in spite of her father's opposition. And Charles at the same time met with a check in Provence. Called in by a party of the magnates of the country, he had imagined himself in a position to lay hands on his nephew's kingdom. But Gerard of Roussillon was mounting guard over the young prince, and in the face of his energetic opposition, Charles was obliged to beat a retreat after having advanced as far as Burgundy (861). At the same time Lothar was making advances to his other uncle, Louis the German, whose friendship he endeavoured to make sure of by ceding to him Alsace, or at least the prospect of possessing it whenever the king of Lorraine should die. Lothar now thought himself strong enough to convoke at Aix a fresh council, which this time declared the marriage contracted with Theutberga null and void, and consequently pronounced the king free to form a fresh union. Lothar, before long, made use of this permission by marrying Waldrada and having her solemnly crowned. But Theutberga, for her part, appealed to the Pope to quash the sentences pronounced against her. Lothar retorted by petitioning the sovereign pontiff to confirm the judgments which had been given. At the same time, in concert with Louis the German, he complained to the Pope of the conduct of Charles the Bald, "who, without any show of right, was seeking to lay hands on the inheritance of his nephews."

Meanwhile Charles was gaining power in his own kingdom. He had just defeated the Bretons under their King Solomon, and suppressed a revolt of his own son Louis the Stammerer, while the magnates who had risen against him in 858–859 were one by one making their submission to him. The invasions by the Northmen indeed were still going on. Paris had again been pillaged in 861. The hordes of the viking Weland, whom Charles had hoped to hire for money and employ against their compatriots in the island of Oscellum, had made common cause with the latter and had ravaged the Seine valley as far as Melun. Charles had discovered a method of resisting them, and from the time of the assembly at Pitres (862) began to put it into practice. It was to have fortified works constructed along the rivers which the Normans ascended, particularly bridges, which should bar the way to the invaders. This new departure in tactics produced fairly good results during the years that followed. In 862, Charles, in this way, cut off the retreat of the bands which had forced their way into the Meaux country, and compelled them to promise to give up the prisoners they had made and to quit the kingdom. During the succeeding years, we find the king taking measures to complete the defences of the valleys of the Seine and Oise. It is true that these precautions did not hinder the Northmen from again burning Paris in 865, and from penetrating as far as Melun in 866. This time Charles could only rid himself of them by paying them ransom. But on the other hand, the Marquess Robert the Strong defeated the Northmen of the Loire on several occasions, and up to his death in the fight at Brissarthe (866) the valour of " the Maccabaeus of France " opposed substantial resistance to the invaders of Anjou and Maine.

In the affair of Lothar, neither Charles nor Hincmar would give way. The king of Western Francia had shewn himself determined strenuously to maintain the fight on behalf of the indissolubility of marriage, and declared that he would hold no further intercourse with his nephew until he should take back Theutberga. He repeated this resolution at the interview which he had with his brother Louis at Savonnières near Toul (November 862), to which Lothar had sent as his representatives several of the bishops of his kingdom. Charles accused his nephew of being a cause of double scandal to the Christian Church by the favour he had shewn to the guilty connexion between Baldwin and Judith, and by marrying Waldrada without waiting for the opinion of the Pope. He called for the assembling of a general council to pronounce definitively on both these questions. In the end, Lothar agreed, so far as Judith's case was concerned, but in the matter of the divorce he declared that he would await the decision of the Pope. Charles was obliged to be content with this reply, and to take leave of his brother, having done nothing more than renew the treaty of peace and alliance concluded in 860 at Coblence.

The death of Charles of Provence (25 January 863) made little change in the respective positions of the sovereigns. The dead man left no children; his heirs therefore were his two brothers, for Louis II does not appear to have recognised the treaty concluded in 858 between Charles and Lothar II, by which the latter was to succeed to the whole of the inheritance. Therefore the two rivals hastened to reach Provence, each being eager to win over the magnates of the country to his own side. The seemingly inevitable conflict was warded off, thanks to an agreement which gave Provence, strictly so-called, as far as the Durance to the Emperor, and to the king of Lorraine the Lyonnais and the Viennois, that is to say the Duchy of Lyons, of which Gerard of Roussillon was governor.

But the question of Theutberga was still not definitely settled, and for the years that followed, it remained the subject of difficult negotiations, on the one hand between the different Frankish sovereigns, and on the other between these sovereigns and the Pope. The situation was eminently favourable to a Pope of the character of Nicholas I, who, in 858 had taken the place of Benedict III on the papal throne. Being petitioned to intervene at once by Theutberga, Lothar, and the opponents of Lothar, he could take up the position of the arbiter of the Christian world. Meanwhile, without deciding the question himself, he resolved to hand over the settlement of it to a great council to be held at Metz at which not only the bishops of Lorraine should be present, but two representatives of the episcopate in each of the kingdoms of France, Germany and Provence. The assembly was to be presided over by two envoys from the Holy See, John, Bishop of Cervia, and Radoald, Bishop of Porto. But Lothar's partisans were on the alert, and were working to gain time. The papal letters carried by the two legates were stolen from them by skilful thieves and they were forced to apply for new ones. While they were waiting, and while, on the other hand, Lothar's absence in Provence to take up the inheritance of his brother delayed the calling of the Council, the emissaries of Gunther and Theutgaud succeeded in bribing Radoald and his colleague. The legates failed to convoke the foreign bishops, and the purely Lotharingian synod held at Metz was a tool in the hands of Gunther. It therefore confirmed the decisions of the assembly of Aix, basing them on the ground of an alleged marriage between Lothar and Waldrada, previous to his union with Theutberga (June 863).

This statement, improbable as being now produced for the first time, did not suffice to appease the righteous anger of Nicholas I when he learned by what methods the case had been conducted. He did not hesitate to quash the decisions of the Council, to condemn Radoald and John, and, irregular as the proceeding was, to depose Gunther and Theutgaud by the exercise of his own authority. On the other hand, Louis II, who had shewn some disposition, at first, to support the Lotharingian bishops, now abandoned his brother, in spite of the interview which he had just had with him at Orbe. Louis the German and Charles the Bald, on the contrary, drew closer together. In February 865, they had an interview at Tusey, where, under colour of renewing their mutual oaths of peace and concord, and of reprehending their nephew, they arranged a treaty for the eventual partition of his lands. The Lotharingian bishops became restive, and drew up a protest to their brethren in Gaul and Provence, in which they declared themselves ready to support their sovereign "calumniated by the malignant." Lothar, equally alarmed, dreading an armed collision with his uncles, and dreading no less that the Pope should pronounce him excommunicate, thought it advisable to have recourse himself to the Holy See, and by the mediation of the Emperor to announce to the Pope that he was prepared to submit to his decision, provided that a guarantee was given him that the integrity of his kingdom should be respected.

Nicholas I was now become the mediator between kings and the supreme judge of Christendom. He immediately despatched a legate, Arsenius, Bishop of Orta, with orders to convey to the three sovereigns the expression of the Pope's will. After an interview with Louis the German at Frankfort, Arsenius reached Lothar's court at Gondreville by the month of July 865, and in the Pope's name, called upon him to take back Theutberga on pain of excommunication. Lothar was obliged to promise obedience. Arsenius then betook himself to Attigny to present to Charles the Bald letters from the Pope, exhorting him to respect his nephew's territory. From thence he went back to Lorraine, bringing with him Theutberga whom he restored to her husband. On 15 August he celebrated a solemn High Mass before the royal pair who were invested with the insignia of sovereignty, before he began his return journey to Rome, on which he was accompanied by Waldrada, who, in her turn, was to answer for her actions before the Pope. The legation had resulted in a triumph for Nicholas. In the presence of the Pope's clearly expressed requirements, peace had been restored between the kings, and Theutberga had regained her rank as queen. Thanks to his own firmness and skill, the Pope had acted as supreme arbiter; not only Lothar, but Charles the Bald and Louis the German had been obliged to bow before him.

Nevertheless, in the succeeding years, it would appear that Lothar conceived some hope of being able to re-open the divorce question and attain his desired object. Waldrada had hardly arrived at Pavia, when without the formality of a farewell, she succeeded in eluding the legate and in returning to Lorraine, where she remained, in spite of the excommunication launched against her by Nicholas I. Besides this, Charles the Bald's attitude towards his nephew became somewhat less uncompromising, doubtless on account of the temporary disgrace of Hincmar, the most faithful champion of the cause of the indissolubility of marriage. The king of the Western Franks even had a meeting with Lothar at *Ortivineas*, perhaps Orvignes near Bar-le-Duc, when the two princes agreed to take up the divorce question afresh by sending an embassy to Rome under the direction of Egilo, the metropolitan of Sens. But the Pope refused point-blank to fall in with their views, and replied by addressing the bitterest reproaches to Charles, and above all to Lothar, whom he forbade ever to dream of renewing his relations with Waldrada. The death of Nicholas I (13 November 867) gave a new aspect to affairs. His successor, Hadrian II, was a man of much less firmness and consistency, almost of a timorous disposition, and much under the influence of Louis II, that is, of Lothar's brother and ally. Thus, while refusing to receive Theutberga, whom Lothar had thought of compelling to accuse herself before the Pope, and while congratulating Hincmar on his attitude throughout the affair, and again proclaiming the principle of the indissolubility of marriage, the new Pope soon relieved Waldrada from her sentence of excommunication. Lothar resolved to go and plead his cause in person at Rome. Hadrian consented to his taking this step, which Nicholas I had always refused to sanction. The only consideration which could arouse Lothar's uneasiness was the attitude of his uncles. The latter, indeed, despite a recent letter from the Pope taking up the position of the defender of the integrity of the kingdoms, had just come to an agreement at St Arnulf's of Metz, that "in case God should bestow on them the kingdoms of their nephews, they would proceed to a fair and amicable division of them " (867 or 868)[1].

However, in the spring of 869, having extracted from Charles and Louis some vague assurances that they would undertake nothing against his kingdom during his absence, even if he married Waldrada, Lothar set out on his journey with the intention of visiting the Emperor in order to obtain his support at the papal court. Louis II was then at Benevento, warring against the Saracens. At first he shewed himself little disposed to interfere, but his wife, Engilberga, proved willing to play the part of mediator, and, in the end, an interview took place at Monte Cassino between Hadrian and Lothar. The latter received the Eucharist from the hands of the Pope, less, perhaps, as the pledge of pardon than as a kind of judgment of God. " Receive this communion," the Pope is reported to have said to Lothar, " if thou art innocent of the adultery condemned by Nicholas. If, on the contrary, thy conscience accuse thee of guilt, or if thou art minded to fall back into sin, refrain; otherwise by this Sacrament thou shalt be judged and condemned." A dramatic colouring may have been thrown over the incident, but when he left Monte Cassino, Lothar bore with him the promise that the question should again be submitted to a Council. This, for him, meant the hope of undoing the sentence of Nicholas I. Death, which surprised him on his way back, at Piacenza, on 8 August 869, put an end to his plans.

His successor, by right of inheritance, was, strictly speaking, the Emperor Louis. But he was little known outside his Italian kingdom, and appears not to have had many supporters in Lorraine, unless perhaps in the duchy of Lyons, which was close to his Provençal possessions. In Lorraine proper, on the contrary, there were two opposed parties, a German party and a French party, each supporting one of the uncles of the dead king. But Louis the German was detained at Ratisbon by sickness.

Thus circumstances favoured Charles the Bald, who hastened to take advantage of them by entering Lorraine. An embassy from the magnates, which came to meet him at Attigny to remind him of the respect due to the treaty which he had made with his brother at Metz, produced no result. By way of Verdun he reached Metz, where in the presence of the French and Lotharingian nobles, and of several prelates, among them the Bishops of Toul, Liège, and Verdun, Charles was solemnly crowned king of Lorraine in the cathedral of St Stephen on 9 September 869. When, a little later, he heard of the death of his wife Queen Ermentrude (6 October), Charles sought to strengthen his position in the country by taking first as his mistress and afterwards as his lawful wife

---

[1] The date 867 is generally accepted. On the other hand, M. Calmette, in *La diplomatie carolingienne*, pp. 195, 399, gives arguments of some force in favour of 868.

(22 January 870) a noble lady named Richilda, a relation of Theutberga, the former queen, belonging to one of the most important families in Lorraine; on her brother Boso Charles heaped honours and benefices.

Neither Louis the German nor Louis II could do more than protest against the annexation of Lorraine to the Western Kingdom, the former in virtue of the Treaty of Metz, the latter in right of his near relationship to the dead king. To the envoys of both, Charles the Bald had returned evasive answers, while he was convoking the magnates of his new kingdom at Gondreville to obtain from them the oath of fealty. But those who attended the assembly were few in number. Louis the German's party was recovering strength. Charles was made aware of it when he attempted to substitute for the deposed Gunther in the see of Cologne, a French candidate, Hilduin. The Archbishop of Mayence, Liutbert, a faithful supporter of the king of Germany, set up in opposition a certain Willibert who ultimately won the day. On the other hand, Charles was more successful at Trèves, where he was able to instal the candidate of his choice.

Meanwhile, Louis the German, having recovered, had collected an army, and, calling on his brother to evacuate his conquest, marched in his turn upon Lorraine, where his partisans came round him to do him homage (spring 870). An armed struggle seemed imminent, but the Carolingians had little love for fighting. Brisk negotiations began, in which the principal part was taken by Liutbert, Archbishop of Mayence, representing Louis, and Odo, Bishop of Beauvais, on behalf of Charles. In the end, the diplomatists came to an agreement based on the partition of Lorraine. The task of carrying it into effect was at first entrusted to a commission of magnates, but difficulties were not long in arising. It was decided that the two kings should meet. But the interview was delayed by an accident which happened to Louis the German, through a floor giving way, and only took place on 8 August at Meersen on the banks of the Meuse. Here the manner of the division of Lothar II's former dominions was definitely settled. The *Divisio regni*, the text of which has been preserved in the Annals of Hincmar, shews that no attention was paid to natural boundaries, to language or even to existing divisions, whether ecclesiastical or civil, since certain counties were cut in two, *e.g.* the Ornois. An endeavour was made to divide between the two sovereigns, as equally as possible, the sources of revenue, *i.e.* the counties, bishoprics and abbeys. Louis received the bishoprics of Cologne, Trèves, Metz, Strasbourg and Basle, with a portion of those of Toul and Liège. Charles, besides a large share of the two last, was given that of Cambrai, together with the metropolitan see of Besançon, and the counties of Lyons and Vienne with the Vivarais, that is to say the lands which Lothar had acquired after the death of Charles of Provence. Without entering into details as to the division of the *pagi* in the north part of the kingdom of Lorraine, from the mouths of the

Rhine to Toul, it is substantially true to say that the course of the Meuse and a part of that of the Moselle formed the border line between the two kingdoms. Thence the frontier ran to the Saône valley, and the limits thus fixed, although not lasting, had distinct influence later in the Middle Ages.

Hardly was the treaty of Meersen concluded, when the brother-kings of Gaul and Germany were confronted by deputies from the Pope and the Emperor, protesting, in the name of the latter, against the conduct of his uncles in thus robbing him of the inheritance which was his by right. Hincmar replied by endeavouring to justify his master, and by dwelling on the necessity of preserving peace in Lorraine; Charles, for his part, bestowed fair words and rich gifts on the Pope. As to Louis the German, he professed himself ready to make over what he had acquired of Lothar's lands to Louis II. These assurances, however, were not followed by any practical result, and Charles spent the latter part of the year in completing the subjection of the southern part of his newly-acquired dominions. Lyons was occupied without a struggle. Only Vienne, which was defended by Bertha, wife of Gerard of Roussillon, who was himself ensconced in a castle in the neighbourhood, made some resistance, surrendering, however, in the end (24 December 870). Charles was recalled to Francia by the rebellion of his son Carloman, who had forsaken his father's expedition in order to collect bands of partisans and ravage his kingdom. Louis the German was at the same time engaged in a struggle with his two sons who had risen against him. Charles confided the government of the Viennois and Provence to his brother-in-law Boso as duke, and turned homewards.

In the meanwhile, a report spread through Gaul and Germany that the Emperor Louis II had been taken prisoner and put to death by Adelchis, Prince of Benevento. In reality the latter had merely subjected his sovereign to a few days' captivity (August 871). But Louis the German and Charles the Bald had lost no time in shewing that each intended to appropriate for himself the inheritance left by the deceased; Louis by sending his son Charles the Fat beyond the Alps, in order to gather adherents, and Charles by setting out himself at the head of an army. However, he went no farther than Besançon, when the two competitors were stopped by the news that the Emperor was still alive. But during the three following years we find both brothers bent on eventually securing the heritage of the king of Italy; Louis the German being supported, it would seem, by the Empress Engilberga, while Charles the Bald, who had rid himself of his rebellious son Carloman, whom he had succeeded in making prisoner and whose eyes he had put out, was trying to form a party among the Roman nobles and those surrounding the new Pope, John VIII, who in December 872 had taken the place of Hadrian. The death of Louis II at Brescia (12 August 875) led to an open struggle between the two rivals.

For a long time the kingdom of Italy had stood considerably apart from the other Carolingian states. Louis the Pious and Lothar had already placed it in a somewhat special position by sending as their representatives there each his eldest son, already associated in the Empire, and bearing the title of king. Since 855 the Emperor had been restricted to the possession of Italy, where he had already received the royal title in 844, and where his coronation as joint-Emperor had taken place (Rome, April 850). Apart from matters concerning the inheritance of his brothers, it does not seem that Louis II held that his office imposed on him the duty of interfering in affairs beyond the Alps. The Emperor had been obliged to devote his chief attention to his duties as king of Italy, and the defence of the country entrusted to him against the attacks of its enemies, particularly the Saracens. But circumstances were too strong for him, and in spite of his activity and energy, Louis II was fated to wear himself out in a struggle of thirty years, and yet neither to leave undisputed authority to his successor, nor finally to expel the Muslims from Italian soil. The royal power had never been very great in the peninsula. The Frankish counts, who had taken the place of the Lombard lords, had quickly acquired the habit of independence. The bishops and abbots had seen their temporal power grow in extent, through numerous grants of lands and immunities. On the other hand, three strong powers, outside the Papal state, had taken shape out of the ancient duchies of Friuli and Spoleto, and in Tuscany. The counts of Frankish origin were reviving the former Lombard title of duke, or the Frankish one of marquess, and regular dynasties of princes, by no means very amenable to the orders of the sovereign, were established at Cividale, Lucca and Spoleto. The March of Friuli, set up between the Livenza and the Isonzo to ward off the attacks of Slavs and Avars, athough its ruler, no doubt, had extended his authority over other countries beyond these limits, had, in the time of Lothar, been bestowed on a certain Count Everard, husband of Gisela, the youngest daughter of Louis the Pious. This man, coming originally from the districts along the Meuse, where his family still remained powerful, was richly endowed with counties and abbeys, and played a distinguished part in the wars against the Serbs, dying in 864 or 865. His immediate successor was his son, Unroch, who died young, and then his second son, Berengar, who was destined to play a conspicuous part in Italy at the end of the ninth century, and who seems from an early date to have thrown in his lot in politics with the partisans of Louis the German and the Empress Engilberga. The ducal family established at Spoleto also came from Francia, from the valley of the Moselle. It was descended from Guy, Count of the March of Brittany under Louis the Pious. His son Lambert, who at first bore the same title, derived from the March, was a devoted adherent of Lothar, and, as such, had been banished to Italy where he died[1].

---

[1] See *supra*, pp. 15, 19–20.

It is this Lambert's son, Guy (Guido) who appears as the first Frankish Duke of Spoleto. Brother-in-law of Siconolf, Prince of Benevento, he contrived to interfere skilfully in the wars among the Lombard princes, betray his allies at well-chosen junctures, and add to his duchy various cities, Sora, Atino, etc., the spoil of Siconolf or his rivals. He died about 858. His son Lambert shewed himself an intractable vassal, some-times the ally of Louis II, and again at open war with him, or fugitive at the court of the princes of Benevento. He was even temporarily deprived of his duchy, which was transferred to a cousin of the Empress Engilberga, Count Suppo. After the Emperor Louis's death, however, Lambert is found again in possession of his duchy, and like his brother Guy, Count of Camerino, is counted among the adherents of Charles the Bald. In Tuscany the ducal family was of Bavarian origin, tracing its descent from Count Boniface who, in the beginning of the ninth century was established at Lucca and was also entrusted with the defence of Corsica. His grandson, Adalbert, succeeded in consolidating his position by marrying Rotilda, daughter of Guy of Spoleto. As to Southern Italy, beyond the Sangro and the Volturno, the Lombard principalities there, in spite of formal acts of submission, remained, like the Greek territories, outside the Carolingian Empire. The power of the Princes of Bene-vento was considerably diminished after the formation of the principality of Salerno, cut off from the original duchy in 848. From the middle of the ninth century, the Gastalds of Capua also affected to consider them-selves independent of the prince reigning at Benevento. The Frankish sovereign could hardly do otherwise than seek to foment these internal dissensions and try to obtain from the combatants promises of vassalage or even the delivery of hostages. But Louis II made no real attempt to compel the submission of the Lombards of Benevento and Salerno, who were firmly attached to their local dynasties and to their independence. If he interfered on several occasions beyond the limits of the States of the Church and the Duchy of Spoleto, it was not as suzerain, but as the ally of the inhabitants in their struggle against the common enemies of all Italy, the Saracens.

These latter, who came from Africa and Spain, were for more than a hundred years to be to the peninsula nearly as great a scourge as the Northmen were to Gaul and Germany. In 827 they had gained a foot-hold in Sicily and four years afterwards (831), taking advantage of the dissensions between the Byzantine governors, they seized Palermo and Messina and made themselves masters of the whole island. In 837 the Duke of Naples, Andrew, set the fatal example of calling them in as allies in his struggle with Sicard of Benevento, to whom he was refusing the tribute he had promised. Thenceforward, in spite of engagements to the contrary, Italian dukes and Greek governors constantly took Muslim pirates into their pay. Other bands having seized various Greek cities such as Taranto, we get the pillage of the towns on the

Adriatic, *e.g.* Ancona (839). In 840 the treachery of the Gastald Pando handed over to them Bari, where they fixed themselves permanently, and it was the Saracens of Bari whom Radelchis of Benevento employed as auxiliaries during his struggle with Siconolf of Salerno. Other pirate crews attempted the siege of Naples, but the city offered a determined resistance, and its duke, Sergius, at the head of a fleet collected from the Campanian ports, won the naval victory of Licosa over the invaders in 846. Repulsed from the Campanian shores, the pirates fell upon the coast nearest to Rome. In order to keep them out of the Tiber, Pope Gregory IV had built a fortress at its mouth. This did not prevent the pirates from landing on the right bank of the river and even pushing their ravages as far as the gates of Rome. Unable to force their way in, they sacked the basilica of St Peter, which was then outside the walls, profaning the tomb of the Prince of the Apostles.

This sacrilege created a profound sensation throughout Christendom. It was, indeed, related that a tempest destroyed the invaders with the precious booty with which they were laden. But the truth appears to be that Louis II, as he was advancing to the rescue of the city, met with a check, and that the Saracens retired unmolested with their spoil. A great expedition organised against them in the spring of the next year (847) by Lothar I and Louis II had no important results. Louis, however, took advantage of being in the south of Italy to put an end by treaty to the contest between Radelchis and Siconolf, definitively separating by a precise frontier line the two principalities of Benevento and Salerno. The Roman suburbs had arisen from their ruins, and Pope Leo IV (847–8) had built a wall round the basilica of St Peter and the quarter on the right bank of the Tiber, enclosing what became "the Leonine City." In 851–2 the Lombards again appealed to Louis II. The latter delivered Benevento from the body of Saracens which had settled down there, but being badly supported by his allies, he was unable to take Bari, the Muslim garrison of which, as soon as the Frankish army had withdrawn, re-commenced its devastating raids into the surrounding country. It was at this time that the Saracens pillaged the famous abbeys of Monte Cassino and St Vincent of Volturno. In 867 the Emperor made a fresh expedition against them, and laid siege to Bari. But it was impossible to reduce the town without the help of a squadron to blockade it from the sea. Louis II, therefore, attempted to secure the aid of the Greek fleet by an alliance with the Basileus, arranging for the marriage of his daughter Ermengarde with the son of Basil, the Eastern Emperor. A Greek fleet did, indeed, appear off Bari, but the marriage not having taken place, it drew off. Louis was not discouraged, and made a general appeal to his subjects in the maritime provinces, even to the half-subjected Slavs to the north of the Adriatic. After many vicissitudes, the town was carried by assault (2 February 871). But the Lombards of Benevento cordially detested their Frankish deliverers, and their prince, Adelchis, feared that the Emperor might take advantage of his success to assert his sovereignty over Southern Italy. In consequence of his hostility, he laid an ambush which threw the Emperor a prisoner into his hands. Adelchis extorted from his captive a promise not to re-enter Southern Italy. A report of the Emperor's death was even current in Gaul and Germany. But Louis II, being quickly set at liberty, obtained from the Pope a dispensation from the oath he had sworn, and renewed the campaign next year (873), without however having attained any advantage. On 12 August 875 he was suddenly carried off by death.

Such was the state of affairs in Italy at the moment when Charles the Bald and Louis the German were preparing to dispute with one another the heritage left by their nephew. The succession question which presented itself, was, it is true, a complicated one. The dead Emperor left only a daughter. The territories which he had ruled, ought, it would seem, to have been divided by agreement between his two uncles. But if the imperial dignity had, since the time of Charlemagne, been considered inalienable from his family, no rule of succession had yet been established, even by custom, which could be applied to it. In practice, it seemed to be bound up with the possession of Italy, and to require as indispensable conditions the election of the candidate, at least in theory, by the Roman people, and his consecration at the hands of the Pope. Now Charles the Bald had on his side the sympathy of John VIII, who claimed that he was only carrying out the wishes already expressed by Nicholas I himself. Charles has been accused of having entangled the Pope by means of offerings and grants. In reality, what John VIII most desired seems to have been a strong and energetic Emperor capable of taking up the task to which Louis II had devoted himself, and of defending the Holy See against the Saracens. Rightly or wrongly, he believed that he had found his ideal in Charles, who was, in addition, well-educated and a lover of letters, and had besides for a long time given his attention to Italy, whither he had been summoned by a party of the magnates at the time of the false report of the death of Louis II. His possession, too, of Provence and of the Viennois, made it possible for him to interfere beyond the Alps more readily than his brother of Germany could do. He took action, besides, with promptness and decision. Hardly had the news of his nephew's death reached him at Douzy near Sedan before he summoned an assembly of magnates at Ponthion near Châlons to nominate his comrades on the expedition. He crossed the Great St Bernard, and had scarcely arrived in Italy when he was met by the envoys of the Pope bearing an invitation to him to come to Rome to be crowned. Louis the German was not inclined to see his brother go to this length without a protest. He despatched his two sons in succession beyond the Alps with an army. Charles the Fat was immediately obliged to beat a retreat. Carloman, more fortunate, succeeded in meeting Charles the Bald on the banks of the Brenta, and, after the Carolingian manner, opened negotiations. Either, as the German annalists say, his uncle got the better of him by deceitful promises, or else he felt himself too weak to fight the matter out. He, therefore, arranged a truce, and returned to Germany without a blow.

Meanwhile Louis the German had made an attack upon Lorraine, having been called in by a disgraced chamberlain, Enguerand, who had been deprived of his office for the benefit of the favourite Boso. Ravaging the country terribly as he went, Louis reached the palace of Attigny on 25 December 875, where he waited for adherents to come in. But the defections on which he had counted did not take place, and the invader, for want of sufficient support, was obliged to retreat and make his way back to Mayence. Charles, meanwhile, had not allowed himself to be turned from his object by the news from Lorraine. He was bent on the Empire. He had reached Rome, and on Christmas Day 875 he received the imperial diadem from the hands of John VIII. But he did not delay long in Rome, and having obtained from John the title of Vicar of the Pope in Gaul for Ansegis, Archbishop of Sens, he began his journey homewards on 5 January 876. On January 31 he was at Pavia, where he had himself solemnly elected and recognised as king of Italy by an assembly of magnates. Leaving Boso to govern this new kingdom, he again set forward, and was back at Saint-Denis in time to keep Easter (15 April). In the month of June, in company with the two papal legates who had come with him from Italy, John, Bishop of Arezzo, and John, Bishop of Toscanella, he held a great assembly of nobles and bishops at Ponthion, when he appeared wearing the imperial ornaments. The council solemnly recognised the new dignity which the Pope had conferred on the king of the West Franks. Charles would have wished also to secure its assent to the grant of the vicariate to Ansegis, but on this point he met with strong resistance. To the same assembly came envoys from Louis the German, demanding in his name an equitable partition of the territories formerly ruled by Louis II. Charles appeared to recognise these pretensions as well-founded. In his turn he sent an embassy to his brother and opened negotiations. They were interrupted by the death of Louis the German, at Frankfort (28 August 876).

The dead king left three sons. In accordance with arrangements which had been made beforehand but often modified in detail, the eldest, Carloman, was to receive Bavaria and the East Mark, the second, Louis, Saxony and Franconia, and the third, Charles the Fat, Alemannia. These dispositions were according to precedent. It is thus difficult to conceive by what right Charles the Bald professed to claim that portion of Lorraine which by the Treaty of Meersen had been allocated to his brother. None the less, it is certain that he hastened to send off emissaries to the country, charged with the business of gaining supporters for his cause, and then set out himself for Metz, Aix-la-Chapelle and Cologne. But Louis the Younger, on his side, had raised an army in Saxony and Thuringia, and sent deputies, although vainly, to call upon his uncle to respect his rights. He himself had recourse to the judgment of God, and when the ordeal proved favourable to his champions, he crossed the Rhine at Andernach. In the meanwhile, fresh envoys bearing proposals of peace sought Charles the Bald on his behalf. His uncle feigned willingness to enter into negotiations. But during the night of 7–8 October, he suddenly struck his camp and began a forward march, hoping to surprise his sleeping enemies in the early dawn. The season, however, was inclement, the roads were soaked with rain, and the cavalry, which was the principal arm of Carolingian forces, could only advance with difficulty. Besides this, a faithful adherent of Louis the Younger in Charles's own camp, had succeeded in warning his master of the *coup-de-main* about to be attempted against him. Thus the imperial army, fatigued by the night march, found the enemy, whom they had thought to surprise, on his guard. The result was a disastrous defeat of the troops of Charles. Numerous prisoners and rich spoil fell to the victor. But it would appear that Louis was not in a position to profit by his advantage, for almost immediately we find him falling back on Aix and Frankfort. Charles, for his part, made no second attempt against him, and shortly afterwards, without any formal treaty having been concluded, peace was restored between the two kings, marked by the liberation of the prisoners taken at Andernach.

Charles the Bald was, besides, absorbed by other anxieties. If his election had been the act of John VIII, the reason was that the Pope needed his help in Italy against the Saracens. Not satisfied with promises of troops and *missi*, he unceasingly demanded Charles's presence in Italy. Two papal legates again approached Charles at Compiègne at the beginning of 877, and finally drew from him a pledge that he would cross the Alps in the course of the summer. The moment, however, was not favourable, for the Northmen were shewing increased activity. In 876 a hundred of their ships had gone up the Seine and threatened the rich abbey of St-Denis, driving the monks to flee to a safer retreat on the banks of the Aisne. Charles the Bald decided to negotiate with them once more, and on 7 May 877 he ordered the collection of a special impost, a *tributum Normannicum*, destined to produce the five thousand pounds of silver needed to purchase the withdrawal of the Northmen from the Seine. On 14 June he assembled the magnates at Quierzy (Kiersy), where he promulgated a celebrated capitulary which has been too long held to be the charter constituting the feudal system, a legislative measure establishing the hereditary nature of fiefs, the deliberate completion of a process of evolution which had been going on from 847, the date at which the Capitulary of Meersen ordered every free man to choose a lord for himself. In 847 what was really in question was a measure to facilitate the levy of the host. In 877 at Quierzy, a whole body of very diverse measures were introduced, their object being to secure the good government of the kingdom, and the proper administration of the private property of the king during his absence, or even in case he should happen to die while on his expedition. The prince, Louis (the Stammerer), was to take his father's place with the assistance of counsellors, the choice of whom shews that the Emperor was not entirely free from distrust of his heir. An article in the capitulary orders Louis not to deprive the son of any count who should die during the campaign of the *honours* enjoyed by the father. Here we have a seal set upon the custom which was becoming more and more general, namely that the honours held by the father should be continued to the son, but at the same time we get the implicit recognition of the sovereign's right to dispose of the fiefs which, in principle, he has granted for life only, a right which Louis might possibly abuse.

Charles, accompanied by Richilda, set out at the end of June. He brought with him only a small number of his chief vassals; others, of whom Boso was one, were to join him a little later at the head of an army which they had received orders to assemble. The Emperor took the St Bernard route, and met John VIII who had advanced as far as Vercelli to receive him. But, at the same time as Charles, Carloman of Bavaria had been crossing the Alps at the head of a powerful army, and now made his appearance in the eastern part of Lombardy. Charles, uneasy at this, hurried on the coronation of Richilda as Empress, and sent her back to Gaul, demanding the hastening forward of the reinforcements which he was awaiting. But his presentiments were realised. The magnates had been irritated to see him depart thus, giving up the struggle with the Northmen, which in the eyes of the Frankish aristocracy was more important than the war against the Saracens. On the other hand they no doubt considered that the expedition was unlikely to provide them with many fiefs and benefices to be conquered beyond the Alps. Thus they made no response to the appeal addressed to them. Boso himself, who the year before, under the influence of Berengar of Friuli and the German party, had married Ermengarde, daughter of the late Emperor Louis II, was opposed to a fresh expedition into Italy, and declined to enter upon the campaign. Some of the most powerful nobles of the Western Kingdom, chosen by Charles to command the relieving army, Bernard, Count of Auvergne, and Bernard, Marquess of Gothia, followed the example set them. Hincmar himself, discontented that the vicariate should have been conferred on Ansegis, shewed himself less loyal than usual, and Prince Louis openly abetted the movement. The one object of the discontented seems to have been to compel Charles to return, and in this they succeeded, for the Emperor lost no time in retracing his way towards Gaul. But on the road he fell sick and on 6 October, in a poor hovel, poisoned, it was said, by his Jewish doctor Zedekiah, he ended, miserably enough, his reign of thirty-seven years.

Historians have often pronounced adversely on the reign, influenced by chroniclers of Louis the German, who accuse his adversary of cowardice and incapacity. But it does not in fact appear that Charles was wanting either in courage or energy. All his contemporaries describe him as a learned man and a friend to letters. He has been reproached with not having succeeded in exacting obedience from his vassals, nor in organising resistance to the Northmen. But it would certainly have been a task beyond human strength to resist the process of evolution, at once economic and social, which gave birth to the feudal system and transformed into hereditary fiefs the benefices which had been granted for life or during pleasure by the early Carolingians. Where Charles the Great had had subjects and functionaries, Charles the Bald has already no more than vassals, and is forced to impoverish himself for their behoof by incessant grants of honours and benefices, lest he should be abandoned by nobles ever ready to transfer their oaths of fidelity to a rival sovereign. Even the bishops, who were usually loyal, had no scruples in taking Charles to task on various occasions, Hincmar being first to set the example. Besides this, the civil wars, whether between the kings or between turbulent counts, and the Northman invasions compelled the free men to gather in groups around magnates or *proceres* strong enough to protect them in time of need. Thus they *commend* themselves to these lords, and in their turn become vassals. This process was at first encouraged by the sovereign, as facilitating the assembling of the host when necessary, and this it is which explains the provisions in the capitulary of 847 ordering every free man to choose himself a lord, the latter being charged with the office of leading his men to war. But an important transformation had besides taken place in the host. The infantry, which in the eighth century had formed the chief strength of the Frankish armies, had given way to cavalry. By the end of the ninth century, the Carolingian armies are almost wholly composed of horse-soldiers. But the mounted warrior cannot be a mere free man, for in order to maintain his steed and his handful of followers he must hold some land or benefice from his lord. He has become the knight, the *miles*, the last rank in the feudal hierarchy. Counts and knights, however, when summoned by the king, shew no great eagerness to respond to the appeal. Constantly the attempts made by Charles to resist the Northmen are brought to nothing by the refusal of his vassals to follow him. Even when the Frankish force is under arms, it is only a sort of *landwehr* or militia, ill-adapted for fighting. The civilised Franks have lost the warlike qualities of their half-barbarous forefathers. It is not with such materials that a king or any other leader could expect to succeed against the bands of the Scandinavians who were trained to warfare and made it their habitual occupation.

CHAPTER III.

THE CAROLINGIAN KINGDOMS (877–918).

THE death of Charles the Bald did not ensure the triumph of Carloman, who was soon forced by an epidemic which broke out in his army to make the best of his way back to Germany. It seemed, however, as if it would be the signal for renewed civil discord in Gaul. When Louis the Stammerer received news at Orville near Laon of the pitiable end of his father, he hastened, without the assent of the magnates, to distribute to such of his partisans as happened to be around him, " honours," counties, estates and abbeys, thus violating an engagement made at Quierzy. Accordingly, when he was about to go into Francia to receive the oath of fidelity from his new subjects, he learned that the magnates, rallying round Boso and the Abbot Hugh, and supported by the widowed Empress Richilda, refused him obedience, and, as a sign of their displeasure, were ravaging the country. Nevertheless, thanks, no doubt, to the mediation of Hincmar, and after some time had been spent in arranging terms, the rebels agreed to a settlement. Richilda was reconciled to her step-son, handing over to him the royal insignia and the deed by which Charles the Bald before his death had nominated his heir. The magnates, whose rights the king promised to recognise, all made their submission. The Abbot Hugh even became one of the most influential counsellors of Louis the Stammerer. On 8 December, after having sternly exhorted the new sovereign to respect the rights of his vassals, Hincmar crowned him King of the West-Franks in the church of Compiègne.

Louis, however, was not the man to carry out his father's imperialist policy, in spite of the opportunity which occurred for it the next year. Anarchy set in more fiercely than ever in Italy. Carloman had obtained from his brothers the cession of their rights over the peninsula, in exchange for those which he possessed over Lorraine in virtue of a partition treaty concluded the year before (877), but he was in no plight to attempt another expedition. Lambert, Duke of Spoleto, and his brother-in-law Adalbert, Duke or Marquess of Tuscany, were making open war upon John VIII, and plainly intended to bring back to Rome the political opponents whom the Pope had formerly expelled, particularly the celebrated Formosus, Bishop of Porto. So John VIII decided upon another attempt to make the Western Kingdom his ally. After having bought a peace from the Saracens, who were still a menace to the Papal States, he embarked on a Neapolitan vessel and landed at Arles, where Boso, who had returned to his former duchy, and his wife Ermengarde, welcomed him with assurances of devotion and in company with him ascended the Rhone as far as Lyons. After somewhat laborious negotiations with Louis the Stammerer, a council presided over by the Pope met at Troyes, at the beginning of autumn. But there were few practical results attained from the assembly; little was settled, except a few points relating to discipline, and the confirmation of the sentence of excommunication against Lambert, Adalbert, and their supporters. John VIII would have wished to see Louis put himself at the head of another expedition against the enemies of the Holy See, whether rebel counts or Saracens: the king, however, seems not to have had the least inclination for such a course, and John VIII was forced to turn to that one among the magnates who, if only by his connexion with Italy, seemed best fitted to take up the task which the Carolingians refused to accept, namely Boso. It was in his company that the Pope re-crossed the Alps, at the end of the year, calling a great meeting of the bishops and lay lords of Northern Italy to assemble at Pavia. In a letter which he addressed at this time to Engilberga, widow of Louis II, he anticipated for her son-in-law the most brilliant prospects. Ermengarde's husband might look forward to the Lombard crown, perhaps even to the imperial one. But Boso himself did nothing to forward the ambitious views of the Pontiff on his behalf. At Pavia, under one pretext or another, he quitted John VIII and made his way back to Gaul.

Louis the Stammerer, who had concluded a treaty at Fouron[1] with his cousins of Germany for the partition of Louis II's inheritance, and being free from anxiety in that quarter, had just resolved upon an expedition against Bernard, Marquess of Gothia, who had not made his submission at the beginning of the reign and still remained contumacious. But a change came over the situation with the death of King Louis on 10 April 879. The leaders of the party, opposed to the Abbot Hugh and to the magnates actually in power, made use of the event to appeal for aid to the foreigner. At the instigation of one of the Welfs, Conrad, Count of Paris, and of Joscelin, Abbot of Saint-Germain-des-Prés, Louis of Saxony entered the kingdom from the west to dispute possession of their father's inheritance with Louis III and Carloman, the two young sons of Louis the Stammerer. He penetrated as far as

---

[1] Three places in Belgium, in the province of Liège, bear the name of Fouron. It cannot be positively ascertained at which of them the conferences took place which led up to the treaty.

Verdun, ravaging the country as he went. But those who took up his cause were few in number. Envoys from the Abbot Hugh, from Boso, and Theodoric, Count of Autun, who were at the head of affairs in the Western Kingdom, had no great difficulty in persuading the king of Germany to abandon his enterprise in return for a promise of the cession of that part of Lorraine which by the Treaty of Meersen fell to the share of Charles the Bald. In the month of September the coronation of the two sons of Louis the Stammerer by his marriage with Ansgarde, took place quietly at Ferrières. But Ansgarde had been afterwards repudiated by her husband, who had taken a second wife named Adelaide, the mother of his son Charles the Simple. The legitimacy of Louis III and Carloman was not universally admitted, discontent still existed, and before the end of 879 the Frankish kingdom was threatened by a new danger. Boso, at the instance of his wife, Ermengarde, who, by birth the daughter of an emperor, was dissatisfied with her position as the wife of a duke, took advantage of the weakness of the kings to re-establish for his own benefit the former kingdom of Charles of Provence (that is, the counties of Lyons and Vienne with Provence) and to have himself proclaimed king of it at an assembly of bishops held at Mantaille, near Vienne. A little later he was solemnly crowned by the Archbishop, Aurelian, at Lyons (autumn of 879).

In the spring of 880 Conrad and Joscelin again called in Louis of Saxony. This second attempt had no better success than the first, and Louis was obliged to return to his own dominions after having concluded with his cousins the Treaty of Ribemont, which again confirmed him in possession of the former kingdom of Lothar II. His tenure of it, however, was somewhat insecure, since the Lyons and Vienne districts were under Boso's control. The Archbishop of Besançon appears to have recognised the usurper. In the north, Hugh, an illegitimate son of Lothar II, had taken up arms and was also endeavouring to make himself independent. Confronted with these dangers, and also with incessant attacks by the Danish pirates, the Carolingian kings felt the necessity for union. By a treaty agreed to at Amiens in the beginning of 880, Louis III was to have Francia and Neustria, Carloman taking Aquitaine and Burgundy, with the task of making head against Boso. None the less, the two kings were agreed in desiring an interview at Gondreville with one of their cousins from Germany, and taking concerted measures against the rebels. It was Charles the Fat, the ruler of Alemannia, who, on his return from Italy whither he had gone to secure his proclamation as king by an assembly of magnates held at Ravenna, met Louis III and Carloman at this last fraternal *colloquium* in June 880. The three sovereigns began by joining forces against Hugh of Lorraine, whose brother-in-law, Count Theobald, was defeated and compelled to take refuge in Provence. The allies then directed their efforts against the latter country. The Count of

Mâcon, who adhered to Boso, was forced to surrender, and the Carolingian kings, pursuing their advance without encountering any resistance, laid siege to Vienne where the usurper had fortified himself. The unlooked-for defection of Charles the Fat put a stop to the campaign. For a long time John VIII, compelled by the desertion of Boso to go back to the policy of an alliance with Germany, had been demanding the return of Charles to Italy. Suddenly abandoning the siege, the king again crossed the Alps in order to go to Rome and there to receive the imperial crown from the hands of the Pope (February 881) while his cousins, unable to subdue Boso at once, returned to their dominions, leaving the task of blockading Vienne to the Duke of Burgundy, Richard the Justiciar, who was own brother, as it happened, to the rebel king of Provence. Queen Ermengarde, who was defending the place, was obliged to surrender a few months later (September 882).

Charles the Fat made no long stay at Rome. As early as February 881 he took the road leading northwards. It is true that the new Emperor made a fresh expedition into Italy at the end of the same year, though he got no farther than Ravenna. Here the Pope came to meet him in order to try and obtain from him measures likely to protect the patrimony of St Peter from the attacks of the dukes of Spoleto. But the death of Louis of Saxony (20 January 882) now recalled the Emperor to Germany. This event made Charles master of the whole Eastern Kingdom, for Carloman of Bavaria, who by an agreement made in 879 with Louis had secured to the latter his whole inheritance, had died in 880. Carloman's illegitimate son Arnulf had been by the terms of the same treaty forced to content himself with the duchy of Carinthia. Hugh of Lorraine, who still under pretext of claiming his paternal heritage had again been indulging in acts of brigandage, had been defeated by Louis some time before his death and constrained to take refuge in Burgundy.

In the Western Kingdom, Louis III of France had died of a fall from his horse on 5 August 882. Carloman, summoned from Burgundy, received the magnates' oaths of fidelity at Quierzy and thus became the sole sovereign of the Western Kingdom. His brief reign is wholly taken up with fruitless struggles against the Northmen. On 12 December 884 he also was carried off by an accident while out hunting. Louis the Stammerer's posthumous son, Charles, known later as the Simple, was by reason of his youth unfit to reign. Thus the Frankish nobles appealed to Charles the Fat, in whose hands were thus concentrated all the kingdoms which had gone to make up the empire of Charles the Great. But the Emperor, though a man of piety and learning, was very far from possessing the activity and vigour demanded by a position now more difficult than ever. For the ravages of the Northmen had redoubled in violence during the preceding years. Established permanently in Flanders, they took advantage of their situation to ravage at once what was formerly Lorraine and the kingdoms of the East and West. A victory gained over them at Thion on the Sambre by Louis of Saxony in 880, had led to no results, for in the same year they burnt Nimeguen, while another band made their way into Saxony. The Abbot Joscelin had in vain attempted to drive out those on the Scheldt, who from their fortified camp at Courtrai made perpetual raids for pillage into the Western Kingdom. Nevertheless, King Louis III won over them at Saucourt in Ponthieu a renowned victory, commemorated by a *cantilène*, a popular song in celebration of it, in the German language which has come down to us. Yet it did not hinder the Danes settled at Ghent from reaching the valley of the Meuse and forming a new entrenched camp at Elsloo. During the winter of 881–882 they burnt Liège, Tongres, Cologne, Bonn, Stavelot, Prüm and Aix, and took possession of Trèves. Walo, the Bishop of Metz, who with Bertulf, Archbishop of Trèves, had put himself at the head of the defenders, was defeated and killed in April 882. At the assembly held at Worms (May 882), Charles the Fat, who was returning from Italy, determined to act with vigour, and gathered a numerous army at the head of which he placed to second his efforts two tried warriors, Arnulf of Carinthia, and Henry, Count or Duke of Thuringia. But on the point of attacking the camp at Elsloo his courage failed. He fell back on the dangerous method, already too often practised by the Carolingians, of negotiating with the invaders. Of their leaders Godefrid (Guðröðr) obtained Frisia as a fief on condition of receiving baptism, and Sigefrid (Sigröðr) was paid to withdraw.

The chief part of the great Northman army then turned to attack the Western Kingdom. By the autumn they were ravaging it up to the gates of Rheims. The aged archbishop, Hincmar, was forced to leave his metropolitan city and flee for refuge to Epernay, where he died on 21 December 882. Carloman succeeded in checking the Danes more than once on the banks of the Aisne and of the Vicogne, but the invasion was not beaten off. Another fortified camp was formed by the Northmen at Condé on the Scheldt. The bands which came forth from it next year seized Amiens, and ravaged the district between the Seine and the Oise without meeting with resistance. Carloman was obliged to negotiate with them, and, thanks to the intervention of Sigefrid, he obtained a pledge that the band in cantonments near Amiens should evacuate the Western Kingdom in consideration of the enormous sum of 12,000 pounds of silver (884). The engagement, moreover, was respected. The main part of the great Northman army crossed over to England, but other bands passed into the kingdom of Lorraine, and a party among them settled down behind the woods and marshes which covered the site of the present town of Louvain.

Such was the position of things at the time when Charles the Fat became sole ruler of the Frankish Empire and the magnates of France and Lorraine came to do homage to their new sovereign at Gondreville near Toul and Ponthion. The beginning of the reign was marked, besides, by several victories gained over the Northmen who had penetrated into Saxony. Other bands were defeated by Count Henry of Alemannia and Liutbert, Archbishop of Mayence. But Hugh of Lorraine had decided that the occasion was a good one for again putting forward his claim to his father's kingdom, with the support of his brother-in-law, the Northman Godefrid. Count Henry, whose task it was to resist them, chose to employ treachery. Godefrid was imprudent enough to consent to an interview in the course of which he was assassinated, and the Franks succeeded in inflicting a check on his leaderless troops. Hugh, being allured to Gondreville under pretext of negotiations, also fell into an ambush. He was blinded, tonsured, and immured in the Abbey of Prüm. His sister, Gisela, Godefrid's widow, was a little later to die as Abbess of the Convent of Nivelles. This partial success was, however, balanced by the defeat suffered in front of Louvain by the army raised in Lorraine and in the Western Kingdom. Charles seemed indeed to be losing his interest in this unceasing war. At the assembly which he held at Frankfort at the beginning of the year 885, his only care seemed to be to procure the recognition of his illegitimate son Bernard's right to succeed him. His wishes, however, were opposed by the magnates. Charles counted on the support of Pope Hadrian III, the successor of John VIII who had been assassinated in 884, but Hadrian died 8 July 885, and this event forced the Emperor finally to give up his project. The successor of the dead Pope, Stephen V, had been elected without consulting Charles the Fat, and so much was the Emperor displeased that he thought it necessary to cross the Alps yet again. But he lingered in the north of the peninsula while his confidential agent, the Arch-Chancellor Liutward, Bishop of Vercelli, went to Rome to negotiate with the Pope. An outbreak of sedition at Pavia nearly cost the Emperor his life, and he decided not to advance farther, but to take the road for Gaul once more, whither he was recalled by the imperious necessity of resisting the Northmen.

Carloman's death had liberated the bands with whom he had treated at Amiens from their pledge to respect the Western Kingdom. Large numbers of the Northmen who had crossed over into England came back during the summer of 885 to rejoin their compatriots at Louvain who, for their part, had got as far as the mouth of the Seine. Other companies, coming from the Lower Scheldt, joined them there On 25 July they entered Rouen, and their fleet, three hundred strong, carrying some forty thousand men, began to push up the Seine. A Neustrian army which attempted to bar the way to the invaders was obliged to beat a retreat without having succeeded in defending the fortified bridge which Charles the Bald had built at Pitres, and the great viking fleet, reinforced by Danes from the Loire, arrived before Paris on 24 November, covering the river's surface for more than two leagues. The city of Paris at this time did not extend beyond the island of the Cité. On the right bank, however, and especially on the left, lay the suburbs with their churches and abbeys, Saint-Merri and Saint-Germain l'Auxerrois to the north, Saint-Germain-des-Prés and Sainte-Geneviève to the south, with the houses, gardens and vineyards surrounding them. Of course no wall enclosed these suburbs. The city itself had been without a rampart in the days of Charles the Bald, since the Roman fortifications there as elsewhere had for long centuries fallen into ruins. Thus the Danes had on several occasions descended on the town and pillaged it without let or hindrance. The last of their incursions dated from 866. But since then Paris had made preparation for resistance. Under the superintendence of Odo, the count, son of Robert the Strong, helped by Bishop Joscelin, the old wall had been rebuilt[1]. Two bridges establishing communication between the island and both banks of the Seine barred the way to the viking ships. One Sigefrid, who seems to have been in command of the expedition, made a demand for himself and his followers of free access to the upper valley of the Seine. Odo and Joscelin refused. A general assault next morning was repulsed with loss, and the Northmen were obliged to undertake a formal siege.

This lasted for long months, varied by attacks upon the bridges and the works defending them on both banks of the river, and also by pillaging expeditions into the neighbouring districts. But the Parisians met the efforts of their assailants with indomitable energy and endurance. On 16 April 886 Joscelin was carried off by sickness. Odo tried a sortie in order to seek for reinforcements; it proved successful, and he made use of his opportunity to send pressing appeals to the Emperor and his counsellors. He then for the second time traversed the enemy lines to re-enter the besieged city. Meanwhile, Charles, on his return from Italy, had held a great assembly at Metz, and had then set out, at a deliberate rate, to go to the succour of the Parisians. Having reached Quierzy he sent forward his best warrior Count Henry of Alemannia, at the head of a detachment of his men. But in attempting to reconnoitre the enemy's camp, Henry fell, with his horse, into one of the fosses dug by the besiegers, and was killed (28 August). His death threw a gloom over his followers, and the relieving detachment which he had been leading fell back. On 28 October the Emperor came up in person before Paris, and the inhabitants could see his army on the heights of Montmartre. But instead of crushing the heathen between his troops and the city walls, Charles once more began negotiations with them. Sigefrid consented to raise the siege, in return for a sum of seven hundred pounds in silver, and permission for his followers to go and winter in Burgundy, with the right to go up the Seine freely. The

---

[1] At the end of the ninth century a fairly general movement took place to restore the walls of cities so as to ensure them against a *coup-de-main* of the Northman bands.

Parisians, however, refused to agree to this last condition and to allow
the viking vessels to pass under the fortified bridges which they had
defended with so much valour. The Danes were obliged to draw their
boats to land to get them above the city by the river bank, but, none
the less, they reached Burgundy, which they ravaged. Sens, in particular,
stood a siege of six months.

In the meanwhile the Emperor fell sick and returned to Alsace. During
the Easter season he held an assembly at Waiblingen near Stuttgart, at
which was present, among others, Berengar, Marquess of Friuli. From
thence he went to Kirchen in the Breisgau, where he was sought out by
Ermengarde, widow of Boso, with her young son Louis. Boso, in spite
of the capture of Vienne and the efforts of the Carolingian kings and their
lieutenants, had succeeded in maintaining his ground in the kingdom he
had created for himself, and died unsubdued (11 January 887). The son
whom he left, Louis, was still almost a child when his mother brought
him to the Emperor. Charles the Fat received him kindly, recognised his
right to succeed his father, and even went through some kind of ceremony
of adopting him. But the young prince was not long to be benefited
by his protection. The discontent of the magnates with the Emperor,
whom they accused of weakness and incapacity, and with the counsellor
by whom he was chiefly guided, his chancellor Liutward, Bishop of
Vercelli, grew greater every day. Charles endeavoured to placate them
by dismissing his chancellor, but their dissatisfaction still continued
undiminished, and at the end of 887 a revolt broke out, facilitated by
Charles's illness and physical incapacity. The rebels, in an assembly
held at Tribur near Darmstadt, formally deposed the Emperor. He
returned to Neidingen on the Danube near Constance, where he made
a pitiable end on 13 January 888, while his former vassals proclaimed in
his room Arnulf of Carinthia, son of Carloman of Bavaria, of illegitimate
birth, it is true, but well known for his warlike qualities, and, in the
eyes of the magnates, the only prince capable of defending the Empire,
or at least the kingdom of Germany, against the enemies threatening it
on every side.

The deposition of Charles the Fat marks the epoch of the final
dismemberment of the Empire of Charlemagne. Even contemporaries
were conscious of this. "Then," said the Lotharingian chronicler,
Regino of Prüm, in a justly famous passage, "the kingdoms which had
been subject to the government of Charles split up into fragments,
breaking the bond which united them, and without waiting for their
natural lord, each one sought to create a king of its own, drawn from
within itself; which thing was the cause of long wars, not that there
were lacking Frankish princes worthy of empire by their noble birth,
their courage, and their wisdom, but because their equality in origin,
dignity and power was a fresh cause for discord. None of them in fact
was sufficiently raised above the rest to make them willing to submit

to his authority." The West Franks elected as king Odo, the valiant defender of Paris. In Italy Berengar, Marquess of Friuli, and Guy (Guido), Duke of Spoleto, contended for the crown. Louis of Provence held the valley of the Rhone as far as Lyons. Finally, a new claimant, the Welf Rodolph, son of Conrad, Count of Auxerre, already duke of "the duchy beyond the Jura" comprising the dioceses of Geneva, Lausanne and Sion, claimed the ancient kingdom of Lorraine, without, however, succeeding in building up more than a " kingdom of Burgundy," restricted to the Helvetian *pagi* and the countries which formed the ancient diocese of Besançon.

The expressions used by Regino must not, however, be understood too literally. The kings whom the new nations " drew from within themselves " were all of the Austrasian race and had their origin in Francia, their families having been for hardly more than two or three generations settled in their new counties. The dismemberment, which began under Louis the Pious and was finally consummated in 888, was by no means caused by a reaction of the different nations within the Carolingian Empire against the political and administrative unity imposed by Charles the Great. The building up of new nationalities may have been largely the work of the chances of the various partitions which had taken place since the Treaty of Verdun. Nevertheless the fact that Louis the German and his heirs had as their portion the populations of Teutonic speech, and Charles the Bald and his successors those of the Romance language, no doubt accentuated such consciousness as these peoples might have of their individuality, a consciousness further strengthened by the antagonism between the sovereigns. Italy, on the other hand, had long been accustomed to live under a king of its own, a little outside the sphere of the other Frankish kingdoms. Besides these more remote causes, we must bear in mind the need which each fraction of the Empire felt of having a protector, an effective head to organise resistance against the Slavs, the Saracens or the Northmen. A single Emperor must often be at too great a distance from the point at which danger threatened. " The idea of the Empire, the idea of the Frankish kingdom recedes into the background, and gives place to an attachment to the more restricted country of one's birth, to the race to which one belongs[1]." Under the influence of geographical situation and of language, or even through the chances of political alliances, new groups had been formed, and each of these placed at its head the man best fitted to defend it against the innumerable enemies who for half a century had been devastating all parts of the Empire.

In spite of this separatist movement, the kinglets (*reguli*) set up in 888 still attributed a certain supremacy to Arnulf as the last representative of the Carolingian family. Odo sought his presence at Worms in

[1] G. Monod. *Du rôle de l'opposition des races dans la dissolution de l'Empire carolingien*, p. 13.

order to place himself under his protection (August 888) before going to Rheims to receive the crown of Western Francia. At Trent, Berengar also took up the attitude of a vassal in order to obtain from Arnulf the recognition of his Italian kingship. Rodolph of Burgundy yielded to the threat of an expedition to be sent against him, and came and made his submission at Ratisbon. A little later, at Worms, it was the turn of young Louis of Provence (894). Doubtless no homage strictly so called was performed, such as would establish between Arnulf and the neighbouring sovereigns a relation of positive vassalage with the reciprocal obligations it entailed. There was, however, a ceremony analogous to that of homage, and the recognition of a kind of over-lordship belonging, at any rate in theory, to the King of Germany. Thus between Arnulf and the rulers of the states which had arisen from the dismemberment of the Carolingian Empire peace seemed assured. But it was less safe against enemies from without and against revolts on the part of the German magnates. Though in 889 Arnulf had received an embassy from the Northmen bearing pacific messages, the struggle had begun again in 891. The Danes had invaded Lorraine and had inflicted on Count Arnulf and Archbishop Sunderold of Mayence the bloody defeat of La Gueule (26 June) balanced, it is true, by the success won by King Arnulf in the same year on the banks of the Dyle. On the other hand, the struggle against the Moravian kingdom founded by a prince named Svátopluk (Zwentibold) was going on amidst alterna-tions of success and failure. In 892 Arnulf, with the assistance of the Slovene duke Braslav, led a successful expedition against the Moravians, but he had been imprudent enough to call to his aid a troop of Hun-garians, thus, as it were, pointing out to the Magyar immigrants from Asia the road into the kingdom of Germany which a few years later was to have such a fearful experience of them. Two years later (894) the death of Svátopluk led to the recognition of Arnulf's authority by his two sons, Moimir and Svátopluk II, and the civil war which before long broke out between them enabled the Franks to intervene successfully in Moravia. But like Charles the Fat, Arnulf was haunted by the dream of wearing the imperial crown. At the opening of his reign the fear of a revolt among the discontented magnates of Swabia had alone prevented him from responding to the appeals made to him by Pope Stephen V (890). Events in Italy now offered him the oppor-tunity of renewing his attempts in that quarter.

The two rivals, Guy and Berengar, who after the deposition of Charles the Fat disputed for the crown of Italy, were each recognised as king by a certain number of adherents. A truce had been arranged between them up to the beginning of the year 889. They used this respite merely to seek support in foreign countries. Berengar, for twenty years the faithful ally of the Eastern Carolingians, received reinforcements from Germany. Guy, after an unsuccessful attempt to secure for himself the crown of the Western Kingdom, had recruited contingents in the district of Burgundy round Dijon, which was his native land. The Italian lords again took sides with one competitor or the other, with the exception of the most powerful of them all, Adalbert, Marquess of Tuscany, who contrived to maintain a prudent neutrality. War then broke out afresh. A bloody battle—a rare event in the ninth century—in which some 7000 men fought on either side was waged for a whole day on the banks of the Trebbia. Berengar, thoroughly worsted, was forced to retreat beyond the Po, where Verona, Cremona and Brescia still remained faithful to him, and to abandon the struggle with Guy. The latter seems not to have troubled himself to follow up his enemy's flight. His victory gave him possession of the palace of Pavia, that is, of the capital of the Italian kingdom. In the middle of February 889, he held a great assembly of bishops there, to whom he solemnly promised that church property and rights should be respected and maintained, and that the plundering raids and usurpations of the magnates should be put down. Then the prelates declared him king, and bestowed on him the royal unction.

For more than half a century, the supreme title of Emperor had seemed to be bound up with the possession of Italy. Guy therefore approached Pope Stephen V, with whom he had hitherto been on good terms, with a demand for the imperial crown. Stephen, however, was not anxious to add to the power of the house of Spoleto, always a menace to the papacy. A more distant Emperor seemed to offer a fairer prospect of safety. He therefore sent a private summons to Arnulf. But as the latter was unable to leave Germany, Stephen V was compelled (11 February 891) to proceed to the consecration of Guy as Emperor. His wife, Ageltrude, was crowned with him, and their son, Lambert, received the title of king and joint-Emperor. Adalbert of Tuscany now resolved on making his official submission to the new ruler. Berengar alone persisted in refusing to recognise him, and maintained his independence in his old domain, the March of Friuli. He even retained some supporters outside its limits who objected to Guy's Burgundian origin and reproached him with the favour which he shewed to certain of his compatriots who had followed him from beyond the Alps, such as Anscar (Anscarius), on whom he bestowed the March of Ivrea. Nevertheless the new Emperor, in the beginning of May 891, held a great *placitum* at Pavia, at which, to satisfy the demands of the prelates, he promulgated a long capitulary enacting the measures necessary to protect church property. On the same occasion, anxious, no doubt, to secure the support of the clergy, he made numerous grants to the bishops.

In September Stephen V died. His successor was the Bishop of Porto, Formosus, an energetic man, but one whose energy had gained him many enemies. In particular he seems to have been on bad terms with Guy, and doubtless considered an Italian Emperor a danger to the

Holy See. He therefore made a fresh appeal to Arnulf. The King of Germany did not come in person, but he sent his illegitimate son, Zwentibold, to whom he entrusted the task of " restoring order " beyond the Alps with the assistance of Berengar of Friuli. Zwentibold allowed himself to be daunted or bribed by Guy, and returned to Germany without having accomplished anything (893). At the beginning of the next year (894) Arnulf resolved to make a descent into Italy himself. He carried Bergamo by assault, and massacred the garrison. Intimidated by this example, Milan and Pavia opened their gates, and the majority of the magnates joined in taking the oath of fidelity to Arnulf. The latter, however, went no further than Piacenza, whence he turned homewards. But on his way back he found the road barred close to Ivrea by the troops of the Marquess Anscar, swelled by a contingent sent by Rodolph, King of Burgundy. Arnulf, however, succeeded in forcing a passage and turned his arms against Rodolph, but without gaining any advantage, as the enemy took refuge in the mountains. Zwentibold was placed at the head of a fresh expedition against the *regnum Jurense*, but was no more successful.

In a word, the brief irruption of Arnulf into Italy had done nothing to alter the situation. Guy remained Emperor. But just as he was about to resume his struggle with Berengar, an attack of haemorrhage carried him off. His successor was his son Lambert who had already been his colleague in the government. But Lambert was young and devoid of energy or authority. Disorder broke out more fiercely than ever, and in the autumn of 895 Formosus again sent a pressing appeal to Arnulf. Again the king of Germany set out, and on this occasion pushed on to Rome. But the population was hostile to him. The resistance was organised by Ageltrude, Guy's widow, an energetic Lombard of Benevento. Arnulf was obliged to carry the city by assault. In February 896 Formosus crowned him Emperor in the basilica of St Peter, and a few days later the Romans were compelled to take the oath of fidelity to him. But his success was to be short-lived. Ageltrude, who had taken refuge in her duchy of Spoleto, held out there in the name of Lambert. Just as he was about to lead an expedition against her, Arnulf fell sick. Thereupon he gave up the struggle and took the road back to his dominions, where, moreover, other disturbances called for his presence. Once he had gone, Lambert lost no time in re-appearing in Pavia, where he again exercised royal power. He also got possession of Milan in spite of the resistance of Manfred, the count whom Arnulf had placed there, and again began hostilities with Berengar. But the two rivals soon agreed upon a treaty, guaranteeing to Berengar the district north of the Po and east of the Adda.

All the rest of Italy was left to Lambert, who again entered Rome with Ageltrude in the beginning of 897. Formosus had died on 4 April 896. After the brief pontificate of Boniface VI which lasted only a fortnight, the Romans had elected Stephen VII. This Pope was a personal enemy of Formosus and, perhaps in co-operation with Lambert, undertook to indict his detested predecessor with a horrible travesty of the forms of law. The corpse of Formosus—if an almost contemporary tradition is to be credited—was dragged from its tomb and clothed in its pontifical vestments and a simulacrum of a judicial trial was gone through. Accused of having infringed canonical rules by his translation from Porto to Rome, of having violated an oath taken to John VIII never to re-enter Rome, and, as a matter of course, condemned, the dead Pope's body was stripped of its vestments and cast into the Tiber. All the acts of Formosus, in particular the ordinations performed by him, were declared null and void. This sinister condemnation brought about a revulsion of feeling, although opinion had been generally somewhat hostile to Formosus. A revolt broke out in Rome, Stephen VII was made prisoner and strangled; some months of confusion followed until finally, the election of John IX (June 898) restored some measure of quiet. In agreement with Lambert, the new Pope took steps to pacify opinion. The judgment pronounced against Formosus was annulled, and the priests who had been deposed as having been ordained by him were restored. A synod, held at Rome, busied itself with measures to secure the good government of the Church and the observance of canonical rule. The prescribed form for the election of a supreme Pontiff was again laid down; the choice was to be made by the clergy of Rome with the assent of the people and nobles in the presence of an official delegated by the Emperor. A great assembly held by Lambert at Ravenna also made provision for the safety of Church property and for the protection of freemen against the oppressions exercised by the counts. But on 15 October 898 the young king lost his life through a hunting accident. Lambert left no heir and Berengar profited by the situation to make himself master of the kingdom of Italy without striking a blow. By 1 December Ageltrude herself acknowledged him, receiving from him a deed confirming her in possession of her property. With the accession of Berengar a new period begins in the history of Italy, not less disturbed than the preceding one, but almost entirely unconnected with the Carolingian Empire and the Kings of Germany.

On his return from Italy in 894 Arnulf was also to find in the western part of his dominions a situation of considerable difficulty. At the diet of Worms in 895, resuming a project which the opposition of his great vassals had forced him to lay aside in the preceding year, he had caused his son Zwentibold to be proclaimed King of Lorraine. Zwentibold was a brave and active prince, often entrusted by his father with the command of military expeditions. Arnulf hoped by this means to protect Lorraine against possible attempts by the rulers of Burgundy or of the Western Kingdom, and at the same time to maintain order, which was often disturbed by the rivalry of two hostile clans who were contending for mastery in the country, that of Count Reginar, inaccurately called the " Long-necked," and that of Count Matfrid. But with regard to the latter object, Zwentibold, who was of a violent and hasty temper, seems to have been but little fitted to play the part of a pacificator. It was not long before he had given offence to the greater part of the magnates. At the assembly of Worms (May 897) Arnulf seemed for a moment to have restored peace between the King of Lorraine and his counts. But no later than next year disorder broke out afresh. Reginar, whom Zwentibold was attempting to deprive of his honours, made an appeal to Charles the Simple, who advanced as far as the neighbourhood of Aix-la-Chapelle. Thanks to the help of Franco, the Bishop of Liège, Zwentibold succeeded in organising a resistance sufficiently formidable to induce Charles to make peace and go back to his own kingdom.

The death of Arnulf (November or December 899) heightened the confusion. He left a son, Louis the Child, born in 893, whose right to the succession had been acknowledged by the assembly at Tribur (897). On 4 February 900, an assembly at Forchheim in East Franconia proclaimed him King of Germany. Some time afterwards in Lorraine the party of Matfrid, with the support of the bishops who resented the dissolute life of Zwentibold and the favour shewn by him to persons of low condition, abandoned their sovereign and appealed to Louis the Child. Zwentibold was killed in an encounter with the rebels on the banks of the Meuse (13 August 900). Louis remained until his death titular King of Lorraine, where he several times made his appearance, but where feudalism of the strongest type was developing. A few years later, civil war again broke out between Matfrid's family and the Frankish Count Gebhard, on whom Louis had conferred the title of Duke and the government of Lorraine. Nor did affairs proceed much better in the other parts of the kingdom, to judge by the few and meagre chronicles of the time. Outside, Louis had no longer the means of making good any claim upon Italy, where Louis of Provence was contending with Berengar for the imperial crown. Germany itself was wasted by the feuds between the rival Franconian houses of the Conradins and Babenberg. The head of the latter, Adalbert, in 906 defeated and killed Conrad the Old, head of the rival family, but being himself made prisoner by the king's officers, he was accused of high treason and executed in the same year (9 September). But the most terrible scourge of Germany was that of the Hungarian invasions. It was in 892 that the Hungarians, a people of Finnish origin who had been driven from their settlements between the Don and the Dnieper, made their first appearance in Germany as the allies of Arnulf in a war against the Moravians. A few years later they established themselves permanently on the banks of the Theiss. In 900 a band of them, returning from a plundering expedition into Italy, made its way into Bavaria, ravaged the country and carried off a rich booty. The defeat of another band by the Margrave Liutpold and Bishop Richer of Passau, as well as the construction of the fortress of Ensburg, intended to serve as a bulwark against them, were insufficient to keep them in check. Thenceforth not a year passed without some part of Louis's kingdom being visited by these bold horsemen, skilled in escaping from the more heavily armed German troops, before whom they were wont to retreat, galling them as they went, with flights of arrows, and at a little distance forming up again and continuing their ravages. In 901 they devastated Carinthia. In 906 they twice ravaged Saxony. Next year they inflicted a heavy defeat on the Bavarians, killing the Margrave Liutpold. In 908 it was the turn of Saxony and Thuringia, in 909 that of Alemannia. On their return, however, Duke Arnulf the Bad of Bavaria inflicted a reverse upon them on the Rott, but in 910 they, in their turn, defeated near Augsburg the numerous army collected by Louis the Child.

It was in the autumn of the following year (911) that the life of this last representative of the Eastern Carolingians came to an end at the age of barely eighteen. He was buried in the Church of St Emmeram at Ratisbon. In the early days of November the Frankish, Saxon, Alemannian, and Bavarian lords met at Forchheim and elected as king Conrad, Duke of Franconia, a man of Frankish race, and noble birth, renowned for his valour. This prince's reign was hardly more fortunate than that of his predecessor. Three expeditions in succession (912–913) directed against Charles the Simple did not avail to drive the Western King out of Lorraine. Rodolph, King of Burgundy, even took advantage of the opportunity to seize upon Basle. Besides this, the Hungarians, in spite of their defeat on the Inn at the hands of Duke Arnulf of Bavaria in 913, continued their ravages in Saxony, Thuringia and Swabia. In 917 they traversed the whole of the southern part of the kingdom of Germany, plundered Basle and even penetrated into Alsace. On the other hand, domestic discords still went on, and the chiefs of the nascent feudal principalities were in a state of perpetual war either with one another or with the sovereign. One of the most powerful vassals about the king, Erchanger, the Count Palatine, had in 913 raised the standard of revolt. Restored to favour for a short time in consequence of the energetic help he gave to Duke Arnulf in the struggle with the Hungarians, he lost no time in giving fresh offence to Conrad by attacking one of his most influential counsellors, Solomon, Bishop of Constance, whom he even kept for some days a prisoner. The sentence of banishment pronounced on him in consequence did not prevent him from continuing to keep the field with the help of his brother Berthold and Count Burchard, or from defeating the royal troops next year by Wahlwies near Lake Constance. To get the better of him Conrad was obliged to have him arrested for treason at the assembly of Hohen Altheim in Swabia and executed a few weeks later with his brother Berthold (21 January 917). But one of the rebels, Count Burchard, succeeded in maintaining possession of Swabia. Conrad was hardly more successful with regard to his other great vassals. One of the most powerful, Henry of Saxony, gave signs from the very beginning of the reign of a hostile temper[1] towards the new sovereign which manifested itself in 915 by an open rebellion, marked by the defeat of the expeditions led against the rebel by the Margrave Everard, brother of Conrad, and by the king himself. In Bavaria, Duke Arnulf had also revolted in 914. Temporarily worsted, and obliged to take refuge with his former foes, the Hungarians, he had re-appeared next year in his duchy. He was forced to submit and to surrender Ratisbon, but he took up the struggle afresh a little later (917) and again became master of the whole of Bavaria.

Conrad and the magnates both lay and ecclesiastical who had remained loyal to him held a great assembly at Hohen Altheim in 916 " to strengthen the royal power," when the severest penalties were threatened against any who should " conspire against the life of the king, take part with his adversaries or attempt to deprive him of the government of the kingdom." When Conrad ended his short reign (23 December 918), recommending the magnates to choose as his successor his former enemy, Henry of Saxony, he was in a position to testify that the magnates had seldom done anything else than transgress the precepts laid down at Hohen Altheim. To split up the realm into great feudal principalities, handed down from father to son and owning little or no obedience to a sovereign always in theory elective,—this was the constantly increasing evil from which Germany was to suffer throughout the whole of the Middle Ages.

The appearance of tribal dukes was not a mere outburst of disorder. Local leaders undertook the defence neglected by the central power, and so duchies, founded upon common race and memories, appeared and grew apart in reaction against Frankish hegemony. In Saxony, left to itself, the Liudolfing Bruno headed from 880 the warfare against Danes and Wends. Bavaria, troubled by Hungarians, found a Duke in Arnulf *c.* 907. Franconia, less harassed and more loyal to the Carolingians, lacked traditions of unity, but in Conrad, the future king, Conradins of the west triumphed over Babenberger rivals in the east. In Lorraine, the Carolingian homeland, even less united, Reginar (a grandson of the Emperor Lothar I) became Duke. Swabia found, under King Conrad I, a Duke in Burchard. Thus everywhere, as local unity met local needs, ducal dynasties arose.

---

[1] The chroniclers of a later period explain this by relating that Conrad had owed his crown only to its refusal by Otto, father of Henry, but the fact is doubtful.

CHAPTER IV.

FRANCE, THE LAST CAROLINGIANS AND THE ACCESSION OF HUGH CAPET. (888–987.)

DESERTED by Charles the Fat, on whom, through a strange illusion, they had fixed all their hopes, the West-Franks in 887 again found themselves as much at a loss to choose a king as they had been at the death of Carloman in 884.   The feeling of attachment to the Carolingian house, whose exclusive right to the throne seemed to have been formerly hallowed, as it were, by Pope Stephen II, was still so strong, especially among the clergy, that the problem might well appear almost insoluble.

It was out of the question indeed, to view as a possible sovereign the young Charles the Simple, the posthumous child of Louis II, the Stammerer.   Even Fulk, Archbishop of Rheims, who was later to be his most faithful supporter, did not hesitate to admit that "in the face of the fearful dangers with which the Normans threatened the kingdom it would have been imprudent to fix upon him then."   Nor, at the first moment, did anyone seem inclined towards Arnulf, illegitimate son of Carloman and grandson of Louis the German, whom the East-Franks had recently, in November 887, put in the place of Charles the Fat.

In this state of uncertainty, all eyes would naturally turn towards Odo (Eudes), Count of Paris, whose distinguished conduct when, shortly before, the Normans had laid siege to his capital, seemed to mark him out to all as the man best capable of defending the kingdom.   Son of Robert the Strong, Odo, then aged between twenty-five and thirty, had, by the death of Hugh the Abbot (12 May 886), just entered into possession of the March of Neustria which had been ruled by his father. Beneficiary of the rich abbeys of Saint-Martin of Tours, Cormery, Villeloin and Marmoutier, as well as Count of Anjou, Blois, Tours and Paris, and heir to the preponderating influence which Hugh the Abbot had acquired in the kingdom, in Odo the hour seemed to have brought forth the man.   He was proclaimed king by a strong party, consisting mainly of Neustrians, and crowned at Compiègne on 29 February 888 by Walter, Archbishop of Sens.

Nevertheless, he was far from having gained the support of all sections. To the people of *Francia* it seemed a hardship to submit to this

Neustrian, "a stranger to the royal race," whose interests differed widely from theirs. The leading spirit in this party of opposition was, from the outset, Fulk, Archbishop of Rheims.

From at least the time of Hincmar, the Archbishop of Rheims, "primate among primates," had been one of the most conspicuous personages in the kingdom. The personal ascendancy of Fulk, who came of a noble family, was considerable; we find him openly rebuking Richilda, widow of Charles the Bald, who was leading an irregular life, and it was he who in 885 acted as the spokesman of the nobles when Charles the Fat was invited to enter the Western Kingdom; again it was he who for the next twelve years was to be the head of the Carolingian party in France. Although on the deposition of Charles the Fat, Fulk had for a moment played with the hope of raising to the throne his kinsman, Guy, Duke of Spoleto, a member of a noble Austrasian family perhaps related to the Carolingians[1], he now no longer hesitated to apply to Arnulf, just as three years before he had applied to Charles the Fat. Accompanied by two or three of his suffragans, he travelled to Worms (June 888) to acquaint him with the position of affairs, the usurpation of Odo, the youth of Charles the Simple, the dangers threatening the Western Kingdom, and the claims which he (Arnulf) might make to the succession. But Arnulf, hearing at this juncture that Odo "had just covered himself with glory" by inflicting, at Montfaucon in the Argonne, a severe defeat upon the Northmen (24 June 888), preferred negotiations with the "usurper." To emphasise his own position of superiority, as successor to the Emperor, he summoned him to Worms, where Odo agreed to hold his crown of him. This was a fresh affirmation of the unity of the Empire of Charlemagne and Louis the Pious without the imperial title, but at the same time it gave a solemn sanction to the kingship of Odo.

Even within his dominions, opposition to Odo gradually gave way. Several of his opponents, among them Baldwin, Count of Flanders, had submitted. But Fulk did not allow himself to be won over. Though he had feigned to be reconciled (November 888), he was merely deferring action till fortune should change sides. For this he had not long to wait. The victory of Montfaucon proved to be a success which led to nothing; the king was forced in 889 to purchase the retreat of a Northman band ravaging the neighbourhood of Paris, and to allow another to escape next year at Guerbigny near Noyon, and was finally surprised by the pirates at Wallers, near Valenciennes, in 891 and routed in the Vermandois. Several of the lords who had rallied to his cause were beginning to abandon him: Baldwin, Count of Flanders, himself had raised the standard of revolt (892). Fulk cleverly contrived to draw together all the discontented and to rally them to the cause of Charles

---

[1] Guy had even been crowned at Langres by its bishop, shortly before the coronation of Odo, but had been obliged to beat a precipitate retreat.

the Simple. The latter, only eight years old in 887, was now thirteen. There were still nearly two years to wait for his majority which, in the Carolingian family, was fixed at fifteen, but the Archbishop of Rheims boldly pointed out " that at least he had reached an age when he could adopt the opinions of those who gave him good counsels." A plot was set on foot, and on 28 January 893, while Odo was on an expedition to Aquitaine, Charles was crowned in the basilica of Saint Remi at Rheims.

Without loss of time, Fulk wrote to the Pope and to Arnulf to put them in possession of the circumstances and to justify the course he had taken. Arnulf was not hard to convince, when once his own pre-eminence was recognised by the new king. But he avoided compromising himself by embracing too zealously the cause of either of the candidates, and thought it better policy to pose as the sovereign arbiter of their disputes. Before long, moreover, Charles, having reached the end of his resources and being gradually forsaken by the majority of his partisans, was reduced to negotiate, first on an equal footing, then as a repentant rebel. At the beginning of 897, Odo agreed to pardon him, and Charles having presented himself to acknowledge him as king and lord, " he gave him a part of the kingdom, and promised him even more." These few enigmatic words convey all the information we have as to the position created for Charles What followed shewed at least the meaning of his rival's promise. Odo having soon afterwards fallen sick at La Fère, on the Oise, and feeling his end near, begged the lords who were about him to recognise Charles as their king.

After his death, which took place on 1 January 898, the son of Louis the Stammerer was in fact acclaimed on all hands; even Odo's own brother, Robert, who had succeeded as Count of Paris, Anjou, Blois, and Touraine, and ruled the whole of the March of Neustria, declared for him.

It thus appeared that after what was practically an interregnum peace might return to the French kingdom. But Charles was devoid of the skill to conciliate his new subjects. His conduct, despite his surname, the Simple, does not seem to have lacked energy or determination; his faults were rather, it would seem, those of imprudence and presumption.

The great event of his reign was the definitive establishment of the Northmen in France, or rather, the placing of their settlement along the lower Seine on a regular footing. One of their chiefs, the famous Rollo, having been repulsed before Paris and again before Chartres, Charles profited by the opportunity to enter into negotiations with him. An interview took place in 911 at St-Clair-sur-Epte, on the highroad from Paris to Rouen. Rollo made his submission, consented to accept Christianity, and received as a fief the counties of Rouen, Lisieux and Evreux with the country lying between the rivers Epte and Bresle and the sea. It was an ingenious method of putting an end to the Scandinavian incursions from that quarter[1].

But it was especially on the eastern frontier of the kingdom that Charles was able to give free scope to his enterprising spirit. The subjects of Zwentibold, King of Lorraine, an illegitimate son of the Emperor Arnulf, had in 898 revolted against him. Charles, called in by a party among them, obtained some successes, but before long had beaten a retreat. But when in September 911 Louis the Child, King of the Germans, who in 900 had succeeded in getting possession of the kingdom of Lorraine, died leaving no children, Charles saw that the moment had come for more decisive interference. Conrad, Duke of Franconia, Louis's successor in Germany, belonged to a family unpopular in Lorraine; Charles, on the contrary, as a Carolingian, could count upon general sympathy. As early as November he was recognised by the Lorrainers as king, and as soon as peace was secured on his western border he was able, without encountering any difficulties, to come and take possession of his new kingdom. We find him already there by 1 January 912, and thenceforward he seems to shew a marked preference for dwelling there. He defended the country against two attacks by Conrad, King of the Germans, and forced his successor, Henry I, to recognise the rightfulness of his authority in an interview which he had with him on a raft midway in the Rhine at Bonn on 7 November 921. His power, both in France and Lorraine, seemed to be firmly established.

This was an illusion. For some time already discontent had been secretly fermenting in the western part of France; the Neustrians were doubtless irritated at seeing the king's exclusive preference for the lords of Lorraine. What fanned their resentment to fury was seeing him take as his confidential adviser a Lorrainer of undistinguished birth named Hagano. In the first place, between 917 and 919, they refused to join the royal *ost* to repel a Hungarian invasion, and in 922, as Hagano continued to grow in favour, and great benefices and rich abbeys were still heaped upon him, they broke into open revolt. Robert, Marquess of Neustria, brother of the late king, Odo, was at the head of the insurgents, and on Sunday, 30 June 922, he was crowned at Rheims by Walter, Archbishop of Sens.

As a crowning misfortune, Charles, at that moment, lost his most faithful supporter. Hervé, Archbishop of Rheims, who had succeeded Fulk in 900 and had boldly undertaken his king's defence against the revolted lords, died on 2 July 922, and King Robert contrived to secure the archbishopric of Rheims, nominating to it one of his creatures, the archdeacon Seulf. Charles gathered an army composed chiefly of Lorrainers, and on 15 June 923 offered battle to his rival near Soissons.

---

[1] For a detailed account see *infra*, chap. XIII.

Robert fell in the fight, but Charles was put to the rout, and attempted in vain to win back a section of the insurgents to his side. The Duke of Burgundy, Raoul (Radulf), son-in-law of King Robert, and, next to the Marquess of Neustria, one of the most powerful nobles in the kingdom, was crowned king on Sunday, 13 July 923, at the Church of St Médard at Soissons by the same Archbishop Walter of Sens who had already officiated at the coronations of Odo and of Robert[1].

Charles's position was most serious. Still it was far from being desperate; besides the kingdom of Lorraine which still held to him, he could count upon the fidelity of Duke Rollo's Normans and of the Aquitanians. He completed his own ruin by falling into the trap set for him by King Raoul's brother-in-law, Herbert, Count of Vermandois. The latter gave him to understand that he had left the Carolingian party against his will, but that an opportunity now offered to repair his fault and that Charles should join him as quickly as possible with only a small escort so as to avoid arousing suspicion. His envoys vouched on oath for his good faith. Charles went unsuspiciously to the place of meeting and was made prisoner, being immured first in the fortress of Château-Thierry, then in that of Péronne.

But the agreement between the new king and the nobles did not last long. Herbert of Vermandois, who in making Charles prisoner seems to have mainly intended to supply himself with a weapon which could be used against Raoul, began by laying hands on the archbishopric of Rheims, causing his little son Hugh, aged five, to be elected successor to Seulf (925); he then attempted to secure the county of Laon for another of his sons, Odo (927). As Raoul protested, he took Charles from his prison and caused William Longsword, son of Rollo, Duke of Normandy, to do him homage; then to keep up the odious farce, he brought the Carolingian to Rheims, whence he vigorously pressed his prisoner's claims upon the Pope. Finally, in 928, he got possession of Laon.

---

[1] For the sake of clearness in the narrative we give here the genealogy of the descendants of Robert the Strong, down to Hugh Capet:

Robert the Strong
Marquess of Neustria
d. 866

Odo
Marquess of Neustria
King of France 888–898

Robert
Marquess of Neustria
King of France 922–923

Hugh the Great
Duke of the Franks
d. 956

Emma = Raoul
Duke of Burgundy
King of France 923–936

dau. = Herbert II
Ct. of Vermandois

Hugh Capet
Duke of the Franks
King of France 987–996

Otto
Duke of Burgundy
960–965

Odo (surnamed Henry)
a priest, then Duke of Burgundy
965–1002

The death of Charles the Simple in his prison at Péronne (7 Oct. 929) deprived Herbert of a formidable weapon always at hand, and Raoul having shortly afterwards won a brilliant victory at Limoges over the Normans of the Loire, seemed stronger than ever.

The Aquitanian nobles recognised Raoul as king, and on the death of Rollo, Duke of Normandy, his son and successor, William Long-sword, came and did homage to him, while for a time his authority was acknowledged even in the Lyonnais and the Viennois, both at that period forming part theoretically of the kingdom of Burgundy. Herbert of Vermandois still held out, but Raoul got the better of him ; entering Rheims by the strong hand he promoted to the archepiscopal throne the monk Artaud (Artald) in place of young Hugh (931), and with the help of his brother-in-law Hugh the Great, son of the late King Robert, he waged an unrelenting war against Herbert, burning his strongholds, and besieging him in Château-Thierry (933–934).

Just, however, as a peace had been concluded between the king and his powerful vassal, Raoul suddenly fell sick (autumn of 935). A few months later he died (14 or 15 January 936).

The disappearance of Raoul, who died childless, once more imposed upon the nobles the obligation of choosing a king. The most powerful of their number was, without question, the Marquess of Neustria, Hugh the Great, son of King Robert, nephew of King Odo and brother-in-law of the prince who had just died. Heir to the whole of the former "March," once entrusted to Robert the Strong, consisting of all the counties lying between Normandy and Brittany, the Loire and the Seine, Hugh was recognised throughout these districts if not as the direct lord, at least as a suzerain who was respected and obeyed. The petty local counts and viscounts, the future rulers of Angers, Blois, Chartres or Le Mans, who were beginning on all hands to consolidate their power, were his very submissive vassals. The numerous domains which Hugh had reserved for himself, his titles as Abbot of St Martin of Tours, of Marmoutier, and perhaps also of St Aignan of Orleans, gave him, besides, opportunities of acting directly over the whole extent of the Neustrian March. He was also Count of Paris, had possessions in the district of Meaux, was titular Abbot of St Denis, of Morienval, of St Valery, and of St Riquier and St Germain at Auxerre, and finally, in addition to all this, bearing the somewhat vague, but imposing title of "Duke of the Franks," Hugh the Great was a person of the highest importance.

But however great was the ascendancy of the "Duke of the Franks" he did not fail to meet with formidable opposition, the chief of it coming from the other brother-in-law of the late King Raoul, Herbert, Count of Vermandois. A direct descendant of Charlemagne, through his grandfather, Bernard, King of Italy (the same prince whose eyes had been put out by Louis the Pious in 818), Herbert also held sway over extensive domains. Besides Vermandois, he possessed in all probability the counties of Melun and Château-Thierry, and perhaps even that of Meaux, to which, a few months later, he was to add those of Sens and Troyes. His tortuous policy had, as we have seen, made him for several years in King Raoul's reign the arbiter of the situation. Ambitious, astute, and devoid of scruples, Herbert was a dangerous opponent, and was evidently little inclined to further the elevation to the throne of the powerful duke of the Franks in whom he had found a persistent adversary.

Such being the situation, the sentiment of loyalty to the Carolingians once more gained an easy triumph. It was conveniently remembered that when Charles the Simple had fallen into captivity, his wife, Queen Eadgifu, had fled to the court of her father, Edward the Elder, King of the English, taking with her Louis her son who was still a child[1]. Educated at his grandfather's court, then under his uncle Aethelstan, who had succeeded Edward in 926, Louis, whose surname "d'Outremer" ("from beyond the sea") recalls his early years, was now about fifteen. There was a general agreement to offer him the crown. Hugh the Great seems from the outset very dexterously to have taken his claims under his patronage, and when Louis landed a few weeks later at Boulogne he was one of the first to go and greet him. On Sunday 19 June 936, Louis was solemnly crowned at Laon by Artaud, the Archbishop of Rheims.

From the very beginning, Hugh the Great sought to get exclusive possession of the young king. First he brought him with him to dispute possession of Burgundy with its duke, Hugh the Black, brother of the

[1] The French Carolingians:

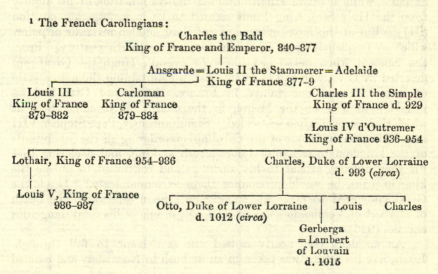

Charles the Bald
King of France and Emperor, 840–877
|
Ansgarde = Louis II the Stammerer = Adelaide
King of France 877–9

Louis III   Carloman   Charles III the Simple
King of France   King of France   King of France d. 929
879–882   879–884
                                          |
                                          Louis IV d'Outremer
                                          King of France 936–954

Lothair, King of France 954–986   Charles, Duke of Lower Lorraine
| d. 993 (circa)
|
Louis V, King of France
986–987   Otto, Duke of Lower Lorraine   Louis   Charles
                        d. 1012 (circa)
                                          Gerberga
                                          = Lambert
                                          of Louvain
                                          d. 1015

late King Raoul : then he drew him in his wake to Paris. But Louis proved to have the same high and independent spirit, the same energetic temper as his father. He shewed this markedly by reviving Charles the Simple's claims to Lorraine, which, in the reign of Raoul, had been re-taken by the king of Germany (925) and reduced to a duchy. Louis invaded it in 938 at the request of its duke, Gilbert (Giselbert). But the results of this firm and decided course were the same as in the case of Charles the Simple. The party of opposition gathered again around Hugh the Great and Herbert of Vermandois, whom a common hostility drew together. The Carolingian's chief support lay in Artaud, Arch-bishop of Rheims.

The rebels marched straight upon Rheims. The place made but a faint resistance, Hugh the Great and Herbert entering it after brief delay. Artaud was driven from his see and sent to the monastery of St Basle, while Herbert procured the consecration in his stead of his own son Hugh, the same candidate whom a few years earlier King Raoul had replaced by Artaud. The rebels proceeded to besiege Laon. Louis defended himself vigorously. In company with Artaud, who had fled from his monastery, he advanced to raise the blockade of Laon. But his bold attempt upon Lorraine had resulted in drawing Otto, the new King of Germany, towards Hugh the Great and Herbert. At their request he entered France, stopping at the palace of Attigny to receive their homage, and for a short time even pitching his camp on the banks of the Seine (940).

Defeated in the Ardennes by Hugh and Herbert, forced to flee into the kingdom of Burgundy, cut off from Artaud (who had been deposed in a synod held at Rheims, and again shut up in the monastery of St Basle, while his rival Hugh obtained the confirmation of his dignity from the Holy See), King Louis seemed to be in a desperate position (941). But at this moment came one of those sudden reversals of policy which so frequently occur in the history of the tenth century. From the moment when he seemed likely to prevail, Hugh the Great was deserted by Otto, who had every interest in maintaining the actual state of instability and uncertainty in France. Louis and Otto had an interview at Visé on the Meuse, in the month of November 942, at which their reconciliation was sealed. Simultaneously, Pope Stephen VIII raised his voice in favour of the Carolingian, ordering all the inhabitants of the kingdom to recognise Louis afresh as king, and declaring that "if they did not attend to his warnings and continued to pursue the king in arms, he would pronounce them excommunicate." Hugh the Great consented to make his submission. Soon afterwards the death of Herbert of Vermandois was to rid Louis of one of his most dangerous enemies (943).

An accident very nearly caused the settlement to fall through. Louis, like his father, was taken in an ambush in Normandy and banded over to Hugh the Great (945). But the latter quickly realised that an attempt at revolution would only end in disappointment, and thought it better policy to obtain from the king the surrender of his capital, Laon.

As soon as he was set at liberty, Louis appealed to Otto. The kings joined in re-taking Rheims, drove out the Archbishop, Hugh of Vermandois, and restored Artaud (946). Then in June 948 a solemn council assembled on German soil at Ingelheim, under the presidency of the Pope's legate, to consider the situation. The kings, Louis and Otto, appeared there side by side. Hugh of Vermandois was excommunicated. Louis himself made a speech, and recalled how " he had been summoned from regions beyond the sea by the envoys of Duke Hugh and the other lords of France, to receive the kingdom, the inheritance of his fathers; how he had been raised to the royal dignity and consecrated by the universal desire and amid the acclamations of the magnates and warriors of the Franks; how then, after that he had been driven from his throne by the same Hugh, traitorously attacked, made prisoner and detained by him under a strong guard for a whole year; how at last in order to recover his liberty he had been compelled to abandon to him the town of Laon, the only one of all the royal residences which the queen, Gerberga, and his faithful subjects had been able to preserve." In conclusion he added that "if anyone would maintain that these evils endured by him since he had obtained the crown had come upon him by his own fault, he would purge himself of that accusation according to the judgment of the Synod and the decision of King Otto, and that he was even prepared to make good his right in single combat." Touched by this remonstrance, the Fathers of the Council replied by the following decision: " For the future, let none dare to assail the royal power, nor traitorously to dishonour it by a perfidious attack. We decide, in consequence, according to the decree of the Council of Toledo, that Hugh, the invader and despoiler of the kingdom of Louis, be smitten with sword of excommunication, unless, within the interval fixed, he shall present himself before the Council, and unless he amends his ways, giving satisfaction for his signal perversity." And, in fact, Hugh the Great, who had not feared even further to expel the Bishop of Laon from his see, was summoned under pain of excommunication to appear at a forthcoming council which was to meet at Trèves in the ensuing month of September. He did not appear and was excommunicated. Not long after, a lucky stroke made Louis again master of Laon (949) and Hugh, again solemnly excommunicated by the Pope "until he should give satisfaction to King Louis," was soon constrained to come and renew his submission (950).

Everything considered, the power of Louis seemed to have been greatly strengthened, when he died suddenly on 10 September 954, as a result of a fall from his horse. This explains why the nobles, Duke Hugh foremost among them, without raising any difficulties chose his eldest son Lothair (Lothar) to succeed him. The latter, then aged about fourteen, was crowned at Rheims on 12 November 954.

Delivered ere long from the embarrassing patronage of Hugh the Great, whom death removed on 17 June 956, Lothair, a few years later, thought himself strong enough to resume the policy of his father and grandfather in Lorraine. He gave secret encouragement to the nobles of that country who were in revolt against Otto II, the new King of Germany, and in 978 attempted by a sudden stroke to recover the ground lost in that direction since the days of Raoul. He secretly raised an army and marched upon Aix-la-Chapelle, where he counted on surprising Otto. The stroke miscarried. Otto, warned in time, had been able to escape. Lothair entered Aix, installed himself in the old Carolingian palace, and by way of a threat, turned round to the east the brazen eagle with outspread wings which stood on the top of the palace. But provisions failed, and three days afterwards he was obliged to beat a retreat. Otto, in revenge, threw himself upon the French kingdom, destroyed Compiègne and Attigny, took Laon and pitched his camp upon the heights of Montmartre. He was only able to burn the suburbs of Paris, and then after having a victorious Alleluia chanted by his priests he fell back upon the Aisne (November 978). Lothair only just failed to cut off his passage across the river, and even succeeded in massacring his camp-followers and taking his baggage. This barren struggle was not, on the whole, of advantage to either sovereign. An agreement took place; in July 980 Lothair and Otto met at Margut on the Chiers on the frontier of the two kingdoms, when they embraced and swore mutual friendship.

It was a reconciliation in appearance only, and a few months later Otto eagerly welcomed the overtures of Hugh the Great's son, Hugh Capet, Duke of the Franks. The death of Otto on 7 December 983 deferred the final rupture. But dark intrigues, of which the Archbishopric of Rheims was the centre, were soon to be woven round the unfortunate Carolingian.

The Archbishop of Rheims, Adalbero, belonged to one of the most important families of Lorraine. One of his brothers was Count of Verdun and of the Luxembourg district. Talented, learned, alert and ambitious, his sympathies as well as his family interests bound him to the Ottonian house. In the same way Gerbert the *scholasticus*, the future Pope Sylvester II, whom a close friendship united to Adalbero, owed the foundation of his fortune and his success in life to Otto I and Otto II. As he had long been a vassal of Otto II, from whom he had received the rich abbey of Bobbio, his devotion was assured in advance to young Otto III who had just succeeded, and to his mother, the Empress Theophano. Lothair having thought well to form an alliance with Henry, Duke of Bavaria[1], young Otto's rival, Adalbero and Gerbert

_____
[1] See *infra*, p. 210.

did not hesitate to plot his ruin. A whole series of obscure letters, with a hidden meaning, often written on a system agreed upon beforehand, were exchanged between Adalbero and Gerbert and the party of Otto III. Hugh Capet was won over to the imperial cause, and a skilful system of espionage was organised around Lothair.

The latter, nevertheless, defended himself with remarkable courage and firmness. He contrived to recruit followers even among the vassals of Hugh Capet, threw himself upon Verdun, surprised the place, and so took captive several Lorraine nobles of Adalbero's kindred who had shut themselves up there. Finally he summoned Adalbero on a charge of high treason before the general assembly to be held at Compiègne on 11 May 985. Unfortunately, all these exertions were in vain; Hugh Capet came up with an army and dispersed the assembly at Compiègne. Not long after the king took a chill and died suddenly on 2 March 986.

Lothair had taken the precaution, as early as 979, to have his son Louis V acknowledged and crowned king. The latter, who was nineteen years of age, succeeded him without opposition. He was about to take up his father's policy with some vigour, and had just issued a fresh summons to Adalbero to appear before an assembly which was to meet at Compiègne, when a sudden fall proved fatal (21 or 22 May 987).

Louis left no children. There remained, however, one Carolingian who might have a legitimate claim to the crown, Charles, brother of the late King Lothair. After a quarrel with his brother, Charles, in 977, had taken service with the Emperor, who had given him the duchy of Lower Lorraine. From that time Charles had taken up the position of a rival to Lothair; in 978 he had accompanied Otto II on his expedition to Paris and perhaps had even tried to get himself recognised as king. But soon there was a complete change; Charles had become reconciled to his brother in order to plot against Otto III. At the same time he had fallen out with Adalbero, and when the succession to the French crown was suddenly thrown open in 987, his prospects of obtaining it seemed from the first to be gravely compromised.

The truth was that for a century past political conceptions had gradually been transformed. Although the kingship had never ceased, even in Charlemagne's day, to be considered as in theory elective, it seemed, up to the time when Odo was called to the throne, that only a Carolingian could aspire to the title of king. The theory of the incapacity of any other family to receive the crown was still brilliantly sustained during the last years of the ninth century by Fulk, Archbishop of Rheims. In a very curious letter of self-justification, which he wrote in 893, he laid it down that Odo, being a stranger to the royal race, was a mere usurper; that the King of Germany, Arnulf, having refused to accept the crown which he himself and his supporters offered him, they had been forced to wait until Charles the Simple, "with Arnulf, the only remaining member of the royal house," should be of an age to ascend the throne, which his brothers, Louis III and Carloman, had occupied. He added that by conferring power on him they had merely observed the principle almost universally known, by virtue of which royalty, among the Franks, had not ceased to be hereditary. Consequently he entreated King Arnulf to interfere for the maintenance of this principle, and not to permit that usurpers should prevail against "those to whom the royal power was due by reason of their birth."

In 987 these principles were far from being forgotten. Adalbero, Hugh Capet himself, according to a contemporary historian, Richer, monk of St Remi at Rheims, declared that "if Louis of divine memory, son of Lothair, had left children, it would have been fitting that they should have succeeded him." Nor shall we find the rights of Charles of Lorraine, brother of King Lothair, denied in principle, and in order to eliminate them it was necessary to have recourse to the argument that Charles by his conduct had rendered himself unworthy to reign.

Another principle had indeed been gradually developing, to the prejudice of hereditary right, namely, that the king, having as his function to defend the kingdom against enemies from without, and to preserve peace and concord within it, ought to be chosen by reason of his capacity. We have seen[1] that Archbishop Fulk himself had deliberately set aside Charles the Simple in 888, "because he was still too young both in body and mind, and consequently unfit to govern." In the same way, the historian Richer makes Adalbero say "that only a man distinguished for valour, wisdom and honour should be put at the head of the kingdom." And in fact, since the death of Charles the Fat, the Carolingians had more than once been supplanted by kings unconnected with their house.

Now even before the succession fell vacant, there was a personage in the kingdom who, as Gerbert wrote in 985, although under the nominal king was in fact the real king. This personage was the Duke of the Franks, Hugh Capet, son of Hugh the Great. With singular skill and perseverance, Hugh the Great, and afterwards Hugh Capet had never in fact ceased to extend through the kingdom, if not their direct domination, at least their preponderating influence. We have seen how, at the accession of Louis IV, Hugh the Great had attempted to act the part of regent of the kingdom. In a charter of the year 936 Louis himself declares that he acts "by the counsel of his well-beloved Hugh, duke of the Franks, who in all our kingdoms holds the first place after me." This guardianship had soon become burdensome to the young king who had freed himself from it, but Hugh had none the less manoeuvred very adroitly to increase his prestige. Having lost his wife, Eadhild, sister

---

[1] See *supra,* p. 71.

of the English King Aethelstan, he had married, about 937, a sister of Otto I, King of Germany.   Soon after, in 943, he had obtained from Louis IV the suzerainty of Burgundy, thus interposing himself between the sovereign and a whole class of his greatest vassals ; a little later he had succeeded in usurping the overlordship of Normandy, and finally in 954 he had attempted to add to it that of Aquitaine.   The new King, Lothair, having allowed this fresh grant to be extorted from him, had even been obliged to go with the duke to lay siege to Poitiers (955).   The attempt, however, had failed, but in 956 on the death of Gilbert, Duke of Burgundy, Hugh directly appropriated his inheritance.   Owner of numerous abbeys and estates dispersed here and there through the kingdom, in Berry, in the Autun district, in that of Meaux and in Picardy, he really did appear as the "Duke of the Gauls" as, some thirty years later, the historian Richer styles him, and his power throwing that of the king into the shade, he had publicly held almost royal courts (*placita*) to which bishops, abbots and counts resorted in crowds.

His son, Hugh Capet, had been obliged to give up Burgundy to his brother Otto, and had tried in vain to secure the Duchy of Aquitaine, of which he had obtained a fresh grant from King Lothair in 960.   But at the same time he saw the power of his rivals much more seriously diminished.   The possessions of Herbert II of Vermandois, who died in 943, had been divided among his sons, and in 987 neither Albert I, titulary of the little county of Vermandois, nor even the Count of Troyes, Meaux and Provins, Herbert the Young, although his territorial power was beginning to be somewhat of a menace, was of sufficient importance to compete in influence with the Duke of the Franks.   But if the duke's authority, when closely examined, might seem to be undermined by the growing independence of several of his vassals, it was none the less very imposing; suzerain, if not immediate holder of all Neustria, including Normandy, of an important part of *Francia*, and titulary of several rich abbeys, the Duke of the Franks, who had on his side the support of Adalbero and Gerbert, might well seem expressly marked out to succeed to the inheritance suddenly left vacant by the death of Louis V.

And this, indeed, was what took place.   The assembly which Louis V at the time of his death had summoned to meet at Compiègne to judge in Archbishop Adalbero's case, was held under the presidency of Duke Hugh.   As was to be expected, it decided that the charges against the prelate were groundless, and, at his suggestion, resolved to meet again a little later at Senlis on the territory of the Duke of the Franks and to proceed to the election of a king.   Adalbero there explained without circumlocution that it was impossible to think of entrusting the crown to Charles, Duke of Lorraine.   "How can we bestow any dignity" he exclaimed (according to the report of the historian Richer who was doubtless present in the assembly) " upon Charles, who is in nowise guided by honour, who is enervated by lethargy, who, in a word, has so lost his judgment as no longer to feel shame at serving a foreign king, and at mismatching himself with a woman of birth inferior to his own, the daughter of a mere knight[1]? How could the powerful duke suffer that a woman, coming from the family of one of his vassals, should become queen and rule over him? How could he walk behind one whose equals and even whose superiors bend the knee before him? Examine the situation carefully, and reflect that Charles has been rejected more by his own fault than by that of others. Let your decision be rather for the good than for the misfortune of the State. If you value its prosperity, crown Hugh, the illustrious duke. Let no man be led away by attachment to Charles, let no man through hatred of the duke be drawn away from what is useful to all. For if you have faults to find in the good man, how can you praise the wicked? If you commend the wicked man, how can you condemn the good? Remember the threatenings of God who says; 'Woe unto them that call evil good, and good evil; that put darkness for light and light for darkness!' Take then as your master the duke, who has made himself illustrious by his actions, his nobility, and his resourcefulness, and in whom you will find a protector, not only of the public weal, but also of your private interests. His benevolence will make him a father to you. Where is the man, indeed, who has appealed to him without finding protection? Who is he who, being deprived of the help of his own people, has not by him been restored to them?" These reasons seemed conclusive, no doubt, to an assembly which asked nothing better than to be convinced. Hugh Capet was proclaimed and crowned at Noyon on Sunday, 3 July 987.

Such were the circumstances attending what is called, improperly enough, the Capetian Revolution. To speak correctly, there was no more a revolution in 987 than there had been a century before when Odo was chosen. In one case as in the other the Carolingian had been set aside because he was considered, or there was a determination to consider him, unfit to govern. If in after years the event of 987 has seemed to mark an epoch in the history of France, it is because Hugh Capet was able enough to hand on his heritage to his son, and because the house of Capet succeeded in retaining power for many long centuries. But this was in some sort an accident, the after-effect of which on the constitution of the State is hardly traceable. It is quite impossible to say in any sense that the kingship became by this event a feudal kingship; neither in this respect nor in any other was the occurrence of 987 of a subversive character; the position of the monarchy in France was to prove itself on the morrow of Hugh Capet's election exactly what it had been in the time of his predecessors.

---

[1] Charles had married the daughter of an unknown knight, the under-vassal of Hugh Capet.

The fact was that since the end of the ninth century, monarchy in France had been steadily losing ground. More and more, the sovereign had found himself incapable of fulfilling the social tasks assigned him, especially, what was most important in the eyes of contemporaries, upon whom lawlessness and disorder pressed intolerably, his task of defending and protecting order and security.

It was the height of the peril from the Northmen that Odo was chosen by the barons, who acclaimed in him the hero of the siege of Paris, the one man capable of making head against the pirates. And indeed it seemed just at first as though he would not fall short of the hopes entertained of him. In June 888 he surprised a whole band of Northmen at Montfaucon in the Argonne district. He had a thousand horsemen at most with him, while the Northmen were ten times as numerous. The impetuous onset of his troops overthrew the enemy; he himself fought in the foremost rank and in the thick of the *mêlée* received a blow from an axe which thrust his helmet back upon his shoulders. Instantly he ran his daring assailant through with his sword, and remained master of the field of battle. But the Northmen returned to the charge. A few weeks later they seized Meaux and threatened Paris. Again Odo hurried up with an army and covered the town. None the less, the Northmen wintered on the banks of the Loing, and in 889 again threatened Paris, when Odo found himself forced to purchase their withdrawal, just as Charles the Fat had done. In November 890 as the Northmen, after ravaging Brittany and the Cotentin, crossed the Seine and marched towards the valley of the Oise, Odo again hastened up to bar their way. He overtook them in the neighbourhood of Guerbigny, not far from Noyon. But the Northmen had a marsh and a brook between them and the king, and the latter was helpless to stay their course. At least he remained with his army on the banks of the Oise to protect the surrounding country. Strongly entrenched in their camp to the south of Noyon, the Northmen spread their ravages far to the north. In the early part of 891 Odo attempted to intercept a band of them returning, laden with booty from Arnulf's kingdom. He hoped to surprise them at Wallers, a few miles from Valenciennes, but once again they escaped him and broke away through the forests, leaving only their spoil in his hands.

Further to the west another contingent might be seen, settled at Amiens, under the leadership of the famous Hasting, in their turn pillaging the country and pushing their ravages as far as Artois. The king's energy shewed signs of slackening; after another failure near Amiens, he allowed himself to be surprised by the enemy in Vermandois where his army was put to flight (end of 891). In 896 he makes no more attempt at resistance, a handful of pirates ravage the banks of the Seine below Paris with impunity, and, ascending the Oise, take up their winter quarters near Compiègne, in the royal "villa" of Choisy-au-Bac.

Throughout the summer of 897 they continued their ravages along the banks of the Seine, while Odo does not appear at all. Finally he was roused from his inaction, but only to negotiate, to "redeem his kingdom." He actually left the Northmen free to go and winter on the Loire! Thus gradually even Odo had shewn himself incapable of bridling them; at first he had successfully resisted them, then, though watching them narrowly, he had been unable to surprise them, and had suffered himself to be defeated by them; finally, he looked on indifferently at their plunderings, and confined himself to bribing them to depart, and diverting them to other parts of the kingdom.

Such was the situation when Odo died, and Charles the Simple was universally recognised as king. The Northmen pillaged Aquitaine and pillaged Neustria, but Charles remained unmoved. Another party went up the Somme, and this was a direct menace to the Carolingian's own possessions. He therefore gathered an army and repulsed the pirates, who fell back into Brittany (898). At the end of that year they invaded Burgundy, burning the monasteries and slaughtering the inhabitants. Charles made no sign, but left it to the Duke of Burgundy, Richard, to rid himself of them as best he might. Richard, indeed, put them to flight, but allowed them to carry their ravages elsewhere. In 903 other Northern bands, led by Eric and Baret, ascended the Loire as far as Tours and burnt the suburbs of the town; in 910 they pillaged Berry and killed the Archbishop of Bourges; in 911 they besieged Chartres, the king still paying no attention. These facts are significant; evidently the king gives up the idea of defending the kingdom as a whole, and leaves it to each individual to cope with his difficulties as he may. When the region where he exercises direct authority is endangered, he intervenes, but as soon as he has diverted the fury of the pirates upon another part of the kingdom, his conscience is satisfied, and his example is followed on all hands.

In 911 Charles entered into negotiations with Rollo, and, as we have seen, the result was that a great part of the Norman bands established themselves permanently in the districts of Rouen, Lisieux and Evreux, but the character which the negotiations assumed and the share that the king took in them are uncertain. In any case, the chief object of the convention of St-Clair-sur-Epte was to put a stop to the incursions by way of the Seine and the Oise; as to the other Norman bands, or the Northmen of the Loire, the king does not concern himself with them, and we shall find them in 924 vociferously demanding a settlement like that of Rollo.

For the rest, the so-called Treaty of St-Clair-sur-Epte however beneficial it may have been, was far from bringing about peace even in the northern part of the kingdom. Though for the most part converted to Christianity, the companions of Rollo were not tamed and civilised in a day. Increased in numbers by the fresh recruits who came in from the north, they more than once resumed their raids for plunder, often in concert with the Northmen of the Loire. And at the same time a new scourge fell upon the country. Troops of Hungarians, having devastated South Germany, Lorraine and Alsace, advanced in 917 into French Burgundy and threatened the very heart of the kingdom. Confronted with this danger, Charles endeavoured to exert himself. But it was now that the utter weakness of the monarchy was made manifest; the barons, ill-pleased with their sovereign, with one accord refused to join the *ost*. Only the Archbishop of Rheims appeared with his vassals, and upon him alone the safety of the kingdom was left to depend.

Thenceforward the Northmen in the north and west, and the Hungarians in the East, harry the country with frenzied pillaging and burning. As long as the king was not directly threatened he remained indifferent and supine: not only did he allow the Normans to devastate Brittany from one end to the other, indeed he had officially permitted them to pillage it in 911, but he allowed them also to go up the Loire, fix themselves at Nantes, burn Angers and Tours, and besiege Orleans (919). The only resistance the spoilers met with in that quarter came, not from the king, but from the Marquess of Neustria, Robert, who in 921 succeeded in driving them out of his duchy at the cost of leaving them at full liberty to settle in the Nantes district. In 923 they plundered Aquitaine and Auvergne, the Duke of Aquitaine and the Count of Auvergne being left to deal with them on their own account. In the same year King Charles himself summoned the Northmen to the north of the kingdom in order to resist Raoul, whom the magnates had just set up in his stead as king. From the Loire and from Rouen the pirates burst forth upon *Francia*; they again went up the Oise and pillaged Artois and the Beauvaisis, so that at the beginning of 924 the threatened lords of *Francia* were forced to club together to bribe them into retiring. Even then the Normans of Rouen would not depart until they had extorted the cession of the whole of the Bayeux district, and doubtless of that of Séez also.

Still the devastastions went on. The Northmen of the Loire, led by Rögnvald also demanded a fief in their turn, and committed fresh ravages in Neustria. Here were the domains of Hugh the Great, King Raoul consequently made no movement. In December 924 the robbers invaded Burgundy, and being repulsed after a determined and bloody struggle, came and fixed themselves on the Seine near Melun. Much alarmed, King Raoul found in *Francia* a mere handful of barons prepared to follow him, Church vassals from Rheims and Soissons, and the Count of Vermandois. These could not suffice. He set off at once for Burgundy to try to recruit additional troops. Duke Hugh the Great, fearing for his own dominions, came and took up a post of observation near the Northmen's entrenchments. But while the king was in Burgundy with difficulty collecting an army, the Northmen decamped without the slightest effort on Hugh's part to pursue them.

The Northmen of Rouen thereupon resumed operations more fiercely than ever; they burned Amiens, Arras and the suburbs of Noyon. Once again directly threatened, the king hurried back from Burgundy and convoked the inhabitants of the district to the *ost*. This time the lords felt the necessity for union, and responded to the king's appeal; all took up arms, the Count of Vermandois and the Count of Flanders among others, and getting possession of Eu they slaughtered a whole band of pirates. Some months later the Northmen surprised the king at Fauquembergue in Artois. A bloody struggle ensued, the king was wounded and the Count of Ponthieu killed, but a thousand Northmen lay dead upon the field. The remainder fled, and indemnified themselves by pillaging the whole of the north of *Francia*.

Just at this time (beginning of 926) the Hungarians fell upon the country, and for a moment even threatened the territory round Rheims. Once again contributions were raised to buy the departure of the Northmen, and, meanwhile, the Hungarians re-crossed the frontier without let or hindrance.

Raoul, however, seemed disposed to make an effort to do his duty as king. In 930, as he was endeavouring to subdue the Aquitanians, who had rebelled against his authority, he met a strong party of Northmen in the Limousin; he pursued them valorously and cut them to pieces. Five years later, as the Hungarians were invading Burgundy, burning, robbing, and killing as they went, Raoul suddenly came up, and his presence sufficed to put the ravagers to flight. The Northmen, for their part, content themselves thenceforward with ravaging Brittany.

But hardly was Raoul dead when the Hungarians grew bolder. Repulsed from Germany in 937, they flooded the kingdom of France, burning and pillaging the monasteries around Rheims and Sens. They penetrated into the midst of Berry, and, traversing the whole of Burgundy, passed into Italy to continue their ravages there. In 951 Aquitaine was devastated in its turn; in 954 having burnt the suburbs of Cambrai, they pillaged Vermandois, and the country round Laon and Rheims, as well as Burgundy.

Against all these incursions, the atrocity of which left a strong impression on the minds of contemporaries, the monarchy did nothing. After having attempted to lead the struggle against the barbarians, it had gradually narrowed its outlook and had thought it sufficient to protect—though even this was in an intermittent way—the territories in which its actual domains lay, leaving to the dukes and counts of other districts the task of providing for their own defence. All care for the public interest was so far forgotten that each man, the king as well as the rest, felt that he had performed his whole duty when he had thrust back the predatory bands upon his neighbour's territory. The conception of a State divided into administrative districts over which the king placed counts who were merely his representatives, had been completely obliterated. The practice of commendation, as it became general, had turned the counts into local magnates, the immediate lords of each group of inhabitants whose fealty they thenceforth transmit from one to another by hereditary right. After 888 not a single legislative measure is found emanating from the king, not a single measure involving the public interest. There is no longer any question of royal imposts levied throughout France; even when the buying off of the Northmen by the payment of a tribute is concerned it is only the regions actually in danger which contribute their quota.

Once entered on this path, the kingdom was rapidly frittered away into fragments. Since the king no longer protected the people they were necessarily obliged to group themselves in communities around certain counts more powerful than the rest, and to seek in them protectors able to resist the barbarians. Besides, the monarchy itself fostered this tendency. From the earliest Carolingian times it had happened more than once that the king had laid on this or that count the command of several frontier counties, forming them under him into a "march" or duchy capable of offering more resistance to the enemy than isolated counties could do. From being exceptional and temporary this expedient, in the course of years, had become usual and definitive. The kingdom had thus been split up into a certain number of great duchies, having more or less coherence, at the head of which were genuine local magnates, who had usurped or appropriated all the royal rights, and on whose wavering fidelity alone the unity of the kingdom depended for support.

In appearance, the sovereign in the tenth century ruled from the mouths of the Scheldt to the south of Barcelona. Some years before the final overthrow of the dynasty we still find the Carolingian king granting charters at the request of the Count of Holland or the Duke of Roussillon, while we constantly see the monasteries of the Spanish March sending delegates to Laon or Compiègne to secure confirmation in their possessions from the king. From Aquitaine, Normandy, and Burgundy, as from Flanders and Neustria, monks and priests, counts and dukes are continually begging him to grant them some act of confirmation. This was because the traditional conception of monarchy with its *quasi* providential authority was thoroughly engrafted in men's minds. But the actual state of things was very different.

The Gascons, never really subjugated, enjoyed an independent existence; though they dated their charters according to the regnal year of the king of France, they no longer had any connexion with him.

To the east of Gascony lay the three great marches of Toulouse, Gothia and Spain. The latter, dismembered from ancient Gothia (whence

came its name of Gothalania or Catalonia) extended over the southern
slope of the Pyrenees beyond Llobregat. Since 875 it had been governed
by the Counts of Barcelona, who, as early as the end of the ninth
century, had gained possession of all the other counties of the March,
those of Gerona, Ampurias, Perelada, Besalu, Ausonia, Berga, Cerdaña,
Urgel, Pailhas and Ribagorza. They had even at last extended their
suzerainty north of the Pyrenees over the counties of Conflent and
Roussillon, which certain counts of their family had succeeded in
detaching from Gothia, in the hope, perhaps—though this is not certain
—of securing for themselves an independent sway[1]. It was a strange
thing, but in these remote parts the king's name—no doubt by the
very reason of his distance—still inspired a certain awe. In 944, we
find the monks of San Pedro de Roda in the county of Ausonia, by the
advice indeed of Sunifred, the Count of Barcelona, coming as far as
Laon to ask of Louis IV a charter expressly recognising their independence, which was threatened by two neighbouring convents. Louis IV
granted them a formal charter by which he takes them under his
protection, and, employing the ancient formula, forbids "all counts,
all representatives of the public power, and all judicial authorities to
come within" their domains. It must be added, however, that the
royal authority does not seem to have been scrupulously respected, for
four years later, the monks of San Pedro and their rivals found it
advisable to come to a compromise, for which, nevertheless, they made
a point of coming to beg the king's confirmation. And in 986 even
the Count of Barcelona reflects that his sovereign owes him protection,
and being attacked by the Musulmans, does not hesitate to appeal to
him. But, as a fact, the March of Spain was almost as completely
independent as that of the Duchy of Gascony. The king's sovereignty
was recognised there, the charters were dated with careful precision
according to the year of his reign, the Count of Barcelona no doubt
came and did him homage, but he had no power of interfering in the
affairs of the country, except in so far as his action was invited.

The March of Gothia, between the Cevennes and the Mediterranean,
the Lower Rhone and Roussillon, had gradually lost its individual
existence and fallen under the suzerainty of the Counts of Toulouse,
whom the records of the tenth century magniloquently style "Princes of
Gothia." They recognised the king's authority, and came to do him
homage; and the charters in their country were dated according to his
regnal year, but further than this the connexion between the sovereign
and his subjects did not extend.

Further north, between the Loire and the ocean, lay the immense

---

[1] We shall even find one of them, at the end of the tenth century, in the time
of King Lothair, taking the title of duke. But the two charters in which they
are thus designated (*Recueil des actes de Lothaire et de Louis V rois de France*, edited
by Louis Halphen) are not perhaps of very certain authenticity.

duchy of Aquitaine, a region never fully incorporated with the Frankish state. From 781 onwards Charlemagne had found himself obliged to form it into a separate kingdom, though subordinate to his own superior authority, for the benefit of his third son Louis the Pious. When the latter became Emperor in 814 the existence of the kingdom of Aquitaine had been respected, and down to 877 the Aquitanians had continued to live their own life under their own king. But at this date their king, Louis the Stammerer, having become King of France, formed the land into a duchy, a measure which, as may easily be imagined, did not contribute to bind it more closely to the rest of the kingdom. The ducal title, long disputed between the Counts of Toulouse, Auvergne and Poitiers, ended, in the middle of the tenth century, by falling to the latter, despite reiterated attempts on the part of Hugh the Great and Hugh Capet to tear it from their grasp. In the course of these struggles King Lothair several times appeared south of the Loire in the train of the Duke of the Franks. In 955 we find him laying siege with Hugh to Poitiers, and in 958 he was in the Nivernais, about to march against the Count of Poitou. Finally, in 979 Lothair took a decisive step, and restored the kingdom of Aquitaine, unheard-of for a century, for the benefit of his young son Louis V, whom he had just crowned at Compiègne. A marriage with Adelaide, widow of the Count of Gevaudan, was no doubt destined in his expectation to consolidate Louis's power. It was celebrated in the heart of Auvergne, in the presence of Lothair himself and of a brilliant train of magnates and bishops. But this attempt at establishing direct rule over Aquitaine led only to a mortifying check. Before three years had passed, Lothair found himself compelled to go in person and withdraw his son from Auvergne. In fact, no sooner was the Loire crossed than a new and strange France seemed to begin; its manners and customs were different, and when young Louis V tried to adopt them, the Northerners pursued him with their sarcasms. And later, when Robert the Pious married Constance, their indignation was aroused by the facile manners, the clothes, and customs which her suite introduced among them. Such things were, in their eyes, "the manners of foreigners." The true kingdom of France, in which its sovereigns felt themselves really at home, ended at the Aquitanian frontier.

To the north of that frontier the ties of vassalage which bound the counts and dukes to the sovereign were less relaxed than in the south. But the breaking-up of the State into a certain number of great principalities had gone forward here on parallel lines. Not counting Brittany, which had never been thoroughly incorporated, and thenceforward remained completely independent, the greater part of Neustria had split off, and since the ninth century had been formed into a March, continually increasing in extent, for the benefit of Robert the Strong and his successors. Francia, in its turn, reduced by the formation of Lorraine to the lands lying between the North Sea and the Channel, the Seine below Nogent-sur-Seine and the lines of the Meuse and Scheldt, was also cut into on the north by the rise of Flanders, and on the west by that of Normandy which at the same time reduced the former area of Neustria by one-third, while to the east the March or Duchy of Burgundy was taking shape in that part of ancient Burgundy which had remained French. The study of the rise of these great principalities is in the highest degree instructive, because it enables us to point out the exact process by which the diminution of the royal power was being effected.

For Flanders it is necessary to go back to the time of Charles the Bald. About 863 that king had entrusted to Count Baldwin, whose marriage with his daughter Judith he had just sanctioned, some counties to the north, among which were, no doubt, Ghent, Bruges, Courtrai and the Mempisc district. These formed a genuine "March," the creation of which was justified by the necessity of defending the country against the northern pirates. The danger on this side was not less serious than from the direction of the Loire, where the March of Neustria was set up, almost at the same time, for Robert the Strong. The descendants of Count Baldwin I not only succeeded in holding the March thus constituted, but worked unceasingly to extend its limits. Baldwin II the Bald (879–918), son of Baldwin I, took advantage of the difficulties with which Odo and Charles the Simple had to struggle to lay hands upon Arras. In the year 900, Charles the Simple having intended, by the advice of Fulk, Archbishop of Rheims, to retake the town, Baldwin II had the prelate assassinated, and not content with keeping Artois, succeeded in fixing himself in the Tournaisis, and in getting a foothold, if he had not already done so, in the county of Therouanne by obtaining from the king the Abbey of Saint-Bertin. His son, Arnold I (918–964) shewed himself in all respects his worthy successor. Devoid of scruples, not hesitating to rid himself by murder of William Longsword, Duke of Normandy, whom he considered dangerous (942) just as his father had done in the case of Archbishop Fulk, Arnold attacked Ponthieu where he got possession of Montreuil-sur-Mer (948). Thus at that time the Flemish March included all the lands lying between the Scheldt as far as its mouth, the North Sea and the Canche, and by the acquisition of Montreuil-sur-Mer even stretched into Ponthieu.

This progressive extension towards the south could not be other than a menace to the monarchy. As in the case of Aquitaine, Lothair endeavoured to check it by a sudden stroke, which on this occasion was at least partly successful. In the first place he was astute enough to persuade Arnold I, now broken in spirit, it would appear, by age and the loss of his eldest son Baldwin, to make him a donation of his duchy (962). It was stipulated only that Arnold should enjoy the usufruct. Three years later on 27 March 965 Arnold died, and immediately Lothair marched into Flanders, and, without striking a blow, took Arras, Douai,

Saint-Amand and the whole of the country as far as the Lys. But he could penetrate no farther; the Flemings, who were determined not to have the king of France for their immediate sovereign, had proclaimed Count Arnold II grandson of their late ruler, with, as he was still a child, his cousin Baldwin Bauce as his guardian. Negotiations were begun between the king and the Flemish lords. Lothair consented to recognise the new marquess who came and did him homage, but he kept Douai and Arras. It was not long, however, before these two places fell back under the rule of the Marquess of Flanders; certainly by 988 this had taken place. Thus the king had succeeded in checking for a moment the expansion of the Flemish March, but had not in any way modified its semi-independence.

We must also go back to the middle of the ninth century in order to investigate the origin of the Duchy of Burgundy. When the Treaty of Verdun (843) had detached from the kingdom of France all the counties of the diocese of Besançon as well as the county of Lyons, Charles the Bald naturally found himself more than once impelled to unite two or three of the counties of Burgundy which had remained French so as to form a March on the frontiers under the authority of a single count. On the morrow of Odo's elevation to the throne (888) the boundaries of French Burgundy, which in the course of the political events of the last forty years had undergone many fluctuations, were substantially the same as had been stipulated by the Treaty of Verdun. At this time one of the principal counties of the region, that of Autun, was in the hands of Richard called *Le Justicier* (the lover of Justice), brother of that Boso who in 879 had caused himself to be proclaimed King of Provence. Here also there was need of a strong power capable of organising the resistance against the incessant ravages of the Northman bands. Richard shewed himself equal to the task; in 898 he inflicted a memorable defeat upon the pirates at Argenteuil, near Tonnerre; a few years later he surprised them in the Nivernais and forced them once again to take to flight. We see him very skilfully pushing his way into every district and adding county to county. In 894 he secures the county of Sens, in 896 he is apparently in possession of the Atuyer district, in 900 we find him Count of Auxerre, while the Count of Dijon and the Bishop of Langres appear among his vassals. He acts as master in the Lassois district, and in those of Tonnerre and Beaune, and is, it would seem, suzerain of the Count of Troyes. Under the title of duke or marquess he rules over the whole of French Burgundy, thus earning the name of "Prince of the Burgundians" which several contemporary chroniclers give him.

At his death in 921 his duchy passed to his eldest son Raoul in the first place, then, when Raoul became King of France (923), to his second son, Hugh the Black. The latter, for some time, could dispose of considerable power; suzerain, even in his father's lifetime, of the counties of the diocese of Besançon, and suzerain also of the Lyonnais, he ruled in addition on the frontiers of the kingdom from the Seine and the Loire to the Jura. But its very size and its want of cohesion made it certain that this vast domain would sooner or later fall apart. Hugh the Black was hard put to it to prevent Hugh the Great from snatching the whole of French Burgundy from him. Soon after the death of Raoul in 936 (July) the Duke of the Franks, bringing with him the young King Louis IV, marched upon Langres, seized it, spent some time at Auxerre, and forced Hugh the Black to cede to him the counties of Langres, Troyes, and Sens. Later, in 943, he obtained from the king the suzerainty of the whole of French Burgundy, thus making Hugh the Black his vassal.

This complex situation, however, did not last long. In 952 Hugh the Black died, and as a result, French Burgundy was separated from the counties of the Besançon diocese and from that of Lyons. For four years Count Gilbert, who was already master of the counties of Autun, Dijon, Avallon and Châlon, was the real duke though he did not bear the title. But he acknowledged the suzerainty of Hugh the Great and at his death in 956 bequeathed him all his lands. Finally, Hugh the Great, in his turn, having died a few weeks later, the duchy regained its individual existence, when after lengthy bickering the two sons of Hugh the Great, Hugh Capet and Otto, ended by agreeing to divide their father's heritage, and Otto received from King Lothair the investiture of the duchy of Burgundy (960).

The formation of the Marches of Flanders and Burgundy, as also that of the March of Neustria, which has already been sufficiently dwelt upon, shew us what was the normal development of things. A count, specially conspicuous for his personal qualities, his valour and good fortune, has conferred on him by the king a general authority over a whole region; he imposes himself on it as guardian of the public security, he adds county to county, and gradually succeeds in eliminating the king's power, setting up his own instead, and leaving to the king only a superior lordship with no guarantee save his personal homage.

And this same formative process, slow and progressive, is to be seen in many of its aspects even in the duchy of Normandy. In 911 at St-Clair-sur-Epte Charles the Simple conceded to Rollo the counties of Rouen, Lisieux and Evreux, and the lands lying between the Epte on the east, the Bresle on the north and the sea to the west. But the Norman duke was not long content with this fief; in 924, in order to check fresh incursions, King Raoul found himself forced to add to it the district of Bayeux, and, no doubt, that of Séez also. Finally, in 933, in order to make sure of the allegiance of William Longsword who had just succeeded his father Rollo, he was obliged to cede also the two dioceses of Avranches and Coutances, thus extending the western frontier of the Norman duchy to the river Couesnon. But these many accretions of territory were not always gained without resistance.   A brief remark of an annalist draws attention in 925 to a revolt of the inhabitants of the Bayeux country, and doubtless more than once the Normans, whose newly adopted Christianity suffered frequent relapses into paganism, must have found difficulty in assimilating the populations of the broad regions placed under their rule.   The assimilation, however, took place rapidly enough for the Norman duchy to be rightly ranked, at the end of the tenth century, as one of those in which centralisation was least imperfect.

On all sides, indeed, the rulers of the marches or duchies, the formation of which we have been tracing, saw in their turn the crumbling away of the authority which they had been step by step extending, and the dissolution of the local unity which they had slowly and painfully built up.   How, indeed, could it have been otherwise ?   No duke had even succeeded in acquiring the immediate possession of all the counties included within his duchy.   The counts who co-existed with him, had originally been subordinate to him, but this subordination could only be real and lasting if the authority of the duke was never for a moment impaired.   On the other hand, when by chance the duke held a large number of counties in his own hands, he was obliged, since he could not be everywhere at once, to provide himself with substitutes in the viscounts, and it was in the natural course of things that these latter should make use of circumstances to consolidate their position, often indeed to usurp the title of count, and finally to set up their own authority at the expense of their suzerains.

Such was the final situation in the March of Neustria.   The most enterprising personage there was the Viscount of Tours, Theobald (Thibaud) the Trickster, who made his appearance very early in the tenth century, and gradually succeeded first in getting himself recognised throughout his neighbourhood, then, before 930, in laying hands on the counties of Chartres, Blois and Châteaudun, thus shaping out for himself within the Neustrian March, a little principality for which he remained in theory a vassal of the Duke of the Franks, while day by day he was emancipating himself more and more from his vassalage.   His son Odo I (Eudes) (975–996) actually attempted to shake it off: in 983, having become joint lord of the counties of Troyes, Meaux and Provins, which had fallen vacant by the death of Herbert the Old, he took up an independent position and treated directly with the king, over the head of the duke, Hugh Capet, whose suzerainty over him had become quite illusory. A more effective overlordship was preserved even at this time by the Duke of the Franks over the county of Anjou, but here again his immediate lordship had ceased, having passed to the viscount, who about 925 had become count.   Slowly and unobtrusively the petty Counts of Anjou worked to extend their own rule, hampered by the neighbourhood of the turbulent Counts of Blois.   With rare perseverance Fulk the Red (died 941 or 942), Fulk the Good (941 or 942–*c.* 960) and Geoffrey Grisegonelle (*c.* 960–987) continued to extend their county at the expense of Aquitaine by annexing the district of Mauges, while in Touraine they set up a whole series of landmarks which prepared the way for their successors' annexation of the entire province. And as at the same time the county of Maine and the county of Vendôme to the west, and the county of Gâtinais to the east had each for its part succeeded in regaining its separate existence, the March of Neustria was hardly more than a memory which the accession of Hugh Capet to the throne was finally to obliterate, for, outside the districts of Orleans, Etampes and Poissy, the Duke of the Franks preserved nothing save a suzerainty which the insubordination of his vassals threatened to reduce to an empty name.

Neustria is perhaps of all the ancient "Marches" the one which shews us most plainly and distinctly the process of the splitting up of the great "regional entities" into smaller units. Elsewhere the course of events was more complex; in Burgundy for instance, where the transmission of the ducal power gave rise, as we have seen, to so much friction and dislocation, a break-up which seemed imminent was over and over again delayed and often definitely averted as the result of a concurrence of unforeseen circumstances. It would have been enough, for instance, if Hugh the Black had not died childless, or, still more, if an understanding had not been arrived at by Hugh the Great and Gilbert, the powerful Count of Autun, Dijon, Avallon, and Châlon, to imperil the very existence of the duchy as early as the middle of the tenth century.

The Dukes of Burgundy were, nevertheless, unable to safeguard the integrity of their dominions. From the very beginning of the ninth century the growing power of the Bishop of Langres had been undermining their rule in the north. Through a series of cessions the Bishop of Langres had succeeded in acquiring first Langres itself, then Tonnerre, then gradually the whole of the counties of which these were the chief towns, as well as Bar-sur-Aube, Bar-sur-Seine, and the districts of Bassigny and the Boulenois, whence at the end of the tenth century the authority of the Duke of Burgundy was wholly excluded. On the other hand, the county of Troyes which, from the days of Richard *le Justicier*, had formed part of the Duchy of Burgundy, before long in its turn had become gradually separated from it. In 936 it had passed into the possession of Herbert II, Count of Vermandois, then into that of his son Robert, from which time the suzerainty of the Duke of Burgundy over the land had appeared tottering and uncertain. On the death of Count Gilbert, Robert openly severed the tie which bound him to the duke, and transferred his homage directly to the king (957), against whom, notwithstanding, he immediately afterwards rebelled. The duke, none the less, continued to regard himself as the suzerain of the Count of Troyes; but his suzerainty remained purely nominal, and the count thenceforward had only one object, that of carving out a principality for himself at the expense both of *Francia* and Burgundy. Robert attempted in vain in 959 to seize Dijon, but succeeded in securing the county of Meaux which by 962 was under his rule. His brother, Herbert II the Old, who succeeded him in 967, and proudly assumed the title of Count of the Franks, found himself ruler not only of the counties of Troyes and of Meaux but also those of Provins, Château-Thierry, Vertus, the Pertois, and perhaps of some neighbouring counties such as Brienne. The latter was, like that of Troyes, a dismembered portion of the Burgundian duchy from which, from the opening of the eleventh century, strip after strip was to be detached, as the county of Nevers, the county of Auxerre and the county of Sens, so that the power of the Duke of Burgundy came to be limited to the group consisting of the counties of Mâcon, Châlon, Autun, Beaune, Dijon, Semur, and Avallon.

The same movement towards disintegration may be observed in the tenth century throughout the whole kingdom of France, shewing itself more or less intensely in proportion as the rulers of the ancient duchies had succeeded in keeping a greater or less measure of control over their possessions as a whole. In Normandy and Flanders, for instance, unity is more firmly maintained than elsewhere, because, over the few counties which the duke or marquess does not keep under his direct control, he has contrived to set members of his own family who remain in submission to him. In Aquitaine, for reasons not apparent, the course of evolution is arrested halfway. In the course of the tenth century its unity seems about to break up, as the viscounts placed by the duke in Auvergne, Limousin, at Turenne and Thouars, with the Counts of Angoulême, Périgueux, and La Marche seem to be only waiting their opportunity to throw off the ducal suzerainty altogether. But despite this, the suzerainty continues intact and is almost everywhere effective, a fact all the more curious as the Duke of Aquitaine hardly retained any of his domains outside the Poitevin region.

But, with more or less rapidity and completeness, all the great regional units shewed the same tendency towards dissolution. *Francia* escapes no more than the rest; but alongside of the county of Vermandois and the counties of Champagne, whether it were the result of chance or, as perhaps one may rather believe, of political wisdom, a whole series of episcopal lordships grow up in independence, which, by the mere fact that their holders are subject to an election requiring the royal confirmation, may prove a most important source of strength and protection to the monarchy. At Rheims as early as 940 Louis IV formally granted the archbishop the county with all its dependencies; about the same time the authority of the Bishop of Châlons-sur-Marne was extended over the entire county of Châlons, and perhaps also that of the Bishop of Noyon over the whole of the Noyonnais. At about the same time (967) King Lothair solemnly committed the possession of the county of Langres into the hands of the Bishop of Langres.

CH. IV

Surrounded as the monarchy was by so many disobedient vassals, it was precisely the existence of these powerful prelates which enabled it to resist. The whole history of the tenth century is filled with the struggles which the kings were forced to wage against the counts and dukes, and with the plots which they had to defeat. But everywhere and always, it was the support, both moral and material, supplied by the Church which enabled them to maintain themselves. The Archbishop of Rheims, from the end of the ninth century, is the real arbiter of their destiny; as long as he supported the Carolingians they were able, in spite of everything, to resist all attacks; on the day when he abandoned them the Carolingian cause was irretrievably lost.

CHAPTER V

FRANCE IN THE ELEVENTH CENTURY.

HUGH CAPET was no sooner elected king than he found himself in the grip of difficulties, amidst which it might well seem that his authority would sink irretrievably. Nevertheless, he shewed every confidence in himself. After having his son Robert crowned at Orleans and granting him a share in the government (30 December 987) he had asked on his behalf for the hand of a daughter of the Basileus at Constantinople, setting forth with much grandiloquence his own power and the advantages of alliance with him. He had just announced his intention of going to the help of Borrel, Count of Barcelona, who was attacked by the Musulmans of Spain; when suddenly the news spread, about May 988, that Charles, Duke of Lower Lorraine, had surprised Laon. Immediately, the weakness of the new king became apparent: he and his son advanced and laid siege to the place, but were unable to take it. In August, during a successful sortie, Charles even contrived to set fire to the royal camp and siege engines. Hugh and Robert were forced to decamp. A fresh siege in October had no better result, again a retreat became necessary, and Charles improved his advantage by occupying the Laonnais and the Soissonnais and threatening Rheims.

As a crowning misfortune, Adalbero, archbishop of the latter city, died at this juncture (23 January 989). Hugh thought it a shrewd stroke of policy to procure the appointment in his place of Arnulf, an illegitimate son of the late King Lothair, calculating that he had by this means secured in his own interest one of the chief representatives of the Carolingian party, and, in despair, no doubt, of subduing Charles by force, hoping to obtain his submission through the good offices of the new prelate. Arnulf, in fact, had pledged himself to accomplish this without delay. Before long, however, it was plain to the Capetian that he had seriously miscalculated. Hardly was Arnulf seated on the throne of Rheims (c. March 989) before he eagerly engaged in schemes to bring about a restoration of the Carolingian dynasty, and about the month of September 989 he handed over Rheims to Charles.

It was necessary to put a speedy end to this state of things, unless the king and his son were to look on at a Carolingian triumph. Nevertheless the situation lasted for a year and a half. Finally, having tried force and diplomacy in turn, and equally without success, Hugh resolved to have recourse to one of those detestable stratagems which are, as it were, the special characteristic of the period. The Bishop of Laon, Adalbero, better known by his familiar name of Asselin, succeeded in beguiling Duke Charles; he pretended to go over to his cause, did homage to him, and so far lulled his suspicions as to obtain permission from him to recall his retainers to Laon. On Palm Sunday 991 (29 March) Charles, Arnulf and Asselin were dining together in the tower of Laon; the bishop was in high spirits, and more than once already he had offered the duke to bind himself to him by an oath even more solemn than any he had hitherto sworn, in case any doubt still remained of his fidelity. Charles, who held in his hands a gold cup of wine in which some bread was steeped, offered it to him, and, as a contemporary historian Richer tells us, "after long reflection said to him: 'Since to-day you have, according to the decrees of the Fathers, blessed the palm-branches, hallowed the people by your holy benediction, and proffered to ourselves the Eucharist, I put aside the slanders of those who say you are not to be trusted and I offer you, as the Passion of our Lord and Saviour Jesus Christ draws near, this cup, befitting your high office, containing wine and broken bread. Drain it as a pledge of your inviolable fidelity to my person. But if you do not intend to keep your plighted faith, abstain, lest you should enact the horrible part of Judas.' Asselin replied: 'I take the cup and will drink willingly.' Charles went on hastily: 'Add that you will keep your faith.' He drank, and added: 'I shall keep my faith, if not may I perish with Judas.' Then, in the presence of the guests, he uttered many other such oaths." Night came, and they separated and lay down to sleep. Asselin called in his men, Charles and Arnulf were seized and imprisoned under a strong guard, while Hugh Capet, hastily summoned from Senlis, came up to take possession of the stronghold. It was to this infamous betrayal that the Capetian owed his triumph over Charles of Lorraine. Death was soon to relieve him of his rival (992).

But Hugh was not at the end of his embarrassments. Arnulf was shielded by his priestly character, and it was clear that neither the Pope nor the Emperor, who had countenanced his intrigues, was disposed to sacrifice him. Hugh at last resolved to accuse him before a Council " of the Gauls," to which he was careful to convoke a majority of pre-lates favourable to the Capetian cause. The council met at Verzy, near Rheims, in the church of the monastery of Saint-Basle (17–18 June 991). In the end, Arnulf acknowledged his guilt, and casting himself upon the ground before the two kings, Hugh and Robert, with his arms stretched out in the form of a cross, he implored them with tears to spare his life. The kings consented. He was raised from the ground, and the assembly proceeded to the ceremony of degradation. Arnulf began by surrendering to the king the temporalities which he held of him, then he placed in the hands of the bishops the insignia of his episcopal dignity. He then signed an act of renunciation drawn up on the model of that of his predecessor Ebbo, who had been deposed under Louis the Pious. In it he confessed himself unworthy of the episcopal office and renounced it for ever. Finally he absolved his clergy and people from the oaths of fidelity which they had sworn to him. Three days later (21 June) Gerbert was elected in his stead.

All seemed ended, and the future of the Capetian dynasty definitely secured. But they had reckoned without the Papacy. Not only, in defiance of the Canons, the Sovereign Pontiff had not been consulted, but his intervention had been repudiated in terms of unheard-of violence and temerity. Arnulf, the Bishop of Orleans, constituting himself, in virtue of his office of "promotor" of the council, the mouthpiece of the assembly, in a long speech in which he had lashed the unworthy popes of his day, had exclaimed : "What sights have we not beheld in our days ! We have seen John (XII) surnamed Octavian, sunk in a slough of debauchery, conspiring against Otto whom he himself had made emperor. He was driven out and replaced by Leo (VIII) the Neophyte, but when the Emperor had quitted Rome, Octavian re-entered it, drove out Leo and cut off the nose of John the Deacon and his tongue, and the fingers of his right hand. He murdered many of the chief persons of Rome, and died soon after. The Romans chose as his successor the deacon Benedict (V) surnamed the Grammarian. He in his turn was attacked by Leo the Neophyte supported by the Emperor, was besieged, made prisoner, deposed and sent into exile to Germany. The Emperor Otto I was succeeded by Otto II, who surpasses all the princes of his time in arms, in counsel and in learning. In Rome Boniface (VII) succeeds, a fearful monster, of super-human malignity, red with the blood of his predecessor. Put to flight and condemned by a great council, he re-appears in Rome after the death of Otto II, and in spite of the oaths that he has sworn drives from the citadel of Rome (the Castle of Sant' Angelo) the illustrious Pope Peter, formerly Bishop of Pavia, deposes him, and causes him to perish amid the horrors of a dungeon. Is it to such monsters, swollen with ignominy and empty of knowledge, divine or human, that the innumerable priests of God (the bishops) dispersed about the universe, distinguished for their learning and their virtues, are to be legally subject ?" And he had concluded in favour of the superior weight of a judgment pronounced by these learned and venerable bishops over one which might be rendered by an ignorant pope "so vile that he would not be found worthy of any place among the rest of the clergy."

This was a declaration of war. The Papacy took up the challenge. John XV, supported by the imperial court, summoned the French bishops to Rome, and also the kings, Hugh and Robert. They retorted by assembling a synod at Chelles, at which it was declared "that if the Pope of Rome put forth an opinion contrary to the Canons of the Fathers, it should be held null and void, according to the words of the Apostle 'Flee from the heretic, the man who separates himself from the Church'" and it was added that the abdication of Arnulf, and the nomination of Gerbert were irrevocable facts, having been determined by a council of provincial bishops, and this in virtue of the Canons, by the terms of which it is forbidden that the statutes of a provincial council should be rashly attacked by anyone (993). The weakness of the Papacy made such audacity possible; a series of synods assembled by a legate of the Pope on German soil, and later at Rheims, to decide in the case of Arnulf and Gerbert, led to nothing (995–996).

But this barren struggle was exhausting the strength of the Capetian monarchy. Hardly had that monarchy arisen when it seemed as if the ground were undermined beneath it. Taking advantage of the difficulties with which it was struggling, Odo (Eudes) I, Count of Chartres, had, in the first place, extorted the cession of Dreux in 991, in exchange for his co-operation at the siege of Laon (which co-operation still remained an unfulfilled promise), then, in the same year, had laid hands upon Melun which the king had afterwards succeeded, not without difficulty, in re-taking. Finally, in 993, a mysterious plot was hatched against Hugh and Robert; the conspirators, it was said, aimed at nothing less than delivering them both up to Otto III, the young King of Germany. Odo was to receive the title of Duke of the Franks, and Asselin the archbishopric of Rheims; possibly a Carolingian restoration was contemplated, for though Charles of Lorraine had died in his prison in 992, his son Louis survived, and was actually in custody of Asselin. All was arranged; Hugh and Robert had been invited to attend a council to be held on German soil to decide upon Arnulf's case. This council was a trap to entice the French kings, who, coming with a weak escort, would have been suddenly seized by an imperial army secretly assembled. A piece of indiscretion foiled all these intrigues. The kings were enabled in time to secure the persons of Louis and of Asselin. But such was their weakness that they were obliged to leave the Bishop of Laon unpunished. An army was sent against Odo, but when he offered hostages to answer for his fidelity, the Capetians were well content to accept his proposals and made haste to return to Paris.

What saved the Capetian monarchy was not so much its own power of resistance as the inability of its enemies to follow up and co-ordinate their efforts. Odo I of Chartres, involved in a struggle with Fulk Nerra, Count of Anjou, and attacked by illness, could only pursue his projects languidly, and had just concluded a truce with Hugh Capet when he died (12 March 996) leaving two young children. The Papacy, for its part, was passing through a fearful crisis; forced to defend itself with difficulty in Rome against Crescentius, it was in no position to take up Arnulf's cause vigorously. The support of the Empire could not but be weak and intermittent; up to 996 Otto III and his mother, Theophano, had more than they could do in Germany to maintain their own authority.

When Hugh Capet died, 24 October 996, nothing had been decided. Supported by some, intrigued against by others, the Capetian monarchy lived from hand to mouth. Uncertain of the morrow, the most astute steered a devious course, refusing to commit themselves heartily to either side. Even Gerbert, whose cause seemed to be bound up with the king's, since he owed his episcopate only to Arnulf's deprivation, took every means of courting the favour of the imperial and papal party. He had made a point of hurrying to each of the synods held by the papal legate in the course of 995 and 996 to decide in Arnulf's case, pretending that he had been passed over immediately after the death of Adalbero " on account of his attachment to the See of St Peter," and entreating the legate for the sake of the Church's well-being, not to listen to his detractors, whose ill-will, he said, was in reality directed against the Pope. Then he had undertaken a journey to Rome to justify himself personally to the Pope, taking the opportunity, moreover, to join the suite of young Otto III who had just had himself crowned there, and succeeding so well in winning his good graces as to become his secretary.

Hugh Capet had hardly closed his eyes when a fresh complication arose. King Robert had fallen in love with the widow of Odo I of Chartres, the Countess Bertha, and had resolved to make her his wife. But Bertha was his cousin, and he had, besides, been sponsor to one of her children, thus the priests and the Pope, who was also consulted, firmly opposed a union which they looked upon as doubly " incestuous." Robert took no notice of their prohibitions, and found a complaisant prelate, Archibald, Archbishop of Tours, to solemnise his marriage, towards the end of 996. This created a scandal. With the support of Otto III, Pope Gregory V, who had in vain convoked the French bishops to Pavia at the beginning of 997, suspended all who had had any share in the Council of Saint-Basle, and summoned the king and all the bishops who had abetted his marriage to appear before him on pain of excommunication.

Alarmed at the effect of this double threat, Robert opened negotiations. Gerbert, naturally, would be the first sacrificed, and, losing courage, he fled to the court of Otto III. The Pope, far from inclining to any compromise, made it plain to the Capetian envoy, the Abbot of St-Benoît-sur-Loire, that he was determined to have recourse to the strongest measures. The unlucky Robert hoped that he might soften this rigour by yielding on the question of the archbishopric of Rheims. As Gerbert had fled, Arnulf was simply and merely restored to his see (January or February 998).

Thenceforward, besides, Arnulf was no longer dangerous. The Carolingian party was finally destroyed. Charles of Lorraine had been several years dead; his son Louis had, it would appear, met with a like fate, or was languishing forgotten in his prison at Orleans; the other two sons, Otto and Charles, had gone over to the Empire (the first in the character of Duke of Lower Lorraine), and no longer had any connexion with France. From this quarter, then, the Capetian had nothing to fear. A fresh revolt of Asselin, the same Bishop of Laon who had so flagitiously betrayed Arnulf, was soon crushed. Only the Papacy refused to be won over as easily as Robert had calculated; as the king refused to separate from Bertha, Gregory V pronounced the anathema against him. But when Gerbert succeeded Gregory V, under the name of Sylvester II (April 999), relations with the Papacy improved, and Robert, to whom Bertha had borne no children, before long separated from her in order to marry Constance, daughter of William I, Count of Arles, and of Adelaide of Anjou (*circa* 1005).

The period of early difficulties was over. But the position of the monarchy was pitiable. From the material point of view, it was limited to the narrow domain which, after many infeudations, remained to it of the heritage of the Carolingians and the March of Neustria. This, in its essence,—not reckoning some outlying possessions, of which the most important was the county of Montreuil at the mouth of the Canche,—consisted in the territories of Paris, Senlis, Poissy, Etampes and Orleans, with Paris and Orleans as chief towns. Within this modest domain the king was only just able to exact obedience; he was unable directly to put an end to the exactions of a petty baron, the lord of Yèvre, who oppressed the Abbey of St-Benoît-sur-Loire with his violence. In the other parts of the kingdom his authority had sunk still lower; the great feudatories openly spoke of him in contemptuous terms; a few years later at the village of Héry in the diocese of Auxerre, almost in his presence, and just after the Peace of God had been proclaimed, the Count of Nevers was not afraid to plunder the monks of Montierender, "knowing well," as a contemporary tells us, "that the king would prefer to use gentle methods rather than force."

The task of Robert the Pious and his successors was to work slowly and unobtrusively, but perseveringly and successfully, to build up afresh the domain and the moral strength of the monarchy which had so greatly declined. The domains were, it is true, not extensive, but a policy of additions and enlargements built up around them a compact and constantly enlarging kingdom. And on the moral side something of the prestige and tradition of the old anointed kings still held the minds of men. The firm but not aggressive rule of the new dynasty skilfully used both sentiment and territorial fact, and did so not only to their own advantage but to that of the land in which they stood for peace and order amid contending vassals.

Little is known to us of the first Capetian kings. Their unimportance was such that contemporaries scarcely think it worth while to mention them. Robert the Pious is the only one of them who has found a biographer, in Helgaud, a monk of St-Benoît-sur-Loire, but he is so artless and indeed so childish a biographer, so reverential an admirer of the very pious and gentle king, so little acquainted with affairs, that his panegyric has very little value for the historian. He paints his hero for us as tall, broad-shouldered, with well-combed hair and thick beard, with eyes lowered and mouth " well-formed to give the kiss of peace," and at the same time of kingly mien when he wore his crown. Learned, disdainful of ostentation, so charitable as to let himself be robbed without protest by the beggars, spending his days in devotion, a model of all the Christian virtues, so much beloved of God that he was able to restore sight to a blind man, such, if we may believe him, was good King Robert, he for whom posterity has for these reasons give the name of the " Pious."

It is hardly necessary to say that this portrait can only have had a distant relation to reality. Doubtless, Robert was a learned king, educated at the episcopal school of Rheims while it was under Gerbert's direction, he knew Latin, loved books, and carried them with him on his journeys. As with all the learned men of the day his knowledge was chiefly theological. He loved church matters, and in 996 the Bishop of Laon, Asselin, could derisively suggest that he should be made a bishop "since he had so sweet a voice."

But the pious king, who was not afraid to persist in the face of anathemas when passion raised its voice in him, who did not hesitate to set fire to monasteries when they hindered his conquests, was a man of action too. All his efforts were directed towards the extension of his domain, and it may be said that he let no opportunity slip of claiming and, when possible, occupying any fiefs which fell vacant or were disputed. This was the case with Dreux, which his father, as we have seen, had been forced to bestow on Odo I, Count of Chartres, and which Robert succeeded in re-occupying about 1015; it was also the case with Melun, which Hugh Capet had granted as a fief to the Count of Vendôme, Bouchard the Venerable, and of which Robert took possession on the death (1016) of Bouchard's successor, Reginald, Bishop of Paris. Some years later (*circa* 1022), when it chanced that Stephen, Count of Troyes, died without children, Robert energetically pushed his claims to the inheritance against Odo II, Count of Blois, who, apparently, had up till then been co-owner, on an equal footing with the deceased count. He did not hesitate to enter upon a struggle with this formidable vassal which, no doubt, would have lasted long if other political considerations had not led the king to yield the point.

It was above all at the time of the conquest of the Duchy of Burgundy that Robert could give proof of the full extent of his energy and perseverance. Henry, Duke of Burgundy, brother of Hugh Capet, died (15 October 1002), and as he left no children, the king might fairly claim to succeed him. He was anticipated by Otto-William, Count of Mâcon, the adopted son of the late Duke, whose connexion with the country gave him great advantages. In the spring of 1003 Robert collected a strong army, and proceeding up the river Yonne, laid siege to Auxerre. He met with desperate resistance. Otto-William's partisans in Burgundy were too strong and too numerous to allow of the question being settled by a single expedition. For nearly two years Robert ravaged the country in every direction, pillaging and burning all that he met with. Otto-William ended by submitting, and before long his son-in-law, Landry, Count of Nevers, after standing a siege of three months, was forced to capitulate at Avallon (October 1005). Then came the turn of Auxerre (November 1005). But a struggle of more than ten years was still necessary before Robert could reduce all the revolted lords to submission, and it was only after having taken Sens and Dijon that he could at last count himself master of the duchy (1015–16).

Following the example of the last Carolingians, Robert endeavoured to push his claims further and to aggrandise himself at the cost of the Empire. As long as the Emperor Henry II lived (1002–1024) relations on the whole remained cordial, indeed in 1006 the two sovereigns co-operated in an expedition to bring their common vassal, Baldwin, Count of Flanders, to his bearings, he having seized Valenciennes. In August 1023 a solemn meeting took place between them at Ivois on the banks of the Meuse. Robert and Henry, each accompanied by a stately train of great nobles and churchmen, exchanged the kiss of peace, heard mass, and dined together and exchanged gifts. They swore mutual friendship, proclaimed the peace of the Church, and resolved to take joint action for the reformation of the clergy. But the interview had no results; almost before a year was over Henry had ceased to live (13 July 1024).

From that time Robert's attitude changed. Having his hands free on the side of Champagne and Burgundy, and rendered bold by success, he contemplated a struggle with the new Emperor, Conrad II of Franconia (1024–1039), for a part of his inheritance. Far-reaching negotiations centring in the king of France, which shew how much his prestige had gradually been heightened, were opened between him, the Duke of Aquitaine, and Odo II, Count of Blois. Nothing less was intended, it would appear, than to proceed to a dismemberment on a large scale of the Germanic Empire. William, Duke of Aquitaine, was to take as his share, or his son's, the Lombard crown, Odo II of Blois was to have the kingdom of Burgundy as soon as Rodolph III should be dead[1], while Lorraine was to be Robert's share. But this passed all

---

[1] For Conrad's claims to the eventual succession to Rodolph see *infra*, Chapter vi. pp. 142–3.

measure, and when it came to carrying out the magnificent programme, obstacles arose which not one of the princes concerned was strong enough to overcome. William of Aquitaine was soon forced to give up the idea of disputing Lombardy with Conrad; Robert's plans miscarried in Lorraine whither Conrad's alarmed partisans hastily summoned their master; and King Rodolph III inclined to the new Emperor. The check was decisive, but surely a considerable step forward had been taken when for several months Robert had succeeded in guiding such a coalition, and had for a time spread terror among the Emperor's faithful Lorrainers.

On the death of Robert the Pious (20 July 1031) the question of the succession came to a crisis. After the example of his father, by whom he had been associated in the government from 987, Robert had taken care in 1017 to crown his eldest son by Queen Constance, then ten years old. But Hugh had died in the flower of his youth in 1025 (September). Two parties had then arisen at court, Robert desiring to have his second son Henry crowned at once, and Queen Constance holding out for a younger son, Robert, whom she preferred to his elder brother. The king's will had prevailed, and Henry had been crowned with great pomp in 1027. But hardly had Robert the Pious closed his eyes when Queen Constance raised the standard of revolt. She succeeded in gaining possession of Senlis, Sens, Dammartin, Le Puiset and Poissy, and won over Odo II of Blois, by the gift of half the town of Sens.

Henry, supported by Robert, Duke of Normandy, defended himself vigorously. He re-took Poissy and Le Puiset, and forced his mother and his brother Robert to make peace. Unfortunately it was purchased by yielding a point which involved a lamentable retrogression. Robert was given the duchy of Burgundy, which Robert the Pious had after so many efforts united to the Royal Domain (1032). At this price the submission of the rebels was dearly bought.

Nor did it avail to put down the revolt. Odo II of Blois refused to disarm. Twice the king besieged him unsuccessfully in Sens (1032–1033); each time he met with fierce resistance and was obliged to retreat. In May or June 1033, despairing of getting the better of this formidable vassal, Henry, in an interview at Deville on the Meuse, made a defensive alliance with the Emperor Conrad, who was Odo's rival for the Burgundian throne, left vacant by the death of Rodolph III, some few months earlier (September 1032). In the end, Odo submitted (1034). But three years later he died, leaving his counties in Champagne to his son Stephen, and the rest of his possessions to his other son Theobald. At once the struggle was renewed, whether through some attempt on Henry's part to lay hands on any portion of the inheritance left by Odo, or simply because Theobald and Stephen thought the opportunity favourable for taking their revenge. A plot was set on foot by them with Odo, the king's youngest brother, the object of which was, briefly, to replace Henry on the throne by Odo. The king contrived to baffle their calculations. Odo, surrounded in a castle, was taken prisoner and immured at Orleans; Stephen was completely routed and put to flight; his ally, the Count of Vermandois, was made prisoner; and finally, against Theobald the king enlisted the help of the Count of Anjou, Geoffrey Martel, by granting him in advance the investiture of Tours which he left it to him to conquer.

On all sides the monarchy had again lost ground. Burgundy had been lost, and it had been necessary to cede the French Vexin to the Duke of Normandy, who had been one of the king's most faithful supporters, as a reward for his services; and finally, the handing over of Tours to Count Geoffrey Martel, who got possession of it in 1044, meant an extension of the Angevin principality, which before long would become dangerous. Moreover the king came out of the crisis so much weakened that, for the future, he had perforce to play a very minor part. While all his feudatories strove without ceasing to round off their territories, he either lived in a pitiable fashion inside his narrow domain, or else interfered in the struggles between his vassals, supporting now one and now another, as need seemed to suggest; such was his poor and his only attempt at a policy.

It was in the west of France that the events of most real importance occurred. Two powers, whose struggles were to occupy the whole of the second half of Henry I's reign, found themselves opposed, namely, the Angevin power and the Norman.

Since the middle of the tenth century, the Counts of Anjou had never ceased to extend their borders at the expense of their neighbours. The terrific Fulk Nerra (987–1040) had throughout his life struggled to bind to one another and to his own lands the new possessions in the midst of Touraine which his predecessors had succeeded in acquiring, as well as to surround Tours with a circle which grew daily narrower. In 994 or 995 he had reached Langeais; about 1005 Montrichard and Montbazon; in 1016 he had inflicted a tremendous defeat on Odo II, Count of Blois, on the plains of Pontlevoy; next year he had built a fortress at Montboyau at only a few miles distance from Tours; in 1026 he had surprised the stronghold of Saumur which for more than a century had been in the hands of the Counts of Blois. Geoffrey Martel, his son (1040–1060), had boldly pushed on the enterprise; taking advantage of the hostility of the new Count of Blois, Theobald III, to King Henry, he had, as we have seen, secured the investiture of Tours from the latter and had proceeded to lay siege to the town. In vain had Theobald and his brother Stephen attempted to raise the blockade; Geoffrey Martel had offered them battle at Nouy, near the village of St-Martin-le-Beau, and here again the Count of Anjou had won a striking victory. Theobald, being taken prisoner, had been forced to cede Tours and the whole of Touraine to the victor (August 1044). At the same time Geoffrey Martel had succeeded in bringing the Count of Vendôme under his suzerainty, and to this the king's consent had not been wanting.

But it was in another direction that the House of Anjou felt itself drawn. The Counts of Maine, hemmed in between Normandy and Anjou, were destined sooner or later to fall under the suzerainty of one or other of their neighbours. As early as the days of Fulk Nerra, the Counts of Anjou had succeeded in bringing them under theirs. Gervase, Bishop of Le Mans, having usurped the guardianship of the young Count Hugh III, Geoffrey Martel had marched against the prelate and put him in prison (1047 or 1048). Thus all things seemed to be moving according to Angevin interests when the king and the Duke of Normandy came upon the scene.

The intervention of the latter had been delayed by serious difficulties within his own borders. Duke Robert the Magnificent (sometimes wrongly called the Devil) had died on pilgrimage in 1035, leaving as successor an illegitimate son, William, barely eight years old. The circumstances favoured the discontented; before long rebellion had been muttering on all sides, and in 1047 it burst forth, headed by Guy, lord of Vernon and Brienne, and by the Viscounts of Coutances and Bayeux. Young William appealed to the king for help, and a battle took place at Val-es-Dunes, to the east of Caen, where Henry fought valiantly in person. It was an utter rout for the rebels, who, after a few attempts at resistance, before long submitted entirely.

The king and the duke then decided upon a joint expedition against the Count of Anjou. Together they invaded Anjou and proceeded to besiege Mouliherne which surrendered (1048). Thus, after having supported the Count of Anjou throughout his struggle with the Count of Blois, the king suddenly changed sides and became his enemy. In 1049 he renewed his attack, and while William flung himself upon Maine, the king invaded Touraine, and even momentarily succeeded in occupying the stronghold of Sainte-Maure where Geoffrey Martel advanced and besieged him.

Three years had not passed before the parts were redistributed. Geoffrey, victorious in Maine, was treating with the king (1052), and the Duke of Normandy saw his late ally take sides against him. In February 1054 the king and the count jointly invaded his duchy. But the attempt did not prosper. The invading army had been divided into two corps; Odo, the king's brother, crossing the Seine, had devastated the Caux country while Henry I and Geoffrey Martel occupied the district of Evreux. William, marching in person to meet the southern army, sent a considerable part of his troops against the northern detachment. Odo allowed himself to be surprised at Mortemer, to the east of Neufchâtel, just as his men were giving themselves up to pillage.

A general rout of the French followed. The news of the defeat discouraged Henry I, who, leaving Geoffrey Martel at grips with the enemy, thought only of withdrawing from the contest as quickly as possible and with the least damage to his own interests.

Geoffrey Martel was obliged to retreat at once. William again invaded Maine, and took up strong positions at Mont-Barbet, near Le Mans, and at Ambrières, not far from the junction of the Varenne with the Mayenne. Soon, however, provisions failed and the duke was obliged to let a part of his army scatter itself into small bodies. When this news reached Geoffrey, who had obtained reinforcements, he hurried up and laid siege to Ambrières. The place held out, giving the Duke of Normandy time to re-assemble his troops and force the Angevin army to retreat. Marching straight upon Mayenne, where the lord, Geoffrey, was one of the chief supporters of Geoffrey Martel, William took the town and carried off Geoffrey of Mayenne to Normandy, where he compelled him to do him homage.

These successes were only temporary. Geoffrey Martel soon recovered the ground lost in Maine, and in 1058, as had happened four years before, in his desire for revenge he persuaded the king to join him in an invasion of Normandy. This time also the campaign, at least in its earlier stages, was unfortunate. Henry I and Geoffrey Martel had barely traversed the Hiémois district, when their rear-guard was surprised just as it was crossing the river Dive at the ford of Varaville. This ford being impracticable through a rising tide, the king and the count could only look on helplessly at the massacre of their troops.

The war went on for some time longer. Negotiations had just been begun when Henry I died suddenly at Dreux on 4 August 1060.

A year before his death, on 23 May 1059, Henry I had been careful to have his son Philip I crowned at Rheims. But Philip, born in 1052, was still a minor, thus Henry had made his brother-in-law Baldwin, Count of Flanders, guardian to the young king, a post which he retained until Philip reached his majority at fifteen years of age at the end of 1066 or the beginning of 1067.

Under Philip, the eclipse of the monarchy only became more complete. It must be said, however, that this eclipse is largely an illusion due to the paucity of our information. Philip was of a very practical turn, and played a part which was somewhat inglorious, but on the whole very profitable to the material interests of his house. The royal power had fallen so low that there could be no question of an aggressive policy, but Philip had at least the art to manoeuvre, and to turn to advantage all circumstances which offered him any opportunity to fish his profit out of troubled waters. Above all, he worked, with much more consistency and perseverance than is usually thought, at the task of enlarging his insignificant domain.

During his father's reign only the county of Sens, vacant through the death without heirs of Count Renard (Reginhard), had been (in 1055) re-united to the crown, an important acquisition, but one for which King Robert himself had prepared the way, by separating in 1015 the county of Sens from the duchy of Burgundy: thus it cost Henry no effort whatever. Philip had no sooner taken the reins than an opportunity arose for him to link together his possessions in the Orléanais and the Sénonais by making himself master of the county of Gâtinais. Geoffrey the Bearded, who bore the title of its Count, and had succeeded his uncle, Geoffrey Martel, in the county of Anjou (1060), had just been imprisoned by his brother Fulk Rechin, who had usurped power in both counties. Philip, without hesitation, joined a coalition formed by the Count of Blois and the lords of Maine against the usurper, and, as the price of peace, exacted the cession of the county of Gâtinais (1068).

A few years later he used the minority of Simon of Crépy, Count of Valois and Vexin, as an opportunity to fall upon his estates. These were very extensive, comprising not only the Vexin and Valois, but the county of Bar-sur-Aube and the territory of Vitry-en-Perthois, which Simon's father, Raoul III of Valois, had acquired by marriage, and, on the north, the county of Montdidier, and Péronne which he had taken from the Count of Vermandois. Entrusting to his vassal, Hugh Bardoux, lord of Broyes, the task of seizing Simon's possessions in Champagne, Philip invaded his other domains in 1075. For two years the struggle went on, almost without a break, fiercely and pitilessly. At last, in the beginning of 1077, the unlucky Simon was forced to beg for peace, and to cede to the king the county of Vexin.

At about the same time, Philip claimed the town of Corbie, which had come to Baldwin of Lille, Count of Flanders, as the dowry of Adela, sister of Henry I of France; and as Count Robert the Frisian refused to surrender it, he entered it by surprise and caused the inhabitants to swear fealty to him. Robert, confronted by an accomplished fact, after a brief attempt at resistance, found no resource but to submit. Corbie was never again to be detached from the royal domain.

Again, in 1101, Philip was to be seen profiting by need of money on the part of Odo-Harpin, Viscount of Bourges, who was about to set off for the Holy Land. The king enlarged the royal domain by purchasing from him an extensive district comprising, besides Bourges, the lordship of Dun-le-Roi.

Nearly all the enterprises of Philip I shew the same character, at once inglorious and practical. His chief efforts were in the direction of Normandy, where two parties confronted each other, on the one hand the King of England, William the Conqueror, and on the other, Robert Curthose, his son. Philip's entire policy consisted in supporting Robert, though he was ready, it would appear, to desert him as often as there seemed any prospect of his becoming dangerous: a course which did not fail to draw from the English chroniclers a charge of engaging in shameless speculation, taking pay from one party for his help and from the other for his withdrawal. In 1076 we find him as far off as Poitiers collecting an army to go to the relief of Dol which William the Conqueror is besieging; then, in 1077 or 1078, he welcomes Robert Curthose and procures his entrance into the stronghold of Gerberoy, on the borders of Beauvaisis and Normandy; he seems ready to help him against his father, when, in 1079, he suddenly changes sides, and goes with William to besiege Gerberoy. A few years later Robert is again at the French king's court, and hostilities are once more begun between the latter and William. In 1087 the people of Mantes having committed depredations on Norman soil, the Conqueror formulates his complaint, and demands that Philip shall hand over to him not only Mantes, but also Pontoise and Chaumont, that is to say, the whole of the Vexin, which, formerly ceded to Robert the Magnificent by Henry I, had since fallen afresh under the suzerainty of the king of France, and had then, as we have seen, been re-conquered by him in 1077. Promptly proceeding from claims to action, William invaded the territory, took Mantes, entered it and set it on fire. It does not appear, however, that he was able to push his advantages much further, for, having suddenly fallen sick, he was forced to have himself brought back to Normandy where, not long after, he died (9 September 1087).

The Conqueror's death made Robert Curthose Duke of Normandy, while his brother, William Rufus, received the English inheritance. A party was at once formed to substitute Robert for his brother on the throne of England; whereupon, as a return stroke, William invaded Normandy. Philip hastened to further a movement which could not fail to injure both brothers, and as William was marching against Robert, he went to the help of the latter prince. Practical as usual, however, Philip contrived to get his support paid for by some fresh concession. In 1089, for instance, as the price of his co-operation in the siege of La Ferté-en-Brai which had gone over to the king of England, he had the domain of Gisors ceded to him; on other occasions he preferred ready money.

His church policy bears the impress of the same character, and is what has chiefly earned for him the bitterest censures of the chroniclers, all of whom belong to the clergy. Reform was in the air, the idea of it was permeating the Church, and its ultimate consequences would have been nothing less than to deprive princes of all power in ecclesiastical appointments. Shocking abuses, indeed, prevailed; the process of appointment had become for princes a regular traffic in ecclesiastical offices. Philip I, notably, had no hesitation in practising simony on a vast scale. But the claims of the reforming party which the Popes, since Gregory VII, had made their own, would have brought about a real political revolution, since kings would have been stripped of all rights over the temporalities of bishops and abbots. If the papal theory had triumphed, all the ecclesiastical baronies of the kingdom, the most constant support of the monarchy, would have been withdrawn from the royal control. Philip fiercely defended what he could not but consider his right.

The question, besides, became further complicated when in 1092 he carried off Bertrada of Montfort, wife of the Count of Anjou, Fulk Rechin, and succeeded in finding a complaisant bishop to solemnise the adulterous marriage. The Pope, Urban II, did not hesitate to excommunicate the king even in his own kingdom, when he presided at the great Council held at Clermont in 1095. The position in which he found himself was too common for Philip to attach any very special importance to it. For the rest, in spite of the reiterated excommunications which Urban II, and later on his successor Paschal II, launched against him, Philip found prelates favourable to him among his clergy. Some were even seen, in the year 1100, who were not afraid openly to oppose the rigorous policy of the Holy See by performing, according to a custom then fairly frequent, a solemn coronation of the king on Whitsunday.

In reality the question of the marriage with Bertrada, that of simony, and the higher question of ecclesiastical elections and investiture were all inter-connected. To avoid a complete rupture, perhaps even a schism, Paschal II saw that it would be more prudent to yield. On the morrow of the Council held at Poitiers in November 1100, at which the Pope's legate had renewed before a large assembly the excommunication pronounced against Philip, the relations between the Pope and the king became somewhat less tense. On both sides something was conceded; in the matter of an episcopal election to the see of Beauvais the king and the Pope sought for common ground; the royal candidate, Stephen of Garlande, whom Manasse, Archbishop of Rheims, had not hesitated to maintain in the face of every comer, was to be consecrated Bishop of Beauvais, while the candidate of the reforming party, Galo, formerly Abbot of St-Quentin of Beauvais, was to obtain the episcopal see of Paris, just then vacant. Philip was to be "reconciled" on condition that he pledged himself to separate from Bertrada. On these bases the negotiations took place. Ivo, the illustrious Bishop of Chartres, who represented in France the moderate party, equally opposed to the abuses of the older clergy and to the exaggerations of the uncompromising reformers, pleaded with Paschal for conciliatory measures. Nor did the Pope remain deaf to his exhortations; on 30 July 1104 the king's case was submitted to a council assembled at Beaugency by Richard, Bishop of Albano, the Pope's legate. The council, unable to agree, came to no decision, but a fresh assembly immediately met at Paris, and Philip having engaged "to have no further intercourse with Bertrada, and never more to speak a word to her unless before witnesses" was solemnly absolved.

In spite of this oath, Philip and Bertrada continued to live together, but for the future, the Pope indulgently closed his eyes. On most of the points raised an agreement was arrived at, and in the beginning of the year 1107 Paschal even travelled through France, had a meeting at St-Denis with Philip and his son, and spoke of them as "the very pious sons of the Holy See."

But already Philip, grown old before his time, was king only in name. Since 1097 he had handed over to his son Louis the task of leading military expeditions, for which his own extreme corpulence unfitted him. It was necessary not only to repress the brigandage to which the turbulent barons of the royal domain were becoming more and more addicted, but above all to make head against the attacks of the King of England, to whom, on his departure for the crusade in 1096, Robert Curthose had entrusted the safe-keeping and government of the Norman duchy. William Rufus, indeed, casting away all restraint, had again invaded the French Vexin, and drawing over to his side Duke William of Aquitaine, threatened to carry his conquests as far as Paris. The situation was all the more dangerous as William Rufus had contrived to gain over several of the barons of the Vexin and a regular feudal coalition was being formed there against the Capetian monarchy. Fortunately, the loyal barons gathered under Louis's banner succeeded in keeping the English king's troops in check, and after an unrelenting warfare of skirmishes and sieges William was forced to retreat and abandon his enterprise (1099).

Admitted about this period, as king-elect and king-designate, to a share in the government, Louis (in spite of the intrigues of Bertrada, who more than once tried to have him assassinated, in order to substitute one of her own children) was now, at nearly twenty years old, in fact the real king. We find him travelling about the royal domain, chastising rebellious vassals, dismantling Montlhéry (1105), seizing the castle of Gournay-sur-Marne, the lord of which had robbed merchants on a royal road (1107), and besieging Chevreuse and Brétencourt. Louis has his own officers and his own counsellors; he intervenes directly in the affairs of the clergy, authorises abbatial elections and administers justice; as it is expressed in a charter of the south of France in 1104 "Philip, king of the French, was still alive; but Louis, his son, a young man of character and courage worthy to be remembered, was at the helm of the kingdom."

Philip was weighed down by disease and felt his end approaching. Like a good Christian he made his confession, then calling around him all the magnates of the kingdom and his friends, he said to them: "The burial-place of the kings of France is, I know, at St-Denis. But I feel myself too heavily laden with sins to dare to be laid near the body of so great a Saint." And he added naïvely, "I greatly fear lest my sins should cause me to be delivered over to the devil, and that it should happen to me as formerly happened, they say, to Charles Martel. I love Saint Benedict; I address my petition to the pious Father of the Monks, and desire that I may be buried in his church at Fleury on the banks of the Loire. He is merciful and kind, he receives sinners who amend, and, faithfully observing his rule, seek to gain the heart of God." He died a few days later at Melun on 29 or 30 July 1108.

It is surprising, on a general view of the Capetian monarchy down to Philip I, that it successfully maintained itself and only encountered trifling opposition easily overcome. Its weakness, indeed, is extreme; it is with difficulty that it proves itself a match for the petty barons within its domain. At the opening of the year 1080 Hugh, lord of Le Puiset, rebelled; and to resist him the king collected a whole army counting within its ranks the Duke of Burgundy, the Count of Nevers, and the Bishop of Auxerre. Shut up in his castle, Hugh defied all assaults. One fine day he made a sortie, whereupon the royal army, stupefied by his audacity, took to its heels; the Count of Nevers, the Bishop of Auxerre and nearly one hundred knights fell into Hugh's hands, while Philip and his followers fled wildly as far as Orleans, without the least attempt to defend themselves.

The resources which the monarchy has at its disposal are even more restricted than of old; the king has to be content with the produce of his farms, with a few tolls and fines, the dues paid by the peasants, and the yield of his woods and fields, but as the greater part of the royal domain is granted in fiefs, the total of all these resources is extremely meagre. They could fortunately be augmented by the revenues of vacant bishoprics to which the king had the nomination, for from the death of one occupant until the investiture of another the king levied the whole revenue and disposed of it at his pleasure. There are also the illicit gains arising from the traffic in ecclesiastical offices, and these are not the least. Yet all these together amount to very little, and the king is reduced either to live in a pitiful fashion, or to go round pleading his "right to bed and purveyance (*procuration*)" to claim food and shelter from the abbeys on his domain.

Surrounded by a little group of knights, and followed by clerks and scribes, the king roved about, carrying with him his treasure and his attendants. This staff, as a whole, had changed but slightly since Carolingian times; there are the same great officers, the Seneschal, the Chamberlain, the Butler, the Constable, the Chancellor, who directed at once the administration of the palace and of the kingdom. But the administration of the kingdom was henceforward hardly more than that of the royal domain. Local administration is now purely domanial, undertaken by the directors of land improvement, the mayors or *villici*, *vicarii* and *prévôts* (*praepositi*) whose duty there, as on all feudal domains, was to administer justice to the peasants and to collect the dues.

CH. V.

At the same time, however wretched may have been his material position, by the very fact that he was king the Capetian[1] had a situation of moral preponderance. The tie of vassalage which bound all the great feudatories of the kingdom to him was not merely a theoretical bond; apart from cases of rebellion they do not, as a rule, fail to fulfil their duties as vassals when called on. We have already seen the Duke of Burgundy and the Count of Nevers come in 1080 and do personal service in Philip I's campaign against Hugh, lord of Le Puiset. In the same way, about 1038 we find the Count of Flanders furnishing troops to the king to suppress the revolt of Hugh Bardoux. When the siege of Dol was about to be undertaken in 1076, the Duke of Aquitaine was required to supply troops. Besides this, in the royal armies contingents of Aquitanians, Burgundians and Champenois are constantly found.

Nor do the great lay and ecclesiastical dignitaries fail to attend in large numbers at the great royal assemblies. If one of them is prevented from coming he sends his excuses, makes known the reasons which hinder him from attending when convoked, and prays that his excuses may be favourably received. "I beg of thee, my lord," writes the Bishop of Chartres to King Robert in 1018, " be not angry that I did not come to Paris to thy court, on Sunday last. I was deceived by the messengers who told me that thou wouldst not be there that day, and that I was summoned to the consecration of a bishop of whom I knew nothing whatsoever. As, on the other hand, I had received no letter on the subject of this consecration, either from thee or from my archbishop, I abstained from attending. If I have committed a fault it arises from my having been misled. My pardon will, I hope, be easily obtained from the royal piety, since even from the point of view of justice the fault is a venial one. With my whole heart I assure thee of my attachment hoping that thou wilt deign to continue to me thy confidence."

[1] Genealogy of Capetian kings after Hugh Capet (cf. p. 75):

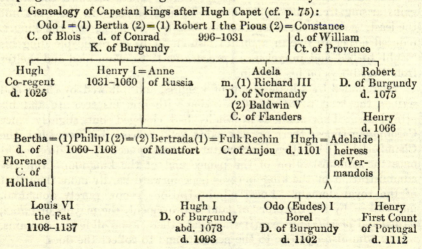

Odo I = (1) Bertha (2) = (1) Robert I the Pious (2) = Constance
C. of Blois   d. of Conrad   996–1031   d. of William
   K. of Burgundy   Ct. of Provence

Hugh   Henry I = Anne   Adela   Robert
Co-regent   1031–1060   of Russia   m. (1) Richard III   D. of Burgundy
d. 1025   D. of Normandy   d. 1075
     (2) Baldwin V
     C. of Flanders   Henry
     d. 1066

Bertha = (1) Philip I (2) = (2) Bertrada (1) = Fulk Rechin   Hugh = Adelaide
d. of   1060–1108   of Montfort   C. of Anjou   d. 1101   heiress
Florence   of Ver-
C. of   mandois
Holland

Louis VI   Hugh I   Odo (Eudes) I   Henry
the Fat   D. of Burgundy   Borel   First Count
1108–1137   abd. 1078   D. of Burgundy   of Portugal
   d. 1093   d. 1102   d. 1112

In a word, it seems as if for the great feudatories there could be no worse misfortune than a formal rupture with their sovereign. In this connexion nothing is more characteristic than the attitude of perhaps the most powerful vassal of Robert the Pious, the celebrated Count of Blois, Odo II, when in about 1022 a dispute arose between him and the king touching the succession in Champagne. Finding what he considers his right attacked by the king, Odo defends himself with a strong hand. On this account Robert considers him guilty of forfeiture, and seeks to have his fiefs declared escheated. At once Odo is terrified, and writes his sovereign a letter full of respect and deference, expressing astonishment only at the measure which the king demands. "For if birth be considered, it is clear, thanks be to God, that I am capable of inheriting the fief; if the nature of the fief which thou hast given me be considered, it is certain that it forms part, not of thy fisc, but of the property which, under thy favour, comes to me from my ancestors by hereditary right; if the value of my services be considered, thou knowest how, as long as I was in favour with thee, I served thee at thy court, in the *ost* and on foreign soil. And if, since thou hast turned away thy favour from me, and hast attempted to take from me the fief which thou gavest me, I have committed towards thee, in defence of myself and of my fief, acts of a nature to displease thee, I have done so when harassed by insults and compelled by necessity. How, in fact, could I fail to defend my fief? I protest by God and my own soul, that I should prefer death to being deprived of my fief. And if thou wilt refrain from seeking to strip me of it, there is nothing in the world which I shall more desire than to enjoy and to deserve thy favour. For the conflict between us, at the same time that it is grievous to me, takes from thee, lord, that which constitutes the root and the fruit of thy office, I mean justice and peace. Thus I appeal to that clemency which is natural to thee, and evil counsels alone can deprive thee of, imploring thee to desist from persecuting me, and to allow me to be reconciled to thee, either through thy familiars, or by the mediation of princes." Such a letter proves, better than any reasonings, how great was the power which respect for royalty and for the obligations of a vassal to his lord, still exercised over minds imbued with tradition.

Moreover, none of the great feudatories who shared the government of the kingdom among them would have been strong enough to overthrow the Capetian dynasty. Independently of the rivalries between great houses, in which their strength was exhausted, the princes found themselves, from the middle of the eleventh century, a little sooner or a little later according to the province they ruled, involved in a struggle with internal difficulties which often paralysed their efforts.

One of the feudal states for which the history is the best known is the

county of Anjou. It has already been seen[1] how under the two counts,
Fulk Nerra (987–1040) and Geoffrey Martel (1040–1060), the county of
Anjou, spreading beyond its frontiers on all sides, had been steadily
enlarged at the expense of its neighbours. The count's authority was
everywhere strong and respected, and as he had his lay vassals and clergy
well in hand, they had a general awe of him. And yet the germs of disintegration were already present. Indeed, in order to provide for the
protection of their territories, and above all to have a basis of attack
against their neighbours, the counts of Anjou had, from the end of the
tenth century, been led to cover their country with a network of strongholds. But to construct the great stone keeps (*donjons*) which at that
time were beginning to take the place of mere wooden buildings, and
to guard them, time, men and money were needed. Therefore, quite
naturally, the counts had not hesitated to grant them out as fiefs, leaving
to their vassals the task of completing and defending them. As a result,
within a short time, the county had come to be filled, not merely with
castles, but with a multitude of lords-castellans handing on the domain
and the fortress from father to son.

In this way, Fulk Nerra, about 994, built the castle of Langeais, and
almost immediately we note that Langeais becomes the seat of a new
feudal family. Hamelin I, lord of Langeais, comes into view about
1030, and when he dies [*c.* 1065] his fief passes to his descendants. A
few years after Fulk built the castle of Montrevault, and immediately
invested Stephen, brother-in-law of Hubert, the late Bishop of Angers,
with it. Here again a new lordship had been founded, as Stephen had
married his daughter Emma to Raoul, Viscount of Le Mans, who succeeded
his father-in-law, and took the title of Viscount of Grand Montrevault,
while close by, on land which had also been received as a fief from Fulk
Nerra by a certain Roger the Old, the fortress and family of Petit
Montrevault had grown up. About the same time Fulk had founded
the castle of Montreuil-Bellay, and again he had without delay enfeoffed
it to his vassal Bellay. A little later Geoffrey Martel had built the castles
of Durtal and Mateflon and enfeoffed them to two of his knights. In
the same way lords-castellans had been installed at Passavant before 1026;
at Maulevrier, at Faye-la-Vineuse, at Sainte-Maure and at Trèves before
1040, all of these being castles built by the count. Everywhere great
families had arisen: here, that of Briollay who had received the castle as a
fief from Fulk Nerra, there, that of Beaupréau, founded by Jocelyn of
Rennes, a soldier of fortune, no doubt singled out by Fulk Nerra. At
this time also had their origin the houses of Chemillé, of Montsoreau, of
Blaison, of Montjean, of Craon, of Jarzé, of Rillé, of Thouarcé and
others. Established in their castles, which secured to them the dominion
of the surrounding flat country, and by that very fact, forming a higher
class among the barons, daily strengthening their position by the marriages

[1] See *supra*, p. 108.

which they concluded among themselves leading to the concentration of several castles in a single pair of hands, the great vassals were only waiting an opportunity to shew their independence. This was supplied by a dispute which arose over the succession.

Geoffrey Martel, dying childless in 1060, had left his county to his eldest nephew, Geoffrey the Bearded, already Count of Gâtinais, whereupon the younger nephew, Fulk Rechin, declaring himself aggrieved, rose in rebellion without delay. Geoffrey the Bearded by his unskilful policy precipitated the crisis; a discontented party growing up in the country gathered itself round Fulk; in the end, Geoffrey was seized and thrown into prison while Fulk gained his own recognition as Count (1068). But in the course of the conflict, which lasted several years, the passions of the great barons who had been called on to take sides in it had been given free play; for months together Fulk was obliged to struggle with the rebels, to go and besiege them in their castles, and to repress their ravages. When at last he succeeded in gaining general recognition, the country, as he himself acknowledges in one of his charters, was a mere heap of ruins.

Even the general submission was only apparent. After 1068 revolts still broke out in all parts of the county. Thus on the death of Sulpicius, lord of Amboise and Chaumont, it was in obedience to threats that Fulk set at liberty Hugh, son and successor of the deceased, who had been given up to him as a hostage. Soon after, the count decided to commit the custody of his castle at Amboise called "The Domicile" to a certain Aimeri of Courron. This choice was distasteful to Hugh's men, five of whom slipped into the donjon, surprised the watchman whom they made prisoner, and planted their master's standard on the tower. Hugh, meanwhile, retired to a fortified mansion which he possessed in the town, and set himself to harass the count's troops. At last Fulk came up, and not daring to try conclusions with his adversary, preferred a compromise with him. Their agreement did not last long, as the unsubdued vassal was merely watching his opportunity to rebel afresh. Suddenly, in 1106, one day when the castellan of "The Domicile," Hugh du Gué, was out hunting in the direction of Romorantin, Hugh of Amboise surprised the castle and destroyed it. The struggle began again: Fulk Rechin, calling to his aid several of his vassals, Aubrey, lord of Montrésor, and Jocelyn and Hugh, sons of the lord of Sainte-Maure, flung himself upon St-Cyr, one of the hereditary possessions of the house of Chaumont and Amboise. Hugh of Amboise, supported by his brother-in-law John, lord of Lignières, retorted by pillaging the suburbs of Tours, and the environs of Loches, Montrichard and Montrésor. In all directions the same situation was reproduced; one day it was the lord of Alluyes, Saint-Christophe and Vallières who rebelled, another day it was the lord of Maillé; again he of Lion d'Angers; in 1097, he of Rochecorbon. A regular campaign was required against Bartholomew, lord of l'Ile-Bouchard, a fortress had to be built at Champigny-sur-Veude, which, by the way, Bartholomew seized and set on fire, taking the garrison prisoners.

Fulk was incapable of resisting so many rebels. Following the example of Philip I, he handed over his military powers to his son, Geoffrey Martel the Younger. Zealous, feared by the barons, in sympathy with churchmen, the young count entered boldly on the struggle with those who still held out. With his father he took La Chartre and burnt Thouars, and was about to lay siege to Candé. But he was killed in 1106, and with him disappeared the only man who might have proved a serious obstacle to baronial independence.

In the other provinces the situation seems to have been almost the same. In Normandy, on the accession of William the Bastard, the mutterings of revolt were heard. Defeated at Val-es-Dunes in 1047, the rebels were forced to submit, but on the smallest opportunity fresh defections occurred. Shut up in their castles, the rebellious vassals defied their sovereign. The revolt of William Busac, lord of Eu, about 1048, and above all, that of William of Arques in 1053 are, in this respect, thoroughly characteristic. The latter fortified himself on a height and awaited, unmoved, the arrival of the ducal army. It attempted in vain to storm his fortress; its position was inaccessible, and the duke was obliged to abandon the idea of taking it by force. In the end, however, he reduced it, because the King of France, hastening up to the relief of the rebel, allowed himself to be deplorably defeated. William of Arques, however, held out to the very last extremity and stood a siege of several weeks before he was reduced by famine.

In 1077, it was Robert Curthose, William the Conqueror's own son, who gave the signal for revolt. This spendthrift complained of want of money. "I have not even the means," he said to his father, "of giving largesse to my vassals. I have had enough of being in thy pay. I am determined now at length to enter into possession of my inheritance, so that I may reward my followers." He demanded that the Norman duchy should be handed over to him, to be held as a fief under his father. Enraged at the refusal he received, he abruptly quitted the Conqueror's court, drawing after him the lords of Bellême, Breteuil, Montbrai and Moulins-la-Marche, and wandered through France in quest of allies and succours. Finally he shut himself up in the castle of Gerberoy, in the Beauvaisis but on the borders of Normandy[1], welcoming all the discontented who came to him, and fortified in his donjon, he bade defiance to the wrath of his father. Once again a whole army had to be levied to subdue him. Philip I of France was called on to lend his aid. But the two allied kings met with the most desperate resistance; for three weeks they tried in vain to take the place by surprise. Robert, in the end, made a sortie; William the Conqueror, thrown from the

[1] See *supra*, p. 112.

saddle, was all but made prisoner; William, his younger son, was wounded; the whole besieging army was ignominiously put to flight (January 1079), and nothing remained for the Conqueror but to give a favourable hearing to his rebel son's promises of submission on his father's pledging himself to leave Normandy to him at his death.

As soon as William the Conqueror had closed his eyes (9 September 1087) and Robert had become Duke of Normandy the barons rose, seized some ducal castles, and spread desolation through the land. The anarchy soon reached its height when the rupture between Robert and his brother William occurred. Thenceforward revolt never ceased within the duchy. Aided by the King of England who sent them subsidies, the rebels fortified themselves behind the walls of their castles and braved the duke's troops; in November 1090 the rebellion spread even to the citizens of Rouen. Weak and fitful as he was in character, even Robert was forced to spend his time in besieging the castles of his feudatories, who, luckily for him, agreed no better with one another than with their duke. In 1088 he besieged and took St Céneri, in 1090 Brionne; in 1091 he besieged Courci-sur-Dive, and then Mont-St-Michel, where his brother Henry had fortified himself; in 1094 he besieged Bréval.

Thus incessantly occupied in defending their authority in their own territories, the Dukes of Normandy, like the Counts of Anjou and like all the other great feudatories of the kingdom, found themselves in a position which made it impossible for them seriously to threaten the power of the Capetian sovereign. Each ruler, absorbed by the internal difficulties with which he had to struggle, followed a shifting policy of temporary expedients. The period is essentially one of isolation, of purely local activity.

Since France was thus split up into fragments, it would be in vain to attempt to give a comprehensive view of it. The more general aspects of civilization, the feudal and religious life of the eleventh century, both in France and in the other countries of Western Europe, will be examined in succeeding chapters. But some information must be given touching the characteristics of each of the great fiefs into which France was then divided, *e.g.* in what manner these states were organised, what authority belonged to the ruler of each of them, who and what were those counts and dukes whose power often counterbalanced that of the king. Owing to the lack of good detailed works on the period, something must necessarily be wanting in any attempt to satisfy curiosity on all these points.

Flanders. On the northern frontier of the kingdom the county of Flanders is one of the fiefs which presents itself to us under a most singular aspect. Vassal both of the King of France for the greater part of his lands, and of the Emperor for the islands of Zeeland, the

"Quatre-Métiers," and the district of Alost, the Count of Flanders in reality enjoyed almost complete independence. "Kings," says a chronicler of the period, William of Poitiers, "feared and respected him; dukes, marquesses and bishops trembled before his power." From the beginning of the tenth century he was considered to have the largest income in the whole kingdom, and in the middle of the eleventh century an Archbishop of Rheims could still speak of his immense riches, "such that it would be difficult to find another mortal possessed of the like." Great was the ascendancy exercised by Baldwin V of Lille (1036–1067); as guardian of Philip I, King of France, he administered the government of the kingdom from 1060 to 1066, and by marrying his eldest son to the Countess of Hainault he succeeded in extending the authority of his house as far as the Ardennes (1050). Robert the Frisian (1071–1093) bore himself like a sovereign prince, he had an international policy, and we find him making an alliance with Denmark in order to counterbalance the commercial influence of England. He gave one of his daughters in marriage to Knut, King of Denmark, and in conjunction with him prepared for a descent upon the British Isles.

The count was even strong enough, it appears, to give Flanders immunity, to a large extent, from the general anarchy. By procuring his own recognition as advocate or protector of all the monasteries in his states, by monopolising for his own benefit the institution of the "Peace of God" which the Church was then striving to spread[1], by substituting himself for the bishops in the office of guardian of this Peace, the count imposed himself throughout Flanders as lord and supreme judge in his state. He peremptorily claimed the right of authorising the building of castles, he proclaimed himself the official defender of the widow, the orphan, the merchant and the cleric, and he rigorously punished robbery on the highways and outrages upon women. He had a regularly organised administration to second his efforts. His domains were divided into *castellanies* or circumscriptions, each centring in a castle. In each of these castles was placed a military chief, the castellan or viscount, along with a notary who levied the dues of the castellany, transmitting them to the notary-in-chief or chancellor of Flanders, who drew into a common treasury all the revenues of the country.

Thus it is not strange that Flanders should have attained earlier than other provinces to a degree of prosperity well worthy of remark. As regards agriculture, we find the counts themselves giving an impulse to important enterprises of clearing and draining in the districts bordering on the sea, while in the interior the monastic foundations contributed largely to the extension of cultivation and of grazing lands. At the same time the cloth industry was so far developed that the home-grown

---

[1] See Huberti, L., *Studien zur Rechtsgeschichte der Gottesfrieden und Landfrieden*, and Vol. v.

wool no longer sufficed to occupy the workmen. Wool from neighbouring countries was sent in great quantities to the Flemish fairs, and
already commerce was bringing Flanders into contact with England,
Germany, and Scandinavia.

Champagne and Blois. The contrast with the territories of the
Counts of Champagne is striking. Here there is no unity; the lands
ruled by the count have no cohesion whatever; only the chances of
succession which at the opening of the eleventh century caused the
counties of Troyes and Meaux to pass into the hands of Odo II, Count
of Blois, Tours and Chartres (996–1037).

The count's power, naturally, suffered from the scattered position of
his lands. The first to unite under his authority the two principalities
of Blois and Champagne, Odo II, has left in history only a reputation
for blundering activity and perpetual mutability. In Touraine, in place
of steadily resisting the encroaching policy of the Counts of Anjou[1], we
find him rushing headlong into one wild enterprise after another, invading Lorraine on the morrow of his defeat by Fulk Nerra at Pontlevoy
in 1016, then joining with reckless eagerness in the chimerical projects
of Robert the Pious for dismembering the inheritance of the Emperor
Henry II (1024), and upon the death of Rodolph III, flinging himself
upon the kingdom of Burgundy (1032). We shall see[2] how the
adventurer fared, how Odo, after a brilliant and rapid campaign, found
himself face to face with the Emperor Conrad, threatened not only by
him but by Henry I King of France, whose enmity, by a triumph of
unskilful handling, he had brought upon himself. A prompt retreat
alone saved him. But it was only to throw himself into a new project;
he at once invaded Lorraine, carrying fire and sword through the country;
he began negotiations with the Italian prelates with a view to obtaining
the Lombard crown, and even dreamed of an expedition to Aix-la-
Chapelle to snatch the imperial sceptre from his rival. But the army
of Lorraine had assembled to bar his way; a battle was fought on
15 November 1037, in the neighbourhood of Bar, and Odo met with a
pitiful end on the field of carnage where his stripped and mutilated body
was found next day.

With the successors of Odo II came almost complete obscurity.
The counties of Champagne and Blois, separated for a brief interval by
his death, then re-united up to 1090 under the rule of Theobald III, go
on in an uneventful course, diminished by the loss of Touraine, which
the Counts of Anjou succeed in definitely annexing.

Burgundy. The history of the duchy of Burgundy in the eleventh
century is hardly less obscure. Its Dukes, Robert I, son of King Robert
the Pious, Hugh and Odo Borel seem to have been insignificant enough, with
neither domains, nor money, nor a policy. Although theoretically they

---

[1] See *supra*, p. 108. [2] Chapter VI, pp. 143–4.

were masters of very extensive territories, they saw the greater part of their possessions slip from under their control to form genuine little semi-independent principalities, such, for example, as the counties of Châlon-sur-Saône and Mâcon, or else ecclesiastical lordships such as the Abbey of Molesme which, before fifty years from its foundation (1075), came to possess immense domains all over the north of Burgundy as well as in southern Champagne.

There is thus no reason for surprise that the Dukes of Burgundy in the eleventh century should play rather a petty part. Robert I (1032–1076) seems, unlike a duke, to have been the type of an unscrupulous petty tyrant such as at this period the lords of the smaller castles too often were. His life was spent in pillaging the lands of his vassals, and especially those of the Church. He carried off the crops of the Bishop of Autun, seized upon the tithes of the churches of his diocese, and swooped down upon the cellars of the canons of St Stephen of Dijon. His reputation as a robber was so well established throughout his country that about 1055 Hardouin, Bishop of Langres, dares not adventure himself in the neighbourhood of Dijon to dedicate the Church of Sennecey, fearing, says a charter, " to be exposed to the violence of the Duke." He hesitates at no crime to satisfy his appetites and his desire for vengeance; breaks into the abbey of St-Germain at Auxerre by armed force, has his young brother-in-law, Joceran, assassinated, and with his own hand kills his father-in-law, Dalmatius, lord of Semur.

His grandson and successor, Hugh I (1076–1079), was far from imitating the example set him, but he was quite as incapable as Robert of establishing any real control over Burgundy, and after having taken part in a distant expedition into Spain to succour Sancho I of Aragon he suddenly carried his contempt for the world so far as to exchange a soldier's restless life for cloistered peace, becoming a monk at the age of twenty-three.

Odo Borel, Hugh's brother (1079–1102), returned to the family tradition and became a highway robber. We have on this subject a curious anecdote, related by an eye-witness, Eadmer, chaplain to Anselm, Archbishop of Canterbury. As Anselm was passing through Burgundy in 1097 on his way to Rome, the duke was informed of his approach and of the chance it afforded of booty worth taking. Allured by the account, Odo, mounting his horse immediately, took Anselm and his escort by surprise. " Where is the Archbishop? " he cried in a threatening tone. Yet at the last moment, confronted by the calm and venerable demeanour of the prelate, some remnant of shame held him back, and instead of falling on him he stood confounded, not knowing what to say. " My lord Duke," said Anselm to him, " suffer me to embrace thee." In his confusion the duke could only reply " willingly, for I am delighted at thy coming and ready to serve thee." It is possible that the good Eadmer has manipulated the incident somewhat, yet it is a significant anecdote: evidently the Duke of Burgundy was looked upon as a common bandit.

Anjou. The county of Anjou presents us with a case intermediary between Flanders which was strong, and already partly centralised, and that of Burgundy which was split up and in a state of disintegration.

It has already been related in detail how, from the middle of the eleventh century onwards, the Count was engaged in the interior of his state in combating a crowd of turbulent barons strongly ensconced in their castles[1]. But in spite of this temporary weakening of the count's authority, the Angevin lands form even in the second half of the eleventh century a coherent whole of which the count is the effective head. Controlling the episcopal see of Angers which could not be filled up without his consent, and finding commonly in the Bishop a devoted and active helper ready to brave Archbishops, Legates, Councils and Popes at his side, secure of the loyalty of the greater number of the secular clergy, master of the chief abbeys also, besides being, as it would seem, rich in lands and revenues, the count, in spite of everything, remains an imposing figure. Under Fulk Rechin (1067–1109), when the spirit of independence among the lesser Angevin fief holders was at its height, the great lords of the county, such as those of Thouarcé or Trèves, were to be found contending for the offices about the count's court which was organised, apparently, on the model of the royal court, in a regular fashion, with a seneschal, a constable and a chaplain (who was also charged with the work of the chancery), chamberlains, cellarers, etc.

Nothing, however, more plainly shews the space which the Counts of Anjou filled in the minds of contemporaries than the considerable body of literature which, throughout the eleventh century and up to the middle of the twelfth gathered round them, by means of which we have come to know them better, perhaps, than even most of their contemporaries did. Few figures, for instance, are stranger or more characteristic of the time than that of Fulk Nerra, whose long reign (987–1040) corresponds with the most glorious part of the formative period of the county. He appears before us as a man ardent and fierce of mood, giving free course to his ambition and cupidity, and governed by a passion for war, then suddenly checking himself at the thought of eternal retribution, and trying by some gift or some penance to obtain pardon from God or the Saints whom his violence must needs have offended. One charter shews him to us too much engrossed in warfare to give a thought to ecclesiastical affairs; in another there is an allusion to his fierce, hasty temper incapable of bearing any contradiction. Does he find himself hampered by a rival? He will not shew himself scrupulous in the choice of means of getting rid of him. In 1025 he lured the Count of Maine, Herbert Wake-dog

---

[1] See *supra*, p. 118 sq.

into an ambush, giving him a rendezvous at Saintes, which, he said, he intended to grant him as a fief in order to put an end to a dispute which had arisen between them. Herbert presented himself unsuspectingly, and was seized and thrown into prison, while the gentle Hildegarde, the Countess of Anjou, planned a similar fate for his wife. Less dexterous than her husband, she missed her stroke, but Herbert remained two years under lock and key and was only set at liberty after the deepest humiliations. A few years before, in 1008, the count of the palace, Hugh of Beauvais, being an obstacle to his designs, Fulk posted cut-throats to wait for him while he was hunting in company with the king and had him stabbed under the very eyes of the sovereign.

Elsewhere, on the contrary, we find him, stricken with fear, making a donation to the Church of St Maurice of Angers, "for the salvation of his sinful soul and to obtain pardon for the terrible massacre of Christians whom he had caused to perish at the battle of Conquereuil," which he had fought in 992 against the Count of Rennes. A charter shews him in 996, just as Tours had been taken, forcing his way into the cloister of St Martin, and suddenly, when he saw the canons wreathing the shrine and the crucifix with thorns, and shutting the gates of their church, coming in haste, humbled and barefoot, to make satisfaction before the tomb of the Saint whom he had insulted. In 1026, when he took Saumur, being carried away, at first, by his fury, he pillaged and burnt everything, not even sparing the church of St Florent; then, his rude type of piety suddenly re-asserting itself, he cried out "Saint Florent, let thy church be burned, I will build thee a finer dwelling at Angers." But as the Saint refused to be won over by fair promises, and as the boat on which Fulk had had his body shipped refused to stir, the count burst out furiously against "this impious fellow, this clown, who declines the honour of being buried at Angers."

His violence is great, but his penances are not less striking; in 1002 or 1003 he set out for Jerusalem. Hardly had he returned when he defiled himself afresh by the murder of Hugh of Beauvais, and again there was a journey to the Holy Land from which neither the perils of an eventful voyage nor the hostility of the infidel could deter him (1008?). Finally, at the end of 1039 when he was nearly seventy years old, he did not hesitate for the sake of his salvation once again to brave the fatigues and dangers of a last pilgrimage to our Saviour's tomb.

All this shews a nature fiery and even savage but constantly influenced by the dread of Heaven's vengeance, and legend has copiously embroidered both aspects. This violent-tempered man has been turned into the type of the most revolting ferocity, he has been depicted as stabbing his wife, giving up Angers itself to the flames, forcing his rebellious son, the proud and fiery Geoffrey Martel, to go several miles with a saddle on his back, and then when he humbly dragged himself along the ground towards him, brutally thrusting him away with his foot, uttering cries of triumph.

He has been made the type of the brave and cunning warrior, capable of performing the most extraordinary feats; for instance, he is represented as overhearing, through a partition wall, talk of an attempt upon his capital, plotted during his absence by the sons of Conan, Count of Rennes. Instantly he gallops without stopping from Orleans to Angers where he cuts his enemies to pieces, and hastens back to Orleans with such speed that there has not even been time to remark his absence. He has been made to figure as the defender of the Pope whom by his marvellous exploits he saves from the fiercest robbers and from the formidable Crescentius himself. Finally, he has been credited with so subtle a brain as to know how to avoid all the traps which the utmost ingenuity of the Infidels could set for him to hinder his approach to the Sepulchre of Christ. Out of this man, on whom the fear of Heaven's wrath would sometimes fall, legend has made the ideal type of the repentant sinner. Not three times, but four or five times he is represented to have performed the pilgrimage to the Holy Land, and is pictured as having himself dragged half-naked, with a cord round his neck, through the streets of Jerusalem, scourged by two grooms, and crying aloud " Lord, have pity upon the traitor!" Does not all this exaggeration of the good as well as the evil in him, these legendary, almost epic, touches, do more to convince us than any argument could, of the strange importance which the Angevins of the period attributed to the person of the count? In comparison with the shadowy figures of the kings who succeed one another on the throne of France, that of a Fulk Nerra stands out in high relief against a drab background of level history.

Normandy. It has been useful, in order to give something like a life-like conception of the great feudatories of the eleventh century, to spend some time over one of the few personalities of the time which we are in a position to know at least in its main outlines. In dealing with the Dukes of Normandy, we may be the briefer because many details concerning them belong to the chapters devoted to the history of England.

More than any other feudal principality, Normandy had derived from the very nature of its history a real political unity. It was not the fact that the chief Norman counties were held as fiefs by members of the duke's own family which secured to the duke, as some continue to repeat, a power greater than was enjoyed elsewhere, for we have already seen that family feeling had no effect in preventing revolts. But the duke had been able to keep a considerable domain in his own hands, and there were hardly any abbeys in his duchy to which he had not the right of nomination, many were part of his property and he freely imposed his own creatures upon them. His word was law throughout the ecclesiastical province of Rouen, and he disposed at his pleasure of all its episcopal sees. Without differing notably from what prevailed elsewhere, the administrative organisation of the duchy was perhaps more stable and regular. The ducal domain was divided into a certain number of

CH. V.

viscounties, with a castle in each of them where a viscount had his seat, who was invested at once with administrative, judicial, and military functions. Military obligations were strictly regulated, each baronial estate owing a certain number of days' service in the field. In a word, Normandy constituted a real state which was, besides, fortunate enough to have at its head throughout the eleventh century, with the exception of Robert Curthose, a succession of brilliant rulers.

Brittany. As under the Carolingians, Brittany continued to form an isolated province, almost a nation apart. Having its own language, a religion more impregnated here than elsewhere with paganism, special customs of its own, and manners ruder and coarser than was usual elsewhere, Brittany in the eyes even of contemporaries seemed a foreign and barbarous land. A priest, called by his duties to these inhospitable regions, looked upon himself as a missionary going forth to evangelise savages, or as a banished man, while the idea of Ovid in his Pontic exile suggested itself readily to such minds as had given themselves to the cultivation of letters.

But in spite of its well-marked characteristics, Brittany did not form a very strong political entity. Already a severe struggle was in progress between the Gallo-Roman population along the March of Rennes, and the Celtic people of Armorica, each group representing its own distinct language. In other respects, the antagonism took the form of a rivalry between the great houses which contended for the dignity of Duke of Brittany. Which among the counts, he of Rennes, or of Nantes, or of Cornouailles had the right to suzerainty? In the eleventh century it seemed for a moment as if the chances of inheritance were about to allow the unification of Brittany to become a fact, and as if the duke might be able to add to the theoretical suzerainty which his title gave him, a direct control over all the Breton counties. Hoel, Count of Cornouailles, after inheriting in 1063 the county of Nantes on the death of his mother Judith of Cornouailles, found himself in 1066 inheritor of the counties of Rennes and Vannes in right of his wife Havoise, sole heiress of her brother the Breton Duke, Conan II. But in order to complete the unification of the duchy it was necessary that the duke should succeed in making himself obeyed on the northern slope of the rocky mass of Brittany. Now the Léon country escaped his control, and he was to exhaust himself in vain efforts to reduce Eon of Penthièvre and his descendants who ruled over the dioceses of Dol, Alet, Saint-Brieuc and Tréguier, and even disputed the ducal dignity with the Counts of Rennes. At a loss for money, and forced to alienate their domains to meet their expenses, neither Hoel (1066–1084), nor his son and successor, Alan Fergent (1084–1112), succeeded in turning Brittany into a unified province.

Aquitaine and Gascony. The destiny of the countries south of the Loire has all the appearance of a striking paradox. While everywhere else the tendency is to the minutest subdivision, the Dukes of Aquitaine, by a policy almost miraculously skilful, succeed not only in maintaining effective control over the unhomogeneous lands between the Loire and the Garonne (with the exception of Berry and the Bourbonnais) but in making good their hold on Gascony which they never again lose, and even for a time in occupying the county of Toulouse and exacting obedience from it. Direct rulers of Poitou, of which district they continue to style themselves counts at the same time that they are known as Dukes of Aquitaine, rulers also of Saintonge (which was for a short time a fief of the Count of Anjou) the dynasty of the Williams who succeed one another in the eleventh century on the Poitevin throne, successfully retained the Counts of Angoulême and la Marche and the Viscount of Limoges in the strictest vassalage, while they compelled obedience from the other counts and viscounts in their dominions. Everywhere or almost everywhere, thanks to perpetual expeditions from one end of his state to the other, the duke presents himself as the real suzerain, ever ready for action or intervention in case of need. In episcopal elections he has contrived to preserve his rights, at Limoges, for instance, as at Poitiers and Saintes, or at Bordeaux after he has taken possession of that town; in the greater part of the episcopal cities he plays an active, sometimes decisive part, often having the last word in the election of bishops.

Few of the rulers of the feudal chiefs at this time knew as they did how to act as the real heads of the state or could manoeuvre more cleverly to extend and maintain their authority. Although praised by a contemporary chronicler, Adémar of Chabannes, for having succeeded in reducing all his vassals to complete obedience, William V (995 or 996–1030) appears to have been above all things a peaceful prince, a lover of learning and *belles lettres*, for which indeed Adémar eulogises him in a hyperbolical strain, comparing him to Augustus and Theodosius, and at the same time to Charlemagne and Louis the Pious. But among his successors, Guy-Geoffrey, called also William VIII (1058–1086), and William IX (1086–1126) were born politicians, unburdened with scruples, moreover, and ready to use all means to attain their ends. By naked usurpation, helped out by a sudden stroke of arms and by astute diplomacy, Guy-Geoffrey succeeded in obtaining possession of the duchy of Gascony, which had fallen vacant in 1039 by the death of his half-brother, Odo, and so ably was his undertaking carried out that Gascony was subdued almost on the spot. His son William IX nearly succeeded in doing as much with regard to the county of Toulouse, some sixty years later, in 1097 or 1098. Profiting by the absence of the Count, Raymond of St-Gilles, on Crusade, he claimed the county in the name of his wife Philippa, the daughter of a former Count of Toulouse, William IV; and notwithstanding that the possessions of Crusaders were placed under the guardianship of the Church and accounted sacred, he invaded his neighbour's territory and immediately took possession of the lands that he coveted. In 1100, on the return of Raymond of St-Gilles, he was forced to restore his conquest. The struggle was only postponed; on the death of Bertrand, son of Raymond, in 1112, he was again to conquer the county of Toulouse, and, this time, refuse to surrender his prey. It took Alphonse-Jourdain, the rightful heir, ten years of desperate strife to gain his point and tear the booty from his terrible neighbour.

This same William IX is besides the very type of a feudal "*bel esprit*," possessed of a pretty wit and apt at celebrating his endless amours and intrigues in graceful, profligate verse, but he was shameless and brazen, trampling the principles of morality underfoot as old-fashioned prejudices, provided that he could indulge his passions. The carrying-off of Maubergeon, the beautiful wife of the Viscount of Châtellerault, whom he claimed to marry without further formalities, in the life-time of his lawful wife, Philippa, and of the Viscount himself, gives one the measure of the man. If we may believe the chronicler, William of Malmesbury, he replied with jests to the prelates who exhorted him to change his manner of living: "I will repudiate the Viscountess as soon as your hair requires a comb," he said to the Bishop of Angoulême, Gerard, who was bald. Being excommunicated for his evil courses, he one day met Peter, Bishop of Poitiers. "Give me absolution or I will kill you," he cried, raising his sword. "Strike," replied the bishop, offering his neck. "No," replied William, "I do not love you well enough to send you straight to Paradise," and he contented himself with exiling him.

Languedoc. Less fortunate and much less skilful than the Dukes of Aquitaine, the Counts of Toulouse nevertheless succeeded in the eleventh century in collecting in their own hands a considerable group of fiefs, all contiguous: they included fiefs within the Empire as well as in France, and stretched from the Garonne to the Alps from the day when Raymond of Saint-Gilles, Marquess of Gothia, had succeeded both his brother William IV in the county of Toulouse (1088) and Bertrand of Arles in the Marquessate of Provence (1094). But even taking Languedoc alone (the county of Toulouse and the Marquessate of Gothia) the unity of the state was only personal and weak, and was always on the point of breaking down. A law of succession which prescribed division between the direct heirs male necessarily involved the division of the component fiefs; besides this, the chiefs of the house of Toulouse had not the continuity of policy necessary if the counts, barons, and citizens, who, within the confines of the principality, were ever seeking to secure a more and more complete independence, were to be held in subjection. They had also to reckon with the rivalry and ambition of two neighbours: the Dukes of Aquitaine, who, as we have seen, sought to lay hands upon the county of Toulouse, and the Counts of Barcelona, who, rulers of Roussillon and in theory vassals of the French crown, were ever ready to contend with the house of Saint-Gilles for the possession of the March of Gothia.

To sum up, if the strength of the feudal tie and the energy or diplomacy of some of the great feudatories prevented France from crumbling into a mere dust-heap of fiefs, contiguous but unconnected, the evil from which the nation was suffering was, none the less, dangerous and deep-seated. The realm was frittered away into principalities which seemed every day to grow further and further apart.

From this general disintegration of the kingdom, the clergy, and especially the bishops, escaped only with the greatest difficulty. Too many members of the episcopate belonged both by birth and tendencies to the feudal classes for them to furnish the elements of a reaction or even to desire it. But there were a few among the mass, who were in a position, either through greater openness of mind, or more genuine culture, to see things from a higher point of view, who succeeded in imposing their ideas above all local divisions, and, while the royal authority seemed bankrupt, were able to exercise in the kingdom some sort of preponderating moral influence. The most illustrious examples are those of two bishops of Chartres, Bishop Fulbert in the time of King Robert, and Bishop Ivo in the time of Philip I.

With Fulbert the whole kingdom seems to have been in perpetual consultation on all manner of questions, even those in appearance most trivial. Does a point in feudal law need clearing up? is there a canonical difficulty to be solved? or a feeling of curiosity to be satisfied? recourse is had to him. About 1020 the Duke of Aquitaine, William the Great, asks him to expound the mutual obligations of suzerain and vassal, and the bishop at once sends him a precise and clear reply, which, he says at the end, he would like to have drawn out further, "if he had not been absorbed by a thousand other occupations and by his anxiety about the re-building of his city and his church which had just been destroyed by a terrible fire." Some years later the public mind throughout the kingdom had been much exercised by a "rain of blood" on the coast of Poitou. King Robert, at the request of the Duke of Aquitaine that he would seek enlightenment from his clergy as to this terrifying miracle, at once writes off to Fulbert, and at the same time to the Bishop of Bourges, seeking an explanation and details concerning previous occurrences of the phenomenon. Without delay Fulbert undertakes the search, re-reads Livy, Valerius Maximus, Orosius, and Gregory of Tours and sends off a letter with full particulars. Next comes the *scholasticus* of St Hilary's of Poitiers, his former pupil, who overwhelms him with questions of every kind and demands with special insistence whether bishops may serve in the army. In reply, his kind master sends him a regular dissertation.

But these are only his lighter cares; he has to guide the king in his policy and warn him of the blunders he makes. About 1010 Robert was on the point of convoking a great assembly to proclaim the Peace of

God at Orleans which at that time was under an interdict.   Immediately Fulbert takes up his pen and writes to the king: " Amidst the numerous occupations which demand my attention, my anxiety touching thy person, my lord, holds an important place.   Thus when I learn that thou dost act wisely I rejoice; when I learn that thou doest ill I am grieved and in fear."   He is glad that the king should be thinking on peace, but that with this object he should convoke an assembly at Orleans, "a city ravaged by fire, profaned by sacrilege, and above all, condemned to excommunication," this astonishes and confounds him.   To hold an assembly in a town where, legally, neither the king nor the bishops could communicate, was at that time nothing short of a scandal!   And the pious bishop concludes his letter with wise and firm advice.

A few years earlier, in 1008, the Count of the Palace, Hugh of Beauvais, the bosom friend of King Robert, had been killed, as we have related, under the very eyes of the sovereign, by assassins placed in ambush by Fulk Nerra, Count of Anjou, who immediately gave them asylum in his dominions.   Such was the scandal, that Fulk was near being proceeded against for high treason, while a synod of bishops sitting at Chelles wished at all events to pronounce him excommunicate on the spot.   Here again Fulbert intervenes, he enjoins clemency upon all, obtains a delay of three weeks, and of his own accord writes to Fulk, though he is neither his diocesan nor his relation, a letter full of kindness, but also of firmness, summoning him to give up the assassins within a fixed time and to come himself at once and make humble submission.

In the days of Ivo the good understanding between the king and the Bishop of Chartres was broken.   But amidst all the religious and political difficulties in which Philip was involved, and with him the whole kingdom, the bishop's influence is only the more evident.   In personal correspondence with the Popes, who consult him, or to whom on his own initiative he sends opinions always listened to with deference, in correspondence with the papal legates whom he informs by his counsels, Ivo seems the real head of the Church in France.   In the question so hotly debated on both sides as to the king's marriage with Bertrada of Montfort[1], Ivo did not hesitate to speak his mind to the king without circumlocution, he sharply rebuked the over-complaisant bishops, acted as leader of the rest, and personally came to an agreement with the Pope and his legates as to the course to be pursued.   He writes in 1092 to the king who had summoned him to be present at the solemnisation of his marriage with Bertrada: "I neither can nor will go, so long as no general council has pronounced a divorce between you and your lawful wife, and declared the marriage which you wish to contract canonical."   The king succeeded in getting this adulterous union celebrated, and in spite of warnings he refused to put an end to it.   Pope Urban II

---

[1] See *supra*, p. 113

addressed to the bishops and archbishops a letter enjoining them to excommunicate this impious man, if he refused to repent. Ivo then appeared as arbiter of the situation. "These pontifical letters," he writes to the king's seneschal, "ought to have been published already, but out of love for the king I have had them kept back, because I am determined, as far as is in my power, to prevent a rising of the kingdom against him."

He was fully informed of all that was said or done of any importance; in 1094 he knew that the king meant to deceive the Pope, and had sent messengers to Rome; he warned Urban II, putting him on his guard against the lies which they were charged to convey to him. Later on, in the time of Pope Paschal II, it was he who finally preached moderation with success, who arranged everything with the Pope for the "reconciliation" of the king. There is no ecclesiastical business in the kingdom of which he does not carefully keep abreast, ready, if it be useful, to intervene to support his candidate for a post, and to give advice to bishop or lord. Not only does he denounce to the Pope the impious audacity of Ralph (Ranulf) Flambard, Bishop of Durham, who in 1102 had seized on the bishopric of Lisieux in the name of one of his sons, but he calls on the Archbishop of Rouen and the other bishops of the province to put an end to these disorders. He does even more, he writes to the Count of Meulan to urge him to make representations without delay, on his behalf, to the King of England whose duty it is not to tolerate such a scandal.

At a period when religion, though ordinarily of a very rude type, was spreading in all directions, and when the gravest political questions which came up were those of Church policy, a prelate who, like Ivo of Chartres, knew how to speak out and to gain the ear of popes, kings, bishops and lords, certainly exercised in France a power of action stronger and more pregnant with results than the obscure ministers of a weak, discredited king.

CHAPTER VI.

THE KINGDOM OF BURGUNDY.

A. *The kingdom of Burgundy down to the annexation of the kingdom of Provence.*

THE unity of the Empire, momentarily restored under Charles the Fat, had, as we have seen, been once more and finally shattered in 888. As in 843, the long strip of territory lying between the Scheldt, the mouth of the Meuse, the Saône and the Cevennes on one hand, and the Rhine and the Alps on the other, was not re-included in France; but the German king was no more capable than his neighbour of keeping it as a whole under his authority. The entire district south of the Vosges slipped from his grasp, and for a moment he was even in danger of seeing a rival put in possession of the whole of the former kingdom of Lothar I.

In fact, very shortly after the Emperor Charles the Fat, abandoned on all hands, and deposed at Tribur, had made a wretched end at Neidingen, several of the great lay lords and churchmen of the ancient duchy of Jurane Burgundy assembled in the basilica of St Maurice d'Agaune, probably about the end of January 888, and proclaimed the Count and Marquess Rodolph king. Rodolph was a person of no small importance. His grandfather, Conrad the Elder, brother of the Empress Judith, count and duke in Alemannia, and his uncle, Hugh the Abbot, had played a prominent part in the time of Charles the Bald, while his father, Conrad, originally Count of Auxerre, had taken service with the sons of the Emperor Lothar about 861, and had received from the Emperor Louis II the government of the three Transjurane dioceses of Geneva, Lausanne and Sion, as well as the abbey of St Maurice d'Agaune. Rodolph had succeeded to this Jurane duchy which now chose and proclaimed him king.

The significance of the declaration was at first far from clear. Still, in the minds of Rodolph and his supporters it must necessarily have involved more than a mere change of style. The Empire, momentarily united, was once more falling apart into its earlier divisions, and there being no one capable of assuming the Carolingian heritage in its entirety, the state of things was being reproduced which had formerly resulted from the Treaty of Verdun in 843. Such seems to have been the idea which actuated the electors assembled at St Maurice d'Agaune ; and Rodolph, without forming a very precise estimate of the situation, left the western kingdom to Odo and the eastern to Arnulf, and set to work at once to secure for himself the former kingdom of Lothar II in its integrity.

At first it seemed that circumstances were in the new king's favour. Accepted without difficulty in the counties of the diocese of Besançon, Rodolph proceeded to occupy Alsace and a large part of Lorraine. In an assembly which met at Toul the bishop of that town crowned him king of Lorraine. But all his supporters fell away on the appearance in the country of Arnulf, the new king of Germany, and Rodolph, after in vain attempting to resist his army, had no choice but to treat with his rival. He went to seek Arnulf at Ratisbon, and after lengthy negotiations obtained from him the recognition of his kingship over the Jurane duchy and the diocese of Besançon, on condition of his surrendering all claims to Alsace and Lorraine (October 888). Thus by force of circumstances the earlier conception of Rodolph's kingship was taking a new form ; the restoration of the kingdom of Lorraine was no longer thought of; a new kingdom, the "kingdom of Burgundy," had come into being.

It was only with reluctance that Arnulf had recognised the existence of this new kingdom. A Caroling, though illegitimate, he might seem to have inherited from Charles the Fat a claim to rule over the whole of the former empire of Charlemagne. Not satisfied that Rodolph should have been forced to humble himself before him by journeying to Ratisbon to seek the confirmation of his royal dignity, he attempted to go back upon the recognition that he had granted. In 894, as he was returning from an expedition to Lombardy, he made a hostile irruption into the Valais, ravaging the country and vainly attempting to come to close quarters with Rodolph, who, a few weeks earlier, had sent assistance to the citizens of Ivrea, a town which the king of Germany had been unsuccessfully besieging. Rodolph took refuge in the mountains and evaded all pursuit. Nor could Zwentibold, Arnulf's illegitimate son, who was sent against him at the head of a fresh army, succeed in reaching him. The dispossession of the king of Burgundy was then resolved on, and in 895 in an assembly held at Worms, Arnulf created Zwentibold "king in Burgundy and in the whole of the kingdom formerly held by Lothar II." But these claims were not prosecuted ; Rodolph maintained his position, and on his death (25 October 911 or 912) his son Rodolph II succeeded unchallenged to his kingdom.

Germany, indeed, since the death of Arnulf in 899 had been struggling in the grip of terrible anarchy. Conrad of Franconia, who in 911 had succeeded Louis the Child, was too busy defending himself against the revolted nobles to dream of intervention in Burgundy. Not only had Rodolph II nothing to fear from this quarter, but he saw a favourable opportunity for retaliation.

On the side of Lorraine it was too late ; the king of Burgundy had been forestalled by the King of France, Charles the Simple, who as early as November 911 had effected its conquest. Rodolph II indemnified himself, it would appear, by attempting to lay hands on the two Alemannic counties of Thurgau and Aargau, the districts lying on the eastern frontier of his kingdom, between the Aar, the Rhine, the Lake of Constance and the Reuss. He was, indeed, repulsed by the Duke of Swabia at Winterthür in 919, but none the less succeeded in preserving a substantial part of his conquests. Other events, however, called his attention and diverted his energies to new quarters.

The state of affairs in Italy was then extremely disturbed. After many rivalries and struggles, both the Lombard crown and the imperial diadem had been placed in 915 upon the head of Berengar of Friuli. But Berengar was far from having conciliated all sections, and at the end of 921 or the beginning of 922 a number of the disaffected offered the Lombard crown to Rodolph. The offer was a tempting one. Though separated from Lombardy by the wall of the Alps, Jurane Burgundy was still naturally brought into constant relations with it; the high road, which from St Maurice d'Agaune led by the Great St Bernard to Aosta and Vercelli, was habitually followed by pilgrims journeying from the north-west into Italy. Besides, owing to their origin, many nobles of weight in the Lombard plain, notably the Marquess of Ivrea, were in personal communication with King Rodolph. Finally, memories of the Emperor Lothar, who had been in possession of Italy as well as Burgundy, could not but survive and necessarily produced an effect upon men's minds.

Rodolph listened favourably to the overtures made him. He marched straight upon Pavia, the capital of the Lombard kingdom, entered the city, and induced the majority of the lay lords and bishops to recognise him as king (February 922). Berengar was defeated in a great battle fought at Fiorenzuola not far from Piacenza on 17 July 923, and forced to fly with all speed to Verona, where he was murdered a few months later (7 April 924). Yet before long Rodolph was forced to change his tone. With their usual instability, the Italian barons lost no time in deserting him to call in a new claimant, Hugh of Arles, Marquess of Provence. Rodolph asked help of the Duke of Swabia, Burchard, whose daughter he had married a few years before, but the duke fell into an ambuscade and was killed (April 926) and Rodolph, disheartened, had no choice but to retrace his steps disconsolately across the Great St Bernard.

Events, however, were soon to convince him that his true interest lay in renouncing the Lombard crown and coming to an understanding with his rival in order to seek the satisfaction of his ambition in another direction.

B. *The kingdom of Provence down to its annexation to the kingdom of Burgundy.*

The wide region lying to the south of Burgundy, between the Alps, the Mediterranean and the Cevennes, had been for several years without a ruler, and was in such a state of confusion and uncertainty as was likely to tempt King Rodolph to seek his advantage there.

In the middle of the ninth century (855) a kingdom had been formed there for the benefit of Charles, third son of the Emperor Lothar. On the death of the young king (863) the inheritance had been divided between his two brothers, and was soon after occupied by Charles the Bald, who entrusted its administration to his vassal Boso (870). The latter, who was of Frankish origin, was among the most influential personages of the Western Kingdom; his sister, Richilda, had been first the mistress and later the wife of the king; he himself, apparently, was an ambitious man, energetic, skilful, and unscrupulous. In 876 he married Ermengarde, daughter of the Emperor Louis II, and secured the favour of Pope John VIII who, on the death of Charles the Bald in October 877, even thought for a moment of drawing him to Italy. Later, on the death of Louis the Stammerer, Boso openly revolted and ventured on having himself crowned king at Mantaille (15 October 879).

Before this date, Boso had been in possession of Provence and of the counties of Vienne and Lyons, and he now obtained recognition as king in the Tarentaise as well as in the Uzège and Vivarais districts and even in the dioceses of Besançon and Autun. But his attempt was premature; the united Carolingians, Louis III and Carloman, supported by an army promptly despatched by Charles the Fat, invaded the country in 880; the war was a tedious one, but at last in September 882 Vienne yielded, and Boso, driven from the Viennois, remained in obscurity till his death (11 January 887).

For more than three years the fate of the "kingdom of Provence" remained in suspense. From the beginning of 888 the public records are dated "in such a year after the death of Boso" or "after the death of Charles" (the Fat). The kingdom of Burgundy had been formed, yet neither Rodolph, its king, nor Odo, King of France, nor Arnulf, King of Germany, all too fully engaged elsewhere, ever thought of laying claim to the vacant throne of Provence.

But if Arnulf were unable to undertake the occupation of the kingdom of Provence, at least it was plainly his interest to further the setting up of a king who would recognise his overlordship and might also serve as a counterpoise to the ambitious and encroaching Rodolph. Now Boso had left a son, still quite young, named Louis, who having been protected and even adopted by Charles the Fat, might be looked upon as the rightful heir of the Provençal throne.   His mother, Ermengarde, set herself energetically to bring about his coronation; in May 889 she repaired to Arnulf's court, and by means of rich gifts secured his help.   Louis's claims, supported also by the Pope, Stephen V, were generally recognised, and towards the end of 890 he was proclaimed king in an assembly held at Valence, and brought under his rule the greater part of the territory lying to the south of Rodolph's dominions.

But the exact nature of his kingship can hardly even be conjectured from contemporary records.   We hear of him only as having journeyed about his kingdom and granted privileges to churches.   Moreover, from the year 900 his energies are diverted to the other side of the Alps, whither he is invited by the lords of Italy, who, weary of their king, Berengar, offer him the crown.   Louis closed with their proposals, as, later on, Rodolph II was to do, marched at once upon Pavia, and there assumed the crown as king of Italy, about the beginning of October 900. Then, continuing his march, he entered Piacenza and Bologna, and in February 901 received the imperial crown at Rome from the hands of Pope Benedict IV.   Some few engagements with Berengar's troops were enough to secure to him the adhesion of the majority of the nobles.

But if Italy was quickly won, it was quickly lost.   Driven from Pavia, which Berengar succeeded in re-entering (902), Louis in 905 made a fresh attempt to thrust out his rival.   But he was surprised at Verona on 21 July 905[1], and made prisoner by Berengar who put out his eyes, and sent him back beyond the Alps.

Thenceforward, the unhappy Louis the Blind drags out a wretched existence within his own dominions.   While continuing to bear the empty title of Emperor, he remained shut up in his town and palace of Vienne, leaving the business of government to his cousin Hugh of Arles, Marquess of Provence, who, holding both the March of Provence and the county of Vienne, acts as master throughout the kingdom.   We find him for instance interfering in the affairs of the Lyonnais, although this district had a count of its own, and again in the business of the church of Valence, the bishop of which see is described as his vassal.   Again, if any question of alliance with a neighbouring king arises, it is he who intervenes.   At the beginning of 924 he has an interview with Raoul, King of France, in the Autunois on the banks of the Loire.   In the same year the Hungarians, who for some time had been devastating the Lombard plain, crossed the Alps and threatened at once the kingdoms

---

[1] This date, accepted by M. Poupardin (*Le Royaume de Provence*, p. 186) and contested by M. Segre (*Archivio storico italiano*, vol. xxxviii. 1906, pp. 442–48) seems to us to have been established by M. Schiaparelli (*Bullettino dell' Istituto storico italiano*, 1908, no. 29, pp. 129–157).

of Rodolph II and Louis the Blind. Again it is Hugh of Arles who
opens communications with Rodolph and concerts with him a common
plan of action against the dreaded barbarians. The two princes joined
their forces to stay the course of the robber bands by penning them
up in a defile, whence, however, they escaped. Hugh and Rodolph
together pursued them to the Rhone and drove them into Gothia.

This concord between Hugh of Arles and King Rodolph was not to
be lasting. We have already seen how Rodolph, called in by the lords
of Lombardy and crowned king of Italy in 922, had the very next year
been abandoned by a large number of his supporters who had offered the
kingdom to the Marquess of Provence. The latter had then come into
collision with Berengar's troops, and had been obliged to pledge himself
to attempt nothing further against him. But when in 926 Rodolph
definitively withdrew from Italy, Hugh embarked from Provence and
landed near Pisa. In the beginning of July 926, at Pavia, he received in
his turn the crown which he was to succeed in retaining for twenty
years without encountering any rival of importance.

About a year later Louis the Blind died. Of his children only one
seemed capable of reigning, Charles Constantine, often held illegitimate[1];
he was Count of Vienne, a district which he had been virtually ruling
since the departure of Hugh. But the new king of Italy, who was still all-
powerful in the kingdom of Provence, was not disposed to favour him.
For several years this state of uncertainty prevailed, and charters were
again dated either by the regnal year of the dead sovereign, or, according
to a formula widely used in times of interregnum, " God reigning, and a
king being awaited."

About 933 events occurred which cleared up the situation. "At this
time," says the Lombard historian Liudprand, "the Italians sent into
Burgundy to Rodolph's court to recall him. When King Hugh heard
of it, he despatched envoys to him and gave him all the lands that he
had held in Gaul before he ascended the throne, taking an oath of King
Rodolph that he would never return to Italy." This obscure passage is
our only source of information as to the agreement arrived at between
the two sovereigns. What was its exact purport it is impossible to say,
but the whole history of the succeeding years goes to prove that the
cession then made consisted of the sovereign rights which Hugh had
practically exercised for many long years in the dominions of Louis the
Blind. It amounted, in fact, to the union of the kingdom of Provence
with that of Burgundy[2].

---

[1] See Previté-Orton, EHR, 1914, p. 705, for the legitimacy of this prince.

[2] It would seem that this treaty (possibly *c.* 931) was not at once effective,
Conrad not being king in the Viennois until *c.* 940, and in Provence until *c.* 948 on
the death of King Hugh. See Previté-Orton, EHR, 1917, p. 347; cf. also *infra*,
p. 156.

C.　*The kingdom of Burgundy and its annexation to the Empire.*

Rodolph II did not long survive this treaty.　He died on 12 or 13 July 937, leaving the government to his young son Conrad, in after years called the Peaceful, and then aged about fifteen at most.

The youth and weakness of the new king were sure to be a temptation to his neighbours.　Apparently Hugh of Arles, King of Italy, planned how he might turn the situation to account, for as early as 12 December 937, we find him on the shores of the Lake of Geneva, where he took to wife Bertha, mother of young Conrad and widow of Rodolph II.　Soon afterwards, he married his son Lothar to Bertha's daughter, Adelaide. The new King of Germany, Otto I, who in 937 had just succeeded his father, Henry I, could not look unmoved on these manoeuvres. Without loss of time he set out for Burgundy, and, as his biographer tells us, "received into his possession the king and the kingdom."　In reality it was a bold and sudden stroke ; Otto, cutting matters short, had simply made young Conrad prisoner.　For about four years he kept him under a strong guard, taking him about with him on all his journeys and expeditions, and when he released him, at about the end of 942, he had made sure of his fidelity.

Thenceforward the king of Burgundy seems to be no more than a vassal of the German king.　When in 946 Otto went to the help of Louis IV[1] d'Outremer, against the aggressions of Hugh the Great, Conrad with his contingent of troops accompanied him.　In May 960 we find him at Otto's court at Kloppen in the neighbourhood of Mannheim.　Gradually the bonds that unite the king of Germany and the king of Burgundy were drawn closer ; in 951 Otto married Adelaide, sister of Conrad, and widow of Lothar, King of Italy ; ten years later he was crowned king of Italy at Pavia, and (2 February 962) received the imperial crown at Rome.　From this time onward, apparently, he looks upon the kingdom of Burgundy as a sort of appendage to his own dominions ; not only does he continue to keep Conrad always in his train (we find him for instance in 967 at Verona), but he makes it his business to expel the Saracens settled at Le Frainet (Fraxinetum) in the district of St-Tropez, and in January 968 makes known his intention of going in person to fight with them in Provence.

Under Rodolph III, son and successor of Conrad, the dependent position of the king of Burgundy in relation to the Emperor, becomes more and more marked.　Rodolph III, on whom even during his life-time his contemporaries chose to bestow the title of the "Sluggard (*ignavus*)," does not seem, at least in the early part of his career, to have been lacking in either energy or decision.　Aged about twenty-five at the time of his accession (993), he attempted to re-establish in his kingdom an authority

[1] See *supra*, Chapter IV. p. 79.

which, owing to the increasing strength of the nobles, was becoming daily more precarious. A terrible rebellion was the result, against which all the king's efforts broke helplessly. Incapable of subduing the revolt, he was obliged to have recourse to the German sovereign. The aged empress, Adelaide, widow of Otto I and aunt of young Rodolph III, hastened to him in 999 and journeyed with him through the country, endeavouring to pacify the nobles.

At the end of the same year, 999, she died, and hardly had two years passed when the Emperor Otto III followed her to the grave (23 January 1002). Under his successor, Henry II of Bavaria, German policy soon shewed itself aggressive and encroaching. In 1006 Henry seized the town of Basle, which he kept for several years; soon afterwards he exacted from Rodolph an oath that before he died he would name him his heir, and ten years later events occurred which placed the king of Burgundy completely at his mercy.

For reasons which are still to some extent obscure, the " Count of Burgundy," Otto-William, and a large group of the lords had just broken out into revolt against Rodolph. In his character of " count of Burgundy " Otto-William was master of the whole district corresponding to the diocese of Besançon, and as he held at the same time the county of Mâcon in the kingdom of France, and was brother-in-law of the powerful bishop Bruno of Langres, and father-in-law of Landry, Count of Nevers, of William the Great, Duke of Aquitaine, and of William II, Count of Provence, he was the most important person in the kingdom of Burgundy. As a contemporary chronicler Thietmar, Bishop of Merseburg, says while the events were yet recent, " Otto-William " though " nominally a vassal of the king " had a mind to live as " the sovereign master of his own territories."

The dispute broke out on the occasion of the nomination of a new archbishop to the see of Besançon. Archbishop Hector had just died, and immediately rival claimants had appeared, Rodolph seeking to have Bertaud, a clerk of his chapel, nominated, and Count Otto-William opposing this candidature in the interest of a certain Walter. The real question was, who was to be master in the episcopal city, the king or his vassal? Ostensibly the king won the day; Bertaud was elected, perhaps even consecrated. But Otto-William did not submit. He drove Bertaud out of Besançon, installed Walter by force, and, as the same Bishop Thietmar relates, carried his insolence so far as to have Bertaud hunted by his hounds in order to mark the deep contempt with which this intruder inspired him. " And," adds the chronicler, " as the prelate, worn out with fatigue, heard them baying at his heels, he turned round, and making the sign of the cross in the direction in which he had just left the print of his foot, let himself fall to the ground, expecting to be torn to pieces by the pack. But those savage dogs, on sniffing the ground thus hallowed by the sign of the cross, felt themselves suddenly stopped, as if by an irresistible force, and turning back, left God's true servant to find his way through the woods to a more hospitable region."

Otto-William was triumphant. Rodolph, having exhausted all his resources, was obliged to ask help of Henry II. An interview took place at Strasbourg in the early summer of 1016. Rodolph made his appearance with his wife, Ermengarde, and two of her sons who did homage to the Emperor. Rodolph himself, not satisfied with renewing the engagement to which he had already sworn, to leave his kingdom on his death to Henry, recognised him even then as his successor and swore not to undertake any business of importance without first consulting him. As to Otto-William, he was declared to have incurred forfeiture, and his fiefs were granted by the Emperor to some of the lords about his court.

Next came the carrying-out of this programme, a matter which bristled with difficulties. The Emperor himself undertook the despoiling of the Count of Burgundy. But entrenched within their fortresses, Otto-William and his partisans successfully resisted capture. Henry could only ravage the country, and being recalled by other events to the northern point of his dominions, was obliged to retreat without having accomplished anything. Thus the imperial intervention had not availed to restore Rodolph's authority. Again abandoned to his own resources, and incapable of making head against the rebels, the king of Burgundy gave ear to the proposals of the latter, who offered to submit on condition that the engagements of the Treaty of Strasbourg were annulled. Just at first, Rodolph appeared to yield. But the Emperor certainly lent no countenance to the expedient, the result of which would be disastrous to himself, and as early as February 1018 he compelled the king of Burgundy, his wife, his step-sons and the chief nobles of his kingdom solemnly to renew the arrangement of Strasbourg[1]. He then directed a fresh expedition against the county of Burgundy. It is not known, however, whether its results were any better than those of the expedition of 1016.

A few years later, when Henry II died (13 July 1024) Rodolph attempted to shake off the Germanic suzerainty, by claiming that former agreements were *ipso facto* invalidated by Henry's death. The latter's successor, Conrad II of Franconia, at once made it his business peremptorily to demand what he looked upon as his rights, and Rodolph

---

[1] This account of the years 1016–18, which are of the first importance in the history of Burgundy, departs very notably from that given by the latest learned authority who has devoted attention to the question, M. René Poupardin, in his study, *Le royaume de Bourgogne*, pp. 126–134. Our account is founded on a fresh study of the text of Thietmar of Merseburg and of Alpert, whose meaning appears to us not to have been always clearly brought out till now. The text of Alpert is, moreover, evidently inexact as to most of the points. Although a contemporary, he has made himself the echo of loose reports denied by other authors.

was forced to submit. He even went as a docile vassal to Rome, to be present at the imperial coronation of the new prince (26 March 1027), and a few months later, at Basle, he solemnly renewed the conventions of Strasbourg and Mayence.

Rodolph III himself only survived this new treaty a few years. On 5 or 6 Sept. 1032 he died, without legitimate children, after having sent the insignia of his authority to the Emperor.

It seemed as though the Emperor Conrad had nothing to do but come and take possession of his new kingdom. The chief opponent of his policy in Rodolph's lifetime, Otto-William, Count of Burgundy, had died several years before in 1026, and the principal nobles of the kingdom had in 1027 come with their king to Basle to ratify the conventions of Strasbourg and Mayence. The course of events, however, was not to be so smooth.

Already, for some time Odo II, Count of Chartres, Blois, Tours, Troyes, Meaux and Provins, the most formidable and turbulent of the king of France's vassals, had been intriguing with the Burgundian lords to be recognised as the successor of King Rodolph. He had even attempted, though without success, to inveigle the latter into naming him as his heir, to the exclusion of his imperial rival. He put himself forward in his character of nephew of the king of Burgundy, his mother being Rodolph's sister, whereas the Emperor Conrad was only the husband of that king's niece[1].

No sooner had Rodolph closed his eyes, than Odo II, profiting by the Emperor's detention at the other end of his dominions, owing to a war against the Poles, promptly crossed the Burgundian frontier, seized upon several fortresses in the very heart of the kingdom, such as Morat and Neuchâtel, and thence marching upon Vienne, forced the Archbishop, Léger, to open the gates and, with a view to being crowned, made sure of

[1] For the sake of greater clearness, a short table of the family of the kings of Burgundy, so far as they concern our narrative, is subjoined :

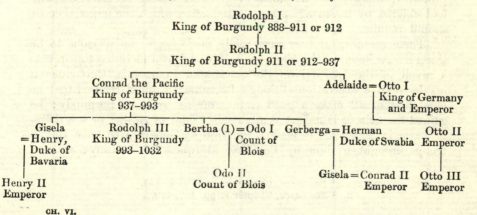

Rodolph I
King of Burgundy 888–911 or 912
|
Rodolph II
King of Burgundy 911 or 912–937

Conrad the Pacific
King of Burgundy
937–993

Adelaide = Otto I
King of Germany
and Emperor

Gisela
= Henry,
Duke of
Bavaria

Rodolph III
King of Burgundy
993–1032

Bertha (1) = Odo I
Count of
Blois

Gerberga = Herman
Duke of Swabia

Otto II
Emperor

Henry II
Emperor

Odo II
Count of Blois

Gisela = Conrad II
Emperor

Otto III
Emperor

his adhesion. The expedition thus rapidly carried out, with a decision all the more remarkable as Odo II had at that very moment to reckon with the hostility of the king of France against whom he had rebelled[1], certainly had the result of deciding a large number of the Burgundian lords, whether willingly or unwillingly, to declare for the Count of Blois. The Archbishop of Lyons and the Count of Geneva pronounced against the Emperor. It was high time for the latter to intervene.

Having secured the submission of the Polish duke, Mesco II, Conrad hastened back and in the depth of winter marched without stopping upon Basle (January 1033). From thence he quickly reached Soleure and then the monastery of Payerne, to the east of Lake Neuchâtel. He took advantage of the Feast of Candlemas (2 February) to have himself solemnly elected and crowned there as king of Burgundy by the nobles who favoured his cause and had come to meet him. From thence he advanced to lay siege to Morat, which was held by the partisans of the Count of Blois. But the cold was so intense and the resistance of the besieged so determined that Conrad was forced to abandon the enterprise and fall back upon Zurich, and from thence return to Swabia until the season should be more favourable.

Luckily for the Emperor, Odo was obliged during the spring of 1033 to make head against Henry I, King of France, who for the second time had made an attempt upon Sens[2], and he was for several months quite unable to follow up his early successes in Burgundy. Some months later hostilities were resumed between Conrad and his rival, but already the latter had begun to cherish new projects, and instead of entering Burgundy he invaded Lorraine and threatened Toul. Conrad replied by an invasion of Champagne. Both parties, having grown weary of the fruitless struggle, decided on opening negotiations. A meeting took place; according to the German chroniclers Odo took an oath to abandon all claims upon Burgundy, to evacuate the fortresses he still held there, and to give hostages for the fulfilment of these promises; finally, he undertook to give the nobles of Lorraine, who had suffered by his ravages, every satisfaction which the imperial court should require.

These promises, if they were really made, were too specious to be sincere. As soon as the Emperor had withdrawn in order to suppress a revolt of the Lyutitzi on the borders of Pomerania, Odo renewed his destructive expeditions through Lorraine. Conrad realised that he must first of all make a good ending of his work in Burgundy; he gained the help of Humbert Whitehands, Count of Aosta; he was therefore able in May 1034 to make a junction at Geneva with some Italian troops brought to him by Boniface, Marquess of Tuscany; without

---

[1] See *supra*, Chapter v. pp. 106–7, 123.
[2] See *supra*, Chapter v. pp. 107, 123.

difficulty he reduced most of the strongholds in the northern part of the Burgundian kingdom, forced the Count of Geneva and the Archbishop of Lyons to acknowledge his authority, and again caused the crown to be placed solemnly upon his head at a *curia coronata* held at Geneva. Morat still held out for the Count of Blois; it was taken by storm and given up to pillage. The cause of the Count of Blois was now lost beyond redemption in Burgundy, and Conrad, recognised by all, or practically all, could promise himself secure possession of his new kingdom.

Meanwhile, Odo, no more successful in his enterprise against Lorraine than in his Burgundian expedition, was soon to meet his death before the walls of Bar (15 November 1037).

From the day that the submission of the kingdom of Burgundy to the Emperor Conrad became an accomplished fact, the history of the kingdom may be said to come to an end. Yet it is not well to take literally the assertions of late chroniclers who sum up the course of events in such terms as these: " The Burgundians, not departing from their habitual insolence towards their king, Rodolph, delivered up to the Emperor Conrad the kingdom of Burgundy, which kingdom had, from the time of the Emperor Arnulf, for more than 130 years, been governed by its own kings, and thus Burgundy was again reduced to a province." But there was really a short period of transition; in fact at an assembly held (1038) at Soleure, Conrad, doubtless feeling the need of having a permanent representative in the kingdom, decided on handing it over to his son Henry. Whatever may have been said on the subject, it appears that Henry was in fact recognised as king of Burgundy; the great lords took a direct oath of fealty to him, and the Emperor doubtless granted him the dignity of an under-kingship, with which the Carolingian sovereigns had so often invested their sons.

But this form of administration did not last long. As early as 4 June 1039 King Conrad died, and now Henry III, the young king of Burgundy, found the kingdoms of Germany and Italy added to his first realm. The title of king of Burgundy was now, however, only an empty form. The domains which the sovereign had at his disposal in Burgundy were so insignificant that during the latter years of Rodolph III the chronicler Thietmar of Merseburg could write in reference to him: " There is no other king who governs thus; he possesses nothing but his title and his crown, and gives away bishoprics to those who are selected by the nobles. What he possesses for his own use is of small account, he lives at the expense of the prelates, and cannot even defend them or others who are in any way oppressed by their neighbours. Thus they have no resource, if they are to live in peace, but to come and commend themselves to the lords and serve them as if they were kings."

The very name of " Kingdom of Burgundy " covered a whole series of territories without unity, without mutual ties, and over which the king's control was quite illusory. Rodolph III, in his latter years, hardly ever so much as shewed himself outside the districts bounded by the valleys of the Saône and the Doubs and between the Jura and the upper course of the Rhône. The greater part of the lords, shutting themselves up within their own domains, made a show of ignoring the king's authority, or else merely deferred their revolt because, knowing the king near at hand, they might fear being constrained by him. "O king!" exclaimed the Chancellor Wipo to Henry III a few years later, "Burgundy demands thee; arise and come quickly. When the master tarries long absent, the fidelity of new subjects is apt to waver. The old proverb is profoundly true 'Out of sight, out of mind.' Although Burgundy is now, thanks to thee, at peace, she desires to view in thy person the author of this peace and to feast her eyes upon the countenance of her king. Appear, and let thy presence bring back serenity to this kingdom. Formerly, thou didst with difficulty subdue it; profit now by its readiness to serve thee."

As a matter of fact, Burgundy could spare her king very well, and the efforts made by Henry III to render his government in these parts a little more effective were to be unavailing. Despite his frequent visits, and the attempts that he made to reduce to obedience his rebellious vassals, notably the Counts of Burgundy and Genevois, Henry III accomplished nothing lasting. On his death (1056), his widow, the Empress Agnes, tried as fruitlessly to restore the royal power by sending Rudolf of Rheinfelden, Duke of Swabia, to represent her in the kingdom. Later on, Henry IV, when he had attained his majority, and after him Henry V in his struggle with the Papacy, met with hardly anything but indifference or hostility in Burgundy as a whole. Henry V's successor, Lothar of Supplinburg, himself supplies the proof of the purely nominal character of his authority in these distant provinces, when, on summoning the lords of Burgundy and Provence to join an expedition which he was preparing for Italy, he exclaims: "At sundry times we have written to you to demand the tribute of your homage and submission. But you paid no heed, thus emphasizing in an indecorous manner your contempt for our supreme power. We intend to labour henceforward to restore in your country our authority, which has been so much diminished among you as to be almost completely forgotten.... Thus we command you to appear at Piacenza, on the Feast of St Michael, with your contingent of armed men."

This summons was to produce no result. The Emperors tried by every means to make their power a reality. Following the example of the Empress Agnes, who had sent Rudolf of Rheinfelden to represent her, Lothar of Supplinburg, and afterwards Frederick Barbarossa were to try the experiment of delegating their authority to various princes of the Swiss house of Zähringen whom they appointed "rectors" or viceroys. This rectorate, soon to be called the Duchy of Burgundia

Minor (lesser Burgundy), was, however, only effective to the east of the Jura, that is, practically over modern Switzerland, and it disappeared in 1217 on the extinction of the elder line of Zähringen. In 1215 Frederick II was to try a return to the same policy, making choice of William of Baux, Prince of Orange, then in 1220 of William, Marquess of Montferrat; from 1237 onwards, he was to be represented by imperial vicars. We shall see the Emperors make an appearance, in an intermittent fashion, in the kingdom and sometimes seeming to re-possess themselves of a more or less real authority in this or that district. Frederick Barbarossa, in particular, after his marriage with Beatrice, the heiress of the county of Burgundy, will appear as unquestioned master in the diocese of Besançon, and be crowned king of Arles in 1178; Frederick II will for a time recover a real power of action in Provence and the Lyonnais; and again in the fourteenth century, Henry VII, strong in the support of the princes of Savoy, will rally to his standard large numbers of the nobles of the kingdom. Charles IV will characteristically go through the empty form of coronation in 1365. But these will be isolated exceptions, leading to nothing.

Incapable of enforcing their authority, the Emperors, from the latter part of the twelfth century onwards, more than once will even meditate restoring the kingdom of Arles, as it is now most frequently called, to its former independence, reserving the right to exact from its new king the recognition of their suzerainty. Henry VI will offer it to his prisoner, Richard Cœur de Lion in 1193; Philip of Swabia to his competitor, Otto of Brunswick in 1207; Rudolf of Habsburg will consider entrusting it in 1274 to a prince of his family, and later on to an Angevin prince, an idea to be revived by Henry VII in 1310.

But all these efforts prove vain. For long centuries the kingdom of Arles remains in theory attached to the Empire, but little by little, this kingdom, over which the German sovereigns could never secure effective control, will crumble to pieces in their hands. Out of its eastern portion the Swiss confederation and the duchy of Savoy will be formed; the kings of France, in the course of the fourteenth century, will succeed in regaining their authority over the Vivarais, the Lyonnais, the Valentinois and Diois, and Dauphiné, successively. To these, a century later, will be added Provence, which had already been long in French hands.

CHAPTER VII.

ITALY IN THE TENTH CENTURY.

THE death of the Emperor Lambert in October 898 dealt a blow to the royal power in North Italy, the *Regnum Italicum* of the tenth century. In place of the born ruler, who had mastered his own vassals and made himself protector of the Papacy, there succeeded Berengar, mild and cheatable. Berengar, too, was weak in resources. His own domains lay awkwardly in the extreme north-east, in Friuli and the modern Veneto, not like Lambert's in the centre ; and he had not like Lambert the support of a large group of the great nobles and bishops who formed the real source of power in Italy. Two magnates in especial were equally faithless and formidable, Adalbert the Rich, Marquess of Tuscany, in the centre, and Adalbert, Marquess of Ivrea, on the western frontier. In vain did Berengar marry his daughter Gisela to Adalbert of Ivrea and give the Tuscan his freedom from the prison to which Lambert had consigned him for revolt. A plot was hatching, when disaster befel king and kingdom.

Already in 898 the Hungarians, or Magyars[1], had raided the present Veneto from their newly-won settlements on the river Theiss. In 899 a larger swarm made its way from Aquileia to Pavia. Berengar, always a gallant warrior, strove to rise to the occasion. From the whole *Regnum Italicum* his vassals came to the number of 15,000 men-at-arms. Before them the outnumbered Magyars fled back, but were overtaken at the river Brenta. Their horses were worn out, they could not escape, and the tradition, perhaps influenced by a sense of tragedy, tells of their proffers refused by the haughty Christians. Yet on 24 September they surprised their heedless foes and scattered them with fearful slaughter. For nearly a year the Lombard plain lay at their mercy, though few fortified cities were taken and they did not cross the Apennines. Amid his faithless vassals, with his land desolated, Berengar submitted to pay blackmail, which at least kept the Magyars his friends if it did not save Lombardy from occasional incursions. The only mitigation of the calamity was the defeat of the Hungarians on the water when in 900 they assaulted Venice under her doge Pietro Tribuno.

[1] See Vol. I. Chapter XII. (A).

Berengar had lost men, wealth and prestige, he was too clearly profitless for his subjects, and the death at Hungarian hands of many bishops and counts left the greatest magnates greater than ever. The plot against him, already begun, gathered strength. It was headed by Adalbert II the Rich of Tuscany, whose wife Bertha, the widow of a Provençal count, was daughter of Lothar II of Lorraine and thus granddaughter of the Emperor Lothar I; and its object was to restore Lothar I's line to Italy in the person of Louis of Provence, grandson of the Emperor Louis II. The Spoletan party, the Empress Ageltrude, and Pope John IX, the old partisan of Lambert, were, it seems, won to the plan, and the hand of the Byzantine princess Anna, daughter of Leo VI, was obtained for the pretender. When Louis came to Italy in September 900, Berengar, faced by a general defection, could only retreat beyond the Mincio, while his rival, surrounded by the magnates, proceeded to Rome to receive the imperial crown in February 901 from the new Pope Benedict IV. But Louis had no great capacity, and the magnates were fickle of set purpose, for, says the chronicler Liudprand in a classic passage, they preferred two kings to play off one against the other. In 902 a counter-change was brought about. Berengar advanced to Pavia, and Louis, who had been unable to get away quickly enough, was allowed to withdraw on taking an oath never to return. Within three years (905), however, Bertha once more tempted her kinsman to invade Italy. He was to be furnished, perhaps, with a Byzantine subsidy[1]. Once more Berengar fled east, this time to Bavaria, for Adalard, Bishop of Verona, his chief stronghold, called in his rival. Louis heedlessly thought himself secure and was surprised and captured (21 July) by Berengar to whom the Veronese citizens, though not their bishop, were always loyal. No risks were taken by the victor, and Louis was sent back to Provence blind and helpless. By an atrocity unlike his usual dealings Berengar at last secured an undisputed throne. Real control over great nobles and bishops he was never to obtain.

While the *Regnum Italicum* lay invertebrate in the hands of the magnates, South Italy was even more disordered and tormented. For sixty years the land had suffered from the intolerable scourge of Saracen ravages. While a robber colony, established almost impregnably on the river Garigliano, spread desolation in the heart of Italy over the Terra di Lavoro and the Roman Campagna, the true base of the Muslims lay in Sicily. There the mixed Berber and Arab population, who had swarmed in under the Aghlabid dynasty of Ķairawān, were on the point of completing the conquest of the Christian and Greek eastern portion of

---

[1] At least the Pseudo-Symeon Magister states (*Ann. Leon. Basil. fil.* cap. 14) that the eunuch Rhodophylus in 904 was taking 100 lbs. of gold " to the Franks." But the other narrators, *e.g.* John Cameniates, *De excidio Thessalonicae*, cap. 59, state that this sum was for the Byzantine army then fighting "the Africans," and in any case it was diverted to ransom the walls of Thessalonica from destruction by the Moslems.

the island, and the brief cessation of their direct raids on the mainland which began *c.* 889 did not last long.

Subdivision and intestine wars for independence and predominance paralysed South Italy in its struggle against the Saracens. The greatest power there was the Byzantine Empire, after Basil I and his general Nicephorus Phocas had revived its power in the West. Two themes were set up in Italy, each under its *strategos* or general[1], that of Longobardia with its capital at Bari which included Apulia and Lucania from the river Trigno on the Adriatic to the Gulf of Taranto, and that of Calabria with its capital at Reggio which represented the vanished theme of Sicily. These detached and frontier provinces, usually scantily supplied with troops and money owing to the greater needs of the core of the Empire, were beset with difficulties occasioned by the hostility of the Italians to the corrupt and foreign Greek officials. The Lombard subjects in Apulia were actively or potentially disloyal; and a long strip of debateable land formed the western part of the Longobardic theme, which was always claimed by the Lombard principality of Benevento, its ancient possessor. Then there were the native Italian states, all considered as its vassals by Byzantium in spite of the competing pretensions of the Western Empire. Three of these, Gaeta, Naples and Amalfi, were coast towns, never conquered by the Lombards, and, like Venice, had long enjoyed a complete autonomy without formally denying their allegiance to East Rome. They were all now monarchies, all trading, and all inclined to ally with the Saracens, who were at once their customers and their principal dread. The three remaining states were Lombard, the principalities of Benevento and Salerno and the county of Capua. The prince of Salerno acknowledged Byzantine suzerainty. Benevento had been conquered by the Greeks in 891, only to be recovered by the native dynasty under the auspices of the Spoletan Emperors of the West, and then conquered by Atenolf I of Capua in 899. This union of Capua and Benevento was the beginning of some kind of order in a troubled land, hitherto torn by the struggle of furious competitors.

It was the Saracen plague, however, which at length brought the petty states to act together. If the invasion of Calabria by the half-mad Aghlabid Ibrāhīm who had conquered Taormina, the last Byzantine stronghold of Sicily, and threatened to destroy in his holy war Rome itself, " the city of the dotard Peter," ended in his death before Cosenza in 902, and civil wars distracted Sicily till she submitted to the new Fātimite Caliphate at Ḵairawān; the Muslims of the Garigliano still ate like an ulcer into the land. The countryside was depopulated, the great abbeys, Monte Cassino, Farfa, Subiaco and Volturno, were destroyed and deserted. At last the warring Christians were so dismayed as to be reconciled, and Atenolf of Capua turned to the one strong power which

[1] See for the system of themes Vol. IV. and its maps.

could intervene and professed himself a Byzantine vassal. Help was long in coming when a warrior Pope stepped in to consolidate and enlarge the Christian league.

Rome had undergone strange vicissitudes since the death of Emperor Lambert, but they had had a clear outcome, the victory of the land-owning barbarised aristocracy over the bureaucratic priestly elements of the Curia. After the death of Benedict IV (903) the revolutions of a year brought to the papal throne its old claimant, the fierce anti-Formosan Sergius III (904–11), over two imprisoned and perhaps murdered predecessors. Sergius owed his victory to "Frankish" help, possibly that of Adalbert the Rich of Tuscany, but he was also the ally of the strongest Roman faction. Theophylact, *vesterarius* of the Sacred Palace and Senator of the Romans, was the founder of a dynasty. He was chief of the Roman nobles; to his wife, the *Senatrix* Theodora, tradition attributed both the influence of an Empress Ageltrude and, without real ground, the vices of a Messalina; his daughter Marozia was only too probably the mistress of Pope Sergius and by him the mother of a future Pontiff, John XI, and finally married the new Marquess of Spoleto, the adventurer Alberic. The power of these and of other great ladies, which is a characteristic of the tenth century, and sometimes their vices, too, won for them the hatred of opposing factions whose virulent report of them has fixed the name of the " Pornocracy " on the debased papal government of that unhallowed day. Two inconspicuous successors of Sergius III were followed, doubtless through Theophylact's and Theodora's choice, by the elevation of the Archbishop of Ravenna to the papal see as John X (914–28). This much-hated pontiff, who like Formosus had been translated to the indignation of the strict canonists, was no mere instrument in his maker's hands. He at once took the lead in the war with the Saracens. The Byzantine regent Zoë was sending a new *strategos*, the patrician Nicholas Picingli, with reinforcements to Bari. From the south Picingli marched in 915 up to Campania, adding the troops of Atenolf's successor at Capua, Landolf I, and of Guaimar of Salerno to his army. Even the rulers of the sea-ports, Gaeta and Naples, appeared in his camp decorated with Byzantine titles. From the north came Pope John and his Romans accompanied by the Spoletan levies under Marquess Alberic. A Byzantine fleet occupied the mouth of the Garigliano, and after a three months' blockade the starving Saracens burst out to be hunted down by the victors among the mountains.

This decisive victory began an era of revival in Southern Italy. Though Calabria and even Apulia remained open to Saracen raids, which recommenced when the Fāṭimite Caliph Mahdī conquered Sicily in 917; though from *c.* 922 onwards Hungarian bands now and again worked their way south; a comparative security was restored. The deserted champaign could be slowly repopulated, the monasteries could claim once more their ravaged possessions and, as the century wore on, be rebuilt.　Not a little of this wanly dawning prosperity was due to the stability which was at last acquired by the princely houses.　The rulers of Capua-Benevento, Salerno and the rest reigned long and transmitted an assured, if not unharassed, dominion to their heirs.　Their thriving was soon shewn in hostility to their Byzantine suzerain.　Picingli's victory had not ameliorated the government of the Italian themes. Calabria, the Greek character of which was being accentuated by the inrush of refugees from Sicily, might only be restive at exactions due to blackmail paid to the Fātimite Caliph for respite from his subjects' raids; but the Lombards, who were predominant in Apulia, hankered for autonomy, and in spite of bribes in cash and titles, were inclined to side with the aggressive prince of Capua.　Landolf I took advantage of the Apulians' discontent and the weakness of the *strategoi*, with their insufficient means and their coast harried by Saracen and Slav pirates.　In concert with Guaimar II of Salerno and the Marquess Theobald I of Spoleto he overran *c.* 927 the greater part of Longobardia and held it some seven years.　Not till the Eastern Empire could ally with a strong king of the *Regnum Italicum* was it possible to oust Landolf and his allies.

The strong king was long in coming.　Berengar indeed received in December 915 the imperial crown from John X, in disregard of Louis the Blind's rights, perhaps in reward for his concurrence in Alberic's assistance at the Garigliano, perhaps to counterbalance the then dangerous might of the Eastern Emperor in the south.　But Berengar was no whit more powerful thereby.　Hungarian raids still occurred and a more persistent enemy began to trouble western Lombardy.　At the close of the ninth century bands of Saracen pirates coming from Spain had established themselves in a fortified settlement on the coast of Provence, on the Golfe du St Tropez, called Fraxinetum, the name of which is preserved in Garde-Freinet.　Thence, as their numbers grew, they conducted terrible raids on the surrounding territory.　Provence was the worst sufferer, but, since the Saracens made the Alps their favourite plundering centre, Italy too was a victim.　The Alpine valleys were desolated, the great roadside abbeys, such as Novalesa, were destroyed.　Bands of pilgrims to the graves of the Apostles at Rome were robbed and massacred, till the intercourse of Italy with the north-west was in danger of ceasing.　Here again the magnates fought in isolation when only a combined effort could root out the evil.　Berengar seems to have done nothing, perhaps he could do nothing, but his discredit naturally increased.

The fickle magnates meanwhile were looking out for another rival king.　Bertha of Tuscany, whose husband Adalbert II was dead, again worked for the restoration of the line of Lothar I and brought in her son by her first marriage, Hugh, Duke of Provence, who ruled his native country during Louis the Blind's incapacity.　This first attempt failed (*c.* 920) and then a group of northern magnates headed by Adalbert of

Ivrea, now husband of Bertha's Tuscan daughter Ermingarde, invited Rodolph II, King of Jurane Burgundy. The accustomed tragicomedy followed. Rodolph came in 922 and was recognised north of the Apennines, while Berengar held out in Verona and won infamy by letting in his Hungarian allies who this time penetrated to Campania. Next year the rivals fought one of the rare pitched battles of the time at Fiorenzuola near Piacenza where Berengar had the worse and the death of 1500 men depleted the scanty ranks of the kingdom's military caste. Thenceforth Berengar vegetated, seemingly under truce, at Verona till his murder by one of his vassals on 7 April 924. He had watched, rather than caused, the anarchy of the realm, just as his lavish grants to the prelates registered rather than caused the cessation of a central government.

Rodolph was not more fortunate. He had two kingdoms, and while he was in Burgundy the Magyars laid Lombardy waste. They burnt Pavia itself in 924 and only left Italy to pass over the Alps and be exterminated by pestilence in Languedoc. The hopes of the house of Lothar revived. Adalbert of Ivrea was dead, and his widow Ermingarde joined with her brother Guido of Tuscany and Lampert, Archbishop of Milan, in calling in once more her half-brother Hugh of Provence. In 925 they revolted, twice repelled Rodolph's efforts at reconquest, and on 6 July 926 elevated Hugh to the throne. In him a strong king had come. Hugh, wily and voluptuous, had his domains and vassals in Provence behind him and a group of magnates in his favour in Italy. He set himself to increase the latter by endowing his Provençal kindred. One nephew, Theobald I, was given the march of Spoleto, another, Manasse, Archbishop of Arles, was later put in charge of three sees *in commendam*. A Provençal immigration set in to the disgust of the Italian nobles. Hugh, who no more than his contemporaries ventured to reconstitute the ancient royal government or to recall the alienations of revenue and administrative functions, did succeed in making the great vassals, as well as the bishops, his nominees.

To be crowned Emperor was the natural goal of Hugh's ambition. Without the protectorate over the Papacy an Italian king had but a maimed dominion in central Italy, and to a mere protection of the Papacy the functions of the Emperor had been reduced since the time of Lambert. Indeed it seems that Hugh came into Italy with the Pope's approval and struck a bargain with him at Mantua in 926. John X was in a dangerous plight. Theophylact was dead, Marquess Alberic was dead, their daughter and widow, the sinister Marozia, led their Roman faction, and had become hostile to the self-willed Pope. If John X probably strengthened himself by obtaining the Spoletan march, which Alberic had held, for his own brother Peter, perhaps in return for Berengar I's coronation, Marozia gained far more power by her marriage to Marquess Guido of Tuscany. In the faction-fighting Marquess Peter was driven from Rome *c.* 927, but a terrible Hungarian raid which lacerated Italy from Friuli to Campania enabled him to re-enter the city. Tradition charged on him an alliance with the raiders. In any case he was slaughtered by the Romans in 928 and his brother the Pope was thrust into prison to die or be murdered without much delay. Marozia now was supreme: "Rome was subdued by might under a woman's hand," says the wrathful local chronicler[1]. Two Popes, so shadowy that they were forgotten in a few years, wore the tiara in turn till in 931 she raised her own son, probably by Sergius III, to the pontificate as John XI. But Marozia was weakened by the death of Guido and looked around her for a potent consort. She found one in Guido's half-brother, Hugh of Italy, then a widower. King Hugh may have been baffled in his original scheme of becoming Emperor by the fall of John X; he had also been drawn off by the Hungarians and a revolt at Pavia. Now, however, he was so firm on his throne as to secure the election of his boy son Lothar II as co-regent. His contract with Marozia is the ugliest episode of the time. He feared his half-brother Marquess Lambert of Tuscany, himself a descendant of Lothar I and a possible rival; and he could not marry his half-brother Guido's widow. Therefore he seized and blinded Lambert, and announced that his two half-brothers were not true sons of Bertha. With the way thus cleared he entered Rome in 932 and married Marozia. But the *senatrix* and her husband miscalculated and did no more than garrison the castle of Sant' Angelo. Before Hugh was crowned the Romans rose against the hated Burgundian foreigner. Their leader was Marozia's own son Alberic, whom she had borne to Alberic of Spoleto, a youth who knew Hugh's treatment of inconvenient relatives. Sant' Angelo was besieged and taken, and although Hugh made his escape Marozia and John XI were imprisoned. Of Marozia no more is said.

The rule of Alberic marks the open and complete triumph of the Roman landed aristocracy over the bureaucratic clerical government of the Papacy. His state resembled the city monarchies of Naples or Gaeta. On him as " prince and senator of all the Romans " was conferred, it seems by popular election, the exercise of the Pope's secular power in Rome and its duchy. Though the act was revolutionary and *ultra vires*, no denial of the Pope's sovereignty was made. It was enough that John XI and his four successors were docile instruments of the prince. Perhaps Alberic dreamed of further change, of reviving a miniature Western Empire, for he tried to win a Byzantine bride, and, even when baffled, surnamed his son Octavian. "His face was bright like his father's and he had old-time worth. For he was exceedingly terrible, and his yoke was heavy on the Romans and on the holy Apostolic See[2]." His stern domination seems to have been a blessing to Rome and its duchy, which he secured, while King Hugh about 938 seized on Ravenna and the Pentapolis which had indeed been ruled by the

---

[1] Benedict. S. Andreae, c. 30.　　　[2] *Ibid.* c. 32.

Italian emperors since the days of Guy (Guido). The turbulent Roman nobles and his own treacherous kindred were kept in order, the submissive churchmen protected by a pious usurper who favoured monastic reform and was the friend of St Odo of Cluny. It was all Alberic could do, however, to maintain himself against the persistent efforts of King Hugh to conquer Rome. A first siege of the city in 933 was a failure, a second in 936 ended in a treaty by which Alberic married Hugh's legitimate daughter Alda. This pacification did not last, although negotiated by St Odo, and in 941 Hugh by bribes and warfare was so successful as just to enter Rome. Somehow he was expelled, "by the hidden judgement of God" according to our only narrator[1]. Yet he would not give up the war until 946 when he had become a king under tutelage. Alberic thenceforth ruled unchallenged till his death in August 954.

Hugh and Alberic had been rival suitors for the alliance of the Eastern Emperor Romanus I Lecapenus, and in 935 Hugh had won the prize, partly through the pressure he could exercise in the south, partly no doubt through an eligibility to which the isolated prince of the Romans could lay no claim. Hugh, by calling off Theobald I of Spoleto, enabled the Byzantines to recover the lost districts of Apulia, and eventually the alliance was sealed by the marriage of Hugh's illegitimate daughter to a Byzantine prince, the future Emperor Romanus II. The two powers suffered in common from the Hungarians and Saracens. Against the Magyars little was done save to pay blackmail, although in 938 some raiding bands as they retreated from Campania, were exterminated by the Abruzzans.   Common action was, however, attempted against the Saracens of Fraxinetum, who, besides their formidable brigandage on the West Alpine passes, raided even as far as Swabia and by sea must have troubled the Byzantines. In 931 the Greeks attacked them and, landing at Fraxinetum, made a slaughter, while it may be that at the same time Hugh's vassals revenged the destruction of Acqui by cutting to pieces the Saracen raiders and occupying for a moment the passes[2]. But no permanent result was obtained. Rather the ravage of the Fraxinetan Saracens grew worse, and in 935 the Fatimites sent a fleet from Africa which stormed Genoa. At last Hugh and Romanus I were roused to a joint campaign. In 942 a Byzantine fleet burnt the Saracens' ships with Greek fire, and blockaded Fraxinetum by sea, while Hugh with his army invested it by land. The Saracens could have been rooted out, when Hugh made a treaty with them: they were to hold the Swabian passes against any attempted invasion by Hugh's exiled nephew-in-law Berengar of Ivrea. Perhaps Italy was somewhat spared in consequence, but the Alps continued the scene of their brigandage.

[1] Liudprand, *Antapodosis*, v. 3.
[2] So we can reconstruct from Flodoard *an.* 931 and Liudprand, *Antapodosis*, iv. 4, which may well refer to the same year.

The fear of invasion had been with Hugh since the beginning of his reign, and in his western policy it was obscurely entangled with his desire to retain Provence. He evidently wished to consider the kingdom of Provence as annexed to his Italian crown after the death of the Emperor Louis the Blind in 928, but in spite of his wide lands and numerous relatives there he could not obtain recognition as sovereign. King Raoul of France also nourished ambitions to rule on the Rhone, and it may be that Hugh hoped to block his way, as well as to buy off an invasion threatened by Rodolph II of Jurane Burgundy, when *c.* 931 he made, on the evidence of Liudprand, a treaty with Rodolph II by which there was ceded to Rodolph II "all the territory Hugh had held in Gaul before he became king of Italy." We may doubt whether this ineffective treaty referred to more than one or two districts; in any case Rodolph II lost them again, and his death in 937 opened out a new prospect[1]. Hugh contrived to marry Rodolph II's widow Bertha himself and to betroth Rodolph's daughter Adelaide to his own son Lothar II. Though the rights of Rodolph's young son Conrad were not disputed, Hugh probably hoped to be the real ruler of Jurane Burgundy, when a greater competitor appeared on the scene.

The German princes had by no means abandoned hopes of Italian conquest since the Emperor Arnulf's death, although the internal troubles of Germany, seconded by Hugh's gifts and embassies, precluded a royal campaign. Duke Burchard of Swabia had aided his son-in-law Rodolph II; in 934 Duke Arnulf of Bavaria suffered defeat in an invasion of the Veneto. But now the German king, Otto the Great, was strong; he was determined to secure his south-western frontier, and perhaps already dreamed of reasserting Arnulf's position and taking the imperial crown. In some way he gained possession of young Conrad and controlled the government of Jurane Burgundy. All that Hugh seems to have kept was the Valley of Aosta, and his lands in Provence.

The perpetual danger of an invasion was increased by the readiness of the magnates to call in a foreign king at any discontent. Although national consciousness was present in Italy, and in a strongly localized form was marked in Rome, the great vassals were still as their ancestors of the ninth century had been, members of the mainly Frankish noble houses which were scattered and endowed throughout Charlemagne's Empire. In Italy they were mostly new-comers, only Italian in their objection to fresh magnates from beyond the Alps. Hugh's safety, on the other hand, lay in the introduction of new men from Provence, his kinsmen and allies, which he could the more readily effect as the magnates he found in possession had struck but short roots since the days of the Emperor Guy. Even so he could not much depend on his nominees; the instinct and the opportunity for feudal turbulence were too strong. Among the bishops the saintly Frank, Ratheri of Verona, had to be deposed for

---

[1] See Previté-Orton, *Italy and Provence*, EHR, 1917, p. 335.

adherence to Duke Arnulf's invasion. In central Italy he could root out the ancient dynasts, but could not implant loyalty to himself. On Lambert's deposition he had given the march of Tuscany to his full brother Boso, once a count in Provence, who in turn vanished in his prisons in 936. Soon after Theobald I of Spoleto died and was replaced by Anscar, son of Adalbert of Ivrea and Hugh's half-sister Ermingarde of Tuscany. This was such a risky appointment in view of the wrongs which Hugh had done to Ermingarde's family that the chronicler Liudprand explains it as intended to remove Anscar from his powerful friends in the north. In any case rumour said that the king stirred up against the new Marquess of Spoleto a Provençal, Sarlio, Count of the Palace, who had married Theobald I's widow. In 940 Anscar was slain in battle, and Hugh then turned on Sarlio whom he forced to take the cowl. The king by now seemed to be finding surer instruments in his own bastard children, of whom the eldest Hubert, Marquess of Tuscany in 936, Marquess of Spoleto and Count of the Palace *c.* 942, kept a firm hand on central Italy, while others were designed for ecclesiastical preferments.

Hugh's astute perfidy alarmed the Italian nobles more and more and especially their greatest remaining chief, Anscar's half-brother, Berengar, Marquess of Ivrea. Everything conspired to make Berengar dangerous and alarmed. He was heir through his mother of the Emperor Berengar I, his wife Willa was daughter of the fallen Boso of Tuscany, his march of Ivrea gave him command of the western gates of the kingdom, and its extent and Anscari's fate pointed him out as Hugh's next destined victim. The story goes that Hugh intended to seize and blind him, but that the Marquess was forewarned by the young co-regent Lothar II, and with his wife fled to Duke Herman of Swabia by whom they were conducted to the German king, Otto the Great. Otto, while he did not actively assist the exile, would not give him up in spite of the redoubled presents of King Hugh, and Berengar was able to plot with the malcontents of Italy for a rebellion. In the meantime Hugh, feeling his throne shake under him, made feverish efforts to recover his vassals' loyalty. Berengar's great domains were distributed among leading nobles: the counts Ardoin Glabrio of Turin, Otbert and Aleram are henceforward in the first rank of magnates; and an unusual number of royal diplomas were issued in 943. But Saracen and Hungarian marauding did not increase Hugh's hold on his subjects. It is clear that besides lay plotters the great prelates and his own kin were ready to revolt. When Berengar saw the time was come, in the mid-winter of 944–5, he made his venture over the Brenner towards Verona, the Count of which, Milo, an old adherent of Berengar I, was in his favour. The decisive moment came when Manasse of Arles, who was in charge of the frontier bishopric of Trent, deserted his uncle. A general defection was headed by Archbishop Arderic of Milan, and Hugh at Pavia could do nothing better than send in April the unhated Lothar II to Milan to appeal to the rebels. The assembly was moved and declared the youth sole king, but, when Hugh tried to escape to Provence with his treasure, Berengar in fear of a new invasion had him intercepted and reinstated in August as nominal joint king. In this humiliating position Hugh remained till April 947 when somehow he gained leave to abdicate and retire to Provence with the treasure with which he still hoped to engineer a fresh invasion. But he died on 10 April 948.

Meanwhile Berengar was ruling, in the name of Lothar II, as "chief councillor of the realm." He seems to have done his best to promote his clerical partisans, but his main reliance was on his fellow magnates. Although no doubt he recovered much of his own domains, he was evidently obliged to buy support by consenting to alienations like that of Turin to Ardoin Glabrio. Even Hubert was left unmolested in Tuscany, if a new Marquess was appointed to Spoleto. How little Berengar was master of the kingdom was shewn when he nominated Manasse of Arles to the see of Milan. The Milanese townsmen elected a rival Adalman, Manasse obtained adherents in the countryside, and the two competitors fought for five years without decisive result. It was, however, in foreign affairs that Berengar's weakness was most obvious. Hugh had been in relations with all his neighbours, Berengar shrank into isolation; Byzantium neglected him, Provence submitted to Conrad of Jurane Burgundy, the *protégé* of Otto the Great, Germany loomed ever more formidably in the north, the Hungarians under their chief Taxis proved in 947 by ravages which reached Apulia that Italy was no better defended than before. Weakness and the greed of wealth which belonged to Berengar's own character brought unpopularity which was exemplified in the accusations that he made a large profit out of the tax levied for blackmail to the Magyars, and that he was the deviser of the sudden death of Lothar II in November 950. Berengar still had sufficient following to secure the election of himself and his son Adalbert as joint kings on 15 December 950, but the disaffected were numerous. Lothar left no son, and his widow Adelaide of Jurane Burgundy with her rich dower was the centre of an opposition in which the bishops, who had suffered under Berengar's exactions, took the leading part. Berengar II's expedient was to ride rough-shod over the ex-queen's rights. Her dower was seized on, she was ill-used and imprisoned, if we may trust later tradition she was required to marry the young King Adalbert. She only gained safety by an adventurous escape to the protection of Bishop Adalard of Reggio, who according to a credible later story consigned her to the impregnable castle of his vassal Adalbert-Atto at Canossa.

This was in August 951, but a champion was already near at hand, whose advent shows that Adelaide's persecution at the hands of Berengar II was not unprovoked. Germany, the most powerful of the kingdoms which arose from the shattered Carolingian Empire, had prospered under the Saxon dynasty and neither her King Otto the Great nor the dukes of her southern duchies, Bavaria and Swabia, were inclined to let slip the opportunity of conquering their wealthy and weak neighbour of Italy. These princes were all near kinsmen, for Henry of Bavaria was Otto's brother and Liudolf of Swabia was Otto's eldest son; but, while Henry and Liudolf who were bitter rivals were imitating the local ambitions of the dukes their predecessors, Otto probably had a greater model in his mind—he would revive the Empire as Arnulf had held it and be suzerain of western Christendom; that he would so win the hand of the beautiful queen he rescued would give an additional attraction to the enterprise. The two dukes, being near at hand, made hasty invasions for their own ends first of all, Henry with some success, Liudolf with failure. Then came Otto at the head of an imposing force, to which both dukes brought contingents. He crossed the Brenner Pass and reached Pavia at the end of September 951, without any resistance being offered him. The churchmen in fact were on his side, led by the versatile Archbishop Manasse, and Berengar II could only flee to one of his castles. But the adhesion of the bishops of the Lombard plain was not enough, and in his triumph Otto's difficulties began. Pope Agapetus, at Alberic's instigation, refused his request to be crowned Emperor, for the Roman prince had no mind to nullify his life's work by introducing a foreign Roman Emperor; and the king's marriage to the rescued Adelaide roused against him a domestic enemy. His son Liudolf, in thorough discontent at the influence of his stepmother and her ally Henry of Bavaria, departed for Germany to scheme revolt. Otto himself followed in February 952, having after all acquired only some half of the kingdom of which he assumed the title. He left his son-in-law Duke Conrad of Lorraine with troops to hold Pavia and continue the war. The king had scarcely gone, however, before Conrad and Berengar II came to terms, both perhaps being well aware how little trust could be placed in the Lombard magnates. Together they came to Otto at Magdeburg in April, but Otto's terms were not so lenient as Conrad imagined. Berengar was received with haughty discourtesy, and dismissed to attend a diet at Augsburg in August, whither he was accompanied by the chief Lombard prelates. There he and Adalbert became Otto's vassals for the *Regnum Italicum* from which they were compelled to cede the marches of Verona, Friuli and Istria to Duke Henry of Bavaria. Thus Otto, although withdrawing from Italy, kept its eastern gateway in German hands.

Berengar II returned to Italy burning with wrath against the bishops and nobles who had caused his disasters and the mutilation of his kingdom. He and his queen Willa earned an evil name for greed and cruelty, since they needed wealth to enrich the enfeebled kingship and were hungry for revenge. Among their lay foes Adalbert-Atto underwent a long vain siege in his castle of Canossa, but the chief sufferers were the churchmen. The series of grants to them, which had continued so persistently under former kings, almost ceases under Berengar. At Milan, Manasse's rival

Adalman was induced to resign, and he himself was dispossessed in favour of a new Archbishop, Walpert. Exiles began to make their way to Otto's court, among them our chief informant about these Italian kings, the chronicler Liudprand, who thereby became the bitter enemy of Berengar II with his house and wreaked his revenge in his historical writings. If there had survived another business-like Italian chronicle, like that of Flodoard for France, Liudprand would have earned more gratitude from posterity than he does for his vivid narrative, his pointed character-sketches, and the brush-like abundance of "local colour" with which he overlays his scanty facts. As it is, in his *Antapodosis* (Retribution) we have a difficulty in obtaining a firm foothold for history amid the crumbling and quaking mass of rancorous, if often contemporary, gossip which Liudprand loves to heap up. Of noble birth, bred at King Hugh's court, and once Berengar II's secretary, he was in the best position to give accurate and full information, but he had a soul above documents. It is hardly his fault that he depended on oral tradition for all events before his own time, for there seems to have been no Italian chronicle for him to use, but he evidently made no record at the time and when he wrote rested wholly on a memory which rejected dates and political circumstances and was singularly retentive of amorous scandal however devoid of probability. He does not even tell in his unfinished work the cause and events of his persecution by Berengar to which he frequently alludes, while sketching with fine precision the diary of his reception at Constantinople whither he first went as Berengar's envoy. For what interested him he could remember and tell to the life. To his credit be it said he was no liar, though he may be found suppressing an unpleasant fact; what he heard he told, and perhaps we may grant him that he gave a ready, and sometimes a determined, belief to the gossip of anterooms and the tradition of wrathful factions. It is unfortunate, for he was a practical statesman, and knew and sometimes reveals the motives of his times.

Berengar had had a free hand in Italy, and had even recovered Verona, because Otto was occupied in German revolts and frontier wars, but in 955 occurred the decisive victory of the Lechfeld in which Otto put an end once for all to Hungarian raids. He had succeeded where all the Italian kings had failed, he had rescued central Europe, and was therefrom with little doubt its destined ruler. His intervention in Italy, Henry of Bavaria being now dead, was renewed by the agency of his reconciled rebel son Liudolf. In 957 the duke made his invasion with the usual rapid success. Berengar II fled, Adalbert was defeated in battle, and all Lombardy had submitted when Liudolf died of fever at Pombia near Lake Maggiore, the first German victor to lose his gains owing to the alien climate of Italy.

The death of Liudolf was followed by the immediate recovery of his lost ground by Berengar. He came back with a new series of bitter feuds to pursue. Walpert of Milan and other prelates fled to Otto, and

Manasse became once more a pluralist by returning to Milan as Berengar's partisan. Among the lay magnates Marquess Otbert went into exile; a general disaffection existed among those who retained their possessions. The king was still eager as Hugh had been before him to amass an imposing royal demesne and to create trusty great vassals. Hitherto central Italy had been faithful to him; now, however, Spoleto seems an enemy, perhaps owing to the new turn of affairs at Rome. On his deathbed in 954 prince Alberic had bound the Romans by oath to elect his son and heir by Alda, John-Octavian, Pope when Agapetus should die. In December 955 the promise was kept and the boy became Pope as John XII. Thus the Pope recovered control of Rome by uniting with the Papacy the chiefship of the strong faction of Alberic. Any design of a permanent principate must have been given up; it was perhaps too anomalous, and it is significant that John renewed the long forgotten habit of dating by the years of the Byzantine Emperors. But the Roman nobles remained in power to the continued subjection of the ecclesiastical bureaucracy. John XII himself was a dissolute boy whose pontificate was a glaring scandal. No gleam of competence redeemed his debauchery, though he was not without secular ambitions. About 959 he made war on the co-regent princes of Capua-Benevento, Paldolf I (Pandulf) Ironhead and Landolf III, with the aid of Marquess Theobald II of Spoleto. He failed, and gave way, for prince Gisulf of Salerno assisted his neighbours; and then Berengar attacked Spoleto on an unknown pretext. Theobald was driven out, and Spoleto taken over by the king possibly to be conferred on his own son Guido. Did Berengar demand the imperial crown? In any case King Adalbert ravaged Roman territory, and John XII was in such straits as to appeal for German intervention, thus strangely shewing how the ancient policy of the Popes could recur in the unclerical son of Alberic.

It was in the summer of 960 that the Pope's envoys, the Cardinal-deacon John and the *scriniarius* Azo, reached Otto the Great in Saxony. The Pope's prayer for help was seconded by the Lombard exiles and by the messages of numerous magnates. Otto was now unembarrassed in other directions, and could resume his old schemes with the knowledge that he would have at last allies and support south of the Apennines. He was not ready to move, however, till August 961, when he crossed the Brenner Pass in force. Adalbert may have attempted to gather troops to bar the defiles north of Verona, but the universal defection of counts and bishops made resistance impossible, and the German king entered Pavia, whence Berengar had fled after spitefully burning the royal palace. Otto and the infant son Otto II whom he had left in Germany were at once acknowledged as co-regent kings of Italy without further ceremony. All their deserted rivals could do was to hold out in strong castles on the spurs of the Alps and in the Apennines where one magnate at least, Marquess Hubert of Tuscany, remained true to them. Otto was able to disregard his enemies while he proceeded through Ravenna, thus avoiding the Tuscan route, to receive the promised imperial crown. On 31 January 962 he encamped on Monte Mario outside Rome, and according to custom certain of his vassals took on his behalf an oath to respect the Pope's rights. The custom was old, but the terms of the oath were new[1], for John XII wished for an ally, not a suzerain, and the German king promised not to hold *placita* or intervene in Rome without the Pope's assent, to restore such alienated papal lands as he should become master of, and to bind whomever he should appoint to rule the *Regnum Italicum* to be the Pope's protector. The Romans disliked a foreigner, and Otto bought his way by elusive promises and fallacious expectations. On 2 February he entered the Leonine city and was crowned with Adelaide in St Peter's by the Pope. A Roman Emperor of the West, successor of Charlemagne, once more existed. It was of evil omen that Otto's sword-bearer stood on guard against his assassination while the sacring was enacted.

On their side Pope John and the Romans swore fealty to the Emperor with an express promise not to aid or receive Berengar and Adalbert. They found that Otto considered the situation changed by his new dignity. It is true that the privilege he granted to the Papacy on 13 February was even more generous than the old Carolingian donations in the matter of territory—for it added a large strip of Spoletan land to Rome and its duchy, the Exarchate, the Pentapolis, the Tuscan territory, the Sabina and the southern patrimonies, not to mention the vaguer supposed donation of 774 which was now confirmed without any clear idea of its meaning. But the pact of 824 was also expressly revived, by which the election of the Pope was submitted to imperial confirmation, and the Emperor's suzerainty in the papal lands was reserved and exercised in Rome itself by his *missus*. The scheme of setting up a vassal king of Italy, if ever really entertained, was abandoned. Although the terms of Otto's oath were not precisely infringed, the change in the spirit of the new treaty was manifest—Pope John had become a subject[2].

There was still Berengar II to conquer, and the Emperor returned to Pavia, driving Hubert of Tuscany into exile on the way. Berengar was holding out in the impregnable castle of S. Leo in the Apennines, queen Willa and her sons in strongholds near the lakes in the north. Willa was now compelled to surrender on terms which allowed her to rejoin her husband: their sons were pressed hard, and Adalbert made his escape to the Saracens of Fraxinetum and Corsica. There he entered into re-

---

[1] Unless the lost charter of Charles the Bald to John VIII really formed a precedent. Cf. *Libellus de imperatoria potestate in urbe Roma* (*M. G. H. Script.* III., p. 722).

[2] This account is based on the view that the *Privilegium Ottonianum* is substantially the text of the privilege granted by Otto to John XII, the existing document being a copy made for the next Pope, Leo VIII.

lations with Pope John who was heartily weary of his new subordination. Meantime Otto was secure in the north, his partisans were placed in power, Liudprand was Bishop of Cremona, Adalbert-Atto Count of Modena and Reggio, Otto's nephew Henry of Bavaria in firm possession of the march of Verona. So the news of the Pope's dubious loyalty only urged the Emperor to finish with Berengar by blockading him in S. Leo in May 963, while he still negotiated with John. The Pope on his side had grounds of complaint, for the Exarchate had not been restored to the Apostolic See on the ground that Berengar must first be conquered. On the other hand Otto had documentary proof that John was trying to rouse the Hungarians against him, and when he heard that Adalbert had been welcomed by John at Civitavecchia he seems to have decided to take the extreme measure of deposing his quondam ally. It was a hazardous course, for in the general belief the Pope could be brought to no man's judgment, and the Romans, even those not of Alberic's faction, resented any diminution of their autonomy. But Otto knew that John XII's scandalous life and government had made men inclined to admit even a Pope's deposition, and were driving his Roman opponents even to alliance with the foreign Emperor. Accordingly in October Otto left a blockading force at S. Leo and marched on Rome, where his partisans rose. John XII and Adalbert fled to Tivoli laden with much church-treasure, and the Romans surrendered. They gave hostages and swore never to elect a Pope save by the choice of Otto and his son. The engagement was novel, going far beyond the Carolingian right to confirm an election and receive the Pope's fealty, but Alberic had already exercised the same power and Otto's imperial crown was unsafe without it. Canonical form was as nearly as possible observed in John's deposition. A synod, in which the Pope's central Italian suffragans predominated, was presided over by the Emperor and attended by the Roman clergy and nobles; John was accused of gross misconduct and was summoned by Emperor and synod to clear himself in person. A brief letter in reply merely threatened with excommunication and suspension any bishops who should elect a new Pope. The synod sent a second summons retorting the threat and criticizing the illiteracy of John whose Latin smacked of the vernacular, but John was not to be found by the messengers. It was clear that the three canonical summonses could not be delivered to the culprit, and Otto now came forward in his own person and denounced John for his breach of fealty to himself. Thereupon on 4 December Emperor and synod declared John deposed and elected the *protoscriniarius*, a layman, Pope as Leo VIII.

Otto was in the full tide of success. Just after Christmas S. Leo at last surrendered and Berengar II and his wife were sent captive to Bamberg where they both died in 966. So Otto confidently dismissed much of his army. But John XII was stronger than he seemed, for his uncanonical deposition and a layman's uncanonical election had roused

qualms among a section of the churchmen, and the Romans were fretting
under their subjugation. A sudden rising failed before the swords of
Otto's tried warriors; yet, when Otto went eastwards to take possession
of the Spoletan duchy, John XII had only to appear before Rome with
troops for the gates to be opened. Pope Leo just escaped with his life,
and John was reinstated. After mutilating his former envoys to Otto,
John and Azo, presumably on a charge of forgery, a synod of the nearest
bishops in February 964 annulled Otto's synod in which most of them
had participated and declared Leo an intruder. Otto, whose *missus* had
been ill-treated, naturally refused to change his policy. While his army
was collecting, however, John XII died on 14 May of paralysis, and the
Romans made a bid for independence by electing a learned and virtuous
Pope, Benedict V. It was a vain manoeuvre. Otto starved out the city,
mutilating all who tried to pass his blockading lines. On 23 June the
surrender was made, and Leo VIII reinstated. Benedict was deposed
and sent to a saintly exile at Hamburg. By now at any rate it was
agreed that Otto's grants to the Popes were only for show, for of all the
lands bestowed by his charter the duchy of Rome and the Sabina alone
were left to the Papacy.

In this way Otto the Great brought into existence the Romano-
Germanic Empire of the West, or, to give it its later and convenient
name, the Holy Roman Empire, compounded by a union of the German
kingdom with the *Regnum Italicum* and with the dignity of Roman
Emperor. It was intended and supposed to be a revival of the Empire
of Charlemagne which had broken up on the deposition of Charles the
Fat, although its title had remained until the fall of Berengar I to express
a protectorate of the Papacy. It was also a reassertion of that claim to
pre-eminence in Western Europe which had been made by Otto's predecessor Arnulf as chief of the Carolingian house. Arnulf's Empire,
indeed, furnishes the transitional form between that of Otto and that of
Charlemagne, for Otto's title implied less than Charlemagne's had.
Otto was considered the lay chief of Western Christendom, its defender
from heathen and barbarians, the supreme maintainer of justice and
peace; but, whereas Charlemagne was ruler of church and state, Otto's
power over the church was protective in its character. The Pope was
unquestioned spiritual chief of Christendom; Otto was at the same time
his suzerain with regard to the papal lands, and his subject as a
member of the Church. The arrangement was only workable because
the Papacy was weak. In secular matters Otto's Empire lacked the
universality of Charlemagne's. Not only were France and Christian
Spain outside its frontiers, but within it the nascent force of nationality
was beginning to make itself felt. The German monarch was a foreigner
in subject Italy, disguised as the fact might be by the absence of national
feeling among the Italian magnates. "He had with him peoples and
tribes whose tongues the people did not know." This meant constant

disaffection, constant suppression. The popular hatred burnt most fiercely at Rome and found utterance in a Roman monk[1]: "Woe to thee, Rome, that thou art crushed and trodden down by so many peoples; who hast been seized by a Saxon king, and thy folk slaughtered and thy strength reduced to naught!"

In the details of government, also, Otto had not the control which Charlemagne exercised. Although the decline of the royal power must not be overrated, especially in Germany, even there feudalism, seignorial independence and state disorganisation, had made great strides. In Italy, where he was too often an absentee, the royal demesne was depleted and the lay vassals were out of hand. Otto met this difficulty by a clever balancing of the two groups by whom he had been called in, the great secular magnates and the bishops. Of these, the first were the Marquesses, a title given in Italy to the ruler of several counties. Towards them Otto was conciliatory; even Hubert in the end was restored to Tuscany, and the Lombards, some four or five in number, were the Emperor's faithful vassals. They were survivors in the struggle for existence among the counts which had raged in the dissolution of the Carolingian order. Under the pressure of civil war, of Hungarian and Saracen ravage, old dynasts had vanished, new had come and had either vanished too, or had remained weakened. In their place or by their side ruled the bishops in the Lombard plain. Since 876 they had been permanent royal *missi* in their dioceses, and thus had at least in name supervision over the counts. Like other magnates the bishops during the years of anarchy had increased their "immunity" inside their domains, by increase of exemptions and jurisdictions and by grants of the profitable royal rights of market and toll and the like, while those domains also grew through the piety or competitive bribery of the kings and nobles. Not least among the sources of the bishops' power was their influence over their cities, inherited from Roman times. In anarchy and disaster they stepped into the breach at the head of their fellow-citizens, whatever civic feeling existed gathered round them, and fragment by fragment they were acquiring in their cathedral cities the "public functions" whether of count or king. In its completed form this piecemeal process resulted in the city and a radius of land round it being excised from its county and removed from the count's jurisdiction. Thus Bergamo, Parma, Cremona, Modena, Reggio and Trieste were at Otto's accession under the rule of their bishops. Otto came as the ally of the bishops and deliverer of the Church. He exercised whether by pressure on the electors or by mere nomination the appointment to vacant sees and great abbeys, and thus gained non-hereditary vassals of his own choice who were the safest supporters of his monarchy. He favoured of set policy these instruments of his power as counter-weights to the feudal magnates. Fresh cities, Asti, Novara, and Penne

[1] Benedict. S. Andreae *Chron.* c. 39.

in the Abruzzi, were wholly given over to their bishops, and the immunities on episcopal lands steadily grew, so that they too were in process of being excised from the counties in which they lay. The work was slowly done by Otto and his successors both in Italy and Germany, but there was no countering tendency. The functions granted were either those of the hereditary counts or those which the kings had been unable to perform. By transference of these to the churchmen Otto and his heirs recovered control of much local government by seeming to give it away, and secured faithful, powerful adherents selected for capacity. Their monarchy came to rest, especially in Italy, on their control of the Church; all the more essential to them therefore became the subjection or the firm alliance of the Papacy.

Scarcely had Otto left Italy when the death of his nominee, Pope Leo VIII, early in 965 endangered his new Empire. The Romans with a show of duty sent an embassy to beg for the exile Benedict as Pope, and Adalbert appeared in Lombardy to raise a revolt. Duke Burchard of Swabia, indeed, defeated Adalbert, and the Romans elected the Bishop of Narni as Pope John XIII at the Emperor's command, but, though John was of Alberic's kindred, the mere fact that he represented German domination enabled rival nobles to raise the populace and drive him into exile. He was not restored till in 966 the news of Otto's descent into Italy with an army provoked a reaction. Punishment was dealt out to the rebels, severer for the Roman enemies of the Pope than for the Lombard rebels against Otto. John XIII's exile seems to have occasioned fresh schemes of the Emperor. Paldolf I Ironhead of Capua-Benevento, with whom the Pope had found an asylum, appeared in Rome in January 967 and was there invested by Otto with the march of Spoleto, at the same time becoming Otto's vassal for his native principality. Otto thus created a central Italian vassal of the first rank, and enlarged his Empire. One motive, no doubt, was the wish to give peace and security to the Spoletan march; but the main purpose was clearly to begin the annexation of South Italy to the *Regnum Italicum*. This design, which was in pursuance of old Carolingian claims, was bound to find resistance in the Eastern Empire. The Byzantines looked on Otto's imperial title as a barbaric impertinence; they considered Capua-Benevento as part of the Longobardic theme; and they were determined to maintain their dominion in Italy.

The Eastern Roman Emperors were always handicapped in their dealings in Italy; their province there was too important to be let go, too remote to be the object of their chief energies. The fall of King Hugh had been followed by outbreaks in Apulia, and at the same time the Saracen raids became a grave danger when the Fāṭimite Caliph Manṣūr once again recovered the revolted colony of Sicily in 947. Calabria was overrun by his troops; even Naples was besieged; and, although in 956 the patrician Marianus Argyrus restored Byzantine authority over subjects and vassals, the peace which suspended, rather than closed, the Saracen war was no more conclusive than the fighting. When a celebrated general Nicephorus Phocas became Emperor in 963 his vigorous effort to succour the last semi-autonomous Greeks of Sicily ended in disaster, and an ignominious peace. Now he found himself on the defensive against the aggression of the new Romano-Germanic Empire and the Latin West. John XIII was trying to revive the decadent Latin Church in south Italy by carving out new archbishoprics for Capua and Benevento from his own Roman province; Otto the Great was acquiring Capua-Benevento as a vassal state. At first it seemed as if an arrangement were possible, for Otto asked for a Byzantine bride, Theophano, daughter of Romanus II, for his son Otto II, whom at Christmas 967 he had caused the Pope to crown co-regent Emperor; and his Venetian envoy promised that Otto would respect the Byzantine dominions in Italy. But in 968 the German monarch made a surprise attack on Apulia and, only after failing to take Bari, did he send Liudprand of Cremona to Constantinople to conclude the marriage-treaty. Otto must have thought it easier to fix the frontier with the territory he claimed already in his possession. The natural effect on the rude and soldierly Nicephorus was to make him badger Liudprand and prepare an expedition. The war was indecisive. The exiled King Adalbert, Nicephorus's Italian ally, could do nothing and eventually fled to French Burgundy where in 975 he died, while his brother Conrad submitted to Otto and received the march of Ivrea. Otto on his side when he warred in person could take no Apulian town and Paldolf Ironhead was captured by the Greeks, who yet were soon defeated again. It was the murder of Nicephorus in December 969 which brought a solution. The new Byzantine Emperor, John Tzimisces, had his hands full in the East; Otto saw the design of conquering Greek Italy was hopeless. By the intervention of Paldolf, released for the purpose, they came to terms, and in April 972 Theophano was married at Rome to Otto II. Events make it clear that Otto kept the suzerainty of Capua-Benevento and abandoned further schemes. Paldolf Ironhead's wide central Italian dominion after all formed a convenient buffer-state for both Empires, no matter to which he was a vassal.

Otto the Great did not long survive the settlement with Eastern Rome, as he died in Thuringia on 7 May 973. His character belongs to German history, but his work affected all Europe. He had created the Holy Roman Empire and in so doing had revived the conception of Charlemagne which moulded the thought and the development of Western Europe. The union of Germany and north Italy was his doing and the fate of both for centuries derives from the bias he gave their history. So, too, in immediate results he closes one era and begins another, for the times of anarchy and moral collapse following the wreck of Charlemagne's Empire come to an end, and a period of revival in government, in commerce and in civilisation is ushered in by the comparative peace he gave. The problem of defence against the barbarian invader, which had baffled the fleeting Italian kings and had contributed to their ruin, was solved. Otto himself crushed the Hungarian hordes for good and all: it was fitting that in his reign the Saracens of Fraxinetum also, who so long preyed on the routes between Italy and France, should be abolished. The impulse to this deliverance was given by a crowning outrage. St Maiolus, Abbot of Cluny, revered throughout the West, was captured in July 972 while crossing the Great St Bernard Pass with a numerous caravan of fellow travellers. The Cluniac monks at once raised the enormous ransom demanded by the Saracens, but the indignation roused by the event and perhaps a hope of so great a booty at length moved the great barons on either side of the Alps to act in concert. The Saracens who had seized St Maiolus were cut off and destroyed, and a federation of nobles led by the counts of Provence and Ardoin of Turin closed in on Fraxinetum itself. The Saracen colony was extirpated. Once more the Alpine passes were free to travellers, save for exactions by the nobles and occasional brigandage[1].

The *Regnum Italicum* could now rest under the shadow of the strong monarchy, untroubled save by the violence of the nobles and the unappeased strife of Roman factions. Otto the Great had nominated in 973 Benedict VI to succeed to the Papacy, but a relative of John XIII and of Alberic, Crescentius, son of a Theodora, thrust in a usurper, the deacon Franco, as Boniface VII in 974. Yet a reaction, perhaps provoked by the true Pope's murder, soon came, and the imperial *missus*, Count Sico, was able to instal the Bishop of Sutri as Benedict VII, although Franco contrived to escape to Constantinople with a quantity of church-treasure. The revolution had not even required a German army, much less an imperial campaign.

Not till December 980 did Otto II (the Red) find leisure or occasion to proceed to Italy. He came to be reconciled with his mother Adelaide, and perhaps to give her some voice in affairs. The young Emperor, then aged twenty-five, was not eminently gifted with a ruler's wisdom; but he was ambitious and energetic, and his ambitions now were directed to that conquest of the south which his father had abandoned. There was much that was tempting in the situation of Byzantine Italy, much that seemed to call for intervention. In answer to the proceedings of Otto the Great an attempt had been made by the Byzantines to unify the administration by transmuting the *strategos* of Longobardia into the *catapan* or viceroy of Italy with a superior authority over the *strategos* of Calabria. This new system was soon put to hard proof. In 969 the Fātimite caliphs conquered Egypt, and thus became hostile neighbours to the East Romans in Syria. War broke out, and spread to the western provinces of both powers. Once more Calabria was ravaged by the

---

[1] The county of Aosta appears to have become again a part of Jurane Burgundy, as a result of this war.

Muslims under the Sicilian emir Abu'l-Ḳāsim in 976 and Apulia suffered in the next year. The only relief given was due to the local payment of blackmail, for the Byzantines, who had begun the war in spirited fashion by the momentary capture of Messina, were paralysed by the campaigns in Syria, by the civil wars which followed Tzimisces' death, and by the disaffection of the Apulians.

Otto the Red succumbed to the temptation. The Saracen danger under Abu'l-Ḳāsim grew ever more menacing and might affect his own dominions. Civil war in the East and disaffection in Italy made the Byzantines weak. He might at one and the same time repel the Muslims and bring the *Regnum Italicum* to its natural limits. In September 981 he had reached Lucera on the Apulian frontier when he was recalled to secure his rear. Paldolf Ironhead had soon extended his central State. When Prince Gisulf of Salerno was dethroned in 973 by a complot of rebellious nobles and his jealous neighbours of Amalfi and Naples, it was Paldolf who overthrew the usurper Landolf, his own kinsman, and restored the old, childless prince as his client. In 977 he succeeded as prince in Salerno. On Ironhead's death, however, in March 981 his great dominion dissolved. One son, Landolf IV, inherited Capua-Benevento, and another, Paldolf, ruled Salerno. Now revolutions broke out. The Beneventans were restive under Capuan rule, and declared Ironhead's nephew Paldolf II their prince while Landolf IV retained Capua: the Salernitans drove out their Paldolf, and introduced the Byzantine ally, Duke Manso III of Amalfi. Otto accepted the separation of Capua and Benevento, but he besieged Salerno, and obtained its submission at the price of recognising Manso. He seemed to have secured a new vassal; he had lost the benefit of surprise and the halo of irresistible success. When with large reinforcements from Germany he marched through Apulia in 982, the towns did not join him, although Bari rebelled on its own account[1], and Taranto surrendered after a long siege. There he heard of the coming of the Saracen foe from whom he claimed to deliver his intended conquest.

Abu'l-Ḳāsim had proclaimed a Holy War and crossed to Calabria. Otto advanced to meet him. At Rossano he left the Empress Theophano and, moving south, captured the Saracens' advance guard in an unnamed town[2]. He met the main body on the east coast, perhaps near Stilo[3]. Headlong courage and no generalship marked his conduct of the battle, for he charged and broke the Saracen centre, without perceiving their reserves amid the hills on his flank. Abu'l-Ḳāsim had been killed, but meanwhile the exhausted Germans were attacked by the fresh troops on their flank and overwhelmed. Some four thousand were slain including

---

[1] It was recaptured by the Byzantines June 983; *Lupus Protospath.* is a year too early in his dates here.

[2] Perhaps Cotrone, see Gay, *L'Italie méridionale et l'Empire byzantin*, p. 337.

[3] Or else the Capo delle Colonne.

the flower of the German nobles; many were made prisoners; the Emperor himself only eluded capture by swimming to a Byzantine vessel, from which in turn he had to escape by leaping overboard when it brought him near Rossano.

With the remnants of his army Otto beat a retreat to Salerno and Rome. As the news spread over the Empire his prestige waned, and a mutinous spirit arose in Italy which was, however, kept in check by the steady adherence of Marquesses and Bishops to the German monarchy. Otto did his best to re-establish his position. In May 983 he held a German Diet at Verona, and there obtained the election as King of Germany of his infant son Otto, whom he thereupon sent north to be crowned. At the same time he made an effort to bring the independent sea-power of Venice to subjection. Venice had prospered exceedingly during the century. Exempt from Hungarian ravage, she had contrived to hold the piracy of the distant Saracens and of the Slavs of Dalmatia in check. She had shaken off Byzantine suzerainty and maintained a privileged intercourse with the *Regnum Italicum*. She had already become the chief intermediary between Constantinople and the West; her wealth, derived partly from her questionable exports of iron, wood and slaves to the Saracens, was growing rapidly. Even when she was obliged to surrender the extra-territoriality of her citizens within the Western Empire to Otto the Great, she obtained in return the perpetuity of her treaty with him. But she had her special dangers. One was the effort of the Doges to erect an hereditary monarchy, like that of Amalfi. The other, caused largely by this effort, was the rise of two embittered factions among the mercantile nobles who held the chief influence in the State. These troubles affected her relations with Otto II, for the aspiring Doge Pietro Candiano IV who had been murdered in 976 had married Gualdrada of Tuscany, niece of the Empress Adelaide. The efforts of Doge Tribuno Menio did indeed result in a hollow reconciliation at Verona in June 983. Otto II restored Venice her privileges with the airs of a suzerain, while Venice tacitly maintained her independence. Hardly was the bargain struck, however, before Otto broke it. The civil discord of Venice had ended in the bitter hatred of the rival families of Caloprini and Morosini. Now Stephen Caloprini fled to Verona and offered to be the Emperor's genuine vassal if restored to Venice as Doge. Otto characteristically seized the chance of conquest. Venice was strictly blockaded by land, and might have been forced to yield had not the Emperor, enfeebled by a foreign climate, died of an over-dose of medicine (four drachms of aloes) on 7 December 983.

Otto had been preparing for new aggression towards the south, where Transemund, the new Marquess of Spoleto, and Aloara of Capua, Paldolf Ironhead's widow, might be relied on. His impatient policy had just been shewn in the promotion of a foreign Pope to succeed Benedict VII, for John XIV had been Peter, Bishop of Pavia and Arch-chancellor of

Italy. The restive Romans, still mindful of the old prohibition of translations, rose against the Lombard Pope at Easter 984. Their leader was that Franco, now once more Boniface VII, who had been let loose with his treasure by the incensed Byzantines. He disgraced himself once more by causing the death of his imprisoned rival, and made himself so hated in his brief and tyrannous pontificate that on his death in 985 the mob outraged his corpse through the streets. He had really bought the Papacy from those who could sell it, the faction led by the house of the Crescentii. By them Alberic's rule of Rome was revived in the person of the "patrician" Crescentius II, son of Crescentius de Theodora. There was, however, a difference; while preserving his autonomous power, Crescentius II avoided a breach with the Empire.

He could take this anomalous position all the more easily because the Empire and the *Regnum Italicum* were in some sort vacant. The child Otto III of Germany was acknowledged as rightful heir, but not as sovereign, in Italy, where the interregnum was filled by admitting the claim of the two crowned Augustas, Theophano and Adelaide, to act for the future Emperor, this constitutional subtlety being made acceptable by the loyalty of Marquesses and Bishops to the German connexion. Otto II's aggressions against Venice and the Byzantines were promptly abandoned, and the peace of the Empire, tempered by the never wholly quiescent local broils, continued its beneficent work. Adelaide was soon thrust aside by Theophano who, Greek though she was, troubled with unruly German magnates and hampered by Slav revolt beyond the Elbe, yet contrived to rule. In 989 she came to Rome, partly to reaffirm the Empire, partly perhaps in rivalry with Adelaide. Crescentius II evidently came to terms, which preserved his patriciate, and she exercised without hindrance all the functions of sovereignty, even being styled Emperor by her puzzled chancery unused to a female reign. It was not, however, all by merit of the adroit and firm-willed lady, for, when a year after her return to Germany she died in June 991, and Adelaide took her place, the fabric of the Empire continued unshaken. The idea of the Ottonian monarchy had captivated men's imagination, the benefits it conferred on lands so recently wretched were indisputable, and the Italian magnates knew their own interests well enough to be persistently loyal.

At the head of the magnates stood Hugh of Tuscany, who for some years had ruled Spoleto as well, thus once more forming a mid-Italian buffer-fief, like that of his father Hubert, or of Paldolf Ironhead. It was Hugh who, when a revolution broke out at Capua on Aloara's death, set up a second son of Paldolf Ironhead's, Laidulf, as prince, and maintained the suzerainty of the Western Empire. At Rome, however, Crescentius II exercised unchallenged sway. Pope John XV had not even the support of the stricter clergy against his lay oppressor, for he himself had a bad name for avarice and nepotism. But intervention by the German monarch became certain. Otto III was now fifteen and of age; his advisers were anxious to put an end to the anomalous formal vacancy of the Empire; and in response to Pope John's invitation the king crossed the Brenner Pass with an army in February 996. No one resisted him, although the inevitable riot between Germans and Italians took place at Verona. At Pavia, where he received the fealty of the magnates, he heard of John XV's death; at the next stage, Ravenna, he was met by a Roman embassy, which submissively requested him to name a new Pope. His choice was as bold as possible; Otto II had only promoted a Lombard; Otto III selected his own cousin Bruno of Carinthia, a youth of twenty-four, who styled himself Gregory V. Thus for the first time a German ascended the papal throne. It must have been gall and wormwood to the Romans, but they made no resistance. On 21 May Otto III was crowned Emperor by his nominee.

Neither Pope nor Emperor was disposed to allow the patriciate to continue. Crescentius II was tried for his offences against John XV, condemned to exile, and then pardoned at the Pope's request. The victory had been so easy that Otto speedily left Italy. Gregory, however, was already in difficulties. He was a rash young man, who was also open to bribes, and the Romans hated their German Pope. In September he escaped from their hands, and Crescentius resumed power. Gregory, safe in Pavia, might excommunicate the usurper and act as the admitted head of the Church. Crescentius did not hesitate to set up an Anti-Pope. His choice was cunning, if hopeless. Otto III, following the steps of his predecessors, had sent to Constantinople to demand the hand of a Greek princess. One envoy died on the mission; the other, John Philagathus, Archbishop of Piacenza, had recently returned with a Byzantine embassy to continue negotiations. This prelate was a Greek of Calabria, who had been the trusted adviser of Theophano and had obtained the independence of his see from Ravenna owing to her influence. Being the tutor and godfather of the Emperor, he might seem a *persona grata* to him. Perhaps he shared Theophano's policy of alliance with the Roman patrician. In any case he accepted Crescentius's offer. But he was everywhere unpopular, a foreigner at Rome, an ingrate further north, and Otto III was resolved. Late in 997 the Emperor returned to Italy with imposing forces. By the usual route of Ravenna he reached Rome with Pope Gregory in February 998. There was no real resistance. John XVI fled to the Campagna to be captured, blinded and mutilated by his pursuers and then made a public spectacle by the revengeful Pope. Crescentius, who held out in the castle of Sant' Angelo, the ancient tomb of Hadrian, soon was taken and executed. Otto and Gregory hoped thus to crush the indomitable independence of the Romans. They only added an injured hero to the traditions of medieval Rome, for Crescentius was widely believed, possibly with truth, to have surrendered upon assurances of safety.

Otto was still in Italy, alternately employed in affairs of Church and

State, and in the pilgrimage and penance dear to his unbalanced character, when Pope Gregory died in February 999. True to his imperial policy, the Emperor selected another non-Roman, Gerbert of Aurillac, the first French, as Gregory had been the first German Pope. Gerbert, now Sylvester II, was the most learned man of his age, so learned that legend made him a magician. Bred in the Aquitanian abbey of Aurillac, he knew both Spain and Italy, but the best of his life had been spent at the metropolitan city of Rheims. There he was renowned as a teacher and had taken eager part in the events which led to the substitution of Hugh Capet for the Carolingian dynasty of France. His reward had been his elevation to the see of Rheims, but this being consequent on the deposition of his predecessor had brought him into collision with the Papacy, and in 997 he gave up the attempt to maintain himself. He had, however, a sure refuge. For long he had stood in close relations to the Saxon Emperors. Known to Otto the Great, he had been given the famous abbey of Bobbio in 982 by Otto II, although the indiscreet zeal he displayed led to his retreat to Rheims again on his patron's death. None the less he had worked in France in the interests of Otto III in the troublous times of the latter's infancy, and as his hold on Rheims grew weaker he had attached himself in 995 to Otto's court. There he speedily became the favoured tutor of the boy Emperor, partly sharing, partly humouring and partly inspiring the visionary schemes of his pupil. In 998 he became again an archbishop, this time of Ravenna, whence he was called to fill the papal chair.

Sylvester II was far too practical a statesman to share in all the dreams of Otto, yet even he seems to have thought of a renovated Roman Empire, very different from the workaday creation of Otto the Great, of an Empire as wide as Charlemagne's which should be truly ecumenic, and no longer an appendage to the German monarchy. Otto's schemes were far stranger, the offspring of his wayward and perfervid nature. Half Greek, half Saxon in birth and training, bred by Theophano and Philagathus and under northern prelates and nobles as well, he not only blended the traditions of Charlemagne's lay theocracy with those of the ancient Roman Empire seen through a long Byzantine perspective, but he also oscillated between the ambitious energy of an aspiring monarch and the ascetic renunciation of a fervent monk. The contradiction, not unexampled at the time, was glaring in an unripe boy, whose head was turned by his dignity and his power. He had his ascetic mentors who fired his enthusiasms, St Adalbert of Prague, St Romuald of Ravenna, St Nilus of Calabria. As the fit seized him he went on pilgrimage or withdrew for austerities to hermitage or monastery. This visionary ruler lacked neither ability nor a policy, however fantastic his aims might be. He believed most fully in his theocracy. He was the ruler of Church and State. The Popes were his lieutenants in ecclesiastical matters. As time went on he emphasised his position by strange titles;

CH. VII.

he was "servant of Jesus Christ," "servant of the Apostles," in rivalry with the *servus servorum Dei* of the Popes. Content with the practical support they received from him in ruling both the Church and Rome, Gregory V tolerated the beginnings of this and Sylvester II submitted at a price to its full development. In a strange, scolding, argumentative diploma Otto III denounced the Donation of Constantine and that of Charles the Bald, the one as a forgery, the other as invalid, and proceeded to grant the Pope eight counties of the Pentapolis hitherto ruled by Hugh of Tuscany. It was a considerable gift, somewhat modified by the fact that Otto intended to make Rome itself his chief capital, and treated the Pope as his vassal. He perhaps saw the revival of the Lombard nobles; he was carried away by the ancient splendours of the Empire, and, proud of his Greek extraction, he hoped to recall the past by a gaudy imitation of its outer forms. Those forms he saw in Byzantium, the continuously Roman. Titles and ceremonies were rudely borrowed. His dignitaries became *logothetes*, *protospathars* and the like: once and again their names were written in the Greek alphabet as an evidence of culture. To gain centralisation and emphasise unity the German and Italian chanceries were fused together, to the muddling of their formal and perhaps of their practical business. Semi-barbarism had a puerile side in the court the German Augustus held at Rome in his palace on the Aventine, and well might the loyal German nobles look askance at the freaks of the Emperor. "He would not see delightful Germany, the land of his birth, so great a love possessed him of dwelling in Italy."

In January 1000 Otto paid his last visit to Germany, whither the deaths of two great ladies, his aunt Abbess Matilda and the aged Empress Adelaide, who had guided the German Government, called him. In July he returned to Italy, for a storm which had long been brewing had burst. It had its principal origin in the prosperity which the Ottonian peace had brought to North Italy. The population had increased, waste and forest were brought under cultivation, trade thrived in the cities. True to Italian tradition the unrest appeared in two separate groups of persons, among the country-side nobles, and among the citizens, but, since the individuals who made up these two groups were largely identical, it was as yet seldom that the effects of their discontents were sharply separated. Under the great vassals of the country-side, the bishops, abbots, marquesses and counts, were ranked the now numerous greater and lesser vavassors, or *capitanei*[1] and *secundi milites*,

---

[1] The *secundi milites* were generally after-vassals without jurisdiction. The *capitanei* included the smaller tenants-in-chief and the greater vavassors. They were possessed of jurisdiction; the same noble might easily hold both of the crown and of another tenant-in-chief. Cf. Schupfer, F., *La società milanese all' epoca del risorgimento del comune* (*Archivio giuridico*, III.), pp. 259–60, 263–4, and Mayer, E., *Italienische Verfassungsgeschichte*, I. pp. 447, 450–1.

who were distinguished not so much by their position in the feudal chain as by the extent of their lands and privileges, but who in general were vassals of the magnates, not of the Emperor. The continued predominance of city-life in Italy, and the terrors of the recent barbarian ravages, had turned large numbers of the *capitanei* and *secundi milites* into inhabitants, either partially or solely, of the cities, where they formed the most powerful class of citizens. Under them were the traders who led the non-noble city-population. All three classes, *capitanei, secundi milites* and plebeians tended to be at odds with one another; there were also signs of a resentment at the bishops' rule which had once been welcomed. Berengar II, at enmity with the bishops, had shewn signs of courting the townsmen when he granted privileges to the men of Genoa collectively; the Milanese, in Otto III's minority, had waged war on their archbishop Landulf II and the great family to which he belonged; the Cremonese obtained from Otto III a diploma which infringed their bishop's fiscal rights and was soon quashed on that account. The movement was contrary to the imperial policy by which the bishops, sometimes of German extraction, were the Emperor's best agents and counter-weights to the restless nobles. Fresh towns, Lodi, Acqui, Piacenza, and Tortona, had been placed completely under episcopal rule; the whole province of Ravenna was made subject to its archbishop's authority by Otto III; lesser privileges in town and country had been continually given piecemeal to the prelates. Yet in the country-side the expedient was losing its value. Prelates in difficulties, prelates of the local noble families, were steadily granting church land by the leases known as *libellariae* to the nobles, thereby impoverishing their churches and strengthening the noble class, and the consequent feudal disorder was only increased by the growing divergence in interest between the magnates, the *capitanei,* and the *secundi milites.* The vast and increasing church estates were being consumed by nominal leases and over-enfeoffment.

Disorder from this cause was already marked under Otto II; Pope Sylvester, as Abbot of Bobbio, had vainly striven to check the system in his abbey; it now led to civil war. Ardoin, Marquess of Ivrea, was probably a relative of Berengar II, but his sympathies lay with the lesser nobles. He and they had profited by spendthrift episcopal grants, and came to bitter feud with Bishop Peter of Vercelli, possibly because he endeavoured to recall them[1]. In 997 they murdered the bishop and burnt the cathedral. Peter's fellow-bishops were up in arms against Ardoin, and Otto III took stringent action. In 998 he enacted that no church *libellaria* should outlast the grantor's life. In 999, in concert with the

[1] This is conjecture. Peter's long captivity among the Saracens after the battle of Stilo (see *supra,* p. 169) must have facilitated usurpations, and Ingo, Peter's predecessor, had certainly dilapidated his see, but Ardoin's immediate grievance may have been owing to his claims on the *curtis* of Caresana, given by Empress Adelaide to the Canons of Vercelli.

Pope, he confiscated Ardoin's lands and condemned him to a life of penitent wandering. At the same time he appointed a stout-hearted German, Leo, to the see of Vercelli, and granted him the counties of Vercelli and Santhià. It was the first grant of entire counties to a bishopric in Lombardy, although parallel to the powers conferred on the see of Ravenna. But Ardoin resisted in his castles, and next year, supported by his accomplices, seems even to have taken the title of king. Otto returned, but was content to drive Ardoin back and to entrust his uprooting to the local magnates. The embers of the revolt against the Romano-Germanic Empire were left to glow. Otto's wishes at this time seem to have turned to the reassertion of the claims of the Holy Roman Empire in the south. Since Abu'l-Ḳāsim's death in his victory over Otto II, the Saracen raids, although they inflicted misery on Calabria and South Apulia, had not been in sufficient force to endanger the Byzantine rule. The catapan Calocyrus Delphinas in 983–4 had subdued the Apulian rebels; nor did Otto III shew any disposition to intervene. But the petty frontier states were a different matter. In 983 the Salernitans had driven out Manso of Amalfi, and under their new prince John II, a Lombard from Spoleto, remained henceforth neutral and disregarded. Their neighbours, however, Capua, Benevento, Naples and Gaeta, were more important for Otto. After a romantic pilgrimage to the famous shrine of Monte Gargano, he sent in 999 the Capuan Ademar, new-made Marquess of Spoleto, to Capua, where Laidulf was deposed and Ademar made prince. At the same time Naples was seized, its Duke John taken captive, and the Duke of Gaeta was bribed into vassalage. These successes, which once more effectively enlarged the Empire, did not last, for in 1000 the Capuans drove out Ademar, substituting Landolf V of the old dynasty, and John of Naples recovered his state and independence. A short campaign of Otto himself next year against Benevento gained at most a formal submission from the Lombard princes. The fact was that the Emperors could never devote enough energy or men to the subjugation of the south, divergent as it was in soil, in organisation, and in habits of life from the Frank-ruled, feudalised and more fertile north.

At the time, indeed, Otto's throne was rocking under him. He had offended the Romans by sparing revolted Tivoli, for which too independent neighbour they nourished a passionate hatred; nor were their desires for their old autonomy and dislike of the Saxon stranger diminished by his imperial masquerade. In February 1001 they broke into revolt and blockaded Otto in his palace on the Aventine, at the same time closing the gates against his troops who were encamped outside the walls under his cousin, Duke Henry of Bavaria and Hugh of Tuscany. After three days Otto prepared a desperate sortie, but at the same time Hugh and Henry entered by treaty with the Romans. Once more they swore fealty, and listened to the Emperor's reproaches, the best proof of the strong illusion under which he laboured: "Are you my Romans? For your sake I have left my country and my kindred. For love of you have I abandoned my Saxons and all the Germans, my own blood. I have led you to the most distant parts of the Empire, where your fathers, lords of the world, never set foot, so as to spread your name and fame to the ends of the earth[1]." And the crowd half believed in the dream. They dragged their leaders out and threw them before the Emperor. His nobles were cooler, and under their persuasions he left the Eternal City, where his escort still remained. It could not be concealed that he had really been driven out by the rebels.

His case was nearly desperate. The German magnates were ready to revolt against the dreamer. St Romuald counselled him to take the cowl. Yet Otto, though a visionary, was resourceful and resolute. He summoned fresh forces from Germany, where Henry of Bavaria kept the princes loyal. He asked once more, and with success, for a Byzantine bride. He vexed Rome whence his men were extracted, and prepared for a siege. But his strength was exhausted. On 23 January 1002 he died at Paterno near the Tiber just as his reinforcements reached him.

All Italy was in confusion. The Germans were obliged to fight their way northwards with the corpse. King Ardoin seized the Italian crown. John Crescentius, son of Crescentius II, ruled Rome as patrician, and Pope Sylvester, who had loyally followed his pupil, was content to return thither despoiled of secular power and soon to die. Hugh of Tuscany was already dead, to the joy of the ungrateful Otto. But the basis of the Holy Roman Empire was still firm. Bishops and Marquesses as a rule were faithful to the Saxon house. If Otto's dreams were over, German supremacy, the fact, remained.

It was not only in the Lombard troubles under Otto III that signs were apparent of the medieval evolution of Italy. His contemporary and friend, Doge Pietro Orseolo II of Venice, was making a city-state a first-rate power at sea. Within a few years Orseolo curbed and appeased the feuds of the nobles, he effected a reconciliation with Germany, he reinstated Venice in her favourable position in the Eastern Empire, and contrived to keep on fair terms with the Muslim world. In 1000 Venice made her first effort to dominate the upper Adriatic and it was successful for the time. The Doge led a fleet to Dalmatia, checking the Slav tribes and giving Venice a temporary protectorate over the Roman towns of the coast. Byzantium was busied in war nearer home and glad to rely on a powerful friend. She soon had occasion for Venice's active help, for the Saracen raids grew once again to dangerous dimensions. In 1002 the caid Ṣafī came from Sicily and besieged Bari by land and sea. The catapan Gregory Trachaniotis was

[1] Thangmar, *Vita S. Bernwardi*, c. 25. But these German accounts glose events. Was the haling of the Roman leaders before Otto a mere piece of ceremonial, suitable to a treaty with the Emperor?

rescued by Venice.   Orseolo II arrived with his fleet, revictualled the town, and fought a three days' battle with the Muslims.   In the end, worsted on both elements, they retreated by night.   They still wasted Calabria and the whole west coast of Italy, yet here too they received a severe check in a naval battle near Reggio in 1005, in which the fleet of the Tuscan trading town of Pisa played the decisive part.   Thus, even before the Holy Roman Empire reached its apogee, the future city-states of North Italy had made their first entry into international politics.

In the security of the frontiers, in the rebirth of civic life, in the resettlement of the country-side, in the renewal of intercourse and commerce, the success of the Ottonian rule was manifest.   Nor were the omens inauspicious in the Church.   During the wretched times of anarchy a demoralisation, analogous to that of which the career of King Hugh bears witness among the magnates, had invaded cathedral and cloister.   The Papacy could be the bone of contention for lawless nobles; a great abbey, like Farfa, could be a nest of murder and luxury in the mid tenth century.   Now at any rate, in the north under Alberic and the Ottos, in the Byzantine south, an improvement, slow and chequered as it might be, had set in.   But in one aim the Ottos had failed, the extension of the *Regnum Italicum* over all Italy.   Sardinia, which vegetated apart ruled by her native "judges" under an all but forgotten Byzantine suzerainty, might be disregarded; but the separation of the south of the peninsula from the north left the Holy Roman Empire imperfect.   It was a case where geographical and climatic influences interacted on historical events and made them, so to say, their accomplices in moulding the future.   South Italy as a whole was always a more barren land than the north, more sunburnt, less well-watered, a land of pasture rather than of agriculture or of intense cultivation, a land of great estates and sparse inhabitants.   Long separated from the main Lombard kingdom by Roman territory, and protected by their mountain defiles, the Lombards of Benevento had fallen apart from their northern kinsmen. Charlemagne had not subdued them; Eastern Rome, by direct conquest and through her client sea-ports, had exercised a potent influence upon them; the Saracens held Sicily.   Throughout the two centuries from 800 to 1000 the schism of the two halves of Italy, which Nature had half prescribed, steadily widened.   Even what they had most in common, the tendency to autonomous city-states, took different embodiment and met a different destiny.   The Norman Conquest only concluded and intensified a probable evolution.

CHAPTER VIII.

GERMANY: HENRY I AND OTTO THE GREAT.

"THE future of the realm," Conrad is said to have declared with his dying words, "lies with the Saxons," and he bade his brother Everard to bear the royal insignia to Henry, the Saxon Duke, as the one man capable of restoring the glory of the German name. The union of Frank and Saxon had given the throne to Conrad on the death of Louis the Child; the same alliance was responsible for the ascendancy of the Saxon dynasty in 919[1]. Everard carried out the last injunctions of the late king, waived his own claim, and caused Henry the Saxon to assume the royal dignity. The election was a purely secular function; for, either from a genuine feeling of his unworthiness or from his dislike of the higher clergy and their secular influence, a dislike which he undoubtedly possessed in the earlier years of his reign, he dispensed with the solemn ceremonials of anointing and coronation offered him by Archbishop Heriger of Mayence. It took place at Fritzlar on the borders of Franconia and Saxony in May 919.

The position of Henry the Fowler[2] was a difficult one. As king he was scarcely more powerful than he was as duke. Saxon and Franconian princes had been present at the election, but there is little reason to believe that the princes of the southern duchies were present or that they acquiesced in the result. Everard, Duke of Franconia, had been chiefly instrumental in raising Henry to the throne, but he had previously been an inveterate enemy to the Saxon house, and his loyalty was only purchased at the price of almost complete independence in his own dukedom. The new king did not at first aspire very high. He had no scheme of governing the whole realm, as the Carolings before him, from one centre through his own officials. He had no choice but to allow the tribes to manage their own affairs according to their own customs and their own traditions. Even his modest ambition to be regarded as the head of a confederate Germany was not yet accepted. Bavaria and

---

[1] Henry's Carolingian descent (he was the great-grandson of Louis the Pious) did not influence the election. He was chosen purely on his own merits.

[2] This name "Auceps" is first given him by the Annalista Saxo in the middle of the twelfth century. Ann. Sax. *M. G. SS.* VI. 594.

Swabia were outside his sphere of authority. Burchard, "no duke, but tyrant, despoiler and ravager of the land" (his unscrupulous disposal of church property had given him a bad reputation among monastic writers) was ruling in Swabia. He had just rid himself of the aggressions of Rodolph II, King of Upper (Jurane) Burgundy, who had attempted to add Swabia to his dominions, by defeating him at Winterthur[1]. At the news of Henry's approach, for it is uncertain whether the king actually entered Swabia, he surrendered unconditionally. Henry allowed him to retain his dukedom, only reserving to himself the right of appointing to bishoprics and the royal domain lying within the limits of the duchy.

Bavaria offered a more difficult task. Arnulf "the Bad," though, like Burchard, he had gained the ill-will of the clergy owing to his habit of appropriating the revenue and property of the Church, was exceedingly popular with the secular nobles. He had been urged, not against his will, to put forward a claim to the throne of Germany, and was only prevented by the antagonism of the clergy from making an immediate attempt to win this end. According to one account Henry was obliged to make two campaigns before he was able to bring Arnulf to terms. However that may be, in 921 he approached Ratisbon (Regensburg), perhaps, as Widukind records, he actually besieged the town; and, by granting particularly favourable conditions, obtained Arnulf's submission. The duke retained the coveted right of appointing to bishoprics within his duchy, a privilege confined to Bavaria alone; in other ways also Bavaria secured a larger measure of independence than was enjoyed by any other German tribe. Almost sovereign powers were given to its duke. Arnulf struck coins, directed his own foreign policy, and dated documents according to the year of his reign.

Henry was not satisfied with the limits prescribed by the Treaty of Verdun; he aimed at the inclusion of Lorraine in the German realm. It was not an easy matter and was only accomplished by untiring patience and by taking advantage of opportunities offered by the ceaseless disturbances in the Western Kingdom. Gilbert (Giselbert), the reigning duke, a versatile and unscrupulous man, sought and obtained the help of the German king when his dominions were overrun by the West Franks. He was reinstated and remained on friendly terms with Henry until, in 920, hostilities broke out between the Eastern and Western Kingdoms. Charles the Simple pushed his way into Germany as far as Pfeddersheim near Worms, but retired on hearing that Henry was arming against him. Gilbert, at this juncture, threw off his allegiance

---

[1] Rodolph, however, partially gained his object. For either on the occasion of his marriage with Burchard's daughter Bertha, or more probably after Burchard's death, at the Council held at Worms in November 926, he added a strip of territory lying to the east of the river Aar, but the extent of which is uncertain, to his dominions in return for the gift to Henry the Fowler of the much coveted Holy Lance. See R. L. Poole, *The Supposed Origin of Burgundia Minor*, EHR, xxx. 51, 1915.

to Henry and assisted Charles in the campaign of the following year. Fighting was however averted: on 7 November 921 the two kings met in a boat anchored in the middle of the Rhine at Bonn. There a treaty was concluded: Henry was formally recognised as king of the East Franks, but Lorraine remained dependent on the Western Kingdom.

During the next years France was immersed in the throes of civil war. First Robert, the younger son of Robert the Strong, and on his death his son-in-law, Raoul (Rudolf), Duke of Burgundy, was set up as rival king to the helpless Caroling, Charles the Simple, who spent most of the remainder of his life in close captivity at Péronne. In the midst of this anarchy Henry sought his opportunity to wrest Lorraine from the Western Kingdom. Twice in the year 923 he crossed the Rhine. In the spring he met Robert and entered into some compact of friendship with him, probably at Jülich on the Roer; later in the year, at the call of Duke Gilbert, who had again changed sides, he entered Lorraine with an army, captured a large part of the country, and was only checked by the appearance of Raoul (Robert had been killed at Soissons in the previous June) with considerable forces. No battle took place, but an armistice was arranged to last until October of the next year and the eastern part of Lorraine was left in Henry's possession. The state of affairs in Lorraine was less favourable to Henry when in 925 he once more crossed the Rhine. Raoul had won a large measure of recognition among the inhabitants and Gilbert, always to be found on what appeared to be the winning side, had come to terms with him. Henry however met with surprisingly little opposition on his way. He besieged Gilbert at Zülpich, captured the town, and soon made himself master of a large portion of the land. Gilbert had no choice but to accept the overlordship of the Saxon king. He was reinstated and was attached more closely to Henry's interests in 928 by receiving his daughter Gerberga in marriage. Raoul bowed to the inevitable: henceforward Lorraine was an integral part of the East Frankish dominion.

In the first six years of his reign Henry had achieved much. He had succeeded in making his authority recognised in the southern duchies and added Lorraine to his kingdom. Content with this recognition he did not seek to interfere further in the affairs of the duchies. It was his policy throughout to leave the administration in the hands of the dukes. Bavaria, as far as we know, he never so much as revisited: Swabia was less isolated, for after the death of Burchard, Herman, a cousin of the Franconian Everard, married his widow and succeeded to the dukedom. The family connexion inevitably brought Swabia into closer relations with the central power.

Henry's own activities were confined almost entirely to Saxony and Thuringia. The weakness of his predecessors had encouraged the audacity of the restless and barbarous neighbours to the north and east of Germany. The Danes ravaged the coast of Frisia: the Wends, inhabiting the land between the Elbe and the Oder, engaged the Saxon nobles in a ceaseless and devastating border warfare: since the accession of Louis the Child a new and still greater peril hung over Germany in the violent inroads of the Magyars.   These barbarians lived for war alone. Though they were addicted to hunting and fishing, they chiefly relied for their subsistence on the spoils of their victories.   Their appearance, made more grotesque and sinister by artificial means, their outlandish war-cries, their dashing onslaught, and their ruthless cruelty combined to strike terror upon those they encountered.   Their unrivalled skill in archery and horsemanship gave them a reputation of invincibility.   For the early years of Henry's reign the Hungarians had remained quiet, but in 924 they once more poured westward into Germany and Italy.   The lack of military organisation and system of defence in Saxony was laid bare. With fire and sword they overran the whole of the province: the people fled before them and hid themselves in the forests: Henry, helpless and unable to offer any resistance, shut himself up in the fortress of Werla at the foot of the Harz mountains.   By an amazing stroke of luck, a Hungarian chief, apparently a person of considerable importance, fell into Henry's hands.   Ransom was refused: the king would only surrender his prize on condition that the invaders would withdraw from Saxony and refrain from molesting him for a period of nine years; for his part, he was prepared to pay a yearly tribute.   The terms were accepted, the Hungarian noble was given up, and for nine years Saxony was rid of the aggressions of her formidable neighbour[1].

The nine years Henry turned to good account.   He was enabled to carry out his schemes of defence undisturbed.   The Saxons were unaccustomed to town life; they lived still, like the Germans of Tacitus, apart in scattered villages and hamlets; a royal fortress or a monastery, the seat of a spiritual or secular prince, alone served as places of meeting for social purposes or the transactions of business.   Fortified towns were all but unknown.   Henry saw the necessity not only of strengthening the existing fortresses but of building and fortifying towns.   Merseburg and Hersfeld, Goslar and Gandersheim were secured within wall and moat. Quedlinburg and Pöhlde are lasting memorials of his constructive activity and prove him not unworthy of the name of " builder of cities " (*Städte-erbauer*) given him by later writers.   The town was to be the centre of all economic and judicial, military and social activity, the position of defence, the place of refuge in time of invasion ; to promote the prosperity of the towns it was ordained that all councils and social gatherings should be held there and that no substantial or valuable buildings should be erected outside the walls.   The country conquered from the Wends Henry divided into military fiefs which he granted out to his *ministeriales.* They were formed into groups of nine tenants, one of whom lived in the

---

[1] The truce appears to have extended only to Saxony and Thuringia, for in 926 we find the Hungarians invading Swabia and Lotharingia.

city to maintain the walls and dwellings in good repair and to take charge of a third of the total produce of the tenement to provide against an emergency. The remaining eight worked in the fields, but in the event of an attack withdrew to the city to defend it against the invader. The establishment of a colony of robbers and bandits on the outskirts of Merseburg is an interesting experiment. It was the condition of their tenure that they should only employ their craft of larceny and plunder against their Slavonic neighbours. In many of these reforms, it is thought, Henry had the example of England before his eyes. England had been alike defenceless and open to the attacks of the Danish invaders until Alfred and his son Edward the Elder adopted measures which not only checked their forward movement but even drove them back and kept them within prescribed limits. In 929 Henry asked his English contemporary Aethelstan for an English princess for his son Otto. The negotiations, which ended in Otto's marriage with Edith, brought Henry into close touch with England and English policy, and it is not difficult to believe that through this connexion he found the pattern on which to model his plans for the defence of his kingdom[1]. The army no less than the system of defence required radical reform. The *heerbann*, corresponding to the Anglo-Saxon fyrd, composed of the freemen—a class which in course of years had considerably diminished in numbers— was untrained and difficult to mobilise. Being an infantry force, it was moreover wholly inadequate to cope with the Hungarian horsemen. Hence it was essential for the Saxons to learn to fight on horseback. The *ministeriales* established on the Wendish marches became the nucleus of the new army. But Henry seems to have exacted knight service whenever possible throughout Saxony and even in the *heerbann*, which continued often to be summoned in times of national danger, the cavalry element gradually became predominant.

Henry tested the mettle of his reorganised army in the campaigns against the Slavs. These restless people dwelling in the forest and swamp lands between the Elbe and the Oder had been intermittently at war with the Germans since the time of Charles the Great. But the warfare had been conducted by the Saxon nobles for private ends and with a view to

---

[1] Lappenberg, I. 365, and Giesebrecht, I. 811, lay stress on the connexion. Cf. the fortresses of Edward the Elder on the Danish border, and also the regulation with respect to the towns. Giesebrecht, *loc. cit.*, restores from Widukind, I. 35, what he believes to be the words of a law of Henry I, *ut concilia et omnes conventus atque convivia in urbibus celebrentur.* Similarly Edward had ordained "that all marketing was to be done 'within port' or market town." *Vide* laws of King Edward I, I. Liebermann, *Die Gesetze der Angelsachsen*, I. 139, *Quod si quis extra portum barganniet, ouerhyrnesse regis culpa sit.* Again, Widukind's statement that of every nine military tenants one should live in the city and the rest mind the fields suggests Alfred's system of keeping one man in the host to every one in the country (*A. S. Chron.* anno 894). Cf. the system of classing the household warriors in three divisions, each of which served in rotation for a period of a month (Asser, ed. Stevenson, c. 100).

enriching themselves by the plunder of their neighbours. Henry the Fowler made the subjection of the Wends a matter of national concern. Four years (928–932) were occupied in their conquest, but every enterprise Henry undertook was crowned with success[1]. First, in a campaign against the Slavs of the Havel country in the depths of winter, he besieged and captured the ice-bound city of Brandenburg and brought the tribe to submission. Thence turning his energies against the Dalemintzi on the lower Elbe, after a siege of twenty days he took by storm their city of Jahna and planted the stronghold of Meissen as a base for further operations in that district. The subjection of Bohemia was a more serious undertaking; for this campaign he sought the help of Duke Arnulf, and for the first time Bavarian and Saxon marched together in the royal army. Wenceslas, the reigning Duke of Bohemia, had entered upon his inheritance at an early age and during a long minority his mother Drahomina, a Lyutitzi by birth, acted as regent; it was her policy of assisting the Wends in their wars against the Germans that brought about the enmity of the German king. When however in 929 (?) Henry and Arnulf entered Bohemia, Wenceslas had assumed the government. He had been brought up to the Christian faith by his grandmother Saint Ludmilla, who by her influence over the young duke had earned the hatred and jealousy of her daughter-in-law and at the latter's instigation had suffered the death of a martyr. Wenceslas, whose pious life and terrible end was to gain for him the reward of canonisation, was prepared to make amends for the imprudent policy of his regent mother; when therefore the German army approached Prague he promptly entered into negotiations. He surrendered his lands, received them back as a fief of the German crown, and agreed to pay a yearly tribute of six hundred marks of silver and one hundred and twenty head of cattle.

But no sooner was peace restored than the Wends, chafing under the German yoke, broke out into revolt[2]. The Redarii were the first to take up arms: they captured the town of Walsleben and massacred the inhabitants. The success was the signal for a general rising. The Counts Bernard and Thietmar, Henry's lieutenants in that district, took prompt action, marched against the fortress of Lenzen on the right bank of the Elbe, and, after fierce fighting, completely routed the enemy on 4 September 929. Many fell by the sword, many, in attempting flight, were drowned in the neighbouring lakes. There were but few survivors of that bloody encounter. Widukind reckons the enemy's losses at the incredible figure of two hundred thousand. Yearly tribute and the

---

[1] For the geography of the Slav campaigns see the Maps No. 26, *a* and *b* of Professor Peisker issued with Vol. II. of this work.

[2] Widukind, I. 36, sums up Henry's achievements against the Slavs before the outbreak of the general revolt of 929 thus: *Cumque vicinae gentes a rege Heinrico factae essent tributariae, Apodriti, Wilti, Hevelli, Dalamanci, Boemi, Redarii et pax esset....*

acceptance of Christianity was the price they paid for their insurrection. In 932 the Lusatians and in 934 the Ukrani on the lower Oder were subdued and made tributary. With these Henry's work among the Wendish tribes is completed. Much still remained to be done but he had laid the foundation for the work of his son Otto, the civilising and the conversion of the people on the eastern frontier.

Even more important were the results of his Hungarian conflict. This warfare was to prove the soundness of his measures of defence and protection, the strength of his new towns, the supreme test of his re-organised army. Cavalry would meet cavalry, not as in the battles with the Wends, horse against foot. In 933 the nine years' truce was at an end. Henry refused the accustomed tribute. The Hungarians lost no time; they swarmed into the West in three armies, one to ravage Italy, another France and Burgundy, and a third to punish Henry for his audacious refusal of tribute. On their way they sought the help of the Dalemintzi, but instead of the expected submissiveness they were received with scorn and derision and were presented with a mongrel dog as a token of their contempt. In Thuringia they divided their forces. One army pushed on westward into Saxony. Henry at once took the initiative, fell on them, slew their leaders, and dispersed the remainder in panic to die from hunger or cold, to be slain by the sword or taken into captivity. He then lost no time in coming up with the other host while still overwhelmed by the fate of their comrades. The battle took place at Riade (perhaps Rittburg on the Unstrut or Ried) near Merseburg on 15 March 933. The seemingly impenetrable masses were broken at the onslaught of the Saxon army, the camp was taken, the remnant of the once feared and invincible army of the Magyars fled back to their own land in panic and confusion. The Danes alone remained unsubdued. They had long pushed beyond the river Eider, the limit fixed by Charles the Great; they had encroached upon Holstein and plundered continually the coast of Frisia. In 934 Henry entered Denmark; Gorm the Old, not venturing to risk a battle, sued for peace which he obtained at the price of the old Eider boundary and the establishment of the march of Schleswig.

Towards the end of his life Henry, largely no doubt owing to the influence of his wife Matilda, became more active in works of piety and in advancing the interests of the Christian Church. He was always a serious churchman and there is evidence that his early hostility to the ecclesiastical power grew less intense in his later years[1]. The Synod of Erfurt in June 932 testifies to his interest in church matters. At his favourite home of Quedlinburg he founded a Church and a nunnery. He

---

[1] The fact that he was, as far as we know, the first German king to make a bishop count over his own city shews that he was not averse to the extension of the secular power of the ecclesiastical party. In 928 he made the Bishop of Toul count in his city.

contemplated, says the Saxon historian Widukind, a visit to Rome, not indeed to seek the imperial crown, for he had declined the honour of coronation even in Germany, but as a pilgrim. Acceptance of Christianity was often imposed by him as a condition of peace on his conquered foes. This was the case at the break-down of the Slav revolt in 928. In 931 (?) baptism was received by the prince of the Obotrites and perhaps by a Danish prince[1], in spite of the hostility of Gorm the Old, who devoted his life to the persecution of the Christians and to stamping out all remnants of Christianity from his dominions.

In the autumn of 935 at Bodfeld in the Harz Mountains, while engaged in a hunting expedition, Henry was struck down with paralysis. Anxious to see the succession decided in his lifetime, he summoned an assembly of nobles at Erfurt in the beginning of 936. Thankmar the eldest son was excluded on the ground that his mother Hatheburg, a Wend, was under a vow to take the veil when Henry sought to marry her; though Henry, the younger and favourite son of Queen Matilda, had claims on the ground that he was born after his father's accession to the German throne, Otto, the elder son, seemed the most fit to carry on the work his father had begun and was accepted as the successor by the assembled princes. At Memleben on 2 July, when nearly sixty years of age, Henry the Fowler succumbed to a second stroke and was buried in his own foundation, the Church of St Peter at Quedlinburg. The chroniclers of the period are unanimous in their praises of Henry's character and achievements. He was a just and farsighted statesman, a skilful and brave general: with foreigners and enemies he was stern and uncompromising, but to his own countrymen he was a lenient and benevolent ruler. He was a keen sportsman, a genial companion. In his own day Henry was recognised as the founder of a new realm. As Duke of Saxony, he was in a good position to inaugurate a new era, for the Saxons were in blood and in customs the purest Germans, the least touched by Frankish influence. It was the work of Henry that prepared the way for the more brilliant and the more permanent achievements of his son and successor.

OTTO I.

Otto came to the throne in the full vigour and idealism of youth (he was born in 912): he was possessed of a high sense of honour and justice, was stern and passionate, inspiring fear and admiration rather than love among his subjects; he was ambitious in his aspirations and anxious to make the royal power felt as a reality throughout Germany. The difference between father and son becomes immediately apparent in the matter of coronation. He had already been elected at an assembly

[1] See note 2, p. 202, in this chapter.

of Saxon and Franconian princes held at Erfurt[1] in his father's lifetime; but not content with this, he laid great stress on the importance of a solemn ceremony which took place early in August at Aix-la-Chapelle, the old Carolingian seat of residence. There the Archbishop Hildebert of Mayence presented the young duke to the assembled multitude of people with the words, "Behold, I bring to you Otto, the elect of God, the chosen of our lord Henry, and now made king by all the princes. If the election is pleasing to you, declare it by show of hands." Immediately the whole people lifted their hands and hailed the new king with clamorous shouts. He was invested at the hands of the Archbishop with the insignia of royalty, the sword with which to strike down the enemies of Christ, the bracelets and cloak, the emblems of peace, the sceptre and the staff by which tokens he is inspired to chasten his subjects and to stretch out the hand of mercy to the servants of God, to widows and orphans. Finally he was anointed and crowned by the Archbishop of Mayence assisted by Archbishop Wikfried of Cologne and by them was led by a special stair to a throne set up between marble pillars where he could see and be observed by all. After the celebration of mass, the company adjourned to the palace for a state banquet at which the dukes officiated, Gilbert of Lorraine as Chamberlain, Everard of Franconia as Steward, Herman of Swabia as Cupbearer, and Arnulf of Bavaria as Marshal. It was a festival of the highest significance; it was a public recognition of the union of the German tribes, the foundation of the German monarchy.

The royal influence was no longer to be confined to the limits of Saxony; while he retained the duchy in his own hands he delegated many of the ducal functions to Herman Billung, a noble connected with the royal house and founder of the later ducal house of Saxony. Another important post was granted to Count Siegfried, who is described as second only to the king among the Saxon chiefs; and on his death it passed to Count Gero. Herman and Gero were the two men who, throughout the reign of Otto, by their untiring efforts not only kept the Wends in check, but established German authority on a firm footing in the marches between the Elbe and the Oder; they relieved the king of a difficult task, enabling him thereby to turn his whole attention to his policy of centralising the government, of extending the royal influence, and later of adding Italy to his dominions and of restoring the imperial title. But these appointments were unpopular in Saxony. Wichmann was jealous of the advancement of his younger brother Herman, and by the selection

---

[1] The passage in Widukind, II. 1: *Defuncto...Heinrico, omnis populus Francorum atque Saxonum iam olim designatum regem a patre, filium eius Oddonem, elegit sibi in principem*, suggests that Otto was formally elected—at Fritzlar or Forchheim it is conjectured—before proceeding to Aix-la-Chapelle for coronation; so Giesebrecht, I. 241, and Köpke-Dümmler, 26. But Waitz, *Verfassungsgeschichte*, VI. 135, n. 3, and Maurenbrecher, *Königswahlen*, 54, n. 3, take these words to refer to the assembly at Erfurt before Henry's death when Otto was designated as the successor.

of Gero, Otto lost the support of his half-brother Thankmar, who in spite of being barred from the throne had hitherto shown himself a loyal subject.   Being akin to Siegfried he had counted on succeeding to his position and estates ; disappointed in this, he joined with Everard in the rebellion of 938.

At the coronation festival at Aix-la-Chapelle the dukes had fully recognised Otto as king and, no doubt with the idea that he would continue his father's policy, had done homage for their dukedoms.   But no sooner had Otto revealed his intentions than they were up in arms.   The trouble began in Bavaria.   Arnulf died in July 937 and his sons refused their homage.   Two campaigns in 938 were necessary to restore the royal authority.   Berthold, Arnulf's brother, formerly Duke of Carinthia, was set over the duchy, but with limited powers.   Otto took to himself the right of nominating to bishoprics and also, now or shortly after, set up Arnulf, son of the late duke, as Count palatine[1] to safeguard the royal interests in the duchy.

Between the two Bavarian campaigns Otto had been called away to deal with a more serious rising in Franconia.   Small raids had been frequent on the borders of Saxony, raids in which Duke Everard had been involved.   In one of these Everard burnt the city of Hellmern and slaughtered the inhabitants; the duke was fined and the abettors of the crime were condemned to the indignity of carrying dogs through the streets of Magdeburg.   But the disturbance was not at an end: the delinquents were emboldened rather than deterred by the lenient treatment they received from Otto at a diet held at Steele on the Ruhr in May, and the petty warfare rose to the dimensions of civil war.   Thankmar, who, as we have seen, had his own reasons to be displeased with Otto's rule, joined forces with Everard : together they captured Belecke on the Möhne and with it the king's younger brother Henry.   But a reaction followed : the discontented Wichmann returned to loyalty and the insurrection in Saxony completely broke down : the fortress of Eresburg, which Thankmar had taken, opened its gates at Otto's approach. Thankmar himself fled to the Church of St Peter where he was slain at the altar, an act of sacrilege of which Otto was entirely innocent. Everard was restored to favour after undergoing a short term of honourable imprisonment at Hildesheim ; but before making his peace he

---

[1] His duties were to act as the king's representative in judicial matters, to take charge of the royal fortresses and lands, and to be responsible for the revenues due from Bavaria.   The object was plainly to set up a counter authority against that of the tribal duke.   Arnulf was the leader of the opposition in Bavaria in 937–8, and was banished as a punishment; his recall and appointment as Count Palatine is characteristic of Otto's generous and lenient treatment of opponents.   The *Cont. Reginonis,* anno 938, the only authority for the Bavarian revolt, speaks of an Everard as the leader of the rebellion, but Erben in *Neues Archiv,* xvi. conjectures on very convincing grounds that the passage *Everhardum Arnolfi filium* should read *Arnolfum Arnolfi filium.*

entered into a secret compact with Henry by which they should, when the opportunity offered, combine against Otto. The crown was to be Henry's reward. Early in the year 939 everything was in readiness. The arrangements were made at a gathering of malcontents at Saalfeld. Gilbert of Lorraine had been drawn into the ranks of the disaffected dukes. All the three leaders, Henry, Everard, and Gilbert, according to Liudprand, Bishop of Cremona, had designs on the throne, trusting perhaps to the fortunes of war to bring one or the other of them to the uppermost. Hostilities broke out in Lorraine. Otto hastened to the scene of action, while the enemy were advancing towards the Rhine near Xanten. The paucity of boats enabled but a small portion of the royalist troops to cross the river before their adversaries came in sight. While the king, with the main body of his army, watched from the opposite bank, this small detachment, perhaps no more than a hundred men, by strategy, by cunning, and by a vigorous attack in front and rear, won a victory on the field of Birthen. It was little short of a miracle, a miracle attributed by the legend to the Holy Lance which Otto held in his hand. This success relieved Otto from all immediate danger. The opposition broke down in Saxony and Thuringia. Dortmund, one of Henry's fortresses, had submitted to the king as he marched towards the Rhine; after the fight at Birthen, in which it was rumoured that Henry had fallen, Merseburg and Scheidungen on the Unstrut alone held out. To the former of these Henry fled after his defeat with but nine followers. After a siege of two months the garrison capitulated and Henry was granted a truce of thirty days to quit Saxony. By the beginning of June the first campaign was over and, says the Saxon historian, "there was rest from civil war for a few days."

The second campaign of the year 939 had a different and more alarming aspect. It received the support of Louis IV (d'Outremer), son of Charles the Simple, who on the death of Raoul of Burgundy had been summoned from his place of refuge at the court of his uncle King Aethelstan and set on the throne of France by Hugh the Great, the powerful Count of Paris. The latter had expected to have things his own way under a king of his own choosing, but soon found he was mistaken. Louis had no intention of being a puppet in the hands of the great duke and at once asserted his independence of action. Within a year of his accession he had alienated from himself all the powerful nobility of France. When, therefore, Louis, in the hope of attaching Lorraine once more to the West Frankish dominions, joined forces with Duke Gilbert, Otto found abundant assistance ready at hand among the discontented feudatories of France. In September he actually entered into some sort of compact with Louis' chief antagonists Hugh the Great, Herbert, Count of Vermandois, William, Duke of Normandy, and Arnold I, Count of Flanders. Henry, the king's brother, liberated from Merseburg, hastened to join Gilbert in Lorraine. Otto, following in hot pursuit, found them garrisoned in the castle of Chèvremont near Liège; he laid siege to the fortress, but was compelled to relinquish it, for Louis was making headway in the neighbourhood of Verdun, where several bishops (perhaps those of Metz, Verdun, and Toul) had submitted themselves to his authority. Otto set out against him, and drove him back to his capital at Laon.

At this point in the campaign the scheming Duke of Franconia openly joined in the revolt. Otto besieged him in the strong fortress of Breisach on the Rhine. An attempt was made to come to terms: Frederick, Archbishop of Mayence, was employed to negotiate with Everard, but he went beyond his powers, conceding more than the king was prepared to yield and Otto refused to ratify the treaty. The effect was to throw the Archbishop into the ranks of the insurgents. He fled privily by night to Metz where he expected to fall in with Henry and Gilbert; but the latter had already started to join forces with Everard: whether Henry accompanied the dukes on the fatal expedition to the Rhine is uncertain; more probably, making Metz his headquarters, he remained behind to organise resistance in Lorraine. Everard and Gilbert made a plundering raid and returned westward, intending to recross the Rhine at Andernach. Part of their army had already crossed the river and the dukes were quietly eating their dinner before crossing themselves, when a body of Franconian troops led by Udo and Conrad Kurzpold, Franconian counts, whose lands had especially suffered from the raid, came up with them. Both the dukes fell in the fight that ensued. Everard was slain by the sword, Gilbert was drowned: according to one account he got into a boat already overloaded with fugitives and the boat capsized; according to another he leapt with his horse into the river and so met his end. By a mere stroke of luck the two leaders of the rebellion were disposed of in a skirmish hardly worthy of the name of battle at a moment when Otto's cause seemed desperate, and when, says Widukind, "there seemed no hope of his retaining rule over the Saxons, so widespread was the rebellion."

The effect was instantaneous. Breisach capitulated: Lorraine was restored to order. Of the remaining leaders, Frederick, after being refused admittance into his own town of Mayence, was captured and punished by a short term of imprisonment; Henry, on hearing the news which deprived him of all hopes of the crown, fled to his old stronghold of Chèvremont but found the gates closed against him; he made his way to France, but finding his cause to be hopelessly lost, yielded himself up to his brother's mercy. Otto with his habitual generosity and magnanimity forgave him everything and took him again into his favour. The royal authority was now firmly established. Henry made one more attempt to overthrow his brother, but it was too late and the conspiracy of 941 collapsed without recourse to arms. The intention had been to assassinate the king at the Easter festival at Quedlinburg: it reached the ears of Otto who proceeded as usual to the feast but with a strong guard, and there seized and executed the whole gang of conspirators. Henry fled, was captured and imprisoned at Ingelheim, but before the end of the year received the king's pardon. The unscrupulous Archbishop of Mayence was also implicated but cleared himself of guilt by receiving the sacrament in public.

The civil wars involved extensive changes in the government of the duchies. During the years which followed the restoration of order, Otto inaugurated and gradually established the policy of attaching the dukedoms more closely to himself by granting them to members of his own family. The administration of Lorraine was in 931 entrusted to a certain Otto, son of Ricwin, and on his death in 944 the duchy was conferred upon Conrad the Red, a kinsman of King Conrad I, who in 947 was married to Otto's daughter Liutgard. Franconia[1], after the death of Everard at the fight of Andernach, the king retained in his own hands. When Duke Berthold died in 947 his duchy of Bavaria passed to the king's own brother Henry, who, after the failure of his last attempt to win the throne in 941, had become one of the loyalest of Otto's subjects and who was already akin to the Bavarian ducal house through his marriage in 938(?) with Judith, the daughter of the old duke Arnulf. Lastly, on the death of Duke Herman in 949, Swabia was given to Otto's son Liudolf, who married Ida, the daughter of the late duke. By these arrangements the ancient supremacy of the Franconian tribe was for ever crushed; but in the southern duchies the order of things remained unchanged, for while granting the dukedoms to his own kinsmen, he maintained the traditions and customs of the tribal duchies by giving the new dukes in marriage to the daughters of the old ducal houses.

In the meanwhile the eastern neighbours of Germany had taken full advantage of the intestine troubles which filled the opening years of the new reign. In the midst of the ducal rebellion of 939 Widukind deplores the numerous enemies that beset his native Saxony, "Slavs from the east, Franks from the south, Lorrainers from the west, and from the north Danes and more Slavs"; he might have added Hungarians from the south-east, for their barbaric hordes swept into Thuringia and Saxony in 937 and 938. They were beaten back and never again ventured into Saxon territory. On the Wendish border there had been ceaseless activity. Fortunately for Otto, the frontier

---

[1] According to von Winterfeld, *Neues Archiv*, xxviii. pp. 510 f., on the authority of a passage in Hrotsvit, *Gesta Oddonis*, 450 ff., Otto did not retain the administration of Franconia in his hands but granted it at this time to his son Liudolf—a boy of eleven years old—who, if this conjecture is correct, would in 949 be Duke of Franconia and Swabia. The evidence however is insufficient to justify this conclusion. For the theory that certain parts of Franconia round the Upper Main and Bamberg were granted to Berthold of Bavaria, see Giesebrecht, *Kaiserzeit*, i. 816 f.

command was in capable hands; Herman Billung and Gero repressed the risings with a firm hand and even extended German influence further eastward. The death of Henry the Fowler had been the first signal for insurrection, in which the Redari seem to have taken the leading part. Henry they had learnt to fear, but Otto was untried and had yet to prove his strength. He hastened back from his coronation at Aix-la-Chapelle and suppressed the rising. The Wends were held in check till the year 939 when Germany was in the throes of civil war, when the total subversion of the royal authority seemed inevitable, and an unrivalled opportunity of throwing off the German yoke presented itself. They made repeated inroads which were beaten off by Gero, and even the king himself, it appears, found time on more than one occasion to enter into the border conflict. In Bohemia, Boleslav, who had in 936 gained the throne by murdering his brother Wenceslas at the gates of the church of Alt-Bunzlau, asserted his independence; and though temporarily checked by a force of Saxons and Thuringians sent against him in 938, he continued to be a source of danger and disturbance till Otto in 950 made an expedition in person to Bohemia and was recognised as overlord. The results, however, of the frontier fighting were on the whole satisfactory. Partly by his own efforts, partly by his keen insight into character which enabled him to select the right men for the work, Otto made progress, extended the German sway as far as the Oder, and prepared the way for the next stage in his Eastern policy, the consolidation of his conquests and the conversion of the conquered peoples to the Christian religion. The newly acquired territory was divided into two marches under the control of Herman and Gero. The tribute and rents accruing from these sources were appropriated to the maintenance of the frontier garrisons, to the establishment of colonies, and to the endowment of churches. In 948, probably on the occasion of the visit of the papal legate Marinus, Bishop of Bomarzo, to Germany, bishoprics were founded at Brandenburg and Havelberg in the province of Mayence, and at Ripen, Aarhus and Schleswig in the metropolitan diocese of Bremen for the organisation of further missionary work.

On the western frontier, also, the state of affairs was troublesome. The possession of Lorraine was by no means entirely a source of strength to the German monarchy. Owing to its position between the East and West Frankish dominions it involved the German king in the everlasting turmoil which characterised the history of France in the tenth century. Moreover Lorraine was always firmly attached to the Carolingian tradition, and there was always a party ready to support the Caroling kings in their attempts to win back the province for the Western Kingdom. There Louis IV was engaged in an incessant struggle to hold his own against a strong coalition of feudal nobles under the leadership of the all-powerful Count of Paris. During the decade 940–950 Otto was busily engaged beyond the Rhine. He lent his aid first to one side, then to the other[1], mediated between them and compelled both parties to realise the weight of his power, the wide scope of his authority, the value of his mediation. In the summer of 940 he entered France to punish Louis for his interference in Lorraine and drove him into Burgundy: but the expedition had daunted neither the spirit nor the enterprise of Louis, who, as soon as Otto was back in Germany, again set out for Lorraine. Otto once more turned westward, but as it was late in the year the kings effected a truce and parted without fighting. For two years Louis was pursued by his relentless adversaries; at last, however, in 942, possibly as a result of the visit of the legate of Pope Stephen VIII who commanded the princes to recognise Louis as their king on pain of excommunication, a solemn assembly took place and a general peace was concluded at a place uncertain but conjectured to be Visé[2] on the Meuse, a few miles north of Liège. A similar obscurity exists with regard to the terms, but it is clear that Louis on his side engaged to desist from interfering in the affairs of Lorraine, while Otto for his part agreed to refrain from assisting the French lords against their king.

This settlement was but transitory, and two years later Otto was again drawn into the affairs of the Western Kingdom. But the position was altered: two of Louis' dangerous opponents, William of Normandy and Herbert of Vermandois, were now dead; for a moment the king and the Count of Paris were on terms of friendship. Then a trivial difference and an accident brought about another change, and Louis was a prisoner in the hands of his powerful feudatory. This was in 944. Hugh, with his valuable prisoner in safe keeping at Laon, sought an interview with Otto. The latter, however, perhaps anxious to abide by the compact of 942, perhaps from a genuine feeling of pity for the luckless king, declined to accept Hugh's overtures and espoused the royal cause. The menace of Otto's displeasure saved Louis: after nearly a year's confinement, he was liberated, but only at the heavy price of losing his one sure stronghold, the fortress of Laon. Louis was free, but without shelter, almost without friends. Gerberga, his queen, made a pressing appeal to her brother. Otto's French campaign in the late summer of 946 met with very limited success. Laon, Rheims, and Senlis were all in turn besieged, but Rheims alone was captured. The two kings then made a plundering raid into Normandy; they even, according to one account, laid siege to Rouen. But in this enterprise they were alike unsuccessful, and Otto made his way back to Germany.

---

[1] Both the antagonists had equal claims, on the ground of kinship, to Otto's friendship; each had married a sister of Otto, Hugh the Great married Hedwig and Louis IV Gerberga, widow of Gilbert of Lorraine.

[2] See Lauer, *Les Annales de Flodoard*, p. 35, n. 5, and *Louis d'Outremer*, p. 83, n. 3. Vouziers on the Aisne has also been conjectured. Cf. Giesebrecht, *Kaiserzeit*, p. 274.

The year 947 was occupied by a series of fruitless assemblies called together to decide a dispute over the archbishopric of Rheims. The two parties in France had each its candidate for the see, and the party uppermost unscrupulously imposed the man of its choice upon the diocese. These transactions, vain as they were, are not without their importance, for they led up to the solemn synod held at Ingelheim on 7 June 948. The legate of Pope Agapetus II, Bishop Marinus of Bomarzo, presided over it. It was an assembly of the highest significance: it was the first occasion since the accession of the Saxon dynasty, since the synod of Hohen Altheim in 916, that a papal legate had appeared in Germany. It was attended by more than thirty bishops, and the two kings Louis and Otto were present in person. The business was not restricted to the Rheims dispute. The discussion on the political question at issue resulted in a canon being passed against attacks on the royal power and a declaration that Hugh should make his submission under pain of excommunication. The dispute over the see of Rheims was decided in favour of Artaud, the candidate of the royal party; his rival Hugh, son of Herbert of Vermandois, was excommunicated. Hugh the Great held the decrees of the synod at defiance; he was excommunicated at the Synod of Trèves (September 948); he continued in his obduracy and carried on hostilities against Louis and his allies Otto and Conrad of Lorraine till 950, when, at a meeting held on the banks of the Marne, he made his submission, restored Laon, and, by his homage, recognised Louis as his lord.

The affairs of France were no sooner settled on a satisfactory basis than a turn of events in Italy provided the occasion for Otto's first expedition across the Alps. The occasion was the death of King Lothar, leaving his widow Adelaide with a title to the Italian throne in her own right, defenceless and soon to be a prisoner in the hands of Berengar, Marquess of Ivrea, who was himself crowned King of Italy at Pavia on 15 December 950. The old connexion between Germany and Italy founded on the Empire of Charles the Great, though it had ceased to be a reality since the death of the Emperor Arnulf in 899, is recalled to memory by many minor incidents in the dark years of the first half of the tenth century. The dukes of Swabia and Bavaria were frequently drawn into the Italian struggles; Berengar of Ivrea, fleeing from the murderous designs of his rival Hugh of Arles, had crossed the Alps, taken refuge in Swabia, and even commended himself to Otto (941), an act which perhaps gave Otto the right to expect an acknowledgment of overlordship from Berengar when the latter ascended the Italian throne in 950. With the opposite faction Otto was also brought into close connexion through Conrad of Burgundy, who had spent his youth at the German court and whose sister Adelaide had married Hugh's son Lothar.

The arrangements for the Italian expedition were settled at the

Easter festival held at Aix-la-Chapelle 30 March 951. Otto formed his plans in close consultation with his brother Henry, now his most trusted adviser, whose brilliant campaigns against the Hungarians, resulting in the acquisition of the march of Aquileia, gave additional weight to his councils. Liudolf, on the other hand, was apparently not taken into the king's confidence: indignant at his exclusion, jealous of his uncle, impetuous and anxious to make a name for himself on his own account, he determined to anticipate his father. He rapidly crossed the Alps with a small army of Swabians; but his expedition was a complete failure and before long he returned to sow the seeds of rebellion, the news of which recalled Otto, who had assumed the title of King of the Lombards at Pavia and taken Adelaide as his wife, in haste to Germany. It was not only disappointment at his failure in Italy that led Liudolf to rebel against his father. Otto's second marriage was not likely to be to his son's advantage; it would lead to a new circle at the court in which he would take but a secondary place; he might even look to being ousted from the succession by the offspring of this new alliance—an event which in fact occurred, for it was Adelaide's son, Otto, who was designated as the successor to the total disregard of the claims of his nephew and namesake, the son of Liudolf. The plans for the rebellion were formed at a Christmas gathering held at Saalfeld; the place is significant, for it was there that Henry had divulged to his friends his designs against Otto in 939. Among the conspirators was Frederick, Archbishop of Mayence, whose implication in the previous rebellions of 939 and 941 was more than suspected. He had been employed as Otto's envoy to the court of Pope Agapetus and the failure of his mission may have led to a rupture with Otto.

The news of this ominous assembly was the immediate cause of Otto's return to Germany. He crossed the Alps in February 952 and by Easter was again in Saxony. Conrad, Duke of Lorraine, was left behind in Italy to complete the overthrow of Berengar. But instead of pursuing the advantage which Otto had already gained, he made terms with Berengar and returned with him to Germany to obtain the king's ratification of his arrangements. They found the court at Magdeburg. Otto was, however, far from satisfied: he had counted on the complete subversion of Berengar. For three days the latter was not permitted to approach the royal presence and even then, through the counsel of Duke Henry, he was "barely granted his life and a safe return to his country." The final settlement with regard to Italy was postponed to a meeting to be held at Augsburg. On 7 August the diet met in the spacious Lechfeld which extended to the south of the city. Franks, Saxons, Swabians, Bavarians, Lombards, and even ambassadors from the Byzantine court attended the gathering, to which a contemporary annalist assigns the imposing Frankish title of *Conventus publicus*. There Berengar and his son Adalbert took the oath of homage and fealty and, by the solemn handing over of the golden sceptre, received back the kingdom of Lombardy as a fief of the German crown. But Duke Henry had his reward for his consistent loyalty at Berengar's expense: the marches of Aquileia and Verona were added to the Bavarian dukedom.

Up to this point there had been no overt act of rebellion on the part of the conspirators. Liudolf and the Archbishop of Mayence had been present at the Augsburg diet; indeed the latter had taken a leading part in the ecclesiastical business transacted there. But as the rebellion matured, the causes of discontent increased. The marked displeasure of Otto at Conrad's management of the affairs of Italy had driven the Duke of Lorraine into the ranks of the malcontents. The appointment of the king's brother Bruno to the post of archchancellor of Italy was an additional grievance to Archbishop Frederick, who had counted upon that dignified sinecure for himself. Whereas Henry had gained by the settlement at Augsburg, Liudolf had received no share in the spoils. Possibly the birth of a child to Adelaide, a boy named Henry who died in infancy, at the end of the year 952, was the decisive event, which determined the outbreak of hostilities.

Otto appears to have been blind to the dangers which surrounded him. It was only while journeying to Ingelheim on his return from Alsace, whither he had gone to visit his wife's relations, that he realised the critical state of affairs. Judging it imprudent to keep the Easter festival, as he had purposed, at so isolated a place as Ingelheim, he turned aside to Mayence; but Mayence proved no less dangerous. He found the gates of the city closed against him and in an unseemly manner he was kept waiting until the Archbishop, who was absent from the city performing his Lenten devotions in retreat, returned to grant him admittance. Liudolf and Conrad also appeared on the scene, and the king was caught in a trap. The conspirators made haste to clear themselves of having any designs against their sovereign; but they acknowledged that it had been their intention to waylay Henry in the event of his coming to Ingelheim for the Easter festival. Even towards the king their attitude was not so peaceable as they had affirmed; by duress they extorted from him some sort of treaty, of which the terms are unrecorded, but the nature may be fairly conjectured. It was no doubt as advantageous to Liudolf as it was detrimental to the interests of Duke Henry. Liudolf was assured of the succession and possibly was even to have an immediate share in the government. Otto was glad to escape at any price. Nevertheless, once safe in Saxony he did not scruple to revoke the treaty. He summoned Liudolf and Conrad to appear before him and ordered them either to hand over their confederates or else to receive the punishment due for their offence. A diet for the discussion of their case was to meet at Fritzlar. The dukes did not present themselves at the diet; they were deprived of their dukedoms, and hostilities began in earnest.

In this rebellion, it is remarkable that the duchies invariably sided against their dukes. The Lorrainers, under the leadership of Adalbero, Bishop of Metz, and Reginar, Count of Hainault, were, almost to a man, loyal to the king and therefore in opposition to their duke, Conrad; whereas in Bavaria the king and his brother Henry met with their bitterest and most dangerous opponents. At first Conrad sought to recover his position in Lorraine; but on the banks of the Meuse, in a desperate battle lasting from noon to sunset, he was defeated, quitted his duchy, and betook himself to Mayence, which henceforth became the headquarters of the insurgents. With an army of Saxons reinforced on the march by troops from Lorraine and Franconia, Otto invested the city. He was soon joined by Henry with his Bavarians. For nearly two months the royal army tried in vain to capture the stronghold of the rebels; every device of siege warfare was employed but all to no account; engines were no sooner brought up to the walls than they were destroyed or burnt; assaults were made upon the gates only to be beaten off with loss by the defenders. At last, wearied by lack of success, Otto made overtures for an armistice and sent his cousin Ekbert as an hostage. But the negotiations came to nothing, and the king's ambassador was won over to the side of the enemy. For Otto the situation was desperate. The defection had spread to Saxony and to Bavaria; in the latter duchy Arnulf, the Count palatine, put himself at the head of a tribal revolt against the rule of Duke Henry. This was perhaps the most serious phase in the rebellion. The Bavarians, led by their duke to assist in the siege of Mayence, went over in a body to the enemy. Leaving the defence of the city in the charge of Conrad, Liudolf hastened with the Bavarian deserters to Ratisbon, seized and plundered the city, and drove Henry's family and adherents from the country. In September Otto abandoned the siege of Mayence with the object of attempting to secure Ratisbon, but in this enterprise he was also doomed to failure. Shortly before Christmas, almost at the end of his resources, he withdrew to Saxony.

Owing to the firm rule of Herman, the insurrection in Saxony had broken down, and Lorraine also remained loyal; but the greater part of Franconia and practically the whole of Swabia and Bavaria had taken up arms against him. So widespread was the disaffection that it has been sometimes regarded as an expression of a national resistance against Otto's imperial policy, as though the interests of Germany were prejudiced by his acquisition of the Italian throne[1]. It is, however, more in accordance with the facts to attribute the civil war rather to tribal than national causes: the separate tribes were rebelling against the authority

---

[1] So von Sybel, *Die neueren Darstellungen der deutschen Kaiserzeit*, pp. 18 f., *Die deutsche Nation und das Kaiserreich*, pp. 32 f., and Maurenbrecher, *Die Kaiserpolitik Ottos I, Historische Zeitschrift*, v. 141, and *Der Ludolfinische Aufstand von 953, Forschungen zur deutschen Geschichte*, iv. 597, but see Giesebrecht, *Kaiserzeit*, i. 828, and Dümmler, *Otto der Grosse*, 212 f., for the opposite view.

of their dukes. It was the duke who was attacked in Bavaria, in Lorraine, and in Saxony. Only in Swabia was Liudolf's personal popularity sufficiently strong to secure the loyalty of the tribe; though even there an anti-ducal party was formed under the leadership of Burchard, a kinsman of the former duke. The inception of the war may be traced to personal causes, to the personal jealousy of the leaders : its support to the tribal opposition to the centralising system of the dukedoms. The issue was decided not by any military exploit, successful campaign, or victory in the field, but by the diversion created by an Hungarian inroad, and by the violent reaction which followed against the party which sought to gain advantage from alliance with the invaders.

The Hungarians had at the outset of Otto's reign, in 937 and in 938, made two abortive attempts to invade Saxony. In 948 and in 949 they had made incursions into Bavaria, but had been beaten off by Duke Henry, who in two campaigns in the following year had successfully carried the war into their own country. Nevertheless, early in the year 954 the Hungarians, who were always ready to turn the intestine troubles of their neighbours to their own advantage, once more poured into Germany. Contemporary historians have laid the charge of inviting the barbarians upon both parties concerned in the struggle, but the occasion was too obvious to require any solicitation. Certain it is, however, that the invaders were eagerly welcomed by Liudolf and Conrad, who supplied them with guides. They swept through Bavaria and Franconia, plundering as they went; they were publicly entertained at Worms on Palm Sunday and loaded with presents of silver and gold. Conrad himself led them on across the Rhine in the hope of regaining his own duchy through their aid. But the raid of the barbarians did nothing to improve the duke's position in Lorraine; they penetrated as far as Utrecht merely laying waste the land as they passed; thence they moved southward through Vermandois, Laon, and Rheims into Burgundy, and the remnant of their band, much reduced in numbers by fighting and disease, returned to their own country by way of Italy.

The invasion was Otto's deliverance. The royal army pressed hard upon the Bavarians, who were forced to crave a truce, which was granted till 16 June when a diet was to be held at Langenzenn, near the present town of Nuremberg, where the case was to be decided. At the diet of Langenzenn, all the leaders of the revolt, realising that their cause was lost, made their appearance. During the proceedings each party accused the other of introducing the Hungarians. The Archbishop of Mayence and Conrad made their submission, but Liudolf remained obdurate; he rode off in the night with his attendants to Ratisbon. The king followed in pursuit, fighting on his way an indecisive engagement at Rosstall. Ratisbon withstood the assault of the royal army. A long siege followed, during which many skirmishes were fought before the walls, and the burghers were reduced to the point of starvation. Finally, after the city had been invested for some six weeks, Liudolf and the citizens obtained a truce, pending a settlement to be arranged at a diet to be held at Fritzlar. Liudolf made a last attempt to rally his cause in Swabia; failing in this, he sought and gained his father's forgiveness. But neither he nor Conrad recovered their dukedoms. As a result of the civil war there were many new appointments to be made. For this purpose a diet was held at Arnstadt on 7 December. The dukedom of Swabia was given to Burchard, probably the son of the old Duke of Swabia of that name and so a first cousin to Queen Adelaide. Lorraine had already been granted to the king's brother Bruno, who in the previous year had succeeded Archbishop Wikfried in the metropolitan see of Cologne. The see of Mayence was also vacant, since the turbulent Archbishop Frederick had died a few weeks before the meeting of the diet. His place was filled by William, Otto's natural son. Bavaria held out until the spring; but Henry was victorious over Herold, the rebellious Archbishop of Salzburg, and the burghers of Ratisbon, again reduced to the extremities of famine, submitted themselves to Otto. So by the end of the spring of 955 Otto was able to return in peace to his native Saxony.

The Hungarians, encouraged by their successful raid of the previous year, made another inroad early in the year 955. It was checked, and Otto received in Saxony what purported to be an Hungarian embassy; in fact its intention was nothing more nor less than to spy out the land, and immediately afterwards Duke Henry sent word that the barbarians had crossed the frontier. Their main body was encamped on the banks of the Lech near Augsburg. The city was defended by its Bishop St Ulric, whose contemporary biographer speaks of the desperate straits to which he was reduced; the city walls were dilapidated and unprovided with towers; it seemed impossible to withstand an assault from an enemy whose numbers are said to have amounted to one hundred thousand horsemen. Yet one day the bishop, arrayed in his pontifical robes, sallied forth, himself unarmed, into the ranks of the enemy and threw them into confusion. On the following day, the feast of St Lawrence (10 August), as the bishop quietly awaited the inevitable counter-attack, he heard the welcome news of Otto's approach. When the news of the invasion reached him Otto had hurried southward with a small band of Saxons. On his march, other troops collected and he reached the neighbourhood of Augsburg with a vast army drawn from all parts of Germany. The host was formed up in eight divisions: three from Bavaria, two from Swabia, and one each from Saxony, Lorraine and Bohemia. The battle was fought in the Lechfeld to the south of the city on the left bank of the river[1].

---

[1] The exact site on which the battle was fought is much disputed. Schäfer in the *Sitzungsberichte der Akademie der Wissenschaften* (Berlin), xxvii. 1905, opposed the old view asserted by Bresslau in *Historische Zeitschrift*, 1897, *Der Ort der Ungarnschlacht*, that the battle was fought in the Lechfeld south of the city on the left bank of the river, and supposes the place to have been on the left bank but north-west of

As on other occasions, legend gives the credit of the victory to the Holy Lance with which Otto was armed. At first the enemy made headway against the Swabian and Bohemian divisions; but the courage and resource of Conrad, the deposed Duke of Lorraine, who fell in the battle, restored the fortunes of the royal army. The victory was complete; and for three days the scattered remnants of the Hungarian hordes were pursued and killed or taken captive. The victory had far-reaching effects both for the conqueror and the conquered. Germany was for ever relieved of the menace of invasion and the Hungarians gave up their restless mode of life and took to a settled and peaceful existence.

The Hungarians were not the only neighbours of Germany who had sought to take advantage of the civil war. The Wends rose in revolt against German rule. In 954 Margrave Gero and Conrad (it is characteristic of Otto to entrust his recent antagonist with a command) won a victory over the Ukrani. Further north, in the district under the authority of Duke Herman, the trouble was more serious; the duke's nephews Wichmann and Ekbert, who had already attempted without success to raise Saxony in revolt against their uncle, now joined with the Wends. No decisive victory determined the fighting, which continued intermittently and with varying success for a period of two years. It was the news of the defeat of the Hungarians on the banks of the Lech which struck the Wends with awe, and compelled them to make an abject submission. They sent messages offering their accustomed tribute: but Otto was not disposed to let them off so lightly. Accompanied by Liudolf and Boleslav of Bohemia, he ravaged their land as far as Recknitz to the west of the Isle of Rügen. Their leader Stoinef was slain: Wichmann and Ekbert fled the country and took refuge at the court of Duke Hugh in France. In 957 Wichmann again appeared in alliance with the Wends, but he was finally defeated in 958 and received a pardon on taking "a terrible oath never to conspire again against Otto or his kingdom."

In Lorraine also there were signs of trouble, but the wise and statesmanlike rule of Bruno restored and maintained peace. Count Reginar of Hainault was at the root of the disturbance; it was his hostility to Conrad that secured the loyalty of Lorraine during the civil war. Apparently he expected reward for his services, and, failing to get it, he stirred up revolts against the authority of Bruno. The archbishop suppressed two risings in 957 and 959 and, as a precaution against disorder in the future, deemed it advisable to divide the duchy into two units of administration: a certain noble of the country named Godfrey had already been placed over the lower, and Frederick, brother of the

Augsburg. Others have suggested yet other possibilities, *e.g.* Wallmenich, *Die Ungarnschlacht auf dem Lechfeld*, chooses the right bank of the river to the south-east of the city and Hadank, *Einige Bemerkungen über die Ungarnschlacht*, 1908, the right bank to the north-east of the city as the spot.

powerful Bishop Adalbero of Metz, was now set over the upper province. To the prudent and judicious policy of the Archbishop of Cologne, it may be added, was due the maintenance of friendly relations with France, and it is no exaggeration to assert that to his support Lothair, on the death of Louis IV in 954, owed his peaceful and uncontested succession in that kingdom.

By the year 960 Otto's rule in Germany was firmly established. The Hungarians were defeated once and for all; the Wends between the Elbe and the Oder were quelled; Lorraine and the Western Kingdom, thanks to Bruno, were at peace. The presence of envoys from foreign courts at his solemn assemblies testifies to the strength of his rule and to the extent of his fame. Romans and Greeks, Saracens and Russians visited his court, bringing him gifts of gold, silver and ivory, balm and precious ointments, and lions, camels, monkeys, and ostriches, animals hitherto unknown in Saxony. All nations of the Christian world, concludes Widukind, looked to the great king in their troubles. So in 959 ambassadors from the Russian Queen Olga, who was baptised in 957, came to Germany to beg Otto to send missionaries to their heathen country. A certain Libertius was ordained bishop for the purpose but died before he could embark on his difficult enterprise; Adalbert from the monastery of St Maximin at Trèves was chosen in his place, but after a year's fruitless endeavour returned to his own country.

So again, John XII, Pope and patrician of Rome, sought Otto's assistance against the oppression of Berengar and his son Adalbert. The project suited Otto's own policy. The conduct of the vassal king of Italy had already earned his displeasure; but unable to go in person he had sent Liudolf, who, since he had lost his dukedom, was in need of employment. A brilliant and successful campaign (956–7) was, however, cut short by the death of its leader. Liudolf died of fever at Pombia and the work was left unfinished. At the appeal of the Pope in 959, Otto prepared to cross the Alps himself. Anxious to secure the throne in his own line in the event of his death during the campaign, he caused his infant son Otto to be elected king at Worms and to be solemnly crowned and anointed in the royal chapel of Charles the Great at Aix-la-Chapelle. Then leaving the boy in charge of William, Archbishop of Mayence, he set out to deliver Italy from its enemies and to receive the imperial crown from the hands of Pope John XII.

Of the last twelve years of his life and reign, the Emperor spent scarcely more than two in Germany. The imperial title brought with it new responsibilities to bear, new difficulties to overcome; the work of his later years was beyond the Alps. Nevertheless, it is unjust to lay to his charge the neglect of Germany, a charge which can be supported against his grandson Otto III. Otto the Great never lost interest, never disregarded the affairs of his original kingdom. At Rome one of his first considerations was the organisation of the Church on the eastern frontier of Saxony, the carrying out of his cherished plan, the foundation of a metropolitan see at Magdeburg.   As early as 955 he had sent Hademar, Abbot of Fulda, to Rome to discuss this project with Pope Agapetus. The jealousy of the Bishop of Halberstadt and of the Metropolitan of Mayence put every obstacle in his path.   But at last, on 12 February 962, he was able to make the final arrangements and obtained from Pope John XII a bull for the erection of an archbishopric at Magdeburg and a bishopric at Merseburg.   It was not, however, until 968 that effect was given to it by the appointment of bishops.   Adalbert, the first Archbishop of Magdeburg, was a man of peculiar interest.   He began life in the monastery of St Maximin at Trèves, for some years he was a notary in the chancery, in 961 he was sent as a bishop to preach the gospel in Russia.   In 966 he became Abbot of Weissenburg in Alsace, and in 968 Archbishop of Magdeburg.   He is also conjectured to be the author of the *Continuation of the Chronicle of Regino of Prüm*[1], and his varied life and profound experience make his work of the highest value for the history of Otto the Great.

The Emperor returned to Germany at the beginning of the year 965. After an absence of more than three years there was much work requiring his attention.   The Wends, again assisted and roused by the turbulent Wichmann, had given much trouble to Otto's vicegerents, Herman and Gero, and the intermittent warfare was only brought to an end in 967 when Wichmann, then in alliance with the Redarii, was defeated and slain. Nevertheless, in spite of the many difficulties in the way, Christianity and German influence had extended very rapidly.   In a campaign in 963 Gero subdued the Lusatians and received the submission and tribute of Mesco, Duke of the Poles, who was also engaged in war with the Wends. Bohemia was on terms of close friendship with Germany when under the younger Boleslav, who appeared in person at Otto's court in 973.   He was zealous in the cause of Christianity and it was through the influence of his daughter Dabravka that Mesco was baptised and missionary work was set on foot for the first time in Poland.   About the same time Harold Bluetooth, King of Denmark, was baptised, and enjoined the Christian faith upon his subjects[2].   The death of Gero, soon after his return from a pilgrimage to Rome in 965, was a set-back to German expansion.   He was the real founder of the German dominion between the Elbe and the Oder, and his place was difficult to fill.   It provided the occasion for the division of the conquered territory into the later system of marches[3].

---

[1] The conjecture now generally accepted is Giesebrecht's, see *Kaiserzeit*, I. 778.

[2] The date of Harold's conversion is disputed.   Waitz, *Heinrich*, I., p. 165, attributes it to the year 934.   But the later date 965 accepted by Dümmler, *Otto der Grosse*, p. 391, seems to be more in accordance with the evidence.   Widukind, III. 65, who gives a detailed account of the conversion, and Adam of Bremen, II. 3, place the event after a successful campaign by Otto against the Danes which must have taken place after the Emperor's return from Italy in 965.

[3] On Gero's death his march was divided into three: (1) the North march under

The death of Archbishop Bruno in the same year deprived the Emperor of another of his most loyal and most valuable governors. In his ducal office he had no successor: the division of the duchy into the provinces of Upper and Lower Lorraine, carried out by Bruno in 959, rendered a duke or archduke over the whole superfluous.

The years 966 to 972 were spent in Italy. Two events which bear upon German history may be recorded; first, the young king Otto II was crowned Emperor at the hands of the Pope John XIII on Christmas Day 967; and secondly, after a long series of negotiations, a Byzantine princess, a niece of John Tzimisces named Theophano, was given in marriage to the young Emperor.

At Christmas 972 Otto the Great was again in Germany. He was honoured by embassies to his court from distant lands, even from the Saracens in Africa. His work, however, was completed, he had outlived his friends and associates. While he was absent in Italy, his son William and his mother Matilda had died (March 968): soon after his return he lost his trusted and loyal servant Herman. He himself did not survive much longer. He died at Memleben, the little town in the Harz Mountains which had also witnessed the death of his father, on 7 May 973, in his sixty-first year. His body was taken to Magdeburg and buried in the cathedral he had built.

The Saxon historian, Widukind, sums up the achievements of his life in the voice of popular opinion: "The people, saying many things in his praise, recalled to mind that he had ruled his subjects with paternal piety, he had liberated them from their enemies, had conquered with his arms the proud Avars, Saracens, Danes, and Slavs; he had brought Italy under his yoke; he had destroyed the temples of his heathen neighbours and set up churches and priests in their place." All this he had accomplished. If he had failed in his attempt to centralise the government of Germany, his failure was due to the inevitable progress towards feudalism and the too deeply rooted tribal traditions. If in this direction his empire fell short of its model, the empire of Charles the Great, in another direction it was conspicuously in advance of it. His work, in the extension of German influence and civilisation and in the progress of Christianity towards the north and east of his dominions, was of permanent value, and stood as the firm basis of future expansion and future development.

one margrave, (2) the East march or March of Lausitz under two margraves, and (3) the Thuringian march, later the March of Meissen, under three margraves

CHAPTER IX.

OTTO II AND OTTO III.

THE stability of the Saxon dynasty is shewn in a marked degree by the way in which son succeeded father almost without question until the direct line breaks off for lack of an heir with Otto III. Otto II, who was born towards the end of 955, had been elected and twice crowned (at Aix-la-Chapelle in May 961 and at Rome on Christmas Day 967) during his father's lifetime. When Otto the Great died in 973, he was universally accepted as his successor. It was not that there was no opposition, but the people of Germany as a whole were satisfied with the ruling family and, in cases of rebellion, were prepared to give their support to the hereditary sovereign. This fact is proved not only in the frequent Bavarian revolts in the reign of Otto II, but also and more remarkably in the attempt of the Duke of Bavaria to wrest the crown from its rightful possessor, the infant Otto III. Otto the Red is described by the chronicler Thietmar as being possessed of fine physical powers; and though at first, through lack of experience, he shunned wise counsel, chastened by troubles he set a rein upon himself and lived nobly for the rest of his days.

During the first seven years of his reign his energies were directed towards Bavaria and Lorraine. Bavaria enjoyed a position of greater independence than any of the other duchies. Its traditions were more deeply rooted; the influence of the old ducal family was stronger. It had ties closely binding it with the other southern duchy, Swabia. Burchard, Duke of Swabia, had died the year of Otto's accession and the new king filled the vacancy by appointing Otto, the son of his half brother Liudolf, former Duke of Swabia. Duke Burchard's widow, Hedwig, was the daughter of Judith, the widow of Henry I of Bavaria, who was always anxious to advance the interests of her family. She and her son Henry, the ruling Duke of Bavaria, resented the favour shewn to Otto, son of Liudolf, and broke into open revolt. In the first struggles we may see an arrangement of parties which remained unchanged throughout the reign. On the one side stand the sons of the children of Otto the Great by his first marriage with Edith, both named Otto, the one just elected to the duchy of Swabia, the other shortly after appointed Duke of Carinthia; to this party the Emperor first turned for support. The Bavarian family, Duke Henry and his cousin Henry, son of Duke Berthold, were the leaders of the opposite faction. Later, it was openly favoured by the Empress Adelaide the queen-mother, who had a somewhat natural aversion to the sons of her stepchildren, for it was these men who had headed the revolt against her husband in 955 just after and largely in consequence of her marriage[1]. In the first rebellion in Bavaria Henry's ambition seems to have aspired to the throne. It was the more serious as he was allied with Boleslav, Duke of the Bohemians, and with Mesco, Duke of the Poles. The plot was however discovered in time; Henry and his chief adviser, Abraham, Bishop of Freising, were summoned under pain of the ban to appear before the Emperor and were imprisoned, Henry at Ingelheim, Bishop Abraham at Corvey; Judith, who was also deeply involved in the conspiracy, entered a convent at Ratisbon.

It was not until the autumn of 975 that Otto was able to take the field against Boleslav of Bohemia to punish him for his share in the Bavarian revolt. In the interval he had been called away to deal with a dangerous incursion of the Danes under Harold Bluetooth who, having crossed the frontier wall, was ravaging the country beyond the Elbe. Otto hurriedly collected an army, marched against the invaders, and drove them back to the wall. He could not pursue his success further for a formidable army of Norwegians under Jarl Hákon blocked his way. But his object was achieved. Harold opened negotiations offering all his treasure; this Otto declined and withdrew to collect a larger army, but when Harold offered not only treasure, but also a tribute and his son as a hostage, his terms were accepted. To strengthen the frontier Otto established a new fortress on the east coast of Schleswig.

Before two years had elapsed, Henry, who well merited his name " the Wrangler," had escaped from his imprisonment at Ingelheim and again broke into revolt. Two brothers, Berthold and Liutpold, of the house of Babenberg, hurriedly mustered the local levies and held him in check until, at the approach of Otto himself, the rebellious duke fled

---

[1] A table will make the relationships clear:

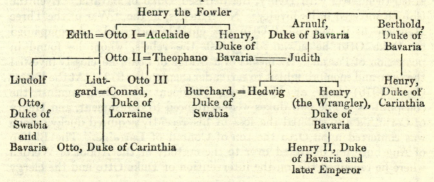

to Bohemia. At an assembly of princes held at Ratisbon in July 976 Henry was deprived of his duchy, which was granted to Otto of Swabia. For the first time the two duchies were united under one ruler; but the Bavaria granted to Duke Otto was not the same Bavaria as Duke Henry had formerly held. Several important changes diminished it in extent and in power; first, Carinthia with the March of Verona was completely severed and formed into a separate duchy which was conferred on Henry, called the younger, son of the old Duke Berthold of Bavaria; secondly, the two brothers, Berthold and Liutpold, were rewarded for their fidelity to the imperial cause. Berthold was made more independent, the Nordgau of Bavaria being formed into a new margravate on the Bohemian frontier, while Liutpold was established on a firmer footing on the East March, which we now know as Austria, where his descendants flourished first as margraves and later as dukes down to the thirteenth century. Certain ecclesiastical changes were made at the same time. The Church in Bavaria was freed from the control of the duke and became directly dependent on the king; large grants were made to the bishops of Salzburg and Passau; and the bishopric of Prague, founded the previous year, was attached to the province of Mayence, thus freeing the ecclesiastical centre in Bohemia from any Bavarian influence.

Boleslav of Bohemia had been a principal accessory to the Bavarian revolts; the campaign of 975 had been without result, so in 977 Otto again took the field against him. Though he himself was successful, his nephew, Duke Otto, in command of an army of Bavarians, met with a disaster. One evening his men were peacefully bathing in the river near Pilsen, when they were surprised by a body of Bohemians who slew many of them and captured much booty. Eventually, however, Boleslav was brought to submission and did homage to the Emperor at Magdeburg (Easter 978). A year later a successful campaign compelled Mesco, Duke of the Poles, to submit to the imperial authority. But while the Emperor was engaged in the punitive expedition in Bohemia, a fresh conspiracy of an alarming nature was set on foot in Bavaria. Henry of Carinthia, and Henry, Bishop of Augsburg, allied themselves with Henry, the deposed Duke of Bavaria. Even the Church wavered in its loyalty. Nevertheless, in the " War of the Three Henries" as it was called, Otto was entirely successful. Accompanied by Duke Otto he advanced against the rebels, whom he found in possession of Passau. By means of a bridge of boats he closely invested the town and soon brought it to surrender (September 977). At the Easter Court (978) held at Magdeburg judgment was given against the conspirators. The two dukes were sentenced to banishment, and Henry of Carinthia also suffered the loss of his recently acquired duchy, which was conferred upon Otto the son of Conrad of Lorraine. The Bishop of Augsburg was delivered over to the custody of the Abbot of Werden where he remained till, on the intervention of Duke Otto and the clergy of his diocese, he was granted his liberty (July). The repeated rebellions in Bavaria occasioned a marked change in the character of the duchy. Its traditions, its independent position, its ruling family were crushed. Henceforth Bavaria like the other duchies takes its place in the national system of Otto the Great. It was also in consequence of the new appointments in Bavaria and of the elevation of the two Ottos to the ducal dignity that the Empress Adelaide who had, in the first years of the reign, exercised considerable influence over her son, now withdrew from court to her native Burgundy. Her place of influence in Otto's councils was afterwards taken by the Empress Theophano.

Lorraine had from the beginning of the reign been a source of trouble to Otto. The lower province, after the death of Duke Godfrey in Italy, had fallen under the direct government of the king. In January 974 Reginar and Lambert (Lantbert), the sons of the banished Count Reginar of Hainault, had attempted to regain their father's possessions and fortified Boussu on the river Haine. Otto advanced into Lorraine, burnt the stronghold, and captured the garrison; but he allowed the brothers to escape. Two years later they reappeared in alliance with Charles, the brother of Lothair, King of France, and Otto, son of the Count of Vermandois. The revolt was, however, suppressed by Godfrey, whom the Emperor had set over the county of Hainault. The next year the troublesome sons of Reginar were reinstated in their paternal inheritance of Hainault, and their ally in the recent rebellion, Charles, the brother of the King of France, was invested with the duchy of Lower Lorraine.

Charles, however, entertained no fraternal feelings for his brother; indeed, Otto's object in granting him the duchy seems to have been a desire to gain an ally in the all too probable event of his coming to blows with the King of France. This appointment, therefore, together with the slight shewn to the Empress Adelaide, whose daughter Emma by her first marriage with Lothar of Italy was now Queen of France, provided ample pretext for Lothair to try to regain Lorraine for the West Frankish crown. So long as a Caroling occupied the Western throne, there was a party in Lorraine ready to transfer their allegiance to him. With so large an army that "their erect spears appeared more like a grove of trees than arms," Lothair marched against Aix-la-Chapelle. When news of the French advance was brought to Otto he refused to believe it possible. Convinced of the truth only when the enemy were at the very gates of the town, he and his wife were compelled to make a hasty retreat to Cologne, leaving the old Carolingian capital in the hands of the enemy. Lothair sacked the palace and reversed the position of the brazen eagle set up on its summit by Charles the Great[1]. He then returned to his own dominions. Otto did not

---

[1] According to Richer III. 71, the eagle was set up by Charles the Great facing the west, signifying that the Emperor was lord of the West Franks as well as the

permit this extraordinary piece of audacity to remain long unpunished. With a large army he crossed the frontier in October, while the French king retreated before him to Etampes. Otto sacked the royal manor of Attigny, passed unchecked through Rheims and Soissons, plundered the palace of Compiègne and eventually appeared on the heights of Montmartre above Paris. But as a fresh army was mustering to resist him, he contented himself with ravaging the country round and then withdrew to Germany. The French army harassed the rear of the retreating army and even fought a slight engagement on the banks of the Aisne. In the next year Lothair involved himself in a local dispute in Flanders, but finally sought an interview with the Emperor at Margut on the Chiers (980), where he agreed to abandon all claim to Lorraine.

During the first seven years of his reign Otto had been fairly successful. He had settled the troubles with which he was confronted in Bavaria at the outset of his reign; he had maintained his position in Lorraine in the face of repeated rebellions and attempts of Lothair to recover it for the West Frankish crown; he had subdued the Danes, the Bohemians, and the Poles. Under his rule the work of conversion of the heathen races on the eastern frontier made rapid progress. Bishoprics were established for Bohemia at Prague, for Moravia at Olmütz and for Denmark at Odense on the island of Fyn. Even the Hungarians, in spite of intermittent warfare in which Liutpold succeeded in extending the East March as far as the Wienerwald, were inclined to be on better terms with Germany and permitted Bishop Pilgrim of Passau to pursue his missionary labours among the heathen Magyars.

The affairs of Germany were at last sufficiently settled to justify the Emperor's absence in Italy. In November 980 he crossed the Alps accompanied by his wife, his infant son (Otto III was born in July 980), and his nephew Otto of Swabia.

The disastrous end of Otto's Italian campaign of 980–983[1] led to revolts all along the German frontier, accompanied by a heathen reaction. Duke Bernard of Saxony on his way to the diet of Verona (983) was summoned back by the news that Svein who had deposed his father, Harold Bluetooth, had overrun the Danish March. The Lyutitzi broke into rebellion, destroyed the churches of Havelberg and Brandenburg and put many Christians to the sword. Hamburg was plundered and burnt by the Obotrites, Zeitz by an army of Bohemians. The faith of Christ and St Peter, says Thietmar, was forsaken for the worship of demons. A combined movement of the Saxon princes

East Franks, and King Lothair turned it to the S.E. indicating that the West Frankish king was lord over Germany. But Thietmar iii. 8 says the opposite. "It was the custom of all who possessed this place to turn it (the eagle) towards their country"; that is, if it pointed east it indicated that the German king was lord of Aix-la-Chapelle.

[1] *Vide supra*, pp. 163–70.

under the Margrave Dietrich, the Archbishop of Magdeburg and the Bishop of Halberstadt succeeded in checking the advance in a battle fought at Belkesheim, just west of the Elbe, but they failed to re-establish German influence or Christianity among the heathen tribes. The work of Otto the Great, carried on so successfully in the earlier years of his son's reign, received a blow from which it did not recover for more than a century.

It only remains to notice the complete reversal of German policy which is marked by the diet held at Verona in June 983. The death of Otto, Duke of Swabia and Bavaria, at Lucca on his way back to Germany necessitated a new arrangement for the southern duchies. His death, combined with the disasters in Germany and Italy, involved the ruin of the party represented by the descendants of Otto the Great's first marriage, the two Duke Ottos, and the ascendancy of what we may call the Adelaide party. The Emperor was not strong enough to stand against the powerful influences of his mother. Not only did he make her regent in Italy, but further he deposed Otto of Carinthia from his duchy which, reunited with Bavaria, he gave to Henry the Younger. The unfortunate Otto was therefore kept from his duchy through no fault of his own, until Otto III, taking advantage of another vacancy in 995, reinstated him in his former dignity. Swabia was granted to Conrad of the Franconian family. At the same diet the infant son of the Emperor was chosen as the successor to the throne.

Misfortune and the Italian climate combined to ruin the Emperor's health. After a short illness he died at Rome on 7 December 983 in his twenty-eighth year and was buried in the church of St Peter.

Otto III, then three years old, was being crowned at the Christmas festival at Aix-la-Chapelle when news arrived of his father's death at Rome. The question of the regency at once arose. It would, according to German practice, fall to Henry the Wrangler, the deposed and im-prisoned Duke of Bavaria, but Byzantine custom favoured the Empress Mother and it was not likely that Theophano would allow her claim to be lightly passed over. Henry, who was immediately set at liberty by the Bishop of Utrecht, took prompt action. Moreover, it soon became evident that he was aiming not at the regency but at the crown. He hurried to Cologne and before his opponents had time to consider the situation, he had taken the young Otto out of the hands of Archbishop Willigis of Mayence. Though he won the support of the powerful Archbishops of Cologne, Trèves and Magdeburg and the Bishop of Metz, yet a strong party in Lorraine collected to withstand him. The strength of this party lay in the influential family of Godfrey, the Count of Hainault and Verdun. His son Adalbero was Bishop of Verdun, his brother, also Adalbero, was Archbishop of Rheims. With the arch-bishop worked the most remarkable man of the tenth century, Gerbert of Aurillac. In 983 Otto II had made him abbot of the Lombard monastery of Bobbio, but disgusted at the lack of discipline of the monks, he had just returned to resume his former work of *Scholasticus* at the cathedral school of Rheims. From his correspondence for these years we can gather how indefatigably he laboured in the interests of the young Otto.

The situation was rendered more complex by the unexpected appearance of Lothair as a candidate for the regency. Perhaps his real motive was to induce Henry to give up Lorraine in return for the abandonment of his claim, which, being upheld by the Lotharingian aristocracy, by his brother Charles, and by Hugh Capet, was sufficiently formidable to cause alarm. Soon he actually made this proposal to Henry and entered into a secret compact with him, by which he agreed to support the duke's claim to the throne in return for the duchy. The Lotharingian nobles, alienated by the altered circumstances, at once prepared to resist Lothair's attempt to occupy the duchy. Verdun fell before the French attack (March 984) and Godfrey, who bravely defended it, was captured. The stout resistance of Godfrey's sons, Herman and Adalbero, prevented Lothair from making further progress, and the hostility of Hugh Capet made it necessary for him to turn his attention to his own kingdom. With the departure of the King of France, the centre of action shifted to the east. In Saxony Henry's efforts met with no success. Though he had himself proclaimed king by his supporters at the Easter festival at Quedlinburg, where he received oaths of fealty from the princes of the Bohemians, Poles and Obotrites, he was formally renounced by an assembly of Saxon princes. Loyal to the representative of the Saxon dynasty, they even prepared to resist the usurper with arms. Failing to reconcile them, though succeeding in staving off a war by a truce, Henry withdrew to his old duchy of Bavaria, where he found himself firmly withstood by his cousin Henry the Younger.

Lothair had made no headway in Lorraine. The loyalty of the Saxons and the energy of Conrad of Swabia and Willigis of Mayence, the leaders of Otto's party, prevented Henry from gaining ground in the other duchies; he was in no position to attempt to win the crown by force of arms. Driven by pressure of circumstances he submitted his claim to a diet of German princes. The assembly which met at Bürstadt near Worms decided unanimously in favour of the young Otto. Henry engaged to deliver the boy to the care of his mother and grandmother at a diet to be held at Rara (perhaps Rohr, near Meiningen) on 29 June. In the interval Henry, supported by Boleslav, prince of the Bohemians, tried his fortunes in Thuringia but with similar lack of success. At the diet of Rara, on the guarantee that he would be compensated with Bavaria, Henry handed over the young king to the charge of Theophano and Adelaide, who had been summoned from Italy. Henry the Younger made some show of resistance at being ousted from his duchy of Bavaria, but a final pacification took place early in the year

985 at Frankfort. Henry was re-established in Bavaria and his cousin was forced to content himself with Carinthia and the March of Verona, now again formed into a separate duchy. At first Theophano and Adelaide acted as joint regents, but the influence of the former soon became predominant. In the administration of the kingdom she was assisted by Willigis, Archbishop of Mayence, who took charge of affairs in Germany during her absence in Italy in 989. The minority fell at a critical time. The death of King Lothair of France in 986, followed a year later by the death of his son, Louis V, without an heir, plunged France into a civil war, during which the opposing parties of Hugh Capet and Charles of Lower Lorraine, the representative of the Carolingian house, each sought to win the help of the regents of Germany. Theophano succeeded in maintaining a neutral attitude ; but the dynastic question was no sooner settled in favour of Hugh, than another hot dispute broke out as the result of the decision of the synod held at the monastery of St Basle de Verzy near Rheims (June 991). The Archbishop Arnulf of Rheims, the natural son of Lothair, was deposed from his see and Gerbert was appointed in his place. Germany was again called upon to play a part in the affairs of France. A synod of German bishops held at Ingelheim in 994 declared against the decisions of St Basle. The controversy dragged on until 998, when Otto solved the problem by making Gerbert Archbishop of Ravenna, thus leaving Rheims in undisputed possession of Arnulf.

Still more serious was the general state of unrest on the Eastern frontier. During the years 985–987 there was continual fighting against the Wends and Bohemians. With the help of Mesco, Duke of the Poles, Meissen was recovered for the Margrave Eckhard. When in 990 a war broke out between the Poles and Bohemians Theophano supported Mesco while Boleslav was allied with the Lyutitzi. The Bohemians, fearing to engage with the Germans, treated for peace. The Saxons acted as mediators but barely escaped destruction through the treachery of the barbarians. It was Boleslav, and not their ally Mesco, who enabled the Saxon army to escape in safety to Magdeburg. On 15 June 991 Theophano died. Adelaide, who now returned from Italy and undertook the regency, had neither the energy nor the statesmanlike qualities of the younger Empress, and the weakness of her rule soon became apparent in the frontier warfare. Brandenburg in 991 became the centre of operations. The young king captured it with the help of Mesco, but no sooner was his back turned than it was reconquered for the Lyutitzi by a Saxon named Kiso. Otto renewed the attack in the following year with the help of Henry of Bavaria and Boleslav of Bohemia; Boleslav, who had succeeded his father Mesco as prince of the Poles, being threatened with a war with the Russians, was unable to accompany the king in person but sent troops to his assistance. But not till the spring of 993 was the fortress recovered, and then not by the ineffectual efforts of his motley army, but by the same means as it was lost, the treachery of Kiso. His faithless conduct brought on an attack of the Lyutitzi; they fell upon and scattered an army sent to Kiso's support under the Margrave Eckhard of Meissen. However, when the king took the field himself they were quickly dispersed. A brief notice of the Quedlinburg annalist informs us of a general rising of the Wends: " All the Slavs except the Sorbs revolted from the Saxons " (994). After a short campaign in the following year Otto seems to have patched up some kind of a truce, and restored order sufficient to permit him to leave Germany, and fulfil his cherished wish of visiting Italy.

Unfortunately the disturbances were not confined to the eastern frontier. In 991 the Northmen, taking advantage of the internal weakness of Germany, renewed their piratical descents on the Frisian coast. In 994 they actually sailed up the river Elbe and carried their devastations into Saxony. In an engagement fought at Stade a small band of Saxons was defeated and their leaders were captured. While the Saxon chiefs lay bound hand and foot on the ships, the Northmen ravaged the country at will. Of the captives, some were ransomed, the Margrave Siegfried effected his escape by making his capturers intoxicated, the remainder, after shameful mutilation, were cast, more dead than alive, upon the shore. The pirates renewed their inroads in the next year, but the defensive measures taken by Bishop Bernward of Hildesheim successfully checked their aggressions.

Our brief summary of the events of the frontier campaigns illustrates the difficulties of the situation in Germany; it shews how fatal and how lasting had been the effects of Otto II's Italian policy, how unwise the high imperial aims of Otto III. Fortunately for the regents the southern duchies had given no trouble since the baffled attempt of Henry the Wrangler to obtain the crown for himself. Changes however had taken place in their administration. On the death of Henry the Younger in 989 Carinthia and the March of Verona had been re-attached to the duchy of Bavaria. But when Henry the Wrangler died in 995, they did not pass with Bavaria to his son Henry, afterwards the Emperor Henry II, but were restored to Otto, the son of Conrad the Red[1].

Otto's first object was to visit Italy. He had taken the government into his own hands in 994 when he was fourteen years of age, but owing to the unsettled state of Germany it was not until 996 that he was able to achieve his purpose. It was after his return from his first expedition across the Alps that he began to develop that ambitious and somewhat fantastic policy, for which perhaps he has been too severely censured. It must be remembered that from his earliest boyhood he had come under the influence of foreigners. The blame must rest equally on all those who had charge of his education. His mother, the Empress Theophano, and his tutor John, Abbot of the monastery of Nonantula, a Calabrian by

---

[1] According to some authorities Otto was not restored to his duchy till 1002.

birth, had taught him Latin and Greek, taught him to despise "Saxon rusticity" and to prefer "our Greek subtility[1]." They had also made him familiar with the elaborate ceremonial of the Byzantine court. His intimacy with Gerbert, when he was still at an impressionable age, had moulded him into the ideals of the Roman Empire.

He was now in 996 Holy Roman Emperor, and the title had for him a greater meaning than for his predecessors. The legend on one of his seals, "renovatio imperii Romanorum," shews clearly that he realised that he was making a change in the imperial position. The change is most apparent in the ordering of the institution where the business of the Empire was transacted, the imperial chancery. Otto the Great had not revived the system which had prevailed under the Carolingians of treating Italy as a part of the Empire under the same administrative machinery. He had established a separate chancery for Italy. Germany and Italy were to be two distinct governments under one ruler. When a vacancy occurred in 994 in the chancellorship of Italy, Otto had appointed his chaplain Heribert. On the death of the German chancellor, Hildibald of Worms, in 998, Heribert was placed at the head of the German chancery also. Otto had departed from the system established by his grandfather and, working on a definite plan, he returned to the Carolingian tradition of a combined chancery for the whole Empire. The two titular heads, the arch-chancellors of Germany and Italy, remained, but their offices were sinecures; the business of the Empire was done by a single chancellor in a single chancery. Equally significant is Otto's choice of counsellors. He completely emancipated himself from the control of those men who had conducted the administration during his minority. Willigis of Mayence, Hildibald of Worms, were replaced by an entirely new body of men. With the exception of the chancellor Heribert, who was appointed Archbishop of Cologne in 999, the men who exercised the most influence at court were foreigners. Gerbert of Aurillac, Marquess Hugh of Tuscany, Peter, Bishop of Como, the arch-chancellor of Italy, form the Emperor's intimate circle of advisers.

The reverential, though perhaps over inquisitive, visit of the Emperor to the tomb of Charles the Great at Aix-la-Chapelle in the year 1000 is symbolic of his attitude and policy. The famous story of the opening of the tomb is recorded by the chronicler of the monastery of Novalesa in Lombardy, who, though writing more than half a century later, gives his information on the authority of Otto, Count of Lomello, who is said to have been present on the occasion. "We entered in," he said, "unto Charles. He was not lying down, as is the manner with the bodies of other dead men, but sat on a certain chair as though he lived. He was crowned with a golden crown, and held a sceptre in his hands, the same being covered with gloves, through which the nails had grown and

---

[1] Gerbert, *Epist.* (ed. Julien Havet), no. 186.

pierced.   And above him was a tabernacle compact of brass and marble exceedingly.   Now when we were come in unto the tomb, we brake and made straightway an opening in it.   And when we entered into it, we perceived a vehement savour.   So we did worship forthwith to him with bended thighs and knees ; and straightway Otto the Emperor clad him with white raiment, and pared his nails, and made good all that was lacking about him.   But none of his members had corrupted and fallen away, except a little piece of the end of his nose, which he caused at once to be restored with gold ; and he took from his mouth one tooth, and built the tabernacle again and departed[1]."

The Emperor's genuine aim was to unite the interests of Germany and Italy.   The appointments of his cousin Bruno (Gregory V) in 996 and of Gerbert (Silvester II) in 999 to the papal chair were intended to advance this end.   But this policy in reality amounted to a neglect of Germany. Since 996 he had spent only a few months on German soil.   It is not surprising, therefore, that he was regarded with distrust.   The older generation of German prelates had their grievance; they disliked his close connexion with the Papacy, they had been ousted from their former influential positions by foreigners and they resented it.   Otto's premature death alone prevented an open outbreak in Germany.   He himself realised that he had set his ambitions too high, that he had sacrificed Germany without gaining any material compensation.   " Are you not my Romans?" he is reported to have said in bitter reproach. " For you I have left my country and my kindred.   For love of you I have abandoned my Saxons, and all the Germans, my own blood...I have adopted you as sons, I have preferred you to all.   For your sake I have brought upon myself the envy and hatred of all.   And now you have cast out your father.   You have encompassed my servants with a cruel death, you have closed your gates against me." These are the words of a disappointed man.   He died in his twenty-second year at Paterno on 24 January 1002 from an attack of the small-pox.   It was his wish that he should be buried in the Carolingian capital.   After fighting a way through the lines of the hostile Romans, his followers succeeded in bringing his body safely to Aix-la-Chapelle, where it was buried in the centre of the choir of the church of St Mary.

---

[1] *Chronicon Novaliciense* III. 32: the truth of this narrative has been much controverted.   The smaller details may have been invented, but the central facts are probably historical and are in part supported by Thietmar [*Chronicon* IV. 46]. See an article by Professor Grauert, *Historisches Jahrbuch*, XIV. 302 f.   At the same time it must be admitted that the chronicler of Novalesa, although truthful, had the inborn gift of romance.

CHAPTER X.

THE EMPEROR HENRY II.

When Otto III, still a youth, expired at Paterno in January 1002, it seemed as if the life work of his grandfather Otto the Great had been completely undone. Animosity pursued the Emperor even after death; for only by hard fighting could his friends succeed in transporting his remains through the plain of Lombardy for interment in Germany. The fate therefore, alike of the Western Empire and of the German kingdom upon which it was based, depended far more than usual upon the qualities of the man who might be called to occupy the vacant throne.

To this grave crisis there was added the misfortune of a disputed succession. Otto III, the last descendant in the male line of Otto the Great, had died unmarried; nor was there any one person naturally destined to succeed him. Descent and election were the two factors by which accession to the throne was legally determined; but the relative influence of these varied according to circumstances. On the present occasion it was election, in practice confined to the magnates, which was bound to be preponderant. For though a candidate was forthcoming from the royal house, he was met at once by powerful opponents. And his claim in itself was not indisputable. The true representative of the Ottos was the son of the late Emperor's only wedded sister Matilda, wife of Ezo, son of Herman, Count Palatine in Lorraine. But this heir was a child, and was the offspring of a marriage which had been deemed unequal. Matilda's son therefore was now passed over in silence. There were also two men who could assert some right to be accepted as head of the Liudolfing house. The one was Otto, Duke of Carinthia, grandson (through his mother Liutgard) of Otto the Great, and son of the famous Conrad, once Duke of Lorraine, who had fallen gloriously at the Lechfeld. To his great position Otto added the personal qualities of dignity and uprightness. He must have been at this time at least fifty years of age. The other was a far younger man, Henry, Duke of Bavaria, son of Duke Henry "the Wrangler," and grandson of that earlier Henry, the younger brother of Otto the Great, who was the first of his family to rule in Bavaria. The present duke therefore was the actual representative in the male line of King Henry "the Fowler," the first of the Saxon kings. As it happened, no rivalry arose between the two kinsmen. For when Henry expressed his readiness to accept Otto as king, the latter declined to come forward and, acknowledging Henry to be the fitter man, urged him to secure election for himself.

But election also was legally necessary; and the magnates were not disposed to let slip the present opportunity of choosing a king at their own pleasure. When therefore the funeral train of the late Emperor reached Augsburg on its way to Aix, Henry, anxious to assert his claim, first took forcible possession of the imperial insignia, and then sought by profuse promises to win over the attendant magnates for the support of his cause, but he met with little success.

Already indeed a formidable rival had appeared. The chief men of Saxony had met at Frohse, and there the Margrave Eckhard of Meissen had revealed his purpose of gaining the throne. He was the foremost warrior of his time; he had fought with distinction against the Saracens in Italy, and at Rome in 998 it was he who had brought about the surrender of the castle of Sant' Angelo and the death of its defender Crescentius. As Margrave of Meissen he had repelled the Wends, reduced Bohemia to vassalage, and restrained the Polish duke Boleslav from assailing the kingdom. Though not of royal descent, he was sprung of an ancient Thuringian stock, and was connected with the Billungs, the new ducal house of Saxony. But a powerful enemy, the Margrave Liuthar of the North Mark, now set himself to frustrate Eckhard's ambitious design. Having secured a sworn promise from most of the Saxon magnates to take no part in electing a king until a further conference, Liuthar secretly visited the Duke of Bavaria, upon whom he urged the necessity of sending an envoy to represent his interests at the postponed meeting. And so skilfully did Henry's emissary, by means of lavish promises, work upon the Saxon nobles when they met at Werla, that he won from them a unanimous recognition of Henry's hereditary right to the throne and a solemn pledge of service. Eckhard's haughty abstention from the meeting had ruined his cause.

By this time a third competitor for the crown was in the field. This was Herman II, Duke of Swabia. Timorous and retiring by nature, Herman had come forward at the suggestion of others. After the obsequies of Otto III had been performed at Aix on 5 April, most of the magnates there present had expressed their disinclination to accept Henry of Bavaria as his successor. In the Duke of Swabia they saw a candidate more to their liking; and certainly Herman's descent from a great Franconian house, one member of which had formerly occupied the throne, and his position as ruler of one of the chief races of Germany were plausible reasons for his elevation. In reality it was his very gentleness of character that recommended him to his proposers, who might hope to find in him a king to be obeyed or not as they pleased.

Through the Duke of Swabia Eckhard hoped to revenge himself upon

Henry. But on his way to Duisburg, where Herman then was, he received an intimation that he would not be admitted to the counsels of the Swabian party. Returning homewards after this second rebuff, he was waylaid at Pöhlde on the night of 30 April by four brothers who cherished a private grudge against him, and was slain.

This tragic event removed a dangerous enemy from Henry's path, but the contention with Duke Herman proved long and bitter. Henry could count upon the magnates of Bavaria, of East Franconia, and of Saxony, while Herman had the support only of those of Swabia and of West Franconia. The Swabian faction, however, was resolute, and the Lorrainers were still doubtful. Archbishop Willigis of Mayence, the mainstay of the last two Emperors, now stood for the principle of legitimate succession. At the beginning of June, Henry, with his Bavarian and Franconian adherents, approached the Rhine at Worms, evaded Herman, and entered Mayence. There his election followed; and on 7 June that act was ratified by his solemn unction and coronation.

This success decided the wavering Dietrich, Duke of Upper Lorraine. But the election had been carried through in haste by a few partisans of the new king; and not only did the Duke of Swabia and his friends remain defiant, but the nobles of Lower Lorraine still held aloof, while those of Saxony took umbrage at their total exclusion from the proceedings at Mayence. To force Herman to submission Henry turned southwards and began to ravage Swabia. But the duke retaliated by assaulting and sacking his own city of Strasbourg, whose bishop had declared for his rival, and refused to be drawn into a decision by battle. Baffled in the South, Henry proceeded to make sure of the rest of the kingdom. In Thuringia, in July, he received full acknowledgment from Count William of Weimar and the other chief men, and gratefully abolished the ancient tribute of swine, due from the Thuringians to the crown. But from the Saxon magnates Henry obtained a less easy recognition. There had assembled to meet him at Merseburg on 23 July a great company of the bishops and counts of Saxony, at whose head stood the Archbishops of Bremen and Magdeburg with their Duke Bernard and the Margraves Liuthar and Gero. Duke Boleslav of Poland also, fresh from an attack on the mark of Meissen made after the death of Eckhard, presumed to appear among them. These men, though they received the new king with deference, were not prepared to offer him an unconditional allegiance. They stood upon their separate rights, and the next day, before any homage was paid, Bernard came forward in their name and in that of the Saxon people to assert their peculiar claims, and to demand of Henry how far he would pledge himself to respect them. Henry replied by extolling the steadfast loyalty of the Saxons to their kings; it was only with their approval that he now came among them as king; and so far from infringing their law he would be careful to observe it at all points, and would do his utmost to fulfil their reasonable wishes. The speech satisfied the magnates; and

17

Duke Bernard taking the sacred lance in his hands, delivered it to the king; their homage and oath of fealty then followed. From Merseburg Henry hastened to Lower Lorraine. In the course of his journey he was joined by his wife Kunigunda, whom he saw crowned queen at Paderborn on 10 August by Archbishop Willigis. A fierce conflict, which broke out between the king's Bavarian followers and the Saxon inhabitants of the city, marred the rejoicings. In Lower Lorraine Henry found no ready acceptance. Two bishops only received him; others hesitated to join them; and Archbishop Heribert of Cologne, indulging a personal grudge, purposely held aloof. At length the prelates concurred in choosing Henry to be king, and after tendering him their oath of fealty, accompanied him to Aix. There, on 8 September, the remaining Lorrainer magnates joined in placing Henry on the coronation chair of his predecessors, and in paying him homage. Nothing therefore was now wanting but the submission of the Duke of Swabia. Herman, however, finding himself now so far outmatched, was already prepared to yield. Through mediators he besought the king's grace for himself and his adherents; and then on 1 October appeared in person before Henry at Bruchsal. On swearing allegiance, Herman was suffered to retain both his duchy and his fiefs, but was required to make good the damage he had caused to the city of Strasbourg.

Henry's title to reign, thus acknowledged in Germany, was also accepted by peoples outside. The Venetians renewed with Henry the treaty of friendship concluded with Otto II. In the vassal state of Bohemia a revolution had lately set up a new ruler who at once sought formal investiture at the hands of Henry. Lastly, from Italy, there came letters and envoys of the imperialist party, urging Henry to intervene in rebellious Lombardy.

Henry of Bavaria, the fifth of his house to occupy the German throne, is known in history as Henry II, both as King and Emperor. He was born on 6 May 973, and had therefore lately completed his twenty-ninth year when he was crowned at Mayence in June 1002. His early life had been moulded by adversity. By the rebellion of his father, Duke Henry "the Wrangler," he had been deprived of his home; and after some time spent under the care of Abraham, Bishop of Freising, he had been sent, still a child, to be brought up at Hildesheim. There he received his first grounding in an education which made him in all ways a cultivated man, well learned both in Holy Scripture and in ecclesiastical lore. He became acquainted at the same time with the methods of church government, as he was meant for the clerical career; but his father's restoration in 985 brought him back to Bavaria. Further training under Bishop Wolfgang of Ratisbon helped to form those decided ideas upon Church and State which afterwards shaped his policy as king. Upon the death of his father in August 995 Henry succeeded without question to the duchy of Bavaria. The last exhortation of the repentant Wrangler to his son had been to remain ever loyal to his king; and by that advice Henry steadily walked during the next six years. Otto III had no more faithful subject than his cousin of Bavaria, who twice accompanied him to Italy, and on the second occasion was instrumental, with Marquess Hugh of Tuscany, in saving him from the wrath of the Roman mob. Moreover, when the German magnates were scheming to dethrone the absent Emperor, Henry refused to take any part in their conspiracy. Until Otto's premature death opened to him the prospect of succession, he had been, as Duke of Bavaria, a just and vigorous ruler.

Of Henry's outward appearance nothing certain is known. Later tradition indeed gives him the attribute of "the Lame," and two varying legends profess to account for the supposed infirmity. A real hindrance, however, was the liability to severe attacks of a painful internal complaint; Henry was in truth a sickly man, and his bodily weakness may have sometimes interfered with his plans. His life and actions were regulated by a strict conscientiousness and by a piety sober and restrained. The Christian faith and its Founder, the saints and their sanctuaries, the German church and its officers, were the objects of his reverence; he punctually attended, and sometimes took part in, the ceremonies of the Church; he was the determined foe of ecclesiastical abuses; and if he shared the prevailing superstition in regard to relics, this was balanced by an ungrudging liberality to the poor and a splendid munificence in the founding and maintenance of religious institutions. With all this, Henry was no mere devotee. He was sociable, and took pleasure in the ordinary amusements of his day; he was not above playing a practical joke on a troublesome bishop, and once even incurred rebuke for encouraging a brutal form of sport. The chase was to him a welcome recreation. Henry was thus utterly unlike Otto III. He loved his ancestral land of Saxony; the glamour of Italy did not entice him away from his proper task as a German king; nor did he entertain any visionary idea of universal dominion under the form of a revived Roman Empire. The whole bent of his mind was practical; his undertakings were limited in scope and were pursued with caution. Prudence indeed was the quality by which he most impressed his contemporaries. Yet he was not without the kingly ideals of his day. He had a passion for law and order; and in his conception of the kingly office he was the guardian of the realm against attack from without and against disturbance within, the champion of the weak and the enemy of all wrong-doers, the defender of the Church and the promoter of its spiritual work. No king before him was more untiring in travel to dispense justice among his people; no ruler could be more stern on occasion in executing judgment on rebels and lawbreakers. In spite of his weak health he did not shrink from taking his full share in the dangers and hardships of a campaign. And with this courage there was joined a royal humanity which could shew mercy to the vanquished. Alike in the limitation of his aims and the steady persistency of his rule, he shewed no little resemblance to the earliest Henry of his race. In moral dignity, it may be safely said, he excelled any monarch of the Saxon house.

The Empire presented a complication of difficulties such as only patience and prudence could overcome. Nearly every province was seething in unrest. Not only were the lay magnates, as ever, at feud with their ecclesiastical neighbours, but each order was rent by quarrels among its own members. Among the clergy of every degree, worldliness and neglect of duty, avarice and loose living, were widely prevalent. It was a heavy task, therefore, that Henry undertook, and he had now to restore by his own efforts the sovereign power in face of men who had hitherto been his equals.

In these adverse circumstances the new reign began, and by them its course was set. The history of the reign is confused; but through it all may be traced the king's unwavering purpose of bringing about a more settled state of things. The large measure of success that he achieved therein entitles Henry to a high place among the sovereigns of Germany; but his zeal for the suppression of ecclesiastical abuses was felt over a wider sphere, and has set him among the reformers of the Western Church. And it is in the ecclesiastical policy that he pursued, combining as it did the political system of Otto the Great with the reforming energy of Henry the Third, and thus linking him with both those monarchs, that the chief interest of his career is to be found.

The beginning of Henry's reign was marked by two grave losses to the Empire; in the South, of the Lombard kingdom; in the East, of the tributary duchy of Bohemia. The former event, indeed, had taken place even before Henry had become a candidate for the throne. For within a month of the death of Otto III Lombardy broke into open revolt; and on 15 February 1002 Ardoin, Marquess of Ivrea, was elected King of the Lombards and crowned in the basilica of St Michael at Pavia.

This new king was nearly related to, if he did not actually spring from, the marquesses of Turin, and was connected also with the late royal house of Ivrea, with whose hereditary March he had been invested about twelve years since. His career as marquess had been a stormy one. During a quarrel with Peter, Bishop of Vercelli, Ardoin had taken that city by assault, and in the tumult the bishop was slain. Soon after, his violence towards Warmund, the Bishop of his own city of Ivrea, had brought down upon him a severe rebuke from Pope Gregory V. Through the influence of Leo, Bishop of Vercelli, Ardoin was summoned to Rome in 999 to answer for his alleged misdeeds. Yet, in spite of papal censure and imperial forfeiture, he had kept fast hold both of his March and of his possessions until the turn of fortune raised him to the Lombard throne[1].

Ardoin may have been in truth little more than a rough soldier. Yet he proved himself a skilful leader in war; and if his reign was unfortunate

---

[1] See *supra*, Chap. VII, pp. 175–6.

it was not through any lack on his part of energy or courage. He certainly inspired his family and his friends with a devotion that shrank from no sacrifice. To the lay magnates he was their champion against the domination of the prelates, some few of whom also, free from German sympathies, were on his side. But it was chiefly the smaller nobles, the *secundi milites* or lesser vavassors, holding their lands at the will of episcopal or secular overlords, and with nothing to hope for from a foreign sovereign, who turned naturally to a native king whose domestic enemies were their own. Beside them stood many of the secular clergy, equally impatient of episcopal control; while lower down were the serfs, the voiceless tillers of church lands, many of whom had obtained their freedom, but all of whom it was now sought to reduce to perpetual bondage. In this endeavour the two bishops of Vercelli, Peter and Leo, had been especially active; and it was the latter who, but a short while before, had drafted the terrible decree of Otto III that no serf of the Church should ever be allowed to issue from his servitude. And to Ardoin therefore these freedmen and bondmen now looked as their only possible saviour.

The revolt, if primarily social, was so far national that it was directed against those elements of authority which leaned on foreign support. The German interest in Lombardy was still strong. Some prelates, the Archbishop of Ravenna and the bishops of Modena, Verona, and Vercelli, were openly hostile to Ardoin from the first; and in agreement with them was the Marquess Tedald, holder of the five counties of Reggio, Modena, Mantua, Brescia, and Ferrara, whose family had risen to eminence by service to the Ottos. But the real soul of the opposition was Leo of Vercelli, a German by birth, whose energetic character, strong intellect, and immense acquirements made him a dangerous enemy. For he was at once an accomplished man of letters, an able lawyer, and a practised man of affairs. Worldly-minded, though zealous for good order in the Church, he was ever eager to advance his material interests; and the disappearance of the imperial system would mean his own utter ruin. His whole energies, therefore, were bent to the overthrow of the national king.

A progress through Lombardy secured Ardoin general acknowledgment, and the administration went on without break. The hostile magnates were helpless; while the rest, whatever their secret inclinations, gave outward obedience to the monarch in possession. But Ardoin's insolent bearing enraged his opponents, and so both sides looked abroad for help. Ardoin sent an envoy to France to obtain a promise of armed support from King Robert; Leo of Vercelli in person, backed by the prayers of other Italian magnates, besought Henry, now recognised as king in Germany, to intervene in Italy. Accordingly, Henry in December 1002 dispatched a moderate force under Duke Otto of Carinthia, in whose hands was the March of Verona, to the aid of his Italian adherents. The latter, headed by Archbishop Frederick of Ravenna and the Marquess

Tedald, were already on their way to join the duke, when Ardoin with superior forces threw himself between the allies, occupied Verona, and seized the mountain passes beyond. A few days later he made a surprise attack upon the enemy in the valley of the Brenta, and routed them with heavy loss. This victory for the time made Ardoin's authority secure.

Only a few weeks after Lombardy had thus asserted its independence, Bohemia was severed from Germany. Boleslav Chrobry (the Mighty), since succeeding his father Mesco as Duke of Poland in 992, had built up a powerful Slav monarchy beyond the Elbe. The various tribes occupying the plains watered by the Oder, the Warta, and the Vistula were united under his rule; he was allied by marriage with the neighbouring princes of Bohemia, Hungary, and Kiev; by the indulgence of the late Emperor he had been relieved of the annual tribute due to the German crown. Through Otto also he had secured from Pope Sylvester II the ecclesiastical independence of his country, with the establishment of Gnesen as a metropolitan see. Only in his vassalage to the Empire was there left any sign of political subjection. Now Boleslav saw an opportunity for enlarging his dominion in the West and achieving full independence. He overran the whole of the East Mark, or Mark of Gero, as far as the Elbe; then, turning southwards, he seized the towns of Bautzen and Strehla, and with the aid of its Slavonic inhabitants gained possession of the city of Meissen itself. Pushing westwards, he occupied the mark of Meissen as far as the White Elster, securing it with Polish garrisons. He had thus mastered all the territory known later as the Upper and Lower Lausitz, and the Elbe had here ceased to be a German river. Then Boleslav appeared at the diet of Merseburg to make sure of his conquest. But his offer to Henry of a large sum for the retention of Meissen was rejected: and Gunzelin, brother of the late Eckhard and half-brother of Boleslav, was invested by the king with the mark of Meissen, while Boleslav himself was allowed to keep only the districts to the east of the Black Elster.

Thenceforth the Polish duke became Henry's determined foe. He found support at once in German disaffection. The Babenberg Henry of Schweinfurt, Margrave of the Nordgau, hitherto a staunch adherent of the king, claimed investiture with the duchy of Bavaria as the promised reward for his aid in the succession contest. Incensed by the king's hesitation in granting the request, the margrave now made common cause with Boleslav, whose own wrath was further inflamed by an assault made upon himself and his followers, though without the privity of the king, on their departure from Merseburg.

And the opportunity soon came to Boleslav for revenge. In Bohemia there had ruled for the last three years, as a tributary of the German crown, his cousin and namesake, Duke Boleslav the Red, a tyrant whose jealousy had sent his half-brothers, Jaromir and Udalrich, with their mother, into exile, and whose cruelty now impelled his subjects to drive him out and to set up his kinsman Vladivoi as duke. While Vladivoi, to secure himself, took investiture from King Henry, the dispossessed prince sought refuge in Poland. But when Vladivoi's own vices brought his rule to an end early in 1003 and the Bohemians recalled Jaromir and Udalrich, the Polish duke intervened by force, drove the two princes a second time into banishment, and reinstated Boleslav the Red. It was not long before the ferocious vengeance which the restored duke took upon his enemies constrained the Bohemians in terror to implore protection from Boleslav of Poland. Seizing the desired occasion, Boleslav craftily enticed his kinsman into his power, caused him to be blinded, and then, hastening to Prague, secured his own acceptance as duke by the Bohemians. The act was an insolent defiance of Henry's authority; but the king, controlling his indignation, sent envoys to Boleslav offering recognition if the duke would acknowledge himself his vassal. Boleslav, however, haughtily rejected the proposal, and for the time Bohemia was lost to the German crown.

Nothing, indeed, could be done as yet for its recovery because of serious trouble in Germany itself. Already, early in the year, Henry had had to suppress disaffection in Lorraine with a strong hand; and now he learnt that the Margrave Henry, secretly aided by the Polish duke, was in open revolt in the Nordgau. From Bavaria the king took vigorous action against the rebel. But the margrave found two unexpected allies in his cousin Ernest of Babenberg and the king's own brother Bruno. Between King Henry and these three men a petty war was waged during the autumn of 1003, of which the Nordgau, the wide district lying north of the Danube between Bohemia and East Franconia, was the scene. Here the Babenbergs were firmly established; but the king's energy soon forced the margrave to forsake his strongholds for lurking places in the country-side. The operations culminated in the siege of Creussen, a fortified town near the sources of the Main, which was valiantly held against the royal forces by Bucco, the brother of the margrave, while the latter himself harassed the besiegers from outside. A surprise attack on his camp drove the margrave into flight, scattered his followers, and delivered Ernest a prisoner into the hands of the king. Thereupon Bucco surrendered Creussen. Boleslav endeavoured first to seduce Gunzelin into betraying Meissen to him, and on his refusal laid waste an entire *gau* west of the Elbe. But this diversion brought no relief to the duke's confederates. The margrave gave up further resistance, and, accompanied by Bruno and other rebels, sought safety with Boleslav. Though hostilities were renewed early in 1004 by a fierce attack by Boleslav upon Bavaria, replied to by Henry with an incursion into the Upper Lausitz, which was frustrated by a change of weather, the confederacy was soon after dissolved. Impelled by remorse, the two German nobles sought forgiveness of the king; Bruno through his brother-in-law King Stephen of Hungary, Margrave Henry of Schweinfurt through powerful friends at home. The margrave suffered imprisonment for some months, but both he and his adherents were spared the forfeiture of their lands. Bruno also was pardoned, and having later been ordained, became his brother's chancellor and eventually Bishop of Augsburg.

With the failure of this domestic revolt Henry was free for action abroad. The recovery of Italy and of Bohemia were equally urgent tasks; but the entreaties of certain Lombard magnates, including a special emissary from the Marquess Tedald and the faithful Leo of Vercelli, prevailed; and Henry, leaving the Saxons and Bavarians to hold Boleslav in check, started from Augsburg late in March at the head of an expeditionary force composed of Lorrainers, Franks, and Swabians, and after severe toil reached Trent on Palm Sunday, 9 April. In the face of this grave peril King Ardoin sent forward to secure the passes, while he himself gathered troops and took post as before in the plain of Verona. Henry thus found his advance checked along the Adige, and turning eastwards into the valley of the Brenta, seized a pass from the Val Sugana by surprise, and pitched camp on the left bank of the river. There he celebrated Easter (16 April). At the critical moment Ardoin had been deserted by most of the Italian leaders, and he had then no choice but to retreat hurriedly to the West. Henry entered Verona, and advanced thence by Brescia and Bergamo to Pavia, being joined at each stage of his march by successive groups of Italian magnates, of whom the Archbishops of Milan and Ravenna, and the Marquess Tedald, were the chief. At Pavia, on Sunday, 14 May 1004, he was elected King of the Lombards, and crowned in St Michael's the following day.

Henry had thus attained his object with surprising ease; and the ceremony he had just gone through, omitted as superfluous by his Saxon predecessors, was the formal annulment of Ardoin's coronation within the same walls two years before. The same afternoon a quarrel on slight cause arose between the Pavese and the Germans, and the citizens, rushing to arms, attacked the palace. Most of the German troops were quartered outside; but the royal partisans within the city rallied to Henry's side, and the assault on the palace was repelled. A furious conflict then ensued; and, as night fell, the royalists for their own protection fired the neighbouring buildings. The troops outside, attracted by the conflagration, stormed the walls in the face of a stiff resistance. The Pavese were now overpowered; numbers were cut down in the streets; and such as continued to fight from the housetops were destroyed along with their dwellings by fire. The slaughter was stopped by Henry's command, but not before many hundreds of the citizens had perished and a great part of their city had been consumed. The survivors were admitted to grace, and either in person or by hostages swore fealty to the king.

The fate of Pavia struck terror throughout Northern Italy. All thought of further resistance was crushed, except in the remote West, where Ardoin in his Alpine castle of Sparone was holding out manfully against a besieging force of Germans. The Lombards generally now made their submission to Henry, who a few days later, at Pontelungo near Pavia, held a general diet for the settlement of the kingdom. But the king's mind was already made up to leave Italy; and he started at the beginning of June on his way to Germany. After receiving, as his last act on Italian soil, the proffer of their fealty from certain Tuscan delegates, he reached Swabia by the middle of the month.

The expedition had in fact failed. For in spite of his coronation, of the homage of the magnates, and of the forced submission of most of the Lombards, Henry had not ventured beyond Lombardy; and even there he left behind him an unsubdued rival and a disaffected people. The horror of the burning of Pavia sank deep into the hearts of the Lombards, for whom he had destroyed the hope of settled order under their native king without giving them a stable government of his own. And for himself the sole advantage he had secured was the renewed assertion of the German claim to the crown of Lombardy.

Want of time was the cause of this meagre result; for Henry could not remain long enough in Italy to effect its settlement without neglecting the peril which menaced Germany from the East. It was necessary before everything to oust Boleslav from Bohemia. Henry gathered an army at Merseburg in the middle of August. The men of Saxony, East Franconia, and Bavaria, who had been exempted from the Italian expedition, were now called upon to serve against their nearest enemy. By gathering boats on the middle Elbe, as though for a direct invasion of Poland, the king hoped to mask his real intention of entering Bohemia from the North. But the flooding of the rivers hindered his movements and gave Boleslav time to prepare his defence. In spite, however, of resistance by the Polish archers, Henry forced his way over the Erzgebirge (Miriquidui), where he was joined by Jaromir, the exiled duke. On the arrival of the Bavarian contingent, which had been delayed, Henry sent forward Jaromir and his Bohemians, with some picked German troops, in order to surprise Boleslav in Prague. Boleslav, however, received timely warning to make his escape. He attempted no further defence, and Jaromir forthwith occupied Prague, where, amid general rejoicing, he was once more enthroned as duke. Henry soon after reached Prague, and solemnly invested Jaromir. In less than a month from the time he set out Henry had made so sure of Bohemia that not only could he send the Bavarians home, but could claim the help of Jaromir for the recovery from Boleslav of the Upper Lausitz. The task proved difficult through the stubborn defence of Bautzen by its Polish garrison; but the surrender of the town at length released the king and his wearied troops from the toils of war.

The recovery of Bohemia closed the earliest stage of Henry's career, a space of nearly three years, during which he had made good his claim to the German throne, and had first tried his strength upon the tasks that lay before him. No striking events, indeed, mark off the reign into definite periods, its course being one of slow and often interrupted accomplishment; yet the three Italian expeditions, made at long intervals, form convenient milestones for recording its progress. Nearly ten years were to elapse before he should again cross the Alps. The interval was occupied by an unceasing struggle in which Henry was able by sheer tenacity to win some success.

The enmity of the Polish duke was a constant menace. Though hostilities with Boleslav were not continuous, yet three actual wars were waged. The campaigns themselves present little of military interest. Whichever side took the offensive, the operations had generally the character of an extensive foray, in which few pitched battles were fought, and decisive results were rarely attained. Boleslav, after losing Bohemia, possessed no chief city the capture of which would have meant his ruin; and thus final victory was only possible for Henry by the seizure or destruction of Boleslav himself. The duke in turn, however successful he might be in the field, could not seriously endanger the German kingdom, though he might enlarge his border at German expense. This he sought to achieve in the region of the middle Elbe. The territory lying to the east of that river, the northern portion of which constituted the East Mark and the southern belonged to the Mark of Meissen, was the usual scene of contention and the prize waiting on its decision. Not without difficulty indeed was Boleslav prevented from winning a foothold on the west of the Elbe. In Henry's absence the jealousies of the Saxon leaders, upon whom lay the duty of defence, hindered united action. Some of them had become secret partisans of Boleslav; some were lukewarm in their service of the king. Especially those ecclesiastical magnates who felt real zeal for the Church were reluctant opponents of a prince who enjoyed the favour of the Roman See, and who had done much to further the cause of Christianity among his own people. A strange act of policy on the part of Henry increased their repugnance to serve against Boleslav. For during the Easter season of 1003 he had received at Quedlinburg envoys of the Redari and of the Lyutitzi, heathen Wendish tribes dwelling in the North Mark and had made a compact with them. None of the Wends had been more stubborn in resistance to the German domination, which they had long ago shaken off; with it had gone their compulsory Christianity. Fear of a fresh subjection and forcible conversion by the sword of Boleslav drove them to negotiate with Henry, to whom they could offer protection on his north-eastern frontier and active help in the field against the Polish duke. These advantages he secured by allowing them to retain their practical independence and still to hold to their heathen religion. The treaty did in fact prove of no small value. Yet this alliance of a Christian king with pagan tribesmen against another Christian prince gave deep offence to many of his subjects; and German warriors saw with impatience the idols of their Wendish associates borne as standards on the march to overcome a foe who held the same true faith as themselves.

Henry was not satisfied merely to regain Bohemia and to stand on the defensive against Polish attack. He aimed at recovering the whole of the lost territory between the Elbe and the Oder, once conquered and Christianised by Otto the Great. After suppressing early in 1005 a rising of the Frisians Henry summoned a general levy at Leitzkau, half-way between Magdeburg and Zerbst, on the farther side of the Elbe; and thence, in the middle of August, the king led his army forward through the East Mark, where he was joined by the Bavarians under their new Duke, Henry of Luxemburg, and by the Bohemians under Duke Jaromir. But the troops, delayed by false guides who entangled them in the marshes about the Spree, were harassed by ambushed attacks of the enemy. Just before the Oder was reached, the Lyutitzi, headed by their heathen images, attached themselves to the royal host. On pitching camp by the Bobra (Bober) near its junction with the Oder, Henry found Boleslav stationed in strong force at Crossen. The discovery of a ford enabled the king to send over part of his troops, whose appearance drove Boleslav into hasty retreat. The march was continued to within two miles of the city of Posen. But the German army was wearied, and now halted to collect supplies. Its want of vigilance, however, while it was scattered in foraging parties, allowed it to be taken unawares and defeated with heavy loss. This reverse, though not the crushing disaster represented by Polish tradition, disposed Henry to accept an offer made by Boleslav to come to terms. Envoys, with the Archbishop of Magdeburg at their head, were sent to Posen to negotiate with the duke; and a peace, the conditions of which are unknown, was established. The treaty, in any case, was hardly flattering to German pride, for at the utmost Henry can have won from Boleslav no more than a recognition of his authority in the Upper and the Lower Lausitz, and a renunciation of the duke's claim to Bohemia.

During the interval of uneasy peace that followed, Henry's attention was claimed on his western frontier. The Frisian coast was being harried by piratical Northmen; Valenciennes had been seized by the count of Flanders; the kingdom of Burgundy was in a state of turmoil. In Burgundy King Rodolph III, the last male of his house, was struggling vainly to uphold the royal authority against a defiant nobility. To Henry, the son of Rodolph's sister Gisela and his nearest heir, the present unsettlement, which imperilled his chance of succeeding to his uncle's crown, was a matter of serious concern. In 1006, therefore, he made his hand felt in Burgundy. The extent of his intervention is unknown; but the fact is clear that he now took possession of the city of Basle. This step, however brought about, was never reversed; and the sequel shewed it as the earliest in a series by which the independence of the Burgundian kingdom was destroyed.

The incursions of the Northmen, this year and the next, into Frisia were left to the local counts to deal with. It was otherwise when the ambitious Count Baldwin IV of Flanders, one of the mightiest vassals of the West Frankish crown, into whose hands had already fallen the castle set up by Otto the Great at Ghent, presumed to violate German territory east of the Scheldt and take forcible possession of the town of Valenciennes. Henry, whose repeated demands for his withdrawal had been ignored by the count, in June 1006 sought a meeting with Baldwin's overlord, King Robert, the result of which was a joint expedition of the two monarchs in September for the recovery of the town[1]. But the undertaking, though supported by Duke Richard of Normandy, the lifelong foe of the house of Flanders, came to naught; and Henry, to retrieve the failure, in the summer of 1007 led a great host to the Scheldt, crossed it, and then proceeded to lay waste the country. At Ghent, upon the supplication of the brethren of St Bavo's, he stayed his hand; but by this time Baldwin was ready to treat. His humble submission soon after, with the surrender of Valenciennes, won for him full forgiveness from the king. He swore peace; and also took an oath of fealty to Henry, by which, as it seems, he became his vassal for the royal castle at Ghent. Two years later, to secure his help against disaffection in Lorraine, Henry granted Baldwin in fief Valenciennes, to which the island of Walcheren was afterwards added. In thus accepting vassalage to the German crown, Baldwin won for the counts of Flanders their first footing beyond the Scheldt.

But while engaged upon this successful enterprise in the West, Henry had been overtaken by disaster on his Eastern frontier. Since the Polish campaign of 1005, he had been at pains to keep the Wends true to their compact, but, in the spring of 1007, he was visited at Ratisbon by a triple embassy from the Lyutitzi, from a considerable town in their neighbourhood, and from Duke Jaromir of Bohemia, which came to denounce the assiduous efforts of the Duke of Poland, by bribes and promises, to seduce them from their allegiance. They declared that, if Henry should remain any longer at peace with Boleslav, he must not count on further service from them. The king, then preparing for the invasion of Flanders, consented, on the advice of the princes, to a renewal of war against Poland. The issue was unfortunate; for the Saxons, the proper guardians of the Elbe and of the Marches beyond, proved utterly wanting. In the absence of the king, Boleslav invaded the Marches in force, wasting a wide district east of Magdeburg, and carrying away captive the inhabitants of Zerbst. The Saxon levies slowly gathered to repel him, and, with Archbishop Tagino of Magdeburg in supreme command, sullenly followed the duke as he returned home. But at Jüterbogk, long before the Oder had been reached, the heart of their leaders failed them, and their retreat enabled the Polish prince to reoccupy the eastern half of the Lower Lausitz, and soon after to secure possession once more of the Upper Lausitz. He had thus regained all the German territory that he had previously held and lost; he had established himself firmly on the west of the Oder; and from the ground thus gained no subsequent efforts of Henry availed to expel him.

---

[1] Cf. *supra*, Chap. v, p. 106.

In another sphere of activity, this same year of mingled success and disaster brought Henry, before its close, a peculiar triumph. This was the establishment, on 1 November 1007, of the new see of Bamberg. The completion of this cherished scheme was at once the fruit of Henry's religious zeal and the witness to his supremacy over the German Church. Nevertheless, it was just his claim to such supremacy in a particular case that involved him soon after in a bitter domestic quarrel, which ran its unhappy course for several years, and, combined with other troubles at home, effectually hindered further action abroad. At this point, then, it is necessary to explain Henry's ecclesiastical policy, upon which his whole system of government was based.

In right of the Crown, Henry had small material means at command to enforce his authority. The obedience due to him as their chosen and anointed king might be readily acknowledged by all his subjects, but was just as readily withheld when it conflicted with private interest. Especially was this the case with the higher nobility. The counts, though still in theory royal officials and responsible to the sovereign for the maintenance of public order in their several districts, had become in fact hereditary territorial magnates, whose offices, like their fiefs and their family estates, usually passed from father to son in regular succession. The privilege of "immunity" which many enjoyed, and the feudal relation now generally subsisting between them and their tenants, still further strengthened their position. These petty potentates however, who should have been the upholders of law, were too often its worst transgressors. Their greed for landed wealth urged them into perpetual feuds with one another or with their ecclesiastical neighbours, while the abuse of their seignorial rights made them the oppressors of the classes below them. In these evil tendencies they had been encouraged by the lax administration of the last two reigns. Yet even more were the greater lay magnates, the dukes and margraves, disposed to regard themselves as hereditary princes. The dukes, in spite of past efforts to reduce their pretensions, were the recognised chiefs of the separate races which made up the German nation, and, like Herman of Swabia, were generally too strong, even in defeat, to be displaced without risk. The margraves, holding an office less venerable, had also won, by effective service on the frontiers, a firm position in the State. Though dukes and margraves alike required investiture by the king, it was rarely that a son was not preferred to his father's place. The control of men so firmly established in power and dignity could be no easy task; yet it now depended upon the vindication of the royal authority whether the nation should preserve its political cohesion, or be split up, like the adjacent kingdoms on the West, into a loose aggregation of almost independent principalities under a nominal sovereign.

It was the second Henry who by his energy postponed for two generations the process of disintegration which set in under Henry IV. To restore the rule of law was his prime object. In the decay, however, of local justice, the Royal, or Palatine, Court, over which the king presided in person, was the only tribunal where redress could be sought against a powerful adversary, or whither appeal could be made from decisions in the inferior courts. Henry knew, as his biographer tells us, that the region left unvisited by the king was most often filled with the complaints and groans of the poor, and he did his utmost, by incessant journeys through the land, to bring justice within reach of all his subjects. In many cases he punished with severity high-born disturbers of the peace. Yet the conditions were now such that the Crown was not strong enough of itself to compel obedience to the law. To make his will prevail, alike in judicial administration and in large measures of policy, he had to secure the co-operation of the magnates assembled in general or provincial diets. At these meetings, which became more frequent under him than under his predecessors, he was generally able, by his fixity of purpose and his skilful address, to win consent to his designs. Even so, however, he was largely dependent for their accomplishment upon such material aid as the good will of the nobles might afford him. There existed no standing army. The national levy could still be summoned by royal command for the defence of the realm; but the only permanent force at the disposal of the king consisted of unfree retainers (*ministeriales*) drawn from the crown lands or from his patrimonial estates. But they were insufficient for making expeditions abroad or for preserving order at home; and it was upon the feudal contingents furnished by the magnates that the monarch had to rely in the last resort.

Furthermore the royal revenues had for years been in steady decline. The immense crown estates, the *villae* on which Charles the Great had bestowed such care, had been broken up and largely dissipated by the later Carolingians, partly through the granting of fiefs to reward their supporters, partly though their lavish endowment of churches and monasteries. And in similar fashion the peculiar royal rights of coinage, tolls, and markets, with others of the same kind, all extremely profitable, had been also freely alienated to laymen and ecclesiastics. In the hands of Otto the Great this practice had been turned to account for the strengthening of the throne; but under his son and grandson it had rather served to establish the local powers in their independence. What crown lands remained to the monarch lay scattered in fragments throughout the kingdom, and were therefore less profitable and more difficult to administer. Henry was a wealthy king, but more through his possession of the great Liudolfing inheritance in Saxony and of the patrimony of his Bavarian ancestors, than through his command of such resources as were proper to the Crown.

Faced then by the growing power of the secular magnates, Henry, if he were to restore the German monarchy, had to seek some surer means than the bare authority of the Crown. But the task was one beyond the powers of a single man, and required the steady action of an ordered administration. This was found in the organisation of the Church. Its dignitaries Henry employed as crown officials, whom he appointed himself. Though the bishops and greater abbots were spiritual chiefs, they were called upon to act also as servants of the king, advising him in council, fulfilling his missions abroad, preserving his peace within their own territories. Further, they, even more than lay princes, had to provide him with military contingents of their vassals, often to follow him in person into the field, sometimes even to conduct his campaigns. And while heavy calls were continually being made upon their revenues for the public need, the right to dispose of their vacant fiefs was frequently claimed by the king for some purpose of his own. More especially did the royal monasteries suffer loss at Henry's hand; for the pious king in several cases did not hesitate at extensive confiscation of monastic lands. Yet these severe measures were not the outcome of caprice or greed, but of a settled policy for the kingdom's weal.

In thus employing the Church Henry resumed the policy adopted by Otto the Great. But while Otto, in using the Church to fortify the throne, had cared little to interfere in matters purely ecclesiastical, Henry sought to exercise over the Church an authority no less direct and searching than over the State. Filled with the ecclesiastical spirit, he set himself to regulate Church affairs as seemed to him best in the Church's interest; and the instinct for order which urged him from the first to promote its efficiency developed at last into a passionate zeal for its reformation.

To achieve his purpose it was essential for Henry to secure an effective mastery over the Church. But only through its constitutional rulers, the bishops, could he, without flagrant illegality, obtain command of its wealth, engage its political services, and direct its spiritual energies. In order, however, to be sure of bishops who should be his willing agents, the decisive word in the appointment to vacant sees must be his. In the Frankish kingdom the old canonical rule that the choice of a new bishop rested with the clergy and laity of the diocese had never been quite forgotten; but from early times the kings had claimed and been allowed the right of confirming or disapproving an episcopal election, and this had been enlarged into the greater right of direct nomination. The claim of the Crown to intervene in episcopal appointments had been fully revindicated by Otto the Great. In a few German dioceses the privilege of free election had been expressly confirmed or granted afresh by charters, yet Otto had never allowed the local privilege to hinder the appointment of any man he desired. The effect of such methods was to fill the bishoprics with royal nominees. Though the procedure was prejudicial to the independence of the Church, yet it freed episcopal elections from those local influences which would have made the bishops mere creatures of the secular magnates, or at best their counterparts in an ecclesiastical disguise.

CH. X.

Otto's practice was followed by Henry, who insisted on his right to nominate the bishops. He made no fresh grants of privilege of free election; he often qualified it by reserving the right of royal assent as at Hamburg, Hildesheim, Minden, Halberstadt, and Fulda, and sometimes he withheld it altogether as at Paderborn. His general practice is fairly illustrated by the case of Magdeburg, which fell vacant four times in the course of his reign. This church had not received from its founder, Otto the Great, the right of choosing its own pastor; and it was by gift of his son, in terms unusually solemn, that the privilege was conferred in 979. Yet Otto II made light of his own charter when, on the first vacancy of the see, he allowed his favourite, the crafty Bishop Gisiler of Merseburg, to supplant the canonically elected nominee. At Gisiler's death in January 1004, the clergy of Magdeburg forthwith unanimously elected their Provost Waltherd. But Henry was resolved that no Magdeburg cleric should occupy the see; and demanded the election of his own attached friend, the Bavarian Tagino. Neither the plea of right nor the humble entreaty of the electors was accepted by the king, whose insistence at length won the consent of Waltherd and his supporters to Tagino's promotion. Through their presence at his investiture by Henry they acquiesced in the reversal of their own previous act. Tagino died in June 1012. Again Henry intervened by sending an envoy, but this time to ask the electors to submit a candidate for his approval. The clergy and vassals of the see once more chose the same candidate, Waltherd, as archbishop. Only with great reluctance did Henry agree, and that upon condition of a fresh election being held in his presence, at which he himself proposed, and the electors concurred in, the nomination of the Provost. Within two months, however, Waltherd was snatched away by death. Next day, the Magdeburg clergy, still anxious to preserve their right, elected Thiedric, a youthful cleric, to the vacant see; and the day following repeated the act. Henry, greatly indignant at this proceeding, determined to enforce his will on the presumptuous Church. He made Thiedric a royal chaplain, and then, coming to Magdeburg, directed another meeting to be held for the election of Gero, one of his chaplains, whom he had designated for the archbishopric. The electors, with an express reservation of their right for the future, obeyed, and Gero was chosen. Yet this reservation appears to have been no hindrance to Henry when, in the last year of his reign, the see of Magdeburg was again vacated by the death of Gero, and he secured the succession of Hunfrid (Humphrey), another royal nominee.

To Henry, therefore, the right of election was useful for giving canonical sanction to a choice made by himself, and the utmost allowed to electors was to name a candidate; thus in course of time most of the German bishoprics were filled by his nominees. Yet Henry's bishops were men far from unworthy of their office. If few of them were learned, the lives of few gave occasion for reproach; if capable men of affairs rather than sound spiritual guides, they were not generally neglectful of pastoral duty; some were even distinguished for evangelical zeal. They were chosen oftenest, it would seem, for their practical capacity, and for a sympathy with his political and ecclesiastical aims gained by long service in the royal chapel or chancery; some, like the historian Thietmar, were chosen for their wealth, part of which they were expected to bestow on their impoverished sees; not a few were recommended by their Bavarian birth. Henry was not the man to dishonour the Church by giving it worthless prelates. Nevertheless, the bishops were his creatures, from whom he demanded obedience; in a word, the Church had to accept a position of strict subordination to the State.

It was not all at once that Henry was able to bring this about. The bishops whom he found in office at his accession owed nothing to him; and even when of proved loyalty they were not inclined to be subservient. Some indeed were openly disaffected. Of such were the Archbishops Heribert of Cologne and Gisiler of Magdeburg, and among bishops, the celebrated Bernward of Hildesheim. Whether indifferent or hostile, however, it was not the spiritual independence of the Church for which most of them were jealous, but for the temporal power and dignity of their own sees. Their sense of ecclesiastical unity was faint; nor did any voice sound from Rome to remind them of their allegiance to the Church Universal. To many even the welfare of their own national branch thereof was of small concern beside the interests of their particular dioceses. Papal impotence left Henry a free hand; and with the rise of a new episcopate the cohesion of the German Church was strengthened and its energies were revived, but only at the cost of its independence. For the bishops learned to acquiesce in Henry's claim to ecclesiastical authority, and zealous churchmen were not slow to enjoin obedience to the Crown as a duty of divine ordinance. But with the Church thus submissive, all fear that the bishops might use their means and their privileges in a spirit defiant of the secular power was removed. They had become, in truth, royal officials; and the more, therefore, that their position was enhanced, the better service could they render to the king. Accordingly, it was with no sparing hand that Henry, following the example of the Ottos, bestowed territory and regalities upon the episcopal churches. His charters reveal also two other special features of his policy. The one is the frequency with which he annexed royal abbeys of the lesser rank to bishoprics, to be held by them as part of their endowment; the other is his extension of the recent practice of giving vacant counties into the hands of prelates. In the former case, the purpose was achieved of turning the smaller religious houses to better account for the service of the State than they could be as isolated corporations; in the latter, advantage was gained for the Crown by the transfer of local authority from secular to ecclesiastical hands, since the bishops were now more amenable to royal control than were the lay counts. Thus the process, by which the bishops

18

became territorial princes, went rapidly forward; although the Crown was strengthened rather than weakened by their exaltation.

It is indisputable that the alliance between the Church and the Monarchy brought immense advantages to both. The former, favoured by the Crown, still further improved its high position. The king, on his side, obtained the services of men highly educated and familiar with business; who could form a counterpoise to the hereditary nobility, and yet could never establish themselves as an hereditary caste; who set an example within their dioceses of upright and humane administration; and who shewed themselves prudent managers of their estates. Besides all which, the revenues of their churches and the military aid of their vassals were at his command. Their corporate feeling as members of a national church had revived; and their general employment in the service of the Crown, which claimed the headship of that church, made them the representatives of national unity on the secular no less than on the ecclesiastical side.

Yet the coalition of the two powers contained the seeds of future calamity to the Church. It was inevitable that bishops so chosen and so employed could not rise to their spiritual vocation. Even within their own dioceses they were as much occupied by secular as by pastoral work. Insensibly they became secularised; and the Church ceased to be either a school of theologians or a nursery of missionaries. At such a price were its temporal advantages secured. Nor was the gain to the Crown without its alloy. For the royal supremacy over the Church depended on the monarch keeping a firm hold on episcopal appointment. That prerogative might become nominal; and during a minority it might disappear. The result in either case would be the political independence of the bishops, whose power would then be all the greater through the favours now lavished upon their churches. This was the latent political peril; and beside it lurked an ecclesiastical danger yet more formidable. Henry had mastered the German Church; and, so long as it remained the national institution he had made it, the tie of interest which bound it to the throne would hold. Yet it was but part of a larger ecclesiastical whole, whose acknowledged head was the Pope. The present thraldom of the Papacy to a local despot made its claim to the obedience of distant churches a shadowy prerogative which could be safely disregarded; but with a future recovery of freedom and of moral influence the pretension of the Roman See to apostolic authority over the Western Church would revive; and the German prelates would have to choose between King and Pope. Within sixty years of Henry's death that question presented itself.

In his government of the Church Henry was accustomed to act both on his own sole authority and in co-operation with the bishops in synod. No sharp distinction is apparent between the matters he decided himself and those he referred to the synods; in general, however, breaches of external order the king dealt with alone, while strictly ecclesiastical questions were more often disposed of in synod.

How vigorously Henry meant to assert his right to regulate Church affairs was seen soon after his accession in his revival of the see of Merseburg. That bishopric, established in 968 by Otto the Great as part of his scheme for evangelising the Wends, had been held by Gisiler for ten years before his elevation to Magdeburg. Such a translation was liable to be impugned as invalid, and the astute prelate therefore induced his patron Otto II and Pope Benedict VII to decree the abolition of Merseburg as superfluous, and to distribute its territory among the neighbouring dioceses, including Magdeburg. Under Otto III Gisiler managed by skilful procrastination to maintain his ill-won position. Henry however made peremptory demand upon Gisiler to vacate the archbishopric and return to Merseburg. The prelate's death before he complied, enabled Henry by the appointment of Tagino to Magdeburg, to bring back the old position. Tagino's first episcopal act was to consecrate Wigbert to the revived Merseburg bishopric, of which the king by his sole act, without reference to synod or to Pope, had thus become the second founder. No less independent was Henry's procedure in settling the ignoble quarrel between two of Germany's noblest prelates over the monastery of Gandersheim. From its foundation by Henry's ancestor Duke Liudolf of Saxony in 842, and after an early subjection to Mayence, this religious house for women had been without question for nearly a century and a half under the spiritual authority of the bishops of Hildesheim. In an unhappy hour Archbishop Willigis claimed jurisdiction over it for Mayence; and the dispute so begun with one bishop was continued later with his successor Bernward, and by him referred for decision to Pope Sylvester II. The papal edict in favour of Hildesheim, when promulgated in Germany, was treated with open disrespect by Willigis. To end the scandal, Henry won the promise of both bishops to abide by his ruling, and then, at a diet in 1006, gave judgment for Hildesheim. The result was loyally accepted by Willigis and his next successor.

This protectorship of the Church led Henry, whom Thietmar calls the Vicar of God on earth, to undertake on its behalf tasks of the most diverse kind. Thus he asserted his right, both to order the due registration of monastic lands, and to require strict observance of German customs in public worship; he took it upon him, not only to enforce ecclesiastical discipline, but to prevent heresy from raising its head. In such matters the synods had a right to speak, although they did so rather as organs of the royal will than as independent church assemblies. For they met upon Henry's summons; he presided over, and took active part in, their discussions; he published their resolutions as edicts of his own. But he called them to account in the tone of a master, and at the very first synod of his reign he rebuked them severely for slackness in their discipline. In pressing for the removal of irregularities Henry certainly shewed himself a conscientious ruler of the Church, but gave no proof of a desire to initiate any far-reaching ecclesiastical reform. His views at this time were bounded by the needs of the German Church; and so strictly national were the synods he convoked that they cared but little whether the measures they agreed upon were in consonance with general church law.

With reform, however, in one wide sphere of organised religion Henry had long shewn his active sympathy. For already, as Duke of Bavaria, he had used his authority to impose a stricter life upon the monasteries of that land. He had thus helped forward the monastic reformation which, beginning in Lorraine in the early decades of the tenth century, had spread eastwards into Germany, and had won a footing in Bavaria through the energy of the former monk, Wolfgang, Bishop of Ratisbon. In his early years Henry had seen the beneficent change wrought in Bavaria, and exemplified at St Emmeram's in Ratisbon. After becoming duke, he had forced reform upon the reluctant monks of Altaich and Tegernsee through the agency of Godehard, a passionate ascetic, whom, in defiance of their privilege, he had made abbot of both those houses. In the same spirit and with like purpose Henry treated the royal monasteries after his accession. They became the instruments of his strenuous monastic policy; while he also, as in the case of the bishoprics, insisted on the right of the Crown to appoint their heads, notwithstanding the privilege of free election which many of them possessed. By this time, however, some of the greater monasteries had acquired immense landed wealth, and their abbots held a princely position. The communities they ruled for the most part led an easy existence. Not a few houses, it is true, did admirable work in art and learning, in husbandry, and in care for the poor. Much of the land, specially reserved to the abbot, was granted out in fief to vassals, in order to acquit his military service to the Crown; but these might also be used against the Crown, if the abbot were not loyal.

Henry's monastic policy was revealed in 1005 by his treatment of the wealthy abbey of Hersfeld. Complaints made to him by the brethren gave him the opportunity for replacing the abbot by the ascetic Godehard of Altaich, who offered the monks a choice between strict observance of the Rule and expulsion. The departure of all but two or three enabled Godehard to dispose of their superfluous luxuries for pious uses, while Henry seized on the corporate lands reserved for the brethren, and added them to the abbot's special estate, which thus became liable to the Crown for greater feudal services. In the end Hersfeld, under Godehard, became again an active religious community. Between 1006 and 1015 Reichenau, Fulda and Corvey were likewise dealt with and with like results. Further, the Crown, by placing several abbeys under one head, was able, out of land hitherto required for the upkeep of abbatial households, to make grants to vassals. In these measures the king was supported by the bishops, some of whom followed his example in monasteries under their control. The result was a general revival of monastic discipline, and a serious curtailment of the resources of the greater abbeys.

The lesser royal monasteries, from whose lands new fiefs could not be granted, needed the king's special protection to keep their independence. Henry had no use for feeble institutions, and subjected seventeen of them to various sees or greater abbeys. If they were not abolished altogether, they were generally transformed into small canonries, while part of their property fell to the bishop.

Henry proclaimed his belief in the episcopal system by the foundation of the see of Bamberg. Near the eastern border of Franconia dwelt a population almost entirely Wendish. Left behind in the general retreat of their kinsfolk before the Franks, these Slavonic tribesmen still kept their own language and customs, and much of their original paganism. Baptised by compulsion, they neglected all Christian observances, while the bishops of Würzburg, to whose diocese they belonged, paid little heed to them. Close by them was the little town of Bamberg, dear to Henry from his boyhood. It was a favourite home with him and his wife, and he resolved to make it the seat of a bishopric. The scheme required the assent of the Bishops of Würzburg and Eichstedt. But Megingaud (Meingaud) of Eichstedt flatly refused to agree, and Henry of Würzburg, though a devoted subject, was an ambitious man, and demanded, in addition to territorial compensation, the elevation of Würzburg to metropolitan rank. After a synod at Mayence (May 1007), at which Bishop Henry was present, had given its solemn approval, envoys were sent to the Pope to secure ratification. By bull issued in June John XVIII confirmed the erection of the see of Bamberg, which was to be subject only to the authority of the Papacy. Würzburg, however, was not made an archbishopric, and Bishop Henry thought himself betrayed. At a synod at Frankfort (1 November 1007) there assembled five German archbishops with twenty-two suffragans, five Burgundian prelates including two archbishops, two Italian bishops, and, lastly, the primate of Hungary. Willigis of Mayence presided, but Henry of Würzburg held aloof. The king, prostrating himself before the bishops, set forth his high purpose for the Church, reminding them of the consent already given by the Bishop of Würzburg. Bishop Henry's chaplain replied that his master could not allow any injury to his church. But the absence of the bishop had displeased many of his colleagues, while the agreement he had made was on record. Thus, finally, the foundation of the see of Bamberg was unanimously confirmed, and the king nominated as its first bishop his kinsman the Chancellor Everard, who received consecration the same day.

Henry's intention to make God his heir was amply fulfilled; he had already endowed Bamberg with his lands in the Radenzgau and the Volkfeld, and he lavished wealth on the new see. Thus Bamberg was among the best endowed of German bishoprics, and the comital jurisdiction, given by Henry to some other sees, can hardly have been withheld here. Yet Everard was for some time a bishop without a diocese. Only in May 1008 did Henry of Würzburg transfer to Bamberg almost all the Radenzgau and part of the Volkfeld. From this moment the new see grew. Just four years later, in May 1012, the now finished cathedral was dedicated in the presence of the king and a great assembly, six archbishops and the patriarch of Aquileia, besides many bishops, taking part in the ceremony with Bishop Everard. Less than a year afterwards, the episcopal rights of Bamberg received the papal confirmation; and the last stage was reached in 1015, when, after the death of Megingaud of Eichstedt, the king was able by an exchange of territory with Megingaud's successor to enlarge the Bamberg diocese to the limit originally planned.

It was to be the fortune of the first bishop of Bamberg to receive a Pope within his own city, and of the second himself to become Pope. Yet even these unusual honours shed no such real glory over the bishopric as did the successful achievement of the purpose for which it was founded. For from Bamberg Christianity spread over a region hitherto sunk in heathenism, and the social arts made way among an uncultured people. A secondary result of its activities, whether intended or not, was the fusion of an alien race with the German population. For a far wider sphere than its actual diocese Bamberg was a wellspring of intellectual energy. Its library grew to be a great storehouse of learning; its schools helped to diffuse knowledge over all Germany. This may have been beyond Henry's aim; yet it was through the Bamberg which he created that the sluggish life of the district around was drawn into the general stream of European civilisation.

The action of dynastic and local politics upon the Church was notably shewn in the queen's own family. Her eldest brother Henry of Luxemburg had been made Duke of Bavaria: a younger brother Dietrich contrived to gain the see of Metz (1005) against Henry's nominee. On the death (1008) of Liudolf, Archbishop of Trèves, a third brother Adalbero, still a youth, was elected successor there. Henry refused his consent and nominated Megingaud; civil war arose and the king's nominee, although approved by the Pope, was kept out of his own city. In Lorraine there were other malcontents to be dealt with, and thence the discontented family of Luxemburg carried the revolt into Bavaria, where Henry had with the consent of the magnates deprived Duke Henry and taken the duchy into his own hands. Dietrich, the Bishop of Metz, supported his brothers, and all Lorraine was plunged into misery. Dietrich of Metz did not return to allegiance until 1012, and even then his brothers Henry and Adalbero kept hold of Trèves. Lorraine was in smouldering strife.

In East Saxony, in the North Mark, and in Meissen the story was the same. Lawless vassals wrought misdeeds, and attempts at punishment brought on rebellion. And behind Saxony lay Boleslav of Poland always ready to make use of local disloyalty. Against him in August 1010 Henry assembled an army of Saxons and of Bohemians under Jaromir. The sickness of the king and many of his troops made this campaign fruitless, and others were as futile. The Saxons were slow to aid; Henry was often busied elsewhere; and when Jaromir was driven from Bohemia his help was lost. Henry, anxious for peace towards the East, recognised the new Duke Udalrich, and Jaromir remained an exile. Thus Bohemia was an ally and the Lyutitzi had long been such. Peace with Poland was therefore easier. And on Whitsunday 1012 Boleslav did homage to Henry at Merseburg, carried the sword before his lord in the procession, and then received the Lausitz as a fief. Boleslav promised help to Henry in Italy whither the king had long been looking: Henry promised a German contingent to Boleslav against the Russians. Henry had gained peace, but Boleslav had won the land he had fought for.

Within the realm Henry's firmness was forming order: he was able to rule through the dukes. In Saxony a faithful vassal, Bernard I, had died (1011) and was succeeded by his son Bernard II. When in Carinthia Conrad (1004–11), Otto's son, died, Henry passed over his heir and nominated Adalbero of Eppenstein, already Margrave there. The next year, with the boy Herman III, Duke of Swabia, died out a branch of the Conradins, and perhaps with Duke Otto of Lower Lorraine, a branch of the Carolingians. To Swabia Henry appointed Ernest of Babenberg, an old rebel (1004) but brother-in-law of Herman, and to Lower Lorraine Count Godfrey of the Ardennes, sprung from a family marked by loyalty and zeal in monastic reform. The duchy of Bavaria he kept in his own hands, and thus all the duchies were safe under rulers either proved or chosen by himself. Upon Godfrey of Lower Lorraine a special burden lay, for Trèves was disaffected and the Archbishop of Cologne was hostile. In the other arch-see of Mayence Willigis died (1011) after thirty-six years of faithful rule. As his successor Henry chose Erkambald, Abbot of Fulda, an old friend in affairs of state and a worthy ecclesiastic. Next year Henry had twice to fill the see of Magdeburg, naming Waltherd and then Gero. Early in 1013, too, died Lievizo (Libentius) of Hamburg, where Henry put aside the elected candidate and forced on the chapter a royal chaplain, Unwan. When (1013) all these appointments had been made, Henry could feel he was master in his own house, and able to turn towards Italy. For a year at least he had felt the call. The years between 1004 and 1014 were in Lombardy a time of confusion. Ardoin had broken out from his castle of Sparone (1005), only to find his authority gone; in the west he had vassals and adherents; some greater nobles, bishops, and scattered citizens wished him well. But he was only the king over the middle and lower classes, and even that only for a small part of the realm.

Yet even so, Henry was only nominally Italian king. Real power rested with the ecclesiastical and secular magnates; and though it might suit prelates and nobles alike to profess to Henry a formal allegiance, few of either order desired his presence among them. To be independent within their own territories was the chief aim of both. The bishops by tradition inclined to the German side. Some few, like Leo of Vercelli, remained steadfast for the German cause from political convictions; while the holders of the metropolitan sees of Milan and Ravenna stood haughtily indifferent to the claims of either king. But if the bishops generally might be counted as in some sort Henry's partisans, this was not true of the great noble families with which they were perennially at strife. Of these, the house of Canossa alone was firmly attached to the German interest; its chief, the Marquess Tedald, and after him his son Boniface, continuing faithful. The rest, the most powerful of whom were those other marquesses who had sprung up in Lombardy half a century before, by accumulating counties and lordships in their own hands, had formed a new order in the State especially inimical to the bishops, although equally ready with them to make outward acknowledgment of Henry. But no class could be less desirous of the reappearance of a sovereign who would be sure to curtail their independence, and, in particular, to check their encroachment on ecclesiastical lands. On the other hand, they had little mind to help Ardoin in regaining an authority which would be exercised over themselves for the benefit of their humbler fellow-subjects. So far as can be discerned, the Aleramids, the progenitors of the house of Montferrat, whose power was concentrated about Savona and Acqui, appear to have played a waiting game; while the Marquesses of Turin, represented by Manfred II, inclined first to the German, and then to the Italian side. Only in the Otbertines, the great Lombard house which held the comital authority in Genoa and Milan, in Tortona, Luni, and Bobbio, whose present head was the Marquess Otbert II, and from which sprang the later dukes of Modena and of Brunswick, can be found some signs of genuine patriotism. But in general, these powerful dynasts, and the lay nobles as a class, had little sense of national duty, and were selfishly content to pursue the old evil policy of having two kings, so that the one might be restrained by fear of the other.

Year after year Ardoin sallied forth from his subalpine fastnesses to attack his enemies and especially the bishops. Leo of Vercelli was forthwith driven out of his city, to become for years an exile. The Bishops of Bergamo and Modena also felt the weight of Ardoin's revenge, and even the Archbishop of Milan, by whom Henry had been crowned, was forced to a temporary recognition of his rival. The Marquess Tedald himself was threatened, while Bishop Peter of Novara only escaped capture by fleeing across the Alps. Yet Ardoin was no nearer being in truth a king. The Apennines he never crossed; the Romagna remained in turmoil. Tuscany obeyed its powerful Marquess.

Henry had never dropped his claim to Italian sovereignty. Royal *missi* were sent at irregular intervals into Lombardy; Italian bishops took their place in German synods; from Italy came also abbots and canons to seek redress at the German throne for injuries done by their bishops. Thus Henry kept alive his pretension to rule in Italy. But he was bound sooner or later again to attempt the recovery of the Lombard crown.

Yet after all it was Rome that now drew Henry once more into Italy. Before the death of Otto III the Romans had repudiated German domination; and soon after that event they had allowed John Crescentius, son of the Patricius slaughtered in 998, to assume the chief authority over the city and its territory, which he ruled thenceforth for ten years. But his power was finally established by the death in May 1003 of Sylvester II, which removed the last champion of the German cause in Rome, and laid the Papacy as well as the city at the feet of the Patricius: he raised three of his nominees in turn to the papal throne. Nevertheless, Crescentius lived in dread of the German king, and spared no pains, therefore, to conciliate him. John died about the beginning of 1012, and with the death a few months later of Sergius IV, his last nominee, there began a struggle between the Crescentian family and the house of the counts of Tusculum, like themselves connected with the infamous Marozia. In the contention that arose for the Papacy, Gregory, the Crescentian candidate, at first prevailed, but had to yield in the end to Theophylact of Tusculum, who became Pope as Benedict VIII. Driven out of Rome, Gregory fled to Germany, and at Christmas 1012 presented himself in pontifical array before Henry at Pöhlde. But the king was not likely to help a Crescentian Pope, and he had already obtained from Benedict a bull of confirmation for the privileges of Bamberg. He now met Gregory's request for help by directing him to lay aside the pontifical dress until he himself should come to Rome.

Honour and interest alike urged Henry to seize the occasion for decisive intervention in Italy. If his promises to return were to remain unfulfilled, the German cause in Lombardy would be lost. So, too, would be his hope of winning the imperial crown, which was to him the symbol of an enhanced authority both abroad and at home. As Emperor he would have a further, though indefinite, claim upon the obedience of his subjects on both sides of the Alps, and would regain for Germany her former primacy in Western Europe. Moreover, through a good understanding with the Papacy, if not by entire mastery over it, he would secure finally his hold upon the German Church and so be able to frustrate the intrigues of Duke Boleslav at the Papal court for recognition as king. During the earlier half of 1013 Henry had therefore sought an agreement with Pope Benedict. Through the agency of Bishop Walter of Spires, a compact, the terms of which are unrecorded, was ratified by mutual oath.

Later in 1013 Henry, accompanied by Queen Kunigunda and many bishops, marched to Italy. Boleslav sent not aid but envoys who intrigued against his lord.

The king reached Pavia before Christmas, while Ardoin withdrew to his fortresses, thus yielding up to Henry nearly the whole of Lombardy without a blow. Then he sent to Pavia offering to resign the crown if he were put in possession of some county, apparently his own march of Ivrea. But Henry rejected the proposal and Ardoin was left in helpless isolation. At Pavia, meanwhile, a throng of bishops and abbots, including the two great champions of monastic reform, Odilo of Cluny and Hugh of Farfa, surrounded Henry, while many lay nobles, even the Otbertines, and others friendly to Ardoin, also came to make submission.

In January 1014 Henry passed on to Ravenna. At Ravenna there reappeared, after ten years of obscurity, Bishop Leo of Vercelli. But beside him stood Abbot Hugh of Farfa, the man who had so firmly upheld in Italy the ideals of monasticism, resolved as ever both to combat vigorously the nobles, especially the Crescentian family who had annexed the possessions of his house, and to make his community a pattern of monastic discipline. Like many others, he had acquired his abbacy by unworthy means: partly in expiation of this offence, partly to get Henry's help against his enemies, he had resigned his office, though still deeply concerned for the prosperity of Farfa. His strenuous character, the moral dignity which placed him at the head of the abbots of Italy, and the identity of his aims for monasticism with those of the king, made Hugh an ally too important to be left aside. In Italy the monasteries supported Henry, and there he shewed them favour, especially Farfa with its command of the road to the south, without any of the reserve he had shewn in Germany.

At Ravenna a synod was convoked, the first business of which was to settle the disputed right to the archbishopric of Ravenna. Adalbert, its actual holder for the last ten years, was generally recognised in the Romagna; but Henry in 1013 had treated the see as vacant, and had nominated thereto his own natural half-brother, Arnold. The intruder, however, failed to establish himself in possession, and now came back to be declared, with the authority of the Pope and the advice of the synod, the rightful archbishop. Thereupon followed the issue in Henry's name of decrees for the suppression of certain ecclesiastical abuses then prevalent in Italy: the simoniacal conferment of Holy Orders, the ordination of priests and deacons below the canonical age, the taking of money for the consecration of churches, and the acceptance by way of gift or pledge of any articles dedicated to sacred use. Of no less serious import for the Church and for the nation at large was the further decree that all bishops and abbots should make returns of the property alienated from their churches and abbeys, of the time and manner of the alienation, and of the names of the present holders. Such a record was a preliminary to any measure of restitution; but this could not fail to arouse the anger of the territorial lords, against whom chiefly it would be directed.

After Ravenna came Rome. On Sunday, 14 February 1014, he made his entry into the city amid applause. Twelve senators escorted the king and queen to the door of St Peter's, where the Pope and his clergy awaited them.

The two chiefs of Western Christendom, whose fortunes were to be closely linked together for the rest of their joint lives, now met for the first time. Benedict VIII was a man of vigorous, though not exalted, character; belonging to the turbulent Roman nobility, raised to the papal throne while yet a layman and after a faction contest, he was not likely to shew any real religious zeal. Though his life was free from scandal, Benedict shone, not as a churchman but as a man of action, whose principal aim was to recover for the Papacy its external dignity and its material power. Already he had repelled the Crescentians from Rome, and taken many of their castles in the Sabina. He had even wrested the duchy of Spoleto out of the hands of John, the elder nephew of the late Patricius. But these enemies, nevertheless, were still formidable, and it was not a mere formality when the Pope demanded of the king, before they entered the basilica, whether he would be a faithful patron and defender of the Roman Church, and be true in all points to himself and his successors. The pledge was heartily given, and then, within the church, Henry offered at the high altar the crown he had worn hitherto as king, and received unction and coronation as Roman Emperor at the hands of Benedict. Queen Kunigunda at the same time was crowned Empress. Soon afterwards the Pope confirmed Henry's acts and canons passed at Ravenna, Adalbert was deposed, and Arnold recognised as Archbishop of Ravenna.

Henry was on the point of starting for the south to force the Crescentii to disgorge the remnant still held of Farfa's lands, most of which Benedict had already regained for the monastery, when a sudden tumult broke out in Rome. After two days' riot the Germans were victorious but, nevertheless, Henry did not venture to remain longer in Rome. Only a week had passed since his coronation and already he had to make sure of his retreat. After another fruitless effort, therefore, to bring the case between the Crescentian brothers and the Abbot of Farfa to legal decision, the Emperor, with the concurrence of the Pope and the judges, as his last act invested Hugh with the possessions claimed from the Crescentii. Having charged Benedict to give actual effect to this decision, the Emperor left Rome.

Nearly two months Henry spent in securing his hold upon Tuscany, the fidelity of which province, as commanding the route between Lombardy and Rome, was of prime importance for him. Since the death in 1012 of the Marquess Boniface, an ineffective ruler and a dissolute man, the March had remained vacant; and Henry now gave it to Rainier, a Tuscan, who had lately, through the influence of the Pope, replaced the Crescentian John as Duke of Spoleto. Since the Marquess of Tuscany enjoyed an authority superior to that of any other lay subject of the Italian crown, the union in a single hand of these two provinces, which had not been held together since the time of the Duke-marquess Hugh "the Great," gave special significance to the choice of Rainier. In the new marquess Henry must have expected to find a stout upholder of the imperial cause. The fact that like Henry he was a generous and enlightened patron of monasticism, probably recommended him to the Emperor. The monastic question was acute in Tuscany as elsewhere and families like the Otbertines, who there held wide territories, had incessant quarrels over property with the ecclesiastical foundations. At Easter 1014 Henry was again in Pavia. In Lombardy, although his authority was not openly disputed, and most of the prelates were on his side, and the secular lords paid outward obedience, disaffection permeated all classes. The Archbishop of Milan held aloof, some of the great families still refused submission, and the hatred of the common people was shewn by their reluctance to furnish supplies. Renouncing therefore any attempt to crush Ardoin by force, Henry sought to strengthen himself by administrative measures. He renewed an institution of Otto the Great by appointing two permanent *missi* for the counties of Pavia, Milan, and Seprio. He thus secured for royal officials the exercise of supreme judicial authority where disaffection was rife, and, significantly enough, Henry now gave an Italian city its first measure of municipal freedom. The Aleramids, who were lords of Savona, had not shewn themselves especially hostile to Henry, and were even now taking some share in the public administration. Yet just at this time the men of Savona obtained through their bishop a royal charter which curtailed the feudal rights of the marquesses over their city, and relieved its inhabitants of many burdensome imposts. But Henry could not stay in Italy to secure the success of his administrative acts; after a month's stay in Pavia he passed on to Verona, and thence to Germany.

Henry's second expedition to Italy, though it fell far short of complete success, ensured the continuance of the Western Empire. It renewed the alliance between the Empire and the Papacy, and it vindicated afresh the pre-eminence of the German monarchy in Western Europe.

But in Lombardy Henry had left his work half done. A hostile population, an alienated nobility, and an uncrushed rival remained as proofs of his failure. And hardly had he recrossed the Alps in June 1014 when a fresh outburst of nationalist fury threatened to overwhelm his adherents. Ardoin at once issued from Ivrea, and attacked Vercelli with such suddenness that the Bishop Leo scarcely avoided capture. The whole of that diocese fell into Ardoin's hands. Thence he went on to besiege Novara, to overrun the diocese of Como, and to bring ruin upon many other hostile places. Though more of a punitive foray than regular warfare, this campaign against the imperialists had yet some of the dignity of a national uprising. For besides the vavassors and small proprietors of his own neighbourhood, not a few nobles in all parts of Lombardy took up arms on Ardoin's behalf. The four sons of the aged Marquess Otbert II, Count Hubert "the Red," a man powerful in the West, with several other counts, and even the Bishop of distant Vicenza, were of the number. These men, assuredly, were not inspired by pure patriotism. But their association for a common purpose with other classes of their fellow-countrymen, under their native king, affords some proof that they had also in view the higher purpose of throwing off an alien yoke.

The fury of the nationalists found vent in ruthless devastation of the episcopal territories, and made them for a few weeks masters of Lombardy. But sudden dismay fell upon them through the unexpected capture of all four sons of the Marquess Otbert, the chief pillar of their cause. Though two soon escaped, the others were sent as prisoners to Germany, whither Leo of Vercelli also now went to arouse the Emperor's vengeance against the insurgent Lombards. At his instigation, Henry struck, and struck hard, at his opponents. At a judicial inquiry held in Westphalia during the autumn, the Lombard law of treason was invoked against the captive Otbertines and their associates still in arms. For having waged war upon their sovereign, they were declared liable to forfeiture. Thereupon, a series of confiscatory charters, mostly drafted by Leo himself, was issued. Though the full penalty was not exacted of the chief offenders, the Otbertine family was mulcted of 500 jugera of land, and Count Hubert the Red of 3000, for the benefit of the see of Pavia; the Church of Como was compensated out of the private inheritance of Bishop Jerome of Vicenza; and to that of Novara was awarded a possession of the archbishopric of Milan. Far more heavily, however, fell the Emperor's hand upon the lesser men. "They had above all grievously afflicted the church of Vercelli," and Bishop Leo was only satisfied with their total forfeiture. To his see, accordingly, were transferred at a stroke the lands of some six score proprietors in the neighbourhood of Ivrea, nearly all men of middle rank.

The recovery of Vercelli itself about this time was an important success, chiefly because it led to Ardoin's death. The spirit which had borne him up through so many vicissitudes sank under this blow; and he withdrew to the monastery of Fruttuaria, where he laid aside his crown to assume the cowl of a monk. There, fifteen months later, on 14 December 1015, he died.

So passed away the last monarch to whom the title of King of the Lombards could be fitly applied. Yet for many months after his abdication the insurgents kept the mastery in Western Lombardy. This struggle is revealed in a series of letters addressed by Leo to the Emperor. They shew Leo, early in 1016, amid serious difficulties. He is backed, indeed, by some of his fellow bishops, as well as by a few powerful nobles; and he can count now upon Archbishop Arnulf and the men of Milan, who are kept true by the presbyter Aribert. But he can hardly maintain himself in his own city; and he appeals to Henry for a German army. He has against him the brother and the sons of Ardoin, the astute Marquess Manfred of Turin with his brother, Alric, Bishop of Asti, and, most dangerous of all, the mighty Count Hubert. These men are intriguing for the support of King Rodolph of Burgundy, and are even negotiating for reconciliation with the Emperor through their friends Heribert of Cologne and Henry of Würzburg. Not only, however, did Leo repel their attack on Vercelli, but, by a successful offensive, he recovered the whole territory of his diocese. Yet the siege of the castle of Orba, which was undertaken at the Emperor's command by Leo with other bishops and some lay magnates, including the young Marquess Boniface of Canossa, ended in an accommodation. At the suggestion of Manfred of Turin, who was anxious for peace, the rebel garrison was allowed to withdraw and the castle itself was burnt.

This agreement was the starting point of serious negotiations. On the one side, the Marquess Manfred and his brother sought the Emperor's favour, while Count Hubert sent his son to Germany as a hostage; on the other, Pilgrim, a Bavarian cleric lately made chancellor for Italy, was sent by Henry into Lombardy to bring about a complete pacification. Pilgrim's success was soon seen in the arrival of Italian envoys at Allstedt in January 1017 to offer greetings to the Emperor. On returning to Germany in the autumn of 1017 Pilgrim left Upper Italy at peace, and the release (January 1018) of the surviving captive Otbertine marked the Emperor's reconciliation with the Lombards.

Leo of Vercelli, indeed, was dissatisfied because no penalty was laid on Count Hubert, and although he secured a grant to his church of the lands of thirty unfortunate vavassors, the vindictive prelate was not appeased until, by a sentence of excommunication issued many months later, he had brought the Count and his family to ruin. Leo's personal victory indicated the political advantage that had been gained by his order over the secular magnates. For the Emperor was bent on forcing the lay nobles into the background by an alliance with the bishops. Hence the great office of Count Palatine, the chief judicial authority of the realm, hitherto always held by a layman, now practically ceased to exist. The granting of palatine rights to bishops, already begun by the Ottos, was continued; similar rights were conferred upon *missi*; while the presidency of the Palatine Court itself was annexed to the royal chancery, and thus invariably fell to a cleric.

In Italy not only did Leo of Vercelli regain his lost influence, but the bishops generally won a new predominance. Yet this predominance was bound up with control from Germany, whence the Emperor directed affairs in Church and State, thus working against Italian independence. The imperial crown enhanced Henry's position in Europe but it added little to his power in Germany; for seven years after his return from

Italy he had to face foreign warfare and domestic strife. Polish affairs claimed him first. Boleslav had not sent his promised help to Italy: he had tried to win over Udalrich of Bohemia. Henry tried diplomacy and on its failure set out on a Polish campaign (July 1015). An elaborate plan of an invasion by three armies did not succeed, and Henry himself had a troubled retreat.

During 1016 Henry was busied in Burgundy, and Boleslav was entangled with Russia, where Vladímir the Great was consolidating a principality. In January 1017 Boleslav attempted negotiations, but as he would make no great effort for peace a new expedition was made in August 1017, this time by one strong army and with the hope of Russian help. Sieges and battles did little to decide the issue and Henry again retreated in September 1017. But now Boleslav was inclined for peace, since Russia although it had done but little was a threatening neighbour. The German princes who had suffered heavily were anxious for peace and at Bautzen (30 January 1018) terms were made: a German writer tells us they were the best possible although not seemly; he speaks of no court service or feudal obligations on Boleslav's part. Moreover he kept the marks he had so long desired. Henry had not gained much military glory but he had the peace which was needed. He kept Bohemia as a vassal; he held firmly the German lands west of the Elbe. For the rest of the reign he had peace with Poland.

On the western frontier Burgundy had steadily grown more disordered since 1006. It was the stepping-stone to Italy and Otto the Great had therefore played the part of a protector and feudal superior to the young King Conrad. This connexion had continued and it, as well as disorder, called Henry to Burgundy. The Welf dynasty had lost its former vigour. Conrad "the Pacific" (937–993) was content to appear almost as a vassal of the Emperors. His son, Rodolph III, far from throwing off this yoke became by his weakness more dependent still. Henry for his part had to support Rodolph unless he meant to break with the Saxon tradition of control in Burgundy and to surrender his inherited claim to succession. But in Count Otto-William, ruler of the counties later named Franche-Comté, he found a resolute opponent. It is probable that Otto-William, himself the son of the exiled Lombard King, Adalbert of Ivrea, aimed at the throne, but in any case, like most of the nobles, he feared the accession of a foreign monarch whose first task would be to curb his independence.

By 1016 the ceaseless struggle between Rodolph and his unruly subjects had reached a climax. Rodolph sought for aid from Henry: he came in the early summer to Strasbourg, again acknowledged Henry's right of succession, and promised to do nothing of importance without his advice. Henry acted at once on his newly won right by nominating to a vacant bishopric.

But the proceedings at Strasbourg were met by Otto-William with defiance, and even the bishop whom Henry had appointed was forced to forsake his diocese. Henry undertook an expedition to reduce Burgundy: it was unsuccessful and was followed by the renunciation of his treaty with Rodolph. The moment, however, that the peace of Bautzen left him safe on his eastern frontier Henry turned to Burgundy again. In February 1018 Rodolph met him at Mayence and again resigned to him the sovereignty which he himself found so heavy. But once again the Burgundian lords refused to acknowledge either Henry's authority in the present or his right to succeed in the future. A fresh expedition failed to enforce his claims, and he never again attempted intervention in person. Possession of Burgundy with its alpine passes would have made the control of Italy easier, but the attempt to secure this advantage had failed.

Thus in four successive years, alternately in Poland and Burgundy, Henry had waged campaigns, all really unsuccessful. His own kingdom meanwhile was torn by domestic strife. Throughout the two Lorraines and Saxony, above all, disorder ruled. In Upper Lorraine the Luxemburg brothers still nursed their feud with the Emperor. But on the death (December 1013) of Megingaud of Trèves, Henry appointed to the archbishopric a resolute great noble, Poppo of Babenberg. Before long Adalbero and Henry of Luxemburg both came to terms. At the Easter Diet of 1017 a final reconciliation was made between the Emperor and his brothers-in-law, which was sealed in November of the same year by the reinstatement of Henry of Luxemburg in the duchy of Bavaria. This submission brought tardy peace to Upper Lorraine, but Lower Lorraine proved as difficult a task.

Since his elevation in 1012, Duke Godfrey had been beset by enemies. The worst of these was Count Lambert of Louvain, whose wife was a sister of the late Carolingian Duke Otto, and whose elder brother Count Reginar of Hainault represented the original dukes of undivided Lorraine. Thus Lambert, whose life had been one of sacrilege and violence, had claims on the dukedom. He was defeated and killed by Godfrey at Florennes in September 1015, but another obstinate rebel, Count Gerard of Alsace, a brother-in-law of those stormy petrels of discontent and strife, the Luxemburgers, remained, only to be overthrown in August, 1017. With all these greater rebellions were associated minor but widespread disturbances of the peace, and not until March 1018 was the province entirely pacified, when, in an assembly at Nimeguen, the Emperor received the submission of the Count of Hainault and established concord between Count Gerard and Duke Godfrey.

But the duke was soon to experience a temporary reverse of fortune. In the far north of his province Count Dietrich of Holland, by his mother (the Empress Kunigunda's sister) half a Luxemburger, had seized the thinly peopled district at the mouth of the Meuse, made the Frisians in it tributary, and, violating the rights of the Bishop of Utrecht, built a castle by the river whence he levied tolls on sea-bound craft. On the bishop's complaint Henry ordered the count to desist and make amends; when he disobeyed, Duke Godfrey and the Bishop (Adalbold) were commissioned to enforce order. But their expedition miscarried; Godfrey was wounded and taken prisoner. Yet the prisoner interceded at court for his captor and peace with friendship was restored.

Saxony was disturbed like Lorraine, but chiefly by private quarrels, especially between lay magnates and bishops. In a diet at Allstedt (January 1017) Henry attempted a pacification. But a rising of the half-heathen Wends brought slaughter on the Christian priests and their congregations, with destruction of the churches. Bernard, Bishop of Oldenburg (on the Baltic), sought but did not get Henry's help, and then Thietmar, brother of the Billung Duke Bernard, revolted. After he had been subdued, his brother the duke himself rebelled, but a siege of his fortress Schalksburg on the Weser ended in a peace. Emperor and duke joined in an expedition against the Wends, reduced the March to order and restored the Christian prince Mistislav over the pagan Obotrites (Obodritzi, or Abotrites). But though civil order was enforced to the north, the Wends remained heathen.

Happily the rest of Germany was more peaceful. In Swabia alone arose difficulty. Ernest, husband of Gisela, elder sister of the young Duke Herman III, had been made duke, but after three years' rule he died in the hunting field (31 May 1015). The Emperor gave the duchy to his eldest son Ernest, and as he was under age his mother Gisela was to be his guardian. But when she soon married Conrad of Franconia the Emperor gave the duchy to Poppo of Trèves, the young duke's uncle. Gisela's new husband, Conrad, afterwards Emperor, head of the house which sprang from Conrad the Red and Liutgard, daughter of Otto the Great, had already one grievance against the Emperor. He had seen in 1011 the duchy of Carinthia transferred from his own family to Adalbero of Eppenstein. Now a second grievance made him Henry's enemy. He had fought alongside Gerard of Alsace against Duke Godfrey: two years later he waged war against Duke Adalbero. For this the Emperor banished him, but the sentence was remitted and Conrad henceforth kept the peace.

Henry's general policy was one of conciliation; as a commander in the field he had never been fortunate, and therefore he preferred moral to physical means. He had learnt this preference from his religion and he well understood how greatly ecclesiastical order could help his realm. In church reform, greatly needed at the time, he took ever more interest as his life went on. One question indeed which came up at the synod of Goslar in 1019 was a foreboding of trouble to come. Many secular priests, serfs by birth, had married free women: it was asked whether their children were free or unfree: the synod at Henry's suggestion declared both mother and children unfree. This decision tended to throw discredit

19

upon marriages which furthered the secularization of the Church. For married clergy often sought to benefit their own families at the expense of their churches. But on the side of reform Henry was greatly helped by the monastic revival which, largely beginning from Cluny, had spread widely in Lorraine. William, Abbot of St Benignus at Dijon, and Richard, Abbot of St Vanne's near Verdun, were here his helpers. William had been called in by the Bishop of Metz: Richard worked in more than one Lorraine diocese. Outside their own order such monks influenced the secular clergy and even the bishops. Simony and worldliness were more widely reproved; Henry would gladly have seen such a reformation spreading and with some such hope he asked the Pope to visit Germany.

Benedict VIII was, it is true, more a man of action than a reformer. He had faced worse foes than the Crescentii at Farfa, for the Saracens under Mujāhid of Denia (in Spain) had (1015) conquered Sardinia and were harrying the Tuscan coasts. He urged on the Pisans and Genoese before their three days' victory at sea (June 1016): a battle which brought the victorious allies into Sardinia. And he had (1016) made use of Lombard rebels and Norman help to try and shake the Byzantine hold upon Southern Italy. But rebels and Normans had suffered defeat and the Byzantines held their own. Benedict might hopefully turn to the Emperor for further help: when on Maundy Thursday (14 April 1020) he reached Henry's favourite Bamberg, he was the first Pope to visit Germany for a century and a half. With him there came Melo, leader of the Apulian rebels, and Rodolph, the Norman leader, who had helped them. Melo was invested with the new title, Duke of Apulia, and held the empty office for the remaining week of his life. Thus Henry entered into the Italian schemes of Benedict. The Pope on his side confirmed at Fulda the foundation of Bamberg, taking it under special papal protection: Henry gave the Pope a privilege nearly identical with that given by Otto the Great to John XII.

The second half of the year 1020 was spent in small campaigns, including one against Baldwin in Flanders, where in August the Emperor captured Ghent. The other was against Otto of Hammerstein, whom we shall mention later. When Henry kept Easter in 1021 at Merseburg he could look on a realm comparatively peaceful. His old opponent Heribert of Cologne had died (16 March 1021) and was replaced by Henry's friend and diplomatist, Pilgrim. Later (17 August) died Erkambald of Mayence, and was succeeded by Aribo, a royal chaplain and a relative of Pilgrim's. The three great sees were now all held by Bavarians. In July a diet at Nimeguen decided on an expedition to Italy. There the Byzantine forces had occupied part of the principality of Benevento, drawing the Lombard princes to their side, and (June 1021) the Catapan Basil seized the fortress on the Garigliano which the Pope had given to Datto, an Apulian rebel. Thus Rome itself was threatened nearly. In

November 1021 Henry left Augsburg for Italy: early in December he reached Verona, where Italian princes joined his Lorrainers, Swabians and Bavarians: among them were the Bavarian Poppo, Patriarch of Aquileia, and the distinguished Aribert, since 1018 Archbishop of Milan. Leo of Vercelli of course was there, and if some lay magnates kept away others made a welcome appearance. Christmas Henry spent at Ravenna and in January moved southwards. Before he reached Benevento Benedict joined him. The army marched in three divisions and the one which Pilgrim of Cologne commanded met with brilliant successes, taking Capua. Henry himself was delayed for three months by the fortress of Troia, built with almost communal privileges by the Catapan in 1018 to guard the Byzantine province and strong enough to surrender on merely nominal terms. But sickness had assailed the Germans and after visiting Rome Henry came in July to Pavia. So far he had made Rome safer and had subjugated the Lombard states. Then in a synod at Pavia (1 August 1022) with Benedict's help he turned to church reform. Clerical marriage, as common in Lombardy as in Germany, was denounced. And the ever growing poverty of the Church was also noted: lands had been alienated and married clerics were trying to endow their families. As at Goslar it was decided that the wives and children of unfree priests were also serfs, and could thus not hold land. These ecclesiastical decrees, meant to be of general force although passed in a scanty synod, the Emperor embodied in an imperial decree. Leo of Vercelli probably drafted alike the papal speech and the imperial decree and he was the first bishop to enforce the canons.

Then in the autumn of 1022 Henry returned to his kingdom. The following Easter he sent Gerard of Cambray and Richard of St Vannes to beg Robert of France to become his partner in church reform. The two kings met (11 August) at Ivois just within Germany. It was agreed to call an assembly at Pavia of both German and Italian bishops: the assembly would thus represent the old Carolingian realm.

But now Germany was not ecclesiastically at peace either within itself or with the Pope. Aribo of Mayence, on the death of his suffragan Bernward of Hildesheim, had revived the old claim to authority over Gandersheim. But Henry had taken sides with the new Bishop, Godehard of Altaich, although his settlement left irritation behind. Aribo had also a more important quarrel with Pope Benedict arising out of a marriage.

Count Otto of Hammerstein, a great noble of Franconia, had married Irmingard, although they were related within the prohibited degrees. Episcopal censure was disregarded: excommunication by a synod at Nimeguen (March 1018), enforced by the Emperor and the Archbishop of Mayence, only brought Otto to temporary submission. Two years later, after rejoining Irmingard, he attacked in revenge the territory of Mayence. At length his disregard of synod and of Emperor alike forced Henry to uphold the Church's law by the sword. But Otto's irregular marriage a few years later raised even greater difficulties. For the present Henry had shewn his ecclesiastical sympathies and his readiness to enforce the Church's decisions even in a field where many rulers disregarded or disliked them. A synod at Mayence in June 1023 separated the pair, whereupon Irmingard appealed to Rome. This appeal was looked upon by Aribo as an invasion of his metropolitan rights, and he persuaded a provincial synod at Seligenstadt to take his view. Here were forbidden all appeals to Rome made without episcopal leave, and also any papal remission of guilt, unless the ordinary penance imposed locally had been first performed. Henry sent the diplomatic Pilgrim of Cologne to explain matters to Benedict, who nevertheless directed a fresh hearing of Irmingard's case, and also significantly sent no pallium to Aribo. In reply the Archbishop called his suffragans to meet at Höchst 13 May 1024; and it was hoped through the Empress Kunigunda to draw thither bishops of other provinces also: meanwhile all the suffragans of Mayence except two signed a remonstrance to the Pope against the insult to their metropolitan. But Benedict died (11 June 1024) before the matter was settled, being succeeded by his brother Romanus, hitherto called Senator of all the Romans by Benedict's appointment, who passed from layman to Pope as John XIX within a day. The new Pope had no religious and few ecclesiastical interests, and the matter of the marriage went no further.

Soon after Benedict Henry himself passed away. During 1024 he had suffered from both illness and the weakness of advancing years; on 13 July the end came. His body was fittingly laid to rest in his beloved Bamberg, itself an expression of the religious zeal which was shewn so strongly and so pathetically in his closing years. Religion and devotion to the Church had always been a leading interest in his active life; as death drew nearer it became an all-absorbing care. The title of Saint which his people gave him fittingly expressed the feeling of his age.

CHAPTER XI.

THE EMPEROR CONRAD II.

WITH the death of Henry II the Saxon dynasty in the male line became extinct; nevertheless under the Ottos the hereditary principle had become so firmly rooted, the Teutonic theory of election so nearly forgotten, that the descendants of Otto the Great in the female branch were alone regarded as suitable successors to the Emperor Henry II. The choice of the princes was practically limited to the two Conrads, the great-grandsons of the first Otto's daughter Liutgard and Conrad of Lorraine. Both were grandsons of Otto, Duke of Carinthia; the future emperor through the eldest son Henry who died young, the other, known as Conrad the Younger, through the third son, also named Conrad, who had succeeded his father in the duchy of Carinthia. This younger Conrad did not inherit the dukedom, which was granted on his father's death in 1011 to Adalbero of Eppenstein, but he acquired nevertheless the greater part of the family estates in Franconia. In wealth and territorial position he was stronger than his elder cousin; moreover, since he had adopted the attitude of Henry II in matters of ecclesiastical politics, he could safely rely on the support of the reforming party in the Church, which, particularly in Lorraine, carried considerable weight under the guidance of Archbishop Pilgrim of Cologne. An orphan[1] with a meagre inheritance, brought up by the famous canonist, Burchard of Worms, Conrad the Elder had little to recommend him beyond seniority and personal character. On late and unreliable authority it is asserted that the late Emperor designated him as his successor[2]; and though it is reasonable to suppose that Henry II should make some recommendation with regard to the succession, it is at least remarkable that he should select a man whose

---

[1] His father died while he was still a child, and his mother married again and took no further interest in the child of her first husband.

[2] Sigebert, *Chron. MGHSS.* vi. 356. Hugh of Flavigny, *Chron.* ii. 16, *MGHSS.* viii. 392. It is accepted as historical by Arndt, *Die Wahl Konrads II*, Diss. Göttingen, 1861, Maurenbrecher, *Königswahlen*, and others; Bresslau, from the silence of contemporaries, and the unreliability of the evidence is led to the conclusion that no such designation was made. (*Jahrbücher, Konrad II*, i. p. 9 f., also in Hirsch, *Jahrbücher, Heinrich II*, iii. p. 356 f.) Harttung, *Studien zur Geschichte Konrads II*, attempts to prove that the younger Conrad was designated by Henry II; but see Bresslau, *Jahrbücher*, Excurs. ii. p. 342 f.

views both in ecclesiastical and secular politics were diametrically opposed to his own. Yet this very fact of his antagonism to the reforming movement induced Aribo, Archbishop of Mayence, and the bulk of the episcopate, jealous and suspicious of the progress of Cluniac ideas in Germany, to throw the whole weight of their influence in support of his candidature. The election took place on the Rhine between Mayence and Worms[1] on 4 September 1024. Before it took place the elder Conrad had a meeting with his cousin and apparently induced him to withdraw from the contest.

Conrad the Elder, left in undisputed possession of the field (for the party of his late rival, the Lorrainers, rather than give him their votes, had retired from the assembly), was elected unanimously, and received from the hands of the widowed Empress Kunigunda, the royal insignia, committed by her husband to her care. The election was a popular one. Princes and people, spiritual and secular, thronged to Mayence to attend the coronation festival. " If Charles the Great himself had been alive and present," writes Conrad's enthusiastic biographer[2], " the rejoicing could not have been exceeded." The ceremony of coronation was performed on 8 September by Aribo in the cathedral of Mayence and was followed by the customary state banquet and by the taking of the oath of fealty by the bishops, nobles, and even, we are told, by other freemen of distinction. One incident marred the general serenity of the proceedings; Conrad's marriage in 1017 with Gisela, the widow successively of Bruno of Brunswick and of Ernest II of Swabia, being within the prohibited degrees, was not sanctioned by the Church. Aribo denied her the crown; and it was only after an interval of some days that Archbishop Pilgrim of Cologne, desirous of making his peace with the king he had opposed, offered to perform the ceremony in his cathedral at Cologne[3].

The princes of Lorraine, among them Gozelo and Dietrich, the Dukes of the lower and upper provinces, Reginar V, the powerful Count of Hainault, and the greater number of the bishops, had, as we have seen, resisted Conrad's election, and after the event had denied him recognition. The bishops adopted this attitude on account of Conrad's lack of sympathy with the movement of reform in the Church; when, however, their

[1] The exact spot is generally said to be Kamba on the right bank of the river near Oppenheim. Schädel (*Die Königsstühle bei Mainz und die Wahl Konrads II,* Progr. Mayence, 1896) believes the place of election to have been on the left bank near Lörzweiler. With Wipo (cap. 2) we can leave it "de vocabulo et situ loci plenius dicere topographis." Anyhow "cis et citra Rhenum castra locabant." Wipo, *loc. cit.*

[2] Wipo, *Script. Rer. Germ.* ed. Bresslau, 1915. See also the editor's preface to this edition. Wipo is the main authority for the reign; probably a Burgundian by birth, he held the office of chaplain to the king, and was an eye-witness of many of the events he records.

[3] So Bresslau, I. pp. 35–37, and Excurs. III. p. 351, following the account of Herman of Reichenau (1024, in Bresslau's ed. of Wipo, p. 94). Other authorities accept the account of the Quedlinburg annals, that Gisela was subsequently crowned by Aribo at the intercession of the princes (Ann. Qued. 1024, *MGHSS,* III. 90).

leader, the Archbishop of Cologne, made his peace with the king, and when Odilo of Cluny, who had, it seems, been present at the election, and had been the recipient of Conrad's first charter (a confirmation of certain lands in Alsace to the Cluniac monastery of Payerne), exerted his influence in Conrad's interest, the bishops were prevailed upon to make their submission. Conrad was therefore able to make his royal progress through Lorraine unhindered.

It was customary for a newly elected king to travel through his kingdom, dispensing justice, settling disputes, ordering peace. Within a year of his coronation (he was back in Mayence at the end of August 1025) Conrad had visited the more important towns of the five great duchies of his kingdom. On his journey through Saxony two significant events occurred; he received the recognition of the Saxon princes and gave a decision against Aribo of Mayence, shewing thereby that he was not to be swayed from the path of justice even in the interests of the foremost prelate of Germany. Before Conrad's election the Saxon princes under their Duke Bernard had assembled at Werla, and there decided on a course of action similar to that which they had pursued on the occasion of the election of Henry II in 1002. They had, it seems, absented themselves from the electoral council, with the object of making their acceptance of the result dependent upon conditions. They required the king to acknowledge the peculiarly independent position, the ancient and barbaric law, of the Saxons. They met him at Minden, where he was keeping his Christmas court. Their condition was proposed and accepted, and their homage, hitherto deferred, was duly performed to their now recognised sovereign[1].

Since the time of Otto III, the jurisdiction over the rich nunnery of Gandersheim had been the cause of a fierce dispute between the bishops of Hildesheim and the archbishops of Mayence. It had been one of the reasons for the breach between Aribo and the late Emperor, who had in 1022 decided in favour of the Hildesheim claim. While Conrad remained in Saxony the matter was brought up before him. The outlook was ominous for Bishop Godehard; Conrad was not likely to give cause for a quarrel with the powerful archbishop to whom he owed his crown, and whom he had already favoured by conferring on him the archchancellorship of Italy, in addition to the archchancellorship of Germany which he had previously held. Moreover, the influential Abbess Sophia, the daughter of the Emperor Otto II, was known to favour the claims of Aribo. On the other hand, Conrad could not lightly reverse a decision made by his predecessor only two years before, and he may also have felt some resentment towards Aribo for the latter's refusal to crown his queen. Postponements and compromises were tried in vain. At last, in March

---

[1] This interpretation of the rather confused evidence is Bresslau's, *i.* 12 and n. 7. Cf. also his edition of Wipo, *Script. Rer. Germ.* 1915, p. 11, n. 1.

1025, at a sparsely attended synod held at Grona, a provisional judgment was given in favour of the Bishop of Hildesheim; the decision was confirmed two years later at a more representative gathering at Frankfort, but it was not until 1030, a year before his death, that Aribo had a meeting with his opponent at Merseburg, and finally renounced his claims which, according to the biographer of Godehard, he confessed that he had raised "partly in ignorance, partly out of malice."

The rebellion, which disturbed the opening years of the new reign, is closely connected with the question of the Burgundian succession and with the revolt in Lombardy. Rodolph III, the childless King of Burgundy, had in 1016 recognised his nephew the Emperor Henry II as the heir to his throne; he maintained however, and probably with justice, that with the Emperor's death the compact became void. Conrad, on the other hand, took a different view of the case; the cession, he argued, was made not to the Emperor but to the Empire, to which he had been duly elected. Against him stood a formidable row of descendants of Conrad the Peaceful in the female line, two of whom, Ernest, Duke of Swabia, whose mother, Queen Gisela, was the niece, and Odo, Count of Blois, whose mother, Bertha, was the sister of Rodolph, aspired to the inheritance. To make his intentions clear Conrad, in June 1025, occupied Basle which, though held by Henry II, actually lay within the confines of the Burgundian kingdom. As his presence was needed elsewhere, he left his wife Gisela, herself a niece of King Rodolph[1], to bring the Burgundian question to a satisfactory issue. The success of her efforts is to be seen in the Burgundian king's refusal to assist Ernest of Swabia in his second revolt (1026), in his submissive attendance at the Emperor's coronation at Rome (Easter 1027), and in his recognition, at Muttenz near Basle, later in the same year, of Conrad's title to succeed to his kingdom. Ernest, whose hopes in Burgundy were shattered by the occupation of Basle, decided to oppose Conrad with arms. He allied himself with Count Welf, with the still disaffected dukes of Lorraine, and with Conrad the Younger who, having heard no more of the proffered rewards by which his cousin had secured his withdrawal from the electoral contest, had openly shewn his resentment at Augsburg in the previous April[2].

In France, Odo of Blois and Champagne was interested in the downfall of Conrad; in Italy, the trend of events moved in the same direction. There the Lombards, taking advantage of the death of Henry II, rose

---

[1] This marriage connexion with the Burgundian house constituted, Poupardin concludes, Conrad's title to be designated by Rodolph and to be chosen by the Burgundian princes, but brought with it no actual right of succession. Cf. Poupardin, *Le Royaume de Bourgogne*, p. 151.

[2] Conrad the Younger stood in the same relation to Rodolph III as did Ernest; his mother Matilda was Rodolph's niece. He appears, however, to have raised no claim to the throne of Burgundy. Cf. Poupardin, *loc. cit.*

in revolt against the imperial domination. The men of Pavia, mindful of the recent destruction of their city at the hands of the late Emperor, burnt the royal palace; the north Italian princes, in defiance of Conrad, offered their crown first to King Robert of France, then, on his refusal, to William V, Duke of Aquitaine, who accepted it for his son. The duke's only hope of success in the dangerous enterprise he had undertaken lay in keeping Conrad engaged in his own kingdom. With this object he set about organising the opposition in Lorraine, France, and Burgundy; he met Robert of France and Odo of Champagne at Tours, and the French king agreed to carry a campaign into Germany. The combination, so formidable in appearance, dissolved into nothing. Robert was prevented by the affairs of his own kingdom from taking the field against Conrad; Odo, engaged in a fierce feud with Fulk of Anjou, was powerless; William of Aquitaine on visiting Italy found the situation there less favourable than he had been led to expect, and thereupon gave up the project; the dukes of Lorraine, no longer able to count on foreign aid, made their submission to the Emperor at Aix-la-Chapelle (Christmas 1025). After the collapse of the alliance, continued resistance on the part of Ernest was useless; at Augsburg early in the next year, through the mediation of the queen, his mother, he was reconciled with Conrad who, to keep him from further mischief, insisted on his accompanying him on the Italian campaign upon which he was about to embark.

It was a wise precaution, and Conrad would have been better advised had he retained his ambitious stepson in his camp; instead he dispatched him to Germany to suppress the disorders which had arisen there in his absence. Welf, obdurate in his disobedience, had attacked and plundered the lands and cities of Bruno, Bishop of Augsburg, the brother of the Emperor Henry II, the guardian of the young King Henry III, and the administrator of Germany during the king's absence in Italy. Ernest, back among his old fellow-conspirators and acting, no doubt, on the advice of his evil genius, Count Werner of Kiburg, instead of suppressing the rebellious Welf, joined with him in rebellion[1]. The second revolt of Ernest was however as abortive as the first; he invaded Alsace, penetrated into Burgundy, but finding to his discomfiture, in Rodolph, not an ally but an enemy, he was compelled to make a hasty retreat to Zurich, whence he occupied himself in making plundering raids upon the rich abbeys of Reichenau and St Gall. Conrad's return soon ended the affair. Ernest and Welf answered the imperial summons to Ulm (July 1027), not however as suppliants for the Emperor's mercy, but, supported by an armed following, with the intention either of dictating their own

---

[1] The attitude of the younger Conrad in this rebellion is ambiguous. Wipo, c. 19, says of him "nec fidus imperatori, nec tamen multum noxius illi." His submission and condemnation to a short term of imprisonment in 1027, mentioned by Wipo, c. 21, proves his implication.

terms or, failing that, of fighting their way to safety. The duke had miscalculated his resources; at an interview with his vassals he discovered his mistake. They were prepared, they said, to follow him as their oath required against any man except the Emperor; but loyalty to the Emperor took precedence to loyalty to the duke. Ernest had no choice but to throw himself on Conrad's mercy; he was deprived of his duchy and imprisoned in the castle of Gibichenstein near Halle. Welf was condemned to imprisonment, to make reparation to the Bishop of Augsburg, and to the loss of a countship in the neighbourhood of Brixen.

Ernest, after less than a year's captivity, was forgiven and reinstated in his dukedom. But the course of events of 1026 was repeated in 1030. Ordered by the Emperor to execute the ban against Count Werner, who had persisted in rebellion, he disobeyed, and was, by the judgment of the princes, once more deprived of his dukedom and placed under the ban of the Empire (at Ingelheim, Easter 1030). After a vain attempt to persuade Odo of Champagne to join him, he and Werner withdrew into the Black Forest, where, making the strong castle of Falkenstein their headquarters, they lived for a time the life of bandits. At last, in August, the two rebels fell in a fierce encounter with the Emperor's troops under Count Manegold.

The rebellions of Ernest, dictated not by any dissatisfaction at Conrad's rule but rather by personal motives and rival ambitions, never assumed dangerous proportions. The fact that even the nobility of Swabia, with few exceptions, refused to follow their duke is significant of the strength and popularity of Conrad's government. The loyalty of Germany as a whole was never shaken. Duke Ernest, a little undeservedly perhaps, has become the hero of legend and romance; he has often been compared with Liudolf of Swabia, the popular and ambitious son of Otto the Great. The parallel is scarcely a fair one; Liudolf rebelled but once and with juster cause; and after his defeat, he lived loyally and died fighting his father's battles in Italy. Ernest, though twice forgiven, lived and died a rebel.

In September 1032 Rodolph III ended a weak and inglorious reign. Conrad had been solemnly recognised as heir by the late king at Muttenz five years before and had been entrusted with the royal insignia, the crown and the lance of St Maurice. Some of the Burgundian nobles had even already taken the oath of allegiance to the German king; but the majority both of the ecclesiastical and secular lords, especially in the romance-speaking district of the south, stood opposed to him. His powerful rival, Odo, Count of Blois and Champagne, had at first the advantage, for Conrad at the critical moment was busily occupied with the affairs of Poland, and when, after the submission of the Polish Duke Mesco, he hastened to Strasbourg, he found a large part of Burgundy already in the hands of the enemy (Christmas 1032). In spite of the severity of the weather, which was sufficiently remarkable to supply the theme of a poem of a hundred stanzas from the pen of Wipo, the Emperor decided to make a winter campaign into Burgundy. He marched on Basle and proceeded to Payerne, where he was formally elected and crowned by his partisans; but the indescribable sufferings of his troops from the cold prevented his further progress, and he withdrew to Zurich.

In the spring, before resuming operations in Burgundy, he entered into negotiations with the French King Henry I, which resulted in a meeting of the two at Deville on the Meuse. What actually took place there is not recorded, but it seems clear that an alliance against Odo was formed between them. Again the affairs of Poland prevented Conrad from completing his task, and on his return thence he found that his adversary had penetrated the German frontier and plundered the districts of Lorraine in the neighbourhood of Toul. Conrad retaliated with a raid into Count Odo's territory and brought him to submission; the latter renounced his claims, agreed to evacuate the occupied districts, and to make reparation for the damage caused by his incursion into Lorraine. The matter was not however so easily settled; not only did Odo not evacuate the occupied parts of Burgundy nor make satisfaction for the harm he had perpetrated in Lorraine, but he even had the audacity to repeat his performance in that country. Conrad determined on a decisive effort; Burgundy was attacked on two sides. His Italian allies, Marquess Boniface of Tuscany and Archbishop Aribert of Milan, under the guidance of Count Humbert of Maurienne, led their troops across the Great St Bernard, and following the Rhone Valley, made their junction with the Emperor, operating from the north, at Geneva. Little resistance was encountered by either army. At Geneva Conrad was again solemnly recognised as king and received the submission of the greater number of Odo's adherents. The town of Morat alone held out defiantly; attacked by the German and Italian forces in conjunction, it was taken by assault and demolished. With it were destroyed the last hopes of Conrad's adversaries; they submitted, and Burgundy, furnishing the Emperor with his fourth crown, became an undisputed and integral part of the imperial dominions. If Burgundy was never a source of much strength or financial profit to the Empire, its inclusion was by no means without its value. Its geographical position as a barrier between France and Italy, and as commanding the western passes of the Alps, made it an acquisition of the first importance. In the last year of his reign Conrad visited his new kingdom. A solemn and well-attended gathering of ecclesiastical and secular nobles assembled at Soleure, and for three days deliberated over the means of establishing peace and organised government in a land, which for many a year had known nothing but lawlessness and anarchy.

The Eastern Frontier.

During the years 1030–1035 Conrad was chiefly occupied with the restless state of the eastern frontier of his kingdom. It is a dreary story of rebellion, ineffective campaigns, fratricidal wars. Poland, Hungary, Bohemia, the Wendish lands to the north-east, demanded in turn the Emperor's attention. Boleslav Chrobry had, during the previous reign, been assiduously building up a strong position for himself in Poland; in the peace of Bautzen (1018) he had been the chief gainer at the expense of the Empire; on the death of Henry II he had taken a further step and boldly assumed the title of king. Conrad was neither strong enough nor at liberty to deal at once with this presumptuous duke; but while at Merseburg in February 1025, he took the wise precaution of securing the loyalty of the neighbouring Slavonic tribes of the Lyutitzi and the Obotrites.

In the summer Boleslav died; his younger son Mesco, having successfully driven his elder brother Otto Bezprim to Russia (or perhaps Hungary), assumed the kingship and the policy of his father. By 1028 his aggressions had become intolerable. The eastern parts of Saxony were raided and plundered; the bishopric of Zeitz suffered so severely that it had to be removed to the better fortified Naumberg, a town of Eckhard of Meissen, near the junction of the Unstrut and the Saale; the Lyutitzi, helplessly at the mercy of the tyrannical Mesco, pleaded for German assistance. Conrad assembled an army beyond the Elbe. But the campaign was a complete failure: the troops were scattered and worn out by long marches through forests and swamps; Bautzen was besieged, but not captured; and the Emperor, despairing of making any headway, withdrew to Saxony. The only success was achieved by Conrad's ally, Břatislav, the son of the Duke of Bohemia, who managed to recover Moravia from the Poles. The death of Thietmar, Margrave of the East Mark (January 1030), was the occasion for another and more serious incursion on the part of the Polish prince, united this time with a band of disloyal Saxons. In the region between the Elbe and the Saale a hundred villages are said to have been destroyed by fire, more than 9000 men and women taken into captivity. The enemy were only beaten off by the courage and resource of Count Dietrich of Wettin.

Conrad was unable to take the matter in hand, for he was engaged in a war with Stephen of Hungary. The relations between the latter country and the Empire had been growing yearly more strained. Werner, Bishop of Strasbourg, Conrad's ambassador to Constantinople in 1027, had been denied a passage through Hungary, and was compelled to take the more hazardous route by sea. The Bavarian nobles, no doubt, gave ample provocation for this hostile attitude by their attempts to extend their possessions across the Fischa, the boundary at that time between Germany and Hungary. According to one account the actual cause for quarrel arose through the Emperor's refusal to grant, at the request of King Stephen, the dukedom of Bavaria to his son Henry (he was the nephew of the Emperor Henry II, whose sister Gisela had married Stephen of Hungary). In 1030 Conrad took the field against him; this, like the Polish campaign, was a miserable disaster. Conrad did no more than ravage the border country as far as the Raab, and retired with an army imperilled by famine, while the Hungarians pursued the retreating Germans and captured Vienna, which celebrated city is now for the first time mentioned under this name. Břatislav, who had gained the only success in the Polish campaign of the previous year, was again conspicuous for his services to the Empire; he defeated the Hungarians and devastated their country as far as the town of Gran. The young King Henry, who as Duke of Bavaria was closely concerned with the affairs of Hungary, was entrusted with the settlement of the quarrel with King Stephen. By the cession of a small tract of country lying between the Fischa and the Leitha he secured, in the spring of 1031, peace and the restoration of Vienna.

Conrad, relieved of danger from Hungary, was at liberty to cope effectively with the troublesome Duke of Poland. Allied with Mesco's banished brother Otto, Conrad organised a combined attack; while he advanced from the west, Otto Bezprim and his protector Yaroslav, Prince of Kiev, were to attack from the east. Mesco, thus threatened from two sides, soon gave way and agreed to the terms stipulated by the Emperor. He was required to surrender the border territory which his father had acquired by the treaty of Bautzen (1018), the prisoners and booty captured in the raids upon Saxony, and also the Upper and Lower Lausitz which were attached respectively to the Meissen and the East Marks. Poland was thus once more confined within the limits of the old duchy as it was before the ascendancy of Boleslav Chrobry. The attack of Bezprim had not synchronised with that of the German troops; it took place after this peace had been concluded. He too, however, was successful; he drove Mesco from the throne, of which he himself took possession, and, by recognising the overlordship of the Emperor, was himself recognised as the lawful duke of Poland. His reign, characterised by the most brutal savagery, was cut short in the next year (1032) by assassination, engineered in part by the enemies he had made in his own circle, in part by the intrigues of the brother he had expelled. Mesco promptly returned from Bohemia, where he had taken refuge with Duke Udalrich. In spite of his apparent willingness to enter into friendly relations with the Emperor, we hear of a renewed outbreak of war before the end of the year. But Conrad was anxious to rid himself of the vexatious business and to be free to make good his claim to the Burgundian crown. He therefore received the duke's submission at Merseburg (1033), and allowed him to retain his dukedom, subject to his feudal superiority and reduced in extent by a strip of territory on the western frontier, which was annexed to the East Mark. The power of Poland was crushed. On Mesco's death in 1034 the country relapsed into an almost chronic state of civil war in which Conrad, wearied with Polish affairs, was careful not to involve himself.

In the meanwhile difficulties had been growing up in the neighbouring country of Bohemia. Udalrich, for some years past, had shewn insubordination to his feudal lord: in 1031 he had refused his help for the Polish campaign; summoned to the diet of Merseburg (July 1033) to answer for his conduct, he had defiantly remained absent. Conrad was too busily engaged with Odo, his rival to the Burgundian throne, to deal himself with his disobedient vassal. He entrusted the task, therefore, to his son Henry, now a promising youth of sixteen years; his confidence was not misplaced, for a single campaign in the summer brought the duke to subjection[1]. At a court held at Werben he was condemned, banished, and deprived of his lands. His brother, the old Duke Jaromir, was dragged from his prison at Utrecht, where he had languished for more than twenty years, to be set again over the duchy of Bohemia. The arrangement was, however, not a permanent one; Udalrich was pardoned at Ratisbon (April 1034), but not content with the partial restoration of his duchy, he seized and blinded his hapless brother. His misdeeds brought a speedy retribution; he died the same year, choked or perhaps poisoned while eating his dinner. Jaromir was disinclined a third time to undertake the title and duties which had brought him only misfortune; at his wish Břatislav, who had on the whole deserved well of Conrad, received the dukedom as a fief of the Empire.

Further north, a feud had broken out between the Saxons and the Wendish tribe, the Lyutitzi, which gave rise to mutual incursions and plundering. At the request of both parties, the Emperor permitted the issue to be determined by the judgment of God in the form of a duel. Unluckily, the Christian champion fell wounded to the sword of the pagan; the decision was accepted by the Emperor, and the Wends, so elated by their success, would have forthwith attacked their Saxon opponents, had not they been constrained by oath to keep the peace and been menaced by the establishment at Werben of a fortress strongly garrisoned by a body of Saxon knights. But the peace was soon broken, the fortress soon captured; and two expeditions across the Elbe (1035 and 1036) were necessary before the Lyutitzi were reduced to obedience. In the first Conrad was seldom able to bring the enemy to an open fight; they retreated before him into the impenetrable swamps and forests, while the Germans burnt their cities, devastated their lands. We have a picture

---

[1] For an examination into the confused chronology of these events and of the conflicting passage in the *Annales Altahenses* see Bresslau, *Jahrbücher* II. Excurs. iii. p. 484 f., and Bretholz, *Geschichte Böhmens und Mährens* (1912), p. 127. Seydel, *Studien zur Kritik Wipos*, Dissertation, Berlin, 1898, places these events a year later, 1034.

from Wipo of the Emperor standing oftentime thigh-deep in the morass, fighting himself and encouraging his men to battle. The punishment, meted out to the prisoners captured in this exploit, leaves an indelible stain on the otherwise upright character of the Emperor. In their heathen fanaticism they had sacrilegiously mutilated the figure of Christ on a crucifix; Conrad avenged the outrage in like fashion. Drawn up before the cross they had dishonoured, their eyes put out, their hands and feet hacked off, they were left to die miserably. The second attack, of which the details are not recorded, appears to have been decisive; the Wends submitted, and had to pay the penalty for their revolt at the price of an increased tribute.

The wisdom of Conrad's diplomacy is perhaps most evident in his relations with his powerful northern neighbour Knut, King of England, Denmark, and, in 1030, Norway. Had Conrad permitted the hostility which had existed under his predecessor to continue, he would have found in Knut a formidable opponent always ready to disturb the stability of the imperial authority on the north-eastern border of Germany. His policy towards Poland, Bohemia, and more especially the Wendish country across the Elbe, could scarcely have met with so large a measure of success. The rulers of Poland and Denmark were closely related; both countries were at enmity with Germany; an alliance between them seemed natural and inevitable. Thus Conrad lost no time in bringing about, through the mediation of Unwan, Archbishop of Bremen, friendly relations with Knut (1025). This alliance was drawn closer some ten years later by the marriage of their children, Henry and Gunnhild, and by the cession to the Danish king of the March and the town of Schleswig. Though the German frontier was thereby brought back to the Eider, the gain outweighed the loss. Knut was zealous for the advancement of the Christian religion; he kept in close touch with the metropolitans of Bremen, Unwan and his successors, and promoted their efforts towards the conversion of the heathen. From Germany he drew churchmen to fill high positions in his English kingdom, as for instance Duduco, Bishop of Wells, and Wichmann, Abbot of Ramsey[1]. Unfortunately, this powerful and useful ally of the Empire survived the treaty of 1035 but a few months: he died in November of the same year, and the Danish ascendancy soon crumbled away under the rule of his successors.

Italy under Conrad II.

We have already noticed how the death of the Emperor Henry II had been the signal in Italy for a general revolt against the imperial authority; for this movement, which found its expression in the burning of the royal palace at Pavia and in the offer of the Lombard crown to a

[1] Cf. Freeman, *Norman Conquest*, II. App. note L. p. 598 f.

French prince, the great noble families of north Italy, the Otbertines, the Aleramids, the Marquesses of Tuscany and of Turin, were mainly responsible. On the other hand the bishops under Aribert, the powerful Archbishop of Milan, stood by Conrad; indeed Aribert with several other bishops, presenting himself before the new king at Constance (June 1025), assured him of his loyalty, of his willingness to crown him king of Italy, and of the warm reception that awaited him when he should set foot across the Alps; other Italian lords appeared a little later at Zurich to perform their homage. Encouraged by these manifestations of loyalty and by the collapse of the attempt of the lay aristocracy to raise a French prince to the throne, Conrad made his plans for an Italian expedition in the ensuing spring. By the route through the Brenner and Verona, in March he reached Milan, where, since Pavia, the old Lombard capital and place of coronation, was still in revolt, he was crowned by Aribert in the cathedral of St Ambrose. The Pavese, fearful of the result of their boldness, had sought pardon from Conrad at Constance, but their refusal to rebuild the palace they had destroyed prevented a reconciliation. Conrad punished them by a wholesale devastation of the surrounding country, and leaving part of his army to complete the subjection of the rebellious city, he passed eastward through Piacenza and Cremona to Ravenna; here his stay was marked by a scene of the wildest uproar. The citizens rose against the German soldiers with the hope that by force of numbers they might succeed in driving them from the town. Their hope was vain; the imperial troops soon gained the upper hand, and Conrad descended from his bedchamber to stop the slaughter of the defeated and defenceless burghers. The incident, related by Wipo, of the German knight who lost his leg in the riot is characteristic of the king's generosity; he ordered the leather gaiters of the wounded warrior to be filled with coin by way of compensation for the loss of his limb.

The heat of the Italian summer drove Conrad northward, to pass some two months in the cooler and more healthy atmosphere of the Alpine valleys. The autumn and winter were spent in reducing to submission the powerful houses of the north-west and of Tuscany. This accomplished, Conrad could proceed unhindered to Rome. The coronation of Conrad and his wife Gisela at the hands of Pope John XIX took place on Easter Day (26 March 1027) at St Peter's in the presence of two kings, Knut and Rodolph, and a vast gathering of German and Italian princes and bishops. Seldom during the early middle ages was an imperial or papal election altogether free from riot and bloodshed. Conrad's was no exception. A trivial dispute over an oxhide converted a brilliant and festive scene into a tumultuous street-fight between the Romans and the foreigners. A synod was held shortly after at the Lateran, in which two disputes were brought up for decision: the one, a question of precedence between the archbishops of Milan and Ravenna, was settled in favour of the former; in the other, the long-standing quarrel between the patriarchs of Aquileia and Grado, the former triumphed; the see of Grado was made subject to the Patriarch of Aquileia, and the Venetians were thereby deprived of their ecclesiastical independence.

In South Italy, Conrad accepted the existing state of things without involving himself further in the complexity of Greek and Lombard politics; he contented himself merely with the homage of the princes of Capua, Benevento, and Salerno. By the summer he was once again in Germany. In a little more than a year the Emperor had succeeded in winning the obedience of the north, the recognition of the south, of Italy, a position with which he might reasonably rest satisfied. An interval of ten years divides the two expeditions of Conrad across the Alps, and the second was made at the request of the Italians themselves. But he had motives of his own for intervention in the affairs of Italy in 1036; his policy had been to strengthen German influence in two ways: first by the appointment of German clergy to vacant Italian bishoprics, and secondly by encouraging the intermarriage of the German and Italian princely houses; so Gebhard of Eichstedt received the archbishopric of Ravenna, while the majority of the suffragan sees in the province of Aquileia and not a few in Tuscany were filled with Germans. The success of the latter policy is exemplified by the marriages of Azzo of the Otbertine family with the Welfic heiress Kunigunda, of Herman of Swabia with Adelaide of the house of Turin, of Boniface of Tuscany with Beatrix, the daughter of Duke Frederick of Upper Lorraine. Such a policy ran counter to the ambition of the Archbishop of Milan, who for his part strove to exercise an overlordship in Lombardy, and, it was said, "disposed of the whole kingdom at his nod." Such a man must be suppressed if Conrad was to maintain his authority in Italy.

The immediate situation, however, which precipitated the Emperor's expedition was due to the feud which had arisen between the smaller and greater tenants, the *valvassores* and the *capitanei*; while the hereditary principle was in practice secured to the latter, it was denied by them to the former. It was customary for the Italian nobles to have houses and possessions in the neighbouring town, where they lived for some part of the year; a dispute of this kind thus affected the towns no less than the country. In Milan one of the vavassors was deprived of his fief by the domineering archbishop. It was sufficient to kindle the sparks of revolution into a blaze; negotiations failed to pacify the incensed knights, who were thereupon driven from their city by the combined force of the *capitanei* and the burghers. The Milanese vavassors, joined by their social equals from the surrounding districts, after a hard fight and heavy losses, defeated their opponents in the Campo Malo between Milan and Lodi. It was at this stage that both parties sought the mediation of the Emperor.

Conrad had watched with interest the turn of events in Italy, and certainly as early as July 1036 decided to visit Italy for the second time. The appeal of the opposing parties, therefore, came very opportunely. "If Italy hungers for law, I will satisfy her," he remarked on receiving the news. He crossed the Brenner in December, spent Christmas at Verona, and reached Milan early in the new year. On the day following his arrival a popular rising occurred which was imputed, not without some reason, to the instigation of Aribert. Lacking confidence in his strength to deal with the situation in the stronghold of his enemies, Conrad decided that all questions of difference should be determined at a diet to be held at Pavia in March. Here numerous complaints were brought against the arrogant archbishop, foremost amongst his accusers being Hugh, a member of the Otbertine family, who held the countship of Milan. The Emperor demanded redress; the archbishop defiantly refused to comply. Conrad, judging his conduct treasonable, took the high-handed measure of thrusting him into prison under the custody of Poppo, Patriarch of Aquileia, and Conrad, Duke of Carinthia. Poppo, however, was not sufficiently watchful of his important prisoner, and suffered for his negligence the displeasure of the Emperor. A certain monk, Albizo by name, had been allowed to share with his lord the hardships of prison; through his agency escape was effected. One night, while the faithful Albizo feigned sleep in the bed of the archbishop, the sheets drawn close over his head to prevent recognition, Aribert in the harmless guise of a monk passed safely through his gaolers, mounted a horse waiting in readiness, and rode in haste to Milan, where he was welcomed with enthusiasm by the patriotic burghers.

With reinforcements brought by his son from Germany Conrad besieged Milan, but without much success; it amounted only to some indecisive fighting, the storming of a few strongholds, the devastation of the surrounding country. But if the siege of Milan produced little military result, it drew forth the most important constitutional act of the reign, one of the most famous documents of feudal law, the edict of 28 May 1037. This celebrated decree solved the question at issue between the greater and the smaller vassals. As in Germany Conrad had shewn himself in sympathy with the small tenants, so in Italy he now secured to them and to their successors the possession of their lands against unjust and arbitrary eviction by their lords. "No vassal of a bishop, abbot, abbess, marquess, count, or of anyone holding an imperial or ecclesiastical fief.....shall be deprived of it without certain and proved guilt, except according to the constitution of our ancestors and by the judgment of his peers." The next two clauses deal with the rights of appeal against the verdict of the peers: in the case of the greater vassals the hearing may be brought before the Emperor himself, in the case of the smaller either before the overlords or before the Emperor's *missi* for determination. Then, the succession of the fief is secured to the son, to the grandson by a son, or, these failing, to the brother. Alienation or exchange without the tenant's consent is prohibited; the Emperor's right to the *fodrum* "as it was taken by our ancestors" is affirmed. Finally, a penalty of a hundred pounds of gold, to be paid half to the imperial treasury, half to the injured party, is enjoined for disobedience. By these concessions the Emperor bound to his interests the strongest and most numerous military class in North Italy, and at the same time struck a blow at the dangerously powerful position of the Lombard episcopate.

The heat of the summer prevented any serious campaigning for some months. The siege of Milan was raised, the army dispersed. The Emperor, however, did not relinquish his efforts to overthrow the Archbishop of Milan; in spite of the remonstrances of his son and many others, he took the unprecedented step of deposing Aribert without reference to an ecclesiastical synod. The Papacy was weak and submissive; John XIX had allowed himself to be inscribed in a document among the *fideles* of the Emperor[1]. He was now dead (1033), and his nephew, a bad man certainly, but not so bad as he is painted in the scurrilous party literature of the succeeding generation, young perhaps, but not the mere boy of twelve he is usually accounted[2], was raised to the pontificate under the name of Benedict IX. He, no doubt, cared little for the duties incumbent on his office; at all events, when he visited the Emperor at Cremona, he made no protest against the uncanonical action of Conrad. Aribert retaliated by organising a conspiracy with Conrad's enemy and late rival for the throne of Burgundy, Odo of Blois. But it soon collapsed; after two incursions into Lorraine, Odo was defeated and killed at Bar on 15 November 1037 by Duke Gozelo. The three Lombard bishops of Vercelli, Cremona, and Piacenza, who were implicated, were banished to Germany.

Towards the end of the year Conrad again took the field, this time with the object of ordering the affairs of the southern principalities. On his march southward the burghers of Parma revolted and were punished by the destruction of their city (Christmas). At Spello the Emperor had another interview with the Pope, who now imposed the sentence of excommunication on the Archbishop of Milan (Easter 1038). It was probably also on this occasion that a constant source of confusion and trouble in the Roman courts was removed; this was the indiscriminate use of Lombard and Roman law, which gave rise to endless disputes between Lombard and Roman judges. The Emperor's edict now established that in Rome and Roman territory all cases should be determined according to Roman law.

[1] "Qualiter nos communi fidelium nostrorum decreto, pape scilicet Johannis et Popponis patriarche venerabilis, Aribonis Moguntini archiepiscopi," etc. Cf. Bresslau I. 148, n. 4.

[2] See the suggestion of R. L. Poole ("Benedict IX and Gregory VI," *Proceedings of the British Academy*, Vol. VIII. p. 217) that Rodulf Glaber misread a statement that Benedict had been Pope *per ann. xii.* for *puer ann. xii.*

Conrad made the initial mistake in 1024 of liberating, at the request of Guaimar, Prince of Salerno, Paldolf (Pandulf) IV of Capua, the wolf of the Abruzzi, as Aimé of Monte Cassino calls him, who had been captured in Henry II's campaign of 1022 and since been held a close prisoner. This act led to the recrudescence of Byzantine power in South Italy, for Paldolf kept on friendly terms with the Greek government. The catapan Bojannes at once set to work to put his valuable ally in possession of his old principality; and in this he was assisted by Guaimar of Salerno, who with lavish grants bought the support of some Norman adventurers under Ranulf. This formidable combination made their first task the capture of Capua. The town fell after a siege of eighteen months; Paldolf V of Teano surrendered and Paldolf IV was restored. This was the situation that Conrad was forced to recognise on his first Italian expedition in April 1027. But Paldolf was not content with the mere recovery of his former possessions. On the death of Guaimar, the only effective rival to his power, he sought to extend his frontiers at the expense of his neighbours. He captured Naples by treachery and drove out its duke, Sergius IV. The latter was restored two years later by the aid of the Norman bands of Ranulf; in reward for this service Ranulf was invested with the territory of Aversa (1030), the nucleus of the Norman power in South Italy, which was to be in the succeeding centuries one of the most important factors in the history of Europe. Ranulf, a skilful but entirely unscrupulous ruler, soon deserted his benefactor and allied himself with Paldolf, who was now at the height of his power. The latter's rule, however, became daily more intolerable; and a body of malcontents, joined soon by the renegade Ranulf, taking advantage of a quarrel between Paldolf and Guaimar IV of Salerno, decided to appeal for the intervention of the Emperors of the East and the West.

No response came from Constantinople. Conrad however, already in Italy, accepted the invitation. Seemingly at Troia[1], the Emperor entered into negotiations with Paldolf, ordered him to restore the property of the Abbey of Monte Cassino which he had seized, and to release the prisoners he had captured. Paldolf on his part sent his wife and son to ask for peace, offering 300 pounds of gold in two payments, and his son and daughter as hostages. The terms were accepted, the first half of the indemnity paid; then the son escaped. Paldolf changed his attitude, refused to carry out the rest of his bargain, and withdrew to the castle of Sant' Agata. Conrad in the meantime entered Capua without resistance and invested Guaimar with the principality. Capua and Salerno were thus once more united in one hand as they had been under Paldolf Ironhead in the days of Otto II. At the same time Conrad officially recognised the new Norman colony at Aversa as a fief of the Prince of Salerno.

---

[1] So Bresslau, ii. p. 307, n. 1, following the notice in the *Ann. Altah.* 1038. But cf. Chalandon, *Hist. de la Domination Normande*, i. 33.

His work in the south completed, the Emperor returned northward. On the march the troops suffered severely from the heat; pestilence broke out in the camp, and many, among them Queen Gunnhild and Herman, Duke of Swabia, perished; Conrad himself was overcome with sickness. Under these circumstances it was impossible to renew the siege of Milan. Leaving, therefore, injunctions with the Italian princes to make an annual devastation of the Milanese territory, the Emperor made his way back to Germany.

Conrad never recovered his strength. At Nimeguen in February 1039 he was overcome by a more severe attack of the gout; in May he was well enough to be removed to Utrecht, where he celebrated the Whitsun festival. But he grew rapidly worse, and died the following day (4 June). His embalmed body was borne through Mayence and Worms to Spires, the favourite city of the Salian emperors, and was buried in the crypt of its cathedral church.

Conrad, once he had gained the mastery in his kingdom, was determined to secure the inheritance to his son; he was not only the first, but by a definite policy the founder, of the Salian dynasty. So at Augsburg in 1026 he designated his youthful son Henry, a boy of nine years old, as his successor; his choice was approved by the princes, and the child was duly crowned at Aix-la-Chapelle in 1028. The theory of hereditary succession seems to have been a guiding principle in the policy of Conrad II. He had suffered himself from the absence of it; for his uncle, the younger brother of his father, had acquired the Carinthian dukedom of his grandfather, and on his death it had passed out of the family altogether to the total disregard not only of his own claims, but also of those of his cousin, the younger Conrad, the son of the late duke. Adalbero of Eppenstein must in his eyes have been looked upon as an interloper. Personal wrongs doubtless biassed his judgment when the Duke of Carinthia was charged with treasonable designs at the Diet of Bamberg in 1035. Adalbero was deposed and sentenced to the loss of his fiefs. The court witnessed a strange scene before the verdict was obtained; the assent of the young King Henry, as Duke of Bavaria, was deemed necessary, and this the latter steadfastly refused to give; he was bound, he afterwards explained, by an oath to Adalbero taken at the instance of his tutor, Bishop Egilbert of Freising. Entreaties and threats availed nothing; the son was obdurate, and the Emperor was so incensed with passion that he fell senseless to the floor. When he recovered consciousness he again approached his son, humbled himself at his feet, and finally, by this somewhat undignified act, gained his end[1]. But the successor to the fallen duke was well chosen; it was the

---

[1] See the letter addressed to Bishop Azecho of Worms in Giesebrecht, II. 712. Cf. also *Neues Archiv*, III. 321.

Emperor's cousin, Conrad, who thus at this late hour stepped into the dukedom of his father (1036)[1].

It was not his aim, however, as sometimes has been suggested, to crush the ducal power. In one instance indeed he greatly strengthened it. A powerful lord was required in the vulnerable border-land of Lorraine; it was a wise step to reunite the two provinces on the death of Frederick (1033) in the hands of Gozelo. In the case of Swabia the hereditary principle prevailed. The rebellious Ernest who fell in the fight in the Black Forest had no direct heir; "snappish whelps seldom have puppies," Conrad remarked on receiving the news of his death; but he had a brother, and that brother succeeded. When the hereditary line failed, Conrad followed the policy of Otto the Great of drawing the dukedoms into his own family; in this way his son Henry acquired Bavaria after the death of Henry of Luxemburg (1026)[2] and Swabia on the death of Herman in Italy (1038).

In Italy, as we have seen, he definitely established by a legislative act the principle of hereditary fiefs for the smaller and greater vassals alike. There is no such decree for Germany; none at least has come down to us. Yet there are indications which suggest that the Emperor, perhaps by legal decision in the courts, perhaps by the acceptance of what was becoming a common usage, sanctioned, indeed encouraged, the growing tendency. Instances multiply of son succeeding father without question or dispute; families become so firmly established in their possessions that they frequently adopt the name of one of their castles. Wipo remarks that Conrad won the hearts of the vassals because he would not suffer their heirs to be deprived of the ancient fiefs of their forbears. Too much weight may not be placed on this statement, but it is certain that Conrad could rely in a marked degree upon the loyalty of the local nobles[3]. In the revolt of Ernest the nobility of Swabia supported not their duke but their king; Adalbero after his deposition found himself unable to raise his late subjects to rebellion. Such loyalty was unusual in the earlier Middle Ages, and it seems a natural conclusion that these knights of Swabia and Carinthia had reason to stand by Conrad. From this rank of society the Emperor reinforced that body of officials, the *ministeriales*, who later came to play so important a part at the courts of the Salian emperors. Conrad's gallant and faithful friend and adviser, Werner, who lost his life in the riot at Rome which followed the imperial coronation, and who earned the honour of a grave beside the Emperor Otto II at St Peter's, is perhaps the first as he is a typical representative of this influential class.

Conrad II is usually depicted as the illiterate layman[4], the complete

---

[1] The Carinthian mark (later, in 1056, the mark of Styria) was severed from the duchy, and bestowed upon Arnold of Lambach.

[2] Elected at Ratisbon, July 1027. [3] See Bresslau, II. 368–374.

[4] "Quamquam litteras ignoraret," Wipo, c. 6.

antithesis to the saintly Henry who preceded him. Undoubtedly he sought from the outset of his reign to emancipate himself from the over-weening power of the Church. He decided questions relating to the Church on his own authority, often without reference to a Church synod. He kept a firm hold on episcopal elections; he appointed his bishops and expected a handsome gratuity from the man of his choice. From Udalrich, elected to the see of Basle in 1025, we are frankly told that "the king and queen received an immense sum of money." Wipo adds that the king was afterwards smitten with repentance, and swore an oath never again to take money for a bishopric or abbacy, "an oath which he almost succeeded in keeping[1]." In truth the oath weighed but lightly on his conscience and affected his practice not at all. If, however, he did nothing to promote, he did little to hinder, reform. More than one of his charters bestows lands on Cluniac houses, and by including the kingdom of Burgundy (a stronghold of the reforming movement) in the Empire, he insensibly advanced a cause with which he was out of sympathy. The leaders of the reforming party, Richard, Abbot of St Vannes at Verdun, and Poppo, Abbot of Stablo (Stavelot), made steady if slow progress in their work, which met with the sympathetic encouragement of the Empress Gisela. The ruins of the picturesque Benedictine abbey of Limburg and the magnificent cathedral of Spires remind us that the thoughts of Conrad, who once at least is described as "most pious," sometimes rose above things merely temporal.

Conrad above all realised the importance of increasing the material resources on which the Empire depended. By careful administration he increased the revenue from the crown lands; he revoked gifts made to the Church by his too generous predecessors, and allocated to himself demesne lands which had fallen into the hands of the dukes. The reign of Conrad was a time of prosperity for Germany; he encouraged the small begin-nings of municipal activity by grants of mint and market rights; the peace was better kept. To Conrad the cause of justice came first among the functions of royalty. A story is told of how the coronation procession was interrupted by the complaints of a peasant, a widow, and an orphan, and how Conrad, without hesitation and in spite of the remonstrances of his companions, delayed the ceremony in order to award justice to the plaintiffs. Stern, inexorable justice is a strong trait in his character. This strong, capable, efficient ruler did much for his country. The allure-ments of Italy, the mysteries of Empire, had led his predecessors to neglect the true interests of Germany. It is to his credit that he restored the strength of the German monarchy and increased enormously the per-sonal influence and authority of the Crown. He prepared the way for his son, under whom the Holy Roman Empire reached the apogee of its greatness.

[1] "In quo voto pene bene permansit." Wipo, c. 7.

CHAPTER XII.

THE EMPEROR HENRY III.

THE reign of Henry III is the summit of the older German imperialism. The path uphill had been made by the persevering energy of the Saxon kings and Emperors; under Henry's successors the Empire rushed, though with glory, into ruin. Henry himself, sane, just, and religious, has the approval of reason, but could never have raised the white-hot zeal, and the fiercer hatred, which burned round the Hohenstaufen.

His father and mother were among those rare men and women who wrest from circumstances their utmost profit. Conrad, trained by adversity, attempting nothing vaguely or rashly, almost invariably attained his object, and left the "East-Frankish" Empire stronger within and without than ever before. His education of his son in state-craft was thorough and strenuous. very early he made him a sharer in his power, and then shewed neither mistrust nor jealousy, even when faced by markedly independent action. Henry, for his part, though he judged adversely some of his father's conduct, honoured him and kept his memory in affection.

Henry's mother Gisela (of the blood of Charlemagne, of the royal house of Burgundy, and heiress of Swabia) used fortune as Conrad used adversity. To power and wealth she added great beauty, force of character, and mind. Her influence is seen in the furtherance of learning and of the writing of chronicles. It was to her that Henry owed his love of books, and she made of her son "the most learned of kings." Gisela's share in public affairs during her husband's reign was considerable, even taking into account the important part habitually assigned to the Emperor's consort. Under Henry III the part of the Empress, Mother or Consort, in the Empire begins to dwindle, and there are indications of misunderstandings later between her and Henry. The chronicler Herman of Reichenau speaks of Gisela dying "disappointed by the sayings of soothsayers, who had foretold that she should survive her son."

Conspicuous in Henry's early circle was his Burgundian tutor, Wipo, the biographer of Conrad and the staunch admirer of Gisela. According to Wipo, a king's first business is to keep the law. Among the influences which were brought to bear upon Henry in his youth, that of Wipo cannot be overlooked.

Henry was a boy of seven when at Kempen, in 1024, Conrad was elected king. In 1026, Conrad, before setting out on his coronation expedition into Italy, named Henry as his successor and gave him in charge to an acute and experienced statesman, Bishop Bruno of Augsburg, brother of the late Emperor and cousin to the Empress Gisela. The energy with which Bruno held views different from those of his brother had, in the last reign, led him into conspiracy and exile. With the same independence in church matters, he, alone in the Mayence province, had taken no part in the collective action of the bishops against Benedict VIII. From such a guardian Henry was bound to receive a real political education. Under his care, Henry attended his father's coronation in Rome. Three months later, Conrad, in accordance with his policy of the absorption of the old national duchies, gave to Henry the Duchy of Bavaria, vacated by the death of Henry of Luxemburg. Then, on Easter Day, 1028, in the old royal Frankish city of Aix-la-Chapelle, Henry, after unanimous election by the princes and acclamation by clergy and people, was, at the age of eleven, crowned king by Pilgrim of Cologne.

In the inscription "Spes imperii" on a leaden seal of Henry's in 1028 Steindorff sees an indication that this election at Aix implied the election to the Empire. He draws attention also to the title "King" used of Henry before his imperial coronation in the Acts emanating from the imperial Chancery in Italy, as well as in those purely German; and to the fact that Henry was never re-crowned as King of Italy. He argues therefore that contemporaries regarded the act of Aix-la-Chapelle as binding the whole of Conrad's dominions, and as a matter of fact this cannot be doubted.

On the death of Bishop Bruno in April 1029, Henry, whose place as its duke was in Bavaria, was placed in charge of a Bavarian, Bishop Egilbert of Freising. Egilbert had in the early years of Henry II's reign taken active part in public affairs, but of late he had devoted himself chiefly to provincial and ecclesiastical duties. Under him Henry played his first part as independent ruler, basing his actions on motives of justice rather than on those of policy. Conrad in 1030 had led an unsuccessful expedition into Hungary; he was planning a new expedition when Henry, " still a child," taking counsel with the Bavarian princes but not with his father, received the envoys of St Stephen and granted peace, " acting with wisdom and justice," says Wipo, " towards a king who, though unjustly attacked, was the first to seek reconciliation."

In 1031 Henry was present with his father in the decisive campaign against the Poles. In 1032 Rodolph of Burgundy died, after a long and feeble rule. Conrad, though he snatched a coronation, had still to fight for his new kingdom against the nationalist and Romance party supporting Odo II (Eudes) of Champagne, and throughout 1032 the imperial diplomas point to Henry's presence with his father, in company with the Empress and Bishop Egilbert. In the following years, Henry was deputed to act against the Slavs of the North-East and against Břatislav of Bohemia. In these, his first independent campaigns, he succeeded in restoring order. In August 1034, Conrad was fully recognised as king by the Burgundian magnates, and in this recognition the younger king was included. Henry had already in the previous year come fully of age, the guardianship of Bishop Egilbert being brought to an end with grants of land in recognition of his services.

The deposition in 1035 of Duke Adalbero of Carinthia led to a curious scene between father and son. In the South the deposition was regarded as an autocratic act (Herman of Reichenau curtly notes that Adalbero "having lost the imperial favour, was deprived likewise of his duchy"); and Bishop Egilbert won a promise from his late ward that he would not consent to any act of injustice against the duke. The princes accordingly refused to agree to the deposition without Henry's consent, which Henry withheld in spite of prayers and threats from Conrad. The Emperor was overcome and finally borne unconscious from the hall; on his recovery, he knelt before Henry and begged him to withdraw his refusal. Henry of course yielded, and the brunt of the imperial anger fell on Bishop Egilbert.

In 1036, at Nimeguen, Henry wedded Kunigunda, or Gunnhild, daughter of Knut, a wedding which secured to Denmark, for over eight hundred years, the Kiel district of Schleswig. The bride was delicate and still a child, grateful for sweets as for kindness. In England songs were long sung of her and of the gifts showered on her by the English people. Her bridal festivities were held in June in Charlemagne's palace at Nimeguen, and on the feast of SS. Peter and Paul (June 29) she was crowned queen. Conrad was soon after called to Italy by the rising of the vavassors against the great lords. Henry was summoned to help, and with him went Kunigunda and Gisela. In August 1038, on the march of the Germans homeward, camp and court were pitched near the shores of the Adriatic. Here a great sickness attacked the host; among the victims was Queen Kunigunda, whose death "on the threshold of life" roused pity throughout the Empire. Her only daughter Beatrice was later made by her father abbess of the royal abbey of Quedlinburg near Goslar.

Another victim of the pestilence was Henry's half-brother Herman, Gisela's second son. His duchy of Swabia devolved on Henry, already Duke of Bavaria. To these two duchies and his German kingship was added, in 1038, the kingship of Burgundy. Then in the spring of 1039 Conrad died at Utrecht.

The position of public affairs at Henry's accession to sole rule was roughly this. There had been added to the Empire a kingdom, Burgundy, for the most part non-German, geographically distinct, yet most useful if the German king was to retain his hold upon Italy. The imperial power in Italy had been made a reality, and an important first step had been taken here towards incorporating the hitherto elusive South, and towards absorbing the new-comers, the Normans. On the north-eastern frontiers of the Empire both March and Mission were suffering from long neglect. Poland had been divided and weakened, and turned from aggression to an equally dangerous anarchy: Bohemia had recently slipped into hostility: Hungary was tranquil, but scarcely friendly. In the North the Danish alliance tended to stability. In the duchies of Germany itself, Lorraine was indeed growing over-powerful, but Bavaria, Swabia and (a few months later) Carinthia were held by the Crown; Saxony was quiescent, though scarcely loyal; in Germany as a whole the people and the mass of fighting landowners looked to the Crown for protection and security. The Church, as under Henry II, was a State-department, and the main support of the throne.

Over this realm, Henry, in the summer of 1039, assumed full sway, as German, Italian, and Burgundian king, Duke of Swabia and of Bavaria, and "Imperator in Spe." The Salian policy of concentrating the tribal duchies in the hands of the sovereign was at its height.

In his father's funeral train, bearing the coffin in city after city, from church-porch to altar, and finally at Spires, from the altar to the tomb, Henry the Pious inaugurated his reign. A young man in his twenty-second or twenty-third year, head and shoulders taller than his subjects, the temper of his mind is seen in his sending away cold and empty the jugglers and jesters who swarmed to Ingelheim for the wedding festivities of his second bride, Agnes of Poitou, and in his words to Abbot Hugh of Cluny, that only in solitude and far from the business of the world could men really commune with God.

The re-establishment of the German kingship, after the disintegration caused by the attacks of Northmen and Magyars, had been a gradual and difficult process. For the moulding of a real unity, not even yet attained, there was need of the king's repeated presence and direct action in all parts of the realm. What Norman and Plantagenet rulers were to do later in England by means of their royal commissioners, judges and justices, the German king had to do in person.

Following in this the policy of his predecessors, Henry opened his reign with a systematic progress throughout his realm, a visitation accompanied by unceasing administrative activity. He had already, before leaving the Netherlands, received the homage of Gozelo, Duke of both Lorraines; of Gerard, the royalist-minded and most energetic bishop of Cambray; and of a deputation of Burgundian magnates who had been waiting on Conrad in Utrecht when death overcame him. He had passed with the funeral procession through Cologne, Mayence, Worms, and Spires. Immediately after the conclusion of the obsequies he returned to Lower Lorraine, to Aix-la-Chapelle and Maestricht, where he remained some eight or nine days, dealing justice to the many who demanded it. Thence he went to

Cologne, the city which competed with Mayence for precedence in Germany; it was already governed by Henry's life-long and most trusted adviser, Archbishop Herman, whose noble birth and strenuous activity contrast strongly with the comparative obscurity and the mildness of Bardo of Mayence.

In the first days of September, accompanied by the Empress Gisela and Archbishop Herman, Henry made his first visit as sole ruler to Saxony, of all the German lands the least readily bound to his throne and destined to play so fatal a part in the downfall of his heir. This weakness in the national bond Henry seems to have tried to remedy by personal ties. The obscure township of Goslar was to be transformed by his favour into a courtly city. Here in the wild district of the Harz was Botfeld, where, now and throughout his life, Henry gave himself up at times to hunting, his only pleasure and relaxation from the toils of state. Near at hand was the Abbey of Quedlinburg, whose then Abbess, the royal Adelaide, he distinguished as his "spiritual mother"; while her successors in turn were Henry's own two daughters, his eldest, Beatrice, niece of the Confessor, and his youngest, Adelaide.

Disquieting news reached Henry in Saxony of events in Bohemia, whose Duke Břatislav had, late in August, returned triumphantly to Prague after a whirlwind campaign throughout the length and breadth of Poland, a land recently made vassal to the Empire, the prince of which, Casimir, an exile in Germany, was the nephew of Herman of Cologne. From Saxony Henry passed through Thuringia towards Bohemia, and there consulted with Eckhard of Meissen, guardian of the Marches against Bohemia, a veteran of staunchest loyalty, in whose wise counsels Henry placed unfailing confidence in spite of his unsuccess in war. There can be no doubt that Henry in Thuringia was at the head of an armed force, and that he meant war with Bohemia; but an embassy with hostages from Břatislav, together, doubtless, with the need for completing the visitation of the German duchies, determined him for the time to peace. So he dismissed his forces, and turned south to Bavaria.

From Bavaria, at the beginning of the new year, 1040, he moved to his mother's native duchy of Swabia; while after his departure Peter of Hungary, ally of Břatislav, sent his Magyars raiding over the Bavarian borders. In Swabia, Henry visited, among other places, the famous monastery of Reichenau, the chief and most brilliant centre of learning in Germany, the home of Herman, the noble cripple, whose genius was extolled throughout Germany, and to whose pen we owe a very large, if not the chief part, of our knowledge both of his times and of Henry himself, a knowledge but little tinged with enthusiasm or sympathy for the king. As he passed through Constance, Henry shews for a moment a touch of human sympathy, as he visited, in the Church of Saint Mary, the tomb of his unfortunate eldest brother, Ernest of Swabia.

At Ulm he summoned his first "Fürstentag," the assembly of princes, bishops, and abbots from all parts of the realm. Here came among others Gunther, the German hermit of the Böhmer Wald, no less notable than any of the great princes, and soon to render a signal service to his king and countrymen in distress. To Ulm there came also the first formal embassy from Italy to the new ruler.

From Ulm Henry passed to the Rhine. He spent April at his palace at Ingelheim, where he received both a formal embassy from his Burgundian kingdom, and more important still, Archbishop Aribert of Milan, his father's stubborn opponent in Italy. Henry had never approved of Conrad's proceedings against him; and the siege of Milan, carried on by Italian princes at Conrad's command, had ceased automatically with Henry's accession. By receiving the explanations and the homage of the archbishop, Henry healed an open wound in the Empire. Thus auspiciously, with an act of justice and reconciliation, he opened the period of his lordship in Italy; thus too closed his inaugural progress through the realm.

During its course had died Henry's cousins, Conrad, Duke, and Adalbero, ex-Duke of Carinthia, after whom, as next heir, he succeeded automatically to the duchy. He was now therefore Duke of Swabia, Bavaria, and Carinthia; of the five great duchies, only Lorraine and Saxony remained apart from the Crown.

The progress through the German lands completed, Henry was free to turn to the Bohemian campaign, the necessity of which had been clearly shewn by the raids of Břatislav's Hungarian ally. Two months more Henry spent, apparently peacefully and piously, after his own heart, in both the Lorraines and in Alsace, at the ancient royal palaces of Nimeguen and Utrecht, at Liège, Metz, Nancy and Moyen-Vic; giving grants to churches; shewing marked favour to the reforming ascetic monasteries; attending, especially, the consecration of the new Minster at Stablo, under Poppo, the pioneer and leader of monastic reform in Germany. Probably it was from Stablo, a scene of peaceful and pious magnificence, that Henry issued the summons for the army to assemble against Bohemia. In July, 1040, at Goslar he again met Eckhard of Meissen, to formulate the plan of campaign. At Ratisbon he joined his forces and proceeded to Cham at the entrance to the Bohemian pass, by which he meant to attack; and on 13 August he broke camp for Bohemia.

The expedition failed speedily and disastrously; his troops were ambushed, their leaders slain. The mediation of the hermit Gunther, and the promise to restore the Bohemian hostages, including Břatislav's son, alone rescued hundreds of German captives. Břatislav was left exultant master of the situation.

Henry, silent and as it were dismissing Bohemia from his mind, retraced his steps through Bavaria. On 8 September he filled up the newly-vacant see of Bamberg by appointing Suidger, a Saxon, who was a few years later, as Clement II, the first of the reforming German popes. Going north, he held an open court, dealing justice, at Allstedt; and received there envoys from Yarosláv, Prince of Kiev. Then at Münster he met the princes, laid before them the Bohemian situation, and dismissed the Bohemian hostage-prince to his own country. This year nature conspired with fortune against Germany The rain fell, the rivers rose, destructive floods swept the country-side, many lost their lives. To crown all, "grapes were scarce and the wine sour."

But Henry's calm attention to other matters by no means meant submission to defeat. At Seligenstadt, in the April of 1041, the princes again met to discuss active measures, and overtures from Bohemia were rejected. Fortune was veering, for Břatisláv was now deprived of his Hungarian ally Peter, who lost his throne by a sudden insurrection and only saved his liberty by flight to Germany, where Henry received him kindly, "forgetting for the sake of God the wrong towards himself." Bohemia, however, he did not forget, but pressed forward his preparations. At Aix, in June 1041, he met the princes and bishops of the West, Gozelo and Godfrey of Lorraine, Herman of Cologne, Poppo of Trèves, Nithard of Liège. At Goslar and at Tilleda, the royal seat in Thuringia, he concerted final measures with Eckhard of Meissen; and on 15 August, the anniversary of his previous expedition, he crossed the Bohemian frontier.

By Michaelmas he was back in Germany a victor. A fortnight later Břatislav followed him to Ratisbon, and there did public homage and underwent public humiliation. Probably Peter also appeared there as a suppliant before Henry. Henceforth Peter was Henry's client and Břatislav Henry's friend. Great was the joy in Germany at this Bohemian victory. With it we can undoubtedly connect the "Tetralogus" of Henry's tutor Wipo, a chant of praise and exhortation to the "fame-crowned King," who "after Christ rules the world," the lover of justice, the giver of peace. It is in the midst of the turmoils and rejoicings of 1041 that the Augsburg Annals record "by his (Henry's) aid and diligence very many excelled in the arts, in building, in all manner of learning."

But in this same year misfortune after misfortune fell upon the land. There were storms and floods. Everywhere the harvest failed and famine reigned. Nor could Henry rest on his oars. The fall and flight of Peter of Hungary had increased, rather than removed, the Hungarian menace, even if it opened new vistas of extended power; while Burgundy, newly in peace, clamoured for attention lest this young peace should die. And although to the great Christmas gathering of princes round Henry at Strasbourg (1041) there came envoys from Obo of Hungary to know "whether might he expect certain enmity or stable peace," it was to Burgundy that Henry first gave his attention. Since his appearance as Burgundian king in 1031 he had not again visited the country.

He kept Christmas (1041) at Strasbourg amid a brilliant gathering of princes; and when immediately afterwards he entered Burgundy, it was at the head of armed vassals. We are told by Herman of Reichenau that the Burgundian nobles made submission, that many were brought to justice, that Henry entered Burgundy, ruled with vigour and justice, and safeguarded the public peace; finally Wipo tells us that "he ruled Burgundy with magnificence."

Some notion of the state of the land before Henry's arrival may be gathered by the history of the archdiocese of Lyons. Here Archbishop Burchard, characterised by Herman of Reichenau as "tyrannus et sacrilegus, aecclesiarum depraedator, adulterque incestuosus," and moreover strongly anti-German, had been cast into prison and chains by Conrad in 1036. The city was then seized upon by a Count Gerard, who, desirous it would appear of playing at Lyons the part played by the "Patrician" at Rome, thrust into the see of Lyons his son, a mere boy. This boy later secretly fled, and since then Lyons had contentedly lacked a bishop.

The filling of the see thus left vacant was one of Henry's first cares in Burgundy: at the recommendation of the Cluniac Halinard of Dijon, who refused the sacred office for himself, it was given to a pious and learned French secular priest, Odulric (Ulric), Archdeacon of Langres. That the peace and order enforced under Henry were after all but comparative may be judged from the murder of Odulric himself only a few years later. There was much to attract Henry in Burgundy; for side by side with its lawlessness and violence were the strivings for peace and holiness embodied in the "Treuga Dei" and in the austerity of Cluny and its monasteries. Henry's approbation of Cluniac ideals is evident, and throughout his whole life he shews real ardour, almost a passion in his striving to realise throughout the Empire that peace founded on religion, upon which the Treuga Dei, if in somewhat other fashion, strove to insist locally.

After some six weeks in Burgundy, he must have heard at Basle on his way back of the havoc played among the Bavarians on the frontier, a week earlier, by the new King Obo of Hungary and his raiders. Henry, himself the absentee duke of the unfortunate duchy, at once handed it over (without waiting, as it would seem, for the formality of an election, as right was, by the Bavarians) to Count Henry of Luxemburg, who was akin to the last Duke Henry of Bavaria, and nephew to the Empress Kunigunda, wife of Henry II. Trusting to the vigour of the new duke to protect Bavaria for the time being, Henry next, a few weeks later, summoned all the princes, including of course Eckhard of Meissen, to Cologne, there to decide upon further steps to be taken with regard to Hungary. They unanimously declared for war.

Some four or five months elapsed before the expedition was launched. From Würzburg, at Whitsuntide, Henry strengthened his hold on his Burgundian realm by dispatching Bishop Bruno to woo for him Agnes of Poitou. A few months he spent in comparative quiet, probably with his mother, in Thuringia and Saxony; then later, in August 1042, he entered Bavaria and started, early in September, on the Hungarian expedition.

It was a success. Henry overcame, not Obo himself, who retired to inaccessible fastnesses, but at least the Western Magyars. He set up a new king, not Peter, but an unnamed cousin of his, and then returned fairly well satisfied to Germany. Directly his back was turned, Obo emerged from his fastness, and the reign of Henry's candidate came to an abrupt end. Yet a lesson against raiding had undoubtedly been given to "the over-daring Kinglet."

The king spent the Christmas of 1042 at Goslar; whither in January came envoys from the princes of the northern peoples. Břatislav of Bohemia came in person, bearing and receiving gifts. The Russians, though they bore back to their distant lord far more magnificent presents than they could have offered, departed in chagrin, for Henry had rejected their offer of a Russian bride. Casimir of Poland also sent his envoys; they were not received, since he himself did not come in person. Lastly Obo too, who had just ejected his second rival king, sent to propose peace. His messengers received an answer ominously evasive.

Early in the following month, at Goslar, the Empress-Mother died. That there had been some measure of alienation between Henry and Gisela is suggested by Wipo's exhortation to Henry to "remember the sweetness of a mother's name," and by his recording in his Tetralogus the many benefits conferred by Gisela on her son; as well as by Herman of Reichenau's acid comment. Yet there is no evidence that the alienation was serious. Henry's grants and charters on his mother's petition are numerous. In all probability he spent with her the only long interval of comparative leisure (1042) that he had enjoyed since his accession; she died whilst with him at Goslar.

Soon after the funeral ceremonies were over, Henry had his first meeting with the King of France, Henry I. Its place and object are obscure; but probably it was on the frontier at Ivois, and it may very well have been in connexion with Henry's approaching marriage with Agnes of Poitou.

The king's mind was now bent on the preparations for yet another Hungarian expedition. Twice Obo sought to evade the conflict. Obo did not, it is true, shew much tact, if indeed he really desired peace; for in his second embassy he demanded that Henry should himself swear to any terms agreed upon, instead of merely giving the oath in kingly fashion by proxy; this request was deemed an insult.

The blow when it came was effective. Henry in the space of four weeks brought Obo to a promise of humble satisfaction, a satisfaction never made effectual, because the promises of Obo were not fulfilled.

Far more important and of solid and lasting advantage to Germany, was the restitution by Hungary of that territory on the Danube ceded to St Stephen "pro causa amicitiae" in 1031.

Since the frontier won by Henry remained until 1919 the frontier between German Austria and Hungary, it is worth while considering it in detail.

The land ceded, or rather restored, was "ex una parte Danubii inter Fiscaha et Litacha, ex altera autem inter Strachtin et ostia Fiscaha usque in Maraha." South of the Danube, that is to say, the Leitha replaced the Fischa as boundary as far south as the Carinthian March. North of the river, the old frontier line seems to have run from opposite the confluence of the Fischa with the Danube to a fortress on the Moravian border, Strachtin or Trachtin. This artificial frontier was now replaced by the river March. Thus among other things was secured permanently for Germany the famous " Wiener Wald."

The realm was now at peace: Burgundy in order, Italy contented (in contrast to the early days of Conrad) with German overlordship, not one of the great princes or duchies of Germany a danger to the realm. The fame or the arms of the king had induced the princes on its borders to seek his friendship and acknowledge his superiority. Nothing remained to mar the public peace save private enmities. To private enemies the king might, without danger to the commonwealth, offer reconciliation. On the "Day of Indulgence" at Constance, in late October 1043, Henry from the pulpit announced to the assembled princes and bishops and to the whole of Germany, that he renounced all idea of vengeance on any who had injured him, and exhorted all his princes, nobles and people in their turn to forget all private offences. The appeal of the king was ordered to be made known throughout the whole land, and this day at Constance became known as the "Day of Indulgence" or "Day of Pardon."

The object was to abolish violence and private war, and so far the attempt bears a strong resemblance to the contemporary Franco-Burgundian institution, the "Truce of God," with which, however, it cannot be confounded, since although the ends were the same, the means were only superficially alike. Since however the "Indulgence" has sometimes been confused with, sometimes considered as deliberately rivalling, this "Treuga Dei," it is worth while to consider some relations and dissimilarities between the two movements.

The "Truce of God" endeavoured to mitigate and limit violence by an appeal to Christian sentiment rather than to Christian principle. The Christian, under heavy church penalties, was to reverence certain days and times regarded as sacred by abstaining on them from all violence not only in aggression but even under provocation. This "Truce" was created in France, the country where private feuds were most general and fiercest, and where therefore there was greatest need of it. Its birthplace was Aquitaine, in the year of Henry's accession; and nowhere was it more eagerly adopted than in Burgundy, where religious zeal burnt whitest and private feuds were most universal and devastating.

Now this "Truce of God" was an addition made to the original proclamation of a Peace of God (*c.* 980), which forbade private violence against non-combatants, by oath and for a fixed time, as contrary to Christian precept. Like most medieval legislation, both " Peace " and "Truce" were largely failures[1]. Henry's "Indulgence" struck at the root of the evil as they had not. The Indulgence, it is true, was not so sweeping as would have been the "Peace of God," because no provision was made for the protection of non-combatants, in case private war did arrive. The "Indulgence," being a pardon of actual enemies, could by its nature refer only to the present and the actual without a word as to the future, although Henry no doubt hoped that the one must entail the other.

Another distinction between the "Treuga Dei" and the "Indulgence" consists in the ecclesiastical character of the former. The "Truce" was conceived by the Church, proclaimed by the Church, its breach punished by heavy ecclesiastical penalties. The "Indulgence" was an example and exhortation from a Christian king to his subjects, compliance being in appearance voluntary, though royal displeasure might threaten him who refused it. But the distinction does not, as some have thought, imply any sort of opposition. Henry approved of the " Truce " as churchmen approved of the "Indulgence." One adversary of the Truce opposed it, indeed, on the ground that by it the Church usurped a royal function. But this was the ultra-royalist Gerard of Cambray, one of the few bishops who did *not* enjoy Henry's favour. On the other hand, the chief supporters of the Truce in Burgundy were the bishops, firm imperialists. Only a year before Henry's visit to Burgundy the Bishops and Archbishops of Arles, Avignon, Nice, Vienne and Besançon, had met Pope Benedict IX at Marseilles and had in all probability obtained his approval for the measure promulgated by the Burgundian synod at Montriond in 1041, extending the time of the Truce to the whole of Lent and Advent. Cluny, whose ideal the king revered as the highest ideal of all monasticism, had, through Abbot Odilo, appealed on behalf of the Treuga Dei to all France and Italy. Within the French part of the Empire, in the diocese of Verdun, Henry's friend the Abbot Richard of St Vannes was a promoter and zealous supporter of the Truce.

To sum up: Henry knew the working of the "Truce": its friends were his friends, its aim was his aim. In the same spirit and with the same object he took a different method, neither identical with, nor an-

---

[1] Cf. Lavisse (Luchaire), *Histoire de France*, ii. 2, pp. 133 ff. and see also Chapter xviii. *infra*, p. 465.

tagonistic to, the sister-movement in the neighbouring Latin kingdoms, but worked independently, side by side with it, in sympathy and harmony, although their provisions were different. Henry was not given to ardours, enthusiasms and dreams. His endeavours to found a public peace on the free forgiveness of enemies shews a real belief in the practicability of basing public order on religion and self-restraint rather than on force. As little can Henry's "Indulgence" be confused with the Landfrieden of a later date, which were in the nature of laws, sanctioned by penalties; not a free forgiveness like Henry's "Pardon."

This year, 1043, which had witnessed in its opening months the homage of the North, in the summer the defeat of Hungary, in the autumn the proclamation of peace between Germans, saw at its close the consummation of the policy by which Henry sought to link the South more closely with the Empire.

His first marriage had allied him with the northern power, whose friendship from that time on had been, and during Henry's lifetime continued to be, of great value to the Empire. His second marriage should strengthen his bond with Italy and Burgundy, and, some have thought, prepare his way in France. From Constance the king journeyed to Besançon, and there, amid a brilliant gathering of loyal or subdued Burgundian nobles, wedded Agnes of Poitou.

Agnes, that "cause of tears to Germany," was a girl of about eighteen, dainty and intelligent, the descendant of Burgundian and Italian kings, daughter to one of the very greatest of the French king's vassals, and step-daughter to another. Her life so far had been spent at the court, first of Aquitaine, during the lifetime of her father Duke William the Pious; then of Anjou, after the marriage of her mother Agnes with Geoffrey the Hammer (Martel). The learning and piety of the one home she exchanged for the superstition and violence of the other. For Geoffrey was certainly superstitious, most certainly violent, and constantly engaged in endeavours, generally successful, to increase his territory and his power at the expense of his neighbours, or of his suzerain, the French king. He and William of Normandy were by far the strongest of the French princes contemporary with Henry, so much the strongest, that a great German historian has seen in the alliance by marriage of Henry with the House of Anjou a possible preparation for the undermining of the French throne and the addition of France to the Empire[1].

The marriage was held in strong disapproval by some of the stricter churchmen on account of the relationship between Henry and Agnes, which, although distant, fell within the degrees of kinship which, by church law, barred marriage[2]. Abbot Siegfried of the reformed monas-

---

[1] Giesebrecht, *Kaiserzeit*, II. p. 375.

[2] Agnes and Henry were great-grandchildren respectively of two step-sisters, Alberada and Matilda, granddaughters of Henry the Fowler. They were descended also respectively from Otto the Great and his sister Gerberga.

tery at Gorze wrote very shortly before to his friend Abbot Poppo of Stablo, who possessed the confidence and respect of Henry, urging him even at the eleventh hour, and at risk of a possible loss of the king's favour, to do all that he possibly could to prevent it. Neither Poppo, nor Bishop Bruno of Toul (later Pope Leo IX), to whom Siegfried addresses still more severe reproaches, nor Henry himself, paid much heed to these representations. The marriage plans went on without let or hindrance: twenty-eight bishops were present at the ceremony at Besançon.

Not only the consanguinity of Agnes with the king, but also her nationality, aroused misgivings in the mind of this German monk. He cannot suppress his anxiety lest the old-time German sobriety shewn in dress, arms, and horse-trappings should now disappear. Even now, says he, the honest customs of German forefathers are despised by men who imitate those whom they know to be enemies.

We do not know how Agnes viewed the alleged follies and fripperies of her nation, thus inveighed against by this somewhat acid German saint. She was pious, sharing to the full and encouraging her husband's devotion to Cluny; she favoured learned men; her character does not however emerge clearly until after Henry's death. Then, in circumstances certainly of great difficulty, she was to shew some unwisdom, failing either to govern the realm or to educate her son.

After the coronation at Mayence and the wedding festivities at Ingelheim, Henry brought Agnes to spend Christmas in the ancient palace at Utrecht, where he now proclaimed for the North the "Indulgence" already proclaimed in the South. So with a peace "unheard of for many ages" a new year opened. But in the West a tiny cloud was rising, which would overshadow the rest of the king's reign. For, in April 1044, old Duke Gozelo of Lorraine died.

Gozelo had eventually been staunch and faithful, and had done good service to Henry's house; but his duchy was over-great and the danger that might arise from this fact had been made manifest by his hesitation in accepting, certainly the election of Conrad, and also, possibly, the undisputed succession of his son. The union of the two duchies of Upper and Lower Lorraine had been wrung by him from the necessities of the kings; Henry now determined to take this occasion again to separate them. Of Gozelo's five sons the eldest, Godfrey, had already during his father's lifetime been duke in Upper Lorraine, and had deserved well of the Empire. He now expected to succeed his father in the Lower Duchy. But Henry bestowed Lower Lorraine on the younger Gozelo, "The Coward," alleging a dying wish of the old duke's that his younger son might obtain part of the duchy. Godfrey thenceforth was a rebel (sometimes secretly, more often openly), imprisoned, set at liberty, deprived of his duchy, re-installed, humbled to submission, but again revolting, always at heart a justified rebel. If, in spite of its seeming successes, Henry's reign must be pronounced a failure, to no one is the failure more due than to Godfrey of Lorraine.

The beginning of the Lorraine trouble coincided with the recrudescence of that with Hungary. Obo, perhaps prevented by nationalist opposition, had not carried out his promises of satisfaction; there was also growing up in Hungary a party strongly opposed to him and favouring Germanisation and German intervention. Preparations for another campaign had been going on strenuously in Germany; by the summer of 1044 they were complete. After a hasty visit to Nimeguen, whither he had summoned Godfrey, and a fruitless attempt to reconcile the two brothers, Henry with Peter in his train set out for Hungary.

With Hungarian refugees to guide him, he was, by 6 July, on the further bank of the Raab. There the small German army confronted a vast Hungarian host, among whom, however, disaffection was at work. In a battle where few Germans fell, this host was scattered; and Hungary was subordinated to Germany. By twos and threes, or by crowds, came Hungarian peasants and nobles, offering faith and subjection. At Stühlweissenburg Peter was restored to his throne, a client-king; and Henry, leaving a German garrison in the country, returned home. On the battlefield the king had led a thanksgiving to Heaven, and his German warriors, at his inspiration, had freely and exultingly forgiven their enemies; on his return, in the churches of Bavaria, Henry, barefoot and in humble garment, again and again returned thanks for a victory which seemed nothing short of a miracle.

It was now that Henry gave to the Hungarians, at the petition of the victorious party amongst them, the gift of "Bavarian Law," a Germanisation all to the good. But Hungary was not being Germanised merely and alone by these subtle influences, by the inclination of its kings and the German party towards things German, nor by the adoption in Hungary of an ancient code of German law. After the battle of the Raab, Hungary was definitely and formally in the position of vassal to Germany; not only its king, but its nobles too, swore fealty to Henry and his heirs; Peter formally accepted the crown as a grant for his lifetime; and Hungary was thenceforth to pay a regular yearly tribute. Obo had been captured in flight and beheaded by his rival. The victory over Hungary seemed even more complete than the victory over Bohemia; the difference in the duration of their effects was partly due to a fundamental difference in the character of the two vassal princes. While Bratislav, a strong man, held Bohemia firmly, and, giving his fealty to Henry, gave with it the fealty of Bohemia; Peter, subservient and cringing to his benefactor, let Hungary slip through his fingers. Within two years he was a blinded captive in his twice-lost kingdom; and Hungary, freed from him, was freed too from vassalage.

This summer saw the gathering of the western clouds. Godfrey of

Lorraine had himself taken part in Henry's former Hungarian campaign, but deeply disappointed by the outcome of the meeting at Nimeguen, had held himself aloof in stubborn disobedience from this last expedition. He now sent envoys to Henry, who declared himself ready to forget the duke's contumacy should he at the eleventh hour consent peaceably to the division of the duchies. But Godfrey would submit to no "wrong," and having failed to move Henry, he began actively and secretly to engage in treason. And here at once becomes evident the peculiar danger to Germany of disaffection in Lorraine. For Lorraine was, in truth, not German as the other German lands were German; and the first ally made by Godfrey was "rex Carlingorum," Henry I of France. His other allies, the Burgundian nationalists of the "Romance" party, were, like himself, of the oft disputed "Middle Kingdom." In his own duchy he prepared for resistance by gaining from his vassals an oath of unlimited fealty for the space of three years to aid him against all men whatsoever.

As yet there had been no overt act of rebellion; but Henry had been given proof of Godfrey's plots, and in the autumn summoned him before a great assembly of the princes in Lower Lorraine itself, at Aix-la-Chapelle. Godfrey could have defied the king and disobeyed the summons; but to do so would have been to acknowledge his guilt. He must have hoped that there was no evidence against him, or that the princes would sympathise with him in his wrongs. He came, was convicted, and condemned to the loss of all the lands, including the duchy of Upper Lorraine and the county of Verdun, which he held in fief from the king. Godfrey now left Aix, and broke into fierce and open rebellion. Arms were distributed to the cities and country people, cities were garrisoned; and the duke fell with fire and sword upon all within reach who were faithful to Henry.

So ended the year that had seen Hungary subdued. Henry, however, did not yet foresee the stubborn nature of the danger that threatened from Lorraine. He spent Christmas 1044 at Spires, "a place beloved by him." It is true that he summoned the princes to consultation over Godfrey's revolt. Yet, after the feast was over, it was only the forces of the neighbourhood that he led against the "tyrant" that threatened them. Even these forces he could not maintain, because of the terrible famine in the land. He succeeded, after a short siege and with the help of siege-engines, in taking and razing Godfrey's castle at Bockelheim, near Kreuznach. The seizure of other castles was entrusted to local nobles, while Henry himself, leaving sufficient men to protect his people against Godfrey's raids, departed to Burgundy.

Here Godfrey's efforts had borne fruit in feuds which had broken out in the preceding year between Imperialist and Nationalist partisans. They ended in victory for the former, for Count Louis of Montbéliard (who had married Henry's foster-sister) with a small force overcame

Godfrey's ally Prince Raynald[1], who was uncle of Henry's queen and son of Count Otto-William, the former head of the anti-German party. When Henry now approached Burgundy, Raynald along with the chief of his partisans, Count Gerald of Geneva, personally made submission to him. Thus died out the last flicker during Henry's life of Burgundian opposition to union with the Empire.

Henry took Burgundy on his way to Augsburg, where he arrived in February 1045, and whither he had summoned the Lombard magnates to discuss with them the affairs of Italy. He kept Easter at Goslar. Here, not wishing to set out for the East without taking steps to protect the West from Godfrey, he handed over to Otto, Count Palatine in Lower Lorraine, his mother's native duchy of Swabia, which he himself had held since 1038.

Otto's mother had been the sister of Otto III. His family was widespread and illustrious. His aunt Abbess Adelaide of Quedlinburg and Gandersheim, and his brother Archbishop Herman of Cologne (who won for that see the right to crown the king of the Romans at Aix) were among Henry's truest friends. His sister, Richessa, had been daughter-in-law of Boleslav the Mighty; his nephew, her son, was Casimir, Duke of the Poles. Another nephew, Henry, succeeded Otto in the Palatinate, and within a year was regarded by some as a fit successor to the Empire. Yet another nephew was Kuno, whom the king first raised to the Bavarian dukedom and afterwards disgraced. The youngest sister, Sophia, about this time succeeded her aunt as Abbess of the important Abbey of Gandersheim; a niece, Theophano, was Abbess of Essen.

Otto himself had been one of the chief of those in the disputed duchy whose loyalty to Henry had drawn upon themselves the vengeance of Godfrey at the beginning of the year. His appointment now to the duchy of Swabia, so long left without a special guardian, and neighbour to Lorraine, recalls the appointment, when trouble threatened from the Magyars, of a duke to Bavaria, neighbour to Hungary. He ruled his new duchy, to which he was a stranger, with success and satisfaction to its people; not, however, for long, for within two years he was dead.

One more step Henry took for the protection of the West from Godfrey. For such (viewed in the double light of Henry's general policy of strengthening the local defence against Godfrey rather than leading the forces of the Empire against him, and of Godfrey's policy of winning the neighbours of Lorraine to his cause) must be considered the grant in this year of the March of Antwerp to Baldwin, son of Count Baldwin V of Flanders. The grant of Antwerp, however, instead of attaching Baldwin to the king's party, increased the power of a future ally of Godfrey's.

[1] Count of four or five counties which afterwards were collectively named Franche Comté. Cf. *supra*, p. 141.

Having thus spent the early months of 1045, from Christmas onwards, in local measures against Godfrey and his allies, Henry after a short visit to Saxony prepared to spend Pentecost with Peter of Hungary. On his way he narrowly escaped death through the collapse of the floor of a banqueting room, when his cousin Bishop Bruno of Würzburg was killed. Henry, notwithstanding this calamity, arrived punctually in Hungary, and on Whitsunday in Stühlweissenburg, in the banqueting-hall of the palace, Peter surrendered the golden lance which was the symbol of the sovereignty of Hungary. The kingdom was restored to him for his lifetime, on his taking an oath of fidelity to Henry and to his heirs. This was confirmed by an oath of fidelity in the very same terms taken by the Hungarian nobles present. After the termination of the banquet, Peter presented to Henry a great weight of gold, which the king immediately distributed to those knights who had shared with him in the great victory of the preceding year.

How far was this scene spontaneous, and how far prepared? The oath taken by the Hungarian nobles, without a dissentient, points to its being prepared; and if prepared, then most certainly not without the co-operation, most probably on the initiative, of Henry. This is what Wipo has in mind when he says that Henry, having first conquered Hungary in a great and noble victory, later, with exceeding wisdom, confirmed it to himself and his successors. But Henry's victory, on which so much was grounded, was a success snatched by a brilliant chance; it could furnish no stable foundations for foreign sovereignty over a free nation.

More than ever Henry appeared as an all-conquering king; and in the West even Godfrey "despairing of rebellion" determined to submit. During July, either at Cologne or at Aix-la-Chapelle or at Maestricht, he appeared humbly before the king, and in spite of his submission was sent in captivity to Gibichenstein, the German "Tower," a castle-fortress in the dreary land by Magdeburg beyond the Saale, very different from his own homeland of Lorraine. "And so the realm for a short time had quiet and peace."

Godfrey was perhaps taken to his prison in the train of Henry himself. For while he had been schooling himself to the idea of peace, the further Slavs, growing restive, had troubled the borders of these Saxon marches on the Middle Elbe. Godfrey's submission perhaps decided theirs; and when Henry with an armed force entered Saxony from Lorraine, they too sent envoys, and promised the tribute which Conrad had imposed on them.

Henry spent the peaceful late summer and early autumn of 1045 in Saxony. For October he had summoned the princes of the Empire to a colloquy at Tribur. The princes had begun to assemble, and Henry himself had reached Frankfort, when he fell ill of one of those mysterious and frequent illnesses which in the end proved fatal. As his weakness increased, the anxiety of the princes concerning the succession to the Empire became manifest. Henry of Bavaria and Otto of Swabia, with bishops and other nobles, met together and agreed, in the event of the king's death, to elect as his successor Otto's nephew Henry, who had followed Otto in the Lorraine palatinate, and was likewise a nephew of the king's confidant, Archbishop Herman, and a grandson of Otto II. The king recovered. Happily for the schemers, he was not a Tudor; but the occurrence must have deepened his regret when the child just at this time born to him proved to be another daughter. This eldest daughter of Henry and Agnes, Matilda, died in her fifteenth year as the bride of Rudolf of Swabia, the antagonist of her brother Henry IV.

The year 1046 opened again, as so many before and after it, with misery to the country people. In Saxony there was widespread disease and death. Among others died the stout old Margrave Eckhard, who, "wealthiest of margraves," made his kinsman the king his heir.

The king, after attending Eckhard's funeral, turned to the Netherlands, where Duke Godfrey's incapable younger brother, Gozelo Duke of Lower Lorraine, was dead[1]; here too Count Dietrich (Theodoric) of Holland was unlawfully laying hold on the land round Flushing, belonging to the vacant duchy.

At Utrecht, where he celebrated Easter, Henry prepared one of his favourite river campaigns against Dietrich. Its success was complete, both the lands and the count falling into Henry's hands. Flushing was given in fief to the Bishop of Utrecht, and Henry, keeping Pentecost at Aix-la-Chapelle, determined to settle once for all the affairs of Lorraine.

The means he used would appear to have been three: the conciliation of Godfrey, the strengthening of the bishops, and the grant of Lower Lorraine to a family powerful enough to hold it. At Aix Godfrey, released from Gibichenstein, threw himself at Henry's feet, was "pitied," and restored to his dukedom of Upper Lorraine. This transformation from landless captive to duke might have conciliated some; but Henry did not know his man. Duke Godfrey's hereditary county of Verdun was not restored, but granted to Richard, Bishop of the city. Lower Lorraine was given to one of the hostile house of Luxemburg, Frederick, brother of Duke Henry of Bavaria, whose uncle Dietrich had long held the Lorraine bishopric of Metz.

At the same assembly there took place an event of importance for the North and in the history of Henry's own house, viz. the investiture of Adalbert, Provost of Halberstadt, with the Archbishopric of Bremen, the northern metropolis, which held ecclesiastical jurisdiction, not only in the coast district of German Saxony, but in all the Scandinavian lands and over the Slavs of the Baltic.

---

[1] For the evidence of Gozelo's death, rather than disgrace, see Steindorff, I. p. 293, note.

Adalbert of Bremen had all virtues and all gifts, save that he was of doubtful humility, humble only to the servants of God, to the poor and to pilgrims, but by no means so to princes nor to bishops; accusing one bishop of luxury, another of avarice. Even as a young man he had been haughty and overbearing in countenance and speech. His father, Count Frederick, was of a stock of ancient nobility in Saxony and Franconia. His mother Agnes, of the rising house of Weimar, had been brought up at Quedlinburg, and valued learning. Adalbert quickly rivalled, or more than rivalled, Archbishop Herman of Cologne in the councils and confidence of the king. He made many an expedition "with Caesar" into Hungary, Italy, Slavonia, and Flanders. He might at Sutri have had from Henry the gift of the Papacy, but that he saw greater possibilities in his northern see. His close connexion with the king caused him to be regarded with suspicion, indeed as a royal spy, by the great semi-loyal Duke of the North, the Saxon Bernard II. It was Adalbert who moved the bishop's seat from Bremen to Hamburg, "fertile mother of nations," to recompense her long sorrows, exposed to the assaults of Pagan Slavs.

But Henry was not only looking northwards. To this same congress he summoned to judgment one of the three great Italian prelates, Widger of Ravenna. He had, before his nomination by Henry to the see, been a canon of Cologne, and although unconsecrated, "had for two years inefficiently and cruelly wielded the episcopal staff." Wazo, the stalwart Bishop of Liège, famous as an early canonist, was one of the episcopal judges chosen, but without pronouncing on Widger's guilt, he significantly denied the right of Germans to try an Italian bishop, and protested against the royal usurpation of papal jurisdiction. This trial is the first sign either of clash between royal and ecclesiastical claims, or of Henry's preoccupation with Italy, where, while these things were doing, church corruption and reform were waging a louder and louder conflict. To Italy Henry was now to pass. Before doing so he once more visited Saxony and the North. At Quedlinburg he invested his little eight-year-old daughter Beatrice in place of the dead Abbess Adelaide, and at Merseburg he held court in June, receiving the visits and gifts of the princes of the North and East, Břatislav of Bohemia, Casimir of Poland and Zemuzil of the Pomeranians.

By the festival of the Nativity of the Blessed Virgin, 8 September 1046, he was at Augsburg, whither he had summoned bishops, lords, and knights to follow him to Italy. The news of the sudden downfall of Peter of Hungary grieved, but did not deter, him. Crossing the Brenner Pass, he reviewed his army before the city of Verona.

When Henry came to Italy (1046), he came to a realm where among the cities of Romagna and the hills of Tuscany a new age was coming into life. He had not visited Italy since he had accompanied his father in 1038, and now the state of things was greatly changed, while his own

policy was different from his father's. Conrad had been at strife with
Aribert, the great Archbishop of Milan, but Henry before he left Germany
made at Ingelheim (1039), as the Milanese historian tells us, " a pact of
peace with the Archbishop, and was henceforth faithfully held in honour
by him." But in 1045, when peace between the populace and nobles of
Milan was hardly restored, Aribert died. Henry rejected the candidate
put forward by the nobles and chose Guido supported by the democracy.
Politics were intertwined with Church affairs, and Henry's dealings with
the Papacy were the beginning of that church reform, which gave Rome
a line of reforming German Popes and led to the Pontificate of Gregory
VII. The story of that progress will come before us later[1], and this side
of the history is therefore here left out. But it was the evil state of
Rome, where the Tusculan Benedict IX, the Crescentian Sylvester III,
and the reforming but simoniacal Gregory VI, had all lately contested
the papal throne and the situation was entangled, that chiefly called
Henry into Italy. By the end of October he was at Pavia, where he held
a synod and dispensed justice to the laymen. At Sutri (20 December
1046) he held a second synod, in which the papal situation was dealt with
and the papal throne itself left vacant. Two days later he entered Rome,
where a third synod was held. No Roman priest was fit, we are told, to
be made a Pope, and after Adalbert of Bremen refused Henry chose on
Christmas Eve the Saxon Suidger of Bamberg, who after " was elected
by clergy and people," and became Clement II.

On Christmas Day the new Pope was consecrated, and at once gave
the Imperial crown to Henry; Agnes was also crowned Empress at the
same time. Then too the Roman people made him " Patrician ": the
symbol of the Patriciate, a plain gold circlet, he often wore, and the
office, of undoubted but disputed importance, gave the Emperor peculiar
power in Rome and the right to control every papal election, if not
to nominate the Pope himself[2]. The new Patrician was henceforth
officially responsible for order in the city; so it was fitting that, a week
after his coronation, he was at Frascati, the headquarters of the Counts
of Tusculum, and that, before leaving for the South, he seized the fortresses of the Crescentii in the Campagna. At Christmas-tide Clement II
held his first synod at Rome, and it was significant of the new era in
church affairs that simoniacs were excommunicated, and those knowingly
ordained by simoniacs, although without themselves paying a price, sentenced to a penance of forty days; a leniency favoured by Peter Damiani
as against those who would have had them deprived. After this the
Empress went northwards to Ravenna, while the Emperor along with the
Pope set out for the South.

[1] In vol. v.
[2] This Patriciate was, in this view, a new departure; it goes back not to the
patriciate of Pepin and Charles the Great but to the patriciate of the Crescentii in
the days of Otto III.

At Capua he was received by Guaimar, recognised by Conrad as Prince of Salerno and also of Capua, from which city Paldolf (Pandulf) IV had been driven out. But Henry restored Paldolf, "a wily and wicked prince" formerly expelled for his insolence and evil deeds. Conrad had also recognised Guaimar as overlord of the Norman Counts of Aversa and of the Norman de Hautevilles in Calabria and Apulia. Now Ranulf of Aversa and Drogo de Hauteville of Apulia, as they went plundering and conquering from the Greeks, were recognised as holding directly from Henry himself[1]. So at Benevento the gates were shut in the Emperor's face and he had to stay outside. Thence he went to join the Empress at Ravenna: early in May he reached Verona and then left Italy. There was trouble in the South, but otherwise he left Italy "in peace and obedience." In the middle of May he was again home in Germany, which during his eight months' absence had also been in quiet.

With Henry's return he steps upon a downward path: the greatness of his reign is over; troubles are incessant and sporadic; successes scanty and small. During his absence Henry I of France, with the approval of his great men and perhaps at the instigation of Godfrey of Lorraine, made a move towards claiming and seizing the duchies of Lorraine. When the unwonted calm was thus threatened, Wazo of Liège wrote to the French king appealing to the ancient friendship between the realms and urging the blame he would incur if, almost like a thief, he came against unguarded lands. Henry I called his bishops to Rheims, reproached them for letting a stranger advise him better than his native pastors, and turned to a more fitting warfare along with William of Normandy against the frequent rebel Geoffrey of Anjou. But in his duchy of Upper Lorraine the pardoned Godfrey was nursing his wrongs: his son, a hostage with Henry, was now dead, and he also heard that his name had not been in the list of those with whom Henry at St Peter's in Rome had declared himself reconciled. Godfrey found allies in the Netherlands, Baldwin of Flanders, his son the Margrave of Antwerp, Dietrich, Count of Holland, and Herman, Count of Mons, all united by kinship and each smarting under some private wrong. Dietrich wished to recover from the Bishop of Utrecht the land round Flushing; Godfrey to recover the county of Verdun from its bishop. It was almost a war of lay nobles against the bishops so useful to Henry in the kingdom. At the moment Henry was busied in negotiations with Hungary and in giving a new duke to Carinthia: this was Welf, son of the Swabian Count Welf, and as his mother was sister to Henry of Bavaria, related to the house of Luxemburg. Now too Henry filled up a group of bishoprics. A Swabian, Humphrey, formerly Chancellor for Italy, went as Archbishop to Ravenna; Guido, a relative of the Empress's, to Piacenza; a royal chaplain, Dietrich (Theodoric), provost of Basle, to Verdun;

---

[1] For the Norman history in detail see vol. **v.**

Herman, provost of Spires, to Strasbourg: another chaplain, Dietrich (Theodoric), Chancellor of Germany, provost of Aix-la-Chapelle, to Constance, where he had been a canon. Metz and Trèves, two sees important for Lorraine, were vacant: to the one Henry appointed Adalbero, nephew of the late bishop, to the other Henry, a royal chaplain and a Swabian.

Henry, now at Metz (July 1047), was thus busy with ecclesiastical matters and the Hungarian negotiations, when he was forced to notice the machinations of Godfrey. Adalbert of Bremen had become suspicious of the Billung Duke Bernard, doubly related to both Godfrey and Baldwin of Flanders. Much was at stake; so Henry quickly made terms with Andrew of Hungary, summoned the army intended for use against him to meet in September on the Lower Rhine, and then went northwards to visit Adalbert. Bernard had always dreaded Adalbert and now, when the Emperor both visited him and enriched him with lands in Frisia, formerly Godfrey's, his dread turned against Henry too. Thietmar, Bernard's brother, was even accused by one of his own vassals, Arnold, of a design to seize the Emperor, and killed in single combat; the feud had begun. Henry's power was threatened, and the succession was causing him further anxiety, so much so that his close friend Herman of Cologne publicly prayed at Xanten, whither Henry had come, for the birth of an heir (September 1047).

The Emperor had begun the campaign by a move towards Flushing, but a disastrous attack from Hollanders, at home in the marshes, threw his army into confusion, and then the rebels took the field. Their blows were mostly aimed at the bishops, but one most tragic deed of damage was the destruction of Charlemagne's palace at Nimeguen: Verdun they sacked and burnt, even the churches perished. Wazo of Liège stood forth to protect the poor and the churches; Godfrey, excommunicated and repentant, did public penance and magnificently restored the wrecked cathedral. In his own city, too, Wazo stood a siege; with the cross in his unarmed hand he led his citizens against the enemy, who soon made terms.

On the return from the Flushing expedition Henry of Bavaria died: after a vacancy of eighteen months his duchy was given to Kuno, nephew of Herman of Cologne. Early in October 1047 Pope Clement II died. Then in January 1048 Poppo, Abbot of Stablo, passed away, the chief of monastic reformers in Germany, who had given other reforming abbots to countless monasteries, including the famous houses of St Gall and Hersfeld.

Against Godfrey Henry held himself, as formerly against Bohemia, strangely inactive. To Upper Lorraine, Godfrey's "twice-forfeited duchy," he nominated "a certain Adalbert," and left him to fight his own battles. Christmas 1047 Henry spent at Pöhlde, where he received envoys from Rome seeking a new Pope; after consultation with his bishops and nobles he "subrogated" the German Poppo of Brixen, and to this choice the Romans agreed. Wazo of Liège, great canonist and stoutest of bishops, had been asked for advice and had urged the restoration of Gregory VI, now an exile in Germany, and, as he held, wrongly deposed. This was one of Wazo's last acts, for on 8 July he died. And the new Pope also died on 9 August 1048. At Ulm in January Henry held a Swabian diet and nominated to the duchy, which had been left vacant for four months, Otto of Schweinfurt, Margrave in the Nordgau, a Babenberg by birth and possibly nephew to Henry's own mother Gisela.

Lorraine remained to be dealt with. In mid-October the two Henries, of France and Germany, met near Metz: France might easily have succoured Godfrey who, spreading "slaughter of men and devastation of fields, the greatest imaginable," had slain his new rival Adalbert. But ecclesiastical matters also pressed; at Christmas the formal embassy from Rome came to speak of the vacant papal throne. They asked for Halinard, Archbishop of Lyons and formerly at Dijon. This prelate, a strict reformer, had refused Lyons in 1041, and asked again to take it later he refused unless he need swear no fealty to Henry. Most German bishops disliked this innovation, but Henry, on the advice of Bruno of Toul, Dietrich of Metz and Wazo of Liège, consented. While archbishop, Halinard had been much in Rome, where he was greatly beloved. But he hesitated long to take new and greater responsibilities, and in the end Bruno of Toul became Pope, and as Leo IX began a new epoch in the Western Church[1].

To Upper Lorraine Henry had given a new duke, Gerard of Chatenois, who, himself of Lorraine, was brother or uncle of the slain Duke Adalbert and related to Henry and also to the Luxemburgers, while his wife was a Carolingian: he was also founder of a dynasty which ruled Lorraine until 1755. The Bishops of Liège, Utrecht and Metz, together with some lay nobles, had been preparing the way for a larger expedition. In the cold winter of 1048–1049, favoured by the lengthy frost, they defeated and slew Count Dietrich, whose brother Florence followed him in Holland. Then came a greater stroke and in this, too, bishops helped, for Adalbert of Bremen was Henry's right hand. He had already dexterously won over the Billungs; but an even greater triumph was the treaty he had brought about with Svein of Norway and Denmark, who had succeeded Magnus in 1047. Svein was in sympathy with the Empire because of his missionary zeal, and now he brought to its aid his sea-power as his fleet appeared off the Netherland coast. England too, which was friendly since Kunigunda's marriage to Henry and had also seen Flanders under Baldwin become a refuge for its malcontents, kept more distant guard; Edward the Confessor "lay at Sandwich with a multitude of ships until that Caesar had of Baldwin all that he would." Thus Baldwin was unable to "aet-burste on waetere." Another kind of aid was given when Leo IX excommunicated Godfrey and Baldwin at

---

[1] See vol. v.

Cologne, where Pope and Emperor kept the feast of St Peter and St Paul (29 June). Godfrey was smitten with fear and, leaving Baldwin in the lurch, surrendered. His life was left him, but liberty and lands he forfeited, "for he merited no mercy because of his cruel deeds." He had claimed two duchies and governed one: he was now for the second time a landless captive. Then, when Henry systematically ravaged Baldwin's lands, he too gave in, came to terms and gave hostages for his faith. So the desolating war was over and there was again, for a short time, peace within the Empire.

Thus the Emperor was free to watch with friendly eye the reforming work of the German Pope as he held a synod at Rheims (3 October 1049). Here appeared not only French bishops in goodly numbers but also English because of the friendliness of Edward with Henry; as the synod was to be "Gallic" there also came to it the prelates of Trèves, Metz, Verdun, Besançon and Lyons. A fortnight later Leo held a German synod at Mayence, attended by a throng of bishops and abbots from all parts of the kingdom. This inner peace Henry secured by outward guard: he urged the Bavarian princes and nobles to watch the Danube; he brought Casimir of Poland to a sworn friendship. Thus he could better face the threatening Hungarian war. Grievous sickness had again attacked him when the birth of an heir gave him a new and dynastic interest in the future.

The young Henry was born on 11 November 1050, at Goslar, the scene of so many events in his life. "In the autumn of this year," says the annalist of Altaich, "the Empress bore a son," and Herman of Reichenau adds "at last." Even before his baptism all the bishops and princes near at hand promised him faith and obedience. At Easter the infant prince was baptised at Cologne and Hugh of Cluny, who was again to be his sponsor at Canossa, was specially summoned to be his sponsor now. In this year Henry completed his work at Goslar, which "from a little mill and hunting-box he made into so great a city." Besides the great new palace he built a church, and set up there canons regular to carry on its work. Two bishops, Benno of Osnabrück and Azelin of Hildesheim, were placed over the work of the new foundation, and soon for ardour in learning and strictness in discipline Goslar had no equal in the province.

After the royal baptism Henry with greater hope for his realm had started on the Hungarian campaign. But the king, Andrew, partly withstood and partly eluded him: the German army could only burn and ravage whole districts until hunger forced their return. Soon after, Adalbert of Austria made a compact with Andrew and peace ensued.

Lower Lorraine still called for Henry's care. Count Lambert of Louvain first gave trouble, and then Richeldis, heiress of Hainault and widow of Herman of Mons, by a marriage with Baldwin's son, the Margrave Baldwin of Antwerp, roused Henry's fear and local strife.

Needed on the Hungarian frontier, Henry took a risky but generous step: he restored to Godfrey of Lorraine a former fief of his in the diocese of Cologne and set him to guard the peace against Baldwin. From this summer of 1051 until his marriage with Beatrice of Tuscany in 1054 Godfrey was outwardly an obedient vassal.

The earlier part of 1052 was marked mainly by ecclesiastical cares and appointments, and then by another Hungarian expedition. The siege of Pressburg was begun, when Andrew induced Leo IX to act the mediator, for which purpose the Pope came to Ratisbon. Andrew had promised the Pope to give all satisfaction and tribute, but when Henry had raised the siege he withdrew the promise. Leo, in just anger, excommunicated him, but Henry could not renew the campaign, which was his last against Hungary. He had other matters, and notably the Norman danger in Italy, to talk over with the Pope. From January 1052 to February 1053 Leo was in Germany: Henry sent off an army to help him in his Italian wars and then quickly recalled it. Leo had to set out with a motley band of his own raising, some sent by their lords, some criminals, some adventurers, and most of them Swabians like himself.

Events were moving towards the deposition of Kuno of Bavaria: since Christmas 1052 he and Gebhard, Bishop of Ratisbon, had been at daggers drawn. The enemies, thus breaking the peace, were summoned to Merseburg at Easter 1053; there Kuno for his violence against Gebhard and "dealing unjust judgements among the people" was deposed by the sentence of "some of the princes." He took his punishment badly, and on returning to the South he, like Godfrey, began to "stir up cruel strife," sparing neither imperialists nor his own late duchy. Bavaria was visited, too, by a famine so sore that peasants fled the country and whole villages were left deserted, and "in those days both great men and lesser men of the realm, murmuring more and more against the Emperor, were saying each to the other that, from the path of justice, peace, divine fear and virtue of all kind, on which in the beginning he had set out and in which from day to day he should have progressed, he had gradually turned aside to avarice and a certain carelessness; and had grown to be less than himself.'

But if the diet at Merseburg saw Kuno turned to an enemy it also saw Svein of Denmark made a friend. In the North, Adalbert's *parvula Bremen* had become almost *instar Romae*. Adalbert's chance lay in the haphazard fashion of the conversion of the Scandinavian nations to Christianity. Before the days of Knut, Bremen had been the missionary centre for the North, although it had not wrought its work as carefully as did the English missionaries under Knut. As Denmark grew more coherently Christian, Bremen began to lose control, and its loss of ecclesiastical prestige meant a loss of political influence to Germany: whether the Danish bishops were consecrated at Rome or even at Bremen they were autonomous. The older alliance between Conrad II and Knut had brought tranquillity to the North in the earlier part of Henry's reign, and in 1049 Svein had sent his fleet to help Henry in the Flemish war. But between 1049 and 1052 the alliance was strained by Adalbert's assertion of his ecclesiastical authority. In 1049 Adalbert had obtained a bull from Leo IX recognising the authority of Bremen over the Scandinavian lands and the Baltic Slavs up to the Peene. Anxious for peace, at first Svein had acquiesced, but when Adalbert reprimanded him for his moral laxity and his marriage with his kinswoman Gunnhild, he threatened war. Yet prudence or maybe religious scruples won the day. Gunnhild was sent home to Sweden and king and bishop made friends (1052). Thus Svein was ready to renew the ancient friendship as useful to Henry against Baldwin as it was to Svein against Harold Hardrada.

In 1052, a papal brief of Leo IX gave Adalbert wider and more definite power to the farthest North and West: Iceland, Greenland, the Orkneys, the Finns, Swedes, Danes and Norwegians, the Baltic Slavs from the Egdor to the Peene, all were definitely put under the ecclesiastical headship of Bremen, as were, indeed, inclusively, all the nations of the North. The Slavs under Godescalc "looked to Hamburg (Bremen) as to a mother": Denmark was submissive: Sweden, at first reluctant, was brought round by a change of kings in 1056: Norway fell in later. It is true that Svein made proposals, approved by Leo IX, for a Danish archbishopric, which would issue in a national Danish church. Adalbert failed to carry out his large scheme of a Northern Patriarchate for Hamburg-Bremen, for which, had he been able to count twelve suffragans, he could have pleaded the sanction of the Pseudo-Isidore. Yet even so he was himself papal legate in the North, and the greatness of Hamburg-Bremen under him is a feature of German history under Henry III.

Early in 1053 at Tribur an assembly of princes elected the young Henry king and promised him obedience on his father's death, but conditionally, however, on his making a just ruler. Thither too came envoys from Hungary, peace with which was doubly welcome because of trouble raised by the ex-Duke Kuno in Bavaria and Carinthia. King Andrew, indeed, would have become a tributary vassal pledged to military service everywhere save in Italy, had not Kuno dissuaded him. Rebellions in Bavaria and Carinthia, intensified by Hungarian help, kept Henry busy for some months. But the duchy of Bavaria was formally given to the young king under the vigorous guardianship of Gebhard. Bishop of Eichstedt. In Carinthia some quiet was gained by the appointment of Adalbero of Eppenstein (son of the former Duke Adalbero deposed by Conrad II, and cousin to the Emperor) to the bishopric of Bamberg, vacant through Hartwich's death. Early in 1054 Henry went northwards to Merseburg for Easter and then to Quedlinburg; Casimir of Poland was threatening trouble, but was pacified by the gift of Silesia, now taken from Břatislav, always a faithful ally.

From Italy had come the news of the Norman victory over Leo IX at Civitate (18 June 1053) which left the Pope an honoured captive in Norman hands; then, when he was eagerly looking for help from the Emperors of both East and West, he died, having reached Rome. Henry, influenced by Gebhard of Eichstedt, had been slow to help the great Pope. But he was to make one more expedition to Italy, not because of Norman successes but because of a new move by his inveterate enemy, Godfrey of Lorraine. The exiled duke had married Beatrice, like himself from Upper Lorraine, foster sister of Henry, and widow of the late Marquess Boniface of Tuscany, whose lands she held. On the side of Flanders the two Baldwins were in rebellion and attacking episcopal territories, and so, after having the young Henry crowned at Aix-la-Chapelle (July 17), the Emperor went to Maestricht. John of Arras had long coveted the castle of Cambray, but was kept out by the bishops, first Gerard and then Liutpert. When Liutpert had gone to Rheims for consecration, John seized the city, ejected the canons, and made himself at home in the bishop's palace. On his return Liutpert found himself shut out not only from his bed but from his city. But Baldwin of Flanders led him home in triumph, and the angry John of Arras turned to the Emperor for help. He offered to lead Henry to Flanders itself, if the Emperor would induce Liutpert, a prelate of his own appointment, to recognise him as holder of the castle of Cambrai. This was the reason why Henry now took the offensive against Baldwin. He invaded Flanders, systematically ravaging it bit by bit; he got as far as Lille, and there the city forced him to halt; siege and hunger made the citizens capitulate and so the Emperor could go home "with glory" as we are told, but with little solid gain. John of Arras, despite Henry's appeal to the bishop, did not gain his longed-for castle. To the South-East there were still Hungarian raids in Carinthia, and in Bavaria Kuno was still ravaging. But the men of Austria (under their old Margrave Adalbert of Babenberg until his death in May 1055) successfully withstood him. Earlier in the year died Břatislav, who had, according to one account, regained Silesia from Casimir of Poland.

Christmas was spent by Henry at Goslar; a little later at Ratisbon in another diet, Gebhard of Eichstedt consented to become Pope, although earlier, when an embassy from Rome had asked for a Pontiff, he had refused. His words "to Caesar" were significant. "Lo, my whole self, body and soul, I devote to St Peter; and though I know myself unworthy the holiness of such a seat, yet I obey your command: but, on this condition, that you also render to St Peter those things which rightfully are his." At the same diet Henry invested Spitignev, son of Břatislav, formerly a hostage at his court, with Bohemia, and received his homage. Then he passed to Italy and by Easter was at Mantua.

In North Italy the Emperor tried to introduce order by holding many royal courts, including one at Roncaglia (afterwards so famous), and by sending special *missi* to places needing them. His enemy Godfrey had fled before a rising of the "plebs," and had naturally gone to join Baldwin of Flanders. Late in May Henry was at Florence, where, along with Pope Victor II, he held a synod. Here too he met Beatrice and her daughter the Countess Matilda. For her marriage to a public enemy she was led captive to Germany, and with her went Matilda. Boniface, her son and heir to Tuscany, "feared to come to Henry" and a few days later died. On his way homewards at Zurich, Henry betrothed his son Henry IV to Bertha, daughter of Otto of Savoy and of Adelaide, Countess of Turin, and widow of Herman of Swabia, brother to the Emperor.

In Germany Henry had to suppress a conspiracy in which Gebhard of Ratisbon, Kuno, Welf and others were probably concerned: according to other accounts it was their knights and not the princes themselves who conspired. But Kuno died of plague, and Welf after deserting his comrades also died. In Flanders Baldwin, now joined by Godfrey, was besieging Antwerp, but was defeated. Death was now removing friends as well as foes, and the loss of Herman of Cologne (February 1055) was a real blow to the Emperor. His successor was Anno, a man not of noble birth, a pupil at Bamberg and Provost at Goslar. At Ivois (May 1056) the Emperor met for the third time his namesake of France, and the matter of Lorraine made the meeting a stormy one, so much so that Henry of France challenged Henry of Germany to single combat. On this the Emperor withdrew in the dead of night. But in Germany itself the disaffected were returning to obedience; not only those who had conspired but Godfrey himself made submission. On the North-East the Lyutitzi were again in arms, and even as Henry was turning northwards against them a great defeat on the Havel and Elbe had made the matter serious, the more so as the Margrave William had been slain. To disaster was added famine, and when all this had to be faced Henry was smitten with illness. Hastily he tried to ensure peace for his son: he compensated all whom he had wronged: he set free Beatrice and Matilda: all those at his court confirmed his son's succession and the boy was commended to the special protection of the Pope, who was at the death-bed. Then 5 October 1056 Henry died: "with him," said men afterwards, "died order and justice." His heart was taken to its real and fitting home in Goslar, while his body rested beside Conrad's at Spires.

The East and North-East throughout Henry's reign had called forth his full energy, and their story is in very large part the story of two men—the Slav Duke Godescalc and the Bohemian Duke Břatislav.

The Bohemian duke was the illegitimate son of Duke Udalrich. When still quite young, "most beautiful of youths and boldest of heroes," he had shewn energy in his reconquest of Moravia from the Poles, and romance in his carrying off the Countess Judith, sister of the Franconian Margrave Otto the White of Schweinfurt, of royal blood.

Břatislav, fresh from his Moravian conquests, had fallen in love with the reported beauty of Judith " fairer than all other maidens beneath the sun," whose good father and excellent mother had confided her to the convent at Zuinprod (Schweinfurt), "to learn the Psalter." Břatislav, desiring her as bride, preferred action to asking; for " he reflected on the innate arrogance of the Teutons, and on the swollen pride with which they ever despise the Slav people and the Slav tongue." So he carried her off by night, on horseback ; and, lest the Germans should wreak vengeance on Bohemia, took her to Moravia.

Břatislav could be as unswervingly faithful as he was audacious and vigorous. His friendship or enmity meant everything to Henry in Bohemia, much elsewhere. Yet, since he was naturally a man of strong ambitions, it was not friendship that he offered.

He had begun his career as the ally of Conrad (against the Poles); and had held Moravia under the joint overlordship of his father and the Emperor. But on his succession to Bohemia in 1037, his horizon was bright with promise. Poland had fallen from aggressive strength into disunion and civil war; the German rulers were absent in Italy. Břatislav saw his opportunity to take vengeance on Poland for old wrongs, and to ensure Bohemia's permanent freedom from the Empire.

In unhappy Poland, Mesco, son of Boleslav the Mighty, had died in 1034, leaving a boy, Casimir, under the guardianship of his German mother, Richessa. While Mesco lived divisions had been fomented and Poland at last partitioned by the Emperor Conrad. Now, first the duchess, and later on her son, when a man, were forced to fly before the violence of the Polish nobles—the duke (says the Polish Chronicle), lest he should avenge his mother's injuries. Casimir wandered through Russia and Hungary, and finally reached Richessa in Germany. Meanwhile Poland was given over to chaos. "Those were lords who should be slaves" says the same chronicle, " and those slaves who should be lords." Women were raped, bishops and priests stoned to death. Upon the distracted country fell all its neighbours, including "those three most ferocious of peoples, the Lithuanians, Pomeranians and Prussians."

Břatislav seized his chance. Sending the war-signal round Bohemia, he fell "like a sudden storm" upon Poland "widowed of her prince." In the South, he took and burnt Cracow, rifling her of her ancient and precious treasures. Up to the North he raged, razing towns and villages, carrying off Poles by hundreds into slavery. He finally ended his career of conquest and slaughter by solemnly transferring, from their Polish shrine at Gnesen to Prague, the bones of the martyred apostle, Adalbert.

While these things were happening Henry became Emperor. In the very year of his accession he prepared an expedition against Bohemia, which did not mature. Herman of Reichenau tells of envoys who came to Henry, in the midst of his preparations for war, bringing with them Břatislav's son as a hostage ; and of a promise made by Břatislav that he himself would soon come to pay homage. This might well, for the time, seem sufficient.

It was in the year 1040 that the first important expedition was launched against Bohemia. Břatislav's intentions were by this time quite clear ; for he had, in the interval, not only demanded from Rome the erection of Prague into an archbishopric, a step which meant the severing of the ecclesiastical dependence of Bohemia upon Germany, but had also formed an alliance with Peter, the new King of Hungary, who had signalised the event by winter raids over the German frontiers.

The wrongs of Poland and of Casimir, and the danger to Germany, were reasons amply justifying Henry's interventions. Preliminary negotiations probably consisted in Henry's ultimatum demanding reparation to Poland, and the payment of the regular tribute to Germany. On Břatislav's refusal, the expedition was launched, but failed (August, 1040).

Henry, humiliated for the moment, was not defeated. He "kept his grief deep in his heart," and the Bohemian overtures were rejected, as we have seen. Even before this refusal, the Bohemians and their ally, Peter of Hungary, were already raiding the frontier.

In 1041 the German forces, which were "very great," advanced more cautiously, and Henry, breaking his way into the country in the rear of its defending armies, found the country-side living as in the midst of peace. It was in August. For six weeks the German forces lived at ease, the rich land supplying them plentifully with corn and cattle. Then, burning and destroying all that was left, and devastating far and wide, "with the exception of two provinces which they left to their humbled foes," the armies towards the end of September moved to the trysting-place above Prague. Meanwhile Austrian knights, under the leadership of the young Babenberger prince, Leopold, made a successful inroad from the South.

Břatislav, unable to protect his land, made ineffectual overtures. Then he was deserted by his own people. The Bishop of Prague, Severus, had been appointed by Udalrich in reward for his skill in catering for the ducal table. This traitor now led a general desertion. The Bohemians promised Henry to deliver their duke bound into his hands. Břatislav perforce made an unqualified surrender. He renounced the royal title, so offensive to German ears; he promised full restitution to Poland; he gave his duchy into Henry's hands. In pledge of his faith he sent as hostages his own son Spitignev and the sons of five great Bohemian nobles. These, if Břatislav failed, Henry might put "to any death he pleased." Henry at last accepted his submission.

Břatislav himself built a way back to Bavaria for the booty-laden invaders; and a fortnight later he himself appeared at Ratisbon, and there before the king and assembled princes and many of his own chieftains, "barefooted, more humiliated now than formerly he had been exalted," offered homage to Henry. His duchy was restored to him, with half the tribute remitted; he was moreover confirmed in the possession of Silesia, seized from the Poles, and then actually in his hands. His own splendid war-horse which Břatislav offered to Henry, with its saddle "completely and marvellously wrought in gold and silver," was given, in the duke's presence, to Leopold of Austria, the hero of the expedition.

Once having sworn fealty, Břatislav maintained it loyally until the close of his life; and his advice on military matters was of great service to Henry. The re-grant of Breslau and the Silesian towns to Poland in 1054 was, however, a great strain even on his loyalty; and in spite of Henry's award, he recovered the lost cities for a time from Casimir, by force of arms, in the following year. Thence he would have proceeded to Hungary, but on his way he died. His successor, Spitignev, although his succession was ratified by Henry, plunged into a riot of animosity against everything German, expelling from Bohemian soil every man and woman of the hated nation, rich, poor and pilgrim.

Duke Casimir of Poland played throughout a less prominent part than his vigorous neighbour. Affairs at home kept him fully occupied; while his close early connexion with Germany, and the memory of the partition of Poland by Conrad, would further deter him from any thought of imitating his father Mesco, who, like Boleslav, had claimed the title of King.

Of his part in events between 1039 and 1041 we know little. With 500 horse, he went to Poland, where he was "gladly received"; he slowly recovered his land from foreigners; and finally (1047) overcame the last and greatest of the independent Polish chiefs, Meczlav of Masovia.

He had secured the greater part of his inheritance; it remained to recover Silesia, seized by Břatislav in 1039 and confirmed to the Bohemian duke by Henry.

It is in 1050 that serious trouble first threatened. In this year, Casimir was definitely accused of "usurping" land granted by Henry to Břatislav; as well as of other, unrecorded, misdemeanours against the Empire. Henry actually prepared an expedition against him, and war was averted only by the illness of the Emperor and the alacrity and conciliatory spirit shewn by Casimir. Coming to Goslar of his own free will, he exculpated himself on oath of the charge of aggression against Bohemia, and consented to make the reparation demanded for the acts of which he was duly judged guilty by the princes. Thence he returned home with royal gifts.

Strife however continued between Casimir and Břatislav; and at Whitsuntide 1054 both dukes were summoned before Henry at Quedlinburg. It is plain that in the meantime Casimir had made good his hold on Breslau; for the town and district are now confirmed to him by Henry, under condition (according to the Bohemian Chronicler) of annual tribute to Bohemia. The dukes departed "reconciled." In the following January Břatislav died, having apparently again temporarily seized Silesia. Peace was eventually ratified between Poland and Bohemia by the marriage of Casimir's only daughter to Břatislav's successor.

In spite of the wanderings of his youth, and the long years spent in conflict, Casimir was a scholar (he is said to have addressed his troops in Latin verse!) and a friend of monks among whom he had been trained. That he was himself a monk at Cluny is a later legend. His last years were spent in the peaceful consolidation through Church and State of what he had so hardly won. He died soon after Henry, in 1058.

The affairs of Hungary in the years 1040–1045 group themselves around King Peter, driven from his realm by the Magyar nobles and restored, but in vain, by Henry. His aid to Břatislav in the first years of Henry's reign had been prompted more by youthful insolence than by any fixed anti-German feeling. He was a Venetian on his father's side and on succeeding his uncle St Stephen in 1039, had promised him to maintain his widow Gisela, sister of Henry II, in her possessions, but after a year or so he broke his faith and she fell into poverty. This marks the time when, along with Břatislav, he began his raids into Germany.

Two such raids, in 1039 and 1040, had been successful, when a rebellion drove him from his realm into Germany. The new government was anti-German and inclined towards paganism, while the new king, Obo, was chosen from among the Magyar chiefs. Peter came, as we have seen, to Henry as a suppliant in August 1041. But Burgundian troubles forced Henry to put Hungary aside and Obo himself began hostilities. "Never before did Hungary carry off so great a booty" from the duchy of Bavaria as now, although a gallant resistance was offered by the Margrave Adalbert of Babenberg, founder of the Austrian house, and his warlike son Leopold. At Easter 1042 Obo was crowned as king.

The puppet-king set up by Henry in his first counter-expedition (1042) was at once expelled, but in 1043, as we saw, Henry obtained solid gain; the land from the Austrian territory to the Leitha and March was by far the most lasting result of all his Hungarian campaigns. The boundary thus fixed remained, but the Hungarian crown could not be brought into any real dependence. A third expedition (1044) restored Peter as a vassal, but by autumn 1046 he had fallen, to disappear in prison amid the depths of Hungary. His cousin Andrew, an Arpad, took his throne. He dexterously used the renascent Paganism, although it was covered over with a veneer of Christianity, and he did not wish for permanent warfare with his greater neighbour. Apologetic envoys gave Henry an excuse for delay and for two years Hungary was left alone. Then the peace was disturbed by Henry's restless uncle, Gebhard of Ratisbon, who (1049) made a raid into Hungary.

In 1050, following raid and counter-raid, Henry "grieving that Hungary, which formerly, by the plain judgment of God, had owned his sway, was now by most wicked men snatched from him," called the Bavarian princes together at Nuremberg, which ancient city now for the first time appears in history. The defence of the frontiers was urged upon them, and next year the Emperor himself invaded Hungary with an army gathered from all his duchies and tributary peoples. Disregarding Andrew's offer, he entered Hungary by the Danube, but when he had to leave his boats he was entangled in the marshes and fighting had small result. The Altaich annalist dismisses the campaign as "difficult and very troublesome."

Shortly afterwards, however, Andrew seems to have made some sort of agreement, but in 1052 Henry had again to make an expedition, though "of no glory and no utility to the realm." Pressburg was besieged for two months before it fell. Then once more came an agreement, made this time by the Pope's mediation. It was only of short duration: Kuno, the exiled Duke of Bavaria, was in arms against Henry and urged Andrew to war. Carinthia was invaded (1054) and the Hungarians returned rejoicing with much booty. The Bavarians themselves forced Kuno into quietness: Henry was busy in Flanders. Thus, inconclusively, ends the story of his relations with Hungary: German supremacy, in fact, could not be maintained.

The darkness in which the great king died was a shadow cast from the fierce and pagan lands beyond the Elbe and the Oder.

The Slavs of the North-East were a welter of fierce peoples, whose hands were of old against all Christians, Dane, German or Pole. Here and there a precarious Christianity had made some slight inroad; but, in general, attempts at subjugation had bred a savage hatred for the name of Christian.

The task of Christian civilisation, formerly belonging to the German kings, was now taken up by Pole and Dane as rivals, in a day of able rulers and of nations welded together by their new faith. Boleslav the Mighty of Poland, an enthusiastic apostle of Christianity, had subdued the Pomeranians and Prussians. After his death his nephew, Knut of Denmark, made his power felt along the Baltic as far as, and including, Pomerania. This extension of his sway was rendered easier by the alliance with Conrad in 1025 and resulted in ten years' peace. But 1035, the year of Knut's death, saw a general disturbance and one of the most savage of recorded Slav incursions.

Among the many Wendish tribes it is necessary to distinguish between the Slavs on the Baltic beyond the Lower Elbe, Obotrites and others, and the inland Slavs beyond the Middle Elbe, the Lyutitzi[1]. The former were more accessible to both Germans and Danes, and as they

[1] See Map 26*a* in vol. II.

lived under princes were partly Christianised and partly though uneasily subject to Germany. But the Lyutitzi, wild and free communities living under elected rulers, were a more savage people. They might be useful as allies against the Poles, whom they hated more than they did the Germans under the tolerant Conrad, but there could be for them nothing approaching even semi-subjection. With them in the years preceding Henry's accession direct conflict had arisen through the avarice of the Saxons, upon whom Conrad had thrown the responsibility of defence. Repeated raids followed and Henry's first trial in arms was against them. Then a campaign in 1036, followed by great cruelty on Conrad's part enforced quiet, which lasted until the end of Henry's reign.

The other Slavs, those of the Baltic, had dealings with the Dukes of Saxony and the Archbishops of Hamburg-Bremen, rather than with the Emperor. Archbishop Albrand (1035–1045) built in Hamburg a strong church and palace as a refuge from Slav raids; Duke Bernard II followed his example with another stronghold in the same city; duke and bishop attended to their respective duties, one of exacting tribute and the other of evangelisation. But there was frequent restlessness and grumbling at tribute demanded by the Duke and episcopal dues demanded by the Bishop of Oldenburg which, until 1160 when the see of Lübeck was founded, was the episcopal centre for the Obotrites; also, when Adalbert (1045) succeeded Albrand, duke and archbishop fell into strife. Bernard looked upon Adalbert as a spy in Henry's service; Adalbert strove to free his see from ducal encroachments. He finished the stone fortifications of Bremen as a protection against Bernard rather than against the Slavs: he added to those of Hamburg, and as further defence built a fortress on the banks of the Elbe, which its garrison made into a robber hold until the outraged inhabitants destroyed it.

In spite of large schemes for a province with more suffragans, Adalbert did little for the Slavs. It was neither archbishop nor Saxon duke who maintained peace among these Slavs of the Elbe, but Duke Godescalc. This remarkable noble was studying at Lüneburg when his father, an Obotrite prince, was murdered for his cruelty by a Saxon. Godescalc at once renounced Christianity and learning alike, and at the head of a horde of Lyutitzi set out to avenge his father's death. Suddenly his heart smote him for the woe and death he was dealing out: he gave himself up to Duke Bernard, who sent him into Denmark. There he took service with Knut and went with him to England. After the deaths of Knut and his sons he came home. He found the Obotrites suffering from a heavy defeat at the hands of Magnus of Norway, in which the family of Ratibor, their leading chief, had been all slain. He was able to regain his father's place and the leadership of the Obotrites. He extended his power as far as the country of the Lyutitzi, and the wide district of the Bremen diocese "feared him as a king" and paid him tribute. With the neighbouring Christian rulers, Scandinavian and German, he kept up a vigorous friendship. It was he who bore the burden of keeping peace, and shortly before Henry's death we find him, the Saxon duke and the Danish king in allied expedition against the Lyutitzi. To the Church, which stood for civilisation, he was also a friend. He established monasteries and canons regular in Lübeck, Oldenburg and elsewhere. Throughout the land he built churches and to their service he summoned missionary priests who "freely did the work of God"; like Oswald in Northumbria he travelled with them and often acted as interpreter. "Had he lived," says the chronicler, "he would have brought all the pagans to the Christian faith." He survived Henry some ten years, being murdered in 1066.

The peace imposed by Conrad upon the Lyutitzi was twice broken under Henry. In 1045 he had to lead an expedition against them, but they promptly submitted and returned to tribute. When ten years later they again broke bounds, Henry sent against them William of the Nordmark and Count Dietrich. At Prizlava, where a ruined castle still overlooks the confluence of Havel and Elbe, the Margrave was ambushed, and both he and Dietrich fell. These tidings reached Henry before his death, and with it the frontier troubles grew more intense.

To this great King and Emperor there has sometimes been ascribed a conscious attempt at a restoration of the Empire of Charlemagne, limited geographically but of world-wide importance through its control of the Western Church from its centre, Rome. But there is little real trace of such a conception on Henry's part, save in the one feature of that ordered rule which was inseparably bound up with Charlemagne's Empire. Too much has been sometimes made of Henry's attitude towards Cluny, and of his marriage with Agnes of Poitou and Aquitaine, as paving the way for the acquisition of France. But this is a mere conjecture based upon a wish to reconcile later German ideals with the work of one of their greatest kings. He did use the sympathy of the Church, and especially of Cluny, in Burgundy, as a help towards the stability of ordered imperial rule, and that was all. It was no new and subtle scheme but an old-established procedure; a piece of honest policy, not a cynical design to trap France by means of piety. Henry's mind was, it is true, pre-occupied with the Middle Kingdom, but there is no trace of any endeavour to pave the way for an eventual re-union under the sceptre of his heirs of the whole Carolingian Empire. There is, however, far stronger basis for the belief that he meant an imperial control over the Papacy than that he aimed at an eventual supremacy over France.

For it is plain that Henry not only un-made and made Popes, but that he accepted the offer of the Patriciate in the belief that it meant control over papal elections, and that he secured from the Romans a sworn promise to give to himself and to his heir the chief voice in all future elections. Whatever the exact force of the Emperor's control, the promise meant that no one could be Pope except with his approval. It put the Roman see almost, if not quite, into the position of a German bishopric. And Henry used the power placed in his hands. Whether the Romans would ever have revolted against Henry's choice we do not know, for his wisdom never put them to the test. But what worked well under Henry at a time when churchmen and statesmen had roughly the same practical aims, although maybe divergent theories, might not work well under a less high-minded ruler under whom Church and State had grown into divergent ideals.

Henry did not aim at imperial aggrandisement; he did not wish to lower the Papacy any more than he wished to conquer France. He was a lover not of power but of order, and order he meant to guard. Moreover he was a man of fact and actuality . he respected law, he respected custom: they must, however, be law and custom that had worked and would work well. He shewed this in his dealings with the Papacy: he shewed it in his dealings with the tribal duchies in Germany. When it is a case of giving a duke to Bavaria, although custom was absolutely on the side of Bavaria in electing its duke, he ignored custom and nominated. He flouted the Bavarian's right of election, not because he thought little of law and custom but because he was concerned with the practical enforcement of order. It was so too with abbots and monasteries; sometimes he allowed free election, sometimes he simply nominated. He was guided by the circumstances, and by the state of the monastery: he always aimed at a worthy choice but cared little how it came about, and corrupt monks were little likely to elect a reforming abbot.

In Germany with its tribal duchies he had no settled policy. A few months after Conrad's death Henry himself was Duke of Swabia, Bavaria and Carinthia, as well as king. He followed his father's policy in uniting the duchies with the Crown unless he saw good reason for the contrary. Hence he gave away one great duchy after another when it seemed good. He gave Bavaria to Henry of Luxemburg when it was threatened by Obo of Hungary; Swabia to the Lorrainer Otto when Godfrey was troubling the neighbouring Lorraine. And he did not fear to raise houses that might become rivals in the Empire if they served the present use. It was so with his patronage of Luxemburgers and of Babenbergs. And yet it must be confessed that Henry's dealings with the duchies were not happy. Bavaria and Carinthia he left largely hostile to the Crown. Lorraine was torn by rebellion because in the case of Godfrey Henry had misjudged his man. Personal genius was lacking, too, in his dealings with the border-land states, although with Bohemia and Hungary he could claim success. And in Burgundy, if anywhere, he did succeed.

Upon internal order he had set his heart. We recall his "Declarations of Indulgence" and the "peace undreamt of through the ages" which followed. Yet the peace was itself precarious, though his example was fruitfully followed afterwards; and Germany, breathing awhile more peacefully during recurring "Landfrieden," had cause to bless the day at Constance.

In himself he seems to have lacked breadth and geniality. with humble fidelity he took up the task of his inheritance: his single-mindedness and purity of character are testified to by all: there were great men whom he chose out or who trusted him: Herman of Cologne, Bruno of Toul (Leo IX), Peter Damiani. Yet he could fail with great men as with smaller: Leo IX towards the end, and Wazo of Liège he misjudged; the difficult Godfrey of Lorraine, whom he failed to understand, wellnigh wrecked his Empire. It was this personal weakness that made him, in his last years, fall below his own high standard, unable to cope with the many difficulties of his Empire. He seems weary when he comes to die. Germany looked back to him, not for the good that he had done, but for the evil which came so swiftly when his day was over.

In Germany he did not build to stand. One great thing he did to change history, and in doing it he raised up the power that was to cast down his son and destroy his Empire. His tomb and his monument should be in Rome.

CHAPTER XIII.

THE VIKINGS.

The term Viking is a derivative of the Old Norse *Vik*, a creek, bay or fjord, and means one who haunts such an opening and uses it as a base whence raids may be made on the surrounding country. The word is now commonly applied to those Norsemen, Danes and Swedes who harried Europe from the eighth to the eleventh centuries, and in such phrases as "the Viking age," "Viking civilisation," is used in a still wider sense as a convenient term for Scandinavian civilisation at a particular stage in its development. It is in this larger sense that the term is used in the present chapter, covering the activities of the Northmen in peace as well as in war. The term Viking in its narrower sense is no more descriptive of this age than "Buccaneering" would be of the age of Elizabeth.

Except along the narrow line of the Eider, Scandinavia has no land-boundaries of importance and is naturally severed from the rest of Europe. Though known to Greek and Roman geographers and historians, it was almost entirely unaffected by Roman civilisation. It was not till the Scandinavian peoples were driven by stress of circumstance to find fresh homes, that they found that the sea instead of dividing them from the rest of Europe really furnished them with a ready and easy path of attack against those nations of North-West Europe who had either neglected or forgotten the art of seamanship.

The history of the Teutonic North from the middle of the sixth to the end of the eighth century is almost a blank, at least in so far as history concerns itself with the record of definite events. During the first half of the sixth century there had been considerable activity in Denmark and Southern Sweden. About the year 520 Chocilaicus, King of the Danes, or, according to another authority, of the Getae (*i.e.* Götar) in South Sweden, made a raid on the territory of the Franks on the Lower Rhine, but was defeated and slain by Theudibert, son of the Frankish king Theodoric, as he was withdrawing from Frisia with extensive plunder. This expedition finds poetic record in the exploits of Hygelac, King of the Geats, in *Beowulf.* Some forty years later there is mention of them in Venantius Fortunatus's eulogy of Duke Lupus of Champagne. They were now in union with the Saxons and made a raid on Western Frisia, but were soon driven back by the Franks. From this time until the first landing of Vikings near Dorchester (*c.* 787), the earliest attacks on the coast of France against which Charles the Great made defence in 800, and the first encounter between the Danes and Franks on the borders of Southern Denmark in 808, we know almost nothing of the history of Scandinavia, at least in so far as we look for information in the annals or histories of the time.

The story of these two hundred years has to some extent been pieced together from scraps of historical, philological and archaeological evidence. Professor Zimmer shewed that it was possible, that the attacks of unknown pirates on the island of Eigg in the Hebrides and on Tory Island off Donegal, described in certain Irish annals of the seventh century, were really the work of early Viking invaders, and that the witness of Irish legends and sagas tends to prove that already by the end of the seventh century Irish missionaries were settled in the Shetlands and Faroes, where they soon came into contact with the Northmen. Evidence for the advance from the other side, of the Northmen towards the West and South, has been found by Dr Jakobsen in his work on the place-names of the Shetlands. He has shewn that many of these names must be due to Norse settlements from a period long before the recognised Viking movements of the ninth century. Archaeological evidence can also be adduced in support of this belief in early intercourse between Scandinavia and the islands of the West. Sculptured stones found in the island of Gothland shew already by 700 clear evidence of Celtic art influence. Indeed archaeologists are now agreed that in the eighth century and even earlier there were trade connexions between Scandinavia and the West. Long before English or Irish, Franks or Frisians, knew the Northmen as Viking raiders, they had been familiar with them in peaceful mercantile intercourse, and it is probable that in the eighth century there were a good number of Scandinavian merchants settled in Western Europe. Their influence on the trade of the West was only exceeded by that of the Frisians, who were the chief trading and naval power of the seventh and eighth centuries, and it is most probable that it was the crushing of Frisian power by Charles Martel in 734 and their final subjection by Charles the Great towards the close of the eighth century which helped to prepare the way for the great Viking advance.

About the year 800 the relations between the North and West Germanic peoples underwent a great change both in character and extent. We find the coasts of England, Ireland, Frisia and France attacked by Viking raiders, while on the southern borders of Denmark there was constant friction between the kings of that country and the forces of the Empire. The question has often been asked: What were the causes of this sudden outburst of hostile activity on the part of the Northmen? Monkish chroniclers said they were sent by God in punishment for the sins of the age; Norman tradition as preserved by Dudo and William of Jumièges attributed the raids to the necessity for expansion consequent on over-population. Polygamy had led to a rapid increase of population, and many of the youth of the country were driven forth to gain fresh lands for themselves elsewhere. Polygamy does not necessarily lead to over-population, but polygamy among the ruling classes, as it prevailed in the North, means a large number of younger sons for whom provision must be made, and it is quite possible that stress of circumstance caused many such to visit foreign lands on Viking raids. Of the political condition of the Scandinavian countries we know very little at this time. We hear however in Denmark in the early years of the ninth century of long disputes as to the succession, and it is probable that difficulties of this kind may have prompted many to go on foreign expeditions. In Norway we know that the growth of the power of Harold Fairhair in the middle portion of the ninth century led to the adoption of a Viking life by many of the more independent spirits, and it is quite possible that earlier efforts towards consolidation among the petty Norwegian kings may have produced similar effects. Social and political conditions may thus have worked together, preparing the ground for Scandinavian activity in the ninth century, and it was perhaps, as suggested above, the destruction of Frisian power which removed the last check on the energy of the populous nations of the North.

The first definite record of Viking invasion is probably that found in the Anglo-Saxon Chronicle (*s. a.* 787), which tells of the coming of Danish ships to England in the days of Beorhtric, King of Wessex. They landed in the neighbourhood of Dorchester and slew the king's reeve. Certain versions of the Chronicle call them ships of the Northmen and tell us that they came from "Herethaland." There can be little doubt that this is the West Norwegian district of Hörthaland, and that " Northmen " here, as elsewhere in the Chronicle, means Norwegians[1]. The term " Danish " is probably generic for Scandinavian, the chronicler using the name of the nationality best known to him. In June 793 the church at Lindisfarne was destroyed, and a year later the monastery of St Paul at Jarrow. In 795 Vikings landed in Skye and visited Lambay Island off Dublin, and in 798 the Isle of Man. These invaders were certainly Norse, for the Irish annalists mention expressly the first arrival of the Danes in Ireland in 849, and draw a rigid distinction between the Norwegian or " white " foreigners and the Danish or " black " ones.

England was not troubled again by Viking raiders until 835, but the attacks on Ireland continued almost without cessation. Iona was

---

[1] Attempts have been made to identify Herethaland with the district of Hardesyssel in Jutland and to prove that these Northmen were Danes, but the weight of evidence seems to the present writer to be all in favour of the identification with Hörthaland. The name Hiruath commonly given to Norway by Gaelic writers is another version of the same name.

destroyed in 802; by 807 the invaders had penetrated inland as far as Roscommon, and four years later they had made their way round the west coast of Ireland as far as Cork. In 821 the Howth peninsula was plundered and during the next few years the rich monasteries of North Ireland were destroyed. By the year 834 the Northmen had visited nearly the whole of the island and no place was safe from their raids. About this time there came a change in the character of the attacks in that large fleets began to anchor in the loughs and harbours and estuaries with which the coast of Ireland abounds. Thence they made lengthy raids on the surrounding country, often staying the whole winter through, instead of paying summer visits only as they had done hitherto. At the same time they often strengthened their base by the erection of forts on the shores of the waters in which they had established themselves.

When the Viking raids were resumed in England in 835 it is fairly certain that they were the work of Danish and not of Norwegian invaders. The Norsemen had found other fields of activity in Ireland, while the Danes who had already visited the chief estuaries of the Frankish coast now crossed to England. At first their attacks were directed towards the southern shores of Britain, but by 841 they had penetrated into Lindsey and East Anglia. London and Rochester were sacked in 842. In 851 the Danes wintered in Thanet and four years later they stayed in Sheppey. The Danish fleet in this year numbered some 350 ships. It was probably this same fleet, somewhat reduced in numbers, which in 852 sailed round Britain and captured Dublin. With the winterings in Thanet and Sheppey the Viking invasions of England had reached the same stage of development as in Ireland. We have passed from the period of isolated raids to that of persistent attacks with a view to permanent conquest.

The mainland of Western Europe was also exposed during these years to attacks of a twofold character. In the first place, trouble arose on the boundary between Southern Denmark and Frankish territory owing to the desire of the Danish kings to extend their authority southward: in the second, constant raids were made along the whole of the shores of Europe from Frisia to Aquitaine.

The friction between the Danes and their neighbours on the south was continuous through the last years of the eighth and the greater part of the ninth century. Charles the Great by his campaigns against the Saxons and Nordalbingians had advanced towards the Danish boundary on the Eider, and the Danes first gave offence in 777 when their king Sigefridus (Old Norse Sigurðr) gave shelter to the Saxon patriot Widukind. Gradually the Frankish power advanced, and in 809 a fort was established at Itzehoe (Esesfeld) on the Stör, north of the Elbe. The Danes also made advances on their side and in 804 their king Godefridus (O.N. Guðröðr) collected a fleet and army at Slesvík (Schleswig). In 808 after a successful campaign against the Obotrites, a Slavonic people in modern Mecklenburg, he constructed a boundary wall for his kingdom, stretching from the Baltic to the Eider. He received tribute not only from the Obotrites but also from the Nordalbingians and Frisians. He was preparing to attack Charles the Great himself when he died suddenly by the hand of a retainer in 810. There can be little doubt that this Godefridus is to be identified with the Gotricus of Saxo Grammaticus and Guðröðr the Yngling of Scandinavian tradition. If that is so, Guðröðr-Godefridus was slain in Stifla Sound (probably on the coast of Vestfold), and was king not only of Denmark, but also of much of Southern Norway, including Vestfold, Vingulmörk, and perhaps Agðir, as well as of Vermland in Sweden.

Later events confirm the evidence for the existence of a Dano-Norwegian kingdom of this kind. In 812 a dispute as to the succession arose between Sigefridus, "nepos" to king Guðröðr, and Anulo (O.N. Óli), "nepos" to a former king Herioldus (O.N. Haraldr) or Harold (probably the famous Harold Hyldetan slain at the battle of Bravalla). Both claimants were slain in fight but the party of Anulo were victorious. Anulo's brothers, Harold and Reginfredus (O.N. Ragnfröðr), became joint kings, and soon after we hear of their going to Vestfold, "the extreme district of their realm, whose people and chiefs were refusing to be made subject to them." Fortune fluctuated between Harold and the sons of Godefridus during the next few years, but Harold secured the support of the Emperor when he accepted baptism at Mayence in 826, with his wife, son and nephew. After his baptism he returned to Denmark through Frisia, where the Emperor had granted him Riustringen as a retreat in case of necessity. An attempt to regain Denmark was frustrated, and Harold probably availed himself of his Frisian grant during the next few years. The next incident belongs to the year 836, when Horic (O.N. Hárekr), one of the sons of Godefridus, sent an embassy to Louis the Pious denying complicity in the Viking raids made on Frisia at that time, and these denials continued during the next few years. In 837 Hemmingus (O.N. Hemmingr), probably a brother of Harold, and himself a Christian, was slain while defending the island of Walcheren against pirates. These two incidents are important as they tend to shew that the Viking raids were rather individual than national enterprises and that there was an extensive peaceful settlement of Danes in Frisia. In addition to the grant of Riustringen the Emperor had assigned (826) another part of Frisia to Roric (O.N. Hrœrekr), a brother of Harold, on condition that he should ward off piratical attacks.

It was during these years that the influence of Christianity first made itself felt in Scandinavia. The earliest knowledge of Christianity probably came, as is so often the case, with the extension of trade. Danes and Swedes settled in Friesland and elsewhere for purposes of trade, and either they or their emissaries must have made the "white

Christ" known to their heathen countrymen. The first definite mission
to the North was undertaken by St Willibrord at the beginning of the
eighth century. He was favourably received by the Danish king
Ongendus (O.N. Angantýr), but his mission was without fruit. In 822
Pope Paschal appointed Ebbo, Archbishop of Rheims, as his legate
among the northern peoples. He undertook a mission to Denmark in
823 and made a few converts. But it was in 826, when King Harold was
baptised and prepared to return to Denmark, that the first opportunity
of preaching Christianity in Denmark really came. With the opportunity
came the man, and Harold was accompanied on his return by Anskar, who
more than any other deserves to be called "Apostle of the Scandinavian
North." Leaving his monastery at Corvey (Corbie) in Saxony, and filled
with zeal to preach the gospel to the heathen, Anskar made many converts,
but Harold's ill-success in regaining the sovereignty injured his mission
in Denmark and, two years later, at the request of the Swedes themselves,
he preached the gospel in Sweden, receiving a welcome at Birca (Björkö)
from the Swedish king Bern (O.N. Björn). After a year and a half's mission
in Sweden, Anskar was recalled and made Archbishop of Hamburg and
given, jointly with Ebbo, jurisdiction over the whole of the northern
realms. Gautbert was made first bishop of Sweden and founded a church
at Sigtuna, but after a few years' work he was expelled in a popular
rising. Little progress was made in Denmark. No churches were
established, but Anskar did a good deal in training Danish youths in
Christian principles at his school in Hamburg.

Anskar's position became a very difficult one when the lands from which
his income was derived passed to Charles the Bald, and still more so when
the seat of his jurisdiction was destroyed by the Danes in 845. Louis
the German made amends by appointing him to the bishopric of Bremen,
afterwards united to a restored archbishopric of Hamburg. Anskar
now set himself to the task of gaining influence first with King Horic,
and later with his successor Horic the Younger. He was so far successful that the first Christian church in Denmark was established at Slesvík,
followed soon after by one at Ribe. He also concerned himself with
Sweden once more, gaining authority for his mission by undertaking
embassies from both Horic and Louis. He obtained permission for the
preaching of Christianity and continued his activities to the day of his
death in 865. Anskar had done much for Christianity in the North.
His own fiery zeal had however been ill supported even by his chosen
followers, and the tangible results were few. Christianity had found a
hearing in Denmark and Sweden, but Norway was as yet untouched. A
few churches had been built in the southern part of both countries, a
certain number of adherents had been gained among the nobles and
trading classes, but the mass of the people remained untouched. The
first introduction of Christianity was too closely bound up with the
political and diplomatic relations of Northern Europe for it to be

otherwise, and the episcopal organisation was far more elaborate than was required.

With the death of Louis the Pious in 840 a change took place in the relations between Danes and Franks. In the quarrels over the division of the Empire Lothar encouraged attacks on the territory of his rivals. Harold was bribed by a grant of the island of Walcheren and neighbouring district, so that in 842 we find him as far south as the Moselle, while Horic himself took part in an expedition up the Elbe against Louis the German. In 847 when the brothers had for the time being patched up their quarrels, they stultified themselves by sending embassies to Horic, asking him to restrain his subjects from attacking the Christians. Horic had not the power, even if he had the desire, but, fortunately for the Empire, Denmark was now crippled by internal dissensions. This prevented any attack on the part of the Danish nation as a whole, but Viking raids continued without intermission.

The first sign of dissension in Denmark appeared in 850, when Horic was attacked by his two nephews and compelled to share his kingdom with them. In 852 Harold, the long-exiled King of Denmark, was slain for his treachery to Lothar, and two years later a revolution took place. We are told that after twenty years' ravaging in Frankish territory the Vikings made their way back to their fatherland, and there a dispute arose between Horic and his nephew Godurm (O.N. Guðormr). A disastrous battle was fought and so great was the slaughter that only one boy of the royal line remained. He became king as Horic the Younger. Encouraged by these dissensions, Roric and Godefridus, brother and son respectively to Harold, attempted in 855 to win the Danish kingdom but were compelled to retire again to Frisia. Roric was more successful in 857 when he received permission from Horic to settle in the part of his kingdom lying between the sea and the Eider, *i.e.* perhaps in North Frisia, a district consisting of a strip of coast-line between the town of Ribe and the mouth of the Eider, with the islands adjacent.

We have now carried the story of the relations between Denmark and her continental neighbours down to the middle of the ninth century, the same period to which we have traced the story of the Viking raids in England and Ireland. Before we tell the story of the transformation which those raids underwent just at this time, we must say something of Viking attacks on the maritime borders of the Continent.

The first mention of raids on the coast of Western Europe is in 800, when Charles the Great visited the coast-line from the Somme to the Seine and arranged for a fleet and coast-guard to protect it against Viking attacks. In 810, probably under direct instruction from the Danish king Godefridus, a fleet of some 200 vessels ravaged Frisia and its islands. Once more Charles the Great strengthened his fleet and the guarding of the shores, but raids continued to be a matter of almost yearly occurrence. The Emperor Louis pursued the same policy as his father, nevertheless by 821 the Vikings had sailed round Brittany and sacked monasteries in the islands of Noirmoutier and Rhé. From 814–833 attacks were almost entirely confined to these districts, and it is possible that these Vikings had their winter quarters in Ireland, where they were specially active at this time. At any rate it was to Wexford that one of these fleets returned in 820. The later years of Louis's reign (from 834) were troubled ones. The Empire was weakened by the Emperor's differences with his sons, and the Vikings had laid a firm hold on Frisia. They were attracted by its rich trade and more especially by the wealth of Dorestad, one of the most important trading cities of the Empire. Before the death of the Emperor in 840, Dorestad had been four times ravaged and the Vikings had sailed up the chief rivers, burning both Utrecht and Antwerp. Their success was the more rapid owing to the disloyalty of the Frisians themselves and possibly to help given them by Harold and his brother Roric, but the exact attitude of these princes and of the Danish king himself toward the raiders it is difficult to determine. There are rather too many protests of innocence on the part of Horic for us to believe in their entire genuineness.

After 840 the quarrels between the heirs of Louis the Pious laid Western Europe open to attack even more than it had been hitherto. In that year the Vikings sailed up the Seine for the first time as far as Rouen, while in 843 they appeared for the first time on the Loire. Here they were helped by the quarrels over the Aquitanian succession, and it is said that pilots, lent by Count Lambert, steered them up the Loire. They then took up their winter quarters on the island of Noirmoutier, where they seemed determined to make a permanent settlement. The invasions in France had reached the same stage of development to which we have already traced them in England and Ireland. It is in connexion with this expedition that we have one of the rare indications of the actual home of the invaders. They are called " Westfaldingi," and must therefore have come from the Norwegian district of Vestfold, which, as we have seen, formed part of the Danish kingdom about this time.

In 843 the Northmen advanced a stage further south. Sailing past Bordeaux they ravaged the upper basin of the Garonne. In the next year they visited Spain. Repelled by the bold defence of the Asturians, they sailed down the west coast of the peninsula and in September appeared before Lisbon. The Moors offered a stout resistance and the Vikings moved on to Cadiz, whence they ravaged the province of Sidonia in southern Andalusia. Penetrating as far as Seville, they captured that city, with the exception of its citadel, and raided Cordova. In the end they were out-generalled by the Musulmans and forced to retreat with heavy loss. Taking to their ships once more they ravaged the coast as far as Lisbon, and returned to the Gironde before the end of the year. It was probably on this expedition that some of the Vikings made a raid on Arzilla in Morocco. After the expedition embassies were exchanged between the Viking king and the Emir 'Abd-ar-Raḥmān II. The Moorish embassy would seem to have found the king in Ireland, and it is possible that he was the great Viking chief Turgeis, of whom we must now speak.

We have traced the development of Viking activity in Ireland and England, for Ireland down to the year 834. It was just at this time that the great leader Turgeis (? O.N. Thorgestr) made his appearance in North Ireland and attempted to establish sovereignty over all the foreigners in Erin and gain the overlordship of the whole country. He conquered North Ireland and raided Meath and Connaught, while his wife Ota (O.N. Auðr) gave audience upon the altar of Clonmacnois. His power culminated in 841, when he usurped the abbacy of Armagh. In 845 he was captured by the Irish and drowned in Lough Owel. By this time so numerous were the invading hosts that the chroniclers tell us "after this there came great sea-cast floods of foreigners into Erin, so that there was not a point without a fleet." In 849 the invasions developed a new phase. Hitherto while the Irish had been weakened by much internecine warfare their enemies had worked with one mind and heart. Now we read: "A naval expedition of seven score of the Foreigners came to exercise power over the Foreigners who were before them, so that they disturbed all Ireland afterwards." This means that the Danes were now taking an active part in the Scandinavian invasions of Ireland, and we soon find them disputing supremacy with the earlier Norwegian settlers. At the same time we have the first mention of intrigues between Irish factions and the foreign invaders, intrigues which were destined to play an important part in the Irish wars of the next fifty years. For a time Dublin was in the hands of the Danes, but in 853 one Amhlaeibh (*i.e.* Olaf), son of the king of Lochlann (*i.e.* Norway), came to Ireland and received the submission of Danes and Norsemen alike, while tribute was given him by the native Irish. Henceforward Dublin was the chief stronghold of Norse power in Ireland.

This Amhlaeibh was Olaf the White of Norse tradition, the representative of that branch of the Yngling family who, according to Ari Fróði, settled in Ireland. Affairs were now further complicated by the fact that many Irish forsook Christianity and joined the Norsemen in their plunderings. These recreant Irish, who probably intermarried with the Norsemen, were known as the Gall-Gaedhil, *i.e.* the foreign Irish, and played an important part in the wars of the next few years. One of their leaders was Caitill Find, *i.e.* Ketill the White, a Norseman with an Irish nickname. Usually they fought on the side of the Norsemen but at times they played for their own hand. Olaf was assisted by his brothers Imhar (O.N. Ívarr) and Auisle (O.N. Auðgísl), and married the daughter of Aedh Finnliath (MacNiall), King of all Ireland. Dublin, Waterford, Limerick and occasionally Cork

were the centres of Norse activity at this time, but there seems to have
been no unity of action among their forces. In 866 Olaf and Auðgísl
made a successful expedition to Pictland, and again in 870–1 Olaf and
Ívarr made a raid on Scotland. Olaf now returned to Norway to assist
his father Goffraidh (O.N. Guðfriðr) and possibly to take part with him
in the great fight at Hafrsfjord against Harold Fairhair. We hear
nothing more of Olaf, and two years later Ívarr, " king of the Norsemen
of all Ireland and Britain," ended his life.

There now appear on the scene Viking leaders of a different family,
which seems to have over-shadowed that of Olaf. They were the sons of
one Raghnall, who had been expelled from his sovereignty in Norway.
Raghnall had remained in the Orkneys, but his elder sons came to the
British Isles, "being desirous of attacking the Franks and Saxons."
Not content with this they pushed on from Ireland across the Canta-
brian sea until they reached Spain. After a successful campaign
against the Moors in Africa they returned to Ireland and settled in
Dublin. So runs the story in the *Fragments of Irish Annals* edited by
Dugald MacFirbis, and there can be little doubt of its substratum of
truth or of the identification of this Raghnall and his sons with the well-
known figures of Ragnarr Loðbrók and his sons. In 877 Raghnall's son
Albdann (O.N. Halfdanr) was killed on Strangford Lough, while
fighting against the Norse champion Baraidh (O.N. Barðr) who was
attached to the house of Olaf.

At this point the *Wars of the Gaedhil with the Gall* notes a period
of rest for the men of Erin, lasting some forty years and ending in 916.
This statement is substantially true. We do not hear of any large fleets
coming to Ireland, and during these years Viking activity seems chiefly
to have centred in Britain. Trouble was only renewed when the success
of the campaigns of Edward the Elder in England once more drove the
Vikings westward.

We have traced the history of the Vikings in England down to
the first settlement in 851 and 855. During the years which followed
there were raids on the south made by Vikings from Frankish territory,
but the great development took place in 866, when a large Danish army
took up its quarters in East Anglia, whence they advanced to York in
867. Northumbria was weakened by dissension and the Danes captured
York without much trouble. This city was henceforward the stronghold
of Scandinavian power in Northern England, and the Saxon Eoforwíc
soon became the Norse Jórvík or York. The Danes set up a puppet
king Ecgberht in Northumbria north of the Tyne and reduced Mercia
to submission. Thence they marched into East Anglia as far as Thetford,
and engaged the forces of Edmund, King of East Anglia, defeating and
slaying him, but whether in actual battle or, as popular tradition would
have it, in later martyrdom is uncertain. The death of St Edmund
soon became an event of European fame, and no event in the Danish

invasions was more widely known and no Danish leader more heartily execrated than Ívarr, their commander on this occasion. After their victory in East Anglia the Danes attacked Wessex. Their struggle with Aethelred and his brother Alfred was long and fierce. In the end Danes and English came to terms by the peace of Wedmore (878), and the ensuing " peace of Alfred and Guthrum" (885) defined the boundary between Alfred's kingdom and the Danish realm in East Anglia. It ran by the Thames estuary to the mouth of the Lea (a few miles east of London), then up the Lea to its source near Leighton Buzzard, then eastwards along the Ouse to Watling Street, somewhere near Fenny or Stony Stratford. The northern half of Mercia was also in Danish hands, their authority centring in the Five Boroughs of Lincoln, Nottingham, Derby, Leicester and Stamford. Northumbria was at the same time under Viking rule, its king until 877 being that Halfdanr (Halfdene) who was killed on Strangford Lough. There can be little doubt that the chief Viking leaders during these years (Halfdanr, Ívarr and Ubbi) were sons of Ragnarr Loðbrók, the greatest of Viking heroes in Scandinavian tradition, but it is impossible to say how much truth there may be in the story which makes their attacks part of a scheme of vengeance for the torture and death of Ragnarr at the hands of Aelle, King of Northumbria. One incident is perhaps of interest in connexion with the family of Loðbrók. When Ubbi was fighting in Devonshire in 878 the English captured from him a raven-banner which, say the *Annals of St Neot*, was woven for the sons of Loðbrók by their sisters.

Though Alfred had secured an enlarged and independent kingdom, his troubles were not at an end, and during the years from 880–896 England suffered from attacks made by raiders issuing from their quarters on the Seine, the Somme and other Continental rivers. The Northumbrian and East Anglian settlers remained neutral on the whole, but they must have been much unsettled by the events of these years, and when they commenced raiding once more, Alfred built a fleet of vessels to meet them, which were both swifter and steadier than the Danish ships. After 896 the struggle between English and Danes was confined almost entirely to those already settled in the island, no fresh raiders being mentioned until 921.

During all this time the Vikings were almost continuously active on the Continent; raids on Frankish territory continued without cessation, and it was only on the Eider boundary that a permanent peace was established by a treaty between Louis the German and King Horic. In 845 a Danish fleet of some 120 vessels sailed up the Seine under the leadership of Reginherus, *i.e.* probably Ragnarr Loðbrók himself. Paris was destroyed and the Viking attack was only bought off by the payment of a large Danegeld. The years from 850–878 have been said, not without justice, to mark the high tide of Viking invasion in Western Frankish territory. We find Danish armies taking up more or less permanent quarters on the Rhine, the Scheldt, the Somme, the Seine, the Loire and the Garonne, prominent among their leaders being one Berno, or Björn Jarnsíða (Ironside), another son of Ragnarr Loðbrók. A curious light is thrown on the effect of these raids upon the peasantry by an incident in 859, when we hear of a rising of the populace between the Seine and the Loire in the hope of expelling the Danes. The annals are not quite clear as to whether it was the Frankish nobles or the Danes who crushed the rising, but the outbreak indicates dissatisfaction with the half-hearted defence of the country by the nobility.

In the years 859–862 a second great expedition to Spain and the Mediterranean took place. Sailing from the Seine under the leadership of Björn Jarnsíða and Hasting (O.N. Hásteinn), they made an unsuccessful attack on Galicia and sailed round the coast through the straits of Gibraltar. They attacked Nekur on the coast of Morocco. There was fierce fighting with the Moors but in the end the Vikings were victorious, and many of the "Blue-men," as they called the Moors, were ultimately carried off prisoners to Ireland, where we hear of their fate in the *Fragments of Irish Annals*. Returning to Spain they landed at Murcia and proceeded thence to the Balearic Islands. Ravaging these they made their way north to the French border, landed in Roussillon, and advanced inland as far as Arles-sur-Tech. Taking to their ships, they sailed north along the coast to the mouth of the Rhone and spent the winter on the Island of Camargue in the Rhone delta. Plundering the old Roman cities of Provence, they went up the Rhone as far as Valence. In the spring they sailed to Italy, where they captured several towns including Pisa and Luna, at the mouth of the Magra, south of the bay of Spezia. The conquest of Luna was famed both in Norman and Scandinavian tradition. It is represented as the crowning feat of the sons of Ragnarr Loðbrók, who captured it under the delusion that they had reached Rome itself. From Luna they sailed back through the straits of Gibraltar and finally returned to Brittany in the spring of 862. The Vikings had now all but encircled Europe with their raids, for it was in the year 865 that the Swedish Rôs (Russians) laid siege to Constantinople.

In France itself the tide began to turn by the end of 865. In November of that year the Vikings finally abandoned Aquitaine, and in the next year the Seine was for a time left free. The tide had now set towards England, and at the same time the Franks commenced fortifying their towns against Viking attack, a policy which was pursued a little later by Edward the Elder in England. For our knowledge of this period we have to rely almost entirely upon the chronicles of various monastic writers compiling their records in isolation from one another, so that it is almost impossible to trace any definite or general design in Viking attacks. The leaders change continually and almost the only constant figure is that Roric, brother of Harold, who was settled in

Friesland.   For some forty years he remained there, now in friendly, now in hostile relations with both Charles the Bald and Louis the German, and he does not disappear from our records until after 873. About the same time Horic the Younger must have died, for we find two new kings reigning simultaneously in Denmark, the brothers Sigefridus and Halbdenus.   Both were probably sons of Ragnarr Loðbrók, the former being the famous Sigurðr Snake-eye and the latter the already-mentioned Halfdanr.

In the year 879 the tide of invasion turned once more towards France, chiefly owing to two causes.   The great attack on England had failed or at least had led to a peaceful settlement, which furnished no outlet for Viking energy, while at the same time affairs in France were once more unsettled.   Charles the Bald died in 877, followed 18 months later by his son Louis the Stammerer, who left two youthful children, Louis and Carloman, and a posthumous son Charles.   Factions arose and the Vikings were never slow to hear and take advantage of them.   When a great fleet which had wintered at Fulham found no opening in England, it crossed to France.   There the young Louis won a decisive victory over it at Saucourt on the Somme, and the victory finds its record in the well-known *Ludwigslied*.   An attack by the Northmen on Saxony and the lower Rhine was more successful.   In a great fight which took place somewhere on the Lüneburg Heath 2 February 880, there fell Duke Bruno of Saxony together with two bishops, eleven counts and eighteen royal vassals.   In 882 the Emperor Charles the Fat came to terms with the Viking leaders, Sigefrid and Guðröðr.   King Guðröðr, who was probably a son of the Harold of Mayence, himself accepted Christianity and was granted lands on the lower Rhine, and at the same time undertook to defend Charles's territory from attack.   King Sigefrid retired with a heavy payment of money.   Guðröðr received his lands on much the same conditions as Charles the Simple granted Normandy to Rollo, but intriguing with the enemies of Charles he aroused hostility and was slain in 885.   He had thrown away the chance of establishing a Normandy in the Low Countries.   Viking rule was now brought to an end in Frisia, and henceforward we hear only of sporadic attacks which continued into the tenth century.   So also from 885 Saxony was free from attack, and when trouble was renewed in the tenth century the attack was not made by sea but across the Eider boundary.

The West Frankish kingdom was still in the midst of the storm. Louis III and Carloman and the local magnates offered a stout resistance, but it seemed impossible to throw off the yoke of the *here* which ravaged the whole country between the Rhine and the Loire. The contest culminated in the great siege of Paris by King Sigefrid in 885-7. The Viking army numbered some 40,000 men with 700 vessels, and it was only through the stout resistance of Count Odo, and Bishop Joscelin and the withdrawal of the Vikings to Burgundy by an arrangement with Charles the Fat, that the siege was raised. With the overthrow of Charles in 887 the West Frankish realm fell into anarchy, and the Vikings ravaged Burgundy and eastern France almost without a check, while Brittany and the Cotentin fared no better. Finally the great *here* concentrated its attack on the valley of the Scheldt. In the autumn of 891 they were defeated on the banks of the Dyle in Brabant by the new King Arnulf, and after more desultory fighting they sailed for England in the autumn of 892. They had been in France some thirteen years, ravaging and plundering, and now for the first time since 840 France was free of the Northmen. In England, after three years' hard fighting, the greater number settled down to a peaceful existence in East Anglia and Northumbria, but a few in whom the spirit of roving was still strong returned to the Seine in 896. Twenty-five years earlier the Vikings had seemed in a fair way to conquer Europe, but now the battle of Edington in England (878), the siege of Paris in France (885–7) and the battle of the Dyle in Germany (891), were significant of failure in these three kingdoms alike.

The West Frankish realm was weakened by the dissensions of the rival kings Odo and Charles the Simple, and soon all the old troubles were renewed. Unfortunately the Annals provide us with very meagre information about events during the next fifteen years, and we know almost nothing about the critical period immediately preceding the cession of Normandy to the Northmen. The Vikings would seem to have settled themselves in the lower basin of the Seine, with Rouen as their centre, and by 910 they appear under the leadership of the famous Rollo (O.N. Hrollaugr). This Viking was probably of Norse origin (the *Heimskringla* describes him as one Hrólfr, son of Rögnvaldr, earl of Möre), though the main body of the settlers were certainly Danes, and he had already made himself a name in England, where he was closely associated with Guthrum of East Anglia. He probably came to France soon after 896 and gradually became the chief person among that band of equals. For some time he carried on a hard struggle with Charles the Simple, and then, towards the end of 911, each party frankly recognised the other's strength. Charles could not oust the Northmen from the Seine valley, while they were unable permanently to extend their settlement, so at St Clair-sur-Epte it was agreed that the part of the Seine basin which includes the counties of Rouen, Lisieux and Evreux, together with the country lying between the rivers Bresle and Epte and the sea, should be left in the hands of the Northmen on condition that they defended the kingdom against attack, received baptism and did homage to Charles for their lands. To these were added in 924 the districts of Bayeux and Séez, and in 933 those of Avranches and Coutances, thus bringing the Normans right up to the Breton border. With the establishment of Normandy, Viking activity was practically at an end in the Frankish kingdom: there were still Northmen on the Loire who ravaged far inland, while the settlers in Normandy freely raided Brittany, but no fresh settlements were made and the Viking *here* had become a recognised part of the Frankish *ost*.

We must now turn our attention to the Danish settlements in England. We have seen that already by the year 880 they had attained the same measure of independence which was granted to Normandy in 911, but their later fortunes were by no means so peaceful or uneventful. The Danes in East Anglia, Mercia and Northumbria were not willing to confine themselves to their settlements, and soon Edward the Elder and his sister Aethelfleda, the "Lady of the Mercians," established a line of fortified towns in Southern Mercia preparatory to an advance on Danish territory. By the year 917 all was ready. Derby fell in that year and Leicester in 918 before the advance of Aethelfleda, while in the same years Northampton, Stamford and Nottingham were captured by Edward, and East Anglia made its submission. By the end of his reign Edward was master of the whole realm, including English, Danes and Norwegians. These last were settled chiefly in Northumbria, where we find towards the close of the ninth and in the early years of the tenth century a line of kings closely associated with the Norse kingdom of Dublin. The Norsemen were often in alliance with the Scots, and matters came to a crisis in 937 when a great confederation of Scots, Strathclyde Welsh, and Norsemen was formed against Aethelstan. The confederates were defeated in the famous battle of Brunanburh (perhaps the modern Birrenswark in Dumfriesshire), and England was freed from its greatest danger since the days of King Alfred and his struggle with Guthrum (O.N. Guðormr) and the sons of Ragnarr Loðbrók. The Norse leaders retired for a time, but trouble was renewed in 940 by an Anlaf (? Olaf Guðfriðson)[1]. Next year the famous Anlaf Sihtricsson (O.N. Olafr Sigtryggson), nicknamed "Cuaran," is found at York. He marched south and endeavoured to conquer the district of the Five Boroughs. King Edmund advanced to their help, and soon drove Anlaf out of Northern Mercia and relieved the Danish boroughs from Norse oppression. During the next twelve years Northumbria was in a state of anarchy. At times Anlaf was acknowledged as king, at others English sovereignty was recognised. Twice during this period Eric Blood-axe, son of Harold Fairhair, appeared as king, but was finally expelled in 954. Later Scandinavian tradition tells us that Aethelstan was on friendly terms with Harold Fairhair, and that when Eric was expelled from Norway in 934 he was welcomed to England by Aethelstan and given charge of Northumbria, where he ruled at York. Edmund was less favourably disposed towards Norwegians and appointed one Olaf in his stead. Ultimately Eric was defeated and killed by his rival. Eric may have been appointed to rule Northumbria after the defeat of Anlaf-Olaf at Brunanburh, while the appointment of Olaf as ruler of Northumbria may refer to the partition of England between Olaf and Edmund in 942. With the expulsion of

---

[1] These Anlafs are variously identified; but cf. *infra*, p. 368.

Eric in 954 (Olaf had already retired to Dublin) Norse rule in Northumbria was at an end.   Henceforward that district was directly under the rule of the English king, and earls were appointed in his name.

We have seen that during these years there was intimate connexion between the Norsemen in Ireland and Northumbria, and that the kings of Northumbria often ruled in Dublin at the same time.   Viking rule in Ireland was in a state of flux.   The chief centres of influence were Dublin and Limerick, but their rulers were often at variance with one another and a succession of great Irish leaders, Niall Glundubh, Muirchertach and Brian Borumha (Boru), made bold and often successful attacks on the Viking strongholds.   Brian was the greatest and most famous of these leaders, and when he became chief king of all Ireland, he built a great fleet and received tribute from Northmen and Irish alike.   His power was threatened by the treachery of his wife Gormflaith, who intrigued with her brother Maelmordha, King of Leinster, and Sigtryggr of the Silken Beard, King of Dublin, against Brian.   A great confederacy of the western Vikings was formed, including Sigurðr, the earl of the Orkneys, and men from the Shetlands, the Western Islands, Man and Scandinavian settlements on the Continent.   Dublin was the rendezvous and thither the great army gathered by Palm Sunday 1014.   Brian had collected a vast army, including Vikings from Limerick, and on Good Friday the two forces met in the decisive battle of Clontarf, just north of Dublin.   For some time the fortune of battle wavered, both Brian and Sigurðr fell, but in the end the Irish were completely victorious, and the Vikings had lost their last and greatest fight in Ireland.   They were not expelled from their settlements, but henceforward they led a peaceful existence under Irish authority and the Norse kingdoms of Dublin, Limerick and other cities either lost all power or ceased to exist.

After the fall of the Northumbrian kingdom in 954 England had peace for some five-and-twenty years, especially under the strong rule of Edgar, but with the weak Aethelred II troubles were renewed and from 980 onwards the whole of the English coast was open to attack.   These raids were the result of a fresh outburst of Viking activity over the whole of the British Isles.   Danes and Norsemen united under one banner and their leader was the famous Olaf Tryggvason.   In 991 after ravaging the east coast Olaf engaged Brihtnoth, the ealdorman of East Anglia, near Maldon.   The struggle was heroic and gave occasion to one of the finest of Old English poems, but Brihtnoth fell, and an ignominious peace was made whereby for the first time since the days of Alfred "Danegeld" was paid to buy off Viking attacks.   Svein Forkbeard now united forces with Olaf and together they besieged London in 994: the siege was a failure, but all southern England was harried and once more a heavy Danegeld had to be paid.   In 995 Olaf went to Norway hoping to gain the kingdom by the overthrow of the tyranny of Earl Hákon, while Svein returned to Denmark. The raids continued but England saw nothing more of King Svein until he returned in 1003 to avenge the ill-advised massacre of St Brice's day. Year after year the kingdom was ravaged, Danegeld after Danegeld was paid, until in 1013 Aethelred fled to Normandy and Svein became King of all England. A few months later he died suddenly at Gainsborough in Lincolnshire (February 1014). His English realm went to his younger son Knut. On the death of Aethelred in 1016, his son Edmund Ironside offered so stout a resistance that for a few months, until his death by treachery, he compelled Knut to share the realm with him. Knut then ruled alone, firmly and well until his death in 1035, having succeeded to the Danish throne also in 1018. On his death the succession was not settled but, after some difficulty, Harold Harefoot succeeded his father in England. He was succeeded in 1040 by his brother Harthacnut (O.N. Harðacnútr), but neither king was of the same stamp as their father and they were both overshadowed by the great Godwin, Earl of Wessex. When Harthacnut died in 1042 the male line in descent from Knut was extinct and, though some of the Danes were in favour of choosing Knut's sister's son Svein, Godwin secured the election of Edward the Confessor, who had been recalled from Normandy and highly honoured by Harthacnut himself. With the accession of Edward, Danish rule in England was at an end, and never afterwards was there any serious question of a Scandinavian kingship either in or over England.

We have now traced the story of Viking activity in its chief centres in the British Isles and the mainland of Europe. A word remains to be said about other settlements in Western Europe, in the Orkneys, the Shetlands, the Western Islands (or as the Norsemen called them "Suðreyjar" (*i.e.* Sodor), the southern islands) and Man, and the Scottish mainland, and then we must turn our attention to Eastern Europe, to the famous Jómsviking settlement in North Germany and to the important but little known movements of the Vikings through Russia down to the shores of the Mediterranean. We have seen how early the Shetlands were settled, and there is no doubt that it was not long before Vikings made their way by the Orkneys round the coast of Scotland to the Hebrides. From the Orkneys settlements were made in Sutherland and Caithness, while Galloway (possibly the land of the Gall-Gaedhil, the foreign Irish) was settled from the Hebrides. In the ninth century the Norse element in the Hebrides was already so strong that the Irish called the islands Innsi Gall (*i.e.* the islands of the foreigners) and their inhabitants were known as the Gall-Gaedhil. Olaf the White and Ívarr made more than one expedition from Ireland to the lowlands of Scotland, and the former was married to Auðr the daughter of Ketill Flat-nose, who had made himself the greatest chieftain in the Western Islands. When Harold Fairhair won his victory at Hafrsfjord he felt that his power would still be insecure unless he gained the submission of these Vikings who belonged to the great families in rivalry with him. He made therefore a mighty expedition to the Shetlands, the Orkneys and the west coast of Scotland, received their submission and gave the Northern Islands to Sigurðr, brother of Rögnvaldr, earl of Möre, as his vassal. Sigurðr's successor Einar, known as Turf Einar because he first taught the islanders to cut peat for fuel, founded a long line of Orkney earls. Warrior and skald, he came into collision with Harold Fairhair, but made his peace on promise of a heavy fine. When the peasants declared themselves unable to pay it, Einar paid it himself and received in return all the *óðal* (the holdings of the freeholders) as his own property. The most famous of the Orkney earls was Sigurðr Loðvesson, who succeeded c. 980. Though he acknowledged the overlordship of Earl Hákon, he ruled with almost independent power, and made himself popular by the return of the *óðal*. After a reign of thirty years he fell fighting for the Viking cause at Clontarf in 1014. Of the Vikings in the Western Islands from Lewis to the Isle of Man we have less definite and continuous record. There was a line of kings in the tenth century, of whom the most famous were Maccus or Magnus and Guðröðr, the son of one Harold. They are found ruling with certain officers known as "lawmen" by their side. The Isle of Man, which had kings of its own, was at times under their authority, at others under that of the kingdom of Dublin. It was probably from the Isle of Man that the extensive Norse settlements in Cumberland and Westmorland were made, and either from here or from Ireland came the various Viking raiders who throughout the tenth century made attacks on Wales. There they founded no permanent kingdom, but left a mark in place nomenclature along the coast from Anglesey to Pembrokeshire and in some districts of South Wales.

From the days of Guðröðr in the beginning of the ninth century to those of Harold Gormson (Bluetooth) in the middle of the tenth, Denmark had paid little heed to her Slavonic neighbours, but the rivalry between Harold Gormson and the Emperor Otto probably turned the Danish king's attention eastwards, and it was in his days that the great Viking settlement of Jómsborg was established at the mouth of the Oder. For many years there had been an important trading centre at Julin on the island of Wollin, where merchants from Scandinavia, Saxony and Russia were settled. Large finds of Byzantine and Arabic coins belonging to the tenth century have been made both in Denmark and in Wollin, bearing witness to the extensive trade which passed through Julin between Denmark and the Orient, using as its high road the broad stream of the Oder and the great Russian rivers. To secure to Denmark its full share in the products of the rich lands south of the Baltic and in the trade with the East, Harold built the fortified town of Jómsborg close to Julin and established there a famous Viking community. He gave them certain laws, and we probably find their substance in the laws given by Palnatóki to his followers in the unhistorical account of the founding of Jómsborg given in *Jómsvíkingasaga* No one under 18 or over 50 was admitted to their fellowship, no woman was allowed in their town, and none of the warriors might be absent for more than three days. They were bound by oaths of fidelity to one another and each must avenge the fall of any of his companions. No word of fear was allowed and all outside news must in the first place be told to their leader. All plunder was divided by lot among the community. The harbour of Jómsborg could shelter a fleet of 300 vessels and was protected by a mole with twelve iron gates. The Jómsvikings played an important part in the affairs of Denmark and Norway in the late tenth and early eleventh centuries, and made many Viking expeditions both in Baltic lands and in the West. In 1043 their stronghold was destroyed by Magnus the Good of Norway. Other Vikings from Denmark made raids still further east than Jómsborg, but the true Viking conquest of those districts was due not to the Danes but to the Swedes.

In the chronicle of the Russian monk Nestor (*c.* 1100) we read how in the middle of the ninth century certain Varangians came from beyond the sea and that one band of them, the Rus, was soon invited to rule among the Slavs and put an end to their mutual quarrels. Their leader Rurik (O.N. Hrœrekr) settled in Novgorod, while two of his men, Askol'd (O.N. Höskuldr) and Dir (O.N. Dyri), sailed down the Dnieper and settled in Kiev. These events probably took place in the half century preceding 862. Twenty years later Kiev was conquered by Rurik's successor Olég (O.N. Helgi), and Kiev, the mother of all Russian towns, was henceforward the capital of the Russian state. From Kiev the Rus advanced down the Dnieper and in 865 ravaged the shores of the Black Sea (soon to be known as the Russian Sea) and the Sea of Marmora. They appeared with a fleet of 200 vessels before Constantinople, but the city was saved by a sudden storm and the greater part of the fleet of the "Rhôs," as Byzantine historians call them, was destroyed. Olég made a more successful attack in 907 with a fleet of 2000 vessels, and the Greeks were forced to pay a heavy ransom. Attacks of this kind continued down to the middle of the eleventh century. At the same time the Rus secured valuable trading privileges from the Eastern emperors and exchanged furs, slaves and honey for the luxuries of the East. From Arab writers we hear of these Rus in districts still further east, on the banks of the Volga and the shores of the Caspian.

Though the point has been hotly contested by Slavonic patriots, there can be no doubt that these Rhos or Rus are really Swedish Vikings. Some of them accompanied a Greek embassy to the Emperor Louis the Pious in 839 and, though they called themselves Rhos, Louis made inquiries and found that they were really of Swedish nationality. They were detained for some time under suspicion of being spies: the Emperor no doubt feared some fresh design against the Empire on the part of the Northmen. A few years later, when the

Vikings attacked Seville (844), an Arab writer calls them Rūs, using probably a name for the Vikings which was already well known in the East.   The descriptions of the life of the ancient Rus, which we find in Greek and Arabic writers, tally in remarkable fashion with those of the Vikings in the West, and archaeological and philological evidence tends to strengthen the belief that their original home was in Scandinavia. Certain types of fibulae found in Western Russia are derived from Scandinavia, and the hoards of Anglo-Saxon pennies and sceatts found there are probably our Danegeld.   One runic inscription, belonging to the eleventh century and shewing evidence of connexion with Gothland, has been found in a burial mound in Berezan, an island at the mouth of the Dnieper.   Professor Braun says that no others have been found because of the rarity of suitable stone.   The names of the Dnieper rapids as given in their Russian form (side by side with the Slavonic) by Constantine Porphyrogenitus (*c.* 950) are undoubtedly Scandinavian in origin.   Exactly how the term Rus came to be applied to the Swedish nation (or a part of it) has been much disputed[1].   Still more difficult is the question of the origin of the term Varangian or Variag, to use the Russian form.   We have seen that it is applied to the whole of the nation of whom the Rus formed part.   It is also given to the guard of the Byzantine emperors.   It is probable that the term Varangians was first applied to the whole of the Scandinavian peoples, but more especially to the Swedes with whom the Slavs had chiefly to deal, and later to the Emperor's guard recruited from these hardy Northerners.   Most famous of such Varangians was the great Harold Hardrada, who after a career of adventure in the East ultimately fell at Stamford Bridge in 1066.

Of the later history of the Scandinavians in Russia we know little, but it is probable that by the year 1000 they were largely Slavised and by the end of the eleventh century they were entirely absorbed by the native element.

We have now traced the main outlines of Viking activity in eastern and western Europe: it remains to say something of their civilisation and its influence on the development of the various countries in which they formed settlements.

During the years of Viking activity the Scandinavian peoples stood at a critical period in the history of their civilisation: side by side with a large element of primitive barbarism we find certain well-developed forms of civilisation, while throughout their activity the Vikings shewed an eager understanding and appreciation of the culture of the older civilisations then prevailing in western Europe.   This strange blend of barbarism and culture finds its clearest illustration in their daily life and in the slow and halting passage from heathendom to Christianity.

---

[1] The form *Rus* is probably the Slavonic version of the Finnish *Ruotsi*, the name given by the Finns to the Swedes generally, and taken from the district of Uppland, known as *Roþr*, with which they were most familiar.

Dr Alexander Bugge has pointed out for us how many characteristic features of Viking life find their closest parallel among uncivilised peoples of the ancient or of the modern world. Their cruelty in warfare finds illustration in their custom of exposing the heads of their enemies outside their camps and towns, or in the strange picture given us in some Irish annals of Danes cooking their food on the field of battle on spits stuck in the bodies of their fallen foes. The custom of human sacrifice was fairly common, while that of cutting the blood-eagle in the back of the fallen foe is well known from the vengeance for their father taken by the sons of Ragnarr Loðbrók. Children were not spared in warfare and were often tossed on the spears of their foes. A curious survival of primitive habit is found in the famous Berserk fury, when men in the heat of battle were seized with sudden madness and, according to the popular belief, received a double portion of strength and lost all sense of bodily pain. There is of course much that is superstitious in this idea, but it finds its parallel in the "running amok" of the races of the Malay peninsula. Side by side with these traits of primitive barbarism we find certain well-developed forms of culture, an extensive commerce, a mastery of the whole art of shipbuilding, and great artistic skill, shewn not only in articles of personal adornment but also in the sculptured memorial stones to be found from Gothland in the East to Man in the West. In warfare their cavalry were skilled, and they understood the construction of siege engines with the whole art of fortification. Above all the Northmen had a genius for law, and few early communities shew their aptitude in the making of laws or such strictness in their observance.

The passage from heathendom to Christianity at this critical period is in some ways even more interesting. We have already seen how in the middle years of the ninth century Christianity was preached in Denmark and Sweden, but it had little effect on the main body of the nations concerned. The best evidence of this is to be found perhaps in the fact that it is in all probability to the ninth and tenth centuries that we owe the poems of the elder Edda, the main source of our knowledge of Old Norse mythology and cosmogony. It is true, no doubt, that in some of these poems we find a note of detachment, touches of irony and even of burlesque, which remind us that the belief in the old gods is passing away, but in the great body of those which deal with the world of the Aesir, there is no question of fading beliefs or of insincere statement. The greater number of the Vikings were undoubted heathen, and like the impious Onlafbald when defying the power of St Cuthbert would have sworn by their great gods Thor and Othin. When the Danes made peace with Alfred in 876 they swore an oath on the holy ring, which would be found on the altar of every heathen temple: such a ring sacred to Thor was taken by the Irish from a temple in Dublin in 996. There was a grove sacred to Thor just north of Dublin and place-names throughout the British Isles and in Normandy bear witness to the worship of this god. At the same time, in religion as in everything else, the Vikings shewed themselves very ready to seize new ideas and, more especially, to avail themselves of any advantages which adhesion to the Christian religion might give. Scandinavian merchants settled in the various European countries were often "prime-signed," *i.e.* received the sign of the cross, preliminary to baptism, which raised them to the rank of catechumens and enabled them to live in trading and social intercourse with Christians, while they did not necessarily proceed to the full renunciation of their heathen faith. Even in the ninth century, when the Danes were fighting the Norsemen in Ireland, we hear how they invoked the aid of St Patrick, thinking that he must take vengeance on those who had done him such injury. When victorious they gave him large offerings, for " the Danes were a people with a certain piety, whereby they could refrain from flesh and from women for a time." As was to be expected in a time of transition from one faith to another, superstition was rife and more than once the Viking hosts fell a prey to it. When the army of Ragnarr Loðbrók was besieging Paris in 845 his followers were attacked by a mysterious sickness: prayer to the heathen gods was unsuccessful, but when, on the advice of a Christian prisoner, they prayed to his God, wisely abstaining at the same time from flesh and mead, the plague was removed. The blending of the old and new is happily illustrated in the sepulchral stones of the Isle of Man and Gothland: here we have stones in the shape of a cross, or with the sign of the cross on them, decorated with scenes from Valhalla or with an inscription praying at the same time for the repose of the dead man's soul and that God may betray those who betrayed him. More than once do we hear of men who believed neither in the heathen gods nor in Christ and had faith in nought but their own strength: the nickname " the godless " is by no means unfrequent among the settlers in Iceland. Throughout the period, however, Christianity made steady advance: by the year 921 we find the Vikings sparing hospitals and churches when sacking Armagh; the great king Olaf Cuaran, who died in 981, spent his old age as a monk in Iona; at one time in the tenth century the primates of York and Canterbury were both of Scandinavian family, and in the later tenth and early eleventh centuries the Roman Church had no more faithful sons than the Normans.

Their general philosophy of life was that every man must rely on himself and his own wisdom; he must place no reliance on others, least of all upon women. The great aim in life is to attain fame and fair speech from men after death. Though their beliefs were strongly tinged with fatalism, this brought no weakening of character or gloom of outlook. "Joyous and happy must every man be until death comes upon him," is the counsel of *Hávamál*, and the highest ideal of the end of life for the hero is found in the picture of Ragnarr Loðbrók who when tortured in the snake-pit goes laughing to his death. With their enemies the Vikings had an evil reputation for cunning and deceit, but the incidents cited in illustration (such as the feigned desire for baptism on the part of a dying leader, which led to the capture of Luna, and the frequent mention of feigned retreats) hardly support this: the enemy were outwitted rather than deceived. Two common but widely different aspects of Viking character are reflected in the portraiture of their two chief gods; on the one side Othin (Odin), whose common epithets are " the wise, the prudent, the sagacious," on the other, Thor, endowed with mighty strength, but less polished and refined. The besetting sins of the Vikings were too great love of wine and women. The rich vine-lands of the Rhine were ceded to the Vikings at their special request, in 885, and one of the best known examples of Viking cruelty is the murder of Archbishop Aelfheah (Alphege) at a drunken orgie in 1012, when he was pelted to death with the skulls of oxen slaughtered for the feast. Many are the references to their immorality. Wandering from country to country they often had wives in each and polygamy prevailed, at least among the leaders. From Ireland in the west to Russia in the east the same story is told. In Ireland we hear of what would seem to be harems for women, while in Russia we are told of the Grand Duke Vladimir, great grandson of Rurik, the founder of the Russian kingdom, that he had more than 800 concubines. Such excesses were unknown in Scandinavia itself. Legitimate wives were esteemed and took part in the national life to an unusual extent. Women at times took part in fighting, and heroic figures are found in the sagas and other historical records: such are Ota (Auðr), the wife of Turgeis, who, as a *völva* or prophetess, gave audience on the high altar at Clonmacnois, and Auðr the Deep-minded, wife of Olaf the White, whose figure stands out clear among the early settlers in Iceland.

In outward appearance the Vikings were marked by a love of "purple and fine raiment." Foreign, and more especially English, clothing was much sought after, and when in 968 the Irish plundered Limerick we hear how they carried off from the Norsemen " their choicest possessions, their beautiful foreign saddles, their gold and silver, their woven cloths of every kind and colour, their silk and satin raiment, beauteous and variegated, both scarlet and green." From John of Wallingford we learn how much attention the Vikings paid to the care of the body, indulging in Sabbath baths and daily hair-combing. The graves of the period have often yielded rich finds of ornaments in silver and bronze, and the geographical distribution of the famous Viking brooches, oval and convex in shape, can be used as an index of the extent of the conquests of the Northmen. The style of decoration is that derived from the interweaving of heads and limbs of animals which is found in Northern Europe in the preceding age, but the influence of Irish art is now often discernible, more especially in the use of spiral and interlacing designs. English and Carolingian influences are also to be traced. The same style of ornamentation is to be found in the memorial stones, as for example in the famous Jellinge stone at the tomb of Gorm the Old in Jutland. Their houses were wooden but often richly decorated with carvings and tapestries. In the latter half of the tenth century we hear how the house of Olaf the Peacock in Iceland was decorated with scenes from the legends of gods and heroes, such as the fight of Loki and Heimdallr, Thor's fishing, and Balder's funeral. Traces of tapestry hangings are found in grave-chambers. The dead chief was often buried in his ship, and ship-graves have been found not only in Norway but also at Groix in Brittany. In Denmark grave-chambers of wood seem to take the place of ship-graves.

Of their ships we know a good deal both from the sagas and from archaeological finds. The Oseberg ship is a vessel for time of peace and coast-navigation only, but in the Gokstad ship we have an example of the ordinary war vessel. It dates from about 900, is of oak, clinker-built, with seats for 16 pairs of rowers, 78 ft. long and 16 ft. broad amidships, with the rudder at the side. The gunwale was decorated with shields painted alternately black and gold, and there was a single sail. In the course of the Viking period their size was greatly increased and in the famous dragon- and snake-boats of Olaf Tryggvason and Knut the Great we hear of 34 and even 60 pairs of oars. The trading vessels probably differed very little from those of war, just as the line of division between merchant and Viking was often a very thin one. Time and again we read how, when merchants visited a foreign land, they arranged a definite time for the conclusion of their business and agreed after that to treat each other as enemies. The most remarkable feature about the Vikings as sailors was the fearless way in which they crossed the open sea, going boldly on such stormy journeys as those to the Hebrides and Ireland, to Greenland, and even to Vinland or America. Hitherto, seamen both in peace and war had confined themselves as much as possible to coasting voyages. The sea was indeed their element, and the phrase which William of Malmesbury uses (quoting probably from an old poem) when describing the failure (after four days' trial) on the part of Guðfrið of Northumbria to settle down at the court of King Aethelstan, "he returned to piracy as a fish to the sea," is probably as true as it is picturesque.

The chief trading centres in Scandinavia itself were Skiringssalr on the Vík in Norway, Hedeby-Slesvík in Denmark, Bjørkø, Sigtuna and Lund in Sweden, besides a great market in Bohuslän on the Götaelv where the three kingdoms met. The chief articles of export were furs, horses, wool and flesh: those of import would consist chiefly in articles of luxury, whether for clothing or ornament. The slave-trade also was of the highest importance: one incident may be mentioned for the vivid light which it sheds on the international character of Viking trade. Once, in the market on the Götaelv, the Icelander Höskuldr bought a female slave from the merchant Gille (a Celtic name), surnamed the Russian (because of his journeys to that country). The slave proved to be an Irish king's daughter made captive by Viking raiders. The Scandinavian countries, like Rome, are very rich in Anglo-Saxon coins, and though many of these must represent our Danegeld, the fact that they are most frequent in Eastern Sweden, on the shores of Lake Mälar and in the neighbourhood of the great waterways connecting Sweden and the Baltic, but above all on the islands of Öland and Gothland, whence, in all probability, very few of the Viking raiders came, would seem to shew that there was extensive peaceful intercourse with England in Viking days. Yet more interesting are the frequent finds of Oriental coins. They first made their way to Scandinavia about the end of the ninth century, and are most common in Sweden. There can be no doubt that the vast majority of these coins reached Sweden overland through Russia, where extensive finds of Arabian coins mark the route along which trade at that time travelled from Asia to the north. The greater number of these coins were minted at Samarcand and Bagdad.

In social organisation the Viking communities were aristocratic. The famous answer of the followers of Rollo when asked who was their lord: "We have no lord, we are all equal," was essentially true, but with their practical genius the Vikings realised that leadership was necessary if any military success was to be gained, and we find throughout their history a series of able leaders, sometimes holding the title of *jarl*, but, if of royal birth, commonly known as kings. That the title did not have its full modern connotation is evident from their numbers and from the frequency with which they changed. When, however, the Vikings established permanent settlements, hereditary kingship became common, and royal houses bore sway in Dublin and other Irish towns: thence a hereditary line of kings was introduced into Northumbria. The rulership of Normandy was hereditary and so possibly was the kingship in East Anglia, but in the districts grouped round the Five Boroughs the organisation was of a different kind, the chief authority resting with the Lawmen. We find frequent mention of these Lawmen both in Scandinavia itself and in those countries where Scandinavian influence prevailed. Originally men skilled in the law, who could state and interpret it when required, they often presided in the Thing or popular assembly and represented the local or provincial community as against the king or his officers, though they do not themselves seem to have exercised judicial functions. They are usually mentioned in the plural number and probably acted as a collective body. In England and the Western Islands they attained a position of yet greater importance. In Man and the Hebrides they became actual chieftains and are mentioned side by side with the kings, while it is probable that they were the chief judicial authorities in the aristocratic organisation of the Five Boroughs and other parts of the Danelaw. They were usually twelve in number, and their presence may be definitely traced in Cambridge, Stamford, Lincoln, York and Chester. The office would seem as a rule to have been hereditary.

The influence of the Vikings varied from country to country, not only according to the political and social condition of the lands in which they settled, but also to some extent according to the nation from which they came. In Ireland the settlements were chiefly Norse, though there is some evidence for the presence of Danes in Cork and Limerick. Here their influence was concentrated in certain important towns on the coast (Dublin, Wexford, Waterford, and the two already mentioned) and the districts immediately surrounding them. Scandinavian influence on Irish place-names is confined almost entirely to these localities and to the harbours and islands which must from time to time have given shelter to their fleets. Intermarriage between the Irish and the Norse settlers began at a very early date, and interesting evidence of it is found in the large numbers of Irish names in the genealogies of the chief Icelandic families preserved in *Landnamabók*. Such intermarriage was frequent, but the strength of the clan system would seem to have enabled the races to continue distinct. Norse words are very rare in Irish, and even when the old Norse kingdoms were shorn of their glory and reduced to dependence, the " Ostmen," as they were called, remained an entirely distinct element in the community, and frequent mention is made of them in the records of the great towns. They still survived at the time of the English conquest, and often both claimed and received privileges entirely different from those accorded to the natives or to the English settlers. In Ireland as in other countries there is no doubt that the Vikings did much harm to religion and to learning, but at the same time they strengthened town-life and developed trade. For many years the trade of Ireland was largely in Scandinavian hands.

Norse influence in Scotland was great, but varied much from place to place. The Orkneys and Shetlands are thoroughly Norse. They formed part of the Norwegian kingdom till 1468, and Norse speech lingered on until the close of the eighteenth century. Place-names are almost entirely of Norse origin and the dialect is full of Norse words. In the system of landholding the udallers are an interesting survival of the old Norse freeholders, whose *óðal* was held on precisely the same free tenure as the Scotch *udal*. The Hebrides were also largely influenced by the Vikings, and it was not till 1266 that Magnus Hákonson renounced all claims of Norway to the islands and to Man. Place-nomenclature both in the names of the islands themselves and of their physical features shews a strong Norse element, and there are many Norse words in the Gaelic of the islands and of the mainland. These words have undergone such extensive changes and corruption in a language so different from their original source that their recognition is a difficult problem. There is at present perhaps a danger of exaggerating this element, the existence of which was long overlooked. Similarly, affinities have been traced between Scandinavian and Gaelic popular tales and folk-lore, but this evidence is of doubtful value to the student of history. As was to be expected, the chief traces of Viking influence on the mainland are to be found in the modern counties of Sutherland (the district south of the Orkneys was so called by the Norsemen), Caithness, Ross and Cromarty, which were for a long time under the authority of the Orkney earls, and in Galloway, which was naturally exposed to attacks from the powerful Norse settlements in Man. The name of this district (perhaps derived from Gall-Gaedhil) possibly bears witness, as we have seen, to the mixed race resulting from their presence, and the evidence of place-names confirms it. In the history of Scotland, as a whole, it is to be remembered that it was the weakening of Pictish power under Norse attack which paved the way for the unification of the land under the rule of Kenneth Mac Alpin.

The Isle of Man bears many and deep marks of its Norse occupation. Here as in the Hebrides the occupation was long and continuous. Attacked by Vikings from the early years of the ninth century, it came first under the rule of the kingdom of Dublin and then of the earls of Orkney. The successors of Godred Crovan, who conquered the island in 1079, took the title of king and were kings both of Man and the Isles (*i.e.* the Hebrides). The chief witnesses to Norse rule are the Manx legal system and the sculptured stones scattered about the island. The highest executive and legislative authority in the island (after the Governor) is still the Tynwald Court, whose name goes back to the Old Norse *þingvöllr* (the open plain where the popular assembly met), and the House of Keys, which is the oldest division of the court, consisted originally of 24 members (a duodecimal notation which constantly recurs in Scandinavian law and polity) chosen by co-option and for life, the office being generally, as a matter of fact, hereditary. These men who have the "keys of the law" in their bosom resemble closely the Lawmen, of whom mention has already been made. All laws to be valid must still be announced from the Tynwald Hill, which corresponds to the *lögberg* or law-hill in the Icelandic *allthing*. When the assembly is held the coroner "fences the court" against all disturbance or disorder, just as in the old Norwegian Gula-thing we hear of *vé-bönd* or sanctuary-ropes drawn around the assembly. Of the sculptured stones we have already spoken more than once: suffice it to say here that in addition to runic inscriptions they often give us pictorial representations of the great scenes in myth and legend, such as the fight of Odin with Fenrir's Wolf and the slaying of the serpent Fafnir by Sigurór. In many ways Man is the district of the British Isles in which we can get closest to the life of the old Viking days.

Cumberland and Westmorland stand somewhat apart from the rest of England in the matter of Viking influence, for they were fairly certainly

colonised by Norsemen from Man and the islands.   The greater number
of the place-names are purely Scandinavian and the local dialects are full
of terms of similar origin.   It is probable that such parts of Lancashire
as shew Viking influence, viz. Furness and Lancashire north of the
Ribble, should be grouped with these districts; south of that river their
influence on place-nomenclature is slight, except on the coast, where we
have evidence of a series of Viking settlements extending to and including
the Wirral in Cheshire.   A twelfth-century runic inscription survives at
Loppergarth in Furness, and the Gosforth cross in Cumberland bears
heathen as well as Christian sculptures.   The parallel existence of hundred
and wapentake and the carucal assessment in Domesday warn us that we
must not underrate the importance of Norse influence.

The Scandinavian kingdom of Northumbria must have been much
smaller than the earlier realm of that name.   Northumberland shews
but few traces of Viking influence, and it is not till we reach Teesdale
that it becomes strongly marked.   From here to the Humber place-
nomenclature and dialect, ridings and wapentakes, carucates and duodecimal notation in the Domesday assessments, bear witness to their
presence from the shores of the North Sea right up to the Pennines.

For the extent and character of the Viking settlements in the district
of the Five Boroughs we have not only the usual (and often somewhat
unsatisfactory) tests of place-names and dialects, ancient and modern,
but also a far more accurate index in the facts recorded in the Domesday
assessment of the eleventh century.   For the northern counties this is
largely non-existent or too scanty to be of any great value, but here it
has its usual fulness of detail.   The chief tests derived from this source
with their respective applications are as follows : (1) The use of the
Danish " wapentake " as the chief division of the county in place of
the English " hundred."   This is found in Derbyshire (with one exception on its southern border), Nottinghamshire, Lincolnshire (with
certain exceptions along the sea-coast which have a curious and unexplained parallel in the Domesday divisions of Yorkshire), Leicestershire, Rutland and one district of Northamptonshire now included in
Rutland.   (2) The assessment by carucates in multiples and sub-
multiples of twelve, which is characteristic of the Danelaw, as opposed
to that by hides arranged on a decimal system.   This we find in the shires
of Derby, Nottingham, Lincoln, Leicester and Rutland (with the above
exception).   In the two N.E. hundreds of Northamptonshire there are also
traces of a duodecimal assessment.   (3) The use of the ore of $16d.$ instead
of that of $20d.$ is found in Derbyshire, Nottinghamshire, Lincolnshire and
Lancashire.   In Leicestershire we are told on the other hand that the
ore was of $20d.$ (4) In Lincolnshire, Nottinghamshire, Derbyshire (and
Yorkshire) we have traces of the use of the Danish " long " hundred
($= 120$), *e.g.* the fine for breaking the king's peace is £8 (*i.e.* 120 ores).
These tests establish Derbyshire, Nottinghamshire, Lincolnshire (Lincoln

and Stamford), Leicestershire and (probably) the whole of Rutland (Stamford), as belonging to the Five Boroughs, and place-names confirm this evidence. The counties to the west and south answer none of the tests, and there is only a slight sprinkling of Danish names in Staffordshire and Warwickshire on their eastern borders. Northamptonshire furnishes a difficulty. Except in the extreme north-east it fails to pass our tests, but Danish place-nomenclature is strongly evident, though it shades off somewhat to the S.W. It resembles Danish East Anglia rather than the district of the Five Boroughs, and it is possible that the boundary of Guthrum's kingdom, which is only carried as far as Stony Stratford in the peace of Alfred and Guthrum, really ran along Watling Street for a few miles, giving two-thirds of that county to the East Anglian realm[1]. While the judicial authority was in the hands of the Lawmen in the Five Boroughs, we hear at the same time of *jarls* in these towns and in Northampton and other places, who lead their forces to war and sign royal charters and documents. Probably to the Danes we owe the organisation of the modern counties of Derby, Leicester, Nottingham, Lincoln (and Stamford), Northampton, Bedford, Cambridge and Hertford.

In East Anglia the tests which we used for the Five Boroughs fail, and we are left with the boundaries of Guthrum's kingdom, certain evidence from place-names, and other miscellaneous facts. A few *holmes* in Bedfordshire, some *holmes*, *biggins* and *tofts* in Hertfordshire, Cambridgeshire, and Huntingdonshire, a "Danish" hundred in Hertfordshire, are almost all the evidence from place-names. Essex shews a few, Suffolk more traces of Danes on the coast, and the latter county has some traces inland, especially in the north. Norfolk is strongly Danish, even if we overlook the doubtful "thorpes," which are so abundant here. The *Historia Eliensis* and other documents tend to shew the presence of a strong Danish element in the population and social organisation of the district around Cambridge. As a whole, however, the Viking impress on East Anglia is much less deep than on Mercia. The difference rests probably on a difference of original organisation, but it is impossible now to define it.

Other features of interest in our social system due to Viking influence may be observed from a study of Domesday and other authorities. Attention has often been called to the number of freeholders in the Danelaw, and it would seem that Lincolnshire, Leicestershire and Norfolk more especially had not been feudalised to any great extent before the Norman conquest. In the other counties the influence of southern custom is more apparent. The "holds" of Northumbria, who rank next after the earls, and the "drengs" of Cumberland, Westmorland, Northumberland and Durham, are undoubtedly of Scandinavian origin. The

---

[1] The Welland is so natural a border that it is very unlikely English authority really came north of it. The hides must remain an unexplained difficulty.

" socmen," a class of free peasants, are most numerous in the Five Boroughs and East Anglia and are only found sporadically in other places.

Our legal system shews again and again the influence of Scandinavian law and custom. The word "law" itself is a Scandinavian term in contrast to the English "doom." We have already mentioned the Lawmen: still more interesting are the "Twelve senior thanes" of Aethelred's laws for the Five Boroughs enacted at Wantage in 997. They have to come forward in the court of every wapentake and to swear that they will not accuse any innocent man or conceal any guilty one. The exact force of this enactment has been a matter of dispute, but there can be little doubt that (in the words of Vinogradoff) such a custom "prepared the way for the indictment jury of the twelfth century." In criminal law the Danes introduced a new conception of crime. The idea of honour in the relationship of members of a military society to one another led to the appearance of a group of crimes whose perpetrators are branded as *nithings*, men unworthy of comradeship with others and, more especially, with their fellow warriors. In the general life of the nation the Danes placed an effective check on learning and literature except during the heroic activities of Alfred the Great, but on the other hand we probably owe to them an extensive development of town-life and of trade and the revival of English naval power. Disastrous as were the Danish wars, there can be little doubt that the Danish settlements were for the ultimate good of the nation.

In the Frankish Empire the only permanent settlement was in Normandy. Scandinavian influence was strong in Frisia and the lower basin of the Rhine (Dorestad was the centre of their commercial activity), but there is no question of influence on law, social organisation or government. In Normandy on the other hand we have a powerful and almost independent State with a full Viking organisation. The history of the Normans does not belong to this chapter. Suffice it to say here that perhaps more than any other of the Vikings they shewed themselves readily able to assimilate themselves to their surroundings, and they were soon Gallicised; nevertheless law and custom, dialect and place-names, still shew their presence clearly.

Of Scandinavian influence in Eastern Europe little can be said owing to our lack of knowledge. Attempts have been made to distinguish Scandinavian elements in the old Russian law and language but without any very definite results, and we must confine ourselves to the points mentioned earlier.

Nothing has been said of Iceland, which was one great field of Scandinavian activity in the ninth and tenth centuries. It was discovered in the middle of the ninth century and soon settled, first by some Norsemen who left their native land under stress of the same conditions as drove others to find fresh homes for themselves in the British Isles and elsewhere, and secondly by other Norsemen (with a considerable admixture of Irish blood) from the Western Islands, who left their settlements there when Harold Fairhair forced them into submission after the battle of Hafrsfjord. In Iceland, Scandinavian law and custom had fullest and freest play for their own development, and we must draw freely on the rich treasures of later Icelandic poetry and prose for our knowledge of the history and civilisation of the Viking age, but Iceland itself lies on the extreme confines of Europe and plays practically no part in the development of Scandinavian influence in Europe in the tenth and eleventh centuries.

Iceland however points for us the moral of Viking civilisation, that when left to develop on its own lines, it ended too often only in social and political anarchy. It is seen at its best when it came into contact with older and richer civilisations. From them it gained stability and strength of purpose, while to them it gave life and vigour when they were fast becoming effete.

CHAPTER XIV.

THE FOUNDATION OF THE KINGDOM OF ENGLAND.

WHEN Offa died in 796, the consolidation of central and south-eastern England into an orderly state under a stable dynasty had continued long enough to make it seem improbable that the work would have to be done a second time. The Mercian kingdom was still far from comprising all England. Wessex and Northumbria were still independent. But in both states the rulers had accepted Mercian brides, and neither seemed sufficiently strong to thwart Mercia's further expansion. Nor was internal faction apparently to be feared. Offa's death brought the crown to Ecgfrith his only son; but though this prince died within a few months of his accession leaving no heir, no struggle arose over the vacant throne. The Mercian witan arranged the succession peaceably among themselves, their choice falling on the aetheling Coenwulf, a member of the royal kindred who seems to have been only distantly related to Offa. This orderly election, if compared with the faction fights which regularly disgraced Northumbria under similar circumstances, is in itself good evidence of the political progress made by Mercia in the eighth century, and Coenwulf's subjects may fairly have looked forward to a further expansion taking place under his leadership.

At Coenwulf's accession the ruler of Wessex was Beorhtric, a weak man who had married Eadburh, Offa's third daughter, and who was almost a Mercian vassal. Of his reign (786–802) little of note is recorded except that it was disturbed one summer by the landing of rovers coming from Hörthaland in Norway on the coast of Dorset. This is the first recorded appearance in England of the so-called Vikings, a most ominous event as the future was to prove. In the Norse sagas the word *vikingr* means a free buccaneer of any nationality, and the phrase "to go in *viking*" denotes freebooting as opposed to trading voyages, both being regarded as equally honourable activities. Not only England but all Western Europe was soon to rue their advent. One other event of Beorhtric's days had far-reaching consequences. In conjunction with Offa he drove into exile an aetheling called Ecgbert, whose father Ealhmund had for a time been under-king in Kent (784–786). This Ecgbert was destined to return and become the ancestor of England's future kings.

In Northumbria in Offa's closing years we also hear of piratical raids. In June 793 heathen men, whether Danish or Norse cannot be decided, ravaged the church at Lindisfarne and captured many of the monks to sell as slaves. Next summer they came again and attacked Wearmouth and Jarrow where Bede had spent his days. These inroads however did not continue, nor can they have disturbed the Northumbrians very much. For the magnates of Bernicia and Deira for many years past had been flying at each other's throats with wearisome monotony. Harryings and burnings had become the rule, and king after king had met with deposition or a violent death. Aethelred, son of Moll, held the throne when the heathen ships appeared. He had married Offa's second daughter, and, like Beorhtric, may be regarded as almost Offa's vassal; but the alliance had brought him little strength. In 796 he was murdered at Corbridge on Tyne. His immediate successor reigned for only twenty-seven days, and then fled making way for Eardwulf, a prince whose reign of ten years (796–806) is merely a chronicle of plunderings and executions ending in his deposition. Clearly it is useless to peer into the gloom and turmoil of the North in these days. One event only seems of importance as it affected the ultimate position of the boundary of England. It was in these years that the Galloway bishopric of Whithern (*Candida Casa*), hitherto subject to York, came to an end, the Picts of this district throwing off their subjection to the English and uniting with the British kingdom of Strathclyde.

Coenwulf ruled over Mercia for a full quarter of a century (796–821). On the whole he shewed himself a man of resource and energy; but his reign was not without its difficulties, and he seems to have been unable to reap any advantage either from the want of enterprise of the West Saxons or from the chaos which reigned among the Northumbrians. In his days nothing occurred to alter the balance of power in England. Mercia remained the leading state; nor is there any record of attacks on its coasts by sea rovers. The king's first recorded activity is a war against the North Welsh, which led to a battle at Rhuddlan. We learn this from the *Annales Cambriae*. As this campaign was followed up later in his reign by another against the South Welsh, it may be useful at this point to say a few words about the general condition of Wales in the years that followed the building of Offa's celebrated boundary dyke. Our information is scanty, but sufficient to prove that the land was subdivided into many chieftaincies or so-called "kingdoms." The most important tribal units, counting from North to South were (1) Gwynedd or North Wales (in Latin *Venedotia*), (2) Powys, (3) Cere-digion (Cardigan), (4) the promontory of Dyfed (in Latin *Demetia*), (5) Ystrad Tywi (the Vale of the Towy), (6) Brycheiniog (Brecknock), (7) Morgannwg (Glamorgan), and (8) Gwent (Monmouthshire). The traditional primacy or overlordship over these and many other smaller units lay with the kings of Gwynedd, whose territories comprised the vales of the Clwyd and Conway, the promontory of Lleyn, the fastnesses of Snowdon and Cader Idris, and the comparatively fertile plains of the Isle of Môn, not yet known as Anglesey, their " principal seat " being at Aberffraw, a small port near Holyhead, whose history goes back to the days of Cadwalader, the contemporary of Oswy. But the superiority of the house of Cunedda, from whom Cadwalader descended, was often merely honorary, and it had long been challenged by princes of South Wales, the *Dextralis pars Britanniae*, as the Welsh termed it. In this, the more spacious and less mountainous half of Wales, a fairly strong principality, later to be known as Deheubarth, was emerging out of conquests made by Seisyll of Ceredigion at the expense of Dyfed, Ystrad Tywi and Brycheiniog. The larger part of these districts in the course of the eighth century were tending to unite under one chief, and already in Offa's day men regarded Dinefwr on the Towy, some fifteen miles east of Carmarthen, as a principal seat or capital, the possession of which carried with it the primacy of South Wales.

For judicial and fiscal purposes most of the tribal units were sub-divided into " cantrefs " of very varying sizes, but on the average rather larger than the English hundreds, each of which in theory was built up of a hundred " trefs " or hamlets. For ecclesiastical purposes there were yet other divisions. Out of the many monastic churches founded in the sixth century four had come to stand out as the most important and had become centres of episcopal organisation. These were Bangor and Llanelwy, otherwise St Asaph, in Northern Wales, Llandaff in Morgannwg, and Mynyw (in Latin *Menevia*), otherwise St David's, in Dyfed. The Welsh Church, too, no longer held aloof from Rome as in earlier days. About 768 it had adopted the Roman Easter, led by Elbodug, a monk of Caer Gybi or Holyhead, and a student of Bede's works. To Wales this peaceful revolution meant as much as the decision come to at Whitby had meant for England a hundred years earlier. With the acceptance of the Roman date for Easter, Wales threw itself open to the influence of the Continent, and not only so, but also to greatly increased intercourse of a non-military character with the English kingdoms. At the date of the fight at Rhuddlan, Elbodug was still living. He died about 809, " chief bishop in the land of Gwynedd." Among his disciples was Nennius, famed as the editor of the *Historia Brittonum*, from which come so many of the folk tales concerning Arthur and the first coming of the Saxons into Britain. Nennius seems to have lived in Deheubarth, probably near the borders of Brycheiniog. He was writing just about the time that Coenwulf ascended the Mercian throne, and his book soon acquired a considerable popularity, not only in Wales, but also in England, Ireland, and Brittany. Nennius wrote shocking Latin, and complains that in-cessant wars and pestilence had dulled the senses of the Britons; but his work, puzzle-headed as it is, shews that the monasteries of Wales still had some learning. He himself refers to Isidore, Jerome, Prosper, and Eusebius, and there are also other indications that some of the Welsh monks of his day were acquainted with parts of the writings of Ovid and Cicero, with Eutychius the grammarian, and Martianus Capella.

The Mercian attack on Wales in 796 was not pressed very far, as Coenwulf soon had other work to do in repressing a rebellion which broke out in Kent. The leader of this revolt was Eadbert Praen, presumably a descendant of the old Kentish kings. For two years he had some success, and then Coenwulf captured and blinded him, and set up his own brother Cuthred instead as under-king of Kent. But this was not all. During the revolt Archbishop Aethelheard had remained loyal to the Mercian cause, in spite of the affront that Offa had put upon the see of Canterbury in 786. Rather than yield to the rebels he had gone into exile, and there exists a letter to the Kentish leaders in which Alcuin pleads for his restoration. In return for this loyal conduct Coenwulf not only restored him to his rights, but agreed with him to undo Offa's work and suppress the recently erected Mercian archbishopric. Aethelheard accordingly journeyed to Rome to lay the matter before Pope Leo III, and having obtained his approval called a synod together at Clovesho in 803 which promulgated the deprivation of Archbishop Higbert and the restoration of the old metropolitan rights of Canterbury. It might have been expected that after this the old alliance between Tamworth and Canterbury would have been effectively restored, but it was not so. Archbishop Aethelheard died in 805, and was succeeded by a Kentish man named Wulfred, an ambitious prelate who resented Mercian control and desired independence for Kent. He soon quarrelled with Coenwulf over questions of property, especially over the nunnery of Minster in Thanet and over the important estate of Harrow in Middlesex. The trouble is said to have extended over six years and to have led to appeals to the Papacy, while it is certain that the archbishop shewed his independence by coining money which does not bear any king's name. These turmoils and Welsh campaigns take up the remainder of Coenwulf's reign; but it must not be supposed that he was altogether unmindful of the claims of the Church. Existing landbooks shew that he was a benefactor to Worcester, and he is also credited with the foundation of Winchcombe Abbey. There is also some evidence that about 813 Wulfred was attempting monastic reforms at Canterbury[1].

Coenwulf died in 821, it is said at Basingwerk in Flint, still occupied with plans for extending the Mercian frontier westwards from Chester to the Conway. His successor was his brother Ceolwulf, who continued the Welsh policy with success, capturing the fort of Deganwy near Llandudno and overrunning Powys. Ceolwulf's accession, however, was not unchallenged, and two years later we find him deposed in favour of a duke called Beornwulf. We are quite in the dark as to Beornwulf's

---

[1] Birch, *Cart. Sax.*, No. 342.

origin and the reasons for his elevation to the throne, but we may suspect the hand of Archbishop Wulfred in the background. For shortly afterwards we find Beornwulf making grants to Wulfred, and the abbess Cwenthryth, Coenwulf's daughter, compelled to resign Harrow to the see of Canterbury. The dispute about the succession between Ceolwulf and Beornwulf marks the beginning of evil days for Mercia. The unity and solidity, which had appeared so well established under Offa, disappears; the Mercian magnates fall a prey to faction, and almost as it were in the twinkling of an eye the supremacy of Mercia is wrecked for ever.

It is time now to turn again to the affairs of Wessex. When Beorhtric died in 802, poisoned, so the tale goes, by his wife, the West Saxon witan saluted as their king that Ecgbert whom Offa and Beorhtric had driven out of England. The choice was most happy; for Ecgbert was a man of experience, who had spent some time in Frankland, and possibly witnessed Charlemagne's Saxon campaigns. He had returned to Wessex about 799, but not before he had marked how the great Frank administered his kingdom. His elevation to the throne clearly meant a less dependent Wessex and so was distasteful to the Mercians. At any rate on the very day of Ecgbert's election the men of the Hwicce took horse and crossed the Upper Thames at Kempsford near Cirencester led by Aethelmund, a Gloucestershire magnate whose estates lay at Deerhurst and Berkeley. They were met by a West Saxon alderman named Weoxtan with the levies of Wiltshire. In the fight which ensued both leaders were killed, but the Mercians had to retreat, after which Ecgbert had several years of peace for organising his kingdom. We know nothing of his acts as an administrator, but in 814 we find him imitating Coenwulf and engaged in expanding his borders westwards at the expense of the Welsh of Cornwall. As the Chronicle puts it, " he laid waste West Wales from eastward to westward," and thenceforth apparently held it as a *ducatus* or dukedom annexed to his *regnum* or kingdom of Wessex, but not wholly incorporated with it. Thus arose that Welsh-speaking duchy or earldom of Cornwall, which almost ever since has formed a quasi-royal appanage in the hands of Ecgbert's successors, and which maintained its distinct nationality to the eighteenth century. The exact stages of its reduction to submission cannot be followed. We only know that in 825 the West Welsh were once more in arms and that Ecgbert again put them down and, as a later document[1] phrases it, " disposed of their territory as it seemed fit to him, giving a tenth part of it to God." In other words he incorporated Cornwall ecclesiastically with the West Saxon diocese of Sherborne, and endowed Ealhstan, his fighting bishop, who took part in the campaign, with an extensive Cornish estate consisting of Callington and Lawhitton, both in the Tamar valley, and Pawton near Padstow. One is naturally

[1] *Crawford Charters*, No. VII.

led to ask, were these three properties really equivalent to a tenth of all Cornwall ; for if so, it is very noteworthy to find such large estate units already evolved as early as 825.   All that can be said in answer is that the evidence of Domesday Book, written 260 years later, does not altogether bear out this conclusion, but yet is more in harmony with it than might have been expected ; for that survey credits these three properties with 130 ploughlands, which is about an eighteenth part of the total ploughlands recorded for all Cornwall.   At any rate, then, we may regard this gift as transferring a very considerable stretch of land, and its effect would be to open up West Wales not a little to English influences.   Little, however, seems actually to have been done in the way of settling West Saxon colonists in the country, if we may judge from the sparsity of the English type of place-name everywhere but in the Tamar valley.   The rest of Cornwall remains to this day a land of " trefs," that is to say, of petty hamlets, bearing such names as Trenance, Tregony and Trevelyan, of which quite a handful are required to form a parish, although this is not called after any one of them, but by the name of the saint to whom the church is dedicated.   Nor would it seem were new local divisions introduced by the conquerors.   The so-called Cornish shires, such as Pydershire or Wivelshire, seem to be really the old Welsh " cantrefs."   The term " shire " must however have been applied to them almost from the first conquest ; for King Alfred's will only sixty years later has an allusion to " Streatnet on Triconshire," that is to say to Stratton near Bude in Triggshire.

The settlement of Cornwall was hardly effected when news came that the Mercians had again invaded Wiltshire.   Ecgbert thereupon led his army eastwards and came up with Beornwulf's forces at Ellandun, a village near Swindon now called Nether Wroughton, but as late as the fourteenth century known as Elynton[1].   A pitched battle ensued in which the Mercians were completely routed.   This victory must be regarded as a turning point in England's development, for it led to a permanent alteration of the balance of power in England in favour of the West Saxons.   To follow up his advantage, Ecgbert at once despatched his son, Aethelwulf, accompanied by Bishop Ealhstan, against Kent, a district which he could claim with some show of reason as he was the son of Ealhmund.   Aethelwulf's march was as successful as his father's.   Baldred, the Kentish under-king, appointed by Mercia, soon fled northwards over the Thames, and thereupon, as the chronicle has it, the men of Kent and Surrey submitted to Wessex, admitting that " they had been wrongly forced from Ecgbert's kin."   Sussex and Essex a few weeks later followed suit ; and finally the East Anglians also rose, and re-established their independence of Mercia, by attacking Beornwulf from the east and slaying him in battle.

No series of events could well be more dramatic than the successive

---

[1] *Feudal Aids* v. 207 ; *Domesday Book,* I. 65 *b.* Elendune.

disasters which brought about the collapse of Mercia in 825. Wessex and Mercia, as it were, changed parts. Within a year the Mercian kingdom dwindled to half its former size, while Wessex expanded so that it may be regarded henceforth as including all England south of the Thames.   Kent, it is true, still retained its individuality in the hands of Ecgbert's son, as an under-kingdom enjoying its own special customs, and as the chief seat of church government; but its affairs were nevertheless directed from Winchester, and the archbishops of Canterbury could no longer look to Tamworth for protection, but were brought much more under West Saxon influences.

For the Mercians the immediate question after 825 was, could they maintain their independence or must they accept Ecgbert as an overlord. They evidently went on with the struggle, but their new king, Ludeca, fared no better than Beornwulf. He fell in battle in 827 with five of his dukes. Wiglaf then succeeded, but likewise made no headway, and soon fled into exile. Meantime Ecgbert, with the help of the East Anglians, overran the Midlands at will, and for the moment was acclaimed lord of all men south of the Humber. In 829 he even projected an attack on Northumbria, and led his army to Dore, a frontier village in the Peak district. The Northumbrian king at this time was Eanred (808–840). He came to Dore and apparently bought off Ecgbert's hostility with offers of homage and perhaps of tribute. Too much has sometimes been made of these episodes. They have even been treated as marking the unification of England under a single overlord, but certainly they had no such result. Ecgbert's position in Mercia was really precarious, and the very next year we find Wiglaf restored to his kingdom. Patriotic West Saxon tradition in later days liked to picture Ecgbert as a " Bretwalda " worthy to be classed with Edwin and Oswy and the other ancient heroes who in Bede's pages stood pre-eminent as wielding an *imperium* before the rise of Mercia; but eulogy must not be mistaken for sober history. It would seem, on the contrary, that Ecgbert's power soon waned, and that Wiglaf's restoration was due to a Mercian revival. The Wessex chronicle gives no hint that Ecgbert was active in Mercia after 830, nor do any Mercian notables attest his landbooks. It has indeed been suggested that the Aethelstan, who ruled East Anglia in Ecgbert's later years, was one of his sons, but this is a guess incapable of proof and hardly in harmony with the independence admittedly enjoyed by the East Anglians shortly afterwards.

Ecgbert's last years are of interest not because of any growth of unity in England but because they witnessed the re-appearance of the Vikings and the consequent rise of a new and grave danger for all the English kingdoms. All through the first quarter of the ninth century Scandinavian long-ships had been harrying Western Scotland and Ireland, coming by way of the Faroe islands and the Orkneys. Beginning in 795 with attacks on Skye, they had in 802 come south to Iona and

Donegal and thence spread east and west along the coasts of Ulster and Connemara.   By 825 they had fairly encircled Ireland and plundered most of its shrines.   In England, on the other hand, no raids are heard of for forty years after the attacks on Lindisfarne and Jarrow in Offa's days, and it was not till 834 that the danger re-appeared as the result of the establishment of Danish exiled chieftains in Frisia, as the Netherlands were then called, by Louis the Pious.   In that year considerable fleets set out from Denmark and the North to attack the Frankish Empire, and coming to the mouths of the Rhine burnt the important Frisian trading ports of Dorestad and Utrecht.   The general situation on the Continent is dealt with in other chapters.   Here we have only to note that a detachment of this force also came to England and entering the Thames ravaged the island of Sheppey.   Two years later the Frisian provinces were again attacked and the town of Antwerp sacked.   Again a small detachment came across to England. This time the raiders landed in Dorset, and Ecgbert himself met them at Charmouth not far from Lyme Regis.   The Vikings had only 35 ships, with crews about 1200 strong, but the fight none the less went against the king, and the victors gained the impression that Wessex was worth attacking.   At any rate in 838 there arrived a larger fleet which came to land in Cornwall.   Once more Ecgbert marched to meet the raiders to find that the Cornish had risen to join them.   Victory, however, lay with the English, the allied Danes and Welsh being put to flight at Hinxton Down, a moor on the west bank of the Tamar near Callington. As a result it would appear that a bishop, definitely subject to Canterbury, was shortly afterwards appointed for Cornwall in the person of one Kenstec, whose see was placed in the monastery of Dinnurrin[1].   This was Ecgbert's last achievement.   He died in the summer of 839.

The accession of his son Aethelwulf, which almost corresponds in point of time with the death of Louis the Pious and the break-up of the Carolingian Empire on the Continent, introduces a new phase into English affairs.   Hitherto the main thread of English history has been concerned with the rivalries between the English kingdoms and with the gradual growth of civilisation and a tendency to union under the auspices of the Church.   But for the next forty years internal progress ceased, and as in Frankland, so in England, the one constant feature of the times was the ceaseless struggle which every province in turn had to wage against Danish invaders.   In 839 the Viking raids could still be regarded as merely a passing inconvenience, and the English people hardly realised the full extent of the danger which threatened them; but from that date the raids grew more persistent and better organised year by year, and it soon became apparent that the object of the invaders was not merely plunder but the complete conquest of the country.

[1] Birch, *Cart. Sax.*, No. 527. Can the latter part of Din-nurrin represent Guerür, the name of the saint buried at St Neots? Asser, c. 74.

Before Aethelwulf died, the heathen fleets had already taken to wintering in England, and in the days of his sons the struggle reached its climax. The Viking armies then penetrated into all parts of the island, ravaging and burning unmercifully, and three of the four English kingdoms, Northumbria, Mercia and East Anglia, one after another succumbed to their onslaughts. At times it even looked as if Wessex, the strongest kingdom of them all, would also go under. Many battles went against its armies and more than once all the shires south of the Thames were overrun. In their hour of trial however the West Saxons found a saviour in the famous Alfred, Aethelwulf's youngest son. Under his leadership they again took courage, and at last beat back the invaders and compelled them to confine their settlements to the northern and eastern portions of the country. The England, which emerged from the struggle, was an entirely changed England. The four kingdoms of Ecgbert's day had been replaced by a division of the country into two well-marked spheres, one of which was English and Christian while the other was Danish in law and custom, and, in part, heathen. The Danish portion, subsequently known as the Danelaw (*Denalagu*), had however little political cohesion, being composed of a large number of petty communities under a variety of independent rulers, some styled kings and others "jarls," who were mutually distrustful of each other, whereas the English portion formed a comparatively compact state, looking for guidance and defence to the house of Ecgbert, which alone survived of the four older royal houses. In the hard-fought struggle much had been lost. Letters and the arts had practically perished; Christianity had received a severe shock, and monastic life had either disappeared or become degraded. But in spite of this partial lapse into barbarism much had also been gained, the new settlers being men of vigorous physique and character and eager to develop trade and industry. Their language, too, and their social and legal institutions were not so different from those of the English as to preclude the hope of amalgamation, and so a situation arose much more favourable than might have been expected for the ultimate unification of the country into a single state, provided that the West Saxon dynasty could retain its vigour and prestige.

The change from Ecgbert to Aethelwulf, just as the period of turmoil began, was by no means a gain for Wessex. The best that can be said for the new king is that he was well-meaning and devout; but he was not the man to intimidate invaders or enlarge his patrimony. He was content to regard Beorhtwulf and Burhred, the kings who ruled in Mercia in his days, as his equals; and, so far as we know, he only once led an army across the Thames, and then not to coerce the Mercians but to assist them in a campaign against the Welsh. Aethelwulf's real bent was towards works of piety, and in later days he was best remembered for his donation to the Church. Landbooks refer to this transaction as a *decimatio agrorum*, and some have connected it with the institution of tithe, but clearly it had quite a different character.   The chronicler Asser, who places the gift in 855, says that the king freed a tenth part of his land from royal dues and dedicated it to God for the redemption of his soul.   This must mean that he gave very considerable properties to the monastic houses of Wessex ; but we are left in the dark whether the king was dealing only with his private booklands, which he had power to dispose of by will, or with all the crown lands in Wessex.   It is noticeable, however, that Aethelwulf is found creating " bookland " in favour of himself, perhaps with his donation in view.   Aethelwulf also maintained close relations with Rome, sending his youngest son, Alfred, on a visit to Pope Leo IV in 853, and himself undertaking the journey thither two years later.   Considering the progress made by the Vikings, the time chosen for his pilgrimage seems most ill advised.   In all parts of England ever since Ecgbert's death the Viking raids had been growing in audacity.   For example, in 841 one force had overrun Lindsey, while in 844 another had slain the king of Northumbria.   In 851 a fleet of no less than 350 ships appeared in the Thames, whose crews burnt Canterbury and then stormed London and put Beorhtwulf of Mercia to flight.   A gleam of success gained this year may perhaps account for Aethelwulf's false confidence, his troops winning a victory at a place called Oakley (*Acleah*)[1] over a contingent of the Danes which had recrossed the Thames to raid in Surrey.   This victory, however, meant little ; for the enemy after their defeat only retreated to East Kent and remained in Thanet over the winter.   This wintering in 851 marks the end of the period of mere raids.   In 855 the outlook became even darker.   Some heathen bands that year harried the province of the *Wreocensaete* along the upper Severn, and others wintered in Sheppey. Aethelwulf, however, was quite blind to the signs of the times.   Instead of returning from Rome as quickly as possible, he remained out of England over a year, and on his way back turned aside to visit the West Frankish King, Charles the Bald.   At his court he committed a further folly, marrying Charles's daughter, Judith, a girl of thirteen.   This high alliance flattered the elderly king's vanity, but the news of it greatly offended his grown-up sons and drove Aethelbald, the eldest, who was acting as regent, to rebel and claim the western parts of Wessex for himself.   Aethelwulf on his return had perforce to acquiesce in this, and for the remainder of his life Wessex was in reality partitioned and Ecgbert's work to a large extent undone.

During the middle years of the century, while the English kingdoms seem to be going down hill, it is interesting to observe the development of an opposite tendency in Wales and Scotland.   In both these Celtic districts rulers of ability appeared and effected some advance in the direction of national unity.   In Wales, the movement first attracts

---

[1] Perhaps Oakley, by Gravesend, the site of several synods, closely adjoining Clovesho.

attention about the time of the battle of Ellandun, when Merfyn the Freckled established a new dynasty in Gwynedd in the place of the ancient house of Cadwallon. Merfyn, however, was completely eclipsed in energy by his son, the celebrated Rhodri Mawr (844–878), who won undying fame among his countrymen by conquering Powys and the greater part of Deheubarth. The unity thus achieved did not, it is true, long endure, but considering that it was attained in the face of constant Viking raids, the feat was undoubtedly a memorable one. In Scotland, a similar task, but on a much larger scale, was undertaken by Kenneth Mac Alpin (844–860). This prince, beginning merely as king of the Dalriad Scots, in a reign of sixteen years not only added the realm of the Picts to his dominions, but also made himself a terror to Northern Bernicia, advancing in his raids into Lothian as far south as Dunbar and Melrose. He may, in fact, be reckoned the true founder of the Scottish kingdom as it was to be known to history, and the first Scot to advance the claim that the frontier of England should be set back from the Forth to the Tweed.

It was in 858, while these events were in progress in the North, that Aethelwulf died, leaving a will, no longer extant, in which it appears that he unwisely recognised the partition of Wessex. This mistake was fortunately remedied in 860, when events enabled his second son Aethelbert to regain Aethelbald's share of the kingdom, and five years later the realm passed entire to yet another brother, Aethelred. The short reigns of Aethelbald and Aethelbert were not without their disasters. In 861 the Vikings sacked Winchester, and in 865 so ravaged East Kent that Archbishop Ceolnoth had to allow clerks to fill the places of monks at Canterbury, while in the rest of the country learning had so decayed that scarcely a scholar remained who could read the mass in Latin. Worse, however, was yet to come. With Aethelred's accession we enter the most stormy period of the ninth century. Fresh swarms of allied sea kings then arrived determined to find homes in England. Our primary authority, the *West Saxon Chronicle*, is silent as to the names of the leaders, but according to later traditions they were Ingwar, Ubba and Halfdene, three brothers who are regarded by the Scandinavian saga writers as sons of the half mythical Ragnarr Loðbrók, in legendary song the greatest of all sea rovers. These chiefs landed first in East Anglia, then ruled by a prince called Edmund. Their immediate object, however, was not to overthrow this king but to obtain horses. In this they succeeded and then, either in 866 or 867, rode round the fens and north across Lindsey to attack Deira, where the usual civil war was in progress between Aelle and Osbeorht, two rival claimants for the Northumbrian throne. Legend tells us that they came to avenge the death of Ragnarr Loðbrók, who is said to have been killed in an earlier raid in Northumbria, but probably they chose Northumbria for attack because its dissensions made it an easy prey. York was quickly taken, and in 867 both Aelle and Osbeorht were killed in a joint attempt to regain it. With their deaths the independence of Deira came to an end; but it would appear that the comparatively unfertile districts of Bernicia did not much attract the invaders, with the result that the country from the Tees northwards to the Scotch boundary remained subject to English princes, seated at Bamborough. These rulers retained for their diminished territories the name of Northumberland, which after this gradually ceases to be applied to the Yorkshire districts actually adjoining the Humber. Their small principality, however, could hardly be regarded as a kingdom, and so they soon dropped the title of king and came to be styled either dukes or later still " high-reeves of Bamborough."

Having secured their footing in the vale of York, the Danes next marched south along the Trent to Nottingham to see whether they could not also establish themselves in the ancient Mercian homeland. Attacked thus in the very heart of his kingdom, Burhred invoked help from the West Saxons; but though Aethelred, who was Burhred's brother-in-law, willingly came to his aid, the allied kings apparently dared not risk a pitched battle, and in 868 the Mercians were reduced to buying a truce by offers of tribute. For the moment this satisfied the Vikings, who withdrew once more to Deira. There they stayed quiet for a year, but in the autumn of 869 they again rode south, perhaps to meet fresh re-inforcements, and after harrying Eastern Mercia from the Humber to the Ouse determined to try their luck against Edmund of East Anglia, whose territories they had spared on landing. Details of their march southwards are missing; but it was doubtless then that the fenland monasteries of Bardney, Medeshamstede, Crowland and Ely, after Worcester the chief centres of Mercian learning and civilisation, were destroyed, and much of Lindsey and Middle Anglia given over again to heathendom. Burhred made no efforts, it would seem, to organise defensive measures for these districts, but a much stouter resistance awaited the Viking forces at Thetford, where they proposed to take up their winter quarters. Again details are very confused and scanty, but it is clear that the English forces were decisively beaten, and we are told that Edmund himself was captured by Ingwar and Ubba and put to death on November 20 at Hoxne in Suffolk by their orders because he refused to abjure Christianity. In the spring of 870 all East Anglia submitted, and there, too, heathendom and the worship of Thor and Woden was partially re-introduced, but their fallen king's memory was so cherished by the vanquished East Anglians that he soon came to be regarded as a saint and martyr, and a generation later the site of his tomb at Bead-ricesworth had grown to be a new Christian centre, which in a short time became famous under the name of St Edmund's Bury.

What became of Ingwar after Edmund's death is not known. It is possible that he returned to Deira to secure his first conquests and went thence to Scotland to assist the Irish Vikings, who, led by Olaf the

White, the Norse king of Dublin, were about this time attacking the Strathclyde Britons. He may even be the Ivarr whose death is reported in the *Annals of Ulster* as occurring in 872. In England, at any rate, he ceases to be heard of, and his place as leader of the Danish army fell to Halfdene, represented as his brother, and to another sea king called Bagseag. These chiefs, by no means satisfied with the territories and booty already won, determined next to invade Wessex and surprise its king by a winter attack. They accordingly set out in the autumn to march by land into the Thames valley, and neglecting London descended late in December on Reading, in Berkshire. Here they set up a fortified camp at the point where the river Kennet joins the Thames. In describing the measures taken to repel this invasion, the *West Saxon Chronicle* suddenly becomes much more detailed, and so it is possible to follow the numerous engagements of the next few weeks with considerable minuteness, and even to gain some idea of the tactics employed. The most favourable encounter to the West Saxons was a fight which took place in January 871 to the west of Reading on the slopes of Ashdown. In this Aethelred fought in person and with the aid of his brother Alfred slew Bagseag and several other Danish leaders. But this success was counterbalanced by a defeat at Basing in Hampshire only a fortnight later, and by yet another disaster in March at a hamlet called Marton on the outskirts of Savernake Forest in Wiltshire.

Amid all this gloom Aethelred's reign terminated. He died about Easter, leaving only infant children, and was buried at Wimborne, one of Ine's foundations in Dorset. Aethelred's death was no real disaster for the West Saxons, for it opened the succession to his brother Alfred, who, in a reign of twenty-eight and a half years (871–899) was destined to prove himself one of the most remarkable characters known to history. Born at Wantage, in Berkshire, the youngest of Aethelwulf's sons by his first wife Osburh, Alfred was a married man just turned twenty-three when he was acclaimed king by the West Saxon magnates. His wife was Ealhswith, daughter of Aethelred Mucel, a leading Mercian duke, who witnesses many of Burhred's landbooks. Before his election Alfred was already known as a prince of courage and energy, who, according to his biographer Asser, had shewn in boyhood a taste for learning, which unfortunately had not been gratified, as he could get no proper masters. His health, however, had never been robust, and he must have taken up his task with many misgivings, having the disasters of eastern England before his eyes. The fate of central Wessex, indeed, seemed hanging by a thread a month later, when the Danes gained another well-contested battle at Wilton ; but as it turned out Alfred was to have a four years' respite. After nine costly encounters, none of which had been at all decisive, the Danes began to think that the conquest of Wessex was too difficult and that Mercia would prove a more remunerative prey Both sides, therefore, as at Nottingham three years before, found themselves anxious to treat, and a peace was patched up on the understanding that the Viking army should abandon its hold on Berkshire and withdraw across the Thames.

This peace shews well the complete want of national feeling in ninth-century England.   It was now the turn of the Midlands to feel the fury of the "army"; but just as Burhred, entangled it would appear in a conflict with the Welsh, had not come forward to help his brother-in-law, Aethelred, in his peril, so now Alfred pledged himself to inactivity while the Vikings laid their plans for the final ruin of Mercia. Their first move was from Reading to London, where they spent the spring of 872, watched by the West Saxons from across the Thames, until Burhred agreed to ransom the town and its dependent districts by the payment of a heavy tribute.   Worcestershire documents which allude to this levy, or *geld* as the Saxons called it, still exist, and also pennies minted by Halfdene at London.   The promise to evacuate south-eastern Mercia was redeemed by the army transferring itself once again to Deira, but it soon came back to Lindsey and encamped for the winter at Torksey on Trent in the immediate vicinity of Lincoln. From this base it could ravage at leisure all the country watered by the tributaries of the Middle Trent, and by the end of 873 it had pushed so far into Mercia that it was able to winter at Repton, revered as the burying place of the Mercian dynasty, only a few miles from Tamworth and Lichfield.   One would like to know details of this campaign and hear more of the fate that overtook Leicester and Nottingham, but unfortunately no native chronicle exists to give vividness to the death struggle of Mercia.   All we know comes from the West Saxon account, which merely states that Burhred's spirit was so entirely broken that in 874 he abandoned his kingdom and fled abroad, dying at Rome shortly afterwards.   His vacant throne was promptly filled by one Ceolwulf, " an unwise king's thegn," but this ruler was little more than a puppet set up with Halfdene's connivance, a *semivir*, as William of Malmesbury terms him, who was forced by the Danes to swear that he would hold his kingdom for the behoof of the army and deliver it up whenever required.   This transaction is pretty good evidence that the Danes had overrun more territory than they could hope to hold, but that their leaders were expecting reinforcements, and anticipated in the near future a need for additional settlements.   The " army " accordingly retired from Repton, and not being united on a common plan broke up into two sections, one of which withdrew to Deira under Halfdene, while the other, under Guthrum, Oscytel and Anwind, sea kings not hitherto mentioned, went to Cambridge.

Halfdene's plan was apparently to regain for York its former dependencies.   He established his base for the winter on the Tyne, and from thence in 875 organised savage raids into every corner of Bernicia, then ruled by Ricsig, and also into the territories of the Picts and Strathclyde

Britons. Nothing permanent was achieved by these devastations, but they have some importance in church history, because they led Bishop Eardulf, who had charge of the shrines of St Aidan and St Cuthbert, to abandon his see at Lindisfarne, so long the spiritual capital of the North, and to set out on an eight years' pilgrimage through the moors of Cumberland and the coasts of Solway in search of a more secure asylum.

And now at last we reach the stage of real colonisation. In 876 Halfdene returned to York and "dealt out" Deira to his followers, "who thenceforward continued ploughing and tilling it." No Danish Domesday Book tells how the allotment of estates was carried out, or what proportion of the English owners preserved their lands, but it must in the main have been a process of imposing Danish warriors on English cultivators, very similar to the settlement of Normans, carried out 200 years later by William the Conqueror, except that the Danish armies contained a large class of freedmen, the so-called *liesings* or "men loosened from bondage," to whom no exact counterpart can be found in the later invasion. This half-free class had to be accommodated with land as well as the fully-free classes, the *holds* and *bonde* who formed the upper and middle grades of Viking society[1], but they were not of sufficient social standing to become independent landowners, being often of alien race and descended from prisoners of war, slaves and bankrupts. How exactly they were dealt with can only be guessed, but it seems not unlikely that they received holdings in the villages similar to those of the English *ceorls*, only that they held them by a distinctly freer tenure as members of the conquering armies. Nor is it fanciful to recognise their descendants later on in the peasant class known as *sochemanni*, who held a position in the society of the eleventh century just above the *villani* or ordinary cultivators, and who are found in very considerable numbers in just those parts of England where the Danes are known to have settled, but not at all or only in trifling numbers elsewhere.

A year later portions of Mercia were similarly colonised. "After harvest," so runs a laconic entry in the *Wessex Chronicle*, "the 'army' went into Mercia, and some part of it they apportioned, and some they delivered to Ceolwulf." No clue is vouchsafed as to the identity of the army concerned, and no names are mentioned either of the leaders or the districts implicated. It is clear, however, from subsequent events that the districts left to Ceolwulf comprised all western Mercia from the Mersey to the Thames, and that the boundary fixed upon ran north and south from near the Peak in Derbyshire to a point just east of Tamworth on the Watling Street, and then along that high-way south-eastwards to the headwaters of the Worcestershire Avon and the Welland and perhaps even further, past Towcester to Stony Stratford on the Ouse. To the east of this boundary Danish customs and law were imposed upon the

[1] Cf. Seebohm, *Tribal Custom*, pp. 240–276.

Mercian villages, and Danish political terminology introduced instead of English. Politically also there was a considerable re-organisation, the land being divided into five districts, each with its own " army " under an independent *jarl*, and each having for its centre a fortified camp, which the settlers could garrison in times of stress. The five centres selected were Lincoln, Stamford, Nottingham, Derby and Leicester, and as the term *burh* at this date still had the meaning of " a fortified place," they soon came to be specially known as the " Five Boroughs."

Meantime in East Anglia and south-east Mercia affairs did not progress so swiftly towards a settlement. The rank and file of the army, which encamped in Cambridge in 875, would doubtless have been well content to form " borough districts " between the Thames and the Welland similar to those which were being set up between the Welland and the Humber, but their leader, Guthrum, coveted Alfred's dominions as well, and when he heard that fresh fleets were in the English Channel attacking the southern coasts of Wessex, he could not resist joining in the enterprise. Already in 875 there is mention of Alfred fighting the Vikings at sea. The next year a fleet appeared off the coast of Dorset over a hundred strong. The chronicler, Aethelweard, alludes to it as a " western army." The bulk of it therefore doubtless came from Ireland, but help reached it from Guthrum. Landing near Poole harbour, the allied vikings proceeded to harry the surrounding districts, and then seized Wareham after out-manoeuvring Alfred's forces. When winter approached, Alfred thought it best to offer terms. The vikings however treacherously deceived him, and, having accepted a sum of money on the condition that they would decamp, slipped out of Wareham suddenly and made a dash for Exeter, with the intention of using it as a base from which to ravage Devon. In 877 the luck turned. While Alfred kept the viking land-force shut up in Exeter, their fleet came to grief in a storm off Swanage. This disaster placed the marauders in a precarious position. Before the end of the year they had to capitulate, and if Aethelweard's account is to be believed, retired to Gloucester. Once more Wessex appeared to be saved. In reality the worst crisis of all was at hand. About midwinter Guthrum threw his whole army unexpectedly upon Wessex, and almost surprised Alfred at Chippenham where he was keeping Christmas. At the same moment Halfdene's brother Ubba, sailing from Dyfed, invaded North Devon. The brunt of Guthrum's invasion fell upon Wiltshire, but other shires also suffered severely, and so great was the general terror that many of the West Saxon leaders fled over sea. Alfred however never despaired ; getting away with difficulty from Chippenham, he retired into the marshlands of Somerset and stockaded himself with Aethelnoth, the alderman of the district, in the island of Athelney at the junction of the Tone and Parret. There he remained on the defensive till the news came that the men of Devon, led by their alderman Odda, had defeated Halfdene's brother. The king then put himself once more at the head of the levies of central Wessex, his men meeting him early in May 878 on the borders of Wiltshire just to the east of Selwood Forest. Two days later he fell upon Guthrum's army at Edington (Ethandun) near Westbury, and so utterly defeated it that a fortnight later at Chippenham a peace was agreed to. The terms arranged were remarkable; for Guthrum not only promised that he would withdraw his army from Wessex, but also that he would accept baptism. The ceremony was accordingly performed in June at Aller near Athelney, the chrismloosing taking place at Wedmore, a village near Glastonbury. The departure of the Danes from Wessex was carried out before long. In 879 we find them at Cirencester, and from that time forward the West Saxons were never again in any serious danger of being conquered by the Northmen.

To the Mercians, in the yet unravaged valley of the Severn, the peace made at Chippenham, often inaccurately called the "Peace of Wedmore," only meant an increase of danger. The move to Cirencester seemed clearly to portend that Guthrum hoped to find satisfaction in Gloucestershire and Worcestershire for his failure in Wessex, and the danger seemed all the greater when it became known, in the summer of 879, that a new fleet of vikings had arrived in the Thames and landed at Fulham. In this predicament the magnates of the Hwicce decided to take an important step. To depend on the puppet king Ceolwulf for defence was clearly useless. They accordingly turned to the victor of Edington, and led by Aethelred of Gloucester their foremost duke, and by Werfrith, the Bishop of Worcester, offered Alfred their allegiance. How many of the leading Mercians supported Aethelred in this submission to Wessex is not recorded. All that can be said is that we find Aethelred after this treated by Alfred to some extent as a vassal and given in charters the title of "Duke of the Mercians." Thus ended the independent kingdom of Mercia.

On the Danes the effect of this politic stroke was immediate. In 880 the province of the Hwicce was evacuated without any fighting, and Guthrum withdrew from Cirencester and marched his army back into East Anglia, while the Fulham fleet returned to Flanders. Next there followed the apportionment of Hendrica, Essex and East Anglia among Guthrum's followers, while in Middle Anglia a second series of boroughs were set up, at Northampton, Huntingdon, Cambridge and Bedford, each ruled by a more or less independent jarl and each with its dependent territory defended by its own "army." Guthrum's own sphere was large enough to be regarded as a kingdom. It had Norwich, Thetford, Ipswich, Colchester and London for head centres, and when first established stretched westwards over half the district of the Cilternsaete. We may guess in fact that it was the creation of Guthrum's new Danish kingdom which first brought about the division of this old

province into the two portions known to us to-day as Oxfordshire and
Buckinghamshire; for the former, when we get information about it in
the eleventh century, shews no signs of Danish colonisation and was
regarded as subject to Mercian law, whereas the latter was then peopled
to a considerable extent by *sochemanni* and was held to be a portion of
the Danelaw.

The followers of Halfdene and Guthrum when once settled proved
fairly peaceable neighbours to Wessex and her Mercian ally, and in the
next two decades only gave trouble on one or two occasions when roused
by the appearance of fresh fleets from abroad. This furnished Alfred
with a much needed opportunity for re-organising his realm, and it is his
great glory that he not only took up the task with patient doggedness,
but shewed himself if possible even more capable as a reformer in peace
than as a leader in war. It is impossible for want of space to follow his
reforms in detail, but a few of the more noteworthy developments due
to his constructive statesmanship may be glanced at. First we may
take his military reforms. These comprised the improvement of his naval
force by the enlistment of Frisians, and the division of the *fyrd*, or
national levy, into two parts, the one to be available as a relief to the
other at convenient intervals, so that the peasant soldiers might have
proper opportunities of attending to the needs of their farms and therefore
less excuse for deserting in the middle of a campaign. But more important than either of these was the gradual creation in all parts of his
kingdom of fortified strongholds, defended by earthworks and palisades
of timber, in imitation of the Danish "boroughs," and the subdivision of
the ancient West Saxon shires into smaller districts of varying size, each
charged with the upkeep of one or more forts. The evidence for this is
found in the many references to the "men of the boroughs" that begin
to appear in the chronicle as the reign proceeds and even in the landbooks, such as the Worcester charter[1], which sets forth how Aethelred,
with Alfred's consent, "worked" a borough at Worcester for the protection of the bishop and monks and granted them the right to take a
scot (*burh-wealles-scaeting*) for its maintenance. This, of course, is a
Mercian instance, but a list[2] of the boroughs of Wessex and of the
hidages assessed on their appendant districts has also chanced to be
preserved, which cannot be of a date much after Alfred's death, and this
mentions some twenty-five strongholds scattered up and down his kingdom.
Of these, the more important along the south coast were Hastings, Lewes,
Chichester, Porchester, Southampton, Wareham, Bridport and Exeter;
and along the north frontier, Barnstaple, Watchet, Axbridge, Bath,
Malmesbury, Cricklade, Wallingford and Southwark (*Suthringa geweorc*).
It seems also likely that the scheme of hidage recorded in this document

[1] Birch, *Cart. Sax.*, No. 579.
[2] *Ibid.*, No. 1335. Maitland treats of this list under the title "The Burghal
Hidage." *Domesday Book and Beyond*, pp. 502–4.

CH. XIV.

was of Alfred's devising; for the figures run smaller than in the eighth century Mercian scheme, though still based on a unit of 1200 hides, and we know of no other occasion so likely to have required a reform of fiscal arrangements as the creation of the borough districts.

Passing to civil reforms the most arduous of all perhaps was the compilation of a fresh edition of the West Saxon laws. For this purpose Alfred examined and sifted not only Ine's earlier dooms but also the laws published by Offa, which unfortunately have not survived to us, and those issued by the Kentish kings. From these he selected what seemed to him to be the most useful, only adding a few new ordinances of his own. There is also good evidence that he took great pains to secure justice for his subjects, and that he was most careful in husbanding and increasing the royal revenue. Most noteworthy, however, of all his reforms was his attempt to revive religion and learning, which had been almost crushed out by the Danish inroads. For this purpose he not only set to work to educate himself in reading and translating Latin, but collected at his court a band of scholars who should give him advice and act as teachers in the schools which he instituted. Some of these he obtained from West Mercia which had not suffered so much as Wessex, some from Wales and Ireland, and some from the Continent. Among them were Werfrith, the Bishop of Worcester, who had helped to bring about the alliance with Aethelred; Plegmund, a Mercian, who, in 890, was chosen Archbishop of Canterbury; Grimbald, a Flemish monk from St Bertin's; John the Old Saxon from Corvey, who became abbot of a monastery founded by Alfred at Athelney; and Asser, a Welsh monk from St David's, who ultimately became Bishop of Sherborne and wrote Alfred's biography. With these men Alfred was on the most intimate terms, and with their help he not only set on foot the celebrated *Anglo-Saxon Chronicle* to record the deeds of his house and nation but also undertook a notable series of translations from Latin into English, in order to place the best authorities on different branches of knowledge within the reach of his subjects. Among the works he selected for this purpose were Bede's *Ecclesiastical History*, Gregory's *Pastoral Care*, Orosius's *History of the World*, and Boethius's *De Consolatione Philosophiae*. All these by good fortune have come down to us, though Alfred's own Handbook is lost, in which he noted down what pleased him most in his reading. Many glimpses however are to be had of the king's own personal views in these works, for the translation is always free; and in them and the Chronicle we have the real starting point of English prose.

Alfred's peaceful reforms were twice interrupted by spells of war. In 885 a viking force attacked Rochester, and this induced Guthrum to break the peace; whereupon the West Saxon fyrd proceeded to besiege London. The upshot was the recapture of that important centre, and such an overthrow of Guthrum's forces that he had to cede the westernmost portion of his kingdom to the English.   The new frontier agreed upon is preserved for us in a document known as " Alfred and Guthrum's Peace."   It went from the Thames east of London "up the river Lea to its source near Luton, then across country to Bedford, and from there up the river Ouse to the Watling Street."   In other words the Danes ceded their portion of the Chilterns and the south-west half of Hendrica including St Albans, and these Alfred handed over to Duke Aethelred as being parts of Mercia.   At the same time Aethelred married Aethelfleda, Alfred's eldest child, who was now about sixteen, and so still further cemented the bond between Mercia and Wessex.   A further clause in the treaty which deserves notice, is the provision for equating the various grades of Englishmen and Danes, should legal questions arise in the ceded district involving a determination of their wergelds.   As to this the treaty laid down the rule that the Danish *bonde*, though in his home across the North Sea only the equal of a *ceorl*, should, in disputes between Saxons and Danes, be regarded as the equal of the Mercian " twelve-hynd man," the *thegn*, as he had come to be called by Alfred's day, while the Mercian *ceorl*, or " twy-hynd man," was only to be regarded as the equal of the half-free *liesing*.   In the case of the *bonde* and the *thegn* the *wer* was to be eight half marks of gold, equivalent, as the ratio of gold to silver was 9 : 1, to £24, and this in live stock meant 240 cows, the cow by Mercian law being valued at 24*d*.   In the case of the *liesing* and the *ceorl* on the other hand the *wer* was to be two hundred Mercian shillings, that is to say 960*d*. or £4, the hundred in this case being the long hundred of six score, and the Mercian shilling being equivalent to 4*d*.   The *wer* of the peasant classes therefore amounted in live stock to 40 cows, or the sixth part of the *wer* of the dear-born military class.   All this, when properly understood, is of considerable interest ; for it enables us to see how greatly Danish society had been modified by the conquest of Eastern England, and how seriously in the Danelaw the Saxon peasants had been depressed by the national defeat, even after some of their disasters had been retrieved and their prestige partially regained.

In 892 a far more dangerous crisis had to be faced when defeats in East Frankland drove another great fleet, led by a chief called Hasting, across the channel to seek lands in England.   Over 800 ships, we are told, set sail from Boulogne and coming to Kent effected lodgements at Appledore near Romney and at Milton near Sheppey, and later on at Benfleet in Essex.   With all his experience Alfred could hardly cope with the emergency, and for three years midland England was in a turmoil. It soon appeared that the aim of the invaders was to get possession of the Severn valley, still the least ravaged part of England, and in pursuit of this object they over and over again dashed across England from their base on the east coast and ravaged Aethelred's dukedom from end to end, one year wintering at Bridgnorth and another at Chester.   In the end, however, Hasting was foiled in all his efforts by the steady co-operation of the West Saxon and Mercian fyrds, and finding in 896 that no real help was to be obtained either from the North Welsh or from the Northumbrian or Midland Danes, he gave up the contest and went back to Frankland.   After this Alfred had peace for the rest of his days. He lived a few years longer, but died on 26 October 899, when still only fifty-one years old[1].

The fifty years following the death of Alfred are the time when the kingdom of England was really established.   Alfred's great work had been to save Wessex from foreign invaders, and then to re-organise what he had saved ; but he had never aimed at conquests beyond his borders. Even over Mercia he had exercised no real sovereignty, and still less over the chieftains of Glamorgan and Gwent, Brecknock and Dyfed, who had sought his protection ; and so he was in no sense king of England or even of half England.   When he died, the territories over which he ruled, and where his laws held good, were confined to the shires south of the Thames, and in the rest of England there were a far greater number of independent principalities than there had been a century earlier. When therefore his eldest son, generally called Edward the Elder to distinguish him from later kings of the same name, was elected to succeed him, it was only the West Saxon magnates who took part in the ceremony, and no one could have predicted that a union of the petty English states would soon be brought about by the West Saxon dynasty. Edward, however, unlike his father, within a few years adopted a policy of expansion in imitation of the earlier Bretwaldas, and fortune so aided him and the three capable sons who afterwards succeeded him in turn, that by 954 the house of Ecgbert had not merely acquired an overlordship of the old pattern but had completely ousted all the other ruling families, whether English or Danish, so that, formally at any rate, there was only one recognised king left in all England.

The events, which produced this far-reaching change, are clear enough in their main outlines, but it is very difficult to arrange them in their proper sequence, as no dates in Edward's reign (899–925) can be fixed with any certainty owing to discrepancies in chronology between the English, Welsh and Irish annals, discrepancies which later historians have attempted to get over by dovetailing the various accounts one into the other, and therefore duplicating not a few of the incidents of the story.   All the sources however agree in stating that Edward's first difficulties arose with his cousin Aethelwald, the younger of the sons of King Aethelred, Alfred's elder brother.   This prince, Aethelhelm his elder brother, and a third aetheling, called Osferth, had under Alfred's will divided between them the royal booklands in Sussex and Surrey. Aethelwald's share comprised Guildford, Godalming and Steyning, all

---

[1] The length of the reigns of Alfred, Edward the Elder and Aethelstan are matters of controversy ; for a recent discussion of the difficulties see M. L. R. Beavan, *Eng. Hist. Rev.* 1917, Vol. XXXII. 517–531.

extensive estates, but this endowment by no means satisfied him, and at the very opening of the new reign he took forcible possession of the newly-built borough of Twyneham, now Christchurch in Hampshire, and also of an old British fortress, which may still be seen, at Badbury Rings near Wimborne. Driven out of these by Edward, he fled to the Yorkshire Danes, who received him as if he were a dispossessed king and offered him their allegiance, being at the moment themselves without a ruler. This led a little later to an alliance between Aethelwald and Eric, King of East Anglia, who had succeeded Guthrum in 890, and the two together, imitating the strategy of Halfdene thirty years before, marched their forces across the Chiltern country to Cricklade on the Upper Thames with the intention of raiding Wiltshire. This invasion met with little effective opposition from Duke Aethelred of Mercia through whose territories it passed, but Edward replied by a bold counterstroke, sending a force from Kent to join the Mercians of London with orders to attack the Danish districts between the river Lee and the river Ouse. The news that the ealdormen of East and West Kent, Sigwulf and Sighelm, were ravaging between the Ouse and the well-known dykes which form such a feature in East Cambridgeshire, soon compelled Aethelwald and Eric to retrace their steps, and this led to a fierce encounter between the two armies at Holme, a hamlet of Biggleswade in Bedfordshire[1]. The English accounts admit that the Danes won the day, but their victory was a hollow one. Both Aethelwald and Eric were killed, and another Guthrum became king of East Anglia, who almost immediately afterwards made a peace[2] at Yttingaford, in the township of Linslade in Buckinghamshire, on the terms that the old treaty between Alfred and Guthrum of 886 should be reconfirmed and that the Danes, in the dioceses of London and Dorchester, should abjure heathendom and pay tithes and other church dues to the bishops.

This campaign not only rid Wessex of a dangerous aetheling but convinced the Danes that Edward and Aethelred were firm in their alliance, and that it was no safe matter to attack them. The result was a period of peace for Wessex, during which Edward shewed himself no unworthy follower of Alfred as a civil ruler. His first care was to finish his father's new minster at Winchester, known in later days as the Abbey of Hyde, and organise it as a college of clerks; and thither, as soon as the church was finished, he removed Alfred's tomb. Much more important however was a scheme, pressed upon him by Archbishop Plegmund, for increasing the number of the West Saxon sees. This was ultimately carried through in 909 on the deaths of Denewulf and

---

[1] The site of this battle has not hitherto been identified, though the hamlet of Holme figures in Domesday Book in seven entries and lies just in the required position on the old North Road.

[2] Liebermann, *Gesetze der Angelsachsen*, pp. 128–135. This undated document is not the actual treaty, but seems to embody its provisions.

Asser, the Bishops of Winchester and Sherborne, Plegmund having journeyed to Rome the year before to obtain the sanction of Pope Sergius III.   By it the two ancient dioceses of Winchester and Sherborne were replaced by five smaller ones, the bishops' seats being fixed at Winchester for Surrey and Hampshire, at Ramsbury near Marlborough for Berkshire and North Wiltshire, at Sherborne for South Wiltshire and Dorset, at Wells for Somerset and at Crediton for Devon and Cornwall.   These ecclesiastical reforms would by themselves be noteworthy and a credit to Edward.   They stand, however, by no means alone, his efforts to put down theft and to improve justice and trade being equally remarkable.   For these we must turn to his laws[1], especially to the dooms issued at Exeter which instructed the witan to search out better devices for maintaining the peace than had hitherto been employed, and to those ordering the king's " reeves " to hold " moots " every four weeks and to see that every man was " worthy of folkright."   This allusion to the moots held by the king's reeves is the first definite indication in the Anglo-Saxon laws of the existence, in Wessex or elsewhere, of any comprehensive system of local courts for areas smaller than the shires.   It does not follow from this that Edward need be regarded as the inventor of these courts, but it shews at any rate that he was active in developing them, a conclusion further borne out by another of his dooms which directs that all buying and selling must take place before a " port-reeve " in a " port."   Here also we have a novel provision notable for its ultimate effects ; for a " port " or urban centre practically meant in most cases a " borough," and so this rule set going a movement which in the end destroyed the military character of the boroughs and converted them into centres of trade and industry.

That Wessex could devote itself for a time to internal reform was largely due to the fact that its boundaries nowhere marched with the Danelaw, but for Mercia as a buffer state the conditions were just the opposite.   There, all round the frontiers there was chronic unrest, so that its duke was kept constantly busy with defensive measures.   In 907 for example he fortified Chester to guard against the Welsh and raiders from Ireland, while in 910–11 he had to meet an invasion of Danes from Yorkshire and the Midlands.   These bands seem to have ravaged all over the dukedom, one force penetrating to the Bristol Avon, and another across the Severn into Herefordshire.   In this emergency Aethelred naturally turned to his brother-in-law for help, and there followed a pitched battle near Tettenhall in Staffordshire in which Edward's forces took a prominent part.   The result was a great defeat for the Danes, no

---

[1] Liebermann, *op. cit.* pp. 138–145. One of these dooms (I Edw. *cap* 2) deserves special remark, as it contains the only mention of "folcland" to be found in the Anglo-Saxon Laws.   Elsewhere the term only occurs twice, in two landbooks, dated 858 and 880 (Birch, *Cart. Sax.*, Nos. 496, 558), dealing with estates in Kent and Surrey.

fewer than three kings, two jarls and seven holds being slain. In fact this victory marks the beginning of the reconquest of the Danelaw.

Shortly after Duke Aethelred died, leaving only a daughter to carry on his line. At the moment his decease made little difference, for his widow Aethelfleda took up the reins of government without opposition, and for nearly eight years (912–919) led the Mercian forces with a skill and energy which few women rulers have ever equalled. In the scanty annals of these years, which speak of her regularly as " the Lady of the Mercians," she is always described as the directing mind, and we are not told the names of the men who assisted her, but one cannot help suspecting that at her right hand there really stood her nephew Aethelstan, the heir to the throne of Wessex, who is known to have been fostered and trained in the arts of ruling by Aethelred. For if this supposition may be hazarded, it will account for the ease with which the Mercian heiress was set aside after Aethelfleda's death, and also for the fact that, when Aethelstan came to be king, he seems to have been as much at home in Mercia as in his ancestral dominions. At any rate throughout Aethelfleda's period of power there was complete accord between herself and her brother, and her first step was to arrange that Edward should take over the defence of the districts that owed obedience to London and Oxford, these being much more easily protected from Wessex than from the Severn Valley. And then began a long-sustained campaign, carried on over several years by the sister and brother in conjunction, with the avowed object of expanding their territories, Edward acting against the Danes from the south and Aethelfleda from the west. Their plan evidently was to keep cautiously moving forward on a regular system, erecting "boroughs" as they went along their frontiers, as Alfred had done in Wessex, to secure their base should they at any moment be forced to draw back. In 913 for example Aethelfleda prepared for an advance in the Trent Valley by erecting boroughs at Stafford and Tamworth, and Edward for an advance in Essex by building two others at Hertford and Witham. In 914 the Danes retaliated by a raid on Luton and a foray into Mercian Cilternsaete as far as Hook Norton, both of which were easily repulsed by Edward, while further north Aethelfleda fortified Warwick in ancient Mercia and Eddisbury in Westerna. In 915 the appearance of a force of vikings from Brittany in the Severn mouth caused some diversion, but Buckingham in Danish Cilternsaete was fortified none the less, and this led next year to the flight of Thurkytel, jarl of Bedford and the capture of his borough.

During these events, some of Aethelfleda's energy was being expended on her Welsh frontiers. We hear of a borough which she built at Chirbury in Shropshire and of an expedition into Brecknock ; but in 917 she returned to the prosecution of the main scheme and got possession of Derby. This meant that the armies of Northampton and Leicester were placed between two fires, and it convinced their jarls that something must be done. Accordingly they in 918 stirred up the jarl of Huntingdon to move his army across the Ouse and entrench himself at Tempsford in the neighbourhood of Holme in the hope of regaining Hendrica. At the same time they organised attacks on two new boroughs which Edward had just erected, one at Towcester in Middle Anglia and the other probably at Wing[1] near Aylesbury. Neither operation was however successful, and even the arrival of the king of East Anglia with considerable reinforcements for the men of Huntingdon failed to make any difference. Guthrum's intervention on the contrary proved his ruin, for Edward made an assault on Tempsford and there slew Guthrum and two of his jarls called Toglos and Mann. This crushing disaster seems to have taken all the fight out of the Danish leaders. We hear of one or two more encounters in Essex in connexion with Colchester and Maldon; and then the Danish resistance collapsed, and the various armies, as it were, tumbled over each other in their haste to make terms with the victorious English. The first chief to come in was Thurferth, the jarl of Northampton, and he was quickly followed by the captains commanding the armies of Huntingdon, Cambridge and East Anglia. All alike agreed to submit without further fighting, and took Edward for their protector and lord on the condition that they and their men should retain their estates and enjoy their national customs. At the same time the army of Leicester without further fighting submitted to Aethelfleda.

Great must have been the rejoicings throughout Wessex and Mercia at the triumphs of 918, but the next year had even greater events in store. It was opened by Edward marching to Stamford and there receiving the submission of the Danes of Kesteven and Holland. There too in June he received the news that Aethelfleda had died at Tamworth. At this juncture a less confident man might have hesitated what step to take. Not so Edward. Without loss of time he marched straight to Tamworth, claiming to be his sister's successor. And thereupon the Mercians also agreed to take him as their lord. This settled, he set out for Nottingham and took possession of it, and a little later he received the submission of the men of Lindsey. Finally embassies arrived from the chief princes of Wales, from Idwal of Gwynedd and Hywel of Deheubarth, the grandsons of Rhodri Mawr, tendering their alliance. Rarely indeed have events moved so quickly. At the beginning of 918 Edward was only one among a great number of princes claiming rule in England; at the close of 919 he was unquestioned superior of all men south of the Humber as well Danish as English.

It is natural to ask why the resistance of the Danes in central and eastern England broke down so rapidly after 911. Many causes may be assigned to account for it, the more obvious being their total lack of cohesion (no jarl helped another until it was too late) and the

---

[1] Wigingamere; cf. *Domesday Book*, i. 146 a. Witehunge.

softening of their manners as Christianity made headway among them. It seems also clear that few of the rank and file cared much by whom they were ruled, as long as they ran no risk of losing the fertile lands won by their fathers forty years before. Land-hunger had brought the vikings to England, not desire for national expansion, and so their ideal was peace, plenty and opportunities for trading, and not political independence. It is well also to remember that at the very moment when Aethelfleda succeeded her husband, the treaty of St Clair-sur-Epte provided a congenial asylum for the more ambitious and wilder spirits, so that from 911 onwards there was a constant drift of English Danes to Normandy, eager to take service under Rollo in the new Frankish Danelaw. A noticeable example of this movement is on record in the *Anglo-Saxon Chronicle*, which tells how Thurkytel, jarl of Bedford, made peace in 914, but a year or two later, with Edward's assistance, "fared over sea with such men as would follow him." This trend of events evidently was not overlooked by Edward, and fairly accounts for the confident way in which he kept pushing forward. Having reached the Humber and Mersey, he might well have paused for a year or two to consolidate what he had won. On the contrary, in the next year he is found advancing as steadily as ever, bent on regaining for Mercia the northern half of the ancient Westerna, the land "betwixt the Mersey and the Ribble," and, in order to control the road from Chester to York, building a fort at Manchester, well within the borders of the Danes of Yorkshire. These Danes had long been a prey to internal dissensions, the old curse of Northumbria, as it were, resting upon them, but they had recently accepted a new king in the person of Regnald of Waterford, an Irish viking, who had first got a footing in Cumberland and then spent most of his time in ravaging the territories of Ealdred, the high reeve of Bamborough, and of Constantine III, King of the Scots (900–942). Edward's bold advance justified itself more rapidly than he could have hoped. In 920, while building a borough at Bakewell in Peakland, he received the homage of all who dwelt in Northumbria, both English and Danes, that is to say of both Regnald and Ealdred of Bamborough. Nor was this all. According to the *Anglo-Saxon Chronicle* there also appeared an embassy from Donald of Strathclyde and from Constantine, saying that the whole nation of the Scots was prepared to take the West Saxon for their "father and lord." Patriotic Scots have mostly challenged the credibility of the annal which makes this assertion, especially as it later became the basis of the claim put forward by the Plantagenet kings of England to suzerainty over Scotland. It seems probable, however, that the embassy really did come to Bakewell, but meant no more than that Constantine and his neighbours wished to offer Edward their congratulations and pave the way for an alliance. It is quite gratuitous to suppose that they held themselves to be in any way submitting to him as vassals in the feudal sense.   In fact, even as regards the Yorkshire Danes, it need not be held that more was meant than that Regnald for the moment wished for peace; and so things remained as long as Edward lived.   He died on 17 July 925 having reigned 26 years.

Edward was succeeded by his son Aethelstan, an equally great organizer and soldier, who ruled for fourteen years (925–939).   The most striking military achievements of his reign were: the actual annexation of the kingdom of York in 926 on the death of Sihtric, Regnald's brother, an expedition beyond the Forth in 933 to chastise King Constantine for taking up the cause of Anlaf Cuaran, Sihtric's son, and the crowning battle of Brunanburh in 937, to be located it would seem at Birrenswark, an old Roman camp in Annandale nine miles north of the Solway.   By this latter victory he broke up a great league of Scots, Strathclyde Britons, Irish vikings, and Danes from Cumberland and Yorkshire, which Constantine had laboriously built up in order to avenge his own wrongs and re-establish a buffer state at York.   These triumphs completely cowed Aethelstan's enemies, and for the moment justified him in assuming the vaunting title of " Rex totius Britanniae " which is found on his coinage.   They also brought him very great renown on the Continent, so that contemporary sovereigns eagerly sought the hands of his sisters, one of them having married Charles the Simple, King of the West Franks, another marrying Hugh the Great, Count of Paris, the father of Hugh Capet, and a third Otto the Saxon, son of Henry the Fowler, who in due time was to found a new line of Roman Emperors.

Meagre as are the annals devoted to Aethelstan's reign in the Chronicle, we can also detect that he applied himself with energy to the work of adapting the institutions, which had hitherto served for the government of Wessex and Mercia, to the conditions of his greatly enlarged realm.   In particular he set about establishing new local machinery in the districts between the Thames and Welland which had longest resisted his father's arms.   Here he adopted the borough system invented by the Danes as the basis of a number of new shires, which are marked off from the older West Saxon shires by being named from a central fortress.   He also in all probability planned a new scheme of hidage for these shires, and further subdivided them for purposes of taxation, police and justice into a number of smaller divisions of varying size, called " hundreds," which continued in use till the nineteenth century.   No absolute proof can be given of this inference; but if the hundreds are counted shire by shire, it will be found that they are artificially arranged so as to form a neatly balanced scheme, in all containing 120 hundreds, and this is only likely to have been introduced in some period of resettlement after a crisis such as followed on Aethelstan's accession.   The term " hundred " moreover soon afterwards appears in the laws.   A table will best shew how the hundreds were distributed, viz. :

Oxfordshire	22	} 40		
Buckinghamshire	18		} 60	
Bedfordshire	12	} 20		
Huntingdonshire (4 double hundreds) ...	8			
Northamptonshire	30			
Cambridgeshire (excluding the Isle of Ely)	15	} 60		
Hertfordshire	9½			
Middlesex	5½	} 15		

Total 120

Similar reorganisation was also carried through further east; for in East Anglia and Essex we can also trace artificial hundred schemes, Essex in 1066 having twenty hundreds and East Anglia sixty, distributed in the proportion of 36 : 24 between Norfolk and Suffolk. In Essex, it would seem, there was also a new assessment of hidage, but not in East Anglia, perhaps because that province had not been actually conquered by force.

Another side of government, to which Aethelstan gave much careful attention, was the better maintenance of the peace as inculcated in his father's dooms. His laws on this head in fact, for their date, are very comprehensive, and it is interesting to find him relying on the feudal relation of lord and man as one means of securing good behaviour. He laid it down, for example, that all lordless men were to be compelled by their kinsmen to find themselves lords, and that the lords were to be responsible for producing their men, if charges were preferred against them. As one doom expressed it, every lord was to keep his men in his suretyship (*fidejussio*) to prevent thieving; and if he had a considerable number of vassals, he was ordered to appoint a reeve (*praepositus*) in each township to look after their behaviour. Another device adopted in Aethelstan's day with the same object was the so-called "*frithgild*," or peace association. This system was set up in the Chilterns and Essex by the advice of the bishops of London and Dorchester and the reeves in those dioceses, but it was also used in other parts. It consisted in grouping men together by tens and hundreds, the members of each group or *frithborh* being mutually responsible for each other's acts, and liable to be fined collectively if one of the group committed a wrong and defaulted. The importance of these new expedients is evident, but it must not be supposed that any attempt was made to apply them uniformly all over the realm. One law indeed was published prescribing a uniform coinage and fixing the number of moneyers for various towns; but it is clear that in the Five Boroughs and in the north Aethelstan as a rule let things alone, and was content to act mainly through the leading Danes who naturally maintained their own customs. For example, in spite of the fact that much of the king's time was devoted to organising shires and hundreds in the south, the more northern Danish provinces preserved their own analogous organisation into "*ridings*" (*i.e.* "third parts") and "*wapentakes*," their reckoning

CH. XIV.

of money in "*marks*" and "*ores*," and their reckoning of land by "*mantals*." The term "*hundred*" indeed was used in the north, but in quite different ways from its uses in Mercia and Wessex. Beyond the Welland it either denoted a sum of 120 ores, and was used as an elliptical expression for 8 pounds of silver or 12 marks, the ore being a sum of 16*d.*, or else it was used as a term of land measurement and denoted 120 *mantals*, the mantal being a unit of cultivation about half the size of the English "*yardland*," ten of them making a ploughland or "*tenmannetale*." Similarly the Northern Danes preserved their own tariff of wergelds, which they stated in "*thrymsas*" or units of 3*d.*, the hold's wergild being 4000 thrymsas, the jarl's 8000, and an aetheling's 15,000.

Aethelstan's successor was his half-brother Edmund, a youth of eighteen, who had fought at Brunanburh. His accession in October 939 was the signal for a tardy attempt to regain independence on the part of the Yorkshire Danes. Led by Wulfstan, whom Aethelstan had made Archbishop of York, they set up Anlaf Guthfrithson, the King of Dublin, as their ruler. By themselves the men of Yorkshire were perhaps no longer formidable; but the revolt quickly spread to the Five Boroughs, and this enabled Anlaf to cross the Welland and attack Northampton. There he was beaten off; but he soon afterwards stormed Tamworth. He was then himself in turn besieged by Edmund at Leicester. The upshot was a truce, by which Edmund acknowledged the Watling Street as his frontier. This was a great loss ; but on Anlaf meeting his death in Bernicia in 941, Edmund at once fell on Anlaf Cuaran, Guthfrithson's cousin and successor ; and in 942 he regained the ancient Mercian frontier, which ran from Dore near Sheffield eastwards to Whitwell near Worksop and so to the Humber. Two years later Anlaf Cuaran fled back to Dublin, and Edmund re-entered York, but feeling himself unequal to maintaining control over the whole of Aethelstan's realm, handed over Cumberland in 945 to Malcolm, King of Scots (942–952), on the condition "that he should be his fellow-worker by land and sea," and keep in control the unruly colony of Norwegians, who by this time had firmly seated themselves round Carlisle.

When not fighting Edmund seems to have been much under the influence of churchmen, especially of Oda, a remarkable Dane whom he promoted to the see of Canterbury, and of Dunstan, a Somersetshire noble a trifle younger than himself, whom he made Abbot of Glastonbury probably in 943. It is to Oda and other bishops, rather than to the king himself, that we must ascribe a measure, of considerable importance for the growth of civilisation, which is found in Edmund's dooms. This is an ordinance which declared that for the future a manslayer's kinsmen, provided they lent the culprit no support after the deed, were not to be held liable to make any amends to the slain man's kin, and conversely that the *maegth* or kindred of the slain man were only to take their vengeance on the slayer himself, who was to be treated by every one as an outlaw and to forfeit all he possessed. Here we have the first recorded attempt in England to put down the time-honoured institution of the blood feud, and to make each man responsible only for his own acts, and to break up the solidarity of the powerful family groups, whose feeling of cousinship often reduced the authority of the state to a shadow. Needless to say the good old custom of following up feuds relentlessly, generation after generation, was at first little abated by this well-meant edict. Its promulgation however marks the spread of a civilising movement which was ultimately to make away with the whole system of private war and wergilds.

Another movement, which was also making gradual progress at this time, and may perhaps therefore be best mentioned here, though it had begun before Edmund's day and was not completed in his reign, concerns the position and functions of the magnates in charge of the shires. All through the centuries of the Heptarchy and down to Alfred's death, each shire, so far as our information goes, had been ruled by its own "scirman," called indifferently either duke, prefect or alderman, most of whom were of royal descent. As soon however as England began to be unified, a demand for wider jurisdictions arose. A shire apiece had been all that the magnates could expect, so long as their king himself ruled only Wessex or Mercia, but their ambitions naturally expanded in proportion with the growth of the kingdom. As the tenth century advanced they accordingly pressed Edward the Elder and his sons more and more to abandon the old scheme of one duke to one shire, and gradually succeeded in getting a new system introduced under which the shires were grouped three or four together with a duke over each group. It must have been a protracted process changing from one system to the other, but the results as they stood in Edmund's day are clear enough, and may be inferred from the lists of magnates who are found attesting his numerous charters. If these be analysed, it is seen that, apart from "jarls" with Danish names, who still ruled districts in the Five Boroughs and beyond the Humber, the total number of dukes attesting at one time is never more than eight, and these can be distributed with moderate certainty over Southern England in the proportion of three to the counties south of the Thames and five to the Midlands and East Anglia[1]. This change, moreover, carried with it another. The new type of dukes could not always be present to preside in the shire-moots. Hence there arose the need for local officials of a lower grade intermediate between the port-reeves and the dukes, a class who seem to be referred to for the first time in the laws of Aethelstan and who ultimately came to be entitled "*scirgerefan*" or shire-reeves[2].

[1] Chadwick, *Studies in Anglo-Saxon Institutions*, p. 188.
[2] The origin of the sheriffs is by no means clear. The term "scirgerefa" is not found in the laws of any of the Anglo-Saxon kings.

This gradual evolution, it need hardly be pointed out, was not altogether in the best interests of the monarchy; for the new dukes had to be given very considerable estates to support their authority, and this meant that the Crown was unable to retain in its own hands sufficient of the newly-won territories to guarantee itself the same territorial superiority over the dukes, as it had formerly possessed in Wessex. Statistics of course cannot be produced to shew the precise distribution of territorial influence, but all indications lead to the conclusion that, everywhere north of the Thames, the Crown had to content itself with a comparatively weak position, especially in East and Middle Anglia, which from 930 onwards were placed in the hands of an aetheling enjoying such a regal endowment that he came to be familiarly known as Aethelstan Half-king.

Responsibility for this development in the direction of feudalism should probably be laid on Aethelstan's shoulders rather than on Edmund's; for Edmund had little opportunity of reconsidering his brother's policy, his career being cut short by assassination when he was still under twenty-five. He left two sons, Eadwig and Edgar, but as these were mere children, the crown was passed on to their uncle Eadred, the youngest son of Edward the Elder. This prince was also short-lived, but his reign of nine years (946–955) remains a landmark, because it witnessed the last attempt made by the men north of the Humber to re-assert their lost independence. In this rising the Danes were led at first by Anlaf Cuaran, their former king, and finally by a viking called Eric, probably Eric Blood-axe, son of Harold Fairhair the unifier of Norway. They also had the support of Archbishop Wulfstan, Edmund's shifty opponent, whom the West Saxon house had vainly tried to bind to their cause by a grant of Amounderness (central Lancashire). The chief incidents of the struggle are reported to have been the deposition and imprisonment of Wulfstan, the burning of Ripon and sundry encounters near Tanshelf, now better known as Pontefract, to secure the ford over the river Aire. In the end however Eric abandoned the struggle, and in 954 Eadred took final possession of Yorkshire and committed it to Oswulf, the high reeve of Bamborough, to hold as a "jarldom." Thus was completed the long process of welding England into a single kingdom with continuous territories stretching from the Forth to the English Channel.

CHAPTER XV.

ENGLAND FROM A.D. 954 TO THE DEATH OF EDWARD THE CONFESSOR.

The task which Alfred's descendants had undertaken of creating an English nation was by no means accomplished in 954. The conquest of the Yorkshire Danes by Eadred and the final expulsion of Eric in that year completed the territorial development of the kingdom, but there still remained the harder tasks of creating a national feeling and a common law ; and even a hundred years later only slight progress can be discerned in either of these important matters. For the moment however the inhabitants of England might fairly congratulate themselves on what had been achieved by the last two generations, and the prospects for the future seemed bright enough. War and the danger of war were over at least for a time ; the country had become consolidated as never before, and the only trouble, which seemed at all threatening, was a certain want of robustness, which was beginning to manifest itself in the royal house. Of this weakness Eadred, despite his energy, was an unmistakeable example. By all accounts he must have been, even from boyhood, a chronic invalid, and his health grew worse as he grew older. It was but little of a surprise then to his subjects that he lived to be only thirty-one, dying at Frome in Somerset somewhat suddenly in 955 while still unmarried.

Eadred's premature death opened the succession to his nephew Eadwig, the son of Edmund, who had been passed over in 946 as too young to rule, and even now was little more than fifteen. From the very first this youth seems to have had an aversion to most of the advisers, who had surrounded his father and uncle, and to have been under the control of a party among the nobles of Wessex who resented the influence which had been exercised at court by Dunstan, the Abbot of Glastonbury, and Eadgifu the young king's grandmother. The result was that quarrels broke out even at the king's coronation, and within a year Dunstan was banished from England and driven to take refuge at Ghent in the abbey of Blandinium. The treatment meted out to Dunstan, together with an unwise marriage made by the king, led to a revolt breaking out in 957, apparently organised by the leading men of the Midlands.   These rebels at once recalled Dunstan, and, supported by Aethelstan Half-king, the great duke of East Anglia, set up Edgar, Eadwig's younger brother, as a rival king.   For a time it seemed as if the unity of England was once more in jeopardy.   Eadwig retained the support of Oda, the Archbishop of Canterbury, and still controlled Wessex ; but the boy Edgar was recognised as king north of the Thames, and in 958 found himself strong enough to secure the bishopric of Worcester for Dunstan, and a little later the bishopric of London as well.   Most fortunately, however, open war was avoided, and in 959 Eadwig died, whereupon Oda abandoned his hostility and Edgar, who was now sixteen, succeeded to the undivided sovereignty.

Edgar's reign, though a period of almost profound peace and therefore dull from the narrative point of view, forms a notable epoch. It lasted some sixteen years (959–975), and is memorable not only for a considerable body of secular legislation but as a period, during which churchmen held the reins of power, and used their influence over the king and the leading nobles to promote a much needed ecclesiastical reform. This reform, whether they deliberately designed it or not, so increased the prestige and popularity of their order that, by the end of the reign, the political power and landed endowments of the English Church were not far from doubled.   Ever since the coming of the vikings, notwithstanding Alfred's remarkable efforts to provide a remedy, the English clergy, both the regulars and the seculars, had remained sunk in a deplorable condition of ignorance and lack of discipline.   Whatever statesmanship had manifested itself under Alfred's successors, had come almost wholly from the warrior and princely classes.   In spite of all their energy in securing the payment of tithes and church dues, few of the bishops or parish clergy had followed high ideals or set any worthy standard before their flocks.   Lax conditions prevailed also among the regular clergy.   Many monasteries had lost their endowments by lay encroachments, and stood practically empty and ruined, while the majority of the foundations which had survived were no longer tenanted by monks living in strict isolation from the world, but by colleges of clerks[1] living under customs which were of varying strictness, but all involving very little of the monk's rigorous discipline.   In monasteries, such as these, the obligations of celibacy, poverty, and the common life prescribed by the Rule of St Benedict were by no means insisted on ; and the clerks who enjoyed the endowments were as often as not married men living with their families in their own houses and dispensing hospitality to their friends with considerable display and luxury.   No doubt there were some devout

---

[1] The English do not seem as yet to have adopted the continental term "canonicus" to distinguish clerks living in communities from the ordinary clergy.   Some term however was clearly needed, and "canon" gradually became current.   A clause in Aethelred's Laws for example, issued *c.* 1008, prescribes specially for "canonicas." Liebermann's *Gesetze*, p. 238.

men among them; but in general their zeal in attending services in their minster churches left much to be desired, and it was difficult to get them even to reside continuously in the neighbourhood of their duties, as they found hunting and travelling about far more to their taste than the solemn chanting of the "canonical hours" for the public weal some six to nine times a day.

Before Edmund's reign few protests had been raised in England over the practical disappearance of strict monasticism. St Oswald's Abbey at Gloucester, founded by Duke Aethelred and the Lady Aethelfleda in 909, the New Minster at Winchester, founded by Edward the Elder as Alfred's memorial, and Milton Abbey in Dorset, founded by Aethelstan, had all been organised as a matter of course as colleges of clerks; while Edmund himself in 944 made a home at Bath for fugitive clerks from Flanders who had been expelled from St Bertin's Abbey at St Omer for refusing to accept reforms. Within the English Church the first men to realise that reform was desirable seem to have been the Danish Archbishop Oda and Aelfheah, who occupied the see of Winchester from 934 to 951. Both these churchmen had relations with the Continent and through them became imbued with the stricter ideas as to clerical and monastic life, which in Aethelstan's time had taken hold of Western Frankland. These ideas in the first instance had emanated either from the famous abbey of Cluny in Burgundy, whence they had spread to Fleury (St Benoît-sur-Loire), regarded in the tenth century as the leading monastery in Neustria, or from Brogne near Namur, whence came St Gerard, who between 939 and 944 reformed the monasteries of Flanders. Several incidents in Oda's career shew that he favoured the new ideas, and wished to spread them in England[1]. In 942 for instance, when appointed archbishop, he decided that he ought himself to become a monk, and sent to Fleury to obtain the monastic habit. Nor was it long before he issued new constitutions for his province, and among them was one insisting that all ordained persons, whether men or women, should observe the rule of chastity. Again a few years later, when his nephew Oswald decided to become a monk, Oda advised him to go and study at Fleury, as the best house in which to prepare himself for his vocation. Bishop Aelfheah's preference for strict monasticism can be traced back still earlier, for we find him already in Aethelstan's reign persuading Dunstan, who was his kinsman, to abandon the idea of marriage and devote himself to a life of asceticism and study. The result was that Dunstan, on his appointment to be abbot of Glastonbury by Edmund, had at once set zealously to work to convert the clerks, over whom he was called to rule, into a more disciplined society by making them share a common dormitory and refectory and

---

[1] The parts played by the chief leaders of the monastic reform in England have been much debated. The views here presented adopt in the main the conclusions reached by Dr J. Armitage Robinson in his two valuable papers, entitled *The Saxon Bishops of Wells* and *St Oswald and the Church of Worcester*.

by refusing to admit any more married men to the community. Glastonbury thus led the way in reform in England, and became a school of
piety and learning in which many men were trained who were to make
their mark in the future. The most remarkable of these was Aethelwold, a native of Winchester. He, like Dunstan, had come as a youth
under the influence of Bishop Aelfheah. At Glastonbury he rose to be
"dean" and Dunstan's right-hand man, and about 950 by the influence of
Eadgifu, the queen mother, he was selected by Eadred to take charge of
Abingdon in Berkshire, one of Ine's foundations, which had become
almost desolate. Very enthusiastic by nature, Aethelwold had hardly
been satisfied with the amount of discipline enforced at Glastonbury.
His first act accordingly, on reaching Abingdon, was to dispatch his
friend Osgar, another of Dunstan's pupils, to Fleury, so that he might
be furnished with first-hand knowledge of what was being done on the
Continent, and then make his abbey a model for England. Backed
by Eadred's patronage Abingdon soon grew to be a large and well
endowed foundation, observing the rule of St Benedict in its most
stringent form. Nor was its progress hindered under Eadwig, who went on
showering benefactions on it notwithstanding Aethelwold's connexion with
Dunstan and the curtailment of his own resources by the revolt of Mercia.

The acceptance of Edgar by the West Saxons gave the advocates of
reform a much freer hand, as the young king from the first relied on
Dunstan as his principal adviser. In 960 he promoted him to the see of
Canterbury, and shortly afterwards proclaimed himself definitely one of
the reforming party by appointing Oswald, Oda's nephew, to the see of
Worcester and Aethelwold to that of Winchester. Though all three
prelates were equally pledged to reform, they set about it in different
ways. Dunstan, though he had a hand in the reform of Westminster
and Malmesbury and perhaps of Bath, thought most of raising the tone
of the laity and the parish priests, and consequently spent much of
his energy in warring against drunkenness and immorality. Aethelwold
on the other hand, holding that the state of the monasteries was the most
crying evil, did little for the laity, and pressed on with a ruthless crusade
throughout Wessex, beginning with Chertsey and the two minsters at
Winchester, by which he hoped to set monks in the shoes of the collegiate
clergy. He seems to have offered the clerks, whether married or not, only
two alternatives, either complete acceptance of a most stringent monastic
vow or instant expulsion, and at the old Minster, when argument proved
of no avail, he actually resorted to violence, calling in lay assistance to
expropriate his opponents from their property. In the Severn valley,
the course pursued by Oswald was more tactful. Relying on example, he
left the clerks of Worcester and Gloucester undisturbed, and merely
established a small house for monks near Bristol at Westbury-on-Trym.
Meanwhile the king started a movement in the Danelaw to refound some
of the great abbeys which had been destroyed in the Danish wars and

which still lay in ruins. The chief of these were Ely, Medeshamstede and Thorney. Thanks to Aethelwold, these were all re-established and filled with monks, Medeshamstede taking the name of Peterborough. A new model abbey also arose at Ramsey in Huntingdonshire about 969. This was the joint work of Bishop Oswald and Duke Aethelwin of East Anglia, a son of Aethelstan Half-king; and it was from Ramsey a few years later that Oswald brought monks first to Winchcombe and ultimately to his cathedral church at Worcester, establishing them in his "familia" side by side with the clerks, whose life interests he respected. Finally, to set the seal on these activities, Aethelwold at Edgar's request translated the Rule of St Benedict into English for the benefit of those who were weak in Latin. He also, with the object of introducing uniformity of practice into the daily life of the monasteries, composed a new rule for English monks, known as the "Regularis Concordia Anglicae Nationis," founded partly on the custom of Fleury and Ghent and partly on the "Capitula" issued in 817 by Benedict of Aniane.

Another side of the ecclesiastical awakening which characterised Edgar's reign is seen in the care with which the reforming prelates set about developing and managing the estates which the laity, encouraged by the king, on all sides pressed upon them. The best evidence of this is found at Worcester, where a number of records still survive shewing how Bishop Oswald personally superintended the administration of the demesnes belonging to his church. Among them are some seventy deeds in which the bishop is seen granting out portions of the episcopal lands to persons whom he describes as his *thegns, knights* or *milites* on condition of faithful service, and side by side with these is preserved a letter, addressed by the bishop to King Edgar, in which he reports in explicit terms exactly what the nature of the bargain was and what were the services which the tenants were to render for their holdings. For the most part these leases, or "land-loans" as they are called, were for the period of three lives, that is to say they were roughly tantamount to ninety-nine year leases, the first tenant having the right to name two successors, after which the land was to revert to the church; but in the meantime the tenants were to pay yearly church-scots, at the rate of a horse-load of corn for each hide of land which they held, to pay toll to the bishop when they bought or sold, to render pannage for their pigs when feeding in the bishop's woods and help their lord in his hunting, to ride on the lord's errands and fulfil all the duties of a knight or, as the letter expresses it, fulfil the "*lex equitandi quae ad equites pertinet.*" What makes these curious records particularly interesting is the clear implication, which they convey, that already the estates of the great English ecclesiastics were taking very much the shape of the baronies of a later day, and that we can discern in these "knights," though they cannot yet be called military tenants, a class who held by a tenure which was almost feudal, and which would easily become "tenure in chivalry" as soon as the tactics of war changed and the time-honoured method of fighting on foot was replaced by reliance on heavy cavalry. These documents in fact shew us how in Edgar's day, side by side with the religious reform, there developed a further drift towards feudalism, an effect of the steady accumulation of land into greater and greater estates. They shew also how prominent a part in this economic evolution may be assigned to the churchmen, for though no other records of estate management have survived, as detailed as those of Worcester, there are plenty of indications that all the ecclesiastical corporations were acting in these matters more or less on uniform lines.

Though the social and religious movements are clearly the most important things that happened in Edgar's reign, it must not be thought that the king remained all his life a mere tool in the hands of the ecclesiastics and had no policy of his own. Like most of his immediate predecessors, he evidently, on coming to manhood, had closely at heart the due maintenance of order in all parts of his realm, and kept constantly amending and sharpening the machinery for enforcing the peace and dispensing justice. His laws no doubt shew the influence of Dunstan in the minuteness with which they deal with tithe and the observance of fasts and festivals, but they are also remarkable for their precise rules as to buying and selling and the pursuit of thieves, as to the maintenance of the suretyship system of *frithborhs* and as to the periods when the various courts were to be held. Specially famous is his ordinance as to the local courts, which contains the first clear proof of a regular division of the shires for judicial purposes into moderate sized units called "hundreds," each with its own tribunal sitting every four weeks. A further step of somewhat doubtful wisdom, as it tended to undermine the royal authority, was to place some of the hundreds, so far as the administration of justice was concerned, under the control of the re-formed monasteries. Considerable districts thereby acquired the status of ecclesiastical franchises, in which the local courts were no longer held in the king's name, and in which the profits of justice went into the coffers of some minster church and not into the king's treasury. The first monastic houses to acquire these franchises, or "sokes" as they were termed in the vernacular (from *sócne*, the Anglo-Saxon term for jurisdiction), were Peterborough and Ely; and there seems no reason to doubt the local traditions, which tell us that they obtained them from Edgar on their first foundation at the instance of Bishop Aethelwold. No formal Latin charters from the king have come down to us attesting these grants, but in either case there are some curious Anglo-Saxon records[1] still existing which more or less explain their nature. From these we can see that Peterborough obtained judicial control over a block of eight hundreds in Northamptonshire, having Oundle as their

---

[1] For Peterborough cf. Birch, *Cart. Sax.* No. 1130 and *Anglo-Saxon Chronicle* E, 963. For Ely cf. Birch, *Cart. Sax.* No. 1267.

chief town, while Ely obtained similar control not only over the two hundreds lying round the monastery, which made up the Isle of Ely, but also over a district of five hundreds in East Suffolk, known as "Wichlawa," having Woodbridge on the Deben as its centre and also comprising Sudbourne with the port of Orford, an estate which Edgar had granted to Aethelwold as a reward for translating the Rule of St Benedict into English. In the "sokes" thus created the essential novelty was not merely the transfer of the king's rights to the monks, but the fact that by the transfer great numbers of men, both small and great, who were in no way the tenants of the monks or under their patronage by "commendation," nevertheless came thus to be subjected to them for police and judicial purposes, and had, if charged with any crime, to appear before officials appointed by them, and became liable to pay to the monks fines whenever they were unfortunate enough to be convicted. In other words the creation of the sokes also created a new kind of lordship, so that the freemen of these districts for the future all had, as it were, three lords over them; first their immediate personal lord, to whom they were tied by commendation; secondly the lord of the hundred, to whom they owed "soke"; and thirdly the king or supreme lord, to whom they owed military service, and to whom they could still appeal as a last resort in judicial matters if the lord of the hundred persistently refused to do them adequate justice.

Here we see no small step taken, at the instance of the ecclesiastics, in the direction of feudalism, one too which was certain to be regarded by the lay magnates as a precedent justifying them in seeking similar franchises for themselves. As yet, however, we have no reason to suppose that Edgar had favoured any laymen in this way; and the only other notable franchise which we can ascribe to him is one which was set up in Worcestershire in favour of Oswald, but which differed from those granted to Aethelwold's foundations in extending only to estates which were already in the bishop's ownership, and to men who were under his lordship as tenants of the see of Worcester. Here again we can produce no genuine Latin charter in witness of Edgar's grant; but none the less we may accept as credible the traditions enshrined in the celebrated but suspect landbook known as *Altitonantis*, and vouched for in the main by the account of Worcestershire given in the Domesday Survey[1]. These authorities, if read together, tell us that Oswald was given a seignorial jurisdiction over about a third of the lands of his see, comprising 300 hides lying scattered in various parts in the valleys of the Severn and the Avon, and that he was further permitted to organise this special area into three new hundreds, which together came to be known as the triple hundred of "Oswaldeslau." The creation of this soke, though in extent of juris- diction a much narrower one than those given to Peterborough and Ely,

[1] Cf. Birch, *Cart. Sax.* No. 1135; *Domesday Book,* I. 172 *b.*, and Maitland, *Domes- day Book and Beyond,* pp. 267–269.

had a very disturbing effect on the local organisation of Worcestershire; for the new hundreds had little geographical coherence and were in every case merely artificial aggregates of land, pieces of them lying interspersed among estates belonging to other lords, and pieces of them being even quite outside the proper bounds of the county and forming detached islands in Gloucestershire. The net result, therefore, was that the hundreds of Worcestershire became a sort of patchwork, and the respective jurisdictions of the king and the bishop remained ever afterwards most awkwardly intermixed. These administrative and legal changes, as well as the general character of his dooms, plainly shew that Edgar was an active ruler, and there can be little doubt that he deserves to share with Dunstan the credit for the peacefulness and increase of civilisation, which marked his reign and made such an impression on his contemporaries. We cannot, however, altogether commend his policy in the matter of the sokes which he created in favour of Aethelwold and Oswald; for he thereby initiated a process which could not fail in the long run to diminish the effectiveness of the central government.

Edgar died in 975, prematurely like so many of his race, being not yet thirty-three, and was buried by Dunstan at Glastonbury. He was twice married and left two sons, Edward a boy of thirteen born of his first wife, and Aethelred aged seven, the child of his second wife Aelfthryth[1]. This Devonshire lady, the sister of the founder of Tavistock Abbey, was filled with ambition for her family, and would not acquiesce in the kingdom passing whole to her stepson, and helped by a party among the Mercian nobility who still cherished a resentment for the hard treatment that had been meted out to the clerks, attempted to obtain recognition for Aethelred. Dunstan, however, with the help of Oswald, who had become Archbishop of York in 971, though still retaining the see of Worcester, supported Edward and caused him to be elected by a witan and crowned at Kingston in Surrey. If the unity of England was to be maintained, this settlement was obviously a wise one, but it only drove the discontented party into more violent action, led by Aelfhere, the duke who had been placed in Edgar's day in control of the Severn valley. Aelfhere probably was opposed to Dunstan's continued control of the king, but his particular grievances seem to have been against Oswald, who had handed over Winchcombe Abbey to Germanus, a monk from Ramsey, and had also tried to displace the clerks from Pershore, a foundation connected with Aelfhere's house. High-born canons, friends and kinsmen of Aelfhere, had thereby lost their incomes and were clamouring for restitution. In judging this movement no reliance can be placed on the accounts of it which have survived, for they originate without exception from the side of the monks and depict all sympathisers with

---

[1] Aelfthryth had been previously married to the eldest son of Aethelstan Half-king. Edgar probably improved his territorial position in East Anglia by marrying her.

the clerks as the blackest scoundrels. The only point that stands out clearly is that Aelfhere and his friends were strong enough to drive out the monks from Evesham and replace their rivals in several of the Worcestershire and Gloucestershire foundations. Meantime a somewhat similar movement had developed in the eastern Midlands in connexion with the lands that had been acquired by Ramsey, Ely and Peterborough. It was alleged that many of them had been taken unjustly from their former owners. Flushed by his successes in the west, Aelfhere came over to support the malcontents, but the fenland abbeys had powerful defenders in Aethelwin, who had founded Ramsey, and in Brihtnoth, the duke of the East Saxons, who had been a liberal benefactor to Ely. These nobles raised armed forces to defend the estates of the monasteries, and eventually Aelfhere and his partisans had to retire discomfited, Aethelwin being ever afterwards styled among the monks in gratitude for his services " the Friend of God." These disputes exhibit Dunstan as no longer equal to the task of maintaining order and were followed almost immediately by his downfall from power. This was brought about in 978 by the murder of the young Edward, a deed done in cold blood at Corfe in Dorset, apparently at the instigation of the ambitious Aelfthryth. If Dunstan had still retained his earlier vigour, he would have promptly taken steps to punish the conspirators; but the murder went unavenged, and Aethelred, though only ten years old, commenced unchallenged a reign which was fated to last for thirty-seven years (978–1016) and bring England untold disasters.

Aethelred's minority was necessarily a long one, but so far as we know without any striking incidents. The leaders of Edgar's time were all ageing and one by one passing into the background. Dunstan lived till 988, but withdrew from court in 980 and spent the rest of his days in dignified retirement, busied with ecclesiastical duties. The rivalry between the monks and clerks cooled down with the deaths of Bishop Aethelwold and Duke Aelfhere some four years later, nor did Oswald or Aethelwin again play parts of importance, although they survived till 992. The ecclesiastical fight ended in a drawn battle, for the canons retained possession of Canterbury and York, of London, Dorchester and Lichfield, of Bury St Edmunds, St Albans and Beverley, and even in Wessex kept some important churches such as Wells and Chichester. As to the king we hear that he was involved in a dispute with Aelfhere's heir, but we do not even know who took charge of his education. His minority in fact would be almost a blank, were it not for some entries in the Chronicle which speak of renewed viking incursions. These began in 980, when raiders made descents on Chester, Thanet and Southampton. The first batch no doubt came from Ireland or Man, the others more probably from Scandinavia; but no one thought them dangerous, even though they were followed by further raids in 982 on Devon and Cornwall. In reality they were the opening of another period of trial for England, and foreshadowed Danish and Norwegian attacks not less dangerous to the security and freedom of Englishmen than those captained by Ingwar and Guthrum in the ninth century.

The position of England about the year 990, when Aethelred attained his majority, might seem at first sight less vulnerable than in Alfred's day. The land was no longer split into rival kingdoms; it had fortresses and ships and the confidence born of former victories. But this impression of unity and strength is misleading. In reality, the West Saxon dynasty had not succeeded in assimilating its conquests further north than the river Welland. In the "Five Boroughs" and in Yorkshire, and still more beyond the Tees, it was from every point of view extremely weak. There is no evidence for example that Edgar, for all his popularity, ever shewed his face in these parts, or that he had estates there bringing in any appreciable revenue, or that he appointed any reeves. Jarls of Danish descent ruled, quite uncontrolled, the half-Danish population in accordance with Danish laws and customs, and only gave their allegiance to the king because they were left alone. Even the Church had failed to reassert itself among the "holds" and "socmen." The sees of York, Lincoln and Leicester were still, as it were, only appendages of Worcester and Dorchester, rarely visited by their bishops, badly endowed and honeycombed with heathen practices only thinly veiled. Nor beyond the Welland had any attempt been made to found any monasteries of the reformed pattern. Little reliance then could be placed on the patriotism of these regions, for should Danish invaders once more get a foothold in the country, the chief land-owners would have much in common with the enemy, and might easily be enticed into joining them.

At the same time it must be remembered that the Scandinavian lands had made in the last century even greater strides towards consolidation than England. Norway under Harold Fairhair (850–933) and his descendants had ceased to be a mere collection of warring chieftaincies, while Denmark under Harold Bluetooth (950–986) had grown into a fairly compact state, and imposed its sway on its neighbours. As stated in the runic inscription on the Jellinge Stone, the famous monument in Jutland which Harold erected in honour of his parents, Gorm and Thyra, he had "won all Denmark and Norway and made the Danes Christians." He had made the "Wick" and the south of Norway a component part of his realm; he had planted Danish outposts in Pomerania and Prussia, he had founded the great stronghold of Jómsborg in Wendland, and he had forced Hákon the Bad to hold northern Norway and the Throndlaw as his vassal. More than this, by his successes he had awakened again the old viking spirit, and set the dragon ships as of old sailing the seas in search of adventure. His closing years were not so successful as his prime. In 975 Hákon had revolted, and in 986 the old king was himself slain fighting against his son Svein, who had thrown off Christianity. His death, however, did not make the Danish power less formidable. The undutiful Svein, Svein Forkbeard, as he was nicknamed, was as able as his father, and bent on reconquering Norway, or failing that extending his realm elsewhere. He had sailed all the seas as a viking and already had his eye on England. There were plenty of reasons then about 990 why Englishmen, had they been well informed about the outside world, should have had forebodings as to the future, and be wondering what manner of leader they had in the young Aethelred.

The first raids, sufficiently serious to test Aethelred's capacity, began in 991, when Olaf Tryggvason, a famous Norwegian exile, who had claims on the throne of Norway, burned Ipswich and defeated and slew Brihtnoth, the duke of the East Saxons, at Maldon. Instead of hastening with all speed to avenge this disaster, Aethelred could think of no better counsel than to bribe the invaders to depart by an offer of £10,000. This was done with the advice of Sigeric, the Archbishop of Canterbury, and other magnates, and precedents could be found for it in Alfred's reign. None the less it was a most unwise expedient, as it gave the raiders the impression that the king was a weakling and that Englishmen were afraid of fighting. Two years later Olaf went harrying along the coasts of Northumberland and Lindsey, and in 994 was joined by Svein, who for the moment had been driven from Denmark by Eric, the King of Sweden. Their design was to pillage London. The citizens, however, put up such a stout defence that the allied princes abandoned the enterprise and betook themselves to Sussex and Hampshire. There they obtained horses and ravaged far and wide. Again Aethelred and the witan thought only of buying a respite, this time with £16,000 and an offer to supply provisions. Having accepted these terms, Olaf came to Andover on a visit to Aethelred in order to be baptised a Christian, and soon afterwards sailed away to claim the throne of Norway. Successful in this adventure, he never afterwards had leisure to trouble England. Not so King Svein. He too sailed away to deal with the Swedes, and for some years was busied in securing his power in Denmark ; but he still kept England in mind, and was only biding his opportunity.

Meantime lesser men continued to make yearly attacks on the coasts of Wessex, and always with such success owing to the quarrels and incompetence of the English leaders that at last Aethelred in despair determined to take some of the vikings into his pay to keep off the remainder. The chief of these was Pallig, a high-born Danish jarl, who had married Svein's sister, Gunnhild. The immediate result, it would seem, was satisfactory, for we hear in the year 1000 of an expedition being led by Aethelred against the Norsemen of Cumberland and the Isle of Man, who had for years been a menace to Yorkshire and the land betwixt the Mersey and the Ribble. The experiment nevertheless was a very risky one, and a year later proved quite ineffective to stop a fresh force of vikings landing in Devon, which ultimately was only bought off with a promise of £24,000 after a triumphant march from Teignton and Exmouth through Somerset and Wiltshire to Southampton Water. Instead of fighting this force Pallig actually joined it with all the ships he could lay hold of, a piece of treachery which enraged Aethelred to such a degree that he lost control of himself and planned a general massacre of the Danes in his service and even of their families. This utterly barbarous and unwise piece of retaliation was carried out on St Brice's day 1002 to the shame of all chivalrous Englishmen, and among the victims was not only Pallig and his son but his wife Gunnhild, Svein's sister, whom Aethelred was holding as a hostage.

The tragedy of Gunnhild's death marks the turning point in Aethelred's reign; for it naturally bred in Svein a desire for vengeance which was only to be satisfied after ten long years of warfare ending in the conquest of England. Of this struggle the Chronicle gives a minute account, but often in such hysterical tones that it is difficult to make out what really happened. Nor can space be given here to unravel its meaning. The bare outlines however are somewhat as follows. In 1003 Svein burnt Exeter, Wilton and Salisbury. In 1004 he sacked Norwich and Thetford, and had some hard tussles with Ulfkytel, the chief Danish jarl in East Anglia. In 1006 he ravaged East Kent, and next spring after wintering in the Isle of Wight plundered right and left through Hampshire and Berkshire. Aethelred meantime had apparently done nothing but hide in Shropshire in the company of a west-country magnate, one Eadric, nicknamed "Streona" or "the Grasper," an evil councillor of whom the Chronicle can hardly speak with patience. As ever Aethelred's one idea was to offer the enemy a ransom. He accordingly patched up a truce, and persuaded Svein to take his forces back to Denmark in return for a tribute of £36,000. At the same time he placed Eadric in possession of the great estates formerly possessed by Aelfhere in the Severn valley, and made him duke of Western Mercia. After this there seems to have been a lull for two years, in which some efforts were made to organise a large naval force for the defence of the country by requiring ships to be furnished from every 300 hides of land; but when this fleet assembled at Sandwich in 1009, the quarrels between its leaders, Brihtric, a brother of Eadric, and Wulfnoth the Child, a powerful Sussex magnate, completely wrecked its utility. In 1010 the Danish fleets were back again, this time led not by Svein in person but by one of his great men, Thorkil the Tall, a famous jarl from Jómsborg. He attacked Ulfkytel, and having defeated him at Ringmere near Thetford harried all the south-east Midlands, penetrating westwards as far as Oxfordshire, and burning in turn Cambridge, Bedford and Northampton. These inland districts, which had not before suffered from the raiders, seem to have been utterly dazed. No leaders could be found to captain the local levies and no shire would help another. The inhabitants simply clamoured for peace on any terms, and so in 1011 a witan

advised Aethelred to offer a still larger ransom, this time no less than
£48,000. It proved difficult, however, to raise so great a tribute. The
disappointed vikings therefore went on ravaging, and a little later
betook themselves to Kent, where they sacked Canterbury, owing to
treachery on the part of the abbot of St Augustine's, and captured the
Archbishop, Aelfheah (Alphege). For some months they held the primate
to ransom, only to murder him in a drunken riot at Greenwich early in
1012. When at last the tribute was got together, the Danish forces
broke up and some went back to Denmark; but Thorkil himself with
a fleet of forty-five ships remained in England and took service with
Aethelred. The plan of setting a thief to catch a thief was evidently to
be tried again; but it met with no more success than in the case of
Pallig, for the news, that Thorkil was obtaining power in England,
immediately brought his overlord Svein upon the scene, bent upon conquering the whole country and outshining his lieutenant.

The plan of attack in 1013 was quite different to the methods hitherto
adopted. Instead of raiding Wessex or East Anglia, Svein directed his
fleet to the Humber, evidently counting on a friendly reception from the
men of the Danelaw. Nor was he disappointed. As soon as he landed
with his son Knut at Gainsborough on the Trent, Uhtred, a son of
Waltheof of Bamborough, who had distinguished himself against the Scots
and become jarl of the Yorkshire Danes, offered him his allegiance, and
shortly afterwards all the men of the Five Boroughs submitted and gave him
hostages. A good base being thus secured, where he could leave his ships
in his son's guardianship, he next marched through Leicestershire across
the Watling Street into Eadric's dukedom and so south to Oxford and
Winchester. Both these boroughs submitted as soon as he appeared,
and it was not till he turned eastwards to London, where Aethelred lay
with Thorkil, that we hear of any resistance. There was a fight, it would
seem, for the possession of London Bridge in which Svein's men were
unsuccessful. Checked for the moment in the east, and uncertain how best
to deal with Thorkil, Svein next proceeded to Bath to secure control of
Western Wessex. A hundred and forty years before this district had been
the scene of Alfred's heroic defence, but its old spirit had long departed.
In a few days it submitted, after which we are told "all the people held
Svein for full king." These sweeping desertions made Aethelred realise
that England as a whole was resolved not to fight for him, and that
Thorkil's forces were hardly likely for long to save him from Svein's
vengeance. He accordingly took ship and sought a refuge in Normandy
at the court of Duke Richard the Good, the brother of his second wife
Emma, whom he had married eleven years before on the very eve of the
fateful massacre of 1002.

Svein's triumph, complete as it seemed, was destined to be only
momentary. He retired to his base on the Trent to keep the Yule-tide
feast with his son Knut, and had the satisfaction of receiving hostages

from the Londoners, but died suddenly in February 1014, before he could be crowned King of England. His death threw the whole Scandinavian world into confusion. The fleet at Gainsborough chose the youthful Knut, though only eighteen, to be king; but he was not Svein's eldest son, and Denmark passed to his brother Harold, while the Norwegians favoured the claims of Olaf the Stout, a cousin of Olaf Tryggvason's, who had been fighting in England with Thorkil, to rule those parts of Norway which had acknowledged Svein's supremacy. In these circumstances it is not surprising to hear that Aethelred was called back to England, and that the jarls who stood round Knut advised a return of the fleet to Scandinavia to enable each man to look after his home interests. Knut therefore sailed away from the Humber, and for a year was occupied in Denmark making terms with his brother.

Meantime a new force arose in England in Edmund, Aethelred's eldest son by his first marriage. Aethelred on his return gave his confidence again to Eadric, and on his advice took steps to punish the men of the Five Boroughs for offering their allegiance to Svein. In pursuit of this object he put to death Sigeferth and Morkere, two of the leading magnates north of the Welland, and added their estates to Eadric's territories. This was just one of those outrages which gained Aethelred the title of the "Redeless" or the "Badly counselled." All additions to the Grasper's power were bitterly resented, and by none more than by Edmund, the heir to the throne. To check Eadric became the fixed purpose of the young prince. He accordingly seized and married Sigeferth's widow, and then marched to the Five Boroughs as the avenger of the lady's wrongs and made himself master of all the lands which Eadric had coveted. This stroke was so popular in the Danelaw, that Edmund at once became a power in the land, but only at the cost of earning the undying hatred of Eadric. What this would entail was seen a few months later when Knut once more appeared in the Channel with a large fleet partly furnished by his brother. This picked force, "which contained neither thrall nor freedman," landed at Wareham without opposition from Aethelred, who was lying ill near Portsmouth, and ravaged at will through Dorset and Somerset. To meet it Edmund and Eadric both gathered forces; but when they came face to face with the enemy in Wiltshire, Eadric promptly went over to Knut. Edmund therefore had to retire over the Thames without fighting, and the whole of Wessex submitted. In the spring of 1016 much the same happened in Mercia. Knut and Eadric came leagued together into Warwickshire, and Edmund in despair was forced to abandon the defence of Middle Anglia. The most he could do was to appeal for assistance to Uhtred, who had his own grievances against Eadric. This caused a momentary diversion; for Uhtred marched through Cheshire to attack Eadric in Staffordshire and Shropshire. But Knut meantime overran the valley of the Ouse, then went unchecked all up the east side of England to the Humber, and eventually appeared before York. When

Uhtred heard of this rapid advance, he turned back from Mercia to repeat the submission which he had formerly made to Svein. Knut, however, instigated by Eadric, connived at his murder by some private enemies, and appointed his own brother-in-law Eric, who had been ruler of part of Norway, to be jarl of Yorkshire in his place. By April the position of affairs was almost the same as it had been before Svein's death. Thanks to Eadric's treachery, all England save East Anglia and the districts immediately round London were in the hands of the invaders. It would seem also that Thorkil had gone over to his countrymen, and so Edmund and Ulfkytel were the only important leaders with whom Knut had still to reckon. It was at this critical juncture that Aethelred died, and Englishmen had to decide whether they would abandon the struggle or choose Edmund as their king in the hope that he might prove a second Alfred and retrieve the national fortunes even at the eleventh hour.

The Londoners to their credit decided for Edmund; and soon the courage of many parts of England began to revive, for Edmund at once shewed his countrymen that he meant to take the offensive. For this purpose he realised that he could not do better than begin where Alfred had set the example. He therefore hurried down to Somerset, leaving London to stand a siege at the hands of the fleet which Knut had brought round from Southampton to Greenwich. His appearance in the west soon brought men to his standard, and in a week or two he was strong enough to advance eastwards to Sherston, near Malmesbury, and attack Thorkil and Eadric, who had been detached by Knut to intercept him. The fight proved indecisive, but Edmund must have had the advantage, as the Danes retreated on London, and left him free to march into the Chiltern country and raise larger forces. With these he relieved London and, after forcing a passage over the Thames at Brentford, had the satisfaction of seeing the Danish fleet retire to the Orwell in search of supplies. Their land-forces meanwhile went into Kent; but again Edmund followed, and having defeated them at Otford drove them into Sheppey and thence into Essex. This series of successes seemed to shew that the luck was turning and led Eadric to pretend at any rate that he wished to change sides. Unluckily Edmund believed him, and allowed him to join his army with a body of men from Herefordshire. The two then moved together into Essex and threw their forces on the Danes at Ashington, near Shoebury. By this time Edmund had far the larger and more confident army, and should have won again; but in the middle of the fight Eadric played the traitor once more and gave Knut a hard-won victory, the list of the slain including the gallant old Ulfkytel of East Anglia and many of the leading men of Eastern Mercia. So costly a defeat forced Edmund once more to fall back westwards. He was, however, by no means beaten, and Knut was by this time convinced that he had better come to terms with him. A meeting was accordingly proposed between the two young kings. This took place under Eadric's auspices at Olney in Gloucestershire, and there it was arranged that the realm should be divided, Edmund taking his ancestral inheritance of Wessex, while Knut obtained all Mercia and the Danelaw, on the condition that he forwent all vengeance on the Londoners and gave them his peace. Knut's object in consenting to this treaty was, no doubt, to obtain a breathing space and allow time for reinforcements to reach him from Scandinavia. It might, however, quite well have opened the way for Edmund to play over again the part of Edward the Elder, now that he had restored the prestige of his house, and won for himself the name of "Ironside" by his audacity and doggedness in an almost desperate situation. Englishmen at any rate now had a rallying point and a leader. Fate, however, willed it otherwise. Only a few weeks after the treaty Edmund died at Oxford unexpectedly, if not by foul play, when still only twenty-two. His loss at once destroyed the reviving spirit of the West Saxons. They might perhaps have turned to Eadwig, Edmund's brother, the sole surviving male of Aethelred's first family, but their dread of the Danes was too great, and so Knut was hailed King of all England early in 1017 without further opposition.

Knut ruled England for eighteen years (1017–1035). Through his mother half a Pole, he was at his accession about twenty-two years old, and already had two sons by an English wife called Aelfgifu of Northampton. His first act, however, was to repudiate this lady and take to wife Emma of Normandy, Aethelred's widow, who was thirteen years his senior. This stroke of policy freed him from all fear of the young Alfred and Edward, her children by Aethelred, who were left at Rouen to be educated as Frenchmen under the charge of their uncle Duke Richard. To his new subjects Knut must have seemed the typical viking raider. He proved, however, altogether different as a king to what men expected. From the very outset he put off the barbarian and did his utmost to make his subjects forget that he was their conqueror. He had of course to take some steps of a drastic kind to secure himself against possible risings and treachery, but, when once his power was fully established, he developed into a most humane and conciliatory ruler, and gave England peace and justice such as it had not enjoyed since the death of Edgar. King at first only of England, in 1018 he acquired Denmark as well by the death of his brother, and ultimately a considerable Scandinavian empire, but he ever considered England his first care and made it his chief residence. A rapid recovery of prosperity therefore followed his accession, and Englishmen had little cause to regret the change of dynasty.

Knut's first task, after sending Edmund's infant sons out of the realm and hunting down their uncle Eadwig, was to appoint a trusty band of dukes, or "earls" as they now come to be called, using the Danish term, to help him in controlling the various provinces of the kingdom. Full details for all England are not available, but the lists of witnesses to his land-books, coupled with entries in the Chronicles, shew that his scheme was somewhat as follows: south of the Thames he kept the bulk of the country in his own hands, leaving, however, an Englishman called Aethelweard in charge of part of Western Wessex. In East Anglia and Yorkshire he relied on Scandinavians, giving the former to Thorkil the Tall and the latter, as already noted, to his Norse brother-in-law Eric, said to be the most chivalrous of the vikings. In Bernicia he left the native line of high-reeves of Bamborough undisturbed, and even put his confidence eventually in the murdered Uhtred's son Ealdred. In Western Mercia he could hardly do otherwise at first than recognise Eadric; but it was impossible to trust such a dangerous turncoat, and so it is not surprising to find that within a year Knut charged him with treachery and allowed Earl Eric to put him to death. In his place Knut set up as Earl of Mercia another Englishman called Leofwine, whose family had great possessions round Lichfield and Coventry, but he apparently did not give him Eadric's great estates in Gloucestershire or along the middle Severn, for shortly afterwards both Worcestershire and Herefordshire appear as separate earldoms. Over these he set Scandinavians, the former district going to his nephew Hákon, the son of Eric, and the latter to Eglaf, son of Thorgils Sprakaleg, whose elder brother Ulf was married to Estrith, Knut's half-sister. What was done in the case of the London districts and the Five Boroughs is not recorded. The names of the above earls, however, sufficiently indicate Knut's general idea, which was to employ English magnates as far as he could, but simultaneously to give sufficient rewards to his more important kinsmen, whether Danish or Norse, so that they in their turn might be able to reward their military followers. As a result a very considerable sprinkling of new Scandinavian families settled in different parts of England, but at the same time there was no systematic forfeiture of lands, and in particular very little ousting of English peasantry to make way for fresh Scandinavian freedmen.

Having once begun a conciliatory policy, Knut adhered to it steadily. In 1018 he held a great *gemot* at Oxford in which he declared his intention of governing in accordance with the law of Edgar, and the same year he paid off the bulk of his Scandinavian forces and sent them back to Denmark, retaining only forty ships in his service, whose crews afterwards came to form a kind of royal body-guard, known as the *huscarls*. The next year he was abroad, securing his hold on Denmark, but signalised his return in 1020 by two acts which shewed still further his trust in his English subjects. The first was the appointment of a Sussex magnate called Godwin to be Earl of Wessex, and the second the issue of a remarkable proclamation declaring that he meant in future to carry on his government in strict conformity with the wishes of the English bishops. Here in fact we have the keynote of his internal policy for the rest of his life. Like Edgar he became a devout son of the Church, a liberal ecclesiastical benefactor and a patron of the monastic or reforming party. More and more he allowed himself to be guided by ecclesiastical advisers, men like Aethelnoth, whom he made Archbishop of Canterbury,

and Lyfing, whom he promoted to be abbot of Tavistock and, later, bishop
of Crediton.　The most notable of his works of piety are perhaps the
rebuilding of the minster of Bury St Edmunds, and its conversion from
a college of canons into a house of monks; the foundation of the monastery
of St Benet at Holme in Norfolk; and the presentation of the port of
Sandwich and other gifts to Canterbury to atone for the murder of Archbishop Aelfheah.　There were few minsters in fact which Knut did not
enrich, for he wished to pose as the great Christian king and civiliser of
his people, and he firmly believed that the Church was the only instrument
which could effect his purpose.

Meantime across the North Sea, Knut was gradually extending his
influence.　In 1022 we hear of an expedition to Witland in Esthonia,
and a little later, of demands on Olaf the Stout that he should hold Norway
as Knut's vassal and pay a tribute.　This led to an alliance between Olaf
and Anund Jacob, the King of Sweden, who together in 1026 invaded the
Danish realm, taking advantage of a dispute which had arisen between
Knut and his brother-in-law Ulf.　The danger brought Knut over to
Denmark.　He found the allied kings ravaging Scania, but so damaged
their fleets in a fight at the mouth of the Helge River that they had to
give up their enterprise.　He next had Ulf put to death, whether justly or
in a fit of passion it is difficult to say, and then in 1028, after a pilgrimage
to Rome to witness the coronation of the Emperor Conrad II, invaded
Norway with a considerable force including an English contingent.　The
result was that Olaf was driven out, his constant efforts since 1015 to
christianise his subjects having rendered him unpopular.　From this time
onwards Knut could call himself King of England, Denmark, Scania,
Witland, and Norway.　Olaf, however, returned in 1030, but only to be
defeated and slain at Stiklestad, near Throndhjem, after which Knut placed
his eldest son Svein in charge of Norway under the guardianship of his
mother Aelfgifu of Northampton.　The remainder of Knut's reign need
not detain us.　The king lived constantly in England and busied himself
energetically with legislation designed to reinforce Edgar's laws and stamp
out any remains of heathenism which still lurked in the country.　It
would seem too that he received some kind of homage from Malcolm II
of Scotland, who in 1018 had driven the Bernician earls out of Lothian
by a decisive victory at Carham.　Knut's interference, however, did not
really retrieve that disaster or prevent the River Tweed becoming henceforth the permanent northern limit of England.

Knut died at Shaftesbury in 1035, when still under forty, and was
buried in the old minster at Winchester.　At once his newly formed
empire fell to pieces.　He had apparently intended that England and
Denmark should remain united under Harthacnut, his son by Emma of
Normandy, even if Svein, his son by Aelfgifu, obtained Norway.　But
the choice of Harthacnut, who was at the moment his representative in
Denmark, did not commend itself either to the corps of *hus-carls* or the

Mercians or the men of Yorkshire or East Anglia. Godwin, the Earl of Wessex, now the most important man in England, alone championed his cause strongly. Nor were the men of Norway willing to bow to Svein. Knut's arrangements, therefore, fell to the ground except in Denmark, and the upshot was that the English witan at Oxford, led by Leofric, the son of Earl Leofwine, who had now become Earl of Mercia, declared for Harold Harefoot, the younger son of Aelfgifu of Northampton, who was in England; while the Norwegians set up Magnus the son of their old national champion Olaf the Stout, and recovered their independence. This settlement of the succession persisted, so far as it affected England, for five years, despite Harold's worthlessness and the strong opposition of Queen Emma and Archbishop Aethelnoth. For Harthacnut remained in Denmark, fully occupied in beating off attacks from Magnus, and Godwin with his partisans, disappointed at his non-appearance in England, deserted his cause. There is nothing, however, to record concerning Harold's reign (1035–1040) except a number of acts of cruelty, the most notable being the murder of Alfred, Queen Emma's eldest son by her first husband King Aethelred, who with his younger brother Edward had been living peaceably in Normandy during the seventeen years of Knut's rule. This young prince landed in England in 1035 with a small following, perhaps to make a bid for the throne, but was seized by Godwin at Guildford and then handed over to Harold, who had him blinded with such barbarity that he died. For this act Godwin got nearly all the blame. Meantime Queen Emma took refuge at Bruges with the Count of Flanders, and it was only in the autumn of 1039 that she at last succeeded in stirring up her son Harthacnut to collect a fleet of some 60 ships for an attack on his half-brother. Before he could reach England, Harold died, whereupon Harthacnut was offered the crown peaceably. He landed at Sandwich in June 1040, but soon shewed himself a bloodthirsty tyrant. He began by imposing a heavy tribute on his new subjects to pay the crews of his fleet. This led shortly afterwards to the harrying of Worcestershire for impeding the king's *hus-carls* in the collection of the tax. A little later he slew Eadulf, the Earl of Northumberland, by treachery and gave his earldom to Siward, the Earl of Yorkshire. He also took to selling vacant bishoprics. Luckily his reign lasted less than two years, terminating with his sudden death in June 1042 at a wedding banquet "as he stood at his drink."

Once more the English magnates had an opportunity of selecting a king, uninfluenced by pressure from an invading army. The choice lay between a Danish or an English succession. If the Danish line was to be maintained, the most promising heir was Knut's nephew Svein, the son of his sister Estrith and the murdered Ulf, whom Harthacnut had left as viceroy in Denmark to contend with Magnus; but if the English line was to be restored, the only possible candidate was Edward, the surviving son of Emma and Aethelred, whom Harthacnut had allowed to return to England. As Earl Godwin was married to Gytha, Ulf's sister, and had been concerned in the death of Edward's brother, Alfred, only a few years before, the West Saxon leader might well have given his support to Svein. He did not however do so, for Svein at the moment was making no headway in Denmark. Accordingly after a short period of indecision, Edward was chosen king by the voice of all the folk of England, and crowned nine months later on Easter Day 1043.

The restoration of Aethelred's line in the person of Edward, known to later generations as Edward the Confessor, freed England from one set of foreign influences, only to introduce another; for Edward, in spite of his direct male descent from Alfred, was half a Norman in blood and almost wholly a Norman in training. When, in 1041, he returned to England, after an exile of more than a quarter of a century, he was already approaching his fortieth year; and he was a man whose habits and ways of thinking had long been fixed. By all who knew him he was accounted a mild-mannered, conscientious person and a confirmed bachelor. He loved hunting, but not fighting. In France a great deal of his life had been spent at Jumièges and other monasteries under the influence of Norman ecclesiastics; and among these surroundings he had acquired a taste for a comparatively cultured life and a tendency to lean on clerics for guidance. He probably thought in French and disliked speaking English, and he was at little pains to conceal the fact that he found the manners of his countrymen uncongenial and their ideas boorish and behind the times. When the English magnates decided to accept him as their king, they probably thought that they had gauged his character and reckoned that with his ignorance of English ways he would be unable to direct affairs, and that all real power would consequently slip by degrees into their hands. Such a forecast, however, was not realised quite in the way the magnates expected. For Edward was no sooner seated on the throne than he began to fill his court with sundry Normans, Flemings and Bretons, who looked for honours and careers in England, and were by no means prepared to play the part of mere courtiers. Their numbers, too, year by year increased, and Edward never hesitated to shew that he preferred their cleverer and more polished society to the ruder ways of English and Danes, however high-born or wealthy. Just at first, of course, he had to rely for support on the native nobles and churchmen, who had favoured his accession, and especially on Earl Godwin, who was by far the most powerful territorial magnate in southern England, and who had been chiefly responsible, with Bishop Lyfing of Crediton, for making him king. Edward, however, was astute enough to perceive that Godwin's predominance was much resented in the Midlands and in the North, and that in every district the great landowners were exceedingly bitter in their jealousies and rivalries, and might easily be pitted one against the other in such a manner that the king might, after all, more or less get his own way if he played his cards skilfully. We find Edward accordingly before long turning for support to Earl Leofric of Mercia and Earl Siward of Northumbria, whenever he felt himself too much in the grip of Earl Godwin.

At the same time he went to work systematically to contrive openings for placing his foreign friends in positions of influence. Being a man without much energy Edward planned no sudden *coup d'état*, nor did he achieve any dramatic success in asserting himself; but he did enough, by persistently adhering to the same tactics, to make his reign a period of continual struggle between rival aspirants for ascendancy in his counsels, and he managed so to manipulate events that a French-speaking element in a few years gained a firm foothold in the ranks of the nobility and in the Church, and gradually acquired considerable territorial influence in many parts of central and southern England. It is, of course, easy to arraign this policy as unpatriotic; and, as it ultimately led to the conquest of England by the Normans, Edward has sometimes been denounced as the most worthless of the old English kings. The introduction from abroad of more civilised manners and ideas was in itself, however, no bad thing, and Edward ought rather to be praised for it. It must be remembered, too, that at the outset of his reign England had clearly fallen behind the Continent in many ways, and required to be reawakened. It seems, then, rather beside the mark to charge Edward with want of patriotism because he attempted to supply new educative influences in the only way open to him, and altogether inaccurate to picture him, as has sometimes been done, as a saintly nonentity entirely at the beck and call of foreign ecclesiastics, and without any policy of his own. The truer picture seems to be that he was neither unpatriotic nor over-saintly, in spite of the grotesque stories handed down about him by monkish biographers of the next generation; he was rather a well-intentioned man of mediocre talent, thrust late in life and unexpectedly into an extremely difficult position, and unfortunately not strong enough to play the king's part with credit to himself or advantage to his subjects.

It is not surprising, then, to find that nothing was done in his long reign of twenty-three-and-a-half years (1042–1066) to weld England together into a more compact state or to retard the growth of feudalising tendencies, and that when he died, leaving no direct heir, the quarrelsome magnates, who had tried unceasingly to overshadow him during his lifetime, held hopelessly divergent views about replacing him.

The outstanding feature of Edward's reign during his earlier years is undoubtedly the constant growth of Godwin's territorial power, and the persistency with which the earl sought to aggrandise himself and his family, not only in his own province of Wessex, but also in Mercia and East Anglia. Godwin's first great success was obtained in 1045, when he induced Edward, in spite of his known preference for celibacy, to marry his daughter Edith and endow her with important estates in many parts of

England. As the king's father-in-law, Godwin thus acquired precedence over the other earls. His ambition, however, was by no means satisfied with this advancement, and we next find him working for the advancement of his sons. Again Edward proved compliant, and Godwin secured in quick succession an earldom in the Severn valley for his eldest son Svein, who had hitherto been content with a subordinate earldom under his father in Somerset and Dorset, another in East Anglia for his second son Harold, and a third in the Midlands for his nephew Beorn. By what means sufficient lands were at the king's disposal to make these promotions possible we do not know. Presumably Edward must have got into his hands most of the estates which Knut had formerly bestowed on his Danish jarls, Eglaf, Hákon and Thorkil the Tall. Some evidence also exists that considerable property was surrendered at this time under pressure by Emma, the queen mother, and also some by the king himself; for later, Harold is found in possession of at least twenty manors in Essex and Hertfordshire which have all the characteristics of crown land, while the king is returned as owning hardly any property in those counties.

Meantime Edward was active, as occasion offered, in introducing his own particular friends into lay and ecclesiastical posts, to act as checks on Godwin's increasing power. The leading clerical examples were Robert, Abbot of Jumièges, one of his closest friends in Normandy, whom he made bishop of London in 1044, and another Norman called Ulf, who became bishop of the wide-spreading diocese of Dorchester. These ecclesiastical appointments passed unresented, as they were set off by others which went to Godwin's party, such as the coadjutorship of Canterbury to Siward, Abbot of Abingdon (who died in October 1048), and the bishopric of Winchester to Stigand, a wealthy landowner in Norfolk and Suffolk, who had been an important king's chaplain in Knut's day and was high in favour with Queen Emma. Less satisfactory to Godwin was the promotion of the king's nephew Ralf to a position of influence. This young Frenchman, who was the son of Goda, Edward's sister, by her marriage with Drogo of Mantes, Count of the Vexin, was given an earldom in Herefordshire which acted as a counterpoise to Svein's earldom; and at the same time two Breton lords, Robert the son of Wimarc and Ralf of Guader near Rennes, were endowed with considerable fiefs in Essex and East Anglia to act as checks on Harold. To distinguish him from Ralf of Mantes this second Ralf is usually styled Ralf the Staller, from the important quasi-military office of constable in the royal household, which Edward also bestowed on him.

Godwin must have realised from these measures that his hold over Edward was precarious, and soon afterwards it was almost destroyed owing to the misdeeds of his son Svein, who first offended the Church by abducting the abbess of Leominster, and then alienated the nobles by murdering his cousin Earl Beorn. Godwin with great stupidity condoned these outrages, but his attempts to shield his son so damaged his influence, even in his own earldom of Wessex, that Edward plucked up courage in 1050, when Eadsige of Canterbury died, to set aside Godwin's kinsman, the elected Aelfric, and promote Robert of Jumièges to be primate of the English Church. Nor could Godwin obtain the bishopric of London, thus vacated, for his friend Spearhafoc of Abingdon, as Robert of Jumièges maintained that his elevation was forbidden by the Pope, and backed the king in appointing another Norman cleric, named William, in his stead.

A definite breach thus arose between Edward and his father-in-law, leading, a year later, to a serious crisis. This developed out of a visit which Eustace, the Count of Boulogne, paid to Edward in 1051. Eustace had recently married the king's sister Goda, the widowed mother of the Earl of Hereford, and he seems to have come to England on an ordinary family visit or perhaps to look after his wife's English lands. His stay with his brother-in-law at the English court went off quietly enough, but on his return journey his retinue provoked a riot at Dover which resulted in some of the count's men being killed, as well as some of the townsmen. Count Eustace regarded this broil as the fault of the burghers, and immediately demanded reparation for the insult; whereupon Edward called upon Godwin in his capacity of earl of the district to punish the men of Dover. Godwin, however, refused. This gave Edward an opportunity of asserting his authority; he accordingly summoned Godwin to appear before a court at Gloucester to defend his action. At the same time Robert of Jumièges advised Edward to rake up against Godwin the old charge that fifteen years before he had been accessory to, if not the prime mover in, the death of Alfred, the king's brother. Godwin, suspecting that the plan was to involve him in a blood-feud, replied by summoning a large force of his own thegns to a rendezvous at Berkeley within easy reach of Gloucester, and by calling upon his sons Svein and Harold also to come with their forces to his help. As a set-off to the attack of the Kentish men on the French count, he also preferred charges against Ralf of Hereford, alleging that Ralf's French followers had been guilty of many acts of cruelty and oppression towards Englishmen, and further, that, following the French fashion, he had erected a private castle in his earldom, which was a danger to English liberties, such a building being quite unexampled on English soil, where the only fortifications hitherto built were the national boroughs maintained in the king's name for defence against the Danes.

When it became known that Godwin had appealed to arms, Earl Leofric of Mercia and Earl Siward of Northumbria also gathered their forces and came south to the support of the king. The upshot was that Godwin found himself outmatched and, fearing defeat, agreed to disband his forces; whereupon the king summoned another witan to meet at

London, which boldly decreed outlawry for Godwin and all his sons. In these circumstances the earl thought it safest to take refuge with his friend Baldwin of Lille, the Count of Flanders, and wait for time to break up the king's party.   He accordingly sailed for Bruges, taking his sons Svein and Tostig with him, the latter of whom had married Baldwin's daughter, while his sons Harold and Leofwine rode for Bristol and took ship to Ireland.

The direction of affairs in southern England after Godwin's departure seems to have fallen largely into the hands of the king's foreign friends. Greedy to obtain a share of Godwin's lands and honours, fresh troops of Normans and Bretons soon came flocking to England, and the king's wife Edith was deprived of her estates and sent in disgrace to the nunnery of Wherwell.   Earl Leofric, however, was by no means backward in pushing his own interests, and used the crisis to consolidate his position in Mercia by obtaining a grant of Beorn's estates for himself, while his son Aelfgar stepped into Harold's shoes as Earl of East Anglia.   As for Svein's estates, in Somerset, Dorset, Devon and the Severn valley, they seem to have passed to a new earl, Odda, whose patrimony lay chiefly in the neighbourhood of Pershore and Deerhurst.

The fall of Godwin's house was thus for the moment pretty complete. His exile, however, lasted but a short time, as a reaction set in when the English thegns realised that Normans and Bretons were the chief gainers by Godwin's absence; and it quickly gathered strength when the news went round that a yet more powerful foreigner than any who had hitherto come was to visit Edward's court.   This was Edward's kinsman William, the young Duke of Normandy.   This prince made little secret of the fact that he regarded himself as a possible claimant to the English throne, should Edward die childless, and those who knew what the Normans were now doing in southern Italy naturally regarded him as coming to England to spy out the nakedness of the land, and shook their heads over his advent.   His visit, as a matter of fact, was quite uneventful; but Edward had none the less blundered, so that in 1052 Godwin found himself in a position to return and claim back his lost possessions. Landing at Southwark, without having met with any effective opposition in the Thames from the king's ships under Earl Ralf and Earl Odda, he found the Londoners actively on his side as were also the prelates of English birth, led by Stigand, who aimed at obtaining the archbishopric of Canterbury.   Neither Leofric nor Siward would now help Edward, and without them he could offer practically little resistance.   The result was a panic among his foreign followers, many of whom, headed by Robert the Archbishop and Ulf of Dorchester, fled from London to a castle in Essex[1], which Robert the son of Wimarc was then building, and

---

[1] Mr Round thinks this castle was at Clavering (*Victoria County History of Essex*, p. 345); but Nayland, the centre of a group of manors lying athwart the

thence by way of the Naze to the Continent. Others fled westward into Herefordshire, hoping to find security in another castle, which Osbern Pentecost, one of Earl Ralf's men, was erecting on the Welsh border, probably at Ewyas. These hurried flights made it clear to everyone that Edward's attempt at independence had failed. A fresh witan accordingly was assembled, which formally outlawed many of the foreigners and restored Godwin and his family to their former possessions. Edith also came back to court from Wherwell, while Stigand obtained the see of Canterbury in the place of the fugitive Robert and proceeded to hold it in plurality with Winchester, not to mention many other preferments, such as canonries, all over his province.

For the rest of his life Edward was never able to shake himself free from the domination of the house of Godwin. The great earl, it is true, did not himself long enjoy his restoration to power. He died in 1053, quite suddenly, while attending a banquet at Winchester. His honours and estates thereupon passed to his second son Harold, his ill-fated eldest son Svein having died a few months earlier at Constantinople while making a pilgrimage to Jerusalem to atone for his crimes.

The character of the reign changes sensibly after Godwin's death. The king still continued fitfully to play the magnates off against each other, reappointing Aelfgar, for example, to the earldom of East Anglia after Harold's transfer to Wessex. But Edward was fast becoming elderly; and as his energy declined, he centred his attention more and more on sport and church matters to the neglect of politics. Harold, on the other hand, though full of ambition and energy, being little over thirty, was more cautious and better liked than his father, and was always careful to keep on terms with Earl Leofric and the Mercians. There was for a time, therefore, a quiet interval, the only incident of note in 1054 being a Northumbrian expedition beyond the Forth undertaken by Earl Siward in the interests of his Scotch grandson Malcolm Canmore. This young prince on the paternal side was great-grandson of Malcolm II, the victor of Carham, and was being kept out of his patrimony by Macbeth, the famous Mormaer (or Earl) of Moray immortalised by Shakespeare. Some years before Macbeth had slain Malcolm's father, Duncan I, and then usurped the crown. For a number of years Malcolm had lived in Siward's household, becoming quite a Northumbrian in speech and education, but by 1054 he was grown up and eager to regain his crown. The expedition was well managed by Earl Siward, who obtained a notable victory at Dunsinane near Perth, but it was not till three years later that Macbeth was killed and Malcolm III (1057–1093) finally set upon the throne. Siward's intervention beyond the Tweed was of great moment for Scotland, as Malcolm's restoration inevitably

Stour which all belonged to Robert, and adjoining Stoke the burying place of the East Anglian ducal house, seems quite as likely to be the site, being much nearer to the Naze.

brought a great access of power to the Anglo-Danish element in the kingdom, and transferred the centre of the realm from the Keltic districts beyond the Forth to the English-speaking province of Lothian. And this in its turn was of great importance to England; for it turned the ambitions of the Scotch kings more definitely southwards, and led them to covet the Tees for their frontier instead of the Tweed.

Siward died in 1055, the year following the fight at Dunsinane. As he had lost his eldest son in that battle and as his younger son Waltheof was still a child, a difficulty arose as to the succession to the Northumbrian earldom. The natural course would have been to select some member of the house of Bamborough for the office, or at any rate some Anglo-Dane possessing territorial influence north of the Humber. Harold, however, considered the appointment an opportunity too good to be lost for extending the influence of his own family. He therefore advised Edward to appoint his brother Tostig to the earldom, in spite of the obvious risk of placing a West Saxon over the Northerners. Edward acquiesced in this plan, partly because he had a real liking for Tostig, and partly because he hoped to pit the brothers against each other and so free himself to some extent from Harold's tutelage. Beyond the Humber Tostig's elevation was accepted at first with sullen indifference, but further south it led at once to trouble, being much resented by Earl Aelfgar, who regarded it as a menace to the Mercian house. Aelfgar's opposition went so far that Harold was able to represent his conduct as treasonable, and in the upshot obtained the consent of a witan to his outlawry. Thereupon Aelfgar, as Harold had done in similar circumstances, withdrew to Ireland, where he soon recruited a fleet manned by adventurous Irish and Danes, and then, eager for revenge, offered his services to the Welsh for an attack on those who had driven him out of England.

The ally to whom Earl Aelfgar turned was Gruffydd (Griffith) ap Llywelyn, prince of North Wales, a remarkable man, who had ascended the throne of Gwynedd in 1039 and gradually extended his sway over Deheubarth and the rest of the Welsh principalities. His power had long been a menace to the men of Herefordshire: in 1052 he had led a raid against Earl Ralf and defeated his forces near Leominster. Having just compassed the death of a dangerous South Welsh rival, Gruffydd was now ready to attack again and was delighted to join forces with Aelfgar. The pair accordingly marched upon Hereford in the autumn of 1055, and having driven off Ralf's levies, who were mounted, we are told, in the French fashion, sacked the borough, and burnt the newly-built minster, at the same time killing several of the canons. The alarm caused in the Severn valley by this exploit was so great that Earl Harold himself had to hurry to the west with assistance. He was unable, however, to punish the invaders, and had to patch up a peace at Billingsley in Archenfield, by which Aelfgar regained his position as Earl of East Anglia.

Two years later, in 1057, Leofric, the old Earl of Mercia, died, and also Earl Ralf. Aelfgar thereupon succeeded to Mercia, but only on the understanding that East Anglia should pass to Harold's brother Gyrth, that sundry Mercian districts near London, such as Hertfordshire and Buckinghamshire, should be formed into a new earldom for Leofwine, another of his brothers, and that Herefordshire should fall to Harold himself. As Somerset and Dorset had been reunited to Wessex upon Odda's death in 1056, these territorial rearrangements meant that the sons of Godwin held the earldoms throughout England with the exception of the curtailed earldom of Mercia, and men began to speculate whether even this exception would be long maintained. The central earldom still formed a good-sized jurisdiction, stretching across the northern Midlands from the Welsh borders to the North Sea, but few could doubt that Harold was aiming at its dismemberment, so that whenever Edward should die there might be no power left in England sufficiently strong to compete with him, if he decided to be a candidate for the throne. This ultimate object, it is true, was not yet avowed; but the thorny question of the succession was beginning to be discussed, as Edward was well over fifty and his only near kinsman was the baby grandson of Edmund Ironside, known to history as Edgar the Aetheling. According to the accepted traditions of the English this child would for many years be far too young to be elected king, and, further, he had no support in the country; for his father had been exiled by Knut in infancy, and having spent almost his whole life in Hungary, had never acquired any territorial position in England. As events turned out, no convenient opportunity for dismembering Mercia occurred ; for Aelfgar, to protect his family's interests, gave his daughter Ealdgyth to Gruffydd in marriage, and so could count on the support of sturdy Welsh allies. Harold, therefore, left him unmolested till his death in 1062, when the Mercian earldom passed to his son Edwin.

Meanwhile King Gruffydd, presuming on his Mercian connexion, kept on harassing Harold's Herefordshire lands. As a counter-blow, early in 1063 Harold made a raid into North Wales and attacked Rhuddlan, hoping to find Gruffydd unprepared. The Welsh king got away by sea, but was not fated to enjoy his good fortune much longer ; for Harold was determined to crush him, and so deprive the young Edwin of the outside support that his father had relied on. To this end Harold summoned Tostig to join him with a Northumbrian levy, and then both brothers pushed into Wales beyond Rhuddlan and chased the Welsh prince from one hill fortress to another. In this extremity Gruffydd was deserted not only by the Mercians but also by his own men, and was shortly afterwards assassinated. His fall, accompanied as it was by the restoration of considerable tracts along the marches to English rule, brought Harold undoubted prestige ; but it must not be supposed that the Welsh were in any sense conquered. Their unity was once more broken up. Within their own borders, however, various Welsh chieftains remained as independent as ever.

During the course of the next year an untoward mishap befell Harold. For some reason or other he had occasion to take a sea trip in the Channel, and, as he was sailing from his paternal seat at Bosham in Sussex towards Dover, a storm caught him and drove his ship ashore on the coast of Ponthieu in France. Guy, the count of the district, when he heard of the wreck, gave orders for Harold's arrest, and being a vassal of William, the Duke of Normandy, handed him over to his overlord at Rouen as a captive. Harold thus became an unwilling guest at the Norman court. As such he accompanied the duke on a campaign into Brittany, but though he was outwardly treated with honour, he was informed that he would not be allowed to return to England unless he would become the duke's man and take an oath to assist William in the future, should he make a claim to the English throne on Edward's death. Seeing no other way of regaining his liberty, Harold had perforce to take the oath demanded of him, whereupon he was permitted to sail for England. On his return he made as little as possible of the misadventure, and no doubt regarded the oath extracted from him by force as of no validity; but he had none the less placed himself in a very false position, considering his own aspirations to be Edward's successor.

Harold came back to find a very disturbed state of affairs in the north of England. For nine years his brother Tostig had been Earl of Northumbria, but he had ruled harshly and had especially provoked discontent by treacherously causing the deaths of Gamel, son of Orm, and Ulf, son of Dolfin, two members of the old Bamborough house, and appropriating their estates. The result was that the kinsmen of the murdered men started an intrigue with the young Edwin of Mercia, and in 1065 broke into open insurrection. A little later they seized York and declared Tostig outlawed. They then elected Morkere, Edwin's younger brother, to be earl in Tostig's place, and putting him at the head of the Northumbrian forces, advanced into Mercia, where they were joined by Earl Edwin and his thegns and also by a body of Welshmen. Marching further south, the combined armies overran in succession Northampton-shire and Oxfordshire, until at last they were met by Harold in the Thames valley. All this time Tostig had remained well out of the way, hunting in Clarendon forest in Edward's company. Harold intervened, it appears, with insufficient forces to risk a battle, and being reduced to negotiate had to accept the conditions demanded by Edwin and his Yorkshire allies.

As a result Morkere was officially recognised by King Edward as earl north of the Humber, whereupon Tostig retired in high dudgeon to Flanders to seek assistance from his father-in-law, Count Baldwin V (1036–1067). As part of the resettlement the youthful Waltheof, the son of Earl Siward, was made Earl of Northamptonshire and Hunting-donshire, as some compensation for the fact that his hereditary claims to Northumberland were a second time ignored. Harold's share in these transactions has sometimes been represented as an act of justice to the Northerners, done at the expense of his family's interests without any real necessity. Be that as it may, Tostig never forgave him for not rendering more effective support, and from this time forward became his bitterest enemy. It certainly looks as if Harold was thinking more of his own interests than Tostig's, and saw in Tostig's fall an opportunity of making the house of Mercia more friendly to himself in the future and less in-clined to oppose him, should he make a bid for the crown. For now it was hardly concealed that Harold and his friends, in the event of the king's death, would seek to set aside the direct line of the house of Alfred and would propose that the house of Godwin should be put in its place. If, however, this was to be effected by general consent, with-out an appeal to force, it could only be by the action of the national assembly, in which Edwin and Morkere and their supporters would have a very influential vote. Harold, therefore, had very good reasons for making terms with them, as it clearly would be more advantageous to him to win the crown by consent than by force.

Questions as to Harold's motives are, however, a problem so complex as to defy our best efforts to unravel them, and all that can be said with certainty is that events were soon to shew that, in abandoning Tostig's cause and favouring the Mercian aspirations, he had taken the most prudent course. For in the winter following Tostig's fall Edward became seriously ill while superintending the building of the new abbey at West-minster, which he had recently founded. And here, in his manor house on the banks of the Thames, he died on 6 January 1066, leaving the succession an open question. To his own contemporaries he was never the saintly person that later historians have depicted, but just a pious and often misguided ruler, who had attempted to bring the English into closer connexion with their continental neighbours than was desirable, and had rather wilfully undermined the insularity of his dominions without knowing how to bring them peace and security. It was only by later generations, who venerated him as the last of the line of Cerdic and Alfred, that he came to be honoured as a saint, and it was only in 1161 that the bull was issued by Pope Alexander III which conferred on him the title of " Confessor " which has become so familiar.

In tracing the political developments under Aethelred, Knut and Edward, little has been said about the economic or social side of English life; but it must not be thought that the period of ninety years from 975 to 1065 was a period devoid of social developments, or that materials are lacking for forming an estimate of the amount and character of the changes which were going on. On the contrary, did space permit, much might be said on such topics as the distribution of wealth and territorial power, the density of the population in different districts, the ranks and grades of society, the methods of tillage and industry, and the condition of the urban centres. Information as to some of these, if not very clear, is comparatively ample; for in addition to the laws and charters and a fair amount of literary evidence, we can use as the groundwork for our picture the very detailed description of England in 1065, which is preserved in the Domesday Survey. Primarily of course this Norman survey is concerned with the condition of the country twenty years later; but the local jurors, who furnished the returns, were also required to state how matters had stood "on the day when King Edward was alive and dead," and there is no reason to doubt the general accuracy of their answers, even though some allowance has to be made for their recollection of the earlier period being somewhat blurred.

The most important feature which stands out in all the sources alike is that there was just as little uniformity in England at the end of the Anglo-Saxon period in social and economic matters as in political conditions. In spite of the fact that the country had been nominally a single kingdom for over a century, each province in 1065 still retained its own traditions and customs in social matters, and there were not only fundamental differences between the English and Danish districts, but also between the valley of the Thames and the valley of the Severn, between Kent and Wessex, between Wessex and Mercia and between the northern and the southern Danelaw. Any attempt, therefore, to give a picture of a typical village or a typical estate would be misleading, for everywhere there were startling variations (even within the limits of a single shire there were frequently several types of organisation) not to speak of differences in nomenclature and differences in land measures and monetary units. There are however some generalisations which can be accepted confidently, and to these we must chiefly confine ourselves.

The first most obvious economic feature is that the density of the population decreased as one passed from east to west. In 1065 Lincolnshire, Norfolk and Suffolk were by far the most thickly populated shires. Were the population of these three counties left out of account, we should be leaving out of account not much less than one-sixth of the whole English nation. The least thickly populated districts south of the Humber and the Ribble were apparently Shropshire, Staffordshire and Cornwall[1], but men were also sparse in Devon and in all parts of the Severn valley. Another clear feature is that the land was much more valuable in the east than in the west, partly of course because of geological differences and the variation of soils, but largely because the denser population of the east facilitated a more intensive working of the land and the maintenance of a far greater head of cattle and sheep. Yet another great contrast between the east and the

---

[1] There is no evidence as to the districts north of the Humber. The Vale of York may have been well populated, but there cannot have been any large number of inhabitants in the great moorland areas.

west, of critical economic importance, arose from the fact that the east was the home of liberty. In the Danish districts the peasantry, whether English or Danish by descent, were far less exploited in the interests of the upper classes than in the English districts. To begin with, there were far fewer actual slaves or "theows" in these parts than elsewhere. In East Anglia the slaves formed only 4 per cent. of the population, whereas in the Midlands they formed 14 to 15 per cent., on the Welsh border 17 per cent. and in Cornwall 21 per cent. But this is not the whole story. In the Danish districts considerable sections of the inferior cultivating classes rendered far lighter dues for their holdings, and performed far fewer services for their lords than in the Midlands or in Wessex. One reason for this was that the overlordship of the soil was far more divided and broken up in the Danelaw than in the south and west. In the Chiltern districts, in Kent and in Wessex generally, it was fairly common for a village to have only one lord; but in the Danelaw, as often as not, four or five lords were concurrently interested in even quite small villages, and it is not impossible to point to instances in which a village was shared between as many as nine or ten. At the same time, in the Danelaw the tie between a lord and his men was far looser as regards a large section of the peasantry than in Mercia or Wessex, for considerable numbers of the classes described in the Domesday Survey as "liberi homines" and "sochemanni" still had the right of choosing their lords and, from time to time, of transferring their allegiance from one lord to another. As the phrase runs in the Domesday Survey, "they could recede from their lord without his license and go with their land where they would." The natural consequence followed that it was difficult for the lord, whose patronage they did acknowledge, to get any burdensome rents or services out of them.

Let us now turn to consider what is known about the ranks of English society outside the Danelaw in the earlier years of the eleventh century. One has to admit that this is an obscure subject, but some direct light is thrown on it by the *Rectitudines Singularum Personarum.* This Anglo-Saxon tract is unfortunately undated, and nothing is known of its origin; but it seems to be a memorandum drawn up by the land-agent of a monastic or episcopal estate, comprising in all probability several villages, in order to keep a record of the services due from the various grades of tenants who were under his management. It is thought to have been put together about 1025, and along with it is found a second tract, which sets forth the duties of the land-agent, calling him at one time a *gerefa* or reeve and at another a *scyrman*. The occurrence of this second term has led some commentators to think that the writer of the tracts might have been a shire-reeve, but *scyrman* carries no such implication, being used indifferently of any official person. The author of the *Rectitudines* begins his treatise by describing the services of the *thegn*. By that term he clearly did not mean a king's thegn or man of much importance, nor did he mean the lord of the estate, who was probably some bishop or abbot, but only a lesser thegn, the *mediocris tainus* of Knut's laws. In the Domesday returns relating to 1065 such lesser thegns are frequently mentioned. They occur most commonly on large ecclesiastical manors, their holdings being termed *tainlands*, and on them lay the burden of providing the military and other services due from the churches to the king. In the *Rectitudines* the thegn's duties are similar, the main ones specified being *fyrdfœreld*, *burhbote* and *brycgeweorc*, that is to say the well-known "trinoda neces-sitas" together with all other burdens arising at the king's ban, such as the provision of ship-service and coastguard service and the building of deer-hays for the king's use when he came into the district. Here then, we seem for the first time in our sources to meet with a definite military tenure, but it differed from the later knight's service in that the thegn fought on foot and not on horse-back, and performed his service on behalf of his lord's estate and not in respect of his own holding. As to the size of the thegn's holding, the *Rectitudines* are silent, but tell us that the thegn was worthy of his book-right. No doubt he was also, as his name implies, a "dear-born" man with a wergeld of 1200 shillings. We cannot, however, picture him as more than a petty squire, for in Domesday the assessment of the "tainland," though sometimes five hides or more, is often no more than one hide. It was not, however, always a compact tenement but might be made up of parcels lying in several villages.

Having described the "thegn," the author of the *Rectitudines* passes next to the *ceorl* class and sets before us three distinct grades, called re-spectively *geneatas*, *geburas* and *cotsetlas*. The differences between them were clearly in the main economic and not due to differences of legal status. In the eyes of the law all alike were *twihyndemen*, and had wergelds of 200 shillings. Even the *cotsetlas*, who were the poorest, paid their "hearthpennies" on Holy Thursday, "as every freeman should." What marked these grades off from one another was the nature of the dues which could be claimed from them by their lords. The *cotsetlas* or cottage tenants, having as a rule no plough-oxen, may probably be re-garded as the lowest of the three in the social scale. They worked every Monday throughout the year for the lord on his *inland*, or demesne portion of the estate, and three days a week at harvest-time. They paid church-scot at Martinmas, but did not normally pay *landgafol* or rent in money. Their holdings in the arable fields were usually five acres more or less. Next in order in the village hierarchy came the *geburas* or boors, whose name itself, used as it is in most Germanic tongues for a peasant of any kind, and still familiar to us in a disguised form in the term "neighbour," seems to imply that they were the commonest and most widespread class[1]. To these tenants our author devotes about a quarter

---

[1] Maitland has contended that the *geburas* were only an insignificant class: cf. *Domesday Book and Beyond*, p. 329. But this opinion ignores the use of the derivative

of his treatise, admitting however that he cannot be very precise about their services, as they varied in details from place to place. Their holdings, described as *gesettesland*, that is, land "set to *gafol*" as contrasted with the *inland* retained by the lord for his own use, were known as "yardlands" or *gyrde*. Each of these comprised a farm-stedding or toft with some thirty acres of arable, scattered in acre and half-acre strips in different parts of the village fields, together with a share in the hay meadows and pastures. In return for their *yardlands* the services of the *geburas* to the lord were far heavier than those of the *cotsetlas*, being three days' work a week on the *inland* from Candlemas (2 February) to Easter, three days' work a week in harvest-time and two days' work a week at other seasons. Moreover, as a part of this week-work (*wicweorc*) they had specially to assist the lord with their own oxen and labour in ploughing his *inland*. They had also to pay divers *gafols* or rents, some in money and some in kind. For example, they might have to feed the lord's hounds, or find bread for his swineherds, while some provided hens and lambs and some paid "honeygafol" and some "ale-gafol." Their beasts also had to lie at the lord's fold from Martinmas to Easter. When first admitted, or set to their holdings, they received an outfit of live-stock and seed from the lord, which had to be returned at their death, a custom which has survived together with the *yardland* in a modified form even to modern times[1] under the name of the *heriot*. Highest in the scale above the *geburas* came the *geneatas*. They were altogether freer men who, though they had to pay *landgafol* and other dues and had to reap and mow for the lord at harvest time, had no fixed week-work to do. The essential feature in fact about their tenure was that their services were occasional and not fixed to definite days. Their main duties were to ride on the lord's errands far and near, to carry loads and do carting when called upon, to reap and mow at harvest time, to act as the lord's bodyguard, to escort travellers coming to the lord, and to maintain the walls and fences round the lord's "burg" or dwelling-house. Exceptional types of rent-paying ceorls are next described, such as the *beo-ceorl* in charge of the lord's hives, and the *gafol-swan* in charge of his pigs; and then to complete the picture we have the various sorts of praedial slaves, the *theowan* or *servi* and *theowan-wifmen* or *ancillae*. Of these unfree hinds

---

words formed from *gebur* in the laws and land-books. In Edward the Elder's dooms, for example, *geburscipe* is the term used to express the village community generally in which a man has his home: cf. Liebermann, *Gesetze*, p. 138, "*on ðam geburscipe þe he on hamfæst wære.*" Similarly an Abingdon charter, dating from 956 or 957, speaks of the three villages adjoining Oxford, called Hinksey, Seacourt and Wytham, as *geburlandes*; cf. Birch, *Cart. Sax.* No. 1002. We know too that in Hertfordshire there were many *geburs* in the district round Hatfield. Cf. Thorpe, *Diplomatarium*, pp. 649–651.

[1] In 1920 considerable heriots were paid to King's College, Cambridge, as lords of the Manor of Ogbourne in Wiltshire, in respect of the transfer of some customary freeholds reckoned to contain $7\frac{1}{2}$ yardlands.

nearly a dozen types are mentioned, such as ox-herds, shepherds, goat-herds, cheese-makers, barn-keepers, woodmen, hedgers and so on; but not much is told about them individually, except details as to the cost of their maintenance.

The remarkable fullness of the details, furnished by the author of the *Rectitudines*, and the great interest of his account as the earliest known picture of a large English landed estate, naturally lead us to speculate how far it is to be considered a valid picture for England generally. The answer seems to be, that it had little application outside Wessex and Mercia, and even in those provinces it is difficult to make it altogether tally with the conditions found in the majority of the counties a generation or two later on, as depicted in the Domesday Survey. It fits best in fact, when compared with Domesday, with the counties along the Welsh border from Gloucestershire to Cheshire; for there is an obvious parallel between these *geneatas* of the *Rectitudines* with their riding services and those *radmanni* or *radchenistres* who were prominent in those counties in 1065, and who were clearly riding men after the style of the "equites" set up by Oswald on the estates of the church of Worcester in Edgar's day. It agrees also remarkably well with an account we have of the labour customs in use at Tidenham in the Forest of Dean, drawn up about 1060[1]. This village lies in the triangle formed by the junction of the Wye with the Severn, and in Edward's reign belonged to the monks of Bath, who had sublet it to Archbishop Stigand for his life. It was an extensive estate divided into several hamlets and was assessed for taxation at 30 hides; nine of these hides were *inland* and twenty-one *gesettesland*, divided into yardlands occupied some by *geneatas* and some by *geburas*. The account speaks of these yardlands as *gyrda gafollandes*; and then sets out the services of the two classes of tenantry, remarking that "to Tidenham belong many labour services," "*to Dyddanhamme gebyreð micil weorc ræden.*" As in the *Rectitudines*, the *geneat's* chief duty was to act as an escort, take messages and do carting, while the *gebur* had not only many *gafols* to render but owed heavy week-work and ploughing services. It looks then as if the *Rectitudines* must apply primarily to this part of Mercia, and as if the tract probably had its origin on one or other of the great church fiefs which dominated the valley of the Lower Severn. On the other hand it is impossible to suppose that the main conditions on the larger ecclesiastical or lay estates in Wessex were not to some extent the same; for *geneat* and *gebur*, *yardland* and *gesettesland*, are all mentioned as West Saxon institutions in the laws of Ine, together with the *gafol geldu*, the lord's *gerefa* and the taking up of land *to weorc and to gafole*. We know too that King Alfred had his *geneatas*, and the abbeys of Glastonbury and Abingdon had their *tainlands* and *geburlands* in the ninth and tenth centuries; while yardlands, half-yardlands and

---

[1] Birch, *Cart. Sax.* No. 928. Seebohm, *English Village Community*, pp. 148–157.

cotlands formed the basis of village organisation in all the southern shires except Kent and Cornwall from the Norman Conquest onwards until rendered obsolete by the enclosures in the eighteenth and nineteenth centuries. We must suppose then that, though *radchenistres* are hardly alluded to at all in Wessex in the Domesday returns (they appear once in Berkshire and twice in Hampshire), they must none the less have existed there in the days of Knut and Edward, and we must account for the silence of Domesday about them by the hypothesis that the jurors for the West Saxon hundreds in 1055 were not asked to distinguish between the two classes of *ceorlas* and therefore merged them together under the vaguer title of *tunesmen*, a term which occasionally appears in Anglo-Saxon documents and which Latin scribes rendered by the word *villanus*. We cannot, however, postulate more than a general similarity of system on the various estates, whether of Wessex or Mercia; for the leading characteristic of rural organisation in England has ever been that each village has been free to regulate its own farming and develop its own special customs as to tenure and tillage. Provided this fundamental limitation is kept steadily in view, we may fairly take the sketch furnished by the *Rectitudines* as an approximately valid picture of all the greater estate-units south and west of Watling Street in the days of Knut and Edward; but at the same time we must remember that the writer of the *Rectitudines* was not attempting a description of the smaller estates of the ordinary thegns. His treatise is clearly restricted to lordly territories, where elaborate differentiation of classes and minute subdivision of services were both natural and feasible. It may well be then that the comparatively heavy rents and services, recorded in the *Rectitudines*, were by no means characteristics of the ordinary thegn's estate, and that it was only on the larger ecclesiastical estates, where the lords had power to bind men's souls as well as their bodies, that the exploitation of the tenantry had been carried to any extreme lengths.

Enough evidence has now been presented to give a general idea of the economic and seignorial relations existing between the landowning classes and the mass of the cultivators in the first half of the eleventh century. One question however of considerable importance still remains to be considered, and that is, had the landlords as a class judicial authority over their tenants merely as landowners? In other words, could they set up petty courts on their estates, similar to the manorial courts of a later day, and compel their men to try their disputes in them, at any rate in matters of civil justice, provided the cases did not involve persons who were tenants under other lords? The evidence at our disposal is perhaps too fragmentary and too lacking in precision to enable us to say how matters stood in all parts of England; but two things at any rate seem clear. First, there certainly was a very considerable number of lords in Edward's day who were holding their own private courts or hallmoots (*halimotes*) in competition with the national hundred moots; and secondly, there was no general law or custom as yet recognised, which entitled landlords to hold such courts, but in all cases, where hallmoots had sprung up, the right to hold them rested on some special grant from the Crown and was in the nature of a franchise or special privilege. The conclusion, that hallmoots had become fairly common institutions by 1050, is not really open to question, being based on the collective evidence of hundreds of passages scattered up and down the Domesday Survey, which tell us that some church magnate or some fairly important layman had enjoyed the privilege of "sake and soke" (*saca et soca*) over this or that estate, or over this or that group of men, in the days of King Edward. But this technical term, which stands for the Anglo-Saxon *saca and socne*, is only a pleonastic phrase for *sócn*; and as we have already seen *sócn* is the Anglo-Saxon term for jurisdiction and implies the right to do justice and, if need be, to hold a court for the purpose.

As it is only possible here to give a few examples of these passages, we must content ourselves with observing that there are very few sections of the survey from which they are entirely lacking, though in different counties they assume different forms. It is clear too that they imply several different types of hallmoots, according as the jurisdiction granted had been extensive or restricted. The simplest but least instructive references to sake and soke are found in certain schedules, which merely record the names of persons who had been entitled to sake and soke under King Edward. For example, we have a list of fifteen persons who had enjoyed the franchise in Kent, a list of nineteen who had enjoyed it in Derbyshire and Nottinghamshire, and a list of thirty-five who had enjoyed it in Lincolnshire. But we cannot from such lists infer with any certainty that these privileged persons had exercised the right over all their lands lying in these counties and still less over their lands in other districts. Elsewhere the information as to sake and soke is more often given in respect of particular places. We read for example under Essex, that Robert, son of Wimarc, the king's staller, had sake and soke over the half-hundred of Clavering; under Suffolk, that Ulwyn of Hedingham had sake and soke over his estates at Lavenham, Burgate and Waldingfield, and under Warwickshire, that Ealdred, the Bishop of Worcester, had sake and soke over seven and a half hides of land at Alveston near Stratford-on-Avon. Or again we are told that the soke was restricted and only applied to some particular class of tenant. For example, at Reedham in Norfolk the Abbot of Holme had sake and soke but only over those who were bound to use his sheepfold (*super hos qui sequebantur faldam*). At Buxhall in Suffolk Leswin Croc had sake and soke but only over his hall and his cottage tenants (*super hallam et bordarios*). In some cases again the soke is attributed not to the immediate landlord but to his overlord. For example, Uggeshall near Dunwich is entered as owned by Osketel Presbyter, but the survey goes on to say "Ralf the Staller had sake and soke over this estate, and over all other estates owned by Osketel."

From these various examples it is easy to see that sake and soke, though not a rare privilege, had not under Edward become a right common to all landowners, for it would be pointless to give lists of those who were exercising it, if all landowners were free to do so. It is clear on the contrary from hundreds of other passages that the wielding of soke was regarded as primarily a royal right, and the general rule of the land still enjoined that all men should attend the hundred moots, and that these should be held under the presidency of officials appointed by the king and the earl, who shared the profits of jurisdiction between them, the king taking two-thirds of the fines and the earl one-third. Further, even where landowners had acquired some measure of soke over their estates, the resulting franchises were regarded primarily as subdivisions carved out of the hundreds by leave of the Crown, and consequently men could still conceive of seignorial justice as being merely a variant of the general scheme of national justice, and not as a distinct and rival type of jurisdiction to be feared by the Crown and suppressed whenever there was an opportunity. There was in fact no idea at all as yet that these franchises constituted encroachments on the powers of the Crown.

If we inquire into their origin we do not find that their existence can be put down chiefly to Edward's being a complaisant ruler, inclined to placate his more ambitious subjects by offering them bribes in the form of judicial concessions. Doubtless, Edward was rather lavish with his grants of sake and soke, and many English writs have survived which testify to his activities in this direction; but there is plenty of evidence to shew that he was no innovator and only followed the practice of his predecessors. For in this connexion we have only to turn to Knut's laws to be convinced that private sokes were plentiful in his day; for, if not, certain famous sections in them which declare that the king ought to have certain important pleas over all his subjects, unless he has expressly granted them away, would be meaningless. Nor does this conclusion depend solely on inferences; for a writ of Knut[1] still survives which was issued about 1020 in favour of the Archbishop of Canterbury, proclaiming to all the king's lieges that the archbishop was to be worthy throughout his lands of *sake and soke, grithbrice, hamsocn, foresteal, infangennethef* and *flymena-fyrmth,* and these specially mentioned rights turn out to be just the very pleas that the laws say ought to be reserved to the king except in very exceptional circumstances. There is nothing about this writ to lead us to question its genuineness. On the contrary it is quite on all fours with Knut's general policy of favouring the Church, and fits in well with some other evidence which shews that this was not the only case in which he was willing to give away the reserved pleas. The evidence which can be quoted to prove this is not indeed contemporary, but seems perfectly trustworthy, and consists in certain later writs issued by Norman

---

[1] Cf. Earle, *Handbook to the Landcharters,* p. 232.

kings which imply that Knut granted his wife Emma sake and soke over eight and a half hundreds in West Suffolk and that the grant carried with it *grithbrice, hamsocn, foresteal, aeberethef, flitwite* and *fihtwite*[1]. From some points of view this grant to his wife is more novel and important than the grant to the archbishop; for it is the earliest clear instance on record of a wide stretch of territory passing into the hands of a lay subject, and shews that sokes had already ceased to be regarded as specially ecclesiastical privileges at least twenty years before Edward came to the throne. None the less this great franchise did ultimately come into the hands of the Church; for Emma's estates were all confiscated in 1043, soon after her son's accession, and this gave Edward the opportunity to transfer the jurisdiction over the eight and a half hundreds to the monks of St Edmund's Bury, who continued to enjoy the franchise right down to the Reformation. How much further back it would be possible to trace these franchises, were documents of Aethelred's reign available, it is impossible to say; but there seems no reason for supposing that Knut was an innovator. Like all rulers he more often than not followed precedents, and after all he had excellent precedents for such sokes as he created in the sokes which Edgar had set up in the tenth century. The really obscure problem is not so much the origin of the larger franchises granted to the magnates, as the origin of the practice of allowing quite small men to exercise sake and soke over petty estates. As to these we can never hope to attain any certainty; but it is interesting to note that the phrase *saca and socne* is even older than the reign of Edgar, being found in a charter issued by Eadwig in 958 which is apparently genuine and which relates to Southwell in Nottinghamshire[2].

[1] Cf. H. W. C. Davis, "The Liberties of Bury St Edmunds," *Eng. Hist. Rev.* 1908, vol. xxiv. pp. 417–423.

[2] Cf. Birch, *Cart. Sax.* No. 1029.

CHAPTER XVI.

THE WESTERN CALIPHATE.

AFTER the successes of Mūsā and 'Abd-al-'Azīz and the occupation of the Iberian peninsula by Hurr the slight resistance of the Christians may be neglected, while we follow the victorious Muslims through Gaul up to the defeat of the Emir 'Abd-ar-Raḥmān at Poitiers by Charles Martel (732). From that date till the accession of 'Abd-ar-Rahmān ibn Mu'āwiya the whole history of Muslim Spain may be said to consist of internal dissensions between Yemenites and Ḳaisites, Syrians and Medinese. 'Abd-al-Malik, an old Medinese chief, was appointed governor of Spain in October 732. He refused to provide some Syrians, who were starving in Ceuta, with the means of crossing over into Spain, but an insurrection among the Berbers in the peninsula compelled him to summon them to his aid. The ragged and starving Syrians fought so fiercely that they routed the Berbers, and then having no desire to return to Africa where they had fared so ill, they revolted and proclaimed Balj as their Emir (741). They sought to inspire terror. They crucified 'Abd-al-Malik, and defeated his sons at Aqua Portora (August 742). The civil war ended with the appointment by the Emir of Africa of Abū-l-Khaṭṭār the Kalbite as governor. He pacified Spain and settled the Syrians along the southern fringe from Murcia to Ocsonoba (Algarve); but the conflict was promptly renewed between Ḳaisites or Ma'addites and Yemenites or Kalbites. The rebels defeated the Kalbites under Abū-l-Khaṭṭār at the battle of Guadalete (745), their leader Thuwāba becoming Emir. On his death war between rival tribes lasted some six years longer.

According to the oldest Arab and Christian chroniclers Asturias was the only part where the Visigoths prolonged their resistance. Some nobles of the south and centre of Spain had taken refuge there with the remnants of their defeated armies. The death of Roderick at Segoyuela[1] led them to elect Pelayo as their king, who took up Roderick's task of heroic resistance. Pelayo retired to the Picos de Europa; there in the valley of Covadonga the Visigoths defeated (718) an expedition led

---

[1] See Vol. II. p. 186, and cf. Vol. II. p. 372.

against them by 'Alḳama, who lost his life in the battle. This victory, all the more remarkable after signal defeats, has been taken as the turning point from which the reconquest of Spain has been dated. National legend has told that Pelayo was chosen king not before this success but as the result of his victory, great if magnified in the telling.

In the north of Aragon and on the frontier of the Basque country (which was for the most part independent) a new centre of resistance arose in 724 under the leadership of Garcia Ximenez, who defeated the Arabs and occupied the town of Ainsa in the district called Sobrarbe. Another independent centre of resistance connected with Sobrarbe must have been formed in Navarre, and its leader according to the oldest records seems to have been Iñigo Arista. But of all this we have only confused and contradictory accounts.

For a century few victories were won over the invaders in the kingdom of Asturias. Its history may be said, according to Visigothic tradition, to have resolved itself into a struggle between king and nobles. The former aimed at an hereditary and absolute monarchy while the latter strove to keep their voice in the king's election and their long-cherished independence. Alfonso I the Catholic, Duke of Cantabria and son-in-law of Pelayo, was the only one to take advantage of the internal conflicts among the Muslims. He made raids through Galicia, Cantabria and Leon, and occupied or laid waste important territories like Lugo. At his death in 756 the Muslim frontier ran by Coimbra, Coria, Toledo, Guadalajara, Tudela and Pampeluna, and the Christian frontier included Asturias, Santander, parts of Burgos, Leon and Galicia. Between these two lines was an area continually in dispute.

Such was the state of Spain on the arrival of 'Abd-ar-Raḥmān ibn Mu'āwiya. He had escaped from the general massacre of the Umayyads, which had been ordered by the Abbasids, by swimming across the Euphrates, and had seen from the opposite bank the slaughter of his thirteen-year-old brother. His faithful freedmen Badr and Sālim, who had been in his sister's service, joined him in Palestine with money and precious stones, and thence he passed to Africa, where he might have lived in peaceful obscurity. But (according to Dozy) " ambitious dreams haunted without ceasing the mind of this youth of twenty. Tall, vigorous and brave, he had been carefully educated and possessed talents out of the common. His instinct told him of his summons to a glorious destiny," and the prophecies of his uncle Maslama confirmed his belief that he would be the saviour of the Umayyads. He believed that he was destined to sit upon a throne. But where would he find one ? The East was lost ; there remained Spain and Africa.

In Africa the government was in the hands of Ibn Ḥabīb, who had refused to recognise the Abbasids and aimed at an independent kingdom. Because of the prophecies favourable to 'Abd-ar-Raḥmān he persecuted him : indeed he persecuted every member of the Umayyad dynasty, and had executed two sons of Caliph Walīd II for some indiscreet remarks which he had overheard. "Wandering from tribe to tribe and from town to town," says Dozy, "'Abd-ar-Rahmān passed from one end of Africa to the other." For some five years it is clear he had never thought of Spain.

At length he turned his eyes towards Andalusia, of which his former servant Sālim, who had been there, gave him some account. Badr went over to Spain, to the clients of the Umayyads, of whom some few hundreds were scattered among the Syrians of Damascus and Ḳinnasrīn in Elvira and Jaen; he bore a letter to them, in which 'Abd-ar-Raḥmān told his plight and set forth his claim to the Emirate as grandson of the Caliph Hishām. At the same time he asked their help and offered them important posts in the event of a victory. As soon as they had received this letter, the chiefs of the Syrians of Damascus, 'Ubaid-Allāh and Ibn Khālid, joined with Yūsuf ibn Bukht, chief of the Syrians of Ḳinnasrīn. It was as much from a sense of their duty as vassals as from hope of office and self-interest that they decided to forward the undertaking. But what means had they at their disposal? They resolved to consult Ṣumail the Ḳaisite, a hero of the civil wars. He put off giving an answer in a matter of such importance, but entertained Badr and the other Umayyads. Afterwards he left for Cordova, where the Emir Yūsuf was collecting forces to punish the Yemenites and Berbers who had revolted at Saragossa. Yūsuf bought the help of the Umayyads for the campaign.

When Yūsuf crossed the Guadalquivir, 'Ubaid-Allāh and Ibn Khālid appeared before him and begged they might first be allowed to get in their crops and then they would join him at Toledo—a request which was granted. Thereupon they urged 'Abd-ar-Raḥmān's cause on Ṣumail, who had just risen from one of his frequent orgies; he was out of temper with Yūsuf and gave way to their demands, and so the Umayyads started on their homeward journey well satisfied. However, as soon as Ṣumail reflected that it would end in the extinction of the independence of the tribal chiefs and of his own authority, he sent messengers to overtake the Umayyads, and informing them that he could not support their master, advised them not to attempt any change of government.

Seeing that all hope was lost of forming an alliance with Ḳaisites, the Umayyads threw themselves into the arms of the Yemenites, who were burning to shake off the yoke of the Ḳaisites. The answer to their call surpassed their expectations. As soon as the subject Umayyads felt sure of the support of the Yemenites and could count on Yūsuf and Ṣumail being engaged in the north, they sent to Tammām in Africa money for the Berbers, who had refused to allow 'Abd-ar-Raḥmān to leave them till a ransom was paid. Then 'Abd-ar-Raḥmān left for Spain and reached Almuñecar in September 755. There 'Ubaid-Allāh and Ibn Khālid awaited him, and put him in possession of the castle of Torrox between Iznajar and Loja.

The receipt of this news made a deep impression on Yūsuf. He had caused distrust by executing three rebel Ḳuraishite chiefs at the instance of Ṣumail, and his resolution to attack the pretender immediately caused the desertion of almost the whole of his army, which was reluctant to undertake a fresh campaign in the depth of winter and in the mountainous district of Regio (Málaga). Yūsuf therefore opened negotiations with 'Abd-ar-Raḥmān. His envoys had an interview with 'Abd-ar-Raḥmān, whom they found surrounded by his little court, in which 'Ubaid-Allāh held the first place; and they offered him on Yūsuf's behalf a safe refuge in Cordova, the hand of Yūsuf's daughter as well as a large dowry and the lands of Caliph Hishām. They shewed him as evidence of good faith a letter from Yūsuf and promised him magnificent presents, left cautiously behind. These terms seemed satisfactory to the Umayyads; 'Ubaid-Allāh was on the point of answering Yūsuf's letter, when the envoy Khālid, a renegade Spaniard, insolently told him that he was incapable of writing a letter like his; 'Ubaid-Allāh's Arab pride was wounded by the Spaniard's reproach, and he gave orders for his arrest. The negotiations were broken off.

As soon as winter was over 'Abd-ar-Raḥmān advanced to Archidona, where the Ḳaisite governor, Jidār, proclaimed him Emir, and entered Seville about the middle of March 756. He then marched out towards Cordova along the left bank of the Guadalquivir, while Yūsuf advanced to Seville along the right bank[1]. On sighting one another the two armies continued their march towards Cordova, still separated by the river. As soon as they reached Mosara, 'Abd-ar-Raḥmān resolved to give battle. By a cunning move he managed to cross the river without any opposition from Yūsuf, a manoeuvre which gave him provisions for his troops. On Friday, 14 May, a sacrificial feast, being the day of the battle of Marj Rāhiṭ[2], which had given the crown to the Umayyads of the East, the combat opened. The cavalry of 'Abd-ar-Raḥmān routed the right wing and centre of the army commanded by Yūsuf and Ṣumail, who each saw the death of his own son. The left wing alone sustained the attack all day until all the notable Ḳaisites had fallen, including their chief 'Ubaid. The victors began to pillage; but 'Abd-ar-Raḥmān forbade it and shewed magnanimity in his treatment of Yūsuf's wife and sons. The Yemenites were offended by his generous behaviour, and formed a plot to kill him. However, he discovered the conspiracy, and no opposition was made to his offering as Imām the Friday prayers in the principal mosque of Cordova. Negotiations were begun, and finally Yūsuf recognised 'Abd-ar-Raḥmān as Emir of Spain in July 756. It was

[1] It was at Colombera or Villanueva de Brenes that the leaders noticed 'Abd-ar-Raḥmān had no banner. Accordingly Abū-ṣ-Ṣabbāḥ, a Sevillan chief, placed his turban on the point of his lance and thus unfurled what became later the standard of the Umayyads in Spain.

[2] See Vol. ii. p. 360.

not long before Yūsuf was slain in battle, and one morning Ṣumail himself was found dead, strangled by order of 'Abd-ar-Raḥmān.

In spite of his growing power 'Abd-ar-Raḥmān had to suppress other revolts, of which the most formidable was that of the Yemenites. In 764 Toledo made its submission. Its chiefs had to pass through Cordova clad in sackcloth, with their heads shaved and mounted on donkeys. But the Yemenites continued restless.

Shortly after 764 the Berbers, who had hitherto kept quiet, rose in arms, headed by a schoolmaster named Shakyā, half fanatic and half impostor, who gave himself out to be a descendant of Ali and Fāṭima. After six years of warfare 'Abd-ar-Raḥmān succeeded in sowing discord among them. He advanced against the rebels, who retreated northwards. Meanwhile the Yemenites and the Berbers of the East advanced towards Cordova. On the banks of the river Bembezar the Yemenites were treacherously left to their fate by the Berbers, and 30,000 perished at the hands of 'Abd-ar-Raḥmān's soldiers. The Berbers of the centre were only subdued after ten years' fighting, when Shakyā was murdered by one of his adherents.

In 777 A'rābī the Kalbite, governor of Barcelona, formed a league against 'Abd-ar-Raḥmān and sent to Charlemagne for help. Charles, who reckoned on the complete pacification of the Saxons, crossed the Pyrenees with an army. A'rābī was to support him north of the Ebro, where his sovereignty was to be recognised, while the African Berbers were to help in Murcia by raising the standard of the Abbasid Caliph, Charles's ally. But this coalition failed. Just as Charlemagne had begun the siege of Saragossa he was called home by the news that Widukind had re-entered Saxony and pushed on to Cologne. On his return to Francia through Roncesvalles the rear-guard of his army was attacked and annihilated by the Basques. There the famous Roland, who was afterwards immortalised in the medieval epic, met his death. 'Abd-ar-Raḥmān reaped the benefit of these successes, which were due to his rebel subjects at Saragossa, to the Basques and to a Saxon prince who did not even know of his existence. He advanced and took possession of Saragossa; he attacked the Basques, and forced the Count of Cerdagne to become his tributary.

These feats were the admiration of the world and evoked from the Abbasid Caliph Manṣūr the following speech concerning 'Abd-ar-Raḥmān: "Although he had no other support to rely on but his statesmanship and perseverance, he succeeded in humbling his haughty opponents, in killing off all insurgents, and in securing his frontier against the attacks of the Christians. He founded a mighty empire, and united under his sceptre extensive dominions which had hitherto been divided among a number of different chiefs." This judgment is an exact description of 'Abd-ar-Raḥmān's life-work.

Detested by the Arab and Berber chiefs, deserted by his followers

and betrayed by his own family, he summoned mercenary troops to his
aid.   Though his policy, which was both daring and treacherous, might
alienate his people's affection, yet it was invariably clever and adapted
to his circumstances.   The very means which he used, violence and
tyranny, were the same as those by which the kings of the fifteenth
century were victorious in their struggle against feudalism.   He had
already traced the outlines of the military despotism, which his successors were to fill in.

His successor Hishām I (788–796) was a model of virtue.   In his reign
the sect of Mālik ibn Anas was started in the East, and the Emir, who
had been commended by Mālik, did his utmost to spread its doctrines,
choosing from its members both judges and ecclesiastics.   When Hishām
died the sect, to which most of the *fakīhs* (professional theologians)
belonged, was already powerful.   It was headed in Spain by a clever
young Berber, Yaḥyā ibn Yaḥyā, who had ambition, enterprise and
experience, along with the impetuosity of a demagogue.

Although the next Emir, Ḥakam, was by no means irreligious, his easy
disposition, his love of the chase and of wine, brought on him the hatred
of the *fakīhs*, which was intensified by his refusing them the influence they
desired.   They were not sparing in their attacks upon him and used as
their tools the *renegados*, who were called *muladíes* (*muwallad* or the
adopted).   The position of these renegades was uneasy ; in religion they
were subject to Muslim law, which punished apostasy with death and
counted any one born a Muslim to be a Muslim.   Socially they were
reckoned as slaves and excluded from any share in the government.   Nevertheless they were able to help the *fakīhs* in bringing about a revolution.

The first rising took place in 805, but was put down by the Emir's
bodyguard.   Then other conspirators offered the throne to Ibn Shammās,
the Emir's cousin, but he revealed the plot, and sixty-two of the conspirators were put to death, while two of them fled to Toledo.   When Ḥakam
was reducing Mérida (806), the inhabitants of Cordova rose a second
time, but he successfully crushed the revolt, beheading or crucifying the
leaders.   Ḥakam now shewed himself even more cruel and treacherous
than before.   His cruelty at Cordova was followed by a massacre at
Toledo.

The Toledans were a people difficult to govern, and under the
headship of the poet Gharbīb, a renegade by birth, they had already
caused alarm to the Emir.   On the death of Gharbīb he appointed as
governor an ambitious renegade from Huesca, 'Amrūs, a man subtle and
dishonest, but a mere puppet in the hands of his master.   He cleverly
won over the Toledans, and was able to build a castle in the middle
of the city, where the Emir's troops were quartered.   An army under
the prince 'Abd-ar-Raḥmān arrived, and the leading Toledans were
invited to a banquet at the castle.   Bidding them enter one by one,

he had their heads cut off in the courtyard of the castle and flung into a ditch. It is impossible to fix the number of those slain on this "day of the ditch," and estimates vary between 700 and 5000.

The impression made by this slaughter kept the people of Cordova quiet for seven years. Moreover, the Emir strengthened his bodyguard with slaves known as "mutes," because they spoke no Arabic. Nevertheless discontent steadily grew among the students and theologians in the quarter of Arrabal del Sur. At length a formidable revolution broke out. In the month of Ramaḍān (May 814) a soldier killed a polisher who refused to clean his sword, and this act was made the pretext for the revolt. A huge mob marched in spite of cavalry charges to the Emir's palace. But Ḥakam with the utmost calmness ordered the execution of some imprisoned *faķīhs*; then after this sacrilege a body of his troops set fire to Arrabal del Sur. The rebels, as he expected, rushed to the help of their families and, attacked on every side, suffered fearful slaughter at the hands of the terrible mutes. Thereupon Ḥakam ordered the expulsion within three days under pain of crucifixion of all the inhabitants of Arrabal del Sur. On reaching the Mediterranean, one body consisting of 15,000 families went to the East, and there after a struggle with the Bedouins seized Alexandria and soon founded an independent kingdom under Abū Ḥafṣ Omar al-Ballūṭī. Another body of 8000 families settled at Fez in Morocco. Ḥakam now issued an amnesty to the *faķīhs* and allowed them to settle anywhere in Spain, except Cordova and its neighbourhood. Yaḥyā even managed to secure his sovereign's favour.

Ḥakam, relentless towards the Toledans and the artisans of Arrabal del Sur, shewed towards the Arabs and Berbers who were of his own race a clemency attributed by Arab historians to remorseful conscience. Some of his verses suggest that he followed the example of 'Abd-ar-Raḥmān: "Just as a tailor uses his needle to join different pieces of cloth, so I use my sword to unite my separate provinces." He maintained the throne of the Umayyads by a military despotism.

At Cordova his son and successor, 'Abd-ar-Raḥmān II (822–852), set a high standard of magnificence. A lover of poetry, mild even to weakness, he let himself be guided by a *faķīh*, a musician, a woman and an eunuch. The *faķīh* was Yaḥyā, the leader of the Arrabal rebellion; he now dominated the Emir, who had given into his hands his own ecclesiastical and judicial functions. The musician was the singer Ziryāb of Bagdad, the pupil of Hārūn ar-Rashīd's famous singer, Isḥāḳ of Mosul, and out of jealousy compelled by him to leave the East. On his arrival in Spain, where 'Abd-ar-Raḥmān II had just ascended the throne, he soon gained the friendship of the sovereign, thanks to his voice, his wit and his wide knowledge of history, poetry, science and art. He became the king of fashion in Cordova as well as the model of good taste, but he did not meddle in politics; they were the province of the

Sultana Ṭarūb, bound to one much like herself, the cruel and treacherous eunuch Naṣr. The son of a Spaniard, Naṣr could speak no Arabic and hated the Christians with the rancour of an apostate. While they governed, the monarch devoted himself to beautifying his capital, which from his time becomes a centre of art and of science for Western Europe.

The country was disturbed: there was the seven years' war between the Maʿaddites and Yemenites in Murcia; there were constant risings of Christians in Mérida; a rebellion, with all the characteristics of a real *germanía* (the later Hermandad, brotherhood), broke out in Toledo, lasting until the city was taken by storm in 837. Then came a new danger: in 844 the Northmen, who were called the *Majūs* by the Arabs, appeared off the coast of Spain. They made a descent on the coast of Galicia and, being repulsed, moved on to Lisbon, Cadiz and up to Seville, but the Emir's troops defeated them and drove them back across the Guadalquivir. In 858 or 859 they returned and sacked Algeciras, carrying their raids along the east coast as far as the Rhone. But they left the coast of Spain as soon as the Muslims began building vessels of the same type as theirs.

But the most formidable difficulty of all came from the Christians. the life of bandits or guerrilla warriors was now impossible for them, and in the cities the path of martyrdom lay plain before them. They were headed by Eulogio and Alvaro. Eulogio belonged to a Cordovan family who detested the Muslims, and was educated at the school of Abbot Spera-in-Deo, where he formed a friendship with Alvaro, a rich young noble of Cordova. As priest at St Zoilo his virtues made him everywhere beloved. He fell under the influence of Flora, the daughter of a Christian mother and so a Christian from birth. Flora was a bold and active champion of militant Christianity; Eulogio made her acquaintance when she escaped from prison and took refuge in the house of a Christian, after she had been accused by her brother and condemned by the *cadi* (*ḳāḍī*) to the punishment of scourging; her personality along with her adventures greatly affected the young priest.

The fanatical hatred of the Muslims was strengthened by the punishment of the priest Perfecto, who was condemned for blasphemy and, owing to the treachery of Naṣr, executed on the feast after Ramaḍān (18 April 850). He prophesied that Naṣr would die within a year, and so it came to pass. For Ṭarūb, who was eager to claim the succession for her son ʿAbdallāh to the exclusion of her step-son Mahomet, compromised Naṣr in a plot to poison the Emir. To this end Naṣr had the poison prepared by the famous doctor Ḥarrānī; but the latter told a woman of the harem, who warned ʿAbd-ar-Raḥmān. Thereupon Naṣr was ordered to drink the poison himself, and the mere fact of his death sufficed to canonise Perfecto. One Isaac, a monk of Tabanos, appeared before the *cadi* and blasphemed the Prophet, which led naturally to his martyrdom on 3 June 851; he was followed by eleven martyrs in less than twelve months. This new kind of rebellion alarmed the government, which put out a decree forbidding Christians to seek martyrdom. A Christian synod was summoned by order of 'Abd-ar-Raḥmān II, who was represented at it by his secretary or *kātib*, Gomez, who, while indifferent to religion, was determined not to confound all Christians with fanatics. The Council pronounced against the martyrs despite the opposition of Saul, Bishop of Cordova, many members only assenting through fear of imprisonment. Eulogio fought hard against its decrees, and on this account was imprisoned with many others. In prison he again met Flora, who was there with another nun, named Maria, and had been threatened by the *cadi* with prostitution. Concealing his love (for such might be termed his affection for Flora), Eulogio exhorted both of them to face their martyrdom. Whilst in prison he worked feverishly at his writings so as to forget his pain, until at length he came forth to practise what he had preached to the two women.

'Abd-ar-Raḥmān died on 22 September 852, and despite Ṭarūb's intrigues Mahomet I ascended the throne. A man of small intelligence, cold-blooded and selfish, he was despised generally for his avarice. But he was supported by the *faḳīhs*, who aimed at making him devout and inspired him with hatred of the Christians, whom he persecuted so terribly that, if we are to believe Eulogio, almost all abjured their faith. But the Emir's intolerance caused the Toledans to revolt; and they advanced as far as Andújar. Reinforced here by an army that Ordoño I of Leon had sent, the rebels gave battle at Guadacelete, but were terribly defeated. Mahomet continued the persecution, while Eulogio and Alvaro persisted in exhorting the people; though lukewarm in Cordova, the Christians were extremely excitable in Toledo, and secured the nomination of Eulogio to the archbishopric in defiance of the refusal of the Emir to give his consent. Mahomet made one last attack on the Toledans and reduced them to submission. Eulogio was charged with concealing an accused Christian, Leocricia, and suffered on 11 March 859. With their death this type of enthusiasm gradually died out, and this painful struggle came to an end.

To return to the Spanish side. After a struggle of twenty years Toledo was placed under the protection of the king of Leon, and extorted a treaty from the Emir who agreed to respect its republican institutions. In Aragon the Beni-Ḳasi, an old Visigothic family, were lords of Saragossa, Tudela, Huesca and the whole of the neighbouring frontier. Throughout a reign of twenty years their chief, Mūsā II, who took the title of Third King of Spain, held his own. In 862 the Emir captured Saragossa and Tudela; but ten years later Mūsā's sons turned out his garrisons. At this time Ibn Marwān founded an independent principality in Mérida and, later, in Badajoz. In 879 an insurrection broke out in Regio under Omar ibn Ḥafṣūn. After a mingled career of robbery and warfare, he became from 884 the leader of the Spanish people in the

south, where his good qualities won him general affection. Meanwhile
Mahomet was succeeded (886) by his son Mundhir (886–888), who, however, was poisoned by his brother 'Abdallāh.

'Abdallāh ascended the throne at a disastrous time. Besides the
revolts already begun, he had to deal with the attempts of the Arab
aristocracy to recover their independence. In Elvira (Granada), where
there were numerous renegades, the Spaniards, whether Muslims or Christians, were called and treated as a low rabble by the Arabs. The result
was a tremendous struggle between the two parties, who fought and
massacred each other for many months.

Meanwhile greater events were happening at Seville. There power
was divided between the Spanish party in the town, represented by the
Beni-Angelino, and the Arab party in the remoter country, led by the
Beni-Ḥajjāj and the Beni-Khaldūn. At the outset of 'Abdallāh's reign
the leader of the Khaldūn was Ḳuraib, a treacherous but able man and
a whole-hearted enemy of the monarchy. He formed a league to capture
Seville and plunder the Spaniards. Under the guidance of Ḳuraib the
Berbers of Mérida and Medellin made a terrible raid on Seville. The
most formidable of the bandits was a Bornos Berber of Carmona, who
was named Tamashecca. Mahomet ibn Ghālib, a gallant renegade from
Écija, offered to make the roads secure if he were allowed to build a
fortress near Siete Torres. He had begun his task when the Ḥajjāj and
the Khaldūn attacked his castle. The Arabs promptly revolted, captured
Carmona, and so filled Seville with alarm. To satisfy them 'Abdallāh
resolved upon the treacherous execution of Ibn Ghālib. As soon as the
renegades knew of the death of Ibn Ghālib, they rose to avenge him.
The prince Mahomet, then at Seville, begged for reinforcements from the
Beni-Angelino, who with some hesitation sent troops to hold the palace.
Every moment the situation became more desperate, and it was only
saved by the timely arrival of Jad, governor of Elvira. The Spanish
party in Seville were afterwards almost all put to the sword by the
Ḥajjāj and the Khaldūn. It was these tribes who reaped full advantage
from the position of affairs, and not the Emir, while Jad's successors were
constantly threatened and even placed under constraint.

Such was the position of affairs in Seville in 891. The rest of Muslim
Spain was quite as independent. The lords of Mentesa, Medina Sidonia,
Lorca and Saragossa only obeyed the Emir when it suited them. The
Berbers had reverted to a system of tribal government. The renegades,
however, maintained their position in Ocsonoba, in Beja and Mértola,
and in Priego. The nobles in the province of Jaen were all in alliance
with Omar ibn Ḥafṣūn. Another independent chief, Daisam ibn Isḥāḳ,
was lord of almost the whole of Todmir (Murcia).

But the Emir's most formidable enemy was still Omar Ibn Ḥafṣūn.
Although the Emir made a truce, Ibn Ḥafṣūn broke it whenever he
chose. When Ibn Mastana of Priego, however, formed an alliance with

some Arabs, Ibn Ḥafṣūn took the side of the Emir. But as his supporters wearied of so temporising a policy, he imprisoned the commander of the Emir's army, and thus caused a complete rupture. Realising that he was virtually master of Spain and imagining that the Arabs and Berbers would refuse to yield him obedience, Omar entered into negotiations for his appointment as emir by the Abbasid Caliph, and through him came into touch with Ibn al-Aghlab, the emir of Africa. As Cordova was now in desperate straits, and his own position even worse, the Emir resolved to stake everything on a single cast, and with the approval of all his supporters attacked the enemy. On Thursday in Holy Week, 16 April 891, the battle began near the castle of Polei (now Aguilar). For the royalists the fortunes of the Umayyads were at stake and they fought desperately. They routed Ibn Ḥafṣūn, while 'Abdallāh sat in his tent and hypocritically recited verses from the Koran expressing his whole confidence in God. He then laid siege to Polei, and soon took it, pardoning the Muslims but slaying the Christians.

The result of the battle of Polei was the surrender of Écija, Archidona, Elvira and Jaen and the restoration of the Emir's authority; but their submission did not last long. In 892 Ibn Ḥafṣūn captured Archidona and Elvira; and to crown his success seized Jaen. In 893, however, he lost Elvira again; in 895 the Emir advanced against Seville, which Ḳuraib ibn Khaldūn successfully defended. Ibn Ḥajjāj, who became master of Seville, made his submission for a brief period and left his son 'Abd-ar-Raḥmān as a hostage in Cordova; shortly after he formed an alliance with Ibn Ḥafṣūn. Because he had become a Christian Omar had been deserted by many of his Muslim subjects, and he therefore gladly made a new confederacy with the Beni-Ḳasi of Saragossa and the king of Leon. The Emir's position was deplorable, though he succeeded in making peace with Ibn Ḥafṣūn (901). In 902 he renewed the war, which went against the allies. In hopes of detaching Ibn Ḥajjāj from the league 'Abdallāh handed over to him his son 'Abd-ar-Raḥmān. Ibn Ḥajjāj was grateful and was reconciled with the Emir. 'Abdallāh advanced from one victory to another. He captured Jaen, and seemed to have greatly improved his position, when he died on 15 October 912.

When 'Abd-ar-Raḥmān III, 'Abdallāh's grandson, ascended the throne of the Umayyads, he found Muslim Spain rent by civil war and menaced by two enemies from outside, the kingdom of Leon and the Fāṭimite Caliphate in Africa. The latter had been founded by the Ismaelites, who were one of the Shī'ite sects, and aimed at forcing their way into Spain, through the preaching of the Mahdī or secret Imām, with the object of establishing a universal monarchy. One of the tools employed by the Fāṭimites seems to have been Ibn Masarra, a philosopher at Cordova. But though he had made proselytes among the common people, he had failed to obtain a following among the *faḳīhs*, and his books were burnt as heretical. The kingdom of Leon, although since Alfonso I it had made no real advance, now took advantage of the revolts in the south to extend its frontier to the Douro and to capture the strongholds of Zamora, Simancas, St Esteban de Gormaz and Osma, which together formed an almost unbreakable barrier against the Muslims. Leonese raids extended to the Tagus and even to the Guadiana. In 901 Aḥmad ibn Muʻāwiya proclaimed himself to the Berbers as the Mahdī. They collected an army and advanced against Zamora, which had been rebuilt by Alfonso III in 893. The Berber leaders, however, were jealous of the power of the Mahdī, who had been victorious in the first battle. They therefore deserted, with the result that Aḥmad ibn Muʻāwiya's army perished and he himself was put to death by the Leonese. This victory, won with the help of Toledo and Sancho of Navarre, gave great impetus to progress in the latter kingdom, which had hitherto been chiefly engaged in combating the Franks. The courage of the Leonese was now raised to such a pitch that they felt strong enough to strike a blow at Muslim civilisation. The life-work of 'Abd-ar-Raḥmān III was to defend that civilisation from the dangers that threatened it on the north and south, but first of all he had to bring his own subjects to obedience.

In dealing with the Spanish party and the Arab aristocracy, he abandoned the tortuous policy of 'Abdallāh in favour of a bolder one which soon won him success. In a few years everything had changed. The chiefs who fought 'Abdallāh were dead, and the aristocracy had no leaders. The Spanish party had lost its first vigour and, although the people were patriotic, they had grown tired of war. Omar, like the Emir, began hiring mercenaries, and these troops were not too heroic, while the lords of the castles were thoroughly demoralised. The struggle had really lost its national character and was becoming a religious war. All these things told in favour of the Emir, whom everyone regarded as the one hope of safety. He vigorously opened the campaign. Within three months he had captured Monteleon and reduced almost all the fortresses of Jaen and Elvira. On the death of Ibrāhīm ibn Ḥajjāj, Aḥmad ibn Maslama was appointed governor of Seville, and he formed an alliance with Ibn Ḥafṣūn. But the Emir laid siege to Seville and defeated Ibn Ḥafṣūn's army, while Seville surrendered 20 December 913. In another campaign against the mountain land of Regio (Málaga) (914) 'Abd-ar-Raḥmān treated the Christians equitably, and this policy was eminently effective; for the commanders of almost all the castles surrendered. That indomitable Spanish hero, Omar ibn Ḥafṣūn, died in 917: he had in the last thirty years often made the throne of the Umayyads totter, but he had failed to secure the freedom of his country or to found a new dynasty; he was, however, spared the sight of his party's ruin. The revolt in Regio lasted another ten years under the sons of Omar. At length in 927 the Emir laid siege to their stronghold, Bobastro, which surrendered on 21 January 928. Ibn Ḥafṣūn's daughter, Argentea, who was a religious devotee, died a martyr, and this was the end of the family. 'Abd-ar-Raḥmān III did not find so much difficulty in putting down the independent Arab and Berber nobles. Ibn Marwān was reduced in 930, and Toledo, the last stronghold of the revolt, followed suit in 932. Arabs, Spaniards and Berbers all submitted to 'Abd-ar-Raḥmān, who thus achieved his object, the fusion of all the Muslim races in Spain and the formation of a united nation.

In 914 Ordoño II, king of Leon, laid waste the district of Mérida and captured the castle of Alanje. 'Abd-ar-Raḥmān III was eager to punish him. In 918 Ordoño II with his ally Sancho of Navarre made an attack on Nájera and Tudela. Sancho captured Valtierra, but 'Abd-ar-Raḥmān's army under the command of the *ḥājib* Badr twice defeated the Leonese at Mutonia. In 920 'Abd-ar-Raḥmān took command of the army in person. By a clever move he seized Osma and then took other places. Meanwhile Sancho had retired, but after a junction with Ordoño II attacked 'Abd-ar-Raḥmān, who found himself in a similar position to Charlemagne's rear-guard at Roncesvalles. At Val de Junqueras the Christians suffered a crushing defeat owing to the mistake they made in accepting battle in the plain. 'Abd-ar-Raḥmān returned to Cordova triumphant. But the Christians did not despair. In 923 Ordoño captured Nájera, while Sancho seized Viguera. But in 924 'Abd-ar-Raḥmān replied by marching in triumph as far as Pampeluna. On the death of Ordoño II, which occurred before this campaign, a civil war broke out between his sons, Sancho and Alfonso IV, while Sancho of Navarre was so far humbled that 'Abd-ar-Raḥmān had leisure to stamp out the rebellion in the south. As he had now attained the height of his ambition, he changed his title and henceforth from 16 January 929 he styled himself *Caliph*, *Amīr al-mu'minīn* (Commander of the Faithful) and *An-Nāṣir lidīn Allāh* (Defender of the Faith).

In Africa he now began a more active policy, and the Maghrawa Berbers, after he had driven the Fāṭimites out of the central part of North Africa (Algiers and Oran), acknowledged his suzerainty. In 931 'Abd-ar-Raḥmān occupied Ceuta, the key to Mauretania.

In the north the civil war left Ramiro II king in the end (932). This warlike monarch marched to the rescue of Toledo, which stood alone in its resistance to the Caliph. He took Madrid on the way, but failed to save Toledo which, as we have already mentioned, surrendered. In 933 he defeated a Muslim army at Osma, but the following year 'Abd-ar-Raḥmān revenged himself by a terrible raid as far as Burgos. Ramiro II formed an alliance with Mahomet ibn Hāshim at-Tujibī, the disaffected governor of Saragossa.

In 937 the Caliph advanced against the allies, capturing some thirty castles. He next turned his arms against Navarre and then against Saragossa, which surrendered. Ibn Hāshim was pardoned owing to his great popularity. Tota (Theuda), the Queen-regent of Navarre, recognised the Caliph as suzerain, so that with the exception of Leon and part of Catalonia the whole of Spain had submitted to 'Abd-ar-Raḥmān III.

From 939 onwards the fortune of war turned somewhat against the Caliph. Carrying out his policy of humbling the great nobles, he had given all the highest civil and military posts to the slaves, who included Galicians, Franks, Lombards, Calabrians, and captives from the coast of the Black Sea ; he had increased their number and compelled the Arab aristocracy to submit to them. In the campaign of 939, during which Najda the slave was in command, the nobles had their revenge on 'Abd-ar-Raḥmān. They allowed themselves to be beaten by Ramiro and Tota at Simancas, and they also were responsible for a terrible defeat at Alhandega, in which Najda was killed and 'Abd-ar-Raḥmān himself narrowly escaped. Their victory did not profit the Christians, however, since Castile, under its Count Fernan (Ferdinand) Gonzalez, the hero of the medieval epic, took advantage of the Caliph's inactivity to declare war on Ramiro II.

During this period Abu Yazīd of the Berber tribe of Iforen came forward to oppose the Fāṭimites in Africa. He declared himself a *khārijī* or nonconformist, and united all the Berbers. He recognised 'Abd-ar-Raḥmān, to whom he gave military help, as the spiritual suzerain of the dominions which he had wrested from the Fāṭimites. But when Abu Yazīd discarded his ascetic sackcloth for more splendid silk, and fell out with the Sunnites (orthodox Muslims), he suffered defeat from the Fāṭimite Caliph Manṣūr, and the Fāṭimite dynasty recovered all the territory it had lost.

The civil war in the north among the Christians ended favourably to Ramiro II. He took Fernan Gonzalez prisoner, and only set him free on swearing fealty and obedience; and forced him further to give up his county and to marry his daughter Urraca to Ordoño, Ramiro's son. Ramiro thus lost the real loyalty of Castile, which henceforth was opposed to León. Ramiro II died in 951 and a war of succession broke out between his sons Ordoño III and Sancho, supported by the Navarrese and his uncle Fernan Gonzalez, who preferred his nephew to his son-in-law. Ordoño III, the final victor in the civil strife, sought peace with the Muslims, and 'Abd-ar-Raḥmān was thus left free to fight the Fāṭimites, whose power was increasing every day. In 955 the fourth Fāṭimite Caliph Mu'izz was planning an invasion of Spain and sent a squadron to Almería, which set fire to all the vessels it encountered and plundered the coast. In 959 'Abd-ar-Raḥmān replied by an expedition against Ifrīkiya (Tunis), but gained no advantage. To leave himself free for Africa he had made peace with Ordoño III; but owing to Ordoño's death in 957 and the accession of Sancho the Fat the calm was broken.

Sancho, who attempted to crush the nobles and to restore the absolute power of his predecessors, was deposed in 958, for reasons which included excessive corpulence, through a conspiracy headed by Fernan Gonzalez. Ordoño IV the Bad was elected king, while Sancho, who was supported by his grandmother, the aged and ambitious Tota of Navarre, sent ambassadors to ask the Caliph of Cordova for aid. The ambassador, whom 'Abd-ar-Raḥmān sent to Navarre, was an excellent Jewish physician who cured Sancho, while by his diplomatic ability he brought to Cordova the rulers of Navarre. They were welcomed there with a splendour that dazzled them. 'Abd-ar-Raḥmān had now at his feet not only the haughty Tota whose valour had guided her armies to victory, but also the son of his enemy, Ramiro II, the other victor of Simancas and Alhandega. To induce the Caliph to renew his attack on Leon, the unfortunate Sancho was obliged to hand over ten fortresses. With the help of the Arabs Sancho, who no longer could claim the name of Fat, took Zamora in 959 and Oviedo in 960. Afterwards he invaded Castile and took Count Fernan prisoner, while Ordoño IV fled to Burgos. At this point 'Abd-ar-Raḥmān fell ill and died on 16 October 961 at the age of seventy, after reigning for forty-nine years.

'Abd-ar-Raḥmān III was the greatest of the Umayyad princes. He saved Andalusia not only from the civil wars but also from the possible foreign domination in the north and south. He established order and prosperity at home and imposed respect and consideration abroad. He encouraged and developed agriculture, commerce, industry, art and science; he beautified Cordova, so that it bore comparison with Bagdad, and he built beside it the city of Az-Zahrā, called after his favourite wife. Outside his realm he contested the command of the Mediterranean with the Fātimites. The Eastern Emperor and the kings of Western Europe opened up a diplomatic friendship with him[1]. To quote the very words of Dozy, our indispensable guide throughout, "But when his glorious reign comes to be studied, it is the worker rather than the work that rouses our admiration. Nothing escaped that powerful comprehensive intellect, and its grasp of the smallest details proved to be as extraordinary as that of the loftiest conceptions. The sagacity and cleverness of this man who by his centralising policy firmly established the unity of the nation and the foundations of his own authority, who by his system of alliances set up a kind of balance of power, whose broad tolerance led him to summon to his council men of different religions, these characteristics are typical of the modern monarch rather than of the medieval caliph."

His successor, Ḥakam II, was pacific, but when Sancho and Garcia of Navarre failed to fulfil their treaties with his father and Fernan Gonzalez

---

[1] It was 'Abd-ar-Raḥmān's own ambassador at the Court of Otto the Great, Recemund, Bishop of Elvira, who suggested to Liudprand the composition of his history, the *Antapodosis*. This is a striking instance of the influence of the Caliphate of Cordova on the culture of the West.

began hostilities, he was forced to prepare for war. Meanwhile Ordoño the Bad implored the Caliph to help him against his brother Sancho, and had a splendid reception at Cordova. As soon as Sancho saw that the Caliph's army was supporting Ordoño, he assured the Caliph that he would fulfil his obligations. Ḥakam therefore broke his promise to Ordoño, who soon died at Cordova. Sancho still refused to carry out the treaty, whereupon Ḥakam declared war on the Christians, and compelled Fernan Gonzalez, Garcia of Navarre and Sancho of Leon to sue for peace; the Catalan counts, Borrel and Miron, followed their example at the same time[1].

Ḥakam was content to leave the Christians to their internal strife. A civil war broke out, during which Sancho died of poison towards 966: he was succeeded by Ramiro III, to whom his aunt, the nun Elvira, was guardian. Under her the kingdom split into pieces. Fernan Gonzalez died in 970, and thenceforth Ḥakam was able to devote himself to literature, his favourite pursuit.

Under him one commanding personality fills the scene of the Caliphate. Mahomet ibn Abī-'Āmir, known to history as Almanzor, belonged to the noble family of the Beni-Abī-'Āmir, and from earliest youth he dreamt of becoming prime minister: natural ability and audacity in action made his dream a reality. From a subordinate official of the *cadi* of Cordova he rose at the age of twenty-six to administer the property of 'Abd-ar-Raḥmān, the son of Ḥakam. By his courtesy and wit he won the favour of the Sultana Aurora, became administrator of her property and shortly after inspector of the mint, in which post he made many friends. Other offices, all of them lucrative, were heaped upon him. He lived in princely grandeur and he soon became popular.

The Fāṭimite danger had disappeared in 969 when Mu'izz moved from Ifrīkiya to the new city of Cairo, but Ḥakam had still to fight the Idrīsids in Morocco, and the war opened up a connexion with the African princes and Berber tribes.

Shortly afterwards the Caliph fell ill, and on 1 October 976 he died. Next day Hishām II took the oath, and his accession raised even higher the power of Ibn Abī-'Āmir who was made vizier, while Muṣhafī, the ex-vizier, was appointed *ḥājib* or prime minister.

The Christians in the north had renewed hostilities at the time of Ḥakam's illness. Ibn Abī-'Āmir undertook the command of an army and returned to Cordova laden with plunder. This triumph made him still more popular in Cordova, and brought about a friendship between him and the commanders of the army.

Soon came the inevitable struggle between the two ministers. On 25 March 978 Muṣhafī was deposed and imprisoned on a charge of embezzlement. All his property was confiscated and after five years of the utmost destitution he was executed.

[1] See for Catalonia *supra*, Chap. IV. pp. 89–90.

Ibn Abī-ʿĀmir was appointed *ḥājib*. His relations with the Sultana Aurora were much criticised in Cordova, and he had to face faction and conspiracy. When his chief enemies, the *faḳīhs*, asserted that he was given over to philosophy, he ordered all the books on that subject in the library of Ḥakam II to be burnt, and in this way he achieved a great reputation for orthodoxy. He had shut up the Caliph in his newly-built palace of Zāhira, adjoining Cordova, and determined to reform the army. But as he could not rely on the Arabs for this task, he brought Berbers from Ceuta in Morocco, whom he loaded with wealth, and unpatriotic Christians from Leon, Castile and Navarre, drawn by high pay. At the same time he carried through the re-organisation of the military system by abolishing the identity of tribes and regiments. Then, to shew the superiority of the army he had created, he turned his arms against the Leonese. He invaded Leon, captured and sacked Zamora (981). Ramiro III of Leon was joined by Garcia Fernandez, Count of Castile, but they were beaten at Rueda to the east of Simancas. He then advanced against Leon, but although he reached its gates in triumph, he failed to take the city. On his return from this campaign he took the title of *Al-manṣūr billah*, "the Victorious by the help of God" (whence his Spanish name of Almanzor is derived), and had royal honours paid him. Owing to the disastrous campaign of 981 the nobles of Leon proclaimed as their king Bermudo II, a cousin of Ramiro III, who being besieged in Astorga sought the aid of Almanzor, but died soon after. Bermudo also asked his help in crushing the nobles, but after giving it Almanzor allowed the Muslim troops to remain in the country. Thus Leon ended by becoming a tributary of Almanzor. He now advanced into Catalonia and took Barcelona by storm on 1 July 985.

Almanzor's tyranny and cruelty at home, however, were making him hated. To make good his position he resolved to enlarge the mosque at great expense. He even worked like an ordinary labourer among a crowd of Christian prisoners. Meanwhile Bermudo II drove out of Leon the Muslim troops who had been left there; but in 987 Almanzor in a terrible raid seized Coimbra and routed all who opposed his march to Leon. He captured the city and only spared one tower to shew posterity its grandeur. After he had also taken Zamora his sovereignty was acknowledged by all the country, while Bermudo kept only the districts near the sea.

Almanzor, already the real ruler, aimed at being even more. For this design he had no fear of the Caliph, who was his prisoner, nor of the army which yielded him blind obedience; but he feared the nation, for whom unreasoning devotion to the dynasty was its very life, and he also feared Aurora, whose affection for him had now turned to hatred. She succeeded in inspiring Hishām II with a semblance of will and energy. She sought the aid of Zīrī ibn ʿAṭīya, the viceroy of

Morocco. Almanzor however managed to see Hishām, reimposed his will upon him, and persuaded the Caliph to issue a decree entrusting to him all affairs of state as formerly. Aurora acknowledged herself defeated and devoted herself to works of piety.

Zīrī's defeat at Ceuta in 998 brought about the end of his power and the transference of all his territory to the Andalusians. At the same time Almanzor attacked Bermudo II for refusing to pay tribute. He penetrated as far as Santiago in Galicia, and after a victorious march returned to Cordova with a crowd of prisoners. These carried on their shoulders the gates of the city, which were placed in the mosque, while the bells of its church were used as braziers.

In 1002 Almanzor went on his last expedition against Castile. Concerning it, the Muslim historians only mention that on his return march from the successful expedition Almanzor's illness grew worse; that he died at Medinaceli in 1002 and was buried there. The *Historia Compostellana* and the *Chronicon Burgense* give much the same account; the latter saying: "Almanzor died in the year 1002, and was buried in hell." But Don Rodrigo Ximenez de Rada, Archbishop of Toledo († 1247), and Lucas, Bishop of Tuy († 1249), tell us that Bermudo II of Leon, Garcia of Navarre and Garcia Fernandez, Count of Castile, formed a league in 998 and attacked Almanzor at Calatañazor, where they inflicted a great defeat on him, and that he died afterwards at Medinaceli from the wounds he had received; and on the return of the Muslim army to Cordova a shepherd miraculously appeared, singing the famous strain: " In Calatañazor Almanzor lost his drum." The appearance in the battle of Bermudo II and Garcia of Navarre, who were already dead, the tale of the shepherd (who was taken for the devil by Christian historians), and the fixing of the date of the battle as 998, induce Dozy to reject the story. But recently Saavedra has attempted to prove the probable truth of the legend. He argues that possibly after the withdrawal of Almanzor through his illness his rear-guard was attacked at Calatañazor; that his not accepting battle and the pursuit by the Christians to the gates of Medinaceli may have been regarded by them as a victory; the anachronisms of the narratives may be due to their having been written two centuries after the event: they failed to be accurate in date and repeated some legendary details which had already gathered round the truth.

But whether this battle was ever actually fought or no, Almanzor, the terrible foe of Christendom, was dead. He was endowed with energy and strength of character; he was idolised by his soldiers whom he led to invariable victory; his love of letters was shewn in a splendid generosity; at the same time, he watched over the material interests of the country and strictly executed justice. In all that he undertook he shewed a clearness of vision which marked his genius. Of his greatness there can be no doubt.

Muẓaffar, Almanzor's son, who took his father's place, won great victories over the Christians and put down some risings. But great changes had occurred in Muslim Spain. Class feeling had taken the place of racial discord, and new sects appeared, advocating innovations in politics and religion. The people were profoundly attached to the Umayyad Caliphate and ardently desired the fall of the ʿĀmirite house of Almanzor. Such was the position of affairs when Muẓaffar died (1008) and was succeeded by his brother ʿAbd-ar-Raḥmān, nicknamed *Sanchuelo*. He was unpopular with the *faḳīhs* and lacked the ability of his father or brother, but he succeeded in obtaining from Hishām II what they had never extorted, his nomination as heir apparent. This brought to a head discontent in Cordova. While *Sanchuelo* was away on a campaign against Alfonso V of Leon, a revolution placed Mahomet II al-Mahdī on the throne, whereupon Hishām II abdicated. Seeing himself deserted, *Sanchuelo* sued for pardon, but on his return to Cordova he was slain (4 March 1009). Mahdī, who was bloodthirsty, and yet lacked courage, alienated both " slaves "[1] and Berbers. When the Berbers proclaimed another Umayyad, Hishām, on Mahdī's passing off Hishām II as dead, he defeated and killed him. A chief, Zawī, however, rallied the Berbers, and the slain man's father, Sulaimān al-Mustaʿīn, was proclaimed Caliph. They formed an alliance with the Castilians. Mahdī was beaten at Cantich, Sulaimān entered Cordova, where the Berbers and Castilians committed every kind of excess; Hishām II returned, only to abdicate in favour of Sulaimān. Mahdī's party, on their side, made an alliance with the Catalan Counts, Raymond of Barcelona and Armengol of Urgel, and defeated Sulaimān at ʿAḳabat-al-baḳar near Cordova, which the Catalans plundered. The Slaves now turned against Mahdī, murdered him, and for the third time proclaimed Hishām II in 1010. Sancho of Castile used the opportunity to recover the fortresses captured by Almanzor. The Berber opposition continued; in 1012 they pitilessly sacked Cordova, houses and palaces were destroyed, and Sulaimān was once more proclaimed Caliph. It was a war of factions, and in 1016 the Slaves entered Cordova. They sought in vain for Hishām II. Sulaimān gave out that he was dead; but apparently he fled to Asia, where he ended his life in obscurity. The welter became more confused, till in 1025 for six months the government was in the hands of a Council of State. In 1027 the Slaves proclaimed the last of the Umayyads, Hishām III al-Muʿtadd. He too failed to satisfy expectations. A revolution broke out in December 1031; Hishām was taken prisoner. The viziers announced the abolition of the Caliphate and declared the government devolved on the Council of State.

Meanwhile in the Christian kingdoms a steady advance had been made. In 1020 Alfonso V of Leon summoned a council to his capital

---

[1] See *supra*, p. 422.

to reform the government, and there issued the *fuero* of Leon and other
general laws.   His son Bermudo III succeeded in 1027, and through
his marriage with a sister of Garcia, Count of Castile, whose other
sister was married to Sancho the Great of Navarre, the relations between
the rulers of the three kingdoms became far more intimate.   Castile,
despite the occasional intervention of Leon, had been independent
since the days of Fernan Gonzalez.   The happy understanding which
prevailed among the Christian states was broken up through the murder
of Garcia of Castile.   Garcia's brother-in-law, Sancho of Navarre, seized
the territories of Castile, and a dispute over the frontier led to war with
Bermudo III of Leon, which was ended by the marriage of Bermudo's
sister with Sancho's eldest son, Ferdinand, the future King of Castile.
On the speedy renewal of the war the Castilians and Navarrese conquered
the whole of Leon, Bermudo only retaining Galicia.   Navarre then
became the dominant power from the frontier of Galicia to the county of
Barcelona, and Sancho ruled over Leon, Castile, Navarre, Aragon and all
the Basque country.   But shortly before his death he divided the kingdom
among his sons.   He left Navarre and the Basque provinces to Garcia,
Castile to Ferdinand, Aragon to Ramiro, and the lordship of Sobrarbe
and Ribagorza to Gonzalo.   Bermudo III continued to reign in Galicia,
but after the death of Sancho (1035) he was defeated at Tamaron by Ferdinand in 1037, who thus united under his sceptre all Leon and Castile.

The counts of Barcelona who succeeded Wifred I had extended
their dominions beyond the river Llobregat and, despite invasions by
Almanzor (986) and his son Muẓaffar, they recovered their lost territory
through their intervention in the civil wars of the Muslims after the fall
of the Almanzors. The break up of the Caliphate was taken advantage of
by Count Raymond-Berengar I (1035–1076), to consolidate his power.

With the fall of the Caliphate there began for Spain the great
period of Christian conquest, when the leadership passed from the
Caliphate to the Christian kingdoms.   The Muslim supremacy had been
due partly to higher military efficiency, which was never recovered
after the collapse of the Caliphate, and even more to the brilliance
of its civilisation compared with the backward condition of the
Northern States.   This Arab civilisation claims especial notice.

The great variety of races in the country hindered the immediate
development of Muslim civilisation, and despite the efforts at union
of 'Abd-ar-Raḥmān III the conflict between the different peoples
and tribes still persisted.   The Arabs refused to regard the Persians,
Berbers and other conquered races as their countrymen, while even
among the Arabs themselves Syrians, Yemenites, and other tribes were
in constant feud.   Inside the tribes there were freemen, divided into
aristocracy and people, and slaves.   Under 'Abd-ar-Raḥmān III
the unbroken struggle with the emirs all but destroyed the Arab

aristocracy. Its place was taken on the one hand by the middle classes, who had amassed much wealth through the great expansion of trade and industry, and on the other hand by a feudal aristocracy of military commanders. The working-men remained under the thumb of the middle classes, and owing to their economic inferiority were stirred occasionally to class hatred. The grants of lands and slaves freely given by the emirs made the dominant aristocracy the wealthiest class, and enabled it to form independent or nearly independent domains. This process may account for the fact that the Arabs and Berbers preferred the country to the cities, whose inhabitants, as in the case of Toledo, Seville and Elvira, were mainly renegades and Mozarabs.

The unfree classes were divided into peasant serfs, whose status was better than under the Visigoths, and household or personal slaves; among the latter the eunuchs who were set apart for the service of the harem enjoyed a privileged position. Occasionally they held the highest appointments, and since they had followers as well as wealth, could intervene effectively in politics. The Slaves[1], who were not only the soldiers but the serfs of the Caliph, held civil as well as military offices, and, as we have seen, on the fall of the Almanzors their political influence was decisive.

The Muladíes (Muwallad) were in an intermediate position. They were mainly descendants of Visigothic serfs who had secured freedom by their profession of Islām. As we have seen, they were viewed with suspicion by Muslims of old standing, and this bitterness caused frequent revolts. From the reign of 'Abd-ar-Raḥmān II their numbers increased owing to the frequent conversions of Mozarabs or Spanish Christians, and their influence on Muslim civilisation was considerable.

The legal status of the Jews improved under the Arabs. The destructive policy of the Visigoths was succeeded by wide toleration and freedom, which was characteristic of the Muslim conquest. In particular the commercial and industrial prosperity of Cordova, which dated from the independence of the Caliph, was due to this liberal policy. The Jew Ḥasdai Ibn Shabrut, who was the treasurer and minister of 'Abd-ar-Raḥmān III and translated the works of Dioscorides, was famous as a diplomatist. Under his influence many of his co-religionists came from the East. They started a Talmudic school which eclipsed the schools of Mesopotamia. The Jews in Cordova adopted the dress, language and customs of the Arabs, and were consistently protected by the Caliphs.

The Mozarabs still kept their government and administration in their own hands under special governors (counts) who were selected by the Caliph. They still kept their *defensor* to represent them at

---

[1] See *supra*, p. 422.

the court of the Caliph.   It is not known whether the *curia* survived ;
but the *exceptor*, who was now a tax-collector, survived, as did also the
censor, who was a judge of first instance, while the count (*conde*) presided over the court of appeal.   He still administered the code (*Fuero
Juzgo*), while transgressions of the law of Islām came before the Muslim
authorities.   The Mozarabs lived in districts apart, and apparently
there was no marked distinction between the Visigothic and Hispano-
Roman elements.   Except for brief periods of persecution, they were
treated tolerantly.

Spain was at first a province of the Caliphate of Damascus with an
emir at its head.   'Abd-ar-Raḥmān I put an end to this dependent position by breaking with the Caliphate of Bagdad, although it was not till
929 that the title of Caliph was assumed by 'Abd-ar-Raḥmān III.   The
Caliph was the supreme temporal and spiritual head.   Sometimes he
was elected by the nobles, but usually it was a hereditary office.   The
hierarchy consisted: of the *ḥājib* or prime minister; of various *wazīrs*
(viziers) or ministers, who were responsible for the various administrative
departments, such as the Treasury and War Office, though they only
communicated with the Caliph through the *ḥājib*; and of the *kātibs* or
secretaries.   The administrative offices together formed the *diwan* and
there were as many offices as public services.   The provinces, which were six
in number apart from Cordova, were under a civil and military governor
called a *wālī*.   In some important cities there were also *wālīs* at the
head of affairs, and on the frontier there was a military commander.

The Caliph administered justice in person ; but as a rule this function was exercised by the *cadis* (*ḳāḍī*) (and in small villages by *ḥākims*).
At their head stood the *cadi* of the *cadis*, who was established at
Cordova.   A special judge, the *Ṣāḥib-ash-shurṭa* or *Ṣāḥib-al-madīna*
(*zal-medina*) heard criminal and police cases, under a procedure simpler
than that of the *cadi*.   The *zabalaquen* or *ḥākim* carried out the
sentences of the *cadi*.   The *muḥtasib* or *almotacén* regulated police,
trade and markets, and intervened in questions of sales, gambling,
weights, measures and public dress.   Cordova had a special judge
(*Ṣāḥib-al-mazālim*), who was appointed by the Emir to hear complaints
of breach of privilege or of offences committed by public officials; Ribera
considers that the *Justicia mayor de Aragon* was set up in imitation of
this functionary.   The usual punishments were fines, scourging, mutilation
and death; this last penalty applied to cases of blasphemy, heresy, and
apostasy.

Besides the taxes on personal and real property (quit rents) paid by
holders of *khums* (State-lands), there was the *azzaque*, a tithe of agriculture, industry and commerce, and also the customs, the head of which
was called *al-mushrif* (*almojarife*).   A census with statistics based on
tribal organisation was drawn up for the assessment of taxation, but
this method of organisation died out on the fall of the Arab aristocracy.

The tribe was the unit of military organisation. Each tribe rallied round its chief and its standard. The soldiers received pay at the end of the campaign at the rate of five to ten gold pieces, and the *baladīs*, who were descended from Mūsā's Arabs, were never summoned except in case of need. Campaigns were generally conducted in the spring and had the character of an *algaras* or raid. The object was booty and with that secured the army invariably retired from any position conquered. The commander-in-chief was called *al-ḳā'id* (*alcaide*); the cavalry was mounted on mules and without stirrups. They used the sword, the pike, the lance and the bow, while their defensive armour consisted of helmets, shields, cuirasses and coats of mail. Their siege weapons were the same as those employed by the Byzantines.

The army underwent many changes in organisation, as the Caliphs became more dependent on foreign troops, and Almanzor completed this process. He substituted the regimental for the tribal division, and thus put an end to the power of the tribal chiefs. There were, moreover, foreign elements; first the Slaves and then the mercenary Christian troops from Leon, Navarre and Castile, who became dangerous to the tranquillity of the country when Almanzor's iron grasp relaxed.

The navy under 'Abd-ar-Raḥmān III, with Almería as its chief harbour, became the most powerful in the Mediterranean. Their raids, under commanders of a squadron called the *Alcaides* of the fleet, extended to Galicia and Asturias, and also to Africa where they attacked the Fāṭimites. In fact, Muslim piracy was the terror of the Mediterranean, and it was from Spain that the colonists of Fraxinetum came[1]. When at the end of the tenth century the Fāṭimite danger disappeared, the Arabs neglected their navy.

The Muslim religion is based on the recognition of one God and of Mahomet as his prophet, and the Caliph is the supreme spiritual head. But among Arabs and Berbers alike grew up many heterodox sects. These made proselytes in Spain, but were not openly professed for fear of the populace. Among orthodox Muslims in Spain the Mālikites were dominant. Fervent Muslims were inclined to asceticism and were called Zāhids. There sprang up regular monasteries, such as those of Ibn Masarra at Montaña and of Ibn Mujāhid of Elvira at Cordova, where apparently they devoted their time to the study of philosophy and other forbidden branches of learning.

The basis of Muslim law was the Koran and the traditions concerning the acts and sayings of the Prophet. These were known as *Sunna*. The chief collection of them, so far as Spain was concerned, was called Al-Muwaṭṭa', composed by Mālik ibn Anas, and contained one thousand seven hundred cases, to which additions were made later.

They had no code, properly speaking, until much later than this

---

[1] See *supra*, pp. 140, 152, 155, 163.

period; but there were special compilations including very heterogeneous subjects, such as prayer, purification, fasting, pilgrimages, sales, the division of inheritances, marriage and so on; and under Mālikite influence these compilations were introduced into Spain.

In the days of the Caliphs Muslim Spain became one of the wealthiest and most thickly populated countries in Europe. Cordova expanded till it contained two hundred thousand houses, and, as we have seen, was greatly embellished in the reigns of 'Abd-ar-Raḥmān II and III, who erected the palace of Az-Zahrā, and under Almanzor who built the palace of Zāhira: another wonderful building was the Mosque, which was begun by 'Abd-ar-Raḥmān I. Cordova was the meeting point of travellers from all over the world, who came to admire the splendour in which the Caliphs lived.

This magnificence was due to the extraordinary growth of industry and commerce. In agriculture a distinct advance was made in the number of small holders, who also stood socially higher than under the Visigoths. The Arabs rapidly assimilated such knowledge of farming as the Spaniards possessed, and added to it the agricultural experience of other Asiatic peoples. The greatest writers on agriculture were Mozarabs; but the Arabs soon learned the lesson taught them, and successfully cultivated the vine on a large scale despite the prohibition of wine. The Muslims introduced the cultivation of rice, pomegranates, cane sugar, and other Oriental products. They started or completed a system of canals for the irrigation of gardens, especially in the provinces of Murcia, Valencia and Granada, and they were devoted to cattle breeding. It is noteworthy that the labourers used the Roman and not the Arab calendar.

Mining of gold, silver and other metals was pre-eminent among industries, the mines of Jaen, Bulche, Aroche, and Algarve being renowned, while the rubies of Béjar and Málaga were famous. The woollen and silk weaving in Cordova, Málaga and Almería was justly celebrated, and in Cordova alone there seem to have been thirteen thousand weavers. Paterna (Valencia) carried the ceramic art to great perfection, and Almería produced glass as well as many kinds of bronze and iron vessels. At Játiva the manufacture of writing-paper out of thread was introduced by the Arabs. Arms for defence and offence were made at Cordova and elsewhere, while Toledo was famous for its swords and armour. Cordova was the home of all kinds of leather industry, and thence was derived the trade term *cordobanes* (cordwainers). Ibn Firnās of Cordova, according to Al-Maḳḳarī, in the ninth century invented a method for manufacturing looking-glasses, various kinds of chronometers, and also a flying machine.

This industrial movement had far-reaching commercial results. Trade was mainly carried on by sea, and under 'Abd-ar-Raḥmān III the most important sources of revenue were the duties on imports and exports.

The exports from Seville, which was one of the greatest river-ports in Spain, were cotton, oil, olives and other local produce. It was peopled, as we have seen, mainly by renegades, who by devotion to business had amassed large fortunes. During the emirate of 'Abdallāh, when Ibn Hajjāj held the sovereignty in Seville, the port was filled with vessels laden with Egyptian cloth, slaves, and singing girls from every part of Europe and Asia. The most important exports from Jaen and Málaga were saffron, figs, wine, marble and sugar. Spanish exports went to Africa, Egypt and Constantinople, and thence they were forwarded to India and Central Asia. Trade was kept up not only with Constantinople, but with the East generally, especially Mecca, Bagdad and Damascus. The Caliphs organised a regular postal service for the government. The necessities of government and of commerce compelled the Arabs to issue a coinage, which, though at first copied from Oriental models, took on later a character of its own. The gold unit was the *dīnār*, and they also used half *dīnārs* and one-third *dīnārs*. The silver unit was the *dirham*, and the copper the *fals* (Latin, *follis*). In time, however, these coins went down considerably in weight and value.

The official language for the government service of Muslim Spain was classical Arabic, the language of the Koran. But the speech of everyday life was a vulgar Arabic dialect, which contained a mixture of various Latin or Romance tongues of the conquered races, and was scarcely understood in the East. Ribera, in his study of the Song Book of Ibn Ḳuzmān, has proved that, even at the court of the Caliphs in Cordova, a vulgar Romance dialect was spoken, which was understood by the *cadis* and the other officials. He explains the existence of this Romance dialect by the probability that the Arabs, who formed the back-bone of the army, must have married Spanish women. Ibn Bashkuwāl, Ibn al-Abbār and other Muslim biographers always praise highly scholars who know Arabic. Thus among the Muslims, as among all the European peoples of that date, there was both a literary language and a language of daily speech. Just as the Mozarabs used Latin and Arabic, so the Spaniards of the North employed Latin in their documents and Romance dialects in their everyday life.

There was no regular system of education, and it is only in 1065 that the first university appears at Bagdad. Up till the reign of Ḥakam government interest in education, according to Ribera, was limited to "maintaining freedom of instruction in opposition to the narrowness of the Mālikite clergy who attempted to monopolise the teaching." Ḥakam II, who was unable to travel to the East, invited Oriental scholars to Cordova, where they gave lectures but received no official recognition. At the end of his life he set aside legacies for the payment of professors in Cordova with an eye to poor students. But this only applied to religious education. The authorities intervened to test the orthodoxy of the teaching, and at first a great impulse was given to the spread of

Mālikite doctrines. But later the *faḳīhs* became exceedingly intolerant of all doctrine which they suspected of heterodoxy. Primary education consisted, as in all Muslim countries, of writing and reading from the Koran, to which the Spanish professors added pieces of poetry and epistolary exercises in composition, and the pupils had to learn by heart the elements of Arabic grammar. Writing was taught at the same time as reading, and to learn writing was compulsory on all. Although education was purely a private matter, yet it was so widely diffused that most Spaniards knew how to read and write, a standard which, as Dozy observes, was still unknown in the rest of Europe. Higher education included, according to Ribera, translations, readings from the Koran and the interpretation of the text; jurisprudence, practical instructions for notaries and judges, the law of succession; branches of religious knowledge; politics, scholastic and ascetic theology; Arabic philosophy, grammar and lexicography; literature, including history, poetry, rhymed prose, stories and anecdotes; medicine, philosophy, astronomy, music, studied in an order which it is impossible to determine.

Undoubtedly poetry was the most popular branch of general culture. Among the Arabs even before the advent of Islām every tribe had a poet, who sang the conflicts, the triumphs and defeats of his tribesmen and, according to Goldziher, had some of the characteristics of the prophet or seer. A copious literature in verse has come down to us from that period, which in its treatment of wars, horses and the wilds has always been a model and a source of inspiration. The chiefs who settled in Spain brought their poets in their train; emirs and Caliphs composed verses, while improvisation was common in the streets and roads. Even the women shared the popular taste, and some of the Caliph's wives and slaves shewed remarkable poetic skill. Moreover, the Caliphs had their court poets, to whom they paid high salaries and shewed the utmost consideration. From primitive themes these writers went on to the love poem. Satire and epigram were also much in use.

Besides poetry the Spanish Arabs diligently studied history and geography, but although they cultivated the short story the drama was unknown to them. Although philosophy was distrusted by the vulgar and its followers filled orthodox theologians with alarm, the highest classes were much addicted to its study in private. Some schools of philosophy, indeed, resembled secret societies. It was certainly through this movement that philosophy found its way into Europe; for the Spanish scholars, who travelled in the East, had read the works of the commentators and translators of the Greek philosophers. Thus the Spaniards served as the channel of communication with the rest of Europe and particularly influenced the development of scholastic philosophy.

Astronomy, like philosophy, was viewed with suspicion by the public, and their efforts to prohibit its study were successful. Despite this fact Muslim Spain produced famous astronomers. More freedom was allowed to the study of pure and applied mathematics, and in medicine Spaniards surpassed the Oriental physicians who had learned their art from Persian Christians, and their influence on medieval medical science was profound. Natural science was another subject studied by their doctors, who were also chemists. The Jews followed attentively these systematic achievements of Arab learning, and more especially its progress in physical and natural science. They, too, influenced the rest of the West.

Side by side with all this progress there was a wide and enthusiastic demand for books. This was due to various causes, such as the cursive character of Arabic writing, which might be compared with the labour-saving device of shorthand, and the employment of linen paper from the earliest times, which was cheaper than papyrus or parchment. More-over the peculiarities of Muslim life, without political assemblies, theatres, or academies, which were the characteristic features of Greece and Rome, made books their sole means of instruction. In the early days of the conquest the Mozarabs preserved their Latin traditions in a Latin form; but with the increase of educated people and the demand for men learned in Muslim law there followed the gradual introduction of books, at first only on legal and theological subjects. The renegades took up the study of their newly adopted language and religion with enthusiasm, and their influence gave fresh impetus to the general appetite for reading. The movement was slow and indecisive at first and only reached its height with the advent of 'Abd-ar-Raḥmān III. Thanks to his establishment of peace and order, learned professors, students from every country, skilled copyists, rich dealers and book-sellers, flocked to Cordova until it became the intellectual centre of the West. The Royal Library was already in the reign of Mahomet I one of the best in Cordova, and 'Abd-ar-Raḥmān III added to it. His two sons Mahomet and Hakam II shewed their dissatisfaction with their father's library by each forming a separate collection, and in the end Hakam II made the three libraries into one vast collection of four hundred thousand volumes. He employed a principal librarian, who had instructions to draw up a catalogue, as well as the best binders, draughtsmen and illuminators. The dispersal of this library at the fall of the Caliphate was a disaster to the West.

Cordova had also its celebrated private libraries. Among women, too, bibliomania became the fashion, and 'Ā'isha, who belonged to the highest society in Cordova, had a notable collection, while women of the lower classes devoted their time to copying the Koran or books of prayers. The Jews, the Mozarabs and the renegades were carried away by the current, and eunuchs acquired considerable learning and even founded libraries.

"The period of these splendid achievements," declares Ribera, the best authority, "was doubtless of short duration. After the rule of Almanzor Cordova was in the throes of civil war, and the Berbers, who formed the majority of the royal army, inaugurated a period of barbarism, plundering and burning palaces and libraries. Wealthy families migrated to the provinces; students and professors fled the capital. Then they formed teaching centres and their enthusiasm for books spread among those populations, who afterwards formed the kingdoms of the Taifas (provincial dynasties)."

Side by side with science and literature the Fine Arts flourished. As we have already seen, Cordova had become the leading city in Spain; the splendour of her buildings and palaces vied even with the court of Bagdad. The architectural methods adopted by the Arabs differed greatly from those of the Romanised Spaniards. The beginnings of Arabic architecture are to be found even before Islām under the Sassanids. From this source the Arabs probably derived not only the gypsum arch embellished with honeycomb cells and pyramids suspended like stalactites, but also the stuccoed walls with their reliefs and decorations which adorn so effectively the interior of Muslim houses. Byzantine influences reinforced those from the Muslim East and affected both the architecture and the scheme of ornamentation, all of which the Spanish Arabs took over bodily, just as they gave Visigothic and classical influences free play in their artistic modelling, the horse-shoe arch, later on so typically Muslim, being of Visigothic origin.

The first period in the development of Hispano-Arabic architecture covers the era of the Caliphate from the eighth to the tenth century, and of it the mosque of Cordova is the most important monument. It was begun in the reign of 'Abd-ar-Raḥmān I and the process of building went on from the eighth to the tenth century. The ground plan of a mosque is rectangular and comprises: a courtyard surrounded by a portico and as a rule planted with trees, with a fountain for the ceremonial ablutions of the faithful; one or more lofty towers of graceful proportions, called *ṣaumaʻa* (but in Spanish known as *alminares*, minarets) which were used by the *muʼadhdhin* to give the call to prayer; and a covered part (*cubierta*) completely surrounding the court-yard and extending much farther in the direction of the *miḥrāb* or niche which faces toward Mecca, while somewhat to the right of this stands the pulpit or *mimbar* from which the *imām* offers prayer. The architectural features of the building are the arches, mainly of the horse-shoe form, though other forms such as the pointed and the lobe-shaped arch were also used, and the cupola resting on its square base; while the columns employed on the early Roman and Visigothic buildings imitated the Corinthian or composite capital, which was afterwards superseded by the Cordovese capital, that flourished until the *Nasarite* or Grenadine style in the last period of Hispano-Muslim architecture. The walls were ornamented with bas-relief plaques in stone or gypsum, the scheme of decoration being sometimes floral and sometimes geometrical on a background usually red or blue. The decoration shewed traces of classical, Visigothic, Syro-Byzantine and Mesopotamian influences.

Painting and sculpture were encouraged by the Spanish Muslims without any restriction save in regard to religion. There are some remarkable examples of representations of animals and persons, among them some glazed vessels at Elvira on which are depicted painted human figures. In metallurgy and ceramics great advances were made, but the glazed tiles or bricks belong to a later period. In bronze work mention should be made of the mosque lamps, and the chest, studded with silver plates of the period of Ḥakam II, which is preserved in the cathedral of Gerona. In furniture immense luxury was displayed; their carpets, silk curtains, divans and cushions gave scope to many industries. With the growth of Muslim influence, buildings for public baths multiplied and at length came to be used even more than in the days of the Romans.

The difference between their family life and that of the Christians was very marked. As is well known, Muslims might have even four lawful wives and as many concubines as they could support : hence the Caliphs and the wealthy had many wives whom they kept in harems. The law gave the first wife the right to secure a promise from her husband that he would not contract a fresh marriage or take concubines. Within the house the woman was subject to the man; but she could dispose of the greater part of his property and appear in the law courts without her husband's leave. She exercised the same authority as he did over the sons, so far as concerned their formal protection, and could obtain divorce for valid grounds. Further, the women enjoyed more liberty in their social relations than is generally supposed. They often walked through the streets with their heads uncovered and attended men's meeting-places like the schools.

The brilliant civilisation of the Caliphate naturally influenced the Christians to the North. This influence was not only due to proximity, but also, contrary to the general view, to frequent community of interests between Christians and Muslims, and especially to Christian slaves who escaped or secured their freedom and on their return home nearly always kept their Arab names. Between Christians and Muslims visits were frequently exchanged and mutual succour given in time of civil war ; they traded together and inter-married not only in the lower but also in the higher classes, including royalty. Such marriages must have been very common, since the Arabs arrived in Spain not as tribes but as bands of warriors. Throughout the later wars the combatants on both sides were apparently a mixture of Muslims and Christians.

When two people come into contact the higher civilisation invariably influences the other. Such indeed was the case of the Arabs in Spain and the Spaniards from the beginning of the ninth to the end of the thirteenth century, when Arab philosophy and science were at their height. In practical life Arab influence was even greater, not only in political but also in legal and military organisation; and this explains why the Christians after the re-conquest of the districts inhabited by Muslims were compelled to respect existing institutions, while they set up analogous systems for the new settlers, as is proved by the charters (*fueros*) granted by the kings of Aragon and Castile to the conquered cities. The literary influence was not so strong. Arabic phrases were common in Leon, Castile, Navarre, and other parts; the Romance languages, which were then in the process of formation, took over a large number of Arabic terms, sometimes making up hybrid words and sometimes pronouncing the Latin words or their derivatives in the Arabic fashion. There were many Moors who understood Romance, particularly in the frontier districts, and they were called *Latin Moors* (*ladinos*) just as many Christians with some knowledge of Arabic (*algarabía*) were called Christians who talked a jargon (*algaraviados*).

The Mozarabs naturally felt Arab influence even more throughout this period. The following passage occurs in the writings of Alvaro of Cordova, the companion of Eulogio, who exhorted the Cordovan martyrs: "Many of my fellow Christians read Arab poetry and stories, and study the works of Mohammedan philosophers and theologians, not with the object of refuting them, but to learn to express themselves in Arabic with greater elegance and correctness. Alas! all our Christian youths, who are winning a name for themselves by their talents, know the language and literature of the Arabs alone; they read and study assiduously their books; at huge expense they form large libraries, and on every occasion they positively declare that this literature merits our admiration."

The Muslim people in turn adopted something of Visigothic culture from the renegades and Mozarabs, particularly in language, administration and the organisation of the arts. The Mozarabs still kept up their old ecclesiastical schools where, under the direction of the Abbots Samson, Spera-in-Deo and others, they carefully kept the Isidorian tradition. The Christian women, who formed an ordinary part of Arab and Berber households, must have added to the force of these influences, which, however, were never so powerful as those exercised by the Muslim over the Christian element.

But, despite the Muslim influence, Christian civilisation with its Visigothic basis continued to grow along its own lines. The political unity of the Visigothic kingdom disappeared with the concentration of Christian resistance at a few isolated points, and in this period there cannot be said to be any national life; in fact, Spain has no real existence: we can only speak of Asturias, Leon, Galicia, Navarre, Castile, and Catalonia. This diversity of states, institutions and nationalities, is the characteristic feature of medieval Spain.

So far as Asturias, Leon and Castile are concerned, the distinction between slaves and freemen still continued, while the latter were subdivided into nobles and plebeians. The nobles were dependent on the king, who gave them grants of land, titles and offices, etc.; from time to time a revolt broke out among these nobles, and this gave rise to a new class of nobles, the *infanzones*, more immediately dependent on the king. In this period, too, first appear the *milites* (*caballeros*), free men who received certain privileges in return for military service, and also the *infanzones de fuero*, nobles of a peculiar kind chosen by the king from inhabitants of cities or boroughs. Some men too put themselves under the protection of nobles, giving personal services and payments in return for it; this protection was known as *encomienda* or *benefactoria*.

The serfs were divided as in the Visigothic period into those belonging to the State (*fiscales*), those owned by ecclesiastics (*ecclesiásticos*) and those who were the property of private individuals (*particulares*). According to their status they might be either personal property (*personales*) or bound to the soil (*colonos*). The latter were indissolubly tied to the soil (*gleba*), so that they were regarded as part of the land like trees or buildings, and were therefore included in contracts for sale or purchase. The status of a serf might be acquired by birth, by debt, by captivity or by voluntary assignment to a lord (*obnoxacion*). These last had a higher status and were called *oblati*. Freedom might be recovered by manumission, which was due to the influence of Christianity and to economic necessities, by revolt or flight; hence arose a class of freedmen with special privileges and more advantages than the primitive serf. By the end of the tenth century these freedmen formed the majority of the population and were known as *juniores*. They spoke of themselves as tenants-in-chief (*de cabeza*), though they were liable to personal service, and were regarded as part and parcel of the inheritance (*heredad*) or ancestral demesne (*solariegos*); even when they worked elsewhere or lived away on an alien plot, they still paid tribute. Such was their condition as it appears in the charter of Leon at the beginning of the eleventh century; but afterwards it steadily improved.

The king was at the head of the government, but his power varied in different cases. He combined legislative and judicial functions, and claimed the sole prerogative of coining money as well as the right to summon his vassals to war (*fonsadera*). There was, however, considerable variation in practice. In the lands directly dependent on the king (*realengas*) he had full jurisdiction over all orders, and was himself their mesne lord. But the nobles sometimes exercised over their own lands an authority that practically superseded the king's. All the inhabitants of the domain were dependent on their feudal lord, some as serfs, others under his patronage. He collected tribute from them, he accepted their personal services; he compelled them to go out on military duty; in a sense he dictated their laws and divided the functions of government between the *judex*, *mayordomus*, *villicus*, and *sagio* who presided over the *concilium*. He could not extend his privileges over lands newly acquired without the express leave of the king. The powers of the king over the lands of ecclesiastical vassals were also limited, while the ecclesiastics had the advantage of setting down their privileges in written documents. Their duties as well as their rights were on the same footing as those of secular feudatories.

The nobles, bishops and abbots could often interfere in lands which were exempt from aristocratic or ecclesiastical control. They were members of the Palatine Office (*oficio palatino*) as well as of the Royal Council and the other councils. They kept in their hands the government and administration of the districts, called *commissa, mandationes, tenentiae*, etc., and in their capacity of counts they were assisted by a vicar and the council of neighbours (*conventus publicus vicinorum*). Such powers intensified their turbulent spirit. They imposed their policy on the crown, interfered in the struggles for the succession, and consequently the monarchy found in them the strongest force in the country. But despite all this there was no *feudal* hierarchy as in France and Germany, since they exercised all their privileges by the favour of the king.

In Leon and Castile we can trace the rise of *behetrías* or collective benefices (*benefactorías collectivas*), "groups of free men who sought the protection of a powerful lord." If they might freely choose their own lord, they were known as *behetrías de mar a mar*, but if their choice were restricted to one family, they were called *de linaje a linaje*. They were never very vigorous, owing to their dependence, but in the tenth century they gave rise to the chartered town or *concejo* which comprised "the inhabitants who had been conquered by the king and were attached to the royal domain, as well those who had recently settled there and were exempt from the jurisdiction of the counts." The reason for the establishment of *concejos* was the necessity of populating the frontier. Since no one would live there owing to its insecurity, the king had to attract inhabitants for chartered towns by granting them privileges. Sometimes all who entered them were declared free men, even if they sprang from the lowest serfs; sometimes they were exempted from services and contributions; sometimes they were allowed some political independence and self-government; sometimes the existing practices and customary exemptions were recognised. These privileges were definitely set forth in the *fuero* or charter of the inhabitants (*carta de poblacion*); of those that have come down to us the charters of Burgos, Castrojeriz, etc., date from the tenth, and those of Nájera, Sepúlveda and Leon from the beginning of the eleventh century. As a rule the organisation of the chartered town depended on the formation of the *concilium* (*concejo*) or assembly of neighbours, which exercised judicial and administrative functions. The Council appointed every year a judge, several assessors, clerks of the market and inspectors, who were entirely dependent on its goodwill. Such were the beginnings of municipal life. Its growth was marked by the gradual absorption by the *concilium* of the powers and prerogatives, which had once belonged to the king and the count; but the king still kept the right to appoint judges who continued side by side with those elected by the council. There were usually distinctions between greater and lesser members of the *concejo*; between nobles (*infanzones*) and citizens, between holders of office (*honoratii*) and simple neighbours (*vicini*), the villagers or townsmen.

Legislation had other sources besides the *Fuero Juzgo* through the new charters granted by the king. The municipality exercised jurisdiction according to custom and tradition in cases which were not expressly included in their charter. Further, the *fueros* of the bishop and the lords contributed an element to the legislation of the period, just as did the municipal councils.

The inhabitants of Leon and Castile lagged far behind the Muslims in point of material comfort. Agriculture, limited as yet by the bare necessities of life, was fostered by the Benedictine monks alone, and for the most part the population confined its energies to war. Industries, however, sprang up at Santiago de Compostela in Galicia round the shrine of St James, and craftsmen began to organise gilds. The salt industry, too, was kept up in Galicia. But there was less freedom of trade than in the preceding period, and taxation generally took the form of duties imposed on the necessaries of life. Money was scarce, and Roman and Gothic types of coin were still current. The official language was Latin; but Romance was already a formed language, although there are no documents extant in the vulgar tongue till the end of the eleventh or the beginning of the twelfth century.

Scarcely anything is known of Aragon and Navarre at this period. In Catalonia, a West Frankish fief, the Franks exercised a profound influence on the organisation of society. Here the counts were landowners, who granted or leased out their lands, and this practice gave rise to the copyholders (*censatarios*), the viscounts and other subordinates of the count. Later, the grant of lands by the king to soldiers, whether in the shape of alods or in that of *beneficia*, led to the formation of a fresh group of free owners. Thus the nobility of Catalonia acquired the full powers of French feudal *seigneurs*. The common law of all three realms was the *Fuero Juzgo*, to which Catalonia added the Frankish capitularies. There were also charters for towns in Aragon and Navarre, but their text has not come down to us, while the *fuero* of Sobrarbe is generally regarded as a forgery. In Catalonia there are extant the *fuero* of Montmell, the town charter of Cardona given by Wifred, and the privilege of Barcelona granted by Berengar-Raymond I.

The history of Spain, so far traced, is very different from that of other Western countries. No land is more marked out by its mere geography and local separations as the very home of rival kingdoms. It fronts towards the sea, and it looks towards Africa: if it borders upon modern France, it is yet separated from it by the almost impassable Pyrenees. It still bore the imperishable marks of Roman rule: it had been flooded by the Teutonic invaders when the Empire fell, and it had been by them even more closely joined to Africa. Then it was again

marked out from the rest of Europe by the Muslim conquest, and Spain
gave a rival to the Eastern Caliphate just as the Franks gave a rival
to the Eastern Emperor. In itself the Iberian peninsula was split up by
many mountain ranges, and marked by startling variations in climate
and soil: it had a unity compatible with the strongest local divergencies.
Thus it was destined for a history strangely apart from other lands: if
at times it drew to itself outside races and outside influences, these in
their turn were moulded into types among themselves both akin and
separate. So, if splendid, it was always weak through its many divisions,
and many contests between Berbers and Arabs, and of Arabs among
themselves. The history of Arab civilisation in Spain intertwines itself
in many links with medieval learning, science and thought, while the
presence of a rival race and rival creed at its very doors gave a special
tinge to Spanish fervour and Spanish faith. In the field of thought,
even in constitutional experiments, Spanish history has thus from early
times a significance far greater than that of its mere events. Even after
its splendour had reached its height the influence of the Moorish kingdom
was not ended. Small Christian states, separated from each other by
physical conditions, had been born in conflict with it, and were sometimes united in enmity against it, sometimes at strife in contest for its
alliance. Thus the later Spanish kingdoms were growing up, but their
day was yet to come.

CHAPTER XVII.

THE CHURCH FROM CHARLEMAGNE TO SYLVESTER II.

THE preceding volume came to an end with the picture of a vast Empire seemingly destined to absorb Europe itself. This volume, on the contrary, has offered little for our consideration save the spectacle of Europe fallen to fragments, of its kingdoms sundered from one another, and of disintegration steadily advancing. The alluring dream of Charles the Great has vanished; after his death no temporal prince was found capable of carrying on his work, and it fell to ruins.

Nevertheless, the root idea which had inspired him still persisted: the idea of the unity of the Christian world, bound together and grouped round a single head, ready to give battle to the infidel, and to undertake the conversion of the barbarians. But it was the Church which now appropriated the idea, and which alone, amidst the surrounding confusion, succeeded in maintaining itself as the principle of order and the power of cohesion. To shew in broad outline how and to what extent the Church succeeded in this design during the disturbed period which preceded the great Church reform of the eleventh century is the object of these few pages which will thus sum up the history.

Under the ever-present influence of scriptural ideals, Charles the Great had really come to see in himself what he was so often called, a new David, or another Solomon, at once priest and king, the master and overlord of the Bishops of his realms; in reducing those Bishops to the level of docile fellow-labourers with him in the work of government, he had believed himself to be working for the consolidation of his own power. But in this matter, as in so many others, the results of his policy had not accorded with his wishes and expectations. The Bishops, having been called upon to take part in affairs of State, were consequently quite ready to busy themselves with them even uninvited, while, on the other hand, by the investment of the Emperor with a semi-sacerdotal character the clergy were encouraged to see in him one of themselves, and, despite his superior position, to look upon him as amenable to their jurisdiction.

This had been clearly perceived as early as the time of Louis the Pious, when, on the morrow of Lothar's usurpation (833), the Bishops, alleging the obligation laid on them by their "priestly office," had plainly asserted their right to examine and punish the conduct of a prince who had incurred guilt by "refusing to obey," as the official record declares, "the warnings of the clergy." For, although Louis the Pious was already looked upon as deposed at the time of the ceremony in St Medard's at Soissons, the course which the Bishops had adopted without hesitation was in point of fact to bring him to trial for his conduct as a sovereign, imposing on him the most humiliating of penances, "after which," as the record concludes, "none can resume his post in the world's army."

Louis the Pious, as already seen[1], did, nevertheless, return to "the world's army," and was even reinstated in the imperial dignity. Yet this decisive action taken by the Bishops in the crisis of 833 shewed clearly that the parts had been inverted. Louis the Pious was the king of the priests, but no longer in the same sense as Charles the Great: he was at their mercy.

The precedent thus set was not forgotten. During the fratricidal struggle which, on the morrow of the death of Louis the Pious, broke out amongst Lothar, Louis the German, and Charles the Bald, the Bishops more than once took occasion to interfere, and to make themselves masters of the situation. In March 842, in particular, when Charles the Bald and Louis the German had encamped in the palace of Aix-la-Chapelle whence their brother had precipitately fled at their approach, the clergy, as Nithard, an eye-witness, relates, "reviewing Lothar's whole conduct, how he had stripped his father of power, how often, by his cupidity, he had driven Christian people to commit perjury, how often he had himself broken his engagements to his father and his brothers, how often he had attempted to despoil and ruin the latter since his father's death, how many adulteries, conflagrations and acts of violence of every description his criminal ambition had inflicted on the Church, finally, considering his incapacity for government, and the complete absence of good intentions in this matter shewn by him, declare that it is with good reason and by a just judgment of the Almighty that he has been reduced to take flight, first from the field of battle, and then from his own kingdom." Without a dissentient voice the Bishops proclaimed the deposition of Lothar, and after having demanded of Louis and Charles whether they were ready to govern according to the Divine Will the States abandoned by their brother, "Receive them," they bade them, "and rule them according to the Will of God; we require it of you in His Name, we beseech it of you, and we command it you."

In thus encroaching on the domain of politics, the Bishops were persuaded that they were only acting in the interest of the higher

[1] See Chapter I. p. 19.

concerns committed to their care. They had gradually accustomed themselves to the idea that the Empire ought to be the realisation upon earth of the " City of God," the ideal city, planned by St Augustine. The study of St Augustine had been the mental food of Bishops, learned clerks and princes themselves, and in their complaints the clergy had always a source of inspiration in the complaints echoed four centuries earlier by St Augustine and his followers. The Empire was hastening to its ruin because religion was no longer honoured, because every man was concerned only for his own interests and was careless of the higher interests of the Church, because instead of brotherliness and concord only cupidity and selfishness reigned unchecked. If the Empire were to be saved, the first thing to be done was to recall every man to Christian sentiments and to the fear of God.

Whatever work of the period we open, whether we go to the letters written at the time by the clergy, or whether we examine the considerations on which the demands made by their synods to the king are based, we shall find the same arguments upon the necessity of reverting to the Christian principles which had constituted the strength of the Empire and had been the condition of its existence. For the deacon Florus, the decadence of the Empire is merely one aspect of the decadence of the Church : at the period when the Empire flourished " the clergy used to meet frequently in councils, to give holy laws to the people "; to-day, he goes on, there is nothing but *conciliabula* of men greedy of lands and benefices, " the general interest is not regarded, everyone is concerned about his own affairs, all things command attention except God." The conclusion of the whole matter is, he says, that " all is over with the honour of the Church " and that " the majesty of the State is a prey to the worst of furies." The same reflections may be found in Paschasius Radbertus, biographer of the Abbot Wala ; the whole of the disorder in the State arises from the disappearance of religion, the imperial power has made shipwreck at the same time as the authority of the Church. Wala's comment, as he made his appearance amidst the partisans of Lothar on the morrow of the penance at St Medard's, is well known : " It is all perfect, save that you have left naught to God of all that was due to Him."

To restore to the " Church of God " and to its ministers the honour that is their due, such is the sheet-anchor which the Episcopate offers to sovereigns. Over and over again during the years that followed the death of Louis the Pious and the partition of Verdun, the Bishops press upon rulers the necessity of acting " with charity," and in cases where any error has been committed, of doing penance, and, as a document of 844 expresses it, " asking the forgiveness of the Lord according to the exhortation and counsel of the priests." And these exhortations bear fruit ; in April 845, while a synod was sitting at Beauvais, the King of France, Charles the Bald, after swearing on the hilt of his sword in the

Name of God and the saints to respect till death the privileges and laws of the Church, admits the right and even the duty of the prelates both to suspend the execution of any measure he might take which should be to the detriment of these privileges and laws, and also to address remonstrances to him, calling upon him to amend any decisions contrary to them.

Strong in this pledge, the prelates of France, a few months later (June 845) ventured to put forward, at the Synod of Meaux, a whole series of claims directed not less against their king than against the whole lay aristocracy, reproaching both alike with hindering the free exercise of religion. Their reproaches were expressed in a language of command, which on this occasion was carried to such a height that the king, with the support of the magnates, resisted.

Nevertheless, the Bishops remained masters of the situation. In the years that follow, making common cause now with the lay aristocracy, they succeed, throughout the various kingdoms which sprang from Charles the Great's empire, in imposing their will upon the sovereigns. They are at once the leaders and the spokesmen of the turbulent vassals, ever ready to league themselves together to resist the king. In an assembly held in August 856 at Bonneuil near Paris, with unprecedented violence they accuse Charles the Bald of having broken all his engagements; they warn him "in charity" that they are all, priests and laymen, of one mind in resolving to see them carried out, and they summon him, in consequence, to amend without delay all provisions to the contrary, concluding this singular "request" with a threatening quotation from the Psalms: "If a man will not turn, He will whet His sword: He hath bent His bow, and made it ready. He hath prepared for him the instruments of death."

We have already seen[1], how two years later this prediction was apparently realised. Louis the German, in response to the appeal of a portion of his brother Charles the Bald's subjects, invaded his dominions and succeeded in occupying a great part of them. Called upon to ratify his usurpation, a group of Bishops from the ecclesiastical provinces of Rheims and Rouen gathered together at Quierzy-sur-Oise, following the suggestions of Archbishop Hincmar, carried matters with a high hand; after having recommended him to meditate upon the duties which a prince owes to the Church, they thought fit to bring to his notice these words from the Psalms: "Instead of thy fathers thou shalt have children," together with the interpretation: "Instead of the Apostles, I have ordained Bishops that they may govern and instruct thee."

Kings working for the maintenance of peace under the aegis of the Church, such was thenceforward the programme of the Episcopate. And by peace is intended the peace of Christendom, the peace of the Church; to disturb it is to infringe the laws of which the Church is the

[1] Chapter II. pp. 36–37.

guardian, and to revolt against the Church itself. Thus in a synod assembled at Metz on 28 May 859, the Bishops of the kingdoms of Western Francia and Lorraine do not hesitate to characterise the attempt of Louis the German to seize upon his brother's lands as a "schism in the Holy Church and in Christendom," adding that he is bound to ask "absolution" for it. A month later in an assembly held at Savonnières (14 June 859) Charles the Bald himself appears to give official recognition to the claims of the clergy; in making a complaint against Wenilo (Ganelon), Archbishop of Sens, who had ventured to crown his brother Louis the German king in his place, he expresses astonishment that a claim should have been set up to depose him, "without the case having been submitted to the judgment of the Bishops, by whose ministry he had been consecrated king, and to whose fatherly admonitions and sentences he had been and ever was ready to submit himself."

The episcopal theory was thus expanded to its utmost limits, as it was about to be stated even more rigorously, and with the greatest boldness by the illustrious Archbishop of Rheims, Hincmar, in numerous treatises and letters or in the decrees of councils which on all hands are allowed to be his work. The theory, very simple in itself, may be brought under these few heads : The king is king because the Bishops have been pleased to consecrate him: "It is rather through the spiritual unction and benediction of the Bishops than from any earthly power that you hold the royal dignity," writes Hincmar to Charles the Bald in 868. The Bishops make kings by virtue of their right to consecrate, and so are superior to them, "for they consecrate kings, but cannot be consecrated by them." Kings, then, are the creatures, the delegates of the Bishops : the monarchy "is a power which is preserved and maintained for the service of God and the Church"; it is "an instrument in the hands of the Church which is superior to it, because she directs it towards its true end." Except "for this special power which the king has at his disposal and which lays upon him special duties, he is but a man like other men, his fellows and equals in the city of God. Like them he is bound to live as a faithful Christian."

The whole trend of this ecclesiastical reaction, thus traced in outline during the half century which followed the death of Charlemagne, was to form a system logically invulnerable but making the monarchy the slave of the clergy. To make head against the unbridled appetites of men the Church claimed as its own the twofold task of maintaining union and concord and of directing the monarchy in the paths of the Lord.

Left, however, to their own resources, and compelled, in addition, to resist the claims and the violent attacks of the lay aristocracy, the Bishops would have been in no position to translate their principles into action. Only a centralized Church, gathered round a single head, could enable them to give practical force to their views, and for this reason, the eyes of an important section of the Bishops were very early directed towards Rome.

This tendency is strikingly shewn in the famous collection of the False Decretals which are still to a great extent an unsolved problem despite endless discussion. They were composed within Charles the Bald's dominions about the year 850 by a Frankish clerk assuming the name of Isidorus Mercator, who, in order to contribute solid support to the prerogatives of the Bishops at once against the arbitrary control of the Archbishops or metropolitans and the attacks of the civil power, did not hesitate to misattribute, to interpolate and rearrange, and thus practically to forge from beginning to end a whole series of pseudo-papal decisions. This collection clearly lays down as a principle the absolute and universal supremacy of the Chair of Peter. It makes the Pope the sovereign lawgiver without whose consent no council, not even that of a whole province, may meet or pronounce valid decrees ; it makes him, at the same time, the supreme judge without whose intervention no Bishop may be deposed, who in the last resort decides not only the causes of Bishops but all "major" causes, whose decision constitutes law even before any other ecclesiastical tribunal has been previously invoked. In this manner, while the Episcopate, freed from the civil authority, is the regulating power within the borders of every State, the Pope appears as the Supreme Head of the whole of Christendom.

Such a theory harmonised too well with the aspirations of the Popes not to find an echo at Rome. They had themselves been trying for some time on parallel lines: to take advantage of the decline of the imperial power to strengthen their own authority, and to claim over the Christian world as a whole that office of supreme guardian of peace and concord which the local Episcopate had assumed for itself inside each of the Frankish kingdoms. The weakness of Louis the Pious and the conflict of interests and of political aims which characterised his reign had been singularly favourable to this project. It has been shewn in a preceding chapter[1] how in 833, when the revolt in favour of Lothar broke out, Pope Gregory IV had allowed himself to be drawn into espousing the rebel cause. Urged on by the whole of the higher Frankish clergy who, though maintaining Lothar's claims on the ground of principle, were, nevertheless, well pleased to be able to shelter themselves behind the papal authority, and, supporting themselves by various texts, pressed upon him the prerogatives attaching to the Chair of Peter, Gregory spoke as sovereign lord. In a letter couched in tart and trenchant language in which the hand of Agobard, Archbishop of Lyons, may probably be traced, he resolutely put forward rights

---

[1] Chapter I. pp. 17–18.

superior to those of any other power whatever. To those Bishops and priests who, loyal to Louis the Pious, had pleaded his orders as a justification for not having hastened to present themselves when summoned by the Pope, Gregory does not hesitate to retort: " Why speak to me of the orders of the Emperor? Are not the orders of the Pope of equal weight? And is not the authority over souls which belongs to the Pope above the imperial rule which is of this world?"

This letter of Gregory IV touched the vital point, since the most formidable obstacle to the centralisation of the Church was the dependence of the body of the clergy in each kingdom upon the different princes among whom the secular rule over Christendom was divided. It was left for Nicholas I (858–867) to make energetic resistance to this danger, and to enable the Papacy to attain that position of supreme headship over the Church which his predecessors had often claimed with theories not hitherto wrought out in practice.

At the outset, a series of sensational events, involving nearly simultaneous struggles with the Carolingian sovereigns and with the Emperor of the East, forced upon Nicholas the choice between a humiliating submission and the offensive in circumstances which, if mishandled, might lead to the gravest consequences. Between these two courses a man of Nicholas I's type could not hesitate. He stood firmly on the rights of the Holy See, and shewed himself resolved on their triumphant vindication.

The first question to be decided was, whether in the important matter of the divorce of Lothar II, King of Lorraine, which has been already under discussion[1], the last word was to rest with the king, supported by a complaisant clergy ready to grant him a divorce, or with the Pope to whom Theutberga, the discarded wife, had appealed. Lothar and the Bishops of his party imagined that they could easily hoodwink the Pope. When Nicholas commissioned two Italian prelates as legates to examine into the matter, and instructed them to hold a council at Metz to which the Bishops of the German, French and Provençal kingdoms were to be convoked as well as the Bishops of Lorraine, Lothar bought over the legates, contrived to exclude the foreign Bishops from the Council, and easily secured the annulment of his first marriage, thanks to the connivance of Gunther, Archbishop of Cologne, and of Theutgaud, Archbishop of Trèves (June 863). Nicholas I replied with a bold stroke. When the two Archbishops reached Rome to announce to the Pope the decisions arrived at, he brought them to trial before a synod composed only of Italian prelates, and declared them deposed (October 863), at the same time quashing the decisions of " this new robber rout of Ephesus," as he called the synod held at Metz.

---

[1] Cf. Chapter II. pp. 38 ff.

That a Pope should venture under such conditions to depose Bishops or Archbishops was a thing unheard of. It was in national or provincial councils that condemnation had been pronounced upon Theodulf, Bishop of Orleans, in 817, and upon the Archbishops Ebbo of Rheims, Agobard of Lyons, Bernard of Vienne and Bartholomew of Narbonne in 835, when the reigning Popes had not even been consulted. But Nicholas I had resolved not to be guided by these precedents. At the same synod in which he pronounced the deposition of the two Archbishops in Lorraine, as if to shew his determination to deal once and for all with all unworthy prelates, he further declared to be deposed Hagano, Bishop of Bergamo, and John, Archbishop of Ravenna, the first being accused of having lent his help to Gunther and Theutgaud, the second of having made common cause with the enemies of the Holy See (October 863). At the same time he announced that a like penalty would be inflicted upon any bishop who did not immediately signify his adhesion to the sentence which he had pronounced. Finally, he threatened with anathema anyone who should contemn on any occasion whatsoever the measures taken by the Pope, the orders given or the sentences pronounced by him.

Thus above the will of kings the will of the Pope asserted itself haughtily and resolutely. Lothar's brother, the Emperor Louis II, appealed to by the deposed prelates to intervene, determined to vindicate the honour of kings, and marched straight upon Rome at the head of his army. But Nicholas I did not yield to the storm. Having ordered fasts and litanies, he shut himself up in the Church of St Peter and awaited in prayer the moment when Louis II should be overawed and brought to give way. The advantage remained with the Pope, and he even came forth from the struggle with a heightened conception of his own power.

The affair of the Patriarch Photius, to be dealt with more at length in the next volume, the controversies arising from which became in the end involved with the Lorraine question, had accentuated the triumphant mood of the Pope. The Patriarch Ignatius, having been banished by order of Bardas the Regent, and Photius, an official of the imperial palace having been put in his place, Nicholas I was requested to sanction what had been done (860). Reports containing a distorted account of the facts were submitted to him, but he resolved that as the first step an inquiry should be held, and despatched two legates. This was inconvenient to Photius and to the court at Constantinople, for they had counted upon the Pope's unconditional acceptance. They succeeded in terrorising the legates and inducing them to preside over a so-called general council at Constantinople, which condemned Ignatius and confirmed his deposition (May 861). Nicholas I, from whom the details of the affair were sedulously concealed, limited himself for the time being to the disavowal of the decrees, the council having been summoned contrary to his orders. But he soon took a higher tone. Being, after long delay, made aware of the facts and of the treachery of the legates, he sent out an urgent summons to a council to meet at Rome, pronounced sentence of deposition on Zachary, Bishop of Anagni, one of the legates, and on Gregory Asbestas, Archbishop of Syracuse, who had consecrated Photius, anathematised the latter, declared Ignatius sole legitimate Patriarch, restored to their offices all the Bishops and clergy deposed for their support of his cause, and declared the deposition of all who had been ordained by Photius (beginning of 863).

This meant war. The Emperor Michael III, surnamed, not without reason, the Drunkard, as soon as he was informed of the measures which had been taken, replied from Constantinople by an abusive letter. Nicholas retorted by insisting before everything else on the immediate restoration of Ignatius whether guilty or innocent, claiming for himself the sole right to judge him afterwards in the name of the authority belonging to the See of Rome, " which confers upon the Pope judiciary power over the whole Church," without his being himself capable of " being judged by anyone." He prohibited the Emperor from interfering with a matter which did not come within the province of the civil authority, "for," he added, "the day of ' king-priests' and ' Emperor-Pontiffs' is past, Christianity has separated the two functions, and Christian Emperors have need of the Pope in view of the life eternal, whereas Popes have no need of Emperors except as regards temporal things" (865). Finally, after a few months, in November 866, as the Emperor Michael refused to give way, Nicholas demanded of him the official retractation and the destruction of the insulting letter of 865, failing which he declared that he would convoke a General Council of the Bishops of the West, when anathema would be pronounced against the Emperor and his abettors.

Stimulated by the conflict, the Pope had thus reached the point, through the logical development of the theories which we have already seen put forward by the Bishops from their standpoint, of so conceiving of his power that he no longer saw in kings and emperors anything more than ordinary Christians, accountable to him for their actions, and as such amenable to his sovereign authority. With all alike he takes the tone of a master. To Charles the Bald he writes in 865 that it is for him to see that one of his (the Pope's) decisions is put in execution, adding that " were the king to offer him thousands of precious stones and the richest of jewels, nothing, in his eyes, could take the place of obedience." He does not fail to remind Charles, as well as Louis the German and Lothar, that the duty of kings is to work for the exaltation of the Church of Rome, " for how think you," he writes to one of them, " that we can, on occasion, support your government, your efforts, and the Churches of your kingdom, or offer you the protection of our buckler against your enemies, if, in so far as it depends on you, you allow that power to be in any degree weakened to which your fathers had recourse, finding in it all the increase of their dignities and all their glory?" Kings should accordingly shew themselves docile to the admonitions of the Pope, as well in the matter of general policy, that is, in the maintenance of concord among princes, as in the concerns of religion, otherwise the Pope will find himself constrained to launch his thunderbolts against them. He does not even admit of any discussion of his orders; in 865 Charles and his brother Louis the German having put forward various pretexts for not sending Bishops from their dominions to the council about to pronounce at Rome upon the incidents arising out of Lothar's divorce, Nicholas wrote them a stinging rebuke, expressing, in particular, his astonishment that they should have dared to question the necessity of sending Bishops when he, the Pope, had demanded their presence. And when, on one occasion, Charles the Bald who, be it said, was docility personified, shewed himself offended by certain rather ungentle reproofs, the Pope sharply replied that, even if his reprimands were undeserved, the king must needs bow to them as Job bowed beneath the chastening of the Most High.

Yet all was not accomplished when kings were restricted in their initiative and were turned into the agents of the Papal will: the clergy, over whom they were deprived of control, had still to be made, in their turn, a docile instrument in his hands. In this way would the work of uniting Christendom be completed.

It is at first sight surprising that it was in this quarter that Nicholas I met with the most vigorous resistance. It came in the main, from the archbishops, at whose expense the work of ecclesiastical consolidation must necessarily be carried out. Yet even they were forced to yield to the iron will of the Pope. The case of Archbishop Hincmar of Rheims is the most conclusive proof of this. In 861, at a synod held at Soissons he had caused his suffragan Rothad, Bishop of that city, whom he accused of insubordination, to be "cut off from the communion of the Bishops." Threatened with deposition when another synod met at Pitres next year (1 June 862) Rothad had lost no time in lodging an appeal to Rome, and, in spite of menaces, had refused to appear before the assembled Bishops. Hincmar, proceeding, nevertheless, with the case, had procured sentence of deposition, and consigned Rothad to a monastery. At once the Pope intervenes with a high hand, insisting before anything else that Hincmar and his suffragans shall reinstate the bishop within thirty days, whatever may be the merits of the controversy, and this under penalty of an interdict. Further, he declares that the cause is to be laid before his own court, and charges the archbishop to dispatch to Rome, also within thirty days, two accredited agents who, together with Rothad, shall submit themselves to the judgment of the Holy See. For month after month,

Hincmar, by various subterfuges, evaded compliance, but in January 865, the Pope decided on bringing the matter to an issue, and the tone adopted by him in announcing the reinstatement of the bishop is that of a master who will tolerate no discussion of his orders. In trenchant language he censures the conduct of Hincmar, publicly reprobates his bad faith, prescribes to him submission pure and simple under pain of excommunication, and since Hincmar has declared that no appeal lay to Rome in Rothad's case, Nicholas does not hesitate to assert that even had the bishop lodged no appeal he could not have been deposed except by the Pope or with his consent. For in all grave matters, and notably those in which Bishops are concerned, the Pope is the sole and sovereign judge: "that which the Pope has decided is to be observed by all."

These general principles which were thus transforming the Church into a vast highly centralised body wholly in the hands of the Pope, were to be unceasingly proclaimed and defined by Nicholas: Every grade of the ecclesiastical hierarchy must yield to the pontifical authority; Archbishops owe their existence to the Pope in virtue of the pallium conferred on them by him; Bishops cannot be judged except by him or in virtue of the authority delegated by him; councils derive their force and their validity from the power and the sanction of the Holy See. Nicholas I thus takes up the position of the False Decretals[1], at the same time setting up, in place of the system of Christendom united around the Emperor, that of Christendom united around the Pope.

But hardly was Nicholas I dead (867) before his ideas seemed as obsolete as those of Charles the Great, and the Papacy found itself obliged to abandon the ideal, which Nicholas himself had only very partially realised, of a confederation of princes exclusively occupied in carrying out his will.

In the first place, the Popes, being themselves temporal princes throughout the Patrimony of Peter, were obliged, from the time of Hadrian II's pontificate (867–872), to provide for the defence of the States of the Church against the terrible risks to which they were exposed by the Saracen invasions. This care, secular in its nature, soon became by force of circumstances their chief preoccupation. The pontificate of John VIII (872–882), though he also was an energetic Pope, consists to a large extent of a series of desperate attempts to organise the defence against the invader, while he makes every possible endeavour to set up an Emperor capable of undertaking the leadership

---

[1] It is, however, a much-disputed question to what extent the papal doctrine was influenced by this famous collection. In "Étude sur les Fausses Décrétales," *Revue d'histoire ecclésiastique*, tome VIII. 1907, pp. 18 et sqq. M. Paul Fournier estimates their influence at practically nothing. His arguments appear to prove his case. It is certain that the papal theory had been formulated in its main outlines before Nicholas had cognizance of the False Decretals.

in this enterprise. And although John VIII still maintains the pretensions of the Holy See at a high level, although he goes so far as to claim the sole right of choosing the Emperor himself, and on two occasions, in 875 and in 881, succeeds in making his view prevail, crowning first Charles the Bald and then Charles the Fat, the horizon of the Papacy nevertheless narrows perceptibly. It becomes less and less feasible for the Popes to exercise over kings as a body a directing and moderating power. Anxiety for their own safety outweighs everything else. Formosus (891–896) is even reduced in 893 to imploring the help of Arnulf, King of Germany, in order to repel the aggressions of the House of Spoleto, as in former days Stephen II had called upon Pepin for succour against the attacks of Aistulf the Lombard.

Taking this course, the Papacy was speedily brought into subjection to those princes and kings over whom it had once claimed to reign. For some time the head of the House of Spoleto, the Emperor Lambert, was, with his mother Ageltrude, the real ruler of Rome. Later, the Papacy fell into the hands of the local aristocracy, and for more than half a century a family of native origin, that of a noble named Theophylact, a chief official of the papal palace, contrived to seize upon the direction of affairs and to make and unmake Popes at its pleasure. Then, when the influence of the direct line of Theophylact began to decline, the Kings of Germany came into the field to dispute with them and with another branch of their family, the Counts of Tusculum, the power of electing the Pope. From 963, the date when Otto I caused a council which he presided over to decree the deposition of Pope John XII, up to the middle of the eleventh century, the Kings of Germany and the Counts of Tusculum turn by turn set up Popes, and thrice at least the lords of Tusculum themselves assumed the tiara. Two sons of Count Gregory, Theophylact and Romanus (the latter being "Senator of the Romans" at the time of his elevation to the papal throne), and later their nephew Theophylact, a child of twelve, successively filled the Holy See, under the names of Benedict VIII (1012–1024), John XIX (1024–1032) and Benedict IX (1032–1044). When the latter grew tired of exercising power, he sold it for cash down to his godfather, a priest named John Gratian, who took the name of Gregory VI.

The prestige of the Papacy could not fail to suffer grievously from these strange innovations, the more so as Popes thus chosen, to be set aside as soon as they ceased to give satisfaction, had, for the most part, little to boast of in the matter of morals, and in any case, seldom inspired much confidence in point of religion. Stephen VI (896–897), too passive a tool in the hands of Lambert of Spoleto and his mother, did not hesitate, in order to recommend himself to them, to disinter the body of his predecessor Formosus, to arraign the corpse before a council, to have it condemned, and stripped of the pontifical ornaments in which it had been beforehand arrayed, to order it to be thrown into the common grave whence it was torn by the populace and cast into the Tiber.   But what is to be said of the Popes of the tenth century? Sergius III (904–911) was well known to be the lover of Marozia, one of the daughters of Theophylact, and had a son by her, whom later she made first a cardinal and then Pope under the name of John XI (931– 936).   The warlike Pope, John X (914–928), owed the tiara to Theophy- lact and Theodora, Marozia's mother[1].   In 955 came the turn of John Octavian, a grandson of Marozia, a youth of sixteen, son of Alberic, "Senator of the Romans," and himself "Senator of the Romans" since the death of his father in 954.   He was raised to the Chair of Peter under the name of John XII (955–964) and completed the debasement of the Papacy by his debauched life and the orgies of which the Lateran palace soon became the scene.

This personal degradation of the Popes, which lasted for nearly a century and a half, had the most untoward results upon the eccle- siastical hierarchy.   The progress made in breaking down the resis- tance of national priesthoods, or that of such a man as Hincmar, through the prestige enjoyed by Nicholas I, could not be maintained by his successors in their very different position.   Suffice it to recall here[2] the violence which in 991 and 993 Arnulf, Bishop of Orleans, and later the prelates assembled in the synod of Chelles, thought fit to use in repelling the interference of Pope John XV, to whom they denied all right of intervention in the matter of the deposition of the Archbishop of Rheims, and even any title to impugn the decisions arrived at by a provincial council.

On the other hand, the Bishops, left to their own resources, were no better able than the Sovereign Pontiff to maintain themselves in the dominant position which they had gradually acquired in the course of the ninth century.   They fell anew into dependence upon the king, or upon the feudal lords who were nearer at hand and even greater tyrants. In the tenth century and in the beginning of the eleventh the Episcopate as a whole is in the hands of the feudal nobility, for whom bishoprics are hardly more than fiefs in which it is allowable to traffic, while many of the Bishops themselves, though contrasted with some striking exceptions, are merely lords with whom everything gives way to temporal interests, and whose importance in certain countries, notably in Germany, is to be computed by the part they play as the rulers of principalities or as the vassals and counsellors of kings.

The Church itself thus appears as the victim of the same anarchy in which lay society is weltering; all evil appetites range unchecked, and, more than ever, such of the clergy as still retain some concern for religion and for the salvation of the souls committed to their charge

[1] On the later unfounded scandals about John X, see Fedele, ASRSP. xxxiv. pp. 75 ff., 393 ff.

[2] Cf. *supra*, Chapter v. pp. 100–102.

mourn over the universal decadence and direct the eyes of the faithful towards the spectre of the end of the world and of the Last Judgment.

Let us, however, avoid laying too much stress upon these allusions to the final cataclysm predicted in the Apocalypse for the period when the thousand years should be fulfilled, during which Satan was to remain bound. Historians have long believed that, as the year 1000 drew near, the populations, numb with terror, and, as it were, paralysed, awaited in painful anxiety, crowded together in the churches with their faces to the ground, the catastrophe in which they believed the world was about to founder. A few passages from contemporaries, wrongly interpreted, account for this erroneous impression. As the thousandth year approached, the people small and great, priests and lay folk, continued the same way of life as in the past, without being alarmed by those apocalyptic threats in which, even after the thousandth year was past, certain gloomy spirits continued to indulge. Before as after the year 1000, as the facts brought together throughout the whole of this volume abundantly prove, feudal society, wholly given up to its warlike instincts and its passion for violence, still went on dreaming of smashing blows to be dealt and great conquests to be achieved.

But out of the excess of evil good was to spring. In proportion as the lay world allowed itself to be thus carried away, and as the Bishops and their clergy suffered the feudal spirit and customs to encroach upon them more and more, the ascetic life came to present an ever stronger and deeper attraction for all truly devout minds. The tenth century, which saw the Chair of Peter filled by a succession of the most unworthy of Popes, saw also the foundation of the Order of Cluny, and the great monastic reforms initiated and spread abroad by the monks of this order. We shall treat more at length in a later volume of this history of this fruitful new departure, which was one day to have a mighty influence on the reform of the Church as a whole. It need only be said here that, by procuring for the modest hermitage which he planted in Burgundy in 910 complete enfranchisement from all temporal control and by placing it under that of the Holy See only, the founder of Cluny, Duke William of Aquitaine, was laying the foundation for the future greatness of the Abbey. Firmly attached to the Benedictine Rule in its primitive purity, strictly subjected to the absolute control of its abbot, Cluny, thanks to its independent position, rapidly became the refuge of faith and the model to be followed. Not only did benefactions flow in for the support of these pattern monks, whose prayers were doubtless held to be of greater efficacy than those of their fellows, but a whole series of monasteries, old and new, begged for the favour of placing themselves under its patronage and of being reckoned among the number of its priories, in order to share in its Rule and in its exemption from secular domination. France was soon covered with convents affiliated to it from

Burgundy to Aquitaine and from Languedoc to Normandy; Italy, Lorraine, Spain, England, Germany, distant Hungary and Poland were won for it.

And at the very time when Cluny was going forth to its early conquests, quite independently and outside the walls of the Burgundian abbey other fires of monastic revival were being kindled. It was at this moment, to cite only one illustrious instance, that Gerard, lord of Brogne, near Namur, suddenly won over by the attraction of monastic life, founded on his own estate a little monastery, where at first he merely thought to end his days in retirement, contemplation and prayer (923). But before long the fame of saintliness, acquired for him and his companions by their strict observance of the Benedictine Rule, brought about the same miracles in Lorraine as the example of Cluny had worked in Gaul. Gerard gained followers throughout Lorraine and Flanders: the ancient monasteries of the land, the chapters already established, reformed themselves under his direction, new abbeys arose on every side reverting, after the example of Brogne, to the wise and holy precepts of St Benedict.

Thus in the shades of the cloister a new religious society is growing up, preparing itself for the struggle, ready to aid in a general reform of the Church so soon as Popes shall arise with enough energy and independence to resolve upon and inaugurate it.

Meanwhile, in the busier world outside, society, even if led by Bishops themselves worldly, was seeking a remedy against violence which brought anarchy and famine in its train. "The Peace of God" was one such attempt, springing up in a world which knew its own disease. From 989 onwards, synods, beginning in Aquitaine and Burgundy where kingly rule was weakest, anathematised ravagers of churches and despoilers of the poor. The movement spread, and sworn promises to keep from violence to non-combatants and the like misdeeds were prescribed and even gladly taken. It is true that, like most medieval legislation, this was only partly effective, and had to be renewed again and again. But it was a triumph of moral power over brute strength, and upon its solid success the reign of order was founded. Thus civil rulers inherited the Church's task. Feudalism became, to some degree, a regulator of its own disorder, and the supplementary "Truce of God" (*c.* 1040) tried to complete what the "Peace" (*c.* 990) had begun.

CHAPTER XVIII.

FEUDALISM.

THE feudal organisation of state and society is the dominant fact of medieval history on its institutional side quite as much as the city-state is the dominant fact of ancient history from the institutional point of view. Such dominant facts cannot be restricted chronologically to a definite period; they arise gradually and give way slowly to new conditions. But it may be said in a general way that the epoch when feudalism formed most characteristically the centre of political and social arrangements comprised the eleventh and twelfth centuries. From the thirteenth century onwards feudal law continued to be appealed to and feudal principles were sometimes formulated even more sharply than before, but the modern State was beginning to assert itself in most European countries in an unmistakable manner and its influence began to modify the fundamental conceptions of feudalism. In our survey of feudal society we shall therefore look for illustrations mainly to the period between the years 1000 and 1200, though sometimes we may have to draw on the materials presented by thirteenth century documents.

The essential relations of feudalism are as unfamiliar to us as the conception of the city-state. In one sense it may be defined as an arrangement of society on the basis of contract. Contracts play an important part in the business life of our time, but we do not think of the commonwealth as based on leases; we do not consider a nation primarily as a number of lords and tenants; we do not take the status of every single person to be determined by obligations as to land; we do not assume that the notions of sovereignty and of citizenship depend on the stipulations of an express or implied contract. In the medieval period under consideration, on the other hand, it would be easy to deduce all forms of political organisation and of social intercourse from feudal contract. The status of a person depended in every way on his position on the land, and on the other hand, land-tenure determined political rights and duties. The public organisation of England, for example, was derived from the fact that all the land in the country was held by a certain number of tenants-in-chief, including ecclesiastical incorporations and boroughs, from the king, while all the rest of the population consisted either of under-tenants or of persons settled on the land of some tenant and amenable to jurisdiction through the latter. In other West-European countries the distribution of the people was more intricate and confused because there had been no wholesale conquest capable of reducing conditions to uniformity, but the fundamental facts were the same. Every West-European country was arranged on the basis of feudal land-tenure.

The acts constituting the feudal contract were called *homagium* and *investitura*. The tenant had to appear in person before the lord surrounded by his court, to kneel before him and to put his folded hands into the hand of the lord, saying: "I swear to be faithful and attached to you as a man should be to his lord." He added sometimes: "I will do so as long as I am your man and as I hold your land" (*Saxon Lehnrecht*, ch. 3). To this act of homage corresponded the "investiture" by the lord, who delivered to his vassal a flag, a staff, a charter or some other symbol of the property conceded. There were many variations according to localities and, of course, the ceremony differed in the case of a person of base status. Yet even a villein received his yard-land or oxgang from the steward of a lord after swearing an oath of fealty and in the form of an "admittance" by the staff, of which a record was kept in the rolls of the manorial court: hence the copyhold tenure of English law.

Tenure conditioned by service was called the *feudum, fief, Lehn*, but sometimes these terms were restricted to the better class of such estates, those held by military service, while the lands for which rents and labour-services were rendered were described as *censivae*, in England *socagia*. The holdings of villeins or rustics (*Bauern, roturiers*) were deemed in law to be at the will of the lord, but in practice were protected by the local custom and generally subjected to quasi-legal rules of possession and inheritance. Although feudal tenure was certainly the most common mode of holding land, it was not the only one. In France and Germany there were still many survivals of *allodial* right, that is of complete ownership, not subject to any conditions of service or payment. In fact, while in northern France there obtained the rule *nulle terre sans seigneur*, that is, the doctrine that all estates were held by feudal law under lords, in southern France, the territory of written law based on Roman books, the contrary was expressed in the words *nul seigneur sans titre*: no lordship was recognised unless proof of title were forthcoming. Many documents shew the constant spread of feudal tenure at the expense of the allodial: the process of feudalisation is, *e.g.*, forcibly illustrated by the inquest as to land-tenures made in 1272 and 1273 by order of King Edward I in Aquitaine: it testified to all sorts of variations in the mode of holding land in these parts; claims to allodial rights are often recorded. But the tendency of the inquest is to impose the burden of services as widely as possible. The circumstances in which the process of feudalisation was going on may be illustrated by the following tale of a Flemish chronicle (Lambert d'Ardres, quoted by Luchaire, *Manuel*, 151). In the beginning of the eleventh century two brothers, Herred and Hacket, possessed considerable allodial estates in Poperinghe, but were persecuted by the Count of Guines and the Count of Boulogne, powerful neighbours, each of whom wanted to obtain feudal suzerainty over these lands. The elder Herred, in order to put an end to these vexations, surrendered his estates to the Bishop of Térouanne and received them back as a hereditary fief (*perpetuum et hereditarium recepit in feodum*), while the junior brother effected a similar release of his part of the estates to the Count of Boulogne.

The dangers of keeping outside the feudal nexus were self-evident: in a time of fierce struggles for bare existence it was necessary for everyone to look about for support, and the protection of the central authority in the State was, even at its best, not sufficient to provide for the needs of individuals. Even in England, where the Conquest had given rise to a royal power possessed of very real authority, and the "king's peace" was by no means a mere word, the maintenance afforded by powerful lords was an important factor in obtaining security.

In any case the feudal nexus originated by such conditions involved reciprocity. The vassal expected gifts and at least efficient protection, and sometimes the duty of the suzerain in this respect is insisted on in as many words; as the French jurist Beaumanoir has it, "the lord is quite as much bound to be faithful to his man as the latter is bound in regard to the lord" (*Coutumes de Beauvaisis*, § 58). If the tenant thought that he was not treated properly, feudal theory allowed him to sever the connexion. He might leave the estate (*déguerpissement*) without any further claim on the part of the lord, but according to French notions he might even do more, namely disavow the subjection to the lord while retaining the estate (*désaveu*). The Assizes of Jerusalem are careful to state the cases of denial of right, in which a vassal may rightfully renounce his obligations in regard to his immediate lord with the natural consequence that henceforth such duties are transferred to the overlord of the one at fault (*Assises de Jérusalem*, "*gager le fief*"). This implied a proof on his part that the lord had not fulfilled his part of the agreement. Though as a matter of fact such a *désaveu* led more often to war than to a judicial process, it was derived from a juridical conception, and expressed the view that the man, vassal or tenant, had definite rights as against his lord. Some of the famous assertions of feudal independence on the part of barons opposed to royal lords are based on this very doctrine of *désaveu* for breach of agreement. Thus the barons of Aragon swore to their king that they would obey and serve him if he maintained the rights, customs and laws of the kingdom, and if not, not. The peers of the Kings of Jerusalem, according to the Assizes, might in case of infringement of their rights lawfully refuse allegiance and offer resistance. The clause of the Great Charter stipulating that a committee of twenty-five barons should watch King John's actions, and in case of his breaking his solemn pledges should make war on him and call on all his subjects to do the same, proceeds from the same fundamental assumption. This view was readily extended from the notion of a breach of agreement between the lord and his tenants to a conception of infringement of laws in general. In this way the feudal view could be made a starting-point for the development of a constitutional doctrine. We may notice this in the case of Bracton. In his treatise on the laws of England, written at the time of Simon de Montfort's supremacy, the English judge, instead of urging with the Roman jurists and with his predecessor Glanvill that the sovereign's will has the force of law, states that kings are not above the law, although they have no single human superior (f. 5 *v.*), and that they ought to be restrained by their peers from breaking the law (f. 34)[1].

The other side of the medal is presented by the duties of vassals in regard to the lord. Close analysis shews that these duties proceed from different sources. There is to begin with a general obligation of fealty, faithful obedience (*fidelitas*) which is owed by all subjects of the lord without distinction of rank, the rustic subjects (*villani*) being especially concerned. This obligation evidently had its roots in the relation between sovereign and subject, and in so far represented rather the gradual decay of sovereign power than the purely contractual side of feudalism; but in so much as fealty became a relation between private lords and their subjects, it was related to the feudal nexus and combined in various ways with the kindred notions of homage and investiture. Homage again, which is distinctly contractual, arises essentially from a contract of service. It proceeds directly from the bond created by free agreement between a leader and a follower, the lord (*hlaford*) and his man. But this contract of service gradually assumed a peculiar form: the personal duties of the servant-retainer are asserted only occasionally, *e.g.* at a coronation ceremony, when great feudatories are made to present dishes and cups, to lead horses, to superintend the arrangements of the bedroom. As a rule, the central duty of the vassal comes to be his military service, regulated according to a certain number of days, generally forty, or a scutage payment in redemption of the latter. Knight service of this kind shades off almost imperceptibly into so-called military serjeanties, that is, services of archers, of garrison soldiers, etc.

---

[1] "Rex autem habet superiorem, id est Deum, item legem, per quam factus est Rex. Item curiam suam, videlicet comites, barones, quia comites dicuntur quasi socii regis, et qui habet socium, habet magistrum, et ideo si rex fuerit sine freno, *i.e.* sine lege, debent ei frenum ponere."

These again are not easily divided from petty serjeanties, in which the menial services are still regarded as characteristic of the bond. In the lists of serjeanties drawn up in the reign of Edward I (published in the volumes of *Feudal Aids* and in the *Testa de Nevill*) we find mentions of cooks, falconers, foresters, etc. In German feudal custom the *ministeriales* correspond to the *servientes* of England and France, but there is a peculiar trait about their condition, namely, that they are distinctly unfree in origin. Some of the greatest warriors of German medieval history came from such unfree stock—Marquard of Anweiler, for instance, who received the March of Ancona as a fief from Emperor Frederick II, was a *ministerialis*, an unfree retainer of the Emperor. As homage creates a relation between man and man, it is not intrinsically bound up with landholding, and a good many of the personal followers and servants of medieval magnates must certainly have lived in the castles of their lords, receiving equipment and arms from them: they saw in the good cheer of the court and in occasional gifts a reward for their personal attendance[1]. But such personal relations tended naturally to strike root in land. If the retainer was at all useful and efficient he expected to be remunerated by a permanent source of income, and such an outfit could only take the shape of a grant of land. On the other hand, when a small landowner sought protection from a magnate, he had generally to throw his tenement into the balance and reassume it as a fief. Thus homage and investiture, although historically and institutionally distinct, grow, as it were, together, and form the normal foundation of feudal contract.

Besides the political colouring of this contract, it assumes a peculiar aspect from the point of view of land law. It gives rise to a significant distinction of two elements in the notion of ownership (*dominium*). Roman property (*dominium*) was characterised during the best period by uncompromising unity. A person having *dominium* over a thing, including an estate in land, had it alone and excluded everyone else. Medieval lawyers, on the other hand, came to deal with plots of land which had normally two owners, a superior and an inferior, one having the direct ownership (*dominium directum*, *dominium eminens*), the other having the useful ownership, the right to exploit the land (*dominium utile*). In England the splitting of the notion of *dominium* was avoided by opposing the tenure in domain to the tenure of service (*tenere in dominio—in servicio*, see, *e.g.*, Notebook of Bracton, case 1436), but the necessity for reckoning with two kinds of right in respect of every holding contributed indirectly to weaken the notion of absolute property in land. Contentions as to

---

[1] Red Book of the Exchequer, 283: Hugh de Lacy's report as to his knights: "Ricardus Brito et ipsi qui post ipsum sunt nominati tenent de domino Hugone sine servitio aliquo quod eis statum est. Quidam de eis sunt mecum residentes et invenio eis necessaria. Et quidam sunt in domibus meis in Wallia et invenio eis necessaria."

land were made to turn principally on *seisin*, protected possession, while the proof of title, which had played an important part in later Anglo-Saxon times, receded, as it were, into the background. Instead of trying to ascertain who the person was who ought to exercise the absolute right of ownership, English courts came to concern themselves with the practical question which of the two litigants had relatively the better right (*ius merum*) in regard to an estate or tenement. From the feudal point of view an estate held as a fief could be freely parcelled out to under-tenants who would become the vassals of the man holding directly of the lord, provided the obligations of that intermediate tenant were not lessened by such a process. Indeed it was not uncommon for tenants to pass on the onerous duties with which the tenement was charged to these under-tenants, who in such a case were called upon to "defend" the land in regard to the superior lord in order that the mesne (*medius*, middle) lord should be able to enjoy his tenure in peace. Various complications arose from such *subinfeudation* in connexion with customary requirements, and it was clearly in the interest of the overlords to restrict such parcelling of fees as much as possible. The English Crown cut short the practice by the statute *Quia Emptores*, which provided that in future the creation of any new fief would involve not subinfeudation but the recognition by the new tenant of immediate dependence on the overlord: thus the grantee of a new fief was placed on the same level as the grantor instead of being subordinated to him.

The incidents arising out of the double claims to land were manifested in a striking manner in cases when the personnel of the contracting parties was changed, more especially when in consequence of the death of the tenant a new representative of the *dominium utile* had to come in. While in the case of a *Thronfall*, as the Germans said, that is, of the demise of the lord, homage and fealty had to be merely renewed, a *Lehnfall*, the demise of the vassal, brought about a temporary resumption of the fief by the direct owner, *i.e.* by the lord: as a rule he was bound to regrant the fief to the right heir, but such a reinvestiture was accompanied by a *relief*, a more or less heavy payment.

The struggle of English barons for reasonable reliefs called forth well-known stipulations of the charters of Henry I and of John. In the case of so-called base holdings the relief had its analogy in the heriot, the surrender to the lord of the best horse or the best ox, and there can be no doubt that this due, which had grown from the custom of surrendering the outfit provided by the lord to his dependent, was originally used quite as much in military fiefs as in villein or socage tenements. In feudal practice, however, the military heriot was absorbed by the relief, while it kept its ground in regard to base tenure.

The resumption of tenancies connected with ecclesiastical offices led, as is well known, to protracted struggles as to rights of investiture between the Church and State. Even when reinvestiture was made dependent on canonical elections, the fiscal interests of the secular power had to be satisfied by the diversion of ecclesiastical revenues for a year or a similar customary period for the benefit of the Crown or of other secular patrons. There were other occasional rights connected with a breach of the continuity of possession, which would not arise out of vacancies in ecclesiastical institutions; such were wardship and marriage, which accrued to the lords in cases when fiefs descended to minors or to unmarried females. These eventualities gave rise to very lucrative rights, and it is a matter of common knowledge to what extent such opportunities were liable to be misused. The English Charters contained provisions against these abuses, but even in their mitigated form these practices were likely to produce much hardship. Special classes of misdeeds arose in connexion with them: we hear of judicial proceedings taken on account of ravishment (kidnapping) of wards and of ravishment of heiresses in order to get the profits, even when the corresponding right belonged to some one else or was contested. From such exactions ecclesiastical tenements were free, and this alone would have sufficed to make the passage of landed property into the hands of the churches undesirable from the feudal point of view. No wonder powerful kings tried to restrict the passage of estates into the "dead hand" (*manus mortua*) of the Church. This was among other things the aim of Edward I's Statute *De religiosis*.

Although these reassertions of the *dominium directum* forcibly shewed that the proprietary rights of the lord were by no means a dead letter, the "useful domain" was protected from wanton interruption by clearly established customs. The *beneficia*, which preceded fiefs in historical evolution, were assumed to be granted for life, but when fiefs developed out of them they nearly always became hereditary. The only exception of any importance is presented by the *beneficia militaria* of French Navarre.

As political subjection was regarded as a matter of contract, the feudal nexus tended towards a disruption of sovereignty, and often led in practice to the formation of numerous political bodies within the boundaries of historical States. This was especially the case in France, Germany and Italy. An authoritative jurist like Beaumanoir summarised the position in the saying, "chaque baron est souverain dans sa baronie"; and the mottoes chosen by some of the French magnates gave expression to an unmeasured feeling of self-sufficiency. The Rohans of Brittany boasted: "prince ne daigne, roi ne puis, Rohan je suis." The seigneur of Coucy, a barony which gave great trouble to the early Capetian kings, disguised his pride by mock humility: "je ne suis ni comte, ni marquis, je suis le sire de Coucy." In Germany the dismemberment of sovereignty was finally recognised by express law in Charles IV's Golden Bull of 1356 in favour of the seven Electors, but it had already been acknowledged in regard to princes in general by Frederick II, and had been acted upon more or less all through the eleventh and twelfth centuries in the course of the protracted feuds between Frankish and Swabian Emperors, on the one hand, and their various vassals on the other. When Frederick Barbarossa went down on his knees, according to tradition, when imploring Henry the Lion of Saxony and Bavaria to stand by him against the rebel Italians, it would have been difficult to say that the Emperor was the sovereign and the duke a mere subject.

A most important consequence of this acknowledgment of sovereign rights on the part of vassals of the Crown lay in the fact that the latter could resort to actual war, when asserting claims or defending infringed interests. The endeavours, which were made by the Church, by royal suzerains and by the barons themselves to restrict and suppress private warfare, are in themselves characteristic of what we should call the anarchy of the times. The end of the tenth century witnessed many attempts to put an end to private wars in France. In consequence of terrible epidemics and bad harvests, which were regarded as signs of divine wrath and incitements to repentance, the magnates of central and northern France met, agreed to renounce private war, and confirmed this resolve by solemn oaths. Gerard, Bishop of Cambrai, objected to this as political; he was much abused by the other members of the congress for holding aloof, and yet, as the chronicler remarks, events proved that he was right, "vix enim paucissimi crimen perjurii evaserunt."

It soon became evident that it was impossible to suppress the pernicious custom entirely. The Truce of God, *treuga Dei*, made its appearance in completion of the Peace of God[1]. The time from Thursday night to Monday morning was considered a time of truce on account of the memories of the Lord's sufferings and resurrection. Churches and churchyards were naturally considered as hallowed and therefore neutral territory. In the South, olive-trees were declared to be exempt from destruction by reason of their vital importance in the economy of the country. The movement for " truce " attained material results under the guidance of the Church in the eleventh and twelfth centuries, and it became even more effective in the thirteenth, when political potentates took it up. Still, even St Louis did not insist on a complete abandonment of the practice of private war by his vassals : he only enforced from all those, who resorted to the last argument of war, submission to certain rules as to its declaration, the beginning of hostilities, their course and so on; the *quarantaine le Roi* was a code as to usage in private war.

To Germany some order was brought by powerful leagues between princes and knights on the one hand, cities on the other. Such leagues were offensive and defensive alliances, and ultimately had recourse to force of arms in order to maintain their position. But as all extensive armaments are apt to do, they prevented the danger and disorder of petty collisions. It was only towards the end of the Middle Ages that

[1] See also Chapter xii. pp. 281—2 and Chapter xvii. p. 457.

something like a peace of the Empire was recognised and to a certain extent secured by the reforms of Maximilian's age. In England the "franchise" or right of private war was suppressed at a very early time. It did not tally with the social order inaugurated by the Norman Conquest, and the king's peace became one of the mainstays of early Common Law. The only period when the real disruption of sovereignty through private war seemed to prevail was the interregnum when Stephen of Boulogne and the Plantagenets struggled for the Crown. But this lapse into anarchy was short, and from the time when Henry II restored order, private war ceased to be recognised as a legal outcome of disputes. Yet the conditions of military contract remained the foundation of government, and this made it possible for opposition to wrong to take the form of armed resistance. The revolt against John, the barons' war against Henry III, the risings of Mortimer and Bolingbroke, the Wars of the Roses, have as their necessary background a society ruled by groups of knights, who considered themselves not merely as subjects, but as peers of the king.

One of the most important consequences of the disruption of sovereignty lay in the alienation of rights of jurisdiction by the central government. As early as the ninth and tenth centuries we observe everywhere the growth of franchises and immunities which break up the ordinary sub-divisions of countries in respect of the administration of justice. The English shires and hundreds, the continental counties and *Grafschaften* are riddled with districts in which the place of the ordinary judges of the land is taken by secular or ecclesiastical magnates or their representatives, among whom the secular judges of ecclesiastical corporations, the *advocati* (*avoués*, *Vogte*), are the most conspicuous. The *Sac* and *Soc* grants of Anglo-Saxon kings, as well as the various privileges of immunity conferred by Carolingian, Franconian and Saxon monarchs, present different steps in the process of political dismemberment. The central authorities merely strove to retain their hold on the most important varieties of jurisdiction, especially judgments as to great crimes, the *Ungerichte*, as they were termed in Germany, for which a man may lose his head and his hand (*Haupt und Hand*), while jurisdiction in minor cases, when a person would only be chastised in skin or hair (*in Haut oder Haar*), were left to local potentates. From similar considerations early English kings tried as much as possible to retain in their hand the great forfeitures. This led eventually to a classification of feudal tribunals according to the amount of jurisdiction acquired by them, some claiming high and some low justice (*haute* or *basse justice*)[1]. The proceedings of *Quo Warranto* instituted by Edward I after his victory over the baronial opposition shew a most exuberant growth of prescriptive rights in regard to the use of gallows, pillory,

---

[1] The medium justice (*moyenne justice*) was a later development and was not generally accepted.

tumbrel, etc. by English noblemen and ecclesiastical magnates. The institution of the *advocaria* (*avouerie*, *Vogtei*), on the contrary, never attained to much importance in England, while it flourished greatly in Germany, France and Flanders. It sprang from the delegation of public power within the territory of an ecclesiastical franchise to a layman, who thereby came to be a kind of policemaster as well as a judge. The ordinary judges, the counts and their subordinates were forbidden to enter the enfranchised district. On the other hand the bishop or abbot at the head of it abstained from the shedding of blood and did not meddle with criminal justice or deal with cases of public coercion: he appointed an advocate who had to arrest criminals, to conduct them before the proper courts, to execute those found guilty, to assist the ecclesiastical lord in cases when force had to be employed for the collection of rents or the taking of distress. These powers ripened in the course of the feudal age to an independent jurisdiction which greatly hampered the freedom of action of the ecclesiastical lord and encroached on his interests. Besides, churches and monasteries often availed themselves of the *advocaria* in order to obtain protection from a powerful neighbour: the surrender of certain rights and sources of income was the price paid for support in those troubled times. No wonder that in the eleventh and twelfth centuries the advocates often became local tyrants at whose hands their clients had to suffer a great deal. This is how, for instance, the Cartulary of St Mihiel in Flanders describes the conduct of a certain Count Raynald, an advocate of the monastery in question: "Count Raynald was the first to commit robberies in our estates under the customary term of *talliatae*; he also put our men into prison and forced them to give up their own by means of torture—he bequeathed this tyranny to his son, the present Raynald. The latter exceeded the malice of his father to such an extent that our men cannot put up any longer with such oppression and leave our estates. They are either unable or do not care to acquit themselves of outstanding rents: he is the only person they are afraid of[1]."

The conflicts between ecclesiastical potentates and their secular "advocates" often led to regular treaties, the so-called *règlements d'avouerie*. The Vogt of the Abbey of Prüm is forbidden to "clip" (*tondere*—clip the hair as for convicts) or to flog anyone except those who are guilty of murder, brigandage or battery, nor has he any part in the *wer-geld* of a man unless he has helped to capture and to judge him. In Echternach the Vogt is excluded from participating in civil trials. In houses appertaining to the garden and the cellar, the laundry and the kitchen of the monks, he is forbidden to hold any pleas or to exact any services, except *pro monomachia* (trial by battle) *et sanguinea percussura* (cf. A. S. *blodwite*) *et scabinis constituendis* (the appointment of popular

---

[1] Cartulary of St Mihiel quoted by Flach, *Origines de l'ancienne France*, I. p. 442

assessors of the tribunals)[1]. The long-standing rivalry between ecclesiastical institutions and their advocates was ultimately composed by the
intervention of the Crown when the latter grew strong. If we turn to
consider the relations between the lord and his vassals, we shall naturally
find that they differ greatly from the relations established at the present
time between the sovereign and his subjects. In the case of the
privileged holders of fiefs, however small, the tie which united them with
their suzerain being one not of general subordination but of limited
obligation, the view that the general will has to prevail over the
particular and can impose rules of conduct upon it did not hold
good. Noble vassals, ecclesiastics possessed of fiefs, and townsmen as
members of municipal corporate bodies were as regards their lords
bound to abstain from certain acts and to perform certain duties. A
systematic treatment of this kind of contractual relation may be found
in a letter of Bishop Fulbert of Chartres to the Duke of Aquitaine
(eleventh century)[2]. The duties which he enumerates are derived more
especially from the oath of fealty, which accompanied the homage
ceremony and was distinct from the fealty of the base and non-
privileged population to be mentioned later on.

The negative duties of the faithful vassal are indicated by the
following terms: *incolume, tutum, honestum, utile, facile, possibile*. The
Benedictine editors of Fulbert's work have explained these expressions
to mean that the vassal undertakes not to assail his lord, not to
reveal his secret, not to endanger the safety of his castles, not to
wrong him in his judicial power, honours and possessions or to put
obstacles in his way which would render what he undertakes difficult or
impossible. On the positive side the vassal is bound to give his lord
advice and aid (*consilium, auxilium*). From the positive obligations of
consilium and *auxilium* various concrete duties are derived. The
principal form of advice (*consilium*) tendered to the lord by his men
consists in their obligation to attend his court. Every lord had a court
of his own, but not every court of this kind was competent to judge all
cases. A feudal distinction has to be drawn in this respect between cases
arising from the feudal nexus and cases of delegated public jurisdiction.
These latter comprised chiefly criminal cases classified, as already pointed
out, under the heads of high and low justice. The privilege of giving
sentence in them and of exercising the fiscal exactions connected with
them accrued only to those among the feudal lords who had obtained
the corresponding franchises through express grant or by force. They
were called *seigneurs justiciers* in France. The more numerous class of
ordinary lords held courts if they had tenants of fiefs, and vassals and
villein subjects under them. These feudal courts took cognizance of all
processes as to land distributed by the lord to his dependents, but also

[1] Quoted by Pergameni, *L'avouerie ecclésiastique belge,* Ghent 1907, pp. 83, 84.
[2] Quoted by Luchaire, *Manuel des institutions françaises,* p. 185.

to a great extent as to pleas concerning the persons of the vassals. The first group of pleas stands out so clearly that there is no special necessity to dwell on its range. It need only be noticed that the proceedings concerning unfree tenures were substantially of the same kind as those affecting free or noble tenancies. A dispute as to the possession of a *villenagium* followed on the same lines as a trial in which a free tenement was the object in dispute, although the latter was naturally much more complex. From the technical point of view, in the first case the trial took place before the peers of the contending parties, who as suitors of the court were its judges, while in the second case the lord or his steward was the only judge and such assessors as were called up had only advisory powers. But as a matter of fact the verdicts of the court were regarded as the expression of legal custom in the second case, and the reservation that the lord might override the customary rules was due to his exceptional position, and not to the ordinary working of manorial courts. A body of legal tradition and of conceptions of equity grew up in the lower social stratum as well as in the upper. This is especially noticeable in the case of English manorial courts, in the composition of which free and unfree elements are generally intermixed in such a way that it is difficult to distinguish between verdicts laid down by the free tenants and those contributed by the villeins. The one really important difference lay in the fact that the villeins had to look for justice to the manorial court in all cases, not only tenurial, but also personal, such as cases of battery, defamation, adultery and the like, while free men and specially men of noble birth were either directly amenable to justice by the medium of the royal tribunals or could, if they appeared before a feudal court, insist on a very strict maintenance of their privileges in view of the supervision of royal courts.

In a sense the circle of tenants constituting the peers' court was a most complete expression of the principle of equality as between allied sovereigns. The decision was formulated strictly by the peers of the contending parties, and this led, in regard to criminal accusations, to the famous doctrine of the Great Charter: "nullus liber homo capiatur vel imprisonetur nisi per judicium parium suorum vel per legem terrae" (sect. 39). The decision of a court of peers was final. An appeal was impossible from the feudal point of view, because it would have meant a revision of the judgment by higher authority, and feudal litigants submitted not to higher authority but to a convention in which they had taken part. There were, however, two cases in which a vassal might seek redress from a source of law superior to the court of peers presided over by his suzerain. If justice was denied to him by this tribunal he could ask the overlord, that is, the suzerain of his immediate lord, to see that justice should be done. This was, however, no appeal as to law or facts, but only an attempt to set the machinery of feudal jurisdiction in motion. The second eventuality occurred when one of the parties to a suit actually contested the justice of a particular decision or sentence. He could in French feudal law attaint or falsify the verdict by pronouncing the formula, " je vous appelle de faux jugement." This meant that he challenged the fairness and honour of the judges, and the result was single combat between the protesting party and one or several of the judges, not a satisfactory solution of the difficulties from our point of view, nor, probably, from that of many judges concerned. There were devices which rendered such attaint hazardous in some cases: the members of the tribunal could pronounce the decision *in corpore*, and in this case the option for the dissatisfied party was to fight them all. In any case this mode of appeal was directed towards the revision of the judgment by God rather than by man, and at bottom did not subvert the principle that a man ought to be judged by his peers and by his peers only. It is hardly necessary to add that the falsifying of judgments has been described here in conformity to strict rules of feudal theory. In practice all sorts of compromises took place. In England, for example, the revision of judgments by higher courts was brought about at a very early stage by the intervention of the king's court, though not without opposition from the barons. An instructive case occurred, for example, in the reign of William the Conqueror. In a trial as to land between Bishop Gundulf of Rochester and Picot, the Sheriff of Cambridgeshire, the county pronounced in favour of the latter, but through the intervention of Odo of Bayeux twelve representatives of the shire were called up to confirm the verdict by oath in the king's court, and ultimately, after a declaration by a monk who had been steward of the estate in question, the unlucky doomsmen were driven either to go through the ordeal of redhot iron or to recant. The indirect way in which the prejudiced intervention of the higher powers took effect in this case is characteristic of the traditional difficulties which stood in the way of downright revision. As on many other occasions, there are threads connecting feudal theory with recent or actual practice, and we may not unreasonably see in the doctrine as to the finality of jury verdicts a modernised offshoot of the older doctrine of the judgment by peers. Of course the differentiation between questions of fact and questions of law has made it possible to concede to juries the highly privileged position which they generally enjoy, but the germ of the corresponding rules is historically connected with the immunity from outside influence which formed one of the most characteristic traits of the feudal judgment by peers[1].

Similar phenomena meet our eye when we come to consider the processes of *legislation* obtaining in the feudal world. It is evident in theory that a baron, being a sovereign, could not be subjected to any will but his own, and that therefore such common arrangements as had

---

[1] Bigelow, *Placita Anglo-normannica*, p. 34.

to be made in medieval society had to be effected on the same lines as modern international conventions. And indeed we find this idea at the root of the feudal doctrine of legislation; in the custom of Touraine-Anjou it was expressed in the following way: "The baron has all manner of justice in his territory, and the king cannot proclaim his command in the land of the baron without the latter's consent; nor can the baron proclaim his command in the land of his tenant without the consent of the tenant[1]."

In consequence of this general principle, all feudal legislation ranging outside the immediate demesne of the single baron takes the shape of a *stabilimentum* (*établissement*) or of an assize enacted in the court of a superior lord with the express or implied consent of his vassals. An ordinance of the Viscount of Thouars (A.D. 1099), for example, instituting a certain annual charge to be paid by the tenants, refers at the close to "the authority and will of the barons of my land" (quoted by Luchaire, *Manuel des institutions françaises*, p. 253). The same notion reappears in ordinances made by much greater potentates, such as the dukes of Normandy, *e.g.* by William the Conqueror, in 1064 (on public peace), by counts of Flanders (Baldwin of Constantinople, in 1199, on usury), by dukes of Brittany (in 1185, on succession to fiefs), even by kings of France and kings of England; Henry II's Assize of the Forest, for instance, begins in the following manner: "This is the assize of the Lord King Henry, the son of Maud, in England, about forest and hunting, by the advice and consent (*per consilium et assensum*) of the archbishops, bishops and barons, earls (*comitum*) and noblemen of England at Woodstock" (Stubbs, Select Ch. 157). Theoretically, the individual consent of each member of the gathering to any decision was needed if it were to bind him, but historically, the legislative assemblies were not merely the outcome of feudal meetings, they were also survivals of more ancient popular assemblies, while, as a matter of practice, the authority of the superior lord and the influence of leading magnates asserted themselves in a much greater degree than would have been allowed from a purely individual point of view. It thus depended very much on circumstances whether centripetal or centrifugal tendencies got the upper hand. The majority principle had not been evolved either, at least during the eleventh, twelfth and thirteenth centuries. As the French historian Luchaire has expressed it, voices were rather weighed than counted. But the idea of a convention made itself felt in a very definite manner, and this point must be noticed as very important in view of subsequent development. The early doctrine of medieval estates is clearly connected with these feudal views on the side both of legislation and taxation. The view that

---

[1] Coutume de Touraine-Anjou, p. 17: Bers si a toutes en sa terre, ne li rois ne puet mettre ban en la tere au baron, sanz son assentement, ne li bers ne puet mettre ban en la terre au vavasor, sanz l'assentement au vavasor; (received in the Établissement de St Louis, I. p. 26. See P. Viollet, *Établissements de St Louis*, II. p. 36).

the nation is not bound to pay a tax to the imposition of which it has not consented through its representatives (the constitutional rule on which the development of Parliament depended later on) certainly has its roots in the feudal maxim that no baron was bound by ordinances in the "establishment" of which he had not taken a part. It is also not alien to our purpose to notice that the distinction between greater and smaller barons suggested by the far-reaching differences, in regard to the appropriation of public power, afforded a germ for the subsequent rise of aristocratic "Second Chambers." The House of Lords, as a court, is a house of peers, and it is not only in England that the prominence of the magnates secured for them a special personal standing in legislative organisation: a curious parallel, all the more instructive because it is supplied by a microscopic state, is presented by the history of Béarn in the Pyrenees. In that *vicomté*, an aristocratic council of twelve hereditary *jurati*, drawn from the most powerful houses of local nobility, appears as the *cour majour* and acts as a standing committee of the full court (*cour plénière*). It had to settle disputes between the viscounts and their vassals and in general to control the current administration of law[1].

A survey of medieval society from the one point of view of contractual relations would, however, be incomplete, one-sided and artificial. In order to be correct it ought to be matched by an examination of the constituent elements combining to form the feudal organisation. Such an examination would have to take each feudal unit singly and to describe the rule of the lord over his subjects as well as the work of these subjects.

The most characteristic type of such a feudal unit is certainly the English *manor*, and I should like to turn now to a study of it which will afford a key to the understanding of similar phenomena in other countries of Western Europe. The manor is a necessary outcome of so-called natural husbandry, providing for the requirements of life by work carried out on the spot, without much exchanging and buying. It is the connecting link in the social life of classes, some of which are primarily occupied with the rough work of feeding, clothing and housing society, while others specialise in defending it and providing for its secular and spiritual government. It presents the lowest and most efficient unit of medieval organisation, and local justice, administration and police are all more or less dependent on its arrangements. Let us look at the different elements of which this historical group is composed.

First of all there is the *economic* element. The manor afforded the most convenient, and even the necessary, arrangements of work and profit in those times. It would be quite wrong to assume that the interests and rights of the many were simply sacrificed to the interests and rights of a few rulers, that the manor was nothing but an estate, cultivated

[1] Cadier, *Les États du Béarn*, quoted by Luchaire, *Manuel*, p. 254.

and exploited for the sake of the lord and managed at discretion by his will and the will of his servants. On the contrary, one of the best established facts in the economic life of the manor was its double mechanism, if one may say so. It consisted, as a rule, of a village community with wide though peculiar self-government and of a manorial administration superimposed on it, influencing and modifying the life of the community but not creating it. This double aim and double mechanism of the manor must be noticed at the outset as a very characteristic feature; it places the manor in a sharp contrast both to the plantations of slaves of the ancient world and to the commercial husbandry of a modern estate struggling for profit as best it may.

Manorial husbandry was all along striving towards *two* intimately connected aims, providing the villagers with means of existence and providing the lord with profits. Hence a dual machinery to attain these aims, both a village community and the lord's demesne.

The *village community* lay at the basis of the whole[1]. It gave rise to a very peculiar system of holding and using land, not to be confused either with the case of the tribal community in which rights are graduated according to the pedigree of a person, or with that of the communalism of the Russian *mir* or of some Hindu settlements, in which land is allotted and redivided according to the requirements and the economic strength of the settlers. The peculiar bent of the English rural community would perhaps be best indicated by the expression "shareholding arrangement" or "community of shareholders." Each of the households settled in the village had a fixed and constant share, or maybe half a share, or a quarter, or the eighth part of a share assigned to it. It stood *in scot and in lot* with the village as a hide or two virgates or one virgate or a bovate, according to the size of the share. By the standard of this hereditary share all rights and duties were apportioned. By the side of the shareholders there generally lived in the village smaller tenants (cottagers, crofters) but they were merely an adjunct to the main body of the tenantry and may be left out of reckoning in our general survey.

The system of communal shareholding was very strikingly illustrated by the treatment of waste and pasture in the medieval village. It was not divided among the tenants, and, though later in legal theory it belonged to the lord, it was everywhere considered by custom as a "common" for the use of the villagers. In most cases it had to be *stinted* to some extent: rules were formulated as to the species and number of beasts to be sent to pasture, as to seasons, and as to precautions against abuses; and these rules can generally be traced to the main principle, that every household has to use the common according to the size of its

---

[1] In parts of the country settled on the system of scattered farms, arable and meadows came naturally to be divided among separate households, but even then a great deal of communalism remained in the management of pasture and wood.

share, so that, for instance, a virgater had the right to send two cows and eight sheep to the pasture, while the owner of a bovate could only send one cow and four sheep, and so on. The use of wood for building purposes, of hedges for fuel, of turf, and other profits drawn from the common and undivided fund of the village, were regulated by rules or by-laws of the same kind. In regard to *meadows*, which were scarce and highly valued, the communalism of the village found a suitable expression in the division of these meadows into a certain number of strips according to the number of households taking part in the community: these strips were then allotted to one after the other of the households in a customary order or by casting lots. The *arable* did not change hands in the same way. As a rule, the strips of the arable were owned by each household in hereditary succession, each generation entering into the rights of the preceding generation in this respect. But, even in the case of the arable, there were many facts to shew that it was considered dependent on the community, though held to a certain extent in severalty by the households. To begin with, the holding in severalty existed on the land only for one part of the year. The tenant had a particular right to it while it was *under crop*, that is, when it had been ploughed up and sown, and while the harvest had not yet removed the proceeds of the individual labour and care which the tiller had bestowed upon it. As most fields were cultivated in medieval England on the three-field or on the two-field system, the households of shareowners obtained private rights over their arable strips while winter corn or spring corn grew on the soil, and these separate rights were marked off by narrow lines of turf between the strips, called *balks*, while the whole of the sown field was protected from the inroads of cattle by a temporary hedge.

But after harvest had been gathered the hedges fell, and the whole field returned to the condition of waste to be used for pasture as a common: a condition which took up the whole of every third year in a three-field and the whole of every second year in a two-field husbandry, besides a considerable part of the years when the field received seed. Private occupation of the strips emerged in this way from time to time from the open common field, an arrangement which not only kept up the principle that the arable was, after all, the property of the village as a whole, but had direct practical consequences in hampering private industry and the use of private capital in cultivation: it rendered, for instance, manuring a very complicated and rather exceptional process. Nor is this all: the householder did not only cease to cultivate his plot as soon as harvest was over, but he had, even before then, to conform in the plan and methods of cultivation to the customs and arrangements of his neighbours. The arable of his holding was generally composed of a certain number of strips in proportion to the importance of his share, and these strips lay intermixed with the strips of other villagers so that every one came to own patches of land, acres and half-acres in all the "shots and furlongs of the village," as the fields were called, and had to wander about in all directions to look after his own. Such an arrangement would be the height of absurdity in any state of society where individual ownership prevails, and this point by itself would be sufficient to shew that what was meant was not a division of claims according to the simple rules of private ownership, so familiar to us, but a communal cultivation in which the arable was divided between the shareholders with as much proportionate fairness as possible. In keeping with this principle, the plan of cultivation, the reclaiming of land, the sequence of seasons for its use for wheat, barley, oats, peas, the time of its lying fallow, for setting up of hedges and their removal, the rules as to sending cattle on to the stubble, and the like, were worked out and put in practice, not by the industry of every single householder, but by the decision of the village as a whole. We may even discover traces of re-divisions, by which the shares of the householders were partitioned anew according to the standard of proportionate importance, though such instances are very exceptional and mostly connected with cases where some confusion had occurred to break up the proper relations of the holdings. If we look at the open-field system as a whole, we must insist upon the fact that the key to its arrangement lies in the principle of shareholding, every household being admitted to a certain proportion of rights according to its share in the community, and being held to corresponding duties.

The village community has, as a rule, a *demesne farm* superimposed on it, and the connexion between the two is very close and intimate. To begin with, the lord's demesne farm draws rents in money and in kind from the plots of the tenants, and it serves as a counting-house for the discharge of these rents. By the side of the counting-house stand barns and stores, where the multifarious proceeds of natural husbandry are gathered as they come in from the holdings. In some manors the dues are arranged to form a complete outfit for the consumption of the lord's household, a farm of one night, of a week, of a fortnight, as the case may be. The manors of the Abbey of Ramsey were bound to render as a fortnight's farm 12 quarters of flour, 2000 loaves of bread, 24 gallons of beer, 48 gallons of malt, 2 sesters of honey, 10 flitches of bacon, 10 rounds of cheese, 10 very best sucking pigs, 14 lambs, 14 geese, 120 chickens, 2000 eggs, 2 tubs of butter, 24 gallons of audit ale. In Lent the bacon and the cheese were struck off and money paid in their stead.

By the help of these accumulated stores, and of funds drawn from money rents and of small leases, the lord keeps a number of servants, and hires some labourers for the cultivation of the home farm, of the orchard and the arable set apart for it, as well as for looking after the buildings, the implements, etc. But the peculiar feature of the manorial arrangement consists in the fact that the demesne farm does not live independently of the village community adjoined to it, does not merely draw profits from it in the way of rents, but actually gets its labour from this village community and thereby builds up its husbandry.

The most important of these services is the *week work* performed by the peasantry. Every virgater or holder of a bovate has to send a labourer to do work on the lord's farm for about half the number of days in the week. Three days is indeed the most common standard for service of this kind, though four or even five occur sometimes, as well as two. It must be borne in mind in the case of heavy charges, such as four or five days' week work, that only one labourer from the whole holding is meant, while generally there were several men living on every holding; otherwise the service of five days would be impossible to perform. In the course of these three days, or whatever the number was, many requirements of the demesne had to be met. The principal of these was ploughing the fields belonging to the lord, and for such ploughing the peasant had not only to appear personally as a labourer, but to bring his oxen and plough or rather to join with his oxen and plough in the work imposed on the village: the heavy plough with a team of eight oxen had usually to be made up by several peasants contributing their beasts and implements towards its composition. In the same way the villagers had to go through the work of harrowing with their harrows, and of carrying the harvest in their wains and carts. Carrying duties, in carts and on horseback, were also apportioned according to the time they took as a part of the week work. Then came innumerable varieties of manual work for the erection and keeping up of hedges, the preservation of dykes, canals, and ditches, the threshing and garnering of corn, the tending and shearing of sheep and so forth. All this hand-work was reckoned according to customary standards as day work and week work. But alongside of all these services into which the regular week work of the peasantry was distributed stood some additional duties. The ploughing for the lord, for instance, was not only imposed in the shape of a certain number of days in the week, but also took the shape of a certain number of acres which the village had to plough and to sow for the lord irrespective of the amount of time it took to do so. This was sometimes termed *gafolearth*. Then again exceedingly burdensome services were required, in the seasons when farming processes are, as it were, at their height, at times of mowing and reaping when every day is of special value and the working power of the farm-hands is strained to the utmost. At that time it was the custom to call up the whole able-bodied population of the manor, with the exception of the housewives, for two, three or more days of mowing and reaping on the lord's fields. To these *boonworks* the peasantry was asked or invited by special summons, and their value was so far appreciated that the villagers were usually treated to meals in cases where they were again and again called off from their own fields to the demesne. The liberality of the lord actually went so far in exceptionally hard straits, as to serve some ale to the labourers to keep them in good humour. In this way the demesne farm throve as a kind of huge parasitical growth by drawing on the strength of the tenantry.

Let us now turn to the second constitutive element of the manor, to what we have called its social aspect in distinction to the economic and to the political aspects. From the social point of view the manor is a combination of classes, and the three main classes are to be found on its soil: the villeins, or as they are sometimes called the customary tenants, the freeholders or free tenants, and the officials and servants of the lord.

The villeins are in the majority. They come from people whose position was by no means uniform. Some of them are the offspring of slaves, some of free men who have lapsed into serfdom through crime or inability to provide the means of existence. Some claim to descend from the *ceorls* of Saxon times, a class of free peasants who were gradually crushed down to rural servitude. Be that as it may, the distinctive features of villeinage are derived from all its original sources and are blended to form a condition which is neither slavery nor self-incurred serfdom nor the subjection of free peasants to their rulers. Three main traits seem especially characteristic of manorial villeinage: the performance of rural services, the inability to claim and defend civil rights against the lord, and the recognition of villeins as free men in all matters concerning the political and criminal law of the realm. Each of these traits deserves some special notice.

The villein is primarily a man obliged to perform rural work for his lord. Every person in the medieval social scheme is bound to perform some kind of work, every one holds by some kind of service or appears as a follower of one who holds by some service. The Church holds some of her lands in return for her obligation to pray and to minister to spiritual needs. The knights and serjeants hold theirs by military service of different kinds. The burgesses and socagers hold in the main by paying rents, by rent service. The villein has to perform agricultural services to his lord. Some such agricultural services may be linked to the tenure of other classes, to the tenure of socagers, burgesses, and even military tenants, but the characteristic *week work* was primarily imposed on the villeins, and though they sometimes succeeded in getting rid of it by commuting it for money payments, these modifications of their status were considered as secondary and exceptional, and generally some traces of the original obligations of agricultural service were left: even privileged villeins had to serve their lord as reeves or rural stewards, had to send their sheep to the lord's fold, had to appear at the bidding of manorial officers to perform one or the other kind of work in the field. The villein was emphatically a man who held by the fork and the flail.

In the early days of feudalism agricultural service must have decided the fate of many people who had good claims to rank as free. In a rough way the really important distinction was this: on one side stood people who were bound to feed the rest and were therefore bound to the glebe, on the other those who were free to go wherever they pleased, provided they performed their military or ecclesiastical duties, and paid their rents. But when once the main social cleavage had taken place, the lawyers had to face a vast number of personal claims and disputes, and they gradually worked out a principle which itself became a basis for social distinctions, namely that the villein, the peasant holding by rural work, had no civil claims against his lord. It was convenient to assume that everything a villein possessed was derived from a grant of his lord and liable to be resumed by him, and though this may by no means be true in point of historical fact, it became as good as true because the king's courts declined to examine and decide civil suits of villeins against their lord. Villeins were left unprotected, and this lack of protection gave birth to a series of customary exactions quite apart from the many instances when a lord simply ill-treated the peasants. A villein had to pay a fine on the marriage of his daughter because she was considered the property of the lord, and this fine was materially increased when she married out of the lordship, as the lord lost his bond-woman and her offspring by such a marriage. On the death of a villein his heir could not enter his inheritance without surrendering a valuable horse or ox in recognition of the claims of the lord to the agricultural outfit of the holding.

As a matter of fact the civil disability of villeins did not amount to a general insecurity of their rights of possession. On the contrary, *the custom of the manor* was elaborately constant and provided for most contingencies of rural life with as much accuracy and nicety of distinction as the law administered in the royal courts. But all these provisions were merely customary rules drawn from facts; they were not binding on the lord, and in one very important respect, the amount and kind of work to be exacted from the peasant, changes and increases occasionally occurred. There was one class of the English peasantry which enjoyed a much better condition, namely the villeins on the so-called *ancient demesne* of the Crown. In manors which had belonged to the kings before the Conquest and had been granted to subjects after the Conquest, the lords had no right to oust the villagers from their holdings and to increase their services at pleasure, but were bound to follow the customs which held good at the time of the transfer of the estates from the Crown. In such manors a recourse to the rural courts was admitted and the peasants were treated as free people in regard to their tenements and services; their tenure became a species of lease or contract, though burdened with base services. This valuable privilege only emphasised with greater sharpness the rightless condition of the rest of the peasantry.

This rightlessness was, however, restricted to the relations of the villeins with their lord. In regard to all third persons and in regard to the requirements of the State they were considered to be free. This is the third marked feature of their condition. Let us remember that the slave of Roman and Saxon times was a thing, an animal at best, that he was supposed to act merely on behalf of his master, that if he committed a theft or slew somebody his master was held responsible for his crime, and that he was not admitted as a warrior to the host and did not pay any taxes to grasping fiscal authorities, though he was estimated at his worth and more than his worth when his master had to pay. All these traits of slavery gradually disappeared when slaves and ceorls were blended in the mould of villeinage. The villein was recognised as having a soul and a will of his own not only in the eyes of the Christian Church but in those of the feudal State. He could enter into agreements, and acquire property in spite of the fact that some authoritative lawyers maintained that he could acquire nothing for himself and that all he had belonged to his lord. He was set in the stocks or hanged for crimes, and the lord had to be content with the loss of his man, as he had not to pay for his felonies. Villeins were grouped in *frithborgs* or *tithings of frankpledge* in order that the peace of the realm and its police might be better enforced. They were not merely taxed by their lords and through their lords, but also had to pay hidage and geld from their own land and fifteenths and twentieths from their own chattels. Altogether the government looked upon them as its direct subjects and did not fail to impose duties on them, though it declined to protect their customary rights against the lord.

The celebrated enactments of Magna Charta as to personal security and rights of property applied primarily to *free men* and to *free tenements*, and of such there were a good many in the manor. Indeed a manor was deemed incomplete without them. Besides the knights and squires or serjeants who held of the lord by military service, there were numerous tenants who stood to him in a relation of definite agreement, paying certain fixed rents or performing certain specified services which, however burdensome, did not amount to the general obligation of rural labour incumbent on the villeins. Many were the tenants, who, without appealing to a charter or a specified agreement to prove their contractual relation to the lord, held their tenements from father to son as if there were a specific agreement between them and the lord, performing certain services and paying certain rents; and this class was the most important of all. These were the *freeholders* properly so termed or, as they were called in many ancient manors, the *sokemen*. Without going into the question of their origin and history, we must emphatically lay down the principle of their tenure in feudal society: it was *tenure by contract and therefore free*. Such was its essence, although in many, perhaps in most cases, the formation of the contract was hidden by lapse of time unto which memory does not run, and indeed hardly amounted to more than a legal presumption. The clear distinction, drawn by the Courts between tenants in a relation of contract with their lord and tenants in a relation of customary subjection, divided sharply the classes of freeholders and villeins and moulded all the details of their personal position. It was not always easy to make out in particular cases to which of the two great subdivisions a person and a holding belonged, and, as a matter of history, the process of pressing the people into the hard and fast lines of this classification was achieved by disregarding previous and more organic arrangements, but undoubtedly this distinction created a mould, which not only worked powerfully to bring some order into feudal society, but set a definite aim before the very class which was depressed by it; to obtain freedom the villeins must aspire to contractual relations with their lords.

We are now concerned with the period when these aspirations were only more or less indefinite ferments of social progress, and the legal distinction still acted as a firm rule. The freeholders sought and obtained protection for their rights in the royal courts and thereby not only acquired a privileged position in regard to holdings, dues and services, but in a sense, obtained an entirely different footing from the villein and were able to step out of the manorial arrangement, to seek their law outside it. This was undoubtedly the case, and the countless records of law suits between lords and tenants tell us of all the possibilities which such a position opened to the freeholders. But it is necessary to realise the other side of the matter, which we may be apt to disregard if we lay too much stress on the legal standing of freeholders in the King's Courts. In all that touched the life and arrangements of the village community underlying the manor, the freeholders were in scot and in lot with the township and therefore on an equal footing with the villeins. In speaking of the management of open field and waste, of the distribution of arable and meadows, of the practices of enclosure and pasture, etc., we did not make any difference between *villeins* and *freeholders*, indeed we have not even mentioned the terms. We have spoken of tenants, of members of the community, of shareholders, and now that we have learnt to fathom the deep legal chasm between the two sections of the tenantry, we still must insist on the fact that both sections were at one in regard to all the rights and duties derived from their agrarian association, appertaining to them as tillers of the soil and as *husbands* of their homes. Both sections joined to frame the by-laws and to declare the customs which ruled the life of the village and its intricate economic practices. And the freeholders had not only to take part in the management of the community but, of course, to conform to its decisions. They were not free in the sense of being able to use their plots as they liked, to manage their arable and pasture in severalty, to keep up a separate and independent husbandry. If they transgressed against the rules laid down by the community, they were liable to pay fines, to get their cattle impounded, to have their property distrained upon. Of course, the processes of customary law were greatly hampered and even modified by the fact that the freeholders had access to the royal courts, and so could challenge the verdicts of the manorial jurisdiction and the decisions of the township in the royal courts. And undoubtedly the firm footing obtained by freeholders in this respect enabled them on many occasions to thwart the petty jurisdiction of their neighbours, and to set up claims which were not in keeping with a subjection to by-laws made by the manorial community. But this clashing of definitions and attributes, though unavoidable in view of the ambiguous position of freeholders, must not prevent us from recognising the second principle of their condition as well as the first; they were not merely tenants by contract but also members of a village community and subjected to its by-laws.

After what has been said of the position of the tenants, we need not dwell very long on the standing of the lord and of his immediate helpers. The lord was a monarch in the manor, but a monarch fettered by a customary constitution and by contractual rights. He was often strong enough to break through these customs and agreements, to act in an arbitrary way, to indulge in cruelty and violence. But in the great majority of cases feelings and caprice gave way to reasonable considerations. A reasonable lord could not afford to disregard the standards of fairness and justice which were set up by immemorial custom, and a knowledge of the actual conditions of life. A mean line had to be struck between the claims of the rulers and the interests of the subjects, and along this mean line by-laws were framed and customs grew up which protected the tenantry even though it was forsaken by the king's judges. This unwritten constitution was safeguarded not only by the apprehension that its infringement might scatter the rustic population on whose labour the well-being of the lord and his retainers after all depended, but also by the necessity of keeping within bounds the power of the manorial staff of which the lord had to avail himself. This staff comprised the *stewards* and *seneschals* who had to act as overseers of the whole, to preside in the manorial courts, to keep accounts, to represent the lord on all occasions; the *reeves* who, though chosen by the villagers, acted as a kind of middlemen between them and the lord and had to take the lead in the organisation of all the rural services; the *beadles* and *radknights* or *radmen* who had to serve summonses and to carry orders; the various warders, such as the hayward, who had to superintend hedges, the woodward for pastures and wood, the sower and the thresher; the *graves* of moors and dykes who had to look after canals, ditches and drainage; the *ploughmen and herdsmen*, employed for the use of the domanial plough-teams and herds. All these *ministri* had to be kept in check by a well-advised landlord, and one of the most efficient checks on them was provided by the formation of *manorial custom*. It was in the interest of the lord himself to strengthen the customary order which prevented grasping stewards and serjeants from ruining the peasantry by extortions and arbitrary rule. This led to the great *enrolments* of custom as to holdings and services, of which many have come down to us from the twelfth, thirteenth and fourteenth centuries; they were a safeguard for the interests both of the tenants and of the lord.

The complex machinery of the manor as the centre of economic affairs and of social relations demanded by itself a suitable organisation. But besides this the manor was the local centre for purposes of police and justice; it had to enforce the king's commands and the law of the realm in its locality. It would be more correct to say that the manor and the village community or township underlying it were regarded as local centres of justice and police, because in these political matters the double aspect of the manor, the fact of its being composed of an upper and a lower half, came quite as plainly to the fore as in its economic working. Indeed, for purposes of justice, taxation, supervision of vagabonds, catching and watching thieves, keeping in order roads, and the like, the government did not recognise as the direct local unit the manor, but the *vill*, the village community or *town*, as the old English term went. The vill had to look after the formation of frankpledge, to keep ward, to watch over prisoners and to conduct them to gaol, to make presentments to justices and to appear at the sheriff's *turn*. This fact is a momentous piece of historical evidence as to the growth of manorial jurisdiction, but, apart from that, it has to be noticed as a feature of the actual administration of justice and police during the feudal period. It may be said that when the central power appealed directly to the population either for help or for responsibility, it did so through the medium not of the manors, but of the ancient towns or townships merged in them.

But there were many affairs delegated to the care of the manor, in which the central power intervened only indirectly. There was the whole domain of petty jurisdiction over villeins, as subjects of the lord, there were the numberless cases arising from agrarian transgressions and disputes, there were disputes between tenants of the same lord in regard to land held from him, there were the *franchises*, that is, the powers surrendered by special grants of the government or by immemorial encroachment of the lords in regard to tolls, market rights, the assize of bread and ale and other matters of commercial police, to the trying of thieves, poachers, and the like. In all these respects the manorial lord was called upon to act according to his standing and warranted privileges. But in no case could he act alone and by himself: he acted in his court and through his court. Originally this court, the *halimote*, the hall meeting, as we may translate the term, dealt with all sorts of affairs: it tried the cases where villeins were concerned, transacted the conveyancing business, enforced the jurisdiction of the franchises. Its suitors were freeholders and villeins alike, and if they did not always act jointly, we have at least no means of distinguishing between the different parts they played. Gradually, however, a differentiation took place, and three main types of courts came into being, the Customary Court, the Court Baron and the Court Leet; but we need not here concern ourselves with the technical distinctions involved by this differentiation of courts.

All these details have a simple and reasonable meaning when we consider them from the point of view of an all-round arrangement of each locality for the settlement of all its affairs, administrative, fiscal, jurisdictional, as well as economic and civil. This confusing variety has to be explained by the fact that, notwithstanding all strivings to make the manor complete and self-sufficient in this petty local sphere, it could not cut itself off from the general fabric of the kingdom. Through the channels which connected it with the central authorities came disturbing elements; the privileges of free tenants, the control over the use of franchises, the interference of royal courts and royal officers. All these factors rendered manorial arrangements more complex and less compact than they might otherwise have been; but, of course, these very elements insured its further development towards more perfect forms of organisation and prevented it from degenerating into despotism or into caste.

The manor is peculiarly an English institution, although it may serve to illustrate Western European society in general. Feudalism, natural husbandry, the sway of the military class, the crystallisation of powers and rights in local centres, are phenomena which took place all over Western Europe and which led in France, in Germany, in Italy and Spain to similar though not identical results. It is interesting to watch how in these bygone times and far-off customs some of the historical traits which even now divide England from its neighbours are forming themselves at the very time when the close relationship between the European countries is clearly visible. The disruption of the nation into local organisms is more complete in France and in Germany than in England, which, through the fact of the Norman Conquest and the early rise of Norman royalty and Norman aristocracy, was welded into a national whole at a period when its southern neighbours were nearly oblivious of national union. Even so, the English manor was more systematically arranged and more powerfully united than the French *Seigneurie* or the German *Grundherrschaft*. The French baron ruled in an arbitrary manner over his serfs and was almost powerless in regard to his free *vassaux*, while the German *Grundherr* had a most confusing complex of social groups to deal with, a complex more akin to the classes of England which existed on the day when King Edward the Confessor was "alive and dead" than to the England of Henry II and

Edward I. The social distinction between the military class and the rural labouring class, the natural husbandry, which dispensed to a great extent with commercial intercourse and money dealings, produced in all western countries the subjection of villeins and the super-imposition of a lord's demesne on the holdings of the working-class. But instead of assuming the form of a union between the lord's demesne and a firmly organised village community, the central economy of the lord had to deal in France with loose clusters of separate settlements, while in Germany the communal element combined with the domanial in all sorts of chance ways, which, though very advantageous in some cases, did not develop without difficulty into a firmly established and generally recognised body of rural custom.

In England things were different. There can be hardly any doubt that through the strong constitution, rooted in custom, of its manor England, in its social development, got quite as much start of its neighbours, as it obtained precedence over them politically through the early growth of parliamentary institutions.

CHAPTER XIX.

LEARNING AND LITERATURE TILL THE DEATH OF BEDE.

BOETHIUS, according to the famous phrase, is the last of the Romans. Between him and the writers who mark the highest point of the Carolingian Renaissance—one may take Einhard as a sample—three centuries intervene. It is the first part of my task to trace the paths along which the torch of learning was carried from the one height to the other.

With what equipment was the journey begun? A reader of the *Saturnalia* of Macrobius cannot fail to be impressed with the abundance and variety of the ancient literature which the literary man at the beginning of the fifth century had at his disposal—sacral, antiquarian, critical—reaching back to the days of Ennius. It may fairly be said that down to the time of Alaric's invasion the Latin literature was intact; and that long after that date, at many educational centres in Italy, Gaul, Spain, Africa, large stores of works now lost to us were preserved and used. Still, the existence of a not inconsiderable part of the literature was bound up with that of Rome: particularly that part which was specifically pagan. Of treatises like those of Veranius on the *Pontifices* or Trebatius Testa *De religionibus* there were probably few if any copies outside the public libraries of the city: no Christian would be at the pains of transcribing them; a single conflagration put an end to them for good and all. What perished during the fifth century we shall never know; but we may be sure that between the days of Macrobius and Boethius there must have been extensive losses.

The works of Boethius are not of a kind to throw much light upon the preservation of Latin literature in his time. Some are versions or adaptations of Greek sources which for the most part still exist. The greatest, the *De consolatione Philosophiae*—in external form resembling the work of an African writer of the previous century, Martianus Capella—witnesses, indeed, to the nobility of the man who wrote it: but the conditions under which it was produced (and for that matter, its whole scope) forbid us to expect from it that wealth of quotation and reference which might have characterised it, had it emanated from the home of Boethius and not from his prison[1].

Among the contemporaries of Boethius there is one, Cassiodorus, of whose literary resources we can form a more precise estimate. It is

---

[1] This statement is not meant to exclude the possibility of the indebtedness of Boethius to earlier writers in the general lines or even in the subject-matter of his work.

Cassiodorus, moreover, whom we must regard as the greatest individual contributor to the preservation of learning in the West. His long life (*c.* 490—583) was enormously effective, both for his own time and for ours. What made it so effective was his conviction that there ought to be an educated clergy. We have seen (I. 570) that in 535-6, under Pope Agapetus, he attempted to found a Christian academy in Rome, avowedly in imitation of those which had existed at Alexandria and Antioch and that which was still active at Nisibis. Failing in this project, he turned to another, which, more modest in its conception, was in reality destined to attain a success far wider, probably, than would have attended the other. The library[1] which he founded for his monks at Squillace (Vivarium, the Calabrian monastery to which he retired about 540), and the handbooks which he compiled for them to serve as a key thereto (*De Institutione Divinarum Litterarum*, and *De Artibus et Disciplinis Liberalium Litterarum*), served to organise the literary side of monastic life. But for the existence of such a sanction for literary culture, it is quite possible that, with the exception of Virgil, no Latin classic would have reached us in a complete form. Not that Cassiodorus specially commends to his monks the study of *belles lettres* or of antiquity for their own sake; such matters are (and this is true of the whole period after Boethius) ancillary to the study of the Bible.

The Bible, therefore, occupies the forefront. There must be, in the first place, examination and comparison of the older versions, both Greek and Latin; and the purest possible text of the standard version, that of Jerome, must be secured. Of the textual labours of Cassiodorus the greatest remaining monument is the *Codex Amiatinus*; the story of its journey from England to Italy in the seventh century is a striking reminder of the wide range of influence which he obtained[2]. Further research is needed to place us in a position to gauge with certainty the extent to which his labours can be traced in the text of the Vulgate Gospels. Upon the fixing of the text of the sacred books follows the ascertaining of their meaning. A valuable companion to the books was provided by Cassiodorus in the shape of a Latin version of the *Antiquities* of Josephus, made at his instigation but not by his own hand. His personal contribution consisted of a voluminous commentary on the

[1] In this connexion the theory put forth in 1911 by the late Dr Rudolf Beer is of surpassing interest. On the evidence of the lists of authors named or used by Cassiodorus, coupled with the old catalogues and extant remains of the Library of Bobbio (founded in 612 by St Columban), he makes it appear probable that there was a great transference of books from Vivarium to Bobbio. Thus the famous palimpsests of which Mai revealed the contents to an astonished world in the early years of the nineteenth century are nothing less than the remnants of the treasure accumulated by Cassiodorus himself.

[2] It is worth mention that quite recently a leaf of a second Cassiodorian Bible has been recovered in the north of England, and other leaves are in private possession.

Psalms, and a more valuable, though incomplete, version of Clement of Alexandria's notes on the Catholic Epistles. His library contained all the best Latin expositors of the fourth and fifth centuries.

His anxiety for the faithful presentation of the Biblical text finds expression in the stress he lays upon "orthography," a term which includes a great deal of what we should call grammar: he recommends the use of a number of older writers on the subject, and his own latest work was devoted to it. Incidentally he speaks of the utility of certain geographical books in connexion with sacred study, and of the Church histories of the fifth-century Greek writers, Socrates, Sozomen, and Theodoret, which he had induced one Epiphanius to render into Latin; we know this translation as the *Historia Tripartita*.

The end of the first division of the *Institutions* deals with the practically useful arts of agriculture (gardening) and medicine. The second part is a summary introduction to the seven Liberal Arts—they are the same for Cassiodorus as for Martianus Capella—Grammar, Rhetoric, Dialectic, Arithmetic, Music, Geometry, Astronomy. The bibliography is here much scantier than in the first book, but even so, some works are named and used which we no longer have. We do not, as was said above, find our author definitely prescribing for his monks the study of the older poets and historians. What we do find is a recognition of the usefulness of secular as well as of sacred learning, an authorisation of the enlargement of the field, an encouragement to make use of all that could be drawn from sources that might subsequently be opened, as well as from those that were at hand.

Thus Cassiodorus did his best to provide tools and to indicate the method of using them. An older contemporary had prepared the workmen and the field. There is no need to recapitulate here what has already been said (I. 537 sqq.) of St Benedict and his Rule. Only it is clear that, but for his work, that of Cassiodorus would not have outlasted more than a few generations. The Rule was, it seems likely, in force at Vivarium itself; but whether this was so or not, and whether or not St Benedict would have accorded a welcome to the scheme of study outlined by Cassiodorus, the fact remains that the ideas of the latter were taken up by the Order and were propagated with more or less activity wherever the Order settled.

There was a third agent in this same century who was a factor of immense importance (though, even more clearly than Benedict, an involuntary factor) in the preservation of ancient learning. This was St Gregory the Great (†604). Gregory was not a "learned" writer. He knew (he says) no Greek: it is doubtful if his writings have been the means of handing down a single reference to an ancient author,—even to a Christian author of the earliest period. His contempt for secular studies is more than once expressed; he is even credited (by John of Salisbury, in the twelfth century) with having burned the library of the

Palatine Apollo. Yet, but for Gregory and his mission of Augustine, there would have been no Aldhelm, no Benedict Biscop, no Bede, no Alcuin, no opening for the enormously important influence of Theodore of Tarsus and of Hadrian the Abbot.

But, this great service apart, his voluminous works were, if not in themselves of great literary value, the progenitors of literature which is of the highest interest. Alfred translated his *Pastoral Care*; Aelfric drew copiously from his *Homilies* on the gospels. His *Moralia* on Job gave occupation to calligraphers and excerptors in Spain and Ireland. Above all, his four books of *Dialogues* formed a model for subsequent writers of the lives of saints as well as a sanction for that mass of miracle and vision literature in which so much of the imaginations and hopes of the medieval peoples is preserved for us.

Thus in the persons of Cassiodorus, Benedict, and Gregory, Italy, which had provided the world with a great literature, furnished also the means by which that literature was to be preserved. It was her last contribution to the cause of learning for many years.

We must turn to the other great fields of western learning, and first to Africa and Spain.

The existence of a flourishing Latin literature in Africa is generally realised : the names of Tertullian, Apuleius, Cyprian, Augustine, Martianus Capella stand out as representative in earlier centuries; something too has been said (i. 322) of the less-known writers of the period of the Vandal kingdom, of Dracontius, almost the last of Christian poets to treat of mythological subjects, and of those (Luxorius and others) whose fugitive pieces have been preserved in the Latin anthology of the *Codex Salmasianus*. We come now to their successors. From Verecundus, Bishop of Junca (†552), we have an exposition of certain Old Testament canticles which are commonly attached to the Psalter and used in the Church services. In this work Verecundus refers his reader to the Natural History of Pliny the Elder, to Solinus, and to a form of the famous *Physiologus*, that manual of allegorised natural history which in later times afforded a multitude of subjects to illuminators and sculptors. From this region and period also comes in all probability a poem on the Resurrection of the Dead and the Last Judgment, dedicated to Flavius Felix (an official to whom some poems in the Salmasian Anthology are addressed). It has been handed down under the names of Tertullian and of Cyprian. Both attributions are out of the question. The author, whoever he was, had written other poems, notably one on the four seasons of the year, to which he alludes. In the resurrection-poem a singular point of interest is that it shews traces of obligation to the ancient *Apocalypse of Peter*.

The two epics of Fl. Cresconius Corippus, the *Johannis*, produced about 550, and the *De laudibus Justini* (*minoris*), of sixteen years later, are from the purely literary point of view the most remarkable achievements of African culture in the sixth century. The first tells the story of the successful campaign of Johannes the *magister militum* against the Moors in 546-8. The other, essentially a court-poem, describes the accession of Justin and the rejoicings and festivities which accompanied it. In both, but especially in the *Johannis*, Corippus has modelled himself upon the antique with extraordinary fidelity, and with undeniable success.

One other production, of small extent but appreciable importance, needs to be noticed before we pass from Africa to Spain. This is a short continuation (extending to but twelve sections) of the catalogue of distinguished Church writers, which, begun by Jerome, perhaps on a model furnished by Suetonius, was continued by Gennadius of Marseilles. An African writer of about 550—it is thought, Pontianus, a bishop—furnished this small supplement. In the next century we shall find Isidore of Seville and his friend Braulio carrying on the work, and, a generation later, Hildefonsus of Toledo, whose outlook is almost confined to his own country. The succession is then broken off, and it is not until the twelfth century that similar compilations again come into fashion.

The extinction of the Vandal kingdom in Africa meant the transference of much literary activity to Spain. There must have been many like the monk Donatus, of whom Hildefonsus tells us that, seeing the imminence of the barbarian invasion, he took ship for Spain with about seventy monks and a large collection of books. Certain it is that towards the end of the sixth century Africa becomes silent, and Spain begins to speak.

Perhaps the first writer in our period whose sphere of influence was Spanish—though it was so by adoption only—is Martin, called of Dumio and of Bracara (Braga), the latter being the see of which he died archbishop in 580. Like the great Martin of Tours he was a Pannonian by birth : but after a pilgrimage to Palestine he chose Galicia and the Arian kingdom of the Suevi as a field for missionary work. He was successful in bringing the Suevi to orthodoxy ; and he seems to have been a man of both strong and attractive personality. There is a distinction about his not very voluminous works. Two of them at least are excerpts from writings of Seneca, the *De officiis* and *De ira*. The first treats of the four Cardinal Virtues, and is addressed to King Miro under the title of *Formula honestae vitae*. It is by far the most widely diffused of Martin's books. The other (which incidentally helps to fill a lacuna in the text of Seneca) is of comparatively rare occurrence. Besides these we have ethical tracts of more definitely Christian complexion, also dedicated to Miro, principally concerned with pride and humility. A collection of sayings of the hermits, and another of conciliar canons, testify to Martin's knowledge of Greek. A brief discourse on the Paschal question states a complicated problem in a strikingly clear form. But of all that we have from him, Martin's instruction for simple people

(*De correctione rusticorum*), addressed to Polemius, Bishop of Asturica, has aroused the greatest interest in modern times. It is indeed a very notable example of the way in which the negative and positive sides of Christian teaching were put before the neophytes of the country districts. Martin begins by setting forth the view of his time as to the origin of the heathen gods. They are devils who fell with Lucifer : therefore all observances which entail any show of reverence towards them are so many denials of the profession of faith made at baptism. He objects— vainly, as time has shewn—to the ordinary names of the days of the week, and to the celebration of the first of January as New Year's day; and further, to the observing of " days of moths and mice " (the object of which was to protect clothes and storerooms from their ravages), to the naming of Minerva over the web on the loom, the lighting of tapers by rocks and springs, and many like usages, which we meet with later in canons of councils and *indiculi superstitionum* : while over and over again the question is asked, " Is this consistent with your promise at the font to renounce the devil and all his works ? " Of the positive side of the teaching more need not be said than that it is admirably adapted to its purpose. It is interesting to find that nearly the whole of the matter recurs in a Homily of Caesarius of Arles († 542), as well as in a tract of the Irish missionary Pirminius of Reichenau (†758), called *Scarapsus*, and in the sermon of St Eligius of Noyon which his biographer St Audoen has either preserved or excogitated. This suggests a question whether Caesarius or Martin is the original source, or whether both may not be utilising a form agreed upon perhaps by a synodical authority.

Let it be recorded, lastly, that Martin of Bracara held in reverence his namesake and fellow-countryman, the saint of Tours, and composed some interesting verses which were inscribed over the south door of the great basilica there.

Before the death of Martin, the life of Isidore of Seville (*c.* 570–636) had begun. He was beyond question the leading transmitter of knowledge in his century. In the twenty books of his *Etymologiae* he brought together a collection of facts (and fictions) which served as the encyclo- paedia of the whole medieval period. It was long in his hands : his friend Braulio of Saragossa could only extract a copy of it, and that in an uncorrected form, by repeated pleadings extending over more than seven years. He seems to have been at work on it up to his death, and it is obviously unfinished. There is neither preface nor peroration ; some sections are unwritten, many references not filled in.

To us its great merit is that it has preserved a number of fragments of early Latin writers : but to many a generation after Isidore its practical utility was immense. It was by far the handiest—and in most cases the only accessible—book in which information about natural history, geography, antiquities, the origins of arts and sciences, could be found, whereas the outlines of the seven liberal arts (which occupy the first three books), the synopsis of history, the elements of religious knowledge, the legal and medical sections, useful as they were, could usually be studied in less compendious form.   In the compilation of the *Etymologiae* a library of very considerable extent was laid under contribution.   Much is derived, no doubt, from hand-books: it is not to be supposed that Isidore possessed the works of an Ennius, a Cinna, a Livius Andronicus, all of whom he cites.   These passages lay ready to his hand in the form of excerpts in various grammatical and critical books, especially in the commentary of Servius on the *Aeneid*.   But, when due allowance has been made for the use of compilations, it is apparent that the range of authors with whom he had a first-hand acquaintance is not despicable.   Lucretius, often cited in the later books (though of course seldom in comparison with Lucan and Virgil), was known to him.   The *Histories* of Sallust and the *Pratum* (and some minor works) of Suetonius are probably the most important of the lost secular works (excluding manuals of rhetoric and grammar) which he can be shewn to have used.   From the *De Republica* of Cicero he makes but one short citation.   It is not apparent that he possessed any specimen of the earliest Christian literature which we do not possess: in his continuation of the literary biographies of Jerome and Gennadius he tells us of many theological writers in his own time who are no more than names to us.

His knowledge of Greek has been doubted, and, I think, with reason.   The evidence for it is almost confined to citations of Greek words to furnish etymologies.   It cannot be shewn that he either owned Greek books or translated from Greek authors for the purpose of his work.

Had he lived long enough to provide the *Etymologiae* with its prologue, it is likely enough that after the manner of the elder Pliny he would have given us the list of the authors on whom he had drawn. As it is, we have to base our estimate of the extent of his library upon a document which leaves a good deal to the imagination.   We have the verses which were painted (probably) on the cornices or doors of his book-presses.   Each of these cupboards, in accordance with a fashion attested by a good deal of archaeological evidence, seems to have been ornamented with a medallion portrait of a famous author, whose worth was celebrated in one or more elegiac couplets.   The number of sections or *tituli* warrants us in reckoning that Isidore owned at least fourteen and perhaps sixteen presses, and we shall be safe in assuming that at this date the contents were in book-form (*codices*) and not rolls (*volumina*). Taking the number of books in each press at 30—not an unreasonable estimate—we reach the very respectable total of 420 or 480 for the whole collection.   As to the contents, the *tituli* suggest that theology predominated.   The secular writers named are few (jurists and physicians) and there is nothing to suggest the presence of works now lost.   That is no more than natural; the effigy on the book-case represents but a fraction of its contents.

Among the remaining writings of Isidore the books *De naturis rerum* and the histories merit special mention. The first is a survey of cosmical phenomena in which, besides extant sources, the *Pratum* of Suetonius is employed (as in the *Etymologiae*). The popular name of the treatise, *Liber rotarum*, is derived from the many circular diagrams with which it was illustrated. In some connexion with it stands an interesting little poem by the Visigoth king Sisebut (612–620) who had asked Isidore to write the treatise, and addressed the poem—chiefly dealing with eclipses—to him, very likely upon receiving the complete book. It is possible that the poem as we have it is but a fragment of a larger work. Sisebut was, we see, a patron of letters and may have been a copious writer, but all that we have from him, besides the poem, is a life of St Desiderius of Vienne, and a few epistles.

Of Isidore's two historical works the first is a Chronicle of the world, divided, in a fashion subsequently adopted and popularised by Bede, into six ages. A brief summary of it is inserted into the fifth book of the *Etymologiae*. For the more recent portions of it the Chronicles of Idatius, of Victor of Tonnensia in Africa, and of John of Biclarum (the last a Spanish contemporary of Isidore himself) have been utilised. The other is a sketch of the history of the Visigoths, Vandals, and Suevi. His commentaries and religious works (with the possible exception of the *Synonyma*, the idea of which he says was suggested to him by a treatise of Cicero) are not important to our present subject.

Isidore's principal friend, Braulio of Saragossa, has left us little besides letters and a few short biographies in the book *De viris illustribus*. He had, however, among his clergy one who ranks as the one considerable Spanish Latin poet of the century. This was Eugenius, who in 647, in spite of Braulio's fervent protests, was removed by King Chindaswinth to preside over the see of Toledo. Chindaswinth, like Sisebut, evidently had some feeling for literature: we find him ordering Eugenius to produce a readable and orthodox edition of the poems of the Arian Dracontius, which were then only current in Spain in a mutilated form. The edition was made, and attained a wide celebrity. Of the works which it comprised, the *Laudes Dei* were turned into a *Hexaëmeron* and somewhat shortened; the *Satisfactio* was abridged and provided with prefaces in prose and verse, and a conclusion: instead of Gunthamund, Theodosius the younger was made to figure as the recipient.

We have, besides this, an original work of Eugenius, which is the metrical portion of a collection of his miscellaneous short writings. The prose half is lost. The poems, in many metres, are for the most part brief. They deal with all manner of subjects, religious and secular. Intrinsically they perhaps hardly deserve mention, but there is a notable fact about them, that they travelled far beyond Spain at an early date.

Aldhelm uses them in the collection of riddles which he embodied in a grammatical tract addressed to "Acircius"[1] (Aldfrid of Northumbria) before the end of the seventh century. Eugenius died in 657.

A pupil of his, who ultimately succeeded to his see (680–690), Julian of Toledo, left works upon theology, history, and grammar. In the first category the book called *Prognosticon futuri saeculi* was by far the most celebrated. The three divisions of which it consists—on death, on the intermediate state of souls and on the final judgment—are made up to a very large extent of "testimonies" from Scripture and from standard writers. Cyprian and Origen are the earliest of these, and Gregory the latest. Augustine is naturally the principal source; Jerome, Cassian, and Julianus Pomerius complete the list. It was to be expected that in a country in which Priscillianism had had great currency, and roused great opposition to the apocryphal literature, Julian should shun all reference to these writings. As his interesting prefatory letter tells us, his main object was to present in a collected form the opinions of Catholic doctors upon the subject he was treating.

The three books *De comprobatione sextae aetatis*, directed against his own countrymen (he was of Jewish extraction), are interesting as proving his acquaintance with Greek patristic literature. He translates passages from the *Demonstratio Evangelica* of Eusebius and from the tract of Epiphanius on Weights and Measures; and, besides these, he makes considerable quotations from Tertullian. The two books of ἀντικείμενα (a noteworthy title) consist of attempts to reconcile contradictory texts of Scripture: they contain no very remarkable citations.

Of more direct interest to us is his history of the rebellion of Duke Paul against King Wamba (673), written in a less conventional style at no great length of time after the events it records. The fashion of writing in rhymed or assonant clauses which is conspicuous in the later chronicles, *e.g.* that called of "Isidorus Pacensis," appears here possibly for the first time to a marked extent.

The fame of this book was naturally confined to Spain. Not so that of the *Ars grammatica*. Both in form and in contents it is remarkable. The form is that of a dialogue between master and pupil; but, as in many later grammars, it is the pupil who puts the questions, the master who answers them. Traube's explanation of this fashion is interesting: he attributes it to a misapprehension. The dialogue form was borrowed from the Greeks, and with it the initials M and Δ, which stood for μαθητής and διδάσκαλος. The accident that the Latin words *Magister* and *Discipulus* have the same initials rendered the inversion of questioner and answerer an easy one.

In respect of its contents, the *Ars Juliani* transmits much matter from older grammarians, Victorinus and Audax, for example. The

---

[1] The *a circio* of the dedication, says Mazzoni (in *Didascaleion* 1914), probably means "(to the ruler of) north-western (Northumbria)."

illustrative quotations are drawn from secular and Christian poets; even authorities contemporary with the writer, as Eugenius of Toledo, are cited. If it be the fact that the grammar was extensively used by Aldhelm within a very short time after its composition, it may be during the lifetime of Julian, we have a striking tribute to the reputation it enjoyed, and a yet more striking evidence of a literary commerce between Spain and Britain: a commerce of which the traces, liturgical and other, have yet to be collected and appreciated.

In liturgy, lastly, important reforms of the Toletan Use are attributed to Julian by his biographer Felix. But details are wanting. In the range of his activity, but not in the permanence of his achievement, Julian surpasses Isidore.

An obscure but interesting figure at this period is the Abbot St Valerius († 695) from whom we have some amusing autobiographical writings. Whether by his own fault, or, as he would have us believe, by that of his neighbours, Valerius was condemned to a very turbulent existence. He was continually being hounded out of some retreat in which he had settled, deceived by his favourite pupils, robbed of his books, and generally victimised. There is a personal note in his narratives which engages the attention. They also supply us with evidence of the existence of at least one rare book in the writer's *milieu*. In one of several visions of the next world which he records is an image which cannot but be derived from a certain Apocalypse of Baruch, now extant only in Greek and Old Slavonic. The seer, a youth named Baldarius, is permitted to watch the rising of the sun from close by. The orb comes up very swiftly and immensely bright; and it is preceded by a huge bird, red in colour but darker towards the tail, whose function is to mitigate the intense heat of the sun by flapping its wings. The bird is the Phoenix, as we learn from *Baruch*, and, so far as is known at present, this particular fable is peculiar to *Baruch*. It is fair to infer the survival of this rare Apocalypse in Spain in the seventh century: whether or not under Priscillianist influence, *non liquet*.

The chain of Spanish writers has now been traced down to the end of the seventh century, and we have seen evidence of the preservation of considerable collections of ancient literature, both pagan and Christian, in the peninsula. Much of this must have had a continuous existence in the country, but much also must have been imported from Africa under the stress of invasion. That same stress now fell upon Spain. The Moorish invasion, culminating in the great defeat of the Christian arms in 711, put an end to literary enterprise for the time. Spain dropped out of the race. But she had made one great contribution to the equipment of European scholarship in the *Etymologiae* of Isidore.

What is the record of the region which we now call France during the corresponding period? The educational apparatus with which she was provided at the beginning of it was as complete as any country could shew. The works of an Alcimus Avitus and of a Sidonius Apollinaris, however exiguous their intrinsic value, are the last links in an unbroken chain reaching back to the rise of the great schools of Gaul. After them comes the break.

The sixth century produced two writers of note who mark it in different ways. Venantius Fortunatus, born in Italy, it is true, but for the best part of his life a resident at Poitiers, is known to the generality as the author of two hymns, the *Pange lingua* on the Cross, the *Vexilla regis* used on Passion Sunday. We have from him, however, a very large mass of poetry besides these. His Life of St Martin of Tours in four books of heroic verse is for the most part merely a paraphrase of the prose Life and Dialogues of Sulpicius Severus. But his eleven books of miscellaneous pieces are full of originality and human interest. They form a chronicle of his friendly relations with the widowed queen of Chlotar I, St Radegund, and others of that house, as well as with Gregory of Tours and many prominent churchmen of France. A considerable number of the poems were sent as letters—thanks for presents and the like. Others are panegyrics, others descriptions of pleasant places: yet others are inscriptions designed for churches, such as commonly form a large ingredient in collections of Christian Latin verse. The best, however, and those from which we gain the most kindly impression of the personality of Fortunatus, are those which were called forth by the deaths of the friends and kindred of Radegund. These are uniformly entitled *Epitaphs*, but their length forbids us to suppose that they can have been inscribed on tombs. They may have been recited; but their real purpose is that of the *Consolationes* of an earlier time. They were meant to be circulated in writing among those whom the death had touched most nearly. These, with his hymns, constitute the best claim of Fortunatus to be remembered as a writer. Yet his skill in handling light verse should not pass unmentioned. His abuse of the river Gers (Egircio, I. 21) and of the cook who appropriated his boat at Metz (VI. 8) are quite worth reading.

Upon the whole the notable thing about Fortunatus is his avoidance of what was becoming a pseudo-classical vein. The form of his poems is old (the elegiac metre predominates), and rococo ornaments in the shape of allusions to mythology are not wanting; but we are impressed by the absence of artificiality, and by the presence of a freshness and simplicity which we miss in Sidonius and Avitus. The poems prepare us for a new epoch, while they have not lost touch with the old.

Of Gregory of Tours († 594), the other famous writer of this century and country, it may be said with more truth that he *had* lost touch with the old. That is, at any rate, his own opinion. A well-known passage in the Prologue to his *History of the Franks* represents his contemporaries as saying, " Alas for our days! for the study of letters is gone from among us." He is, moreover, given to apologising on his own account for his "rustic" and incorrect style. This, to be sure, is a common pose, and it has been held that in Gregory's case it is but a pose, and that the copyists of his works are responsible for many of the *monstra* we encounter in them. Yet can this be so? does not the particularity with which he specifies mistakes—false concords, misuse of prepositions and of cases—go to shew that he at least was in earnest? Certainly his self-accusations are borne out by every page of his writings. He had read some good authors, in particular Virgil; he knew some books which no longer exist. In a little tract which deals mainly with astronomy he shews considerable acquaintance with that science, and quotes a lost chronicler, Julius Titianus. He had, too, a collection of Latin lyric poetry, which he lent to his friend Fortunatus. And it is possible (though not very relevant to our present purpose) that he knew some Syriac: a Syrian (there were not a few then resident in France, and one became bishop of Paris) helped him to translate the legend of the Seven Sleepers from Syriac into Latin. This, however, is little more than a curiosity: Gregory certainly made no use of Syriac literature. His lament is undoubtedly justified: "Periit studium litterarum a nobis." The gulf between him and Fortunatus, in respect of command of correct Latin, is immense.

To dwell upon the value of the *Historia Francorum* would be quite out of place here, where we are thinking of Gregory as a link in the transmission of ancient knowledge. It is more relevant to suggest in passing a comparison between this and the next national history that was written—that of Bede; for the slight work of Isidore hardly comes into consideration. In Gregory we see letters on a level confessedly low; in Bede a height has been reached which is rivalled only, in these centuries, by the best work of the Carolingian Renaissance.

The popularity of Gregory's *History* in medieval times was far inferior to that of his hagiological writings, which furnished much material to the compilers of breviaries and to such writers as Jacobus de Voragine. Besides the seven which he himself enumerates, dealing with St Julian of Le Mans, St Martin of Tours, the Martyrs, the Confessors, and the Anchorites, there is one—the *Miracles of St Andrew*—which may be confidently assigned to him, and which is perhaps more important than any of the others to the historian of Christian literature. It is our best source for the knowledge of a second or third century Greek romance, the *Acts of Andrew*; once eagerly read, but ultimately condemned by the Church, and only transmitted to us in fragments, and expurgated epitomes, such as this of Gregory. Not that Gregory read it in Greek. He had before him, no doubt, a complete Latin version, made, it is likely, for Manichaeans to read: since, in Manichaean circles, the apocryphal romances about the Apostles were adopted as substitutes for the Canonical Acts. Not long after Gregory's date—it may be even in his lifetime—a complete orthodox collection of abstracts of these Acts, with others added to them, was put together, probably in France, in which the *Miracles of Andrew* were incorporated. We know it under the misleading name of the *Apostolic History of Abdias*. The investigation of its origin, and the determination of its text, have not as yet been completely carried out. As a source of inspiration for artists and romancers it deserves (though it does not usually obtain) a special recognition among the literary documents of its time.

I shall be pardoned for passing over the feeble efforts of the continuators of Gregory's *History* (the so-called Fredegarius and the rest) in favour of two writings which attest at once the survival of a knowledge of Greek in France and an extremely low standard of culture. The one is known as the *Barbarus Scaligeri* (from its style and its first editor). It is a Chronicle of the world, rendered from an almost contemporary Greek original in a fashion and in a Latin of which it is difficult to exaggerate the badness. The other is a very similar version, made by the aid of a glossary, of the *Phaenomena* of Aratus, and of a Commentary thereon. It can be dated by the fact that Isidore is used in it, and that Bede uses it. Did we not possess the Greek original of this extraordinary work, many passages of it would defy interpretation. The literalness is extreme: Ἀράτου Φαινόμενα appears as *Arati ea quae videntur*. This we might perhaps unravel, but we should be more than ready to suspect corruption in the phrase "*in quo apud Diodorum*" which is the rendering of ἐν τῷ πρὸς Διόδωρον, or in this "*nihil aliud quorum Eudoxi videntur facere*," which is the equivalent of μηδὲν ἕτερον τῶν Εὐδόξου φαινομένων ποιήσαντα. Nevertheless, absurd as is the interpreter's achievement, his very attempt is creditable and interesting. We have no clue to the identity of the man who made it, nor to the part of France in which he lived.

It has been transmitted to us in more than one copy, as well as in a revised form due to a scholar of the Carolingian period. The *Barbarus* of Scaliger survives in but one manuscript, which is not impossibly the autograph of the translator.

There is another writer, of southern France, who is the centre of an unsolved problem—Virgilius Maro Grammaticus. That he must be reckoned to France seems now to be the accepted view, though the evidence at command is scanty. An obscure phrase in which he says that he will set forth "*bigerro sermone*" the letters of the alphabet, is taken to contain the name which survives as Bigorre, and to point to the south-west of France: a plainer indication is his reference to the Gauls as "*nostri*." Importance is also rightly attached to the fact that Abbo of St Germain in the tenth century calls him *Tolosanus*. That he was a Christian, and a Catholic—not an Arian—may be regarded as certain. But, though he gives us a great many other details about himself, his teachers, and his contemporaries, hardly one of them can be taken seriously.

Upon a first reading of his works (they are wholly devoted to grammatical subjects, and consist of two series of *Epitomae* and *Epistles*) the reader feels that he is confronted with a piece of pure mystification.   A striking, but yet fairly typical example of the extravagances we encounter is the passage in which he describes, on the authority of a certain Virgil of Asia, the " twelve Latinities."   The first of these is the *usitata*, that in which (ordinary) Latin writings are " inked " (*atramentantur*).   Of the eleven others, ten, it is safe to say, have never been used either by Virgilius or anyone else.   The second, called *assena* or *notaria*, may possibly be intended to mean the Tironian notes ; it employs a single letter for a whole word.   But the *lumbrosa*, which expands a single word into four or five, the *sincolla*, which condenses a whole line into two syllables, and the rest of the series, correspond to nothing in heaven or earth[1].

Not only is the vocabulary of Virgilius abnormal ; the authors whom he cites have left no trace anywhere else.   There is a Cicero, and a Horace ; there are three Virgils and three Lucans, and so on : but none of them are identical with those known to fame.   There are, too, numerous grammarians, of whom Aeneas, Galbungus, and Terrentius are among the most prominent ; but what is told of them does not carry conviction to the mind.   Galbungus and Terrentius disputed for fourteen consecutive days and nights as to whether *ego* had a vocative. Regulus of Cappadocia and Sedulius of Rome went without food and sleep for a similar period while they were discussing the inchoative and frequentative forms of the verb : three soldiers in the employ of each were in attendance ready to arbitrate by force of arms if required.

In all, some ninety writers and teachers are named or quoted.   Do they correspond to anything that ever existed ?   Of late a suggestion has found favour that they represent an academy which had its headquarters at Toulouse, and that the great names of Cicero, Lucan, Virgil and so on, were adopted by its members, just as Charlemagne and his friends called themselves David, Homer, Flaccus, and Naso.   Perhaps, it is added, the Carolingian fashion was a conscious imitation of the Tolosan.   If this be the truth of the matter, it is surely very strange that while we do hear of Virgilius himself before the end of the seventh century, no single trace of any of his " authorities " has ever been pointed out.   Moreover, he claims a high antiquity and a wide range of influence for his school of thought : he traces his writers back to the time of Romulus, nay, even to the days before the Flood.   Some of them lived at Troy, others in Egypt, Arabia, India.   The variety, again, of books which he quotes is large ; there are poems, histories, epistles, orations, as well as works on grammar ; far too many—supposing them to be

---

[1] A notion recently broached that Arabic influence is discernible in his nomenclature of metres (and numerals) has yet to be sifted.

real—to have disappeared without leaving some sign. In short, the complete isolation of Virgilius compared with his pretensions enforces the belief that his authorities like his Latinities are from first to last impositions pure and simple. Such imposition—I allude to the invention of authorities—was an expedient not unknown to the world of grammarians and scholiasts. The tract of the African Fulgentius (cent. vi.) *De dubiis nominibus* contains, side by side with genuine passages from Plautus and other early writers, quotations which, it is agreed, are fabrications of Fulgentius's own. A scholiast on the *Ibis* of Ovid helps himself over the difficulties of the poem (and they are many) by explanatory tags which he fathers upon Propertius, Lucretius, Homer, Callimachus, etc., etc. The procedure in both cases is not easily distinguishable from that of Virgilius.

It is curious to find that in spite of all this he was taken seriously. Not only does Aldhelm († 709) quote him, but also Bede, a man less likely to be attracted by eccentricity, and so do almost all the Irish grammarians of the Carolingian period—a point which will demand further attention. To the later Middle Ages he was quite unknown; we have no manuscripts or quotations after the eleventh century[1].

We have not yet approached the question of the date at which he lived. Zimmer in an elaborate investigation (published posthumously) contends for the fifth to sixth centuries. His main thesis is that western Gaul had, both commercially and intellectually, a profound influence upon Ireland long before the age of Patrick. He seeks to shew, in particular, that the grammatical theories of Virgilius affected the language and methods of Irish writers. He finds traces of them in the *Amra* or panegyric on St Columba († 597), that obscure Irish poem by Dallan Forgaill, of which we have but a series of enigmatical fragments glossed by successive commentators. He believes that he has found actual mention of Virgilius in Irish books under the name of *Ferchertne file*; and he lays stress on the undoubted fact that our manuscript authorities for the text of Virgilius shew traces of transmission through Irish channels. The text, long preserved in Ireland, he would suggest, passed to the Continent in the train of the Irish missionaries. To our grammarian, too, he would refer the epigrams in which Ennodius (473–521) ridicules "a certain foolish man who was known as Virgilius."

Clearly much of this argument is inappreciable by those ignorant of Celtic languages. To the general contention one objection has been urged which makes its appeal to a wider circle, and which, if upheld, must do away with the greater part of Zimmer's hypothesis. It is that Virgilius makes use of the *Etymologies* of Isidore of Seville († 636). If so, he takes his place in the seventh century, after Isidore and before Aldhelm. An examination of the long list of passages cited by Manitius from the *Etymologies*, and supposed by him to have been

---

[1] An abridged text of 1465 in a Bodleian MS. (D'Orville 147) is an exception.

CH. XIX.

borrowed thence by Virgilius, has failed to convince me that Virgilius, and not Isidore, is the borrower. Practically all the passages contain derivations of words (*legitera = littera* and the like). They are thoroughly germane to the manner of Virgilius; nor is it a consideration of any weight that Isidore nowhere names Virgilius as his source, for in this respect his practice is by no means consistent. In short, though it may be shewn on other grounds that Zimmer has placed Virgilius too early, I cannot think that his theory is invalidated by the appeal to Isidore; and I feel justified in provisionally adopting his date.

Ireland has been named, and will for a time engage our whole attention; but before we leave France and Virgilius, a word must be said of a book which has perhaps a claim to be regarded as a product of his school. At least it reminds us of him by its language and by its solemn absurdity. The work in question is the *Cosmography* of "Aethicus Ister." I use inverted commas because it is not certain that the form "Aethicus" is what was intended by the author of the text, who may have meant to write "Ethicus" and have used that word as a synonym for "philosopher." The *Cosmography* comes to us in the shape of an abstract or series of extracts from a larger work, purporting to have been made by St Jerome (or at least by a "Hieronymus presbyter"). In spite of the efforts of Wuttke to uphold this attribution and to identify the places and peoples who are mentioned, it is not possible to regard Aethicus as anything but a romancer or to put him earlier than the seventh century. His wild Latin, full of *hapax legomena*, elaborate alliteration and short assonant clauses, his fables about countries, tribes, and creatures, partly borrowed from Solinus and the Alexander-romances, but largely peculiar to himself, and his display of absurd learning (exemplified by the bogus Scythian alphabet with which he ends his book), all stamp him as a charlatan. He probably wrote in France: it seems that the first writer who quotes him is Frankish—one of the continuators of the chronicler who is called Fredegarius.

At the same time, it would be no surprise to learn that he had Irish connexions. Indeed, definite allusions to Ireland have been pointed out in his writings and in those of Virgilius. Aethicus represents himself as having crossed from Spain to Ireland, and having studied the books (*eorum volumina volvens*) which he found there (a phrase which may reasonably be taken to imply that Ireland enjoyed a reputation for culture in his time)[1]. The two passages adduced from Virgilius are both of doubtful import. One says that in the composition and elocution of the....the verb holds the first place. The statement is true of Irish, and the word represented by dots is given in the manuscripts as *hi bonorum, hiborum, in iborum*, respectively. The conjecture *Hibernorum* lies ready to hand; yet the possibility of *Hiberorum* or *Iberorum* must

---

[1] For all that, he says of the island "Inperitos habet cultores, et instructoribus habet destitutos habitatores." (p. 19, Wuttke.)

be considered, especially as we have seen that Virgilius elsewhere mentions the speech of his neighbours, the Basques. The other passage, in which he quotes a verse by one Bregandus Lugenicus, has been thought to contain an Irish tribal name. But strong collateral evidence is needed to bring this out of the category of Virgilius's ordinary mystifications.

We now approach the problem of the classical culture of Ireland. How, when, and whence did it come into being? Many generations of scholars have been contented to regard the mission of Patrick (in 430–460) as marking the accession of Ireland to the world of learning. It has been realised, indeed, that Patrick himself was no scholar, but he has been thought of as the parent of scholars, the progenitor of the great monastic schools which sprang up all over Ireland in the sixth century— Clonard (520), Clonmacnois (544), Clonfert (*c.* 550), Bangor (*c.* 560). Before Patrick (or at least before Palladius), it has been commonly believed, Ireland, lying outside the sphere of Roman political influence, was also untouched by Roman culture. A readjustment of this view has become necessary. Patrick was not the Apostle of Ireland in the sense that before he landed there were no Christians in the island. Apart from such results as may have attended the obscure mission of Palladius (whom Zimmer would identify with Patrick), there were pre-Patrician churches and pre-Patrician saints. It would indeed be strange, if at a time when Christianity was highly organised and flourishing both in Britain and in western Gaul—countries in active intercourse with Ireland—there had been no sporadic evangelisation, no formation here and there of small Christian communities. As a matter of fact there are in the undoubted writings of Patrick allusions to existent Christianity, and in particular to men who, we gather from Patrick's language, possessed a higher degree of culture than he did. There is, too, a persistent tradition (though the documents which contain it are not of the earliest) that certain saints, Ailbe, for instance, and Declan, were in Ireland before Patrick.

Into the precise value of this tradition I cannot attempt to inquire; to do so would be to exaggerate its importance for our purpose. I should be giving the impression that missionary enterprise was the sole factor in bringing the learning of the Continent into Ireland. This would be a mistake. We have seen that stress has been laid in recent years by Zimmer upon the commercial relations which undoubtedly linked the island with Gaul, as well as with Britain; while yet more recently, attention has been called to a definite statement by an anonymous writer, evidently of Gaul, such as has not been hitherto producible: to the effect that in the early years of the fifth century an exodus of scholars from the Continent took place under the pressure of barbarian invasion, which affected the area under consideration.

The Huns, says our new authority, began that devastation of the whole

Empire which was carried on by the Vandals, Goths, and Alani; "and owing to their ravages, all the learned men on this side the sea fled, and in the countries beyond sea, namely, Ireland, and wherever else they betook themselves, brought to the inhabitants of those regions an enormous advance in learning." This statement, printed from a Leyden manuscript as long ago as 1866, was, it seems, only noticed by Zimmer at the end of his life. The importance of it may be over-estimated, but cannot be denied. For the first time we have definite testimony that the culture of Bordeaux, Toulouse, Autun, Lyons—in other words, the best learning attainable in the West—did actually make its way in some shape into Ireland. And we have, besides, the reminder which was needed, that the missionaries were not solely or primarily the channels by which it came. The words throw light upon Patrick's own challenge to the *rhetorici* who knew not the Lord; but, more than all, they supply an explanation of the undoubted presence in Ireland in the sixth century of a certain type of learning. The fact that that learning was widely and rapidly diffused over the country was due in no small degree to this, that it went hand in hand with evangelisation. Had missionary effort not been there to prepare the soil, it is impossible to suppose that men would have been found so ready to study the grammar and rhetoric of Latin, or the elements of Greek. But when these were presented to them as part of the apparatus of the new faith, they were assured of a reception, and subsequently gained citizenship by their own merits.

It will not be possible to call attention to every indication of higher learning in Ireland; but it will be worth while to devote some space to the vexed question, how far this learning included a knowledge of Greek.

The question is not, it must be premised, a simple one. We must remember, on the one hand, that some of the most striking specimens of Irish Greek learning were produced on the Continent, and on the other, that, in and after the lifetime of Theodore and Hadrian (668–690) when Greek was made accessible to the English, there is a possibility of English influence upon Ireland. In any case it remains the most reasonable account of the knowledge of Greek on the part of a Johannes Eriugena or a Sedulius Scottus, that it was acquired in Ireland and transferred thence to the Continent.

In the first place, we can hardly doubt that Graeco-Latin glossaries had made their way to Ireland in very early times. The occurrence of Greek words in Irish writings of the sixth century is best accounted for on this hypothesis. We meet with such Greek words in the hymn *Altus prosător* of Columba, in that of St Sechnall on Patrick and in more than one of those in the Bangor Antiphonary. Their *raison d'être* from the point of view of the writers of these compositions is to deck the page. They are the spangles on the cloak, no essential part of the fabric, and they do not by themselves necessarily imply a knowledge of the structure of the Greek language on the part of those who use them. They may mean little more than does the use of Greek letters for colophons—the ΦΙΝΙΘ ΔΕΩ ΓΡΑΘΥΑC of a Breton monk in 952, and the like. Yet as a fact they probably do mean more. It seems likely that with the glossaries (taking the word glossary as the equivalent of a bare vocabulary) there came to Ireland a more valuable guide to the Greek language, in the shape of a manual containing conversations and narratives, fables of Aesop, *dicta* of the Emperor Hadrian, stories of the Trojan war, compiled as far back as the year 207. We have it under the formidable modern title of *Hermeneumata Pseudo-Dositheana*. It has been transmitted through "insular" channels, and was in the hands of Sedulius Scottus in the ninth century, as is thought, before he left Ireland for the Continent. The suggestion has been made that this and other Greek writings were brought to Ireland by Byzantine monks taking refuge from the Iconoclastic persecution about the middle of the eighth century: but of such refugees there is small trace. Certain entries in Martyrologies, and the existence of a "Greek church" at Trim in Meath, have been adduced in favour of the hypothesis, but no such evidence as can be called conclusive. There seems, moreover, no reason why a monk should have brought the *Hermeneumata* with him, whereas it is just the book that is likely to have formed part of the equipment of a fifth century rhetorician from Gaul.

Instances have been brought forward of Irishmen who were clearly acquainted with Greek. We will examine them briefly. Pelagius is the foremost, both in date and in eminence. He came to Italy about the year 400, and it is on record that in 415 he took part in a controversy at Jerusalem which was carried on in Greek. It will be allowed that, even granting that Pelagius was Irish and not British by extraction, he had every opportunity of acquiring Greek after he had left Ireland.

We find, next, that the commentary of Theodore of Mopsuestia upon the Psalms was preserved and transcribed in a revised and shortened Latin form at Bobbio. The actual work of translation and revision has been ascribed to St Columban. That point is doubtful: but the commentary was certainly studied by Irish writers on the Continent, and it is possible that the translation was actually made upon Irish soil. It had a wide influence. The researches of Dr Robert M. L. Ramsay and Dr J. Douglas Bruce have demonstrated the use of it by English glossators of the Psalter (perhaps by Bede himself) down to the eleventh century.

In a gospel book of the eighth century at Würzburg is a note to the effect that Mosuin Mac Armin (Abbot of Bangor, who died in 610) learned by heart a Paschal *computus* drawn up by a Greek sage— probably Theophilus of Antioch. Coupled with the presence of Greek words in the antiphonary of Bangor, this statement has a certain force, and it should be noticed that the date of Mosuin excludes the possibility of Theodorian influence from Canterbury and England. What is not excluded is the possibility that the *computus* lay before him in a Latin version.

The Schaffhausen manuscript of Adamnan's *Life of Columba*, written at Iona before 714, has in it the Lord's Prayer in Greek, and in Greek letters. This is an example of importance, though, like those that follow, it is post-Theodorian in date, and is accordingly liable to a certain discount.

Sedulius Scottus had in his possession in the ninth century a collection of apophthegms called *Proverbia Graecorum*. We have them only in Latin, preserved in the *Collectanea* of Sedulius in a manuscript at Cues, quoted copiously in an English source, the tracts of the famous " Yorker Anonymus," and alluded to in a letter of one Cathvulf to Charlemagne[1]. Their Latinity is Celtic, and they may safely be regarded as a Greek collection rendered into Latin on the soil of Ireland.

To Ireland also we probably owe the excerpts we possess of Macrobius's important treatise on the differences and conformities of the Greek and Latin verb, a book for the understanding of which a knowledge of Greek is indispensable. One of our manuscripts attributes the selection of the excerpts to a Johannes, thought to be the great Eriugena (Erigena). The line of transmission has insular connexions. Similarly, quotations from the lost *Peplus* of Theophrastus, dealing with the origin of the alphabet, appear in a Laon manuscript of the school of Eriugena and in a commentary on Martianus Capella derived from that same school. That these imply the use of a Greek source, not necessarily of a complete text of the *Peplus*, cannot be doubted.

In addition to this evidence, it will be useful, I think, to consider a class of examples as yet not utilised in the investigation of this question. They consist of traits in Irish literature (principally Latin) which are drawn according to all appearance from some of the obscurer apocryphal writings—writings which are not known to have existed in Latin. This evidence, again, is not unambiguous. Some of our sources, notably the Latin Lives of Irish saints, are of late date. Yet that fact is no real bar to their testimony; for whatever they have absorbed in the way of reminiscence of old learning was acquired before the exodus of Irishmen to the Continent. In the interval between that exodus and the compilation of the Lives, Ireland, harried by the Northmen and deserted by its scholars, had ceased to be a learned country. These Lives, as their most recent editor, Dr Plummer, has shewn, contain much that is pre-Christian, and little that is characteristic of the later medieval period. This is true also of such documents in the Irish language as will be cited.

First among the supposed sources I will place the *Acts of Philip*. The Western Church knew absolutely nothing of the sensational Greek

[1] The title occurs (crossed out) in an early catalogue of the library of Lincoln Minster.

romance which passes under that name. According to the Latins, Philip died a peaceful death like John the Evangelist. In Ireland we find traces of a different tradition. The *Passion* in the *Leabhar Breac* interpolates the martyrdom into a version of the Latin Acts. The Irish writing called the *Evernew Tongue*[1] is a kind of apocalypse in which the tongue of the Apostle, cut out nine times by his persecutors, discourses to assembled multitudes. In the life of St Boece is an incident strongly reminiscent of the Greek Acts: a wolf brings a kid to the saint, as a leopard does to the Apostle. In Muirchu's life of St Patrick (not later than 699) is another possible reminiscence. A magician is whirled up into the air and dashed on the ground. It may be a version of the fate of Simon Magus, but it does rather strikingly resemble passages in the Eastern Acts of Philip and of Peter and Andrew[2].

In the life of St Berach there is a story of a druid killed at the window of his cell by the arrow of a hunter. Pilate, in an exclusively Greek legend, meets his end in precisely the same way. The climax of the Greek book known as the *Rest of the words of Baruch* is that when the Jews have resolved to stone the prophet to death, a stone pillar is made to assume his form, and their attacks are directed against it until Jeremiah has finished his last directions to his disciples. In the Irish life of St Brendan, a follower of the saint is attacked: a stone is made to put on his appearance, and the man escapes. In the Greek *Testament of Abraham* a striking incident is that a tree utters words of praise to God and prediction of Abraham's death. In the life of St Coemgen a tree sings to him. In the same *Testament* is the story of a calf, slaughtered at Mamre for the entertainment of the three angels, being restored to life and running to its mother. This miracle figures in several of the Lives, *e.g.* that of St Ailbe.

Evidence that apocryphal literature unknown to the rest of Europe was read in Ireland is furnished by the Irish *Vision of Adamnan*, which quotes a form of the story of the death of Mary only found now in Syriac. The same Vision makes use of an apocalypse, as yet not identified, which is also quoted in a (Latin) Reichenau manuscript of Irish connexion now at Carlsruhe. The Irish tale of the *Two Sorrows of Heaven* is another document based on an *apocryphon* which it is safe to say belongs to Eastern Christendom. In it Enoch and Elias prophesy to the souls of the blessed, which (as in certain Greek apocalypses) are in the form of birds, the terrors of the end of the world.

Of the writings I have mentioned so far, the literature of the

---

[1] *Eriu*, 1905, p. 96.

[2] Other traces of reading have been pointed out in Muirchu, which may be mentioned here: an allusion to Abraham's conversion to a belief in the true God, possibly derived from Josephus; and an apparent reminiscence of a line of Valerius Flaccus, as well as clear evidence of a knowledge of Virgil. The occasional use of Greek words (*e.g. antropi*) may be merely "glossarial" learning.

English Church of the seventh and eighth centuries betrays no know-ledge. There are others, now to be noticed, for example, the *Book of Enoch*, of which this cannot be said. A non-Irish insular manuscript of the eighth century has preserved a fragment of a Latin version of *Enoch*. In Ireland we find, in the *Saltair na Rann*, a number of names of angels which are pretty certainly derived from the same book. There, too, are episodes taken from a *Life of Adam*, but whether they are to be traced to a Western or to an Eastern text has not as yet been made clear. In the "Gelasian" list of apocryphal books the *Testament of Job* is mentioned, which probably implies the existence of a Latin version. An unpleasing trait which occurs in this *Testament* is adopted in the Life of St Mochua. It would not be difficult to shew by examples from the Irish Lives of Saints that the legends of the Infancy of our Lord were familiar in the country; but these were so widely diffused that the demonstration would add nothing to our present purpose. Let it be recorded, lastly, that the Reichenau manuscript cited above shews, in one of the fragmentary Homilies which it contains, undoubted knowledge of the obscure *Apocalypse of Thomas*[1], and that a fragment of an Irish service-book in the Vatican Library presents us with a Lection from a Gospel attributed to James the Less. Both Apocalypse and Gospel are con-demned in the "Gelasian" decree.

It has seemed worth while to set forth this class of evidence in some detail. Without detail, indeed, its force is inappreciable. The upshot of it is that the Eastern legendary literature was domiciled in Ireland to such an extent that it coloured the imaginations and contributed to the stock-in-trade of hagiologists and seers; and this familiarity with a branch of Eastern literature is not negligible as a confirmation of other indications that in the sixth and seventh centuries a knowledge of Greek was far from uncommon in Ireland.

Apart from Greek, which after all must be regarded as the fine flower of their learning, what did the normal culture of Irish scholars amount to? The scanty list of their Latin writers between the end of the sixth and the beginning of the eighth century—between Columba († 597) and Adamnan († 704)—includes besides penitentials, lives of saints, and hymns of no very marked excellence, several writings which are without rival in their time. The *Altus prosător*, Columba's great alphabetic hymn, and the playful poem in short Adonic lines by Columban, cannot fail to impress the reader, the former in virtue of its achievement, the latter by the background of learning which it implies. The *Altus* has something of the learnedness and intricacy of Celtic decorative art: Columban's poem, with its allusions to Sappho and Danaë, is the work of a man who merits the name of scholar. The

---

[1] This is true also of the Anglo-Saxon Homilists. What is practically a version of the Apocalypse is contained in the *Vercelli Book*; and two other Homilies, in a Blickling and a Hatton MS. respectively, make copious use of it.

second half of the seventh century gives us a treatise—that known as Augustine *De mirabilibus Scripturae*—which, alike for its Latinity and for the wide reading of its author, deserves respect. "Augustine" has some acquaintance with ancient history, gathered from such sources as the Eusebian Chronicle and from Josephus; he is a student of Jerome, and seems to have read books on medicine and natural history. His allusions to Ireland, fewer in number than we could have wished, add a pleasant flavour to his book. Aileran the Wise, not far from this author in date, has left a tract on the interpretation of the names of our Lord's ancestors according to the flesh, in which there is not much sound philology.

At the end of the same century we have Adamnan. His two undoubted works, the account of Arculf's pilgrimage to Palestine, and the Life of Columba, are intrinsically two of the most precious books of their time. The value of the tract on the Holy Places to the archaeologist and topographer needs no exposition. It is worth much, also, as exemplifying the interest in all sorts of knowledge which characterised the Irish scholars of the day. The Life of Columba—less a biography than a collection of anecdotes—preserves a picture of that saint and seer which will never lose its charm. Evidence of Adamnan's grammatical studies, and of his knowledge of Greek (or at least of Greek words), abounds in this book; but there is a third work, a set of notes on the *Bucolics* and *Georgics* of Virgil, which, if it could be proved to be his, would be plain evidence of his distinction as student and as teacher. It is in the form of excerpts from three earlier commentaries, those of Philargyrius, Titius Gallus, and Gaudentius, which seem to have been written down by a class at the dictation of Adananus. Whether or not this Adananus was the Abbot of Hy, this work is an undoubted product of Irish scholarship. It witnesses to these facts: that the scientific study of "grammar," as the Romans understood it, was carried on by the Irish at a time when it was dead in continental Europe: and that complete texts of ancient commentaries on Virgil had made their way into the hands of an Irishman.

Exaggerated language has no doubt been used about the learning of the Irish, and about their share in the preservation of classical literature. When allowance has been made for this, it remains incontestable that, during the latter part of the seventh century, it was in Ireland that the thirst for knowledge was keenest, and the work of teaching was most actively carried on. There the Latin language (and in a less degree the Greek) was studied from the scholar's point of view. To the Irish, we must remember, Latin was no inheritance: they had not heard it commonly spoken among them: their knowledge of it was book-knowledge. They had to treat it very much as we do now—more nearly, perhaps, as it was treated in the sixteenth and seventeenth centuries, when it was the recognised medium of communication for scholars of all countries. We need not, however, insist that the great body of the classical Latin literature which we now possess was preserved to us by the exertions either of the Irish or of the English, to whom the lamp of learning passed next in order. No doubt, whatever the Irish came across in the way of ancient literature they welcomed and treasured, but it is not to be supposed that they ever acquired in their native land a very large mass of such writings. It was when, impelled in the first instance by missionary zeal, and later by troubled conditions at home, they passed over in large numbers to the Continent, that they became instrumental in rescuing fragments of the literature which they had already learned to value. It is reserved for the palaeographers of the next few decades to shew how many of our Latin classics betray the existence of an "insular" stage in the line of their transmission. An important class of scribal errors is due to the fact that a copyist of the Middle Ages or of the Renaissance was using an archetype in "Scriptura Scottica," in the insular script, in which the peculiar forms, say, of *r* and *s* misled him. Sometimes these errors affect the whole body of manuscripts of a given author, and in these cases it is obvious that we owe the preservation of the text to an insular scribe. A leading instance, as Traube has shewn, is furnished by the *History* of Ammianus Marcellinus.

We shall have occasion to revert to the work of the Irish on the Continent. The time has now come for us to pass from Ireland to Great Britain. It will be worth while to inquire what, apart from vague modern panegyric, is to be known of the state of learning in the British Church before the coming of Theodore.

The small tract of the British bishop Fastidius is the only monument assignable to the fifth century. In the sixth we have the writings ascribed to Gildas, the *Epistle*, undoubtedly his, the *Lorica*, and the penitential Canons. We have, too, the *Hisperica Famina*. Little, if anything else, has been credited to Britons of this period. For any further information about the leading lights of the British Church we have to depend upon traditions committed to writing at a far later time, and in particular upon the lives of the saints, which are of exactly similar complexion with those of the Irish; embodying a modicum of fact wrapped in a sparkling tissue of wonders.

Fastidius may be dismissed with a word : he has no trait that can be identified as British. Gildas, as his *Epistle* attests, was a man of education. The writers whom we may credit him with having known are, indeed, not recondite, but they are of good quality : Virgil, Persius, Claudius (?Claudian), Jerome, Orosius, Rufinus. Such books as these, then, were accessible in Britain ; was there more than this ? The *Epistle* affords no evidence of the study of languages other than Latin ; Greek and Hebrew words occur in the *Lorica*, but—whether this be of Gildas's composing or no—they need imply no more than the use of a glossary.

The same is true of the *Hisperica Famina*. Whoever were the authors of that strange and attractive *farrago*, glossarial learning was to them synonymous with culture. Literary success meant the forging of phrases that should only just not defy interpretation. When, however, we find in a Bodleian manuscript (Auct. F. 4. 32), written in Wales about 887, passages from the Bible in Greek (and Latin) it is possible that we may be in the presence of a relic of British learning independent of Theodore's influence. The volume comes to us from Glastonbury, one of the few places where Celtic and English learning had a chance of blending; and, as Bradshaw says, "it passed out of British into Saxon hands in the tenth century, during St Dunstan's lifetime, when the old animosity had given way to a much more friendly feeling between the races." When we remember how sharp the animosity had been, we shall be more ready to acknowledge the probability that the pedigree of this solitary evidence of the study of Greek in Britain may be wholly independent of the school of Canterbury.

The truth of the matter is probably this, that in the period with which we are concerned there was learning in Britain, and learning of the same standard that then existed in Ireland; but that it was confined to a smaller area, that its products were fewer and that they have perished more completely. There must surely be some foundation for the stress laid by the Irish hagiographers upon the intercourse between the saints of Ireland and of Britain. Over and over again we find that the former go for instruction to the latter: they sit at the feet of David, Cadoc, Gildas. Gildas visits Ireland, as he visits Brittany; in the life of St Brendan it is said that he, Gildas, had a missal written in Greek letters, which Brendan, ignorant of the characters, was miraculously enabled to read at sight. It is, if I mistake not, the one mention of Greek in these late lives,—a fact which adds something, be it but a feather-weight, to the credit of the tale, apart from the miracle. In the Breton and Welsh lives we hear of the school of St Iltut (Illtyd) at Llantwit Major, and, through the mist of words with which modern writers have enwrapped the "first of British Universities," we discern something comparable to the monastic schools of Clonard and the Irish Bangor. For Brittany at least Llantwit was a mother of teachers. From her went forth Paul Aurelian (St Pol-de-Léon), Samson, Leonorius; and they went qualified to Christianise the Bretons, if not to educate them. Of their studies at Llantwit no first-hand record survives; but a few ancient Welsh books, a famous Juvencus at Cambridge, and a Martianus Capella, probably written at St David's and now among Archbishop Parker's manuscripts at Corpus Christi, may safely be accepted (though not earlier than the ninth century) as representing the kind of culture attainable in such a school. And the beautiful story of St Cadoc's intercession for the soul of Virgil, uncertain as is the date of it, gives a glimpse of the attitude of some Britons towards the great literature of

Rome that at least harmonises well with evidence of a better kind emanating from Ireland.

Thus our knowledge of early British culture is scanty. It rests largely upon conjecture and inference. It is not so with the first beginnings of learning among the English. Whereas no English scholar or writer can be named before 668, the next half century produces two who would be remarkable in any age—Aldhelm and Bede. Nor is there any room for doubt that these men owe their learning to Theodore and Hadrian. For, even if there be a Celtic strain in Aldhelm's education, as there surely is in his style, we must remember in the first place that the very fact of an Englishman's taking to literary pursuits is a novelty; and in the second place that we have this Englishman's own testimony (in his letter to Eahfrid) to the enormous influence of Theodore and Hadrian in the work of education: an influence not confined to England, for it was potent enough to attract the scholars of Ireland. In Bede no admixture of Celtic influence is traceable: he is simply the supreme product of the normal teaching of his day. What, then, did Theodore and Hadrian bring with them to this country? They brought the permanent equipment of learning in the shape of books. They also brought the knowledge and enthusiasm which secured that the books should be used to profit. In these two men the culture of East and West was concentrated. Theodore of Tarsus had studied in the schools of Athens, and very little of his life had been spent in Italy. Hadrian was of African extraction and abbot of a monastery near Naples: he had absorbed all that Italy could furnish, and was possessed of Greek as well. Through him we are linked with the ancients. The *Institutions* of Cassiodorus are responsible for the existence of a man with such qualifications. Unproductive of written monuments as Italy was at this time, its monks had not, thanks to Cassiodorus, lost all touch with the education of an earlier day. It is to Hadrian that we must attribute the greatest share of achievement in the educational work which now began in England. Less could be done by Theodore, occupied as he was with administration and organisation, and often absent on journeys to distant parts of the island.

With them an Englishman must be joined in our grateful remembrance—the man who spent his life and substance in the labour of bringing to us the actual palpable treasures of art and learning—Biscop, surnamed Benedict, Abbot of Wearmouth. It was he who accompanied Theodore and Hadrian to England; he was himself returning from his third journey to the tombs of the Apostles. On every subsequent expedition (and he made four more) he brought back in quantities books of every kind[1], pictures, and vestments, to say nothing of the masons and the musicians whom on several occasions

[1] The only book of a secular kind specified—indeed, the only one specified at all except a Bible—was a book on cosmography of admirable workmanship which

he induced to come and work upon his buildings and to teach his monks. Is it not a fair inference from the facts that the influence of Theodore and Hadrian went for something here? Whether or no, Biscop's work was just what was wanted to supplement theirs and to ensure its continuance after their removal.

We do not find these intellectual fathers of the English race figuring as writers. This is a slight matter. Their effectiveness as teachers and the importance of their literary equipment are attested by the works of the first generation of English scholars. Both Aldhelm and Bede are able to use books on grammar and prosody in large numbers: they know the standard poets, both heathen and Christian, and have access, it seems, even to contemporary Spanish writers. The great Latin fathers, and such other books as were valued for their bearing on the Scriptures, doubtless formed the bulk of the libraries which now began to be formed at Canterbury, York, Wearmouth, and perhaps Malmesbury. To put it shortly, within the space of a few years England was placed on a level with the Continent (and with Ireland) in respect of the apparatus of learning. There was this great difference between them, that on the Continent the tools were lying neglected, in England they were in active use.

It is not, perhaps, necessary to describe in any detail the literary monuments of the first age of our literature: the age of which Aldhelm marks the youth and Bede the prime. The subject is well-worn: little that is new can be offered in a general survey. The central fact is that at the beginning of the eighth century England was the home of the one great writer of the time, and was a source of light to the whole of the West. In Bede's *Ecclesiastical History* we have a book of real literary excellence, as well as an invaluable historical source. In his other works, some of which have outlived their period of greatest usefulness, especially his commentaries, he provided sources of information which were at once welcomed as superior to anything then available, and which retained their popularity until the thirteenth century at least[1].

The lifetime of Bede tides over the first third of the eighth century. The last third sees the beginning of the Carolingian Renaissance. The middle third, compared with its neighbours, is a barren time so far as regards the production of writings of abiding value.

Indeed, when one has named Boniface, with the small group of English writers who were his contemporaries, and Virgilius of Salzburg, almost all is said. Boniface and his circle bear witness, in their letters

Ceolfrid gave to King Aldfrid in exchange for some lands. (Bede, *Vitae Abbatum*, 15.) This may possibly have been the *Christian Topography* of Cosmas Indicopleustes, from which we undoubtedly find an excerpt in Latin in a manuscript given by King Aethelstan to the see of St Cuthbert (CCCC. 183).

[1] See also Vol. II. p. 574.

and in their poems, to the sound learning imparted in the great English schools. What they wrote has some flavour of the elaboration characteristic of Aldhelm as distinguished from Bede. The acrostic and the riddle are in favour: Boniface even copies, in his verses to Duddus, the "figured" poem of Publilius Optatianus, in which certain letters picked out of the lines form a pattern or picture, and also compose distinct lines or sentences. It is more to the purpose however to draw attention to the frequent requests for books which Boniface prefers to his friends in England, the fruit of which we may perhaps see now in some of the small but precious group of manuscripts still preserved at Fulda. Among the treasures of the Würzburg library too are books with English connexions: in one is mention of a Worcester abbess[1]. The presence of others may be due to the Irish missionary and martyr Kilian († 689), among them the unique copy of the works of the heretic Priscillian, or, as Dom Morin now inclines to think, of his companion Instantius. It is thought, I may add, that the Graeco-Latin *Codex Laudianus* of the Acts has made the journey between Britain and the Continent twice. First brought to England by Theodore and Hadrian, and there used by Bede, it travelled to Germany with some members of the Bonifacian circle, and found a home there till the seventeenth century, when a second Archbishop of Canterbury, Laud, was instrumental in bringing it once again to this country along with many other spoils of German libraries.

It will eventually be possible, thanks to the work of the great palaeographers of our own time, to write a history of the transmission of ancient literature, and to trace its influence upon individual authors of the early Middle Ages by the help of our rapidly growing knowledge of the styles of writing peculiar to the great centres of learning, monastic and other, and by the indications, which single manuscripts are gradually being induced to yield, of their own parentage and wanderings. But the time for attempting this is not yet: many monographs have to be written and multitudinous details correlated; and the reader of a survey such as this must be content to be told that the cloud which hangs over the literary life of the sixth, seventh, and eighth centuries is in process of being thinned: it is beyond hope that it can be wholly dispersed.

One other name demands notice before we close our review of pre-Carolingian literature. Virgilius, Bishop of Salzburg, has made a considerable figure in many a text-book in the capacity of an enlightened cosmographer; or of an early martyr of science, persecuted and silenced by clerical obscurantists because of his belief in the Antipodes. We have not a line of his writing: our only life of him makes no allusion to his secular learning: all that we know of this side of him is confined to a couple of lines in a letter of Pope Zacharias to St Boniface, and to

[1] The MS. is of Jerome on Ecclesiastes (cent. vi): the owner was Abbess Cuthsuuitha (690–700).

the epithets Geometer and Solivagus[1] which were applied to him, the former by the Annals of the Four Masters when recording his death, the other by an authority as yet untraced. Pope Zacharias, answering a complaint of Boniface, says, " with regard to the perverse and wicked doctrine which he has spoken, against God and his own soul ; if it be made clear that he admits it,—that there is another world and other men, or sun and moon, beneath the earth (*sub terra*)—you must hold a council, deprive him of priestly rank, and expel him from the Church." This brief and rough characterisation has been made to bear the interpretation that Virgilius had published a philosophical treatise setting forth the view that there are Antipodes, possibly in dependence upon Martianus Capella's teaching. Or, it is put more modestly that he had given expression to this view in his lectures. It will be seen that the words of Zacharias contain nothing to support (and nothing to bar) this explanation. Another has been advanced which has never become fashionable, but which, I think, deserves to be weighed. It is that Virgilius had in his mind not Antipodes, but dwellers below the surface of the earth. In the twelfth century, as William of Newburgh tells us, a green boy and girl appeared at Woolpit in Suffolk, who were members of an underground race. They called their world the land of St Martin (perhaps Merlin was the real name) and told how it was lighted—not, it is true, by another sun and moon,—and how it was a Christian land and had churches. Any one who has read much of Scandinavian or Celtic fairy-lore will realise that the beliefs he finds there about the underground people are just such as could be described by Pope Zacharias's phrase. Were it not for the epithet Geometer, which does seem to imply an interest in science, I should be strongly inclined to give the preference to this second explanation of Virgilius's erroneous doctrine.

[1] It seems to have been assumed that the word is connected with *Sol*: but does it in fact mean more than " the lone wanderer " ?

CHAPTER XX.

LEARNING AND LITERATURE TILL POPE SYLVESTER II.

Only a few years before the death of Bede, Alcuin was born, and in Alcuin we have the principal link between the vigorous learning of these islands and that, hardly yet born, of Central Europe. The main facts of the connexion are familiar. Alcuin, educated in the traditions of York, left England at about the age of fifty, on a mission to Rome to receive the archiepiscopal pall for Eanbald of York, and in 781 met Charlemagne at Parma and was invited by him to come to his court as soon as his errand should be accomplished. With the exception of one interval spent in England, the rest of Alcuin's life was passed on the Continent. It ended in 804.

Meanwhile England had begun to be the prey of Danish invasion. Exactly when the library of York, which Alcuin describes so glowingly in an often-quoted passage of his poem on the Saints of the Church of York, was destroyed, we do not know; but that this was a time of destruction, that a whole literature in the English vernacular was wiped out, and that the stores of ancient learning, accumulated in the North by Benedict Biscop and in the South by Theodore and Hadrian, were scattered, is certain. Only waifs and strays remain to attest the height which art and learning had attained here, and the value of the treasures that had been imported. The Lindisfarne Gospels and the Ruthwell Cross on the one hand, and the *Codex Amiatinus* (happily retrieved by its parent country before the catastrophe) on the other, are outstanding examples.

Between the departure of Alcuin for the Emperor's court and the revival of English letters under Alfred, England, disunited and ravaged, makes no contribution to the cause of learning.

Interest is centred upon that same court of Charlemagne. Here for a time lived Paul the Deacon and Peter of Pisa, both representatives of Italy, where learning, if inert, was not dead. Incomparably the more important figure of the two is that of Paul, chiefly in view of two pieces of work, his abridgment of the Glossary of Pompeius Festus, and his History of the Lombards. Both are precious, not for style, but for the hard facts which they preserve. About half of the glossary of Festus, itself an abridgment of the work of Verrius Flaccus, has survived only in a sadly damaged Naples manuscript: without it, and what Paul has rescued of the remainder, our knowledge of archaic Latin would be far fuller of gaps than it is. His epitome was a mine, too, for later writers, who drew from it strange forms to adorn their pages. In virtue of his other great work, Paul has earned the name of the Father of Italian history. Neither of these books was written at the instance of the Emperor, who employed Paul in educational work and in the compilation of a set of Homilies for use in church.

Paul was something of a verse-writer, and some fables of his are by no means without merit; but both he and Peter were chiefly valued by their patron as teachers of grammar. We have writings of both of them on this subject, a subject touched by almost every one of the great scholars of the period we have been and shall be reviewing; Aldhelm, Bede, Boniface, Alcuin, not to mention a crowd of minor names, Irish and Continental. Especially in the Carolingian age, when serious efforts were afoot to raise the standard of education, were grammatical manuals of frequent occurrence. Their compilers used the works of recent predecessors and of more ancient writers in varying degrees, commonly contributing little of their own, save perhaps the order and arrangement of the material[1]. No detailed review of these writers will be attempted in this chapter; but they deserve mention, and honourable mention, since they ministered to the first needs of a fresh and very numerous generation of scholars.

In leaving Paul the Deacon, it is worth while to remark that he expressly disclaims knowledge of Greek (and Hebrew), and to note that Greek does not figure very conspicuously in the works of most of the important scholars in Charlemagne's own circle, though we can see that it was known to more than one of them. There may have been some few Greek books accessible to them: between 758 and 763 Pope Paul I had sent some to Pepin; " the grammar of Aristotle, of Dionysius the Areopagite; a geometry, an orthography " says the Pope, obscurely enough. But we do not fall on the track of these again.

The knowledge that Charlemagne revived education and learning in his empire is common property. I shall not dwell upon his methods, but rather upon the individual men whom he gathered about him to do the work, and upon the results they achieved. Three have already been mentioned, and I do not think it is insular prejudice which inclines me to regard Alcuin as the central figure.

He was not a great writer: interesting as are his letters and his poems, none of them can be rated high as literature. But as an organizer and administrator, and as a personally attractive man, he stands in the

---

[1] Smaragdus of St Mihiel (c. 820) takes illustrations from the vernacular, an interesting point.

first rank. Socially we can see that he must have been very acceptable; in the common phrase of to-day, he had a genius for friendship. In promoting the revival of education he had this advantage over his helpers, that alone among them he was possessed of the traditions and methods of a long-established and thriving school.

The mass of writing for which he is responsible is very large. There are Biblical commentaries, not more distinguished for originality than those of Bede: treatises upon the Adoptionist heresy which sprang up in his time in Spain, and upon the Trinity, accounted his best theological work. There is a liturgical *corpus*, of great importance in the history of worship, of which a Homiliary, a Lectionary, and a Sacramentary are the chief members. Of a revision of the text of the Latin Bible due to him there is a constant tradition which we need not doubt, though we possess no record of the imperial order under which it is said to have been undertaken, and there are few allusions to it in Alcuin's own writings. Moreover, the task of distinguishing the Alcuinian text from other current types is beset with difficulties. There is also a series of educational manuals: we have those on Grammar, Rhetoric, and Dialectic, and there seem to have been others. They were not popular for long, and were not intrinsically very valuable. Still, they were pioneer work, and as such they doubtless had an influence not to be despised.

As to his own range of reading, apart from the theology which ranked as standard in his time, something must be said. The mass of verse which we have from him shews his knowledge of such authors as Virgil—some study of whom may be assumed in the case of everyone with whom we shall be concerned—Statius, Lucan, and of the Christian poets Juvencus, Prudentius, Arator, Sedulius and others who, like Virgil, were read by all who read at all. His list of the writers who were to be found in the library at York is instructive though incomplete (it omits, for example, Isidore); but it contains few names which ceased to be familiar in later centuries. Of theologians, Victorinus and Lactantius, of poets, Alcimus Avitus, of grammarians Probus, Focas, Euticius Pompeius, Cominianus, are those who became comparative rarities in and after the twelfth century. The most learned of Alcuin's letters are those that relate to astronomy, in which the Emperor was interested. In one of them he asks for a copy of Pliny's *Natural History* to help him to answer certain queries, and elsewhere in his correspondence he quotes Vitruvius and alludes to Dares Phrygius as if he knew the Trojan History current under that name. He is also credited with the introduction of a few texts to the Continent—the spurious correspondences of Alexander the Great with Dindimus, king of the Brachmani, and of St Paul with Seneca. If not very important, both of these became excessively popular: more so than the *Categoriae* of Augustine, the transmission of which is also due to Alcuin.

His knowledge of Greek is a matter of controversy, but at least he can quote the Psalter and the Epistles to elucidate a point of grammar.

A remark may be permitted here which is applicable to most of the individual cases we shall meet. Those who had learnt the grammar and machinery of the Greek language were not few in number (and I see no reason for excluding Alcuin's name from the list), but when they had learnt it and were in a position to use Greek books, there were no Greek books for them to use. Literally, as we shall see, hardly any beyond a few copies of parts of the Bible—Psalter, Gospels, Epistles. In other words, there was very little matter which they did not already possess in a form easier to be used and considered equally authoritative. Hence the study was unpopular; it involved great labour, and had little to offer save to those who coveted abstruse learning and took pleasure in the process of acquiring it. For all that, the tradition of the supreme excellence of Greek learning was slow to die; and in every generation some individuals were attracted by it, though the difficulties they had to encounter increased as time went on.

Alcuin's abbey of St Martin at Tours played a great part in the diffusion of that form of writing, the Carolingian minuscule, which was the vehicle of transmission of the main bulk of the ancient literature. Obscured for a time—ousted, indeed—by the Gothic scripts of the later Middle Ages, it emerged again at the revival of learning, took perhaps a more refined shape at the hands of the humanists, and became the parent of the common " Roman " type in which these lines will be read. That the introduction of this clear and beautiful script is one of the most remarkable and beneficial of the reforms of Charlemagne's age, whoever has had to do with Merovingian, Beneventan, or Visigothic hands will readily allow. It would be pleasant if we could point to it as an enduring trace of the influence of Alcuin, as has been commonly done. The trend of expert opinion, however, is against this attribution. The traditions of writing in which Alcuin was brought up were insular, and so good an authority as Traube pronounces that the great Anglo-Saxon scholar had no share in forming the hand of the scriptorium of Tours.

The pupils of Alcuin did not fail to follow his methods and to propagate sound learning to the best of their ability. We shall revert to them and their work. It is now time to leave the great teacher and to notice a few other leading members of the court circle.

Einhard, Theodulf, and Angilbert are three figures of great interest. The *Vita Karoli* of the first may be unhesitatingly named as the best piece of literature which the Carolingian revival produced. As is well known, it follows the lines of an ancient model, Suetonius's Lives of the Caesars, and especially that of Augustus. A copy of Suetonius, the parent, it seems, of all that we have, was at Fulda: Servatus Lupus of Ferrières writes for a transcript of it in later years. This MS Einhard

must have studied closely and wisely ; from it he derives the plan and proportions, and the method of narration, in his biography. Succinct, clear,
and picturesque, inspired with a sagacious perception of the greatness of
its subject, it is a really worthy monument to the Emperor. "Nardulus"
is an attractive personality as revealed in this work, and in the letters
and poems of his friends. His own letters are rather jejune business-
documents for the most part. A mention of Vitruvius is almost the
only detail of literary interest ; there is evidence, besides, of acquaintance
with the letters of Pliny, and, elsewhere, with the *Germania* of Tacitus.
More characteristic than the correspondence is his narrative of the
translation or theft of the relics of SS. Marcellinus and Peter, which he
procured from Rome for his abbey of Michelstadt. It is the classical
instance of these pious conveyances, and an early one in the series. Of
the documents which throw light upon Einhard's personality and his
domestic relations, the best are the letters of condolence written to him
by Servatus Lupus on the death of his wife. That Einhard took part
in the compilation of the very valuable Lorsch annals—anonymous, as is
the rule with that class of records—has been denied, but is affirmed by
weighty opinion. His poems, and his lost work on the Saxons, can have
no more than a bare mention here.

Theodulf, Spaniard by birth and education, ecclesiastic and statesman,
Bishop of Orleans and Abbot of Fleury, stands out as by far the most
skilful versifier—I think I would say poet—of his time. He has an
astonishing facility in the elegiac metre. A very large mass of his
writing has survived, though the only manuscript of the longer poems
has disappeared since Sirmond printed them. If one were asked to
single out the most successful piece, perhaps that addressed *To Judges*
has the strongest claim. In this he describes an official journey of
inspection which he took with Leidrad (afterwards Archbishop of Lyons)
through Gallia Narbonensis. At one place he introduces an incident
which is rather characteristic of his manner. Some one who wishes to
curry favour with him calls him aside and offers him a piece of plate,
evidently of antique workmanship : it is worn with age, and has in the
centre a representation of Hercules and Cacus surrounded with others
which shew Hercules and the snakes and the Twelve Labours : on the
outside are the fight with Nessus and the deaths of Lichas and Hercules,
as well as the story of Antaeus. Other suitors proffer Eastern fabrics
with beasts woven upon them, and so forth. I call this characteristic,
for we find several similar descriptions of works of art in the poems, as,
for example, the Seven Liberal Arts depicted on a dish, and a picture,
designed by Theodulf himself, of the Earth in the form of a woman
suckling a child, and surrounded by many symbolic attributes. These
things are interesting in themselves and as affording evidence of the
survival of classical traditions and monuments.

Another ingenuity in which he evidently took pleasure, is the introduction of place-names in large numbers. Many distichs are made up of these: here is one enumerating some of the rivers which watered Charlemagne's dominions:

> Rura Mosella Liger Vulturnus Matrona Ledus
> Hister Atax Gabarus Olitis Albis Arar[1].

He does not even shun Bagdad:

> Si veniat Bagatat, Agarenis rebus onusta.

As amusing as any is his poem on the court (xxv), where he tells how Nardus (Einhard), Erkambald, and Osulf might serve (being all of a size, and that not great) as the three legs of a table, and how, when the poem is read aloud, a wretched Scot (possibly Clement the Irishman, the palace schoolmaster) will be in a miserable state of temper and confusion.

Two pieces of his verse, and only two, were at all commonly copied in later centuries: an extract from his Preface to the Bible finds a place in some thirteenth century Vulgates, and a part of his Palm Sunday hymn, " Gloria, laus, et honor," remains in use in the original and in vernacular versions.

What has been said of his facility in the writing of elegiac verse implies his close study of older models, particularly of Ovid. His compatriot Prudentius was also a well-read source. But on the whole his range of classical reading does not comprise unfamiliar names. We do not learn much from him about the preservation of ancient literature.

A word in conclusion as to his work on the revision of the text of the Bible. That he undertook a recension of it is not to be doubted, and it is generally agreed that we have, at Le Puy and at Paris (*B.N. Lat.* 9380), two copies, more or less faithful, of that recension. That he made it by the help of old Spanish manuscripts is also the prevailing view: it is probable enough that fragments of some of these survive at Orleans, whither they came from his abbey, Fleury. But neither was it a very remarkable piece of work in itself, nor did it exercise upon the history of the text an influence approaching that attributed to the contemporary Alcuinian revision.

Angilbert—Homer, as he was called—influential as he was personally, takes on the whole a secondary place among the writers. If the fragment of an epic poem on Charlemagne and Pope Leo, which contains a celebrated description of the Emperor and his family out hunting, be not his (but it probably is) there is not much to preserve his name as an author. But as Abbot of St Riquier he was zealous in collecting books —over 200 of them—for his monastery, and, if we may judge by the names of authors whom Mico had at disposal, there was a strong contingent of Latin poets amongst them.

---

[1] Roer, Moselle, Loire, Volturno, Marne, Lès near Montpellier, Danube, Aude, Gave, Lot, Elbe, Saone. This characteristic reappears in the German Renaissance.

Only a systematic history of literature could undertake to name the minor figures of this or of subsequent periods. It must suffice here to select a few men and books that stand out from a crowd which begins to thicken rapidly.

Alcuin, dying in 804, was the first after Paul the Deacon to disappear. Einhard and the rest were considerably younger men, and Einhard lived till 840. Before we take up the direct line of succession to Alcuin, we will devote a few words to one who stood outside the circle that has been engaging our attention, and who was just about coeval with Einhard. This is Agobard, Archbishop of Lyons (769–840). Like Theodulf he was a Spaniard. It is no part of my purpose to trace his career or catalogue his many tracts: three points only shall be noted as germane to the subject of this chapter. First, he was instrumental in preserving, in a manuscript which he gave to a church at Lyons, and which is now at Paris, a very large proportion of the extant works of Tertullian. Next, though he shews no interest in classical learning, it is curious to find that he had some knowledge of Jewish lore. In his fierce attack on the Jews he quotes Rabbinic teaching about the seven heavens, and also some form of the Jewish libel on our Lord which is commonly called the *Toledoth Jesu*. Lastly, two of his tracts have a bearing on folklore: one of them denounces the current belief in *Tempestarii*, people who could produce storms at will: the other tells of a mysterious epidemic which had induced people in the district of Uzès to revert to pagan observances. These, two of which are no doubt small matters, are samples of the odds and ends of strange information which may be picked up from the literature of the time.

The most influential of the *diadochi* of Alcuin was perhaps his pupil Magnentius Hrabanus Maurus (Raban) (784–856), Abbot of Fulda for twenty years (822–842) and from 847 Archbishop of Mayence. He was no original genius, but a great channel of learning, which he transmitted through compilations in the form of commentaries and of an encyclopaedia founded on Isidore. The achievement which his contemporaries admired most was his book *In Praise of the Holy Cross*. This too is closely modelled on an older book, the panegyric on Constantine by Publilius Optatianus Porphyrius. Pages of capital letters in which some are picked out in red, meet the eye, and it is realised that the red letters not only have their proper part in the text, but also form some device or picture, and that they make up some sentiment or verse independently. Such *carmina figurata*, of terrible ingenuity and infinitesimal value, were popular throughout these centuries.

Raban Maur not only found a precious library at Fulda, but increased it substantially. It can have had few rivals in quality by the time he left it. To Fulda we owe, it appears, the preservation of Suetonius, of Tacitus, of Ammianus Marcellinus, to name three leading examples: it has been shewn, too, that Raban had access to Lucretius.

The mention of this library affords an occasion for speaking, though in the briefest terms, of the others which competed with it on the Continent: Lorsch, Reichenau near Constance, St Gall, Corbie in Picardy, St Riquier, Fleury on the Loire, Bobbio and Monte Cassino in Italy. These, I imagine, are all indisputably to be placed in the first class. Of them be it remembered that Fulda, Reichenau, St Gall, and Bobbio owe their being to these islands: Boniface, Pirminius, Gallus, Columban were their founders. How much further our list should stretch no two people would agree; but it would be absurd to omit the libraries of Tours, Rheims, St Denis, Mayence, Cologne, Trèves, Corvey in Westphalia (daughter of Corbie), Würzburg, Laon, Liège; or that of Verona, to which the archdeacon Pacificus († 846) added more than 200 volumes. Each of these had its importance as school or storehouse, and some, like St Gall, Würzburg, and Verona, have kept together a surprisingly large proportion of their ancient possessions up to the present day. Not so all those which were first named. The books of Fulda, of which we have a catalogue, made late in the sixteenth century, have very largely disappeared. Lorsch is better represented, in the libraries of the Vatican and elsewhere, Reichenau at Carlsruhe, Corbie at Paris, Petrograd, and Amiens, Fleury at Rome and Orleans, Bobbio at Rome, Milan, Turin, Vienna and Bamberg.

Among them these houses produced a great proportion of the ninth century manuscripts which exist to-day, and anyone who will be at the pains to examine Chatelain's *Paléographie des Classiques Latins* or Sabbadini's account of the rediscovery of the classics at the Renaissance will realise how much of what we have is due to the scribes who lived between, say, 800 and 950.

There are three Latin authors of the first class, Virgil, Terence, and Livy, of whom the whole or a considerable portion have survived in manuscripts of the classical period. Neglecting fragments, it may be said that the earliest copies of Caesar, Sallust, Lucretius, Juvenal, Persius, both Plinies, Tacitus, Lucan, Suetonius, Martial, the greater part of Cicero, all date from the Carolingian Renaissance. There is, of course, something to be set against this immense debt: what, we ask, has become of the archetypes which the scribes of the ninth century used? It is to be feared that, once transcribed, they were cast aside as old and useless[1], and few of them allowed to live on even as palimpsests, for vellum was not so scarce as it had been. Still, the fact remains that they *were* copied, and that in such numbers as attest a vivid and widespread interest in the best literature that was accessible.

In Walafrid (Walahfridus) Strabo or Strabus, the pupil of Raban Maur, we have another scholar of the direct Alcuinian succession. His career was not a long one (808–849), but the amount, and in some respects the

---

[1] There was some excuse for this. Books written in short lines, in capital letters, with the words undivided, cannot be read with ease or comfort.

quality of his work, is remarkable. The *Glossa Ordinaria*, an abridgment of patristic commentaries on all the books of the Bible, a predecessor of the Synopsis Criticorum of more modern times, was his great monument. In the twelfth century no monastic library of any consideration lacked a set, and even the smallest owned a few of the principal volumes. It is no more than a compilation, from sources which still exist, but it was a source of primary importance to students of the Bible for many years.

Walafrid's poetry is more interesting to us than the gloss. There is a good deal of it, but only two pieces shall be selected for special mention. *De imagine Tetrici* is notable for its subject (which is the equestrian statue of Theodoric removed from Ravenna to Aix-la-Chapelle by Charlemagne in 801), and also for its form; it is a dialogue between the poet and *Scintilla* (roughly, his genius), which is succeeded by a remarkable description of the Emperor Louis the Pious and his train. *De cultura hortorum* is the first of medieval Georgics. Those who have seen it will at least remember the epilogue, addressed to Grimaldus of St Gall, in which Walafrid says: "Think of me when you are sitting in your walled garden under the shade of a peach tree.

> Dum tibi cana legunt tenera lanugine poma
> Ludentes pueri, scola laetabunda tuorum,
> Atque volis ingentia mala capacibus indunt
> Grandia conantes includere corpora palmis."

The lines are not "great poetry," but the picture is pleasant.

A group of three writers whose works bear on the preservation of Roman literature shall next be noticed.

The first part of the ninth century (805–862) is covered by the life of Servatus Lupus, Abbot of Ferrières, whose letters, not uncelebrated, are by far the most remarkable of his writings. The frequent requests he makes for books, and especially classical books, have long since attracted attention. From Einhard he borrows Aulus Gellius and the rhetorical works of Cicero; from Altsig of York, Quintilian; from another he tries to get Livy; from the Abbot of Fulda, Suetonius in two small volumes. He owns and has read Caesar; he quotes Horace, and may have had some other Latin lyrics. A line which he cites as Horace's, (Meos dividerem libenter annos), is not to be found in Horace now.

Mico of St Riquier seems to have compiled his work on prosody about the year 825. It is a collection, arranged alphabetically, of lines from upwards of thirty poets, pagan and Christian, exemplifying the scansion of particular words, the name of the source being written beside each. One could hardly have a more convenient key to the contents of the St Riquier library as regards Latin verse. The list need not be set out in full here, but a few remarks may be made. The *Aratea* both of Cicero and of Germanicus and the medical poem of Q. Serenus Sammonicus, to which Lucretius may be added, count as rarities. We miss Calpurnius and Nemesianus, who were known to the Carolingian court, and

Macer—perhaps last mentioned as extant by Ermoldus Nigellus, a notable court-poet. The absence of Catullus, Tibullus and Propertius is not surprising; the first and last evidently did not emerge till a good deal later. Tibullus, however, does occur in an interesting ninth-century list of books written in a grammatical manuscript at Berlin (Santen. 66).

Hadoardus gives another aspect of the picture. We know nothing of him but that he calls himself a presbyter and obviously lived in an establishment—most likely monastic—where he had a good library at command. He put together a collection of moral, religious and philosophical excerpts which has survived in one manuscript. Its distinguishing feature is that a large part consists of extracts from the philosophical writings of Cicero. Hadoardus had no more of these than we have; the *Republic* was not known to him. Cicero is useful to him merely as a moralist, and he expunges from his extracts the personal and historical allusions, so that what we thank him for is little more than the evidence he supplies as to the existence in his time of the collected philosophical works in very much their present shape.

It is long since I have made any reference to Spain. The little that can now be said must be confined to the Christian writers: I cannot touch on the great literary and scientific achievements of the conquering Moors. And the Christian writers were not very remarkable. A mass of matter connected with the Adoptionist heresy appeared at the end of the eighth century. The question at issue (recalled by the *Filioque* clause): Was the Son of God Son by adoption, as opposed to eternal generation? was affirmed by Felix of Urgel and Elipandus of Toledo and, outside Spain, denied by Alcuin. Within the country Beatus wrote against Elipandus, but he would hardly have been remembered for that alone. He is remembered, however, both by patristic students and by those interested in art, as the compiler of an immense commentary on the Apocalypse from sources which are some of them lost and valuable. Copies of this (to which Jerome on Daniel is almost always added), profusely illustrated, are the chief monuments of Spanish art for the ninth and following centuries. The designs of the pictures were transmitted with almost Chinese fidelity from one scriptorium to another: among them is a map of the world which has a special place of its own in geographical history.

In the middle of the ninth century a pair of Cordovan writers emerge to whom a few words must be devoted: Paulus Albarus, a converted Jew, and Eulogius (Eulogio), Archbishop of Toledo, who died a martyr in 859. The writings of Eulogius are chiefly concerned with the martyrs of his own time, and with polemic against the Prophet; those of Paul include a life of Eulogius and a good deal of indifferent verse. Their main importance is, no doubt, for Spanish history, and they are mentioned here principally in virtue of a passage in the life of Eulogius which bears on general literature. In 848, says Paul, Eulogius brought back from certain monasteries a number of books. Virgil, Horace, Juvenal, Avienus are specially named, and also the epigrams of Adelelmus, who is no other than our English Aldhelm. The fact that Aldhelm was read in Spain in the ninth century is worth noting. We remember how Aldhelm himself at the end of the seventh century read Julian of Toledo and Eugenius.

A chapter of history yet unwritten will most likely disclose many unsuspected threads of connexion between Ireland, Britain, and Spain. In the making of it the rôle of the liturgiologist will be an important one.

We return to Central Europe. A good deal of space in the last chapter was devoted to Greek learning and to Irish culture. Now that we have passed to the middle years of the ninth century, both subjects come before us again. Their representatives are in the first instance Johannes Scottus Eriugena and Sedulius Scottus, but these are only the protagonists. There was a crowd of minor personages, some few of whom will claim separate notice. The testimony of the time is that imperial and royal courts and the palaces of the great ecclesiastics were thronged with needy "Scotti," all learned in their various ways, all willing to teach, and all seeking (not always in the most dignified terms) shelter and maintenance. Heiric of Auxerre, writing about 876, represents the influx of Irish scholars as due to the enlightened liberality of Charles the Bald. "Ireland, despising the dangers of the sea, is migrating almost *en masse* with her crowd of philosophers to our shores, and all the most learned doom themselves to voluntary exile to attend the bidding of Solomon the wise." But this was not the sole or even the chief reason. As the rhetoricians of Gaul had been driven into Ireland by one set of invasions, so now the Irish were driven out of it by another, that of the Scandinavian pirates who had already done so much mischief in England. We cannot doubt that lamentable destruction of books took place in Ireland too, but we know little or nothing about established libraries there.

We first hear of John the Scot at the court of Charles the Bald in 845, and his first continental writing was on predestination against Gottschalk (851). Not very long after, in 858–860, he made his first important translation from Greek, of the works called of Dionysius the Areopagite. The copy he used was most likely one which in 827 the Greek Emperor, Michael, had given to the Abbey of St Denis[1]. Hilduin, Abbot of that house, had done his best to establish the identity of the patron of the Abbey with the Areopagite, and the identification was commonly accepted throughout the medieval period.

It is generally agreed that John knew Greek before he left Ireland. This would make it natural to commit to him the task of rendering the very difficult language and matter of Dionysius into Latin. But the

---

[1] Now at Paris (B. N. Gr. 437).

contents were such as were certain to attract him. He was a philosopher born, and the blend of Neo-Platonism and Christianity in these writings was exactly suited to his temperament. He performed his work in a way that excited the wonder of a very competent scholar at Rome: for in 860 the translation was sent to Pope Nicholas, and he referred it for an opinion to his librarian Anastasius, who had done much work of the kind. Anastasius marvels how a man from a remote and barbarous land could have attained such mastery of Greek; Irish learning was evidently an unknown thing to him.

In his dedications of his version to the Emperor, and also in a good many of his occasional poems, John ventures upon original Greek verse composition: here he is at his weakest, both as poet and as prosodist; the scansion is surprisingly bad. The Dionysius was followed by the *Ambigua* of Maximus (ἄπορα εἰς Γρηγόριον περὶ φύσεων), also a difficult text to translate and not one of much importance. Most likely no other philosophical text (if we except the *Solutiones* of Priscianus Lydus, as to which there is doubt) came into John's hands. He made no other translations, but turned to the composition of his last and greatest work, to which he gave a Greek title, περὶ φύσεων μερισμοῦ (867). Little copied, for it soon became suspect of pantheism, it is the most original piece of speculative thought which these centuries have to shew. Nothing so remarkable probably was put forth until Anselm came.

Other works by John to which no precise date has been assigned are his excerpts from Macrobius on the verb, which preserve all we have of a very valuable book, a fragmentary commentary on St John's Gospel in which he makes use of the Greek text, and commentaries on Martianus Capella and Boethius. We still await a critical edition of the whole of the works of this very marked scholar and thinker. It is unfair to judge of his personality from silence, but the fact remains that there is no written tribute to any but his intellectual gifts.

Sedulius Scottus is found at Liège about 848, and after a lapse of ten years becomes untraceable. In him we have no original thinker, but a writer of some skill, a most industrious compiler and transcriber, and a lover of ancient literature. His book *De rectoribus Christianis* addressed to Lothar II, interspersed with pieces of verse in many metres (after the fashion of Boethius) and with copious quotations from the *Proverbia Graecorum* (see p. 504), is his best original composition. There are, too, many fugitive pieces of verse, some addressed to his patrons, one or two to his Irish companions, others descriptive of works of art, for example, a silken pall embroidered with a long series of scenes from the life of St Peter. Under the head of compilations we reckon his collections on St Matthew and on the Pauline Epistles (the former as yet unprinted) and his Commentaries on grammatical works, Priscian, Donatus, Eutychius. In the last-named, which was very likely written in Ireland, he uses that tract of Macrobius on the verb, of which John has been the chief preserver.

There is also in the library of the hospital of Cues (Cusa) near Trèves a manuscript of a commonplace book of his of very remarkable character. It has supplied us with pieces of Cicero's orations against Piso and for Fonteius which are wanting in our other copies, and of Vegetius, Porphyrio, and Lactantius. Partly perhaps because of the many Greek passages in his works, Lactantius was little read or copied between the ninth and the fifteenth century. To Sedulius however these were no deterrent; he collects some of them at the end of a Greek psalter which we have of his transcribing. A remark of Traube's will be in place here: "I hazard the guess," he says, "that wherever Greek passages survive in Latin works, they are to be referred to Irish influence."

The manuscripts transcribed by Sedulius and his circle remain to be noticed. Those which are most confidently ascribed to his hand are the Psalter just mentioned, which is signed by him (it is now in the Arsenal Library at Paris, and was once at St Nicholas's Abbey at Verdun), and a Graeco-Latin copy of the Pauline Epistles at Dresden, of which the *Codex Augiensis* at Trinity College, Cambridge, is a transcript. There are besides at St Gall a Priscian, perhaps brought from Ireland, and a Gospels in Greek and Latin (known as Δ), and there is a famous book at Berne (363) containing our oldest copy of Horace's Odes. In these we find, scribbled on margins, Irish names, and names of others, such as Hartgar of Tongres, Gunther of Cologne, Hilduin, Hincmar, etc., whom we know to have been connected with Sedulius. His own name also occurs not unfrequently.

Of the less distinguished members of the band of Irish scholars, Dunchad or Duncant has been asserted and also denied to be the author of a Comment on Martianus Capella (not printed). Common to this, and to John the Scot's comment on the same author, is a fragment of the lost *Peplus* of Theophrastus, which is also copied in a Laon manuscript (444) written by an Irish teacher, Martin of Laon († 875). This book contains a Graeco-Latin glossary, and, *inter alia*, Greek verses by Martin himself, no better and no worse than those of John.

νυν ληγε νεανισκε λεγειν, δος δεσματα χιλσιν (χείλεσιν)

is the last line, and a fair sample.

Room must be found here for a word about glossaries. They were the indispensable tool of any who aspired to a knowledge of Greek, and were used by others who had no real grasp of the language but desired to be thought Greek scholars. The two chief Graeco-Latin glossaries go by the names of Cyrillus and Philoxenus respectively. The prime authority for the text of *Cyrillus* is an ancient manuscript in the Harleian collection (5792) which came from the hospital of Cues. We now know that Laon 444, written by Martin, is a copy of it, and this means that in the ninth century it was at or near Laon. It was not, however, written in France, but most likely in Italy: its archetype is conjectured to have been a papyrus book. *Philoxenus* depends upon a ninth century manuscript at Paris, and this too is referred to the neighbourhood of Laon, or at least to the north of France.

Fergus was another of the Irish circle; he was the writer of part of the St Gall Gospels (Δ). Yet another, of whom we know little more than the name, was Elias, a connecting link between the Irish and their most distinguished continental pupil, Heiric of Auxerre.

Heiric learned what Greek he knew from an Irish teacher or teachers at Laon; he also sat under Lupus of Ferrières, and at his lectures took down excerpts from Valerius Maximus and Suetonius. Elias supplied him with the text of two collections of apophthegms, one current under the name of Caecilius Balbus. A manuscript now at the abbey of Melk in Austria preserves (with autograph notes by Heiric) another set of extracts which is particularly interesting as including some from Petronius. The copy from which these were taken is now divided between the libraries of Berne and Paris.

His own works are not epoch-making: commentaries on some of the poets, which supplied material to his pupil Remigius, and a long life of St Germanus of Auxerre in verse. In this he makes considerable parade of his Greek, intercalating into his dedications many words which he got from the works of Dionysius the Areopagite. He makes such experiments in lyric metres as shew him to have been a student of the Odes and Epodes of Horace, and he is credited with being the first of his time to pay much attention to these poems, which were always far less popular than the Satires and Epistles.

Those who have studied the commentaries of Heiric award to them higher praise for real soundness of learning than to those of Remigius. But the name of the latter lived on, and Heiric's did not. Remigius learnt of Dunchad as well as of Heiric, and taught at Rheims for Archbishop Fulk, and at Paris. He lived on into the tenth century, and, it is said, had Odo of Cluny among his pupils. The tale of his writings is a long one, consisting almost entirely of commentaries upon grammarians, poets, and books of the Bible. A tract on the Mass and a glossary of proper names in the Bible, both ascribed to him, went on being copied down to the end of the Middle Ages. Few of the many Bibles of the thirteenth century are without the *Interpretationes Nominum*.

This is perhaps the place to mention the mythographers. Two anonymous collections of stories of the ancient gods and heroes, very baldly told, were printed by Mai from Vatican manuscripts of the tenth and eleventh centuries, along with a later one which does not concern us. The second of these mythographers copies a good deal of matter from the first, and has been, not quite certainly, identified with Remigius. The first quotes authors as late as Orosius, and mingles tales from Roman history with his mythology. Neither attained a wide circulation, but they deserve a word in virtue of their attempts to hand on the ancient legends and throw light on the allusions to them in classical literature.

By the end of the ninth century, it is probably true to say that the Irish stimulus had worked itself out. Had a steady supply of Greek texts been available, one cannot doubt that men would have been found to make use of them, but, it must be repeated, no new material was coming in. Byzantium despised the West and did not care to enlighten it. The Greek monasteries of Southern Italy seem never to have attracted any attention in the north. The chief scholar at Rome, Anastasius Bibliothecarius, died in 897 and left no successor. Something more needs to be said of what he had accomplished. Nearly all his translations, which are not few, were made at the request of friends or of the Pope. He revised John's Dionysius and provided it with scholia rendered from Greek. He put into Latin the Acts of two Councils, that of 787 and that in which Photius was deposed and Ignatius restored to the patriarchate. For John the Deacon, who was designing a large Church history, he translated the Chronography of Nicephorus and copied extracts from the chronicles of George the Syncellus and of Theophanes, the three together forming what was known as the *Chronographia tripartita*, not to be confused with the *Historia tripartita* that was made for Cassiodorus. It is an imposing list, and there is more than this to his credit.

The excursions made into Greek literature in the tenth century are almost negligible. In the middle of it Leo of Naples produced a version of an Alexander-romance for Duke John of Naples from a manuscript he had brought from Constantinople. It marks a stage in the spread of that most influential romance. Later on we encounter another type of Greek scholar, the man thoroughly familiar with the spoken language, in Liudprand of Cremona, diplomat and historian.

It is not pretended that what has been said here of the study and influence of Greek in these centuries is a complete survey. The gaps will be obvious to experts. The province of liturgy, for instance, has not been touched, and there is much in early tropers and other service books which goes to shew that forms were borrowed from the Byzantines. That the litanies of the Saints first appeared in Greek, transmitted from Rome late in the seventh century to England by a Greek-speaking Pope, is a proposition recently maintained by that great scholar Edmund Bishop. Hagiography, again, would easily fill a chapter of its own. We do not yet know all that was done by eastern monks, driven westward by the Iconoclastic troubles, in the way of translation of Acts of Saints, or more generally in the diffusion of their language. Further—a small matter, this, perhaps—it would be worth while to collect the instances in which western scribes have employed the Greek alphabet for their titles and colophons; it is mainly a piece of harmless parade, but is not wholly insignificant. Irishmen, Bretons, and Spaniards were fondest of the practice, though it is not confined to them. Yet another class of documents in which the use of rare Greek words became a fashion are the charters of the tenth century, especially those made in England.

This love of a bizarre vocabulary, which we have noticed before, crops up again and again almost to the end of our period. About 830 we have the strange poem of Lios Monocus, a Breton, who uses the *Hisperica Famina.* About 896, Abbo of St Germain appends to his two books of verse on the siege of Paris by the Northmen a third which is nothing but a series of conundrums, unintelligible from the first without a gloss. A hundred years later our English chronicler Fabius Aethelweard puts the Anglo-Saxon Chronicle into a very crabbed Latin with tags of verse and sesquipedal compounds of his own devising.

It is a relief to turn from these oddities to some writings which have an appreciable value as literature. Gottschalk or Godescalcus, monk of Orbais (805–869), fills an enormous space in the dogmatic history of his time. He paid dear enough to Hincmar of Rheims for the errors of his doctrine, and his tragic story has been remembered by many who forget how grim was his view of election and reprobation: Christ did not die to save all men, but only the elect.

Only in somewhat recent times have certain lyrics of his been brought to light which make him a more sympathetic character. There is a lightness about them not very common; lightness, not of tone, for they are plaintive, but of touch:

> Ut quid iubes   pusiole
> quare mandas   filiole
> carmen dulce   me cantare
> cum sim longe   exul valde
>   intra mare?
> O cur iubes canere?

Yet more recently Gottschalk has been accepted as the author of a poem very famous for six or seven centuries after him, the Eclogue of Theodulus. (Theodulus is no more than Gottschalk, God's slave, turned into Greek.) This Eclogue is a colloquy between Truth (Alithia) and Falsehood (Pseustis) with Reason (Phronesis) for umpire. Falsehood cites a number of incidents from pagan mythology, giving a quatrain to each. Truth caps every one with a contrast from the scriptures. The verdict is a foregone conclusion. In length and subject the poem was admirably fitted to be a school-book, and as a school-book it survived well into the Renaissance period.

In 874 died Hathumoda, first Abbess of Gandersheim. Agius her friend, a monk of Corvey (?), wrote a long prose life of her, and also a dialogue in elegiac verse between himself and her nuns. Rather exalted language has been used about the beauty of this poem, but its ease and simplicity and truth of feeling do mark it out among the productions of its time. It is not however distinguished for originality of thought or excellence of technique.

> Mathias et Barnābas, Tǐmŏthēus, Apollo
> Silvanus, Titus, Theophilus, Gaïus

is not a good couplet, but

> Te iam portus habet: nos adhuc iactat abyssus:
> Te lux vera tenet: nos tenebrae retinent:
> Tu cum virginibus comitans, quocunque eat Agnus
> Lilia cum violis colligis atque rosas

are better lines, and typical of what has been praised in the poem.

Opinion is still unsettled as to whether Agius and a writer known as *Poeta Saxo* are identical. Agius would not gain greatly were his claim established: the poem is nothing but a versification of prose sources (Annals and Einhard) on the life of Charlemagne.

The community of St Gall, as may be guessed from the frequent mention of it in these pages, has a wonderful record for the preservation of ancient literature. It is scarcely less remarkable for its own literary productions. Two of its writers shall have special notice now.

The first is Notker Balbulus, the Stammerer (840–912). Several other Notkers of St Gall followed him, the most famous of whom was Notker Labeo († 1022), translator into German of Boethius and much else. But this first Notker is considerably more important, principally on two grounds. One was the development of a form of church poetry known as the Sequence. The essence of it was this. It had become the fashion to prolong to an exaggerated extent the singing of the word Alleluia where it occurred at the end of antiphons. The melodies of such Alleluias were fixed, but were exceedingly hard to remember. Taking the hint from a Jumièges service-book that had been brought to St Gall, Notker fitted the Alleluias with words appropriate to the Church season or feast, putting as a rule a syllable to each note of the long wandering melody. Thus there grew up a new form of poem, non-metrical at the outset, which in later years became bound by stricter rules, and which exercised a great influence upon secular poetry. In Notker's hands it was wholly conditioned by the tune to which it was set. The one example of it that is widely known in this country is the funeral sequence, *Media in vita*, "In the midst of life," whether that is truly Notker's work or not.

He is also famous as the author of the book of reminiscences of Charlemagne called *Gesta Karoli* and long current simply as the work of the "Monk of St Gall." It is now recognised as Notker's. Alas! we possess only a part of it, but what we have is one of the few books of the period which can really be read with pleasure. There is not much plan in it; it is in the main Notker's recollections of stories told to him in his youth by an old warrior Adalbert who had fought for the Emperor, and by Adalbert's son Werinbert, a cleric, and also by a third informant whose name has been lost with the preface and the third book of the *Gesta*. It was written down at the request of Charles the Fat, who when staying at St Gall in 883 had been greatly delighted with Notker's tales of his great-grandfather and his father. Almost all the picturesque anecdotes that we have of Charlemagne come from this book; tales of war and peace, of embassies from the East and what they brought, of the Emperor's dealings with his clergy, behaviour in church, dress, are to be found here, many doubtless true, others shewing the beginning of a Charlemagne mythology. The loss of the third book is particularly exasperating, for in it were promised recollections of the hero's every-day conversation.

Much more might be said of Notker, of his letters, his poems, his humour, his treatise on the study of the Fathers (a parallel to the Institutions of Cassiodorus), but proportion must be observed, and we must bid farewell to a man both gifted and amiable.

Our second St Gall author is Ekkehard, the first of five persons of that name who are prominent in the Abbey's annals. He died in 973. Early in life he began the work by which he has deserved to be remembered, the short epic of Waltharius. It is a heroic tale, a single episode in a warrior's career. Waltharius escapes with his love from the Hungarian court in which both he and she were kept as hostages, is pursued and successfully defends himself against great odds. The story ends happily, and none of the Latin poems of all this age is better worth reading. There is little of the flavour of a school exercise about it, and there is a great deal of the freshness of the best romances in the vernacular.

With the exception of the *Gesta Karoli*, most of the writings we have touched upon recently have been in verse. We will give a few paragraphs to some of the remaining poets. John the Deacon, a Roman, writing in 875, gives us a curious versification of a curious old piece called the *Caena Cypriani*, and mingles it with personal satire. The whole thing is a *jeu d'esprit*, written, as Lapôtre has shewn, on the occasion of the coronation of Charles the Bald at Rome, and was recited at a banquet where were present various notabilities (Anastasius the Librarian among them) who are smartly hit off.

Hucbald of St Amand's Eclogue in praise of baldness, produced about 885, must be passed with averted eye. Every word of its 146 lines begins with the letter C.

The early part of the tenth century gives us two anonymous books of some slight celebrity, the *Gesta Berengarii*, a panegyric on that Emperor by an Italian who knew some Greek, and the *Ecbasis captivi* by a monk of Toul, "the oldest beast-epic of the Middle Ages." Animals are the actors, and tales in which they figure are woven together not without spirit. But more famous in respect of the sex of the writer and of the vehicle she has employed are the works of Hrotsvitha, a nun of Gandersheim who wrote about 960. They are collected into three books

whereof the first consists of poems on the lives of the Virgin and certain
other saints (the grotesque legend of Gengulphus of Toul is among them),
the second of six so-called comedies, the third of a short epic on Otto I:
another, on the origins of Gandersheim, is preserved separately. The
comedies are the unusual feature. They are written in no strict metre
but in a rhythmical prose, and treat of episodes from saints' lives. They
are avowedly intended to extol chastity, as a counterblast to the mis-
chievous writings of Terence. We have here the earliest of Christian
dramas (dramatic only in form, for Hrotsvitha would never have sanctioned
the acting of them) and as such they would in any case be interesting;
but they are not without merit. Short and easily read, their plots are
not ill-chosen, and the dialogue moves quickly. There is even a touch
of humour here and there, as when, in *Dulcitius*, the Roman persecutor
makes love to the pots and pans in the kitchen, under the illusion of their
being Christian girls, and gets covered with soot.

In one or two cases the sources employed are interesting. The first
poem of the first book deals with the life of the Virgin and the Infancy
of Christ, and is drawn from an apocryphal Gospel, in a text usually
fathered upon Matthew, but here upon James the Lord's brother. The
second, on the Ascension, is from an unidentified Greek text translated
by a bishop John. One of the plays is an episode from the Acts of
St John the Evangelist.

It must be said once again that this chapter is not a text-book or a
history, but a survey, of the literature of two centuries. So far it has
been mainly occupied with what by a stretch of language might be called
belles lettres: but these form only a small fraction of the whole bulk of
writings which have come to us from the years 800 to 1000. To leave
the rest unglanced at would be outrageous. Five headings seem to comprise the greatest part of what it is really essential to notice: Theology,
Hagiography leading over to History, the Sciences and Arts, and books
in vernacular languages.

In the enormous department of Theology we find two great categories,
Commentaries on the Scriptures and controversial writings. Liturgy and
Homiletics we must leave untouched. From the commentators we have
a huge bulk of material, but with very few exceptions, it is wholly un-
original. Like Bede, these men compiled from earlier authors. The
Glossa Ordinaria, already noticed, is typical. Angelomus of Luxeuil,
Haymo of Halberstadt, Raban Maur, are compilers of this class. For
anything like originality we must look to John the Scot and to Christianus
" Druthmarus " of Stavelot, who wrote (in 865) on St Matthew's Gospel:
but even he is distinguished rather by good sense than by brilliancy.

Five principal controversies occupied the minds and pens of the church
writers. At the beginning of our period we have two: the Adoptionist,
in which Elipandus and Alcuin were the foremost figures, and the Iconoclastic. The latter produced a remarkable group of books. The Icono-

clastic cause met much opposition, but also some support, in the West. The *Libri Carolini* against images, written at the Emperor's order (whether or no Alcuin had a hand in them is not settled), are the work of a well-read man who draws interesting illustrations from pagan mythology and contemporary works of art. Claudius, Bishop of Turin, was also a hot Iconoclast in deed and in word. We have only extracts from the treatise he wrote, but we have replies to it from an Irishman, Dungal, and from Jonas of Orleans. Dungal, who quotes the Christian poets very largely, especially Paulinus of Nola, prefixes to his books some fragments from Claudius, and says that the whole work was one-third as long again as the Psalter: he seems to think that this aggravates the offence.

The middle of the ninth century saw two more great disputes. One is that on Predestination, in which the monk Gottschalk, who took the most rigid view, was forcibly silenced, scourged, and imprisoned by Hincmar of Rheims, and written against by John the Scot and Paschasius Radbert of Corbie, to name only two of a large group. Radbert was a man of very wide reading and had one of the best libraries of the time at his command. He is one of the very few who quote Irenaeus *Against Heresies*. The other dispute concerned the Eucharist. Radbert is here again to the fore, in defence of the view which, developed, is the faith of Rome. Ratramn, also of Corbie, wrote in a strain which made the Reformers of the sixteenth century claim him as an early champion on their side.

We have other interesting matter from Ratramn's pen; a treatise against the errors of the Greeks, and a letter to one Rimbert, who had inquired what was the proper view to take of the race of Cynocephali, tribes of dog-headed men believed to inhabit parts of Africa. St Christopher, it is not generally realised, was of this race, and the conversion of one of them is also related in the eastern Acts of SS. Andrew and Bartholomew. Ratramn, who does not cite these examples, answers Rimbert with good sense. If what is reported of the Cynocephali is borne out by facts, they must be looked upon as reasonable and redeemable beings.

The controversy with the Greeks is the fifth and last of these to be mentioned here. Besides Ratramn's book, there is an important contribution to it by Aeneas of Paris.

To Hagiography the Carolingian Renaissance gave an immense stimulus. The founding of a multitude of abbeys and the building of great churches and the stocking of them with relics of ancient martyrs, begged, bought or stolen from Rome, were operative causes. Einhard's story of the translation of SS. Marcellinus and Peter is one classic to which relic-hunting gave birth, Rudolf of Fulda's about St Alexander is another, this last because passages from the *Germania* of Tacitus are embodied in it. There was, besides, the natural wish to possess a readable life of many a patron saint whose doings had been forgotten or else were only chronicled in barbarous Latin of the seventh century. Lives

CH. XX.

invented or rewritten in response to this wish bulk very large in the *Acta Sanctorum*. Not unimportant are the versified Passions and Lives which perhaps begin with Prudentius and Paulinus of Nola and are carried on by Fortunatus (St Martin), Bede (St Cuthbert), Heiric (St Germanus), Notker (St Gall) and a whole host of *anonymi*. All these, fiction or fact, have their interest, but are of course much inferior to the rare contemporary biographies such as those of St Boniface by Willibrord and of St Anschar by Rimbert.

The mention of these leads naturally to the single biographies of uncanonised persons. Charlemagne, we have seen, is the subject of the two best. Those of Louis the Pious by the "Astronomus" and by Thegan have nothing of the charm and skill of Einhard and Notker. Nearest to them is a British writing, the first to be mentioned after a long interval of silence, Asser's life of Alfred.

Of others, that of Eigil by Candidus, a Fulda production of about 840, and that of John of Gorze by Abbot John of Metz have distinct interest. Agnellus's collections on the Archbishops of Ravenna, full of archaeological lore (839), and some of the lives of Popes in the *Liber Pontificalis*, perhaps due to the pen of Anastasius the Librarian, supply us with many facts we are glad to have, but do not pretend to be artistic biographies.

History writing takes three other principal forms. There is the world-chronicle, of which Freculphus of Lisieux and Regino of Prüm (near Trèves) and, later, Marianus Scotus, give examples; there are the annals, commonly connected with a religious establishment, such as those of Lorsch; and there is the episodic, telling of some particular campaign or the rise of some great church. To this last class belongs Nithardus († 844), natural son of Angilbert by Charlemagne's daughter Bertha, and successor (ultimately) to his father as lay-abbot of St Riquier. He writes four short books in clear and simple prose, on Louis the Pious and the quarrels of Lothar, Charles the Bald, and Louis the German—a strictly contemporary record. Incidentally he has preserved, by transcribing the terms of the Oath of Strasbourg, the oldest piece of French and one of the oldest pieces of German which we have. The church of Rheims had two historians. Flodoard (also author of some immense poems) begins in the mists of antiquity and carries the story down to about 966. Richer, whose book is extant (at Bamberg) in the author's autograph, dedicates his history to Gerbert; he devotes small space to early history and much to his own time: his narrative ends in 995. Widukind of Corvey is another name that cannot be passed over: his *Gesta Saxonum* in four books run to the year 973, but by the 16th chapter of the first book he has reached 880, so that his also must rank as a history of his own time. Of all these chroniclers and observers Liudprand of Cremona is by far the smartest. His spiteful pictures of the Byzantine court are not easily to be paralleled: he has a real turn for satire and for vivid description, and the gaps in his text are very much to be deplored.

Of those who treat of the Arts and Sciences the grammarians are probably the most numerous. I have renounced the idea of noticing each Irishman or Frank who has left us an *Ars*, but I would find a place here for mention of two Epistles, separated in time by a full century, which are largely grammatical in subject and epistolary only in form. They serve mainly as displays of their authors' reading. One is by Ermenrich of Ellwangen to Grimald of St Gall (854), the other by Gunzo of Novara to the monks of Reichenau (965) *à propos* of a monk of St Gall who had rashly criticised his Latin. They are tedious compositions, but have their importance.

The writers on Geography are few. Dicuil, an Irishman (825), draws largely upon ancient sources, but adds something about Iceland and the Faröe Islands that depends upon the observations of compatriots who had been there. The famous voyages of Ohthere and Wulfstan, inserted by Alfred into his Orosius, though they are in the vernacular, must find mention under this head. Other quasi-geographers are the translators of Alexander's letter to Aristotle, and other matter on the Marvels of the East. They probably fall within our period, but the best copies we have of them—Anglo-Saxon versions illustrated with pictures—may be of the eleventh century.

Medicine meant chiefly *materia medica*, collections of recipes, and spells. The Latin version of Dioscorides, and the recipes and charms current under the names of Apuleius and Sextus Placidus, were prime authorities. Little new work was produced.

No idea of the progress made in Music can be given, but by a specialist: it must suffice here to name Notker, Hoger, and Hucbald of St Amand as the leading exponents.

Astronomy and Mathematics remain. Both were ancillary to church purposes, the settling of the Calendar and especially the determination of Easter. Bede's were the text-books which were perhaps found most useful generally, and that of Helperic of Auxerre (*c.* 850) had a wide circulation. But we may neglect every name that appears in connexion with Mathematics in favour of that of Gerbert of Aurillac, who died as Pope Sylvester II in 1003. He is the last really outstanding figure. Everything that he wrote and did has distinction, and he demands a somewhat extended notice. Born at Aurillac (Cantal) he spent the years 967–970 in Spain with Hatto, Archbishop of Vich. From 970 to 972 he was with the Emperor: for the next ten years (972–982) he was master of the cathedral school at Rheims, and Richer devotes many pages to telling us what he taught there. In 982 he was made Abbot of Bobbio, the literary treasures of which were no doubt a great attraction to him: in 991 he became Archbishop of Rheims, in 998 of Ravenna. In the following year he passed to the Chair of Peter. His political

activities, which were great, we will pass over, and deal only with his
literary interests, as they are revealed in his letters and in other sources.
The letters most instructive from this point of view are mostly written
from Bobbio.   To Archbishop Adalbero of Rheims he says (*Ep.* 8),
"Procure me the history of Julius Caesar from Adso, Abbot of Montièrender, to be copied, if you want me to furnish you with what I have,
viz. the eight books of Boethius on Astrology and some splendid geometrical diagrams."   To Abbot Gisalbert (*Ep.* 9): "The philosopher
Demosthenes wrote a book on the diseases and treatment of the eyes,
called Ophthalmicus.   I want the beginning of it, if you have it, and also
the end of Cicero pro rege Deiotaro."   Rainard, a monk, is asked for
M. Manlius *De astrologia* (who is thought by Havet not to be the poet
Manilius, but Boethius) and for some other books.   Stephen, a Roman
deacon, is to send Suetonius and Symmachus.   "The art of persuasive
oratory (*Ep.* 44) is of the greatest practical utility.   With a view to it
I am hard at work collecting a library, and have spent very large sums
at Rome and in other parts of Italy, and in Germany and the Belgian
country, on scribes and on copies of books."   To a monk of Trèves
(*Ep.* 134): "I am too busy to send you the sphere you ask for: your
best chance of getting it is to send me a good copy of the Achilleis of
Statius."   The monk sent the poem, but the sphere was again withheld.
Such extracts shew the catholicity of Gerbert's tastes.   Richer tells the
same tale; he runs through the Seven Liberal Arts, and shews what
methods and books Gerbert used in teaching each of them.   In Mathematics his chief innovation seems to have been the revival of the use of
the abacus for calculations, and the employment, in connexion with it,
of an early form of the "Arabic" (really Indian) numerals from 1 to 9,
without the zero.   He also wrote on mathematical subjects, though,
perhaps, no signal discovery stands to his credit.   Besides all this he was
a practical workman.   William of Malmesbury describes in rather vague
terms an organ made by him which was to all appearance actuated by
steam.   To the same excellent author and to Walter Map we owe all the
best of the many legends that have gathered about Gerbert; of the
treasure he found at Rome, guided to it by the statue whose forehead
was inscribed "Strike here," of the fairy whom he met in the forest near
Rheims, and of his death.   He, like Henry IV of England, was not to
die but in Jerusalem.   His Jerusalem was the basilica of Sta Croce in
Gerusalemme at Rome.   It may be worth while to end this sketch of
him with a correction.   We are commonly told that the sixth or seventh
century uncial manuscript of the *Scriptores Gromatici*, the Roman writers
on land-measurement, which is now at Wolfenbüttel, and is known as the
Codex Arcerianus, was Gerbert's.   This is denied by his latest editor,
Boubnov, though he allows that the book was at Bobbio in the tenth
century.
    Our last topic is that of books in vernacular.   For practical purposes

this unscientific expression means the Celtic and Teutonic families of speech; our period has nothing to shew for the Romance languages. Most of what it seemed needful to say about Celtic literature in connexion with learning has found a place in the chapter preceding this. It must be borne in mind that the evolution of fresh native literatures independent of learning transmitted by books is foreign to our subject; the fact that the really native product is in itself the best worth reading is irrelevant here. Famous poems such as the *Tain Bo Cuailnge* and *Beowulf*, and the *Dream of the Rood*, therefore have to be passed over, and such parts of the old Northern *corpus* of poetry as critics allow to be anterior to the year 1000.

Infinitely the largest place in these two centuries is occupied by the Anglo-Saxon writings. A certain number of poems assigned to the latter part of the eighth century are on themes derived from books. The *Andreas* of the Vercelli manuscript is from a text which is only forthcoming in scanty fragments of Latin, though we have it in Greek: there was also once a poem on the adventures of St Thomas in India, but it has disappeared; it was too fabulous for Aelfric to use as the basis of his Homily on the Apostle. Other Acts of Saints are drawn upon in the poems called *Elene* and *Juliana*. We have not the original that lies behind the *Dialogue of Salomon and Saturn*, but there was one, presumably in Latin, and a strange book it must have been. The *Phoenix* is in part at least a rendering of a poem attributed to Lactantius. One of the Genesis-poems—that which is called Genesis B, and has been said to be anglicised from Old Saxon—is held to be under obligations to the poems of Alcimus Avitus. The ninth century Homilies of the Vercelli and Blickling manuscripts, as has been said, present versions of and allusions to the Apocalypse of Thomas. The source oftenest employed for sermons is not unnaturally the homily-book of Gregory the Great, to whom Christian England owed so much.

The end of the same century sees King Alfred's work: he puts into the hands of his clergy and people Gregory, Orosius, Bede, and Boethius, and infuses into Orosius and Boethius something of his own great spirit. He did not seek to make his people or his priests erudite, but to fit them for the common duties of their lives: we find little curious learning in what he wrote or ordered to be written. And in the work of Aelfric, nearly a hundred years later, I seem to see an equally sober and practical, yet not prosaic, mind. His sermons, whether he is paraphrasing Gregory on the Sunday Gospels, or is telling the story of a saint from his Acts, appear to be exactly fitted to their purpose of leading simple men in the right way: skill in narrative, beauty of thought, goodness of soul, are there.

Whatever Aelfric it was who composed the Colloquy for schoolboys, he, too, was gifted with sympathy and freshness. It gives some pictures of ordinary life and manners which have long been popular, and with good reason.

Of some books and fragments which concern matters not theological, it is hard to say whether they fall just within or just outside our period. Such are the medical receipts, the leechdoms and the descriptions of Eastern marvels already alluded to; such too the dream-books, the weather prognostics, the version of the story of Apollonius of Tyre. Byrhtferth of Ramsey, almost the only author of this class whose name has survived, wrote partly in Latin and partly in the vernacular upon "computus," Calendarial science, shortly before the year 1000, when he anticipates the loosing of Satan.

There was a time when it would have been proper to say that important remains of Welsh poetry far older than A.D. 1000 were in existence. That time is past, and it is recognised that the poems of Taliesin and the rest are not of the first age. Glosses and small fragments of verse are the oldest things we have in Welsh. Ireland has more, but of the documents—so far as they have not been noticed already—which bear on learning, a great many can only be dated by the linguistic experts, and unanimity is no more the rule among the scholars than among the politicians of the Celts.

There are, it has been said, Irish versions of the *Aethiopica* of Heliodorus, of the *Thebaid* of Statius and of the *Odyssey*. To the first no date is assigned; it is not in print, and for all one can tell it may have been made from a printed edition: the second appears to be a medieval abstract in prose: the only published text that represents the third is a short prose tale. It has some traits (as of the dog of Odysseus recognising him) which are not derivable from Latin sources, and read like distorted recollections of the Greek; but the main course of the story is wholly un-Homeric. Nor is it claimed as falling within our period. I cite this as a specimen of exaggerations that are current. They are wholly uncalled for. Nobody doubts the reality of the ancient learning of Ireland. It is safe to predict that sober and critical research will not lessen but increase our sense of the debt which the modern world owes, first to Ireland and after her to Britain, as the preservers and transmitters of the wisdom of old time.

I end this chapter, as I began it, with these islands; and as I write, just such a storm hangs over them as that which, breaking, drove Alcuin from their shores eleven centuries ago; and just such destruction is being wrought in the old homes of learning, Corbie, and St Riquier, Laon and Rheims, as the Vikings wrought then. But the destroyers of to-day are no Vikings. They are, and the more is the pity, men of a race which has done a vast deal for learning; that has brought to light things new and old. They are undoing their own work now: they have robbed the world of beauties and delights that never can be given back. It will be long before any of the nations can forgive Germany; longer still, I earnestly hope, before she can forgive herself.

CHAPTER XXI.

BYZANTINE AND ROMANESQUE ARTS.

WHEN Constantine rebuilt the city which we still call Constantinople as a new Rome in the East, doubtless mixed methods in architecture were resorted to. The more important buildings of his official architects must have been in the current Roman manner. Secondary buildings and ordinary dwellings would, however, have been constructed according to local customs, and a modified style must soon have resulted here, as earlier had been the case in Alexandria, and in other Greek and Roman cities of the East. The later Roman architecture became more and more changed through these contacts with the East, not only in structure but in the decorations and the underlying ideals which governed both. It is this mixed product which formed the Byzantine architecture, and has been so named by modern students from the old name of the new capital of the Empire.

As through recent explorations we come to know more of the building modes practised in Egypt, North Africa, Syria, Asia Minor and Mesopotamia, that is, throughout eastern Christendom, it becomes increasingly difficult to cover them all with the one narrow word Byzantine. In Syria, for instance, the builders had much fine stone at command, but little or no brick or timber, and here, in consequence, everything architectural tended to be turned to stone. In Constantinople the common stone was a good, easily cutting, white marble, and this was liberally used in association with excellent burnt bricks of thin flat shape. In Egypt there was a little fine limestone and much mud for bricks, which were frequently, for secondary purposes, used in an unburnt condition.

The term Byzantine properly applies to the style of building developed in the new imperial capital, but some such word as Byzantesque seems to be required to describe inclusively those many varieties of building practised in the Christian East, which were yet more or less the members of a common tradition.

In the fourth century, when the new capital was built, the style was still Roman and the point of view was mainly pagan. Byzantine architecture developed step by step as the Empire became Christianised; and two hundred years later, during the reign of Justinian, the Byzantine style was fully established. We may put the emergence of the style about the middle of the fifth century, that is half-way between the reigns of Constantine and Justinian.

In the East from a very early time ordinary building works were for the most part done with sun-dried mud bricks. In hot, dry countries this forms a fairly good material. Besides this use of crude bricks there had come down a still simpler way of building by aggregations of clay. The mud, even when subdivided into crude bricks, adhered so thoroughly when put together in a mass with liquid mud in the joints, that a type of structure was developed which was homogeneous; the roofs and floors being of the same materials as the walls, and continuous with them. The chambers, large or small, were cells in a mass-material. Such a method of building was common to the valleys of the Nile and the great rivers of Western Asia. Burnt bricks were in turn developed from mud bricks by an extension of the method found so successful in making pottery. Such bricks were often used for special purposes in combination with the crude bricks from an early time. The building forms made use of in typical Byzantine architecture largely depended on the use of brick, which may be regarded as the bringing together of small units well cemented so as to form continuous walls and vaults. Burnt bricks were usually set in so much mortar, the bricks being thin and the joints thick, that the whole became a sort of built concrete. The mortar in a wall, in fact, must frequently have been much more in quantity than the bricks.

Arising doubtless out of primitive ways of forming mud roofs, it became customary later to construct vaults of mud bricks, and then of burnt bricks, by leaning the courses against an end wall so that the vault was gradually drawn forward from the end of a given chamber in inclined layers. Each layer was thus supported by the part already done and no centring was required. Domes came to be erected in a somewhat similar way. A rod or a cord being attached to the centre so as to be readily turned in any direction, a dome was reared on its circular base, a course at a time, the curvature being determined by the length of the rod or cord. About 1670 Dr Covel described this method of procedure, and it is still practised in the East, although skilled dome builders are now but few.

If a dome is not set over a circle, but over an octagon or a square, a troublesome question arises in regard to the angles. Where the chamber is small, and especially in the case of the octagonal form, the work can easily be jutted out in the angles so as roughly to conform to the circular base required for the dome. When, however, a square area is large, some regular solution becomes necessary. The angles of the square may be cut off by diagonal arches so as to form an octagon. If such arches are so built as to continue back into the angles forming little vaults, on a triangular base, they are called squinches. In such cases as these the base of the dome is governed by the width across the chamber, but it is possible to plan a dome on the diagonal dimensions of the area to be covered so as to spring out of the angles. In this case it is clear that the dome as seen from within gradually expands from the four lowest points and spreads on the walls as it grows upward, forming concave triangles having curved lines against the four walls. These pieces of the domical surface running down into the angles are called pendentives. When the circular basis required for the dome is formed by these pendentives it is possible to set a complete semispherical dome on them, and there will be a break in the curvature where such a dome springs from the pendentives; or it is possible to carry on the curvature of the pendentives, forming in this case a flatter dome with the surface continuous to the angles. The first would be a dome on pendentives, and the other we might call a pendentive dome. Again a third variety is obtained by building a circular ring of wall, a "drum," above the pendentives, and on that the dome at a higher level. This was a later fashion. It is rather difficult to see the geometry of all this without a model; but if an apple be cut into halves, and then one half is laid on its cut surface and four vertical cuts are made in pairs opposite to one another so as to reduce the circular base to a square, we shall obtain a model of a dome with continuous pendentives.

The methods of building ordinary vaults with inclined courses as described above were practised in Egypt in the early dynasties, and also in Mesopotamia. Evidence is accumulating which suggests that domes, even domes with pendentives, were used in these countries long before the Christian era. A dome with pendentives has been found over an Egyptian tomb which seems to have been built about 1500 years B.C. When Alexander built his new Greek capital in Egypt it must have been a city of brick buildings covered with vaults, save for a few chief structures which were built in the usual manner of Greek temples. A Latin author, writing about the year B.C. 50, says that the houses of Alexandria were put together without timber, being constructed with vaults covered over with concrete or stone slabs. The scarcity of timber in Egypt, the cause behind the development of vaulted structures, is again brought before us in a letter written by St Gregory to Eulogius, the Patriarch of Alexandria, in regard to timber which was sent to him all the way from Italy. It was doubtless from the new Hellenistic capital, and possibly from Western Asia as well, that the art of building vaulted structures spread to Pompeii and Rome. Later, it was almost certainly from Alexandria that Constantinople obtained the more developed traditions of brick building by which it was possible to erect the great church of St Sophia. It seems to be equally true that decorative ideas and processes were largely derived from Alexandria. In addition to the facts mentioned in the first volume, reference may be made to a painted catacomb chamber at Palmyra illustrated by Strzygowski, who assigned it to the third century. Amongst the subjects are Victories carrying medallions like those on consular ivories of the fifth century. There are also panels representing geometrical arrangements of marble, and a cornice imitating modillions in a formal perspective on the flat. This is practically identical with a "cornice" band made up of flat morsels of marble of different colours at Salonica. At Ravenna again there are angels in mosaic which are certainly derived, as Strzygowski himself pointed out, from such medallion-bearing Victories as those of Palmyra. Alexandria would be the best common centre for places so far apart as Salonica, Ravenna and Palmyra, and the painted catacomb at the latter place may be taken to represent Alexandrian art of the fifth century. Catacomb burial itself most probably originated in Alexander's city. Recent explorations in Asia reveal how wide was the saturation of late Hellenistic and early Christian art in the East. Alexandria was the great emporium for distributing works of art over the civilised world.

Two early churches, both perhaps of the fifth century, may be taken as types, one of the circular plan and the other of the basilican. The former, the church of St George at Salonica, is a domed rotunda having a very thick wall in which a series of recesses are, as it were, excavated, while a bema with an apse projects to the eastward. The circular "nave" thus follows the tradition of many Roman tomb buildings as, for instance, that of St Helena at Rome; this constitutes indeed the martyrion type of church. The rotunda of Salonica may be earlier than the bema attached to it and may have been erected in the fourth century; the masonry of the wall is of small stones with bonding courses of brick, a late Roman fashion. The dome, which is about eighty feet in diameter, was encrusted within with mosaics of which large portions still remain. Eight great panels contained martyrs standing in front of architectural façades. These are, it may be supposed, the courts of paradise. The saints are in the attitude of prayer; and some ivories shew St Menas of Alexandria in a similar way. One of these ivories has the background filled by an architectural composition which is remarkably like those of the Salonica mosaics. Here are round pediments filled with shells, lamps hanging between pairs of columns, curtains drawn back, and birds. Mr Dalton has spoken of the architectural façades which derive from the scenes of the theatre as "in a Pompeian style," and has remarked that the free use of jewelled ornament on columns and arches is an oriental feature. It is not to be doubted that these mosaics derive from the art of Alexandria. The recesses of the interior are also covered with mosaic; this church must have been a wonderfully beautiful work. The dome is covered externally by a low pitched roof.

The basilican church mentioned above is St John of the Studion at Constantinople, which was built about 463 and is now in a terribly ruined condition. It is rather short and wide and had two storeys of marble columns on either hand, the lower tier supporting a moulded marble beam, forming the front of a gallery floor, and the upper tier aiding to carry the roof. A really structural gallery of this kind is a beautiful feature. The most perfect part of this church is now the columnar front of the narthex. The columns and entablature are of marble elaborately carved. This carving, in accordance with a principle which afterwards became still more marked, is sharply cut into the general block-form of the mouldings and capitals, the serrated edges of the leaves are in sharp triangular forms, and details are accentuated with holes formed by a drill. On the white marble and under the bright light this delicately fretted surface decoration tells like pierced work; indeed a little later it became customary to undercut much of the surface patterns so that the capitals were surrounded by a thin layer of pierced pattern work only attached here and there to the background; the result was often wonderfully vivid and delightful. Marble door frames were set between the columns of the narthex, forming a screen; this, like all such expedients in Byzantine architecture, is done in a perfectly direct and simple manner. Without pretence and without bungling the builders did what was required in a free and great way; but it was done in noble materials under the guidance of a fine tradition. Byzantine architecture at its best gives us a romantic feeling of freedom with a classical sense of order; it followed a law of liberty.

Another typical building is the church of SS. Sergius and Bacchus at Constantinople, built about 526. The plan of the central area is an octagon with semicircular recesses projecting from the alternate sides; there are eight strong piers but the interspaces are set with columns which bear a marble entablature forming a gallery beam which follows the tradition just described. The outer walls form a square, from which to the eastward projects the apse of the bema. The central area is covered by a dome which is protected by leadwork but not by any independent roof. The church of S. Vitale at Ravenna closely resembles that of SS. Sergius and Bacchus, but it has hemicycles of columns projecting from every side of the octagon except where the bema opens to the east.

Both these churches were built before Justinian essayed the colossal task at St Sophia, which became one of the greatest building triumphs in the whole history of architecture. The reign of Justinian was a time of astonishing architectural activity; nothing of the kind was to be experienced again, until the twelfth and thirteenth centuries marked, by the erection of countless cathedrals, another flood-time of art. The superb plan of St Sophia must have been led up to by a great number of experiments in smaller churches, many of which have been destroyed unrecorded. The church of Sergiopolis, the ruins of which still exist has great hemicycles of columns on either side of the " nave," and Wulff has recorded two fragmentary plans from ruined churches at Tralles, one of which had some affinity with the church at Sergiopolis, while the other had a great apse from which five apsidal niches projected.

Then again the churches of St Irene and of the Holy Apostles, the latter of which was later than St Sophia, were both experiments in form and in the equilibrium of domes. The Church of Christ (the Holy Wisdom, St Sophia) at Constantinople, has from the moment of its erection been the most famous church in the world. It was only a century old when Arculf brought an account of it to the West, and from that day to this its reputation has been unchallenged. It was the supreme effort of the greatest emperor-builder of the Christian era. It seems to be more individual and original and less related to other buildings of its kind in scale, power and splendour than is any other great architectural work. As M. Choisy has said, " It is a conception marvellous in its audacity— the science of effect, the arts of counterpoise, and of noble decoration can be pushed no further." This wonderful structure was begun on 15 January 532 ; it was completed in six years and dedicated at Christmas 537 : an astonishing effort. The dome soon fell, but it was rebuilt and the church was re-dedicated at Christmas 563.

It is a vast domed hall, surrounded by other halls forming aisles and having two storeys, while the central area rises to the dome. The more organic parts of the structure like the columns, door and window frames, are all of porphyry and of marbles, some white, some coloured. All the rest is rough brickwork entirely covered over within by a precious plating of fine marbles and mosaics of pattern-work and figures on gold backgrounds. There must be whole acres of these encrustations of marble and mosaic. Procopius says, " The entire vaulting is covered with gold, but its beauty is even surpassed by the marbles which reflect back its splendour." On the exterior the structure is bare and plain. It was probably partially sheeted with marble ; the great windows are filled with marble lattices. The domes are covered with lead applied directly upon the brickwork. The central dome was much flatter as first built than it is at present. Expanse rather than height was aimed at. In front of the church was a great square court surrounded by arcades, and many other enclosures full of trees formed quiet precincts around the cathedral. From the description of the Court poet, Paul the Silentiary, recited in 563, at the opening ceremony after the fallen dome had been rebuilt, we may form some picture of the splendour of the great building when complete with all its necessary furniture. The stalls of the priests in the apse were plated with silver. The iconostasis was also of silver, while the altar was of gold set with precious stones, and sheltered by a ciborium, or canopy, of silver—" a silver tower, on fourfold arches and columns, furnished with an eight-sided pyramid, a globe and cross above wrought with many a loop of twining acanthus." On the central axis in front of the iconostasis was the ambo, having a flight of steps to the east and another to the west. It rose from the midst of a circular screen of columns which enclosed also the place for the singers. On the beam which rested on the columns stood many standards bearing lamps, " like trees." The ambo itself had a canopy, and the whole was formed of precious marbles, silver and ivory. On the elevated floor of this ambo the Emperors were crowned. It was the prototype of the " pulpitum" set up at Westminster where the English kings were crowned.

"Who shall describe the fields of marble gathered on the pavement and lofty walls of the church? Fresh green from Carystus, and many-coloured Phrygian stone of rose and white, or deep red and silver; porphyry powdered with bright spots, green of emerald from Sparta, and Iassian marble with waving veins of blood-red on white; streaked red stone from Lydia and crocus-coloured marble from the hills of the Moors. Celtic stone like milk poured out on glittering black; the precious onyx like as if gold were shining through it, and the fresh green from the land of Atrax, a mingled harmony of shining surfaces. The mason also has fitted together thin pieces of marble figuring intertwining curves bearing fruit and flowers, with here and there a bird sitting on the twigs. Such adornment surrounds the church above the columns. The capitals are carved with the barbed points of graceful acanthus; but the vaulted roof is covered over with many a little square of gold, from which the rays streaming down strike the eyes so that men can scarcely bear to look."

The church was dedicated and re-dedicated at Christmas, and the axis of the church points exactly to the point of sunrise on Christmas Day. It must have been at the very moment of sunrise that the doors of the completed church were thrown open.

The poet says, " At last the holy morn had come, and the great door of the new-built temple ground on its opening hinges. And when the first beam of rosy light, driving away the shadows, leapt from arch to arch, all the princes and people hymned their song of praise and prayer, and it seemed as if the mighty arches were set in heaven."

The architects were two artists from Asia Minor, Anthemius of Tralles and Isidorus of Miletus. They were the most famous builders of the age, and Anthemius with a younger Isidorus, nephew of the other, is said to have built also the Church of the Holy Apostles.

The square area covered by the central dome of St Sophia is more than one hundred feet in each direction; it is prolonged, east and west, by two vast semicircles, making a length of considerably more than two hundred feet. From the eastern semicircle open three smaller apses, and to the west open two apses and a central square compartment. All this is unobstructed area, one colossal chamber. At the sides of the square central space, and around the four corner apses, stand magnificent monolithic columns of porphyry, and of marble, green spotted with white. These columns with their arches support the gallery floor above the aisles. Over them again rise other columns which bear the lateral walls supporting the dome. The dome itself is pierced around its base by forty windows through which a flood of light pours into the vast space.

On the pendentives are still four colossal six-winged cherubim of mosaic, which probably formed part of the first decoration. Similar creatures are painted in the nearly contemporary MS. of Cosmas the traveller. The dome probably had a figure of Christ in a circle at the summit and the rest of its surface sprinkled with stars. Right and left on the vault of the bema are still two great angels with wings which reach to their feet. On the vault of the apse itself are also some remains, although much injured and now obscured by paint, of a large figure of the seated Virgin holding in her arms the Saviour who gives the benediction. Probably these are works executed after the Iconoclastic interval.

Anthony, a Russian pilgrim (*c.* 1200), says that Lazarus the image-painter first painted in the sanctuary of St Sophia the Virgin with Christ in her arms and two angels. Now a celebrated artist of this name was one of those who suffered at the Iconoclastic persecution; he was imprisoned and tortured but he survived to replace over the great gate of the palace called Chalce the image of Christ. Bayet, who quotes the story from the life of Theophilus, speaks of this with some doubt as a monastic legend (*Byz. Art*, p. 124). This very figure, however, is mentioned within fifty years of the time required in an edict of Leo the Wise known as the Book of the Prefect. In this it is ordained that the perfumers of the city should have their shops between the Milion and the "Venerated image of Christ which surmounts the Portico of Chalce, to the end that the incense should rise toward the image." Further Dr Walsh, who was chaplain to our embassy at the Porte about 1820, writes in a little book entitled *Essays on Ancient Coins*, "There stood till very late in Constantinople an inscription over the gate of the palace, called Chalce. Under a large cross sculptured over the entrance to the palace were the following words, 'The Emperor cannot endure that Christ should be represented (graphes) a mute and lifeless image graven on earthly materials, but Leo and his young son Constantine have at their gates engraved the thrice blessed representation of the Cross, the glory of believing monarchs.'" A plain cross had evidently replaced the original image; later, possibly under Michael II, a crucifix was again placed over the gateway. Doubtless a similar alteration was made in St Sophia and other churches, and of one of these we still have ample evidence. The fine conch over the apse of the church of St Irene in Constantinople has only a large plain cross, erect on a stepped base set on a gold background. In St Sophia at Salonica there is a similar plain cross over the apse, and both these are almost certainly of the Iconoclastic period.

After this short description of the central classical example of Byzantine art, St Sophia, Constantinople, it is impossible to attempt any account of other individual buildings. At Salonica there is a wonderful group of churches, including the superb basilica of St Demetrius. In Asia Minor there are a great number of ruined churches, many of which must have been built during the reign of Justinian. One important group of ruins comprising a monastery and a palace, Ḳasr ibn Wardān, has only recently been discovered. The church in Isauria described by Dr A. C. Headlam is now famous as a step in development. Later researches by Sir William Ramsay and Miss Bell, and the German excavations at Priene, Miletus and Ephesus, have brought to light an immense body of new material. Syria is crowded with ruined churches, many of which were built in the great sixth century. A well-equipped American expedition, which lately worked over the ground, has added greatly to our knowledge of the period. Still further east in Mesopotamia and Armenia there are many interesting buildings, some of which are still used for Christian worship. In Egypt and the Sūdān the Christian ruins are at last receiving attention, and an Austrian expedition has excavated the convent of St Menas near Alexandria. The excavations at Bawit and Saḳḳara have brought to light a wonderful series of capitals and other sculptured stones. Many of these seem to be prototypes of forms well known in Constantinople and Ravenna. One or two second-rate capitals of this kind have recently been added to the British Museum, but the best have gone to Berlin, where there is a very fine collection of Christian art, and to Boston. To the age of Justinian belong the monastery and church of St Catherine under Mount Sinai, where still as when Procopius wrote, "monks dwell whose life is only a careful study of death." It is a compact square fort surrounded by high walls, within which is a large church half filling up the space, the rest being occupied by a few narrow lanes of small dwellings. The Egyptian monasteries are of this type, and that of Sinai was doubtless built by masters from Egypt. The plan of the church has an Egyptian characteristic in a chapel across the east end outside the apse. The church is basilican with granite columns and a wooden roof. On the old timbers were found three inscriptions, which shewed that the monastery was finished between 548 and 562. In the apse is a much injured mosaic of the Transfiguration which is probably of the age of the church. Besides the celebrated enamelled door, which probably dates from the eleventh century, are some carved wooden doors, which De Beylié thinks belonged to the original work. The inscriptions spoken of above mention Justinian, "our defunct empress Theodora," and Ailisios the architect.

During the last generation an enormous body of evidence for Christian art in North Africa has been recorded by French scholars. One of the latest discoveries is a beautiful baptistery at Timgad, which had the floor and the basin of the font with its curb-wall continuously covered with mosaic. It may be mentioned here that parts of a mosaic floor, from what must have been a baptistery at Carthage, are now in the British Museum. This shews a stag and a hind drinking from the waters of paradise, recalling the verse: "As the hart panteth after the water brooks."

On the shores of the Adriatic and in Italy are many pure Byzantine works of the sixth century. One is the splendid basilica of Parenzo with its atrium and baptistery complete. It has a great number of beautiful carved capitals which were certainly imported from Constantinople. There are also some fine mosaics. The most remarkable of these is one covering the external surface of the west wall above the atrium roof. It shewed the Majesty enthroned amidst the seven candlesticks. This may remind us that Justinian encrusted the west external wall of the basilica of the Holy Nativity at Bethlehem with a great mosaic of the birth of Christ. Such external mosaics were quite common on Byzantine churches. At Parenzo, as also at Ravenna, and in St Sophia itself, there is much ornamental plastering of the sixth century.

At Ravenna is a large group of buildings, some of the age of Justinian, others both earlier and later. S. Vitale has already been mentioned. The delightful small cruciform tomb-chapel of Galla Placidia has some fifth century mosaics. There are also two large baptisteries and two magnificent basilican churches with their splendid mosaics. Here also is the very curious tomb of Theodoric with its monolithic covering shaped like a low dome.

One of the chief treasures preserved in this city is a superb ivory throne, a work of the fifth century, with panels carved with subjects from the Old and New Testaments. This is almost certainly an Alexandrian work. Somewhat similar panels, preserved at Cambridge and in other museums, suggest that more than one of such thrones had been made.

In Rome there are several remnants from the age of Justinian, chief amongst which are the choir enclosures of S. Clemente. At Milan, on the north side of S. Lorenzo, is a beautiful chapel with mosaics in apsidal recesses. One is of Christ and the Apostles, which is executed in a very grey scheme of colour, largely black and white, with some blue and green; the nimbus of Christ is white. Although so simple these mosaics are most beautiful. At Naples there is a baptistery with very fine but fragmentary mosaics, which date perhaps from the end of the fifth century.

Byzantine mosaic decoration was one of the noblest art-forms ever developed. Enormous areas were covered by perfectly coherent and co-ordinated schemes of pictorial teaching, and a solemn majesty was unerringly attained; while the splendour of the gold backgrounds suffused the whole with a glowing atmosphere.

The types of Christian imagery which are found in the Byzantine mosaics of the fifth and sixth centuries were probably drawn from Egyptian Christian sources. It has been suggested that these types may have originated in Palestine, and that the paintings and mosaics of the great churches built there by Constantine largely influenced the schemes of imagery in the rest of Christendom may not be doubted. It is improbable, however, that Palestine was a school of iconographical invention; whereas

Egypt seems to have been a glowing hearth of pictorial activity from the Hellenistic age onwards.

Early Christian iconography must have been developed at an active Hellenistic centre. Jerusalem was hardly this, and Palestinian art for the most part must have been an offshoot of that of Alexandria. It is probable that painted rolls and books were the chief sources, from which the types to become familiar in paintings and mosaics were spread abroad.

The codex form of book, which seems at an early time to have become specially associated with Christian literature, was almost certainly an Egyptian innovation. According to Sir Maunde Thompson, codices of vellum, of the third century and earlier, have been found in Egypt, and this form of MS. " was gradually thrusting its way into use in the first centuries of our era.... The book form was favoured by the early Christians. In the fourth century the struggle between the roll and the codex was finished." Some fine book-bindings, which may even be as early as the sixth century, have lately been found in Egypt. The noble *Codex Alexandrinus* of the fifth century, now in the British Museum, is an Egyptian book. So also, almost certainly, is the once beautiful, but now almost destroyed, pictured book of Genesis called the Cotton Bible. The writing of this volume is very like that of the *Codex Alexandrinus* and of a great number of papyrus fragments. It also seems to date from the fifth century, and furthermore its pictures have some affinities with others in an Alexandrian chronicle of the world on papyrus, which has been published by Strzygowski, while they have a closer likeness to other painted books which have been judged to have been produced in Alexandria, such as illuminated volumes of Dioscorides and of Cosmas the traveller, and a roll of Joshua. Many points in the miniatures with which the Cotton Genesis was crowded bear out this view of its origin. Thus, two of those relating to Joseph in Egypt shew a group of pyramids in the background; a third had well-drawn camels; and another the burial of a body wrapped like a mummy. It has been proved by Dr Tikkanen of Helsingfors that this MS. or a duplicate of it, was used by the mosaic workers at St Mark's, Venice, at the end of the twelfth century, for the designs from early Bible history which fill the domes of the narthex. Twenty-six of those relating to the Creation were accurately enlarged copies of as many miniatures from the now terribly injured book, and these subjects, designs of great dignity and grace, can consequently be restored. Other pictures in the volume which relate to Lot, Abraham and Joshua, were again very similar to the series of mosaics executed in Sta Maria Maggiore in Rome about A.D. 440, and, indeed, the types found in the Cotton Genesis seem to have had an almost canonical importance. Their influence can be traced far down in the Middle Ages, and even the Biblical pictures of Raphael still retained some reminiscence of them. One characteristic of the Cottonian MS. is the appearance in the miniatures of impersonations of such ideas as the Seven Days of Creation, and the Four Rivers of the Garden; the former being represented as seven angels, and the latter as four reclining figures with urns. The Soul breathed into man is depicted in the form of a winged Psyche. The Creator is shewn as Christ, " by Whom all things were made."

Another famous book of Genesis at Vienna, having pictures painted below the text on pages of purple vellum, is almost certainly later than the Cottonian book, and although there are obviously some links between them, the Vienna designs seem to stand outside the Alexandrian circle. Two other books on purple, which have much in common with the Vienna book, are the codices of Rossano and Sinope. All three may probably be dated about A.D. 500, and may have been painted at Constantinople. The magnificent Dioscorides, which is dated *c.* 512, is almost certainly an Alexandrian book. Its fine, clear drawings of plants may be copied from a more classical original. The Joshua Roll of the Vatican is probably sixth century and of Alexandrian origin.

Several of the mosaics at Ravenna have characteristics similar to the miniatures in these Egyptian books, and it may be regarded as certain that it was not only at St Mark's, Venice, that the designs for mosaics were taken from such sources. Indeed, it must be more and more recognised that such compositions were very often drawn out of authorities almost as fixed as the texts which they illustrated. All religious art, and Byzantine art especially, has in a large degree been the handing on of a tradition. The outlines of these iconographical schemes must have been suggested by theologians[1]. They were certainly not the result of a free play of artistic fancy.

A number of figured textiles which have been found in Egypt are also very interesting in regard to the treatment of their subjects. Some are merely painted or dyed and others are woven and embroidered. Three pieces of the dyed work in the Victoria and Albert Museum have designs of the Annunciation, the Nativity and the Miracles of Christ. These, again, are interesting as giving us versions of well-known types of the subjects, and suggest that these designs also had their character impressed upon them in Egypt. For instance, they closely resemble others found on the ivory throne at Ravenna, and this similarity reinforces the argument in favour of that famous work having been made in Alexandria, which was the great mart for objects in carved ivory[2].

A favourite scheme of ornamentation on the Christian textiles found in Egypt is the imitation of jewelling. Especially is this the case with the Cross; and the jewelled cross, which appears again and again in the mosaics of Rome, Ravenna and Constantinople, would also seem to have been an Egyptian invention. Recently many wall-paintings have been

---

[1] As in some later Italian works, such as in the Spanish Chapel at Florence. See Wood Green, J., *Sta Maria Novella*, pp. 150 ff.　　　[2] See Vol. I. Chapter xxi.

exposed by excavation in Egypt and here, also, well-known types, like the Majesty and the Ascension, have been found.

It has not been possible to speak of the quality of Byzantine art but only of certain leading facts in its history. As a whole it was a wonderful movement of return to first principles in regard to structures and to the free expression of feeling in what we call decoration. Roman art was very largely official, grandiose, and a matter of formulas. The Roman artist was as closely imprisoned in conventions as we ourselves are. Then came a time and an influence which led the people to build what they wanted only by the rules of common sense, and to draw for decorative art fresh draughts from the springs of poetry.

So art was transformed and a great cycle of a thousand years was entered on. Early Christian, Byzantine, Romanesque and Gothic are all incidents in its mighty sweep, and before it was spent great cathedrals had been built all over Europe.

Having followed, so far as our space will allow, the main stream of Christian art while flowing through Constantinople and the East, we must now try to trace the broader facts of its development in the West.

It is not to be doubted that, until the eastern civilisation was checked by the Arab conquests in the seventh century, its art had been the true heir of the ages, and that the great upheaval put a stop to its proper progress, and then threw it back in many broken eddies over western Europe. In our first volume we saw that early Christian art was a phase of Roman art modified by eastern ideas. In western Europe, for the early Christian period, there were in the main three influences at work, in the culture of which art is one aspect: the native stock, the Romano-Christian tradition, and the steady, unceasing pressure of oriental ideas. In mentioning the latter we do not try to beg any " Byzantine question." It would doubtless be true to say conversely that the West influenced the East, but here and now we are only concerned with the West and the action of external forces upon it.

In reaction against claims which have been urged for oriental influence in Christian art, Commendatore Rivoira has lately made a powerful plea for a further consideration of the part played by Rome and Italy as the main source of western Christian art, but he confessedly does this rather in regard to structural architecture than to the pictorial and plastic matters which form so great a part of any complete architecture. Further, in regard to the structures, his contention in many cases only avails to shew that those eastern customs, which some earlier writers had thought came in with Byzantine art, had already been taken over by Roman builders. And it must never be forgotten that Roman art itself was only one branch of a widespread Hellenistic culture the prime centre of which was Alexandria.

Quite recently a whole new phase of Roman art has been coming into view, that is, the form of it which was developed rather in the provinces than in the capital. An enormous body of this Roman provincial art has been revealed by French researches in North Africa, and the study of local antiquities in Italy, France, Spain, South Germany, and even Britain, shews how far this little-known art had developed or degenerated from the standards of the Augustan age. This art is rude and redundant, shewing a ferment of undisciplined ideas, and in it we may find many of the germs of the Christian architecture of the West which, by a true instinct, has been called Romanesque.

Probably the best centre in which to study provincial Roman art is Trèves, where a perfectly arranged museum is crowded with smaller monuments, while many large ones are still extant in the streets. Among the latter are a magnificent basilica, now a church, a great city gate, the Porta Nigra, and a ruined palace, usually called that of Augustus, although apparently it must belong to the fourth century. The monuments in the museum comprise a great number of important, richly sculptured, tombs, some of which are of the sarcophagus form, while others are like small towers crowned by a pyramid, with a sculptured finial at the apex, a form which recalls many a Romanesque tower and spire built centuries later. They themselves seem to derive from the mausoleum of Halicarnassus. The sloping surfaces of the pyramidal coverings are roughly carved into leafage arranged like scales, and the rest of these monuments is adorned with a profusion of sculptured figures and pattern-work. The large plain surfaces are frequently covered by what, in later art, we should call diaper patterns, that is, recurring arrangements of lozenges, octagons and circles, combined so as to cover the field and with the interspaces filled in with simply-carved leafage. This type of ornamentation is practically unknown in classical Roman architecture. It was doubtless taken up from the East, and it is the precursor of a kind of decoration, which thenceforth was to be common for many centuries; indeed, the covering of flat vertical surfaces with roughly cut patterns in low relief is typical of the art of the " Dark Ages." It may be noted that the surface patterns, and even the figure sculptures, on the monuments of Trèves were painted with bright colours, and hence it seems probable that the elaborate braided and chequered ornamentation of our own Saxon crosses was completed by colouring.

What we have found best illustrated at Trèves must have been characteristic, in greater or lesser degree, of all the cities of western Europe[1]. Even in London, at the Guildhall and British Museums, there are fragments which shew that a similar type of architecture prevailed here. Amongst the stones are some which clearly belong to tombs with pyramidal coverings like those mentioned above, and other stones, some of which belong to small columns, have diaper pattern-work. These fragments

[1] Even in Britain the lion dug up at Corbridge (Corstopitum) is a striking example.

probably belonged to the tombs of the rich merchants of Londinium. The coins of Roman Britain shew a similar likeness to those of Trèves, which in the fourth century was the capital of the western section of the Empire. In the museum at Sens are important remnants of a façade, which was largely decorated with boldly designed vine foliage of a curiously "Romanesque" character.

Romanised Europe was a soil well prepared for the upspringing of Romanesque art, and many centres, down to the end of the twelfth century, shew us how the old monuments were turned to for inspiration and guidance. In some places there was hardly any interruption of continuity; in others the conquering peoples from the North (although they entered into that which they could not properly understand or use) could not help crude imitation when they themselves had to build. The problem of architectural history is now less one of inquiry as to sources than a question as to the vigour of building impulse. An energetically expanding school always gathers from everything it may reach, but a declining school does not know how to use even what it has. When the Romanesque movement in architecture was under way, the Roman background was searched, and at the same time the current customs of the more powerful art of the East were drawn upon.

In the fifth century, western Europe had a vast system of splendid roads linking up a great number of provincial Roman cities. Many of them were burned and ruined, but few can have been destroyed. Even in Britain these Roman cities were sights to wonder at, as the poem on the ruins of Bath witnesses, and Bede tells us how the citizens of Carlisle guided St Cuthbert round the city shewing him the walls and a fountain of marvellous workmanship constructed formerly by the Romans. In Rome itself the early Christian tradition was being continued, and there, as at Ravenna and Milan, at Lyons and Arles, Byzantine influences were all the time being absorbed and passed on to the West.

The third strain in Romanesque art was the barbaric element in the blood and traditions of the people. After the Roman and Byzantine influences, which came from the Church, had been absorbed and transformed, the art began to put on more and more of a barbaric character. This was especially the case in the West after the Danish irruptions. Some of the stone carvings wrought in England during the tenth century were extremely savage in their character.

A school of art, which should be of extraordinary interest to us, is that which arose in Northumbria in the second half of the seventh century, but was soon to disappear. There is ample documentary record of the culture of the time when Wilfrid and Benedict Biscop built churches and formed monastic libraries, and when Bede wrote his famous history. Some remnants of Wilfrid's churches yet remain, and Bede tells us how they were decorated by paintings forming a consistent series of Biblical types and story. These paintings were brought from Rome, and the fortunate discovery of the painted walls of Sta Maria Antiqua in that city, which were decorated by Greek artists just at the time that Benedict Biscop was making his collection, suggests very clearly what these pictures must have been like. It cannot be doubted that they were of eastern origin. Many works of art, which we still fortunately possess, have been attributed to the same age, but some of them are so remarkable as compared with other works of that time on the Continent that Commendatore Rivoira and Professor Cook of Yale have argued with great detail that they could not have been produced at that time. At Ruthwell and Bewcastle, on either side of the Scottish border, are the shafts of two tall standing crosses elaborately sculptured with figures and pattern-work, with long inscriptions in runes, and, in the case of Ruthwell, with Latin inscriptions as well. Rivoira, approaching the question from the Italian point of view, and with a wide knowledge of European art, would assign them to the twelfth century, and Professor Cook argues that they were probably erected by King David of Scotland about 1140[1].

These noble cross shafts, however, are only the most famous of a large class of monuments of more or less the same type, which must belong to about the same period. If they have to be dated in the twelfth century, the Irish crosses also, as is recognised by the critics just named, cannot be earlier. Such a scheme in all its implications would make a tremendous alteration in British archaeology. On the other hand, the early dates of some of the Saxon works are so firmly established that they cannot even be attacked. Such are large numbers of early Saxon coins, some of which bear devices analogous to the decorations of the crosses, while others, like the coins of Offa, have fine heads. Others, again, like a coin of Peada, have runes of similar form to those on the crosses. If a selection of such coins was published in comparison with the crosses, much that has been said as to the improbability of the early date of these would have to be ruled out. We also possess the splendid illuminated text written and decorated at Lindisfarne very early in the eighth century, with its braided ornamentation, symbols of the four evangelists, and other designs which closely resemble the ornament and symbols on the crosses. There is also the noble *Codex Amiatinus*, once owned by Abbot Ceolfrid, and taken with him as a present for the Pope when he left England for Rome in 716, which has some points of resemblance. It has further been shewn that the Latin inscriptions, which describe the sculptures on the Ruthwell Cross, are in an alphabet of a semi-Irish character resembling the letters of the Lindisfarne book, while the runic inscription of this cross contains a version of the old English poem on the Dream of the Holy Rood, which Dr Bradley attributes to the authorship of Caedmon. Another monument, the date of which has not been

[1] See Baldwin Brown, G., *The Arts in Early England*, Vol. v. 1921.

attacked, is the shrine of St Cuthbert now at Durham, which is recorded to have been made in 698. Some designs incised on it, which include figures of Christ, angels, and apostles, together with symbols of the evangelists, a cross and inscriptions, are again singularly like the designs found upon the two great cross shafts. The runes on the Bewcastle cross formed a memorial inscription, which is terribly decayed, and doubt is cast on the readings, first made in 1856, by which it appeared that it was set up to Alchfrid, son of Oswy, about the year 670. On the other hand, the name Cyneburh, which was the name of Alchfrid's wife, has often been read by many independent observers, including Kemble, in 1840. Even the presence of the name Alchfrid is admitted by Viator, the Runic scholar, but Professor Cook claims that the form is feminine and cannot apply to Alchfrid. Thus the question stands for the moment, but when, by comparative illustration, it has been shewn that the objection to the early date of the art of these wonderful monuments must fall to the ground, then we may anticipate that much of the opposition to the interpretation of the runes will also disappear. At the least the certain name of Cyneburh will be given its due weight. The present writer has no doubt at all that these crosses were set up by a powerful Northumbrian ruler in the seventh century. Professor Cook even expresses a doubt as to whether these shafts were parts of crosses at all, which to English scholars will seem like doubting whether a torn volume was ever a book. His work, however, is valuable as stating the case for the extremist reaction. In regard to the sculptures on the Ruthwell cross, it has been shewn that they have affinities with the subjects on the Byzantine ivory throne at Ravenna, which was probably made in Alexandria, and with some Coptic works. Now the second half of the seventh century was exactly the time when Rome itself had become almost completely Byzantinised. The church of Sta Maria Antiqua, before mentioned, belongs to this time. It is no accident that it was just at this moment that a Greek from Tarsus, Theodore by name, became Archbishop of Canterbury. The sculptures on the Ruthwell cross include the Crucifixion, the Annunciation, Christ healing the blind man, Christ and the Magdalene, and the Visitation on one side; on the other, the flight into Egypt, SS. Paul and Anthony the hermits, breaking bread in the desert, Christ worshipped by " beasts and dragons," St John Baptist, and the symbols of the evangelists. A third cross shaft, hardly less remarkable, that of Acca, now at Durham, is accepted by Rivoira as being of the eighth century. It is difficult for an English student to understand why two should be taken away and the other left.

Saxon works of a different kind, but not less noteworthy, are the silver Ormside cup, the celebrated Alfred jewel and the vestments of Bishop Frithstan, now at Durham, which were embroidered at Winchester about the year 912. It may be remembered that William of Malmesbury says that the daughters of Edward the Elder were skilful needlewomen, and it is not unlikely that these exquisite works came from this royal school of art. It may be pointed out that one of the designs on the Durham embroideries is the Right Hand of God. Now this same device also appears on the Wessex coinage of Edward the Elder, and on the sculptured Rood of Romsey Abbey, which probably filled the central space on the west front of the church with figures of the Virgin and St John on either hand of the Crucified Figure, above which the Hand appears. A similar group, much defaced, may still be seen on the west front of the little church at Hedbourne Worthy, close to Winchester.

Anglo-Celtic art has been very much neglected, but in Great Britain and Ireland we have an enormous number of sculptured monuments which certainly have high interest for the history of art in Europe during the dark ages. It may seem an extravagant claim, but if the productions of the Anglian school are recognised, it will appear to be, at its Northumbrian centre especially, the first Teutonic school of Christian art. This is allowed for literature; poems like Caedmon's were not written in Gaul, but it has hardly even been suggested for sculpture, metalwork, and other crafts. It is agreed that the later school formed by Charlemagne became the centre for west European culture; yet, after all, Charlemagne gathered up the Northumbrian traditions, and Alcuin was but a follower of Wilfrid and Ceolfrid.

The Irish crosses are less competent in execution than the finest of the Anglian works, and the same is true of other forms of Irish art. The large number and the good preservation of the Irish crosses, however, give them considerable importance. On them we find sculptures which carry on the early Christian tradition in a very remarkable way. The designs must, for the most part, have been copied from quite early painted books of Eastern origin, and from ivories and other small works. The subjects are of the Crucifixion, and of Christ the Judge, with many scenes from the life and miracles of Christ, together with "types" from the Old Testament. Favourite types of Christ are the offering of Isaac, and David protecting the sheep by slaying the lion. Over the Crucifixion of a cross at Monasterboice is Moses with his uplifted arms supported by two companions. The life of David as a type of Christ is given in several scenes on some of the crosses. Another subject which occurs very frequently is the meeting of SS. Anthony and Paul in the desert. The ideals were clearly monastic, and those who had the crosses set up looked reverently back to the hermits of the Egyptian desert.

Much in Carolingian Romanesque art was directly derived from the Roman monuments; indeed, it must have been thought by Charlemagne and his Court that Roman architecture was being continued just as the Empire was being resumed. Romanesque, we may say, is "Holy Roman architecture." A letter of Einhard's exists, which was sent together with an ivory model of a column shaped according to the rules

of Vitruvius, and it is significant that the earliest existing text of
Vitruvius, the Harley MS. in the British Museum, is also Carolingian.
The doorway of Charles the Great's church at Aix-la-Chapelle, recently
exposed, has a large architrave of classical form. This doorway might
well be a work of the fourth century A.D., and so might some of the bronze
doors, and the pine-cone fountain. The mouldings of the interior had
classical forms, and old Corinthian capitals, which were probably brought
from Italy, were re-used in the arches of the gallery storey. Of course
there was no thought of any archaeological distinction between what was
Roman and what was Byzantine; the great fact was that barbarism
took up the arts of civilisation, and it must have been thought that
Rome was being renewed by the efforts of Charlemagne. This Carolingian Renaissance gives us an invaluable example of a conscious building
up of a school of art.

In Italy many buildings, like the baptistery at Florence, shew a
deliberate attempt to be classical. In France, also, we meet with the
same intention. At Langres, once a Roman town, the fine cathedral
church (twelfth century) is wonderfully Roman in many particulars.
The buttresses between the chapels at the east end are in the form of
fluted Corinthian pilasters. In the interior the nave arches rise from
similar fluted pilasters with Corinthian capitals; the triforium has fluted
pilasters rising to a horizontal string moulding; beneath is a bold band
of scroll carving of a classical type; and many of the columns have the
classical entasis. At Bourges, another Roman town, the elaborate
doorways of the north porch have finely carved lintels of scroll work
and foliage, which must have been practically copied from a Roman
original. At Autun the direct influence of the Roman gateway, which
is still standing, can be traced in the details of the cathedral. At
Arles, St Gilles, Le Puy, and in dozens of other places a similar transference from Roman prototypes is apparent in Romanesque architecture.
The Romanesque type of tower, with a low, square spire, with scale
ornaments cut into the sloping surfaces, must largely derive from the
late Roman tombs like those of Trèves above described. Even Roman
methods of construction, like concreted rubble walling, small facing
stones, and courses of tiles set in arches, persisted until the eleventh and
twelfth centuries.

The second great strain in Romanesque art was formed by the
constant inflow of eastern ideas and decorative objects, as well as of
monks and artists. After Justinian reconquered Italy, fragments of the
land remained dependencies of the Eastern Empire until the eighth century. In Rome itself during this time Art became almost completely
Byzantinised. There are several beautiful Byzantine capitals and slabs
in Rome which were imported from Constantinople, and the round church
of St Theodore on the Palatine belongs to this time. Even a brick-
stamp of Pope John (A.D. 705) is inscribed with Greek letters.

The monument which most clearly witnesses to the presence of the East in the West is the church of Sta Maria Antiqua, excavated about twenty years ago out of the *débris* at the foot of the Palatine Hill. It is in the Forum, on the right in going to the Coliseum. It was an old Roman building, which was transformed into a church early in the seventh century, being a large, high hall having lateral chambers formed into chapels. The walls were partly covered with a plating of marble, and all the rest was adorned with paintings, which, for the most part, are still in good condition. The paintings are inscribed mostly in Greek with some Latin. A stone of the ambo had a bilingual inscription: † John Servant of the Theotokos. The art-types are obviously eastern, and the saints depicted are both eastern and western. There are paintings of the Crucifixion, the Majesty, the enthroned Virgin and Child, the Annunciation, Nativity, Daniel in the Lions' Den, and many others. In the apse of the chapel is a large figure of Christ between two six-winged tetramorphs. The background of this subject is divided into an upper portion painted black, and a lower part divided vertically into four parts alternately red and green. The Crucifixion is very like another in a Syrian book now at Florence. On either hand of the Cross are the two soldiers, by one of whom is inscribed Longinus. On the Syrian Gospel, which was written in 586 by the monk Rabula, the similar figure of the soldier is named ΛΟΓΙΝΟC. The resemblances are altogether so remarkable that it cannot be doubted that this very Syrian MS. or a similar one was the direct source for the wall painting. It has been already pointed out by Mr Dalton that a curious pattern which is found at Sta Maria Antiqua, like a row of overlapping coins, occurs again also in the Codex of Rossano, another book which is possibly of Syrian origin, and it occurs again in a Syrian book at Paris. The coincidences are so striking that it becomes evident that some oriental books must have been directly used as the sources for the designs in the church. It has often been pointed out that the mosaics of Sta Maria Maggiore must have been drawn from some book of Genesis painted in the East. Several of the mosaics in Ravenna follow a similar canon, and so again do some fragmentary Genesis pictures in Sta Maria Antiqua itself. Further, it has been proved by Tikkanen, as before mentioned, that the Genesis mosaics at St Mark's, Venice, were accurately copied from the Cotton Genesis, a book which almost certainly was painted in Alexandria in the fifth century. In these instances we get examples of what was happening all the time. Books from the East, especially ancient books, were regarded as authorities; sacred designs were not made up at will, but were handed forward as traditions. Doubts have been raised by Ainalov as to whether the important Crucifixion picture of Rabula's Gospel is not much later than the rest of the book, but the finding of it repeated at Sta Maria Antiqua proves that it is probably at least as old as the painting there. Other fragmentary paintings suggest that there was a series of subjects drawn from the New Testament with their "types" from the Old Testament set against them. Now Bede tells us categorically that a series of pictures representing such types was brought from Rome by Benedict Biscop to adorn his monastery. Thus paintings, embodying theological conceptions, originated in the East and were carried to Northumbria. Already in the Rossano book Christ appears as the Good Samaritan, who aids the traveller and carries him to the inn. This is a conception which is fully worked out in the superb late twelfth century stained glass window at Sens. In the painted book of Cosmas the Indian traveller, a sixth century Alexandrian work, there are several pairs of types, thus the Sacrifice of Isaac, the escape of Jonah from the Whale, and the Translation of Elijah, typify the Crucifixion, Resurrection and the Ascension of Christ. All these types reappear on the sculptures of the Irish crosses. Of course such "types" are found in the catacomb paintings, but in these the idea had not been systematised.

From the time of Charlemagne until the generation in which Gothic architecture was to emerge, Germany led in the arts. This is less obvious in architecture, but when the arts are considered as a whole it must be admitted. The carved ivories of the Carolingian school form a magnificent series, and the metal-work, enamels and manuscripts are as noteworthy. If we regard all the splendid works of art wrought in North Italy, Germany, North France and England, we may see that the Romanesque was an essentially Teutonic movement. The Gothic arose in France when the people had been sufficiently saturated with the new Romance spirit. The Romanesque looked back to Rome and Byzantium, the Gothic faced forward to the new world. The French kingdom was born while Gothic architecture was being formed.

Until the beginning of the twelfth century the centres of Romanesque art were in the neighbourhood of the lower Rhine and in Lombardy.

The most advanced piece of figure art wrought early in the twelfth century is the noble bronze font now at Liège, the work of an artist of Huy. This has completely shaken off barbarism, it is clear and sweet in expression, the sort of thing we should like to call modern if modern people could rise to it. A study of the bronze works at Hildesheim, wrought under the direction of the great Bishop Bernward, shews that the bronze workers of Huy derived their traditions from the artists of Hildesheim, as those doubtless followed the men who worked for Charlemagne at Aix two centuries earlier still. At Hildesheim the doors and the celebrated bronze column were made about the year 1075. On the square base of the latter are little figures of the four rivers of Paradise. This may remind us of the bronze pine cone at Aix which has the names of the rivers of Eden inscribed on its four sides. The four rivers occur again on a most beautiful bronze font of the thirteenth century in the cathedral. Again, on the bronze column there is a group of people listening to Christ, which is plainly the prototype of another group on the Liège font. Thus the traditions of the bronze workers were handed on to Dinant, which in turn inherited from Huy and became the chief European centre for bronze working.

It is impossible here to give a separate account of the many Romanesque schools of art, or even of architecture, which flourished between the Carolingian Renaissance and the emergence of Gothic art in the twelfth century. In Italy, Germany, and France there was constant effort and practically continuous development towards one unforeseen end, the formation of the highly specialised type of art which we call Gothic. All three countries contributed valuable ideas to the commonwealth of art and continuously reacted on one another. The master impulse in architecture was that by which the builders set themselves to explore the possibilities of vaulting and the interaction between vaulting and planning. This may have been brought about in part by the desire to guard against fire, but it was fed by the gradual spread of Byzantine customs over the West.

In western Europe during the Carolingian age the churches were planned in various forms. The central type of plan, varieties of which are the circle, the polygon and the equal-armed cross, is represented by the Palatine chapel at Aix-la-Chapelle. Germigny, near Orleans, is a square with apses projecting on every side. The large abbey church of St Croix, Quimperlé, of the eleventh century, is circular with square projections in the four directions.

Simple churches of this fashion were built in England. At Hexham one of these was built by Wilfrid, and King Alfred built another at Athelney. Several later Saxon churches had a big tower forming the body of the structure with an apse opening from its east side and another extension towards the west; such "tower churches" must have been simplifications of the central type. The close association of the central tower, the western version of the Byzantine dome, with the idea of the church has not been fully worked out, but it led to a general insistence on the central tower, or lantern, in Romanesque churches. Beneath these towers, at the crossing of the central span and the transepts, the choirs were placed.

The monk Reginald, one of the Durham chroniclers, describes the "White Church" (the cathedral) at Durham built by Bishop Aldhun in 1099 thus: "There were in the White Church, in which St Cuthbert had first rested, two stone towers, as those who saw them have told us, standing high into the air, the one containing the choir, the other standing at the west end of the church, which was of wonderful size. They carried brazen pinnacles set up on top, which aroused both the amazement of all men and great admiration." The still earlier abbey church at Ramsey, built about 970, was cruciform with a central tower, and at the west end a smaller tower. Again, when in the description of the Confessor's church at Westminster we are told that the *domus principalis arae* was of great height, it possibly means the choir with the lantern tower, and that the actual site of the altar in the apse of the eastern limb was considered as attached to this dominating central feature. In some later Romanesque churches in France, as at Issoire, Clermont, and elsewhere, parts of the transept on either side of the lantern tower are lifted above the general body of the work, thus adding to the importance of the central structure.

A central tower seems a more or less obvious arrangement, as a matter of design, where it rises at the centre of a cruciform plan, and it has sometimes been explained as a device for simplifying the intersection of the roofs. Several Norman churches, however, like the one at Iffley, have a tower rising over the choir of a long, simple, unaisled church, a little to the east of the middle of its length. Here again the tower is as typically the church as the hall is the house.

The central type of plan persisted also in palace chapels. Charlemagne's chapel was repeated at the palace of Nimeguen near the mouth of the Rhine. The palace of Goslar has a chapel with a plan resembling that of Germigny mentioned above. William of Malmesbury has a curious note to the effect that a cathedral church built at Hereford at the end of the eleventh century was copied from the church at Aix. In the forest of Loches is a royal chapel, built in the reign of Henry II, which is circular in form. At the palace of Woodstock was another circular chapel, and a Norman chapel at Ludlow castle, which still exists, is also of this form. The English circular and polygonal chapter-houses of cathedrals, of which that at Worcester is a Norman example, must either have been adopted from such circular chapels or from the baptisteries of some of the old Saxon cathedrals. There seems to have been such a baptistery at Canterbury, and we are told that it was used for meetings as well as for its primary purpose.

The transepts of a church were an obvious means of enlarging the interior space, and as they gave a symbolic form to the plan they became normal parts of Romanesque structure. Sometimes they were of single span, at others they had one or two aisles, and from their eastern sides projected chapels, usually apses. Another type of Carolingian plan had apses at both ends of the main span. A ninth century drawing for the plan of the monastery at St Gall is of this form. And this arrangement was for long a favourite one in Germany. It doubtless conformed to ritual requirements. In England the Saxon cathedral at Canterbury and the abbey church at Ramsbury were of this type.

A plan which persisted longer was one with three parallel apses at the east end, the larger apse terminating the central space being flanked by two others at the end of the side aisles. This form of church early became the usual one in Normandy. The abbey church at Bernay, built *c.* 920, had transepts, and three parallel apses to the east. This plan was again repeated in the great abbey church at Jumièges, which was itself copied by Edward the Confessor for his fine new church in the Norman manner, built at Westminster from about 1050. Some remnants of it which still exist are enough to shew that the plan was a very accurate copy of its prototype, so much so, that it appears that Norman workmen must have been brought here to do it. The same tradition was followed at Durham, Lincoln, and many other important churches. Both Westminster and Jumièges had vestibules and triforium storeys; these were old customary features which tended to disappear. Charlemagne's church at Aix has a fine vaulted gallery over the aisle which surrounds the central space: and we are told of the Confessor's church at Westminster that there were, both above and below, chapels dedicated to the saints. In such cases the triforium evidently fulfilled a function. Later it became a mere formal survival, although the triforium of the later church at Westminster was probably used for the great congregations at coronations. Many of the German Romanesque churches have structural galleries at the sides of the choir, and many Norman churches had galleries at the ends of the transepts. At Canterbury, Lincoln and Christ Church the transepts seem to have had upper storeys over their whole extent, forming chapels. Vestibules mentioned above must represent the narthex of Eastern churches. The church of St Remi at Rheims had in the tenth century a vaulted work which occupied nearly half the nave. Immense vaulted porches still exist at Vézelay, St Benoît-sur-Loire and other places, and the tradition of a western porch has left its mark on some of the English Romanesque churches, as Ely and Lincoln. In Germany the western bay was usually carried up higher than the nave roof between two western towers, making thus an impressive west end externally.

Quite generally crypts were also constructed beneath the choirs of Romanesque churches; deriving from the early *confessio* beneath the altar, they frequently became of great size. Often, in the German and Lombard churches, they were but little buried in the ground, but the eastern limbs of the churches were raised high above them, and approached by many steps. This arrangement is often very dignified and impressive. A great seven-branched candlestick usually stood in the middle of the platform beyond the steps. Many of the German Romanesque churches had rounded ends to the transepts as well as to the eastern limb, the crossing being thus surrounded by three apsidal projections. This is a well-known Byzantine type, and St Mary in the Capitol at Cologne is an early and noble example in the West; Tournai cathedral is another. This form of plan was handed on to the early Gothic of North France, at Noyon and Soissons, and it persisted long in Germany. The thirteenth century church at Marburg has similar semi-octagonal apses in three directions, a short nave, no longer than the transepts, and a chapel at each of the four re-entering angles. It is practically a church of the central type, and is certainly a very beautiful plan.

Another very beautiful scheme of planning is found in a church at Angers, which has a wide vaulted nave extended and supported by a series of large apsidal recesses or chapels along each side. This type is again followed at Orvieto cathedral.

The most perfect plan for a great church would seem to be that in which the central eastern apse is surrounded by an ambulatory from which small circular-ended chapels open out—one, three, four, five or seven. This is the plan which was adopted in the main line of progress into Gothic, and it continued to be used right through the Middle Ages. This fine scheme probably dates from Carolingian days, and three important churches, at Tours, Dijon and Le Mans, were built in this form at the end of the tenth century. Churches of the same type were built in England, first for the abbey of St Augustine, Canterbury, and the cathedrals of Winchester and Gloucester, during the last quarter of the eleventh century. An apse was an essential member of a great church during the Romanesque period. In its centre the bishop had his throne lifted high above the altar as ruler of the assembly; this broken remnants at Norwich still shew. The planning of a great church implied the dealing with several common factors which might be variously combined, The nave might be one, or three, or five spans wide ; there might be a transept of one, two, or three spans, and the eastern limb might have a simple apse, or parallel apses, or an ambulatory and a series of radiating chapels. The position of towers was another factor to be considered. Their positions were partly, doubtless, a matter of choice, but largely they were conditioned by structural requirements. A great single tower at the west end, as at Ely, will stop the thrusts of the inner arcading as well as the more usual pair of towers. In French churches towers were frequently put at the transepts also, and Winchester cathedral seems to have been intended to have transeptal towers. In Germany towers are often seen on either side of the apse. At Tournai four towers built around the crossing against the transepts support the central lantern, making a most impressive group of five spire-capped towers. At Exeter two massive towers stand over small square transepts. A third great controlling factor in the design of churches was that of vaulting. The possibilities of rearing vaults were explored in all sorts of ways. All three spans might have barrel vaults, or those over the aisles might be quadrants rising higher against the nave than where they fell on the aisle walls. The bays might be vaulted transversely, a favourite device in Burgundy, or they might be covered by a combination of longitudinal and transverse vaults interpenetrating and forming " groined " vaults. This last became the standard form for the vaults of churches in northwestern Europe, and the tradition was carried forward into Gothic. The use of this scheme allowed of high windows in every bay, and concentrated the thrusts at intervals above the piers of the inner arcades. One school of French Romanesque experimented with a series of domes covering square compartments, and the curious church at Loches has its nave covered by stone pyramidal erections like low pitched spires. It has hardly been realised how many of the greater " Norman " churches in England were vaulted, especially their eastern limbs and transepts. The eastern limb of the great abbey church of St Albans, begun about ten years after the Conquest, was vaulted. Durham and Lincoln cathedrals were vaulted throughout, by the middle of the twelfth century. The abbey churches of Gloucester, Pershore and Tewkesbury all seem to have had vaulted choirs and transepts; so probably had Canterbury cathedral, Winchester cathedral, St Paul's cathedral, Reading abbey and Lewes priory churches and many others. Frequently the nave was covered with a wooden ceiling while the eastern half of the church was vaulted. At Peterborough such a ceiling, delightfully decorated with bold pattern-work, still exists. This church and others had such ceilings throughout. The " glorious choir " at Canterbury had a specially famous painted ceiling. It is noteworthy that even in quite small churches the chancels were frequently covered with vaults, while the rest of the structure had wooden roofs.

Many modifications were made in the planning of great churches to accommodate the vaults, and a remarkable contrivance became common towards the end of the twelfth century for the purpose of supporting the high central vaults. This was the flying buttress, a strong arch built in the open air, rising from the lower walls of the aisles, and butting against those of the clerestory. Such buttresses were greatly developed in Gothic architecture, but their invention is due to Romanesque builders. Another great invention, which was of primary importance for the development of Gothic, seems to have been made towards the end of the eleventh century. This was the method of erecting vaults by first building a series of skeleton arches (ribs) diagonally across each bay, and then covering this subdivided space with a lighter web of work. In England the method was used at Durham, and this is the first well-authenticated instance in the west of Europe. Other examples, which are said to be earlier, are known in Italy.

The general movement, which was to pass over an invisible frontier into what we call Gothic architecture, was characterised by a search for more vigorous and clear solutions of structural problems, a gathering up of the wall masses into piers and buttresses and the vaults into ribs. The whole medieval process in architecture from, say, the time of Charlemagne to the time of the Black Death, was an organic development. One phase in the progress may be traced in the tendency to break up piers and arches into a series of recessed orders or members; that is, they widen by degrees in a step-like profile. This held the germ of the change from a square pier set in the direction of the wall into one placed diagonally. Such membering of arches and piers easily led to sub-arching, that is, the including of two or more smaller arches under a larger one; and this again was to lead up to the development of tracery. The process also early shewed itself in a liking for alternation.

A nave arcade, for instance, was often planned with a more or less square pier and then a column alternately. In some German churches square piers alternately wider and narrower may be seen.

The pointed arch has been known from time immemorial. It was generally adopted by Saracen builders from the seventh century, and it became well known in the West from the eleventh. It proved especially useful in adjusting the many difficulties which arose in applying vaulting to compartments of various sizes and shapes. And further, it was used as a strong structural form before it was generally admitted into the architectural code. Thus, as ever, the aesthetic delight of one century was found in the structural device of an earlier one.

The cusping of arches fell in with the general tendency toward subordination and grouping. The cusped arch had a distant origin in the shell forms carved in the arched heads of the niches, which were common in Hellenistic architecture. Byzantine and Arab builders simplified the scalloped edge of this shell into a series of small lobes set within the containing arch. Such cusped arches were passed on to the North-West by the Moors. The special centre for their distribution seems to have been the south-east of France, where the delight in cusped arches is very noticeable at Clermont, Vienne and Le Puy. The forms of trefoiled arches appear in the North as early as the tenth century in the ornaments of illuminated books, and probably they were handed on in this pictorial form long before they entered into real structures. Architecture and sculpture often followed where painting led. Circular windows had been used by the Romans and are frequently found in Romanesque work. Both circular and quatrefoil openings were probably known in the West from Carolingian days. The quatrefoil became popular as a form of cross. Ordinary windows, when grouped into pairs with a circle above, formed the point of departure for the development of the traceried window.

From the early days of Christian art glazing of various colours arranged in patterns had been used. Doubtless the beautifully patterned casements of Arab art were, like so much else, taken over from the Byzantine school. The jewelled lattices of Romance must have been suggested by the use of coloured glass. At some time in the great Carolingian era, which we are only now beginning to appreciate, painting was added to the morsels of coloured glass, and they were joined together by thin strips of lead rather than by some ruder means. These two steps of development brought into being the stained glass window proper. From this time windows were conceived as vast translucent enamels of which the leads formed the divisions. The agreement of style between the earliest known stained glass windows and Romanesque enamels is so close that we may not doubt the near kindred of the two arts. The earliest windows still extant, like those of St Denis (*c.* 1140–50), were probably designed by some enameller.

For long the style of German Byzantine enamels may be traced in the glass of Le Mans, Chartres, and Strasbourg, and for the most part the code of imagery had been worked out by enamel-workers and illuminators of books before it was adopted for stained glass.

There was a great expansion in the production of sculpture and its application to architecture during the twelfth century, and an enormous increase of power in dealing with it. Here again, however, all the great types and traditions of treatment seem to have been invented or rather developed by the Carolingian schools. For instance, there are two delightful small impersonations of Land and Sea carved amongst the early Gothic sculptures of the west front of Notre Dame at Paris. Such impersonations derive directly from Romanesque ivories and illuminated books of the German school and thence may be traced to Alexandrian art. In the Carolingian age imagery had, for the most part, been on a small scale, in metal-work and ivory, but some of it had been of great beauty in conception and of masterly execution. By the middle of the twelfth century several notable schools of architectural sculpture had been developed in Italy, France, and Spain. In England beginnings were made towards the development of what became a special English tradition; the west front treated as a background for an array of sculptured figures having reference to the Last Judgment. Some remnants found at York and others extant at Lincoln are evidence for this.

Sculpture, stained glass, and the large schemes of painting which covered the interiors of Romanesque churches, were very largely inspired by painted books. These illuminated volumes are almost the most wonderful products of the whole Romanesque period. What the book of Kells is to Irish art, and the Lindisfarne book to the Anglo-Celtic school of Northumbria, is well known. Several superb Carolingian volumes are just as remarkable, and this pre-eminence of the book was sustained until the end of our period. Some hundred splendid books and rolls written and painted in the twelfth century are marvels of thoughtful invention and skilful manipulation. At this time types and symbols were still dealt with in the great manner; many of the designers at work seem to have had the imagination of Blake with ten times his power of execution. For example, take the designs of an "Exultet" roll in the British Museum; the first painting is Christ majestically enthroned; then comes a group of rejoicing angels; then the interior of a basilica shewn in section with nave and aisles and in the midst a colossal *Mater Ecclesia* standing between groups of clergy and people; the next is Mother Earth, a woman's figure half emerging from the ground, nourishing an ox and a dragon; further on is the Crucifixion with its "type," the passage of the Red Sea; and near the end, after a flower garden with bees, the Virgin and Holy Child. This appears to be an Italian work of the middle of the twelfth century.

The artists of Charlemagne made use of mosaic in large schemes of decoration. The vault, an octagonal dome in form, over the central area of the palace chapel at Aix-la-Chapelle was covered by a simple but splendid design of the sort which modern designers find it so hard to imitate. The first rapture of all these things can never be recovered. On a starry ground was set a great Figure of the throned Majesty, and beneath were the twenty-four elders forming a band around the base of the dome. The ancient church of Germigny in France still has in its apse a mosaic of rather crude workmanship but similar in ability of design. Here two colossal cherubim with expanded wings guard the ark of the New Covenant, and above in the centre is the Right Hand of God. The floor of the chapel at Aix was also covered with coarse mosaic, and mosaic floors were common in the Romanesque churches of Germany, Lombardy and France. The mosaics of both walls and floors in Italy are too many and too well known to require mention. In France one or two floor mosaics still remain. The most perfect one is in the church of Lescar in the south. This was laid down in 1115. Two panels are preserved in the Cluny Museum of the beautiful mosaic floor of the abbey church of St Denis (*c.* 1150).

The internal walls and ceilings of Romanesque churches were (by custom) painted entirely with scriptural pictures and large single figures of saints, all set out according to traditional modes of arrangement and with schemes of teaching. In Germany several large churches retain, in a more or less restored condition, an almost complete series of such paintings. One of the most notable is the basilican church at Brunswick. But the most striking of all is, probably, the church at Hildesheim, where the flat boarded ceiling is entirely occupied by an enormous Jesse-tree, the ramifying branches of which spread over the whole nave. In Italy many painted churches of Romanesque date still exist, as, for instance, the church of San Pietro a Grado near Pisa. In France the church of St Savin has preserved its paintings most completely. Here, and in the many traces of paintings in a Byzantine tradition which are to be found on the walls and vaults of the cathedral of Le Puy, may be seen sufficient evidence to suggest what the idea of interior architectural painting was during the Romanesque epoch. A Romanesque church was intended to be as fully adorned with paintings as was a Byzantine church, and, indeed, the traditions of the two schools flowed very much in a common stream from one source. It was the same in England, as is shewn by fragments at Pickering, St Albans, Norwich, Ely, Romsey, Canterbury, and other places. We probably think of our "Norman" churches as rude and melancholy, but if we picture for ourselves all the colour suggested by the fragmentary evidences which exist, and furnish again by imagination the vistas of the interior with their great coronae of lights, the gilded roods, and embossed altar-pieces, the astonishing nature of these vast and splendid works will fill our minds with somewhat saddening reflections. Archaeology is no minister to pride.

LIST OF ABBREVIATIONS OF TITLES
OF PERIODICALS, SOCIETIES, ETC.

(1) The following abbreviations are used for titles of periodicals:

AB.   Analecta Bollandiana. Brussels.
AHR.   American Historical Review. New York and London.
AKKR.   Archiv für katholisches Kirchenrecht. Mayence.
AM.   Annales du Midi. Toulouse.
AMur.   Archivio Muratoriano. Rome.
Ang.   Anglia. Zeitschrift für englische Philologie. Halle a. S. 1878 ff.
Arch. Ven.   Archivio veneto. Venice, 1871–90, continued as Nuovo archivio veneto.
             Venice. 1891 ff.
ASAK.   Anzeiger für schweizerische Alterthumskunde. Zurich.
ASHF.   Annuaire-Bulletin de la Société de l'histoire de France. Paris.
ASI.   Archivio storico italiano. Florence. Ser. i. 20 v. and App. 9 v. 1842–53.
             Index. 1857. Ser. nuova. 18 v. 1855–63. Ser. iii. 26 v. 1865–77.
             Indices to ii and iii. 1874. Suppt. 1877. Ser. iv. 20 v. 1878–87.
             Index. 1891. Ser. v. 49 v. 1888–1912. Index. 1900. Anni 71 etc.
             1913 ff. in progress. (Index in Catalogue of The London Library,
             vol. i. 1913.)
ASL.   Archivio storico lombardo. Milan.
ASPN.   Archivio storico per le province napoletane. Naples. 1876 ff.
ASRSP.   Archivio della Società romana di storia patria. Rome.
BCRH.   Bulletins de la Commission royale d'histoire. Brussels.
BHisp.   Bulletin hispanique. Bordeaux.
BISI.   Bullettino dell' Istituto storico italiano. Rome. 1886 ff.
BRAH.   Boletin de la R. Academia de la historia. Madrid.
BZ.   Byzantinische Zeitschrift. Leipsic.
CQR.   Church Quarterly Review. London.
CR.   Classical Review. London.
DZG.   Deutsche Zeitschrift für Geschichtswissenschaft. Freiburg-i.-B.
DZKR.   Deutsche Zeitschrift für Kirchenrecht. Leipsic.
EHR.   English Historical Review. London.
FDG.   Forschungen zur deutschen Geschichte.
HJ.   Historisches Jahrbuch. Munich.
HMC.   Historical Manuscripts Commission's Publications. London. 1883 ff.
HVJS.   Historische Vierteljahrsschrift. Leipsic.
HZ.   Historische Zeitschrift (von Sybel). Munich and Berlin.
JA.   Journal Asiatique. Paris.
JB.   Jahresberichte der Geschichtswissenschaft im Auftrage der historischen
             Gesellschaft zu Berlin. Berlin. 1878 ff.

JSG.	Jahrbuch für schweizerische Geschichte. Zurich.
JTS.	Journal of Theological Studies. London.
MA.	Le moyen âge. Paris.
MIOGF.	Mittheilungen des Instituts für österreichische Geschichtsforschung. Innsbruck.
NAGDG.	Neues Archiv der Gesellschaft für ältere deutsche Geschichtskunde. Hanover and Leipsic.
NRDF.	Nouvelle Revue historique du droit français. Paris.
QFIA.	Quellen und Forschungen aus italienischen Archiven und Bibliotheken. Rome.
RA.	Revue archéologique. Paris.
RBAB.	Revue des bibliothèques et des archives de la Belgique. Brussels.
RBén.	Revue bénédictine. Maredsous.
RCel.	Revue celtique. Paris.
RCHL.	Revue critique d'histoire et de littérature. Paris.
RH.	Revue historique. Paris.
RHD.	Revue d'histoire diplomatique. Paris.
RHE.	Revue d'histoire ecclésiastique. Louvain.
Rhein. Mus.	Rheinisches Museum für Philologie. Frankfurt-a.-M.
RN.	Revue de numismatique. Paris.
ROC.	Revue de l'Orient chrétien. Paris.
RQCA.	Römische Quartalschrift für christliche Altertumskunde und Kirchengeschichte. Rome.
RQH.	Revue des questions historiques. Paris.
RSH.	Revue de synthèse historique. Paris.
RSI.	Rivista storica italiana. Turin.
SKAW.	Sitzungsberichte der Kaiserlichen Akademie der Wissenschaften. Vienna. [Phil. hist. Classe.]
SPAW.	Sitzungsberichte der kön. preussischen Akademie der Wissenschaften. Berlin.
TRHS.	Transactions of the Royal Historical Society. London.
VV.	Vizantiyski Vremennik. St Petersburg (Petrograd).
ZCK.	Zeitschrift für christliche Kunst. Düsseldorf.
ZKG.	Zeitschrift für Kirchengeschichte. Gotha.
ZKT.	Zeitschrift für katholische Theologie. Gotha.
ZR.	Zeitschrift für Rechtsgeschichte. Weimar. 1861–78. Continued as
ZSR.	Zeitschrift der Savigny-Stiftung für Rechtswissenschaft. Weimar. 1880 ff.
ZWT.	Zeitschrift für wissenschaftliche Theologie. Frankfurt-a.-M.

(2)   Among other abbreviations used (*see General Bibliography*) are:

AcadIBL.	Académie des Inscriptions et Belles-Lettres.
AcadIP.	Académie Impériale de Pétersbourg.
AllgDB.	Allgemeine deutsche Biographie.
ASBen.	*See* Mabillon and Achery *in Gen. Bibl.* IV.
ASBoll.	Acta Sanctorum Bollandiana.
BEC.	Bibliothèque de l'École des Chartes.
BGén.	Nouvelle Biographie générale.
BHE.	Bibliothèque de l'École des Hautes Études.
Bouquet.	*See* Rerum Gallicarum etc. *in Gen. Bibl.* IV.
BUniv.	Biographie universelle.
CIG.	Corpus Inscriptionum Graecarum.
CIL.	Corpus Inscriptionum Latinarum.

Coll.
    textes.   Collection des textes pour servir à l'étude et à l'enseignement de l'histoire.
CSCO.   Corpus scriptorum christianorum orientalium.
CSEL.   Corpus scriptorum ecclesiasticorum latinorum.
CSHB.   Corpus scriptorum historiae Byzantinae.
DCA.   Dictionary of Christian Antiquities.
DCB.   Dictionary of Christian Biography.
DNB.   Dictionary of National Biography.
EcfrAR.   École française d'Athènes et de Rome.   Paris.
EETS.   Early English Text Society.
EncBr.   Encyclopaedia Britannica.
FHG.   Müller's Fragmenta Historicorum Graecorum.
Fonti.   Fonti per la Storia d' Italia.
KAW.   Kaiserliche Akademie der Wissenschaften.   Vienna.
MEC.   Mémoires et documents pub. par l'École des Chartes.
MGH.   Monumenta Germaniae Historica.
MHP.   Monumenta historiae patriae.   Turin.
MPG.   Migne's Patrologiae cursus completus.   Ser. graeca.
MPL.   Migne's Patrologiae cursus completus.   Ser. latina.
PAW.   Königliche preussische Akademie d. Wissenschaften.   Berlin.
RC.   Record Commissioners.
RE³.   Real-Encyklopädie für protestantische Theologie, etc.
Rec.
    hist.Cr.   Recueil des historiens des Croisades.
RGS.   Royal Geographical Society.
RHS.   Royal Historical Society.
Rolls.   Rerum Britannicarum medii aevi scriptores.
RR.II.SS.   *See* Muratori *in Gen. Bibl.* iv.
SGUS.   Scriptores rerum Germanicarum in usum Scholarum.
SHF.   Société d'histoire française.
SRD.   Scriptores rerum Danicarum medii aevi.

In the case of many other works given in the General Bibliography abbreviations as stated there are used.

Abh.	Abhandlungen.	kais.	kaiserlich.
J.	Journal.	kön.	königlich.
Jahrb.	Jahrbuch.	mem.	memoir.
R.	Review, Revue.	mém.	mémoire.
Viert.	Vierteljahrschrift.	n.s.	new series.
Z.	Zeitschrift.	publ.	publication.
antiq.	antiquarian, antiquaire.	roy.	royal, royale.
coll.	collections.	ser.	series.
hist.	history, historical, historique, historisch.	soc.	society.

GENERAL BIBLIOGRAPHY.

I. DICTIONARIES, BIBLIOGRAPHIES AND GENERAL WORKS OF REFERENCE.

For modern historical works co-operate or in series see Section V.

Allgemeine deutsche Biographie (histor. Kommission bei d. kön. Akademie der Wissenschaften zu München). Ed. Liliencron, R. von, and Wegele, F. X. Leipsic. 1875–1910. (AllgDB.)

Allgemeine Geschichte in Einzeldarstellungen. Ed. Oncken, W. Berlin. 1379–93. (Series by various writers, *cf. sub nom.*) (Oncken.)

Annuario bibliografico della storia d' Italia. 1902 ff.

Balzani, U. Le cronache italiane del Medio Evo. 3rd edn. Milan. 1909.

Bibliothèque de l'École des Chartes. Paris. 1839–1900. (BEC.)

Bibliothèque de l'École des Hautes Études. Paris. 1839 ff. (BHE.)

Biographie nationale de Belgique. Brussels. 1866, in progress. Acad. Roy. des sciences, des lettres et des beaux arts.

Biographie universelle, ancienne et moderne. (Michaud.) Paris. 1854–65. 45 vols. [Greatly improved edn. of earlier work, 1811–28, and supplement, 1832–62.] (BUniv.)

Cabrol, F. Dictionnaire de l'archéologie chrétienne et de la Liturgie. Paris. 1901. 2nd edn., 1907, in progress.

Calvi, E. Bibliografia generale di Roma medioevale e moderna. Pt I. Medio Evo. Rome. 1906. Suppt. 1908.

Capasso, B. Le fonti della storia delle provincie napolitane dal 563 al 1500. Ed. Mastrojanni, E. O. Naples. 1902.

Ceillier, R. Histoire générale des auteurs sacrés et ecclésiastiques. 23 vols. Paris. 1729–63. New edn. 14 vols. in 15. Paris. 1858–69.

Chevalier, C. U. J. Répertoire des sources historiques du moyen âge. Bio-bibliographie. Paris. 1883–8. Rev. edn. 2 vols. 1905–7. Topo-bibliographie. Montbéliard. 1894–1903.

Dahlmann, F. C. and Waitz, G. Quellenkunde der deutschen Geschichte. 8th edn. Herre, P. Leipsic. 1912.

Dictionary of National Biography. Ed. Stephen, L. and Lee, S. 63 vols. London 1885–1901. 2nd edn. 22 vols. 1908–9. 1st suppt. 3 vols. 1901. 2nd suppt 3 vols. 1912. (DNB.)

Du Cange, C. du Fresne. Glossarium mediae et infimae Latinitatis. Edns. of Henschel, 7 vols., Paris, 1840–50, and Favre, 10 vols., Niort, 1883–7.

Encyclopædia Britannica. 11th edn. Cambridge. 1911. (EncBr.)

Ersch, J. S. and Gruber, J. G. Allgemeine Encyklopädie der Wi enschaften und Künste. Berlin. 1818–50. (Ersch-Gruber.) [Incomplete.]

Grässe, J. G. T. Lehrbuch einer allgemeinen Litterärgeschichte aller bekannten Völker der Welt von der ältesten bis auf die neueste Zeit. Leipsic. 4 vols. 1837–59.

Gröber, G. Grundriss der romanischen Philologie. 2 vols. Strasbourg. 1888–1902. 2nd edn. Vol. I. 1904–6.

Gross, C. Sources and Literature of English History from the earliest times to about 1485. London. 1900. 2nd edn. enl. 1915. (Gross.)

Hardy, T. D. Descriptive Catalogue of materials relating to the Hist. of Great Britain and Ireland to end of reign of Henry VII. 3 vols. 1862–71. (Rolls.)

Hastings, J. and Selbie, J. A. Encyclopaedia of Religion and Ethics. Edinburgh and N. York. 1908, in progress.

Herre, P. (Hofmeister, A. and Stübe, R.) Quellenkunde zur Weltgeschichte. Leipsic. 1910.

Herzog, J. J. and Hauck, A. Real-Encyklopädie für protestantische Theologie und Kirche. 3rd edn. 24 vols. Leipsic. 1896–1913. (RE³.)

Keene, H. G. An Oriental Biographical Dictionary, founded on materials collected by Beale, T. W. New and revised edn. London. 1894.

Lees, B. A. Bibliography of Mediaeval History. (400–1500.) London. 1917. (Historical Assoc. Leaflet 44.)

Lichtenberger, F. Encyclopédie des Sciences religieuses. 13 vols. Paris. 1877–82.

Maigne d'Arnis, W. H. (pub. Migne). Lexicon manuale ad scriptores mediae et infimae Latinitatis. Paris. 1866.

Manzoni, L. Bibliografia statutaria e storica italiana. 3 vols. Bologna. 1876. 2nd edn. enl. 1892. i. i, ii. Bibl. d. statuti etc. dei municipii. ii. Bibl. storica municipale etc. A–E. [No more publ.]

Meister, A. Grundriss der Geschichtswissenschaft zur Einführung in das Studium der deutschen Geschichte des Mittelalters und der Neuzeit. Vol. i (1). Leipsic. 1906. Vol. i (2) and ii (1–8). 1907. 2nd edn. 1912 ff., in progress. (Meister.)

Molinier, A. Les Sources de l'histoire de France des origines aux guerres d'Italie (1494). 6 vols. Paris. 1901–6.

Monod, G. Bibliographie de l'hist. de France depuis les origines jusqu'en 1789. Paris. 1888.

Nouvelle Biographie générale, depuis les temps les plus reculés jusqu'à nos jours, avec les renseignements bibliographiques. Sous la direction de J. Ch. F. Höfer. Paris. 1854–66. 46 vols. in 23. (BGén.)

Oudin, Casimir. Commentarius de scriptoribus ecclesiae antiquae illorumque scriptis tam impressis quam manuscriptis adhuc extantibus in celebrioribus Europae Bibliothecis a Bellarmino etc. omissis ad annum MCCCCLX. 3 vols. Frankfurt-a.-M. and Leipsic. 1722.

Paetow, L. J. Guide to the study of Medieval History (University of California Syllabus Series, No. 90). Berkeley, California. 1917.

Paul, H. Grundriss der germanischen Philologie. 2nd edn. 3 vols. Strasburg. 1896 ff.

Pauly, A. F. von. Real-Encyklopädie der klassischen Alterthumswissenschaft. Vienna. 1837–52. Ed. Wissowa, G. Stuttgart. 1894–1903. New edn. 1904, in progress. (Pauly-Wissowa.)

Pirenne, H. Bibliographie de l'hist. de Belgique. Brussels and Ghent. 1893. 2nd edn. 1902.

Potthast, August. Bibliotheca historica medii aevi. Wegweiser durch die Geschichtswerke des europäischen Mittelalters bis 1500. Berlin. 2nd edn. 2 vols. 1896.

Rivista storica italiana. Rome. Turin. Florence. 1884 ff., in progress. [Contains quarterly classified bibliography of books and articles on Italian history.]

Thompson, E. M. Introduction to Greek and Latin Palaeography. London. 1912.

Vacant, A. Dictionnaire de la Théologie. Paris. 1899 ff.

Victoria History of the Counties of England. London. 1900 ff., in progress. (Vict. Co. Hist.)

Waitz. *See* Dahlmann.

Wattenbach, W. Deutschlands Geschichtsquellen im Mittelalter bis zur Mitte des XIII. Jahrhunderts. Berlin. 1858. 7th edn. Dümmler, E. 2 vols. Stuttgart and Berlin. 1904.

Wetzer, H. J. and Welte, B. Kirchenlexikon oder Encyklopädie der katholischen Theologie. 1847-60. 2nd edn. Kaulen, F. Freiburg-i.-B. 1882-1901. Index, 1903. (Wetzer-Kaulen.) French transl. Goschler, I. 26 vols. 1869-70.

II. ATLASES AND GEOGRAPHY.

Baudrillart-Vogt-Rouziès. Dictionnaire d'histoire et de géographie ecclésiastique Paris. 1911, in progress.

Droysen, G. Allgemeiner historischer Handatlas. Bielefeld. 1886.

Freeman, E. A. Historical Geography of Europe (with Atlas). London. 1881. 3rd edn. revised and ed. Bury, J. B., 1903.

Kretschmer, K. Historische Geographie von Mitteleuropa. 1904. (In Below's Handbuch, *see* v *below.*)

Longnon, A. Atlas historique de France depuis César jusqu'à nos jours. (Text separate.) Paris. 1912.

Muir, R. Philips' New Historical Atlas for students. 2nd edn. London. 1914.

Poole, R. L. (ed.). Historical Atlas of Modern Europe. Oxford. 1902. [With valuable introductions.]

Putzger, F. W. Historischer Schul-Atlas. Ed. Baldamas, A. and others. 34th edn. Bielefeld, Leipsic. 1910.

Saint-Martin, V. de (and others). Nouveau dictionnaire de Géographie Universelle. 7 vols. Paris. 1879-95. Supplement by Rousselet, L. 2 vols. 1895-7. [Contains short bibliographies.]

Schrader, F. Atlas de géographie historique. Paris. New edn. 1907.

Spruner-Menke. Hand-Atlas für die Geschichte des Mittelalters und der neueren Zeit. Gotha. 1880. (3rd edn. of Spruner's Hand-Atlas etc. Ed. Menke, Th.)

(For place-names :—)

Bischoff, H. T. and Möller, J. H. Vergleichendes Wörterbuch der alten, mittleren und neuen Geographie. Gotha. 1892.

Deschamps, P. Dictionnaire de Géographie (suppt. to Brunet, J. C. Manuel du Libraire). Paris. 1870. 2nd edn. 2 vols. 1878-80.

Grässe, J. G. T. Orbis Latinus. Dresden. 1861. Ed. Benedict, F. Berlin. 1909. [Part I only.]

Martin, C. T. The Record Interpreter. London. 1892. 2nd edn., 1910 (for British Isles).

III. CHRONOLOGY AND GENEALOGY.

(Chronology :—)

Art de vérifier les dates et les faits historiques, L'. 2ᵉ partie. Depuis la naiss. de J.-C. 3rd edn. Paris. 3 vols. 1783 ff., and other edns. and reprints. Also 4th edn. by Saint-Allais. 1818-19. 18 vols. (Art de v.)

Belviglieri, C. Tavole sincrone e genealogiche di storia italiana dal 306 al 1870. Florence. 1875. Rptd. 1885.

Bond, J. J. Handybook of Rules and Tables for verifying Dates. London. Last edn. 1875.

Calvi, E. Tavole storiche dei comuni italiani. Pts I-III. Rome. 1903-7. I. Liguria e Piemonte. II. Marche. III. Romagna. [Also useful bibliographies.]

Gams, P. B.   Series episcoporum ecclesiae Catholicae (with supplement).   Ratisbon. 1873, 1886.

Ginzel, F. K.   Handbuch der mathematischen und technischen Chronologie.   Vol. I. Leipsic.   1906.   Vol. II.   1911.

Grotefend, H.   Taschenbuch der Zeitrechnung des deutschen Mittelalters und der Neuzeit.   3rd enlarged edn.   Hanover.   1910.

—— Zeitrechnung des deutschen Mittelalters und d. Neuzeit.   2 vols.   Hanover. 1891–8.

Ideler, C. L.   Handbuch der mathematischen und technischen Chronologie.   2 vols. Berlin.   1825.   New edn.   Breslau.   1883.

Lane-Poole, S.   The Mohammedan Dynasties.   London.   1894.

Mas Latrie, J. M. J. L. de.   Trésor de chronologie, d'histoire et de géographie pour l'étude des documents du moyen âge.   Paris.   1889.

Nicolas, Sir H. N.   The Chronology of History.   London.   Best edn.   1838.

Poole, R. L.   Medieval Reckonings of Time.   (Helps for Students of History.) S.P.C.K.   London.   1918.

Ritter, Carl.   Geographisch-statistisches Lexicon.   8th edn.   Penzler, J.   2 vols. Leipsic.   1894–5.

Rühl, F.   Chronologie des Mittelalters und der Neuzeit.   Berlin.   1897.

Savio, F.   Gli antichi vescovi d' Italia dalle origini al 1300.   Il Piemonte.   Turin. 1899.   La Lombardia.   Pt I.   Milano.   Florence.   1913, in progress.

Schram, R.   Hilfstafeln für Chronologie.   Vienna.   1883.   New edn.   Kalendario-graphische und chronologische Tafeln.   Leipsic.   1908.

Searle, W. G.   Anglo-Saxon Bishops, Kings and Nobles.   Cambridge.   1899.

Stokvis, A. M. H. J.   Manuel d'histoire de généalogie et de chronologie de tous les États du globe etc.   3 pts.   Leyden.   1888–93.   Vol. II.   2 pts.   Europe.

Stubbs, W.   Registrum sacrum Anglicanum.   Oxford.   1897.

Wislicenus, W. F.   Astronomische Chronologie.   Leipsic.   1895.

(*Note:*—Much information in such works as Gallia Christiana; Ughelli, Italia Sacra; for which see IV.)

(NUMISMATICS :—)

Corpus nummorum italicorum.   Vols. I–XV, in progress.   Rome.   1910 ff.

Engel, A. and Serrure, R.   Traité de Numismatique du Moyen Âge.   2 vols. Paris.   1891–4.

Grueber, H. A.   Handbook of the Coins of Great Britain and Ireland in the British Museum.   London.   1899.

Hill, G. F.   Coins and Medals.   (Helps for Students of History.)   S.P.C.K. London.   1920.   [Excellent bibliographical guide.]

Luescher von Ebengreuth, A.   Allgemeine Münzkunde und Geldgeschichte des Mittelalters und der neueren Zeit.   1904.   (Pt 5 of Below's Handbuch, *see* v.)

Macdonald, G.   The Evolution of Coinage.   Cambridge.   1916.

(GENEALOGY :—)

(*Note:*—*Caution is necessary in consulting Genealogies of the* 10*th century.*)

Cokayne, G. E.   Complete Peerage of England, Scotland, Ireland, Great Britain and the United Kingdom.   8 vols.   Exeter.   1887–98.   (G. E. C.)   2nd edn. enl. Gibbs, V.   London.   1910, in progress.

Fernandez de Bethencourt, F.   Hist. genealógica y heráldica de la Monarquia Española, Casa Real y Grandes de España.   Madrid.   1897 ff., in progress.

Foras, E. A. de, and Maréschal de Luciane.   Armorial et Nobiliaire de l'ancien Duché de Savoie.   Vols. I–IV.   Grenoble.   1863–1902.

George, H. B.   Genealogical Tables illustrative of Modern History.   Oxford.   1873. 5th edn., Weaver, J. R. H., rev. and enl.   1916.

Grote, H. Stammtafeln mit Anhang calendarium medii aevi. (Vol. ix of Münz-studien.) Leipsic. 1877.

Guasco di Bisio, F. Dizionario feudale degli antichi stati sardi e della Lombardia dal-l' epoca carolingica ai nostri tempi (774–1909). 5 vols. Biblioteca della Soc. Storica subalpina. Vols. 54–58. Pinerolo. 1911.

Institut héraldique de France. Le Nobiliaire universel. 24 vols. Paris. 1854–1900.

Litta, P. (and continuators). Famiglie celebri italiane. 11 vols. Milan and Turin. 1819–99. 2nd series. Naples. 1902 ff., in progress.

Moreri, L. Le grand dictionnaire historique. Latest edn. 10 vols. Paris. 1759. English version, Collier, J., with App. London. 1721.

Voigtel, T. G. and Cohn, L. A. Stammtafeln zur Gesch. d. europäischen Staaten. Vol. i. Die deutschen Staaten u. d. Niederlande. Brunswick. 1871.

See also L'Art de vérifier les dates (*above*).

IV. SOURCES AND COLLECTIONS OF SOURCES.

Achery, L. d'. Spicilegium sive collectio veterum aliquot scriptorum. 13 vols. Paris. 1655 (1665)–77. New edn. Barre, L. F. J. de la. 3 vols. Paris. 1723.

Acta Sanctorum Bollandiana. Brussels. 1643–1770. Paris and Rome. 1866, 1887. Brussels. 1894 ff. (ASBoll.)

Altnordische Saga Bibliothek. Ed. Cederschiöld, G., Gering, H. and Mogk, E. 7 vols. Halle. 1892–8.

Anglo-Saxon Chronicle. Ed. Plummer, C. 2 vols. Oxford. 1892–9. Transl. Gomme, E. E. C. (with notes). London. 1909. Giles, J. A. 2nd edn. London. 1912.

Archivio Storico italiano. *Cf. List of Abbreviations* (1). ASI. (Useful Index in Catalogue of The London Library, vol. i, 1913.)

Biblioteca Arabico-Hispana. Ed. Codera and Ribera. 10 vols. Madrid and Sara-gossa. 1883–95.

Biblioteca della Società storica subalpina. Pinerolo, etc. 95 vols. 1899 ff., in progress. [Contains charters and monographs.]

Bibliotheca rerum Germanicarum. Ed. Jaffé, P. 6 vols. Berlin. 1864–73. (Bibl.rer.German.)

Birch, W. de G. Cartularium Saxonicum (A.D. 430–975). 3 vols. London. 1885–93. Index of personal names, 1899.

Böhmer, J. F. Regesta imperii. 11 vols. (New edn. in several parts by various editors.) Innsbruck. 1877 ff.

    Vol. i. Regesten unter den Karolingern. Ed. Mühlbacher, E. 2nd edn. Lechner, J. 1908 ff.

    Vol. ii. Regesten unter...d. sächsischen Hause. Ed. Ottenthal, E. von. 1893 ff., in progress.

Bouquet. *See* Rerum Gallicarum...scriptores.

Camden Society, Publications of the. London. 1838, in progress. Now publ. by the R. Hist. Soc. (Camden.)

Chartes et diplômes relatifs à l'histoire de France. Publ. AcadIBL. Paris. 1908 ff., in progress.

Collection de chroniques Belges inédits. Publ. par l'ordre du gouvernement. 44 vols. Brussels. 1858–74.

Collection de documents inédits sur l'histoire de France. Paris. 1835 ff., in progress.

Collection de textes pour servir à l'étude et à l'enseignement de l'histoire. Paris. 1886 ff., in progress. (Coll. textes.)

Corpus scriptorum christianorum orientalium. Ed. Chabor, J. B. and others. Paris, Rome and Leipsic. 1903 ff. (CSCO.)

Corpus scriptorum ecclesiasticorum latinorum. Vienna. 1866, in progress. (CSEL.)

Corpus scriptorum historiae Byzantinae. Bonn. 1828–97. (CSHB.)

Domesday Book. Ed. Farley, A. and Ellis, H. 4 vols. London. 1783–1816. (RC.) Vols. 1, 2, contain text. Vol. 3, introd. and indices. Vol. 4, Exon. Domesday and Inquisitio Eliensis.

Duchesne, L. Fastes épiscopaux de l'ancienne Gaule. Paris. 1894, in progress.

Dugdale, Wm. Monasticon Anglicanum. 3 vols. London. 1655–73. 2nd edn. Vol. i. 1682. 2 addit. vols. by Stevens, J. 1722–3. New enlarged edn. by Caley, J., Ellis, H., Bandinel, B. 6 vols. in 8. 1817–30. Repr. 6 vols. 1846. (Dugdale.)

Early English Text Society, Publications of the. London. In progress. (EETS.)

España Sagrada. Ed. Florez, Risco, and others. 51 vols. Madrid. 1747–1879.

Fonti per la storia d' Italia. Publ. Istituto storico italiano. Genoa, Leghorn and Rome. 1887 ff., in progress. (Chronicles, 29 vols. Letters, 6 vols. Diplomas, 6 vols. Statutes, 7 vols. Laws, 1 vol. Antiquities, 2 vols.) (Fonti.)

Gallia Christiana. 16 vols. Paris. 1715–1865.

Gallia Christiana novissima. Albanis, J. H. and Chevalier, C. U. J. Montbéliard and Valence. 1895 ff., in progress.

Geschichtschreiber der deutschen Vorzeit etc. Ed. Pertz, Wattenbach and others. New series. Leipsic. 1884, in progress. [German Translations.]

Graevius, J. G. and Burmannus, P. Thesaurus antiquitatum et historiarum Italiae etc. 30 vols. Leyden. 1704–25.

——— Thesaurus antiq. et histor. Siciliae, Sardiniae, Corsicae etc. 15 vols. Leyden. 1723–5.

Guizot, F. P. C. Collection des mém. relatifs à l'hist. de France depuis la fondation de la monarchie française jusqu'au 13ᵉ siècle. Paris. 1823–35. [French Translations.]

Haddan, A. W. and Stubbs, W. Councils and Ecclesiastical Documents relating to Great Britain and Ireland. Ed. after Spelman and Wilkins. 4 vols. Oxford. 1869–78.

Haller, J. Die Quellen zur Gesch. der Entstehung des Kirchenstaates. Leipsic and Berlin. 1907. *In* Quellensammlung zur deutschen Geschichte. Ed. Brandenburger, E. and Seeliger, G.

Hinschius, P. Decretales Pseudo-Isidorianae et Capitula Angilramni. Leipsic. 1863.

Historiae patriae monumenta. *See* Monumenta historiae patriae.

Jaffé, Phil. Regesta pontificum Romanorum ab condita ecclesia ad annum post Christum natum 1198. Berlin. 1851. 2nd edn. Wattenbach, W., Loewenfeld, S., Kaltenbrunner, F., Ewald, P. Leipsic. 1885–8. 2 vols. (Jaffé.)

Kehr, P. F. Regesta Pontificum Romanorum, in progress. Italia Pontificia. Vol. i. Rome. ii. Latium. iii. Etruria. iv. Umbria etc. v. Aemilia. vi. Liguria (Lombardy, Piedmont, Genoa). Berlin. 1906–14.
Brackmann, A. Germania Pontificia. Vol. i, i, ii. Salzburg. Berlin. 1910–11.

Kemble, J. M. Codex diplomaticus aevi Saxonici. 6 vols. London (Engl. Hist. Soc.). 1839–48.

Liber Censuum de l'église romaine. Ed. Fabre, P. and Duchesne, L. Vol. i. 1889–1910. Vol. ii in progress. EcfrAR.

Liber Pontificalis. 3 vols. Rome. 1724–55. Ed. Duchesne, L. 2 vols. Paris. EcfrAR. 1884–92. (LP.) Ed. Mommsen, Th. MGH. Gesta Pontif. Romanorum. Vol. i to 715. 1898.

Liebermann, F. Die Gesetze der Angelsachsen. 3 vols. Halle-a.-S. 1898–1916.

Mabillon, J. Annales Ordinis S. Benedicti. 6 vols. 1703–39. 2nd edn. Lucca. 1739–45.

Mabillon, J. and Achery, L. d'. Acta Sanctorum ord. S. Benedicti [A.D. 500–1100]. 9 vols. Paris. 1668–1701. Repr. Venice. 1733–40. (ASBen.)

Mansi, J. D. Sacrorum conciliorum collectio. Florence and Venice. 1759–98. 31 vols. Repr. Martin, J. B. and Petit, L. Paris. 1901, in progress.

Marrier, M. and Quercetanus (Duchesne), A. Bibliotheca Cluniacensis. Paris. 1614.

Mémoires et documents publiés par l'École des Chartes. Paris. 1896 ff.

Migne, J. P. Patrologiae cursus completus. Series graeca. Paris. 1857–66. 161 vols. in 166. (MPG.) Indices, Cavallera, F. Paris. 1912.

—— —— Series latina. 221 vols. Paris. 1844–55. Index, 4 vols. 1862–4. (MPL.)

Mirbt, C. Quellen zur Geschichte des Papsttums und des römischen Katholizismus. 2nd edn. Freiburg, Tübingen and Leipsic. 1901. 3rd edn. enl. 1911.

Monumenta Germaniae Historica. Ed. Pertz, G. H., Mommsen, Th. and others. Hanover. 1826 ff. New edns. in progress. Hanover and Berlin. (MGH.) Index, 1890.

 Auctores Antiquissimi. 15 vols. in many pts. 1876 ff. (Auct. ant.) Vols. ix, xi, xiii form Chronica minora (saec. iv, v, vi). Ed. Mommsen, Th. 1892–8.

 Deutsche Chroniken (Scriptores qui vernac. lingua usi sunt). i–vi. 1892 ff., in progress.

 Diplomata imperii. Fol. i. 1872. [All published; contains Merovingian diplomas.]

 Diplomata Karolinorum. Die Urkunden d. Karolinger. i. 1906 ff., in progress.

 Diplomata regum et imperatorum Germaniae. Urkunden d. deutschen Könige und Kaiser. Vols. i–iv. 1879 ff., in progress.

 Epistolae. i–vii 1, in progress. (iii–vii 1 are Epistolae Karolini aevi, i–v 1.)

 Epistolae saec. xiii e regestis pontificum Romanorum. i–iii.

 Gesta pontificum Romanorum. i. 1898, in progress.

 Leges. i–v. 1835–89. Fol.

 Legum sectiones quinque. 4º.
  Sect. i. Legum nationum Germanicarum. i, ii 1, v 1. 1902 ff., in progress.
  Sect. ii. Capitularia regum Francorum. i–ii complete. 1883, 1897.
  Sect. iii. Concilia. i–ii complete. 1893 ff.
  Sect. iv. Constitutiones etc. i–v, vi 1, viii 1. 1893 ff.
  Sect. v. Formulae Merovingici et Karolini aevi. 1886. Complete.

 Libelli de lite imperatorum et pontificum (saec. xi, xii). i–iii. 1891 ff.

 Libri confraternitatum. 1884.

 Necrologia Germaniae. i–iii, v 2. 1884–1913, in progress.

 Poetae Latini medii aevi (Carolini). i–iv, 1. 1881 ff., in progress.

 Scriptores. 30 vols. in 31. Fol. 1826–96. And 4º. Vols. xxxi, xxxii 1903, 1913. (Script.) In progress.

 Scriptores rerum Langobardicarum et Italicarum. 1878.

 Scriptores rerum Merovingicarum. i–vii. 1885–1920, in progress.

Monumenta historiae patriae. 19 vols. Fol. 2 vols. 4º. Turin. 1836 ff., in progress. (MHP.)

Monumenta historica Britannica. Ed. Petrie, H. and Sharpe, T. London. 1848.

Muratori, L. A. Rerum Italicarum scriptores. 25 vols. Milan. 1723–51. Supplements: Tartini, J. M., 2 vols., Florence, 1748–70, and Mittarelli, J. B., Venice, 1771, and Amari, M., Biblioteca arabo-sicula and Appendix. Turin and Rome. 1880–1, 1889. Indices chronolog. Turin. 1885. New enlarged edn. with the chronicles printed as separate parts. Carducci, G. and Fiorini, V. Città di Castello and Bologna. 1900, in progress. (RR. II. SS.)

—— Antiquitates italicae medii aevi. 6 vols. Milan. 1738–42. Indices chronolog. Turin. 1885.

Ouvrages publiés par la Société de l'histoire de France. Paris. 1834 ff., in progress.

Record Commissioners, Publications of the. London. 1802–69. (RC.)

Recueil des historiens des croisades. AcadIBL. 1844 ff. Historiens occidentaux (vols. 1–5), Hist. orientaux (vols. 1–5), Hist. grecs (2 vols.), Documents arméniens (2 vols.) [detailed list in Catalogue of The London Library]. (Rec. hist. Cr.)

Regesta chartarum Italiae. Publ. by K. Preuss. Histor. Instit. and Istituto storico italiano. Rome. 1907 ff., in progress.

Rerum Britannicarum medii aevi scriptores. (Chronicles and Memorials of Great Britain and Ireland during the Middle Ages.) Published under direction of the Master of the Rolls. (Various editors.) London. 1858 ff. (Rolls.) [For convenient list see Gross, App. C.]

Rerum Gallicarum et Franciscarum scriptores. (Recueil des hist. des Gaules et de la France.) Ed. Bouquet, M. and others. 23 vols. 1738–1876. Vols. i–xix re-ed. by Delisle, L. 1868–80, and vol. xxiv, 1894. New series. 4°. 1899, in progress. (Bouquet.)

Scriptores rerum Danicarum medii aevi. Ed. Langebek, I. 9 vols. Copenhagen. 1772–1878. (SRD.)

Scriptores rerum Germanicarum in usum scholarum. Hanover. 1839 ff. Fresh series. 1890 ff., in progress. 8°. [Contain revised editions of many of MGH in Fol. edn.] (SGUS.)

Selden Society, Publications of the. London. 1888 ff.

Stevenson, J. Church Historians of England. 8 vols. London. 1853–8. (Translations.)

Stubbs, W. Select Charters and other illustrations of English Constitutional History to the reign of Edward I. Oxford, 1870, and many repts. 9th edn. revd, Davis, H. W. C., 1913. Translation, 1873.

Stumpf, K. F. Die Reichskanzler vornehmlich des x, xi und xii Jahrhunderts. 3 vols. Innsbruck. 1865–83.

Theiner, A. Codex diplomaticus dominii temporalis S. Sedis. 3 vols. Rome. 1861–2.

Ughelli, F. Italia sacra. 2nd edn. Coleti, N. 10 vols. Venice. 1717–22.

Vic, C. de, and Vaissete, J. J. Histoire générale de Languedoc. New edn. Dulaurier, E. 16 vols. Toulouse. 1872–1904.

Watterich, J. M. Pontificum Romanorum qui fuerunt inde ab exeunte saeculo ix usque ad finem saeculi xii, vitae. 2 vols. Leipsic. 1862.

V. MODERN WORKS.

Alzog, J. Universalgeschichte der Kirche. Mainz. 1841. Best edn. 10th by Kraus, F. X. 1882. Transl. (from 9th German edn.) Pabisch, F. J. and Byrne, T. S. Manual of Church History. 4 vols. Dublin. 1895–1900.

Baronius, Cæs. Annales Ecclesiastici una cum critica historico-chronologica P. A. Pagii, contin. Raynaldus, O. Ed. Mansi, J. D. Lucca. 34 vols. 1738–46. Apparatus, 1 vol. Index, 4 vols. 1740, 1757–9. New edn. Bar-le-duc. 1864–83.

Below, G. von, and Meinecke, F. Handbuch der mittelalterlichen und neueren Geschichte. Munich and Berlin, 1903 ff., in progress. *See below*, Redlich.

Bernheim, Ernst. Lehrbuch der historischen Methode und der Geschichtsphilosophie. Leipsic. (5th and 6th enlarged edn.) 1908.

Bresslau, H. Handbuch der Urkundenlehre für Deutschland und Italien. Leipsic 1889. Vol. i. 2nd edn. enlarged. 1912.

Brown, G. B. The Arts in Early England. 5 vols. London. 1903 ff., in progress.

Brunner, H. Deutsche Rechtsgeschichte. 2 vols. Leipsic. 1887–92. Vol. i. 2nd edn. 1906.

—— Grundzüge der deutschen Rechtsgeschichte. 6th edn. Munich and Leipsic. 1913. [Excellent bibliographies.]

Bryce, J. The Holy Roman Empire. Enl. edn. London. 1907.

Bury, J. B. A History of the Eastern Roman Empire from the fall of Irene to the accession of Basil 1 (802–867). London. 1912.

Caetani, L. C. (Duca di Sermoneta). Annali dell' Islam. Vols. i–x. Milan. 1905 ff.

Cambridge History of English Literature, The. Ed. Ward, A. W. and Waller, A. R. 14 vols. Cambridge. 1907–14.

Carlyle, R. W. and A. J. A history of Mediaeval Political Theory in the West. Edinburgh and London. 1903 ff., in progress.

Dozy, R. P. A. Hist. des Mussulmans d'Espagne de 711–1110. 4 vols. Leyden. 1861. Transl. Stokes, F. G. Spanish Islam: a hist. of the Moslems in Spain. Introd. and notes. London. 1913.

—— Recherches sur l'hist. polit. et litt. de l'Espagne pendant le moyen âge Vol. i. Leyden. 1849 [all pubd]. 3rd edn. enl. with app. 2 vols. Paris, Leyden. 1881.

Ebert, A. Allgemeine Geschichte der Litteratur des Mittelalters im Abendland. 3 vols. Leipsic. 1874–87. 2nd edn. of vols. i and ii. 1889.

England, A History of, in seven volumes. Ed. Oman, C. London. 1905 ff.

—— The Political History of. Ed. Hunt, W. and Poole, R. L. 12 vols. London. 1905 ff. (*Cf. sub nom.*)

Ficker, G. and Hermelink, H. Das Mittelalter. 1912. Vol. 2 of Handb. d Kirchengesch. für Studirende. Ed. Krüger, G. 4 vols. Tübingen. 1907 ff.

Finlay, G. Ed. Tozer, H. F. History of Greece, b.c. 146 to a.d. 1864. 7 vols. Oxford. 1877.

Flach, J. Les origines de l'ancienne France. xe et xie siècles. Vols. i–iv. Paris. 1886–1917.

Fleury, Claude. Histoire ecclésiastique. 20 vols. Paris. 1691–1720. Continued to end of 18th century under Vidal, O. Many editions. [Orig. edn. to 1414. 4 add. vols. by Fl. to 1517, pub. Paris, 1840.]

Fustel de Coulanges, N. D. Histoire des Institutions politiques de l'ancienne France. Completed and ed. Jullian, C. 6 vols. Paris. 1888-92.

Gay, J. L'Italie méridionale et l'Empire byzantin. (867–1071.) EcfrAR. 1904.

Gebhardt, B. Handb. d. deutschen Gesch. 2 vols. Stuttgart. 1891–2.

Geschichte der europäischen Staaten. Ed. Heeren, A. H. L. and Ukert, F. A. Hamburg and Gotha. 1819–98. (Series by various writers, *cf. sub nom.*) (Heeren.) Contin. ed. Lamprecht, K. Allgemeine Staatengeschichte. (Lamprecht.)

Gibbon, Edward. The History of the Decline and Fall of the Roman Empire. 1776–81. Ed. in 7 vols. by Bury, J. B. 1896. Latest edn. 1909 ff. (Bury-Gibbon.) [Notes essential especially for bibliography.]

Giesebrecht, W. von. Geschichte der deutschen Kaiserzeit. Vols. i–v. Brunswick and Leipsic. 1855–88. i–iii (5th edn.). Leipsic. 1881–90. iv (2nd edn.). Brunswick. 1899. vi (ed. Simson, B. von). Leipsic. 1895.

Gieseler, J. C. L. Lehrbuch der Kirchengeschichte. Bonn. 3 vols. 1824 ff. and 6 vols. in 5, 1828–57. Transl. Davidson, S. 5 vols. Edinburgh, 1854, and Cunningham, Text-book of Ecclesiastical History. Philadelphia. 3 vols. 1836.

Gregorovius, F. Geschichte der Stadt Rom im Mittelalter. 8 vols. Stuttgart. 1859–72. (Translated from 4th edition by Mrs A. Hamilton. London. 1894–1902. 8 vols. in 13.)

Harnack, G. C. A. Dogmengeschichte. Tübingen. 1905. 5th edn. 1914. (Grundriss d. theolog. Wissenschaften, iv, 3.)

Hartmann, L. M. Geschichte Italiens im Mittelalter. i–iv 1. Gotha. 1897–1915, in progress. (No. 42 of Heeren.)

Hauck, A. Kirchengeschichte Deutschlands. 5 vols. Leipsic. 1887–1920. Vols. 1–4. 4th edn. 1906–13. Vol. 5. 2nd edn. 1911–20.

Hefele, C. J., contin. Hergenröther, J. A. G. Conciliengeschichte. 9 vols. Freiburg-i.-B. 1855 ff. 2nd edn. 1873 ff. French transl. Delarc, O. 1869. New Fr. transl. Leclercq, H. i–viii 1. Paris, in progress. 2nd edn. 1914 ff., in progress.

Hinojosa, E. de. Estudios sobre la historia del derecho español. Madrid. 1903.

Histoire de la nation française. Ed. Hanotaux, G. Vol. I 1. Géographie humaine de la France, by Brunhes, J. Paris. 1921.

Historia Generale de la España. By members of Real Acad. de la Hist. Ed. Cánovas del Castillo, A. Madrid. 1892 ff., in progress.

Holdsworth, W. S. A history of English Law. 3 vols. London. 1903-9. 2nd edn. 1914-15.

Jahrbücher der deutschen Geschichte bis 1250. Berlin and Leipsic. 1862 ff., in progress Kön. Akad. d. Wissenschaften (Munich).

Jahrbücher des deutschen Reiches unter dem sächsischen Hause. (Ed. Ranke, L. v.) 3 vols. Berlin. 1837-40.

Jorga, N. Transl. Powles, A. H. The Byzantine Empire. London. n.d. [For bibliography appended.]

Köhler, G. Die Entwicklung des Kriegswesen und der Kriegsführung in der Ritterzeit von der Mitte des 11 Jahrhunderts bis zu den Hussitenkriegen. 3 vols. Breslau. 1886-90.

Kraus, F. X. Ed. Sauer, J. Geschichte der christlichen Kunst. Freiburg-i.-B. and St Louis, Minnesota. 1896-1908. 2 vols. in 3.

Langen, J. Geschichte der römischen Kirche. 4 vols. Bonn. 1881.

Lavisse, E. (and others). Histoire de France jusqu'à la Révolution. 9 vols. in 18. Paris. 1900-11.

Lavisse, E. and Rambaud, A. Histoire générale du IVᵉ siècle jusqu'à nos jours. 12 vols. Paris. 1893-1900. Vols. I, II.

Lloyd, J. E. History of Wales. 2 vols. London. 1911.

Luchaire, A. Hist. des Institutions monarchiques de la France sous les premiers Capétiens. (987-1180.) Paris. 1883-5.

—— Manuel des Institutions françaises; période des Capétiens directs. Paris. 1892.

Macdonald, M. History of France. 3 vols. London. 1915.

Manitius, M. Gesch. der lateinischen Literatur des Mittelalters. Munich. 1911. (Vol. 9 ii of Handb. d. klassischen Altertums-Wissenschaft, ed. Müller, J. E. P. v.)

Meitzen, P. A. Siedelung und Agrarwesen der Westgermanen und Ostgermanen, der Kelten, Römer, Finnen und Slawen. 4 vols. Berlin. 1893-6.

Milman, H. H. History of Latin Christianity. London. 1854-5. Rev. edn. 9 vols. 1867.

Moeller, C. Hist. du moyen âge depuis la chute de l'empire romain jusqu'à la fin de l'époque franque (476-950). Paris and Louvain. 1898-1905. 2nd edn. with index. Louvain. 1910.

Moeller, W. Hist. of the Christian Church (A.D. 1-1648). Transl. Rutherfurd and Freese. 3 vols. London. 1892-1900. Vol. I. (1-600.) London. 1902.

Mosheim, J. L. von. Institutionum historiae ecclesiasticae antiquae et recentioris libri 4. 4 vols. Helmstedt. 1755. Transl. Murdock, J., ed. Soames, H. 1841. Rev. edn. 1850.

Mühlbacher, E. Deutsche Geschichte unter den Karolingern. Stuttgart. 1896. (*In* Zwiedineck-Südenhorst's Bibliothek deutscher Geschichte.)

Müller, K. Kirchengeschichte. Vols. I, II. Freiburg-i.-B. 1892.

Muratori, L. A. Annali d' Italia. 12 vols. Milan. 1744-9. Also other editions and reprints.

Neander, August. Allgemeine Geschichte der christlichen Religion und Kirche. 6 vols. in 11. Hamburg. 1825-52. Transl. Torrey, J. General History of the Church. 9 vols. London. 1847-55.

Oman, C. A history of the Art of War. The Middle Ages. London. 1898.

Palgrave, F. The Hist. of Normandy and of England. 4 vols. London. 1851-64. New edn. Cambridge. 1919-21.

Pargoire, J. L'Église byzantine de 527 à 847. Paris. 1905. (*In* Bibliothèque de l'enseignement de l'hist. ecclésiastique.)

Pertile, A. Storia del diritto italiano dalla caduta dell' impero Romano alla codificazione. 6 vols. 2nd edn. Del Giudice, P. Turin. 1892–1902. Index. Eusebio, L. Turin. 1893.

Petit de Julleville, L. Histoire de la langue et de la littérature françaises. 8 vols. Paris. 1896–1900.

Pirenne, H. Histoire de Belgique. 5 vols. Brussels. 1900–21. 3rd edn. in progress.

Pollock, F. and Maitland, F. W. The history of English Law before Edward I. 2 vols. Cambridge. 1895. 2nd edn. 1898.

Previté-Orton, C. W. Outlines of Medieval History. Cambridge. 1916. 2nd edn. 1921.

Quentin, H. Les Martyrologes historiques du Moyen Âge. Étude sur la formation du martyrologe romain. Paris. 1908. (Études d'hist. des dogmes et d'ancienne littérature ecclésiastique.)

Ranke, L. von. Weltgeschichte. 9 vols. Leipsic. 1881–8. 2nd edn. 1895.

Redlich, O. and Erben, W. Urkundenlehre. Pt I. 1907. IV, 1 of Below's Handbuch (*see above*).

Richter, G. and Kohl, H. Annalen d. deutschen Gesch. im Mittelalter. 3 pts in 5. Halle a. S. 1873–98.

Romano, G. Le dominazioni barbariche in Italia. (395–1024.) (Storia polit. d' Italia.) 1909.

Schaube, A. Handelsgeschichte der romanischen Völker des Mittelmeergebiets bis zum Ende der Kreuzzüge. (Below and Meinecke, Handbuch, *see above*.) Munich and Berlin. 1906.

Schupfer, F. Manuale di storia del diritto italiano. Città di Castello. 1904.

Sismondi, J. C. L. de. Hist. des républiques italiennes du moyen âge. Paris. 1809–18 (and later edns.).

Storia letteraria d' Italia scritta da una Società di Professori. Milan. 1900 ff.

Storia politica d' Italia scritta da una Società d' amici. 8 vols. Ed. Villari, P. Milan. 1875–82. (By various writers, *cf. sub nom.*)

Storia politica d' Italia scritta da una Società di Professori. Vols. I–VIII. Milan, in progress. (By various writers, *cf. sub nom.*)

Stubbs, Wm. Constitutional history of England. 3 vols. Oxford. 1874. (Frequently reprinted.) French transl. (with notes and studies). Lefebvre, G. and Petit Dutaillis, Ch. Paris. 1907. English transl. of notes etc. Studies and Notes supplementary to Stubbs' Constitutional History. Vol. I. Rhodes, W. E. Manchester. 1908. Vol. II. Waugh, W. T. 1914.

Tiraboschi, G. Storia della letteratura italiana. 2nd edn. Modena. 1787–94.

Vinogradoff, P. Roman Law in Mediaeval Europe. London and New York. 1909. [Excellent bibliographies.]

Viollet, P. Histoire du droit civil français. 3rd edn. Paris. 1905.

—— Histoire des institutions politiques et administratives de la France. 3 vols. Paris. 1890–1903.

Waitz, G. Deutsche Verfassungsgeschichte. 8 vols. Kiel. 1863–78. 2nd and 3rd edns. Berlin. 1880–96.

Weltgeschichte in gemeinverständlicher Darstellung. Ed. Hartmann, L. M. Vol. IV. Das Mittelalter bis zum Ausgang der Kreuzzüge. Hellmann, S. Gotha. 1920.

Werminghoff, A. Geschichte der Kirchenverfassung Deutschlands. I. Hanover and Leipsic. 1905.

Zeller, J. Hist. d'Allemagne. Paris. 1872–91. Vols. 1–9. [No more pub.]

CHAPTERS I, II, III.

LOUIS THE PIOUS AND THE CAROLINGIAN KINGDOMS.

I. BIBLIOGRAPHIES.

Dahlmann-Waitz. Quellenkunde. (8th edn. 8vo.) p. 224 sqq. *See ib.*
Molinier. Les sources de l'hist. de France. Fasc. i. pp. 211–236. *See Gen. Bibl.* i.
Wattenbach. Deutschlands Geschichtquellen. (7th edn.) p. 198 sqq. *See ibid.*

II. ORIGINAL AUTHORITIES.

(1) Contemporary Annals.

Numerous documents and texts, collected particularly in vols. vi, vii, viii and ix of
Bouquet, Recueil des hist. des Gaules etc. *See Gen. Bibl.* iv. The best editions
in MGH; especially 4to series:
    Epistolae aevi Karolini. Ed. Dümmler, E. and Hampe, K. 1892 ff. In progress.
    Poetae latini aevi Carolini. Ed. Dümmler. 1881 ff. 4 vols. In progress.
The most important texts are the following:
    Agobardi Opera. MPL. civ.
    Annales Bertiniani. Ed. Waitz, G. SGUS. 1883.
    Annales Fuldenses. Ed. Kurze, F. *Ibid.* 1891.
    Annales Regni Francorum et Annales quae dicuntur Einhardi. Ed. Kurze, F.
        Ibid. 1895.
    Annales Vedastini (874–900). Ed. de Simson, B. *Ibid.* 1909.
    Ermoldus Nigellus. In honorem Hludowici imperatoris libri iv. Ed. Dümm-
        ler. MGH. Poet. Lat. ii.
    Hincmarus. Opera. Ed. Sirmond. Paris. 1649. Reproduced MPL. cxxv,
        cxxvi.
    —— De ordine Palatii. Ed. Prou, M. Paris. 1884. (Valuable for the
        introduction, translation, and notes.)
    Lupus Ferrariensis abbas. Epistolae. Ed. Dümmler. MGH. Epistolae vi.
    Nithardus. Historiarum libri iv. Ed. Müller, E. SGUS. 1907.
    Paschasius Radbertus. Vita Walae (Epitaphium Arsenii) et Vita Adalhardi.
        Ed. Mabillon. ASBen. Vol. iv. *See Gen. Bibl.* iv. *Also* ed. Dümmler
        (for the Epitaphium Arsenii) in Abh. PAW. 1899–1900.
    Regino Prumiensis abbas. Chronicon. Ed. Kurze, F. SGUS. 1890.
    Theganus. Vita Hludowici imperatoris. Ed. Pertz, G. MGH. Script. ii.
    Vita Hludowici imperatoris, ascribed to the Astronomer. *Ibid.*

(2) Documents.

Boehmer, J. F.   Regesta chronologico-diplomatica Karolorum.   Frankfort.   1833.
Capitularia Regum Francorum.   Ed. Boetius and Krause.   2 vols.   MGH.   1893–97.
Mühlbacher, Eng.   Die Register des Kaiserreichs unter den Karolingern (751–918).   2nd edition.   Innsbrück.   1908.
Poupardin, R.   Recueil des actes des rois de Provence, 855–928.   AcadIBL.   Paris.   1920.
Sickel, Th. von.   Acta regum et imperatorum Karolinorum digesta et enarrata.   2 vols.   Vienna   1867.

III. MODERN WORKS.

(1) Criticism of Authorities.

All the texts of the period have been the subject of many works on special points for the most part drawn upon and referred to in the editions mentioned *supra*.   A full bibliography will be found in the works of Potthast, Wattenbach, Dahlmann-Waitz and Molinier (*see Gen. Bibl.*).   Only the most important which refer both to the biography and political career of the original authors and to the historical value of their works are here mentioned.

Agobard.
    Foss, R.   Leben und Schriften Agobards Erzbischof von Lyon.   Gütersloh.   1897.
    Marcks, J.-Fr.   Die politisch-kirchliche Wirksamkeit des Erzbischofs Agobard von Lyon.   Leipsic.   1888.
    Rozier, L.   Agobard de Lyon.   Montauban.   1891.
Annales Bertiniani:
    Büchting, E.   Glaubwürdigkeit Hincmars von Reims im III Teile der sogenannten Annalen von S. Bertin.   Halle.   1887.
Einhard:
    Bacha, E.   Étude biographique sur Eginhard.   Liège.   1888.
    Kurze, Fr.   Einhard.   Berlin.   1899.   8vo.
    Bondois, Marg.   La translation des saints Marcellin et Pierre.   Étude sur Einhard et sa vie politique de 827 à 834.   Paris.   1907.
Lupus of Ferrières:
    Levillain, L.   Etude sur les lettres de Loup de Ferrières.   BEC.   1901–2.
Monod, G.   Études critiques sur les sources de l'histoire carolingienne.   I, Les annales carolingiennes.   Bk. I.   Des origines à 829.   Paris.   1898.
Nithard:
    Meyer von Knonau, G.   Ueber Nithards vier Bücher Geschichte.   Leipsic.   1866.
    Küntzemüller, O.   Nithard und sein Geschichtswerk.   Guben.   1873.
Paschasius (Radbertus):
    Rodenberg, C.   Die Vita Walae als historische Quelle.   Göttingen.   1877.
Regino:
    Schulz, P.   Zur Glaubwürdigkeit des Chronik des Abtes Regino von Prüm.   Hamburg.   1897.

(2) General Works.

Calmette, J.   La diplomatie carolingienne du traité de Verdun à la mort de Charles le Chauve (843–877).   Paris.   1901.
Drapeyron, L.   Essai sur la séparation de la France et de l'Allemagne aux IXe et Xe siècles.   Paris.   1870   (Superficial.)

Dümmler, E. De Arnulfo Francorum rege. Berlin. 1852.

—— Gesch. des ostfränkischen Reiches. 2nd edn. 3 vols. Leipsic. 1887–8. (Jahrbücher d. deutsch. Gesch.) (The standard authority for the whole period 840–918.)

Faugeron, H. P. De fraternitate seu colloquiis inter filios et nepotes Hludowici Pii (842–882). Rennes. 1868.

Favre, E. Eudes, comte de Paris et roi de France. Paris. 1893.

Fustel de Coulanges, N. D. Les transformations de la royauté pendant l'époque carolingienne. Paris. 1892.

Gfrörer, A. F. Geschichte der ost- und westfränkischen Karolinger. Freiburg. 1848. 2 vols. (Greatly out of date so far as criticism of the texts is concerned, but still quoted for general views.)

Giesebrecht, W. Gesch. der Kaiserzeit. I. Leipsic. 1881. *See Gen. Bibl.* v.

Harnack, O. Das karolingische und das byzantinische Reich. Göttingen. 1880.

Himly, Aug. Wala et Louis le Débonnaire. Paris. 1849.

Kleinclausz, A. L'empire carolingien. Ses origines et ses transformations. Paris. 1902.

Lapôtre, A. L'Europe et le Saint-Siège à l'époque carolingienne. I, Le pape Jean VIII. Paris. 1895.

Lesne, Abbé E. La hiérarchie épiscopale en Gaule et en Germanie depuis la réforme de saint Boniface jusqu'à la mort de Hincmar. Lille. 1905. (Important for Hincmar and his political theories.)

Lilienfein, H. Die Anschauungen von Staat und Kirche im Reiche der Karolinger. Heidelberg. 1902.

Lot, F. and Halphen, L. Le règne de Charles le Chauve. Part I (840–851). Paris. 1909.

Monod, G. Du rôle de l'opposition des races et des nationalités dans la dissolution de l'empire Carolingien. Annuaire de l'École des Hautes Études. 1896.

Mühlbacher, E. Deutsche Geschichte unter den Karolingern. Stuttgart. 1896.

Parisot, R. Le royaume de Lorraine sous les Carolingiens (843–923). Paris. 1899.

Phillips, G. Beiträge zur Gesch. Deutschlands vom Jahr 887 bis 936. Abh. der Akad. v. München. 1841.

Richter, G. and Kohl, H. Annalen des deutschen Reichs im Zeitalter der Karolinger. *See Gen. Bibl.* v.

Rintelen, K. Gesch. Ludwigs des Kindes und Konrads I. FDG. III.

Simson, B. Jahrbücher des fränkischen Reichs unter Ludwig dem Frommen. 2 vols. Leipsic. 1874–6. (Jahrbücher d. deutsch. Gesch.)

Warnkönig, L. A. and Gérard, P. A. F. Hist. des Carolingiens. Brussels. 1862. (Somewhat out of date but useful for general views.)

Wenck, W. B. Das fränkische Reich nach dem Vertrage von Verdun (843–861). Leipsic. 1851.

—— Die Erhebung Arnulfs und der Zerfall des karolingischen Reiches. Leipsic. 1852.

(3) Monographs and Biographies.

Amelung, K. Leben und Schriften des Bischofs Jonas von Orléans. Dresden. 1888.

Barthélemy, A. de. Les origines de la maison de France. RQH. XIII.

Bourgeois, E. Le capitulaire de Kiersy-sur-Oise (877). Paris. 1885.

Calmette, J. Étude sur les relations de Charles le Chauve avec Louis le Germanique et l'invasion de 858–859. MA. 1899.

—— De Bernardo sancti Guillelmi filio. Toulouse. 1902.

Doizé, J.　Le gouvernement confraternel des fils de Louis le Pieux, et l'unité de l'Empire.　MA.　1898.

Dümmler, E.　Ueber die sudöstlichen Marken des fränkischen Reichs unter den Karolingern.　(795–907.)

Gasté, A.　Les serments de Strasbourg.　Paris.　1888.

Halphen, L.　La pénitence publique de Louis le Pieux à Saint-Médard de Soissons. Bibliothèque de la Faculté des lettres de Paris, fasc. xviii.

Hirsch, F.　Die Schenkung Kaiser Karls des Kahlen für Papst Johann VIII und der Libellus de imperatoria potestate in urbe Roma, in FDG.　xx.

Hirsch, Paul.　Die Erhebung Berengars I von Friaul zum König in Italien. Strasbourg.　1910.

Lokys, G.　Die Kämpfe der Araber mit den Karolingern bis zum Tode Ludwigs II. Heidelberg.　1906.

Lot, F.　Mélanges carolingiens.　MA.　1904–8.

—— La grande invasion normande de 856–862.　BEC.　1908.

—— Une année du règne de Charles le Chauve.　Année 866.　MA.　1902.

—— De quelques personnages du ixe siècle qui ont porté le nom de Hilduin. MA.　1903.　Cf. BEC.　1904–5.

Mabille, C.　Le royaume d'Aquitaine et ses marches sous les Carlovingiens. Toulouse.　1870.　In Vic, C. de, and Vaissete, J. J.　Hist. générale de Languedoc.　New edn.　ii.　*See Gen. Bibl.* iv.

Noorden, C. von.　Hinkmar, Erzbischof von Reims.　Bonn.　1863.

Pfister, Christian.　L'archevêque de Metz Drogon.　Mélanges Paul Fabre.　Paris. 1902.

Poupardin, R.　Le royaume de Provence sous les Carolingiens (855–933?).　Paris. 1901.

—— Études sur l'histoire des principautés lombardes de l'Italie méridionale et leurs rapports avec l'empire franc.　MA.　1906–7.

Pouzet, P.　La succession de Charlemagne et le traité de Verdun, in Mélanges Carolingiens.　Paris.　1890.

Prou, M.　Les Monnaies carolingiennes de la Bibliothèque nationale.　Paris.　1896.

Pückert, W.　Aniane und Gellone.　Diplomatisch-kritische Untersuchungen zur Geschichte der Reformen des Benediktinerordens im ix und x Jahrhundert. Leipsic.　1899.

Richterich, J.　Papst Nikolaus I.　Bern.　1903.

Schottmüller, R.　Die Entstehung des Stammesherzogthums Bayern am Ausgang der karolingischen Periode.　Berlin.　1868.

Schrörs, H.　Hinkmar, Erzbischof von Reims.　Freiburg.　1884.

Sickel, W.　Die Verträge der Päpste mit den Karolingern und das neue Kaisertum. DZG.　xi, xii.

Trog, H.　Die Schweiz vom Tode Karls des Grossen bis zum Ende des burgundischen Reiches.　Basle.　1889.

Vogel, W.　Die Normannen und das fränkische Reich bis zur Gründung der Normandie (799–911).　Heidelberg.　1906.

CHAPTER IV.

FRANCE, THE LAST CAROLINGIANS AND THE ACCESSION OF HUGH CAPET, 888–987.

1. SPECIAL BIBLIOGRAPHIES.

Very complete bibliographies will be found at the beginning of the works of MM. Eckel, Favre, Lauer and Lot mentioned below.

2. ORIGINAL DOCUMENTS.

The charters of the kings of France will be brought together in Chartes et diplômes, *see Gen. Bibl.* IV. Already published: Recueil des actes de Louis IV, roi de France, 936–954. Ed. Lauer, Ph. Paris. 1914. Recueil des actes de Lothaire et de Louis V, rois de France, 954–987. Ed. Halphen, L. and Lot, F. Paris. 1908. A few may be found also in Bouquet. IX. *See Gen. Bibl.* IV.

3. AUTHORITIES.

Abbo, monk of Saint-Germain-des-Prés. De bellis Parisiacae urbis. Ed. Taranne, N. R. Paris. 1834. With French transl. MGH. Poetae lat. aevi carol. IV. Ed. Winterfeld, P. V.
Annales Vedastini. Simson, B. de. Hanover. SGUS. 1909.
Dudo of Saint-Quentin. De moribus et actis primorum Normanniae ducum. Ed. Lair, J. Caen. 1865.
Flodoard. Annales. Ed. Lauer, Ph. Coll. textes. 1906. *See Gen. Bibl.* IV.
—— Historia Ecclesiae Remensis. Ed. Waitz. MGH. Script. XIII. Lejeune. Rheims. 1854. 2 vols.
Gerbert. Letters. Ed. Havet, J. Paris. Coll. textes. 1889.
Regino. Chronicon. Ed. Kurze. Hanover. SGUS. 1890.
Richerus. Historiae. Ed. Waitz. Hanover. *Ibid.* 1877.

4. MODERN WORKS.

(a) GENERAL.

Eckel, A. Charles le Simple. Paris. 1899. BHE. 124.
Favre, E. Eudes, comte de Paris et roi de France 882–898. Paris. 1893. BHE. 99.
Flach, J. Les origines de l'ancienne France. Xᵉ et XIᵉ siècles. *See Gen. Bibl.* V. 4 vols. have appeared. (An original work, but confused and open to question.)
Heil, A. Die politischen Beziehungen zwischen Otto dem Grossen und Ludwig IV von Frankreich, 936–954. Berlin. 1904.
Kalckstein, C. von. Gesch. des französischen Königthums unter den ersten Capetingern. I. Der Kampf der Robertiner und Karolinger. Leipsic. 1877. (Out-of-date.)

Lauer, Ph. Robert I et Raoul de Bourgogne, rois de France, 923–936. BHE. 188. Paris. 1910.

—— Le règne de Louis IV d'Outre-mer. BHE. 127. 1900.

Lippert, W. König Rudolf von Frankreich. Leipsic. 1886.

Lot, F. Les derniers Carolingiens : Lothaire, Louis V, Charles de Lorraine, 954– 991. BHE. 87. 1891.

—— Études sur le règne de Hugues Capet et la fin du xe siècle. BHE. 147. 1903.

Pfister, C. in Lavisse, E. Histoire de France. ii, pt 1. 1903. *See Gen. Bibl.* v.

Schoene, C. Die politischen Beziehungen zwischen Deutschland und Frankreich in den Jahren 953–980. Berlin. 1910.

(*b*) Monographs and Special Treatises.

Haskins, Ch. H. The Normans in European history. Boston and New York. 1915.

Lair, J. Études critiques sur divers textes des xe et xie siècles. Paris. 1899. 2 vols. (Audacious critical work on texts.)

—— Étude sur la vie et la mort de Guillaume Longue-Épée, duc de Normandie. Paris. 1893.

Lot, F. Fidèles ou vassaux ? Essai sur la nature juridique du lien qui unissait les grands vassaux à la royauté depuis le milieu du ixe jusqu'à la fin du xiie siècle. Paris. 1904. (Full of information on the territorial development of France from the middle of the ninth century.)

Lüttich, R. Ungarnzüge in Europa im 10 Jahrhundert. Berlin. 1910.

Mabille, E. Le royaume d'Aquitaine et ses marches sous les Carolingiens. Vic, C. de, and Vaissete, J. J. Histoire de Languedoc. New edn. ii. 1870. pp. 277–323. *See Gen. Bibl.* iv.

Merlet, R. Les comtes de Chartres, de Châteaudun et de Blois aux ixe et xe siècles. Mém. de la Soc. archéolog. d'Eure-et-Loir. xii. 1897.

Parisot, R. Les origines de la Haute-Lorraine et sa première maison ducale (959– 1033). Paris. 1909.

—— Histoire de Lorraine. Vol. i. Paris. 1899.

Pirenne, H. Histoire de Belgique. i. 3rd edn. Brussels. 1909.

Prentout, H. Essai sur les origines et la fondation du duché de Normandie. Paris. 1911.

—— Étude critique sur Dudon de Saint-Quentin et son Histoire des premiers ducs normands. Paris. 1916.

Vanderkindere, L. La formation territoriale des principautés belges au moyen âge. 2 vols. Brussels. 1902.

Viollet, P. La question de la légitimité à l'avènement de Hugues Capet. Mém. AcadIBL. xxxiv, pt 1. 1892. pp. 257–288.

Vogel, W. Die Normannen und das fränkische Reich bis zur Gründung der Normandie, 799–911. Heidelberg. 1906.

CHAPTER V.

FRANCE IN THE ELEVENTH CENTURY.

1. SPECIAL BIBLIOGRAPHY.

Halphen, Louis. La France sous les premiers Capétiens, 987–1226. RSH.
Vol. xiv. 1907. pp. 62–88. (A bibliographical review of works published
up to 1907.)

2. ORIGINAL DOCUMENTS.

(a) Charters of the Kings of France.

See Bibl. c. iv, 2. Some in Bouquet. x, xi.
For Philip I, Prou, M. Recueil des actes de Philippe Ier roi de France 1059–
1108. Paris. 1908.
For Robert the Pious, a short calendar only, by Pfister, Chr. *See below,* 4 (*b*).
For Henry I, a full calendar, by Soehnée, F. Catalogue des actes de Henri Ier
roi de France 1031–1060. Paris. 1907. BHE. 161.

(b) Charters of the Great Feudatories etc.

Certain provincial histories mentioned below (those of Halphen, L. for Anjou,
of Latouche, R. for Maine, and Petit, E. for Burgundy) contain the catalogue of the
charters of some of the great feudatories.

3. AUTHORITIES.

(a) General Works.

Molinier, A. Les sources de l'histoire de France des origines aux guerres d'Italie.
See Gen. Bibl. i. Vol. ii. 1902. (A critical bibliography of all the chroniclers
and all the collections of letters.)
Recueil des historiens des Gaules et de la France. (Bouquet.) *See Gen. Bibl.* iv.
Vols. x–xvi. Paris. 1760 ff. (Contains the text of the principal authorities,
but many of the texts included have been re-published in modern times, with
a critical examination. See Molinier, *op. cit.*)

(b) Principal Authorities.

Adalbero, bishop of Laon. Satirical poems. Ed. Hückel, G. A. (In Université
de Paris. Bibliothèque de la Faculté des Lettres. Vol. xiii. 1901. pp.
49–184.)

Ademar of Chabannes. Chronicle. Ed. Chavanon, J. 1897. Coll. textes, *see Gen. Bibl.* IV. For critical notes on this text see Halphen, L. Remarques sur la chronique d'Adémar de Chabannes, RH. 98. (1908.) pp. 294–308.

Chronicon Namnetense. Ed. Merlet, R. Paris. 1896. Coll. textes.

Fulbert, bishop of Chartres. Letters in Bouquet x and MPL. 141. For the chronology of these letters see Pfister, Chr. De Fulberti Carnotensis episcopi vita et operibus. Nancy. 1885.

Gerbert. Letters. Ed. Havet, J. 1889. Coll. textes.

Gesta consulum Andegavorum. Edd. Halphen, L. and Poupardin, R. Chroniques des comtes d'Anjou et des seigneurs d'Amboise, pp. 25–171. 1913. *Ibid.*

Guibert of Nogent. Monodiae. Ed. Bourgin, G. Paris. 1907. *Ibid.*

Helgaldus. Epitoma vitae Roberti regis. Bouquet. x. pp. 99–117.

Ivo, bishop of Chartres. Letters. MPL. 162.

Miracula S. Benedicti. Ed. Certain, E. de. Les miracles de Saint Benoît. Paris. 1858. SHF.

Ordericus Vitalis. Historia ecclesiastica. Ed. Le Prévost, A. and Delisle, L. Paris. 1838–55. 5 vols. SHF.

Richerus. Historiae. Ed. Waitz, G. Hanover. 1877. SGUS.

William of Jumièges. Gesta Normannorum ducum. Ed. Marx, J. Rouen and Paris. 1914. Soc. de l'hist. de Normandie.

William of Poitiers. Gesta Guillelmi ducis. Ed. Duchesne, A. Hist. Normann. Scriptores. pp. 178–213. MPL. 149, col. 1216–1270.

4. MODERN WORKS.

(a) GENERAL.

Flach, J. Les origines de l'ancienne France. *See Bibl.* c. IV. (On vol. III and IV see Halphen, L. RH. Vol. 85. 1904. pp. 271–235. And vol. 129. 1918. pp. 90–6.)

Glasson, E. Hist. du droit et des institutions de la France. Vol. IV. Paris. 1891. (A compilation of moderate value.)

Halphen, L. La lettre d'Eude II de Blois au roi Robert. RH. 97 (1908). pp. 287–296.

Lot, F. Fidèles ou vassaux? *See Bibl.* c. IV, 4 (*b*).

Luchaire, A. Manuel des institutions françaises. Période des Capétiens directs. Paris. 1892.

—— Les premiers Capétiens 987–1137. Paris. 1901. (Lavisse II. 2. *See Gen. Bibl.* V.)

Viollet, P. Histoire des institutions politiques et administratives de la France. II, III. Paris. 1898–1903. (Original and suggestive, has good bibliographies.)

(b) WORKS ON THE CAPETIAN DYNASTY.

Fliche, A. Le règne de Philippe Iᵉʳ roi de France, 1060–1108. Paris. 1912.

Lot, F. Les derniers Carolingiens. *See Bibl.* c. IV, 4 (*a*).

—— Études sur le règne de Hugues Capet et la fin du xᵉ siècle. *See Bibl.* c. IV, 4 (*a*).

Luchaire, A. Hist. des institutions monarchiques de la France sous les premiers Capétiens. 987–1180. 2 vols. Paris. 1883. 2nd edn. 1891.

Monod, B. Essai sur les rapports de Pascal II avec Philippe Iᵉʳ, 1099–1108. Paris. 1907. BHE. 164.

Pfister, Chr. Études sur le règne de Robert le Pieux, 996–1031. Paris. 1885. BHE. 64.

(c) The Chief Provincial Histories.

Anjou :
  Halphen, L. Le comté d'Anjou au xi⁰ siècle. Paris. 1906. (Contains
    a bibliography.)
Brittany :
  La Borderie, A. Le Moyne de. Histoire de Bretagne. Vol. iii. Paris.
    1899. (Uncritical.)
Burgundy :
  Kleinclausz, A. Quomodo primi duces Capetianae stirpis Burgundiae res
    gesserunt 1036–1162. Dijon. 1902.
  —— Histoire de Bourgogne. Paris. 1909. (Very brief but containing
    a bibliography.)
  Petit, Ernest. Histoire des ducs de Bourgogne de la race capétienne.
    Vols. i, ii. Paris. 1885–8.
Champagne and Blois :
  Arbois de Jubainville, H. d'. Histoire des ducs et comtes de Champagne.
    Vol. i. Paris. 1859. (Old-fashioned.)
  Landsberger, J. Graf Odo I von der Champagne (Odo II von Blois, Tours
    und Chartres). Berlin. 1878. (Inadequate.)
  Lex, L. Eudes comte de Blois, de Tours, de Chartres, de Troyes et de
    Meaux (995–1037) et Thibaut son frère. Troyes. 1892. (Superficial.)
Flanders :
  Pirenne, H. Histoire de Belgique. Vol. i. 3rd edn. Brussels. 1909.
Gascony :
  Jaurgain, J. de. La Vasconie. Pau. 1898–1902. 2 vols. (A genealogical
    compilation, rather uncritical.)
Languedoc :
  Vic, C. de, and Vaissete, J. J. Histoire de Languedoc. New edn. 1872–
    1904. *See Gen. Bibl.* iv. (With considerable additions by the new
    editors, especially A. Molinier.)
Maine :
  Latouche, R. Histoire du comté du Maine pendant le x⁰ et le xi⁰ siècle.
    Paris. 1910. BHE. 183.
Normandy :
  Böhmer, H. Kirche und Staat in England und in der Normandie im 11 und
    12 Jahrhundert. Leipsic. 1899.
  David, C. W. Robert Curthose Duke of Normandy. Cambridge, Mass.
    1920. Harvard hist. studies. 25.
  Davis, H. W. C. and Whitwell, R. J. Regesta regum Anglo-Normannorum. i.
    Regesta Willelmi Conquestoris et Willelmi Rufi, 1066–1100. Oxford. 1913.
  Freeman, E. A. History of the Norman Conquest of England. 3rd edn.
    Oxford. 1877. 5 vols.
  Haskins, C. H. The Normans in European history. Boston and New York.
    1915.
  —— Norman Institutions. Cambridge, Mass. 1918. Harvard hist.
    studies. 24. (Capital.)
  Marion, M. De Normannorum cum Capetianis pacta ruptaque societate. Paris.
    1892.
  Valin, L. Le duc de Normandie et sa cour, 912–1204, étude d'hist. juridique.
    Paris. 1910.
Poitou :
  Richard, A. Histoire des comtes de Poitou. 778–1204. Paris. 1903. 2 vols.
    (Uncritical.)

CHAPTER VI.

THE KINGDOM OF BURGUNDY.

1. SPECIAL BIBLIOGRAPHIES.

Very complete bibliographies will be found in the works of MM. Fournier, Jacob and Poupardin, cited below.

2. ORIGINAL DOCUMENTS.

(a) CHARTERS OF THE KINGS OF PROVENCE AND BURGUNDY.

Some in Bouquet. IX. *See Gen. Bibl.* IV.

Recueil des actes des rois de Provence, 855–928. Ed. Poupardin, R. Paris. 1920. (Chartes et diplômes AcadIBL.)

Recueil des actes des rois de Bourgogne, in preparation.

I diplomi italiani di Lodovico III e di Rodolfo II. Ed. Schiaparelli, L. Rome. 1910. (Fonti.)

(b) CHARTERS OF THE GREAT FEUDATORIES ETC.

See the bibliographies in the works of M. Poupardin.

3. AUTHORITIES.

There is no original authority devoted exclusively to the history of Burgundy. We are reduced to the information furnished incidentally by the chroniclers of neighbouring kingdoms, which will be found to be enumerated in the bibliographies referring to them.

4. MODERN WORKS.

(a) GENERAL.

Flach, J. Les origines de l'ancienne France. Vol. IV. 1917. pp. 361–450. *See Gen. Bibl.* V.

Fournier, Paul. Le royaume d'Arles et de Vienne. Paris. 1891.

Gingins la Sarra, F. de. Mém. pour servir à l'hist. des royaumes de Provence et de Bourgogne jurane. Lausanne. 1851–3. 2 vols. (Uncritical and at the present day useless.)

Hofmeister, A. Deutschland und Burgund im früheren Mittelalter: eine Studie über die Entstehung des Arelatischen Reiches und seine politische Bedeutung. Leipsic. 1914.

Jacob, Louis. Le royaume de Bourgogne sous les empereurs franconiens 1038–1125. Paris. 1906.

Philipon, J. Le second royaume de Bourgogne. Annales Soc. d'émulation de l'Ain, ann. 1895–1906 et sqq. (Deals chiefly with the historical geography.)

Poupardin, R. Le royaume de Provence sous les Carolingiens (855–933?). Paris. 1901. BHE. vol. 131.

—— Le royaume de Bourgogne (888–1038). Étude sur les origines du royaume d'Arles. Paris. 1907. BHE. vol. 163.

Terrebasse, A. de. Œuvres posthumes. Vol. ii. Hist. de Boson et de ses successeurs. Vienne. 1875. (Unfinished and somewhat superficial.)

(*b*) MONOGRAPHS.

Hüffer, G. Die Stadt Lyon und die Westhälfte des Erzbisthums in ihren politischen Beziehungen zum deutschen Reich und zur französischen Krone von der Gründung des 11ten burgundischen Königreichs bis zur Vereinigung mit Frankreich. Münster. 1878.

Kallmann, R. Die Beziehungen des Königreichs Burgund zu Kaiser und Reich von Heinrich III bis auf die Zeit Friedrichs I. JSG. vol. xiv. 1889. pp. 1–107.

Kiener, Fritz. Verfassungsgesch. der Provence seit der Gothenherrschaft bis zur Errichtung der Konsulate, 510–1200. Leipsic. 1900.

Manteyer, Georges de. La Provence du premier au douzième siècle. Études d'hist. et de géogr. politique. Paris. 1908. MEC. viii.

—— Les origines de la maison de Savoie en Bourgogne 910–1060. La paix en Viennois et les additions à la Bible de Vienne. Grenoble. 1906. (Repr. with addns fr. Mélanges d'archéol. et d'hist. xix. École franç. à Rome. 1899. MA. ser. ii, v and sep. Paris. 1901. Bulletin de la Soc. de statistique de l'Isère. xxxiii. Grenoble. 1904.)

Poole, R. L. Burgundian Notes. EHR. xxvi (1911), pp. 310–17, xxvii (1912), pp. 299–309, xxviii (1913), pp. 106–12, xxx (1915), pp. 51–6.

Previté-Orton, C. W. Italy and Provence, 900–950. EHR. vol. xxxii (1917), pp. 335–347.

—— Charles Constantine of Vienne. EHR. vol. xxix (1914), pp. 703–6.

Renaux, C. Humbert Ier dit Aux-Blanches-Mains, fondateur de l'État de Savoie et le royaume de Bourgogne à son époque 1000–48. Carcassonne. 1906.

Steyert, A. Nouvelle histoire de Lyon et du Lyonnais. 3 vols. Lyon. 1895–9.

Trog, E, Rudolf I und Rudolf II von Hochburgund. Basle. 1884.

Wyss, G. von. Herzog Rudolf, der Sohn Königs Rudolfs II von Burgund und der Königin Bertha. Anzeiger f. schweizerische Gesch. xvi, pp. 357–362.

CHAPTER VII.

ITALY IN THE TENTH CENTURY.

I. BIBLIOGRAPHIES.

Romano, G., Le dominazioni barbariche in Italia (*see Gen. Bibl.* v), contains useful bibliographies at the head of the notes on the several chapters. The quarterly lists of books and periodical literature which appear in the Rivista storica italiana (*see Gen. Bibl.* i) are indispensable. An account of the narrative sources is in Balzani, U., Le cronache italiane del Medio Evo (*see Gen. Bibl.* i), while Potthast, A., Bibliotheca historica Medii Aevi (*see Gen. Bibl.* i), is indispensable for editions of the sources, and the critical literature upon them. Sources and modern works on the subject which have some relation to German history are listed in Dahlmann-Waitz (*see Gen. Bibl.* i). Molinier, A., Les sources de l'histoire de France, Part i, Divisions i and ii (*see Gen. Bibl.* i), is valuable for such of the sources as concern French history. Prof. Bury in the appendices to his edition of Gibbon's Decline and Fall of the Roman Empire, vols. v and vi (*see Gen. Bibl.* v), gives a bibliography of the Byzantine sources of the period. For South Italy, Capasso, B., Le fonti della storia delle provincie napolitane, 2nd edn. by Mastrojanni, E. O. (*see Gen. Bibl.* i), gives an exhaustive list of the sources. The bibliography of Gay, J., L'Italie méridionale et l'empire byzantin (*see Gen. Bibl.* v), is a convenient handlist. Poupardin, R., gives an excellent account of the South Lombard chronicles and cartularies in his Études sur l'histoire des principautés lombardes de l'Italie méridionale et de leurs rapports avec l'empire franc, Paris, 1907, and lists much of the sources and modern works on Northern Italy in the bibliographies of his Royaume de Provence and Royaume de Bourgogne (*see below,* iii, A). Regional bibliographies are to be found in such works as Kretschmayr, H., Geschichte von Venedig, vol. i (*see below,* iii, B) and Davidsohn, R., Geschichte von Florenz, vol. i (*see below,* iii, B). For the Veneto published sources up to 1885 are to be found in Cipolla, C., Fonti edite della storia della regione veneta, in Monumenti storici of R. Dep. Veneta....di stor. pat., Ser. iv. Miscellanea, vol. ii, 1883 and vol. iii, 1885.

II. SOURCES AND CRITICISM.

A 1. CHRONICLES ETC.

[Reprints of most of these are to be found in Migne, Patr. Lat. *See Gen. Bibl.* iv.]

Annales Barenses. Ed. Pertz, G. H. MGH. Script. v.

Annales Beneventani I. Ed. Pertz, G. H. MGH. Script. iii. p. 173 ff., col. 1.

Annales Beneventani II. *Ibid.* col. 3.

 (New edn. of both Beneventan Annals by Bertolini, O. BISI. 40.)

Annales Casinates breves. Ed. Pertz, G. H. MGH. Script. iii.

Anonymus Barensis. Ed. Muratori. RR.II.SS. Ed. i. Vol. v.

Arnulfus Mediolanensis. Rerum sui temporis libri quinque. Ed. Wattenbach, W. MGH. Script. viii.

Atto episcopus Vercellensis. Epistolae. *In* Attonis opera. Ed. Burontius. Verona. 1768.

Auxilius presbyter. In defensionem sacrae ordinationis papae Formosi Libellus prior et posterior. Ed. Dümmler, E. Auxilius und Vulgarius. pp. 59, 78. Leipsic. 1866.

—— Libellus in defensionem Stephani episcopi (Neapolitani) et praefatae ordinationis. *Ibid.* p. 96.

—— Libellus de ordinationibus a Formoso papa factis. Ed. Mabillon. Vetera analecta. Paris. 1723. (Also excerpts in Dümmler, *op. cit.*, p. 117.)

—— Libellus super causa et negotio Formosi papae seu Liber cuiusdam requirentis et respondentis. Ed. Mabillon. *Op. cit.*

—— Tractatus qui Infensor et Defensor dicitur de eadem quaestione. Ed. Mabillon. *Op. cit.*

Benedictus de S. Andrea. Chronicon. Ed. Zucchetti, G. (with Libellus de imperatoria potestate in urbe Roma). (Fonti.) Rome. 1920. *Also* ed. Pertz, G. H. MGH. Script. III.

Biblioteca arabo-sicula. Ed. Amari, M. Published as supplement to Muratori. RR.II.SS. Vol. I, pt 2. Turin and Rome. 1880–1, 1889. (Contains the Arabic sources of Sicilian history.)

Bruno episcopus (Querfurtensis). Vita quinque fratrum Poloniae. Ed. Kade, R. MGH. Script. XV.

Carmina Mutinensia. Ed. Winterfeld, P. v. MGH. Poetae Latini. Vol. III.

Catalogi abbatum Nonantulanorum. Ed. Waitz, G. MGH. Script. Langob. et Ital.

Catalogi regum Italicorum Oscelenses. *Ibid.*

Catalogi regum Langobardorum et Italicorum Brixiensis et Nonantulanus. *Ibid.*

Catalogus comitum Capuae. *Ibid.*

Catalogus imperatorum, regum Italicorum, ducum Beneventanorum et Spoletinorum Farfensis. *Ibid.*, and in Balzani, U., Chronicon Farfense, vol. I.

Catalogus regum Langobardorum et ducum Beneventanorum. Ed. Waitz, G. MGH. Script. Langob. et Ital.

Catalogus regum Langobardorum et Italicorum Lombardus. *Ibid.*

Catalogus regum Tuscus. *Ibid.*

Chronica S. Benedicti Casinensis. Ed. Waitz, G. MGH. Script. Langob. et Ital. pp. 478–88.

Chronicon Amalphitanum. Ed. Muratori, L. A. Antiq. Ital. I. pp. 207–16.

Chronicon Novaliciense. Ed. Cipolla, C. In Monumenta Novaliciensia vetustiora, vol II. (Fonti.) Rome. 1901.

Chronicon Salernitanum. Ed. Pertz, G. H. MGH. III.

Chronicon Vulturnense. Ed. Muratori, L. A. RR.II.SS. 1st edn., vol. I, pt 2. New edn., Federici, V., in Fonti. 1925 ff. in progress. (Largely consists of charters.)

Constantinus VII Porphyrogenitus. De administrando imperio. Ed. Bekker, I. CSHB. Bonn. 1840.

—— De thematibus. *Ibid.*

Cronaca siculo-saracena di Cambridge. Ed. Cozza-Luzi, G. Doc. p. servire alla storia di Sicilia, Series IV, 2. Palermo. 1890.

Donizo. Vita Mathildis comitissae. Ed. Bethmann, L. MGH. Script. XII.

Eugenius Vulgarius. De causa Formosiana libellus. Ed. Dümmler, E., in Auxilius und Vulgarius (*see below*, III, C), p. 117.

—— Epistolae et carmina. *Ibid.*, and in MGH. Poetae Latini, IV, 1, with title Eugenii Vulgarii Sylloga. Ed. Winterfeld, P. v.

Flodoardus. Les annales de Flodoard. Ed. Lauer, P. (Coll. textes.) Paris. 1906.

—— De Christi triumphis apud Italiam. *Ibid.*

Gesta Berengarii imperatoris. Ed. Winterfeld, P. v. MGH. Poetae Latini, IV, 1, and by Dümmler, E. Halle. 1871.

Gesta episcoporum Cameracensium. Ed. Bethmann, L. MGH. Script. iv.
Gregorius Catinensis. Chronicon Farfense. Ed. Balzani, U. 2 vols. (Fonti.)
Rome. 1903. (Largely consists of charters.)
Hrotsvitha. Panegyricus Ottonis magni. Ed. Barack, K. R., in Die Werke von
Hrotsvitha. Nuremberg. 1890. *Also* in MGH. Script. iv.
Hugo abbas Farfensis. Destructio Monasterii Farfensis.
—— Relatio constitutionis domni Hugonis abbatis.
—— Exceptio relationum de monasterii Farfensis diminutione.
—— Querimonium ad imperatorem.
All ed. Balzani, U., in Chronicon Farfense, vol. i. (Fonti.) Rome. 1903.
Invectiva in Romam pro Formoso papa. Ed. Dümmler, E., in Gesta Berengarii
imperatoris. Halle. 1871.
Johannes Canaparius. Vita...S. Adalberti episcopi Pragensis. Ed. Pertz, G. H.
MGH. Script. iv.
Johannes Diaconus. Chronicon Venetum. Ed. Monticolo, G., in Cronache vene-
ziane antichissime, vol. i. (Fonti.) Rome. 1890.
Johannes Diaconus Neapolitanus. Translatio S. Severini. Ed. Waitz, G. MGH.
Script. Langob. et Ital. pp. 463-5.
Johannes Italus. Vitæ S. Odonis abbatis Cluniacensis. Ed. Duchesne, A., in
Marrier, M., and Quercetanus (Duchesne), A., Bibliotheca Cluniacensis (*see Gen.
Bibl.* iv). Reprinted in MPL. cxxxiii. Excerpts, ed. Heinemann, L. v., in
MGH. Script. xv. 2.
Johannes X Papa (Archiepiscopus Ravennatis). Epistulae. Il rotolo opistografo
del principe Antonio Pio di Savoia. Ed. Ceriani, A. and Porro, G. Milan.
1883. *Also* in NAGDG. ix, p. 515, xi, p. 599.
Landulphus Senior. Mediolanensis historiae libri iv. Ed. Wattenbach, W. MGH.
Script. viii.
Leo episcopus Ostiensis [also Leo Diaconus and Leo Marsicanus]. Chronica monasterii
Casinensis. Ed. Wattenbach, W. MGH. Script. vii. (Includes charters.)
Liber censuum S. Romanae Ecclesiae (Cencius Camerarius). *See Gen. Bibl.* iv.
Liber Pontificalis. *See Gen. Bibl.* iv.
Liudprandus episcopus Cremonensis. Antapodosis.
—— Historia Ottonis.
—— Relatio de legatione Constantinopolitana.
All ed. by Becker, J., in SGUS. 3rd edn. Hanover. 1915.
Lupus Protospatarius Barensis. Annales Barenses. Ed. Pertz, G. H. MGH.
Script. v.
Monumenta ad Neapolitani ducatus historiam pertinentia. Ed. Capasso, B. 3 vols.
Naples. 1881-92. (Contains both chronicle and documentary sources.)
Necrologio dei SS. Ciriaco e Nicola. Ed. Egidi, P., in Necrologi e libri affini della
Provincia romana, vol. i, p. 3. (Fonti.) Rome. 1908.
Odilo abbas Cluniacensis. Epitaphium Adelheidae imperatricis. Ed. Pertz, G. H.
MGH. Script. iv.
Orestes patriarcha Hierosolymitanus. Vita S. Sabae iunioris. Ed. Cozza-Luzi, G.,
in Studi e documenti di storia e diritto. xii. Rome. 1890.
—— Vitae SS. Christophori et Macarii. Ed. Cozza-Luzi, G., in Studi e documenti
di storia e diritto. xiii. Rome. 1892.
Petrus Damianus. Vita S. Romualdi fundatoris ordinis Camaldulensium. Ed.
Cajetanus, C., in Petri Damiani opera. Vol. ii. Rome. 1608. Excerpts, ed.
Waitz, G., in MGH. Script. iv.
Petrus Subdiaconus. Libellus miraculorum S. Agrippini episcopi Neapolitani. Ed.
Waitz, G. MGH. Script. Langob. et Ital. pp. 463-5.
Radoynus. Vita et translatio S. Pardi episcopi Lucerini. Ed. Waitz, G. MGH.
Script. Langob. et Ital. pp. 589-90.

Ratherius episcopus Veronensis. Epistolae. Ed. Ballerini, P. and H., in Ratherii Opera. Verona. 1765.

Regino abbas Prumiensis. Chronicon cum continuatione. Ed. Kurze, F. SGUS. Hanover. 1890.

Rodulfus Glaber. Historiarum sui temporis libri v. Ed. Prou, M. (Raoul Glaber. Les cinq livres de ses histoires, in Coll. textes.) Paris. 1886.

—— Vita S. Guilelmi I abbatis S. Benigni Divoniensis. Ed. Mabillon. ASBen. vi. Pt i. (*See Gen. Bibl.* iv.) Excerpts, ed. Waitz, G. MGH. Script. iv.

Romualdus Salernitanus. Annales. Ed. Garufi, C. A., in Muratori. RR.II.SS. New edn., vol. vii, pt i, in progress. Città di Castello. 1914 ff. *Also* ed. Arndt, W. MGH. Script. xix.

Sylvester II papa. Epistolae. Ed. Havet, J., in Lettres de Gerbert. (Coll. textes.) Paris. 1889.

Syrus. Vita S. Maioli abbatis Cluniacensis. First recension. Ed. Mabillon. ASBen. v. Second recension. ASBoll. 11 Mai. ii. 663–84.

Thangmarus. Vita Bernwardi episcopi Hildesheimensis. Ed. Pertz, G. H. MGH. Script. iv.

Thietmarus Merseburgensis episcopus. Chronicon. Ed. Kurze, F. SGUS. Hanover. 1889.

Vita S. Eliae junioris. ASBoll. 17 Aug. iii.

Vita S. Eliae Spelaeotae. ASBoll. 11 Sept. iii.

Vita S. Lucae abbatis Armenti. ASBoll. 13 Oct. vi.

Vita S. Nili junioris. ASBoll. 26 Sept. vii.

Vita S. Vitalis Siculi. ASBoll. 9 Mart. ii.

Widukindus monachus Corbeiensis. Rerum gestarum Saxonicarum libri iii. Ed. Kehr, K. A. 4th edn. SGUS. Hanover. 1904.

Willelmus monachus Clusensis. Chronicon monasterii S. Michaelis de Clusa. Ed. Provana, L. A. MHP. Script. iii.

A 2. DIPLOMATA ETC.

Letters of the Popes are printed in various volumes of Migne, Patrologia Latina (see for list, Molinier, A., Les sources de l'histoire de France, Ire partie, i, pp. 278, 283, 284). Charters of Roman churches are edited in ASRSP. vols. xvi–xxx. Rome. 1893–1907.

Beltrani, G., Documenti Longobardi e Greci per la storia dell' Italia meridionale nel medio evo. Rome. 1877.

Biblioteca della società storica subalpina, directed by Gabotto, F. In progress. Pinerolo etc. 1899 ff. (Some 95 volumes have been published, mostly of Piedmontese charters up to A.D. 1300.)

Chronicon S. Sophiae Beneventi. Ed. Ughelli. Italia Sacra. 2nd edn. Coleti. Vol. x, pt 2. (*See below.*) (Really a cartulary, following Annales Beneventani. *See above,* A 1.)

Codex diplomaticus Caietanus (in Tabularium Casinense). 2 vols. Monte Cassino. 1887–91.

Codex diplomaticus Cavensis. Ed. Morcaldi, M., Schiani, M., de Stephano, S. 8 vols. Naples and Milan. 1873–93.

Codex diplomaticus Longobardiae. MHP. xiii. Turin. 1873.

Codice diplomatico Barese. Publ. by Comm. prov. di archeol. e storia patria di Bari. (Apulian charters.) Vols. i to viii. In progress. Trani. 1896 ff.

Constitutiones et Acta publica imperatorum et regum. Tom. i. Ed. Weiland, L. (MGH. Legum Sect. iv. *See Gen. Bibl.* iv.)

Fantuzzi, M. Monumenti ravennati de' secoli di mezzo. 6 vols. Venice. 1801–4.

Gaddoni, S. and Zaccherini, G.   Chartularium imolense.   2 vols.   Imola.   1912.
Gattola, E.   Historia abbatiae Casinensis.   Venice.   1734.
—— Ad historiam abbatiae Casinensis accessiones.   Venice.   1734.
Hartmann, L. M.   Ecclesiae S. Mariae in Via Lata tabularium.   2 vols.   Vienna.
   1895.
Jaffé, P.   Regesta pontificum Romanorum.   2nd edn., Wattenbach, W.   *See Gen.*
   Bibl. IV.
Kehr, P. A.   Regesta pontificum Romanorum.   Italia Pontificia.   *See Gen. Bibl.* IV.
Memorie e documenti per servire all' istoria della città e stato di Lucca.   11 vols. in
   14.   Lucca.   1813–84.
Monumenta ad Neapolitani ducatus historiam pertinentia.   Ed. Capasso, B.   3 vols.
   Naples.   1881–92.
Muratori, L. A.   Antiquitates medii aevi.   *See Gen. Bibl.* IV.
—— Trattato delle Antichità Estensi.   Modena.   1717–40.
Ottenthal, E. v.   Ein ineditum Ottos I für den Grafen von Bergamo von 970.
   MIOGF. XVII.   p. 35.   Innsbruck.   1896.
Poupardin, R.   Études sur les institutions...des principautés lombardes etc.   (*See*
   below, III, C.)
Regesta Chartarum Italiae, publ. by K. Preuss. Histor. Institut and Istituto storico
   italiano.   12 vols.   In progress.   Rome.   1907 ff.   (Mostly central Italian
   charters.)
Regesto di Farfa, compilato da Gregorio di Catino.   Ed. Giorgi, I. and Balzani, U.
   5 vols.   Rome.   1879–1914.
Regesto Sublacense del secolo XI.   Ed. Allodi, L. and Levi, G.   Rome.   1885.
Regii Neapolitani Archivi Monumenta.   6 vols.   Naples.   1846–61.
Schiaparelli, L.   I diplomi di Guido e di Lamberto.   (Fonti.)   Rome.   1906.
—— I diplomi di Berengario I.   *Ibid.*   Rome.   1903.
—— I diplomi italiani di Lodovico III e di Rodolfo II.   *Ibid.*   Rome.   1910.
—— I Diplomi di Ugo e di Lotario, di Berengario II e di Adalberto.   *Ibid.*   Rome
   1924.
Sickel, T. v.   Die Urkunden Konrad I, Heinrich I und Otto I.   (MGH.   Diplo-
   mata, I.)   Hanover.   1879–84.
—— Die Urkunden Otto des II.   (*Ibid.*   Vol. II, pt 1.)   Hanover.   1888.
—— Die Urkunden Otto des III.   (*Ibid.*   Vol. II, pt 2.)   Hanover.   1893.
Tafel, L. F. and Thomas, G. M.   Urkunden zur älteren Handels- und Staats-
   geschichte der Republik Venedig.   (Fontes Rerum Austriac. II.   Vols. XII–XIV.)
   Vienna.   1856–7.
Theiner, A.   Codex diplomaticus dominii temporalis S. Sedis.   Vol. I.   Rome.   1861.
Trinchera, F.   Syllabus Graecarum membranarum.   Naples.   1865.

B 1.   CRITICISM ON CHRONICLES.

Besides the prefaces to the several editions cited above under A 1, valuable
general introductions are to be found in Balzani, U., Le cronache italiane nel medio
evo (*see Gen. Bibl.* I), and in Wattenbach, W., Deutsche Geschichtsquellen (*see Gen.*
Bibl. I).   For detailed lists of the critical literature on each source up to 1895, see
Potthast, A., Bibliotheca historica Medii Aevi (*see Gen. Bibl.* I), and on some sources
up to 1900 see Molinier, A., Les sources de l'histoire de la France, Pt I, 1 (see *Gen.*
Bibl. I).   For Liudprand, Köpke, R. A., De vita et scriptis Liudprandi episcopi
Cremonensis commentatio historica, Berlin, 1842; Dändliker, C. and Müller, J. J.,
Liudprand von Cremona und seine Quellen (in Büdinger, Untersuchungen zur
mittelalterlichen Geschichte), Leipsic, 1871; Becker, J., Textgeschichte Liudprands
von Cremona (in Bd. III, 2 of Traube-Lehmann, Quellen und Untersuchungen zur
lateinische Philologie des Mittelalters, Munich, 1905 ff.); and Fedele, P., in Ricerche

per la storia di Roma e del papato nel secolo x (*see below*, III, B), are specially important. For the chronicles of Southern Italy see Hirsch, F., De Italiae inferioris annalibus saeculi decimi et undecimi, Berlin, 1864; and Poupardin, R., Études sur l'histoire des principautés lombardes etc. (*see above*, under I). For the critical literature on Venetian sources see Kretschmayr, H., Geschichte von Venedig, vol. I, pp. 385 ff. (*see below*, III, B).

B 2. CRITICISM ON DIPLOMAS.

Bresslau, H.   Handbuch der Urkundenlehre für Deutschland und Italien.   *See Gen. Bibl.* v.

Buzzi, G.   La curia arcivescovile e la curia cittadina di Ravenna dall' 850 al 1118.   BISI. 35, p. 7.   Rome.   1915.

Kehr, P.   Die Urkunden Ottos III.   Innsbruck.   1890.

Poole, R. L.   Lectures on the History of the Papal Chancery down to the time of Innocent III.   Cambridge.   1915.   (An invaluable introduction.)

Poupardin, R.   Étude sur la diplomatique des princes lombards de Bénévent, de Capoue et de Salerne.   (École française de Rome, Mélanges d'archéol. et d'histoire, XXI, p. 115.)   Paris.   1901.

Sackur, E.   Das römische Paktum Ottos I.   NAGDG. XXV. p. 409.   Hanover and Leipsic.   1900.

Schiaparelli, L.   I diplomi dei re d'Italia, ricerche storico-diplomatiche.

—— I diplomi di Berengario I.   BISI. 23, p. 1.   Rome.   1902.

—— I diplomi di Guido e di Lamberto.   *Ibid.* 26, p. 7.   Rome.   1905.

—— I diplomi di Lodovico III.   *Ibid.* 29, p. 105.   Rome.   1908.

——- Un diploma inedito di Rodolfo II per la chiesa di Pavia.   Alcune note sui diplomi originali di Rodolfo II.   *Ibid.* 30, p. 7   Rome.   1909.

—— I diplomi di Ugo e di Lotario.   *Ibid.* 34, p. 7.   Rome.   1914.

   (All valuable for the history of the reigns.)

Sickel, T. v.   Das Privilegium Otto I für die Römische Kirche vom Jahre 962.   Innsbruck.   1883.

—— Erläuterungen zu den Diplomen Otto II.   MIOGF. Ergänzungsband II. p. 77.   Innsbruck.   1886.

—— Erläuterungen zu den Diplomen Otto III.   MIOGF. XII. pp. 209, 369.   Innsbruck.   1891.

Simson, B. v.   Zum Privilegium Ottonianum für die Römische Kirche.   NAGDG.   XV. p. 577.

Smidt, W.   Das Chronicon Beneventani monasterii S. Sophiae.   Berlin.   1910.

Voigt, A.   Beiträge zur Diplomatik der langobardischen Fürsten von Benevent, Capua und Salerno.   Göttingen.   1902.

III.   MODERN WORKS.

A. GENERAL.

Böhmer-Ottenthal.   Böhmer, J. F.   Regesta Imperii.   II.   Unter den Herrschern aus dem sächsischen Hause 919–1024. Lieferung I. [Otto I.] Ed. Ottenthal, E. v.   *See Gen. Bibl.* v.

Bryce, Lord.   The Holy Roman Empire.   *See Gen. Bibl.* v.

Dümmler, E.   Gesta Berengarii Imperatoris.   Halle.   1871.

Fietz, C.   Geschichte Berengars von Ivrea.   Leipsic.   1870.

Gibbon, E.   The Decline and Fall of the Roman Empire.   Ed. Bury, J. B.   *See Gen. Bibl.* v.

Giesebrecht, W. v.   Geschichte der deutschen Kaiserzeit.   Bd. I, Theil II, Das Kaisertum der Ottonen.   *See Gen. Bibl.* v.

Hartmann, L. M. Geschichte Italiens im Mittelalter. Band III, Hälfte II. 1911. And Band IV, Hälfte I. 1915. *See Gen. Bibl.* v.

Hauck, A. Kirchengeschichte Deutschlands. Pt III. *See Gen. Bibl.* v.

Kehr, P. Zur Geschichte Ottos III. HZ. LXVI (n.s. 30), p. 385. Munich and Leipsic. 1891.

Köpke, R. and Dümmler, E. Jahrbücher der deutschen Geschichte. Otto der Grosse. Munich. 1876. *See Gen. Bibl.* v.

Manitius, M. Deutsche Geschichte unter der sächsischen und salischen Kaisern (911–1125). Stuttgart. 1889.

Mayer, E. Italienische Verfassungsgeschichte von der Gothenzeit bis zur Zunftherrschaft. 2 vols. Leipsic. 1909.

Muratori, L. A. Annali d' Italia. *See Gen. Bibl.* v.

Pivano, S. Stato e Chiesa da Berengario I ad Arduino (888–1015). Turin. 1908.

Poupardin, R. Le royaume de Provence sous les Carolingiens. (BHE.) Paris. 1901.

—— Le royaume de Bourgogne (888–1038). (BHE.) Paris. 1907.

Provana, L. Studi critici sovra la storia d' Italia a' tempi del re Ardoino. Turin. 1844.

Romano, G. Le dominazioni barbariche in Italia (395–1024). *See Gen. Bibl.* v.

Uhlirz, K. Jahrbücher der deutschen Geschichte. Otto II und Otto III. Bd. I, Otto II. Leipsic. 1902. *See Gen. Bibl.* v.

Villari, P. L' Italia da Carlomagno alla morte di Arrigo VII. Milan. 1910. Engl. transl. Mediaeval Italy from Charlemagne to Henry VII. London. 1910.

Wilmans, R. Jahrbücher des Deutschen Reichs unter der Herrschaft...Otto's III. (Ranke's Jahrbücher, Bd. II, Abtheil. II.) Berlin. 1840. *See Gen. Bibl.* v.

B. REGIONAL.

Amari, M. Storia dei Musulmani di Sicilia. 3 vols. Florence. 1854–72.

Besta, E. La Sardegna medioevale. 2 vols. Palermo. 1908–9.

Brown, H. F. Venice, an historical sketch of the republic. 2nd edn. London. 1895.

Camera, M. Memorie storico-diplomatiche dell' antica città e ducato di Amalfi. Salerno. 1876–81.

Carabellese, F. L'Apulia ed il suo comune nell' alto medio evo. (Documenti e monografie del Comm. prov. di archeol. e storia patria, VII.) Bari. 1905.

Cipolla, C. Compendio della storia politica di Verona. Verona. 1900.

Davidsohn, R. Geschichte von Florenz. Bd. I. Berlin. 1896. Ital. transl. Storia di Firenze, Le Origini (with valuable illustrations). Florence. 1907–12.

Di Meo, A. Annali critico-diplomatichi del regno di Napoli della mezzana età. 8 vols. Naples. 1795–1819.

Dina, A. L'ultimo periodo del principato longobardo e l'origine del dominio pontificio in Benevento. Benevento. 1899.

Duchesne, L. Les premiers temps de l'État Pontifical. 3rd edn. Paris. 1911.

Fedele, P. Ricerche per la storia di Roma e del papato nel secolo X. ASRSP. XXXIII, p. 177, and XXXIV, pp. 75 and 393. Rome. 1910, 1911.

Federici, G. B. Degli antichi duchi e consoli o ipati della città di Gaeta. Naples. 1791.

Gay, J. L'Italie Méridionale et l'Empire Byzantin (867–1071). *See Gen. Bibl.* v.

Giulini, G. Memorie spettanti alla storia, al governo e alla descrizione della città e della campagna di Milano nei secoli bassi. 2nd edn. 7 vols. Milan. 1854–7.

Gregorovius, F. Geschichte der Stadt Rom im Mittelalter. *See Gen. Bibl.* v.

Hodgson, F. The Early History of Venice from the foundation to the conquest of Constantinople. London. 1901.

Kretschmayr, H. Geschichte von Venedig. Vol. I. (Heeren's Series.) Gotha. 1905.

Lenel, W. Die Entstehung der Vorherrschaft Venedigs an den Adria. Strasbourg. 1897.

Lumbroso, G. Sulla storia dei Genovesi avanti il 1100. Comenti. Turin. 1872.

Moreres, M. Gaeta im frühen Mittelalter. Gotha. 1911.

Previté-Orton, C. W. Early History of the House of Savoy. Cambridge. 1912.

Romanin, S. Storia documentata di Venezia. Vol. I. Venice. 1853.

Savio, F. Antichi vescovi d' Italia. Piemonte. Turin. 1899.

—— —— Lombardia, Pt I (Milano). Florence. 1913.

Schipa, M. Storia del principato di Salerno. ASPN. XII. pp. 79, 209, 513, 740. Naples. 1887.

—— Storia del ducato di Napoli. *Ibid.* XVII. pp. 103, 358, 587, 780. XVIII. pp. 41, 247, 463, 621. XIX. pp. 3, 231, 445. Naples. 1892, 1893, 1894.

Sickel, W. Alberich II und die Kirchenstaat. MIOGF. XXIII. p. 50. 1902.

C. Special Subjects.

Allen, R. Gerbert, Pope Sylvester II. EHR. VII. p. 625. 1892.

Baudi di Vesme, B. Il re Ardoino e la riscossa italica contra Ottone III e Arrigo II. Bibl. Soc. stor. subalpina VII, Studi eporediesi, p. 1.

Bentzinger, J. Das Leben der Kaiserin Adelheid Gemahlin Ottos I während der Regierung Ottos III. Diss. Breslau. 1883.

Bloch, H. Beiträge zur Geschichte des Bischofs Leo von Vercelli und seiner Zeit. NAGDG. XXII. p. 11. 1897.

Bresslau, H. Jahrbücher des Deutschen Reiches unter Konrad II. Band I, Excurs IV, Zur Genealogie und Geschichte der hervorragendsten Dynastengeschlechter Ober- und Mittelitaliens im 11 Jahrhundert. Leipsic. 1879. (Jahrb. d. deutsch. Gesch.) *See Gen. Bibl.* V.

Buzzi, G. Ricerche per la storia di Ravenna e di Roma dall' 850 al 1118. ASRSP. XXXVIII. p. 107. Rome. 1915.

—— Per la Cronologia di alcuni pontefici dei secoli X–XI. ASRSP. XXXV. p. 611. Rome. 1912.

Carutti, D. Il conte Umberto I (Biancamano) e il re Arduino. Rome. 1888.

Ciccaglione, F. Le istituzioni politiche e sociali dei ducati napoletani. Naples. 1892.

Cipolla, C. Della supposta fusione degli Italiani coi Germani nei primi secoli del Medio Evo. Rendiconti del r. Accad. dei Lincei. Classe di Scienze morali, storiche e filologiche. Series V. Vol. 9. pp. 329, 369, 517, 567. Rome. 1900.

—— Di Audace Vescovo d'Asti. Miscell. stor. ital. XXVII. (2nd ser. XII.) p. 133. Turin. 1889.

—— Di Brunengo Vescovo d'Asti. Miscell. stor. ital. XXVIII. (2nd ser. XIII.) p. 297. Turin. 1890.

—— Di Rozone Vescovo d'Asti. Mem. Accad. Scienze di Torino, scienze morali, storiche e filologiche. 2nd ser. XLII. p. 3. Turin. 1892.

Desimoni, C. Sulle marche d' Italia e sulle loro diramazioni in marchesati. Atti della Società Ligure di storia patria. XXVIII. p. 1. Genoa. 1896.

Dresdner, A. Kultur- und Sittengeschichte der italienischen Geistlichkeit im 10 und 11 Jahrhundert. Breslau. 1890.

Dümmler, E. Auxilius und Vulgarius. Quellen und Forschungen zur Geschichte des Papstthums im Anfange des zehnten Jahrhunderts. Leipsic. 1866.

Fedele, P. La battaglia del Garigliano dell' anno 915. ASRSP. XXII. p. 181. 1899.

—— Sull' origine dei Frangipane. *Ibid.* XXXIII. p. 493. 1910.

Ficker, J.   Forschungen zur Reichs- und Rechtsgeschichte Italiens.   4 vols.
    Innsbruck.   1868–74.
Franke, W.   Romuald von Camaldoli und seine Reformtätigkeit zur Zeit Ottos III.
    Berlin.   1913.
Gaudenzi, A.   Il monastero di Nonantola, il ducato di Persiceto e la chiesa di
    Bologna.   (BISI.   36, p. 7; 37, p. 313.)   Rome.   1916.
Halphen, L.   Études sur l'administration de Rome au Moyen Âge (751–1252).
    (BHE.)   Paris.   1907.
——   La cour d'Otton III à Rome, 998–1001.   École franç. de Rome, Mélanges
    d'archéologie et d'histoire.   xxv.   p. 349.   Paris.   1905.
Hampe, K.   Die Berufung Ottos des Grossen nach Rom durch Papst Johann XII (in
    Historische Aufsätze Karl Zeumer zum 60 Geburtstag dargebracht).   Weimar.
    1900.
Handloike, M.   Die lombardischen Städte unter der Herrschaft der Bischöfe und die
    Entstehung der Comunen.   Berlin.   1883.
Hartmann, L. M.   Zur Wirtschaftsgeschichte Italiens im frühen Mittelalter.
    Gotha.   1904.
Hegel, C.   Geschichte der Stadtverfassung von Italien seit der Zeit der römischen
    Herrschaft bis zum Ausgang des zwölften Jahrhunderts.   2 vols.   Leipsic.
    1847.
Hofmeister, A.   Markgrafen und Markgrafschaften im italischen Königreich von
    Karl dem Grossen bis auf Otto den Grosse.   MIOGF.   Ergänzungsband vii.
    p. 258.   Innsbruck.   1906.
Lüttich, R.   Ungarnzüge in Europa.   Berlin.   1910.
Lux, C.   Pabst Silvesters II Einfluss auf die Politik Kaiser Ottos III.   Breslau.
    1898.
Manfroni, C.   Storia della marina italiana dalle invasioni barbariche al trattato di
    Ninfeo (400–1261).   Leghorn.   1899.
Patrucco, C.   I Saraceni nelle Alpi occidentali e specialmente in Piemonte.   Bibl.
    della Soc. stor. subalpina.   xxxii.   p. 319.   Pinerolo.   1908.
Poole, R. L.   The Names and Numbers of Medieval Popes.   EHR.   xxxii.   p. 470.
    1917.
——   The Counts of Tusculum, App. to Benedict IX and Gregory VI.   Proceedings
    of the British Academy.   Vol. viii.   1917.
Poupardin, R.   Étude sur les institutions…des principautés lombardes de l'Italie
    méridionale (ixᵉ—xiᵉ siècles), suivie d'un catalogue des actes des Princes de
    Bénévent et de Capoue.   Paris.   1907.
Previté-Orton, C. W.   Italy and Provence 900–950.   EHR.   xxxii.   p. 335.   London.
    1917.
Rieger, K.   Die Immunitätsprivilegien der Kaiser aus dem sächsischen Hause für
    italienische Bisthümer, 7ᵗᵉʳ Jahresbericht über das k.k. Franz-Josef Gymnasium
    in Wien.   Vienna.   1881.
Salvioli, G.   L' immunità e le giustizie delle chiese in Italia.   (Atti e Memorie delle
    rr. deputazioni di storia patria per le provincie modenesi e parmensi.   Ser. iii.
    Vols. v, p. 29, and vi, p. 1.)   Modena.   1888, 1890.
——   Le nostre origini.   Studi sulle condizioni fisiche, economiche e sociali
    prima del mille.   (Storia economica d' Italia nell' alto medio evo.)   Naples.
    1913.
Schaube, A.   Handelsgeschichte der romanischen Völker des Mittelmeergebiets bis
    zum Ende der Kreuzzuge.   *See Gen. Bibl.* v.
Schultz, J.   Atto von Vercelli, 924–961.   Diss.   Göttingen.   1885.
Schupfer, F.   La società milanese all' epoca del risorgimento del comune.   (Archivio
    Giuridico, iii, pp. 115, 252, 460, 732; iv, 309; v, 40.   Bologna.   1869–70.)
Segre, A.   Note Berengariane.   ASI.   1906.   ii.   p. 442.

Solmi, A. Stato e chiesa secondo gli scritti politici da Carlomagno fino al Concordato di Worms. Modena. 1901

—— Studi storici sulle istituzioni della Sardegna nel medio evo. (Biblioteca della società storica sarda. Ser. II. Vol. II.) Cagliari. 1917.

Tamassia, N. Chiesa e popolo. Note per la storia dell' Italia precomunale. (Archivio Giuridico, LXVII (n.s. VII), p. 300.) Modena. 1901.

—— Raterio e l' età sua. (Studii giuridici dedicati e offerti a Francesco Schupfer. II. p. 85.) Turin. 1898.

Vogel, A. Ratherius von Verona und das zehnte Jahrhundert. 2 vols. Jena. 1854.

CHAPTER VIII.

GERMANY· HENRY I AND OTTO I.

I. BIBLIOGRAPHY.

A very full account of the authorities will be found in Giesebrecht, Kaiserzeit. *See Gen. Bibl.* v. Vol. I. 1881.
Dahlmann-Waitz. Quellenkunde. *See Gen. Bibl.* I.
Potthast, A. Bibliotheca historica medii aevi. *See ib.*
Wattenbach, W. Deutschlands Geschichtsquellen. *See ib.*

II. DOCUMENTS.

Constitutiones et Acta Publica Imperatorum et Regum. I. Ed. Weiland, L. 1893. MGH. Leg. (IV).
MGH. Diplomatum I: Conradi I, Heinrici I et Ottonis I Diplomata. Ed Sickel, Th. 1879–84.
Böhmer. Regesta Imperii. *See Gen. Bibl.* IV.
Stumpf. Reichskanzler. *See ib.*

III. AUTHORITIES.

(Adalberti) Continuatio Reginonis. MGH, Script. I and SGUS. Ed. Kurze. 1890.
Adami Gesta Hammaburgensis Ecclesiae Pontificum. MGH, Script. VII and SGUS. Ed. Lappenberg. 1876. Re-ed. Schmeidler. 1917.
Annales Augienses. MGH, Script. I.
—— Colonienses. *Ib.*
—— Corbeienses. *Ib.* III, and in Jaffé, Bibliotheca rer. German. I.
—— Einsidlenses. MGH, Script. III.
—— Hersfeldenses. These are preserved only in six derived compilations, viz.:—
    Annals of Quedlinburg, Weissenburg, and Hildesheim, all printed in MGH, Script. III, the last also in SGUS, ed. Waitz, 1878; the Annals of Ottenbeuern in MGH, Script. v, and of Niederalteich in *Ib.* xx, and SGUS, ed. Giesebrecht and ab Oefele, E. L. B. 1868; and lastly the Annals of Lambert of Hersfeld, MGH, Script. III, and SGUS, ed. Holder-Egger, 1894.
—— Lobienses. MGH, Script. XIII.
—— S. Maximini Trevirensis. *Ib.* IV.
—— Sangallenses Maiores. *Ib.* I.
—— Weingartenses. *Ib.*
Annalium Alamannicorum Continuatio Sangallensis Tertia. *Ib.*
Epitaphium Adalheidae imperatricis auctore Odilone. *Ib.* IV.
Flodoardi Annales. *Ib.* III and Coll. textes. Ed. Lauer. 1905.
Gerhardi Vita Oudalrici Episcopi Augustani. MGH, Script. IV.
Hrotsvithae Carmen de Gestis Oddonis I Imperatoris. *Ib.* IV, and SGUS. Ed. Winterfeld. 1902.

Liudprandi opera. MGH, Script. III, and SGUS. Ed. Dümmler. 1877. Re-ed. Becker. 1915.
    Antapodosis.
    Historia Ottonis.
    Relatio de Legatione Constantinopolitana.
Richeri Historiarum Libri IV. MGH, Script. III, and SGUS. Ed. Waitz. 1877.
Ruotgeri Vita Brunonis Archiepiscopi Coloniensis. MGH, Script. IV, and SGUS. Ed. Pertz. 1841.
Thietmari Chronicon. MGH, Script. III, and SGUS. Ed. Kurze. 1889.
Vita Johannis Gorziensis auctore Johanne abbate S. Arnulfi. MGH, Script. IV.
—— Matildis Reginae. *Ib.*
—— Matildis Reginae antiquior. *Ib.* X.
Widukindi Rer. Gest. Saxonicarum Libri III. MGH, Script. III, and SGUS. Ed. Waitz, 1882, and re-ed. Kehr, 1904.

IV. MODERN WORKS.

(a) General.

Bryce. Holy Roman Empire. *See Gen. Bibl.* v.
Fisher, H. A. L. The Medieval Empire. 2 vols. London. 1898.
Giesebrecht, L. Wendische Geschichten aus den Jahren 780-1182. 3 vols. Berlin. 1843.
—— W. von. Kaiserzeit. Vol. I. *See Gen. Bibl.* v.
Hauck, A. Kirchengeschichte Deutschlands. Vol. III. *See Gen. Bibl.* v.
Köpke, R. A. and Dümmler, E. L. Kaiser Otto der Grosse. Jahrb. d. deutsch. Geschichte. Leipsic. 1876. *See Gen. Bibl.* v.
Manitius, M. Deutsche Geschichte unter den sächsischen und salischen Kaisern (911-1125). Stuttgart. 1889.
Maurenbrecher, W. Gesch. der deutschen Königswahlen vom 10 bis zur Mitte des 13 Jahrhunderts. Leipsic. 1889.
Ranke. Weltgeschichte. *See Gen. Bibl.* v.
Richter and Kohl. Annalen d. deutsch. Gesch. Vol. III. *See ib.*
Riezler, S. Geschichte Bayerns. Gotha. 1878.
Sybel, H. von. Die deutsche Nation und das Kaiserreich. Düsseldorf. 1862.
Waitz. Deutsche Verfassungsgeschichte. *See Gen. Bibl.* v.
—— Jahrb. d. deutsch. Reiches unter Heinrich I. Jahrb. d. deutsch. Geschichte. Leipsic. 1885. *See Gen. Bibl.* v.
Zeller, J. Histoire d'Allemagne. Vol. II. *See Gen. Bibl.* v.

(b) Special.

Bresslau, H. Der Ort der Ungarnschlacht. HZ. XCVII. 1906.
Caro, G. Der Ungarntribut unter Heinrich I. MIOGF. XX. 1899.
Erben, W. Zur Fortsetzung des Regino von Prüm. NAGDG. XVI. 1891.
Grund, O. Kaiser Otto des Grossen angeblicher Zug nach Dänemark. FDG. II. 1871.
Hadank, K. Einige Bemerkungen über der Ungarnschlacht, 955, in Delbrück-Festschrift. Berlin. 1908.
Heil, A. Die polit. Beziehungen zwischen Otto d. Gr. und Ludwig IV von Frankreich. 936-954. (Eberings Historische Studien 46.) Berlin. 1904.
Heinemann, O. von. Gesch. Braunschweigs und Hanovers. Vol. I. Gotha. 1884.
—— Margraf Gero. Brunswick. 1860.
Hofmeister, A. Die Heilige Lanze. In Gierke's Untersuchungen. XCVI. 1908.

Hofmeister, A. Deutschland und Burgund im früheren Mittelalter. Leipsic. 1914.

Keutgen, F. Untersuchungen über den Ursprung der deutschen Stadtverfassung. Leipsic. 1895.

Kirchhoff, A. Über den Ort der Ungarnschlacht von 933. FDG. VII. 1867.

Löher, F. Die deutsche Politik König Heinrichs I. Munich. 1857.

Maurenbrecher, W. Der Ludolfinische Aufstand von 953. FDG. IV. 1864.

—— Die Kaiserpolitik Ottos I. HZ. v. 1861.

Merkert, P. Kirche und Staat im Zeitalter der Ottonen. Diss. Breslau. 1905.

Mystakidis, B. A. Byzantinisch-deutsche Beziehungen zur Zeit der Ottonen. Tübingen. 1892.

Parisot, R. De la cession faite à Louis d'Outremer par Otton I de quelques pagi de la Lotharingie. Ann. de l'Est et du Nord. II. 1906.

Pflugk-Harttung, J. von. Das Bisthum Merseburg unter den sächsischen Kaisern. FDG. XXV. 1885.

Rodenburg, C. Die Städtegründungen Heinrichs I. MIOGF. XVII. 1896.

Rommel, O. Der Aufstand Herzog Ludolfs von Schwaben in den Jahren 953 u. 954. Eine Untersuchung seiner politischen Bedeutung. FDG. IV. 1864.

Schäfer, D. Die Agrarii Milites des Widukind. SPAW. 1905.

—— Die Ungarnschlacht. HZ. 1897.

—— Die Ungarnschlacht von 955. SPAW. 1905.

Uhlirz, K. Geschichte des Erzbistums Magdeburg unter den Kaisern aus sächsischem Hause. Magdeburg. 1887.

Wallmenich, W. von. Die Ungarnschlacht auf dem Lechfelde. Munich. 1907.

Wendt, G. Die Germanisierung der Länder östlich der Elbe. (Progr. Liegnitz.) 1884.

Winterfeld, P. von. Die Aufhebung des Herzogtums Franken. NAGDG. XXVIII. 1903.

CHAPTER IX.

GERMANY: OTTO II AND OTTO III.

I. BIBLIOGRAPHY.

See Bibliography to Chapter VIII.

II. DOCUMENTS.

MGH. Constitutiones et Acta. I. *See Bibl.* c. VIII.
—— Diplomatum II. Ottonis II and III Diplom. Ed. Sickel, Th. 1888.
See also Bibliography to Chapter VIII.

III. AUTHORITIES.

See for references Bibl. c. VIII.

Adami Gesta.
Annales Colonienses, Corbeienses, Einsidlenses, Hersfeldenses, Lobienses, S. Maxi-
mini Trevirensis.
Epitaphium Adalheidae.
Gerberti Epistolae. Ed. Havet, J. Coll. textes. 1889.
Gerhardi Vita Oudalrici.
Gesta Episcoporum Cameracensium. MGH, Script. VII.
Richeri Hist.
Thietmari Chron.
Vita Bernwardi Episcopi Hildesheimensis auct. Thangmaro. MGH, Script. IV.
—— Burchardi Ep. Wormatiensis. *Ib.*
—— Heriberti Archiep. Coloniensis auct. Lantberto. *Ib.*
—— Johannis Gorziensis. *See Bibl.* c. VIII.

IV. MODERN WORKS.

(a) GENERAL.

Jahrb. d. deutsch. Reiches. *See Gen. Bibl.* v. Otto II. Giesebrecht, W. 1840.
—— Otto III. Wilmans, R. 1840.
Jahrb. d. deutsch. Geschichte. *See Gen. Bibl.* v. Otto II und Otto III. Uhlirz, K.,
vol. I (Otto II). Leipsic. 1902.
And see Bibl. to c. VIII, IV (*a*).

(b) SPECIAL.

Allen, R. Gerbert. Pope Silvester II. EHR. VII. 1892.
Erben, W. Excurse zu den Diplomen Ottos III. MIOGF. XIII. 1892.
Grössler, H. Begründung der Christlichen Kirche in dem Lande zwischen Saale und
Elbe. Z. d. Ver. für Kirchengesch. d. Provins Sachsen. 1907.
Kehr, P. Zur Geschichte Ottos III. HZ. LXVI. 1891.
—— Die Urkunden Ottos III. Innsbruck. 1890.
Lux, C. Papst Silvester II. Einfluss auf die Politik Kaiser Ottos III. Breslau. 1898.
Moltmann, J. Theophano die Gemahlin Ottos II in ihrer Bedeutung für die Politik
Ottos I und Ottos II. Schwerin. 1878.

Schulte, W. Die Gründung des Bistums Prag. HJ. xxii. 1901.

Sickel, Th. von. Erläuterungen zu den Diplomen Ottos II. MIOGF, Ergänzungs-band ii. 1888.

—— Erläuterungen zu den Diplomen Ottos III. MIOGF. xii. 1891.

—— Uhlirz, K., Fanta, A. Excurse zu Ottonischen Diplomen. MIOGF, Ergänz. ii. 1888.

Uhlirz, K. Untersuchungen zur Gesch. Kaiser Otto II. MIOGF, Ergänz. vi. 1901.

—— Über die Herkunft der Theophanu. BZ. iv. 1895.

—— Die Kriegszüge Kaisers Otto II nach Böhmen 976 u. 977. Verein für Gesch. der Deutschen in Böhmen. Festschrift. Prague. 1902.

—— Die Errichtung des Bistums Prag. *Ib.* Mittheilung. xxxix.

—— Die Interventionen in den Urkunden des Königs Otto III. NAGDG. xxi. 1896.

CHAPTER X.

THE EMPEROR HENRY II.

A. FOR GERMANY.

I. Documents.

Giesebrecht. Kaiserzeit, II. *See Gen. Bibl.* v. 5th edn. 1835. Quellen und Beweise. Briefe, Nos. 1–4.

Jaffé, P. Bibl. rer. Germanicarum. *See Gen. Bibl.* IV. Vol. III. Ep. Moguntinae. 1866. Nos. 21–29. v. Ep. Bambergenses. 1869. Nos. 2–7.

MGH. Constitutiones et Acta. I. 1893. Ed Weiland, L. (*a*) Constitutiones, pp. 57–81. (*b*) Acta Varia, Nos. 437, 438.

—— Diplomata. III. Ed. Bresslau, H. and Bloch, H. 1900–3. (*a*) For Henry II, Nos. 1–534 (510–534 spurious). (*b*) For Kunigunda, Nos. 1–4.

II. Authorities.

(*a*) *Contemporary.*

Adalboldi Vita Heinrici II. (Only to 1004.) MGH, Script. IV, 679–695.

Alpertus. De Diversitate Temporum Lib. II. *Ibid* 702–723.

Annales:

> Altahenses Maiores; I, auct. Wolfherio, B. (899–1032.) MGH, Script xx, 785–791. Corbeienses, Einsidlenses, Heremi (Einsiedeln), Hildesheimenses, Continuatio, all *ibid.* III. Laubienses, Leodienses, *ibid.* IV. Quedlinburgenses, Continuatio, *ibid.* III. Sangallenses Maiores, *ibid.* I.

Thietmari (bp. of Merseburg) Chronicon. Ed. Kurze, F. SGUS 1889. Bk IV, cc. 49–54, and V–IX.

Vitae:

> Adalberonis II (bp. of Metz), auct. Constantino Abbate. MGH, Script. IV.
> Bernwardi (bp. of Hildesheim), auct. Thangmaro. *Ibid.* Continuatio, auct. Wolfherio. *Ibid.* XI.
> Burchardi (bp. of Worms), auct. Anonymo. *Ibid.* IV.
> Godehardi (bp. of Hildesheim), auct. Wolfherio. (*a*) Prior. (*b*) Posterior. *Ibid.* XI.

(*b*) *Later.*

Adamus Bremensis. Gesta Hammaburgensis Eccles. Pontif. MGH, Script. VII. Also SGUS. Ed. Weiland, L. 1876. Bk. II.

Gesta Episc. Cameracensium. MGH, Script. VII. Bk. III

Herimannus Augiensis Monachus (Contractus). Chronicon (O.C.–1054). *Ibid.* v.

Rudolfus Glaber. Francorum Hist. Lib. v. Ed. Prou, M. Raoul Glaber. Les cinq livres de ses hist. Coll. textes. 1886. Extracts in MGH, Script. VII.

Vitae:

> Cunigundis, auct. Anon. *Ibid.*
> Heinrici II Imp., auct. Adalberto. MGH, Script. IV.
> Heriberti (archbp. of Cologne), auct. Lantberto. *Ibid.*
> Meinwerci (bp. of Paderborn), auct. Anon. *Ibid.* XI.
> Popponis Abbatis, auct. Everhelmo Abbate. *Ibid.*
> Ricardi Abbatis, auct. Anon. *Ibid.*
> Wolfgangi (bp. of Ratisbon), auct. Othlone. *Ibid.* IV.

III. Modern Works.

(a) General.

Allgemeine Deutsche Biographie. *See Gen. Bibl.* i.

Bresslau. Urkundenlehre. Vol. i. *See Gen. Bibl.* v.

Giesebrecht. Kaiserzeit. Bk. vii. Befestigung des Reichs durch Heinrich II. *See Gen. Bibl.* v.

Hauck, A. Kirchengeschichte. Vol. iii. 1906. *See Gen. Bibl.* v.

Jahrbücher des deutschen Reichs unter Heinrich II. i. Ed. Hirsch, S. 1002–1006. 1862. ii. Ed. Pabst, H. 1007–1014. 1864. iii. Ed. Bresslau, H. 1014–1024. 1875. (Jahrb. d. deutsch. Gesch.) *See Gen. Bibl.* v.

Maurenbrecher, W. Gesch. der deutschen Königswahlen vom 10 bis 13 J. 1889.

Nitzsch, K. W. Gesch. des deutschen Volkes. Ed. Matthäi, 2nd edn. i, pp. 385–396. 1892.

Ranke. Weltgeschichte. Vol. iii. *See Gen. Bibl.* v.

Richter, G. and Kohl, H. Annalen der deutschen Gesch. im Mittelalter. iii, i (4). *See Gen. Bibl.* v.

Schultze, W. In Handbuch der deutschen Gesch. Ed. Gebhardt, B. i (§ 52). 1891. (Wiederherstellung des Ottonischen Systems.)

(b) Special.

Cohn, A. Kaiser Heinrich II. 1867.

Foltz, K. NAGDG. iii. 1877. (For Henry's seals.)

Matthäi, G. Die Klosterpolitik Kaiser Heinrichs II. Diss. Göttingen. 1877.

Müller, R. Aribo von Mainz. 1881.

Schnurer, G. Erzbischof Pilgrim von Köln. Diss. Münster. 1883.

Zeissberg, H. Die Kriege Heinrichs II mit Herzog Boleslav von Polen. Vienna. SKAW. lvii, pp. 265 ff. 1868.

B. FOR ITALY.

I. Documents.

Ficker, J. Forschungen. iv. 1874. *See below,* iii (a).

Galletti, P. L. Del Primicero della Santa Sede Apostolica. App. de' Documenti. 1776.

Jaffé. Regesta. Ed. Wattenbach. *See Gen. Bibl.* iv. i. (Silvester II—Benedict VIII.)

Leo of Vercelli. Letters and other Writings. Ed. Bloch, H. NAGDG. xxii. 1896.

Mansi. Concilia. xix.

MGH. Constitutiones. i. Constit. 27, 30, 33, 34.

—— Diplomata. iii. (a) For Henry, many charters for Italy in the general series. (b) For Ardoin, Nos. 1–10.

MHP. Chartarum i, Nos. 202–257. 1836. ii, 73–95. 1858.

Muratori, L. A. Delle Antichità Estensi. Ed. Italiana. i. 1717.

Provana, L. G. Studi critici sovra la storia d' Italia a' tempi del re Ardoino. Ap. pp. 331–395. 1844.

II. Authorities.

Adalboldi. *See above.*

Ademari (Cabannensis) Hist. Lib. iii, c. 37. MGH, Script. iv.

Amatus of Salerno. Ystoire de Li Normant. Ed. Delarc, O. 1892.

Annales in MGH, Script.:
> Beneventani, Casinenses, Cavenses, Hildesheimenses Continuatio, Quedlin-burgenses Continuatio. *All in* iii; Barenses and Lupus Protospatharius. *In* v.

Arnulfi Gesta Archiepisc. Mediolanensium. Bk. i, cc. 14–20; ii, 1. MGH, Script. viii, 1–31.

Catalogi Regum Italiae et Imperatorum. (6 Lists.) *Ibid.*

Chron. Novaliciense. *Ibid.* vii.

Hugonis Abbatis Farfensis Opuscula:—Destructio Monasterii Farfensis. De diminutione Monasterii Farfensis. *Ibid.* xi.

Johannis Diaconi Chronicon Venetum. *Ibid.* vii. 1–33. Also in Fonti. *See Gen. Bibl.* iv. (Cronache Veneziane i.) Ed. Monticolo, G. B. 1890.

Leonis Ostiensis Chronica. MGH, Script. vii.

Liber Pontificalis. ii. *See Gen. Bibl.* iv.

Rudolfus Glaber. *See above,* ii (*b*).

Thietmar *See above.* For Italy:—Bk. iv, c. 54; v, 24–26; vi, 4–8; vii, 33; viii, 2, 24.

III. Modern Works.

(a) *General.*

Delarc, O. Les Normands en Italie depuis les premières invasions jusqu'à l'avènement de St Grégoire VII. 1883.

Ficker, J. Forschungen zur Reichs- und Rechtsgesch. Italiens. Innsbruck. 1868–1874.

Gay, J. L'Italie méridionale. *See Gen. Bibl.* v.

Giesebrecht. *See above.*

Gregorovius. *See Gen. Bibl.* v.

Hartmann. Gesch. Italiens. iv, i. 1915. Bk. vi, c. 5. *See Gen. Bibl.* v.

Hauck. *See above.* Bk. vii, c. 3.

Jahrbücher d. deutsch. Gesch. *See above,* iii (*a*).

Mann, H. K. Lives of the Popes in the Early Middle Ages. 5 vols. in 6. 1902–10.

Muratori. Annali. *See Gen. Bibl.* v.

Romano, G. Dominazioni. *Ibid.*

(b) *Special.*

Bloch, H. Beiträge zur Gesch. des Bischofs Leo von Vercelli und seiner Zeit. NAGDG. xxii. pp. 13–136. (1896.)

Bresslau, H. Jahrbücher, Konrad II. i. Excurse, i, v, vi. 1879. *See above,* iii (*a*).

Carutti, W. Il Conte Umberto I e il re Ardoino. Bk. ii, cc. 1–5. 1888.

Darmstaedter, P. Das Reichsgut in der Lombardei und Piemont 568–1250. 1896.

Dresdner, A. Kultur- u. Sittengeschichte der italienischen Geistlichkeit im 10 und 11 Jahrhundert. 1890.

Holtzmann, R. Die Urkunden König Arduins. NAGDG. xxv.

Loewenfeld, S. Leo von Vercelli. Diss. Göttingen. 1877.

Provana, L. G. Studi critici sovra la storia d' Italia a' tempi del re Ardoino. 1844.

Schwartz, G. Die Besetzung der Bistümer Reichsitaliens unter den sächsischen und salischen Kaisern. 1913.

CHAPTER XI.

THE EMPEROR CONRAD II.

1. BIBLIOGRAPHIES.

Full bibliography in Giesebrecht's Kaiserzeit (*see Gen. Bibl.* v), vol. II, and a shorter but useful one in Hampe's Deutsche Kaisergeschichte.

Dahlmann-Waitz. Quellenkunde. *See Gen. Bibl.* I.

Potthast, A. Bibliotheca historica medii aevi. *See ib.*

Wattenbach, W. Deutschlands Geschichtsquellen. *See ib.*

2. DOCUMENTS.

MGH. Constitutiones et Acta Publica Imperatorum et Regum. I. Ed. Weiland. 1893.

MGH. Diplomatum IV. Conradi II Diplomata. Ed. Bresslau, H., Wibel, H. and Hessel, A. 1909.

Jaffé. Regesta pontificum Romanorum. *See Gen. Bibl.* IV.

Stumpf. Die Reichskanzler. *See Gen. Bibl.* IV.

3. AUTHORITIES.

Adami Gesta Hammaburgensis Ecclesiae Pontificum. MGH, Script. VII, and SGUS. Ed. Schmeidler. 1917.

Ademarus Cabannensis. Chronicon Aquitanicum et Francicum. MGH, Script. IV.

Amatus Casinensis. Historia Normannorum. Ed. Delarc, O. (Soc. de l'histoire de Normandie.) Rouen. 1892.

Annales Altahenses Maiores. MGH, Script. XX, and SGUS. Ed. Giesebrecht, W., and Oefele, E. L. B. ab. 1868.

Annales Corbeienses. MGH, Script. III, and Jaffé, Bibliotheca rer. German. I.

Annales Hildesheimenses. MGH, Script. III, and SGUS. Ed. Waitz. 1878.

Annales Laubienses. MGH, Script. IV.

Annales Leodienses. *Ib.* IV.

Annales Quedlinburgenses. *Ib.* III.

Annales S. Emmerammi. *Ib.* XVII.

Annales Sangallenses Maiores. *Ib.* I, and the portion relating to the reign of Conrad II in Bresslau's edition of Wipo. (SGUS, 1915.)

Anselmus. Gesta episcoporum Leodiensium. MGH, Script. VII.

Arnulfus Mediolanensis. Gesta Archiepiscoporum Mediolanensium. MGH, Script. VIII, and in Muratori, Script. Rer. Ital. IV. 1st edn.

Chronicon S. Michaelis Virdunensis. MGH, Script. IV.

Chronicon Novaliciense. *Ib.* VII, and SGUS. Ed. Pertz. 1846.

Chronicon Suevicum universale. MGH, Script. XIII, and portions relating to the reign of Conrad II in Bresslau's edition of Wipo. (SGUS, 1915.)

Cosmas Pragensis. Chronicae Bohemorum libri III. MGH, Script. IX.

Florentius Wigorniensis monachus. Chronicon. Ed. Thorpe. Eng. Hist. Soc. 1848-9, and in Petrie, Mon. Hist. Brit. [For Canute's letter describing the Coronation of Conrad II.]

Gesta episcoporum Cameracensium. MGH, Script. VII.

Gesta Treverorum. *Ib.* VIII.

Herimannus Augiensis monachus. Chronicon. *Ib.* v, and the portion relating to the reign of Conrad II in Bresslau's edition of Wipo. (SGUS, 1915.)

Hugo Flaviniacensis. Chronicon Virdunense. MGH, Script. VIII.

Leo Marsicanus. Chronica monasterii Casinensis. *Ib.* VII.

Rodulphus Glaber. Francorum historiae libri v. MGH, Script. VII, and Coll. textes. Ed. Prou, M. 1886.

Sigebertus Gemblacensis. Chronographia. MGH, Script. VI.

Vita S. Bardonis archiepiscopi Moguntini. *Ib.* IX.

Vita Burchardi episcopi Wormatiensis. *Ib.* IV.

Vita S. Godehardi episcopi Hildenesheimensis prior auctore Wolfherio. *Ib.* XI.

Vita S. Kunigundae imperatricis. *Ib.* IV.

Vita S. Leonis (IX) auctore Wiberto archidiacono Tullensi coaetaneo, in Watterich, Rom. Pontificum vitae I, and Muratori, Script. Rer. Ital. III. 1st edn.

Vita S. Meinwerci episcopi Paderbornensis auctore monacho Abdinghofensi anonymo. MGH, Script. XI.

Vita Odilonis abbatis Cluniacensis auctore Jotsaldo Sylviniacensi monacho. *Ib.* XV.

Vita S. Popponis abbatis Stabulensis. *Ib.* XI.

Vita S. Stephani regis primi et apostoli Ungarorum maior. *Ib.* XI.

Wiponis opera. Gesta Chuonradi etc. *Ib.* XI, and SGUS. Ed. Bresslau. 1915. (This edition includes extracts from the other principal sources for the reign of Conrad II, *i.e.* from the chronicle of Herman of Reichenau, from the annals of St Gall, and from the Swabian world chronicle.)

4. MODERN WORKS.

(*a*) GENERAL.

Bresslau, H. Jahrbücher des deutschen Reichs unter Konrad II. Leipsic. 1879–1884.

Chalandon, F. Histoire de la Domination Normande en Italie et en Sicile. Vol. I. Paris. 1907.

Giesebrecht, W. von. Kaiserzeit. Vol. II. *See Gen. Bibl.* v.

Gregorovius, F. History of the City of Rome. Vol. IV. *See Gen. Bibl.* v.

Hampe, K. Deutsche Kaisergeschichte im Zeitalter der Salier und Staufer. 2nd edn. Leipsic. 1912.

Hauck, A. Kirchengeschichte Deutschlands. Vol. III. *See Gen. Bibl.* v.

Maurenbrecher, W. Geschichte der deutschen Königswahlen vom 10 bis zur Mitte des 13 Jahrhunderts. Leipsic. 1889.

Ranke, L. von. Weltgeschichte. *See Gen. Bibl.* v.

Richter and Kohl. Annalen der deutschen Geschichte. Vol. III. *See Gen. Bibl.* v.

Waitz, G. Deutsche Verfassungsgeschichte. *See Gen. Bibl.* v.

(*b*) SPECIAL.

Arndt, W. Die Wahl Conrads II. Diss. Göttingen. 1861.

Blümcke, O. Burgund unter Rudolf II. Diss. Greifswald. 1869.

Bresslau, H. Excurse zur den Diplomen Konrads II. NAGDG. XXXIV. 1908–9.

—— Die Kanzlei Kaiser Konrads II. Berlin. 1869.

—— Über die Zusammenkunft zu Deville zwischen Konrad II und Heinrich I. Jahrbuch d. Gesellschaft für Lothringische Geschichte u. Altertumskunde. VIII. 1907.

Dieterich, J. R. Die Polenkriege Konrads II und der Friede von Merseburg. Giessen. 1895.

Harttung, J. Studien zur Geschichte Konrads II. Bonn. 1871.

Jacob, L. Le Royaume de Bourgogne sous les empereurs Franconiens. Paris. 1906.

Ladewig, P. Poppo von Stablo und die Klosterreform unter den ersten Saliern. Berlin. 1883.

Nusch, A. Kaiser Konrad II in der deutschen Sage-Poesie. Speier. 1875.

Papst, H. Frankreich und Konrad II in den Jahren 1024 und 1025. FDG. v. 1865.

Pfenniger, M. Kaiser Konrads II Beziehungen zu Aribo von Mainz, Pilgrim von Köln und Aribert von Mailand. Progr. Bresslau. 1891.

Pflugk-Harttung, J. von. Untersuchungen zur Geschichte Konrads II. Stuttgart. 1890.

Posse, O. Die Markgrafen von Meissen und das Haus Wettin. Leipsic. 1881.

Previté-Orton, C. W. The Early History of the House of Savoy. Cambridge. 1912.

Scheffer-Boichorst. Heinrichs II Itinerar im J. 1024 u. d. Stellung d. Sachsen z. Thronfolgefrage. MIOGF. vi. 1885.

Schreuer, H. Wahl und Krönung Konrads II. HVJS. xiv.

Seydel, W. Studien zur Kritik Wipos. Diss. Berlin. 1898.

Wagner, F. Die Wahl Konrads II zum römischen König. Diss. Göttingen. 1871.

Wahnschaffe, U. Das Herzogtum Kärnten und seine Marken im 11 Jahrhundert. Klagenfurt. 1878.

Weingartner, L. Die Vereinigung Burgunds mit dem deutschen Reich. Progr. Budweis. 1880.

CHAPTER XII.

THE EMPEROR HENRY III.

I. SOURCES.

(a) REGESTA, COLLECTIONS ETC.

Constitutiones et acta publica imperatorum et regum. Ed. Weiland, L. Vol. I.
MGH, Leges. *See Gen. Bibl.* IV.

Die Urkunden Heinrichs III. Ed. Bresslau, H. MGH, Diplomata regum et
imperatorum, V, 1.

Dahlmann-Waitz. Quellenkunde. *See Gen. Bibl.* I.

Jaffé. *Ib.* IV.

Mansi. *Ib.*

Stumpf, K. F. *Ib.*

(b) CHRONICLES ETC.

[Editions of most of these, besides those expressly mentioned, are in MGH,
Script. *See Gen. Bibl.* IV.]

Adamus. Gesta Hammaburgensis ecclesiae pontificum. Ed. Lappenberg, J.M. SGUS
(*see Gen. Bibl.* IV), and in MGH, Script. VII. (Especially useful for Adalbert of
Bremen and the Slavs of the North-East.)

Annalista Saxo. Ed. Pertz, G. H. MGH, Script. III.

Annales Magdeburgenses. *Ib.* XVI. (This and the Ann. Saxo were probably compiled,
for 1037–1043, from Herman of Reichenau's lost Gesta Chuonradi et Heinrici
imperatorum.)

—— Altahenses maiores. Ed. Oefele, E. L. B. ab, in SGUS, 2nd edn. 1891, and MGH,
Script. XX. (Valuable.)

—— Augustani. MGH, Script. III.

—— Beneventani. *Ib.* (p. 173 ff.)

—— Corbeienses. *Ib.*

—— Laubienses. *Ib.* IV.

—— Leodienses. *Ib.*

—— Pragenses. *Ib* III.

—— Romani. *Ib.* V. (Unreliable.)

—— Sangallenses Maiores, pars altera genuina. Ed. Arx, I. V. *Ib.* I. (For Bohemia
and Hungary.)

Anonymus Haserensis. De episcopis Eichstetensibus. Ed. Bethmann, L. C. *Ib.* VII.
(For Gebhard of Eichstedt, Victor II.)

Anselmus Leodiensis. Gesta episcoporum Traiectensium et Leodiensium. Ed.
Köpke, R. *Ib.* VII. (For Bishop Wazo of Liège.)

Arnulphus Mediolanensis. Rerum sui temporis libri quinque. Ed. Wattenbach, W.
Ib. VIII. (Important for Lombardy.)

Bertholdus. Annales sive chronicon. Ed. Pertz, G. H. *Ib.* V. (Continuator of
Herman of Reichenau.)

Bonitho. Liber ad amicum. Bibl. rer. German. Vol. II. *See Gen. Bibl.* IV. (*c.* 1085. Unreliable.)

Brief von Abt Berno von Reichenau. Ed. Strehlke, E. in Archiv für Kunde österreichischer Gesch. xx, p. 189. (Written to Henry III after battle of the Raab in 1044.)

Bruno ep. Signiensis. Vita S. Leonis IX. Ed. Watterich. Vol. I. *See Gen. Bibl.* IV. (Written at command of Pope Gregory VII.)

Chronicae Polonorum. Ed. Szlachtowski, J. and Köpke, R. MGH, Script. IX.

Cosmas Pragensis. Chronicon Boemorum. Ed. Köpke, R. *Ib.*

De ordinando pontifice, Auctor Gallicus. Ed. Dümmler, E. MGH, Libelli de lite, I. (Hostile to Henry. Written between death of Clement II and election of Damasus II.)

Ekkehardus Uraugiensis. Chronicon universale. Ed. Waitz, G. MGH, Script. VI.
—— Chronicon Wirzeburgense. Ed. Waitz, G. *Ib.*

Epistola Gozechini scholastici. Ed. Mabillon, J. Vetera Analecta (folio), p. 437. Paris. 1723. (Written in 1066.)

Gesta episcoporum Cameracensium. Ed. Bethmann, L. MGH, Script. IV. (For John of Arras and Flanders.)

Helmoldus presbyter Bozoviensis. Cronica Slavorum. Ed. Schmeidler, B. SGUS. 2nd edn. Hanover. 1909.

Herimannus Augiensis (H. Contractus or Herman of Reichenau). Chronicon. Ed. Pertz, G. H. MGH, Script. V. (To 1054. One of the chief sources.)

Lampertus Hersfeldensis. Annales. Ed. Holder-Egger, O. SGUS. 1894. (Of mediocre value.)

Landulphus Senior. Mediolanensis Historiae libri IV. Ed. Wattenbach, W. MGH, Script. VIII.

Leo ep. Ostiensis (also Leo Diaconus and Leo Marsicanus). Chronica monasterii Casinensis. Ed. Wattenbach, W. *Ib.* VII.

Liber Pontificalis. *See Gen. Bibl.* IV.

Petrus Damianus. Liber Gratissimus. Ed. Heinemann, L. v. MGH, Libelli de lite, I. (Written in 1052)

Rodulfus Glaber. Historiarum sui temporis libri V. Ed. Prou, M. (Raoul Glaber, Les cinq livres de ses histoires.) Coll. textes. 1886. *See Gen. Bibl.* IV.

Vita Bennonis II ep. Osnabrugensis auct. Nortberto abbate Iburgensi. Ed. Bresslau, H. SGUS. 1902.

Vita Guntheri Eremitae. Ed. Pertz, G. H. MGH, Script. XI.

Wibertus. Vita S. Leonis IX papae. Ed. Watterich. Vol. I. *See Gen. Bibl.* IV.

Wipo. Gesta Chuonradi. Proverbia. Tetralogus. Ed. Bresslau, H. SGUS. 3rd edn. 1915.

II. MODERN WORKS.

(a) GENERAL HISTORIES.

Büdinger, M. Oesterreichische Geschichte. Leipsic. 1858.

Giesebrecht. Gesch. d. deutsch. Kaiserzeit. Vol. II. 5th edn. 1885. *See Gen. Bibl.* V.

Hauck. Kirchengesch. Deutschlands. Vol. III. 3rd edn. 1906. *Ib.*

Nitzsch, C. W. Gesch. des deutschen Volkes. Ed. Matthäi, G. v. 2nd edn. 1892.

Schäfer, D. Deutsche Geschichte. Vol. I. Jena. 1910.

Werminghoff. Kirchenverfassung. 1905. *See Gen. Bibl.* V.

(*b*) Works on Henry III and his time.

Drehmann, J. Papst Leo IX und der Simonie. (In Goetz's Beiträge zur Kultur-gesch. des Mittelalters und der Renaissance.) Leipsic. 1908.

Höfler, C. A. C. v. Die deutschen Päpste. Ratisbon. 1839.

Polzin, H. Die Abtswahlen in den Reichsabteien von 1024–1056. Greifswald. 1908.

Raumer, G. W. v. Regesta Historiae Brandenburgensis. Berlin. 1836.

Steindorff, E. De ducatu qui Billingorum dicitur in Saxonia origine et progressu. Berlin. 1863.

—— Jahrb. des deutschen Reiches unter Heinrich III. 2 vols. Leipsic. 1874–81. (Jahrb. d. deutsch. Gesch.) *See Gen. Bibl.* v.

Steindorff, F. Königtum und Kaisertum Heinrichs III.

Stenzel, G. A. H. Gesch. Deutschlands unter d. fränkischen Kaisern. Leipsic. 1827.

Strehlke, E. De Heinrici Imp. bellis Ungaricis. Berlin. 1856.

Wedemann, M. Gottfried der Bärtige, seine Stellung zum fränkische Kaiserhaus und zur römische Curie. Leipsic. 1876.

Will, C. Die Anfänge der Restauration der Kirche im ix Jahrhundert. Marburg. 1859–64.

CHAPTER XIII.

THE VIKINGS.

[In the case of countries whose general history during this period is dealt with in other chapters this bibliography confines itself almost entirely to works devoted specially to the subject of the chapter. General bibliographies will be found in Vol. II, ch. 19 and Vol. III, chs. 1–2–3, 4, 5, 8 and 14–15.]

1. THE VIKING MOVEMENT GENERALLY.

(a) ORIGINAL AUTHORITIES.

Adamus Bremensis. Gesta Hammenburgensis Ecclesiae Pontificum. MGH. Script. VII.
Ari Froði. Islendingabók. Ed. Golther, W. Altnordische Saga Bibliothek. Vol. I. Halle. 1892.
Dudo S. Quintini. De Moribus et actis primorum Normanniae ducum. MPL. 141.
Ermoldus Nigellus. Narratio Metrica de Baptismo Haraldi Danorum regis. SRD. Vol. I, pp. 398–424.
Gulielmus Gemeticensis. Historia Normannorum. MPL. 149.
Odd Snorrasøn. Saga Olafs Konungs Tryggvasunar. Ed. Munch, P. A. Christiania. 1853. Transl. Sephton, J. London. 1895.
Rembertus, S. Vita Sancti Anscharii. SRD. Vol. I, pp. 427–95.
Saxo Grammaticus. Historiae Danicae libri XVI. Ed. Holder, A. Strasbourg. 1898.
Snorri Sturluson. Heimskringla. Ed. Jónsson, F. 9 parts. Copenhagen. 1893–1901. Transl. Morris, W. and Magnússon, E. 4 vols. London. 1893–1905.
Sveno Aggonis filius. Regum Daniae Historiae. SRD. Vol. I, pp. 42–64.

Anonymous.

Af Upplendinga Konungum. Ed. Rafn, C. C. Fornaldar Sögur. Vol. II, pp. 101–6. Copenhagen. 1829.
Ágrip af Noregs konungasögum. Ed. Dahlerup, V. Copenhagen. 1880.
Corpus Poeticum Boreale. Ed. Vigfússon, G. and Powell, F. York. 2 vols. Oxford. 1883.
Danske Runemindesmærker. Undersøgte og tolkede af Wimmer, L. F. A. Vols. I–IV. Copenhagen. 1895–1908.
Diplomatarium Norvegicum. Aktstykker vedrørende Norges forbindelse med de Britiske Øer. Ed. Bugge, A. Vol. I. Christiania. 1910.
Edda, Die prosaische. Ed. Wilken, E. Bibliothek der ältesten deutschen Litteratur-Denkmäler. Vols. XI, XII. Paderborn. 1877–82. Transl. Dasent, G. W. Stockholm. 1842.

Edda, Die Lieder der. Ed. Sijmons, B. and Gering, H. 2 vols. *Ibid.* Vol. vii. Halle. 1888–1906. Transl. Bray, O. Mythological Poems. London. 1908.

Egils Saga Skallagrímssonar. Ed. Cederschiöld, G. etc. Altnordische Saga Bibl. Vol. iii. Halle. 1894. Transl. Green, W. C. London. 1893.

Encomium Emmae Reginae Daniae et Angliae. (SRD. ii, pp. 472–502.)

Erbyggjasaga. Ed. Gering, H. Altn. Saga Bibl. Vol. vi. Halle. 1897.

Færeyinga Saga. Ed. Rafn, C. C. Copenhagen. 1832. Transl. Powell, F. York. London. 1896.

Fagrskinna, Nóregs konunga tal. Ed. Jónsson, F. Copenhagen. 1902–3.

Flateyjar-bók. Ed. Vigfússon, G. and Unger, C. R. 3 vols. Christiania. 1860–8.

Flóamannasaga. Ed. Vigfússon, G. and Möbius, T. Fornaldar Sögur. Leipsic. 1860.

Friþjofs Saga ins frockna. Ed. Larsson, L. Altn. Saga Bibl. Vol. ix. Halle. 1901.

Gaungu-Hrólfs saga. Ed. Rafn, C. C. Fornaldar Sögur. Vol. iii, pp. 235–364. Copenhagen. 1830.

Gunnlaugs Saga Ormstungu. Ed. Mogk, E. Altn. Saga Bibl. Vol. i. Halle. 1886.

Hervarar Saga ok Heiþreks konungs. Ed. Rafn, C. C. Fornald. Sögur. Vol. ii, pp. 513 ff. Copenhagen. 1829.

Knytlinga saga. Fornmanna Sögur. Vol. xi, pp. 177 ff. Copenhagen.

Landnamabók. Ed. Jónsson, F. Copenhagen. 1900.

Laxdæla Saga. Ed. Kálund, K. Altn. Sag. Bibl. Vol. iv. Halle. 1896. Transl. Press, M. A. C. London. 1899.

Njáls Saga. Ed. Jónsson, F. Altn. Saga Bibl. Vol. xiii. Halle. 1908. Transl. Dasent, G. W. 2 vols. Edinburgh. 1861.

Norges undskrifter med de ældre Runer. Ed. Bugge, S. Christiania. 1891–1903.

Olafs Saga hins helga. Ed. Keyser, R. and Unger, C. R. Christiania. 1849.

Olafs Saga Tryggvasonar. Fornmanna Sögur. Vols. i–iii. 1825–8.

Ragnars Saga Loðbrókar. Ed. Rafn, C. C. Fornald. Sögur. Vol. i, pp. 235–310. Copenhagen. 1829.

Ragnars sonum, Ðáttr af. Ed. Rafn, C. C. Fornald. Sögur. Vol. i, pp. 343–60. Copenhagen. 1829.

Runverser. Ed. Brate, E. Antiq. Tidskr. för Sverige. Part 10. Stockholm. 1887–91.

(b) Modern Works.

Almgren, O. Vikingatidsgrafvar i Sagån vid Sala. Fornvännen. 1907. pp. 1–19. Stockholm.

—— Vikingatidens grafskick i verkligheten och i den fornnordiska litteraturen.

Arne, T. J. Sveriges förbindelsen med Östern under Vikingetiden. Fornvännen. 1911. pp. 1–66.

Bugge, A. Norse Elements in Gaelic Tradition. Christiania. 1900.

—— Vikingerne. 2 series. Christiania. 1904–6. Transl. 1st series. Hungerland. 1908.

—— Vesterlandenes Inflydelse paa Nordboernes i Vikingetiden. Christiania. 1905.

—— Die nordeuropäischen Verkehrswege etc. Vierteljahrschrift f. Soz. u. Wirtsch. Gesch. Vol. iv, part 2, pp. 227–77. Leipsic. 1906.

—— Havelok og Olav Tryggvason. Aarb. f. nord. oldk. og hist. 2nd series. Vol. xxiii, pp. 233–72. Copenhagen. 1908.

—— Norges Historie. Vol. i. Part ii. Christiania. 1909–10.

—— Sandhed og digt om Olav Tryggvason. Aarb. f. nord. oldk. 2nd series. Vol. xxv, pp. 1–34. Copenhagen. 1910.

Chadwick, H. M.   The Cult of Othin.   Cambridge.   1899.

Craigie, W. A.   The Religion of Ancient Scandinavia.   London.   1906.

Dozy, R. P. A.   Recherches sur l'histoire et la littérature de l'Espagne.   2 vols. 3rd ed.   Leyden.   1881.

Fabricius, A.   Normannertogene til den spanske Halvø.   Aarb. f. nord. oldk. og hist.   2nd series.   Vol. XIII, pp. 75–160.   Copenhagen.   1897.

——   L'ambassade d'al-Ghazal auprès du roi des Normands.   Actes du 8ᵐᵉ Congr. Intern. des Orientalistes.   2ᵐᵉ partie, pp. 119–131.   Leyden.   1893.

Friesen, Otto v.   Historiska Runinskrifter.   Fornvännen.   1909.   pp. 57–85.

Gustafson, G.   Norges Oldtid.   Christiania.   1906.

Hildebrand, E.   Anglo-sachsiska mynt i svenska Kongl. myntkabinettet.   Stockholm. 1846.

Hildebrand, H. O. H.   Svenska folket under Hednatiden.   Stockholm.   1872.

——   Sveriges medeltid.   3 vols.   Stockholm.   1879–1903.

Jónsson, F.   Den oldnorske og oldislandske Literaturs Historie.   Vols. I–III. Copenhagen.   1894–1902.

Jørgensen, A. D.   Den nordiske Kirkes Grundlæggelse.   Copenhagen.   1874–8.

Keary, C. F.   The Vikings in Western Christendom.   4 parts.   London.   1891.

Keyser, J. R.   Nordmændenes private liv i Oldtiden.   Transl. Barnard, M. R. London, 1868.

Maurer, K. (C. von).   Die Bekehrung des norwegischen Stammes.   2 vols.   Munich. 1855–6.

——   Vorlesungen über altnord. Rechtsgeschichte.   3 vols.   Christiania.   1907–8.

Mawer, A.   The Vikings.   Cambridge.   1912.

Montelius, O.   Sveriges Historia intill tjugonde Seklet.   Vol. I.   Stockholm. 1903.

——   Kulturgeschichte Schwedens.   Leipsic.   1906.

Müller, S.   Vor Oldtid.   Copenhagen.   1897.   Transl. Jiriczek, O. L.   2 vols. Strasbourg.   1897–8.

Munch, P. A.   Det Norske Folks Historie.   Vols. I and II.   Christiania.   1852–3.

Nansen, F.   In Northern Mists.   Transl. Chater, A. G.   2 vols.   London.   1911.

Niedner, F.   Islands Kultur zur Wikingerzeit.   Jena.   1913.

Olrik, A.   Nordisk Aandsliv i Vikingetid og Tidlig Middelalder.   Copenhagen. 1907.   Trans. Ranisch, W.   Heidelberg.   1908.

Rosenberg, C.   Nordboernes Aandsliv.   Vol. I.   Hedenold.   1878.

Rydbeck, O.   Ett silfverfynd från Vikingatiden.   Fornvännen.   1906.   pp. 136– 90.   Stockholm.

Sars, J. E.   Udsigt over den Norske Historie.   1st part.   Christiania.   1873.

Schoenfeld, E. D.   An nordischen Königshöfen zur Vikingerzeit.

Schück, H. and Warburg, K.   Illustrerad Svensk Litteraturhistoria.   1st part. Stockholm.   1896.

Steenstrup, J. C. H. R.   Normannerne.   4 vols.   Copenhagen.   1876–82.

——   Danmarks Sydgrænse.   Copenhagen.   1900.

——   Danmarks Riges Historie.   Vol. I.   Copenhagen.   1907.

Storm, G.   Ragnar Lodbrok og Gange Rolv.   Kritiske Bidrag til Vikingetidens Historie I.   Christiania.   1878.

Vedel, E.   Bornholmske Undersøgelser.   Aarb. f. nord. oldk. og hist.   2nd ser. Vol. V, pp. 1–77.   Copenhagen.   1890.

Weinhold, C.   Altnordisches Leben.   Berlin.   1856.

Worsaae, J. J. A.   Den danske Erobring af England og Normandiet.   Copenhagen. 1863.

——   La civilisation Danoise à l'époque des Vikings.   Mém. de la Soc. Roy. des antiq. du Nord.   1878–83.   pp. 91–130.   Copenhagen.

Worsaae, J. J. A. Minder om de Danske og Nordmændene i England, Skotland og Irland. Copenhagen. 1851. Transl. London. 1852.
See also :
> Viking Club. Saga-Book (Proc. and Papers). London. 1896 ff. Year Book. London. 1909 ff.

2. THE VIKINGS IN ENGLAND.

(*a*) Original Authorities. (*See* Bibliography of Chapters 14–15.)

(*b*) Modern Works.

Björkman, E. Scandinavian Loan-words in Middle English. 2 parts. Halle. 1900–2.
—— Nordische Personennamen in England. Halle. 1910.
—— Zur englischen Namenkunde. Halle. 1912.
Clapham, J. H. The Horsing of the Danes. EHR. **xxv**, pp. 287–93. London. 1910.
Collingwood, W. G. Remains of the Pre-Norman Period in Cumberland. Vict. Co. Hist. Cumberland. **i**, pp. 253–93.
—— Some Manx names in Cumbria. Cumb. and Westm. Antiq. and Arch. Soc. Trans. Vol. **xiii**, pp. 403–14. Kendal. 1895.
—— The Battle of Stainmoor in Legend and History. Cumb. and Westm. Antiq. and Arch. Soc. Trans. Vol. **ii**. New series. pp. 231–41. Kendal. 1902.
—— Anglian and Anglo-Danish Sculpture in the North Riding of Yorkshire. Yorks. Arch. Soc. Journ. Vol. **xix**, pp. 265–413.
—— Scandinavian Britain. London. 1908.
Duignan, W. H. Notes on Staffordshire Place Names. Oxford. 1902.
—— Warwickshire Place-names. Oxford. 1912.
Farrer, W. Introd. to Domesday Book of County of Lancaster. Vict. Co. Hist. Vol. **i**, pp. 269–82. London. 1906.
Fergusson, R. The Northmen in Cumberland and Westmoreland. London. 1856.
Gaythorpe, H. The Runic tympanum at Pennington. Cumb. and Westm. Antiq. and Arch. Soc. Vol. **iii**. New series. pp. 373–9. Kendal. 1903.
Haigh, D. H. Coins of the Danish Kings of Northumberland. Arch. Aeliana. New Series. Vol. **vii**, pp. 21–77. Newcastle-upon-Tyne. 1876.
Lindkvist, H. Middle-English Place-names of Scandinavian Origin. Uppsala. 1912.
McClure, E. British Place-names in their Historical Setting. London. 1910.
Mawer, A. The Scandinavian Kingdom of Northumbria. Essays presented to William Ridgeway. pp. 306–14. Cambridge. 1913.
Moorman, F. W. The Place-names of the West Riding of Yorkshire. Thoresby Society. Leeds. 1910.
Mutschmann, H. Place-names of Nottinghamshire. Cambridge. 1913.
Round, J. H. Introd. to Northamptonshire Domesday. Vict. Co. Hist. North-amptonshire. Vol. **i**, pp. 257–98. London. 1902.
—— The Domesday Ora. EHR. **xxiii**, pp. 283–5. 1908.
Skeat, W. W. Place-names of Cambridgeshire. Camb. Antiq. Soc. Cambridge. 1901.
—— Place-names of Hertfordshire. East Herts. Arch. Assoc. Hertford. 1904.
—— Place-names of Bedfordshire. Camb. Antiq. Soc. Cambridge. 1906.
—— Place-names of Huntingdonshire. Camb. Antiq. Soc. Cambridge. 1906.
—— Place-names of Suffolk. Cambridge. 1913.
Stenton, F. M. Introd. to Derbyshire Domesday. Vict. Co. Hist. Vol. **i**, pp. 293–326. 1905.

Stenton, F. M.   Introd. to Nottinghamshire Domesday.   Vict. Co. Hist.   Vol. i, pp. 207–46.   1906.

—— Introd. to the Leicestershire Domesday.   Vict. Co. Hist.   Vol. i, pp. 277–305.   1907.

—— Introd. to the Rutland Domesday.   Vict. Co. Hist.   Vol. i, pp. 121–36. 1908.

—— Aethelward's account of the last years of King Alfred's reign.   EHR. xxiv, pp. 79–84.   1909.

—— Types of Manorial Structure in the Northern Danelaw.   Oxf. Studies in Legal History.   Oxford.   1911.

Stephens, G.   En Yorkshire Liste over danske-engelske Mandsnavne.   Copenhagen. 1881.   Cf. Yorks. Dialect Soc. Trans.   1906.

Streatfeild, G. S.   Lincolnshire and the Danes.   London.   1884.

Vinogradoff, P.   English Society in the Eleventh Century.   Oxford.   1908.

Walker, B.   Place-names of Derbyshire.   Part i.   Derbyshire Arch. Journal. 1914.

Wyld, H. C. and Hirst, T. O.   Place-names of Lancashire.   London.   1911.

—— Old Scandinavian Personal Names in England.   Mod. Lang. R.   Vol. v, pp. 289–96.   Cambridge.   1910.

3.   THE VIKINGS IN THE FRANKISH EMPIRE.

(*a*) Original Authorities. (*See* Bibliographies to Vol. ii, ch. 18 and chs. 1–3, 4, 5, 8 of this Vol.)

(*b*) Modern Works.

Delarc, O.   Les Normands en Italie.   Paris.   1883.

Du Chatellier, P. and Le Pontois, L.   La Sépulture Scandinave à Barque de l'Île de Groix.   Bulletin de la Soc. Arch. du Finistère.   Vol. xxxv.   Quimper.   1908.

Fabricius, A.   Danske minder i Normandiet.   Copenhagen.   1897.

Heinemann, D. von.   Die Niederlage der Sachsen etc.   Mitteil. d. Vereins f. Hamb. Gesch.   3rd Year.   pp. 58–65.   Hamburg.   1881.

Heinemann, L. von.   Geschichte der Normannen in Unteritalien.   Vol. i.   Leipsic. 1894.

Jakobsen, J.   Stednavne og Personnavne i Normandiet.   Danske Studier.   1911. 2de Hæfte.   pp. 59–84.

Lair, J.   Les Normands dans l'île d'Oscelle.   Mém. de la Soc. hist. et arch. de Pontoise et du Vexin.   Vol. xx.   1898.

—— Le siège de Chartres par les Normands.   Caen.   1902.

Lot, F.   Grande invasion normande, 856–62.   BEC.   Vol. lxix, pp. 1–62.   1908.

Mabille, E.   Les invasions des Normands dans la Loire.   BEC.   Vol. xxx, pp. 149–54, 425–60.   1869.

Peigné-Delacourt, A.   Les Normans dans le Noyonnais.   Noyon.   1868.

Vogel, W.   Die Normannen und das fränkische Reich.   Heidelberg.   1906.

4.   VIKINGS IN SCOTLAND AND THE ISLES AND WALES.

(*a*) Original Authorities. (*See also* under other countries.)

Annales Cambriae.   Ed. J. Williams ab Ithel.   Rolls.   London.   1860.

Brut y Tywysogion.   Ed. J. Williams ab Ithel.   Rolls.   1860.

Chronicles of the Picts, Chronicles of the Scots etc.   Ed. Skene, W. F.   Scott. Record Publ.   Edinburgh.   1867.

Chronicon regum Manniae et Insularum.   Ed. Munch, P. A.   Christiania.   1860.

Orkneyinga Saga.   Ed. Vigfússon, G.   Rolls.   1887.   Transl. Dasent, G. W. London.   1894.

(b) MODERN WORKS.

Allen, J. R. and Anderson, J. The Early Christian Monuments of Scotland. Edinburgh. 1903.

Anderson, J. Viking graves in Islay. Proc. Soc. Antiq. Scotland. N. ser. Vol. II, pp. 51–89. Edinburgh. 1880.

—— Silver Brooches found at Skaill, Orkney. Proc. Soc. Antiq. Scot. N. ser. Vol. III, pp. 286–98. Edinburgh. 1881.

—— Notice of Bronze Brooches and Personal Ornaments from a Ship-Burial of the Viking Time etc. Proc. Soc. Antiq. Scot. 4th ser. Vol. V, pp. 437–50. Edinburgh. 1907.

Brate, E. Runinskrifterne på Ön Man. Fornvännen. 1907. pp. 20–34 and 77–95. Stockholm.

Bugge, S. Nordiske Runeindskrifter og billeder paa Mindesmærker paa øen Man. Aarb. f. nord. oldk. og hist. 2nd ser. Vol. XIV, pp. 229–62. Copenhagen. 1899.

Dietrichson, L. and Meyer, J. Monumenta Orcadica. Christiania. 1906.

Goudie, G. The Celtic and Scandinavian Antiquities of Shetland. Edinburgh. 1904.

Henderson, G. The Norse Influence on Celtic Scotland. Glasgow. 1910.

Jakobsen, J. The Dialect and Place Names of Shetland. Lerwick. 1897.

—— Shetlandsøernes Stednavne. Aarb. f. nord. oldk. og hist. 2nd ser. pp. 55–258. Copenhagen. 1901.

Kermode, P. M. C. Manx Crosses. London. 1907.

Lloyd, J. E. History of Wales. 2 vols. London. 1911.

MacBain, A. Norse elements in the topography of the Highlands and Isles. Trans. Gaelic Soc. of Inverness. Vol. XIX, pp. 217–45. Inverness. 1894.

Moore, A. W. History of the Isle of Man. 2 vols. London. 1900.

—— Manx Names. London. 1903.

Neilson, G. Brunanburh and Burnswark. Scottish Hist. Rev. Vol. VII, pp. 37–55. See also pp. 212–14 and 431–6. Glasgow. 1910.

Olsen, M. Om Sproget i de Manske Rune-indskrifter. Christiania. 1909.

Orkney and Shetland Miscellany. Ed. Johnston, A. W. and Amy. Vols. I and II. 1907–9. (In progress.)

Thomas, F. W. L. On Islay Place Names. Proc. Soc. Antiq. Scot. Vol. IV. New series. pp. 241–76. Edinburgh. 1882.

Watson, W. J. Place-names of Ross and Cromarty. Inverness. 1904.

5. THE VIKINGS IN IRELAND.

(a) ORIGINAL AUTHORITIES.

Annales Inisfalenses. Ed. O'Conor, C. Rerum Hibernicarum scriptores veteres. Vol. II. Buckingham. 1825.

Annales Tigernachi. Ed. O'Conor, C. *Ibid.* Vol. II. 1825.

Annals of Ireland by the Four Masters. Ed. O'Donovan, J. Vols. I and II. Dublin. 1851.

Annals of Ireland. Three fragments. Ed. O'Donovan, J. Dublin. 1860.

Annals of Ulster. Ed. Hennessy, W. M. Vol. I. Dublin. 1887.

Cellachan of Cashel, The victorious career of. Ed. Bugge, A. Christiania. 1905.

Chronicon Scotorum. Ed. Hennessy, W. M. Rolls. 1866.

Duald MacFirbis. On the Fomorians and the Norsemen. Ed. Bugge, A. Christiania. 1905.

War of the Gaedhil with the Gaill Ed. Todd, J. H. Rolls. 1867.

(b) Modern Works.

Bugge, A. Nordisk Sprog og nordisk Nationalitet i Irland. Aarb. f. nord. oldk. 2nd series. Vol. xv, pp. 279–333. Copenhagen. 1900.
—— Contributions to the History of the Norsemen in Ireland. 3 parts. Christiania. 1900.
—— Bidrag til det Sidste Afsnit af Nordboernes Historie i Irland. Aarb. f. nord. oldk. 2nd series. Vol. xix, pp. 248–315. Copenhagen. 1904.
Coffey, G. A pair of brooches and chains of the Viking period. J. Roy. Soc. Antiq. Ireland. Vol. xii. 5th series. pp. 71–3. Dublin. 1903.
Craigie, W. A. The Gaels in Iceland. Proc. Soc. Antiq. Scot. Vol. vii. New series. pp. 247–64. Edinburgh. 1897.
Curtis, E. The English and Ostmen in Ireland. EHR. xxiii, pp. 209–19. 1908.
Haliday, C. The Scandinavian Kingdom of Dublin. Dublin. 1884.
Joyce, P. W. Origin and History of Irish Names of Places. Two ser. Dublin. 1875. 3rd series. 1914.
Mogk, E. Kelten und Nordgermanen im 9. und 10. Jahrhundert. Leipsic. 1896.
Petersen, Th. A Celtic reliquary found in a Norwegian Burial-mound. Det Kgl. Norske Videnskabers Selskabs Skrifter. 1907. No. 8. Trondhjem.
Stokes, G. T. Ireland and the Celtic Church. pp. 251–306. 1899.
Vogt, L. J. Dublin som Norsk By. Christiania. 1906.
Zimmer, H. Über die frühesten Berührungen der Iren mit den Nordgermanen. SPAW. pp. 279–317. 1891.
—— Keltische Beiträge. Z. für Deutsches Alt. Vols. xxxii, xxxiii, xxxv. Berlin. 1888–91.

6. THE VIKINGS IN RUSSIA AND EASTERN EUROPE GENERALLY.

(a) Original Authorities. For full Russian bibliography see Thomsen, below.

Constantinus Porphyrogenitus. De administrando imperio. Works. Vol. iii. CSHB.
Jómsvíkingasaga. Ed. C. af Petersens. Copenhagen. 1882.
Nestor. Russiske Krønike. Ed. Smith, C. W. Copenhagen. 1869.

(b) Modern Works.

Archäologischer Anzeiger. Jahrb. des Archäol. Instituts. Berlin. 1906. Cols. 117–18.
Bugge, A. Novgorod som varjagisk By. Nordisk Tidsskrift. 1906.
Kunik, A. A. Die Berufung der schwedischen Rodsen durch die Finnen und Slawen. St Petersburg. 1844.
Marquart, J. Osteuropäische und ostasiatische Streifzüge. Leipsic. 1903.
Roos, W. The Swedish part in the Viking expeditions. EHR. vii, pp. 209–23. 1892.
Steenstrup, J. C. H. R. Venderne og de Danske. Copenhagen. 1900.
Thomsen, V. The Relations between Ancient Russia and Scandinavia. Oxford. 1877.
—— Ryska Rikets Grundläggning genom Skandinaverne. Stockholm. 1882.
Worsaae, J. J. A. La colonisation de la Russie etc. Mém. de la Soc. roy. des antiq. du nord. Nouv. série. 1872–7. pp. 73–198. Copenhagen.

CHAPTERS XIV AND XV.

ENGLAND FROM A.D. 796 TO A.D. 1066.

I. ORIGINAL SOURCES.

(a) CHRONICLES, ANNALS, BIOGRAPHIES, SAGAS ETC.

(i) *Contemporary.*

Abbo of Fleury. Vita S. Edmundi. (Memorials of St Edmund's. *See below,* ii.) Vol. I.

Aelfric. Vita S. Aethelwoldi. (Chron. Abingdon. *See below,* ii.) Vol. II.

Anglo-Saxon Chronicle. Ed. Plummer. *See Gen. Bibl.* IV. Also ed. Thorpe, B 2 vols. Rolls. 1861.

Annales Cambriae. Ed. Williams, J. ab Ithel. Rolls. 1860.

Annales Lindisfarnienses (A.D. 532–993), et Annales Dunelmenses (A.D. 995–1199). Ed. Pertz, G. H. MGH. Script. XIX. 1866.

Asser. Life of King Alfred, together with the Annals of St Neots, erroneously attributed to Asser. Ed. Stevenson, W. H. Oxford. 1904.

Cnutonis Regis Gesta sive Encomium Emmae. Ed. Pertz, G. H. MGH. Script. XIX. 1866.

Ethelwerd's Chronicle. Ed. Petrie, H. Monumenta hist. Brit. *See Gen. Bibl.* IV, 499–521. Transl. Giles, J. A. New edn. London. 1900.

Vita Edwardi Regis. Ed. Luard, H. R. Lives of Edward the Confessor. 387–435. *See below,* ii.

Vita Oswaldi Archiep. Eboracensis auct. anonymo. Ed. Raine, J. Historians of the Church of York. I. *See below,* ii. (The life opens with an account of Archbp. Oda. pp. 400–410.)

Vita S. Dunstani auctore B. Ed. Stubbs, W. Memorials of St Dunstan. pp. 3–52. *See below,* ii.

(ii) *Later.*

Bremen, Adam of (d. *c.* 1076). Gesta Hammenburgensis Ecclesiae pontificum. Ed. Lappenberg, J. M. and Pertz, G. H. MGH. Script. VII. 1346.

Chronicon abbatiae Rameseiensis. Ed. Macray, W. D. Rolls. 1886.

Chronicon monasterii de Abingdon. Ed. Stevenson, J. 2 vols. Rolls. 1858.

De obsessione Dunelmi et de probitate Uchtredi Comitis. Ed. Hinde, J. H. Symeonis Dunelmensis opera. I. Surtees Soc. London. 1868.

Durham, Symeon of. Opera omnia. Ed. Arnold, T. 2 vols. Rolls. 1882–5.

Eadmer. Vita Odonis archiepiscopi Cantuariensis. Ed. Wharton, H. Anglia Sacra. 1691. Vol. II. Ed. Mabillon. ASBen. *See Gen. Bibl.* IV. Vol. VII.

—— Vita Oswaldi. *See below.* Hist. of Church of York. Vol. II.

Fornmanna Sögur. 12 vols. Copenhagen. 1825–37. Latin translation, Scripta
historica Islandorum. 12 vols. Copenhagen. 1828–46.
Heimskringla by Snorro Sturlasson. Ed. Jónsson, F. 4 vols. Copenhagen. 1893–
1901. Transl. Morris, W. and Magnússon, E. The Stories of the Kings of
Norway, called the Round World. 4 vols. London. 1893–1905.
Historians of the Church of York and its Archbishops. Ed. Raine, J. Rolls.
3 vols. 1879–94.
Liber Eliensis. Ed. Stewart, D. J. Anglia Christiana Soc. London. 1848.
Liber Monasterii de Hyda. Ed. Edwards, E. Rolls. 1866.
Lives of Edward the Confessor. Ed. Luard, H. R. Rolls. 1858.
Malmesbury, William of. De gestis Pontificum Anglorum Libri quinque. Ed.
Hamilton, N. E. S. A. Rolls. 1870.
—— De gestis Regum Anglorum Libri quinque. Ed. Stubbs, W. Rolls. 1887–9.
Memorials of St Dunstan. Ed. Stubbs, W. Rolls. 1874.
Memorials of St Edmund's Abbey. Ed. Arnold, T. 3 vols. Rolls. 1890–6.
Osbern. Vita S. Elphegi. Ed. Wharton, H. Anglia Sacra. 1691. ii. MPL. 149.
1853. 371–94.
Saxo Grammaticus. Gesta Danorum. Ed. Holden, A. Strasbourg. 1886.

(b) Laws.

Liebermann, F. Gesetze der Angelsachsen. ZSR. 3 vols. Halle. 1898–1916.
Vol. i contains the texts, with German translations. Vol. ii, pt i a dictionary and concordance; pt ii a glossary. Vol. iii introductions to each text
and notes.
Owen, A. Ancient Laws and Institutes of Wales. 2 vols. RC. 1841.

(c) Landbooks, Wills etc.

Birch, W. de G. Cartularium Saxonicum. *See Gen. Bibl.* iv.
Earle, J. A hand-book to the land charters and other Saxonic documents. Oxford.
1888.
Facsimiles of ancient Charters in the British Museum. Ed. Bond, E. A. 4 pts.
London. 1873–8.
Facsimiles of Anglo-Saxon Manuscripts. Ed. Sandars, W. B. 3 pts. Ordnance
Survey Office. Southampton. 1878–84.
Harmer, F. E. Select English Historical Documents of the ninth and tenth cen-
turies. With translations. Cambridge. 1914.
Heming. Chartularium ecclesiae Wigorniensis. Ed. Hearne, Thomas. 2 vols.
Oxford. 1723.
Kemble, J. M. Codex diplomaticus aevi Saxonici. *See Gen. Bibl.* iv.
Napier, A. S. and Stevenson, W. H. The Crawford collection of early charters etc.,
now in the Bodleian library. Oxford. 1895.
Stevenson, W. H. and Duignan, W. H. Anglo-Saxon Charters relating to Shrop-
shire (A.D. 664–1004). Shropshire Archaeol. and Nat. Hist. Soc. Trans. 4th
series. i, 1–22. Shrewsbury. 1911.
Thorpe, B. Diplomatarium Anglicum aevi Saxonici. A collection of English char-
ters from A.D. 605 to William the Conqueror, with a translation of the Anglo-
Saxon. London. 1865.

(d) Fiscal Surveys and Economic Tracts.

De institutis Londoniae. Printed in Liebermann's Gesetze, vol. i, 232–7, and in
Thorpe's Ancient Laws etc., i, 300–3.
Domesday Book. *See Gen. Bibl.* iv.

Gerefa: or The duties of a reeve. Ed. Liebermann, F. Anglia. 1886. ix, 251–66. Also printed by Cunningham, English Commerce, vol. I, 571–6. *See below*, II (*a*), and in Liebermann's Gesetze, vol. I, 453–5. *See above*, I (*b*).

Inquisitio Comitatus Cantabrigiensis; subjicitur Inquisitio Eliensis. Ed. Hamilton, N. E. S. A. Royal Soc. of Literature. London. 1876.

Rectitudines Singularum personarum. Printed in Liebermann's Gesetze, I, 444–53, and in Thorpe's Ancient Laws etc., I, 432–41.

The Burghal Hidage. Printed by Birch, Cart. Sax. III, 671; and discussed by Maitland, F. W., Domesday Book and Beyond. Cambridge. 1897.

The County Hidage. Printed by Morris, R., Old English Miscellany, p. 145, EETS. 1872, and Gale, T., Hist. Britannicae Scriptores xx. 2 vols. Oxford. 1687–91. Vol. I, App., p. 748; and discussed by Maitland, Domesday Book and Beyond.

(*e*) Ecclesiastical Canons and Monastic Rules.

Haddan and Stubbs. Councils. Vol. III. Anglo-Saxon England to 870. *See Gen. Bibl.* IV.

The Regula Canonicorum of Chrodegang, Bishop of Metz. MPL. 89. 1057–1120.

The Regularis Concordia, or De consuetudine Monachorum. Ed. Dugdale, Monasticon. Vol. I, pp. xxvii–xlv, and Logeman, W. S. Anglia. 1891–3. xiii, 365–454; xv, 20–40.

The Rule of St Benet. Latin and Anglo-Saxon interlinear Version. Ed. Logeman, H. EETS. 1888.

Thorpe, B. Ancient Laws and Institutes of England. With an English Translation of the Saxon. RC. 1840.

Wilkins, D. Concilia Magnae Britanniae et Hiberniae. A.D. 446–1718. 4 vols. London. 1737.

(*f*) Poems, Sagas, Homilies etc., illustrating Social Life.

Aelfric's Colloquium. Ed. Thorpe, B. Analecta Anglo-Saxonica. pp. 18–36. London. 1868.

—— Homilies, with English version. Ed. Thorpe, B. Aelfric Soc. 2 vols. London. 1844.

—— Lives of the Saints. Ed. Skeat, W. W. EETS. 2 vols. London. 1881–1900.

Bibliothek der angelsächsischen Poesie. Ed. Grein, C. W. M. 4 vols. Göttingen. 1857–64. New edn. by Wülker, R. P. 3 vols., 4 pts. Cassel. 1883–98.

Corpus Poeticum Boreale. Ed. and transl. by Vigfússon, G. and Powell, F. York. 2 vols. Oxford. 1883.

Egils Saga. Ed. Jónsson, F. Copenhagen. 1886–8. Transl. Green, W. C.: The Story of Egil Skalla-Grimsson. London. 1893.

Leechdoms, Wortcunning and Starcraft of Early England. Ed. Cockayne, O. 3 vols. Rolls. 1864–6.

Njals Saga. Ed. Jónsson, F. Altnordische Saga Bibliothek (No. 1381). Vol. xiii. Halle. 1908. Transl. Dasent, G. W.: The Story of Burnt Njal. 2 vols. Edinburgh. 1861. 1 vol. London. 1900.

Origines Islandicae. Sagas relating to the early history of Iceland. Ed. and transl. by Vigfússon, G. and Powell, F. York. 2 vols. Oxford. 1905.

The Blickling Homilies of the Tenth Century, with English Version. Ed Morris, R. EETS. 1880.

Wulfstan. Sammlung der ihm zugeschriebenen Homilien. Ed. Napier, A. S. Pt I. Berlin. 1883.

II. MODERN WORKS.

(a) GENERAL.

Adams, H. and others.   Essays on Anglo-Saxon Law.   Boston   1876.
Brown, G. Baldwin.   The Arts in Early England.   *See Gen. Bibl.* v.
Cambridge History of English Literature.   *See Gen. Bibl.* v.
Cunningham, W.   The Growth of English Industry and Commerce.   Last edn.
    Cambridge.   1910.
Dugdale, W.   Monasticon Anglicanum.   *See Gen. Bibl.* iv.
Hodgkin, T.   Political History of England to 1066.   London.   1906
Hunt, W.   The History of the English Church from its foundation to the Norman
    Conquest.   London.   1899.
Kemble, J. M.   The Saxons in England.   London.   1849.   Ed. Birch, W. de G.
    2 vols.   1876.
Lloyd, J. E.   History of Wales.   *See Gen. Bibl.* v.
Makower, F.   Constitutional History of the Church of England.   Berlin.   1894.
    Transl. Upton.   London.   1895.
Maurer, Konrad.   Angelsächsische Rechtsverhältnisse, kritische Überschau der
    deutschen Gesetzgebung.   Munich.   1853–6.
Medley, D. G.   A Student's Manual of English Constitutional History.   Oxford.
    4th edn.   1907.
Oman, C.   England before the Norman Conquest.   London.   1910.
Ramsay, J. H.   The Foundations of England.   2 vols.   London   1898.
Social England.   By various writers.   Ed. Traill, H. D. and Mann, J. S.   Illus-
    trated edn.   London.   1901.
Stubbs, W.   Constitutional History.   *See Gen. Bibl.* v.   Registrum Sacrum.   *Ib.* iii.
Vict. Co. Hist.   *See Gen. Bibl.* i.

(b) SPECIAL TREATISES.

Adams, G. B.   Anglo-Saxon Feudalism.   AHR.   vii.   11–35.   1901.
Andrews, C. M.   The Old English Manor.   Baltimore.   1892.   EHR.   x.   137–41.
    1895.
Ballard, A.   The Domesday Boroughs.   Oxford.   1904.
—— The Domesday Inquest.   London.   1906.
Bateson, M.   Rules for Monks and Secular Canons after the revival under King
    Edgar.   EHR.   ix.   690–708.   1894.
Beaven, M. L. R.   The beginning of the year in the Alfredian Chronicle 866–887.
    EHR.   xxxiii.   328–42.   1918.
—— The Regnal dates of Alfred, Edward the Elder, and Athelstan.   EHR.   xxxii.
    517–31.   1917.
—— King Edmund I and the Danes of York.   EHR.   xxxiii.   1–9.   1918.
Björkmann, E.   Nordische Personennamen in England in alt- und frühmittel-
    englischen Zeit.   Halle.   1910.   (Morsbach's Studien zur engl. Philologie,
    xxxvii.)
Böhmer, H.   Kirche und Staat in England und in der Normandie.   Leipsic.   1899.
    Pt i, chap. 2, Die Englische Kirche im Jahre 1066.
Bugge, A.   Vikingerne.   2 vols.   Copenhagen.   1904–6.
—— Vesterlandenes Indflydelse paa Nordboernes og särlig Nordmundenes ydre
    Kultur, Levesaet og Samfundsforhold i Vikingetiden.   Christiania.   1905.
—— Norse settlements round the Bristol Channel.   Christiania.   1900.
Cam, H. M.   Local Government in Francia and England (768–1034).   London.   1912.
Chadwick, H. M.   Studies on Anglo-Saxon Institutions.   Cambridge.   1905.
Clapham, J. H.   The Horsing of the Danes.   EHR.   xxv.   287–93.   1910.

Collingwood, W. G. Scandinavian Britain. London. 1908.
Davis, H. W. C. Cumberland before the Norman Conquest. EHR. xx. 61–3. 1905.
—— The Liberties of Bury St Edmund. EHR. xxiv. 417–31. 1909.
—— The Anglo-Saxon Laws. EHR. 418–31. 1913.
Demarest, E. B. The Firma Unius Noctis. EHR. xxxv. 78–89. 1920.
—— The Hundred-Pennies. EHR. xxxiii. 62–72. 1913.
Dietrich, E. Abt Aelfrik. Zeitschrift für die Historische Theologie. xxv. 487–594. xxvi. 163–256. Gotha. 1855–6.
Du Chaillu. The Viking Age. New York. 1890.
Ekwall, E. Scandinavians and Celts in the North-west of England. Lund. 1918.
Flom, G. T. Scandinavian Influence on Southern Lowland Scotch. New York. 1900. (Columbia Univ. Germanic Studies. i, No. 1.)
Gaskoin, C. J. B. Alcuin, his life and his work. London. 1904.
Green, J. R. The Conquest of England, A.D. 829–1071. London. 1899.
Haskins, C. H. A charter of Canute for Fécamp. EHR. xxxiii. 342. 1918.
Hilderbrand, B. E. Anglo-sachsiska mynt i svenska kongliga myntkabinettet funna i Sveriges jord. Stockholm. 1881.
Howorth, Sir H. H. Ragnall Ivarson and Jarl Otir. EHR. xxvi. 1–19. 1911.
Keary, C. F. The Vikings in Western Christendom, A.D. 789–888. London. 1891. (Chap. xii deals with England.)
Larson, L. M. The King's Household in England before the Norman Conquest. Madison. 1904. (Bulletin of Univ. of Wisconsin.)
—— The Political Policies of Cnut as King of England. AHR. xv. No. 4. 1910.
—— Canute the Great. London. 1912.
Lees, B. A. Alfred the Great. New York. 1915.
Liebermann, F. Zur Geschichte Bryhtnoths, des Helder von Maldon. Archiv für das Studium der neueren Sprachen. ci. 15–28. Brunswick. 1898.
—— The National Assembly in the Anglo-Saxon Period. Halle. 1913.
—— Einleitung zum Statut der Londoner Friedensgilde unter Aethelstan; in Mélanges Fitting. ii. 77–104. Montpellier. 1908.
—— On the Instituta Cnuti aliorumque Regum Anglorum. Trans. RHS. New Ser. Vol. vii. 77–109. 1893.
Maitland, F. W. Domesday Book and Beyond. Cambridge. 1897.
—— Surnames of English Villages. Archaeol. Rev. iv. 233–40. London. 1889.
—— The Origin of the Borough. EHR. xi. 13–19. 1896.
Maurer, K. Ueber das Wesen des ältesten Adels der deutschen Stämme. Die Angelsachsen. Munich. 1846.
—— Das Vapnatak der Nordischen Rechte. Bartsch's Germania. xvi. Vienna. 1871.
Mawer, A. The Vikings. Cambridge. 1913.
Morris, W. A. The Frankpledge System. (Hammond Hist. Ser. xiv.) New York. 1910.
—— The Origin of the Sheriff in the Anglo-Saxon Period. EHR. xxxi. 20–49. 1916.
Munch, P. A. Det norske Folks Historie. Vols. i–iii. Christiania. 1852–63.
Pearson, K. A Myth about Edward the Confessor. EHR. xxv. 1910.
Plummer, C. The Life and Times of Alfred the Great. Oxford. 1902.
Reid, R. R. Barony and Thanage. EHR. xxxv. 161–200. London. 1920.
Rietschel, S. Untersuchungen zur Geschichte der germanischen Hundertschaft. ZR. xli. Weimar. 1907.
Robinson, J. A. The Saxon Bishops of Wells. Brit. Acad. Supplemental Papers. iv. 1919.
—— St Oswald and the Church of Worcester. *Ibid.* v. 1919.
—— The Coronation Order in the Tenth Century. JTS. Vol. xix. pp. 56 and 72.

Roeder, F.   Die Familie bei der Angelsachsen.   Pt I. Mann and Frau.   Halle. 1899.

Round, J. H.   The Tertius Denarius of the Borough.   EHR.   xxxiv.   62–4.   1919.

—— The Officers of Edward the Confessor.   EHR.   xix.   1904.

Sackur, E.   Die Cluniacenser in ihrer kirchlichen und allgemein-geschichtlichen Wirksamkeit bis zur Mitte des elften Jahrhunderts.   Halle.   1892, 1894.

Searle, W. G.   Anglo-Saxon Bishops, Kings and Nobles.   Cambridge.   1899.

—— Onomasticon Anglo-Saxonicum.   Cambridge.   1897.

Seebohm, F.   The English Village Community.   London.   1883.

—— The Tribal System in Wales.   London.   1895.

—— Tribal Custom in Anglo-Saxon Law.   London.   1902.

Steenstrup, J. C. H. R.   Normannerne.   4 vols. Copenhagen.   1876–82.   Vol. iii. Viking Kingdoms in the British Isles.   Vol. iv. Danish institutions in England.

Stenton, F. M.   Aethelwerd's account of the last years of King Alfred.   EHR. xxiv.   79–84.   1909.

—— The Supremacy of the Mercian Kings.   EHR.   xxxiii.   433–52.   1918.

—— The Danes at Thorney Island in 893.   EHR.   xxvii.   1–12.   1912.

—— Gudmundeslaech.   EHR.   xx.   697–9.   1905.

—— William the Conqueror.   London.   1908.

—— The Early History of Abingdon Abbey.   Oxford.   1913.

—— Types of Manorial Structure in the Northern Danelaw.   Oxford.   1910.

Stephens, G.   The Old Northern Runic Monuments of Scandinavia and England. 4 vols.   London and Copenhagen.   1866–1901.

Stevenson, W. H.   A Latin Poem addressed to King Athelstan.   EHR.   xxvi. 482.   1911.

—— Fragments of a Worcester chartulary drawn up about the year 1000.   Lord Middleton's MSS.   HMC.   1917.

—— Yorkshire Surveys and other Eleventh Century Documents in the York Gospels.   EHR.   xxvii.   1912.

—— An alleged Son of King Harold Hardrada.   EHR.   xxviii.   1913.

—— Trinoda Necessitas.   EHR.   xxix.   1914.

Streatfeild, G. S.   Lincolnshire and the Danes.   London.   1884.

Taranger, A.   Den Angelsaksiske Kirkes Indflydelse paa den norske (Norske Historiske Forening).   Christiania.   1890.

Taylor, C. S.   The Origin of the Mercian Shires.   Bristol and Glouc. Archaeol. Soc. Trans.   xxi.   32–57.   Bristol.   1898.

—— The Danes in Gloucestershire.   *Ibid.*   xvii.   68–95.   1892.

Toke, L. A. St A.   The date of Dunstan's birth.   Appendix to The Bosworth Psalter.   Ed. Gasquet, A. H. and Bishop, E.   London.   1908.

Vinogradoff, P.   The Growth of the Manor.   London.   1905.

—— English Society in the Eleventh Century.   Oxford.   1908.

—— Transfer of Land in Old English Law.   Harvard Law Review.   xx.   532–48. 1907.

—— Folkland.   EHR.   viii.   1–17.   1893.

—— Romanistische Einflüsse im angelsächsischen Recht, das Buchland.   Mélanges Fitting.   ii.   499–522.   Montpellier.   1908.

White, C. L.   Aelfric, a new study of his life and writings.   Boston.   1898.

Williams, L. F. R.   History of the Abbey of St Albans.   London.   1917.

Worsaae, J. J. A.   Minder om de Danske og Nordmœndene i England, Skotland og Irland.   Copenhagen.   1851.   English transl. London.   1852.

Zinkeisen, F.   The Anglo-Saxon Courts of Law.   Political Science Quarterly.   x. 132–44.   Boston.   1895.

—— Die Anfänge des Lehngerichtsbarkeit in England.   Berlin.   1893.

CHAPTER XVI.

THE WESTERN CALIPHATE.

I. SPECIAL BIBLIOGRAPHIES.

Brockelmann, C.   Geschichte der arabischen Litteratur.   2 vols.   Weimar.   1898.
Casiri, M.   Bibliotheca arabico-hispana Escurialensis.   2 vols.   Madrid.   1760.
Derenbourg, H.   Les manuscrits arabes de l'Escurial.   Paris.   1884.
Dozy, R.   Notice sur quelques manuscrits arabes.   Leyden.   1847.
Guillén Robles, F.   Catálogo de los manuscritos árabes existentes en la Biblioteca Nacional de Madrid.   Madrid.   1889.
Ḥaji Khalifa.   Lexicon bibliographicum et encyclopaedicum.   Ed. Flügel.   7 vols. Leipsic and London.   1835–58.
Pons Boigues, F.   Ensayo bio-bibliográfico sobre los historiadores y geógrafos arábigo-españoles.   Madrid.   1898.
—— Dos obras importantísimas de Aben Hazam [Ibn Ḥazm].   In Homenaje a Menéndez Pelayo.   Vol. I, p. 509.   Madrid.   1899.
Ribera, J. y Asín, M.   Manuscritos árabes y aljamiados de la Biblioteca de la Junta para ampliación de estudios e investigaciones científicas.   (Bibl. J. amp. estud.) Madrid.   1912.
Wustenfeld, F.   Die Geschichtsschreiber der Araber und ihre Werke.   Göttingen. 1882.

II.   MANUSCRIPTS.

'Abd-Allah ibn 'Abd-al-Wāḥid al-Fihrī of Alpuente.   Formulary of notarial acts. MS 11.   Bibl. J. amp. estud.   See above, I.
'Alī ibn Yahyā ibn al-Ḳāsim.   Formulary of notarial acts.   MS 5.   Bibl. J. amp. estud.   See above, I.
Ibn Ḥayyān.   Kitāb al-muqtabis fī akhbār al-Andalus.   Arabic MS 592 of the Bib. Nac. of Madrid, Oxford, Cat. II, 137 and R. Acad. de la Hist. of Madrid.
Ibn al-Khatīb.   Iḥāṭa.   MS 1673 of El Escorial (1668 Cat. Casiri), 27–33 of Bib. Nac. Madrid and of R. Acad. de la Historia.
Al-Khushanī.   History of the ḳāḍīs of Cordova.   MS of Bodl. Oxford, II, 2582. Ed. Ribera, J., in Centro de Estudios históricos, Madrid.   1914.

III.   ORIGINAL AUTHORITIES.

1.   Arabs.

Ibn 'Abd-al-Ḥakam.   History of the conquest of Spain.   Arabic text and transl. Jones, J. H.   London.   1858.   Spanish transl. in Akhbar majmu'a.
Ibn Aḍarī [Ibn al-'Idhārī].   Historias de Al-Andalus.   Transl. Fernandez y González, F.   Granada.   1862.
—— Al-Bayano-l-Mogrib.   Ed. Dozy, R.   Leyden.   1848–51.   Transl. Fagnan, E. Argel.   1901–4.
Akhbār Majmū'a.   Crónica anónima del siglo XI.   Transl. and annotated Lafuente Alcántara, E.   Madrid.   1867.

Anonymous. Fatho-l-Andalus. Historia de la conquista de España. Transl. González, J. Argel. 1889.

Ibn al-Athīr. Chronicon quod Perfectissimum inscribitur ad fidem codicum Berolinensis, Musei Britannici et Parisinorum. Ed. Tornberg, C. J. 14 vols. Leyden. 1867–76.

Ibn Baṭūṭā. Voyages de Ibn Batoutah. Texte arabe et traduction par Defrémery et Sanguinetti. Paris. 1853.

Bibliotheca arabico-hispana. Ed. Codera and Ribera. Madrid-Saragossa. 1883–95. 10 vols.

    I–II. Aben Pascualis Assila. (Dict. biographicum.) 1883.

    III. Adh-Dhabbī. Desiderium quaerentis historiam virorum populi Andalusiae. (Dict. biographicum.) 1885.

    IV. Aben Al-Abbar [Ibn al-Abbār]. Almocham. 1886.

    V–VI. Aben Al-Abbar. Tecmila. Complementum libri Assilah. 1887–9.

    VII–VIII. Aben Alfaradhī. Hist. virorum doctorum Andalusiae. 1891.

    IX–X. Abu Bequer ben Khair. Index librorum de diversis scientiarum ordinibus. Saragossa. 1895.

Ibn Ḥazm. Ḳitāb al-faṣl fi-l-milal wal-ahwā wan-niḥal. Critical hist. of religions, sects and schools. 5 vols. Cairo. 1321 heg.

Idrīsī. Description de l'Afrique et de l'Espagne par Edrisi. Ed. Dozy, R. and de Goeje, M. Leyden. 1866. Spanish transl. Blazquez, A. Madrid. 1901.

Ibn Khaldūn, Les prolégomènes de. French transl. and notes, De Slane. 3 vols. Paris. 1863–8.

—— Histoire des Berbères et des dynasties musulmans de l'Afrique septentrionale. De Slane. Algiers. 1852–6.

Ibn Khallikān. Ibn Challikan vitae illustrium virorum nunc primum arabice edidit. Wüstenfeld, F. Göttingen. 1835–43. Also edited by De Slane. Vies des hommes illustres de l'Islamisme en arabe par ibn Khallikan. Paris. 1838–42. [Incomplete.] English transl., De Slane. Biographical dictionary. Paris-London. 1843–71.

Ibn al-Ḳūṭīya. Hist. de la conquête de l'Espagne par les Musulmans. Trad. Cherbonneau, A. JA. 5th series. VIII, n. 32. 1856.

Al-Maḳḳarī. The history of the Mohammedan dynasties in Spain. Transl. with critical notes, De Gayangos, P. London. 1840–3.

—— Analectes sur l'histoire et la littérature des Arabes de l'Espagne. Arabic text. Ed. Dozy, Dugat, Krehl and Wright. 2 vols. Leyden. 1855–61.

An-Nuwairī. Historia de los musulmanes de España y Africa. Texto árabe y trad. española. Gaspar Remiro, M. Granada. 1917–19.

Roudh el-Kartas [Rauḍ al-Ḳirṭās]. Hist. des souverains du Maghreb (Espagne et Maroc) et Annales de la ville de Fès. Trad. Beaumier, A. Paris. 1860. (Pub. Ministère des Affaires étrangères.)

Ash-Shahrastānī. Book of Religions and philosophical Sects. Ed. Cureton, W. 2 vols. London. 1842.

Tecmila [Takmila]. Apendice a la ed. Codera de la "Tecmila" de Ibn Al-Abbār. Ed. Alarcón, M. and Palencia, A. González. Madrid. 1915.

Jacut [Yāḳūt]. Geographisches Wörterbuch. Ed. Wüstenfeld, F. Leipsic. 1866.

—— Dictionary of learned men. Ed. Margoliouth. 2 vols. Leipsic-London. 1907.

2. Latin.

Alvaro of Cordova. Opera. MPL, CXXI. Paris. 1852.

Anales Compostelanos. In España Sagrada, XXIII.

Anonimo latino. In Esp. Sagr. VIII. Ed. Tailhan, P. L'Anonyme de Cordoue. Paris. 1885. (Attributed to Pacense.)

Bofarull (P. y F.). Colección de documentos inéditos del Archivo general de la Corona de Aragón. 40 vols. Barcelona. 1847–1910.

Caetani, L. Chronographia islamica. Paris. 1912. (In prog.)

—— Annali dell' Islam. Milan. 1906 ff. (In prog.)

Cronicón Albeldense. Esp. Sagr. xiii.

Cronicón de Alfonso III. Esp. Sagr. xiii. Also ed. Villada, Z. García. Madrid. 1918.

Cronicón Burgense. Esp. Sagr. xxiii.

Cronicón Conimbricense. Esp. Sagr. xxiii.

Cronicón Lusitano. Esp. Sagr. xxiii.

Cronicón del Pacense. *See above*, Anonimo latino.

Cronicón del Silense. Esp. Sagr. xvii.

España Sagrada. *See Gen. Bibl.* iv.

Eulogio of Cordova. Sancti Eulogii Cordubensis opera...eiusque vita per Alvarum Cordubensem, omnia Ambrosii Morales scholiis illustrata. Alcalá de Henares. 1574.

Historia Compostellana. Esp. Sagr. xx.

Leo Africanus. Africae descriptio ix libris absoluta. Lugduni Batavorum. 1632.

Lucas Tudensis. Chronicon mundi ab eius origine usque ad eram 1274. In Hispaniae illustratae scriptores varii, vol. 4. Frankfort. 1603–8.

Pelayo. Chronicon Regum Legionensium. Esp. Sagr. xiv.

Sampiro. Chronicon. Esp. Sagr. xiv.

Samsón. Apologeticum. Esp. Sagr. xi.

Speraindeo. Apologeticum. *See above*, Eulogio, Mem. Sanct. Bk. i.

—— Epistola ad Alvarum. Esp. Sagr. xi.

Ximénez de Rada, R. Historia Arabum. In Hist. Saracenica by Elmacinus. Ed. Latin. T. Erpenii. Lugduni Batavorum. 1625.

IV. MODERN WORKS.

1. General.

Altamira, R. Hist. de España y de la civilización española. 4 vols. 2nd edn. Barcelona. 1911.

De Boer, T. J. The hist. of Philosophy in Islam. Transl. Jones, E. R. London. 1903.

Catálogo de las monedas árabes del Museo Arqueológico Nacional. Madrid. 1892.

Cerdá de Villarestain, M. Catálogo de las monedas arábigo-españolas. Madrid. 1861.

Codera y Zaidin, F. Tratado de Numismática arábigo-española. Madrid. 1879.

—— Cecas arábigo-españolas. Revista de Archivos, Bibliotecas, Museos. 1874.

—— Articles on numismatic and epigraphic topics in BRAH.

—— Paleografía árabe. BRAH, xxxiii. 1898.

—— Las fuentes árabes en el vocabulario de los dialectos españoles desde el siglo viii al xii. Discurso de recepción en la R. Ac. Española. Madrid. 1910.

Derenbourg, H. La science des religions et de l'Islamisme. Paris. 1886.

Dozy, R. Histoire des Musulmans d'Espagne jusqu'à la conquête de l'Andalousie par les Almohades. 4 vols. Leyden. 1861. Spanish transl. de Castro, F. [Poor]; and de Fuentes, M. S. (Calpe). Madrid. 1920. English transl. Stokes, F. G. Spanish Islam: a history of the Moslems in Spain. London. 1913.

—— Recherches sur l'histoire et la littérature de l'Espagne pendant le Moyen Âge. 3rd edn. 2 vols. Leyden. 1881.

—— Essai sur l'histoire de l'Islamisme. Chauvin, V. Leyden. 1879. (Transl. from the Dutch.)

—— Introduction au Al-Bayano-l-Mogrib par Ibn Aḍarī. Leyden. 1848–51.

—— Dict. détaillé des noms des vêtements chez les arabes. Amsterdam. 1845.

Dozy, R.   Lettre à M. Fleischer sur le texte d'Al-Maḳḳarī.   Leyden.   1871.
Dugat, G.   Hist. des Philosophes et des Théologiciens musulmans.   (De 632 à 1258.)   Paris.   1878.
—— Cours complémentaire de géographie, histoire et législation des états musulmans.   Paris.   1873.
Gauthier, L.   La philosophie musulmane.   Paris.   1900.
De Goeje, M.   Descriptio Al-Magribi sumpta ex libro regionum Al-Jacubi.   Lugduni Batavorum.   1860.
Goujet, A.   L'Art arabe.   Paris.   1893.
Horten, M.   Die philosophischen Systeme der spekulativen Theologen im Islam.   Bonn.   1912.
Huart, C.   Littérature arabe.   Paris.   1902.
Jusué, E.   Tablas de reducción del cómputo musulmán al cristiano y viceversa.   Madrid.   1903.
Lampérez, V.   Hist. de la Arquitectura cristiana española en la Edad Media.   2 vols.   Madrid.   1908.
Lavoix, E.   Catalogue des monnaies musulmans de la Bibliothèque National.   Paris.   1891.
Leclerc, L.   Hist. de la Médecine arabe.   Paris.   1876.
Macdonald, B. D.   Development of Muslim Theology, Jurisprudence and Constitutional Theory.   New York.   1903.
—— Muslim Jurisprudence.   Hartford.   1900.
—— The religious attitude and life in Islam.   Chicago.   1909.
Marcel, J.   Paléographie arabe.   Paris.   1828.
Menéndez Pelayo, M.   Hist. de los heterodoxos españoles.   Vol. i.   Madrid.   1880.
Munk, S.   Mélanges de Philosophie juive et arabe.   Paris.   1879.
Saladin, H. et Migeon, G.   Manuel d'art musulman.   Paris.   1902.
Sawas Pacha.   Étude sur la théorie du droit musulman.   2nd edn.   Paris.   1902.
Schmolders, A.   Essai sur les écoles philosophiques chez les arabes.   Paris.   1842.
Seybold, C. F.   Zur spanisch-arabischen Geographie.   Halle.   1906.
Simonet, F.   Hist. de los mozárabes de España.   Madrid.   1903.
—— Glosario de voces ibéricas y latinas usadas entre los mozárabes.   Madrid.   1888.
Sprenger, A.   A Dictionary of the technical terms used in the sciences of the Musulmans.   Bengala.   1854.
Van Vloten, G.   Recherches sur la domination arabe.   Le chiitisme et les croyances messianiques sous le Khalifat des Omayades.   Amsterdam.   1894.
Vives, A.   Monedas de las dinastias arábigo-españolas.   Madrid.   1893.

2. Monographs, Biographies and Special Treatises.

Amador de los Rios, R.   Inscripciones árabes de Córdoba.   Madrid.   1871.
Asin Palacios, M.   La indiferencia religiosa de la España musulmana según Abenhazam.   Cultura Española.   Madrid.   1907.
—— Abenmasarra y su escuela.   Madrid.   1914.
—— La escatología musulmana en la Divina Comedia.   Madrid.   1919.
—— Investigacion de los origenes del pensamiento extra-religioso y heterodoxo en la Hist. crítica de los religiones de Abenhazam el Cordobés.   (In progress.)
Bofarull, P.   Los Condes de Barcelona vindicados.   Barcelona.   1836.
Braga, T.   La invasión de los árabes en España y su influencia en el desenvolvimiento de la población libre.   (Revista dos Estudos livres.   1884.)
Carreras y Candi, F.   Relaciones de los Vizcondes de Barcelona con los árabes.   In Homenaje a Codera, p. 207.
Chabás, R.   Los mozárabes de Valencia.   In El Archivo.   Valencia.   1891.
—— Los mozárabes valencianos.   BRAH, xviii.

Codera y Zaidin, F. Estudios críticos de Hist. árabe española. Saragossa. 1903. Madrid. 1917. Vols. vii–ix de la Colección de Estudios árabes.

—— Embajadores de Castilla encarcelados en Córdoba en los últimos años de Alhaquem II. BRAH, xiv. 1889.

—— Campaña de Gormaz en el año 364 de la hégira. *Ibid.*

—— Los Benimeruán de Mérida y Badajoz. Revista de Aragón. Saragossa. 1904.

—— Noticia de los Omeyas de Alandalus por Aben Hazam. BRAH, xiii. 1888.

—— Embajada de príncipes cristianos en Córdoba en los últimos años de Alhaquem II. BRAH, xiii. 1888.

—— La batalla de Calatañazor. BRAH, lvi. 1910. 197–200.

Cotarelo, E. El casamiento de Almanzor con una hija de Bermudo II. España Moderna. 1903.

Díaz-Jimenez, J. Immigración mozárabe en el reino de León. El monasterio de Abellar o de los Santos mártires Cosme y Damian. BRAH, xx. 1892. 123 ff.

Dozy, R. Le Calendrier de Cordoue de l'année 961. Texte arabe et ancienne traduction latine. Leyden. 1873.

Fabricius, A. K. La première invasion des Normands dans l'Espagne musulmane en 844. Lisbon. 1892.

—— La connaissance de la Péninsule espagnole par les hommes du Nord. Lisbon. 1892.

Fernández Guerra, A. Fortalezas del guerrero Omar ben Hafson hasta ahora desconocidas. Boletín histórico. Madrid. 1880.

Gaspar Remiro, M. Historia de Murcia musulmana. Saragossa. 1905.

—— Cordobeses musulmanes en Alejandría y Creta. Homenaje a Codera, p. 217.

Gayangos, P. Memoria sobre la autenticidad de la Crónica llamada del Moro Rasis. Mem. RAH, viii. 1850.

Goldziher, I. Die Zahiriten. Leipsic. 1884.

—— Le dogme et la loi de l'Islam. French transl. Arin. Paris. 1902.

Gómez Moreno, M. Excursión a través del arco de herradura. Cultura española. 1906.

—— Iglesias mozárabes. Arte español de los siglos ix–xi. Madrid. 1919.

Guillén Robles, F. Málaga musulmana. Málaga. 1880.

De Osma, G. J. Apuntes sobre cerámica morisca. 3 vols. Madrid. 1906–11.

Pons Boigues, F. Apuntes sobre las escrituras mozárabes toledanas existentes en el Archivo Histórico Nacional. Madrid. 1897.

Ribera y Tarragó, J. La enseñanza entre los musulmanes españoles. Saragossa. 1893.

—— Bibliófilos y bibliotecas en la España musulmana. 2nd edn. Saragossa. 1896.

—— Orígenes del Justicia mayor de Aragón. Saragossa. 1897. Colección de estudios árabes, iii.

—— El Cancionero de Ibn Quzmān. Discurso de recepción. R. Ac. Esp. 1912.

—— [La épica entre los musulmanes españoles.] Discurso en la R. Ac. Hist. Madrid. 1915.

Saavedra, E. La mujer mozárabe. Conferencia. Madrid. 1904.

—— Estudio sobre la invasión de los árabes en España. Madrid. 1892.

—— Pelayo. Conferencia. Madrid. 1906.

—— Abderrahmen I. Monografía histórica. Revista de Archivos, Bibliotecas y Museos. Madrid. 1910.

—— La batalla de Calatañazor. Mélanges Hartwig Derenbourg, p. 335. Paris. 1909.

Ureña, R. La influencia semita en el derecho medieval de España. Madrid. 1898.

—— Familias de jurisconsultos : Los Benimajlad de Córdoba. Homenaje a Codera, p. 251.

Velázquez Bosco, R. La Arquitectura de la Edad Media en Europa. Madrid. 1894.

—— Medina Azzahra y Alamiriya. Madrid. 1912.

CHAPTER XVII.

THE CHURCH FROM CHARLEMAGNE TO SYLVESTER II.

I. DOCUMENTS AND SOURCES.

(*a*) Councils.

Concilia aevi Karolini. Ed. Werminghoff, A. (Vol. ı to 842 alone published.) MGH. Leges. Sect. III. Concilia II, 1. 1906–8.
Mansi. XIV–XIX. *See Gen. Bibl.* IV.

(*b*) Papal Letters.

Calendars:
Jaffé, P. Regesta. *See Gen. Bibl.* IV. New edn. Wattenbach. Vol. I. Leipsic. 1887.
Kehr, P. F. Regesta pontificum Romanorum. *See Gen. Bibl.* IV.

Editions :
MGH. Epistolae v and seq. (Epistolae Karolini aevi. Vol. III and seq.) Corresp. of Nicholas I. Vol. VI (IV), pt 2, fasc. I. Ed. Perels. 1912. Corresp. John VIII. Vol. VII (v), pt 1. Ed. Caspar, E. 1912. *See Gen. Bibl.* IV.
MPL. Parts of 102–142.

(*c*) Papal Decretals.

Burchard of Worms. Decretum. MPL. 140. *See Gen. Bibl.* IV.
Decretales Pseudo-Isidorianae et Capitula Angilramni. Ed. Hinschius, P. *See Gen. Bibl.* IV.

(*d*) Capitularies.

Capitularia regum francorum. Ed. Boretius and Krause. MGH. Leges. Sect. II, 1, 2. *See Gen. Bibl.* IV.

(*e*) Letters of Prelates.

MGH. Epist. Karolini aevi, *ut sup.* MPL, *ut sup.* Bouquet, VI–XI. *See Gen. Bibl.* IV.

(*f*) Canonical and Polemical Treatises.

(Among others especially) Agobard. MPL. 104. *See Gen. Bibl.* IV.
Hincmar. *Ibid.* 125–126.

(*g*) Chronicles (*specially bearing on Papal History*).

Duchesne, Liber pontificalis. *See Gen. Bibl.* IV.
Watterich, J. M. Pontificum romanorum...vitae. *See Gen. Bibl.* IV. (Extracts from chronicles etc. Convenient, though incomplete, handbook if checked by later edns. of texts cited.)

II. MODERN WORKS.

(*a*) General.

(*See also Gen. Bibl.* v for Church Histories.)

Duchesne, L. Les premiers temps de l'État pontifical. 3rd edn. Paris. 1911.

Gregorovius, F. Stadt Rom. *See Gen. Bibl.* v.

Hartmann, L. M. Gesch. Italiens. *See ib.* Vol. iii, 1 and 2.

Hauck, A. Kirchengesch. Vol. ii–iii. *See ib.*

Hefele, C. J. Hist. des conciles, transl. Leclercq. *See ib.* Vol. iv, 1, 2. (Contains full bibliographical notes.)

Hinschius, P. Das Kirchenrecht der Katholiker und Protestanten in Deutschland. 6 vols. Berlin. 1869–97.

Kleinclausz, A. L'empire carolingien, ses origines et ses transformations. Paris. 1902.

Lilienfein, H. Die Anschauungen von Staat und Kirche im Reich der Karolinger. Heidelberg. 1902. (Heidelberger Abhandlungen zur mittleren und neueren Geschichte, i.)

Luchaire, A. Les premiers Capétiens. Lavisse, Hist. de France. ii, 2. *See Gen. Bibl.* v. (Specially for the Peace and Truce of God.)

Romano, G. Le dominazioni barbariche in Italia, 395–1024. *See Gen. Bibl.* v.

Werminghoff, A. Kirchenverfassung Deutschlands. *See Gen. Bibl.* v. Vol. i.

—— Verfassungsgeschichte der deutschen Kirche im Mittelalter. 2nd edn. Leipsic and Berlin. 1913. (Meister's Grundriss. The two latter, though summaries, contain valuable bibliogr. information.)

(*b*) Monographs.

Bourgeois, E. Le capitulaire de Kiersy-sur-Oise (877). Étude sur l'état et le régime politique à la fin du ixe siècle d'après la législation de Charles le Chauve. Paris. 1885.

Calmette, J. La diplomatie carolingienne du traité de Verdun à la mort de Charles le Chauve. (843–877.) Paris. 1901. BHE. 135.

Davenport, E. H. The False Decretals. Oxford. 1916.

Dümmler, E. Gesch. des ostfränkischen Reichs. 2nd edn. 3 vols. Leipsic. 1887–8 (Jahrb. d. deutsch. Gesch.)

Duval, F. Les terreurs de l'an mille. Paris. 1908.

Ebers, G. J. Das Devolutionsrecht vornehmlich nach katholischem Kirchenrecht. Stuttgart. 1906. (Kirchenrechtliche Abh. Vol. 37.)

Fournier, P. Étude sur les Fausses Décrétales. RHE. vii. 1906. 1–4 et viii. 1907. 1. (Indicates principal authorities on the False Decretals up to 1906.)

Greinacher, A. Die Anschauungen des Papstes Nikolaus I über das Verhältnis von Staat und Kirche. Berlin. 1909.

Himly, A. Wala et Louis le Débonnaire. Paris. 1849.

Huberti, L. Studien zur Rechtsgesch. der Gottesfrieden u. Landfrieden. Vol. i. Die Friedensordnung in Frankreich. Ansbach. 1892.

Imbart de la Tour, P. Les élections épiscopales dans l'Église de France du ixe au xiie siècle. Paris. 1890.

—— Les paroisses rurales dans l'ancienne France du ive au xie siècle. Paris. 1900. (Repr. from RH. Vols. lx, lxi, lxiii, lxvii, lxviii.)

Koeniger, M. Burchard I von Worms und die deutsche Kirche seiner Zeit. Munich. 1905.

Lapôtre, A. L'Europe et le Saint-Siège à l'époque carolingienne. Vol. ɪ (no more pub.): Le pape Jean VIII. Paris. 1899.

—— De Anastasio bibliothecario. Paris. 1889.

Lesne, E. La hiérarchie épiscopale, provinces, métropolitains, primats en Gaule et Germanie depuis la réforme de Saint Boniface jusqu'à la mort d'Hincmar (742–882). Paris. 1905. (Mém. et travaux des Facultés catholiques de Lille. ɪ.)

—— Hincmar et l'empereur Lothaire. RQH ʟxxvɪɪɪ.

Lot, F. Études sur le règne de Hugues Capet et la fin du xᵉ siècle. Paris. 1903. BHE. 147.

—— La question des Fausses Décrétales. RH. xcɪv (1907). pp. 290–9.

Lot, F. et Halphen, L. Le règne de Charles le Chauve. Vol. ɪ (no more pub.). Paris. 1909. BHE. 175.

Manteyer, G. de. La Paix de Dieu en Viennois. *In* Les Origines de la maison de Savoie en Bourgogne etc. Grenoble. 1906. *See Bibl. c.* vɪ, 4 *b.*

Noorden, C. v. Hinkmar, Erzbischof von Rheims. Bonn. 1863.

Parisot, R. Le royaume de Lorraine sous les Carolingiens (843–923). Paris. 1898.

Poupardin, R. Le royaume de Bourgogne, 888–1038. Paris. 1907. (For the hist. of the Peace and Truce of God in Burgundy.)

Richterich, J. Papst Nikolaus I. Berne. 1903 (dissertation).

Rocquain, F. La papauté au moyen âge (pp. 4–74 : Nicolas Iᵉʳ). Paris. 1881.

Roy, J. Saint Nicolas I. Paris. 1899. (Collection " Les saints.")

—— Principes du pape Nicolas Iᵉʳ sur les rapports des deux puissances. *In* Études d'histoire de moyen âge dédiées à Gabriel Monod (pp. 95–105). Paris. 1896.

Sackur, E. Die Cluniacenser in ihrer kirchlichen und allgemeingeschichtlichen Wirksamkeit bis zur Mitte des elften Jahrhunderts. 2 vols. Halle. 1892–4.

Schrörs, H. Hinkmar, Erzbischof von Reims. Sein Leben und seine Schriften. Freiburg-i.-B. 1884.

Sickel, Th. Das Privilegium Otto I für die römische Kirche vom Jahre 962. Innsbruck. 1833. (For later literature on this subject cf. Dahlmann-Waitz, 8th edn., No. 4817.)

Sickel, W. Die Verträge der Päpste mit den Karolingern. DZG. xɪ (1894). pp. 301–91. xɪɪ (1895), pp. 1–43.

—— Die Kaiserkrönungen von Karl bis Berengar. HZ. n.s. xʟvɪɪ (1899), pp. 1–38.

—— Kirchenstaat und Karolinger. HZ. n.s. xʟvɪɪɪ (1900), pp. 389–409.

Simson, B. Jahrb. des fränkisches Reichs unter Ludwig dem Frommen. 2 vols. Leipsic. 1874–6. (Jahrb. der deutschen Gesch.)

Weise, G. Königtum und Bischofswahl im fränkischen und deutschen Reich vor dem Investiturstreit. Berlin. 1912.

CHAPTER XVIII.

FEUDALISM.

I. EDITIONS OF SOURCES.

Assises de Jérusalem. Ed. Beugnot, A. A. Rec. des hist. des croisades, Lois. Vols. 1, 2. AcadIBL. 1841–2.

Beaumanoir, Ph. de Remi, Sieur de. Coutumes de Beauvaisis. Ed. Salmon. 1899–1900.

Bracton, H. de. De legibus et consuetudinibus Angliae. London. 1640. Ed. Woodbine, G. E. Haven, Conn. (Yale Hist. publ.) 1915. In progress.

Bracton's Notebook. Ed. Maitland, F. W. 3 vols. London. 1887.

Établissements de St Louis. Ed. Viollet, P. 4 vols. Soc. de l'hist. de France. 1881–6.

[Glanville, Ranulphus de.] Tractatus de legibus et consuetudinibus Regni Angliae. London. 1604. Transl. Beames, J. London. 1812.

Libri feudorum. Das Langobardische Lehnrecht. Ed Lehmann, K. Göttingen. 1896.

Placita Anglo-Normannica. Bigelow, M. M. London. 1879.

Placitorum Abbreviatio. RC. 1821.

Sachsenspiegel. Des Sachsenspiegels 1ter und 2ter Theil. Ed. Homeyer, C. G. Berlin. 1827 2nd edn. 3 vols. 1835–44. 1ter Theil. 3rd edn. 1861.

Select Charters. Ed. Stubbs, W. See Gen. Bibl. IV.

Select Passages from the works of Bracton and Azzo. Ed. Maitland, F. W. Selden Soc. Vol. 8. 1895.

Select Pleas in Manorial and other Seignorial Courts. Ed. Maitland, F. W. Selden Soc. Vol. 2. 1889.

Statutes of the Realm (1235–1713). 11 vols. RC. 1810–28. Second rev. edn. (1235–1899). 14 vols. 1888–9. Index etc. 2 vols. 1899. (15th edn.)

II. MODERN AUTHORITIES.

1. On England.

Ashley, W. J. Introduction to English Economic History and Theory. Vol. I. Pts 1, 2. London. 1888–93. Pt 1. 3rd edn. 1894.

Ballard, A. The Domesday Inquest. London. 1906.

Cunningham, W. The Growth of English Industry and Commerce during the Early and Middle Ages. 4th edn. 3 vols. Cambridge. 1905–7.

Holdsworth, W. S. History of English Law. See Gen. Bibl. V.

Maitland, F. W. Domesday Book and Beyond. Cambridge. 1897.

—— The Constitutional History of England. Cambridge. 1908.

Pollock, F. and Maitland, F. W. History of English Law. See Gen. Bibl. V.

Round, H. Feudal England. London. 1905.

Seebohm, F.   The English Village Community examined in its relation to the manorial and tribal systems.   London.   1883.   4th edn.   1890.

Stubbs, W.   Constitutional Hist. of England.   5th edn.   1896.   Vols. I and II. *See Gen. Bibl.* v.

Vinogradoff, P.   The Growth of the Manor.   London.   1905.   3rd edn.   1920.

—— Villainage in England.   Oxford.   1892.

—— English Society in the Eleventh Century.   Oxford.   1908.

2.   On France and Neighbourlands.

Brissaud, J. B. M. F.   Cours d'histoire générale du droit français, publique et privé.   Paris.   1904.   Transl. Howell, R.   Hist. of French Private Law. Boston.   1912.

Esmein, A.   Cours élémentaire d'histoire du droit français.   6th edn.   Paris.   1905.

Flach, J.   Les origines de l'ancienne France.   x^e et xie siècles.   I–III.   *See Gen. Bibl.* v.

Fustel de Coulanges.   Le bénéfice et la féodalité.   (Hist. des Institutions.)   *See Gen. Bibl.* v.

Holzmann, R.   Französische Verfassungsgeschichte von der Mitte des 9^n Jahrh. bis zur Revolution.   (Below's Handbuch.)   1910.

Luchaire, A.   Manuel des institutions françaises.   *See Gen. Bibl.* v.

Pergameni, C.   L'avouérie ecclésiastique belge.   Ghent.   1907.

Pirenne, H.   Histoire de Belgique.   I, II.   Brussels.   1909.

Seignobos, C.   Le régime féodal en Bourgogne jusqu'en 1360.   Paris.   1882.

Tanon, L.   Histoire des justices des anciennes églises et communautés monastiques de Paris.   1883.

Viollet, P.   Histoire des institutions politiques et administratives de la France. *See Gen. Bibl.* v.

—— Histoire du droit civile français etc.   *See Gen. Bibl.* v.

3.   On Germany and Neighbourlands.

Inama-Sternegg, K. v.   Deutsche Wirtschaftsgesch.   3 vols.   Leipsic.   1879–1901. Vol. I.   2nd edn.   1909.

Knapp, G. F.   Grundherrschaft und Rittergut.   Leipsic.   1897.

Kötzschke, R.   Deutsche Wirtschaftsgesch. bis zum 17 Jahrh.   Leipsic.   1908.

Lamprecht, K.   Deutsches Wirtschaftleben im Mittelalter etc.   3 vols. in 4. Leipsic.   1886.

Maurer, G. L. v.   Geschichte der Mark, Hof- Dorf- und Stadtverfassung und der öffentlichen Gewalt.   Munich.   1854.   2nd edn.   Kunow, H.   Vienna.   1896.

Mayer, E.   Deutsche u. französische Verfassungsgesch. vom 9–11 Jahrhundert. 2 vols.   Leipsic.   1399.

Meister, A.   Deutsche Verfassungsgeschichte.   Leipsic.   1907.   (Meister II, pt 3. *See Gen. Bibl.* III.)   2nd edn.   1913.

Schröder, R.   Lehrbuch der deutschen Rechtsgesch.   Leipsic.   1889.   5th edn. 1907.

Sering, M.   Agrarwesen und Erbrecht in Schleswig und Holstein.   Berlin.   1908.

Stemann, C. L. E.   Geschichte des öffentlichen und Privat-Rechts des Herzogthum Schleswig.   Copenhagen.   1866.

Waitz, G.   Deutsche Verfassungsgeschichte.   v–viii.   *See Gen. Bibl.* v.

Wittich, W.   Die Grundherrschaft in Nordwestdeutschland.   Leipsic.   1896.

4. VARIOUS.

Erslev, K. Valdemarernes Storhedstid. Studier og Omrids. (1157–1375.) Copenhagen. 1898.

Hildebrand, H. O. Sveriges Medeltid. 3 vols. in 4. Stockholm. 1879–1903.

Hinojosa, E. de. Historia general del derecho español. Vol. i. (Visigoths.) Madrid. 1887.

Meitzen, A. Ansiedelungen und Agrarwesen der Römer, Germanen, Kelten und Slaven. 4 vols. Berlin. 1896.

Modderman, A. E. J. Die Reception des römischen Rechts. Jena. 1875.

Pertile, A. Storia del diritto italiano della caduta dell' impero Romano alla codificazione. Bologna. 1868. 6 vols. Padua. 1873–87. 2nd edn. Turin, partly ed. Del Giudice, P. 1891–1902. Index, ed. Eusebio, L. Turin. 1893.

Steenstrup, J. C. H. R. Studier over Kong Valdemars Jordbog. Copenhagen. 1874.

Taranger, A. Udsigt over der Norske Rets Historie. 1898.

Vinogradoff, P. Roman Law in Medieval Europe. London and New York. 1909.

CHAPTERS XIX AND XX.

LEARNING AND LITERATURE.

I. SOURCES.

For texts of authors alluded to the main sources are:
MPL. *See Gen. Bibl.* IV.
MGH. Poetae Latini aevi Carolini I–IV, 1. Edd. Dümmler, Traube, v. Winterfeld.
See Gen. Bibl. IV.
Monumenta Moguntina, Mon. Alcuiniana, Mon. Carolina (in Bibl. rerum Germanic.
ed. Jaffé, P., vols. 3, 6, 4). Berlin. 1864–73. *See Gen. Bibl.* IV.
España Sagrada. *See Gen. Bibl.* IV.

II. MODERN WORKS.

(a) GENERAL OUTLINES.

Manitius, M. Lateinische Literatur des Mittelalters. *See Gen. Bibl.* V. Pt I. Von Justinian bis zur Mitte des 10ten Jahrhdts.
Traube, L. Vorlesungen und Abhandlungen. Vol. I. Zur Paläographie u. Handschriftenkunde. Ed. Lehmann, P. and Boll, F. Vol. II. Einleitung in die lateinische Philologie d. Mittelalters. Ed. Lehmann, P. Munich. 1909–11.
—— ' O Roma nobilis,' Philolog. Untersuchungen aus dem Mittelalter. Munich. 1891. (Abh. d. kgl. Bayr. Akad. d. Wissenschaft. I. Kl. XIX.) *Also separately.*
—— Perrona Scottorum, ein Beitrag z. Überlieferungsgesch. (Sitzungsberichte d. kgl. Bayr. Akad. d. Wissenschaft.) 1900.

(b) MONOGRAPHS ETC. *(For Chap. XIX.)*

Articles in JTS (XIII, 512 ff. and refs.) by Ramsay, R. M. L., Bright, J. W. and Douglas Bruce, J.
Atkinson, R. The Passions and Homilies from Leabhar Bréac Text, tr. and glossary. Todd lect. S. 2. I, II. London. 1885–7.
—— and Bernard, J. H. The Irish Liber Hymnorum. (Henry Bradshaw Soc. vols. XIII, XIV.) 1898.
Bannister, H. M. JTS, IX. 1908, p. 437.
Beer, R. In Wiener Studien. 1911.
Boswell, C. S. An Irish Precursor of Dante. London. 1908.
Bradshaw, H. Collected Papers. Cambridge. 1889.
Bruyne, D. de. Fragments retrouvés d'Apocryphes Priscillianistes. RBén. 1917.
Bury, J. B. Life of St Patrick and his place in History. London. 1905.
Flamion, J. Les Actes apocryphes de l'Apôtre André. 1911.
Goetz, G. and Loewe, A. G. Corpus glossariorum Latinorum. 7 vols. Leipsic. 1888 ff.
Gougaud, L. Les Chrétientés celtiques. Paris. 1911.
Haddan and Stubbs. Councils. *See Gen. Bibl.* IV.

Hellmann, S. Sedulius Scottus. In Traube-Lehmann, Quellen u. Untersuchungen z. latein. Philologie d. Mittelalters, ɪ, 1. Munich. 1906.

Maas, E. W. T. Commentariorum in Aratum reliquiae. Berlin. 1898.

Plummer, C. Vitae Sanctorum Hiberniae. 2 vols. Oxford. 1910.

Roger, M. L'Enseignement des lettres classiques d'Ausone à Alcuin. Paris. 1905.

Stokes, W. Lives of the Saints from the Book of Lismore. Oxford. 1890. (Anecdota Oxon.)

Thilo, G. and Hagen, H. Servii Grammatici quae feruntur in Vergilii carmina commentarii. 3 vols. in 4. Leipsic. 1881–1902.

Turner, C. H. Early Worcester Manuscripts. Fragments of 4 Books photographically reproduced. Oxford. 1916. (New Palaeographical Soc. pl. 158, 159.)

Virgilius Maro Grammaticus. Ed. Huemer, J. Leipsic. 1886.

—— Stangl, T. Virgiliana. Die grammatischen Schriften des Galliers Virgilius Maro...untersucht. Munich. 1891.

Zimmer, H. Westgallien und Irland. SPAW. 1909–10.

—— Pelagius in Irland. Berlin. 1901.

(For Chap. XX.)

Berger, S. Hist. de la Vulgate. Paris. 1893.

Bishop, E. Liturgica Historica. Oxford. 1918.

Gerbert (Sylvester II). Lettres de Gerbert. Ed. Havet, J. 1889. Coll. textes. See *Gen. Bibl.* ɪv.

—— Gerberti opera mathematica. Ed. Boubnov, N. Berlin. 1899.

Haupt. Analecta in Hermes. ɪɪɪ. 221.

Hellmann. *See above.*

Hrotsvitha. Ed. Strecker, K. Bibl. Script. med. aevi. Leipsic. 1906.

Keil, H. Grammatici Latini. 7 vols. and suppl. Leipsic. 1857–78.

Lapôtre, A. Le Souper de Jean Diacre (École franç. à Rome, Mélanges d'archéologie et d'histoire, Rome, 1901, p. 305).

Leo of Naples (archipresbyter of Constantinople). Ed. Landgraf, G. Erlangen. 1885.

Lindsay, W. M. Articles in Classical Quarterly and Classical Review. 1915 ff.

Merugud Uilix maicc Leirtis: the Irish Odyssey. Ed. Meyer, K. London. 1886.

Poole, R. L. Illustrations of the history of Medieval Thought and Learning. 2nd edn. London. 1920.

Rand, E. K. Johannes Scottus. In Traube-Lehmann, Quellen u. Untersuchungen z. latein. Philologie d. Mittelalters. ɪ, 2. 1907.

Ratramnus on Cynocephali. ZWT, xxɪv. 61 and MGH, Epistolae vɪ, 155.

Theodulus. Ed. Ostermacher. Urfahr-Linz. 1902.

CHAPTER XXI.

BYZANTINE AND ROMANESQUE ARTS.

GENERAL AUTHORITIES.

Ainalov, D. V.   Ellinisticheskiya osnovy vizantiyskago iskusstva.   St Petersburg. 1900.

Allen, J. R.   The Monumental History of the Early British Church.   London. 1892.

Anderson, J. E.   The Early Christian Monuments of Scotland (1892).   Ed. Allen, J. R.   Edinburgh.   1900.

Antoniades, E. M.   Ἔκφρασις τῆς Ἁγίας Σοφίας.   3 vols.   Athens.   1907–9.

Bastard, A. de.   Peintures et ornements des manuscrits.   Paris.   1832–69.

Bayet, C.   L'Art Byzantin.   2nd edn.   Paris.   1904.

Bell, G. L.   Churches and monasteries of the Ṭūr 'Abdīn etc.   (Zeitschr. f. Geschichte d. Architektur, Beiheft 9.)   Heidelberg.   1913.

Birch, W. de G.   History, Art and Palaeography of the MS styled the Utrecht Psalter.   London.   1886.

—— Latin Psalter in the Univ. Lib. of Utrecht.   London.

Boinet, A.   La miniature carolingienne.   Paris.   1913.

Brown, G. Baldwin.   The Arts in Early England.   *See Gen. Bibl.* **v.**   (Vol. 5 is on the Ruthwell and Bewcastle Crosses.)

Butler, H. Crosby.   American Archaeological Expedition to Syria, 1899–1900. Part II.   Architecture and other arts.   New York.   1903.

Cattaneo, R.   L'Architettura in Italia dal sec. VI al mille circa.   Venice.   1888. Transl. Curtis, J., Architecture in Italy etc.   1896.

Dalton, O. M.   Byzantine Art and Archaeology.   Oxford.   1911.

Dehio, G. and Bezold, G. v.   Die kirchliche Baukunst des Abendlandes.   7 vols. Stuttgart.   1884–1901.

Delisle, L.   *See* Bibliographie des Travaux de M. Léopold Delisle.   Lacombe, P. Paris.   1902.

Diehl, C.   Les mosaïques de Sainte-Sophie de Salonique (Monuments et Mémoires, AcadIBL. XVI, 1).   Paris.   1908.

—— Manuel de l'Art byzantin.   Paris.   1910.

Enlart, E.   Manuel d'Archéologie française dep. les Temps mérovingiens jusqu'à la Renaissance.   Part I.   Architecture.   2 vols.   1902–4.   2nd edn. vol. I. Paris.   1917.

George, W. S.   The Church of St Eirene at Constantinople.   (Notes etc. by van Millingen, A. and others.)   London.   (Byzantine Research Fund.)   1912.

Heissenberg, A.   Grabeskirche u. Apostelkirche.   2 pts.   Leipsic.   1908.

Humann, G.   Zur Geschichte der karolingischen Baukunst.   (Studien zur deutschen Kunstgeschichte.)   Strasbourg.   1909.

Jackson, T. G.   Byzantine and Romanesque Architecture.   London.   1921.

Kondakoff, N. P.   Histoire de l'art byzantin.   Éd. franç.   2 vols.   Paris.   1886–91.

—— (*And other works.*)

Kraus, F. X.   Geschichte des christlichen Kunst.   Vol. I and vol. II, 1te Abth. Freiburg-im-Breisgau.   1895–7.

Lasteyrie, R. de.   L'Architecture religieuse en France à l'époque romane.   Paris. 1912.

[Omont, H.] Peintures et initiales de la première Bible de Charles le Chauve. Paris. n.d.

—— Peintures et initiales de la seconde Bible de Charles le Chauve. Paris. n.d.

Porter, A. K. Mediaeval Architecture: its conditions and development. New York. 1909.

Ramsay, Sir W. and Bell, Miss G. L. The thousand and one churches. 1909.

Reber, F. v. Der karolingische Palastbau. 2 pts. (In Abhandlungen d. Akad. München.) Munich. 1891–2.

Rivoira, G. T. Le origini d' architettura lombarda e d. sue principali deriv. nei paesi d' oltr' Alpe. 2 vols. Rome. 1901–7. Transl. Rushforth, G. McN. Lombardic Architecture etc. 2 vols. London. 1910.

Rushforth, G. McN. S. Maria Antiqua. (Papers of the British School at Rome.) 1902.

Schultz, R. W. and Barnsley, S. H. The monastery of St Luke of Stiris etc. London. 1901.

Strzygowski, J. (with Crowfoot, J. W. and Smirnov, J. I.). Kleinasien, ein Neuland d. Kunstgesch. Leipsic. 1903.

—— Orient oder Rome. Beiträge zur Geschichte der spätantiken u. frühchristlichen Kunst. Leipsic. 1901.

—— (*Many other works.*)

Tafrali, O. Topographie de Thessalonique. Paris. 1913.

Texier, C. F. M. and Pullan, R. P. Byzantine Architecture. London. 1864.

Tikkanen, J. J. Die Psalterillustration im Mittelalter. Helsingfors. 1895 ff.

—— Die Genesismosaiken von S. Marco in Venedig. Helsingfors. 1899.

Uspenski, Th. I. O vnov' otkrytykh mozaikakh v tserkvi Sv. Dimitriya v Soluni (Izvêstiya russk. arkh. Instituta v Konstantinopolê, xiv). Sofia. 1909.

Van Millingen, A. (and others). Byzantine Churches in Constantinople. London. 1912.

Venturi, A. Storia dell' Arte Italiana. Milan. 7 vols. 1901–15.

Viollet-le-Duc, E. E. Dictionnaire raisonné de l'Architecture française du xi⁰ au xvi⁰ s. Paris. 1858–68. Index, Sabine, H. 1889.

Warner, G. F. and Wilson, H. A. The Benedictional of Saint Aethelwold, Bishop of Winchester 963–984. (The Roxburghe Club.) Oxford. 1910.

Wilpert, J. Die römische Mosaiken u. Malereien der kirchlichen Bauten v. 4 bis 13 Jhdt. 2nd edn. 4 vols. Freiburg-im-Breisgau. 1917.

Wulff, O. Altchristliche u. byzantinische Kunst. i. Berlin-Neubabelsberg. 1918.

Zimmermann, E. H. Die Buchmalerei in karolingischer u. ottonischer Zeit. (K.K. Zentral-Kommission f. Kunst- u. historisch. Denkmäle.) Vienna. 1910.

CHRONOLOGICAL TABLE

OF

LEADING EVENTS MENTIONED IN THIS VOLUME

463 Death of St Patrick.
c. 490–583 Cassiodorus.
576–636 Isidore of Seville.
594 Death of Gregory of Tours.
597 Death of Columba.
    Augustine's mission in Kent.
604 Death of St Gregory the Great.
615 Death of Columban.
690 Death of Benedict Biscop.
704 Death of Adamnan.
709 Death of Aldhelm.
732 Victory of Charles Martel over the Saracens at Poitiers.
735 Death of Bede (most probable date).
756 'Abd-ar-Raḥmān ibn Mu'āwiya, emir of Spain.
c. 787 First landing of the Vikings in England.
796 Death of Offa of Mercia.
c. 800 The invasions of the Northmen begin.
802–825 The Northmen establish themselves in Ireland.
802–839 Reign of Ecgbert as king of Wessex.
804 Death of Alcuin.
814–840 Reign of Louis the Pious.
817 *Divisio Imperii.*
822 Death of St Benedict of Aniane.
824 Promulgation of the *Constitutio Romana.*
825 Conquest of Cornwall by Ecgbert.
    Collapse of Mercia.
826 St Anskar's first mission to Scandinavia.
827–831 Saracen conquest of Sicily.
833 The Field of Lies.
834 The Norsemen attack the Frankish Empire in force.
835 Resumption of Viking raids upon England.
840 Death of Einhard.
840–855 Reign of Lothar I.
840–876 Reign of Louis the German.
840–877 Reign of Charles the Bald.
841 Battle of Fontenoy (25 June).
841–891 Height of the Viking invasions.
842 Oath of Strasbourg (14 Feb.).
843 Sack of St Peter's at Rome by the Saracens.
    Treaty of Verdun (Aug.). Division of the Frankish Empire.
844–860 Kenneth Mac Alpin of Scotland

845–882 Hincmar, archbishop of Rheims.
847 Pope Leo IV walls the Leonine City.
c. 850 Pseudo-Isidorian Decretals.
  Rurik, the Scandinavian, of Russia.
851 The Danes first winter in Thanet.
855 Death of the Emperor Lothar I and division of his lands.
855–869 Reign of Lothar II in Lorraine.
855–875 Reign of the Emperor Louis II in Italy.
856 Death of Raban Maur.
857 Photius, Patriarch of Constantinople.
858–867 Pope Nicholas I.
859–862 Second expedition of the Norsemen to Spain and the Mediter-
    ranean.
864 St Cyril and St Methodius among the Moravians.
867 Schism of East and West in the affair of Photius.
868 Death of Ratramn.
869 Death of Lothar II (8 Aug.).
  Charles the Bald crowned king of Lorraine (6 Oct.).
  Martyrdom of St Edmund.
c. 870 Harold Fairhair founds the kingdom of Norway.
870 Submission of East Anglia to the Northmen.
  Partition of Lorraine at Meersen (8 Aug.).
871 Battle of Ashdown.
871–899 Reign of Alfred the Great.
872–882 Pope John VIII.
874 The Norse begin to settle in Iceland.
875 Death of the Emperor Louis II (12 Aug.).
  Imperial Coronation of Charles the Bald (25 Dec.).
876 Death of Louis the German (28 Aug.).
  Colonisation of Northumbria by the Danes.
877 Settlement of the Five Boroughs.
  Assembly of Quierzy (14 June).
  Death of Charles the Bald (6 Oct.).
878 Battle of Edington.
  Peace between Alfred and Guthrum at Chippenham (the so-called
    Treaty of Wedmore).
879–887 Boso, king of Provence.
880 Treaty of Ribemont (all Lorraine ceded to Germany).
c. 880 Death of John Scottus (Erigena).
881–887 Charles the Fat as Emperor.
882 Death of Hincmar, archbishop of Rheims (21 Dec.).
  Murder of Pope John VIII. Triumph of Roman nobles.
884 Union of the Frankish kingdoms under the Emperor Charles the
    Fat.
885 Recapture of London by Alfred, and Alfred and Guthrum's Peace.
885–887 The Northmen besiege Paris.
887 Final disruption of the Empire of Charles the Great.
887–899 Arnulf, king of Germany.
888–898 Odo, king of France.
888–911 or 912 Rodolph I, king of Jurane Burgundy.
c. 890 The Saracens seize Fraxinetum.
891 King Arnulf defeats the Northmen near Louvain.
895 The Magyars settle in Hungary.
896 Arnulf crowned Emperor.

898–923 Reign of Charles the Simple of France.
899–911 Reign of Louis the Child of Germany.
899–925 Reign of Edward the Elder.
900 The Hungarian ravages begin.
901 Louis (the Blind), now king of Italy, receives the Imperial Crown.
910 Foundation of Cluny.
911–918 Conrad I of Germany.
911 Convention of St Clair-sur-Epte, and definitive establishment of the Northmen in France.
    Beginning of the reconquest of the Danelaw.
    Charles the Simple gains Lorraine.
912–919 Aethelfleda, Lady of the Mercians.
914–929 Pope John X.
915 Defeat of the Saracens at the Garigliano.
919–938 Henry I (the Fowler), king of Germany.
922 Revolt of France from the Carolingians.
925–939 Reign of Aethelstan.
925 Lorraine finally united to Germany.
926–945 Reign of Hugh of Provence in Italy (d. 948).
927–941 Odo, abbot of Cluny.
928–936 St Wenceslas (Václav), duke of Bohemia.
929 Death of Charles the Simple.
    'Abd-ar-Raḥmān III declares himself Caliph in Spain.
c. 931–933 Treaty for the union of Burgundy and Provence.
932–954 Alberic, ruler of Rome.
933 Defeat of the Hungarians at Riade (15 Mar.).
935 Death of Gorm the Old, king of Denmark.
935–970 Fernan Gonzalez, count of Castile.
936 Carolingian Restoration (Louis d'Outremer) in France.
936–973 Reign of Otto the Great.
937 Battle of Brunanburh.
939 Rebellion of the German dukes.
939–946 Reign of Edmund of England.
943 Dunstan made abbot of Glastonbury.
946–955 Reign of Eadred of England.
947 The Kalbite dynasty of Sicily founded.
950 Berengar II crowned king of Italy.
951–952 First expedition of Otto the Great to Italy.
953–954 Second rebellion of the German dukes.
954 England under one king.
954–994 Maiolus, abbot of Cluny.
954–986 Reign of Lothair in France.
955 Defeat of the Hungarians in the Lechfeld (10 Aug.).
955–963(4) John XII (Octavian), Pope.
959–975 Reign of Edgar the Peaceable of England.
960 Final establishment of Otto's rule in Germany.
960–988 Dunstan, archbishop of Canterbury.
961–964 Otto's second expedition to Italy.
962 Otto the Great, Emperor of the West.
963 Deposition of Pope John XII (4 Dec.), and election of Leo VIII, the Emperor's nominee.
966–972 Otto's third expedition to Italy.
968 Adalbert, first archbishop of Magdeburg, appointed.
969 Conquest of Egypt by the Fatimites.

970–1035 Sancho the Great, king of Navarre.
972 Marriage of Otto II and Theophano.
  Capture of Frainet (Fraxinetum).
973–983 Otto II, Emperor of the West.
975–978 Reign of Edward the Martyr of England.
977 War of the three Henries.
978–1002 Almanzor, prime minister in Spain.
978–1016 Reign of Aethelred the Unready.
980 Renewal of Scandinavian invasions of England.
c. 980–1040 *Peace of God.*
982 Otto II defeated by the Saracens. Revolt of the Wends from Germany.
983 Otto II nominates a Lombard Pope (John XIV), the first to take a papal name.
983–991 Regency of Theophano.
983–1002 Otto III, Emperor of the West.
985–996(8) Crescentius II, patrician of Rome.
987–996 Hugh Capet, king of France.
c. 989 Vladímir of Russia becomes Christian.
991–1009 Peter Orseolo II, doge of Venice.
992–1025 Boleslav (Boleslaw) Chrobry, duke of Poland.
994–1049 Odilo, abbot of Cluny.
996 Otto III nominates a German Pope (Gregory V).
996–1037 Reign of Robert the Pious of France.
999 Otto III nominates a French Pope (Sylvester II).
1000 The Hungarians become Christian under St Stephen.
  Foundation of the archbishopric of Gnesen for Poland.
1000–1025 Burchard, bishop of Worms, canonist.
1001 St Stephen crowned king of Hungary.
  Foundation of the archbishopric of Gran for Hungary.
1002 Death of the Emperor Otto III (23 Jan.).
  Massacre of St Brice's Day.
  Saracens defeated at Bari by the Venetians.
1002–1012 John Crescentius (III), patrician of Rome.
1002–1014 Reign of Ardoin of Ivrea in Italy.
1002–1024 Reign of Henry II, Emperor of the West.
1003 Death of Pope Sylvester II (Gerbert).
1004 Henry II crowned king of the Lombards at Pavia.
  Richard, abbot of St Vannes.
1007 Establishment of the see of Bamberg.
1007–1029 Fulbert, bishop of Chartres.
1012 Murder of Archbishop Alphege (Aelfheah).
1012–1024 Benedict VIII (of Tusculum), Pope.
1012–1044 Counts of Tusculum supreme in Rome.
1013 Triumph of Svein in England.
1014 Death of Svein (Feb.).
  Imperial coronation of Henry II at Rome.
  Defeat of the Vikings at Clontarf by Brian Boru.
1016 Death of Edmund Ironside.
  Revolt of Melo in Apulia.
1017–1035 Reign of King Knut the Great.
1018 Treaty of Bautzen.
1024 Death of Pope Benedict VIII.
  Death of Henry II.

1024–1039 Reign of Conrad II the Salic.
1027 Conrad II crowned Emperor at Rome.
1030 Ranulf becomes count of Aversa.
1031 Abolition of the Caliphate in Spain.
1031–1060 Reign of Henry I of France.
1032 Death of Rodolph III of Burgundy.
Ferdinand I, first king of Castile.
1033–1034 Acquisition of Burgundy by Conrad II.
1034–1058 Reign of Casimir I of Poland.
1035 Foundation of the State of Aragon by Ramiro I Sanchez.
1035–1076 Raymond-Berengar I of Barcelona.
1037 Conrad's *Constitutio de feudis* for Italy.
1037–1055 Břatislav I, duke of Bohemia.
1038 (?) Conrad II declares Roman Law the territorial law of Rome.
1038 Death of St Stephen of Hungary.
1039 Death of Conrad II (4 June), and accession of Henry III as king of Germany, Italy, and Burgundy.
Beginning of the *Truce of God.*
1042 Accession of Edward the Confessor.
1042–1048 Wazo, bishop of Liège.
1043 The "Day of Indulgence."
William de Hauteville, count of Apulia.
1046 Henry III's coronation as Emperor; he reforms the Papacy. Synod of Sutri.
1046–1047 Pope Clement II (Suidger of Bamberg).
1049 Death of Odilo, abbot of Cluny.
1049–1054 Pope Leo IX (Bruno of Toul).
1053 Battle of Civitate.
Death of Earl Godwin.
1054 Battle of Dunsinane.
Schism of East and West.
1055–1057 Pope Victor II.
1056 Death of Henry III and succession of Henry IV.
1060–1108 Reign of Philip I of France.
1066 Death of Edward the Confessor.
1079 First Norse king of the Isle of Man.

NOTE

For the transliteration of Slavonic names there has been adopted the scheme given in the *Proceedings of the British Academy,* Vol. VIII; for Oriental names that used in the publications of the Royal Asiatic Society.

INDEX

Aar, river, 26, and Burgundy, 136, 180 *note*

Aargau, seized by Rodolph II, 136

Aarhus, see of, founded, 192

Abacus, revived by Gerbert, 536

Abbasid Caliphs, 413, 419; in Africa, 410, 413

Abbo of St Germain, 497, 529

'Abdallāh, becomes Emir of Spain, 418 sq.; 420; 433

'Abdallāh, son of Ṭarūb, 416

'Abd-al-Malik, Governor of Spain, 409

'Abd-ar-Raḥmān, Emir of Spain, 409

'Abd-ar-Raḥmān I, ibn Mu'āwiya, Emir of Spain, early life of, 410; enters Spain, 411; becomes Emir, 412 sq.; 415; independent of the Caliphate of Bagdad, 430; builds a mosque at Cordova, 432, 436

'Abd-ar-Raḥmān II, Emir of Spain; as prince, 414; reign of, 415 sqq.; the Spanish March and, 8; the Vikings and, 317, 416; social conditions under, 429, 432

'Abd-ar-Raḥmān III, Emir of Spain; and the Spanish party, 419 sqq.; takes the title of Caliph, 421; wars with Leon, 420 sqq.; with Navarre, 421; African policy, 421 sqq.; character and death of, 423; library of, 435; trade and society under, 428, 431 sq.

'Abd-ar-Raḥmān, son of Ḥakam II, 424

'Abd-ar-Raḥmān, son of Ibn Hajjāj, 419

'Abd-ar-Raḥmān, "Sanchuelo," 427

Abdias, Apostolic History of, 497

Aberffraw, 342

Abingdon, abbey at, 374, 404; abbots of, *see* Aethelwold, Siward, Spearhafoc

Abotrites. *See* Obotrites

Abraham, Bishop of Freising, imprisoned, 205; 218

Abraham, Testament of, 505

Abruzzans, the, 155

Abruzzi, the, bishopric in, 166; Paldolf of Capua in, 268

Abū Ḥafṣ Omar al-Ballutī, 415

Abulaz. *See* Ḥakam I

Abu'l-Kāsim, Sicilian emir, 169, 176

Abū-l-Khaṭṭār, Governor of Spain, 409

Abu-Marwān, at Saragossa, 8

Abū-ṣ-Ṣabbāḥ, cited, 412 *note*

Abu Yazīd, Berber chief, 422

Acca, cross of, 555

Acircius, identified, 493 *note*

Acqui, 240; see of, 175

Adalard, Abbot of Corbie, 2, 12

Adalard, Abbot of Saint-Bertin, 35 sqq.

Adalard, Bishop of Reggio, 158

Adalard, Bishop of Verona, aids Louis (the Blind), 149

Adalard, Count Palatine, 3

Adalbero, Archbishop of Rheims, 80, 209; charged with treason, 81 sqq.; correspondence of, 81; 536; death of, 99

Adalbero, Archbishop of Trèves, 238, 248

Adalbero, Bishop of Laon. *See* Asselin

Adalbero, Bishop of Metz, 197; 200

Adalbero (III), Bishop of Metz, 293

Adalbero, Bishop of Verdun, 209 sq.

Adalbero of Eppenstein, Bishop of Bamberg, 297

Adalbero of Eppenstein, Duke of Carinthia; made Duke, 239, 249, 253; deposed, 269 sq., 274; death of, 277; 297

Adalbert, King of Italy, 158; submits to Otto I, 159, 195; wars with Otto I, 160 sqq.; escapes to the Saracens, 162; leads revolt, 166 sq.; death of, 167; 201; 247

Adalbert, Provost of Halberstadt, made Archbishop of Bremen, 289 sq.; declines Papacy, 291; Duke Bernard and, 293 sq., 305; negotiates treaty with Svein, 294; strained relations with Svein, 296 sq.; ecclesiastical ambitions of, 297, 305 sq.

Adalbert, monk, missionary to Russia, 201 sq.; Archbishop of Magdeburg, 202

Adalbert, Archbishop of Ravenna, 242 sq.

Adalbert, St, Bishop of Prague, xvi sq.; 173; 300

Adalbert, Duke of Upper Lorraine, 293 sq.

Adalbert I, Duke (Marquess) of Tuscany, 48; war with John VIII, 55 sq.

Adalbert II, the Rich, Marquess of Tuscany, submits to Emperor Guy, 65; plots against Berengar I, 148 sq.; Sergius III and, 151

Adalbert, Marquess of Ivrea, 148; and Rodolph II, 136, 152 sq.; 157

Adalbert-Atto, of Canossa; and Queen Adelaide, 158 sq.; Count of Modena and Reggio, 163

Adalbert of Babenberg, 68

Adalbert, of Babenberg, Margrave of Austria, 295; 298; 303

Adalbert, veteran of Charles the Great, 530

Adalbold, Bishop of Utrecht, 249

Adalman, contests see of Milan, 158; resigns, 160

Adam, Life of, 506

Adamnan, Abbot of Hy (Iona), *Life of Columba* by, 504, 507; 506

Adamnan, Vision of, 505
Adananus. *See* Adamnan
Adela, wife of Baldwin of Lille, Count of Flanders, 111
Adelaide, Empress, marries Lothar II, King of Italy, 140, 156, 158, 194; marries Emperor Otto I, 140 sq., 159, 162, 195, 205 *note*; Otto II and, 168, 207, 209; Otto III and, 171, 210 sq.; sole regent, 211; Bavarian family and, 205; retires from court, 207; her party, 205, 209; regent in Italy, 209; death of, 141, 143 *note*; 174
Adelaide, wife of Louis II the Stammerer, 57, 77 *note*
Adelaide, wife of Louis V, 91
Adelaide, Abbess of Quedlinburg, 276, 290; Abbess of Gandersheim, 287
Adelaide, daughter of Henry III, Abbess of Quedlinburg, 276
Adelaide of Anjou, 104
Adelaide of Turin, marries Herman of Swabia, 265; marries Otto of Savoy, 299
Adelaide, heiress of Vermandois, 116 *note*
Adelchis, Prince of Benevento, 46, 50
Adelelmus. *See* Aldhelm
Adémar of Chabannes, cited, 129
Ademar, Marquess of Spoleto, made Prince of Capua, 176
Adige, river, Henry II checked at, 224
Adoptionism, heresy, 516, 523, 532 sq.
Adso, Abbot of Montièrender, 536
Aedh Finnliath (Mac-Niall), King of Ireland, 317
Aegilwi, mother of Judith, 13
Aelfgar, Earl of East Anglia, 394 sq.; allies with the Welsh, 396; Earl of Mercia, 397
Aelfgifu of Northampton, 386, 388 sq.
Aelfheah (Alphege), Archbishop of Canterbury, murder of, 331, 383; 388
Aelfheah, Bishop of Winchester, 373 sq.
Aelfhere, 378 sq., 382
Aelfric, Archbishop elect of Canterbury, 393
Aelfric, Abbot of Eynsham, 488, 537
Aelfthryth, 378 and *note*, 379
Aelle, King of Northumbria, 319, 350 sq.
Aeneas of Paris, 533
Aesop, fables of, in Ireland, 503
Aethelbald, King of Wessex, revolts from his father, 349 sq.; disastrous reign, 350
Aethelbert, King of Wessex, 350
Aethelfleda, Lady of the Mercians; marries Aethelred, 359; wars with Danes and Welsh, 363 sq.; 323; death of, 364; 365; 373
Aethelheard, Archbishop of Canterbury, 343
Aethelhelm, attacks Edward the Elder, 360
Aethelmund, 344
Aethelnoth, alderman, 355
Aethelnoth, Archbishop of Canterbury, 387, 389
Aethelred I, King of Wessex, 350; and Vikings in Mercia, 351; 319; at battle of Ashdown, 352
Aethelred II, King of England; birth of, 378; minority of, 379 sq.; buys off the Danes,

381 sq.; 324; massacre of St Brice's Day, 382; 325; flight to Normandy, 383; return of, 384; death of, 385; laws of, 338
Aethelred of Gloucester, Duke of Mercia; allies with Alfred, 356 sqq.; receives land ceded by Guthrum, 359; and Aethelwald's rising, 361; war with Welsh and Danes, 362 sq.; founds Gloucester Abbey, 373; death of, 363
Aethelred, King of Northumbria, 341
Aethelred Mucel, 352
Aethelstan, ruler of East Anglia, 346
Aethelstan, King of Wessex; in Mercia, 363; wars of, 366; 323; reforms of, 366 sqq.; 77, 83; 183
Aethelstan Half-King, Duke of East Anglia; 370; 378 *note*; Edgar's revolt, 372; founds Ramsey Abbey, 375
Aethelwald, attacks Edward the Elder, 360 sq.
Aethelweard, Fabius, cited, 355, 529
Aethelweard, of West Wessex, 387
Aethelwin, Duke of East Anglia, 375, 379
Aethelwold, Abbot of Abingdon; made Bishop of Winchester, 374; monastic reforms of, 374 sq.; translates rule of St Benedict, 375, 377; obtains church franchises, 376 sqq.; death of, 379
Aethelwulf, son of Ecgbert, King of Wessex, 352; subdues Kent, 345 sq.; becomes King, 347 sq.; his Donation, 348 sq.; visits Rome, 349; death of, 350; 39
Aethicus Ister, *Cosmography* of, 500
Africa, 'Abd-ar-Rahmān I in, 410 sq.; Fātimite Caliphate in, 419, 424, 431; 'Abd-ar-Rahmān III and, 421 sq.; learning and letters in, 488 sq.; art and architecture in, 539, 547, 552; trade with, 433
Agapetus I, Pope, 486
Agapetus II, Pope, obstructs Otto I, 159; dies, 161; 194 sq.; 202
Ageltrude, Empress, 65 sqq., 149, 454
Aghlabid dynasty, the, of Kairawān, 149 sq.
Agius, biographer of Hathumoda, 529 sq.
Agnellus, biographer, 534
Agnes of Poitou, Empress; 287, 292; early life of, 283 sq.; marries Henry III, 275, 280, 291, 306; Burgundy and, 146
Agnes, wife of Geoffrey Martel, 283
Agnes of Weimar, 290
Agobard, Archbishop of Lyons, partisan of Lothar, 17, 19, 448; deposed, 20, 450; writings of, 520; cited, 9 sq.; 12
Agoût, river, the, 31
Aguilar. *See* Polei
Ahmad ibn Maslama, Governor of Seville, 420
Ahmad ibn Mu'āwiya, claims to be the Mahdi, 420
Aidan, St, shrine of, 354
Ailbe, Irish saint, 501; life of, 505
Aileran the Wise, 507
Ailisios, architect, 547
Aimé of Monte Cassino, cited,
Aimeri of Courron, 119
Ainsa, 410
Aire, river, 370

A'isha, 435
Aisne, battle of the, 208
Aistulf, King of the Lombards, 454
Aix-la-Chapelle, burnt by Danes, 59; captured by Lothair, 80, 207; assemblies at (814) 3; 2; (817) 6, 9 sqq.; (831) 15 sq.; (836) 20; (837) 21; (860) 39; (861) 40, 42; Judith at, 14; 19, 25, 28, 52, 68; Otto I crowned at, 187 sq.; 195; Otto II crowned at, 201, 204; Otto III crowned at, 209; Otto III buried at, 214, 216; Henry II acknowledged at, 218; Dukes of Lorraine submit at, 257; Henry III crowned at, 269, 273, 287; 275, 278; Godfrey of Lorraine deposed at, 286; Godfrey of Lorraine restored at, 289; Henry IV crowned at, 298; Charlemagne's brazen eagle at, 207 *note*; his palatine church at, 557, 560 sqq., 567; his tomb at, 213 sq.; bronzes at, 559; Theodoric's statue at, 522
'Akabat-al-bakar, battle of, 427
Alan Fergent, Duke of Brittany, 128
Alanje, 421
Albano, Bishop of. *See* Richard
Albdann. *See* Halfdanr.
Alberada, ancestress of Agnes of Poitou, 283 *note* 2
Alberic, Marquess of Spoleto, 151 sq., 153 sq.
Alberic, Senator of the Romans, rules in Rome, 154 sq.; opposes Otto I, 159; death of, 161; 166, 168, 171, 178, 455
Albert I, Count of Vermandois, 83
Albizo, aids Aribert of Milan's escape, 266
Albrand, Archbishop of Bremen, 305
Alchfrid, son of Oswy, 555
Alcuin, 514 sq., 520; works of, 516; letters of, 343, 515; opposes Adoptionism, 523, 532; and images, 533; 488, 514 sqq., 520, 556
Alda, wife of Alberic of Rome, 155
Aldfrid, King of Northumbria, 493, 510 *note*
Aldhelm, Bishop of Sherborne, 488, 493 sq., 499, 510 sqq., 515, 524
Aldhun, Bishop of Durham, 560
Aldric, Bishop of Le Mans, 18
Alemannia, given to Charles the Bald, 13, 16; invaded, 16; 21; given to Charles the Fat, 51; ravaged by Hungarians, 69; 134; counts of, *see* Conrad, Henry; *see also* Swabia
Aleram, Count, 157
Aleramids, the, 240, 244, 264
Alet, 128
Alexander, St, translation of, 533
Alexander the Great, letters to Dindimus, 516; romance of, 528; letter to Aristotle, 535
Alexander III, Pope, 399
Alexandria; architectural influence of, 539, 541 sq., 549, 551, 558, 566; Convent of St Menas near, 547; ivory carving of, 548, 550, 555; painting and decoration of, 549 sq., 558 sq.; learning at, 486; Bedouins at, 415; patriarch of, *see* Eulogius
Alfonso I, the Catholic, King of the Asturias, 410, 420

Alfonso III, King of Leon, 420
Alfonso IV, King of Leon, 421
Alfonso V, King of Leon, 427 sq.
Alfred, King of Wessex, 348; visits Leo IV, 349; at battle of Ashdown, 352; accession of, 352; wars with Guthrum, 183, 319, 329, 355 sq.; 358; reforms in Wessex, 357 sq.; "Alfred and Guthrum's Peace," 359, 361; builds Athelney church, 560; death of, 360; will of, cited, 345; memorial minster to, 361, 373; literary work of, 535, 537; revival of learning under, 514; Asser's life of, 534; house of, 399; 323; 338; 404; 488
Alfred, son of Aethelred, 386; murdered, 389 sq.; 393
Algarve. *See* Ocsonoba
Algeciras, 416
Algiers, 421
Alhandega, battle of, 422 sq.
Ali, 413
'Alkama, 410
Aller, Guthrum baptised at, 356
Allstedt, Italian envoys at, 246; 249; 278
Alluyes, rebellion of lord of, 119
Al-Makkarī, cited, 432
Almanzor (Mahomet ibn Abī-'Āmir), vizier in Spain, 424; invades Leon, 425 sq.; 427; 428; reorganises the army, 431; death of, 426; 435
Almería, 422, 431 sq.
Almuñecar, 411
Aloara, wife of Paldolf Ironhead, 170 sq.
Alost, district of, and Flanders, 122
Alpaïs, daughter of Louis I, 3
Alpert, chronicler, 142 *note*
Alphege. *See* Aelfheah
Alphonse-Jourdain, Count of Toulouse, 130
Alps, the, 11, 20 sq.; Saracens in, 152, 155; 161; Saracens driven from, 168; Otto I crosses, 194 sq.; 240, 264 sq.
Alric, Bishop of Asti, 246
Alsace, given to Charles the Bald, 13; 18; given to Louis the German, 18; invaded by Hungarians, 69, 87; surrendered by Rodolph I of Burgundy, 135; invaded by Ernest of Swabia, 257; counts of, *see* Gerard
Altaich, abbey, 236; annals of, 295, 304; abbot of, *see* Godehard
Alt-Bunzlau, murder of Wenceslas at, 192
Altitonantis, land-book, 377
Altsig of York, 522
Altus prosātor, hymn, 502, 506
Alvaro, 416 sq.; 438
Alveston, 406
Amalfi, independence of, 150; 169; duke of, *see* Manso III
Amboise, lords of. *See* Hugh, Sulpicius
Ambrières, siege of, 110
Amhlaeibh. *See* Olaf the White
Amiénois, the, 16
Amiens, captured by Vikings, 59 sq., 85, 88; treaty of, 57; MSS. at, 521
Ammianus Marcellinus, *History* of, 508; 520

Amounderness, 370

Ampurias, county of, 90

'Amrūs, Governor of Toledo, 414

Anagni, Bishop of. *See* Zachary

Anastasius the Librarian, 525, 528, 531, 534

Ancona, pillaged by Saracens, 49; march of, 462

Andalusia, 411, 423

Andernach, 52, 190

Andover, 381

Andreas, 537

Andrew, King of Hungary, 293; makes peace, 295, 297, 303 sq.; relations with the Pope, 296

Andrew, Duke of Naples, 48

Andrew, St, Acts of, 496, 533

Andrew, St, Miracles of, 496 sq.

Andújar, 417

Angelomus of Luxeuil, 532

Angers, 76; Louis I at, 9; 12; Vikings at, 33, 87; relations to Anjou, 125 sqq.; church at, 562

Angilbert (Homer), Abbot of St Riquier, 25, 517, 519, 534

Anglesey. *See* Môn

Anglo-Saxon Chronicle, set on foot, 358; put into Latin, 529; cited, 365

Angoulême, independence of, 97; and Aquitaine, 129; bishop of, *see* Gerard

Angoumois, the, 31

Anjou, independence of, 95; growth of, 107 sqq., 118-20, 125-7; counts of, *see* Fulk, Geoffrey

Anlaf (? Olaf Guðfriðson), 323

Anlaf Guthfrithson. *See* Olaf Guðfriðson

Anna, wife of Louis of Provence, 149

Annales Cambriae, cited, 341

Annals of the Four Masters, cited, 513

Annals of Ulster, cited, 352

Anno, Archbishop of Cologne, 299

Anscar, Marquess of Ivrea, 65 sq.

Anscar, Marquess of Spoleto, 157

Ansegis, Archbishop of Sens, 51, 53

Anselm, Archbishop of Canterbury, 124; 525

Anselm, Archbishop of Milan, 11

Ansgarde, wife of Louis the Stammerer, 57, 77 *note*

Anskar, 6; Archbishop of Hamburg, 314; Bishop of Bremen, *ib.*; *Life* of, 534

Anthemius of Tralles, 545

Anthony, Russian pilgrim, 546

Antioch, Academy at, 486

Antwerp, March of, 287. *See* Baldwin, Marquess of

Antwerp, siege of, 299; sacked by Vikings, 316, 347

Anulo (Óli), "nepos" to Heriolbus, King of Denmark, 313

Anund Jacob, King of Sweden, 333

Anwind, Viking leader, 353

Aosta, pass of, 11; pilgrim route to, 136; 156, 168 *note*. *See* Humbert, Count of

Apennines, the, 161; Berengar II in, 162 sq.; 240

Apocalypse, of St John, Beatus's commentary of, 523

Apocalypses, used by Irish writers, 504 sqq.; used in Africa, 488; used in Spain, 494

Apocrypha, used by Irish writers, 504 sqq.; used by Hrotsvitha, 532. *See also* Apocalypses

Apollonius of Tyre, 538

Appledore, 359

Apuleius, 488

Apuleius, medical writer 535

Apulia, and the theme of Longobardia, 150; and the Saracens, 151, 176; and the Byzantine Empire, 152, 155, 166 sq., 169; 250, 292; duke of, *see* Melo; *see also* Longobardia

Aqua Portora, 409

Aquileia, Hungarians defeated in, 195; March of, added to Bavaria, 196; patriarch of, 238, 265, *and see* Poppo

Aquitaine, 1; assigned to Pepin, 3, 10, 16; expedition against, 17; assigned to Charles the Bald, *ib.*, 21, 23, 24; 27; revolts in, 31 sqq.; assigned to Charles the Young, 34; given to Carloman, 57; 76; Hugh Capet and, 83; pillaged by Northmen, 86 sqq., 316, 320; independence of, 91, 97, 128-30; "Truce of God" in, 281, 457; land tenure in, 459 sq.; kings of, *see* Charles, Louis, Pepin; dukes of, 468; *see* Guy-Geoffrey, William

A'rābī the Kalbite, Governor of Barcelona, 413

Arabic influence on Virgilius Maro Grammaticus, 498 *note*

Arabic numerals, used by Gerbert, 536

Arabs, ch. XVI, and Louis I, 6; and Eastern art, 551; and Western art, 565; *see also* Saracens

Aragon, 410, 417, 428, 433; institutions of, 430, 441, 460; kings of, *see* Ramiro, Sancho

Arator, poet, 516

Aratus, *Phaenomena* of, 497

Archibald, Archbishop of Tours, 103

Archidona, 412, 419

Architecture, ch. XXI

Architecture, Byzantine, development of, from Roman, 539; tradition of, 543, 550 sq.; under Justinian, 544 sqq.; Eastern influences in, 541 sq., 547; influence of, upon Romanesque, 553 sqq., 557 sq., 560, 562; influence of, upon Gothic, 560, 565

Architecture, Gothic, rise of, in France, 559, 562; rise of, in Italy and Germany, 560; ground plan in, 563; characteristics of, 563 sqq.

Architecture, Greek, in Alexandria, 541; Gothic cusping and, 565

Architecture, Hispano-Arabic, 436

Architecture, Norman, 561; in England, 562 sqq., 567

Architecture, Roman, 551, 553; development of, into Byzantine, 539, 550; into Romanesque, 556 sq., 565

Architecture, Romanesque; in Western Europe, 552 sq., 556 sqq.; influence on Gothic, 563 sq.

Arculf, pilgrimage of, 507, 544

Ardennes, the, 78, 122; count of, *see* Godfrey

Arderic, Archbishop of Milan, 157

Ardoin, Marquess of Ivrea, King of Lombardy, revolts, 175 sq.; King of Lombardy, 177, 220; his party, 221, 240; first war with Henry II, 222, 224, 239; attacks Lombard bishops, 240, 244 sq.; second war with Henry II, 242, 244; death of, 245; sons of, 246

Ardoin Glabrio, Count (Marquess) of Turin, 157 sq.; defeats the Saracens, 168

Arezzo, Bishop of. *See* John

Argentea, 420 sq.

Argenteuil, 2; Viking defeat at, 93

Arians, 489

Aribert, presbyter of Milan, 246; Archbishop of Milan, 251, 259; supports Conrad II, 264; his ambitions, 265 sq.; deposed by Conrad II, 267, 277; excommunicated, 267; reconciled to Henry III, 277; death of, 291

Aribo, Archbishop of Mayence, 250 sq.; supporter of Conrad II, 254 sq.; Arch-chancellor of Italy and of Germany, 255

Ari Fróði, cited, 317

Aristotle, 535

Aristotle, Grammar of, 515

Arles, kingdom of, and the Empire, 147; counts of, *see* Fulcrad, William; archbishops of, 282; *see* Manasse; art and architecture in, 553, 557

Arles-sur-Tech, Vikings at, 320

Armagh, abbacy of, usurped by Turgeis, 317; 330

Armengol, Count of Urgel, 427

Armenia, architecture in, 547

Armorica, Celtic population of, 128

Arnold, Archbishop of Ravenna, 242 sq.

Arnold I, Count of Flanders, 92, 189

Arnold II, Count of Flanders, 93

Arnold of Lambach, given the Carinthian Mark, 270 *note* 1

Arnold, vassal of Thietmar, 293

Arnstadt, diet of (954), 199

Arnulf, Emperor, Duke of Carinthia, 58 sq.; proclaimed King of Germany, 62 sqq., 71 sq.; war with Moravia, 64 sqq.; invades Italy, crowned Emperor, 66, 454; Rodolph I of Burgundy, 135; defeats the Vikings, 322; death of, 68; 164

Arnulf the Bad, Duke of Bavaria, 69 sq., 205 *note*; defeated in the Veneto, 156; Henry the Fowler and, 180, 184; Otto I and, 187; death of, 188

Arnulf, Archbishop of Milan, 245 sq.

Arnulf, Archbishop of Rheims, 99; imprisoned, 100; abdicates, 101 sq., 211, 455; restored, 103 sq.

Arnulf, Bishop of Orleans, 101, 455

Arnulf, Count in Lorraine, 64

Arnulf, son of Arnulf the Bad, Count palatine in Bavaria, 188

Aroche, mines at, 432

Arrabal del Sur, 415

Arras, burnt by Northmen, 88; added to Flanders, 92; recaptured, *ib.*

Arsenal Library, Paris, MS. in, 526

Arsenius, Bishop of Orta, 42

Art, ch. XXI; in the Eastern Empire, 538 sqq.; in the West, 551 sqq.; in Muslim Spain, 436 sq. *See* Architecture, Mosaic, Illuminated MSS.

Artaud (Artald), Archbishop of Rheims, 76 sqq.; 194

Artois, seized by Baldwin II, 92

Arzilla, Viking raid on, 317

Ashdown, Battle of, 352

Ashington, 385

Asia Minor, architecture in, 539, 541, 545 sqq.

Askol'd (Höskuldr), in Kiev, 327

Asselin (Adalbero), Bishop of Laon, 100 sqq., 102, 104 sq.

Asser, Bishop of Sherborne, 358; 361; chronicler, cited, 349; biographer of Alfred, cited, 352, 534

Assize of the Forest, 471

Asti, city of, 165; bishop of, *see* Alric

Astorga, siege of, 425

"Astronomus," life of Louis the Pious by, 534

Asturias, Visigoths in, 409 sq.; 431; 438; kings of, *see* Alfonso, Pelayo

Asturica, Bishop of. *See* Polemius

Atenolf I, Count of Capua, Prince of Benevento, 150

Athelney, 355; Abbey of, 358; abbot of, *see* John; Alfred's church at, 560

Atino, added to Spoleto, 48

Attigny, Louis I at, 12; 24, 34; Louis the German at, 36, 51; Charles the Bald at, 42, 44; Otto at, 78, 80; Otto II at, 208

Atuyer, added to Burgundy, 93

Aubrey, lord of Montrésor, 119

Audax, grammarian, 493

Audoen, St, 490

Auðgisl (Auisle), brother of Olaf the White, 317 sq.

Auðr (Ota), 317, 331

Auðr, the Deep-Minded, 325, 331

Augsburg, Louis the German at, 17; Hungarians near, 69; 199; diet at (952), 159, 195; bishops of, *see* Bruno, Henry, Ulric; Henry II at, 216, 224; Conrad the Younger at, 256, 257; Conrad II names Henry III his heir at, 269; Henry III at, 287, 290; annals of, cited, 278

Augustine, author of *De mirabilibus Scripturae*, 507

Augustine, St, of Canterbury, mission to the English, 488

Augustine, St, of Hippo, the *City of God*, 445, 488; *Catagoriae* of, 516

Auisle. *See* Auðgisl

Aulus Gellius. *See* Gellius, Aulus

Aurelian, Archbishop of Lyons, 57

Aurora, Sultana, 424 sqq.

Ausonia, county of, 90

Austrasia, 23, 27

Austria. *See* East Mark

Autun, given to Pepin, 10; 97; counts of, *see* Gilbert, Moduin, Theodoric; diocese of, 124; Boso of Provence and, 137; learning in, 502; cathedral of, 557

Auvergne, pillaged by Northmen, 87; Louis V at, 91; 97; count of, *see* Bernard

Auxerre, besieged, 106; 97; count of, *see* Conrad

Auxerrois, the, 24

Avallon, given to Pepin, 10; Burgundy and, 94, 97; captured by Robert the Pious, 106; count of, *see* Gilbert

Aversa, given to Ranulf, 268; made a tenure in chief, 292

Avienus, 524

Avignon, Bishop of, 282

Avitus, Alcimus, 495, 516, 537

Avon (Bristol), river, 362

Avon (Worcs.), river, 354

Avranches, ceded to Normans, 94, 322

Axbridge, 357

Azelin of Hildesheim, 295

Azo, *scriniarius*, envoy to Germany, 161, 164

Az-Zahrā, 423, 432

Azzo, an Otbertine Marquess, marries heiress of the Welfs, 265

Babenberg, House of, 68, 70, 205, 222 sq., 294, 301, 307. *See* Bamberg

Badajoz, 417

Badbury Rings, 361

Badr, *ḥājib*, 421

Badr, slave of 'Abd-ar-Raḥmān I, 410 sq.

Bagdad, caliphate of, 430; university at, 433; coins from, in Sweden, 333

Bagseag, Viking leader, 352

Bakewell, 365

Baldred, under-king of Kent, 345

Baldric, *missus*, 6

Baldwin I Iron-arm, Count of Flanders, and Judith, 39, 41; 92

Baldwin II the Bald, Count of Flanders, submits to Odo, 72; 92

Baldwin III, son of Arnold I of Flanders, 92

Baldwin IV, Count of Flanders, takes Valenciennes, 106, 227 sq.; takes Ghent, 228; loses Ghent, 250

Baldwin V, of Lille, Count of Flanders, 111; 287; guardian of Philip I, 110, 122; joins Godfrey of Lorraine, 292 sqq.; submits to Henry III, 295; 297; again revolts, 298; 299; ally of Earl Godwin, 394, 398

Baldwin VI, son of Baldwin V of Flanders, granted March of Antwerp, 287, 292; marries Richeldis of Hainault, 295; revolts, 298

Baldwin IX, of Constantinople, Count of Flanders, 471

Baldwin Bauce, and the Flemish March, 93

Balearic Islands, ravaged by Vikings, 320

Balj, Emir, 409

Ballon, battle at (845), 31

Bamberg (Babenberg), see of, established,

229, 237 sq., 241, 250; bishops of, *see* Adalbero, Clement II, Everard, Hartwich; Benedict VIII visits, 250; Henry II buried at, 252; diet of, 269; MSS. at, 521, 534; 163, 299; *see also* Babenberg

Bamborough, high-reeves of, 351, 387; *see* Ealdred, Oswulf, Waltheof; House of, 396, 398

Bangor (Ireland), monastic school of, 501, 509; abbot of, *see* Mosuin Mac Armin; Antiphonary of, 502 sq.

Bangor (Wales), 342

Barbarian invasions, flight of scholars to Ireland before, 501 sq.

Barbarus Scaligeri, chronicle, 497

Barcelona, 413; Saracens at, 8, 13; Bernard in, 14; Almanzor in, 425, 428; privilege of, 441; counts of, and Gothia, 89 sq., 130. *See* Berengar-Raymond, Borrel, Raymond, Raymond-Berengar, Sunifred, Wifred

Bardas, 450

Bardney, monastery of, 351

Bardo, Archbishop of Mayence, 276

Barðr (Baraidh), kills Halfdanr, 318

Baret, Viking leader, 86

Bari, Saracens at, 49; capital of Longobardia, 150; attacked by Otto I, 167; rebellion in (982), 169; besieged by Ṣafī (1002), 177 sq.

Bar-le-Duc, battle of, 123, 145, 267

Barnstaple, 357

Bar-sur-Aube, added to Langres, 96; 111

Bar-sur-Seine, added to Langres, 96

Bartholomew, Bishop of Narbonne, deposed, 20, 450

Bartholomew, lord of l'Ile-Bouchard, 119 sq.

Bartholomew, St, Acts of, 533

Baruch, Apocalypse of, 494

Baruch, Rest of the Words of, 505

Basil, catapan, 250 sq.

Basil I, Eastern Emperor, 49, 150

Basing, battle at, 352

Basingwerk, death of Coenwulf at, 343

Basle, added to Burgundy, 69; seized by Henry II, 141, 227; 143 sq.; seized by Conrad II, 256; 259; diocese of, 45; bishop of, *see* Udalrich

Basques, revolt of, 8; independence of, 410; defeat Charles the Great, 413; under Navarre, 428; language of, 501

Bassigny, 27; 96

Bath, 357; 404; 553; Edmund's foundation at, 373 sq.; Svein at, 383

Bautzen, taken by Boleslav, 222; recovered by Henry II, 225; peace with Poland at, 247 sq.; 260 sq.; besieged by Conrad II, 260

Bavaria, assigned to Lothar, 3; to Louis the German, 10, 13, 21; 23; 27; 34; to Carloman, 51; invaded by Hungarians, 69 sq., 198; given to Otto of Swabia, 206; revolts in, against Otto I, 188, 197 sqq., 205; against Otto II, 204 sq.; against Otto III, 204; relations to Germany, 179 sqq., 207; and Swabia, 204; Church of, 205, 236; Law of, 284. *See also*

Nordgau; dukes of, *see* Arnulf, Berthold, Henry, Kuno, Otto; kings of, *see* Carloman, Lothar, Louis

Bawit, excavations at, 547

Bayeux, district of, ceded to Northmen, 87, 94 sq., 322; viscount of, 109

Beadricesworth, 351

Béarn, constitution of, 472

Beatrice, wife of Frederick Barbarossa, 147

Beatrice, Abbess of Quedlinburg, 274, 276, 290

Beatrice, marries Boniface of Tuscany, 265; marries next Godfrey of Lorraine, 296, 298; captive in Germany, 299

Beatus, opponent of Adoptionism, 523

Beaugency, Council of (1104), 113

Beaumanoir, *Coutumes de Beauvaisis*, of, 460, 464

Beaune, district of, subject to Burgundy, 93, 97

Beaupréau, family of, in Anjou, 118

Beauvais, Synod of, 445; bishops of, *see* Odo, Stephen

Beauvaisis, Coutumes de. See Beaumanoir

Bede, the Venerable, 510 sqq.; *Ecclesiastical History* of, 358, 496, 511, 553, 559; Life of St Cuthbert by, 534; mathematical works of, 535; works used by, 492, 497, 499; 488; 515; 532; 537

Bedford, 356, 359; captured by Wessex, 363; burnt by Danes, 382

Bedfordshire, hundreds of, 367; Scandinavian influence in, 337

Bedouins, 415

Bego, Count of Paris, 3

Beja, 418

Béjar, 432

Belecke, captured by Everard, 188

Belgium, part of, ceded to Louis the German, 16; ceded to Charles, 21

Belkesheim, battle at, 209

Bellême, lord of, 120

Belley, diocese of, 39

Bembezar, river, 413

Benedict, St, of Aniane (Witiza), monastic reformer, 1, 3 sq., 375

Benedict, St, of Nursia; Order of, 441, 456 sq., 487; Rule of, 4; 375, 377

Benedict III, Pope, 29

Benedict IV, Pope, 138; 149; 151

Benedict V, the Grammarian, Pope, 101, 164, 166

Benedict VI, Pope, 168

Benedict VII, Pope, 168

Benedict VIII (Theophylact), Pope, 241; 273; 454; character, 243, 250; visits Germany, 250; at Synod of Pavia, 251; death, 252

Benedict IX (Theophylact), Pope, and Conrad II, 267; 291; and the "Truce of God," 282; sells the Papacy, 454

Benedict Biscop, Abbot of Wearmouth, 488, 510 sq., 514, 553, 559

Beneventan script, 517

Benevento; Salerno separated from, 48; Saracens in, 44, 49; joined to Capua, 150; 152; separated, 169; Otto III and, 176;

178; Byzantines in, 250 sq.; Conrad II and, 265; Henry III and, 292; see of, 167; princes of, *see* Adelchis, Atenolf, Grimoald, Landolf, Paldolf, Radelchis, Sicard, Sico, Siconolf

Benfleet, 359

Beni-Abī-'Āmir, house of, 424, 427, 429

Beni-Angelino, the, in Seville, 418

Beni-Hajjāj, the, in Seville, 418 sq.

Beni-Ḳasi, the lords of Saragossa, 417, 419

Beni-Khaldūn, the, in Seville, 418

Benno, Bishop of Osnabrück, 295

Beorhtric, King of Wessex, and the Vikings, 311, 340; death of, 344

Beorhtwulf, King of Mercia, 348; defeated by Vikings, 349

Beorn, Earl, 392; murdered, *ib.*, 394

Beornwulf, King of Mercia, 343 sqq.; defeated by Ecgbert, 345; slain, 345

Beowulf, 309, 537

Berach, St, Life of, 505

Berbers, in Africa, 424 sq.

Berbers, in Spain, 428 sq., 435 sq., 442; 438; defeated by Syrians, 409; revolt at Saragossa, 411; revolts under Shakyā, and A'rābī, 413; under Emir Hakam, 415; raid Seville, 418; Ibn Hafsun and, 419; desert the Mahdī, 420; submit to 'Abd-ar-Rahmān III, 421; rise against Mahomet II, 427

Berengar I, Emperor, King of Italy, Marquess of Friuli, 47, 53, 62; claims Italy, 63 sqq.; defeated, 65; makes treaty with Lambert, 66; King of Italy, 67 sq., 138 sq.; crowned Emperor, 152; death of, 136, 153; policy of, 148 sq., 152 sq.; 157; *Gesta Berengarii*, 531

Berengar II, King of Italy, Marquess of Ivrea, 155; rebels against Hugh, 157, 194; rule of, in Italy, 158, 194; submits to Otto I, 159, 195; attacked by Liudolf, 160, 201; attacked by Otto I, 161; besieged, 162; exile and death of, 163

Berengar, Count of Toulouse, 17

Berengar-Raymond I, Count of Barcelona, 441

Berezan, Runic inscription at, 328

Berga, county of, 90

Bergamo, captured by Arnulf, 66; Henry II at, 224; bishop of, 240; *see* Hagano; see of, 165

Berkeley, 344; 393

Berkshire, 382, 405

Berlin, MS. at, 523; art treasures at, 547

Bermudo II, King of Leon, 425 sq.

Bermudo III, King of Leon, 428

Bern. *See* Björn, King of Sweden

Bernard, King of Italy, 3 sq., 9; revolt of, 11 sq.; 19, 77

Bernard, Archbishop of Vienne, 20, 450

Bernard, Bishop of Oldenburg (on Baltic), 249

Bernard I Billung, Duke of Saxony; and the Danes, 208 sq.; and Henry II, 217 sq.; death of, 239

Bernard II Billung, Duke of Saxony, 239; revolts, 249; Conrad II and, 255; Adalbert of Bremen and, 290, 293, 305

Bernard, Marquess of Gothia, 53, 56

Bernard, Count, 184

Bernard, Count of Auvergne, 53

Bernard, Count of Septimania, 8, 13 sqq., 16 sq.; executed, 31

Bernard, illegitimate son of Charles the Fat, 60

Bernay, Abbey of, 561

Berne, MSS. at, 526 sq.

Bernicia, feud with Deira, 341; invaded by Scots, 350; spared by Vikings, 351; Halfdene's invasion of, 353 sq.; 368

Bernier, grandson of Charles Martel, 2

Berno. *See* Björn Jarnsîða

Bernward, Bishop of Hildesheim, 233; 559; withstands the Vikings, 212; dispute with see of Mayence, 235, 251

Berry, 83; pillaged by Northmen, 86; invaded by Hungarians, 88; 129

Bertaud, elected to see of Besançon, 141

Bertha, betrothed to Henry IV, 299

Bertha, widow of Rodolph II, marries Hugh of Arles, 140, 156; 180 *note*

Bertha, wife of Odo I of Blois, and of Robert the Pious, 103 sq., 116 *note*, 143 *note*, 256

Bertha, wife of Adalbert II of Tuscany, 149, 152 sqq.

Bertha, wife of Gerard of Roussillon, 46

Bertha, daughter of Charles the Great, 2, 534

Berthold, 69; executed (917), 70

Berthold of Babenberg (Bamberg), 205; given Margravate of Nordgau, 206

Berthold, Duke of Carinthia, 205 *and note*, 206; becomes Duke of Bavaria, 188; death of, 191

Bertrada of Montfort, wife of Philip I, 113 sq., 116, 132

Bertrand of Arles, Marquess of Provence, 130

Bertrand, Count of Toulouse, 130

Bertulf, Archbishop of Trèves, 59

Besalu, county of, 90

Besançon, Boso of Provence and, 137; Henry III married at, 283; see and diocese of, 45, 63, 93 sq., 135; 147; disputed election to, 141; archbishops of, 57; 282; 295. *See* Bertaud, Hector, Walter

Besse, Island of, 33

Bethlehem, Church of the Nativity at, 548

Beverley, monastery of, 379

Bewcastle, cross at, 554 sq.

Bezprim. *See* Otto Bezprim

Bible, study of the, 486, 517, 525, 527, 532; textual revisions of, by Alcuin, 516, 519; by Theodulf, 519; *Glossa Ordinaria* to, 522, 532; Cotton MS. of, 549 sq.

Bigorre, 497

Billingsley, 396

Billung, house of, 216; *see also* Bernard, Herman, Wichmann

Birca. *See* Björkö

Birrenswark, 323, 366

Birthen, battle at (939), 189

Biscop. *See* Benedict Biscop

Björkö (Bjørkø), (Birca), Anskar at, 314; trading centre, 332

Björn, King of Sweden, 314

Björn Jarnsîða (Berno Ironside), Viking chief, 35, 320

Black Forest, Ernest III of Swabia killed in, 270

Black Sea, 327; 422

Blaison, house of, 118

Blandinium, Abbey of, 371, 375

Blickling Hall, Norfolk, MS. at, 506 *note*, 537

Blois, ravaged by Vikings, 33; seized by Theobald the Trickster, 95; united to Champagne, 123; counts of, *see* Odo, Theobald, William

Bobastro, 420

Bobbio, Abbey of, Gerbert at, 173, 175, 210; Otbertines at, 250; Greek learning at, 503; library and MSS. of, 486 *note*, 521, 536; abbot of, *see* Sylvester II, Pope

Bobra (Bober), river, Henry II at, 227

Bodleian Library, MS. in, 509

Bockelheim, castle of, 286

Boece, St, Life of, 505

Boethius, *De Consolatione Philosophiae*, 358, 485; 525; 536 sq.

Bohemia, and Louis the German, 10; subject to Henry I, 184; under Otto I, 192–202; Henry the Wrangler in, 206, 210 sq.; war with the Poles, 211; revolution in, 218; severed from Germany, 220, 222 sq., 224; church in, 206, 222; *and see* dukes of, Boleslav, Břatislav, Jaromir, Spitignev, Udalrich, Vladivoi, Wenceslas

Bohuslän, market at, 332

Bojannes, catapan, 268

Boleslav, Duke of Bohemia, submits to Otto I, 192; at war with the Wends, 200

Boleslav the Younger, Duke of Bohemia, 202; aids Bavarian revolt, 205 sq; Henry the Wrangler and, 210; war with the Poles, 211

Boleslav the Red, Duke of Bohemia, 222 sq.

Boleslav (Bolesław) Chrobry (the Mighty), Duke of Poland, son of Mesco, 211, 216 sq., 261, 304; revolts from the Empire, 222 sq.; seizes Bohemia, 223; attacks Bavaria, 223; loses Bohemia, 225, 227; plots with Henry's enemies, 226, 238; makes peace with Henry, 227; regains his conquests, 228, 239; does homage, 239; intrigues with Papacy, 241; wars with Henry II renewed, 247; peace made at Bautzen, 247, 260; spreads Christianity, 304

Bolingbroke, revolt of, 466

Bologna, Louis (the Blind) at, 138

Bomarzo, bishop of. *See* Marinus

Boniface, St, 511 sqq.; 515; 521; 534

Boniface VI, Pope, 66

Boniface VII (Franco), Pope, misdeeds of, 101, 168; death of, 171

Boniface, Marquess of Tuscany, 48; invades Africa, 8

Boniface, Marquess of Tuscany, 243

Boniface, of Canossa, Marquess of Tuscany etc., 144, 240, 246; in Burgundy, 144, 259; marriage of, 265, 298

Boniface, Marquess of Tuscany, 299

Bonn, burnt by Danes, 59; Henry I and Charles the Simple at, 74, 181

Bonneuil, assembly at, 446

Bordeaux, culture of, 502; dukes of Aquitaine and, 129; Vikings at, 316

Borrel, Count of Barcelona, 99, 424

Boru. *See* Brian Borumha

Bosham, 398

Boso, King of Provence, 45 sq.; 51; marries Ermengarde, 53; Louis the Stammerer and, 55 sq.; takes royal style, 57 sq., 137; death of, 62, 137

Boso, Abbot of St Benoît-sur-Loire, 14

Boso, Count in Provence, Marquess of Tuscany, 157

Boston, Mass., art treasures at, 547

Botfeld, in the Harz, 186, 276

Bouchard the Venerable, Count of Vendôme, 105

Bouin, pirates at, 7

Boulenois, the, added to see of Langres, 96

Boulogne, 359; counts of, 460. *See* Eustace

Bourbonnais, the, independent of Aquitaine, 129

Bourges, acquired by Philip I, 111; archbishop of, 86; *see* Odo-Harpin; cathedral of, 557

Boussu, destroyed by Otto II, 207

Bozna, Župan of the Croats, 7

Bracara, archbishop of. *See* Martin

Brachmani, king of. *See* Dindimus

Bracton, English jurist, cited, 461 sq.

Braga. *See* Bracara

Brandenburg, besieged and captured by Henry I, 184; bishopric founded in, 192; church burnt, 208; Lyutitzi at, 211 sq.

Braslav, Slovene Duke, 64

Břatislav, Duke of Bohemia, 299; recovers Moravia from the Poles, 260, 299 sq.; defeats the Hungarians, 261; marries Judith, 299 sq.; succeeds to Bohemia, 262, 300; invades Poland, 276, 300; war with Henry III, 276, 301; 277, 301; second war, 278, 301; does homage, 278, 301 sq.; 285; 290; restores Silesia, 297 sq., 302; death of, 298, 302

Braulio of Saragossa, 489 sq.; works of, 492

Brecknock, tribal unit, 341 sq., 360; invaded by Aethelfleda, 363

Bregandus Lugenicus, 501

Breisach, besieged by Otto I, 190

Bremen, fortification of, 305; diocese of, 192, 289; archbishop of, 217; *see* Adalbert, Albrand, Anskar, Lievizo, Unwan; jurisdiction of see of, 296 sq.

Brendan, St, Life of, 505, 509

Brenner Pass, the, Berengar II crosses, 157; Otto I crosses, 159, 161; Otto III crosses, 172; Conrad II crosses, 264, 266; Henry III crosses, 290

Brenta, river, Hungarian victory on, 148; Ardoin's victory on, 222; Henry II on, 224

Brentford, 385

Brescia, death of Louis II at, 46; county of, 221; Henry II at, 224; counts of, *see* Boniface, Suppo, Tedald

Breslau, restored to Poland, 302

Bresle, river, 73; Norman boundary, 322

Brétencourt, Louis VI at, 114

Breteuil, lord of, 120

Bretwalda, title applied to Ecgbert, 346

Bréval, siege of (1094), 121

Brian Borumha (Boru), King of Ireland, and the Vikings, 324

Bridgenorth, Vikings in, 359

Bridport, 357

Brienne, Charles the Bald and Louis the German at, 36; lord of, *see* Guy

Brihtnoth, Duke of Essex, 379; slain, 324, 381

Brihtric, 382

Briollay, family of, in Anjou, 118

Brionne, besieged (1090), 121

Brissarthe, fight at (866), 41

Bristol, 394

Britain, literary connexion with Spain, 494; learning in, before Theodore, 508 sqq.; literary connexion with Brittany, 509; Roman provincial art in, 552; Northumbrian art in, 553 sqq.

British Museum, art treasures in, 547 sqq., 552, 566

Brittany; 398; 471; revolts against Louis I, 8 sq., 14, 19, 27; wins independence, 30 sqq., 35, 40, 91, 128; Vikings in, 86, 316, 320, 322 sq.; 363; literary connexion with Britain, 509; Greek learning in, 528 sq.; kings, dukes, of, *see* Alan, Conan, Erispoë, Hoel, Morvan, Nomenoë, Solomon, Wihomarch; counts of March of, *see* Guy, Lambert, Louis, Robert

Brixen, bishop of. *See* Poppo

Brogne, abbey of, 373, 457

Broyes, lord of. *See* Hugh

Bruchsal, Herman of Swabia submits at, 218

Bruges, and the Flemish March, 92; 389; 394

Brunanburh, battle of, 323, 366

Bruno, Archbishop of Cologne, appointed archchancellor of Italy, 196; receives Lorraine, 199; policy of, 200 sq.; death of, 203

Bruno, Bishop of Augsburg, 224, 257; revolts against Henry II, 223; 273; attacked by Welf, 257 sq.; guardian of Henry III, 273; death of, 273

Bruno, Bishop of Langres, 141

Bruno, Bishop of Toul. *See* Leo IX, Pope

Bruno, Bishop of Würzburg, 288

Bruno, Duke of Saxony, killed on Lüneburg Heath (880), 321; 70

Bruno of Brunswick, husband of Empress Gisela, 254

Bruno, of Carinthia. *See* Gregory V, Pope

Brunswick, dukes of, 240; Basilican church of, 567

Brycheiniog. *See* Brecknock
Bucco [of Schweinfurt], 223
Buckingham, fortified, 363
Buckinghamshire, Danes in, 357; hundreds of, 367; 397
Bulche, mines at, 432
Bulgaria, and Louis I, 6 sq.
Burchard, Archbishop of Lyons, 279
Burchard, Bishop of Worms, canonist, 253
Burchard, Duke of Swabia, 69 sq.; 156; at Winterthür, 136, 180
Burchard, Duke of Swabia, 205 *note*; defeats King Adalbert (965), 166; leads anti-ducal party, 198; receives dukedom, 199; death of, 204
Burgate, 406
Burgos, 410, 421, 423, 440
Burgundia Minor, Duchy of, 146–7
Burgundy, ancient province, part of, given to Charles the Bald, 13, 16, 21, 23 sq.
Burgundy, French Duchy of, 36, 65; allotted to Carloman, 57; duchy under Richard *le Justicier*, 58, 93; Northmen in, 61 sq., 86 sqq., 321 sq.; 75; 77; Hugh the Great its suzerain, 83; formation of duchy, 93 sq.; decline of duchy, 96 sq.; conquered by Robert the Pious, 105 sq.; given to Duke Robert I, 107 sq.; 111, 115, 116, 167; in the XI century, 123 sqq.; architecture in, 563; dukes of, *see* Gilbert, Henry, Hugh, Odo Borel, Otto, Raoul, Richard, Robert
Burgundy, Kingdom of Jurane, Chap. VI. A; founded, 63, 134 sq.; 66; annexation of Basle, 69; annexation of Aargau etc., 136, 180 *and note*; cession to, by Hugh of Italy, 139, 156; union with Provence, 139, 158; 153, 156; loss of Aosta, 156; kings of, *see* Rodolph; *see also* Jurane Burgundy, Duchy of
Burgundy, Kingdom of, after union with Provence, Chap. VI. c; 78; 123; Raoul acknowledged in, 76; recovery of Aosta, 168; Hungarians in, 198; 207; loss of Basle, 141, 227; intervention of Henry II, 141 sq., 227, 247 sq.; annexed to the Empire by Conrad II, 142–5, 256, 258 sq., 271, 273 sq.; Ernest of Swabia in, 257; rule of Henry III, 145 sq., 274 sq., 279, 282 sq., 286–7, 306 sq.; Romance party in, 285 sqq.; rectorate of, 146 sq.; as Kingdom of Arles, 147; kings of, *see* Conrad, Frederick, Henry, Rodolph; rectors of, *see* Rudolf, William of Baux, William of Montferrat
"Burgundy," County of (Franche-Comté), formation of, 93 sq., 141 sq.; 146; 147; 247; 287 *note*; counts of, *see* Frederick, Otto-William, Raynald; *see also* Franche-Comté
Burhred, King of Mercia, 348; buys off the Vikings, 351; driven from Mercia, 353
Bürstadt, assembly at, 210
Bury St Edmunds, 351; monastery of, 379, 388, 408

Buxhall, 406
Byrhtferth, of Ramsey, 538
Byzantine Empire. *See* Empire, Eastern

Cader Idris, 342
Cadiz, Vikings at, 316, 416
Cadoc, St, 509
Cadolah, Marquess of Friuli, 7
Cadwalader of Gwynedd, 342
Cadwallon, house of, 350
Caecilius Balbus, 527
Caedmon, poet, 554, 556
Caena Cypriani, 531
Caesar, MSS. of, 521 sq., 536
Caesarius of Arles, 490
Cairo, 424
Caithness, Viking settlements in, 325, 335
Caitill Find (Ketill the White), leader of the Gall-Gaedhil, 317
Calabria, theme of, 150; and Saracen raids, 151, 176, 178; and the Byzantine Empire, 152, 166, 168; 422
Calatañazor, battle of, 426
Callington, 344
Calocyrus Delphinas, catapan, 176
Caloprini, the, of Venice, 170
Calpurnius, 522
Camargue, Vikings at, 320
Cambrai, see of, 45; attacked by Hungarians, 88; seized by John of Arras, 298; see of, 45; bishops of, *see* Gerard, Halitgar, Liutpert
Cambridge, Vikings at, 353, 355; *burh* of, 356; submits to Edward the Elder, 364; burnt by Danes, 382; King's College, 403 *note*; ivories at, 548
Cambridgeshire, hundreds of, 367; Scandinavian influence in, 334, 337
Camerino, count of. *See* Guy
Campagna, the Roman, revolt in, 4; Saracens in, 149
Campania, Picingli in, 151; Hungarians in, 153 sqq; *see* Terra di Lavoro
Campo Malo, battle of, 265
Candé, and Anjou, 120
Candiano, Doge of Venice, *see* Pietro
Candidus, life of Eigil by, 534
Canossa, Hugh of Cluny at, 295
Canossa, house of, 240; marquesses of, *see* Adalbert-Atto, Boniface, Tedald
Cantabria, raided by Alfonso I, 410; duke of, *see* Alfonso I
Canterbury, burnt by Vikings, 349; monks of, 350, 379; sacked by Danes, 383; Abbot of St Augustine's, 383; library at, 511; cathedral at, 561 sq., 564, 567; St Augustine's Abbey at, 563; see of, 388; archbishops of, 407; *see* Aelfheah, Aelfric, Aethelheard, Aethelnoth, Anselm, Augustine, Ceolnoth, Dunstan, Eadsige, Oda, Plegmund, Sigeric, Theodore, Wulfred
Cantich, battle of, 427
Cantref, Welsh fiscal unit, 342, 345
Capitularies, Frankish, 441

Capua, independent, 48; united to Benevento, 150, 152; vassal to Otto I, 166 sq.; separated from Benevento, 169; Otto III and, 176; separated from Salerno, 169; taken by Henry II, 251; reunited to Salerno, 268; Conrad II and, 265, 268; Henry III and, 292; see of, 167; princes of, Ademar, Atenolf, Guaimar, Laidulf, Landolf, Paldolf

Cardigan, tribal unit, 341

Cardona, charter of, 441

Caresana, granted to canons of Vercelli, 175

Carham, 388

Carinthia, 7; assigned to Louis the German, 10; duchy of, 58; ravaged by Hungarians, 69, 298, 304; separated from Bavaria, 206; reunited, 209; again separated, 212; dukes of, see Adalbero, Arnulf, Berthold, Conrad, Henry, Otto, Welf

Carinthian Mark (Styria), separated from the Duchy, 270 note 1; margraves of, see Adalbero, Arnold

Carlisle, Norwegians in, 368; Roman remains at, 553

Carloman, King, son of Louis the German, 50; receives Bavaria and East Mark, 51; attacks Lombardy, 53; retreats, 55; death 58; 62

Carloman, King of France, 56, 321; crowned, 57; death of, 58; 59 sq.; 77 note

Carloman, son of Charles the Bald, 46

Carlsruhe, MSS. from Reichenau at, 505 sq., 521

Carmona, 418

Carniola, 7

Carolingian minuscule, 517

Carthage, 8; baptistery at, 547

Casimir, Duke of Poland, exiled, 276, 300; Henry III and, 280; 290; 295; 301 sqq.; given Silesia, 297 sq., 302; regains Poland, 302; strife with Bohemia, 302 sq.

Caspian Sea, and the Rus, 327

Cassian, 493

Cassiodorus, 485 sqq., 510, 528, 530

Castile, opposed to Leon, 422; invaded by Sancho, 423; by Almanzor, 425 sq.; conquers Leon, 428; Arab influence in, 438; society in, 441; kings and counts of, see Ferdinand, Fernan, Garcia, Sancho

Castrojeriz, 440

Catalonia (Gothalania), and Barcelona, 89 sq.; and Languedoc, 130; 424; Almanzor in, 425; independence of, 422, 438; towns in, 441; see Barcelona

Cathvulf, letter to Charlemagne from, 504

Catullus, 523

Caux, district of, 109

Ceadrag, Prince of the Obotrites, 7

Centullus, Duke of the Gascons, 8

Ceolfrid, 510 note, 554, 556

Ceolnoth, Archbishop of Canterbury, 350

Ceolwulf I, King of Mercia, 343 sq.

Ceolwulf II, King of Mercia, 353 sq., 356

Cerdaña (Cerdagne), 90; count of, 413

Ceredigion. *See* Cardigan

Cervia, bishop of. *See* John

Ceuta, 409, 421, 425 sqq.

Châlons-sur-Marne, 24, 36, 50; bishop of, 97

Châlon-sur-Saône, 11, 21, 26, 97; independence of, 124; count of, see Gilbert

Cham, pass of, 277

Champagne, 97, 111; succession in, 117; united to Blois, 123; invaded by Conrad II, 144; counts of, see Odo, Stephen; see also Troyes

Champigny-sur-Veude, 120

Charlemagne (Charles the Great), erects a brazen eagle at Aix, 207; his tomb entered by Otto III, 213 sq.; 'Abd-ar-Rahmān I and, 413; the Vikings and, 310, 312, 315; letter from Cathvulf to, 504; Theodoric's statue and, 522; revival of learning under, 514 sqq.; art under, 556 sq., 559; *Life of*, by Einhard, 517 sq., 534; epic upon, by Angilbert, 519; *Gesta* of, by Notker, 530 sq., 534; *Libri Carolini* against images, 533; mentioned, 22; 50; 254; 344; 421; 443

Charles the Bald, Emperor, 13; 16 sq.; at Prüm, 18 sq.; inheritance of, 21; dealings with Lothar I, 22, 23 sqq., 30 sqq., 444; oath of Strasbourg, 25 sq.; share by Treaty of Verdun, 27 sq.; Lothar II and, 35 sq., 39–44; Louis the German and, 36 sqq., 42, 45, 50 sq., 534; in Provence, 40, 46; King of Lorraine, 44 sqq.; Emperor, 51–53, 454, 531; the Northmen and, 30 sqq., 35 sq., 40, 52 sqq.; the Bretons and, 30–33, 35, 40; the Church and, 455 sqq., 451 sq.; learning and, 524; death of, 53, 321; character of, 54; descendants of, 63, 73 note

Charles the Fat, Emperor, 46; 50; 531; receives Alemannia, 51; meets Louis III and Carloman, 57; King of Italy, 57; becomes Emperor, 58, 454; ruler of all Francia, 58; the Northmen and, 59 sqq., 321 sqq.; deposed, 62, 71

Charles IV, Emperor, and Burgundy, 147; Golden Bull of, 464

Charles (the Young), made King of Aquitaine, 34 sqq.

Charles the Simple, King of France, 57 sq.; and Reginar, 68; reign of, 71 sqq.; marriage of, 366; the Vikings and, 73, 321 sq.; gains Lorraine, 74, 180; imprisoned, 75; 181; death of, 76; descendants of, 77 note; 82

Charles, King of Provence, 34, 38 sqq.; death of (863), 41, 57, 137

Charles, Duke of Lower Lorraine, 77 note; 81; 83 sq., 207; secures Laon and Rheims, 99 sq.; plots against Otto III, 81, 210; civil war with Hugh Capet, 211; death of, 100, 102

Charles, son of Charles, Duke of Lower Lorraine, 77 note, 104

Charles Constantine, Count of Vienne, 139

Charles Martel, 28, 310, 409

Charmouth, Vikings at, 347

Chartres, Rollo at, 73, 86; seized by Theobald the Trickster, 95; Odo II and, 123; stained glass at, 566; bishops of, 116; *see* Fulbert, Ivo; counts of, *see* Odo, Theobald

Chateaudun, seized by Theobald the Trickster, 95

Château Thierry, Charles the Simple imprisoned at, 75; 76 sq.

Chaumont, claimed by William the Conqueror, 112; lords of, *see* Hugh, Sulpicius.

Chelles, synods at (993), 102, 455; (1008), 132

Chemillé, house of, in Anjou, 118

Chertsey, Abbey of, 374

Cheshire, 404

Chester, 343; 359; 365; 379; Scandinavian influence at, 334; fortified, 362

Chèvremont, siege of (939), 190

Chevreuse, Louis VI at, 114

Chichester, 357; monastery of, 379

Chilterns, 361, 385; Danes in, 359; *frithgild* in, 367; village-lords in, 401

Chindaswinth, King of the Visigoths, 492

Chippenham, Alfred defeated at, 355; treaty of, 356

Chirbury, 363

Chlotar I, King of the Franks, 495

Chocilaicus (Hygelac), King of the Getae, 309

Choisy-au-Bac, Northmen at, 85

Christchurch (Hants.), 361

Christ Church (Oxford), 562

Christianity, introduced among Wends, 192, 238; decline among Wends under Otto II, 208, 226; progress of, among Slavs, 304 sqq.; spread of, in Scandinavia, 6 sq., 313 sqq., 329

Christianus Druthmarus of Stavelot, 532

Chrodegang, Saint, 4

Chronicon Burgense, cited, 426

Chronographia Tripartita, 528

Church, the, Chap. xvii.; and Louis I, 4 sq.; and Louis the German, 36 sq.; States of, 48; conflict with the state, 290; mortmain, 464; Roman-Greek controversy, 533. *See* Rome, Papacy, the respective states, and Cluniac Movement

Cicero, 343, 491 sq., 521 sqq., 526, 536

Cilternsaete, 363

Cinna, 491

Cirencester, Danes at, 356

Cividale, 47

Civitate, Leo IX defeated at, 298

Clarendon, forest, 398

Claudius (? Claudian), 508

Claudius, Bishop of Turin, iconoclast, 533

Clavering, 394 *note*, 406

Clement II, Pope (Suidger), 291, 293; Bishop of Bamberg, 277 sq.

Clement of Alexandria, 487

Clement the Irishman, 519

Clermont, church at, 561, 565

Clermont, Council of (1095), 113

Clonard, monastic school at, 501, 509

Clonfert, monastic school at, 501

Clonmacnois, monastic school at, 501; Auðr at, 317, 331

Clontarf, battle of (1014), 324, 326

Clovesho, synod of, 343

Cluniac Movement, 236; 250; 253; 456 sq.; opposed by Conrad II, 254, 271; favoured by Henry III, 277, 279, 282, 306; and by Agnes of Poitou, 284; in England, 373 sqq., 387 sq.

Cluny, Abbey of, 303, 456, 567; and the "Truce of God," 282; abbots of, *see* Hugh, Maiolus, Odilo, Odo

Clwyd, vale of, subject to Kings of North Wales, 342

Coblence, 26, 35; treaty of (860), 37, 41

Codex Alexandrinus, 549

Codex Amiatinus, 486, 514, 554

Codex Arcerianus, 536

Codex Augiensis, 526

Codex Laudianus, 512

Codex Salmasianus, 488

Codex Sangallensis (Δ), 526 sq.

Coemgen, St, life of, 505

Coenwulf, King of Mercia, 340 sq.; relations with Wales, 341 sqq.; with Kent and Canterbury, 343

Coimbra, 410, 425

Coinage, by Archbishop of Canterbury, 343; under Aethelstan, 367

Colchester, *burh* at, 356, 364

Colmar, Louis I at, 18

Cologne, 45; 275 sq.; 279; 295; 413; burnt by Danes, 59; Otto II at, 207; library of, 521; Church of St Mary in the Capitol at, 562; see of, 287; archbishops of, 209; 239, *see* Anno, Bruno, Gunther, Heribert, Herman, Hildebold, Pilgrim, Wikfried, Willibert

Colombera, 412 *note*

Columba, St, 499, 502, 506; *Life of*, *see* Adamnan

Columban, St, 486 *note*, 503; 521; poem by, 506

Cominianus, grammarian, 516

Como, diocese overrun by Ardoin, 244 sq.; bishop of, *see* Peter

Compiègne, assemblies at (816), 6; (823), *ib.*; (857), *ib.*, 8, 18; (985), 81; (987), 83 sq.; Louis I at, 14 sq., 18; 19; 30 *note*; Odo crowned at, 71; plundered by Otto II, 80, 208; Northmen at, 85; 89

Conan, Count of Rennes, 127

Conan II, Duke of Brittany, 128

Condé, Northmen encamp at, 59

Conflent, county of, 90

Connaught, raided by Turgeis, 317

Connemara, Vikings in, 347

Conquereuil, battle of, 126

Conrad I, King of Germany, Duke of Franconia, reign of, 69 sq., 74, 135; 179; 191

Conrad II, of Franconia, Emperor, early years, 249, 253; elected King of Germany, 254 sq.; opponent of Cluniac views, 254;

marriage with Gisela, 143 *note*, 249, 254; relation with Lorraine, 254 sqq.; relation with Saxony, 255; conquers Burgundy, 106 sq., 123, 142 sq., 144 sq., 256, 258 sq.; 262; 273 sq.; Lombards revolt against, 256 sq.; campaigns against Mesco II, 260 sqq.; 273, 300, 302; war with Hungary, 261, 273; subdues the Lyutitzi, 262 sq., 288, 308; relations with Knut, 263; enters Italy, 264, 268; crowned at Rome, 256, 264; second visit to Italy, 265 sqq.; deposes Aribert, 267; relations with South Italy, 265, 267 sq.; 292; imprisons Burchard of Lyons, 279; death of, 145, 269; his arrangements for the succession, 269, 273; aims and policy of, 269 sqq., 272; establishes hereditary principle in Italy, 266 sq.; in Germany, 269 sq.

Conrad, Duke of Carinthia, 239; 253; 269

Conrad the Younger, Duke of Carinthia, ecclesiastical views of, 253; ally of Ernest III of Swabia, 256; denied the duchy, 239, 253, 269; granted the duchy, 270; 266; death of, 277

Conrad the Red, Duke of Lorraine, 191, 194, 205 *note*; 212; 215; 249; 253; in Italy, 159, 195; rebels, 196 sqq.; death of, 200

Conrad [the Franconian], Duke of Swabia, 209; supports Otto III, 210

Conrad the Peaceful, King of Burgundy, 139 *note*; 143 *note*; 158; 194; and Otto I, 140, 156, 247; descendants of, 256, 143 *note*

Conrad, son of Berengar II, Marquess of Ivrea, 167

Conrad, Count of Auxerre, 35, 37; acquires the Jurane Duchy, 134

Conrad, Count of Paris, 56 sq.

Conrad, lay Abbot of Jumièges, 14 sq., 35; Count and Duke in Alemannia, 134

Conrad Kurzpold, Count in Franconia, 190

Conrad the Old, killed by Adalbert, 68

Conradin, house of, 68, 70, 239

Constance, wife of Robert the Pious, 104, 107

Constance, Italian bishops submit to Conrad II at, 264; Ernest of Swabia buried at, 276; "Day of Indulgence" at, 281; bishops of, *see* Dietrich, Solomon

Constantine the Great, 539

Constantine VII, Porphyrogenitus, Eastern Emperor, 546; cited, 328

Constantine III, King of Scots, 365 sq.

Constantinople, 395; 433; 548; Liutprand at, 160, 167; Boniface VII at, 168; embassy from Conrad II to, 260; General Council (861) at, 320, 327; besieged by the Rus, 320, 327; Roman architecture in, 539; Byzantine style, 539 sq.; Alexandrian influence on architecture of, 541 sq.; Church of St John of the Studion at, 542 sq.; Church of SS. Sergius and Bacchus, 543; Church of St Irene, 544, 546; Church of Holy Apostles, 544 sq.; Church of St Sophia at, 541, 543 sqq.; palace of Chalce at, 546; liturgical influences of, 528; MS. from, 528; patriarchs of, *see* Ignatius, Photius

Constitutio (817), the, *see Divisio Imperii*

Constitutio Romana (824), the, 5, 29

Conway, vale of, 342 sq.

Coptic art, 555

Corbie, monastery of, 2, 12, 15; abbots of, *see* Adalard, Wala; library of, 521, 538; town of, claimed by Philip I, 111

Corbridge on Tyne, Aethelred murdered at, 341; Roman relic at, 552 *note*

Cordova, 411 sqq.; 419; 421; Vikings raid, 316; revolt against Ḥakam, 414; 'Abd-ar-Raḥmān II at, 415; Christians in, 417; Navarrese embassy at, 423; Ibn Abī-'Āmir at, 424; Almanzor at, 426; revolution in, 427; importance of, 429 sq., 432 sq., 435; 523; mosque of, 436; bishop of, *see* Saul

Cordova, Caliphate of, founded, 421 sqq.; independent of Bagdad, 421, 430; abolished, 427; caliphs of, *see* 'Abd-ar-Raḥmān, Ḥakam, Hishām, Mahomet, Sulaiman

Corfe, King Edward murdered at, 519

Coria, 410

Corippus, Fl. Cresconius, poet, 488 sq.

Cork, and the Northmen, 312, 317, 334

Cormery, abbey of, 71

Cornouailles, Count of. *See* Hoel

Cornwall, made a duchy subject to Wessex, 344 sq.; Vikings raid, 347; 379; bishopric founded in, 347; society in, 400 sq., 405. *See also* Wales, West

Corsica, pirates at, 8; Saracens in, 162

Corvey (New Corbie), monastery of, 7, 15, 236, 314, 358; Bishop Abraham at, 205; library of, 521

Cosenza, Ibrāhīm defeated at (902), 150

Cosmas Indicopleustes, 511 *note*; 546, 549, 559

Cotentin, the, ravaged by the Vikings, 322

Cotrone, 169 *note*

Cotton Bible, 549 sq., 558

Coucy, lords of, 464

Couesnon, river, 94

Count Palatine, office of, 188 *note*; in Italy, 246; counts, *see* Adelard, Arnulf, Erchanger, Henry, Herman, Otto; *see also* Palace, Counts of the

Courci-sur-Dive, siege of (1091), 121

Courtrai, Norman camp at, 59; in the Flemish March, 92

Coutances, ceded to Normans, 94, 322; Viscount of, 109

Covadonga, battle of, 409

Coventry, 387

Cracow, burnt by Břatislav, 300

Craon, house of, in Anjou, 118

Crediton, see of, 362; bishop of, *see* Lyfing

Cremona, Conrad II at, 264, 267; city and see of, 165, 175; bishops of, 267, *see* Liudprand

Crescentii, the, 241, 243, 250, 291. *See* Crescentius

Crescentius I, de Theodora, and Boniface VII, 168, 171
Crescentius II, and the Papacy, 103, 127; 171; executed, 172, 216
Crescentius III, John, 177, 241
Crescentius, John, Duke of Spoleto, 243
Creussen, siege of, 223
Cricklade, 357, 361
Croats, Župan of the. *See* Bozna
Cromarty, Scandinavian influence in, 335
Crossen, Boleslav Chrobry at, 227
Crosses, Saxon, 552, 554 sqq.; Irish, 556
Crowland, monastery of, 351
Cues (Cusa), MSS. at, 504, 526
Cumberland, Eardulf tours through, 354; Regnald in, 365 sq.; ceded to the Scots, 368; Aethelred's invasion of, 381; Norse settlements in, 326; Scandinavian influence in, 335 sqq.
Cunedda, house of, 342
Cuthbert, St, 553; shrine of, 354, 555, 560
Cuthred, King of Kent, 343
Cuthsuuitha, Abbess of Worcester, 512 *note*
Cwenthryth, Abbess, 344
Cyneburh, wife of Alchfrid, 555
Cyprian, St, 488, 493
Cyrillus, Glossary of, 526

Δ (*Cod. Sangallensis*), Gospels, 526 sqq.
Dabravka, daughter of Boleslav the Younger, 202
Daisam ibn Ishāk, 418
Dalemintzi, the campaign of Henry I against, 184; 185
Dallan Forgaill, *Amra* of, 499
Dalmatia, frontiers of, 6; Venice and, 177
Dalmatius, lord of Semur, 124
Dalriad Scots, 350
Damascus, 411, 433; Caliphate of, 430
Damasus II, Pope (Poppo of Brixen), 293 sq.
Dammartin, taken by Queen Constance, 107
Danelaw, 348, 354 sqq., 359, 361; reconquest of, 362 sqq., 365 sq., 370, 380; causes of its fall, 364 sq.; institutions of, 334, 348, 354, 359, 367 sqq., 400 sq.; monasteries of, 374 sq., 380; invaded by Svein, 383 sq.; ceded to Knut, 386 sq.; *see also* Denmark, Vikings
Danes. *See* Denmark, Vikings
Daniel, St Jerome on, 523
Danube, 223; and Hungarian frontier, 281, 295; invasion by way of, 304
Dares Phrygius, Trojan history of, 516
Datto, Apulian rebel, 250
Dauphiné, restored to France, 147
David, King of Scots, 554
David, St, 509
"Day of Indulgence" or "Day of Pardon." *See* Indulgence
Declan, Irish saint, 501
Deerhurst, 344, 394
Deganwy, captured by Ceolwulf, 343
de Hauteville, house of, in Italy, 292
Deheubarth, principality of, 342, 364, 396; conquered by Rhodri Mawr, 350

Deira, feud with Bernicia, 341; Vikings conquer, 350 sq., 353; colonised by the Vikings, 354
De Laudibus Justini (*minoris*), 488 sqq.
Demosthenes, *Ophthalmicus* of, 536
Denewulf, Bishop of Winchester, 361 sq.
Denmark, early history of, 309 sqq.; relations with the Franks, 6 sq., 312 sqq.; civil wars in, 315; invaded by Henry the Fowler, 185; the Jómsvikings and, 326 sq.; Otto II and, 205, 208; subdues Norway, 380; repels the Swedes, 388; allies with Flanders, 122; Christianity in, 314, 329; civilisation of, 328 sqq. *See* Scandinavia, Vikings. Kings of, *see* Chocilaicus, Godefrid, Gorm, Guðröðr, Harold, Harthacnut, Horic, Knut, Magnus, Ongendus, Oscar, Reginfredus, Roric, Sigefrid, Sigurðr, Svein
Derby, 319, 355; captured by Aethelfleda, 323, 363
Derbyshire, 406; Scandinavian influence in, 336
De Religiosis, English statute, 464
Desiderius, St, of Vienne, 492
Deville, interview at (1033), 107, 259
Devon, invaded by Vikings, 319, 382
Dicuil, Irish geographer, 535
Dietrich (Theodoric), Chancellor of Germany, provost of Aix, made Bishop of Constance, 293
Dietrich of Luxemburg, Bishop of Metz, 238, 289, 294
Dietrich (Theodoric), provost of Basle, made Bishop of Verdun, 293
Dietrich, Duke of Upper Lorraine, 217, 254, 256 sq.
Dietrich, Margrave of the North Mark, 209
Dietrich, Count of Holland, 248 sq.
Dietrich (Theodoric), Count of Holland, 289; allies with Godfrey of Lorraine, 292; slain, 294
Dietrich, Count of Wettin, repels Mesco II, 260
Dietrich, Count, 306
Dijon, county in French Burgundy, 93, 97; taken by Robert the Pious, 106; 124; church at, 563; abbey of, *see* St Benignus; count of, *see* Gilbert
Dinant, bronze-work at, 560
Dindimus, King of the Brachmani, 516
Dinefwr, 342
Dinnurin, see of, established, 347 *and note*; bishop of, *see* Kenstec
Dionysius, St, the Areopagite, 515, 524, 527 sq.
Dioscorides, medical writer, 535; illuminated MS. of, 549 sq.; translated, 429
Dir. *See* Dyri
Divisio Imperii, the, 9 sqq., 13, 23, 27
Dnieper, river, and the Rus, 327 sq.
Dol, siege of (1076), 112, 116; 128; metropolitanate of, 33 *note*
Dome, history and use of, 540 sq., 543 sqq., 560, 563
Domesday Book, 345, 377, 400

Donald, of Strathclyde, 365
Donatus, African monk, 489; grammarian, 525
Donegal, Vikings in, 347
Dorchester, Vikings near, 310 sqq.; church dues in diocese of, 361; canons of, 379; see of, 380; bishop of, *see* Ulf
Dore, 368; Ecgbert at, 346
Dorestad, Vikings at, 20, 316, 338, 347
Dorset, Vikings on coast of, 340, 347, 365; Danes ravage, 384; 392; 394; 397
Dortmund, submits to Otto I, 189
Douai, taken from Flemish March, 92 sq.
Doué, 1
Douro, river, 420
Douzy, Charles the Bald at, 50
Dover, 393
Dozy, cited at, 423, 426, 434
Dracontius, African poet, 488; poems edited by Eugenius, 492
Drahomina, mother of Duke Wenceslas, 184
Dream of the Rood, 537, 554
Dresden, MS. at, 526
Dreux, ceded to Odo I, Count of Chartres, 102; recovered, 105; death of Henry I at, 110
Drogo, illegitimate brother of Louis I, 2, 12, 18 sq., 22; Archbishop of Metz, 12, 29 sqq.
Drogo of Mantes, Count of the Vexin, 392
Drogo de Hauteville, 292
Dublin, captured by Danish Fleet (852), 312; Norse stronghold, 317 sq., 324; Scandinavian influence in, 329 sq., 333 sq.; kings of, *see* Olaf, Sigtryggr
Duddus, verses by Boniface to, 512
Dudo, cited, 311
Duduco, Bishop of Wells, 263
Duisburg, 217
Dukes, in Germany, 70, 179 sq., 191, 197, 229, 239, 270; in Italy, 47 sq.; in France, 89–95; in England, 369
Dunbar, Kenneth MacAlpin at, 350
Duncan I, King of Scots, 395
Dunchad (Duncant), 526 sq.
Dungal, Irish theologian, 533
Dun-le-Roi, acquired by Philip I, 111
Dunsinane, battle of, 395
Dunstan, St, Archbishop of Canterbury, Abbot of Glastonbury, 368, 373 sq.; banished, 371; recalled, 372; Bishop of Worcester and London, 372; made Archbishop, 374; influence of, 376, 378; fall of, 379, 509
Durham, 511 *note*; Shrine of St Cuthbert at, 354, 555, 560; Acca's cross at, 555; Frithstan's vestments at, 555 sq.; Cathedral of, 560, 562, 564; Scandinavian influence at, 337; bishops of, *see* Aldhun, Ranulf
Durtal, castle of, 118
Dyfed (Demetia), tribal unit, 341 sq., 355; 360
Dyle, river, Danes defeated on, 64, 322
Dyri (Dir), settles in Kiev, 327

Eadbert Praen, revolt of, in Kent, 343
Eadburh, marries Beorhtric of Wessex, 340
Eadgifu, Queen, 371
Eadgifu, wife of Charles the Simple, 77, 366
Eadhild, wife of Hugh the Great, 82, 366
Eadmer, chaplain to Anselm, cited, 124
Eadred, King of England, 370 sq., 374
Eadric Streona (the Grasper), Duke of West Mercia, 382 sq.; feud with Edmund, 384 sq.; death of, 387
Eadsige, Archbishop of Canterbury, 393
Eadulf, Earl of Northumberland, 389
Eadwig, 370, 374, 408; becomes King of England, 371; revolt against, 372
Eadwig, son of Aethelred, 386
Eahfrid, Aldhelm's letter to, 510
Ealdgyth, 397
Ealdred, high reeve of Bamborough, 365
Ealdred, son of Uhtred, 387
Ealdred, Bishop of Worcester, 406
Ealhmund, King of Kent, 340, 345
Ealhstan, Bishop of Sherborne, 344 sq.
Ealhswith, wife of Alfred, 352
Eanbald, Archbishop of York, 514
Eanred, King of Northumbria makes terms with Ecgbert, 346
Eardulf, Bishop of Lindisfarne, 354
Eardwulf, King of Northumbria, 341
East Anglia, revolts from, Mercia, 345; independent position of, 346; conquered by Vikings, 312, 318, 348, 350 sq., 355 sq.; colonised, 322 sqq., 356; submits to Edward the Elder, 364; hundreds of, 367; semi-independence of, 370; invaded by Danes, 382; 385, 387; society in, 333, 337 sq., 401; kings and earls of, *see* Aelfgar, Aethelstan, Aethelwin, Edmund, Eric, Guthrum, Gyrth, Harold, Thorkil
East Franks, the, 7, 69 sq., 179, 181, 191; and Arnulf, 62, 71; *see also* Franconia
East Mark (of Bavaria), or Austria, given to Carloman, 51; given to Liutpold of Babenberg, 206; extensions of, 208, 261, 281, 303; 298, 301, 303; margraves of, *see* Adalbert, Leopold, Liutpold
East Mark (of Saxony), with Lausitz (Lusatia), conquest of, 192, 202 *and note*; 208; 211 sq.; conquered by Boleslav Chrobry, 222, 226; Henry II in, 227; Conrad II and, 261 sq.; margraves of, *see* Gero, Thietmar; *see also* Lausitz, Lusatians
Ebbo, Archbishop of Rheims, mission to the Danes, 6, 314; Louis the Pious and, 18; deposed, 20, 30, 450; Bishop of Hildesheim, 32
Ebro, river, 413
Ecbasis Captivi, 531
Ecgberht, King of Northumbria, 318
Ecgbert, exiled by Offa and Beorhtric, 340; made King of Wessex, 344; subdues Cornwall, 344 sq.; defeats Beornwulf, 345; subdues Kent, 345; invades Mercia, 346; threatens Northumbria, 346; defeats the Vikings, 347; death of, 347
Ecgfrith, King of Mercia, 340

Echternach, 467

Ecija, 418 sq.

Eckhard, Margrave of Meissen, 222; recovers Meissen, 211 sq.; claims crown of Germany, 216; career, 216; slain, 217

Eckhard, Margrave of Meissen, 260; adviser of Henry III, 276 sqq., 279; death of, 289

Eddisbury, 363

Edgar, 324, 370; 380; becomes King of England, 372; ecclesiastical reforms of, 372 sqq.; temporal legislation, 376 sqq., 387 sq., 408; death of, 378

Edgar the Aetheling, 397

Edington, battle of, 322, 356

Edith, marries Edward the Confessor, 391; 394 sq.

Edith, wife of Otto I, 183, 204, 205 *note*

Edmund, King of Wessex, and Danish revolt, 368; cedes Cumberland to the Scots, 368; relations to the Church, 368 sq., 373

Edmund, St, King of East Anglia, 318, 350 sq.

Edmund (Ironside), King of Wessex, 397; feud with Eadred, 384; war with the Danes, 385; death of, 386

Edward the Elder, King of Wessex, 77; 360 sq.; 373; 555 sq.; revolt against, 361; erects new sees, 362; legislation of, 362; 183 *note*; 369; 402 *note*; wars with Danes, 183, 318, 320, 323, 363 sq.; lord of Mercia, 364

Edward the Martyr, King of England, reign and death of, 378 sq.

Edward the Confessor, King of England, early years, 325, 386, 389; character and policy, 390 sqq., 399; relations with the Empire, 294; breach with Godwin, 393 sqq.; succession question, 397 sq.; death of, 399

Edward I, King of England, and land tenures in Aquitaine, 459 sq.; and English serjeanties, 462; *quo warranto* inquest, 466

Edwin, Earl of Mercia, 397; intrigue against Tostig, 398

Egdor. *See* Eider

Eggideus, Count, 11

Egilbert, Bishop of Freising, 269, 273 sq.; guardian of Henry III, 273; Adalbero's deposition, 269, 274

Egilo, Archbishop of Sens, 43

Eglaf, Earl of Herefordshire, 387, 392

Egypt, 433; Fātimites in, 168; architecture in, 539, 541, 547; iconography in, 548 sqq.; textile ornament, 550

Eichstedt, see of, 237; bishops of, *see* Megingaud, Victor II (Gebhard)

Eider (Egdor), river, and Danish encroachments, 185, 263, 309, 312 sq.; Horic and, 315, 319, 321; Slav border, 297

Eigg, attacked by pirates in the 7th century, 310

Eigil, life of, by Candidus, 534

Einar (Turf Einar), Earl of Orkney, 326

Einhard, 522, 533, 556; *Vita Karoli* of, 517 sq.; 519 sq.; 530; 534

Ekbert, cousin of Otto I, 197

Ekbert, nephew of Herman, Duke of Saxony, raises rebellion, 200

Ekkehard of St Gall, 531

Elbe, 6; Vikings ascend the, 212; Poles seize the, 222; Polish schemes for, 226; 260, 262, 304; German defeat on, 299, 306

Elbodug of Caer Gybi, 342

Election, to Bishoprics, 232 sqq., 307; to Duchy of Bavaria, 279, 307; to Papacy, 291, 293 sq., 306 sq.

Electors (of the Empire), 464

Elene, A.S. poem, 537

Elias, Irish scholar, 527

Eligius, St, of Noyon, 490

Elipandus of Toledo, Adoptionist, 523, 532

Elisachar, Chancellor, 3; Abbot, 8, 12, 15

Ellandun (Nether Wroughton), battle of, 345

Elsloo, Danish camp at, 59

Elster, Black, river, boundary of Poland, 222

Elster, White, river, reached by Poles, 222

Elvira, 411; Ibn Hafsūn and, 418 sq.; conquered by 'Abd-ar-Raḥmān III, 419; civilisation of, 429, 437; bishop of, *see* Recemund

Elvira, nun, and Ramiro III, 424

Ely, monastery of, 351, 562 sq., 567; refounded, 375, 379; soke of, 376 sq.

Emma, wife of Aethelred, 383; marries Knut, 386, 388 sq.; 392, 408

Emma, wife of Louis the German, 19

Emma, wife of Lothair of France, 207

Emma, wife of Raoul, King of France, 75 *note*

Emma, daughter of Stephen, lord of Montrevault, 118

Empire, Eastern (Byzantine), in South Italy, 150, 178; 166 sqq.; 268; and Berengar II, 158; and Henry II, 250 sq.; relations to the Western Empire, 6, 167; to Venice, 177; to Sardinia, 178; to Caliphs of Cordova, 423, 431, 436; literary connexion with Ireland, 503; with the West, 528; Liudprand on, 534 sq.; Emperors of, *see* Basil, Constantine, John Tzimisces, Justin, Justinian, Leo, Michael, Nicephorus, Romanus, Theodosius

Empire, Holy Roman. *See* Empire, Western

Empire, Western, or Holy Roman, Chap. I, 443 sq.; division of, 28 sq.; in Italy, 34, 47, 50 sq., 58; union under Charles the Fat, 59; dismemberment, 62 sq.; in Italy, 65 sqq., 138, 149, 152 sqq.; renewed as Holy Roman Empire by Otto I, 162, 164 sq.; schemes of Otto III, 173 sq., 213; history of, from 962, Chaps. VII, VIII, IX, X, XI, XII; Emperors of, *see* Arnulf, Berengar, Charlemagne, Charles, Conrad, Frederick, Guy, Henry, Lambert, Lothar, Louis, Otto

Engeltrude, wife of Pepin, 13

Engilberga, Empress, wife of Louis II, 44, 46 sq., 56

England, kingdom of, foundations and union, 360, 370 sq., 380, 391; law and institutions, 362, 366 sqq., 369, 375 sqq., 386 sq.; attacked by Vikings, 59, 183, 310 sqq., 318 sqq., 322 sqq., 379 sqq.; conquest of, by Svein, 382 sqq.; by Knut, 384 sqq.; social history of, 399 sqq.; learning and literature in, 510 sqq.; literary connexion with Spain, 511, 524; art in, 555 sqq.; kings of, *see* Aethelred, Eadred, Eadwig, Edgar, Edward, Harold, Harthacnut, Henry, John, Knut, Richard, Stephen, Svein, William

Enguerand, chamberlain, 51

Ennius, 485, 491

Ennodius, epigrammatist, 499

Enoch, Book of, 506

Ensburg, fortress of, 69

Eon of Penthièvre, 128

Epernay, Hincmar dies at, 59

Ephesus, excavations at, 547

Epiphanius, *Historia Tripartita* of, 487

Epiphanius, on Weights and Measures, 493

Epte, river, 73, 94, 322

Erchanger, Count Palatine, 69; executed, 70

Eresburg, fortress of, submits to Otto I, 188

Erfurt, Synod of (932), 185; assembly at (936), 186 sq.

Eric, Viking leader, 86

Eric, jarl of Yorkshire, 385, 387

Eric, King of East Anglia, 361

Eric, King of Sweden, 381

Eric Blood-Axe, King of Yorkshire, 323 sq., 370 sq.

Erispoë, Breton king, 33, 35

Erkambald, 519

Erkambald, Abbot of Fulda, made Archbishop of Mayence, 239, 250

Ermengarde, Empress, 5; death of, 12

Ermengarde, wife of Lothar I, 12

Ermengarde, daughter of the Emperor Louis II, 49; wife of Boso, 53, 56 sqq., 62, 137 sq.

Ermengarde, wife of Rodolph III, 142

Ermenrich of Ellwangen, 535

Ermentrude, wife of Charles the Bald, 35, 44

Ermingarde, wife of Adalbert of Ivrea, 153, 157

Ermoldus Nigellus, 523

Ernest II, of Babenberg, Duke of Swabia; revolts against Henry II, 223; made Duke, 239; death of, 249; 254

Ernest III, Duke of Swabia, 249; first revolt of, 257; second revolt of, 256 sqq.; imprisoned, 258; last revolt of, 258, 270, 276

Erzgebirge, Henry II crosses the, 225

Essen, Abbess of. *See* Theophano

Essex, 392; 394; 406; submits to Wessex, 345; colonised by Vikings, 356; attacked by Edward the Elder, 363; institutions of, 367; Danes in, 385; Scandinavian influence in, 337; duke of, *see* Brihtnoth

Estrith, daughter of Svein, 387, 389

Etampes, and the Capetians, 96, 104; 208

Ethandun. *See* Edington

Eu, Northmen slaughtered at, 88; lord of, *see* William Busac

Eucharistic controversy, in ninth century, 533

Eudes. *See* Odo

Eugenius II, Pope, 5

Eugenius, Archbishop of Toledo, 492 sqq., 524

Eulogio (Eulogius), Archbishop of Toledo, 416 sq.; 438; 523 sq.

Eulogius, Patriarch of Alexandria, 541

Eusebius, St, 343, 493, 507

Eustace, Count of Boulogne, 393

Euticius Pompeius, grammarian, 516

Eutychius, grammarian, 343, 525

Everard, Bishop of Bamberg, 237 sq.

Everard, Marquess of Friuli, 47

Everard, Duke of Franconia, brother of Conrad I, 70, 179, 181, 187; rebellion of, 188 sqq.; death of, 190

Evernew Tongue, 505

Evesham, monastery of, 379

Evreux, granted to Rollo, 73, 86, 94, 322; invaded by Henry I, 109

Ewyas, castle of, 395

Exeter, 357, 362; Vikings in, 355; 382; cathedral of, 563

Exmouth, 382

Exultet roll in British Museum, 566

Ezo, son of Herman Count Palatine in Lorraine, 215

Fabius Aethelweard. *See* Aethelweard

Fakihs, chap. xvi

Falkenstein, Ernest of Swabia at, 258

False Decretals, 448, 453 *and note*

Faremoutier, 2

Farfa, 250; Abbey of, destroyed, 150; disorder in, 178; Henry II and, 243; abbot of, *see* Hugh

Faroe Islands, Irish missionaries in, 310; Vikings in, 346; 535

Fastidius, bishop and writer, 508

Fātima, 413

Fātimite Caliphate, 150 sqq., 166, 168; 421 sqq., 431; *see also* Africa

Fauquembergue, battle at (925), 88

Faye-la-Vineuse, fief of Anjou, 118

Felix, biographer of Eusebius, 494

Felix of Urgel, Adoptionist, 523

Ferdinand, King of Castile and Leon, 428

Fergus, writer of St Gall Gospels, 527

Fernan (Ferdinand) Gonzalez, Count of Castile, 422 sqq.; 428

Ferrara, county of, 221

Ferrières, coronation at, 57; abbot of, *see* Servatus Lupus

Feudal Aids, cited, 462

Feudalism, chap. xviii, in England; *temp.* Aethelstan, 367, 369 sq.; *temp.* Edgar, 375 sqq.; *temp.* Knut, etc., 401 sqq.; in Spain, 439 sq.; 457; 393

Fez, 415

Fidejussio, 367

Fiefs, in Francia, 54; in France, 116 sqq.; in Italy, 174 sq.; in Germany, 229; succession to in Italy and Germany, 266, 270; in France, 53

Field of Lies, the. *See Lügenfeld*

Filioque clause, 523

Fiorenzuola, Berengar defeated at (923), 136, 153

Fischa, boundary between Germany and Hungary, 260 sq., 281

Five Boroughs, 319, 355, 367, 369, 380; revolt, 368; welcome Svein, 383 sq.; Scandinavian influence in, 333 sq., 336 sqq. *See* Derby, Leicester, Lincoln, Nottingham, Stamford

Flaccus, Valerius, 505 note

Flanders, Normans in, 58; March of, 92 sq., 97; growth of, 121 sqq.; 398; counts of, 389, *see* Arnold, Baldwin, Robert

Flavius Felix, 488

Flemish March. *See* Flanders

Fleury, Abbey of, St Benoît-sur-Loire, 104, 115, 562; and monastic reform, 373 sqq.; Biblical MS. from, 519; library of, 521; abbots of, 103, *see* Boso, Theodulf

Flodoard, historian of Rheims, 534

Flora, 416 sq.

Florence, Count of Holland, 294

Florence, Spanish Chapel in, 550 note; baptistery at, 557; Syrian MS. at, 558

Florennes, Lambert of Louvain killed at, 248

Florus of Lyons, political writer, 10, 28, 445

Flushing, captured by Dietrich of Holland, 289; given to Bishop of Utrecht, 289, 292; Henry III defeated at, 293

Focas, grammarian, 516

Fontenoy (Fontanetum), battle of, 24 sq.

Forchheim, assembly at (900), 68, (911), 69

Formosus, Pope, Bishop of Porto, 56, 65 sqq., 454

Forth, Firth of, English frontier, 350, 366, 370, 395

Fortunatus, Venantius, poet, 309, 495, 496, 524

Fouron, treaty made at, 56

France (West Franks, Western Francia), kingdom of, Chaps. II, III, IV, V; 27 sqq., 134; relations to Germany, 211; and the Vikings, 310, 315 sq., 319 sqq.; kings of, *see* Carloman, Charles, Henry, Hugh, Lothair, Louis, Odo, Philip, Raoul, Robert; dukes of, *see* Hugh; allodial right in, 459 sq.; baronies in, 464; private wars in, 465; learning and letters in, 494 sqq.; literary influence on Ireland before St Patrick, 498, 501; Romanesque architecture in, 557; *see also* Western Kingdom

Franche-Comté, 247, 287 *note*; *see also* Burgundy, County of

Francia (Franks), undivided kingdom of, Chaps. I, II; disruption of, 26 sqq.; re-

united under Charles the Fat, 58; final disruption of, 62 sq.; kings of, *see* Charles, Charlemagne, Chlotar, Louis, Pepin, Theodoric, Theudibert; *see also* Franks

Francia [Western]; given to Louis III, 57; Odo and, 71; Hugh Capet and, 83, 104; Northmen invade, 87 sq.; limits of, 91 sq.; disintegration of, 97

Franco, deacon. *See* Boniface VII

Franco, Bishop of Liège, 68

Franconia, given to Louis the Younger, 51; duchy of, 70; revolt in, 188; administered by Otto I, 191; rebels, 197; invaded by Hungarians, 198; Conrad the Younger in, 253; dukes of, *see* Conrad, Everard; *see also* East Franks

Frankfort, assembly at (823), 6, (885), 60; 17; 42; 51; synod at, 237; assembly at, 256; Henry III's illness at, 288

Franks, the, Chaps. I, II, 27 sqq.; 420; 422; *see also* Francia

Frascati, Henry III at, 291

Fraxinetum. *See* Le Frainet

Freculphus of Lisieux, chronicler, 534

Fredegarius, chronicler, 497, 500

Frederick Barbarossa, Emperor, and Burgundy, 146 sq.; and Henry the Lion, 465

Frederick II, Emperor, and Burgundy, 147, 462, 464

Frederick, Archbishop of Mayence, rebellion of, against Otto I, 190 sq., 195 sq.; submits, 198; death of, 199

Frederick, Archbishop of Ravenna, 221, 224

Frederick, brother of Adalbero of Metz, Duke of Upper Lorraine, 201

Frederick II, Duke of Upper Lorraine, 270

Frederick of Luxemburg, Duke of Lower Lorraine, 289

Frederick, Count, 290

Freising, bishop of. *See* Egilbert

Friesland. *See* Frisia

Frisia, Viking raids on, 7, 20, 32, 185, 210, 227, 309 sqq.; 338; given to Harold, 313; Louis the Pious and, 347; given to Lothar, 26; given to Roric, 315; given to Godröðr, 59, 315, 321; Alfred and, 357; end of Viking rule in, 321; revolts against Henry II, 227; the count of Holland and, 248; see of Bremen and, 293

Frithstan, vestments of Bishop, 555 sq.

Fritzlar, coronation of Henry the Fowler at, 179; diet of (953), 196, (954), 199

Friuli, March of, 47; ceded to Germany, 159; marquesses of, *see* Berengar, Cadolah, Everard, Unroch; *see also* Aquileia, Verona

Frohse, assembly at, 216

Frome, 371

Fruttuaria, monastery of, 245

Fuero Juzgo, Spanish Code, 430, 441

Fulbert, Bishop of Chartres, 116, 131, 468

Fulcrad, Count of Arles, 31

Fulda, bishopric of, 232; abbey of, 236; Benedict VIII at, 250; MSS. at, 512, 517, 520 sq.; abbots of, 522, *see* Erkambald, Hademar, Raban Maur

Fulgentius, *De Dubiis Nominibus*, 499
Fulham, Vikings at, 321, 356
Fulk, Archbishop of Rheims, 527; and Charles the Simple, 71 sqq.; opposes Odo, 72 sq., 81 sq.; assassinated, 92
Fulk Nerra, Count of Anjou, builds castles, 118; Odo of Chartres and, 102, 257; Hugh of Beauvais and, 132; career of, 118, 125 sqq.
Fulk Rechin, Count of Anjou, 125; and Geoffrey the Bearded, 111, 119 sq.; and Bertrada, 113
Fulk the Red, Count of Anjou, 95
Fulk the Good, Count of Anjou, 96
Furness, Scandinavian influence in, 336
Fyn, 208
Fyrd, reformed by Alfred, 357; besieges London, 358; repels the Vikings, 360

Gaeta, independence of, 150; 151; Otto III and, 176
Gainsborough, Svein and Knut at, 325, 383 sqq.
Galicia, raided by Alfonso I, 410; Vikings in, 320, 416; Bermudo III in, 422; 428; 431; 438; 441; 489
Gall-Gaedhil, the, in Ireland, 317; in the Hebrides, 325
Galloway, Vikings in, 325, 335; Picts in, 341
Gallus, St, 521
Gallus, Titius, commentator on Virgil, 507
Galo, Bishop of Paris, election of, 113
Gamel, son of Orm, 398
Gandersheim, fortifications of, 182; disputed jurisdiction over the monastery of, 235, 251, 255 sq.; abbesses of, *see* Adelaide, Hathumoda, Sophia
Ganelon (Wenilo), Archbishop of Sens, 32, 37, 447
Garcia, King of Navarre, 423 sq., 426
Garcia, King of Navarre, 428
Garcia Fernandez, Count of Castile, 425 sq.
Garcia II, Count of Castile, murdered, 428
Garcia Ximenez, 410
Garde-Freinet. *See* Le Frainet
Garigliano, river, Saracens on, 149 sqq.; catapan Basil on, 250
Garnier, Count, 2
Garonne, river, and the Vikings, 316, 320
Gascony, revolt in, 8; given to Pepin, 10; independence of, 89 sq.; subject to Aquitaine, 129; dukes of, *see* Centullus, Lupus, Odo, Sancho, Séguin, William
Gâtinais, independence of, 96; added to royal domain, 111
Gaudentius, commentator on Virgil, 507
Gautbert, first Bishop of Sweden, 314
Gauzbert, Count, family of, 35
Geats. *See* Götar
Gebhard, Archbishop of Ravenna, 265
Gebhard, Bishop of Eichstedt. *See* Victor II
Gebhard, Bishop of Ratisbon, 296, 299, 303
Gebhard, Duke of Lorraine, 68
Gelasius I, Pope, canon of, 506

Gellius, Aulus, 522
Genesis, A.S. poems upon, 537; Cotton MS. of, 549 sq.; Vienna MS. of, 550
Geneva, Conrad II at, 144 sq., 259; diocese of, 38, 63, 134; count of, 144; *and see* Gerald
Geneva, Lake of, 15, 140
Gengulphus of Toul, legend of, 532
Gennadius of Marseilles, 489, 491
Genoa, stormed by Fātimites (935), 155; Otbertine counts of, 240; Sardinia and, 250
Geoffrey Martel, Count of Anjou, 126, 283, acquires Tours, 108; war with William of Normandy, 109 sq., 292; rule of, 118 sq.
Geoffrey the Bearded, Count of Anjou, 111, 119
Geoffrey Grisegonelle, Count of Anjou, 96
Geoffrey Martel the Younger, Count of Anjou, death of, 120
Geoffrey, lord of Mayenne, 110
George, Greek priest, 6
George the Syncellus, chronicler, 528
Gerald, Count of Geneva, seizes Lyons, 279; 287
Gerard, Bishop of Angoulême, 130
Gerard, Bishop of Cambrai, 251, 275, 282, 298, 465
Gerard of Chatenois, made Duke of Upper Lorraine, 294
Gerard, Count of Alsace, 248 sq.
Gerard, Count of Paris, 24
Gerard, Count of Vienne (Girard of Roussillon), regent in Provence, 34, 41, 46
Gerard, St, of Brogne, reforms Flemish monasteries, 373, 457
Gerberga, wife of Gilbert of Lorraine, 181; wife of Louis d'Outremer, 79, 193
Gerberga, wife of Herman Duke of Swabia, 143 *note*
Gerberoy, siege of (1078), 112, 120
Gerbert of Aurillac. *See* Sylvester II, Pope
Germanicus, 522
Germanus, Abbot of Winchcombe, 378
Germanus, St, of Auxerre, *Life* of, 527
Germany (East Franks), Chaps. II, III, VIII, IX, X, XI, XII; 23; kingdom of, 26 sqq., 62 sq.; and Hungarian invasions, 69, 87 sq.; 70; 135; royal power in, 165 sq., 187, 229 sq.; relations to the Church, 231–36; chancery of, 213; allodial right in, 459; *ministeriales* in, 462; baronies in, 464; leagues in, 465 sq.; art in, 552, 559; kings of, *see* Arnulf, Carloman, Charles, Conrad, Henry, Louis, Maximilian, Otto, Philip, Rudolf; *see also* East Franks
Germigny, church at, 560 sq., 567
Gero, Archbishop of Magdeburg, 232, 239
Gero, Margrave, conquers the Wends, 187, 192, 200, 202
Gero, Margrave of the East Mark, 217, 222
Gerold, Count of the Eastern March, 4
Gerona, 8; county of, 90; cathedral of, 437
Gers, river, 495

Gervase, Bishop of Le Mans, 109
Gesta Berengarii, 531
Getae. *See* Götar
Gharbīb, 414
Ghent, Danes at, 59; 92; taken by Baldwin IV, 228; castle built by Otto I, 228; captured by Henry II, 250; Dunstan at, 371. *See* Blandinium, abbey of
Gibichenstein, Ernest of Swabia imprisoned at, 258; Godfrey of Upper Lorraine imprisoned at, 288 sq.
Gilbert (Giselbert), Duke of Lorraine, 78; and Henry the Fowler, 180 sq., 187; rebels against Otto I, 189 sq.; drowned, 190
Gilbert (Giselbert), vassal of Charles the Bald, 31 sq.
Gilbert of Burgundy, Count of Autun, etc., 83, 94, 96
Gildas, writings of, 508 sq.
Girard of Roussillon. *See* Gerard, Count of Vienne
Gironde, river, and the Vikings, 316
Gisalbert, Abbot, 536
Gisela, Empress of Conrad II, 264; 273; 276; 294; guardian to Ernest of Swabia, 249; marries Conrad II, 249, 254; Burgundy and, 256; favours Cluniac movement, 271; influence of, 272; Henry III and, 280
Gisela, daughter of Charles the Great, 2
Gisela, wife of Henry the Wrangler, 143 *note*, 227
Gisela, daughter of Louis the Pious, 47
Gisela, Abbess of Nivelles, 60
Gisela, wife of Stephen of Hungary, 261, 303
Gisela, wife of Adalbert of Ivrea, 148
Giselbert. *See* Gilbert
Gisiler, Bishop of Merseburg, Archbishop of Magdeburg, 232 sq., 235
Gisors, acquired by Philip I, 112
Gisulf, Prince of Salerno, resists John XII, 161; dethroned, 169; restored, *ib.*
Glamorgan, tribal unit, 341, 360
Glanvill, English legist, 461
Glastonbury, Abbey of, 374, 378, 404, 509; abbot of, *see* Dunstan
Gloria, laus et honor, hymn, 519
Glossa Ordinaria to the Bible, 522, 532
Gloucester, 393; Vikings in, 355; Abbey of St Oswald, 373; cathedral, 563 sq.
Gloucestershire, 387, 404
Gnesen, metropolitan see founded at, 222; relics removed to Prague from, 300
Goda, sister of Edward the Confessor, 392 sq.
Godalming, 360
Godefrid. *See* Guðröðr
Godehard, Abbot of Altaich, Tegernsee and Hersfeld, 236; Bishop of Hildesheim, 251, 255 sq.
Godescalc, Obotrite noble, 297, 299, 305
Godescalcus. *See* Gottschalk
Godfrey, Duke of Lower Lorraine, 200, 207
Godfrey, Count of the Ardennes, Duke of Lower Lorraine, 239, 248 sq.

Godfrey, Duke of Upper Lorraine, 278; 307; resents the division of the Duchy, 284 sq.; allies with France and Burgundy, 286, 292; deposition and revolt of, 286 sqq.; submission and restoration of, 288 sq.; renewed disaffection of, 292 sq.; second deposition of, 293 sqq.; liberated, 296; marries Beatrice of Tuscany, 296, 298; joins Baldwin of Flanders, 299
Godfrey, Count of Hainault and Verdun, 207, 209 sq.
Godred Crovan, Man conquered by, 335
Godurm. *See* Guðormr
Godwin, Earl of Wessex, 387, 389; house of, 397; accession of Edward the Confessor, 389 sq.; 325; his ambitions, 391 sq.; quarrel with Edward, 393 sqq.; outlawed, 394; restoration and death of, 395
Goffraidh. *See* Guðfriðr
Golden Bull, 464
Goldziher, cited, 434
Gomez, 417
Gondreville, Lothar II at, 42; 45; 57; 59 sq.
Gonzalo, lord of Ribagorza, etc., 428
Gorm, the Old, King of Denmark, makes peace with Henry I, 185; opposes Christianity, 186; tomb of, 332, 380
Gormflaith, wife of Brian Borumha, 324
Gorze, abbot of. *See* Siegfried
Goslar, fortification of, 182; synod of, 249, 251; Henry III at, 276, 278, 287, 295, 298 sq.; Břatislav at, 280; Henry IV born at, 295; cathedral, 295, 299; Casimir at, 302; palace of, 561
Götar (Getae, Geats), 309
Gothalania. *See* Catalonia
Gothia, given to Charles the Bald, 16; Catalonia and, 89; Toulouse and, 90, 130; Hungarians in, 139; marquesses of, *see* Bernard, Raymond; *see also* Septimania
Gothland, memorial stones of, 310, 328 sq.; Anglo-Saxon coins found at, 333
Gotricus. *See* Guðröðr the Yngling
Gottschalk (Godescalcus), of Orbais, 524, 529, 533
Gournay-sur-Marne, castle of, 114
Gozelo, Duke of Lower Lorraine, 254, 256 sq.; kills Odo II, 267; acquires Upper Lorraine, 270, 275; at Aix, 278; death of, 284
Gozelo the Coward, Duke of Lower Lorraine, 284, 289
Grado, see of, 265
Gran, Hungarians defeated at, 261
Granada, 432
Greek, Language and Literature, knowledge of, 489, 491, 493, 496 sq., 507 sqq., 515, 517, 528; in Ireland, 502 sqq., 524 sqq.; in England, 502 sqq., 529; in ninth century, 524 sqq.; glossaries, 526
Greek Church, at Trim, 503
Greenwich, Danes at, 383
Gregory I, Saint, the Great, Pope, **541**; writings of, 358, 487 sqq., 493, **537**

Gregory IV, Pope, and the Emperor, 6; and Lothar, 17 sq.; fortifies the Tiber, 49; on the lay power, 448 sq.

Gregory V, Pope (Bruno of Carinthia), accession of, 172, 214; Otto III and, 174; council of St Basle, 103; Ardoin and, 220; death of, 173

Gregory VI, Pope, 291, 294, 454

Gregory VII, Pope, 291

Gregory Asbestas, Archbishop of Syracuse, 451

Gregory, candidate for Papacy (1012), 241

Gregory, Count of Tusculum, xvii, 454

Gregory Trachaniotis, catapan, 177

Gregory of Tours, *History of the Franks* of, 495 sq.

Grimaldus of St Gall, 522, 535

Grimbald, 358

Grimoald, Prince of Benevento, 8

Groix, Scandinavian influence at, 332

Grona, Synod at, 256

Gruffydd (Griffith) ap Llywelyn, Prince of North Wales, 396; marries Ealdgyth of Mercia, 397; attacks Wessex, 396 sq.; death of, 397

Gundacelete, battle of, 417

Guadalajara, 410

Guadalete, battle of, 409

Guadalquivir, river, 411 sq., 416

Guadiana, river, 420

Guaimar II, Prince of Salerno, 151 sq.

Guaimar III, Prince of Salerno, 268

Guaimar IV, Prince of Salerno, 268, 292

Gualdrada, wife of Pietro Candiano IV, 170

Guðfrið of Northumbria, 332

Guðfriðr (Goffraidh), 318

Guðormr (Alfred's foe). *See* Guthrum

Guðormr (Godurm), 315

Guðröðr the Yngling (Godefridus, Gotricus), King of Denmark, 312 sq., 315; 326

Guðröðr, King of the Western Isles, 326

Guðröðr (Godefrid), Viking leader, granted Frisia, 59, 315; slain, 60, 321

Guerbigny, Northmen at, 72, 85

Guerür, St, 347 *note*

Guido, Marquess of Tuscany, 153 sq.

Guido, son of Berengar II, 161

Guido, Archbishop of Milan, 291

Guido, Bishop of Piacenza, 292

Guildford, 360, 389

Guines, Count of, 460

Gundrada, granddaughter of Charles Martel, 2

Gundulf, Bishop of Rochester, 470

Gunnhild, sister of Svein, 381 sq.

Gunnhild of Sweden, 297

Gunnhild (Kunigunda), daughter of Knut, marries King Henry son of Conrad II, 263, 274, 294; death of, 269, 274

Gunthamund, Vandal king, 492

Gunther, Archbishop of Cologne, 526; and Theutberga, 39; deposed, 42, 45, 449 sq.

Gunther, hermit of Böhmer Wald, 277

Gunzelin, made Margrave of Meissen, 222; 223

Gunzo of Novara, 535

Guthrum (Guðormr), King, wars with Alfred, 353, 355 sq., 358 sq.; settles in East Anglia, 319, 322 sq., 356 sq.; death of, 361

Guthrum, King of East Anglia, 361, 364

Guy (Guido), Emperor, Duke of Spoleto, King of Italy, 63 sqq.; Emperor, 65; death of, 66; 72; 155 sq.

Guy, Duke of Spoleto, 48

Guy, Count of the March of Brittany, 47

Guy, Count of Camerino, 48

Guy, lord of Vernon and Brienne, 109

Guy, Count of Ponthieu, 398

Guy-Geoffrey, Duke of Aquitaine. *See* William VIII

Gwent, Welsh tribal unit, 341, 360

Gwynedd. *See* Wales, North

Gyrth, Earl of East Anglia, 397

Gytha, wife of Earl Godwin, 389

Hacket, allodial estates of, 460

Hademar, Abbot of Fulda, 202

Hadoardus, 523

Hadrian, Emperor, 503

Hadrian the Abbot, 488, 502, 510 sqq., 514

Hadrian II, Pope, 43, 46, 453

Hadrian III, Pope, 60

Hafrsfjord, battle at (872), 318, 325, 339

Hagano, favourite of Charles the Simple, 74

Hagano, Bishop of Bergamo, 450

Hainault, given to Godfrey, 207; counts of, *see* Reginar

Hakam I, Emir of Spain, 8, 414 sq.

Hakam II, Caliph of Cordova, reign of, 423 sq.; patron of learning, 425, 433, 435; 437

Hákon the Bad, Earl (Jarl) of Norway, 324, 326, 380; aids Harold Bluetooth, 205

Hákon, Earl of Worcestershire, 387, 392

Halbdenus. *See* Halfdanr

Halberstadt, bishops of, 202, 209, 232

Halfdanr (Irish, Albdann; O.E., Halfdene), King of Northumbria, attacks Northumbria, 319, 350, 357; enters Mercia, 351; enters Wessex, 352; 361; at London, 353; ravages Bernicia, 353 sq.; King of Denmark, 321; death of, 318 sq.

Halfdene. *See* Halfdanr

Halicarnassus, mausoleum of, 552

Halinard of Dijon, 279; Archbishop of Lyons, 294

Halitgar, Bishop of Cambrai, 6

Hamburg; see of, founded, 7, 314; destroyed by Danes, 31, 314; burnt by Obotrites, 208; fortifications at, 305; 232; Archbishop of Bremen at, 290, 297; archbishops of, *see* Adalbert, Albrand, Anskar, Lievizo, Unwan

Hamelin I, lord of Langeais, 118

Hampshire, plundered by Danes, 381 sq., 405

Harðacnútr. *See* Harthacnut

Hardesyssel, 311 *note*

Hardouin, Bishop of Langres, 124

Harleian MSS., 526

Harold, King of Denmark, baptism of, 6 sq., 313 sq.; death of, 315 sq.; 321

Harold, King of Denmark, succeeds Svein, 384

Harold Fairhair, King of Norway, 311, 323, 370; conquests of, 325 sq., 339, 380

Harold Gormson (Bluetooth), King of Denmark, baptism of, 186, 202; submits to Otto II, 205, 326; deposed, 208, 380

Harold Hardrada, King of Norway, 297, 328

Harold Harefoot, King of England, 325, 389

Harold Hyldetan (Herioldus, O.N. Haraldr), King of Denmark, 313

Harold, King of England; Earl of East Anglia, 392 sq.; outlawed, 394; succeeds to Earldom of Wessex, 395 sq.; obtains Herefordshire, 397; war with Welsh, 396 sq.; oath to William, 398; Morkere's revolt, 398 sq.

Harrānī, 416

Harrow, 343 sq.

Hartgar of Tongres, 526

Harthacnut (Harðacnútr), King of Denmark, 388; becomes King of England, 325, 389

Hartwich, Bishop of Bamberg, 297

Hārūn ar-Rashīd, Abbasid Caliph, 415

Harz, 276

Hasdai ibn Shabrut, Jewish diplomatist, 429

Hasting (Hásteinn), Viking leader, 320, 359

Hastings, 357

Hatfield, 402 *note*

Hatheburg, wife of Henry I, 186

Hathumoda, first Abbess of Gandersheim, 529 sq.

Hatto, Archbishop of Vich, 535

Hatton, MS. at, 506 *note*

Havel, river, Germans defeated on, 299, 306

Havelberg, bishopric founded in, 192; church burnt, 208

Havoise, wife of Hoel of Cornouailles, 128

Haymo of Halberstadt, 532

Hebrew, knowledge of, 508, 515, 520

Hebrides (Suðreyjar), the, Viking settlements in, 324 sqq.; Scandinavian influence in, 324 sqq.; 333 sq. *See also* Western Isles

Hector, Archbishop of Besançon, 141

Hedbourne Worthy, 556

Hedeby-Slesvik, trading centre, 332

Hedwig, widow of Burchard, Duke of Swabia, revolts, 204; 205 *note*

Hedwig, wife of Hugh the Great, 83, 193 *note*

Heiric of Auxerre, 527, 534; cited, 524

Helgaud, biographer of Robert the Pious, 105

Helge, river, 388

Heliodorus, *Aethiopica* of, 538

Hellmern, burnt by Everard, 188

Helperic of Auxerre, 535

Hemmingus (Hemmingr), killed at Walcheren (837), 313

Hendrica, 356, 359, 364

Henries, War of the Three, 206

Henry I, the Fowler, King of Germany, 70,
74, 205 *note*, 215, 220; election of, 179; policy of, 179 sqq., 182 sqq.; the Church and, 185 sq.; death of, 186

Henry II, Emperor, succeeds Henry the Wrangler in Bavaria, 143 *note*, 176 sq., 205 *note*, 212, 218 sq.; struggle for the crown of Germany, 215 sqq.; crowned at Mayence, 217; opposition in Saxony, 216 sqq.; birth, character, and policy, 218 sq.; loss of Lombardy, 218, 220 sqq.; loss of Bohemia, 218, 222 sq.; quarrel with Poland, 222 sq.; becomes King of Lombardy, 224; recovers Bohemia, 225; allies with heathen Wends, 226; makes peace with Boleslav, 227; Burgundy and, 141 sq., 143 *note*, 227; Flanders and, 106, 228; losses to Poland, 228; resources of the Crown, 229 sq.; ecclesiastical policy, 231 sqq., 241, 242, 246, 249 sq., 253; second visit to Italy, 239 sqq.; crowned Emperor, 243; makes peace in Italy, 246; intervenes in Burgundy, 247 sq., 256; Benedict VIII and, 250; third visit to Italy, 250 sq., 268; death of, 142, 252; succession to, 253 sq.; 261

Henry III, Emperor, Duke of Bavaria, 270, 273 sq.; 279, 287, 307; Duke of Swabia, 270, 273 sq.; 287, 307; Duke of Carinthia, 277; King, 269, 273; relations with Hungary, 261, 273; war with, 278 sqq., 285, 288; 295 sqq., 303 sq.; relations with Bohemia, 262, 273; 276 sqq., 299 sqq.; relations with Burgundy, 273; King of Burgundy, 145 sq., 274, 278 sq.; relations with Lorraine, 284, 286 sqq.; settlement of, 289 sq.; further trouble with, 292 sqq.; first visit to Italy, 266 sq., 277; second visit, 290 sqq.; becomes Emperor and Patrician, 291, 306; last visit, 298 sq.; at Diet of Bamberg, 269, 274; relations with Flushing and Flanders, 289, 293, 297 sq.; marriage policy, 283, 306; marries Gunnhild, 263; marries Agnes, 275, 280, 283; ecclesiastical policy, 275, 277, 291, 306; aims and achievements, 306 sqq.; death of, 299

Henry IV, Emperor, born, 295; elected king, 297; made Duke of Bavaria, 297; crowned, 298; Burgundy and, 146; Rudolf of Swabia and, 289

Henry V, Emperor, and Burgundy, 146

Henry VI, Emperor, and Burgundy, 147

Henry VII, Emperor, and Burgundy, 147

Henry I, King of France, loses Burgundy etc., 107 sq.; wars with vassals, 107–10, 143 sq.; 123; meets Conrad II, 259; Henry III, 280; 294; 299; threatens Lorraine, 285, 292; death of, 110

Henry I, King of England, 121; charter of, 463

Henry II, King of England, 466, **471**

Henry III, King of England, 466

Henry IV, King of England, 536

Henry, Duke of Bavaria, 186; 188; given March of Verona, 159, 196; rebellions against Otto I, 189 sqq.; marriage of, 191, 204; defeats the Hungarians, 195, 198; the Bavarian revolt, 197, 199; death of, 160; 205 *note*

Henry [II], the Wrangler, Duke of Bavaria, 218; revolts against Otto II, 204 sq.; deprived of his Duchy, 206; attempts to supplant Otto III, 80, 209 sqq.; submits, 210; joins Otto III before Brandenburg, 211; death of, 212, 218

Henry of Luxemburg, Duke of Bavaria, 238, 248; and the Lyutitzi, 227; death of, 270

Henry of Luxemburg, Duke of Bavaria, 279, 289, 292 sq., 307; death of, 293

Henry (Odo), Duke of Burgundy, 75 *note*, 106

Henry the Younger, Duke of Carinthia, 205 and *note*, 206; Duke of Bavaria, 209; opposes Henry the Wrangler, 210; cedes Bavaria to him, 210 sq.; death of, 212

Henry the Lion, Duke of Saxony, 465

Henry, Archbishop of Trèves, 293

Henry, Bishop of Augsburg, 206

Henry, Bishop of Würzburg, 237 sq., 246

Henry of Schweinfurt, Margrave of Nordgau, claims Bavaria, 222; revolts, 223 sq.

Henry, Count of Alemannia, 60 sq.

Henry, Count Palatine in Lower Lorraine, 287; chosen successor to Henry III, 289

Henry, Count (or Duke) of Thuringia, 59

Henry, son of Otto I, 196

Henry, son of Stephen of Hungary, denied the Dukedom of Bavaria, 261

Henry, son of Otto Duke of Carinthia, 253

Herbauges, Count of. *See* Reginald

Herbert the Young, Count of Troyes, 83

Herbert the Old, Count of Troyes, 95, 97

Herbert II, Count of Vermandois, 76 sq., 96; 189; and Charles the Simple, 75 sq.; and the Vikings, 87 sq.; death of, 78, 83

Herbert Wake-dog, Count of Maine, 125 sq.

Hereford, Earls of. *See* Eglaf, Ralf; cathedral at, 561

Herefordshire, invaded, 362, 385, 387, 395 sqq.

Herethaland. *See* Hörthaland

Heribert, Archbishop of Cologne, chancellor, 213, 246; and Henry II, 218, 233; death of, 250

Heriger, Archbishop of Mayence, 179

Herioldus. *See* Harold Hyldetan

Herman Billung, Duke of Saxony, 187; subdues the Wends, 192, 202; 197; death of, 203

Herman I, Duke of Swabia, 143 *note*; 157; 187; marriage of, 181; death of, 191

Herman II, Duke of Swabia, claims crown of Germany, 216 sq.; sacks Strasbourg, 217 sq.; submits to Henry II, 218

Herman III, Duke of Swabia, 239, 249

Herman IV, Duke of Swabia, marriage of, 265, 299; death of, 269 sq., 274

Herman, Archbishop of Cologne, 278; 289; 293; and Henry III, 276, 287, 308; and Adalbert of Bremen, 290; death of, 299

Herman, Bishop of Strasbourg, 293

Herman, Count Palatine in Lorraine, 215

Herman, Count of Mons, 292, 295

Herman of Reichenau, 276; cited, 254 *note* 3, 272, 274, 279 sq., 295, 300

Herman, son of Godfrey of Verdun, 210

Hermandad, 416

Hermeneumata Pseudo-Dositheana, 503

Herold, Archbishop of Salzburg, 199

Herred, allodial estates of, 460

Hersfeld, fortification of, 182; abbey of, 236, 293; abbot of, *see* Godehard

Herstall, Louis the Pious at, 2, 6

Hertford, *burh* at, 363

Hertfordshire, 392, 397, 403; hundreds of, 367; Scandinavian influence in, 337

Hervé, Archbishop of Rheims, 74, 87

Héry, village of, 104

Hexham, church at, 560

Hieronymus presbyter, 500

Higbert, Archbishop of Mercia, deprived, 343

Hildebert, Archbishop of Mayence, 187

Hildebold, Archbishop of Cologne, 3

Hildefonsus of Toledo, 489

Hildegarde, Countess of Anjou, 126

Hildesheim, Everard imprisoned at, 188; Henry II educated at, 218; bronzes at, 559; church at, 567; see of, 232, 235, 255 sq.; bishops of, *see* Bernward, Ebbo, Godehard

Hildibald of Worms, Chancellor of Germany, 213

Hilduin, 45

Hilduin, Abbot of St Denis, 524, 526; banished, 15 sq.; joins Lothar, 24

Hincmar, Archbishop of Rheims, 30, 32; 526; prevents a council, 37; Lothar II's marriage, 39, 41, 43; 46; 53 sqq.; Gottschalk, 529, 533; views on monarchy, 446 sqq.; the papacy, 452 sq.; 455; death of, 59; annals of, 45

Hinksey, 402 *note*

Hinxton Down, Vikings defeated at, 347

Hiruath. *See* Hörthaland

Hishām, Caliph of Damascus, 411 sq.

Hishām I, Emir of Spain, 414

Hishām II, Caliph of Cordova, 424 sqq.; disappearance of, 427

Hishām III, al-Mu'tadd, Caliph of Cordova, 427

Hishām, son of Sulaimān al-Musta'īn, 427

Hisperica Famina, 508 sq., 529

Historia Campostellana, cited, 426

Historia Tripartita, 528. *See* Cassiodorus

Höchst, synod at, 252

Hoel, Count of Cornouailles, becomes Duke of Brittany, 128

Hoger, musician, 535

Hohen Altheim, assembly of (916), 69 sq., 194

Holland (in England), submits to Edward the Elder, 364

Holland, counts of. *See* Dietrich, Florence

Holme (Beds.), battle of, 361

Holme (Norf.), monastery of St Benet, 388, 406

Holstein, Danes in, 185

Homer. *See* Angilbert

Homer, *Odyssey* of, 538
Hook Norton, 363
Horace, 522, 524, 526 sq.
Horic (Hárekr), King of Denmark, 20, 313; and Anskar, 314; attacks Louis the German, 31 sq., 315 sq., 319
Horic the Younger, King of Denmark, 314; accession of, 315; death of, 321
Hörthaland, Vikings from, 311, 340
Höskuldr, the Icelander, 333
Höskuldr. *See* Askol'd
Howth, plundered by Vikings, 312
Hoxne, St Edmund martyred at, 351
Hrabanus Maurus, Magnentius. *See* Raban Maur
Hroerekr. *See* Roric, Rurik
Hrolfr. *See* Rollo
Hrollaugr. *See* Rollo
Hrotsvitha, nun of Gandersheim, 531 sq.; cited, 191 *note*
Hubert, Marquess of Tuscany and Spoleto, 157 sq., 161; exiled, 162; restored, 165; 171
Hubert, the Red, Count, 245 sq.
Hubert, brother of Theutberga, Duke of Jurane Burgundy, 38 sq.
Hucbald of St Amand, 531, 535
Huesca, 414, 417
Hugh of Arles, King of Italy; Marquess of Provence, 136, 138 sq., 152; crowned at Pavia, 139, 153; plans to acquire Burgundy, 140, 156; Alberic of Rome and, 154 sq.; alliance with Byzantium, 155; relations with Burgundy and Germany, 156 sq.; fall of, 157; death of, 158
Hugh Capet, King of France, 75 *note*, 80 sqq.; crowned, 84; relations with Aquitaine, 91; and Burgundy, 83, 94; and Neustria, 95 sq.; reign of, 99 sqq.; plots against Otto III, 210; civil war with Charles of Lower Lorraine, 99 sq., 211; death of, 103
Hugh, King, son of Robert the Pious, 107
Hugh of Vermandois, Archbishop of Rheims, 75 sq., 78 sq., 194
Hugh, Abbot of Cluny, 275, 295
Hugh, Abbot of Farfa, 242 sq.
Hugh, Abbot of Saint-Germain, 35, 37; Abbot of Saint-Bertin, *ib.*, 55 sqq.; death of (886), 71, 134
Hugh the Great, Duke of the Franks, Count of Paris, 75 *note*; 193 *note*; 366; possessions of, 76; policy of, 77 sq., 82 sq., 192; captures Louis IV, 79, 193; excommunicated, 79, 176; the Vikings and, 87 sq.; Aquitaine and, 91; Burgundy and, 94, 96; 189; death of, 80
Hugh the Black, Duke of Burgundy, 77, 93 sq., 96
Hugh I, Duke of Burgundy, 124
Hugh, Marquess of Tuscany, rules Spoleto, 171, 244; at Rome, 176, 219; adviser of Otto III, 213; death of, 177
Hugh, Otbertine Marquess, Count of Milan, 266
Hugh of Beauvais, Count of the Palace, 126, 132

Hugh III, Count of Maine, 109
Hugh, Count of Tours, 8
Hugh Bardoux, lord of Broyes, 111, 116
Hugh du Gué, castellan, 119
Hugh, lord of Le Puiset, 115 sq.
Hugh, lord of Amboise and Chaumont, 119
Hugh, illegitimate brother of Louis the Pious, 2; 12; 19
Hugh, illegitimate son of Lothar II, 57 sq., 60
Hugh, son of the lord of Sainte-Maure, 119
Hugh of Flavigny, chronicler cited, 253 *note* 2
Humber, the, 351, 355, 400; Edward the Elder's power reaches, 365; Svein enters, 383 sq.
Humbert Whitehands, Count of Aosta and Maurienne, 144, 259
Humphrey, Archbishop of Ravenna, 292
Hunfrid (Humphrey), Abp. of Magdeburg, 232
Hungarians (Magyars), the, 64; invade Germany, 68 sqq., 74, 182, 191; 195; and France, 87, 185; in Burgundy and Provence, 138 sq., 185; in Italy, 148 sq., 151 sqq., 154 sq., 158, 182, 185; in Languedoc, 153; defeat of, on the Lechfeld (955), 160, 168, 198 sqq., 201; defeat of near Merseburg (933), 185; Christian missions to, xvi, 208; alliance with Poles, 222. *See also* Hungary
Hungary, relations with Germany, 260 sq., 273, 276 sqq., 279 sqq., 285, 287 sq., 295 sqq., 298, 300 sq., 303-5, 397; kings of, *see* Andrew, Obo, Peter, Stephen
Huns, 501
Huntingdon, *burh*, 356; jarl of, 364
Huntingdonshire, hundreds of, 367; earl of, *see* Waltheof; Scandinavian influence in, 337
Hurr, 409
Huy, 559
Hwicce, men of, 344, 356
Hy, abbot of. *See* Adamnan
Hyde, abbey of, 361, 373
Hygelac, King of the Geats, 309
Hywel, Prince of Deheubarth, 364

Ibn Abī-'Āmir. *See* Almanzor
Ibn al-Abbār, cited, 433
Ibn al-Aghlab, Emir of Africa, 419; *see also* Ibrāhīm
Ibn Anas. *See* Mālik ibn Anas
Ibn 'Atīya. *See* Zīrī ibn 'Atīya
Ibn Bashkuwāl, cited, 433
Ibn Bukht. *See* Yūsuf ibn Bukht
Ibn Firnās, 432
Ibn Ghālib. *See* Mahomet ibn Ghālib
Ibn Habīb, 410
Ibn Ḥajjāj. *See* Ibrāhīm ibn Ḥajjāj
Ibn Hāshim at-Tujībī. *See* Mahomet ibn Hāshim at-Tujībī
Ibn Isḥāk. *See* Daisam ibn Isḥāk
Ibn Khaldūn. *See* Ḳuraib ibn Ḳhaldūn
Ibn Khālid, 411
Ibn Ḳuzmān, poet, 433

Ibn Marwān, Prince of Mérida and Badajoz, 417

Ibn Marwān, 421

Ibn Masarra, 419, 431

Ibn Mastana, 418

Ibn Muʻāwiya. *See* ʻAbd-ar-Raḥmān I

Ibn Mujāhid, 431

Ibn Shammās, 414

Ibn Yaḥyā. *See* Yaḥyā ibn Yaḥyā

Ibrāhīm, Aghlabid Emir of Africa, 150, 419

Ibrāhīm ibn Hajjāj, 419 sq., 433

Iceland, settlement of, 338 sq.; 535

Iconoclastic controversy, 528, 532 sq.; influence of, upon art, 546

Ida, wife of Liudolf of Swabia, 191

Idatius, chronicler, 492

Idrīsids, 424

Idwal, Prince of Gwynedd, 364

Iffley, church at, 561

Iforen, Berber tribe, 422

Ifrīkīya (Tunis), 422, 424

Ignatius, Patriarch of Constantinople, 450, 528

Illtyd. *See* Iltut

Illuminated MSS., mosaics based upon, 549 sq.; English and Irish crosses and, 544 sqq.; architectural decoration and, 565 sq.

Iltut, St, school of, 509

Imhar. *See* Ívarr

Inden, monastery of, 4

India, trade with, 433

Indulgence, Day of, 281 sqq., 284, 307

Ine, King of Wessex, founder of Abingdon, 374; laws of, 358, 404

Ingelheim, Louis I at, 16, 22; council at (948), 79, 194; Henry I of Bavaria imprisoned at, 191; Otto I at, 196; Henry II of Bavaria imprisoned at, 205; Synod at, 211; Ernest of Swabia banned at, 253; Henry III married at, 275, 284; Henry III receives Aribert of Milan at, 277

Ingo, Bishop of Vercelli, 175 *note*

Ingwar. *See* Ívarr

Iñigo Arista, 410

Inn, river, Hungarians defeated on, 69

Instantius, heretic, 512

Investiture, 459; of Church fiefs, 463 sq.

Iona (Hy), Vikings in, 311, 330, 346; 504

Ipswich, *burh* at, 356, 381

Ireland, Vikings in, 346 sq., 310 sqq., 317 sq., 324, 330, 346 sq.; Harold and Leofwin in, 394; Aelfgar in, 396; Scandinavian influence in, 343; Gallic influence in, 498 sqq., 501; learning and literature in, 501 sqq., 524 sqq., 538; literary connexion with Spain, 524; art in, 556; kings of, *see* Aedh, Brian

Irenæus, St, 533

Irmingard, wife of Otto of Hammerstein, 251 sq.

Isaac of Tabanos, 406

Ishāk of Mosul, 415

Isidore, St, 343, 438, 489, 497, 499 sq., 516;

Etymologiae of, 490 sqq.; 520; other works of, 492

Isidorus Mercator. *See* Pseudo-Isidore

Isidorus of Miletus, 545

Isidorus Pacensis, chronicler, 493

Ismaelites, 419

Issoire, church at, 561

Istria, March of, ceded to Germany, 159

Italy, kingship of Bernard, 3; Lothar made King of, 5, 15, 20, 26; Louis I and, 3, 7, 11; under Louis II, 34, 47–50; Charles the Bald becomes King of, 51; dispute for the crown of, 63 sqq.; becomes an independent kingdom, 67; invaded by Hungarians, 88; under Rodolph II, 136, 153; under Louis III, 138, 149; under King Hugh, 139, 153–57; the Byzantine Empire and, 150 sq., 155, 166 sqq., 176; in the 10th century, ch. VII; Vikings in, 320; Empress Adelaide regent in, 209; Otto III visits, 212; chancery of, 213 sq.; reign of Ardoin, 220 sqq., 240; Henry II and, 218, 224; 239 sqq., 243, 246; 250 sq.; 268; Conrad II and, 256 sq.; 264, 268; 265 sqq.; hereditary succession in, 266 sq.; baronies in, 464; Henry III's first visit to, 266 sq., 277; second, 290 sqq.; 306; last, 298 sq.; Art in, 547 sq., 552; learning and letters in, 485 sqq., 528; kings of, *see* Adalbert, Ardoin, Berengar, Bernard, Carloman, Charlemagne, Charles, Conrad, Guy, Henry, Hugh, Lambert, Lothar, Louis, Otto, Rodolph; *see also* Lombardy

Itzehoe (Esesfeld), Frankish fort at (809), 312

Ívarr (It. Imhar, O.E. Ingwar), son of Ragnarr Loðbrók, in Northumbria, 350; at Thetford, 319, 351; in Scotland, 351 sq. (cf. 318, 325); death of, 318, 352

Ívarr (Ir. Imhar, O.E. Ingwar), brother of Olaf the White, in Ireland. 317 sq.; in Scotland, 325 (cf. 351 sq.); death of, 318, 352

Ivo, Bishop of Chartres, 113, 131 sqq.

Ivois, meeting of Robert the Pious and the Emperor Henry II at, 106, 251; meeting of Henry I and Henry III at, 280; (1056) 299

Ivrea, 66; besieged, 135; bishop of, *see* Warmund; March of, 65, 157, 167; under Ardoin, 220, 244; marquesses of, *see* Adalbert, Anscar, Ardoin, Berengar, Conrad

Jacobus de Voragine, 496

Jad, governor of Elvira, 418

Jaen, 411, 418 sqq., 433; mines at, 432

Jahna, capture of, by Henry I, 184

James, St, apocryphal *Gospel of*, 532

James the Less, Gospel of, 506

Jaromir of Bohemia, 222 sq.; made Duke of Bohemia, 225; aids Henry II against Boleslav, 227 sq.; driven from Bohemia, 239; restored, 262

Jarrow, destroyed by Vikings, 311, 341, 347

Jarzé, house of, in Anjou, 118

Jativa, 432
Jellinge, stone, 332, 380
Jerome, Bishop of Vicenza, 245
Jerome, St, 343, 493; 500; 507 sq.; 512 *note*; 523; his catalogue of church writers, 489, 491
Jerusalem, 126; 536
Jérusalem, Assises de, 460 sq.
Jews, in Spain, 429, 435
Jidār, 412
Job, Gregory on, 488
Job, Testament of, 505
Jocelyn, son of the lord of Sainte-Maure, 119
Jocelyn of Rennes, in Anjou, 118
Joceran, brother of Robert I of Burgundy, 124
Johannes, *magister militum,* 489
Johannes Scottus (Eriugena), 502, 504, 524 sqq., 527, 533
Johannis, poem, 488 sq.
John the Evangelist, St, Acts of, 532
John VIII, Pope, 46; and Charles the Bald, 50 sqq.; and Louis II, 55 sq., 137; and Charles the Fat, 58; assassinated, 60; 67; Papal theory of, 453 sq.
John IX, Pope, 67; aids Louis of Provence, 149
John X, Pope, 455; Archbishop of Ravenna, 151 sq.; Hugh of Provence and, 153; death of, 154
John XI, Pope, 151, 154, 455
John XII (John Octavian), Pope, 101; and Otto I, 161 sqq., 201 sq.; deposed, 163, 454 sq.; restored, 164
John XIII, Pope, 166 sqq., 203
John XIV (Peter, Bishop of Pavia), Pope, 101, 170 sq.
John XV, Pope, 101, 455; and Crescentius II, 171; death of, 172
John XVI (Philagathus), Pope, fate of, 172; 173, 212
John XVIII, Pope, 237
John XIX (Romanus), Pope, 252, 264, 267, 454
John, King of England, 461, 466
John Tzimisces, Eastern Emperor, 167, 169, 203
John II, Prince of Salerno, 176
John, Duke of Naples, 176, 528
John, Duke of Spoleto. *See* Crescentius, John
John, Archbishop of Ravenna, 450
John, Bishop, and a Greek book of the Ascension, 532
John, Bishop of Arezzo, 51
John, Bishop of Cervia, 42
John, Bishop of Toscanella, 51
John, Abbot of Athelney, 358
John, Abbot of Metz, 534
John, Abbot of Nonantula. *See* John XVI, Pope
John, Cardinal deacon, 101, 161, 164
John Crescentius, son of Crescentius II. *See* Crescentius III

John Gratian. *See* Gregory VI, Pope
John Octavian. *See* John XII, Pope
John Philagathus. *See* John XVI, Pope
John of Arras and Cambrai Castle, 298
John, lord of Lignières, 119
John of Biclarum, chronicler, 492
John Cameniates, cited, 149 *note*
John the Deacon, 528, 531
John of Gorze, *Life* of, 534
John of Salisbury, cited, 487
John of Wallingford, cited, 331
Jómsborg, fortress of, 326 sq., 380, 382
Jonac, 17
Jonas, Bishop of Orleans, 14, 533
Joscelin, Bishop of Paris, Abbot of Saint-Germain-des-Prés, 56 sq., 59; death of, 61, 321
Josephus, *Antiquities* of, 486; 505 *note*; 507
Joshua, illuminated roll of, 549 sq.
Jouy, Louis II retreats from, 37
Judith, wife of Henry I of Bavaria, 191, 204, 205 *and note*
Judith of Cornouailles, mother of Hoel, 128
Judith, Empress, 13 sqq., 16, 18 sqq., 22, 24, 35
Judith, daughter of Charles the Bald, 39, 41, 92, 349
Judith of Schweinfurt, 299 sq.
Julian, Archbishop of Toledo, 493 sq., 524
Julian, St, of Le Mans, 496
Juliana, Anglo-Saxon poem, 537
Julianus Pomerius, 493
Julianus Titianus, chronicler, 496
Jülich, meeting of Robert and Henry the Fowler at, 181
Julin, trading centre, 326
Jumièges, ravaged by Danes, 32; Edward the Confessor at, 390; service book of, 530; Abbey of, 561 sq.; abbots of, *see* Conrad, Robert
Junca, Bishop of. *See* Verecundus
Jurane Burgundy, duchy of, 38, 63, 134; dukes of, *see* Conrad, Hubert, Rodolph. *See also* Burgundy, kingdom of Jurane
Justin II, Eastern Emperor, 488 sq.
Justinian I, Eastern Emperor, Byzantine architecture under, 539 sq., 534 sqq., 547 sq., 557
Jüterbogk, Henry II retreats from, 228
Juvenal, 521, 524
Juvencus, poet, 516; MS. of, 509

Kaisites (Ma'addites), 409, 411, 416
Kalbites. *See* Yemenites
Kamba, Conrad II elected at, 254 *note*; *cf.* Kempen
Kasr ibn Wardān, ruins at, 547
Kells, Book of, 566
Kempen, Conrad II elected king at, 273; *cf.* Kamba
Kempsford, Mercian defeat at, 344
Kennet, river, Vikings on, 352
Kenneth Mac Alpin, founds the Scottish kingdom, 335, 350
Kenstec, Bishop of Dinnurin, 347

Kent, 401, 405 sq.; under-kingdom of, re-
volts against Coenwulf, 343; subject to
Wessex, 345 sq.; Vikings in, 349 sq.; 359;
382 sq., 385; kings of, *see* Baldred, Cuth-
red, Ealhmund
Kesteven, submits to Edward the Elder, 364
Ketill Flatnose, chieftain of the Western
Islands, 325
Ketill the White. *See* Caitill Find
Khālid, 412
Kiburg, Count of. *See* Werner
Kiersy. *See* Quierzy
Kiev, Varangians settle in, 327; alliance
with Poles, 222; princes of, *see* Olég,
Vladimir, Yaroslàv
Kilian, Irish missionary, 512
Kingston, 378
Ḳinnasrīn, 411
Kirchen, Charles the Fat at, 62
Kiso, takes Brandenburg, 211 sq.
Kloppen, Otto I at, 140
Knut, King of Denmark, 122
Knut, King of England, Denmark and Nor-
way, 305; 383; succeeds Svein, 384;
renews Danish invasions, 384 sq.; King
of England and Denmark, 325, 332, 386 sq.;
alliance with Conrad II, 263, 296 sq., 304;
visits Rome, 264, 388; policy in Church
and State, 387 sq., 407 sq.; war with Nor-
way, 388; laws of, 402, 407; death of,
388
Kunigunda, Empress of Henry II, 218, 241,
248, 252, 254, 279
Kunigunda, Queen of Henry III. *See* Gunnhild
Kunigunda, Welfic heiress, 265
Kuno, Duke of Bavaria, 287; made Duke,
293; deposed, 296; intrigues in Hungary,
297 sq., 304; death of, 299
Ḳuraib ibn Khaldūn, 418 sq.
Ḳuraishites, 412

La Chartre, taken by Fulk Rechin, 120
Lactantius, theologian and poet, 516, 526,
537
La Fère, Odo at, 73
La Ferté-en-Brai, 112
La Gueule, Danish victory at, 64
Laidulf, Prince of Capua, 171; 176
La Marche, independence of, 97; subject to
Aquitaine, 129
Lambay Island, Vikings at (795), 311
Lambert of Spoleto, Emperor, King of Italy,
65, 454; succeeds Guy, 66, 148 sq.
Lambert, Duke of Spoleto, 48, 55 sq.
Lambert, Marquess of Tuscany, 154
Lambert, Count of Nantes (Breton March), 2
Lambert, Count of the Breton March
(Nantes), 15 sq., 19 sq., 31, 47 sq., 316
Lambert (Lantbert), Count of Louvain, 207,
248
Lambert, Count of Louvain, 295
Lambert d'Ardre, chronicler, cited, 460
Lampert, Archbishop of Milan, 153
Lancashire, Scandinavian influence in, 336

Lance, Holy, 180 *note*; 189, 200, 218; of
Burgundy, 258; of Hungary, 288
Landfrieden, 282, 307
Landolf, usurps principality of Salerno, 169
Landolf I, Prince of Capua-Benevento,
151 sq.
Landolf III, Prince of Capua-Benevento,
161
Landolf IV, Prince of Capua-Benevento, 169
Landolf V, Prince of Capua, succeeds Ademar,
176
Landry, Count of Nevers, 104, 106, 141
Landulf II, Archbishop of Milan, 175
Langeais, Fulk Nerra at, 108, 118; lord of,
see Hamelin
Langenzenn, diet at, 198
Langres, and Burgundy, 93 sq., 96; bishopric
of, 97; cathedral of, 557; bishops of, *see*
Bruno, Hardouin
Languedoc, 130; Hungarians in, 153; *see
also* Gothia, Toulouse
Lantbert. *See* Lambert
Laon, Empress Judith at, 14; 75, 77; be-
sieged by Hugh the Great, 78, 193;
restored to Louis IV, 79, 194; taken by
Otto II, 80; 89 sq.; captured by Charles
of Lorraine, 99; recaptured, 100, 102; 190;
Hungarians near, 198; MSS. at, 504, 521,
526, 538; Greek taught at, 527; bishop
of, *see* Asselin
Lassois, subject to Burgundy, 93
Lateran, Synod at, 264
Lausanne, diocese of, 38, 63, 134
Lausitz, March of, created, 202 *note*; con-
quered by Boleslav, 222 sq., 225; recovered,
227; again lost, 228, 239; surrendered by
Mesco, 261; *see also* East Mark, Lusatians
Lavenham, 406
Law, Bavarian, 284
Law, Canon, xviii, 132, 163, 232, 251 sq.,
290; *see also* False Decretals
Law, Lombard, superseded by Roman Law
in Rome, 267; amended by Conrad II, 266
Law, Mozarabic, 430, 441
Law, of Wessex, reformed by Alfred, 358;
by Edward the Elder, 362; by Aethelstan,
367
Law, Roman, to supersede Lombard Law
in Rome, 267; sovereign's powers, 461;
ownership, 462
Law, Saxon, 217, 255; *Lehnrecht* of, 459
Lawhitton, 344
Lazarus, Byzantine painter, 546
Lea, river, 319, 359
Leabhar Breac, 505
Lechfeld, the Hungarians defeated on, 160,
199 sq., 215; Diet of Augsburg at (952),
195
Le Frainet (Fraxinetum), Saracens at, 140,
152, 155, 162; extirpated, 168; 431
Leicester, 319, 353; *burh* of, 355; see of,
380; submits to Aethelfleda, 323, 363 sq.;
besieged by Edmund, 368
Leicestershire, Svein in, 383; Scandinavian
influence in, 336 sq.

Leidrad, Archbishop of Lyons, 518
Leinster, king of. *See* Maelmordha
Leitha, district ceded to Hungary, 261; recovered, 281, 303
Leitzkau, Henry II musters at, 227
Le Mans, 33, 36; bishops of, *see* Aldric, Gervase; viscount of, *see* Raoul; church at, 563; stained glass at, 566
Lenzen, Wends defeated at, 184
Leo III, Pope, 4, 343, 519
Leo IV, Pope, 29; walls Leonine city, 49; 349
Leo VIII, Pope, 101; election of, 163; driven out, 164; reinstated, *ib.*; death of, 166
Leo IX, Pope (Bruno, Bishop of Toul), 280, 284; becomes Pope, 294; in Italy, 296; see of Bremen, 297; defeated at Civitate, 298
Leo VI, the Wise, Eastern Emperor, 546
Leo, Bishop of Vercelli, enemy of Ardoin, 220; invites Henry II to Italy, 221, 224; pro-German, and exiled, 240; at Ravenna, 242; again expelled from Vercelli by Ardoin, 244; goes to Germany, 245; correspondence, 245; recovers Vercelli, 246; synod of Pavia, 251
Leo of Naples, 528
Leo, *nomenclator*, executed, 5
Leocricia, 417
Leofric, Earl of Mercia, 389, 391, 393 sqq., 397
Leofwine, son of Godwin, outlawed, 394; given earldom, 397
Leofwine, Earl of Mercia, 387, 389
Leominster, 396
Leominster, Abbess of, 392
Leon, Kingdom of, raided by Alfonso I, 410; raided by Toledo, 417; southward expansion of, 419 sqq.; war with Castile, 422; invaded by Almanzor, 425; conquered by Castile and Navarre, 428; 423, 425, 438 sq., 441; kings of, *see* Alfonso, Bermudo, Ferdinand, Ordoño, Ramiro, Sancho
Leon, city of, 440
Leonorius, missioner to Brittany, 509
Leopold, Margrave of Austria, 301 sqq.
Le Puiset, taken by Queen Constance, 107; lord of, *see* Hugh
Le Puy, Biblical MS. at, 519; paintings at, 567; architecture at, 557, 565
Lescar, church at, 567
Leswin Croc, 406
Lewes, 357; priory at, 564
Leyden, MS. at, cited, 502
Libentius. *See* Lievizo
Liber Pontificalis, 534
Liber Rotarum, 492
Libertius, missionary to Russia, 201
Libri Carolini, against images, 533
Lichfield, 387; canons of, 379
Licosa, naval battle of (846), 49
Liège, 33, 525; burnt by Danes, 59; besieged, 293; library of, 521; font at, 559 sq.;

bishopric of, 45; bishops of, 44, 294, *see* Franco, Nithard, Wazo
Lievizo (Libentius), Archbishop of Hamburg-Bremen, 239
Lignières, lord of. *See* John
L'Ile-Bouchard, lord of. *See* Bartholomew
Lille, siege of, by Henry III, 298
Limburg, Abbey of, 271
Limerick, and the Northmen, 317, 324, 331, 334
Limoges, 17, 34; battle at, 76; and Aquitaine, 129
Limousin, the, Northmen defeated in, 88; 97
Lincoln, 319, 334, 355; see of, 380; cathedral, 562, 564, 566
Lincolnshire, 400, 406; Scandinavian influence in, 336 sq.
Lindisfarne, raided by Vikings, 311, 341, 347; abandoned by Eardulf, 354; Gospels of, 514, 554, 566; bishop of, *see* Eardulf
Lindsey, Vikings in, 312, 349 sqq., 353, 381; pagan revival in, 351; submits to Edward the Elder, 364
Lion d'Angers, lord of, 119
Lios Monocus, Breton poet, 529
Lisbon, Vikings at, 316, 416
Lisieux, granted to Rollo, 73, 86, 94, 322; bishopric of, seized by Ranulf Flambard, 133
Lithuanians, attack Poland, 300
Liudevit, Slovene Prince, 7
Liudolf, Archbishop of Trèves, 238
Liudolf, Duke of Saxony, 235
Liudolf, Duke of Swabia, 204, 205 *note*; invades Italy, 159 sq.; marriage of, 191; rebellion, 196 sqq., 258; reconciliation, 199; death, 160, 201
Liudolfings, House of, 215, 230
Liudprand, chronicler, cited, 139, 149, 156 sq., 189; at the court of Otto I, 160; Bishop of Cremona, 163; sent to Constantinople, 167; his *Antapodosis*, 423 *note*, 528, 534 sq.
Liutbert, Archbishop of Mayence, 45, 60
Liutgard, wife of Conrad of Lorraine, 191, 205 *note*, 215, 249, 253
Liuthar, Margrave of North Mark, 216 sq.
Liutpert, Bishop of Cambrai, struggle with John of Arras, 298
Liutpold, Margrave in Bavaria, 69
Liutpold of Babenberg, 205; Margrave of Austria, 206, 208
Liutward, Bishop of Vercelli, 60, 62
Livius Andronicus, 491
Livy, 521 sq.
Llanelwy. *See* St Asaph
Llantwit Major, school at, 509
Lleyn, promontory of, 342
Llobregat, river, 90, 428
Lobbes, annalist of, 25
Loches, attacked by Hugh of Amboise, 119; chapel at, 561; church at, 563
Lodi, see of, 175
Loire, river, 35, 40, 128; Northmen on, 60, 86 sq., 312, 320 sqq.; 76 *note*

Lombards, the, 7, 47 sqq., 150, 152, 176, 178; 422; kings of, *see* Aistulf; *see also* Longobardia

Lombardy, 27, 53; and Conrad II, 106 sq.; and Rodolph II, 136 sq.; invaded by Hungarians, 148, 153; raided by Saracens, 152; Otto I and, 165, 196; Henry II intervenes in, 218; *see also* Italy

Lomello, Count of. *See* Otto

London, sacked by Danes, 312; stormed by Vikings, 349; ransomed, 353; in Guthrum's kingdom, 356; captured by Alfred, 358; 363; repels the Danes, 324, 381; accepts Svein, 383 sq.; makes Edmund king, 385; besieged by Knut, 385; 387; 394; St Paul's Cathedral, 564; canons of, 379; Church dues in diocese of, 379; 361; bishops of, *see* Dunstan, William

Longobardia, theme of, 150, 152, 166, 168

Loppergarth, runic inscription at, 336

Lorca, 418

Lorica, ascribed to Gildas, 508

Lorraine (Lotharingia), 27; given to Lothar II, 34; 36, 38, 41, 43; contest for, 44 sq.; partition of, 45; invasion of, 51 sq.; Carloman and, 55; cession of, 57; Northmen in, 58 sq., 64; claimed by Rodolph of Burgundy, 63, 135; Zwentibold, King of, 67 sq.; under Charles the Simple, 68 sq., 74 sq., 78, 87; invasion by Louis d'Outremer, 78, 189 sq.; conquest by Henry the Fowler, 78, 180 sq.; Hungarians in, 87, 182 *note*; under Otto I, 189 sqq., 192 sq.; given to Bruno, 199 sqq.; invasions of, by Lothair, 80, 207 sqq.; disaffection against Henry II, 223, 228; Robert the Pious and, 106 sq.; relations with Burgundy, 135, 144 sq.; Church reform in, 236, 250, 253; opposed to Conrad II, 254, 256 sq.; ravaged by Odo of Blois, 123, 144 sq., 259, 267; divided into two, 200 sqq., 203; reunited, 270; made into two Duchies, 284; Henry III in, 277; romance party in, 285; revolt of Duke Godfrey, 286 sqq.; settlement of, 289 sq.; kings, dukes, etc. of, *see* Arnulf, Bruno, Charles, Conrad, Gebhard, Gilbert, Lothar, Louis, Otto, Reginar, Zwentibold

Lorraine, Lower, given to Charles, 207; Henry II in, 218; Henry III in, 275; dukes of, *see* Charles, Frederick, Godfrey, Gozelo, Otto

Lorraine, Upper, dukes of, *see* Adalbert, Dietrich, Frederick, Gerard, Godfrey, Gozelo

Lorsch, 16; annals of, 518, 534; library of, 521

Lörzweiler, Conrad II elected near, 254 *note* 1

Lothair, King of France, 77 *note*, 80; invades Lorraine, 207 sq.; 210; death of, 81, 211

Lothar I, Emperor, and Bavaria, 3; King of Italy, 5, 13, 20; the succession, 10, 13; marriage of, 12; rebels, 14 sqq., 17, 444; 448; claims the Empire, 18; restores Louis I, 19; 21; proclaimed Emperor, 10, 22; relations with his brothers, 22 sqq., 32 sqq., 534; with Gilbert, 34; relations with the Church, 29 sq., 444; relations with Vikings, 315; death of, 34

Lothar III, of Supplinburg, Emperor, 146

Lothar II, King of Lorraine, inheritance of, 34 sq.; 36 sqq.; divorce of, 38 sqq., 449 sqq.; death of, 44; 525

Lothar II, son of King Hugh, 140; joint-king of Italy, 154, 157; death of, 158, 194

Lotharingia. *See* Lorraine

Lothian, invaded by Scots, 350; 388; influence of, 396

Louis I (the Pious, or the Debonnaire), Emperor, accession of, 1 sqq.; the Church, 4 sq., 444; the Vikings, 313, 315, 327; the succession, 9 sqq.; second marriage of, 12 sq.; revolts of his sons, 14 sqq.; humiliation, 18, 444, 448 sq.; restoration, 19; death, 22; in Walafrid's poem, 522; *lives* of, 534

Louis II, Emperor, King of Italy, 34, 38; obtains Provence, 41; the Pope and, 42 sqq., 50, 450; 44 sq.; death of, 46, 50; reign in Italy, 47–50; 53, 134, 137, 149

Louis III (the Blind), Emperor, son of Boso, 62 sqq.; in Italy, 68, 138, 149; king of Provence, 138; captured at Verona, *ib.*, 149; 152; death of, 139, 156

Louis II (the German), King of Germany, 3, 29, 34; and the succession, 10, 13; rebels, 14 sqq.; pardoned, 15, 18, 19; deprived of territory, 21 sq.; relations with Lothar I, 23 sqq., 32 sq., 444; relations with Lothar II, 35, 40, 42 sqq.; and Charles the Bald, 36 sqq., 42, 50 sq., 446 sq., 534; and the Pope, 43, 451 sq.; and Lorraine, 44 sqq.; and Italy, 46 sq., 49 sq.; death of, 46, 51; 63; 314

Louis the Younger, son of Louis the German, 33 sq.; King of Saxony, 51 sq.; invades France, 56 sq.; death of, 58; 59

Louis the Child, King of Germany, 68; death of, 69; 74, 136

Louis, King of Bavaria. *See* Louis the German

Louis II (the Stammerer), King of France, Duke of Maine, 35, 40, 53; King, 55; death of, 56, 321; marriages, 57; 77 *note*

Louis III, King of France, 56; crowned, 57; struggle with the Northmen, 59, 321; death of, 58; 77 *note*

Louis IV d'Outremer, King of France, crowned, 77; policy of, 78; Otto I and, 189 sqq., 192 sqq.; death of, 79, 201

Louis V, King of France, made King of Aquitaine, 91; death of, 81, 211

Louis VI, King of France, 114

Louis, St, IX, King of France, 465

Louis, King of Aquitaine. *See* Louis I, Emperor

Louis, Abbot of Saint-Denis, 35
Louis, Count of Montbéliard, 287
Louis, son of Charles, Duke of Lower Lorraine, 77 *note*, 102, 104
Louvain, Northmen encamp at, 59 sq.
Louviers, treaty of (856), 35
Lübeck, see of, 305 sq.
Lucan, 491, 516, 521
Lucania, in the theme of Longobardia, 150
Lucas, Bishop of Tuy, 426
Lucca, 47; Otto, Duke of Swabia, dies at, 209
Lucera, Otto II at, 169
Lucretius, 491, 520 sqq.
Lucy, Hugh de, knights of, 462 *note*
Ludeca, King of Mercia, 346
Ludlow Castle, 561
Ludmilla, St, 184
Lügenfeld, the, 18
Lugo, wasted by Alfonso I, 410
Luna. *See* Luni
Lund, trading centre, 332
Lüneburg, 305; battle near, 321
Luni, Otbertines in, 240; Vikings at, 320, 331
Lupus, Duke of Champagne, eulogy of Venantius Fortunatus on, 309
Lupus of Ferrières, 527
Lupus of Gascony, banished, 8
Lusatians, the, submit to Henry I, 185; subdued by Otto I, 202. *See also* Lausitz
Luton, 359; Danish raid upon, 363
Luxemburg, family of, 292; 307; in Lorraine, 238, 248, 294
Luxorius, African poet, 488
Lyfing, Abbot of Tavistock, made Bishop of Crediton, 388; Edward the Confessor and, 390
Lyonnais, the. *See* Lyons, county of
Lyons, county of, 27, 93; duchy of, 34, 41, 44; given to Charles the Bald, 45 sq.; claimed by Boso, 57, 137; Hugh of Arles, 138; restored to France, 76, 147; archbishopric of, 279; synod of Rheims, 295; culture of, 502; MS. from, 520; art and architecture, 553; see of, 379; archbishops of, 295; *see* Agobard, Aurelian, Burchard, Halinard, Leidrad, Odulric
Lyutitzi, revolt of the, 144; rebel against Otto II, 208; and Brandenburg, 208, 211 sq.; ally with Henry II, 226 sq., 228, 239; ally with Conrad II, 260, 305; revolt of, 262 sq., 288, 305; revolt again, 299; *see* Wiltzi; *see also* Slavs, Wends

Ma'addites. *See* Ḳaisites
Macbeth, Earl of Moray, 395
Maccus (Magnus), King of the Western Isles, 326
Macer, 523
Mâcon, 26, 97; independence of, 124; under Otto-William, 141; counts of, 57 sq.; *see* Otto-William, Warin
Macrobius, *Saturnalia* of, 485; on the verb in Greek and Latin, 504, 525

Madrid, 421
Maelmordha, King of Leinster, 324
Maestricht, 275, 298
Magdeburg, city, Berengar submits to Otto I at, 159, 195; 188; Otto I buried at, 203; Boleslav submits to Otto II at, 206; three Henries condemned at, 206; 211
Magdeburg, metropolitan see of, founded, 202; 232; archbishops of, 209, 217; *see* Adalbert, Gero, Gisiler, Hunfrid, Tagino, Thiedric, Waltherd; provost of, *see* Waltherd
Maghrawa Berbers, 421
Magna Carta, 461, 463, 469, 479
Magnus. *See* Maccus
Magnus the Good, King of Norway, 294; 389; defeats the Obotrites, 305; destroys the Jómsvikings, 327
Magnus Hákonson, King of Denmark, 334
Magyars. *See* Hungarians, Hungary
Mahdī, Ahmad ibn Mu'āwiya claims to be the, 420
Mahdī, Fātimite Caliph, 151
Mahomet I, Emir of Spain, 416 sq.; 435
Mahomet II, al-Mahdī, Caliph of Cordova, 427
Mahomet ibn Abī-'Āmir. *See* Almanzor
Mahomet ibn Ghālib, 418
Mahomet ibn Hāshim at-Tujībī, governor of Saragossa, 421
Mahomet, son of 'Abd-ar-Rahmān III, 435
Maillé, rebellion of lord of, 119
Maine, given to Pepin, 18; seized by Lambert, 31; duchy of, 35; independence of, 96; subject to Anjou, 109 sq.; dukes and counts of, *see* Herbert, Hugh, Lambert, Louis II, Robert
Maiolus, St, Abbot of Cluny, 168
Mälaga. *See* Regio
Mälar, Lake, Anglo-Saxon coins from, 333
Malcolm, King of Scots, receives Cumberland, 368
Malcolm II, King of Scots, 388, 395
Malcolm III (Canmore), King of Scots, 395
Maldon, 364; battle of, 324, 381
Mālik ibn Anas, 414, 431
Mālikites, Muslim sect, 414, 431 sqq.
Malmesbury, 357; abbey of, 374; library at, 511
Man, Isle of, Vikings in, 311, 324 sqq., 329, 379, 381; Scandinavian influence in, 333 sqq.
Manasse, Archbishop of Arles, 153; deserts Hugh, 157; Archbishop of Milan, 158 sqq.
Manasse, Archbishop of Rheims, 113
Manchester, fortified, 365
Manegold, Count, 258
Manichaeans, and religious romances, 496 sq.
Manfred II, Marquess of Turin, 240, 246, 264
Manfred, Count of Milan, 66
Manilius, poet, 536
Manlius, M., *De Astrologia*, 536
Mann, *jarl*, 364

Manor, the, 472 sqq.; French and German analogies, 483
Manso III, Duke of Amalfi, chosen Prince of Salerno, 169; driven out, 176
Mansūr, Abbasid Caliph, 413
Mansūr, Fātimite Caliph, 166, 422
Mantaille, Boso becomes King of Provence at, 57, 137
Mantes, claimed by William the Conqueror, 112
Mantua, Hugh of Provence and John X at, 153; county of, 221; Henry III at, 298
Map, Walter, cited, 536
Marburg, church of, 562
Marcellinus and Peter, SS., relics of, 518, 533
March, river, Hungarian frontier, 281, 303
March, the North, *see* North Mark; the East, *see* East Mark, Lausitz, March of; the Thuringian, *see* Meissen, March of
Margoil. *See* Margut
Margut (Margoil), 80, 208
Maria, nun, 417
Marianus Argyrus, in South Italy, 166
Marianus Scotus, 534
Marinus, Bishop of Bomarzo, 192, 194
Marj Rāhit, battle of, 412
Marmora, Sea of, and the Rus, 327
Marmoutier, abbey of, 71; abbot of, *see* Hugh the Great
Marne, river, meeting on (950), 194
Marozia, Senatrix, wife of Alberic, of Spoleto, 151, 455; wife of Guido of Tuscany, 153; wife of Hugh of Italy, 154; 241
Marquard of Anweiler, 462
Marseilles, 282
Martial, 521
Martianus Capella, 343, 485, 487 sq., 504, 509, 513, 525 sq.
Martin, St, of Tours, 489 sq., 495 sq.
"Martin, Land of St," 513
Martin of Dumio, Archbishop of Bracara, 489 sq.
Martin of Laon, 526
Marton, battle at, 352
Maslama, 410
Mateflon, castle of, enfeoffed, 118
Matfrid, Count of Orleans, 8; exiled, 15, 19 sq.
Matfrid, Count, 68
Matilda, Abbess, 174
Matilda, wife of Henry the Fowler, 185 sq.; 203
Matilda, ancestress of Agnes of Poitou, 283 *note* 2
Matilda, Countess of Tuscany, 299
Matilda, sister of Otto III, 215
Matilda, wife of Conrad Duke of Carinthia, 256
Matilda, daughter of Henry III, marries Rudolf of Swabia, 289
Matthew, St, apocryphal *Gospel of,* 532
Maubergeon, Viscountess of Châtellerault, 130
Mauges, district of, added to Anjou, 96

Maulevrier, fief of Anjou, 118
Mauretania, 421
Maurice, St, lance of. *See* Lance, Holy
Maurienne, Count of. *See* Humbert
Maursmünster, monastery, 3
Maximilian, King of the Romans, 466
Maximus, *Ambigua* of, 525
Mayence, 16, 25 sqq., 51, 275 sq.; Harold of Denmark baptised at, 7, 313; convention at, 143; Otto I at, 196 sq.; Henry II at, 217 sq., 248; synods at, 237, 252, 295; Conrad II crowned at, 254; Agnes crowned at, 284; see of, 206, 235, 255 sqq.; library of, 521; archbishops of, *see* Aribo, Bardo, Erkambald, Frederick, Heriger, Hildebert, Liutbert, Raban Maur, Sunderold, William, Willigis
Mayenne, taken by William of Normandy, 110; lord of, *see* Geoffrey
Meath, raided by Turgeis, 317
Meaux, 446; district of, 16, 40, 76 sq., 83; captured by Northmen, 85; Odo II and, 123
Mecca, 433
Meczlav of Masovia, 302
Medellin, 418
Medeshamstede, monastery of, 351; refounded, 375. *See* Peterborough
Media in Vita, sequence, 530
Medinaceli, 426
Medina Sidonia, 418
Medinese, 409
Mediterranean Sea, command of, 423, 431
Meersen, conferences at (847), 31, 52; (851), 32, 37; Treaty of (870), 45, 51, 57
Megingaud, Archbishop of Trèves, 238, 248
Megingaud (Meingaud), Bishop of Eichstedt, 237 sq.
Meissen, fortification of, 184; recovered by Eckhard, 211; captured by Boleslav, 222; lost, *ib.*; further attempt on, 223
Meissen, March of, created, 202 *note*; attacked by Boleslav of Poland, 217, 222; given to Gunzelin, 222; Boleslav's designs upon, 226, 238; Upper Lausitz attached to, 261; margraves of, *see* Eckhard, Gunzelin
Melk, MS. at, 527
Melo, Duke of Apulia, 250
Melrose, Kenneth Mac Alpin at, 350
Melun, Vikings at, 40; besieged (991), 102; recovered, 105; death of Philip I at, 115
Memleben, death of Henry I at, 186; death of Otto I at, 203
Mempisc district, the, 92
Menas, St, of Alexandria, ivories of, 542
Mentesa, 418
Mercia, Kingdom of, extent at Offa's death, 340; extension westward, 343; conflict with Wessex, 344; decline of, 345 sq.; conquered by Vikings, 348, 351, 353; colonised by Vikings, 354 sq.; submits to Wessex, 356, 360; kings of, *see* Beorhtwulf, Beornwulf, Burhred, Ceolwulf, Coenwulf, Ecgfrith, Ludeca, Offa, Wiglaf

Mercia, Dukedom of, 356, 359 sq., 384; 387; 397; and Aethelwald's rising, 361; wars with Welsh, 362 sqq.; wars with Danes, 362 sqq.; lady of, *see* Aethelfleda; Edward the Elder, lord of, 323, 364; recovered by Edmund, 368; revolt against Eadwig, 372, 374; faction favours Aethelred, 378; ceded to Knut, 386 sq.; society in, 337, 401, 404; dukes and earls of, *see* Aelfgar, Aelfhere, Aethelfleda, Aethelred, Eadric Streona, Edwin, Leofric, Leofwine

Mercia, archbishops in, suppressed, 343; *see* Higbert

Merfyn the Freckled, King of North Wales, 350

Mérida, 414, 416, 418, 421; independence of, 417

Merlin, 513

Merovingian script, 517

Merseburg, fortification of, 182 sq.; siege of (939), 189; see of, founded, 202; revived, 235; assembly at, 217, 222; Henry II musters at, 225; Boleslav makes peace at, 239; Henry II at, 250; Mesco II submits at, 261 sq.; Diet of (1033), 262; Diet of (1053), 296; 256; 297; bishops of, *see* Gisiler, Thietmar, Wigbert

Mersey, 354; Edward the Elder's power reaches, 365

Mértola, 418

Mesco I, Duke of the Poles, submits to Otto I, 202; aids Bavarian revolt, 205; submits to Otto II, 206; war with Bohemia, 211; 222

Mesco II, Duke of Poland, 144, 258 sq., 302; suceeds Boleslav the Mighty, 260; wars with Conrad II, 260 sq.; driven out by Otto Bezprim, 261; succeeds Otto, 261; submits to Conrad II, 261 sq.; death of, 262, 300

Mesopotamia, 436; architecture in, 539, 541, 547

Messina, seized by Saracens, 48; by Byzantines, 169

Metz, council at, 41 sq.; Treaty of, 43, 45; 44; 52; 190; assemblies at, 447; 61; synod of, 449; see of, 45; bishops of, 209; 250; 294 sq.; *see* Adalbero, Dietrich, Drogo, Walo; abbot of, *see* John

Meuse, river, 46 sq., 59, 68, 134; Conrad of Lorraine defeated on, 197; mouth of, seized by Count of Holland, 248 sq.

Mézières, 27

Michael II, Eastern Emperor, 524, 546

Michael III, the Drunkard, Eastern Emperor, 451

Michelstadt, Abbey of, 518

Mico of St Riquier, 519, 522 sq.

Middle Angles, King of. *See* Peada

Middle Kingdom, 286; *see* Lorraine. *See also* Burgundy

Middlesex, hundreds of, 367

Milan, and Arnulf and Lambert, 66; Lothar II sent to, 157; Otbertines in, 240; *missi* sent to, 244; favours Henry II, 246;

Conrad II crowned at, 264; siege of, 266 sqq., 277; counts of, *see* Hugh, Manfred; MSS. at, 521; Church of St Lorenzo at, 548; art and architecture in, 553; see of, contested, 158; lands of, seized, 245; precedence of, 264; archbishops of, 224, 240, 244; *see* Adalman, Anselm, Arderic, Aribert, Arnulf, Guido, Lampert, Landulf, Manasse, Walpert

Miletus, excavations at, 547

Milo, Count of Verona, 157

Milton (Dorset), Abbey of, 373

Milton (near Sheppey), 359

Minden, bishopric of, 232; Saxons acknowledge Conrad II at, 255

Ministeriales, German, 230, 270, 462

Minster, nunnery of, 343

Miriquidui. *See* Erzgebirge

Miro, King of the Suevi, 489

Miron, Catalan Count, 424

Missi, 5, 6, 9, 29, 162, 165, 168, 240, 244, 246, 266, 299

Mistislav, Prince of the Obotrites, 249

Mochua, St, Life of, 506

Modena, 221; counts of, *see* Adalbert-Atto, Boniface, Tedald; dukes of, 240; see of, 165; bishops of, 221, 240

Moduin, Bishop of Autun, 18

Moimir, Moravian prince, 64

Molesme, Abbey of, its importance, 124

Môn (Anglesey), 342; Norse names in, 326

Monasterboice, 556

Monasticism, Muslim, 431; Christian, in Spain, 441; in Europe, 457. *See* Cluniac Movement

"Monk of St Gall." *See* Notker Labeo

"Monk of Toul," 531

Mons, Count of. *See* Herman

Mont-Barbet, William of Normandy at, 110

Montbazon, Fulk Nerra at, 108

Montbéliard, Count of. *See* Louis

Montboyau, fortress of, 108

Montbrai, lord of, 120

Montdidier, county of, 111

Monte Cassino, Lothar II and the Pope at, 44; Abbey of, 49, 150, 268; library of, 521

Monte Gargano, Otto III at, 176

Monteleon, 420

Montfaucon, Northmen defeated at (888), 72, 85

Montferrat, marquesses of, 240. *See* William

Montfort, Simon de, 461

Montièrender, monastery of, 104; abbot of, *see* Adso

Montjean, house of, in Anjou, 118

Montlhéry, dismantled (1105), 114

Montmartre, 61; Otto II at, 80, 208

Montmell, *fuero* of, 441

Montrésor, attacked by Hugh of Amboise, 119; lord of, *see* Aubrey

Montreuil, county of, 104

Montreuil-Bellay, castle of, 118

Montreuil-sur-Mer, added to Flanders, 92

Montrevault, castle of, built by Fulk Nerra, 118; lords of, *see* Roger, Stephen

Montrichard, Fulk Nerra at, 108; Hugh of Amboise at, 119
Montriond, synod of, 282
Mont-St-Michel, siege of (1091), 121
Montsoreau, house of, 118
Morat, seized by Odo II, 143; besieged by Conrad II (1033), 144 sq., 259
Moravia, struggles in, 31, 64, 68; conquered by Břatislav, 260, 299; bishopric for, 208; princes of, *see* Moimir, Svatopluk
Moray, Earl of. *See* Macbeth
Möre, Earl of. *See* Rögnvaldr
Morgannwg. *See* Glamorgan
Morienval, abbey of, 76
Morkere, 384
Morkere, Earl of Northumbria, 398
Morocco, 424, 426
Morosini, the, of Venice, 170
Mortemer, Odo defeated at, 109
Mortimer, revolt of, 466
Mortmain, 464
Morvan (Murmannus), Breton leader, 8 sq.
Mosaic, at Ravenna, 542, 548, 550; at Salonica, 542; in St Sophia, 544 sqq.; in North Africa, 547 sq.; in Milan and Naples, 548; in St Mark's, 549 sq., 558; in Sta Maria Maggiore, 549, 558; in France, 567; at Aix, 567; Byzantine, sources of, 548 sqq.
Mosara, 412
Moselle, river, 21, 46; Harold penetrates to (842), 315
Mosuin Mac Armin, Abbot of Bangor, 503 sq.
Mouliherne, siege of (1048), 109
Moulins-la-Marche, lord of, 120
Mouzon, 27
Mozarabs, 429 sq., 432 sq., 435, 438
Muirchertach, Irish leader, and the Vikings, 324
Muirchu, Life of St Patrick, 505
Mu'izz, Fātimite Caliph, 422, 424
Mujāhid of Denia, conquers Sardinia, 250
Muladies (Muwallad), class in Spain, 414, 429
Mundhir, Emir of Spain, 418
Münster, meeting at, 278
Murcia, 409; Vikings at, 320; discontent in, 413, 416; irrigation of, 432
Mūsā, conqueror of Spain, 409, 431
Mūsā II, "Third King of Spain," 417
Mushafī, ḥājib in Spain, 424
Muslims (in Spain), ch. xvi; boundary (in 756), 410; (in 912), 420; law and institutions, 431 sqq.
Mutonia, 421
Muttenz, Rodolph III makes Conrad II his heir at, 256, 258
Muwallad. *See* Muladies
Muzaffar, son of Almanzor, 427 sq.
Mynyw. *See* St David's

Najda, slave general, 422
Nájera, 421, 440
Nantes, plundered, 30, 33; added to Brittany, 33; 128; Vikings at, 87; counts of, *see* Hoel, Lambert

Naples, besieged by Saracens, 49; independence of, 150; 151; besieged by Caliph Mansūr, 166; 169; Otto III and, 176; captured by Paldolf IV, 268; MS. at, 514; baptistery at, 548; dukes of, *see* Andrew, John, Sergius
Narbonne, Bishop of. *See* Bartholomew
Nardulus, Nardus. *See* Einhard
Narni, Bishop of. *See* John XIII, Pope
Nasr, 416
Naumberg, bishopric of Zeitz removed to, 260
Navarre, 410, 421 sqq., 425, 438, 441; conquers Leon, 428; military tenure in, 464; kings of, *see* Garcia, Sancho
Nayland, 394 *note*
Naze, the, 395
Neidingen, death of Charles the Fat at, 62
Nekur, attacked by Vikings, 320
Nemesianus, 522
Nennius, author of *Historia Brittonum*, 342
Nestor, Russian chronicler, cited, 327
Nether Wroughton (Ellandun), battle at, 345
Neustria, given to Louis III, 57; March of, 71, 73; 83; and the Northmen, 86 sq.; formation of the March, 91 sq., 94; decay of the March, 95 sq.; 104; marquesses of, *see* Hugh, Odo, Robert
Neustrians, 23, 27, 74
Nevers, given to Pepin, 10; count of, *see* Landry
Newburgh, William of, cited, 513
Niall Glundubh, Irish leader, and the Vikings, 324
Nice, Bishop of, 282
Nicephorus, *Chronography* of, 528
Nicephorus Phocas, Eastern Emperor, in Italy, 150; as Emperor, 167
Nicholas I, Pope, 40 sqq., 449 sqq.; 525; claims of, 452 sq.; 455
Nicholas Picingli. *See* Picingli
Nile, river, architecture in valley of, 540
Nilus, St, of Calabria, 173
Nimeguen, 13; assemblies at, 15, 21, 248; burnt by Vikings, 59; diet at, 250; synod at, 251; Henry III married at, 274; meets dukes of Lorraine at, 284 sq.; Charlemagne's palace at, 293, 561
Nisibis, academy at, 486
Nithard, Bishop of Liège, 278
Nithard, Abbot of St Riquier, historian, 24 *note*, 444, 534
Nivelles, convent of, 60; abbess of, *see* Gisela
Nivernais, the, Northmen defeated in, 93
Noirmoutier, Viking settlement at, 316
Nomenoë, Breton King, 9, 30 sq.; death of, 33
Nonantula, John, Abbot of. *See* John XVI, Pope
Nordalbingians, the, campaign of Charles the Great against, 312; submit to Denmark, 313
Nordgau of Bavaria, made a margravate, 206; war in (1003), 223; margraves of, *see* Berthold, Henry, Otto

Norfolk, 392, 400; hundreds of, 367; Scandinavian influence in, 337

Normandy, foundation of, 73 sq., 92, 94 sq., 97, 322; Hugh the Great suzerain of, 83; Henry I and, 108 sqq.; Philip I and, 111 sq.; revolts in, 120–1; Danes from England in, 365; Scandinavian influence in, 330, 333, 338; government of, 127 sq.; dukes of, *see* Richard, Robert, Rollo, William

Normans, the, 86 sqq.; beginnings of their power in South Italy, 268; 296; at battle of Civitate, 298; *see also* Normandy

Northampton, *burh*, 356; submits to Aethelfleda, 323, 363 sq.; attacked by Anlaf, 368; burnt by Danes, 382

Northamptonshire, 398; hundreds of, 367; Scandinavian influence in, 336 sq.; earl of, *see* Waltheof

North Mark, 202 *note*; 238; margraves of, *see* Dietrich, Liuthar, William

Northmen. *See* Vikings

Northumberland, earls of, *see* Eadulf, Siward

Northumbria, kingdom of, 340 sq.; disorders under Eardwulf, 341; conquered by Vikings, 318 sqq., 322 sqq., 333, 348 sq., 350 sqq.; raided by Olaf, 381; art and learning in, 553 sqq.; continental art and, 556, 559; Scandinavian influence in, 336 sq., *see* Bernicia, Deira, Northumberland, Yorkshire; kings of, *see* Aelle, Aethelred, Aldfrid, Eanred, Eardwulf, Ecgberht, Halfdanr; earls of, *see* Morkere, Siward, Tostig

Norway, assists Denmark against Otto II, 205; Vikings of, 311; 327; *see* Vikings; subject to Denmark, 380; Christianity in, 313 sq.; civilisation of, 328 sqq.; *see* Scandinavia; kings of, *see* Hákon, Harold, Knut, Magnus, Olaf, Svein

Norwich, *burh*, 356, 382; cathedral, 563, 567

Notker Balbulus, Sequences and *Gesta Karoli* of, 530 sqq.; life of St Gall by, 534; as a musician, 535

Notker Labeo, 530

Nottingham, Vikings at, 319; 323; 351, 353; *burh* of, 355, 364

Nottinghamshire, 406; Scandinavian influence in, 336 sq.

Nouy, battle of (1044), 108

Novalesa, Abbey of, destroyed, 152; chronicler quoted, 213 sq.

Novara, besieged by Ardoin, 244; see of, 165, 245; bishop of, *see* Peter

Novgorod, settlement in, by Rurik, 327

Noyon, Hugh Capet crowned at, 84; Northmen at, 85, 88; bishopric of, 97; cathedral, 562

Nuremburg, first mention of, 304

Oakley, battle of, 349

Obo, King of Hungary, 278, 303; raids Bavaria, 279 sq., 303; 307; defeat and death of, 285

Obodritzi. *See* Obotrites

Obotrites (Abotrites, Obodritzi), 6 sq., 31, 313; and Christianity, 186, 249, 304; burn Hamburg, 208, 249; allies of Conrad II, 260; princes of, *see* Ceadrag, Godescalc, Mistislav, Slavomir

Ocsonoba (Algarve), 409, 418; mines at, 432

Oda, Archbishop of Canterbury, 368, 372; church reformer, 373

Odda, alderman, 355

Odda, granted Svein's earldom, 394, 397

Odense, bishopric founded at, 208

Oder, river, and Otto I's supremacy, 192; and Boleslav's state, 222; a trade route, 326

Odilo, Abbot of Cluny, 242, 255; and the "Truce of God," 282

Odo (Eudes), King of France, Marquess of Neustria, 75 *note*; Count of Paris, 61, 321; made king, 63, 71 sq.; 81; 84 sqq.; death of, 73

Odo, Bishop of Bayeux, 470

Odo, Bishop of Beauvais, 45

Odo, St, Abbot of Cluny, 155, 527

Odo (Henry), Duke of Burgundy. *See* Henry

Odo Borel, Duke of Burgundy, 123 sq.

Odo, Duke of Gascony, 129

Odo (Eudes) I, Count of Chartres, Blois, etc., 95, 102, 143 *note*

Odo (Eudes) II, Count of Blois and Champagne, 105 sq.; relations of, with Robert the Pious, 117; policy of, 123; claims Burgundy, 143 sq.; 256 sqq.; 262; 273; overcome by Conrad II, 259; death of, 107, 145, 267

Odo, Count of Orleans, 14

Odo, Count of Troyes, 35 sqq.

Odo, son of Robert the Pious, 108 sq.

Odo-Harpin, Viscount of Bourges, 111

Odoacer, 39

Odulric (Ulric), Archdeacon of Langres, made Archbishop of Lyons, 279; murdered, 279

Offa, King of Mercia, 340, 343; laws of, 358; coins of, 554

Offa's Dyke, 341

Ogbourne, 403 *note*

Ohthere, voyages of, 535

Olaf the Peacock, in Iceland, 332

Olaf the Stout, King of Norway, 384, 388 sq.

Olaf Tryggvason, King of Norway, Viking leader, in East Anglia, 324; 332; 381; 384

Olaf the White (Amhlaeibh), Norse King of Dublin, 317 sq., 351 sq.; in Scotland, 325

Olaf (Olafr, Anlaf) Guðfriðson, King of Dublin and York, 323, 368

Olaf (Olafr) Sigtryggson (Anlaf Sihtricsson), "Cuaran," driven from York, 323, 366, 368; revolts, 370; death of, 330

Öland, Anglo-Saxon coins in, 333

Oldenburg, see of, 305 sq.; bishop of, *see* Bernard

Olég (Helgi), Kiev conquered by, 327

Olga, Russian Queen, 201

Olmütz, bishopric founded at, 208

Olney (Glouc.), 385

Omar ibn Hafṣūn, 417 sqq.; death of, 420
Ongendus (Angantýr), King of Denmark, 314
Optatianus Porphyrius, Publilius, "figured" poems of, 512, 520
Oran, 421
Orange, Prince of. *See* William
Orba, siege of, 246
Orbe, interviews at, 34, 42
Ordoño I, King of Leon, 417
Ordoño II, King of Leon, 421
Ordoño III, King of Leon, 422
Ordoño IV, the Bad, King of Leon, 423 sq.
Orford, 377
Origen, 493
Orkneys, the, Vikings in, 318, 325 sq., 346; Scandinavian influence in, 334 sq.; earls of, *see* Einar, Sigurðr
Orleans, 14, 16 sq., 19; Charles the Bald at, 32; Vikings' raids on, 33, 87; 36; importance of, 96, 104, 111; interdicted, 132; MSS. at, 519, 521; bishops of, *see* Arnulf, Jonas, Theodulf; counts of, *see* Matfrid, Odo
Ormside Cup, the, 555
Ornois, the, 27; partition of, 45
Orosius, *History of the World* of, 358; 508; 527; 535, 537
Orseolo, Doge of Venice. *See* Pietro Orseolo
Orta, Bishop of. *See* Arsenius
Ortivineas (? Orvignes), 43
Orvieto, cathedral of, 563
Orwell, river, 385
Osbeorht, 350 sq.
Osbern Pentecost, 395
Osburh, wife of Aethelwulf, 352
Oscar, Danish king, 32
Oscellum, 35 sq., 40
Oscytel, 353
Osferth, 360
Osgar, 374
Osketel Presbyter, 406
Osma, 420 sq.
Osnabrück, Bishop of. *See* Benno
Osulf, 519
Oswald, Bishop of Worcester, 374 sq.; at Fleury, 373; management of his estates, 375, 377 sq., 404; Archbishop of York, 378
Oswaldeslau, 377
Oswulf, high reeve of Bamborough made jarl of Yorkshire, 370
Ota. *See* Auðr
Otbert, Marquess and Count, 157, 161
Otbert II, Marquess, 240, 244
Otbertines, House of, 240, 242, 244 sqq., 264 sqq.
Otford, 385
Otto I, the Great, Emperor, King of Germany, 78, 101; seizes Burgundy, 140, 156; 143 *note*; 157; in Italy, 158 sq., 194, 201 sq.; defeats the Hungarians, 160; King of Italy (961), 161; becomes Emperor, 162, 201; drives out Berengar, 163; rule of, 164; reign of, 164 sqq., 186 sqq.; marriage of, 183, 195, 366; the organisation of the Empire, 213; builds castle at Ghent, 228;

founds archbishopric of Magdeburg, 232; *missi* of, revived, 244; Burgundy, 247; Cordova, 423 *note*; deposes John XII, 455; death of, 167, 204; descendants of, 143 *note*, 204, 205 *note*, 209, 215; epic upon, 532; compared with Henry II, 230 sq.
Otto II, Emperor, King of Germany, 101, 143 *note*, 195, 205 *note*; King of Italy, 161; marriage of, 167, 203; coronations of, 201, 203 sq.; Bavarian revolts, 204 sq.; subdues the Danes, 205; War of the Three Henries, 207; attacked in Lorraine, 80, 207; invades France, 80, 208; in Italy, 168 sq., 208; defeat by Saracens, 169 sq.; relations with Venice, 170; progress of Christianity under, 208 sq.; heathen reaction, 209, 212; see of Magdeburg, 232; death of, 80, 170, 209
Otto III, Emperor, King of Germany, 143 *note*, 205 *note*; born, 208; education, 173, 212 sq.; minority of, 80 sq., 171; Bavarian revolt against, 204; struggle for regency of, 209 sqq.; recovers crown from Henry the Wrangler, 210; begins to rule, 212; advisers of, 213; relations with France, 102 sq.; wars in the east, 211; and north, 212; enters Italy, 172, 176 sq., 212; reorganises the chancery, 174, 213; decree on serfdom, 221; opens Charles the Great's tomb, 213 sq.; neglects Germany for Italy, 173–4, 214; death of, 141, 177, 214 sq.; succession to, 215 sq.
Otto IV, Emperor, of Brunswick, 147
Otto Bezprim, Duke of Poland, 260 sq.
Otto, Duke of Burgundy, 75 *note*, 83, 94
Otto, Duke of Carinthia, 204, 205 *note*, 206, 239, 252; deposed and reinstated, 209, 212; declines the crown of Germany, 215 sq.; sent to Italy, 221
Otto, son of Ricwin, Duke of Lorraine, 191
Otto, Duke of Lower Lorraine, 77 *note*, 104, 239, 248
Otto, Duke of Saxony, 70 *note*
Otto, Duke of Swabia and Bavaria, 195, 204, 205 *note*; 206; in Italy, 208 sq.
Otto of Schweinfurt, Margrave of Nordgau, 299; made Duke of Swabia, 294
Otto, Count Palatine in Lower Lorraine, made Duke of Swabia, 287, 289, 307
Otto, Count of Hammerstein, 250 sqq.
Otto, Count of Lomello, 213
Otto, Count of Savoy, Marquess of Turin, 299
Otto, son of Count of Vermandois, 207
Otto-William, Count of Mâcon, "Count of Burgundy," 106, 141 sq., 247 sq.; death of, 143
Oundle, 376
Ouse, river, 319, 359, 384
Ovid, 343; 519; scholiast on the *Ibis* of, 499
Oviedo, 423
Owel, Lough, Turgeis drowned in, 317
Oxford, placed under defence of Wessex, 363; Danes in, 383; 386 sq., 389, 398

Oxfordshire, under Mercian Law, 357; hundreds of, 367; Danes in, 382 sq.

Pacificus, archdeacon, and Verona library, 521
Paderborn, assembly at (815), 6; Kunigunda crowned at, 218; bishopric of, 232
Pailhas, county of, 90
Palace, Counts of the. *See* Hugh of Beauvais, Sarlio; *see also* Count Palatine
Palatine. *See* Count Palatine
Paldolf I (Pandulf) Ironhead, Prince of Capua-Benevento, 161; receives Spoleto, 166; death of, 169
Paldolf II, Prince of Benevento, 169
Paldolf IV, Prince of Capua, recovers Capua and takes Naples, 268; driven out and restored, 292
Paldolf V of Teano, Prince of Capua, 268
Paldolf, Prince of Salerno, 169
Palermo, seized by Saracens, 48
Palestine, 489; 'Abd-ar-Raḥmān I in, 410; art in, 549 sq.
Palladius, St, missioner to Ireland, 501
Pallig, Viking leader, 381 sq.
Palmyra, catacomb at, 541 sq.
Pampeluna, 8, 410, 421
Pando, Gastald, 49
Pange Lingua, hymn, 495
Pannonia, 7
Papacy, and the False Decretals, 448, 453 *and note*; and temporal rulers, Chap. XVII, and archbishops, 452 sq.; appeals to, *ib.*; kings of Germany, 454; counts of Tusculum, 454; degradation of, in 9th century, 454 sq.; degradation of, in 10th century, 101 sq., 151, 154, 161, 163, 171, 455; provincial churches, 455, *see Liber Pontificialis*; Popes, *see* Agapetus, Alexander, Benedict, Boniface, Clement, Eugenius, Formosus, Gelasius, Gregory, Hadrian, John, Leo, Nicholas, Paschal, Paul, Sergius, Stephen, Sylvester, Urban, Valentine, Zacharias
Papal States, 5, 29, 154, 162, 453
Parenzo, basilica at, 548
Paris, 2, 25; 85; 104; plundered by Vikings, 35, 40; siege of (845), 330; siege of (885), 60 sqq., 321 sq., 529; assembly at, 113; Otto II at, 208; MSS. at, 519 sqq.; 525 sqq.; cathedral of, 566; Remigius teaches at, 527; bishops of, 496, *see* Galo, Joscelin, Reginald; counts of, *see* Bego, Conrad, Gerard, Hugh, Odo, Robert
Parma, revolt and destruction of, 267; Alcuin at, 514; see of, 165
Parrett, river, 355
Paschal I, Pope, 5 sq., 314
Paschal II, Pope, and Philip I, 113 sq, 133
Paschasius Radbertus, political writer and theologian, 10, 12, 14, 445, 533
Passau, captured by Otto II, 206; see of, 206; bishops of, *see* Pilgrim, Richer
Passavant, fief of Anjou, 118
Paterna (Valencia), 432

Paterno, death of Otto III at, 177, 214
Patriciate, importance of, 291, 306
Patrick, St, and Irish learning, 501; 502; 505
Patrimony of Peter. *See* Papal States
Paul, St, letters of, to Seneca, 516
Paul I, Pope, sends Greek books to Pepin, 515
Paul Aurelian (St Pol-de-Léon), 509
Paul the Deacon, 514 sq., 520
Paul, Duke, revolt of, 493
Paul the Silentiary, cited, 544 sq.
Paulinus of Nola, poet, 533 sq.
Paulus Albarus of Cordova, 523
Pavia, 43, 51; assembly at (878), 56; 60; Guy crowned at, 65; submits to Arnulf, 66; Rodolph II crowned at, 136; Louis (the Blind) crowned at (900), 138; 149; 154; Otto I at, 140, 159, 195; Hungarians at, 148, 153; Otto III at, 172; Berengar II crowned at, 194; Ardoin crowned at, 220; Henry II crowned at, 224; massacre in, 224; Henry II at, 242, 244; *missi* for, 244; forfeitures granted to, 245; synods at, 251; 291; diet at, 266; Imperial palace at, burnt, 257, 263 sq.; bishop of, *see* John XIV, Pope
Pawton, 344
Payerne, monastery of, 144, 255; Conrad II crowned King of Burgundy at, 259
"Peace of God," 282, 457, 465
Peada, King of Middle Angles, 554
Peene, river, and see of Bremen, 297
Pelagius, at Jerusalem, 503
Pelayo, King of Asturias, 409 sq.
Pembrokeshire, Viking influence in, 326
Penne, see of, 165
Pentapolis, the, seized by King Hugh, 154; given to the Pope, 162, 174
Pepin, the Short, King of the Franks, 454; 515
Pepin I, King of Aquitaine, 3, 8, 13; receives Gascony and Toulouse, 10; rebellion of, 14 sqq.; expedition against, 17; receives Maine, 18 sqq.; death of, 21
Pepin II, King of Aquitaine, 21 sqq., 27; relations with Charles the Bald, 31 sq., 33 sqq.
Perelada, county of, 90
Perfecto, 416
Périgueux, counts of, 97
Péronne, meeting of Lothar and Charles the Bald at (849), 32; Charles the Simple at, 75 sq., 181; added to Valois, 111
Pershore, 394; Abbey of, 378, 564
Persians, 428, 435
Persius, 508, 521
Peter, Apocalypse of, 488
Peter and Andrew, Acts of, 505
Peter, King of Hungary, 276; allies with Břatislav, 301, 303; deposed, 278, 280, 303; restored, 285; 288, 290, 303
Peter, Marquess of Spoleto, 153; killed by the Romans, 154
Peter, Bishop of Como, 213
Peter, Bishop of Novara, 240

Peter, Bishop of Pavia. *See* John XIV, Pope
Peter, Bishop of Poitiers, 130
Peter, Bishop of Vercelli, 175, 220
Peter Damiani, 291, 308
Peter of Pisa, 514
Peterborough, monastery of, 375, 379, 564; soke of, 376. *See* Medeshamstede
Petrograd, MSS. from Corbie at, 521
Petronius, 527
Pfeddersheim, Charles the Simple at, 180
Philargyrius, commentator on Virgil, 507
Philip, Acts of, in Ireland, 504 sq.
Philip I, King of France, 110 sqq.; excommunicated, 113; Ivo, Bishop of Chartres, and, 131 sqq.; death of, 114
Philip II, of Swabia, King of the Romans, 147
Philippa, wife of William IX of Aquitaine, 129
Philoxenus, 526
Phœnix, A.S. poem, 537
Photius, Patriarch, 450, 528
Physiologus, 488
Piacenza, Louis the Blind at, 138; death of Lothar II at, 44; Conrad II at, 264; see of, 175; bishop of, 267; *see* Guido
Picingli, Nicholas, *strategos,* 151 sq.
Pickering, paintings at, 567
Picos de Europa, 409
Picot, Sheriff of Cambridgeshire, 470
Picts of Galloway, unite with Strathclyde, 341; conquered by Kenneth Mac Alpin, 350; raided by Olaf, 318; raided by Halfdene, 353 sq.
Pietro Candiano IV, Doge of Venice, 170
Pietro Orseolo II, Doge of Venice, 177 sq.
Pietro Tribuno, Doge of Venice, 148
Pilate, Pontius, legend of, 505
Pilgrim, Archbishop of Cologne, Chancellor for Italy, 246; 250 sqq., 253 sqq., 273
Pilgrim, Bishop of Passau, 208
Pilsen, Otto, Duke of Swabia, defeated near, 206
Pirminius of Reichenau, Irish missionary, 490, 521
Pisa, growing importance of, 178; and Sardinia, 250; captured by Vikings, 320; Church of S. Pietro a Grado, near, 567
Pitres, Vikings at, 35; assembly at (862), 40; synod at (862), 452; fortified, 60
Plegmund, Archbishop of Canterbury, 358, 361 sq.
Pliny, the Elder, *Natural History* of, 488, 516, 521
Pliny, the Younger, *Letters* of, 518, 521
Poeta Saxo, identity of, 530
Pöhlde, fortified by Henry I, 182; Eckhard of Meissen slain at, 217; Emperor Henry II meets Gregory at, 241; Henry III at, 293
Poissy, 96, 104, 107
Poitiers, Judith at, 15; Vikings at, 33; siege of (955), 83, 91; Philip I at, 112; Council of (1078), 113; Aquitaine and, 129; battle of (732), 409; bishop of, *see* Peter
Poitou, 31; and Aquitaine, 129; "rain of blood" in, 131

Poland, Christian missions to, 202; extent of, 222, 261 sq.; wars with Henry II, 223, 225 sqq., 239, 247; partitioned by Conrad II, 273, 300, 302; 143 sq.; submits to Henry the Wrangler, 210; war with Bohemia, 211; loses Moravia, 260, 299; dukes of, *see* Boleslav, Casimir, Mesco, Otto Bezprim
Pol-de-Léon, St. *See* Paul Aurelian
Polei (Aguilar), 419
Polemius, Bishop of Asturica, 490
Pombia, Liudolf dies of fever at, 160, 201
Pomeranians attack Poland, 300; prince of, *see* Zemuzil
Pompeii, vaulted structures at, 541
Pompeius Festus, Glossary of, 514 sq.
Pontefract, 370
Pontelungo, Diet at, 225
Ponthieu, 16; 398; and the Flemish March, 92; count of, *see* Guy
Ponthion, palace of, 36, 50; assembly at (876), 51
Pontianus, African bishop, 489
Pontlevoy, battle at (1016), 108, 123
Pontoise, claimed by William the Conqueror, 112
Poperinghe, allodial estates at, 460
Poppo, Bishop of Brixen. *See* Damasus II, Pope
Poppo of Babenberg, Archbishop of Trèves, 248; given Duchy of Swabia, 249; 278
Poppo, Patriarch of Aquileia, 251, 265, 266
Poppo, Abbot of Stablo (Stavelot), 271, 277, 284, 293
Porchester, 357
Porphyrio, 526
Porto, bishop of. *See* Formosus, Radoald
Portsmouth, 384
Posen, Henry II defeated near, 227
Powys, 341; invaded by Ceolwulf, 343; conquered by Rhodri Mawr, 350
Prague, Henry I meets St Wenceslas at, 184; see of, 206, 208, 301; bishops of, *see* Adalbert, Severus; Boleslav of Poland at, 223; Jaromir invested Duke at, 225; relics removed from Gnesen to, 300
Predestination, controversy on, 524, 533
Pressburg, siege of, 296, 304
Priego, 418
Priene, excavations at, 547
Priscian, grammarian, 525 sq.
Priscianus Lydus, 525
Priscillian, heretic, 512
Priscillianism, 493 sq.
Privileges, given to John XII by Otto I, 162; given to Benedict VIII by Henry II, 250
Prizlava, battle at, 306
Probus, grammarian, 516
Procopius, cited, 544 sq.
Propertius, 523
Prosper, referred to by Nennius, 343
Provence, apportioned to Charles the Bald, 16, 24; rebellion against Lothar I in, 31; kingdom of, formed, 34, 137 sq.; attacked by Charles the Bald, 40; partition of, 41,

137; 42; seized by Charles the Bald, 46, 137; 50; Boso, King of, 57 sq.; relations with Burgundy, 137 sq.; united to Burgundy, 139; annexed to France, 147; Saracens in, 152, 155, 168; under King Hugh, 156, 158; plundered by Vikings, 320; marquessate of, 130; county of, 147; kings of, *see* Boso, Charles, Louis; marquesses of, *see* Bertrand, Hugh; counts of, *see* William

Proverbia Gaecorum, 504, 525
Prudentius, poet, 516, 519, 534
Prüm, burnt by Danes, 59; abbey of, 18, 34, 60, 467
Prussians attack Poland, 300
Pseudo-Isidore, 297, 448
Pseudo-Symeon Magister, 149 *note*
Pydershire, 345
Pyrenees, 90, 441; Charles the Great crosses, 413

Quarantaine le Roi, 465
"Quatre-Métiers," the, and Flanders, 122
Quedlinburg, and Henry the Fowler, 182, 185 sq.; plot against Otto I at, 190 sq.; Henry the Wrangler proclaimed king at, 210; compact with Wends at, 226; Henry III at, 297, 302; abbey of, 276, 290; abbesses of, *see* Adelaide, Beatrice; Quedlinburg Annals, cited, 212, 254 *note* 3
Quentovic, pillaged, 30
Quia Emptores, English statute of, 463
Quierzy (Kiersy), assemblies at (820), 8; (857), 36; (877), 52 sq., 55; 58; 61; 446; Louis I at, 19, 21
Quimperlé, abbey of St Croix at, 560
Quintilian, 522
Quo Warranto, inquest of, 466

Raab, river, Conrad II reaches, 261; Henry III's victory on, 284
Raban Maur (Magnentius Hrabanus Maurus), Abbot of Fulda, Archbishop of Mayence, 19, 520 sq., 532
Rabula, Syrian Gospels of, 558
Radbert, Paschasius. *See* Paschasius
Radegund, St, Queen of Chlotar I, 495
Radelchis, Prince of Benevento, 49
Radenzgau, given to see of Bamberg, 237 sq.
Radoald, Bishop of Porto, 42
Raghnall. *See* Ragnarr Loðbrók
Ragnarr Loðbrók, Viking hero, legends of, 318 sqq., 329 sqq., 350; identified with Raghnall, 318; with Reginherus, 319
Ragnfröðr. *See* Reginfredus
Rainard, monk, 536
Rainier, Duke of Spoleto, made Marquess of Tuscany, 243 sq.
Ralf of Guader, the Staller, 392, 406
Ralf of Mantes, Earl of Herefordshire, 392 sqq., 396 sq.
Ramiro, King of Aragon, 428
Ramiro II, King of Leon, 421, 422 sq.
Ramiro III, King of Leon, 424; defeat and death of, 425

Ramsbury, Abbey of, 561
Ramsbury, see of, 362
Ramsey, abbey founded at, 375, 378 sq., 475, 560; abbot of, *see* Wichmann
Ranulf, Count of Aversa, 268, 292
Ranulf (Ralph) Flambard, Bishop of Durham, 133
Raoul (Radulf, Rudolf), King of France, Duke of Burgundy, 75, 181; and the Northmen, 87 sq.; 93; 138; 156; death of, 76
Raoul III, Count of Valois, 111
Raoul, Viscount of Le Mans, 118
Raphael, Biblical pictures of, 549
Rara (perhaps Rohr), Diet at, 210
Ratbold, Bishop of Verona, 11
Ratheri, Bishop of Verona, 156
Ratisbon (Regensburg), meeting of Rodolph I and Arnulf at, 64, 135; besieged by Henry the Fowler, 180; taken by Liudolf, 197; besieged by Otto I, 198 sq.; convent at, 205; assembly of princes at, 206; Wendish embassy at, 228; St Emmeram's, 236; Břatislav does homage at, 278, 301; Leo IX at, 296; Victor II at, 298; bishops of, *see* Gebhard, Wolfgang
Ratramn, of Corbie, 533
Ravenna, assemblies at (880), 57; (898), 67; 58; seized by King Hugh, 154; Otto I at, 162; Otto III at, 172; Henry II at, 242; 251; synod at, 242 sq.; Conrad II and massacre at, 264; art and architecture in, 547, 553; mosaics at, 542, 548, 550; Church of S. Vitale at, 543, 548; Church of Galla Placidia at, 548; statue of Theodoric at, 521; tomb of Theodoric at, 548; ivory throne at, 548, 550, 555; see of, 175 sq., 240, 242, 264; archbishops of, 534; *see* Adalbert, Arnold, Frederick, Gebhard, Humphrey, John, John X, Sylvester II, Widger
Raymond, Count of Barcelona, 427
Raymond-Berengar I, Count of Barcelona, 428
Raymond of St Gilles, Count of Toulouse 129 sq.
Raynald, "Prince," Count of Burgundy, 287
Raynald, Count, 467
Reading, Vikings at, 352 sq.; Abbey, 564
Recemund, Bishop of Elvira, 423 *note*
Recknitz, raided by Otto I and Boleslav, 200
Rectitudines Singularum Personarum, 401 sqq.
Redarii (Wends), the, revolt of, 184, 192, 202, 226
Red Book of the Exchequer, cited, 462 *note*
Reedham, 406
Reggio, capital of the theme of Calabria, 150; Moslem defeat near (1006), 178
Reggio (in Lombardy), county of, 221; counts of, *see* Adalbert-Atto, Tedald; see of, 165; bishop of, *see* Adalard
Reginald of Durham, chronicler, 560
Reginald, Count of Herbauges, 20
Reginald, Bishop of Paris, 105

Reginar (Rainier), chamberlain, 11 sq.
Reginar, the Long-Necked, Duke of Lorraine, 68, 70
Reginar III, Count of Hainault, supports Otto I, 197; rebellion of, 200
Reginar IV, Count of Hainault, 207, 248
Reginar V, Count of Hainault, 254
Reginfredus (Ragnfröðr), joint King of Denmark, 313
Reginherus. *See* Ragnarr Loðbrók
Regino of Prüm, 25, 62 sq., 534
Regio (Málaga), 412, 417, 420, 432 sq.
Regnald of Waterford, King of York, 365 sq.
Regularis Concordia Anglicae Nationis, 375
Reichenau, Abbey of, 236, 257, 276; 535; library of, 505 sq., 521
Remigius, 527
Renard (Reginhard), Count of Sens, 111
Rennes, 14, added to Brittany, 33 ; March of, 128; counts of, 126, *see also* Conan
Renovatio Imperii Romanorum, 213
Repton, 353
Retz, added to Brittany, 33
Rhaetia, given to Charles the Bald, 13
Rhé, monastery of, sacked, 316
Rheims, Stephen IV at, 4; Louis I crowned at, 5; province of, 16; 59; Odo at, 64; Charles the Simple crowned at, 73; Robert I crowned at, 74; 75 sq.; captured by Hugh the Great, 78; recaptured by Louis IV, 79, 193; Lothair crowned at, 80; Hungarians threaten, 88; episcopal lordship of, 97 sq.; captured by Charles of Lorraine, 99; synod at (996), 102; Gerbert of Aurillac *scholasticus* at, 80, 173, 210; dispute concerning see of, 75–78, 194; Hungarians at, 193; Otto II at, 208; French bishops meet at, 292; Leo IX's synod at, 295; 298; historians of, 534; library of, 521; Remigius teaches at, 527; 538; Church of St Remi at, 562; archbishops of, *see* Adalbero, Arnulf, Artaud, Ebbo, Fulk, Gerbert, Hervé, Hincmar, Hugh, Manasse, Seulf
Rhine, river, 18, 21 sq., 23, 26 sq., 34, 37, 46, 52; interview between Charles the Simple and Henry I on, 74 ,181; 134, 136; 189 sq.; Hungarians cross, 198; raid of Chocilaicus on, 309; and Viking raids, 321; 331; Scandinavian influence in lower basin of, 338
Rhodophylus, the eunuch, 149 *note*
Rhodri Mawr, King of North Wales, 364; conquers Powys, 350
Rhone, river, 26 sq., 38, 56, 139, 146, 259, 416
Rhôs. *See* Rus
Rhuddlan, battle at, 341; 397
Riade (? Rittburg), Hungarian defeat at (933), 185
Ribagorza, 90, 428; lord of, *see* Gonzalo
Ribble, 400
Ribe, church at, 314
Ribemont, Treaty of (880), 57
Ribera, cited, 430, 433, 435

Richard I, King of England, 147
Richard, Duke of Normandy, 228, 383, 386
Richard *le Justicier*, Duke of Burgundy, 58, 86, 93
Richard, Bishop of Albano, 113
Richard, Bishop of Verdun, 289, 292
Richard, Abbot of St Vanne's, 250 sq., 271, 282
Richeldis, of Hainault, marries Baldwin of Antwerp, 295
Richer, Bishop of Passau, 69
Richer, historian of Rheims, 534; cited, 82 sq., 535 sq.
Richessa, 287, 300
Richilda, wife of Charles the Bald, 45, 53, 55, 72
Ricsig, ruler of Bernicia, 353 sq.
Rillé, house of, in Anjou, 118
Rimbert, letter from Ratramn to, 533
Rimbert, *Life of St Anskar* by, 534
Ringmere, Danish victory at, 382
Ripen, see of, founded, 192
Ripon, burnt, 370
Riustringen, granted to Harold of Denmark, 313
Robert the Strong, Marquess of Neustria, 35, 40, 71, 75 *note*, 91
Robert I, King of France, Marquess of Neustria, 73; King, 74, 181; killed at Soissons, 75, 87
Robert II the Pious, King of France, 91, 99 sqq.; marriage of, 103 sq.; domain of, 104 sqq.; character of, 105; Fulbert and, 131 sq.; Ardoin and, 221; joins Henry II against Flanders, 106, 228; Henry II and, 251; 257
Robert I, Duke of Burgundy, son of King Robert II, 107, 123 sq.
Robert Curthose, Duke of Normandy, 111 sq., 114, 120 sqq., 128
Robert the Magnificent (or the Devil), Duke of Normandy, 107; dies, 109
Robert the Frisian, Count of Flanders, 111, 122
Robert, Count of Troyes, 96 sq.
Robert, son of Wimarc, 392, 394, 406
Robert, Abbot of Jumièges, Bishop of London, 392; Archbishop of Canterbury, 393 sqq.
Rochecorbon, lord of, 119
Rochester, raided by Danes, 312; attacked by Vikings, 358; bishops of, 367; *see* Gundulf
Roderick, King of the Visigoths, 409
Rodolf, Norman leader in South Italy, 250
Rodolph I, King of Jurane Burgundy, 63 sq., 66, 134 sq.; seizes Basle, 69; 143 *note*
Rodolph II, King of Jurane Burgundy, 135 sq.; King of Italy, 136, 153; Treaty with King Hugh, 139, 156; death of, 140, 156; 143 *note*; 180
Rodolph III, King of Burgundy, 106 sq.; 227; 246 sqq.; 264; reign of, 140 sqq.; makes Henry II his heir, 141, 256; acknowledges Conrad II's title, 142 sq., 256,

258; refuses support to Ernest of Swabia, 257; death of, 123, 143, 258
Rodrigo Ximenez de Rada, Archbishop of Toledo, 426
Roger the Old, lord of Petit Montrevault, 118
Rögnvald, Northman, leader, 87
Rögnvaldr, Earl of Möre, 322, 326
Rohan, Breton house of, 464
Rohr (Rara), Diet at, 210
Roland, 413
Rollo (Hrollaugr, Hrolfr), Duke of Normandy, settles in Normandy, 73, 75, 86, 322 sq., 365; death of, 76
Romagna, 240
Romance language, the, 27
Romanus I Lecapenus, Eastern Emperor, 155
Romanus II, Eastern Emperor, 155; 167
Romanus, Senator of all the Romans. *See* John XIX, Pope
Rome, 4 sq., 28 sq., 31, 43; Louis II crowned at, 47; sacked by Saracens (846), 49; Charles the Bald crowned at, 51; 56; Council at (865), 452; Charles the Fat crowned at, 58; Arnulf crowned at, 66; trial of Formosus in, 67; Louis the Blind crowned at, 138, 149; Otto I crowned at, 140, 162; factions in (903-28), 151, 153 sq.; rule of Alberic, 154 sq.; rule of John XII, 161 sqq.; siege of, 164; disaffection in, 164 sq., 168; Otto II crowned at, 167, 204, 388; dies in, 209; rule of Crescentius II in, 171 sq.; Otto III crowned at, 172; as capital, 174; revolt of, 176 sq.; rule of Crescentius III in, 177, 241; Henry II and, 241, 243, 251; Conrad II crowned at, 143, 264; Roman law to prevail in, 267; Henry III and, 291, 306; Alfred and Aethelwulf in, 349; Burhred dies at, 353; Christian academy at, 486; Alcuin at, 514; Byzantine art in, 557 sq.; vaulted structures at, 541; churches at: Sta Croce in Gerusalemme, 536; St Helena, 542; S. Clemente, 548; Sta Maria Maggiore, 549, 558; Sta Maria Antiqua, 554 sq., 558 sq.; St Theodore, 557
Romsey Abbey, Rood of, 556; paintings at, 567
Romuald, St, of Ravenna, 173, 177
Roncaglia, court at, 298
Roncesvalles, 8, 413, 421
Roric (Hroerekr), brother of Harold, King of Denmark, settles in north Frisia, 313, 315 sq., 320 sq.
Roscommon, Viking raids in (807), 312
Ross, Scandinavian influence in, 335
Rossano, Otto II at, 169 sq.; purple MS. at, 550, 558 sq.
Rosstall, skirmish at (954), 198
Rothad, Bishop of Soissons, 452 sq.
Rothaid, daughter of Charles the Great, 2
Rothfeld, the, 18
Rotilda, daughter of Guy of Spoleto, 48
Rouen, assembly at (824), 6; Northmen

at, 32, 60; 316; granted to Rollo, 73, 86, 94, 322; 87 sq., 127; siege of (946), 193; 386; 398
Roussillon, county of, 90, 130; Vikings in, 320
Rudolf of Habsburg, King of the Romans, 147
Rudolf of Rheinfelden, Duke of Swabia, 146, 288
Rudolf, brother of Judith, 14 sq.
Rudolf of Fulda, 533
Rueda, battle of, 425
Rufinus, 508
Rurik (Hroerekr), settles in Novgorod, 327
Rus, in Russia, 327 sq.; besiege Constantinople, 320, 327
Rūs, Vikings, 328
Russia, and Otto I, 201; war with Poland, 211, 239, 247; Otto Bezprim flees to, 260; and Henry III, 280; relations to Scandinavia, 326 sqq.; 338; grand duke of, *see* Vladimir
Russian Sea. *See* Black Sea
Ruthwell, cross at, 514, 554 sq.
Rutland, Scandinavian influence in, 336 sq.

Saalfeld, plots against Otto I at, 189, 195
Saavedra, cited, 426
Sabina, the, and the Papacy, 162, 164, 243
Safī, caid, besieges Bari (1002), 177
St Aignan of Orleans, Abbey of, 76
St Albans, 359; monastery, 379, 564, 567
St Amand, taken from Flemish March, 93
St Arnulf's of Metz, 43
St Asaph (Llanelwy), church of, 342
St Basle, monastery of, of Verzy, 78; Council of, 100, 103, 211
St Bavo, Ghent, monks of, 228
St Benet, Holme, monastery of, 388
St Benignus, Dijon, Abbot of. *See* William
St Benoît-sur-Loire. *See* Fleury
St Bernard pass, Great, 136; crossed by Charles the Bald, 53; Maiolus captured at, 168; Tuscans and Lombards cross, 259
St Bertin, Abbey of (at St Omer), 92, 358, 373; abbots of, *see* Adalard, Hugh
St Brice's day, massacre of, 382
St Brieuc, 33 *note*; 128
St Clair-sur-Epte, treaty of (911), 73, 86, 94, 322, 364
St Cyr, seized by Fulk Rechin, 119
St David's (Mynyw), church of, 342, 358, 509
St Denis, 2, 19; 25; abbey of, 30 *note*; 76; library of, 521, 524; abbots of, *see* Hilduin, Louis; Paschal II and Philip I at, 114; stained glass at, 565; mosaic at, 567
St Edmund's Bury. *See* Bury St Edmunds
St Emmeram, church of (Ratisbon), 69, 236
Saintes, 126; Aquitaine and, 129
St Esteban de Gormaz, 420
St Florent, church of, at Saumur, 126
St Gall, Abbey of, 257, 293, 561; library of, 521, 526; literary productions of, 530 sq.; "Monk of," *see* Notker Labeo

Ste Geneviève, 61
St Germain-des-Prés, Abbey of, 61; abbots of, *see* Hugh, Joscelin
St Germain l'Auxerrois, Abbey at Paris, 61
St Germain of Auxerre, Abbey, 76, 124; abbot of, *see* Hugh
St Germer de Flay, 30 *note*
St Gilles, Romanesque architecture in, 557
S. Leo, castle of, Berengar II besieged in, 162 sq.
St Martin of Tours, Abbey of, 71; Fulk Nerra and, 126; calligraphy at, 517
Ste Maure, 109; fief of Anjou, 118
St Maurice d'Agaune, Abbey of, 134 sq., 136
St Maurice of Angers, church of, 126
St Médard, monastery, 18, 444 sq.
St Merri, church of, 61
St Mihiel, cartulary of, 467
St Neots, 347 *note*
St Omer, Abbey of St Bertin at. *See* St Bertin
Saintonge, 31; and Aquitaine, 129
St Oswald, Abbey of, Gloucester, 373
St Quentin, 35
St Remi, Abbey, Charles the Simple crowned at, 73
St Riquier, 14; Abbey of, 35, 76; abbots of, *see* Angilbert, Nithard; library of, 519, 521 sq., 538
St Savin, church at, 567
St Stephen of Dijon, church of, 124
St Valery, Abbey of, 76
St Vannes, abbot of. *See* Richard
St Wandrille, ravaged by Danes, 32
St Zoilo, 416
Sakkara, excavations at, 547
Salerno, principality of, 48 sq., 150, 152, 265; united to and separated from Capua, 169; Otto II at, 169 sq.; 176; reunited to Capua, 268; separated from Capua, 292; princes of, *see* Gisulf, Guaimar, John, Landolf, Manso, Paldolf, Siconolf
Salian Dynasty, founded by Conrad II, 253, 269
Sālim, 410 sq.
Salisbury, 382
Sallust, 491, 521
Salonica, decoration at, 542; Church of St George at, 542; Church of St Sophia at, 546; Church of St Demetrius, 546
Saltair na Rann, 506
Salzburg, see of, 206; archbishops of, *see* Herold, Virgilius
Samarcand, coins from, in Sweden, 333
Sampson, Abbot, 438
Sampson, missioner to Brittany, 509
Sancho, Count of Gascony, 33
Sancho I, King of Aragon, 124
Sancho, Count of Castile, 427
Sancho the Fat, son of Ramiro II, 421; King of Leon, 422 sqq.
Sancho II, King of Navarre, 420 sq.
Sancho III, the Great, King of Navarre, 428
Sanchuelo. *See* 'Abd-ar-Rahmān

Sandwich, Edward the Confessor's fleet at, 294; 382; 388 sq.
San Pedro de Roda, monastery of, 90
Sant' Agata, castle of, 268
Santander, 410
Sant' Angelo, castle of, 154; Crescentius II captured in, 172, 216
Santhià, granted to see of Vercelli, 176
Santiago de Compostela, 426, 441
Saône, river, 26, 46, 134, 146
Sappho, alluded to by Columban, 506
Saracens, the, Chap. xvi; menace of, 8, 28 sqq., 33 sq., 44, 47 sqq., 453; conquer Sicily, 48, 150; capture St Peter's, 49; attacks of, 50, 52 sq.; peace made with, 56; 63; in Provence, 140, 152; in Italy, 149 sqq., 155, 166 sq.; driven from Provence, 168; defeat Otto II, 169 sq.; renewed attacks, 176 sq.; defeats, 178; at Otto's court, 201, 203; in Sardinia, 250; the Vikings and, 316 sqq., 320; architecture of, 565
Saragossa, 8, 411, 413, 417 sqq.
Sardinia and Louis I, 6; and the Saracens, 8, 250; and the Byzantine Empire, 178
Sarlio, Count of the Palace, Marquess of Spoleto, 157
Sassanids, 436
Saucourt, Northmen defeated at, 59, 321
Saul, Bishop of Cordova, 417
Saumur, captured by Fulk Nerra, 108, 126
Savona, counts of, 240, 244; men of, 244
Savonnières, interview at (859), 447; assembly at (862), 41
Savoy, duchy of, formed, 147
Saxon dynasty, founded, 179; 215, 218; end of, 253, 269; *see also* Liudolfings
Saxons, the, 23, 26, 179; ally with Vikings, 310; Charles the Great and, 312; Slavs revolt from, 208, 212; plot with Boleslav, 226, 228; Widukind's history of, 534
Saxony, Widukind in, 413; Viking invasions of, 7, 31, 59 sq.; 212; 321; ceded to Louis the German, 16, 18; 22; 25; given to Louis the Younger, 51 sq.; duchy of, 70; invaded by Hungarians, 69, 182, 185, 198; under Henry the Fowler, 181 sqq.; under Otto I, 187 sq., 191, 197 sq.; supports Otto III against Henry the Wrangler, 210; accession of Henry II, 216 sqq.; accession of Conrad II, 255; raided by Mesco II, 260 sq.; war with Lyutitzi, 262; Henry III and, 276 sq., 288; dukes of, *see* Bernard, Bruno, Herman, Liudolf, Otto; king of, *see* Louis
Scaliger, edits the *Barbarus*, 497
Scandinavia, early history of, 309 sqq.; spread of Christianity in, 6 sq., 313 sq.; civilisation of, 328 sqq.; trade of, 332 sq.; influence of, in Russia, 328; in Ireland, 334; in Scotland, 335; in Man, *ib.*; in England, 366 sqq. *See* Denmark, Norway, Sweden, Vikings
Scania, 388
Schalksburg, besieged, 249

Scheidungen, fortress of, 189
Scheldt, river, 26, 34, 92, 228; Danes settle on, 59 sq., 320; 322
Schleswig, Danish fleet at, 312; March of, founded, 185; Christianity in, 314; bishopric founded at, 192; ceded to Denmark, 263, 274; Otto II and, 205
Scholasticus, office in Rheims cathedral, 80, 210, 535
Schweinfurt, branch of Babenberg family. See Bucco, Otto, Henry
Schweinfurt (Zuinprod), convent of, 300
Scotland, Vikings in, 318; 325; 346 sq.; extended to the Tweed, 350; 388; homage question with England, 365, 388; southern influence in, 395 sq.; Scandinavian influence in, 334 sq.; kings of, see Constantine, David, Duncan, Kenneth, Malcolm
Scriptores Gromatici, 536
Scythian, bogus alphabet, 500
Seacourt, 402 *note*
Sechnall, St, hymn by, 502
Sedulius Scottus, poet, 502 sqq., 516, 524 sqq.
Séez, ceded to Northmen, 87, 94, 322
Segoyuela, 409
Segre, river, 8
Séguin, Duke of Gascony, 8
Seine, river, 7, 16, 21, 24 sq.; Northmen in, 31 sq., 35, 40, 52, 59 sqq., 73, 85 sqq., 316, 319 sq., 322; 78, 315
Seisyll of Ceredigion, 342
Seligenstadt, synod at, 252; peace refused to Bohemia at, 278
Semur, subject to Burgundy, 97; lord of, *see* Dalmatius
Seneca, 489; epistles of St Paul to, 516
Senlis, assembly at, 83; 100, 104; seized by Queen Constance, 107; besieged (946), 193
Sennecey, church of, 124
Sens, 36; besieged by Danes, 62; 77; attacked by Hungarians, 88; Burgundy and, 93 sq.; taken by Robert the Pious, 106, 111; besieged (1032), 107, 144; reunited to royal domain, 111; window at, 559; archbishops of, *see* Ansegis, Egilo, Ganelon, Walter
Seprio, county of, 244
Septimania, secured to Charles, 24; count of, *see* Bernard; *see also* Gothia
Sepúlveda, 440
Serbs, the, 47
Serenus, Q., Sammonicus, 522
Serfdom, 221, 249, 251, 401, 469, 477 sqq.
Sergiopolis, church at, 543
Sergius II, Pope, 29
Sergius III, Pope, 151, 362, 455
Sergius IV, Pope, 241
Sergius, Duke of Naples, 49
Sergius IV, Duke of Naples, 268
Servatus Lupus, Abbot of Ferrières, 517 sq., 522
Servius, on the *Aeneid*, 491
Seulf, Archbishop of Rheims, 74 sq.
Seven Sleepers, legend of, 496

Severn, 362 sq., 387, 394, 396, 400; valley invaded, 359 sq.
Severus, Bishop of Prague, 301
Severus, Sulpicius, biographer of St Martin, 495
Seville, 412, 418 sqq., 428, 432; captured by Vikings, 316, 328, 416
Sextus Placidus, medical writer, 535
Shaftesbury, 388
Shakyā, Berber leader, 413
Shi'ites, Muslim sects, 419
Sheppey, raided by Vikings, 312, 347, 349; Danes in, 385
Sherborne, diocese of, 362; Cornwall incorporated in, 344; bishops of, *see* Aldhelm, Asser, Ealhstan
Sherston, 385
Shetlands, the, Irish missionaries in, 310; Viking settlements in, 324 sqq.; Scandinavian influence in, 334
Shropshire, Aethelred in, 382; Danes in, 384
Sicard, Prince of Benevento, 48
Sicily, Saracens in, 48, 149–166, 177 sq.
Sico, Count, imperial *missus*, 168
Sico, Prince of Benevento, 8
Siconolf, Prince of Salerno, 48 sq.
Sidonia, ravaged by Vikings, 316
Sidonius Apollinaris, poet, 495
Sidroc, the Viking, 35
Siegfried, Saxon Count, 187
Siegfried, Saxon Margrave, 212
Siegfried, Abbot of Gorze, 283
Siete Torres, 418
Sigeferth, 384
Sigefrid (Sigröðr), Viking leader, 59, 61, 321
Sigefridus (Sigurðr), King of Denmark, 312
Sigefridus, "nepos" to Godefridus, King of Denmark, 313
Sigefridus. *See* Sigurðr Snake-Eye
Sigeric, Archbishop of Canterbury, 381
Sighelm, alderman of West Kent, 361
Sigtryggr, of the Silken Beard, King of Dublin, plots against Brian, 324
Sigtuna, church founded at, 314; trade at, 332
Sigurðr Snake-Eye (Sigefridus), King of Denmark, 321
Sigurðr, Earl of Orkney, 324, 326
Sigurðr Loðvesson, Earl of Orkney, 326; death of, 324, 326
Sigwulf, alderman of East Kent, 361
Sihtric, King of York, 366
Silesia, transferred from Břatislav to Casimir, 297 sq., 301 sqq.
Simancas, 420, 422 sq.
Simon Magus, 505
Simon of Crépy, Count of Valois and Vexin, 111
Sinai, St Catherine's monastery at, 547
Sinope, Purple MS. at, 550
Sion, diocese of, 38, 63; given to Conrad of Auxerre, 134; *see also* Valais, the
Sisebut, King of the Visigoths, 492
Sithiu (Saint-Bertin), 14

Siward, Abbot of Abingdon, coadjutor of Canterbury, 392

Siward, Earl of Yorkshire and Northumberland, 389, 391, 393 sqq.; death of, 396

Skiringssalr, trading centre, 332

Skye, Vikings in, 311, 346

Slaves, the, party in Spain, 422, 427, 429, 431

Slavomir, Prince of the Obotrites, 7

Slavs, the, 7, 16, 47, 49, 63; and Louis the German, 10, 27, 30 sq., 36; and Henry I, 183; and Henry III, 304; *see also* Bohemia, Croats, Lusatians, Lyutitzi, Moravians, Obotrites, Poland, Russians, Serbs, Slovenes, Sorbs, Wends, Wiltzi

Slesvik. *See* Schleswig

Slovenes, at Compiègne, 6; 7; *see also* Liudevit

Smaragdus of St Mihiel, grammarian, 515 *note*

Snowdon, 342

Sobrarbe, 410, 428, 441

Socrates, Church historian, 487

Soissons, Louis the Pious at, 18 sq., 444; battle at (923), 74, 181; Otto II at, 208; synod of (861), 452; cathedral, 562; bishop of, *see* Rothad

Soleure, Conrad II at, 144; assembly at (1038), 145, 259

Solinus, 488

Solomon and Saturn, Dialogue of, 537

Solomon, Breton king, 40

Solomon, Bishop of Constance, 69

Solway, Eardulf's journey through, 354

Somerset, invaded by Vikings, 382; Danes in, 384; Edmund in, 385, 392, 394, 397

Somme, river, 315; and the Vikings, 319 sq.

Sophia, daughter of Otto II, Abbess of Gandersheim, 255

Sophia, niece of Otto III, Abbess of Gandersheim, 287

Sora, added to Spoleto, 48

Sorbs, the, 7, 212

Southampton, 357, 379, 382, 385

Southwark, 357, 394

Southwell, 408

Sozomen, Church historian, 487

Spain, and Louis I, 8; and the Vikings, 316, 318, 320; Muslims in, ch. xvi; society in, 428 sqq., 439 sqq.; learning and letters in, 433 sqq., 489 sqq., 523 sq.; literary connexions with Britain, 494; with England, 511, 524; with Ireland, 524; Adoptionism in, 516, 523; Roman art in, 552; emirs of, *see* 'Abdallāh, 'Abd-ar-Rahmān, Ḥakam, Hishām, Mahomet, Mundhir; *see* Mūsā; *see also* Cordova, Caliphs of

Spanish March, disturbances in, 3, 8. *See* Barcelona, Catalonia

Sparone, Ardoin at, 224, 239

Spearhafoc, Abbot of Abingdon, 393

Spello, Conrad II at, 267

Spera-in-Deo, Abbot, 416, 438

"Spes Imperii," 273

Spires, 275; Conrad II buried at, 269; cathedral of, 271; diocese of, 27; bishop

of, *see* Walter; Henry III at, 286; Henry III buried at, 299

Spitignev, Duke of Bohemia, succeeds his father Břatislav, 298, 302

Spoleto, duchy of, 47 sq., 58; 66, 454; 161; given to Paldolf I, 166; joined to Tuscany, 157, 171, 243; Crescentians lose, 243; dukes and marquesses of, *see* Ademar, Alberic, Anscar, Guy, John Crescentius, Lambert, Paldolf, Peter, Rainier, Sarlio, Suppo, Theobald, Transemund, Winichis

Spree, river, marshes of, 227

Squillace, monks at, 486

Stablo (Stavelot), 59; abbey of, 277; abbot of, *see* Poppo

Stade, battle with Vikings at, 212

Stafford, *burh* of, 363

Staffordshire, Danes in, 384; Danish names in, 337, 400

Stamford, occupied by the Danes, 319, 355; recaptured by Edward the Elder, 323, 364; Scandinavian influence in, 334, 337

Statius, 516, 536, 538

Stavelot. *See* Stablo

Steele, Diet of (938), 188

Stellinga, the, 26

Stephen II, Pope, 71, 454

Stephen IV, Pope, 4 sq.

Stephen V, Pope, 60, 64 sq., 138

Stephen VII, Pope, 67, 454

Stephen VIII, Pope, 78

Stephen, King of England, 466

Stephen, St, King of Hungary, xvii, 223, 260, 303; war with Conrad II, 260 sq., 273, 281

Stephen, Count of Champagne, 107 sq.

Stephen, Count of Troyes, 105

Stephen of Garlande, Bishop of Beauvais, 113

Stephen, lord of Grand Montrevault, 118

Stephen Caloprini, and Otto II, 170

Stephen, Roman deacon, 536

Steyning, 360

Stifla Sound, death of Godefridus at, 313

Stigand, Bishop of Winchester, 392, 394; becomes Archbishop of Canterbury, 395, 404

Stiklestad, 388

Stilo, battle of, 169

Stoinef, Wendish chief, 200

Stony Stratford, and the Danish boundary, 319, 337, 354

Strachtin (Trachtin), 281

Strangford Lough, death of Halfdanr on, 318

Strasbourg, 23, 25; Treaty of (1016), 142 sq., 247; sacked, 217 sq.; Conrad II at, 258; Hungarian envoys at, 278; Oath of, 25 sq., 534; stained glass at, 566; see of, 45; bishops of, 217; *see* Herman, Werner

Strathclyde, kingdom of, Picts of Galloway, unite with, 341; attacked from Ireland, 352; raided by Halfdene, 353 sq.; in league against Aethelstan, 366

Strehla, taken by Boleslav, 222

Stühlweissenburg, Peter of Hungary restored at, 285, 288
Styrian Mark, formed, 270 *note* 1
Subiaco, abbey of, destroyed, 150
Sūdān, architecture in, 547
Sudbourne, 377
Suðreyjar. *See* Hebrides
Suetonius, 489, 491 sq., 520 sqq., 527, 536; a model for Einhard, 517 sq.
Suevi, John of Biclarum's history of, 492; conversion of the, 489; king of, *see* Miro
Suffolk, 392, 400, 406, 408; hundreds of, 367; Scandinavian influence in, 337
Suidger, Bishop of Bamberg. *See* Clement II, Pope
Sulaiman, al-Musta'in, Caliph of Cordova, 427
Sulpicius, lord of Amboise and Chaumont, 119
Sumail, the Ḳaisite, 411 sq.; murdered, 413
Sunderold, Archbishop of Mayence, 64
Sunifred, Count of Barcelona, 90
Suppo, Count, cousin of Empress Engilberga, Duke of Spoleto, 48
Suppo, Count of Brescia, 11
Surrey, submits to Wessex, 345
Susa, pass of, 11
Sussex, submits to Wessex, 345; plundered by Danes, 381
Sutherland, Viking settlements in, 325, 335
Sutri, Henry III at, 290 sq.
Svatopluk (Zwentibold), King of Moravia, 64
Svatopluk II, Moravian prince, 64
Svein Forkbeard, King of Denmark, deposes Harold Bluetooth, 208, 380 sq.; driven from Denmark, and raids England, 381; conquest of England, 324, 382 sqq.; death of, 325, 384
Svein, King of Denmark and Norway, nephew of King Knut, treaty with Henry III, 294, 296 sq., 325, 389 sq.
Svein, King of Norway, son of Knut, 388 sq.
Svein, Earl, 392 sq.; outlawed, 394; death of, 395
Swabia, revolt in, 64; ravaged by Hungarians, 69, 182 *note*; duchy of, 70, 179; 136, 144, 204; Saracens advance into, 155; relations with Henry I, 180 sq.; with Otto I, 197 sq.; with Italy, 136, 194; with Bavaria, 204, 206; granted to Conrad, 209; refuses support to Duke Ernest against Conrad II, 258; Henry III in, 276; dukes of, *see* Burchard, Conrad, Ernest, Henry, Herman, Liudolf, Otto, Rudolf; *see also* Alemannia
Swanage, Viking defeat off, 355
Sweden, early history of, 309; preaching of Anskar in, 314; Viking expeditions from, 327 sq.; civilisation in, 328 sqq.; kings of, *see* Anund, Björn, Eric; bishop of, *see* Gautbert; *see also* Scandinavia
Switzerland, French, 38
Sylvester II, Pope (Gerbert of Aurillac), career of, xvii, 535 sq.; *scholasticus* at Rheims, 80, 210, 535; Abbot of Bobbio, 80, 173, 175, 210, 535; correspondence

of, 81, 536; Archbishop of Rheims, 101, 103, 173, 210, 534; Archbishop of Ravenna, 173, 210; Pope, 104, 173 sqq., 214; Otto III and, 210, 213; Bohemian church and, 222; Willigis and, 235; death of, 177, 241, 536
Sylvester III, Pope, 291
Symmachus, 536
Syracuse, Archbishop of. *See* Gregory
Syria, Muslim power in, 168 sq.; architecture in, 539, 547; MSS. from, 558
Syrians, 409, 411, 428, 436; in France, 496; influence in Ireland, 505

Tacitus, 518, 520 sq., 533
Tagino, Archbishop of Magdeburg, 228, 232
Tagus, river, 420
Taifas, 436
Tain Bo Cuailnge, 537
Taliesin, poems of, 538
Tamaran, battle of, 428
Tamashecca, 418
Tammām, 411
Tamworth, *burh* of, 363 sq., 368
Tanshelf, 370
Taormina, conquered by Saracens, 150
Taranto, seized by Saracens, 48; siege of (982), 169
Tarentaise, diocese of, 39; Boso acknowledged king in the, 137
Tarūb, Sultana, 416 sq.
Tavistock, Abbey, 378; abbot of, *see* Lyfing
Taxis, Hungarian chief, 158
Tedald, Marquess (of Canossa), 221 sq.; 224; 240
Tees, river, boundary of Northumberland, 351, 396
Tegernsee, Abbey of, 236; abbot of, *see* Godehard
Teignton, 382
Tempestarii, belief in, 520
Tempsford, 364
Terence, 521, 532
Terouanne, Bishop of, 460
Terra di Lavoro, Saracens in the, 149; *see* Campania
Tertullian, 488, 493; MS. of, 520
Testa de Nevill, cited, 462
Tettenhall, battle near, 362
Tetralogus, by Wipo, 278, 280
Tewkesbury Abbey, 564
Thames, river, 344, 346, 348 sq., 352, 354 sqq., 359 sq., 385
Thanet, Vikings winter in, 312, 349; renewed raids, 379
Thankmar, 186; rebels, 188
Thegan, life of Louis the Pious by, 534
Theiss, river, Hungarians settle on, 148
Theobald I, Marquess of Spoleto, 152 sq., 155, 157
Theobald II, Marquess of Spoleto, 161
Theobald, Count, 57
Theobald the Trickster, Viscount of Tours, Count of Blois, 95
Theobald III, Count of Blois, 107 sq., 123

Theobert, Count, 13
Theodora, Empress, 547
Theodora, mother of Crescentius, 168
Theodora, *Senatrix*, wife of Theophylact, 151, 455
Theodore, *primicerius*, executed, 5
Theodore, Archbishop of Canterbury, 488, 502, 504, 508 sqq., 511 sq., 514, 555
Theodore, of Mopsuestia, 503
Theodoret, Church historian, 487
Theodoric, statue of, 521; tomb of, 548
Theodoric I, King of the Franks, 309
Theodoric, Count of Autun, 57
Theodoric, illegitimate brother of Louis I, 2, 12
Theodosius II, Eastern Emperor, 492
Theodrada, daughter of Charles the Great, 2
Theodulf, Bishop of Orleans, Abbot of Fleury, 2, 11 sq., 450, 517 sq.
Theodulus. *See* Gottschalk of Orbais
Theophanes, chronicler, 528
Theophano, Empress, 80, 103, 169, 172 sq., 205 *note*, 207, 212; marries Otto II, 167, 203; joint regent for Otto III, 171, 209 sq.; dies, 171, 211
Theophano, Abbess of Essen, 287
Theophilus of Antioch, 503
Theophrastus, *Peplus* of, 504, 526
Theophylact, Senator of the Romans, 151, 153, 454 sq.
Theophylact of Tusculum. *See* Benedict VIII, Pope
Theophylact of Tusculum. *See* Benedict IX, Pope
Thessalonica, siege of, 149 *note*
Thetford, Viking victory at, 318, 351; *burh* at, 356, 382
Theuda. *See* Tota
Theudibert I, king of the Franks, 309
Theutberga, wife of Lothar II, 38 sqq., 41 sqq., 449
Theutgaud, Archbishop of Trèves, 39, 42, 449 sq.
Thiedric, Archbishop elect of Magdeburg, 232
Thietmar, Bishop of Merseburg, cited, 141, 145, 204, 207 *note*; 208; 214 *note*; 233, 235
Thietmar, Margrave of East Mark, 260
Thietmar, brother of Bernard II (Billung), revolts, 249, 293
Thietmar, Count, 184
Thion, Vikings defeated at (880), 59
Thionville, assemblies at (831), 6, 12, 16; (835), 20
Thomas, Apocalypse of, 506 *and note*, 537
Thomas, St, in India, 537
Thor, worship of, restored, 351
Thorgestr. *See* Turgeis
Thorgils Sprakaleg, 387
Thorkil the Tall, 382 sqq.; deserts, 385; earl of East Anglia, 387, 392
Thorney, Abbey of, 375
Thouarcé, fief of Anjou, 118, 125

Thouars, viscounty of, 97, 471; town of, burnt, 120
Thousand, the Year, 456
Three Henries, War of the, 206
Throndlaw, subjected to Denmark, 380
Thurferth, *jarl* of Northampton 364
Thurgau, county of, seized by Rodolph II, 136
Thuringia, given to Louis the German, 16, 18; 22 sq.; ravaged by Hungarians, 69, 182, 185; Henry the Fowler and, 181; Henry the Wrangler in, 210; Henry II acknowledged in, 217; tribute of swine, 217; Henry III in, 276, 278; duke of, *see* Henry
Thurkytel, *jarl* of Bedford, 363, 365
Thuwāba, Emir, 409
Thyra, 380
Tibullus, 523
Tidenham, 404
Tilleda, royal seat in Thuringia, 278
Timgad, baptistery at, 547
Tivoli, John XII and Adalbert at, 163; revolt of, 176
Todmir, 418
Togloss, *jarl*, 364
Toledo, 410 sq., 413 sq., 416 sq., 420 sq., 429, 432; massacre of, 414; use of, 494; archbishops of, *see* Eugenius, Eulogio, Julian, Rodrigo Ximenez
Toledoth Jesu, 520
Tone, river, 355
Tongres, burnt by Danes, 59
Tonnerre, subject to Burgundy, 93, 96
Torksey, Vikings at, 353
Torrox, castle, 411
Tortona, Judith at, 18; Otbertines in, 240 see of, 175
Tory Island, 310
Toscanella, bishop of. *See* John
Tostig, outlawed, 394; Earl of Northumbria, 396 sq.; driven from earldom, 398
Tota (Theuda), Queen of Navarre, 421 sqq.
Toul, Rodolph I of Burgundy crowned at, 135; threatened by Odo of Blois, 144, 259; bishopric of, given to Louis the German, 45 sq.; bishop of, made count, 185 *note*; bishops of, 44; *see* Bruno; "Monk of Toul," 531
Toulouse, sieges of (844), 31; (849), 33; county of, given to Pepin, 10; March of, 89 sq.; wars with Aquitaine, 129 sq.; state of, 130; supposed academy at, 498; 502; counts of, *see* Alphonse-Jourdain, Berengar, Bertrand, Raymond, William
Touraine, and Anjou, 96, 108 sq., 123; custom of, 471
Tournai, cathedral at, 562 sq.
Tours, ravaged by Vikings, 32, 86 sq.; 33; abbey of Saint-Martin at, 76; given to Geoffrey Martel, 108 sq.; attacked by Hugh of Amboise, 119; Odo II and, 123; Fulk Nerra at, 126; library at, 521; church at, 563; counts of, *see* Hugh, Odo, Theobald; archbishop of, *see* Archibald

Towcester, 354, 364
Towy, Vale of (Ystrad Tywi), 341 sq.
Tralles, churches at, 543 sq.
Tramoyes (Ain), assembly at (835), 20
Transemund, Marquess of Spoleto. 170
Trebatius Testa, *De Religionibus*, 485
Trebbia, river, battle on (889), 65
Tref, Welsh fiscal unit, 342, 345
Tréguier, 33 *note*, 128
Trent, river, Vikings follow, 351; Mercian
    advance in, 363
Trent, city, 21; Berengar at, 64; see of,
    157; Henry II at, 224
Treuga Dei. See Truce of God
Trèves, 17; captured by Danes, 59; council
    at (948), 79, 194; disaffection at, 238;
    diocese of, 45; library of, 521, 536;
    Romanesque art at, 552, 557; archbishops
    of, 209, 295; *see* Adalbero, Bertulf, Henry,
    Liudolf, Megingaud, Poppo, Theutgaud
Trèves, fief of Anjou, 118, 125
Tribuno Menio, Doge of Venice, 170
Tribur, assemblies at (887), 62; (897), 68;
    (1045), 288; (1053), 297
Triconshire (Triggshire), 345
Trieste, see of, 165
Triggshire, 345
Trim, supposed Greek church at, 503
Troia, 251, 268
Troyes, added to Burgundy, 93; recaptured,
    94; under Odo II, 105; council of (878),
    56; counts of, *see* Herbert, Odo, Robert,
    Stephen; *see also* Champagne
Truce of God, 279, 281 sqq., 457, 465
Tudela, 410, 417, 421
Tunis. *See* Ifrīkīya
Turenne, viscounty of, 97
Turgeis (? Thorgestr), Viking chief, 317
Turin, marquesses and house of, 220, 240,
    265; *see* Ardoin Glabrio, Manfred; MSS.
    from Bobbio at, 521; bishop of, *see* Clau-
    dius
Tuscany, 47 sq.; Henry II and, 240, 243 sqq.;
    Saracens and, 250; reduced by Conrad II,
    264; marquesses etc. of, *see* Adalbert,
    Boniface, Boso, Guido, Hubert, Hugh,
    Lambert, Matilda, Rainier
Tusculum, counts of, 241, 291, 454; *see*
    Gregory
Tusey, interview at (865), 42
Tuy, bishop of. *See* Lucas
Tweed, river, English frontier, 350, 388, 395
Two Sorrows of Heaven, 505
Twyneham, 361
Tynwald Hill, Isle of Man, 335

'Ubaid-Allāh, 411 sq.; death of, 412
Ubbi (Ubba), 319, 350 sq., 355
Udalrich, Bishop of Basle, 271
Udalrich, Duke of Bohemia, 222 sq., 239,
    247, 260, 299; revolt and deposition of,
    262; death of, 262
Udo, Franconian count, 190
Uggeshall, 406
Uhtred, jarl of Yorkshire, 383 sq., 387

Ukrani, the, submit to Henry I, 185; de-
    feated by Gero and Conrad (945), 200
Ulf, Knut's brother-in-law, 387 sqq.
Ulf, Bishop of Dorchester, 392, 394
Ulf, son of Dolfin, 398
Ulfkytel, 382, 385
Ulm, Ernest of Swabia submits at, 257;
    diets at, 276 sq., 294
Ulric, Bishop of Augsburg, 199
Ulster, Vikings in, 347
Ulwyn of Hedingham, 406
Umayyads, massacred by Abbasids, 410; in
    Africa, 410; in Spain, 411 sq., 415, 419.
    See Spain, Emirs of; Cordova, Caliphs of
Unroch, Marquess of Friuli, 47
Unwan, Archbishop of Hamburg-Bremen,
    239, 263
Urban II, Pope, excommunicates Philip I,
    113, 132 sq.
Urgel, county of, 90, 427; count of, *see*
    Armengol
Urraca, 422
Utrecht, Hungarians reach, 198; Udalrich
    imprisoned at, 262; Conrad II dies at,
    269; Henry III at, 275, 284, 289; plun-
    dered by Vikings, 316, 347; bishops of,
    209, 249, 289, 292, 294; *see* Adalbold
Uzège, 27; Boso recognised in, 137
Uzès, paganism in, 520

Valais, the, invaded by Arnulf, 135; *see
    also* Sion
Val de Junqueras, 421
Valence, assembly at (890), 138; Hugh of
    Arles and, 138; Vikings at, 320
Valencia. *See* Paterna
Valenciennes, 33; seized by Baldwin IV,
    106, 227 sq.
Valentine, Pope, 5
Valentinois, the, united to France, 147
Valerius, St, works of, 494
Valerius Maximus, 527
Val-es-Dunes, battle of (1047), 109, 120
Valois, 111; counts of, *see* Raoul, Simon
Val Sugana, Henry II in, 224
Valtierra, 421
Vandals, in Africa, 489; John of Biclarum's
    history of, 492; king of, *see* Guntha-
    mund
Vannes, and Breton revolts, 8 sq.
Varangians, the, in Russia, 327 sq.
Varaville, defeat of Angevins at (1058), 110
Vaulting, history and use of, 540; Gothic
    development of, 560 sqq., 564
Vegetius, 526
Vendôme, independence of, 96; and Anjou,
    109; count of, *see* Bouchard
Veneto, the, raided by Hungarians, 148
Venice, Hungarians repulsed at, 148; inde-
    pendence of, 150; growth and danger of,
    170; under Orseolo II, 177 sq.; doges of,
    see Pietro, Tribuno; treaty with Otto II,
    170, 218; and Henry II, *ib.*; loss of eccle-
    siastical independence, 265; St Mark's
    at, 549 sq., 553

Ver, synod of (844), 29 sq.
Veranius, on the *Pontifices*, 485
Verberie, 14, 36
Vercelli, pilgrim route to, 136; taken by Ardoin, 220, 244; lost, 245; see of, 175 *note*, 176, 245; bishops of, 267; *see* Ingo, Leo, Liutward, Peter
Vercelli Book, 506 *note*; 537
Verdun, 57; captured by Lothair, 81, 210; sacked, 293; Treaty of (843), 26 sqq., 30, 93, 135; county of, 286, 289, 292; count of, *see* Godfrey; St Nicholas's Abbey at, 526; see of, 289; bishops of, 295; *see* Adalbero, Dietrich, Richard
Verecundus, Bishop of Junca, 488
Vermandois, county of, Northmen in, 72, 85; Hungarians in, 88; 83, 97, 198; counts of, 108, 207; *and see* Albert, Herbert, Hugh
Vermland, under Danish rule, 313
Vernon, lord of. *See* Guy
Verona, 65; Berengar I murdered at, 136, 153; Louis the Blind surprised at, 138, 149; Berengar II at, 157; 160 sq.; German Diet at (983), 170, 208, 209; Otto III at, 172; captured by Ardoin, 222; Henry II at, 224, 244, 251; Conrad II at, 140, 264, 266; Henry III at, 290; library at, 521; bishops of, 221; *see* Adalard, Ratbold, Ratheri; count of, *see* Milo
Verona, March of, added to Bavaria, 159 sq., 163, 196; added to Carinthia, 206; to Bavaria, 209; to Carinthia, 211; to Bavaria, 212
Verrius Flaccus, 514
Verzy. *See* St Basle
Vestfold, under Danish rule, 313, 316
Vexilla Regis, hymn, 495
Vexin, added to Normandy, 108; acquired by Philip I, 111 sq.; invaded by William Rufus, 114; counts of, *see* Drogo, Simon
Vézelay, church at, 562
Vicenza, bishop of. *See* Jerome
Vich, Archbishop of. *See* Hatto
Victor II, Pope (Gebhard, Bishop of Eichstedt), 297 sq.
Victor of Tonnensia, chronicler, 492
Victorinus, grammarian, 493, 516
Vienna, first mention of the name, 261; captured by Hungarians, 261; MSS. from Bobbio at, 521; MS. of Genesis at, 550
Vienne, 19; given to Charles the Bald, 45 sq.; ruled by Boso, 57, 137; siege of (882), 58, 137; Louis the Blind at, 138; cusping at, 565; archbishops of, 282; *see* Bernard; counts of, *see* Charles Constantine, Gerard
Viguera, 421
Vikings, chap. XIII; meaning of, 309, 340; in Frisia and Saxony, 20, 212, 227; in Spain, 316, 318, 320, 416; civilisation of, 329 sqq., 365
Vikings (Danish), chap. XIII, 311; ravage Frisia, 347; invade England, 311 sq., 323 sq., chap. XIV, 379 sqq; *see* Danelaw,

England, York; invade Ireland, 317; *see* Vikings (Irish); invade France, 31 sqq., 35, 40, 52 sqq., 57 sqq., 86 sqq.; besiege Paris, 60 sqq., 529; 63 sq., 72; foundation of Normandy, 73, 86, 322; *see* Normandy
Vikings (Irish), 311 sq., 317, 362, 368, 379; attack Strathclyde, 351 sq.; raid Dorset, 355; in league against Aethelstan, 365 sq.; flight of Irish scholars from, 524; *see* Dublin, kings of
—— (Norwegian), 311; in England, 311, 340, 346 sqq., 368, 380; in Ireland, 311 sq., 317
Villanueva de Brenes, 412 *note*
Villeloin, abbey of, 71
Vingulmörk, under Danish rule, 313
Vinland, Viking expedition to, 332
Virgil, 486, 491, 496, 505 *note*, 507 sqq., 516, 521, 524
Virgilius, Bishop of Salzburg, 511; and the antipodes, 512 sq.
Virgilius Maro Grammaticus, 497 sqq.; date and influence of, 499 sqq.
Visé, interview at (942), 78, 193 *and note*
Visigothic script, 517
Visigoths, in Asturias, 409; in Spain, 429 sq., 432; 436; 438; John of Biclarum's history of the, 492; kings of, *see* Chindaswinth, Roderick, Sisebut, Wamba
Vistula, river, and the Poles, 222
Vitruvius, 516, 518, 557
Vitry-en-Perthois, territory of, 111
Vivarais, the, 27, 45; Boso acknowledged as king in, 137; united to France, 147
Vivarium, monastery of, 486
Vladímir, the Great, Grand Duke of Russia, 247, 331
Vladivoi, Duke of Bohemia, 222 sq.
Volga, river, and the Rus, 327
Volkfeld, given to see of Bamberg, 237 sq.
Volturno, abbey of, destroyed, 49, 150

Wahlwies, battle at (914), 69
Waiblingen, assembly at (887), 62
Wala, 2, 12, 14 sq., 445
Walafrid (Walafridus) Strabo (Strabus), *Glossa Ordinaria* of, 521 sq., 532
Walcheren, Vikings at (837), 313; granted to Harold, 25, 315; added to Flanders, 223
Waldingfield, 406
Waldrada, and Lothar II, 38, 40 sqq.
Wales, divisions of, 341 sq.; Church of, and Rome, 342; Vikings in, 326; 347; attacked by Mercia, 341 sqq., 353; defeated by Mercia, 396 sqq.; Marches of, 401, 404; learning in, 509; literature of, 538
Wales, North (Gwynedd, Venedotia); 360; 362; 397; Coenwulf's war with, 341, 343; extent and overlordship of, 341 sq., 350; submits to Wessex, 364; princes of, *see* Gruffydd, Idwal, Merfyn, Rhodri Mawr
Wales, South, Coenwulf's war with, 341; expansion of, 341; 396
Wales, West (Cornwall), settlement of, by Ecgbert, 344 sq.; assists Vikings, 347

Walīd II, Caliph of Damascus, 411
Wallers, Northmen victorious at, 72, **85**
Wallingford, 357
Walo, Bishop of Metz, 59
Walpert, Archbishop of Milan, 160
Walsleben, captured by Wends, 184
Walter, elected to see of Besançon, 141
Walter, Bishop of Spires, 241
Walter, Archbishop of Sens, 71, 74 sq.
Waltheof of Bamborough, 383
Waltheof, 396; made Earl of Northampton-
    shire and Huntingdonshire, 398 sq.
Waltherd, Provost of Magdeburg, 232, 239
Wamba, King of the Visigoths, 493
Wantage, 338; 352
Wareham, 357; captured by Vikings, 355;
    Knut lands at, 384
Warin, Count of Mâcon, 14, 24
Warmund, Bishop of Ivrea, 220
Warte, river, and the Poles, 222
Warwick, fortified, 363
Warwickshire, 337, 384, 406
Watchet, 357
Waterford, Norse in, 317; Danes in, 334
Watling Street, 319, 337, 354, 359, 368, 383,
    405
Wazo, Bishop of Liège, canonist, 290; pre-
    serves peace between France and Ger-
    many, 292, and sack of Verdun, and siege
    of Liège, 293; death of, 294
Wearmouth, Vikings raid, 341; library at,
    511; abbot of, *see* Benedict Biscop
Wedmore, 356; Peace of, 319, 356
Weimar, Count of. *See* William
Weland, the Viking, 40
Welf, house of, 35, 56; in Burgundy, 134,
    247
Welf, Count, 13
Welf, Count, 256 sqq.
Welf, Count, made Duke of Carinthia, 292,
    299
Welland, river, 354 sq., 380
Wells, see of, 362; bishop of, *see* Duduco;
    canons of, 379
Wenceslas, St, Duke of Bohemia, 184;
    murder of, 192
Wends, the, Saxony ravaged by, 182, 184 sq.,
    191 sq.; defeat of, 200 sqq.; revolt of,
    208 sq.; war with Otto III, 211 sq.; ally
    with Henry II, 226 sq., 228; in Bamberg
    district, 237; rising of, 249; 262; *see also*
    Dalemintzi, Lusatians, Lyutitzi, Obo-
    trites, Redarii, Sorbs, Ukrani, Wiltzi
    and Slavs
Wenilo. *See* Ganelon
Weoxtan, 344
Werben, Udalrich of Bohemia deposed at,
    262; fortress of, 262
Werden, abbot of, 206
Werfrith, Bishop of Worcester, 356, 358
Werinbert, 530
Werla, fortress of, Henry I at, 182; assemblies
    at, 216, 255
Werner, Count of Kiburg, 257 sq., 270
Werner, Bishop of Strasbourg, 260

Wessex, kingdom of, 340 sq.; rivalry
    with Mercia, 344 sqq.; subdues Cornwall,
    344 sq.; subdues Kent, 345 sq.; struggles
    with Vikings, 319, 348, 350, 352 sqq., 358;
    partitioned, 349 sq.; freed from the Danes,
    356; subjection of Mercia to, 356, 360; 364;
    reformed by Alfred, 357; new sees erected
    in, 361; progress against the Danes, 362 sqq.,
    law and institutions, 362, 366 sq., 369;
    Eadwig in, 372; Knut in, 384; retained
    by Edmund, 386; society in, 401, 404 sq.;
    kings of, *see* Aethelbald, Aethelbert,
    Aethelred, Aethelstan, Aethelwulf, Alfred,
    Beorhtric, Eadred, Ecgbert, Edmund,
    Edward, Ine
Wessex, earldom of, 387, 397; earls of,
    see Godwin, Harold
Westbury-on-Trym, monastery at, 374
Westerna, 363, 365
Western Islands (Suðreyjar), *see* Hebrides;
    kings of, *see* Guðröðr, Ketill, Maccus
Western Kingdom, the, 28, 31 sq., 35; Louis
    the German invades (858), 36; Lorraine
    added to, 45; *see also* France
West Franks, the; *see* France
Westminster, Abbey of, 374, 399, 545,
    560 sqq.
Westmorland, Norse settlements in, 326;
    Scandinavian influence in, 335, 337
West Saxon Chronicle, cited, 350, 352, 354
Wettin, Count of. *See* Dietrich
Wexford, Viking fleet in (820), 316; Danes
    in, 334
Wherwell, nunnery of, 394 sq.
Whitby, synod of, 342
Whithern, bishopric of, 341
Whitwell, 368
Wichlawa, 377
Wichmann, Abbot of Ramsey, 263
Wichmann, brother of Herman, Duke of
    Saxony, 187 sq.
Wichmann, nephew of Herman, Duke of
    Saxony, raises rebellion among the Wends,
    200; defeated and slain, 202
Wick, conquered by the Danes, 380
Widger, Archbishop of Ravenna, trial of,
    290
Widukind, Saxon hero, in Denmark, 312;
    invades Saxony, 413
Widukind of Corvey, Saxon historian, 534,
    cited, 183 note, 184, 186, 187 note, 190 sq.,
    201, 203
Wienerwald and the East March (Austria),
    the, 208, 281
Wifred I, Count of Barcelona, 428, 441
Wigbert, Bishop of Merseburg, 235
Wight, Isle of, Danes in, 382
Wiglaf, King of Mercia, exiled, 346; re-
    stored, 346
Wihomarch, Breton leader, 9
Wikfried, Archbishop of Cologne, 187, 199
Wilfrid, St, Bishop of York, 553, 556, 560
Willa, wife of Berengar II, 157, 159, 162;
    exile and death of, 163
William I (the Conqueror), King of England,

(the Bastard), Duke of Normandy; in Normandy, 283; 471; wars with Anjou, 109; 292; revolt in Normandy, 120; visits England, 394; Harold's oath, 398; King of England, 111 sq., 120 sq.

William II (Rufus), King of England, 112, 121

William, Archbishop of Mayence, appointment of, 199; 201; death of, 203

William Longsword, Duke of Normandy, 75; does homage to Raoul, 76; murder of, 92; 94; 189

William, Duke of Aquitaine, founder of Cluny, 456

William V (the Great, the Pious), Duke of Aquitaine, 106 sq., 129, 131, 141; accepts crown of Lombardy for his son, 257, 263; 283

William VIII (Guy-Geoffrey), Duke of Aquitaine, 129

William IX, Duke of Aquitaine, 114, 129 sq.

William, Marquess of Montferrat, Rector of Burgundy, 147

William, Margrave of Nordmark, 306; slain, 299

William of Baux, Prince of Orange, Rector of Burgundy, 147

William I, Count of Arles, 104

William II, Count of Provence, 141

William, Count of Blois, 14

William IV, Count of Toulouse, 129 sq.

William, Count of Weimar, 217

William, Bishop of London, 393

William, Abbot of St Benignus, Dijon, 250

William of Arques, revolt of, 120

William Busac, lord of Eu, 120

William of Gellone, 13

William of Jumièges, cited, 311

William of Malmesbury, cited, 130, 332, 353, 536, 555, 561

William of Poitiers, cited, 122

Willibert, Archbishop of Cologne, 45

Willibrord, St, in Scandinavia, 314

Willibrord, *Life of Boniface* by, 534

Willigis, Archbishop of Mayence, 209, 213, 235; supports Otto III, 210 sq.; and Henry II, 217; crowns Kunigunda, 218; at Synod of Frankfort, 237; death of, 239

Wilton, 382; battle of, 352

Wiltshire, invaded by Mercians, 345; invaded by Guthrum, 355; attacked by Aethelwald, 361; invaded by Vikings, 382, 384

Wiltzi, the, 6, 184 *note* 2; *see* Lyutitzi

Wimarc, 392

Wimborne, 352

Winchcombe Abbey, 343, 375, 378; abbot of, *see* Germanus

Winchester, 395; sacked by Vikings, 350; Svein at, 383; new minster of, 361, 373 sq. (*see* Hyde, abbey of); diocese of, 362; old minster of, 374, 388; royal school of art at, 555 sq.; cathedral of, 563 sq.; bishops of, *see* Aelfheah, Aethelwold, Denewulf, Stigand

Wing, *burh* at, 364

Winichis, Duke of Spoleto, 4

Winterthür, Rodolph II repulsed at (919), 136, 180

Wipo, Chronicler, cited, 254 *notes* 1-3, 259, 263 sq., 270 sq., 273, 279, 280, 288; tutor of Henry III, 272; Chancellor, 146; author of *Tetralogus*, 278, 280

Wirral, the, Scandinavian influence in, 336

Witan, of Mercia, 340; of Wessex, 344, 362; of England, 378, 381 sq.

Witham, *burh* at, 363

Witiza. *See* Benedict of Aniane

Witland, 388

Woden, worship of, restored, 351

Wolfenbüttel, MS. at, 536

Wolfgang, Bishop of Ratisbon, 218, 236

Wollin, island of, trade at, 326

Woodbridge, 377

Woodstock, assize of, 471; palace of, 561

Woolpit, apparition at, 513

Worcester, cathedral and see of, 343, 351, 374 sq., 380, 561; bishops of, *see* Dunstan, Ealdred, Oswald; charter, 357; estate-management of, 375, 404; franchise of, 377 sq.; abbess of, *see* Cuthsuuitha; earl of, *see* Hákon

Worcestershire, 387, 389

Worksop, 368

Worms, 25 sq.; 72; 275; assemblies at (829), 13; 23; (882), 59; (894), 64; (895), 67, 135; (897), 68; council at (926), 180 *note*; Louis the Pious at, 17, 21 sq.; diocese of, 27; Hungarians at, 198; Otto II crowned at, 201

Wreocensaete, ravaged by Vikings, 349

Wulfnoth, the Child, 382

Wulfred, Archbishop of Canterbury, 343; and Beornwulf's accession, 344

Wulfstan, Archbishop of York, 368, 370

Wulfstan, voyages of, 535

Würzburg, 279; library and MSS. at, 503, 512, 521; see of, 237; bishops of, *see* Bruno, Henry

Wytham, 402 *note*

Wyvelshire, 345

Xanten, 189, 293

Yaḥyā ibn Yaḥyā, 414 sq.

Yaroslav, Prince of Kiev, 261, 278

Year Thousand, the, 456

Yemenites (Kalbites), 409, 411 sqq., 416, 428

Yèvre, oppressive baron of, 104

York, captured by Danes, 318, 350, 353; monastery of, 379; 566; library at, 511, 514, 516; Alcuin and, 514; see of, 341, 380; archbishops of, *see* Eanbald, Wilfrid, Wulfstan; Scandinavian influence in, 334; kings, earls, etc. of, *see* Eric, Morkere, Olaf, Regnald, Sihtric, Siward, Tostig, Uhtred

Yorker Anonymus, 504

Yorkshire, kingdom and earldom of, 361; 365; 383 sq.; 387; 398; 400; annexed to

Wessex, 366; revolts from Edmund, 368; conquered by Eadred, 370; Scandinavian influence in, 336

Ystrad Tywi, tribal unit, 341 sq.

Yttingaford, 361

Yūsuf ibn Bukht, Emir, 411 sq.; slain, 413

Yütz, assembly at (844), 30 sq.

Zacharias, Pope, and Virgilius of Salzburg, 512 sq.

Zachary, Bishop of Anagni, 451

Zāhids, Muslim sect, 431

Zāhira, 425

Zähringen, house of, and Burgundy, 146 sq.

Zamora, 420, 423, 425

Zawī, Berber chief, 427

Zedekiah, Jewish doctor, 54

Zeeland, and Flanders, 121

Zeitz, burnt by Bohemians, 208; bishopric removed to Naumberg, 260

Zemuzil, prince of the Pomeranians, 290

Zerbst, captured by Boleslav, 228

Zīrī ibn 'Atīya, viceroy of Morocco, 425 sq.

Ziryāb of Bagdad, 415

Zoë, Byzantine Empress-regent, 151

Zuinprod. *See* Schweinfurt

Zülpich, siege of (925), 181

Zurich, Conrad II at, 144, 259, 264; Ernest of Swabia at, 257; Henry IV betrothed at, 299

Zwentibold, Moravian prince. *See* Svatopluk

Zwentibold, illegitimate son of Arnulf, 66; King of Lorraine, 67 sq.; killed, 68, 74; 135

Map 28 a & b

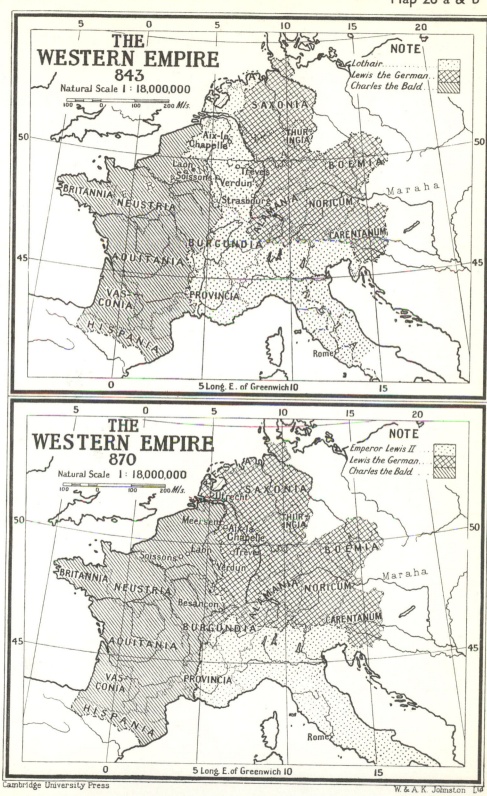

MAP 29
France
in 987

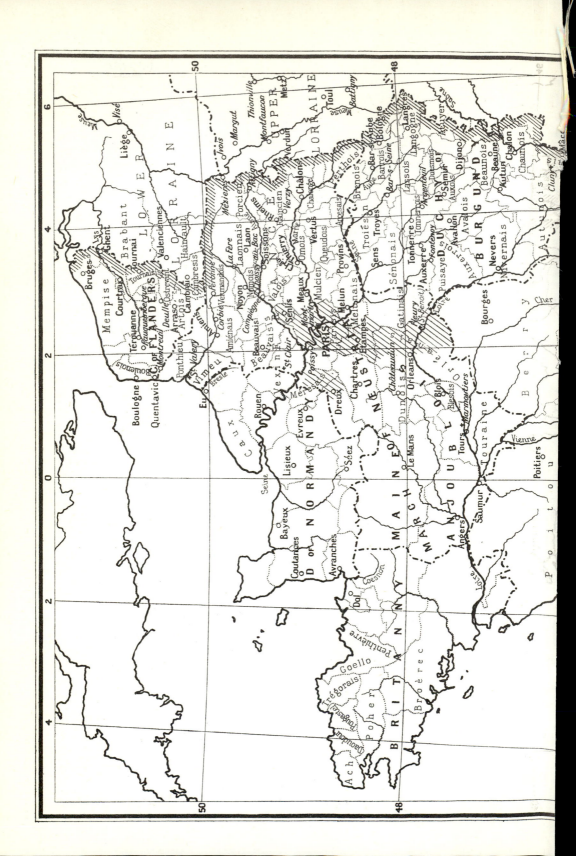

Map 29

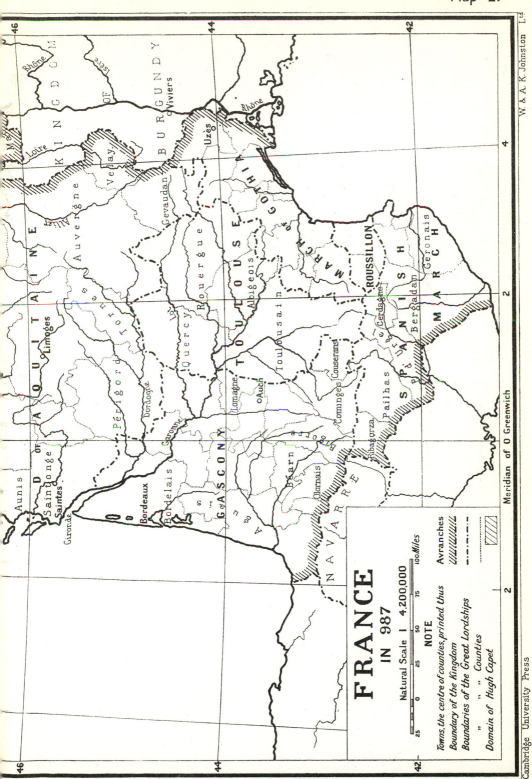

FRANCE
IN 987

Natural Scale 1 : 4,200,000

25   0   25   50   75   100 Miles

NOTE

Towns, the centre of counties, printed thus   Avranches
Boundary of the Kingdom
Boundaries of the Great Lordships
"   "   "   Counties
Domain of Hugh Capet

Cambridge University Press
W. & A. K. Johnston Ltd

Meridian of 0 Greenwich

KINGDOM OF BURGUNDY

AQUITAINE

TOULOUSE

GOTHIA

SPANISH MARCH

GASCONY

NAVARRE

ROUSSILLON

Rhône
Isère
Rhône
Mer
Loire
Allier
Viviers
Uzès
Velay
Auvergne
Gévaudan
Rouergue
Albigeois
Limousin
Limoges
Périgord
Dordogne
Quercy
Lot
Garonne
Lomagne
Auch
Toulousain
Comminges
Couserans
Bigorre
Pailhas
Ribagorza
Cerdagne
Bergadan
Gerônais
Béarn
Oloron
Aunis
Saintonge
Saintes
Gironde
Bordeaux
Bordelais
Agenais

MAP 30

North-Western France
in the 11th century
Inset:
Environs of Paris

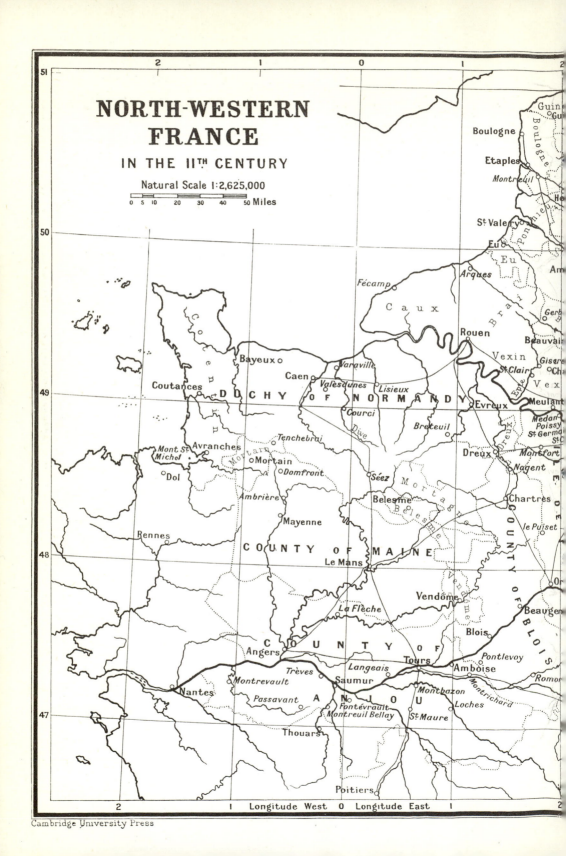

NORTH-WESTERN FRANCE

IN THE 11TH CENTURY

Natural Scale 1:2,625,000

0 5 10 20 30 40 50 Miles

Guin·Gu

Boulogne

Boulogne

Etaples

Montreuil

St Valery

Ponthieu

Eu

Am

Eu

Eu

Fécamp

Arques

Bray

Caux

Gerb

Rouen

Beauvais

Côten

Vexin

Gisore·Cha

Bayeux

Varaville

St Clair

Vex

Caen

Valesdunes

Lisieux

Coutances

DUCHY OF NORMANDY

Evreux

Meulant

Courci

Medan

Poissy

St German

St C

Dive

Breteuil

Dreux

Mont St Michel

Avranches

Tenchebrai

Séez

Mortagn

Montfort

Mortain

Mortain

Domfront

Belesme

Dreux

Nagent

Dol

Belesme

Chartres

Ambrière

le Puiset

Mayenne

Rennes

COUNTY OF MAINE

Vendome

Le Mans

Or

Vendôme

COUNTY OF BLOIS

La Flèche

Beauge

Blois

COUNTY OF

Angers

Tours

Pontlevoy

Trèves

Langeais

Amboise

Montrevault

Saumur

Romor

Nantes

Montbazon

Montrichard

Passavant

ANJOU

Loches

Fontévrault

Montreuil Bellay

St Maure

Thouars

Poitiers

Map 30

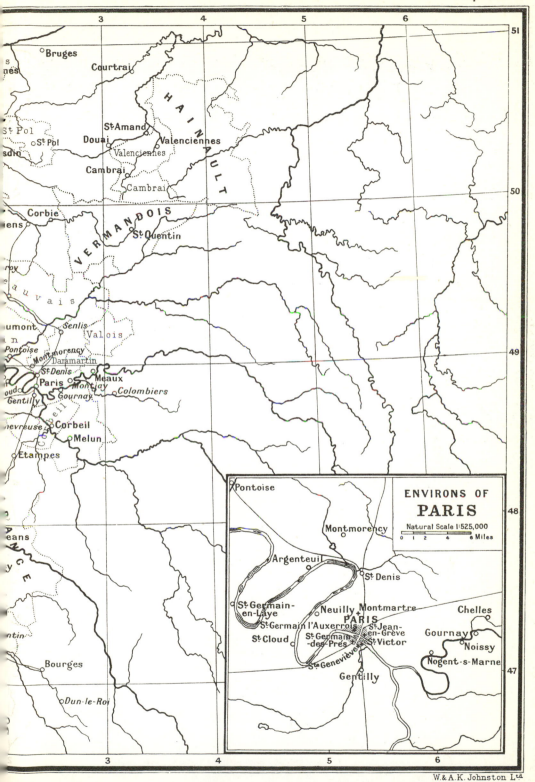

Bruges
Courtrai
HAINAULT
St Pol
St Pol
sdin
St Amand
Douai
Valenciennes
Valenciennes
Cambrai
Cambrai
Corbie
ens
VERMANDOIS
St Quentin
roy
auvais
umont
Senlis
n
Valois
Pontoise
Montmorency
Dammartin
St Denis
Paris
Meaux
Montjay
Colombiers
Gournay
Gentilly
eil
oud
evreuse
Corbeil
Melun
Etampes
FRANCE
eans
Bourges
ntin
Dun-le-Roi

ENVIRONS OF
PARIS
Natural Scale 1:525,000
0 1 2 4 6 Miles

Pontoise
Montmorency
Argenteuil
St Denis
St Germain-
en-Laye
Neuilly Montmartre
PARIS
St Germain l'Auxerrois
St Jean-
en-Grève
St Cloud
St Germain
-des-Prés
St Victor
St Geneviève
Gentilly
Chelles
Gournay
Noissy
Nogent-s-Marne

W.& A.K. Johnston Ltd

MAP 31

Burgundy
at the beginning of the
11th century

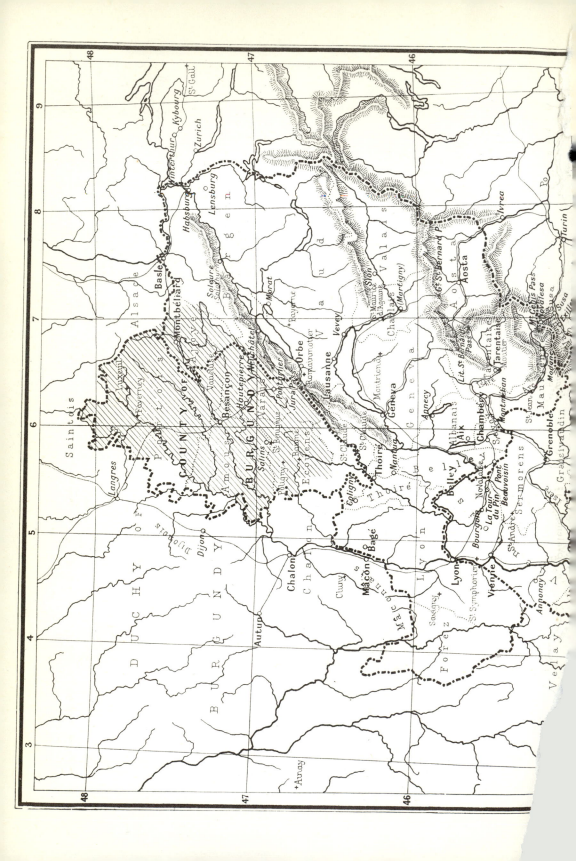

Map 31

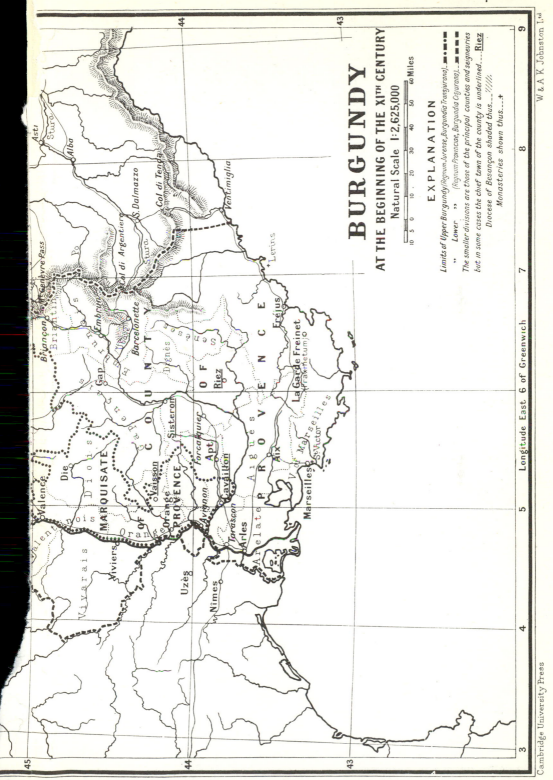

BURGUNDY

AT THE BEGINNING OF THE XITH CENTURY

Natural Scale 1:2,625,000

10 5 0 10 20 30 40 50 60 Miles

EXPLANATION

Limits of Upper Burgundy (Regnum Jurense, Burgundia Transjurana)...
" " Lower " (Regnum Provinciae, Burgundia Cisjurana)...
The smaller divisions are those of the principal counties and seigneuries
but in some cases the chief town of the county is underlined.... Riez
Diocese of Besançon shaded thus....////.
Monasteries shown thus...+

W & A K Johnston L.rd

Longitude East 6 of Greenwich

MAP 32

Italy
at close of 10th century
Inset: **Rome**

approximate plan before
A.D. 1084

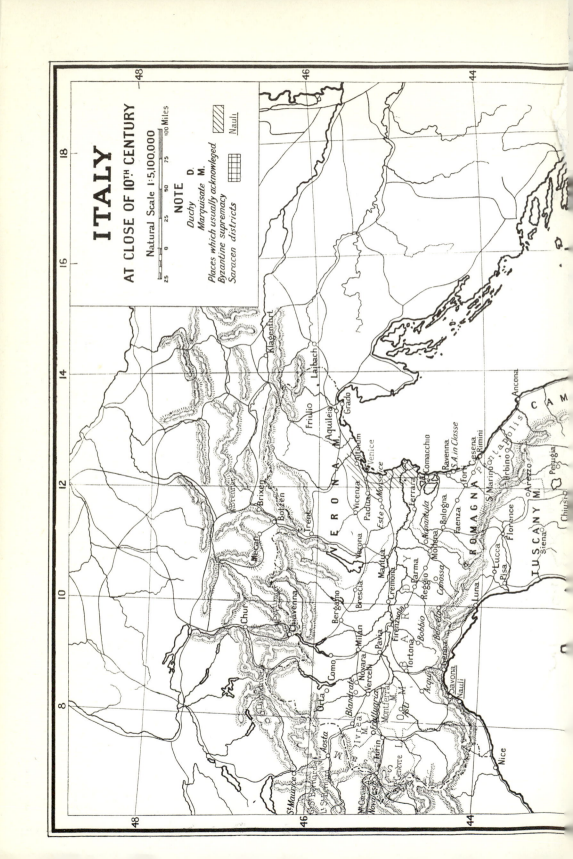

ITALY

AT CLOSE OF 10TH CENTURY

Natural Scale 1:5,100,000

NOTE

Duchy   D.
Marquisate M.
Places which usually acknowleged
Byzantine supremacy
Saracen districts

Nauli

Map 32

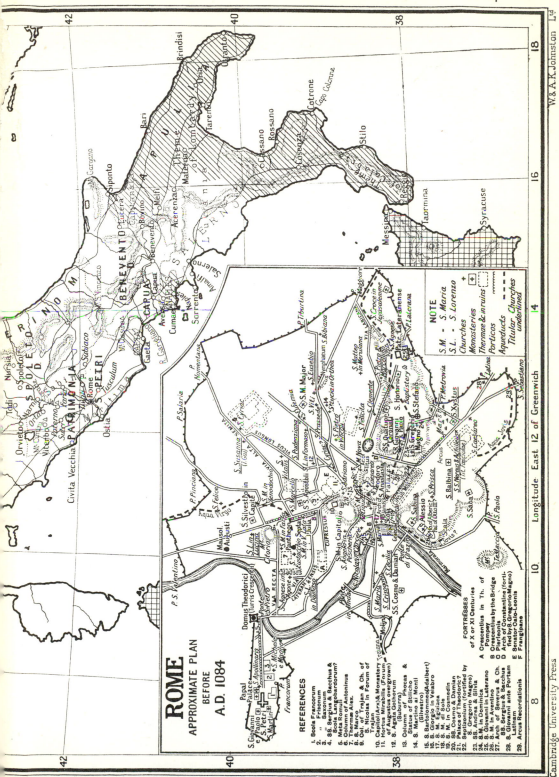

Map 33

Germany
in the 10th and 11th centuries

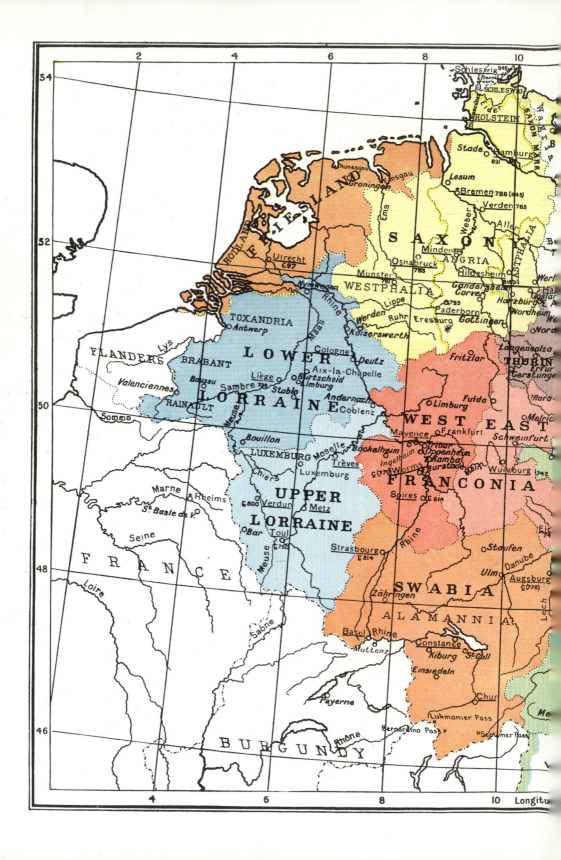

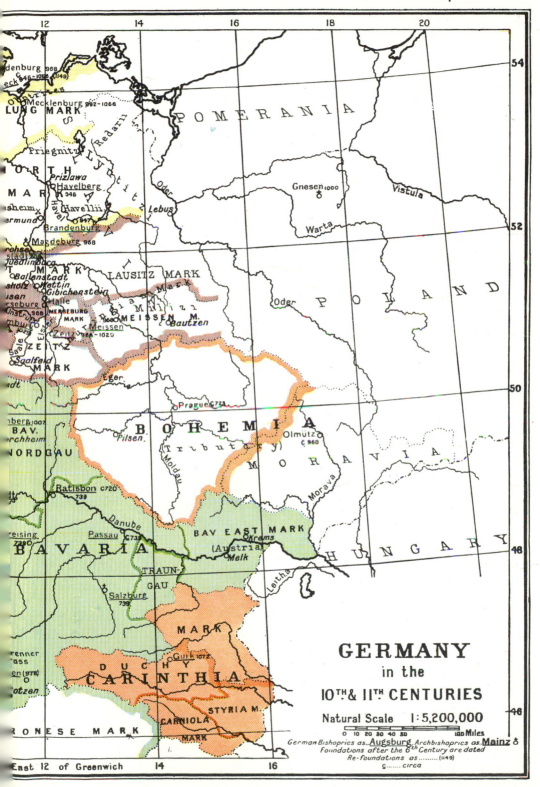

Map 33

POMERANIA

denburg 968
eck 946-1058 (1149)

Mecklenburg 992-1066

LUNG MARK

Redarii

Lyutici

Priegnitz

ORTH

MARK

Prizlawa
Havelberg 946
Havellii 947

heim
mund

Brandenburg

Magdeburg 968

Havel

Lebus

Oder

Gnesen 1000

Vistula

Warta

POLAND

rohsa
stadt
Quedinburg

T MARK

Ballenstadt
Wettin
Gibichenstein
Halle
MERSEBURG
MARK

Zeitz 968-1029

LAUSITZ MARK

Silesia Mark

Milzi

MEISSEN M.

Meissen

Bautzen

Oder

ZEITZ

Saalfeld
MARK

Saale

Eger

BOHEMIA

Prague c724

Pilsen

(Tributary)

Olmütz
c 960

MORAVIA

Morava

nberg 1007
rchheim

BAV.

NORDGAU

Ratisbon c720
739

Moldau

eising

Passau c739

Danube

BAVARIA

reising

BAV EAST MARK
Krems

(Austria)
Melk

HUNGARY

Leitha

TRAUN-
GAU

Salzburg
739

renner
ass
en (978)

otzen

MARK

Gurk 1072

DUCHY
CARINTHIA

STYRIA M.

CARNIOLA

MARK

RONESE MARK

GERMANY
in the
10TH & 11TH CENTURIES

Natural Scale 1:5,200,000

0 10 20 30 40 50   100 Miles

German Bishoprics as Augsburg Archbishoprics as Mainz
Foundations after the 6th Century are dated
Re-foundations as .... (1149)
c ... circa

Map 34

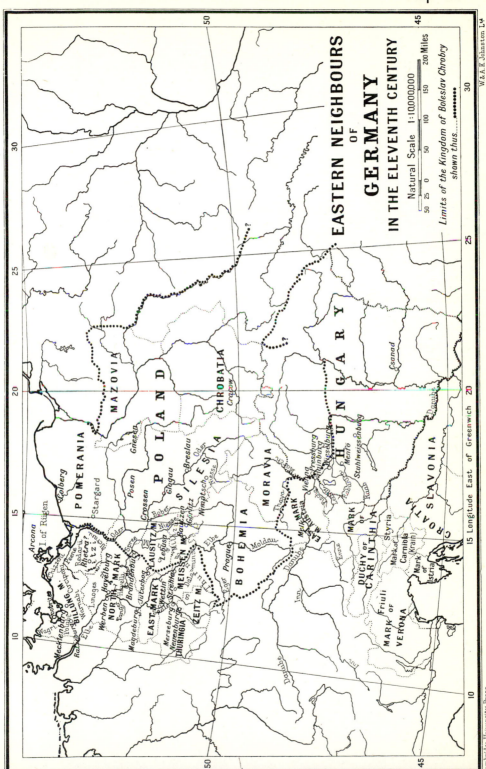

EASTERN NEIGHBOURS
OF
GERMANY
IN THE ELEVENTH CENTURY

Natural Scale 1:10,000,000

50 25 0 50 100 150 200 Miles

Limits of the Kingdom of Boleslav Chrobry
shown thus......●●●●●●●

W.& A.K.Johnston L^{td}

POMERANIA

MAZOVIA

POLAND

CHROBATIA
Cracow

SILESIA

Gnesen

Posen

Breslau

Crossen

Glogau

Oder

Neisse

Bober

Kamptschlau

Arcona

I. of Rügen

Colberg

Stargard

Stargard

Mecklenburg

Oldenburg

Ratzeburg

Wagri

Elbe

Linoges

Rhetra?

Radasü?

Havel

Havelberg

Brandenburg

Spree

Lebusi

LAUSITZ

BILLUNG M.

NORTH MARK

Werben

Magdeburg

EAST MARK

Merseburg

Naumburg

Strehla

THURINGIA

ZEITZ M.

MEISSEN

Wettin

Dalaminze

Görlitz

BOHEMIA

Eger

Prague

Elbe

Moldau

Inn

Danube

Danube

MORAVIA

Thaya

EAST MARK

Inn

Meurn

Wels

Ens

MARK
OF
CARINTHIA

DUCHY OF
CARINTHIA

Styria

Mark of
Carniola
(Krain)

MARK
OF
VERONA

Mark
of
Istria

Friuli

HUNGARY

Raab

Wieselburg

Ödenburg

Steinamanger

Stuhlweissenburg

Raab

Danube

CROATIA

SLAVONIA

Csanad

15 Longitude East of Greenwich

Cambridge University Press

Map 35

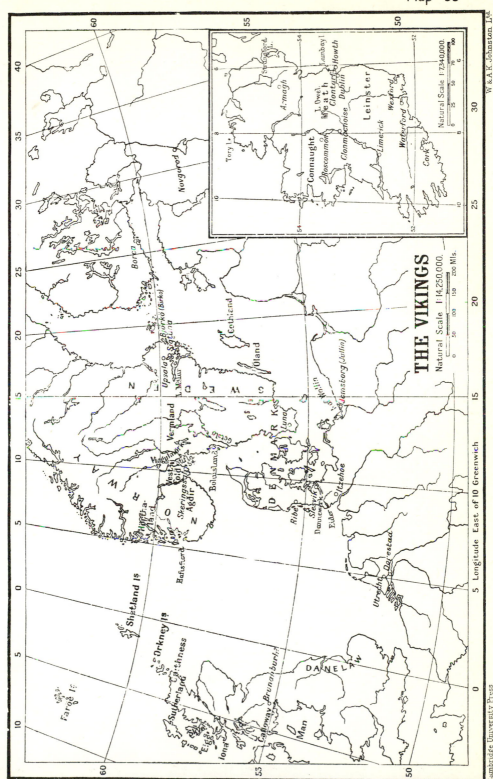

THE VIKINGS

Natural Scale 1:14,250,000.

Cambridge University Press

W & A.K.Johnston Ltd.

Map 36

England

circa A.D. 900

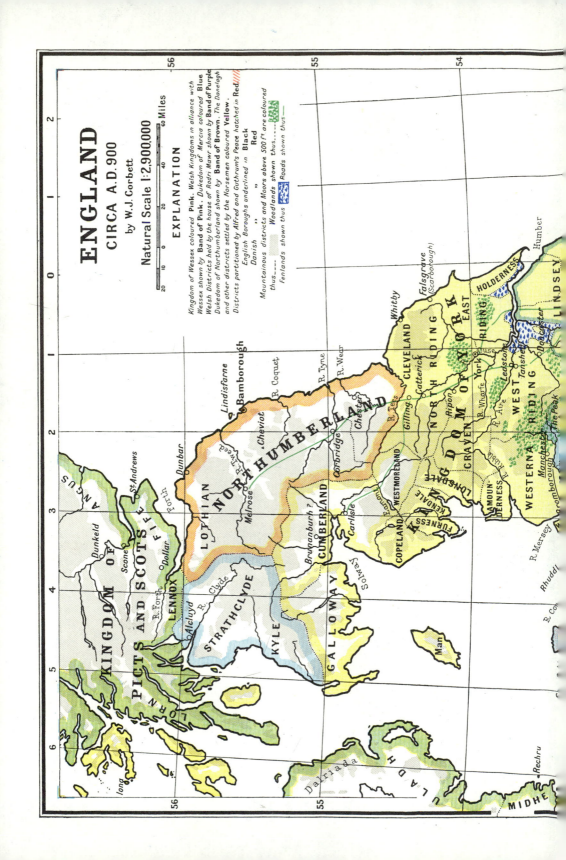

ENGLAND

CIRCA A.D. 900

by W.J. Corbett

Natural Scale 1:2,900,000

20   10   0   10   20   30   40   50   60 Miles

EXPLANATION

Kingdom of Wessex coloured **Pink**. Welsh Kingdoms in alliance with
Wessex shown by **Band of Pink**. Dukedom of Mercia coloured **Blue**.
Welsh Districts held by the house of Rodri Mawr shown by **Band of Purple**.
Dukedom of Northumberland shown by **Band of Brown**. The Danelagh
and other districts settled by the Norsemen coloured **Yellow**.
Districts partitioned by Alfred and Guthrum's Peace hatched in **Red**.
English Boroughs underlined in **Black**
Danish   "   "   "   **Red**
Mountainous districts and Moors above 500 f.t are coloured
thus----   Woodlands shown thus----
Fenlands shown thus----   Roads shown thus----

Iona

KINGDOM OF

PICTS AND SCOTS

Dunkeld
Scone
Dollar
R.Forth
LENNOX
Alcluyd
R.Clyde
STRATHCLYDE
KYLE

LORN

Dalriada

ULADH

MIDHE

Rechru

FIFE
St.Andrews
ANGUS
R.Forth
Forth
Dunbar
LOTHIAN
Melrose
R.Tweed
Cheviot

NORTHUMBERLAND

Lindisfarne
◎Bamborough
R.Coquet
R.Tyne
R.Wear

Corbridge
Chester
R.Tees

Brunanburh ?
Carlisle
CUMBERLAND
GALLOWAY
Solway
Man
R.Mersey
Rhuddl
R.Con

COPELAND
FURNESS
KENDALE
COPELAND
WESTMORELAND
R.Eamont
AMOUN-DERNESS
LONSDALE
CRAVEN
WESTERN
RIDING
Ribble
Manchester
R.Ribble
Gromborough? The Peak

Whitby
Falsgrave
(Scarborough)
CLEVELAND
Gilling◦
Catterick
NORTH RIDING
Ripon◦
R.Wharfe
R.Aire
York◦
Ledstone
Tanshelf
EAST RIDING
Driffield
HOLDERNESS
Humber
LINDSEY

KINGDOM OF YORK

56
55
54

2   1   0   1   2   3   4   5   6

Map 36

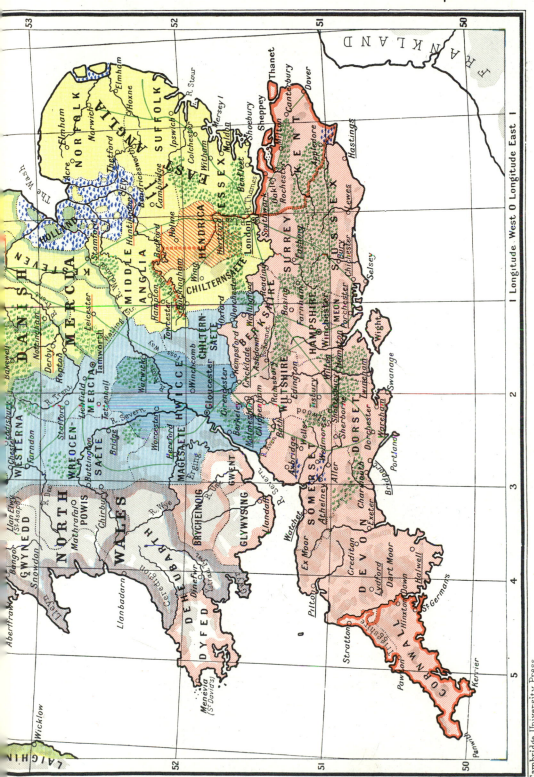

MAP 37

Spain

to illustrate the era of the
Umayyads

Inset: Spain

at the death of Alfonso I.

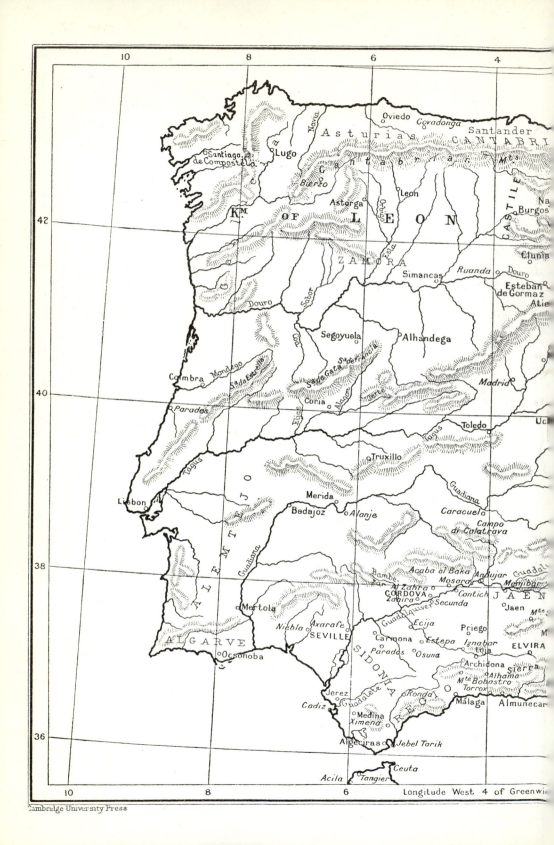

Map 37

SPAIN
to illustrate the
ERA OF THE UMAYYADS

Natural Scale 1 : 4,800,000

0 10 20 30 40 50   100 Miles

SPAIN
at the death of
ALFONSO I.

Christians   Mohammedans

W & A.K. Johnston Ltᵈ